Communications
in Computer and Information Science 194

Ezendu Ariwa   Eyas El-Qawasmeh (Eds.)

Digital Enterprise and Information Systems

International Conference, DEIS 2011
London, UK, July 20 – 22, 2011
Proceedings

Springer

Volume Editors

Ezendu Ariwa
London Metropolitan Business School
London Metropolitan University
Eden Grove - EG4.06, London N7 8EA, UK
E-mail: e.ariwa@londonmet.ac.uk

Eyas El-Qawasmeh
King Saud University
Information Systems Department
Riyadh 11543, Saudi Arabia
E-mail: eyasa@usa.net

ISSN 1865-0929 e-ISSN 1865-0937
ISBN 978-3-642-22602-1 e-ISBN 978-3-642-22603-8
DOI 10.1007/978-3-642-22603-8

Springer Heidelberg Dordrecht London New York

Library of Congress Control Number: 2011931778

CR Subject Classification (1998): H.3, H.4, C.2, I.2, H.5, J.1

Typesetting: Camera-ready by author, data conversion by Scientific Publishing Services, Chennai, India

Printed on acid-free paper

Springer is part of Springer Science+Business Media (www.springer.com)

Message from the Chairs

The International Conference on Digital Enterprise and Information Systems (DEIS 2011), co-sponsored by Springer, was organized and hosted by the London Metropolitan University, UK, during July 20–22, 2011, in association with the Society of Digital Information and Wireless Communications. The DEIS conference series is planned as a major event in the area of digital enterprise and information systems, and serves as a forum for scientists and engineers to meet and present their latest research results, ideas, and papers in the diverse areas of digital information, data processing, enterprises, computer science, and related topics in this area.

DEIS 2011 included guest lectures and 70 research papers for presentation in the technical session. This meeting was a great opportunity to exchange knowledge and experience for all the participants who joined us from around the world to discuss new ideas in the areas of digital enterprises, digital businesses and other applications related to digitalization. We are grateful to London Metropolitan University, UK, for hosting this conference. We use this occasion to express our thanks to the Technical Committee and to all the external reviewers. We are grateful to Springer for co-sponsoring the event. Finally, we would like to thank all the participants and sponsors.

Ezendu Ariwa
Jan Platos
Eyas El-Qawasmeh

Preface

On behalf of the DEIS 2011 conference, the Program Committee and London Metropolitan University, UK, we welcome you to the proceedings of The International Conference on Digital Enterprise and Information Systems (DEIS 2011) held at London Metropolitan University.

DEIS 2011 explored new advances in digital enterprise including digital econcoy, digital management products, business technology intelligence, software applications, computer systems, and digital information and data communications technologies. It brought together researchers from various areas of software engineering, information sciences, and enterprise businesses to address both theoretical and applied aspects of digital information and computer systems. We hope that the discussions and exchange of ideas will contribute to advancements in the technology in the near future.

The conference received 200 papers, out of which 73 were accepted, resulting in an acceptance rate of 37%. The accepted papers are authored by researchers from 27 countries covering many significant areas of digital information and enterprise business. Each paper was evaluated by a minimum of two reviewers.

Finally, we believe that the proceedings document the best research in the studied areas. We express our thanks to London Metropolitan University, UK, Springer, the authors and the organizers of the conference.

Hocine Cherifi

Organization

General Chair

Ezendu Ariwa	London Metropolitan University, UK

Program Chairs

Jan Platos	VSB Technical University of Ostrava, Czech Republic
Eyas El-Qawasmeh	King Saud University, Saudi Arabia

Program Co-chairs

Yoshiro Imai	Kagawa University, Japan
Renata Wachowiak-Smolikova	Nipissing University, Canada

Proceedings Chair

Hocine Cherifi	Université de Bourgogne, France

Publicity Chair

Maitham Safar	Kuwait University, Kuwait
Zuqing Zhu	University of Science and Technology of China, China

Table of Contents

Cryptography and Data Protection

Embedded Systems and Software

Biquitous Computing, Services and Applications

E-Commerce

Information Technology Management

E-Business Applications and Software

Critical Computing and Storage

Computational Intelligence

Distributed and Parallel Applications

Digital Management Products

Image Processing

Digital Enterprises

XML-Based Languages

Mobile Commerce

User Interfaces, Visualization and Modeling

e-Commerce Strategy & Implementation

E-Technologies

Digital Libraries

Data Mining

Miscellaneous Topics on Digital Enterprise and Information Systems

Combining Mediated and Identity-Based Cryptography for Securing E-Mail

Sufyan T. Faraj Al-Janabi and Hussein Khalid Abd-alrazzaq

College of Computer, University of Anbar,
Ramadi, Iraq
sufyantaih@ieee.org, hu_albasri@yahoo.co.uk

Abstract. This work aims to exploit a distinguished method of the public key cryptography which is known as Identity-Based Cryptography (IBC) to solve the usability problem of secure e-mail systems. The public key is taken from general information (such as e-mail address) of the recipient and thus does not require access to any certificate to validate the key. To increase the system strength, the identity-based cryptography is combined with mediated cryptography to enable the cancelation of any key that is being exposed or suspicious. In addition, all the operations of decryption and signature are controlled (without the ability to fraud or detect secret) by the authorized person to prevent hackers and non-authorized parties from using or manipulating of the system. This proposal includes the deployment of the combined method for Mediated Identity-Based Cryptography.

Keywords: e-mail security, identity-based cryptography, mediated RSA, public-key infrastructure.

1 Introduction

Email is one of the essential applications of the Internet. More than a hundred million electronic messages traverse the world's computer networks every day, most of this electronic mail is vulnerable. Securing email has always been an important issue and a subject of growing concern for the researchers and the users, where the volume of email grows continuously. Various standards and products have been created. Securing E-mails with encryption is introduced broadly by many experts, and they are successful in security matters. Several algorithms are designed for encryption and decryption. But intruders or hackers are still trying to find solutions in order to break these algorithms and retrieve the plaintext. For this reason, it is always desirable to find better ways to raise the security level for email and eliminate the increased risk of hackers.

Most of available secure e-mailing systems relies on public key cryptography for key management and signature issues. However, most people continuously fail in protecting themselves, despite the long time that has passed on the availability of systems that based on public-key infrastructure (PKI). The main reason for this is that PKI is just too difficult for the average user. A well-known difficulty with the use of public key cryptographic systems is the verification and distribution of the public

E. Ariwa and E. El-Qawasmeh (Eds.): DEIS 2011, CCIS 194, pp. 1–15, 2011.

keys. Therefore; it requires a tremendous overhead in terms of setting up a public key. A relatively new trend of research in this direction is to use Identity-Based Cryptography (IBC) in securing e-mail systems so that to make them easier for use by users. IBC facilitates easy introduction of public key cryptography by allowing an entity's public key to be derived from an arbitrary identification value, such as email address. Thus, it greatly reduces the need for public key certificates. However, IBC techniques are not compatible with popular public key encryption algorithms. On the other hand, mediated cryptography or mediated RSA (mRSA) achieves simple splitting of RSA private key between the user and a Security Mediator allowing fine-grained control of users' security privileges. However, mediate cryptography relies on public key certificates to manage public keys. In this paper, we present an interesting combination of IBC and mediated cryptography for securing e-mail systems. In addition, a secure e-mail system based on this hybrid security technique has been developed and tested.

The remaining of this paper is organized as follows: Section 2 contains some background of public key cryptography. Section 3 presents theoretical background of IBC. Then, a general description of the proposed system is given in Section 4. The proposed hybrid security techniques is described in Section 5. Next, Section 6 outlines the operation of the system. Finally, the paper is concluded in Section 7.

2 Public Key Cryptography

Public key cryptography requires the receiver's public key. As a consequence, before sending any message, the sender should obtain this public key. Moreover, he should make sure that the public key he obtains is indeed the correct one. This introduces two important steps in real life implementation, fetching the public key and verifying it. It may seem that the second step is the difficult one. However, there is a simple solution that allows one to verify a public key is public-key certificates. At the most basic level, a public-key certificate is simply a message that asserts: "The public key of user Bob is upk_B", to make sure that the certificate is genuine. It needs to be signed [1].

To use a public key that is contained in a digital certificate, a user queries the public repository where the certificate can be found and retrieves the certificate. Because a public key may be valid for quite a while, it is often necessary to check such a public key for validity before using it. A much more difficult problem when using such certificates is the management of trust. This is related to what guarantee can be given to trust the owner of the verification key [2].

2.1 Public Key Infrastructure

The Public Key Infrastructure provides the digital certificates that can identify the individual's identity. The digital certificate is used to offer level of security that means each person must present the digital certificate which contains the public key to check from the identity. PKI is the combination of hardware, software, encryption technology, people, and policies. The PKI consist of many parts, which are [2, 3]:

- *Certification Authority (CA):* CA is to oversee the generation, distribution, renewal, revocation and suspension of the digital certificates.

- *Register Authority (RA):* RA is accredited that it must be trustworthy, it is responsible for assurance all procedures executed is corresponded within the followed policy and all requirements of issuance and verifies are provided accordant for local policy.
- *Certificate Revocation Lists (CRLs):* A CRL is a time stamped list identifying revoked certificates which is signed by a CA.
- *Certificate Repositories:* It is a system or distributed systems that stores certificates and CRLs and serves as a means of distributing these certificates and CRLs to end-entities.

2.2 Security-Mediated Cryptography

Security-mediated cryptography is an approach for fast certification revocation centered about the concept of an on-line semi-trusted mediator (SEM) [4]. It is used to help the client in completing sign and decrypt message where the client must first obtain message-specific token from SEM. Without this token the client cannot use his/her private key. The security mediated approach has many advantages such that, the full operation cannot accomplish without acceptance of SEM. Thus, it reduces or eliminates need to certification revocation The SEM uses to immediate revocation of user's ability to sign or decrypt the message. The SEM itself not gain any useful information because it is only able partially to decrypt or sign the message. The main idea behind mRSA is the splitting of an RSA private key into two parts as in threshold RSA, one of the two is given to user and other given to SEM, no one can use knowledge half-key (its own part) to derive another half [4, 5].

3 Identity-Based Cryptography (IBC)

In 1985, Shamir introduced the concept of identity (ID) based cryptosystems that may offer a nice solution to some important practical security problems. This concept is used to eliminate the complexity of using digital certificates. In, identity-based cryptography (IBC), the public key of a user can be derived from public information that uniquely identifies the user. It allows a party to encrypt a message using the recipient's identity as a public key. and the corresponding private key is generated by a trusted third party called the *Private Key Generator* (PKG). ID based cryptosystems are advantageous over the traditional public key cryptosystems (PKC) as they avoid the need of certified public key register [6, 1]. In 2001, Boneh and Franklin gave a practical Identity-Based Encryption scheme that relies on the bilinear Diffie-Hellman problem for its security. It uses a complicated mathematical transformation called the Tate pairing [7, 8].

This can be described as follows: Let G_1 be a cyclic group generated by P, whose order is a prime q, and G_2 be a cyclic multiplicative group of the same order. The discrete logarithm problems in both G_1 and G_2 are hard. Then e: $G_1 \times G_1 \rightarrow G_2$ is a pairing which satisfies the following properties [9, 10]:

1. Bilinear: $e\,(P_1 + P_2, Q) \;=\; e\,(P_1, Q)\; e\,(P_2, Q)$
2. Bilinearity: $e(aP, bQ) = e(P, Q)^{ab}$ for all $P, Q \in G_1$ and $a, b \in Z_q^*$.

3. Non-degeneracy: *If* $P \in E[n] \backslash O$, then there exists $Q \in E[n]$ such that $e(P,Q) \neq 1$. If $e(P,Q) = 1$ for all $Q \in E[n]$ then $P=O$ and also that if $e(P,Q) = 1$ for all $Q \in E[n]$ then $P = O$.
4. Computability: There is an efficient algorithm to compute $e(P,Q)$ for all $P, Q \in G_1$.

3.1 Some of Computational Problems

Some computational problems have the property that they are of suitable hardness to be used to create public-key algorithms that get their cryptographic strength from the difficulty of the hard problem. The following are some computational problems which depend on Diffie-Hellman problem:

The Decision Diffie-Hellman Problem. The decision Diffie-Hellman problem (DDHP) was invented in 1998 by Boneh which is related to the discrete log assumption, where is: given g, g^a, g^b, and x, determine whether or not $x = g^{ab}$. One obvious way to solve this problem is to determine b solving the CDHP[1] and then to calculate $(g^a)^b = g^{ab}$, and then compare this value of g^{ab} to the given value of x [1].

Definition. Let G be a group and $g \in G$. The Decision Diffie-Hellman problem (DDH) is given a quadruple $(g, g^a, g^b, g^{ab}) = (g, g^a, g^b, g^c)$ of elements in $\langle g \rangle$ to determine whether or not $g^c = g^{ab}$ [11].

The decisional Diffie–Hellman (DDH) is a computational hardness assumption about a certain problem involving discrete logarithms in cyclic groups. It is used as the basis to prove the security of many cryptographic protocols, such as Cramer–Shoup cryptosystems.

The Bilinear Diffie-Hellman Problem. The bilinear Diffie-Hellman problem (BDHP) generalizes the CDHP to groups with a pairing. Where, Let $\mathbb{G}_1$, $\mathbb{G}_2$ be two groups of prime order q. Let $\hat{e} : \mathbb{G}_1 \times \mathbb{G}_1 \rightarrow \mathbb{G}_2$ be a bilinear map and let P be a generator of $\mathbb{G}_1$. The BDH as follows: Given (P, aP, bP, cP) for some $a, b, c \in \mathbb{Z}_q^*$ compute $\hat{e}(P,P)^{abc} \in \mathbb{G}_2$.The BDHP is no more difficult than calculating discrete logarithms. BDHP can be solved if we can calculate the discrete logarithm of cP in $\mathbb{G}_1$ to find value of c or if we can find it by calculating the discrete logarithm of $\hat{e}(P,cP) = \hat{e}(P,P)^c$ in $\mathbb{G}_2$, then we can calculate $\hat{e}(aP,bP)^c = (\hat{e}(P,P)^{ab})^c = \hat{e}(P,P)^{abc}$. In other side, the $f_P : \mathbb{G}_1 \rightarrow \mathbb{G}_2$ is defined by $f_P(Q) = \hat{e}(P,Q)$ which is an isomorphism of groups, If any one of these isomorphisms turns out to be invertible then BDH is easy that is we can easily calculate, $f_P^{-1}(\hat{e}(P,Q)) = Q$ [7, 1].

---

[1] Sometimes the Diffie-Hellman Problem (DHP) is called the computational Diffie–Hellman problem (CDHP) to more clearly distinguish it from the DDHP.

The Decision Bilinear Diffie-Hellman Problem. The decision bilinear Diffie-Hellman problem (DBDHP) generalizes the DDHP. The DBDHP can be described as follows: Let $\mathbb{G}_1$, $\mathbb{G}_2$ be two groups of prime order q. Let $\hat{e} : \mathbb{G}_1 \times \mathbb{G}_1 \rightarrow \mathbb{G}_2$ be a bilinear map and let P be a generator of $\mathbb{G}_1$, the decisional bilinear Diffie–Hellman (BDH) problem is to determine, given g, $A = aP, B = bP, C = cP$ *and* $X = \hat{e}(P,P)^x$, determine whether or not $X = \hat{e}(g,g)^{abc}$ for hidden values of a, b, c and x [12].

3.2 The Fujisaki-Okamoto Transform

A technique, invented by Fujisaki and Okamoto in 1999 which is widely known to be able to generically transforms a public-key encryption algorithm with fairly weak properties into one which is secure against chosen ciphertext attacks. [13].

In particular, if we have $\mathcal{E}_{pk}(M,\sigma)$, where $\mathcal{E}_{pk}$ is a public-key encryption algorithm that encrypts the plaintext M using the random input σ and the public key pk. If $\mathcal{D}$ is the decryption function that corresponds to $\mathcal{E}_{pk}$, and let H_1 and H_2 are cryptographic hash functions. The encryption algorithm $\mathcal{E}'_{pk}$ that is resistant to chosen-ciphertext attacks is:

$$\mathcal{E}_{pk}(M,\sigma) = (\mathcal{E}_{pk}(\sigma, H_1(c,M)) . H_2(\sigma) \oplus M) = (C_1, C_2) = C$$

where

$$C_1 = \mathcal{E}_{pk}(\sigma, H_1(\sigma, M))$$
$$C_2 = H_2(\sigma) \oplus$$

The decryption is:

1. Calculate $\mathcal{D}_{pr}(C_1) = \sigma$.
2. Calculate $H_2(\sigma) \oplus C_2 = M$.
3. Set $r = H_1(\sigma, M)$ and check that $\mathcal{E}_{pk}(\sigma, r) = C_1$

This transformation can be used to create a more secure scheme from a less secure algorithm [14, 1].

3.3 Formal Definition Identity-Based Cryptography

Formally, an IBC protocol is a family of algorithms, usually consisting of four algorithms. An identity-based encryption (IBE) scheme consists of: Setup, Private key Extraction (Generation), Encryption, Decryption. An IBE scheme can be described using the following steps [15]:

- *Setup:* This algorithm is run by the key generation center, which generates the common system parameters together with the master secret key, (*msk*). The system parameters include a description of the message space M, the ciphertext space C and the identity space I and the master public key (*mpk*). They are publicly known while the master secret key is known only to the private key generator (PKG).

- *Key Extraction (Derivation):* This algorithm is run by the key generation center on behalf of a user that requests his own private key, after checking that the user matches his claimed identity, then takes as input an identity $id \in$ I together with the system parameters and the master secret key (*msk*) and returns a private key of the user (*usk*), using the master secret key. The identity *id* is used as the public key while (*usk*) is the corresponding private key.
- *Encryption:* This algorithm takes as input an identity $id \in$ I and a message $M \in$ M and produces a ciphertext $C \in$ C encrypted under the public key *id* using the master public key (*mpk*).
- *Decryption:* This is a deterministic algorithm which takes as input a ciphertext $C \in$ C, the private key (*usk*) of the corresponding identity *id* and the system parameters. It returns the message *M*.
- If use identity-based signature (IBS) scheme then replace the Encryption and Decryption with Sign and Verify:
- *Sign:* Using its private key *usk*, sender creates a signature σ on the message *M*.
- *Verify:* Having obtained the signature σ and the message *M* from sender, the verifier checks whether σ is a genuine signature on *M* using sender's identity and the PKG's public key. If it is so, he returns "*Accept*". Otherwise, he returns "*Reject*".

4 Description of the Proposed System

The basic idea in this proposed system is to replace the traditional public key cryptography with IBC and combine it with mediated cryptography technique to build secure email system. The proposed design goals of this email security system are as follows:

1. To provide a secure and robust email system that can resist hacker attacks by using more enforced methods
2. To make the secure email system easier to user, and provide more usability and flexibility.
3. To reduce the need to certificates and use simple method to distributed key (by using IBC where use user's email address as public key), and provide immediate revocation of public key (by using the SEM).
4. To design a system that is more convenient for the establishments and organizations through enabling monitoring by administrators.

4.1 General Structure

The main part of the system has been designed as an email client that is used for secure messaging. Two methods have been used to provide the security, which are: IBC and mediated cryptography. Each one of them is composed of parts that work together to achieve the aims. By combining IBC and mediated cryptography, the hybrid system consists of three parts. The first part is used for generating private keys from public information (public key) and public parameters and it is called the Generation Center (GC). It has three functions: generating public parameters

(Parameters Generation Center or PGC), generating the private key from a public key which be often email address (Private Key Generation Center or PKGC), and dividing the private key into two parts and giving one for user and other for the SEM. The GC is considered the trusted authority where it knows all keys of users. Hence, any compromise of it will expose the system to destruction. The second part is SEM which completes decrypting/signing for user and it has the half of the user's private key. SEM takes all the halves of the users' private keys from PKGC and stores them in the database. The client is the third part of the designed system, which should download the parameters before requesting his private key from PKGC in order to use the system. Figure 1 illustrates the general structure of the system.

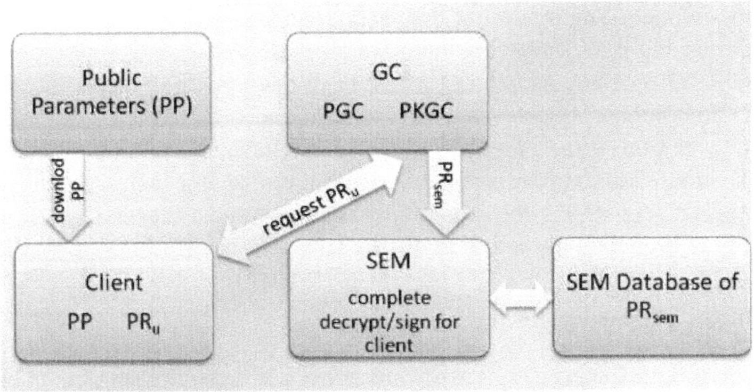

Fig. 1. General Structure of System

Since the private key in this method is generated by PKGC, therefore, the system must provide a way to distribute the private key. There are two options for implementation:

- Providing the key remotely, by sending request and receive respond include private key. In this exchange will use session key to protect the key.
- Providing the key directly (manually), that requires presence of the personal to take the key hand by hand.

When dealing with the large scale environment the first option is more appropriate to use in the proposed system. In this case the PKG will need session key. In addition, other cryptographic algorithms will be used to achieve the required security services, such as the AES cipher that is used as symmetric key algorithm.

4.2 Private Key Distribution

Delivering private key to user should be performed secretly. Keys distribution protocols are necessary to establish a secure channel, where there is a need to session key (secret key) to achieve that. This secret key is transferred with the use of PKGC's public key. The authentication process is accomplished by using the message digest algorithm. The user must send his/her email address as definition of identifies, this method does not guarantee the credibility, but guarantee the response will be send to this address. This method prevents the forgers from benefit impersonation of another user because they cannot arrive to email contents. The user should obtain the email address of PKGC to can send request. This process executes between user and PKGC, as in following steps (See Figure 2):

1- The user (email client) must first obtain the public system parameters to be able to generate the ciphertext of message request by IBE.
2- The user generates the session key which is used by a PKGC. Then the email client creates request that includes: user's email address, timestamp, session key and message digest of (email address, time stamp and session key). The message digest is added to detect any change in request (integrity). This request is encrypted with public key of PKGC by using IBE (PKGC's public key is the email address). The request is then sent. The session key should be kept secret in order to using it in decrypting the private key.
3- The PKGC receives the request message, it decrypts the request to extract session key, and computes the message digest for request to compare with message digest which was sent. If true, then the PKGC generates the user's private key depending on the email address that is appended in the message as corresponding public key. The PKGC constructs the responding message and encrypts it using the session key by using any symmetric algorithm (the AES is used in our implementation), and signs it by using PKGC's private key. After that it sends the result to user by using the email address.
4- After receiving the message from PKGC, the user decrypts it by the same session key to retrieve the private key, then user verifies the sign using the public key.

5 The Proposed Hybrid Cryptographic Technique

To apply IBC in secure email, we must use the signature with the encryption, but the problem is not all the schemes use the same method to generate the private key. This means that the private key almost in any scheme is not similar to that generated by other scheme. Consequently, the user needs two private keys, one for encryption and other for signature. For this reason, the schemes must be chosen carefully to be compatible with each other to have the same algorithms (setup, extract) which are used in GC. These hybrid techniques which combine between identity-based encryption (IBE), identity-based signature (IBS), and mediated cryptography can be the best choice to solve the problem of usability in secure email.

One of the most promising hybrid techniques is the one that combines between Boneh-Franklin Identity-based Encryption (BK-IBE) and Sakai-Ogishi-Kasahara Identity-Based Signature (SOK-IBS) with mediated cryptography. The BF scheme cannot be used for signature service; therefore, the SOK scheme is used to do this service. Both schemes depend on identity information as public key and both have similar algorithms for setup and extract. The required modification will be applied on extraction of the private key to be split into two parts. In signature algorithms, the sign algorithm will also be shared between user and SEM. This means that it will perform in two steps. Although the verification algorithm is required only by the recipient, it must be modified to be compatible with modified signature algorithm. Since the need to the private key will be only in decryption, the change in BF scheme will be only on the decryption algorithm without modifying on encryption algorithm.

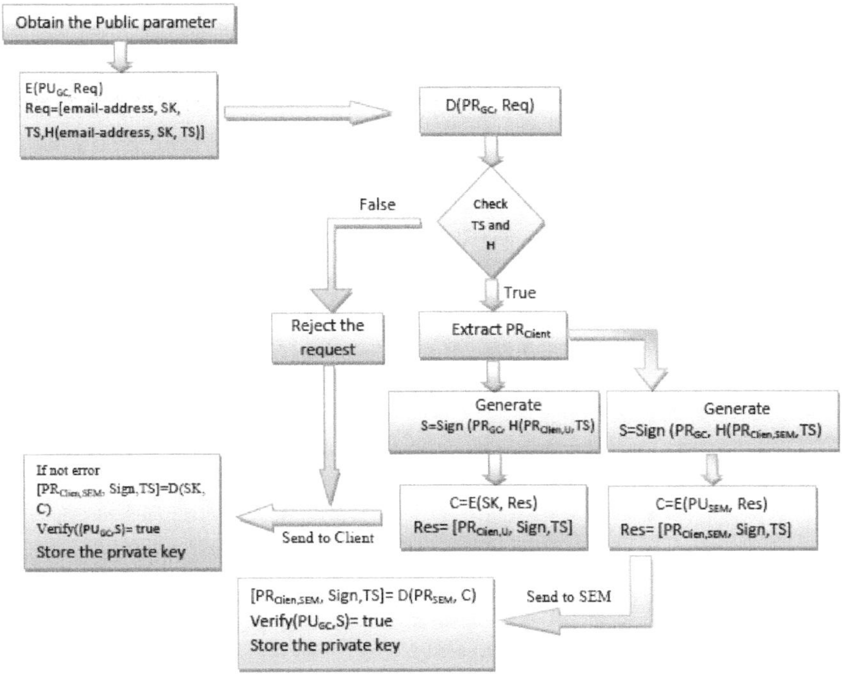

Fig. 2. Private Key Distribution

5.1 Mediated BF-IBE Scheme

This scheme consists of three parties: GC, SEM, and users. It also contains four algorithms: Setup, Extract, Encrypt and Decrypt. The GC governs the SEM and a SEM can serve many users. Two of the algorithms, Setup and Encrypt, are analogous to those in the original BF scheme. The others, Extract and Decrypt, provide the mediated cryptography capability. These four algorithms are described as follows:

- **Setup:** Let P be a generator of G. Pick a random $s \in \mathbb{Z}_p^*$ and set $P_{\text{pub}} = sP$. Choose cryptographic hash $H_1:\{0,1\}^* \rightarrow \mathbb{G}_1$, $H_2: \mathbb{G}_T \rightarrow \{0,1\}^n$, $H_3 : \{0,1\}^n \times \{0,1\}^n \rightarrow \mathbb{Z}_p^*$, $H_4 : \{0,1\}^n \times \{0,1\}^n \rightarrow \mathbb{Z}_p^*$, The master secret is s and the public parameters are the similar use in BF Full scheme, $(q, E/\mathbb{F}q, p, \mathbb{G}_1, \mathbb{G}_T, \hat{e}, n, P, P_{pub}, H_1, H_2, H_3, H_4)$.

- **Extract:** Given an identity ID, PKGC chooses a random number s_u from $\mathbb{Z}_p^*$, computes $Q_{id} = H_2(id)$, $D_{user} = s_u Q_{id}$ and $D_{sem} = (s - s_u)Q_{id}$. D_{user} is sent secretly to the user whose identity is ID as his private key and (D_{sem}, id) is sent to the SEM.

- **Encryption:** The sender encrypts the message M with id of recipient as public key as in the following step (similar original algorithm):

1) Calculate $Q_{id} = H_1(id)$.
2) Pick a random $\sigma \in \{0,1\}^n$.
3) Calculate $r = H_3(\sigma, M)$.
4) Calculate $C_1 = rP$.
5) Calculate $C_2 = \sigma \oplus H_2(\hat{e}(Q_{id}, P_{pub})^r)$.
6) Calculate $C_3 = M \oplus H_4(\sigma)$.

The Ciphertext is $C = (C_1, C_2, C_3)$.

- **Decryption:** To decrypt the message, the recipient must obtain agreement of SEM. This algorithm passes through two parties (user, SEM), after receiving the message the recipient sends some information to SEM in order to complete calculation the remaining half of decryption. As in the following steps:
  User:

  1) Pick a random number $x \in \mathbb{Z}_p^*$
  2) Calculate $D_1 = \hat{e}(D_{user}, rP)^x$
  3) Calculate $D_2 = x(rP)$

  The user sends (D_1, D_2) to SEM
  SEM:
  4) Calculate $D_3 = D_1\, \hat{e}(D_{sem}, D_2)$
  Return D_3 to user
  User:

  5) Calculate $K = (D_3)^{\frac{1}{x}}$
  6) Calculate $\sigma = C_2 \oplus H_2(k)$
  7) Calculate $M = C_3 \oplus H_4(\sigma)$.
  8) Calculate $r = H_3(\sigma, M)$.
  9) Calculate rP. If $C_1 \neq rP$ then reject the ciphertext as invalid.

5.2 Mediated SOK-IBS Scheme

This scheme is based on the SOK-IBS scheme. It also consists of three parties: GC, SEM, and users. In addition, it has four algorithms: Setup, Extract, Sign and Verify. Two of the algorithms, Setup and Extract, are analogous to those in Mediated BF-IBE scheme. The others, Verify and Sign, are different which provide the mediated signature's capability. They are described as follows:

- **Setup:** Let P be a generator of G. Pick a random $s \in \mathbb{Z}_p^*$ and set $P_{pub} = sP$. Choose cryptographic hash H_1: $\{0,1\}^* \rightarrow \mathbb{G}_1$, H_2: $\mathbb{G}_T \rightarrow \{0,1\}^n$, $H_3 : \{0,1\}^n \times \{0,1\}^n \rightarrow \mathbb{Z}_p^*$, $H_4 : \{0,1\}^n \times \{0,1\}^n \rightarrow \mathbb{Z}_p^*$. The master secret is s and the public parameters are the similar use in BF Full schema, $(q, E/\mathbb{F}q, P, \mathbb{G}_1, \mathbb{G}_T, \hat{e}, n, P, P_{pub}, H_1, H_2, H_3, H_4)$.

- **Extraction:** Given an identity *ID*, PKGC chooses a random number s_u from $\mathbb{Z}_p^*$, computes $Q_{id} = H_2(id)$, $D_{user} = s_u Q_{id}$ and $D_{sem} = (s - s_u)Q_{id}$. D_{user} is sent secretly to the user whose identity is *ID* as his private key and (D_{sem}, *id*) is sent to the SEM.

- **Signature:** To sign a message m, the user must cooperate with the SEM to do that, solely with help of the SEM, the user can generate a valid signature. Initialy the user must send information to SEM in order to enable complete signature message. As in the following steps:
  User:

  1) Calculate $SHA = H(M)$
  2) Choose random number u_1 and Calculate $U_1 = u_1 P$.

  The user sends (U_1, *SHA, id*) to SEM.
  SEM:
  3) Calculate $H = H_1(SHA)$
  4) Choose random number u_2 and Calculate $U_2 = u_2 P$.
  5) Calculate $U = U_1 + U_2$.
  6) Calculate $h = H_2(SHA, U, id)$.
  7) Calculate $S_{sem} = hD_{sem} + u_2(P_{pub} + H)$.

  Return (U, S_{sem}) to user
  User:
  8) Calculate $H = H_1(SHA)$
  9) Calculate $h = H_3(SHA, U, id)$.
  10) Calculate $S_{user} = hD_{user} + u_1(P_{pub} + H)$.
  11) Calculate $S = S_{sem} + S_{user}$.

  The Signature is $\sigma = (U, S)$.

- **Verification:** Given a signature $\sigma = (U, S)$. on message *M* under *ID*, a verifier performs the following:
  1) Calculates $SHA = H(M)$
  2) Calculates $H = H_1(SHA)$
  3) Calculates $Q_{id} = H_1(id)$
  4) Calculates $h = H_3(SHA, U, id)$.
  5) If $\hat{e}(P, S) = \hat{e}(P_{pub}, hQ_{id})\hat{e}(U, P_{pub} + H)$, then he/she accepts the signature.

6 System Operation and Implementation

In order to use the system, the SEM and all users must obtain the public parameters from GC. When any user (Alice) wants to send the message to another one (Bob), they must execute the following procedures (See also Figure 3):

1. Alice sends request to get her private key from PKGC.
2. Alice generates the message digest for the email message and signs it using her private key with help of SEM.
3. Alice generates session key (one-time key) as a key for a symmetric algorithm (AES).

4. Alice encrypts the email message by symmetric cryptography using session key.
5. Alice encrypts the session key using Bob's identity (email address) as a public key by Identity-Based Cryptography.
6. Alice sends a message that includes (encryption message, signature, and encryption session key).
7. Bob receives the message that he cannot decrypt without his private key; therefore, he sends request to get his private key.
8. Bob decrypts the session key using his private key with help the SEM.
9. Bob decrypts the message using the session key by the same symmetric algorithm (AES).
10. Bob verifies the signature using Alice's public key and generates message digest for email message to compare with that sent.

In the next messages of the session, Alice and Bob continue sending and receiving the messages without a need to contact with GC. This means that the same procedure is used but without steps 1 and 7.

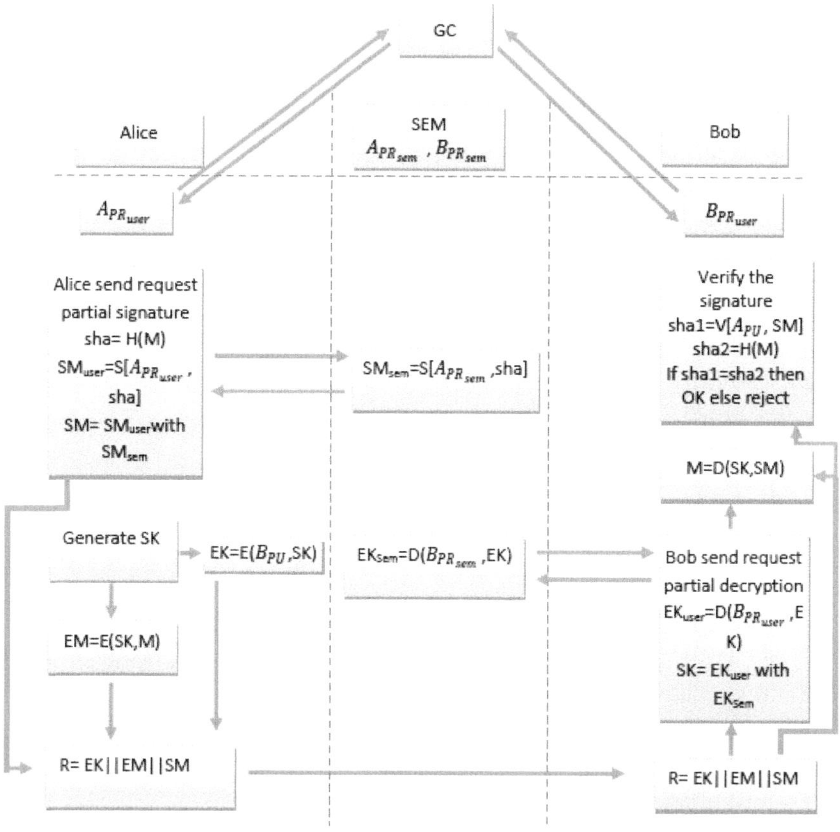

Fig. 3. Procedures of System Operations

The system was implemented using Visual C# programming language. This language gives to programmer the flexibility to build large systems efficiently. The system uses the standard SMTP and POP3 internet protocols to send and receive emails through the email server. Anyone must have an access to an email server that supports SMTP and POP3 to use the system by creating a user account and mailbox on the server. Using the email account, together with developed secure-email software, a user can send and receive messages securely over the internet. The developed software can get email messages, store them for future reference, show them to user, let him/her organize them, and let him/her write and send own messages.

The architectural parts needed to implement this application are: SMTP, POP3, GC, SEM, and Client with suitable Graphical User Interface (GUI). The GUI must be used to provide a secure and simple means of messaging via email. These messages are received and sent using ordinary email methods (SMTP and POP3) but with adding the required security services. Each part of the developed system has its own interface to enable users or administrators to prepare the setting correctly. Figure 4 illustrates the application main window. It contains the basic options to manage the email (inbox, sent, draft) and also to display the message. When the received message is encrypted, it must be decrypted before reading. The decryption is performed directly after requesting to show the message. A flag has been added before sending to indicate whether the message is encryption or not. Figure 5 shows the window used to compose and send new messages and attachments. This window has the option of cryptography which enable users to choose methods and enter private and session keys to perform encryption and signatures.

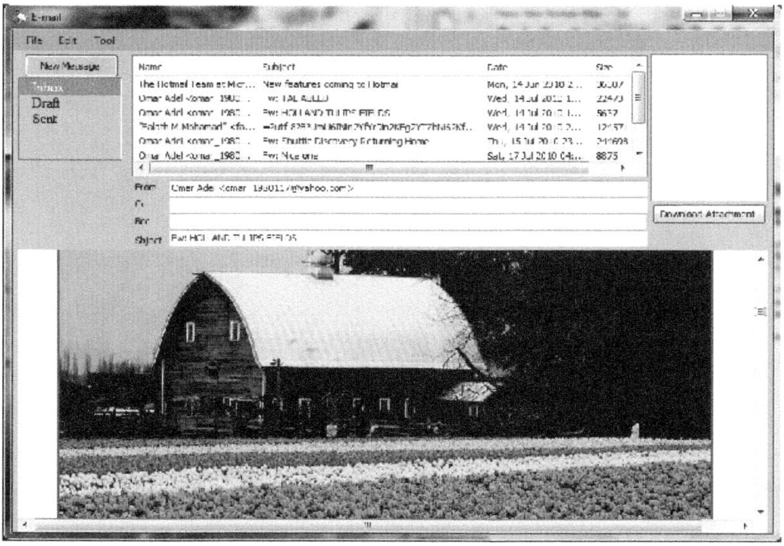

Fig. 4. Main Window of the Application

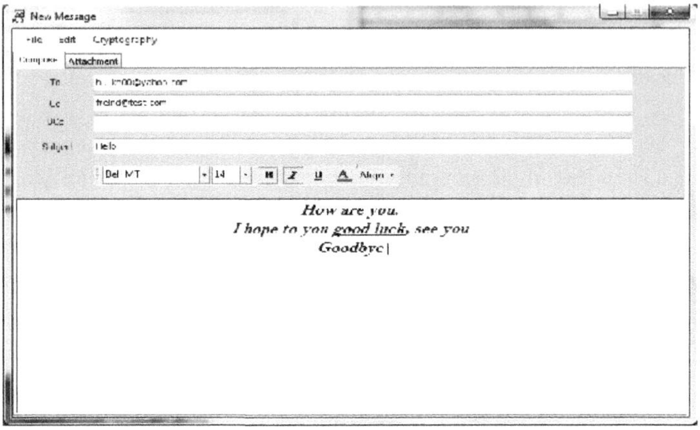

Fig. 5. The Window to Compose New Message

7 Conclusions

The developed hybrid secure email system has very good characteristics. Using Mediated cryptography has given a choice of keeping users under control to prevent any unauthorized person from using the system. This could be very useful for organizations. The hybrid cryptographic scheme used has shown to be of higher speed and more efficiency compared with mRSA. Indeed, the proposed system does not need to use key rings for public keys of users (as in PGP) because the public key is the e-mail address of the user.

References

1. Martin, L.: Introduction to Identity-Based Encryption. Artech House Inc., Boston (2008)
2. Kuhn, D., Hu, V., Polk, W., Chang, S.: Introduction to Public Key Technology and the Federal PKI Infrastructure. National Institute of Standards and Technology (NIST). U.S. Government Publication (2001)
3. Vacca, J.R.: Public Key Infrastructure: Building Trusted Applications and Web Services. Auerbach Pub. (2004)
4. Boneh, D., Ding, X., Tsudik, G., Wong, C.: A Method for Fast Revocation of Public Key Certificates and Security Capabilities. In: SSYM 2001 Proceedings of the 10th Conference on USENIX Security Symposium, vol. 10. USENIX Association, CA (2001)
5. Koga, S., Imamoto, K., Sakurai, K.: Enhancing Security of Security-Mediated PKI by One-time ID. Kyushu University. In: 4th Annual PKI R&D Workshop, pp. 176–189 (2005)
6. Guan, Z., Cao, Z., Zhao, X., Chen, R., Chen, Z., Nan, X.: WebIBC: Identity Based Cryptography for Client Side Security in Web Applications. School of Electronics Engineering and Computer Science, Peking University (2008)
7. Boneh, D., Franklin, M.: Identity-Based Encryption from the Weil Pairing. In: Blakely, G.R., Chaum, D. (eds.) CRYPTO 1984. LNCS, vol. 196, pp. 47–53. Springer, Heidelberg (1985)

8. Martin, L.: Identity-Based Encryption: A Closer Look. The ISSA J. (September 2005)
9. Agarwal, A., Shrimali, V., Das, M.: GSM Security Using Identity-based Cryptography. Institute of Information and Communication Technology, India (2009)
10. Yong, Y., Yang, B., Sun, Y.: ID-Based Threshold Signature and Mediated Signature Schemes. IEEE Computer Society, Los Alamitos (2007)
11. Galbraith, S.: Mathematics of Public Key Cryptography. University of Copenhagen, Denmark, Version 0.6
12. Abdalla, M., Kiltz, E., Neven, G.: Generalised Key Delegation for Hierarchical Identity-Based Encryption. IET Information Security (July 2008)
13. Fujiski, E., Okamoto, T.: Secure Integration of Asymmetric and Symmetric Encryption Schemes. In: 19th Annual International Cryptography Conference, California, USA (1999)
14. Yang, P., Kitagawa, T., Hanaoka, G., Zhang, R., Matsuura, K., Imai, H.: Apply Fujiaski-Okamoto to Identity-Based Encryption. In: 16th International Symposium (AAECC-16) Algebraic Algorithms and Error-Correcting Codes, Las Vegas, USA (2006)
15. Joye, M., Neven, G.: Identity-Based Cryptography. IOS Press, Amsterdam (2009)

Privacy-Enhanced Deniable Authentication E-Mail Service

JuHee Ki[1], Jung Yeong Hwang[2], DaeHun Nyang[3], Dong Hoon Lee[4], and Jongin Lim[4]

[1] Information Security PD Team, KEIT, Daejeon, Korea
eye@keit.re.kr
[2] Knowledge-based Information Security Department, ETRI, Daejeon, Korea
videmot@etri.re.kr
[3] Information Security Research Laboratory, Inha University, Incheon, Korea
nyang@inha.ac.kr
[4] CIST, Korea University, Seoul, Korea
{donghlee,jilim}@korea.ac.kr

Abstract. E-mail brings us lots of conveniences. Especially with help of PGP and S/MIME, it gives both confidentiality and message/origin authentication. However, in some cases for strong privacy, a message sender will not want to let others know even the fact that he sent a message to a recipient. Very recently, Harn and Ren proposed a fully deniable authentication scheme for E-mail where a sender can repudiate his or her signature. In this paper, however, their deniable authentication scheme is proved not to be fully deniable. To resolve this deniability problem, we suggest a designated verifier signature scheme to support strong privacy, and construct a privacy-enhanced deniable authentication E-mail scheme using the designated verifier signature scheme. Compared with the Harn and Ren's scheme, the proposed scheme has a simple cryptographic structure and can be easily realized with the existing secure E-mail systems.

Keywords: E-mail, authentication, Deniable Authentication, Strong Designated Verifier Signature, Anonymity.

1 Introduction

Nowadays E-mail systems have been widely used as one of the most convenient communication tools. E-mail systems enable us to perform a variety of transactions with rapidity in the delivery of messages. However, a simple use of E-mail service exposes users to serious security risks. Basically, E-mail systems should guarantee user authentication and message confidentiality. In addition, they should provide users with sufficient privacy in performing business transactions over the public internet. In some cases, a sender does not want to let others know even the fact that a message was sent from the sender to a recipient in an authenticated way. Security-enhanced E-mail systems such as S/MIME [1]

E. Ariwa and E. El-Qawasmeh (Eds.): DEIS 2011, CCIS 194, pp. 16–29, 2011.

and PGP [2] using cryptographic mechanisms provide confidentiality and origin/data authenticity but not the sender's deniability property for a message [3].

In the cryptography society, to guarantee a signer's deniability, a notion of the designated verifier signature (DVS) has been introduced [4]. Even when the verifier reveals his or her verifying key, he/she cannot convince others to believe the origination of the signature, i.e., the signature was generated by a signer in the DVS setting. For improving the versatility of a DVS, a "strong" version of DVS (sDVS) was introduced [5]. Under the strong DVS, the deniability of the basic DVS is still maintained but the public verifiability on a DVS is not permitted any more. Instead, only a specific verifier designated by a signer can check the validity of a signature using the private key which is known only to the designated verifier.

Recently, without the help of the DVS, Harn and Ren proposed an interesting construction of a deniable authentication (DA) E-mail scheme [3] using a novel technique with the existential forgeability of a signature.

1.1 Our Contributions

In this paper, we try to prove that Harn and Ren's DA scheme has vulnerability in terms of deniability, that is, the transcripts generated by an E-mail sender is reasonably distinguishable from those generated by a receiver assuming the chosen cipher text attacks (CCA) [6], [7]. Since Harn and Ren's scheme uses a public-key encryption scheme as the underlying primitive, it is important to guarantee the security against CCA for the public-key encryption scheme. Because of various attack possibilities such as computer viruses, malicious software, misconfigurations of related systems, and lost/stolen portable devices, CCA may not be hard to assume [6], [7]. RSA-OAEP [8] is the best-known public key encryption scheme with the CCA-security. To cope with the attack, a CCA-secure public key encryption scheme is strongly recommended to be used. For example, However, with the CCA-secure encryption scheme, Harn and Ren's protocol is shown not to be deniable any more owing to the well-formness requirement of cipher texts.

In addition, we propose a robust deniable authentication scheme that works on the concept of a strong DVS. This scheme can be easily implemented on the existing E-mail systems. In principle, our scheme is simple but provides the perfect deniability and private verifiability in a strict sense. Nobody can distinguish a signature generated by a sender from one by a receiver even when the sender and the receiver's keys are revealed. Also, except a designated receiver, nobody is able to verify a given E-mail message. Furthermore, exposure of a sender's secret key does not compromise private verifiability which is only given to a designated verifier. A signature in our proposal is very short, and consists of one hash value and one group element. Also, the required operations are just exponentiation and multiplication, and cryptographic hashing. And thus, our signature scheme can be easily realized with the existing secure E-mail systems, for example PGP and S/MIME, which already have such cryptographic operations.

1.2 Related Works

Many efforts have been taken to provide the e-mail system with enhanced security services as well as the basic security services such as authenticity and confidentiality. Sun et al. constructed a secure E-mail protocol to achieve perfect forward secrecy [9]. Unfortunately, this protocol was found to have flaws [10]. Kim et al. suggested two improved protocols based on Sun et al.'s protocol [11], but Yoon et al. showed that one of their protocols are susceptible to two impersonation attacks [12]. Regarding the DA protocol, Deng et al. presented two DA protocols with the communication model of [13]. However, Zhu et al. showed that these protocols are vulnerable to the person-in-the-middle attack and modified the protocols. Also, very recently, Harn and Ren proposed a construction of deniable authentication (DA) scheme for e-mail system [3].

Meanwhile, the concept of DVS was introduced and constructed in [14] to provide deniable signature, and a number of DVS schemes have been studied [15-18]. A variety of cryptographic techniques based on RSA, discrete logarithm, or bilinear map parameters have been used for the construction of DVS schemes. A generic construction of DVS schemes using bilinear maps was proposed [16]. As noted in [19], the basic functionality of a DVS can be achieved by a ring signature with two ring members. However, the method is not sufficient for achieving stronger security properties for sDVS because the secret key of a verifier is not required to verify the authenticity of a signature. The sDVS scheme that Jakobsson et al. briefly discussed in [14] was formally defined in [20] and strengthened in [16]. An sDVS scheme does not permit public verifiability of a DVS. Instead, only a verifier designated by a signer can verify a signature on a message with his or her own secret key.

Various extensions of the standard DVS scheme such as an identity-based DVS and multi-designated verifier signature have been proposed [15], [17], [18], [21].

1.3 Organization

In Section 2 we briefly review the Harn-Len's DA scheme and show its vulnerability in terms of deniability. In Section 3 we explain a security model for a DVS scheme, and present our DVS scheme and prove it achieves three main security properties in the security model. In Section 4 we propose an efficient DA E-mail scheme using the proposed DVS scheme and present that the proposed DA E-mail scheme achieves the desired security properties. We compare our DA schemes with that of other DA schemes in terms of the performance in Section 5. We conclude in Section 6.

2 Vulnerability of the Harn-Ren DA E-Mail Scheme

We briefly review the Harn and Ren's DA E-mail scheme [3] and point out vulnerability in this scheme. In the following description, we use "||" to represent the message concatenation. The Harn-Ren DA scheme is described as follows:

This scheme has two participants, sender Alice and receiver Bob. The scheme makes use of a signature scheme for the sender and a public-key encryption scheme for the receiver. Assume that (x_A, vk_A) is the key pair of Alice, which is used for signing, and (x_B, pk_B) is the key pair of Bob, for the message encryption. In order to transmit an E-mail message m, Alice and Bob proceed as follows:

(1) Alice picks a one-time secret key k uniformly at random, and computes $c = pE_{pk_B}(k)$ using the Bob's public key pk_B. She also generates a signature $\sigma = sign_{x_A}(c)$ by her private key x_A, and computes $H_k(m//T)$ which is the one-way hash value by a keyed hash function H. Alice sends $\{\sigma, c, H_k(m//T), m, T\}$ to Bob.

(2) After receiving the message $\{\sigma, c, h{=}H_k(m//T), m, T\}$ sent by Alice, Bob checks if the received signature σ is a valid one on c using the public verification key vk_A. If the signature is valid then Bob decrypts the ciphertext c using his private key x_B, that is, recovers $k = pD_{x_B}(c)$. He then checks if the time-stamp T is valid. If T is valid then Bob computes $h'{=}H_k(m//T)$ and checks if $h' = h$. If the values are the same then the received e-mail message is authenticated.

As shown in [3], the deniability of the above scheme relies on an interesting property, existential unforgeability of the underlying signature scheme. To simulate a valid transmission message, a receiver first generates a signature on a random message using a publicly-known forgery algorithm and then decrypts the random message to compute a key k for the underlying hash function $H_k()$ using his decryption key.

However, it will be unreasonable to assume that the random message retains a correct format for a given specific public-key encryption algorithm. In order to show this vulnerability more concretely, we consider a simple example with the well-known RSA-OAEP public-key encryption scheme which is proven to be CCA-secure [8]. The CCA-security means that a ciphertext does not reveal any meaningful information of the plaintext, even to an adversary who can decrypt adaptively chosen ciphertexts except a challenge ciphertext, both before and after this challenge ciphertext is available [6], [7].

The RSA-OAEP public key scheme is described as follows: Let (n, e) and d be the Bob's public and private keys. The scheme uses two hash functions $G_1:\{0,1\}^{k_0}\rightarrow\{0,1\}^{k-k_0}$ and $G_2:\{0,1\}^{k-k_0}\rightarrow\{0,1\}^{k_0}$, where k, k_0, and k_1 are pre-defined parameters.

- **Encryption:** For a given message m, pick a random value $r\in\{0,1\}^{k_0}$ and then compute $s = (m/|0^{k_1})\oplus G_1(r)$ and $t = r\oplus G_2(s)$, and then return a ciphertext $c = (s||t)^e$.

- **Decryption:** For a given a ciphertext c, compute $c^d = (s||t)^{ed} = s||t$. Parse this as $s = (m/|0^{k_1})\oplus G_1(r)$ and $t = r\oplus G_2(s)$. Compute $r = t\oplus G_2(s)$ and $M = s\oplus G_1(r)$. If the k_1 least significant bits of M is 0^{k_1} then return m from M. Otherwise, return NULL. Here, $\oplus$ be the bitwise eXclusive OR operation.

Note that the decryption algorithm of the RSA-OAEP scheme confirms the well-formness of a ciphertext by checking the existence of 0^{k_1} before recovering a plaintext. As mentioned previously, a ciphertext computed from the Harn-Ren simulation method is simply a random message. It will be hard to expect the existence of 0^{k_1} in the random message. Since the CCA-security model assumes that an adversary can access the decryption oracle, if this ciphertext is queried to a decryption oracle then an adversary can easily check that the ciphertext is generated from the simulation method executed by a designated verifier, not a signer. This shows that the deniability of the Harn-Ren DA scheme cannot be guaranteed when combined with a CCA encryption scheme.

Since public key encryption schemes are required to achieve the CCA-security for confidentiality [6], [7], [22], the Harn-Ren DA scheme may not be sufficient for a practical deployment.

3 Our Primitive for a DA E-Mail Scheme

We formally review and present a DVS scheme which is used as a basic primitive for our DA E-mail protocol.

3.1 Security Notion for a DVS Scheme

A DVS scheme consists of KeyGen for generating keys, Sign for signing a message, and Vrfy for verifying a signature. Here, KeyGen and Sign are probabilistic polynomial-time (PPT) algorithms and Vrfy is a deterministic polynomial-time algorithm.

- **KeyGen** takes as input a security parameter κ and outputs a pair of public and private keys for a user U, i.e., (sk_U, pk_U).
- **Sign** takes as inputs a private signing key sk_S and the public key of a designated verifier pk_V, and a message m, and then outputs a signature σ. This is denoted by $\sigma \leftarrow$ **Sign**(sk_S, pk_V, m).
- **Vrfy** takes as input a signature σ, a message m and a signer's public key pk_S and a designated verifier's secret key sk_V, and then outputs 1 (valid) or 0 (invalid). This is denoted by $b \leftarrow$ **Vrfy**(σ, m, pk_S, sk_V).

We consider three secuirty properties, unforgeability and non-transferability, and strong-anonymity for a DVS scheme. As noted in the literature [23], unforgeability and non-transferability are corresponding to 'unforgeabiltiy' and 'anonymity' for a ring signature with a ring of two members, respectively.

Unforgeability. This notion means that any party who cannot access private keys of a signer and a designated verifier cannot generate a signature of which the designated verifier can check the validity of the signature. Next, we formally define this notion.

A DVS scheme $\sum$ is said *existentially unforgeable* under chosen message attacks (EUF-CMA) if no PPT adversary F has a non-negligible advantage in the following game:

For a security parameter κ, a challenger C runs **SetUp** to generate pairs of private and public keys for each user. An adversary F gets all the public keys. The adversary F is allowed to access to the following **Sign** and **Vrfy** oracles to make queries adaptively. Here, "adaptively" means that the adversary can make a query reflecting the answers of oracle queries.

- **Corrupt**. On a query $<pk_U>$, return the corresponding secret key sk_U.
- **Sign**. On a query $<(pk_S, pk_V), m>$, return $\sigma \leftarrow$ **Sign**(sk_S, pk_V, m).
- **Vrfy**. On a query $< \sigma, (pk_S, pk_V), m >$, return $b \leftarrow$ **Vrfy**(σ, m, pk_S, sk_V).

Finally, F outputs $((pk_S, pk_V), m', \sigma')$. Assume that σ' on $((pk_S, pk_V), m')$ is valid, i.e., $1 \leftarrow$ **Vrfy**$(\sigma', m', pk_S, sk_V)$.

F succeeds in the above game if the following two conditions hold: (1) Any of pk_S and pk_V has not been queried to **Corrupt** oracle. (2) The tuple (pk_S, pk_V, m') is not the same as any of the tuples queried to **Sign** oracle. The event of the success is denoted by Suc_{Forg}. The EUF-CMA advantage of F for $\sum$ is defined by $\mathbf{Adv}_{F,\sum}^{\text{EUF-CMA}}(k) = \Pr[\text{Suc}_{\text{Forg}}]$.

Non-Transferability. Intuitively, *non-transferability* captures that any party except a signer and a designated verifier cannot identify the real generator of a DVS. A DVS scheme $\sum$ is said *non-transferable* if no PPT adversary has a non-negligible advantage to distinguish the distribution of signatures generated from real executions of the scheme and those from the simulation algorithm **Sim** where **Sim** takes as inputs a designated verifier's secret key, a signer's public key and a message, and then outputs a signature. More specifically, we consider the following game between a challenger C and an adversary F: For a security parameter κ, the challenger C runs **SetUp** to generate pairs of private and public keys for users. The adversary F gets all the public keys. This adversary is given access to the following oracles to make queries adaptively. Here, "adaptively" means that the adversary can make a query reflecting the answers of oracle queries.

- **Corrupt**. On a query $<pk_U>$, return the corresponding secret key sk_U.
- **Sign**. On a query $<(pk_S, pk_V), m>$, return $\sigma' \leftarrow$ **Sign**(sk_S, pk_V, m).
- **Vrfy**. On a query $< \sigma, (pk_S, pk_V), m >$, return $b \leftarrow$ **Vrfy**(σ, m, pk_S, sk_V).

When F submits $((pk_S, pk_V), m)$ as a challenge, the challenger C picks a bit $b \in \{0,1\}$ uniformly at random. If $b = 0$ then return $\sigma \leftarrow$ **Sign**(sk_S, pk_V, m) and, otherwise, $\sigma \leftarrow$ **Sim**$((pk_S, sk_V), m)$. The signature σ is given to the adversary F. Finally, F outputs a guess bit b'.

F succeeds in the above game if $b = b'$. We note that F can get secret keys for the challenge public keys pk_S and pk_V. The event of the success is denoted by Suc_{NT}. The advantage of F for $\sum$ is defined by $\mathbf{Adv}_{F,\sum}^{\text{NT}}(k) = |\Pr[\text{Suc}_{\text{NT}}]-1/2|$. Alternatively, the above notion can be defined by using the "anonymity" for a ring signature with a ring of two members [23].

Strong-Anonymity. The notion of *signature privacy* means that the validity of a signature associated with a designated verifier must be confirmed only with the designated verifier's secret key, where the adversary does not have an access to the signing key. This notion is also known as *strongness* in the literature [15, 24]. In order to enhance the signature privacy, we introduce a stronger notion called *strong-anonymity* which allows an adversary to access even a signing key. In other words, strong-anonymity captures that the validity of a signature associated with a designated verifier should be confirmed only with the designated verifier's secret key, even when a signing key to be used to generate the signature is exposed in the future. As known in the literature, some DVS schemes achieve only signature privacy, not strong-anonymity. Next we formally define this notion.

For a security parameter κ, a challenger C runs **SetUp** to obtain pairs of private and public keys for users. An adversary F gets the public parameters. The adversary F is given access to the following oracles to make queries adaptively. Here, "adaptively" means that the adversary can make a query reflecting the answers of oracle queries.

- **Corrupt**. On a query $<pk_U>$, return the corresponding secret key sk_U.
- **Sign**. On a query $<(pk_S, pk_V), m>$, return $\sigma' \leftarrow$ **Sign**(sk_S, pk_V, m).
- **Vrfy**. On a query $<\sigma, (pk_S, pk_V), m>$, return $b \leftarrow$ **Vrfy**(σ, m, pk_S, sk_V).

When F submits $((pk_S, pk_V), m_0, m_1)$ as a challenge, the challenger C picks a bit $b \in \{0,1\}$ uniformly at random. Return $\sigma \leftarrow$ **Sign**(sk_S, pk_V, m_b) to the adversary F. We assume that F is already aware of the private signing key sk_S by querying pk_S to **Corrupt** oracle. Finally, F outputs a guess bit b'.

F succeeds in the above game if (1) $b = b'$ (2) pk_V has never been queried to **Corrupt** oracle, and (3) $(\sigma, (pk_S, pk_V), m)$ has never been queried to **Vrfy**. The event of the success is denoted by Suc_{SA}. The advantage of F for $\sum$ is defined by $\mathbf{Adv}_{F,\Sigma}^{SA}(k) = |\Pr[Suc_{SA}]-1/2|$.

3.2 Our DVS Scheme

We propose our DVS scheme as follows. Assume that p is a prime number, G is a mathematical group of order p and g is a random generator of G. Let $H_1 : \{0, 1\}^* \rightarrow Z^*_p$ and $H_2 : \{0, 1\}^* \rightarrow \{0, 1\}^l$ be cryptographic hash functions.

- **KeyGen.** On input a security parameter κ, it picks $x_U \in Z^*_p$ and computes $pk_U = g^{x_U}$ and then outputs $(sk_U = x_U, pk_U = g^{x_U})$ as a pair of public and private keys for a user U. The user may be a signer or a designated verifier.
- **Sign.** On inputs a private signing key $sk_S = x_S$ and a public of a designated verifier $pk_V = g^{x_V}$, and a message m, and picks $r \in Z^*_p$, and computes $W = g^r \in G$, $h = H_1(W//pk_S//pk_V)$, and $K_1 = (pk_V)^{x_S} = g^{x_V x_S}$, $K_2 = pk_V^{(x_s+hr)} = g^{x_V(x_s+hr)} \in G$, and $\tau = H_2(K_1//K_2//W//m)$. It then outputs a signature $\sigma = (W, \tau)$.
- **Vrfy.** On inputs a signature $\sigma = (W, \tau)$ and a a message m and a signer's public key pk_S and a designated verifier's secret key $sk_V = x_V$, it computes $h = H_1(W// pk_S//pk_V)$, $K_1' = g^{x_V x_S}$, and $K_2' = (W^h \cdot pk_S)^{x_V}$ and a hash value $\tau' = H_2(K_1'//K_2'//W//m)$. It then checks if $\tau' = \tau$. If the equaltiy holds then output 1 (valid), and otherwise, 0 (invalid).

It is easy to see that the DVS scheme constructed above is correct. We will prove that this scheme achieves three security properties, unforgeability and non-transferability, and strong-privacy in the security model in Section III. The CDH (Computation Diffie-Hellman) problem in G is defined as follows: Let G be a finite group whose order is prime p and g a random generator of G. For a given (g, g^a, g^b), the CDH problem is to compute $g^{ab} \in G$, where a and b are picked uniformly in Z^*_p. A DDH (Decision Diffie-Hellman) problem in G is defined as follows: Let G be a group whose order is prime p and g a random generator of G. The DDH problem is to decide, given a tuple of values $(\alpha = g^a, \beta = g^b, \gamma)$ for random $a,b \in_R Z^*_p$, whether γ is g^{ab} or not.

Theorem 1. *If the CDH problem is intractable in G then the above DVS scheme is existentially unforgeable in the random oracle model.*

Proof. We prove that we can construct an efficient CDH-solver S to a random CDH problem, (g, g^a, g^b) using a forger attacking our DVS scheme in the unforgeability game. First, S initializes the DVS scheme running **SetUp** and generating pairs of private and public keys for users. S guesses the public keys of a signer and a designated verifier that the forger will output for a final forgery. Denote these keys by $pk_S = g^a$ and $pk_V = g^b$. Even though the simulator S cannot learn the secret keys or exponents a and b corresponding to the public keys, we show that this simulator can correctly answer to oracle queries as follows.

For a **Sign** $<(pk_S, pk_V), m>$ query, the simulator outputs a random number σ which is selected from $\{0,1\}^l$ uniformly at random. Note that this simulation is correct because we consider the random (hash) oracle model and a signature is defined as a hash output in our scheme. For a **Corrupt** query $<pk_U>$, if $pk_U = pk_S$ or $pk_U = pk_V$ then the simulator aborts, and otherwise, returns the corresponding secret key sk_U. For a verification query, **Vrfy** $< \sigma=(W,\tau), (pk_S,pk_V), m >$, if $< (pk_S,pk_V), m >$ was queried to the **Sign** oracle and σ was returned as an answer to this query then the simulator outputs 1 (valid), and otherwise, 0 (invalid). On a hash oracle query, if the query has been issued then S finds the previous answer and returns it. Otherwise, S picks a random number and returns it.

When the forger outputs a final forgery, $\sigma = (W,\tau)$ on m for (pk_S,pk_V), the simulator proceeds as follows: The simulator finds out the pre-image $K_1//K_2//W//m$ to τ in the hash lists such that $\tau = H_2(K_1//K_2//W//m)$, and then outputs K_1 as a solution of the given CDH problem .

A signature is defined as a hash output in our scheme. Since we assume the use of a random hash function and the hash outputs are distributed uniformly at random as presented, we can assume that there is no meaningful relation among hash outputs and so signatures. The given simulation for hash outputs is perfect except negligible failures caused from natural collision. If the simulator is able to guess the target public keys correctly then an abortion of the presented simulation does not occur. The probability of this correct guess is $1/q(q\text{-}1)$ where q is the number of total public keys generated for users. Note that q is upper-bounded by a polynomial in the security parameter. Hence, the solver can solve the CDH problem with the advantage of a forger attacking our DVS scheme. □

Theorem 2. *The above DVS scheme is non-transferable.*

Proof. We show that we can construct a simulator **Sim** such that no PPT adversary has a non-negligible advantage in distinguishing the distribution of signatures generated from real executions of the constructed DVS scheme with a signing key and that from the simulator **Sim** with a designated verifier's secret key. Define **Sim** by $(W, \tau) \leftarrow$ **Sim**(pk_S, sk_V, m), where for a message $m \in \{0,1\}^*$, $r \leftarrow_R Z^*_p$, $W \leftarrow g^r$, $K_1 = (pk_S)^{x_V}$, $K_2 = (pk_S\ W^h)^{x_V}$, and $\tau \leftarrow H(K_1//K_2//W//m)$. Since $K_1 = (pk_S)^{x_V} = g^{x_V x_S} = (pk_V)^{x_S}$ and $K_2 = (pk_S W^h)^{x_V} = g^{x_V x_S} g^{x_S\ rh} = pk_V^{(x_S+hr)}$, the distribution of (W, τ) is identical in the **Sim** and **Sign** algorithms.

Theorem 3. *If the DDH assumption holds in G then the above DVS scheme achieves the strong-anonymity in the random oracle model.*

Proof. We prove that we can construct an efficient DDH-solver ***S*** using an adversary ***F*** attacking the strong-anonymity of our DVS scheme. Assume that a random DDH problem, (g, g^a, g^b, T) in the group G is given. The goal of ***S*** is to guess whether $T = g^{ab}$ or not.

To simulate the attack environment for the strong-anonymity game, ***S*** initializes the DVS scheme running **SetUp** and generating pairs of private and public keys for users. ***S*** guesses the public key of a designated verifier that the forger will output as a final forgery. Set this key by $pk_V = g^b$. All public keys are given to the adversary ***F***. In addition, by the definition of the strong-anonymity game, all signers' private keys except a designated verifier's private key are given to the adversary. Next, even though ***S*** cannot learn the secret key, i.e., b corresponding to the designated verifier's public key $pk_V = g^b$, we show that ***S*** can correctly answer to oracle queries as follows. Assume that, for consistency, ***S*** manages lists and respond with answers using the lists.

- For a **Sign** $<(pk_S, pk_V), m>$ query, the simulator outputs a random number σ which is selected from $\{0,1\}^l$ uniformly at random. Note that this simulation is correct because we consider the random (hash) oracle model and a signature is defined as a hash output in our scheme.
- For a **Corrupt** query $<pk_U>$, if $pk_U = pk_S$ or $pk_U = pk_V$ then the simulator aborts, and otherwise, returns the corresponding secret key sk_U.
- For a **Vrfy** $< \sigma=(W,\tau), (pk_S,pk_V), m >$ query, if $< (pk_S,pk_V), m >$ was queried to the **Sign** oracle and σ was returned as an answer to this query then the simulator outputs 1 (valid), and otherwise, 0 (invalid).
- For a hash oracle query, if the query has been issued then S finds the previous answer and returns it. Otherwise, S picks a random number and returns it.

Assume that ***F*** outputs $((pk_S, pk_V), m_0, m_1)$ as a challenge. The simulator ***S*** selects a bit $b \in \{0,1\}$ uniformly at random and then proceeds as follows: We note that ***S*** is aware of the secret key x_S corresponding to pk_S. Compute $W = g^a$, $h = H_1(W// pk_S//pk_V)$, $K_1 = pk_V^{x_S} = g^{bx_S}$, $K_2 = K_1 T^h$. If $b = 0$ compute and then return $\tau = H_2(K_1//K_2//W//m_0)$, and otherwise, i.e., if $b=1$ then $\tau = H_2(K_1//K_2//W//m_1)$. If $b = b'$ then ***S*** outputs 1, which means $T = g^{ab}$, and otherwise, 0.

It is obvious that the given simulation for hash outputs is perfect. Since we assume the use of a random hash function and the hash outputs are distributed uniformly at random, there exists no meaningful relation among hash outputs and so signatures. If $T= g^{ab}$ then the presented simulation is perfect without abortion. If the simulator S is able to guess the target public key correctly then no abortion occurs in the presented simulation. The probability of this correct guess is $1/q_{pk}$ where q_{pk} is the number of total public keys generated for users and q_{pk} is upper-bounded by a polynomial in the security parameter. Hence, the solver can efficiently solve the DDH problem with the advantage of an adversary attacking the strong-anonymity of our DVS scheme.

4 Our DA E-Mail Scheme

In this section, we present a novel efficient DA scheme to achieve robust deniable authentication for E-mail services. Our DA scheme provides not only deniable authentication but also strong privacy for validity of E-mail transmission messages.

4.1 Construction

The main idea of our construction essentially is based on the DVS scheme which is presented in the previous section. The DVS scheme makes use of two types of Diffie-Hellman (DH) key agreement methods [25] between a mail sender and a designated verifier or receiver. In contrast to the Harn-Ren DA scheme which is based on a complex combination of signature and encryption schemes, our approach is simple but quite efficient.

Next, we describe our scheme concretely. Let G be a multiplicative group of prime order p and g be a random generator of G, and let H_1 :$\{0, 1\}^* \rightarrow Z^*_p$ and H_2 :$\{0,1\}^* \rightarrow \{0,1\}^l$ be collision-resistant cryptographic hash functions.

Initialization Phase. For each user U, a pair of a secret key and its corresponding public key is defined as in the DVS scheme: $(x_U, pk_U = g^{x_U})$. We assume that anyone can obtain an authentic public key generated by a party in a pre-defined manner, e.g., via PKI (Public Key Infrastructure).

Communication Phase. The communication procedure between two users, sender Alice and recipient Bob, is described as follows: Let TS be a time-stamp. Assume that Alice has an E-mail message EM=Filename||TS||Data||EOF to be sent. Let pk_S and pk_V be the public keys of Alice and Bob for the DVS scheme, respectively.

•Sender: To generate a certified transmission message for the designated receiver Bob, Alice generates a Header and a Body for a transmission message as follows.

(1) Generation of a Header. Alice picks a random session key SK and encrypts it using the Bob's public encryption key *pek*. Denote the ciphertext of SK by $E_{pek}(SK)$.

(2) Generation of a Body. Alice first generates a DVS on EM by using the DVS scheme presented in Session 3.2. Alice picks a random $r \in Z^*$ and computes $W = g^r \in G$, $h = H_1 (W// pk_S//pk_V)$ and two keys $K_1 = g^{x_V x_S}$ and $K_2 = pk_V^{(x_S+hr)} = g^{x_V(x_S+hr)} \in G$ and

then $\tau = H_2(K_1//K_2//W//TS//\text{EM})$, where TS is a time-stamp. Let $\sigma = (W, \tau)$. She then generates a ciphertext of EM, $\mathbf{C}_{\text{SK}}(\text{EM})$. Let

$$\text{TM}= \text{E}_{pek}(\text{SK})||TS||pk_S//pk_V||\mathbf{C}_{\text{SK}}(\text{EM}).$$

Finally, Alice transmits TM to Bob.

• Receiver: To verify the validity of a given E-mail transmission message $\text{TM}=\text{E}_{pek}(\text{SK})||TS||pk_S//pk_V||\text{C}_{\text{SK}}(\text{EM})$, the designated verifier Bob proceeds as follows: (1) First, parse TM into three parts, session-key, signature, and message. (2) Check the validity of the DVS, $\sigma = (\tau,W)$ included in the signature part as follows: Check if the given timestamp T is valid. If valid, then compute $h=H_1(W//pk_S//pk_V)$, $K_1' = g^{x_V x_S}$, $K_2'=(W^h\cdot pk_S)^{x_V}$ and $\tau' = H_2(K_1'//K_2'//W//\text{EM})$, and then check if $\tau' = \tau$. If the equality holds then the authentication is valid, and otherwise, invalid. (3) If the DVS is valid then recover the session key from $\text{E}_{pek}(\text{SK})$ using the Bob's secret decryption key corresponding to pek. (4) Using this session key, decrypt the encrypted E-mail message. If the time stamp in the decrypted message is equal to TS for the DVS then the decrypted message is valid.

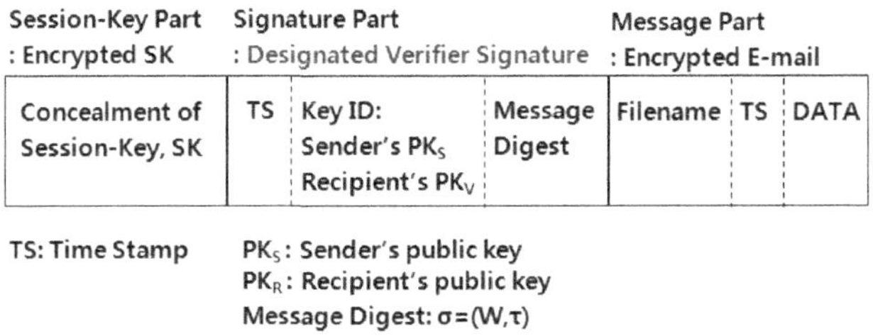

Fig. 1. The Structure of our E-mail Message

4.2 Security

We show that the proposed DA e-mail scheme is secure, that is, it achieves unforgeability, deniable authentication (or non-transferability), and strong-privacy. Throughout the description, hash values are assumed to be distributed uniformly at random.

Unforgeability. A valid transmission message consists of EM, σ, T where T is a time-stamp, and $\sigma = (W, \tau)$, $W = g^r$, $\tau = H_2(K_1//K_2//W//T//\text{EM})$, $K_1 = g^{x_V x_S}$ and $K_2 = pk_V^{(x_S+hr)} = g^{x_V(x_S+hr)}$ for random $r \in Z^*_q$. In order to generate a forged transmission message, an adversary must generate a forged DVS, $\sigma = (W, \tau)$. An adversary is not allowed to access the sender's secret key x_S or the receiver's secret key x_V. In addition, since other valid transmission messages are randomized by an ephemeral number r, it is infeasible for an adversary to learn meaningful information by manipulating known valid messages. We can formally prove that the proposed scheme is unforgeable under the existential-unforgeability of the underlying DVS scheme.

Deniable Authentication. Using the non-transferability of the underlying DVS scheme we can easily show that the proposed scheme has deniable authentication. By the non-transferability, both the message sender and the designated receiver are able to generate a signature. Because of this possibility for generation of a signature, the sender can deny the signature claiming that the receiver generated this signature.

The receiver, however, is able to confirm that the message is originated from the signer or the sender, if the receiver or the verifier has not generated the signature.

Strong-Privacy. By the strong-anonymity of the underlying DVS scheme, the validity of a signature cannot be publicly checked by only a designated verifier or a receiver. Since a transmission E-mail message is encrypted with a session key, any useful information regarding the origination or the validity of an E-mail cannot be revealed from the transmission in our DA E-mail scheme. .

5 Performance Comparison

In this section we show that our scheme is efficient with respect to performance, that is, the signature length and computation overhead by comparing other DA E-mail schemes with our scheme. (Refer to Table 1.)

Table 1. Performance Comparison

	Signature Length	Comput. Overhead	
		Sign	Vrify
[HR08]	$2L_l + 1L_{hash}$ (or $1L_l + 1L_{hash}$)	$1E_{1024}$	$1E_{RSA}$ (or $3E_{1024}$)
Ours	$1L_G + 1L_{hash}$	$2E_{160}$	$2E_{160}$

Our signature consists of a group element and a hash value. When 80-bit security level is considered, the signature length of our scheme is only 320 bits with an elliptic curve group of 160-bit prime order p. In the DA E-mail scheme of [3], since the ElGamal signature or the textbook RSA signature scheme can be assumed to make use of 1024-bit parameter, $L_l = 1024$ and so the signature bit-length is 2048+160=2208 or 1024+160=1184. Thus, our signature length is about 73% shorter than that of the scheme [3]. To generate a signature our scheme performs two exponentiations with 160-bit exponents but the scheme of [3] performs one exponentiation with 1024-bit exponents. Thus, our scheme is about 60% faster than that of the scheme [3]. To verify a signature our scheme performs two exponentiations with 160-bit exponents but the scheme of [3] performs one (for RSA) or two (for ElGamal) exponentiations with 1024-bit exponents.

6 Conclusion

We remarked about the security of Harn-Ren's deniable authentication scheme in the aspect of practice and theory, and propose a privacy-enhanced deniable authentication scheme for E-mail services. Our scheme has several desirable security features including strong verifiability in a strict sense and deniability for privacy. Our DVS scheme generates a very short signature whose length is only 320-bit with elliptic curve groups, and requires a sender to do only two exponentiations and a receiver only one exponentiation. In terms of compatibility, it can be easily realized with known secure E-mail systems such as PGP and S/MIME.

References

1. S/MIME: Secure Multipuepose Internet Mail Extensions, `http://www.rsasecurity.com/standards/smime/`
2. OpenPGP: An Open Specification for Pretty Good Privacy, `http://www.ietf.org/html.charters/openpgp-charter.html`
3. Harn, L., Ren, J.: Design of Fully Deniable Authentication Service for E-mail Applications. IEEE Communications Letters 12(3), 219–221 (2008)
4. Jakobsson, M., Sako, K., Impagliazzo, R.: Designated Verifier Proofs and Their Applications. In: Maurer, U.M. (ed.) EUROCRYPT 1996. LNCS, vol. 1070, pp. 143–154. Springer, Heidelberg (1996)
5. Saeednia, S., Kramer, S., Markovitch, O.: An Efficient Strong Designated Verifier Signature Scheme. In: Lim, J.-I., Lee, D.-H. (eds.) ICISC 2003. LNCS, vol. 2971, pp. 40–54. Springer, Heidelberg (2004)
6. Dolev, D., Dwork, C., Naor, M.: Non-malleable Cryptography. SIAM Journal on Computing 30(2), 391–437 (2000)
7. Rackoff, C., Simon, D.: Non-interactive Zero-Knowledge Proof of Knowledge and Chosen Ciphertext Attack. In: Feigenbaum, J. (ed.) CRYPTO 1991. LNCS, vol. 576, pp. 433–444. Springer, Heidelberg (1992)
8. Fujisaki, E., Okamoto, T., Pointcheval, D., Stern, J.: RSA-OAEP is secure under the RSA assumption. J. of Cryptology 17(2), 81–104 (2004)
9. Sun, H., Hsieh, B., Hwang, H.: Secure E-mail Protocols Providing Perfect Forward Secrecy. IEEE Communications Letters 9(1), 58–60 (2005)
10. Dent, A.W.: Flaws in an E-mail Protocol of Sun, Hsieh, and Hwang. IEEE Communications Letters 9(8), 7180–7719 (2005)
11. Kim, B.H., Koo, J.H., Lee, D.H.: Robust E-mail Protocols with Perfect Forward Secrecy. IEEE Communications Letters 10(6), 510–512 (2006)
12. Yoon, E.J., Yoo, K.Y.: Cryptanalysis of Robust E-mail Protocols with Perfect Forward Secrecy. IEEE Communications Letters 11(56), 372–374 (2007)
13. Aumann, Y., Rabin, M.O.: Authentication, enhanced security and error correcting codes. In: Krawczyk, H. (ed.) CRYPTO 1998. LNCS, vol. 1462, pp. 299–303. Springer, Heidelberg (1998)
14. Jakobsson, M., Sako, K., Impagliazzo, R.: Designated Verifier Proofs and their Applications. In: Maurer, U.M. (ed.) EUROCRYPT 1996. LNCS, vol. 1070, pp. 143–154. Springer, Heidelberg (1996)

15. Huang, X., Susilo, W., Mu, Y., Zhang, F.: Short (Identity-Based) Strong Designated Verifier Signature Schemes. In: Chen, K., Deng, R., Lai, X., Zhou, J. (eds.) ISPEC 2006. LNCS, vol. 3903, pp. 214–225. Springer, Heidelberg (2006)
16. Laguillaumie, F., Vergnaud, D.: Designated Verifiers Signature: Anonymity and Efficient Construction from any Bilinear Map. In: Blundo, C., Cimato, S. (eds.) SCN 2004. LNCS, vol. 3352, pp. 105–119. Springer, Heidelberg (2005)
17. Laguillaumie, F., Vergnaud, D.: Multi-designated Verifiers Signatures. In: López, J., Qing, S., Okamoto, E. (eds.) ICICS 2004. LNCS, vol. 3269, pp. 495–507. Springer, Heidelberg (2004)
18. Zhang, J., Mao, J.: A Novel ID-Based Designated Verifier Signature Scheme. Information Sciences 178, 733–766 (2008)
19. Rivest, R., Shamir, A., Tauman, Y.: How to Leak a Secret. In: Boyd, C. (ed.) ASIACRYPT 2001. LNCS, vol. 2248, pp. 552–565. Springer, Heidelberg (2001)
20. Saeednia, S., Kramer, S., Markovitch, O.: An Efficient Strong Designated Verifier Signature Scheme. In: Yazıcı, A., Şener, C. (eds.) ISCIS 2003. LNCS, vol. 2869, pp. 40–54. Springer, Heidelberg (2003)
21. Susilo, W., Zhang, F., Mu, Y.: Identity-based Strong Designated Verifier Signature Schemes. In: Wang, H., Pieprzyk, J., Varadharajan, V. (eds.) ACISP 2004. LNCS, vol. 3108, pp. 313–324. Springer, Heidelberg (2004)
22. Cramer, R., Shoup, V.: Design and Analysis of Practical Public-Key Encryption Schemes Secure against Adaptive Chosen Ciphertext Attack. SIAM Journal on Computing 33(1), 167–226 (2003)
23. Bender, A., Katz, J., Morselli, R.: Ring Signatures: Stronger Definitions, and Constructions Without Random Oracles. In: Halevi, S., Rabin, T. (eds.) TCC 2006. LNCS, vol. 3876, pp. 60–79. Springer, Heidelberg (2006)
24. Lee, J., Chang, J.K., Lee, D.H.: Forgery attacks on Kang et al.'s Identity-Based Strong Designated Verifier Signature Scheme and its improvement with security proof. Computers and Electrical Engineering 35, 49–53 (2009)
25. Diffie, W., Hellman, M.: New Directions in Cryptography. IEEE Transactions on Information Theory 22(6), 644–654 (1976)

Chaotic Image Encryption Using Bézier Curve in DCT Domain Scrambling

Ahmed A. Abd El-Latif, Xiamu Niu, and Ning Wang

School of Computer Science and Technology,
Harbin Institute of Technology 150080, Harbin, China
ahmed_rahiem@yahoo.com

Abstract. In this paper, an extended sequence using chaotic map and Bernstein form Bézier curve to improve the chaotic key sequence is presented. Based on this sequence, we perform the scrambling in DCT domain with variable control parameters. To further enforce the security, the gray values of image pixels are diffused using keystream extracted from the extended key sequence of the chaotic map and the plainimage. As a result, the algorithm resists the chosen-plaintext/chosen-ciphertext/known-plaintext attacks, as diffusion depends on the plainimage. Moreover, experimental results and analysis confirm a high security level using the proposed scheme.

Keywords: Image encryption, Chaotic maps, Bézier curve, DCT domain.

1 Introduction

Image encryption is the process of realigning the original image into a new image that is non-recognizable in appearance, disorderly, and unsystematic [1]. It is challenging task which is quit different from text encryption due to some intrinsic properties of images such as high redundancy and bulky data capacity, which are generally diffuclt to handle by using traditional techniques. Recently, chaos theory has received ever increasing research interests from cryptographers. This is because of the fact that, chaotic systems have many important cryptographically desirable features, such as high sensitivity to initial conditions/parameters, long periodicity, high randomness and mixing [2-5]. Moreover, chaotic maps are easy to be implemented by microprocessors and personal computers. Therefore, chaotic cryptosystems generally are expected to have high speed with low cost, which makes them better candidates than many traditional ciphers for multimedia data encryption.

Till now, a number of chaos-based cryptographic schemes have been proposed. The core majorty of these encryption systems consists of one or several chaotic maps serving the purpose of either just scrambling the image or shuffling the image in the spatial domain and subsequently masking the resulting shuffled image [6-10]. It is noted, however, that many of these schemes encrypt the image in spatial domain. Indeed, spatial domain encryption has drawbacks in that it keeps the statistical characteristics of image intact after scrambling. So, it is not secure to perform the scrambling in a spatial domain as the attacker can utilize the characteristics of

E. Ariwa and E. El-Qawasmeh (Eds.): DEIS 2011, CCIS 194, pp. 30–41, 2011.

encrypted image to recover the plainimage. Additionally, in diffusion operation, the pixels gray values are masked to enhance the statistical characteristics of the image. If the keystream used in the mixing operation is determined only by the key and independent of plainimage as in [7-10], then such algorithms cannot resist the chosen-plaintext (CP) and known-plaintext (KP) attacks [11,12,14].

To cope with these problems, we introduce an efficient image encryption algorithm based on chaotic systems in DCT domain scrambling. First, an extended sequence using chaotic map and Bernstein form Bézier curve to improve the chaotic key sequence is presented. Then, we perform the scrambling in DCT domain to withstand the security threats of a spatial domain scrambling. Two chaotic maps are used to perform the scrambling effect: chaotic cat map is utilized to scramble the DCT coefficients, while the control parameters are randomly generated using a chaotic logistic map. To further enforce the security, the diffusion operation is done to diffuse the gray values of image pixels using the keystream extracted from the chaotic map and the plainimage.

The rest of this paper is organised as follows: Section 2 present the basic theory of the encryption scheme. The proposed image encryption scheme is introduced in Section 3. Section 4 is devoted to experimental analysis and discussion. Finaly, the conclusion is drawen in Section 5.

2 Preliminaries

2.1 Bézier Curve

A Bézier curve is a 2D or 3D parametric curve of degree n defined on $n+1$ points $P_0, \ldots, P_n$ whose points $x(t)$ are defined by [13]

$$x(t) = \sum_{i=0}^{n} p_i \cdot B_i^n(t) \tag{1}$$

where $p_i \in R^3$, $t \in [0,1]$, and $i=0,\ldots, n$

The p_i are called control points; the B_i^n are Bernstein polynomials, which are given by:

$$B_i^n(t) = \binom{n}{i} (1-t)^{n-i} t^i \tag{2}$$

The main properties of Bézier curve are illustrated as follows [13]:

1. **Affine invariance**: Bézier curve is invariant under affine maps.
2. **Convex hull property** For $u \in [0,1]$, Bézier curve lies in the convex hull of the control polygon
3. **Endpoint interpolation** Bézier curve passes through P_0 and P_n.
4. **Symmetry** Bézier curve defined by control polygon $p_0 p_1 \ldots\ldots p_n$ is the same as the curve defined by control polygon $p_n p_{n-1} \ldots\ldots p_0$, they only differ in the direction in which they are traversed.

2.2 Chaotic Maps

A chaotic map is a dynamic system that can be easily denoted by mathematical equations [14]. Generally, for a chaotic map, the initial value acts as its input, the control parameters determine its action, and the output is the sequence produced by the iterated maps, as shown in Fig. 1. It has some typical properties suitable for data encryption. Given the initial value, the chaotic map generates the sequence with random properties. The sequence is sensitive to the initial value, that is, two initial values with a slight difference will cause great differences after multiple iterations. Additionally, the sequence is very sensitive to the control parameters, that is, different parameters produce different sequences as shown in Fig. 1, and a chaotic map is similar to a cipher. The initial value of the chaotic map is regarded as the plainimage, the control parameters as the key and the output sequence as the cipherimage.

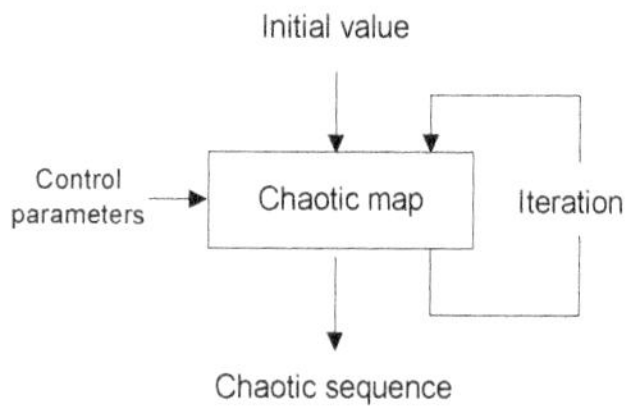

Fig. 1. General architecture of a chaotic map

2.2.1 Chaotic Cat Map

The cat map is a 2D map that maps the unit square onto itself in a one-to-one manner. It is defined by the following matrix equation [7]:

$$\begin{bmatrix} x_{i+1} \\ y_{i+1} \end{bmatrix} = \begin{bmatrix} 1 & u \\ v & uv+1 \end{bmatrix} \begin{bmatrix} x_i \\ y_i \end{bmatrix} (\text{mod } N) \tag{3}$$

where u and v are positive integers. (x_i, y_i) and (x_{i+1}, y_{i+1}) are the i -th and the i+1-th states, respectively.

2.2.2 Chaotic Logistic Map

The Logistic is one of the simplest nonlinear chaotic discrete systems that exhibit chaotic behavior and is defined by the following equation [8]:

$$x_{n+1} = \lambda x_n (1 - x_n), n \geq 0 \tag{4}$$

where x_0 is initial condition, λ is the system parameter and n is the number of iterations. The research shows that the map is chaotic for $3.57 < \lambda < 4$ and $x_{n+1} \in (0,1)$ for all n.

2.3 Extended Chaotic Sequence by Bézier Curve

Assume that $\{x_1^i, x_2^i, x_3^i, \ldots\ldots, x_n^i, \ldots\ldots\}$, $(i = 0, 1, 2, \ldots., L)$ are known chaotic sequences, and supposc the sequences have the same dimension D and $\{s_1, s_2, s_3, \ldots\ldots\ldots\}$ is a chaotic sequence with one or D dimension. Then, we can get an extended chaotic sequence $\{x_1, x_2, x_3, \ldots\ldots\ldots\}$ as follows:

$$x_n = \sum_{i=0}^{L} x_n^i \cdot B_i^n(s_n), n = 1, 2, \ldots\ldots \tag{5}$$

when $\{s_1, s_2, s_3, \ldots\ldots\ldots\}$ is one dimension or

$$x_n^j = \sum_{i=0}^{L} x_n^{i,j} \cdot B_i^n(s_n^j), n = 1, 2, \ldots\ldots, j = 1, 2, \ldots., D \tag{6}$$

when $\{s_1, s_2, s_3, \ldots\ldots\ldots\}$ is D dimensions.

For example, we can show an extended chaotic sequence of the chaotic logistic map (Eq. 4) using formula (5) for D=1.

2.4 The 2-D Discrete Cosine Transform and Its Inverse

Let $f(x, y)$, for $x = 0, 1, 2, \ldots\ldots\ldots, M-1$ and $y = 0, 1, 2, \ldots\ldots\ldots, N-1$, denote an $M \times N$ image. The 2-D Discrete Cosine Transform (DCT) of *f, denoted* by $F(u, v)$, is formulated as [15]

$$F(u,v) = \frac{2}{\sqrt{MN}} c(u)c(v) \sum_{x=0}^{N-1} \sum_{y=0}^{M-1} f(x,y) \cos\left[\frac{\pi(2x+1)u}{2N}\right] \cos\left[\frac{\pi(2y+1)u}{2M}\right] \tag{7}$$

For $u = 0, 1, 2, \ldots\ldots\ldots, M-1$ and $v = 0, 1, 2, \ldots\ldots\ldots, N-1$, where

$$C(k) = \begin{cases} \frac{1}{\sqrt{2}} & for \quad k=0 \\ 1 & otherwise. \end{cases}$$

The 2-D Inverse Discrete Cosine Transform (IDCT) is computed in a similar fashion. The 2D IDCT of $F(u, v)$ is formulated as

$$f(x,y) = \frac{2}{\sqrt{MN}} \sum_{x=0}^{N-1} \sum_{y=0}^{M-1} c(u)c(v)F(u,v) \cos\left[\frac{\pi(2x+1)u}{2N}\right] \cos\left[\frac{\pi(2y+1)u}{2M}\right] \tag{8}$$

3 The Proposed Image Encryption Method

In this section, we propose an efficient image encryption algorithm. The algorithm consists of two procedures: firstly, the pixels of plainimage are scrambling in DCT domain using the chaotic cat map with variable control parameters; Secondly, the scrambled image pixels are diffused using keystream extracted from the chaotic map and the plainimage. The detailed encryption algorithm is described as follows:

1: Pixel-chaotic-shuffle in DCT domain with variable control parameters

Step 1: Evaluate the DCT $F(i, j)$ of the plainimage $f(i, j)$.

Step 2: Generate the control parameters u and v of the chaotic cat map for permutation according to the following Eq.

$$\begin{cases} u = floor(x(K) * 2^{24}) \bmod N \\ v = floor(x(K) * 2^{48}) \bmod 2^{24} \bmod N \end{cases} \tag{9}$$

where $x(K)$ is the state of the extended chaotic logistic map after K iterations

Step 3: Relocate the resulting image $F(i, j)$ using chaotic cat map with variable control parameters defined by Eq. (3).

Step 4: Take inverse DCT to get final scrambled image.

2: Diffusion method of the shuffled image with keystream dependence

Step 1: Let $Sc(i, j)$ be the final scrambled/shuffled image obtained.

Step 2: Arrange the pixels of scrambled image $Sc(i, j)$ from left to right and then top to bottom, we get sequence $Sc(1), Sc(2), \ldots\ldots, Sc(N \times N)$.

Step 3: Perform the diffusion operation as illustrated below:

i. Repeat ii to iv for k=1 to $N \times N$.

ii. Iterate Eq. (4) for N_0 times to get rid of the transient effect, where N_0 is a constant.

iii. Evaluate modified key $\phi(k)$ using the values of the currently operated pixel and the modified current state of chaotic map based Bernstein function as:

$$x_k = (\sum_{i=0}^{3} x_k^i \cdot B_i^n(s_n)) \tag{10}$$

$$\varphi(k) = (x_k + \frac{Sc(k-1)}{256}) \tag{11}$$

$$\phi(k) = \left(floor(\beta \cdot \varphi(k) + \beta)^2 \right) \bmod 2^L \tag{12}$$

where $L = \log_2 G$ *and* G is the number of possible gray levels in image pixels. For example, L is 8 if the plainimage is a 256 gray-scale image. β is the control parameter

iv. Calculate pixel gray value $C(k)$ of cipherimage as

$$C(k) = Sc(k) \oplus \phi(k) \tag{13}$$

Step 4: Arrange the sequence of encrypted pixels $C(1), C(2), \ldots\ldots, C(N \times N)$ into a 2D cipherimage $C(i, j)$.

The decryption process is similar to encryption, except that the scrambling and the diffusion stages are performed in reversed order. This means that the cipherimage is first operated by the inverse diffusion process to remove the diffusion effect. Then the pixels are relocated in a manner just opposite to that performed in encryption. This reverse pixel relocation process is guaranteed as the chaotic cat map is invertible as shown:

$$\begin{bmatrix} x_i \\ y_i \end{bmatrix} = \begin{bmatrix} 1 & u \\ v & uv+1 \end{bmatrix}^{-1} \begin{bmatrix} x_{i+1} \\ y_{i+1} \end{bmatrix} (\bmod N) \tag{14}$$

If multiple permutation and overall rounds are done in encryption, the same number of rounds should be performed in decryption. With the correct key, the final reconstructed image is exactly the same as the original plainimage, without any distortion.

4 Experimental Results and Analysis

Here, the proposed encryption algorithm is applied to various plainimages like *Lena*, *Baboon*, *Peppers*, *Cameraman*, *Barbara*, *Boat* and *Airplane* of 256×256 size. Among them, the plainimages of *Lena*, *Cameraman*, *Elaine*, *Boat* and their respective histograms are shown in Fig. 2. As can be seen in this figure that the gray value distributions of plainimages are not uniform. The initial conditions and system parameters taken for experimentation are: $\lambda = 3.9, x_0 = 0.3, \beta = 99$. The results of shuffling scheme are shown in Fig. 3.

The cipherimages of *Lena*, *Cameraman*, *Elaine*, and *Boat* using proposed encryption algorithm and their histograms are shown in Fig. 4 respectively. It is clear from the Fig. 4(a)-(d) that the cipherimages are very much indistinguishable and appears like a noise. Moreover, as seen in Fig. 4(e)-(h) that the distribution of gray values of the cipherimages is fairly uniform and much different from the histograms of the plainimages shown in Fig. 2(e)-(h). Therefore, we can hardly do any statistical analysis to decrypt encrypted images because the histograms changed greatly by the proposed scheme. In addition, the cost of whole encryption is approximately 2.1 s, which is acceptable for security.

4.1 Key Space Analysis

The key space is the total number of different keys that can be used in the encryption. For a secure image encryption, the key space should be large enough to make brute force attacks infeasible [2-4]. In the proposed algorithm, secret key consists of

$$K + 2 \text{ } \textit{initial parameters} \text{ } , 0 \le Sc(0) \le 255 \text{ }, \lambda \in [3.9, 4] \text{ }, 0 < \beta < 256 \text{ } N_0 \ge 1 \text{ }.$$

And all the variables are declared as Matlab type *long* which is scaled fixed point format with 15 digits precision for *double*. After considering the permitted range of all initial conditions and parameters involved, the key space comes out to be $256 \times 254 \times$ (4-3.9) $\times (10^{14})^8 \times$ K+2$\times$ $N_0 \approx$ 1.3 $\times 10^{120}$. Thus, the key space of the proposed algorithm is extensively large enough to resist the exhaustive brute-force attack.

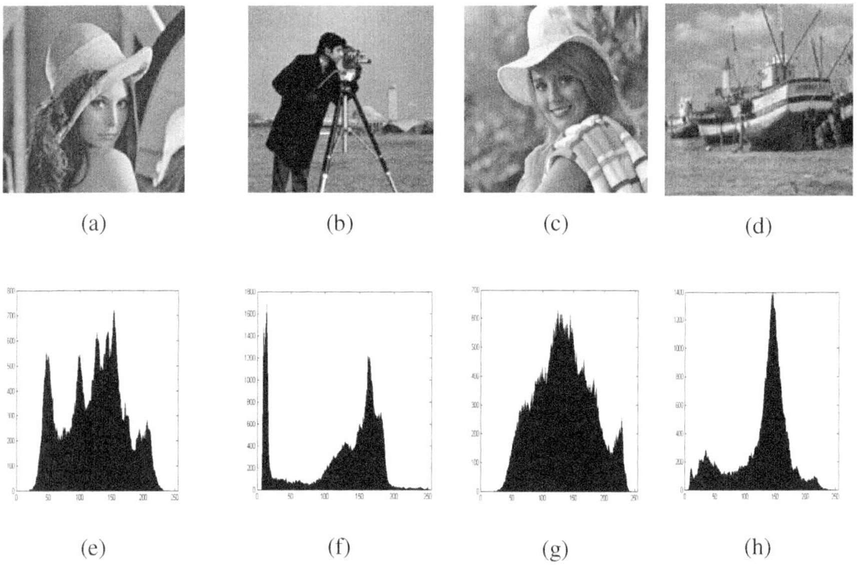

Fig. 2. Plainimages and their histograms (a) *Lena* (b) *Cameraman* (c) *Elaine* (d) *Boat* (e) histogram of *Lena* (f) histogram of *Cameraman* (g) histogram of *Elaine* (h) histogram of *Boat*

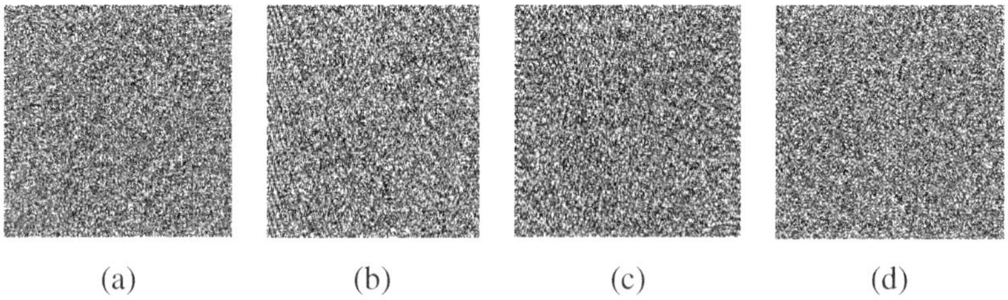

Fig. 3. Scrambled images (a) *Lena* (b) *Cameraman* (c) *Elaine* (d) *Boat*

4.2 Key Sensitivity

An efficient encryption algorithm should be sensitive to secret key i.e. a small change in secret key during decryption process results into a completely different decrypted image [4]. In the proposed algorithm, an incremental change in key; even of the order of $(\Delta =)$ 10^{-10}, results into completely unrecognizable decrypted image. The cipherimages shown in Fig. 5 is decrypted using $\beta + \Delta$, $x_0 + \Delta$, $Sc(0)+1$, $\lambda + \Delta$ separately, the resultant decrypted images shown in Fig. 5 are unrecognizable and noise like. Hence, it can be said that the proposed algorithm has high sensitivity to secret key.

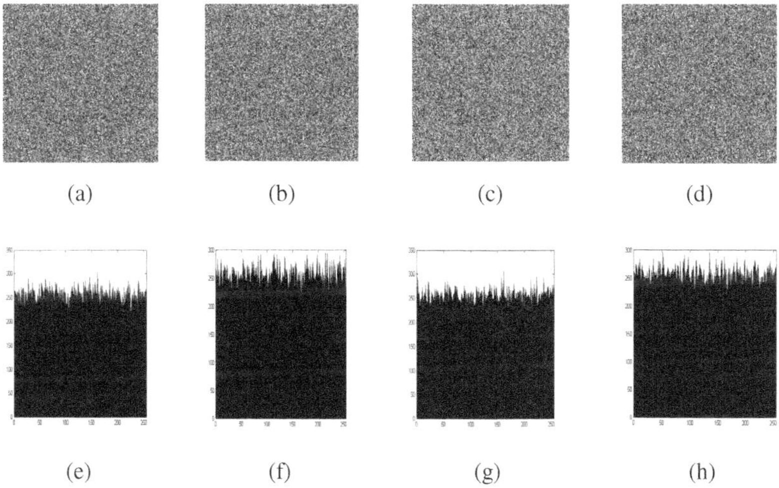

Fig. 4. Ciphered images and their histograms (a) *Lena* (b) *Cameraman* (c) *Elaine* (d) *Boat* (e) histogram of *Lena* (f) histogram of *Cameraman* (g) histogram of *Elaine* (h) histogram of *Boat*

4.3 Correlation Coefficient Analysis

In most of the plainimages, there exists high correlation among adjacent pixels. It is mainstream task of an efficient image encryption algorithm to eliminate the correlation of pixels [2-5]. Two highly uncorrelated sequences have approximately zero correlation coefficient. The correlation coefficient between two adjacent pixels in an image is determined as:

$$r_{xy} = \frac{\sum_{i=1}^{N} (x_i - E(x))(y_i - E(y))}{\sqrt{\sum_{i=1}^{N} (x_i - E(x))^2}\sqrt{\sum_{i=1}^{N} (y_i - E(y))^2}} \quad (15)$$

where $E(x) = mean\ (x_i)$ and x, y are gray values of two adjacent pixels in the image. In the proposed algorithm, the correlation coefficient of 1000 randomly selected pairs of vertically, horizontally and diagonally adjacent pixels is determined.

The average of several correlation coefficients in plainimages and cipherimages in three directions are listed in Table 1 and Table 2, respectively. The values of correlation coefficients show that the two adjacent pixels in the plainimages are highly correlated to each other, whereas the values obtained for cipherimages are close to 0, or may be negligible correlation between the two adjacent pixels in it. This shows that the proposed algorithm highly de-correlate the adjacent pixels in cipherimages.

(a) (b) (c) (d) (e)

Fig. 5. Key sensitivity: (a) decrypted images with correct key (b) $\beta + \Delta$ (c) $x_0 + \Delta$ (d) $Sc(0)+1$ (e) $\lambda + \Delta$

Table 1. Correlation coefficient of two adjacent pixels in plainimages

Test images	Vertical	Horizontal	Diagonal
Lena	0.9492	0.9691	0.9288
Pepper	0.9788	0.9830	0.9592
Cameraman	0.9342	0.9629	0.9222
Elaine	0.9652	0.9724	0.9384
Boat	0.9076	0.9405	0.8658
Airplane	0.9763	0.9715	0.9505

Table 2. Correlation coefficient of two adjacent pixels in cipherimages

Test images	Vertical	Horizontal	Diagonal
Lena	0.00051	0.00129	0.00102
Pepper	0.00010	0.00048	0.00014
Cameraman	0.00109	0.00042	0.00140
Elaine	0.00057	0.00194	0.00118
Boat	0.00026	0.00027	0.00103
Airplane	0.00318	0.00090	0.00262

4.4 Information Entropy Analysis

Information theory is the mathematical theory of data communication and storage founded in 1949 by C.E. Shannon [16]. Modern information theory is concerned with error- correction, data compression, cryptography, communications systems, and related topics. To calculate the entropy $H(m)$ of a source m, we have:

$$H(m) = \sum_{i=0}^{2^N-1} P(m_i)\log_2 \frac{1}{P(m_i)} \ bits \tag{16}$$

Where $p(m_i)$ represents the probability of symbol m_i and the entropy is expressed in bits. Let us suppose that the source emits 2^8 symbols with equal probability, i.e., $m = \{ m_0, m_2, \ldots\ldots, m_{255} \}$ after evaluating Eq. (16), we obtain its entropy $H(m) = 8$, corresponding to a truly random source. Actually, given that a practical information source seldom generates random messages, in general its entropy value is smaller than the ideal one. However, when the messages are encrypted, their entropy should ideally be 8. If the output of such a cipher emits symbols with entropy less than 8, there exists certain degree of predictability, which threatens its security.

The values of entropies obtained for plainimages and cipherimages are given in Table 3. The entropy values for cipherimages are very close to the ideal value 8. This implies that the information leakage in the proposed encryption process is negligible and the encryption algorithm is secure against the entropy based attack.

Table 3. The entropy analysis of plainimages and cipherimages

Test images	Plainimage	Cipherimage
Lena	7.4433	7.9975
Cameraman	7.0097	7.9977
Elaine	7.4841	7.9974
Boat	7.1640	7.9976
Airplane	6.7794	7.9973
Pepper	7.5842	7.9973

4.5 Resistance to *KPA/CPA/CCA* Attacks

In the proposed algorithm, the control parameters of permutation are randomly generated from key of map (4). A tiny different key results in distinct control parameters and non-identical permuted images. Moreover, the keystream $\phi(k)$ used in diffusion operation is extracted from key of map (4) and (5) and it also depends on plainimage. Different keystreams are generated in diffusion operation when different plainimages are encrypted using proposed algorithm. Therefore, the known-plaintext (*KP*), chosen-plaintext (*CP*) and chosen-ciphertext (*CC*) attacks are not applicable in case of proposed encryption algorithm. Hence, the proposed algorithm can resist the *KPA/CPA/CCA* attacks.

4.6 Comparisons with Other Chaos-Based Algorithms

In this section, we will compare our proposed algorithm with other chaos-based algorithms. Here, we mainly focus on the security consideration. The test image is a

256 gray-scale "*Lena*" image with a size of 256× 256 and the results are shown in Table 4. From Table 4 we can see that our algorithm has a better security performance when compared with other algorithms.

Table 4. Comparison results with other chaos-based encryption algorithms

Considered items		Encryption scheme			
		Gao *e. al.* 2008	Behnia *et al.*2008	Zhang *et al.* 2005	proposed
Key sensitivity		Yes	Yes	Yes	Yes
Correlation coefficients	Horizontal	-0.0142	0.0038	0.0286	0.00129
	Vertical	-0.0074	0.0023	0.0203	0.00051
	Diagonal	-0.0183	0.0004	0.0197	0.00102
Information entropy		N/A	7.9968	N/A	7.9975
Key space		2^{233}	2^{260}	2^{129}	1.3×10^{120}
Chaotic system employed		Chen's chaotic system	Coupled chaotic system	Hybrid of CNN and Logistic map	Chaotic cat map and logistic map

5 Conclusion

In this work, an efficient encryption algorithm for secure digital images is proposed. The algorithm is based on the concept of scrambling the pixel's positions and changing the gray values of the image pixels. To perform the scrambling of the plain image's pixels, a scrambled scheme with variable control parameters through 2D Cat transform is suggested in DCT transform domain. The control parameters of scrambling are randomly generated using a 1D Logistic map to enforce the secrecy of the images. The diffusion operation of the scrambled image is done using extended chaotic sequence generated through 1D Logistic and Bernstein function. All the simulation and experimental analysis show that the proposed image encryption system has very large key space, high sensitivity to secret keys, better diffusion of information in the ciphered images and low correlation coefficients. Hence, the proposed image encryption algorithm has high level of security with less computation and is more robust towards cryptanalysis.

Acknowledgment

This work is supported by the National Natural Science Foundation of China (Project Number: 60703011, 60832010, 60671064), the Chinese national 863 Program (Project Number: 2007AA01Z458), The Research Fund for the Doctoral Program of Higher Education (RFDP: 20070213047) and the Fundamental Research Funds for the Central Universities (Grant No.HIT.NSRIF.2009050).

References

1. Ye, G.: Image Scrambling Encryption Algorithm of Pixel Bit Based on Chaos Map. Pattern Recognition 31, 347–354 (2010)
2. Amin, M., Faragallah, O.S., Abd El-Latif, A.A.: A Chaotic Block Cipher Algorithm for Image Cryptosystems. Commun. Nonlinear Sci. Numer. Simulat. 15, 3484–3497 (2010)
3. Kocarev, L., Galias, Z., Lian, S. (eds.): Intelligent Copmuting Based on Chaos. Springer, Heidelberg (2009)
4. Amin, M., Abd El-Latif, A.A.: Efficient Modified RC5 Based on Chaos Adapted to Image Encryption. Journal of Electronic Imaging 19(1) (January 2010)
5. Wang, Y., Wong, K.-W., Liao, X., Xiang, T., Chen, G.: A Chaos-Based Image Encrypttion Algorithm With Variable Control Parameters. Chaos, Solitions and Fractals 41, 1773–1783 (2009)
6. Behnia, S., Akhshani, A., Mahmodi, H., Akhavan, A.: A Novel Algorithm For Image Encryption Based On Mixture Of Chaotic Maps. Chaos, Solitons & Fractals 35, 408–419 (2008)
7. Chen, G., Mao, Y., Chui, C.K.: A Symmetric Image Encryption Scheme Based on 3D Chaotic Cat Maps. Chaos, Solitions and Fractals 21, 749–761 (2004)
8. Pareek, N.K., Patidar, V., Sud, K.K.: Image Encryption Using Chaotic Logistic Map. Image Vision Comput. 24, 926–934 (2006)
9. Gao, T., Chen, Z.: Image Encryption Based on a New Total Shuffling Algorithm. Chaos, Solitions and Fractals 38, 213–220 (2008)
10. Gao, T., Gu, Q., Chen, Z.: A New Image Encryption Algorithm Based on Hyper-Chaos. Phys. Lett. A 374(4), 394–400 (2008)
11. Rhouma, R., Belghith, S.: Cryptanalysis of a New Image Encryption Algorithm Based on Hyper-Chaos. Phys. Lett. A 372, 5973–5978 (2008)
12. Wang, K., Pei, Zou, L., Song, A., He, Z.: On The Security of 3D Cat Map Based Symmetric Image Encryption Scheme. Phys. Lett. A 343(6), 432–439 (2005)
13. Salamon, D.: Curves and Surfaces for Computer Graphics. Springer Science+ Business Media, Inc. (2006)
14. Lian, S.: Multimedia Content Encryption: Techniques and Applications. Taylor & Francis Group, LLC (2009)
15. Acharya, T., Ray, A.K.: Image processing: Principble and Applications. John Wiley & Sons, Inc., Chichester (2005)
16. Shannon, C.E.: Communication Theory of Secrecy System. Bell Syst. Tech. J. 28, 656–715 (1949)

Improving Hybrid Cryptosystems with DNA Steganography

Mohammad Reza Najaf Torkaman, Pourya Nikfard, Nazanin Sadat Kazazi, Mohammad Reza Abbasy, and S. Farzaneh Tabatabaiee

Faculy of Computer Science and Information System, Universiti Teknologi Malaysia (UTM), Kuala Lumpur, Malaysia
{rntmohammad2,sknazanin2,npourya2, ramohammad2,ftseyedeh2}@live.utm.my

Abstract. There exists a big demand for secure electronic communications while the expertise level of attackers increases rapidly and that causes even bigger demands and needs for an extreme secure connection. An ideal security protocol should always be protecting the security of connections in many aspects, and leaves no trapdoor for the attackers. Nowadays, one of the popular cryptography protocols is hybrid cryptosystem that uses symmetric and public key cryptography to change secret message. In available cryptography protocol attackers are always aware of transmission of sensitive data. Even non-interested attackers can get interested to break the ciphertext out of curiosity and challenge, when suddenly catches some scrambled data over the network. In this paper we discuss about the disadvantages of asymmetric algorithms in cryptography protocol. Furthermore, this paper proposes new cryptography protocol based on DNA steganography to reduce the usage of public cryptography to exchange session key. In this protocol session key between sender and receiver is hidden by DNA data hiding technique. Therefore, the attackers are not aware of transmission of session key through unsecure channel. Finally, the strength point of the DNA steganography is discussed.

Keywords: Cryptography; Steganography; Cryptography protocols; DNA steganography.

1 Introduction

Cryptography is the science and art of secret writing [1][2][3]. It studies some mathematical techniques and provides mechanisms necessary to provide aspects related to information security like confidentiality, data integrity, entity authentication, and data origin authentication [3].

Symmetric algorithms are cryptosystems that either a secret key will be shared for both encryption and decryption [4][5]. The algorithms of symmetric cryptosystems are very strong against possible attacks, but mainly weakness of symmetric cryptosystems is brute-forcing the secret key. This characteristic creates the biggest critical act in any cryptosystem that uses symmetric algorithms which is distribution of the shared secret between the two parties like DES algorithms [5] [6].

E. Ariwa and E. El-Qawasmeh (Eds.): DEIS 2011, CCIS 194, pp. 42–52, 2011.

Asymmetric algorithms use different values for encryption and decryption and do not need to share secret between two parties. Each party only has to keep a secret of its own. The earliest foundation of asymmetric algorithms known as public key cryptosystems comes from key exchange problem of symmetric algorithms. In 1976, Whitfield Diffie and Martin Hellman proposed a method were the sender and receiver do not have to share a secret. That was the first work on hybrid cryptosystem [4][7][3].

1.1 Key Management in Cryptography

To create the best cryptosystem, it is feasible to use symmetric algorithms since they are extremely fast in process and secure in algorithms comparing to asymmetric algorithms. However, the distribution of the secret key over an insecure channel is one of the most challenging topics in cryptosystems [1][8][9][4][6][7][5][10][11].

Here on wards, this paper will express viable information on how to incorporate symmetric algorithms with other methods to provide a new method that holds a strong security in many aspects. There are several steps in key management of a cryptosystem. The main ones are: Key generation, Key distribution, and Key revocation [12].The distribution of the key is the critical step since it is the most interest of Eve to intercept and catch the key. If the cryptosystem uses the strongest algorithm with best generated key but distribution of the key has lack of security, the overall security of that cryptosystem would be zero. Diffie Hellman algorithm was the establisher of key distribution over insecure channels [13].

1.2 Public Key Methods_ Hybrid Cryptosystem

The best existing method for a cryptosystem to provide best security possible seems to be hybrid cryptosystems. They are called hybrid because they are a mixture of symmetric and asymmetric algorithms, using security and speed of symmetric together with asymmetric strength in secure key distribution, authentication, etc.

1.2.1 Security and Implementation Issue of Public Key Methods Affecting Hybrid Cryptosystems

Public key methods have much strength but there are lots of drawbacks to these cryptosystems. The following is a short list of these drawbacks:

1. Public key methods are very low in speed [4]. The usage of symmetric algorithms has decreased this problem but this still is an issue in asymmetric role.
2. The asymmetric algorithms are very vulnerable to chosen-plaintext attacks. This attack is effective because of the fact that encryption key is published [4][14][15].
3. Another consideration in asymmetric algorithms is algorithmic attacks. Even though factoring n is known as nearly impossible calculation, but researchers have shown the possibility of this attack especially with the growth of technology and speed of computer's processors [16].

4. Although the database that holds the value of the public keys are very secured and only authorized user can modify it, there still exists a high risk of Eve's chance in modifying the data of the database[4].
5. Man-in-the-Middle-Attack is the most popular attak to public key cryptosystem[4]. Interlock Protocol [17] has been proposed to solve this problem but there are still big arguments against the efficiency and effectiveness of this protocol [18].
6. Certification Authorities (CA) were a solution to public key distribution. But there still exists critical issues for this method as well, such as the terms certificate, trust, how to choose the authority on top of everyone, and how much of a time period that authority is trusted [4].

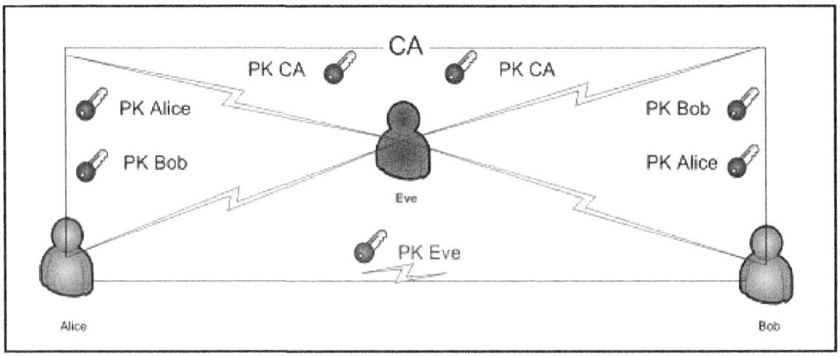

Fig. 1. Conventional Hybrid Cryptosystem

1.3 Steganography

Steganography is the science and art of information hiding. Cryptography and Steganography have same mission with different method, the former changes the content but latter covers the existence of the information. In Greek's literature, Steganography means "covered writing" [19].

The famous traditional story of Steganography is known as Simmons' Prisoner's Problem. Two of the prisoners are planning for an escape; they have to discuss the plan without getting the attention of the guards. The only practical way for them is by having a normal insusceptible communication that carries the message in a hidden way [20].

In Steganography's ancient history, Histiaeus in 5th century BC used a steganography technique to send his message by tattooing shaved head of a slave and sending him as a carrier when the hair grew back. Another historical story is a reinvention of a Chinese old method of secret writing by an Italian mathematician using a paper mask that holds some holes and will be put on a blank page, the holes should be filled up with letters of the secret message, and when the mask is removed, the blank spaces between letter will be filled up with other letters to make a normal sentence so the message looks differently, but when the mask is put back, the letters of the secret message will be distinct. The mask is shared between two parties. [30]

Every method that includes Steganography uses an algorithm that embeds the data into a carrier and employs a detector function that retrieves back the embedded information. The embedding function has to use a secret key that only authorized parties are aware of. The function detects and recovers the message using the secret key. The hardest part in embedding the data is to not to create any detectable changes in carrier media while embedding. The most important point here is although detection of embedded data and secret data does not necessarily results to recovering it, but the risk of the chance of attacker's success is very high, hence avoiding obvious modifications is a must. The other important point to consider is that avoiding detectable changes does not guarantee invisibility of embedded data [22].

Some requirements of Steganography are *capacity*, *imperceptibility*, and *robustness*. Where, each concentrates respectfully on: the biggest amount of data that can be embedded in the carrier, avoiding unauthorized detection of embedded data, and strength of embedded data against being removed or damaged by operations done on the carrier like copy, cut, paste, etc[20].

1.4 DNA-Steganography

Nowadays, scientists work on different kind of Steganography algorithms to ameliorate the security of system. There are many Steganography algorithms to hide the secret data in to the host carrier. DNA Steganography is one of the cutting edge techniques in this area.

Basic concepts of the DNA Steganography are based on the properties of natural DNA sequences in the cell. In molecular biology, genetic information is stored in deoxyribonucleic acid which is known as DNA in the cells. DNA is made by four nucleotides which are thymidine (T), cytidine (C), guanosine (G), and adenosine (A). These bases are linked by backbone of DNA strands which are sugar components and phosphate groups. This backbone identifies the direction of the DNA strands [23].

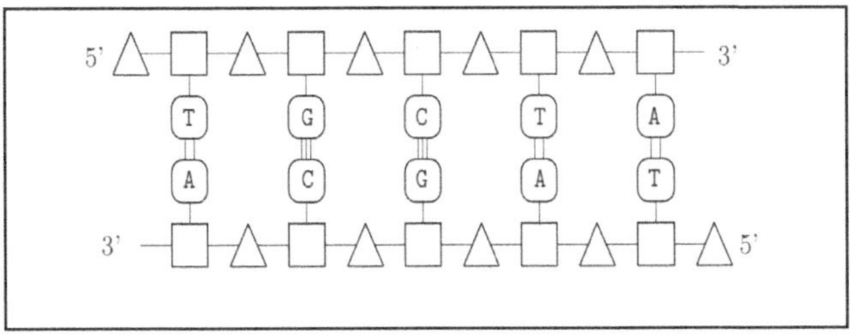

Fig. 2. The Backbone of DNA strand [23]

Each single strand is linked by hydrogen bond to make the DNA double strand. The standard situation of nucleotides allows to make a hydrogen bind between C and G; or A and T. This complementarily standard rule is known as Watson-Crick base-pairing. C and G are bonded by triple hydrogen bond, although A and T are linked by double hydrogen bond. This complementarily concept is the fundamental issue in genetic activities that leads to double DNA strands are twisted together and make DNA double helix. The mixture of these basic nucleotides which are thymidine (T), cytidine (C), guanosine (G), and adenosine (A) make the long polymer strands which able to make massive amount of combinations of DNA double helix that stores the every living features and properties of creatures such as human and mammal.

Some of the DNA data hiding approaches is based on biological properties of natural DNA sequences [24, 25, and 26]. That means that scientists work on real molecular DNA. Although, these works are very worthwhile and introduced new area of data hiding approaches, they have some drawbacks. One of the most popular disadvantages of natural DNA-based data hiding is the biological errors like mutation and difficulty of implementation of DNA system. Fortunately, Shiu proposed three different data hiding method based on DNA-coding technology. He claimed that his algorithm is robust and do not need equipped laboratory. In fact, DNA reference sequence S is elected and sample message N is combined with it to produce final data hiding result (S'). Furthermore, he compared these three algorithm based on capacity and payload. DNA reference sequence can be selected from different DNA database. One very important DNA database is EBI that provides vital genetic information [27].

2 The Proposed Protocol: Cryptography-Steganography Protocol

As discussed earlier, public key methods have much strength but there are lots of drawbacks to these cryptosystems. We are proposing a method for best security possible using a combination of cryptographic and steganography techniques. The method answers to requirements of a secure communication while defeating most of the popular attacks known up until today. The purpose of the proposed protocol is reducing the usage of public key cryptography.

The structure of proposed algorithm is combinational of concepts of cryptography and steganography. Available cryptography protocols use potential advantages of symmetric and public cryptography. As we know, symmetric-key cryptography is strong in terms of their algorithms and asymmetric-key cryptography can be used to protect symmetric algorithm by distributing its key. However, because of the nature of cryptographic algorithms the attacker is always aware of transmission of sensitive data. Even a non-interested attackers can get interested to break the ciphertext out of curiosity and challenge, when suddenly catches some scrambled data over the network, and who knows, this might be some vital information of a an organization! So the problem still is how to distribute the secret key of symmetric algorithms.

By using steganography we propose to hide the existence of transmission of message and by that we mean a hidden key distribution. Steganography needs a secret key, which is distributed among two parties for every establishment of new communication, for embedding the data. The steganography technique in this paper is DNA-based algorithm to change secret messages.

Every DNA Steganography algorithm has its secret key to extract real message from the carrier. We can use some different techniques to transfer the steganography key. In this paper we do not want to focus on approach to exchange DNA steganography, but we can use hybrid cryptosystem based on DNA Steganography which is proposed in NajafTorkaman's paper [28]. Sender and receiver use following protocol to exchange the session key.

For the first communication,

1. Alice communicates with Bob to share a secret key (DNA steganography key).
2. Bob receives the steganography key and uses it to embed the symmetric key in a DNA stream
3. Alice receives the DNA stream, extracts the symmetric key and the symmetric connection is established.

For all next communications,

1. Alice embeds a new symmetric key in a DNA stream, sends it to Bob.
2. Using the same DNA Steganography key, Bob extracts the symmetric key and generates a symmetric connection.

The following figure demonstrates a graphical representation of the proposed protocol:

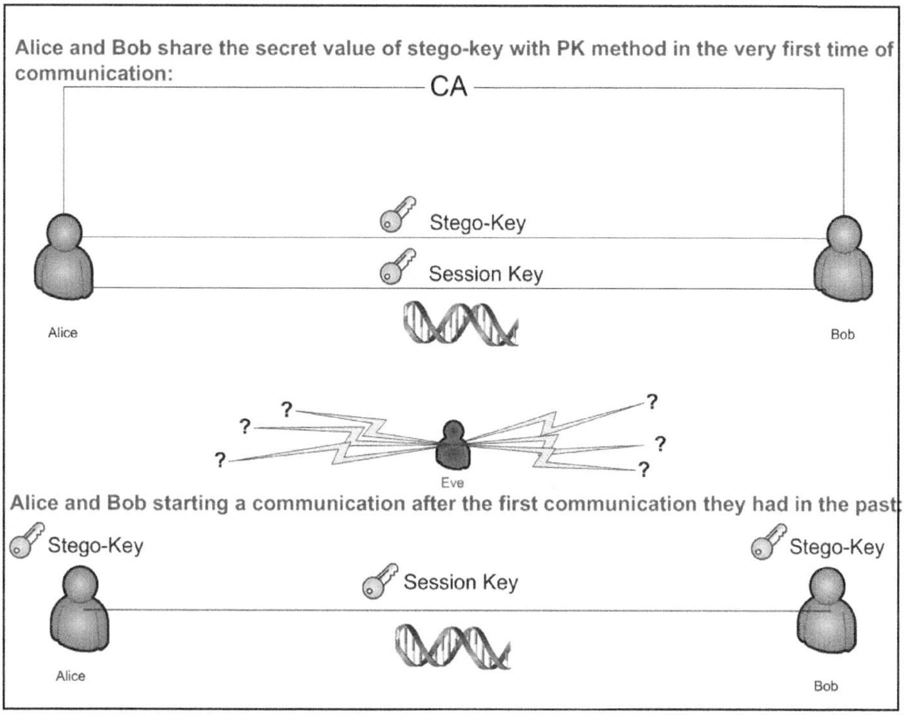

Fig. 3. Proposed method – hybrid cryptosystem integrated with DNA Steganography

2.1 Proposed DNA Steganography

The background knowledge of proposed algorithm in this section to hide the session key is based on Shiu experiment [27]. In fact there are different DNA sequences on diverse DNA bank web sites like EBI database (European Bioinformatics Institute) [29]. Proposed algorithm use the EBI DNA bank to extract 163 million DNA based sequences.

There are two major rules in this DNA steganography process. The first rule is the DNA coding technology rule that is kept secret among the sender and receiver. DNA coding technology is the approach to convert binary data to DNA string. The second rule of this DNA-based steganography is DNA complementary rule is also kept secret in sender and receiver side. There are six major complementary rules for each letter of DNA sequence. For all letter x, C(x), C(C(x)), C(C(C(x))) is not equal.

AT	TC	CG	GA
AT	TG	GC	CA
AC	CT	TG	GA
AC	CG	GT	TA
AG	GT	TC	CA
AG	GC	CT	TA

Fig. 4. Six major complementary rules for each DNA sequence

Furthermore, our DNA coding technology rules to convert binary data to DNA string in this paper is based on table following rules. 00 is converted to AA, 01 converted to T, 10 converted to C, 11 converted to GG, 0 converted to A, and 1 converted to G.

The DNA-based data hiding algorithm is divided to two main part sender and receiver process. Sender follows some steps to conceal binary data in the DNA sequence. First, sender extracts reference sequence from EBI database which is available publicly or uses DNA coding technology to convert any binary data and make reference DNA sequence. For example the reference sequence is S= 'CGTATCGAATCGATGCAGAT'. In this example secret message is M='10001101'. As we can see the length of reference sequence is 20 and the length of secret message is 8. Use any random generator to make 8 integer random numbers which are from 1 to 20. After implementation of this pseudo code in MATLAB software the output of sender algorithm is s'= 'CGATGATCGGATCGAATGCA' , Sender can send this DNA string in public channel to receiver.

$S=s_1+s_2+s_3+\ldots+s_m=$ CGTATCGAATCGATGCAGAT
$M=m_1+m_2+m_3+\ldots+m_p=$ '10001101'
$A=\{A_1+A_2+A_3+\ldots+A_p\}=\{1, 3, 4, 6, 9, 11, 13, 16\}$

```
function S'=hide(S,M,A)
x= size(S,2); // get the length of reference sequence
y= size(A,2); // get the length of set of random number
 for i=1:x
  for j=1:y
if (i== A(j) && M(j)==1 )
   S'(i)= C(s(i))    // use complementary rule
```

```
else if  (i== A(j) && M(j)==0 )
      S'(i)= s(i);
else
S'(i)=  C( C(s(i))) // use complementary rule
     end
end
end
```

Receiver knows about complementary rule and the DNA reference sequence S. He uses this pseudo code to find original secret message. As we mentioned C(s(i)) is complementary based on complementary rule . The output of this pseudo code is M which is the original secret message.

```
function S'=extract(S, S')
i=1;
j=1;
x= size(S',2);
for i=1:x
 if (s(i)==s(i'))
      M(j)= 0;
      j=j+1;
 else (s'(i)== C(s(i)))
    M(j)= 1;
  j=j+1;
end
end
```

In connection establishment, sender and receiver transfer steganography key which is complementary rules. This transformation process can be done with different kind of current cryptography or DNA cryptography algorithms. After that session key of communication is transferred by proposed DNA steganography.

2.1.1 Strength of Proposed DNA Steganography

In proposed DNA steganography, as we mentioned there are six main complementary rules for each letter in DNA sequence. The strength point of steganography algorithm is DNA reference sequences which are selected from EBI database. There are almost 163 million DNA sequences. It is impossible for the attacker to get knowledge about existence of a secret message concealed in the DNA sequence. In case the attacker knows that a secret message is embedded in the DNA sequence, it is unfeasible to guess the correct sequence among 163 million DNA sequences. Therefore the probability of finding the original secret message from 163 million DNA sequences is:

$$\frac{1}{1.63\times 10^{8}} \times \frac{1}{6}$$

Proposed DNA steganography algorithm is based on the third algorithm of shiu [27] and he compared different DNA steganography based on capacity and payload.

This algorithm has some properties. The first property is using DNA reference sequence from EBI database. Therefore, it is impossible to find correct message among 163 million DNA sequences. The second property is its capacity which is equal to selected DNA string (|S|) that means the payload of this algorithm is zero. Table 1 shows the comparison between proposed algorithm and two other DNA data hiding method which are presented in Shiu's papper [27].

Table 1. A comparison of the different DNA data hiding methods

DNA data hiding method	Capacity	Payload
Insertion	$\lvert S\rvert + \frac{\lvert M\rvert}{2}$	$\frac{\lvert M\rvert}{2}$
Complementary pair	$\lvert S\rvert + \lvert M\rvert(K + 3\frac{1}{2})$	$\lvert M\rvert(K + 3\frac{1}{2})$
Algorithm of this paper	$\lvert S\rvert$	0

3 Conclusion

One of the popular cryptography protocols to exchange secret message is hybrid cryptosystems. They are called hybrid because they are a mixture of symmetric and asymmetric algorithms. Based on the information of this paper, public cryptography brings many disadvantages when used in key distribution protocols. Therefore, in this paper we proposed to reduce the usage of asymmetric cryptography and introduced a new cryptographic-steganography protocol. The main advantage of proposed cryptography protocol was using DNA steganography techniques to hide secret session key which is transferred among sender and receiver throughout unsecured channel. In proposed protocol attackers are not aware of exchanging session key which is hidden by DNA data hiding method. The strength point of the DNA steganography algorithm is using DNA reference sequences which are selected from EBI database. We have almost used 163 million DNA sequences from EBI database. It is impossible for attackers to find whether or not there are secret message concealed in DNA sequences. Even if attackers know a secret message is embedded in DNA sequences, it is unfeasible to guess the correct sequence among 163 million DNA sequences.

Acknowledgment

We would like to thank Professor Keith Martin of Information Security Group at Royal Holloway, University of London for many remarkable discussions on modern cryptography techniques and key management issues.

References

[1] Willett, M.: Cryptography old and new. Science Direct, Computers & Security, 177–186 (1982)
[2] Lin, H.S.: Cryptography and Public Policy. Journal of Government Information, 135–148 (1998)
[3] Alia, M.A., Yahya, A.: Public–Key Steganography Based on Matching Method. European Journal of Scientific Research, 223–231 (2010)
[4] Schneier, B.: Applied Cryptography. John Wiley & Sons, New York (1996)
[5] Kumar, S., Wollinger, T.: Fundamentals of Symmetric Cryptography. Embedded Security in Cars, 125–143 (2006)
[6] Burke, J., McDonald, J., Austin, T.: Architectural support for fast symmetric-key cryptography. In: Architectural Support for Programming Languages and Operating Systems. Association of Computing Machinery (2000)
[7] Mohapatra, P.K.: Public-Key Cryptography, Crossroads (2000)
[8] Knudsen, L.R.: Block ciphers-analysis, design, applications, Doctor Philosohy, Aarhus University (1994)
[9] Stinson, D.: Cryptography: Theory and Practice (discrete mathematics and its applications). CRC Press, Boca Raton (1995)
[10] de Canniere, C., Biryukov, A., Preneel, B.: An introduction to Block Cipher Cryptanalysis, pp. 346–356 (2006)
[11] Vignesh, R.S., Sudharssun, S., Kumar, K.J.J.: Limitations of quantum & the versatility of classical cryptography: a comparative study. Environmental and Computer Science, 333–337 (2009)
[12] Chaeikar, S., Razak, S., Honarbakhsh, S., Zeidanloo, H., Zamani, M., Jaryani, F.: Interpretative Key Management (IKM), A Novel Framework. Computer Research and Development, 265–269 (2010)
[13] Diffie, W., Hellman, M.E.: New Directions in Cryptography. IEEE Transactions on Information Theory, 644–654 (1976)
[14] Tzeng, W.G.: Common modulus and chosen-message attacks on public-key schemes with linear recurrence relations. Information Processing Letters, 153–156 (1999)
[15] Izmerly, O., Mor, T.: Chosen ciphertext attacks on lattice-based public key encryption and modern (non-quantum) cryptography in a quantum environment. Theoretical Computer Science, 308–323 (2006)
[16] Aboud, S.J.: An efficient method for attack RSA scheme. IEEE Applications of Digital Information and Web Technologies, 587–591 (2009)
[17] Rivest, R.L., Shamir, A.: How to Expose an Eavesdropper. Communications of the ACM, 393–395 (1984)
[18] Bellovin, S.M., Merritt, M.: An attack on the Interlock Protocol when used for authentication. IEEE Information Theory, 273–275 (1994)
[19] Johnson, N.F., Jajodia, S.: Exploring Steganography: Seeing the Unseen. IEEE, 26–34 (1998)
[20] Lenti, j.: Steganographic Methods. Periodica Polytechnica, 249–258 (2000)
[21] Fridrich, J., Du, R.: Secure Steganographic Methods for Palette Images. LNCS, pp. 47–60. Springer, Heidelberg (2000)
[22] Phoenix, S.: Cryptography, trusted third parties and escrow. Bt Technol. Journal 32, 45–62 (1997)
[23] Watson, J., Crick, F.: Molecular structure of nucleic acids: a structure for deoxyribose nucleic acid. JAMA (1993)

[24] Leier, A., Richter, C., Banzhaf, W., Rauhe, H.: Cryptography with DNA binary strands. BioSystems 57, 13–22 (2000)
[25] Manacher, G.: A new linear-time on-line algorithm for finding the smallest initial palindrome of the string. Journal of the ACM 22, 346–351 (1975)
[26] Shimanovsky, B., Feng, J., Potkonjak, M.: Hiding Data in DNA. In: Petitcolas, F.A.P. (ed.) IH 2002. LNCS, vol. 2578, pp. 373–386. Springer, Heidelberg (2003)
[27] Shiu, H., Ng, K., Fnag, J.F., Lee, R., Huang, C.: Data hiding methods based upon DNA sequences. Information Sciences 180, 2196–2208 (2010)
[28] Najaftorkaman, M., Shanmuham, B., Abbasy, M., Ordi, A.: Hybrid Cryptosystem with DNA Technology. In: International Conference on Information Security and Artificial Intelligence, vol. 1, pp. 1460–1464 (2010)
[29] European Bioinformatics Institute, http://www.ebi.ac.uk/
[30] Cheddad, A., Condell, J., Curran, K., Kevitt, P.M.: Digital image steganography: Survey and analysis of current methods. Signal Processing 90, 727–752 (2010)

Data Hiding Method Based on DNA Basic Characteristics

Mohammad Reza Abbasy, Azizah Abdul Manaf, and Shahidan M.A.

Advanced Informatics School (AIS), International Campus,
Universiti Teknologi Malaysia (UTM), Kuala Lumpur
ramohammad2@live.utm.my,
{azizah07,mshahidan}@ic.utm.my

Abstract. The main target of this paper is to propose an algorithm to implement data hiding in DNA sequences to increase the complexity by using software point of view. By utilizing some interesting features of DNA sequences, the implementation of a data hiding is applied. The algorithm which has been proposed here is based on binary coding and the complementary pair rules. Therefore, DNA reference sequence is chosen and also a secret message M is hidden into it. After applying three steps, M´´´ is come out. Finally, M´´´ is sent to the receiver. When the receiver takes the M´´´, the process of identifying and extracting the original message M, which has been hidden in DNA reference sequence, begins. In addition, security issues are demonstrated to inspect the complexity of the algorithm.

Keywords: DNA sequence; data hiding; DNA base pairing rules; complementary pairing rules; DNA binary coding.

1 Introduction

In order to protect data through the unsecure networks like the Internet, using various types of data protection is necessary. One of the famous ways to protect data through the Internet is data hiding. Because of the increasing number of Internet users, utilizing data hiding or Steganographic techniques is inevitable. Eliminating the role of the intruder and authorizing the receiver, are eventual goals of these techniques.

Thus, the role of data hiding has become more eminent nowadays. Before employing biological properties of DNA sequences, usually embedding a secret message into the host images was the traditional way of data hiding [1, 2, 3, 4, and 5].

Unfortunately, this had some liabilities. The most important ones was the detection of the distortions of the image when the host image changed to some degrees. This spot was the best spot to start the wholly detection of the secret message through the image. By advent of biological aspects of DNA sequences to the computing areas, new data hiding methods have been proposed by researchers, based on DNA sequences [6, 7, 8, 9, and 10]. The key portion of their work is, utilizing biological characteristics of DNA sequences.

In order to convert binary data into amino acids as a DNA sequence, the base pairing rules must be used. Synthesizing nucleotides in real environment (biology) is done in constant rules:

E. Ariwa and E. El-Qawasmeh (Eds.): DEIS 2011, CCIS 194, pp. 53–62, 2011.

- Purine **A**denine (A) always pairs with the pyrimidine **T**hymine (T)
- Pyrimidine **C**ytosine (C) always pairs with the purine **G**uanine (G)

Always, those rules are done naturally because the opportunities to synthesize hydrogen bonds between A and T (two bonds), and also between C and G (three bonds) is different, basically (hydrogen bonds have been shown with dotted lines in Fig1). These concepts are named Watson-Crick base pairing rules when they discovered DNA's fundamental structure as a Noble prize [13].

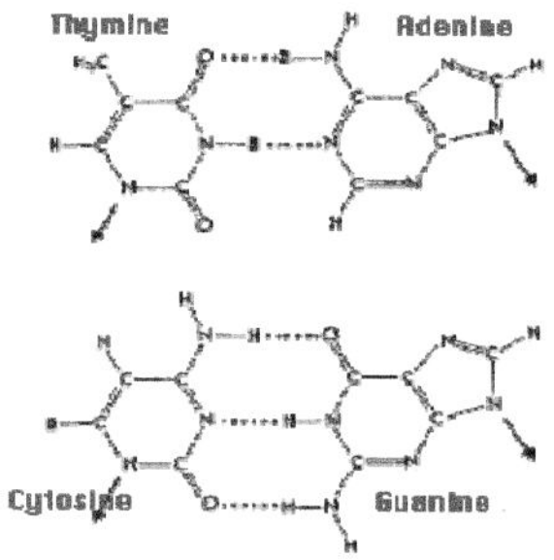

Fig. 1. Synthesizing basic nucleotides naturally

In binary computing area, it is possible to change the natural rules by own decision. For example, in biology A is synthesized to T while we can assume A to C or A to G, and so on, as we prefer. Increasing the complexity of the algorithm is the main purpose of the changing the rules. In this paper, the authors consider A=00, T=01, C=10, and G=11 to convert binary message to DNA sequences.

A way to increase the complexity is complementary pair rule. Complementary pair rule is a unique equivalent pair which is assigned to every nucleotides base pair. As an example, complementary rule is applied on strand in below [16]:

Complementary rule: ((AC) (CG) (GT) (TA))
DNA strand: AATGC
Applying complementary rule on DNA strand: CCATG

Increasing the complexity is the main purpose of using those rules, in this paper. It means that, finding the original message by intruder needs extra calculations because there are four basic alphabets therefore four likelihood of complementary rule for every DNA sequences. So, the final number of possible those rules are 4×3×2×1=24. On the other hand, the possibility to happen a correct guess is $\frac{1}{24}$.

Extra information and findings for some basic definitions can be obtained in molecular biology reference books [11, 12, and 13].

2 Related Works

For the purpose of clarifying the algorithm in current paper, introducing some backgrounds of the knowledge is necessary [8, 11, 12, and 13]. The most important part of each DNA base data hiding algorithm is, manipulating four letters which has been called as nucleotides in biology. The letters are A, C, G, and T.

Any composition from them will make a sequence. For instance, two DNA sequences have been appeared in [16]. They mentioned sequences from European Bioinformatics Institute (which is known as EBI Database) [15] for the purpose of extracting DNA sequences of Litmus and Balsaminaceae. So, Litmus with 154 nucleotides and Balsaminaceae with 2283 are shown in below, respectively:

Litmus:
"ATCGAATTCGCGCTGAGTCACAATTCGCGCTGAGTCACAATTCG
CGCTGAGTCACAATTGTGACTCAGCCGCGAATTCCTGCAGCCCCG
AATTCCGCATTGCAGAGATAATTGTATTTAAGTGCCTGCTCGATA
CAATAAACGCCATTTGACC".

Balsaminaceae:
"TTTTTATTATTTTTTTTCATTTTTTTCTCAGTTTTTAGCACATATCA
TTACATTTTATTTTTTCATTACTTCTATCATTCTATCTATAAAATCG
ATTATTTTTATCACTTATTTTTCTAATTTCCATATTTCATCTAATGA
TTATATTACATTAAAGAAATCG".

Even though data can be shown by DNA nucleotides, but representing to binary was emerged in 1999 by Rauhe and et al. [17]. They represented numbers by using binary DNA sequences in figure 1. The creativity of their work was in how they could separate binary sequences from each other.

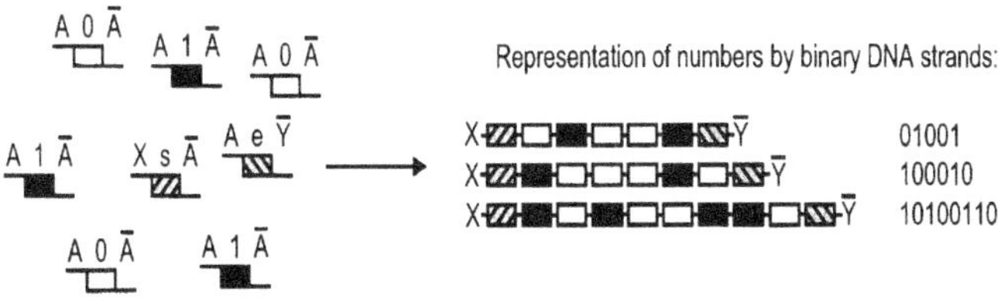

Fig. 2. Assembly of DNA binary strands [8]

All binary sequences are illustrated in form of s{0|1}e. An arbitrary DNA bits has been concatenated between two terminations, s and e, as start and end, respectively. Annealing and ligation are the way of concatenating DNA bits between s and e. Both of terminations and DNA bits have been made by annealing complementary oligonucleotides. In order to concatenate on both sides, having sticky ends (A, $\bar{A}$, X, $\bar{Y}$) are necessary. The sticky end A($\bar{A}$) acts as a variable for correct concatenation of bits and terminations. For subsequent cloning, the sticky ends X and $\bar{Y}$ should be used.

In 2000 Leier and et al. [8] brought a robust technique by utilizing a special key strand. They called it, primer. Primer has key role to decrypt a coded strand. Using a public DNA strand was utilized as a reference sequence in their DNA based encryption technique. In this scheme, the receiver must also be informed about the reference sequence. Namely, the receiver will receive a selected primer and an encrypted strand. The intruder is not able to decrypt the binary data without knowing about both of primer and reference strand, certainly. A primer is a complementary subset from a sort of DNA strand. Normally, the primer is called a short substring. For example, assume S is a DNA strand:

S= "ATGCTTAGTTCCATCGGAGACTAATGGCCTA" and "two primers ATCAA and GATTAC". So "ATCAA and GATTAC are complementary substring of TAGTT and CTAATG", correspondingly. Definitely, a complementary rule is needed to handle the manipulations, correctly. For this reason, they defined a complementary rule which is A-T, T-A, C-G, and finally G-C.

Accomplishing those states in biology is done by a series of chemical mechanisms to combine primers with a DNA strand. Indicating the right position of the primers also is shown by a fluorescent chemical substance. When hybridization occurs among primers and substrings of the reference DNA reference sequence, it will become bright, obviously. Except bright places, remaining are dim sections. The exact message of bright portion is binary data '1' and naturally, a dim portion is referred to the binary data '0'. So, according to the above, the proper output of the hybridization is:

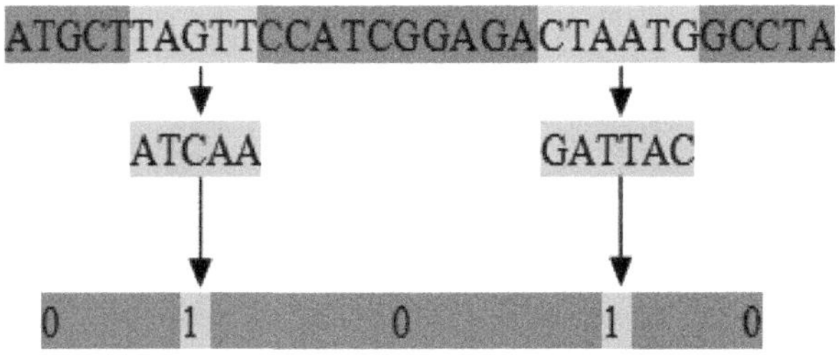

Therefore, the final secret message in form of binary is "01010". If the sender prefers to complicate that proposed technique, it can send one part of primers to the legitimate receiver. For the purpose of recovering primers, the receiver must apply PCR. PCR is another chemical scheme which has been known as Polymerase Chain Reaction, scientifically. It can recover primers correctly [16].

Considering a certain substring from DNA sequence as a character was proposed by Peterson in 2001 [9]. By substituting three successive nucleotides as a character, he could hide data in DNA sequence, appropriately. For instance, 'A'=GGC, 'B'=ATG, and so on. So, for this scheme we face to 64 symbols that can be possibly encrypted.

The main liability of this method is the frequency for both of 'E' and 'I' in an English message. Because of those holes, an intruder can apply a cryptanalysis technique base on frequencies of the most repetitive letters in English and subsequently extracts the secret message, simply.

The next scheme in 2002 [18] needs some backgrounds before explaining. An arrangement of nucleotides determines a protein. The responsibility of the proteins is almost every activity in cells. Transcription is the process by which RNA is created, an intermediary copy of the instruction contained in DNA. Naturally, RNA has four bases. They are adenine (A), cytosine (C), uracil (U) and guanine (G). The RNA copy is related to mRNA (abstract of messenger RNA) by throwing away the coming among sequences of RNA. On mRNA, each codon has three nucleotides for the purpose of representing which amino acid must be assigned in the next position. All different amino acids have been listed in Table 1. They are: Phe, Leu, Ile, Val, Ser, Pro, Thr, Ala, Tyr, His, Gln, Asn, Lys, Asp, Glu, Cys, Trp, Arg, Met and Gly. Each codon binds a set of three nucleotides into an anticodon which is called tRNA molecule (transfer RNA). The responsibility of the tRNA is, translating nucleic acid into protein. Totally, there are forty separate tRNA molecules which each one has a binding for one of amino acids, as represented in Table 1.

Apposite tRNA is bound to codon on the mRNA. When the STOP codon was seen, the translation is completed, and then a protein is released. Because of the codon redundancy, Shimanovsky et al. [18] utilized from that feature to hide data in mRNA. In general, each mRNA codon has been composed of three nucleotides. The likely nucleotides are: ‘U’, ‘C’, ‘A’, and ‘G’. Therefore, there are many different probable combinations to form each mRNA codon, whereas in Table 1, there are only twenty different amino acids. It is because of some codons might be mapped to the same amino acids. For instance, the codons ‘UUA’, ‘CUU’, ‘CUA’ and ‘UUG’ are mapped to the same amino acid Leu.

Table 1. The mapping of codon to amino acid [18]

UUU →Phe	UCU →Ser	UAU →Tyr	UGU →Cys
UUA →Leu	UCA →Ser	UAA →Stop	UGA →Stop
CUU →Leu	CCU →Pro	CAU →His	CGU →Arg
CUA →Leu	CCA →Pro	CAA →Gln	CGA →Arg
AUU →Ile	ACU →Thr	AAU →Asn	AGU →Ser
AUA →Ile	ACA →Thr	AAA →Lys	AGA →Arg
GUU →Val	GCU →Ala	GAU →Asp	GGU →Gly
GUA →Val	GCA →Ala	GAA →Glu	GGA →Gly
UUC →Phe	UCC →Ser	UAC →Tyr	UGC →Cys
UUG →Leu	UCG →Ser	UAG →Stop	UGG →Trp
CUC →Leu	CCC →Pro	CAC →His	CGC →Arg
CUG →Leu	CCG →Pro	CAG →Gln	CGG →Arg
AUG →Ile	ACC →Thr	AAC →Asn	AGC →Ser
AUG →Start	ACG →Thr	AAG →Lys	AGG →Arg
GUC →Val	GCC →Ala	GAC →Asp	GGC →Gly
GUG →Val	GCG →Ala	GAG →Glu	GGG →Gly

Feasibility of embedding information in the mRNA codon is because of the redundancy. For example, if the codon must be encrypted with ‘UUA’, while the secret message if four, it is possible to use the codon ‘UUG’ in order to replace the original. It is feasible because ‘UUG’ is the fourth codon of all the codons whose mapping amino acid is Leu. Even though previous replacement does not have any effect on the results of transcription, but it modifies the nucleotides of the original sequence, that might probably trigger unidentified consequences.

Although the previous beginning schemes utilize distinct biological features for hiding data in DNA sequences, they are not cost-effective and efficient to employ. In this paper, we apply a scheme to hide data in DNA strands based on a software point of view to improve them.

3 Proposed Method

This section is divided into two phases. The first one is, embedding and the second one is, extracting the original message.

3.1 *Phase 1*: Embedding Secret Message

In order to explain embedding phase, separating the phases into some successive and vivid sub-phases, is the best way of proposing current method. In below, sub-phases have been shown, respectively.

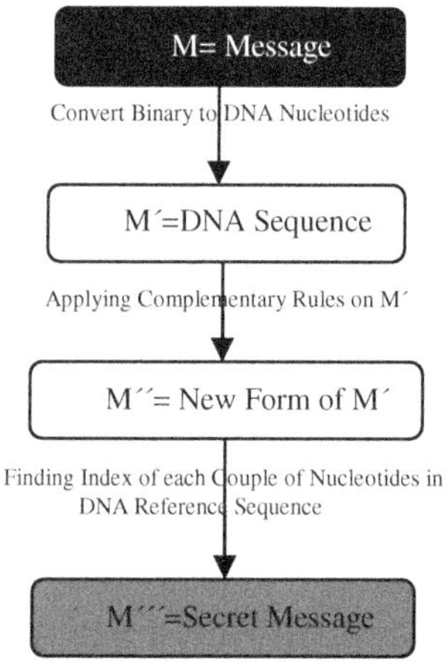

Fig. 3. Phase 1: Embedding secret message

Obviously, there is an original message M which the sender decides to send via a network to another client who is called receiver. So, there are three sub-phases to provide the final form of M which is M´´´ and send it to receiver. The first sub-phase is, converting by DNA base pairing rules. The product is M´. M´ contains nucleotides sequences. By applying DNA base pairing rules, the message can convert from binary to DNA sequence. Not only DNA base pairing helps to encrypt the message from binary to DNA sequence but also it is applied to decrypt the secret message to original one, truly.

The next (second) sub-phase is, applying complementary rules. Increasing the complexity is the real and exact purpose of this step. By applying the complementary rules, the new form of the M´ which is M´´ emerges. Now, M´´ is appeared. As mentioned before, both of sender and receiver have a DNA reference sequence from a large number of possibilities base on EBI [14] or NCBI [15] database. It means that, they have selected the same DNA reference sequence, exactly. The exact role of the third sub-phase is, extracting the index of each couple nucleotides in DNA reference sequence, numerically. When all the indexes have been extracted, M´´´ has been made, properly. M´´´ is precisely the secret message with some changes through the embedding phase. Now, sender can send the message (M´´´) to receiver.

Clarification of the current phase is continued by demonstrating an example, step by step. In this example, assume original message M=100111000011 should be sent to the receiver.

DNA Reference Sequence:
$AT_1CG_2AA_3TT_4CG_5CG_6CT_7GA_8GT_9CA_{10}CA_{11}AT_{12}TC_{13}GC_{14}GC_{15}TG_{16}AG_{17}TG_{18}AA_{19}CC_{20}$
M=100111000011

Sub-phase$_1$ $_{(A=00,\,T=01,\,C=10,\,G=11)}$: M´= CTGAAG
Sub-phashe$_2$ $_{((AC)\,(CG)\,(GT)\,(TA))}$: M´´= GATCCT
Sub-phase$_3$ (*Indexes*): M´´´=8137

Now, embedding phase is finally completed. Then, sender sends 8,13,7 to the receiver. In the next section, the receiver will apply the extracting phase for extracting the original message by using three consecutive phases.

3.2 *Phase 2*: Extracting Original Message

Now, receiver takes the secret message in form of some numbers. For the purpose of extracting the original message from DNA reference sequence, phase two with its sub-phases will extract the original message, correctly.

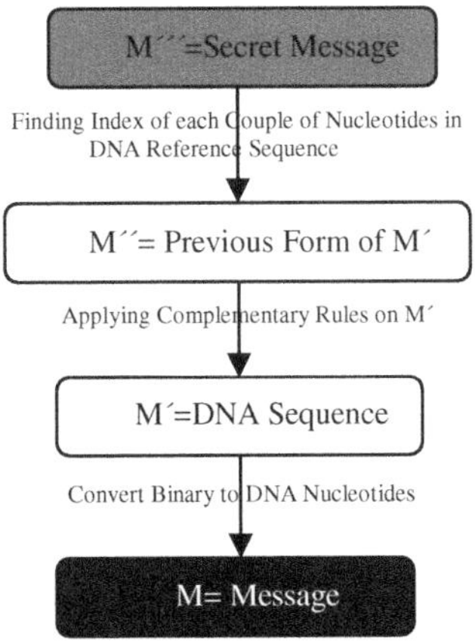

Fig. 4. Phase2: Extracting original message

So, the first sub-phase manipulates the M´´´. Because of the nature of the secret message which is some sorts of numbers (exact positions (indexes) of the original message on DNA reference sequence), extracting the message starts by finding the indexes on DNA reference sequence one by one according to the numbers which sender has sent in form of the current secret message. M´´ is the exact product of the first sub-phase. Consequently, the second sub-phase applies complementary rules on M´´ in order to extracting M´, correctly. The importance of the M´ is the form of it. M´ is the last form of message, based on DNA nucleotides. Converting the M´ to the M is the third sub-phase. Transforming from DNA nucleotides to the binary is the responsibility of the last sub-phase. Now, the receiver has truly extracted the original message M.

Those steps are demonstrated through the example in below:

DNA Reference Sequence:

$AT_1CG_2AA_3TT_4CG_5CG_6CT_7GA_8GT_9CA_{10}CA_{11}AT_{12}TC_{13}GC_{14}GC_{15}TG_{16}AG_{17}TG_{18}$ $AA_{19}CC_{20}$

M´´´=8137

Sub-phase$_{1\ (Indexes)}$: M´´= GATCCT
Sub-phase$_{2\ ((AC)\ (CG)\ (GT)\ (TA))}$: M´= CTGAAG
Sub-phase$_{3\ (A=00,\ T=01,\ C=10,\ G=11)}$: M=100111000011

So, the receiver extracted the original message, accurately by using a simple algorithm. In the next section, security and liabilities of the algorithm will inspect, briefly.

4 Security Issues

In terms of security, each intruder must be aware from the following information, correctly. Without this fundamental information, possibility of extracting original message is near to zero, scientifically. They are:

- DNA reference sequence: there are 163 million DNA reference sequence on EBI database. Therefore, the likelihood of making a doing well conjecture by attacker is $\frac{1}{24}$.
- Binary coding rule: as mentioned, the sender is free to select any equivalent binary form for every nucleotide. It means that, A can be '00', '01', '10', or '11'; C can be '00', and so on. In other words, all the binary coding rules are 4×3×2×1=24. So, the likelihood of making correct guess by attacker is $\frac{1}{24}$.
- Complementary pairing rule: like binary coding rule, there is 4×3×2×1=24 complementary alphabet among basic nucleotides. Therefore, the possibility of making successful attack is $\frac{1}{24}$.

Eventually, the final probability of making a correct and successful guess by attacker is $\frac{1}{163\times10^6}\times\frac{1}{24}\times\frac{1}{24}$.

5 Conclusion

Considering DNA characteristics brings new ideas in data hiding. DNA sequences are potential to implement new data hiding techniques or even transforming previous schemes to new one. In this paper, a reference DNA sequence has been shared between sender and receiver. Not only this DNA reference sequence can be retrieved from EBI [15] or NCBI [14] databases but it can also be simply selected from any database. Therefore, by considering any sort of database, there are 163 million targets to select it. Virtually, guessing the correct DNA sequence by attacker is unachievable.

The crucial feature of the DNA sequences is visibility. Finding secret message in a DNA sequence is difficult because the visibility of the sequences is very low. Therefore, attacker can not find out whether this sequence is a fake or not. In comparison with previous techniques, such as in images, not only implementing this method is not difficult but also it is formidable to detect, as well.

Acknowledgment. We would like to express our appreciation to Universiti Teknologi Malaysia (UTM) for providing financial support for this research.

References

1. Chang, C.C., Lin, C.C., Tseng, C.S., Tai, W.L.: Reversible hiding in DCT-based compressed images. Information Sciences 177 (2007)
2. Chang, C.C., Wu, W.C., Chen, Y.H.: Joint coding and embedding techniques for multimedia images. Information Sciences 178 (2008)
3. Huang, C.H., Wu, J.L.: Fidelity-guaranteed robustness enhancement of blind-detection watermarking schemes. Information Sciences 179 (2009)
4. Tsai, H.H., Sun, D.W.: Color image watermark extraction based on support vector machines. Information Sciences 177 (2007)
5. Tseng, H.W., Hsieh, C.P.: Prediction-based reversible data hiding. Information Sciences 179 (2009)
6. Chang, C.C., Lu, T.C., Chang, Y.F., Lee, R.C.T.: Reversible data hiding schemes for deoxyribonucleic acid (DNA) medium. International Journal of Innovative Computing, Information and Control 3 (2007)
7. Clelland, C.T., Risca, V., Bancroft, C.: Hiding messages in DNA microdots. Nature 399 (1999)
8. Leier, A., Richter, C., Banzhaf, W., Rauhe, H.: Cryptography with DNA binary strands. BioSystems 57 (2000)
9. Peterson, I.: Hiding in DNA, Muse (2001)
10. Shimanovsky, B., Feng, J., Potkonjak, M.: Hiding data in DNA. In: Petitcolas, F.A.P. (ed.) IH 2002. LNCS, vol. 2578, pp. 373–386. Springer, Heidelberg (2003)
11. Alberts, B., Bray, D., Lewis, J., Raff, M., Roberts, K., Watson, J.D.: Molecular Biology of the Cell. Garland Publishing, New York (1994)
12. Lehninger, A.L., Nelson, D.L., Cox, M.M.: Principles of Biochemistry. Worth, New York (2000)

13. Watson, J., Hopkins, N., Roberts, J., Steitz, J.: Molecular Biology of the Gene, 4th edn. Benjamin Cummings, Menlo Park (1987)
14. National Center for Biotechnology Information, http://www.ncbi.nlm.nih.gov/
15. European Bioinformatics Institute, http://www.ebi.ac.uk/
16. Shiu, H.J., Ng, K.L., Fang, J.F., Lee, R.C.T., Huang, C.H.: Information Sciences 180(11) (June 1, 2010)
17. Rauhe, H., Vopper, G., Banzhaf, W., Howard, J.C.: (1999)
18. Shimanovsky, B., Feng, J., Potkonjak, M.: Hiding data in DNA. In: Petitcolas, F.A.P. (ed.) IH 2002. LNCS, vol. 2578, pp. 373–386. Springer, Heidelberg (2003)

Influence of Access Pattern on Performance of NAND-Based Storage

Ilhoon Shin

NowonGu GongleungDong, Seoul National University of Science and Technology, Building 3, 207, Seoul 139-743, South Korea
ilhoon.shin@snut.ac.kr

Abstract. NAND flash memory lacks an over-write operation, and NAND-based storage deploys flash translation layer (FTL), which emulates the over-write with out-of-place updates. The performance of NAND-based storage is mainly determined by the performance of the FTL, which significantly varies according to access pattern. The present work aims to identify key attributes of access pattern which favors for the FTL. If the key attributes are identified, file systems can be modified to generate NAND-friendly access pattern. The performance evaluation results through trace-driven simulations shows that the request size is the most critical factor that impacts on the performance.

Keywords: access pattern, NAND-friendliness, flash translation layer, NAND flash memory.

1 Introduction

NAND flash memory is small-form, lightweight, shock-resistant, and energy-efficient compared to hard disk, and thus it has been widely used for mobile devices. As the cost per bit of NAND flash memory is steeply decreasing, even PC and laptop recently start to deploy NAND as a form of SSD (Solid State Drives). However, it is not as successful as in the mobile market because of its expensive price and relatively low write performance. Thus, there have been various researches to improve the write performance of NAND-based storage. Most of them focused on the internal design of NAND-based storage such as sector mapping schemes of FTL (Flash Translation Layer) [1-6]. Whereas these approaches are advantageous in that it does not require modifying file systems, a performance improvement is restricted. For example, the pure page mapping scheme [1] that delivers the best performance is not easy to be deployed for TB (Terabytes) sized SSDs because of considerably large memory consumption. Both the block mapping scheme [2] and the BAST (Block Associative Sector Translation) scheme [3] are vulnerable against a random write pattern. The FAST (Fully Associative Sector Translation) scheme [4] causes a serious computation overhead, which results in a degraded performance [5, 6].

The effective way to improve the write throughput of large sized NAND-based storage is to utilize the external file systems. If file systems generate NAND-friendly access pattern, even a simple FTL can deliver a good performance. The issue is what pattern is NAND-friendly. In this work, we identify the prime attributes to determine

E. Ariwa and E. El-Qawasmeh (Eds.): DEIS 2011, CCIS 194, pp. 63–69, 2011.

NAND-friendliness. The candidate attributes are request size, page-alignment and skewed write probability. As to the representative sector translation schemes, we study the influence of these attributes on the performance.

The rest of the paper is organized as follows. Section 2 describes NAND flash memory and the representative sector mapping schemes. The candidate attributes are explained in section 3. Section 4 presents an experiment results, and a conclusion is drawn in section 5.

2 Flash Translation Layer (FTL)

NAND flash memory consists of blocks and pages. A block is generally 128 KB in size and consists of multiple pages. A page is generally 2 KB in size. NAND flash memory is a kind of EEPROM (Electrically Erasable Programmable Read Only Memory). In order to update a cell, the cell should be erased first. The unit of the erase operation is a block, whereas the unit of the read/write operation is a page. Implementing an in-place update is therefore almost impossible because the erase operation clears the entire block. Therefore, NAND flash memory deploys a special firmware called FTL, which emulates the over-write operation with an out-of-place update.

In the out-of-place update, the physical location of the sector becomes different on a write request. Thus, FTL maintains the mapping table between logical sectors and their physical locations. The mapping table is usually kept in main memory for a fast access, which is a main source of memory consumption of FTL.

By the mapping unit, FTL is classified to page mapping [1], block mapping [2], and hybrid mapping [3, 4]. The block mapping performs the write in a block unit. Even when modifying a sector, the entire block that the sector belongs to is copied to other clean block. Thus, the write performance is seriously damaged. The page mapping performs the write in a page unit. The page mapping utilizes clean pages maximally and delivers a good write performance. However, the mapping table size is large because the number of mapping table entries is the same with the number of pages of NAND.

The hybrid mapping scheme combines the page mapping and the block mapping. It uses several blocks as write buffer, which is called log blocks. Log blocks are managed by page mapping to efficiently utilize the clean space, while the other data blocks are managed by block mapping. The requested data are written to the associated log blocks. If there is no available log block or no clean pages in the associated log block, a victim log block is merged with the associated data blocks. The BAST scheme [3] associates a log block with only one data block. Thus, log blocks may be frequently merged with under-utilized in the random write pattern, which hurts the write performance seriously. The FAST scheme [4] allows a log block to be associated with multiple data blocks to utilize the log blocks. It copes well with the random write pattern. However, a computation overhead of finding the location of the sector is considerable because the sectors that belong to the same block can be distributed across multiple log blocks. As FTL is executed by the low-speed internal controller, the considerable computation overhead degrades the performance seriously [5, 6].

3 Attributes That Determine NAND-Friendliness

The approaches to improve the write performance with the efficient sector mapping schemes are limitedly effective. The effective way is for file systems to generate NAND-friendly access pattern. It is clear that the sequential access is NAND-friendly because NAND does not support the over-write operation. Thus, the representative NAND flash file systems such as JFFS2 and YAFFS inherits log-structured file systems that assume the underlying storage is append-only log and generate only sequential writes. However, PC and server generally deploy EXT3, NTFS, or FAT file systems that issue the over-write requests. We therefore need to find a way to generate the NAND-friendly access pattern with the traditional file systems.

The goal of the work is to find critical attributes except the sequential writes that influence on the NAND performance. The candidate attributes are request size, page alignment, and skewed write probability. The request size is selected because the block mapping scheme and the BAST scheme may deliver a good performance when the request size is as large as a block. If the request size is a prime factor that determines NAND-friendliness, the format tool of the traditional file systems should be changed to use a large allocation unit.

Second, the page alignment is selected because unaligned requests may hurt the NAND performance. For example, if a 2KB sized write request is issued and it is page-aligned, one page write operation is performed in the best case. However, if it is unaligned, at least two page write operations should be performed. If the page alignment influences seriously on the performance, the partition and the format tools should be changed to keep NAND page alignment.

Third, the skewed write probability is selected because the hybrid sector mapping scheme that uses write buffer prefers the write requests to be concentrated. If the skewed write probability is a key factor, the file block allocation scheme should be modified to separate hot block (metadata, directory, small files, and so on) from cold block (multimedia data blocks).

4 Experiment Result

Since the influence of each attribute may be different according to the sector mapping schemes and the sector mapping scheme of NAND-based storage is usually unknown, we use a trace-driven simulation which implements the representative sector mapping schemes.

The simulator counts NAND read, write, and erase operations while handling the write requests from trace files, and finally prints the average write throughput. The latency of NAND read, write, and erase operations is assumed as Table 1 according to the Hynix NAND specification [7].

Traces were generated varying request size, page-alignment, and skew of write probability. The target partition was 8 GB in size, and the total amount of written bytes was 64 GB. The implemented sector mapping schemes are the block mapping, the page mapping, the BAST, and the FAST scheme. In the BAST and in the FAST scheme, 3% of the entire space is assumed to be used as log blocks.

Table 1. Latency of NAND operations

NAND Operation	latency
Page Read	30 us
Page Write	200 us
Block Erase	2 ms

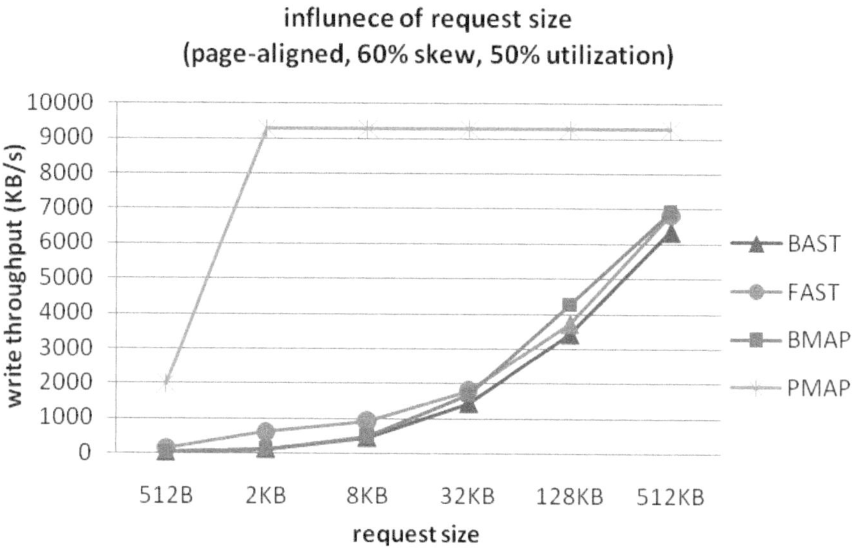

Fig. 1. The influence of request size

Fig. 1 shows the influence of request size. X axis of the figure is the request size, which varies from 512 bytes to 512 KB. Y axis is the average write throughput. The write requests are NAND page-aligned and only 50% of the partition was used. 60% of the write requests occurred in the 40% of the used region. The page mapping scheme and the block mapping scheme are denoted as PMAP and BMAP, respectively. The result shows the request size considerably influences on the write throughput. Except the page mapping scheme, the throughput is continuously improved as the request size increases. Especially, the improving ratio of the block mapping scheme is high. The block mapping scheme delivers a higher throughput than the hybrid mapping schemes when the request size exceeds NAND block size (128 KB). The performance of the page mapping scheme is greatly improved when the request size is the same with NAND page size (2 KB). However, if the request size is greater than 2KB (mapping unit), the performance of the page mapping scheme is the same, regardless of the request size. Conclusively, the request size should be at least greater than the mapping unit, and it is more beneficial to increase the average request size as possible.

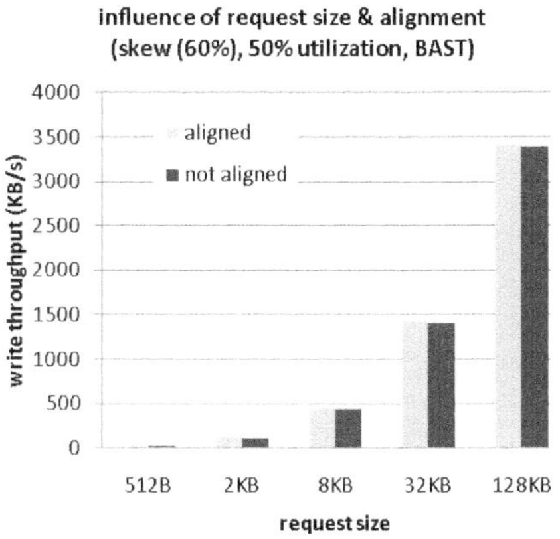

Fig. 2. Influence of page-alignment (BAST)

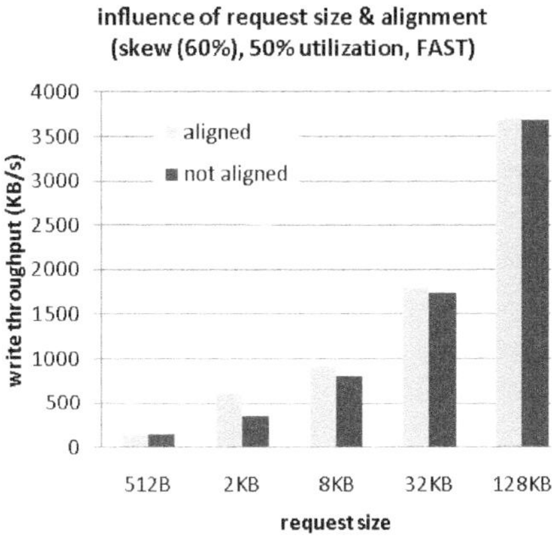

Fig. 3. Influence of page-alignment (FAST)

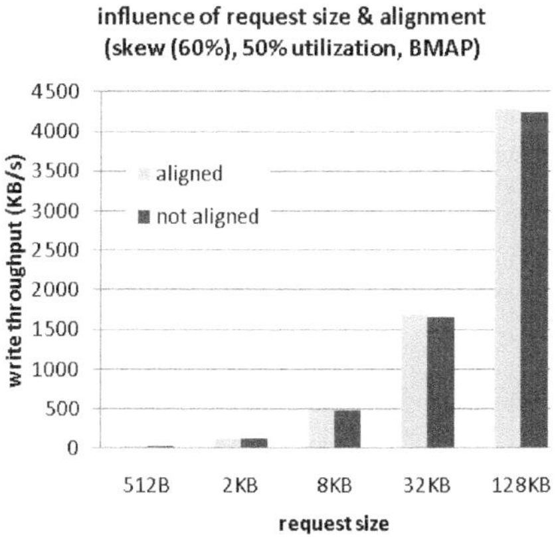

Fig. 4. Influence of page-alignment (BMAP)

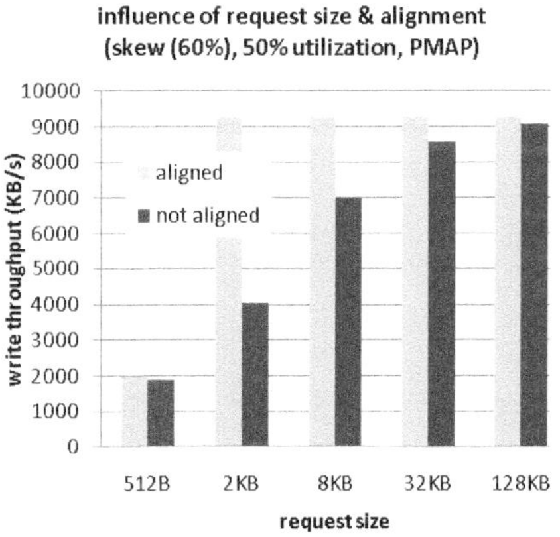

Fig. 5. Influence of page-alignment (PMAP)

Figures 2-5 show the influence of page-alignment of the BAST, the FAST, the block mapping, and the page mapping, respectively. X axis of each figure is the request size, which varies from 512 bytes to 128 KB. Y axis is the average write throughput. 50% of the whole partition was used, and 60% of the write requests occurred in the 40% of the used region. The results show that the page-alignment influences on the performance, and however its influence is not as critical as the request size, except the page mapping scheme. The performance degradation cased by unaligned requests is not serious in the hybrid scheme and in the block mapping scheme. In the page mapping scheme, its influence is serious when the request size is 2KB. However, the influence decreases as the request size increases. Thus, in the system that uses un-aligned partitions, it is required to increase the request size.

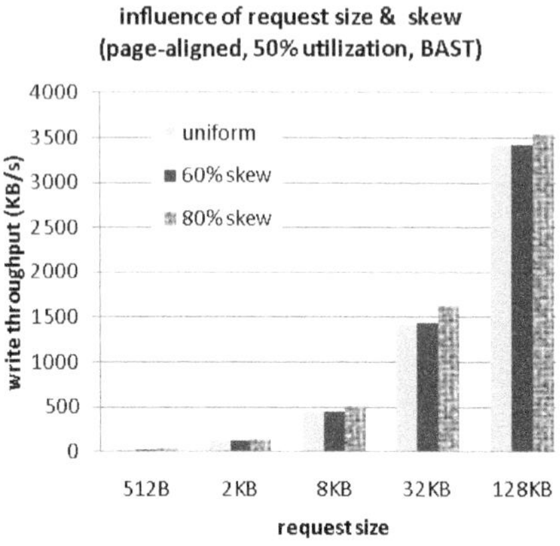

Fig. 6. Influence of skewed write (BAST)

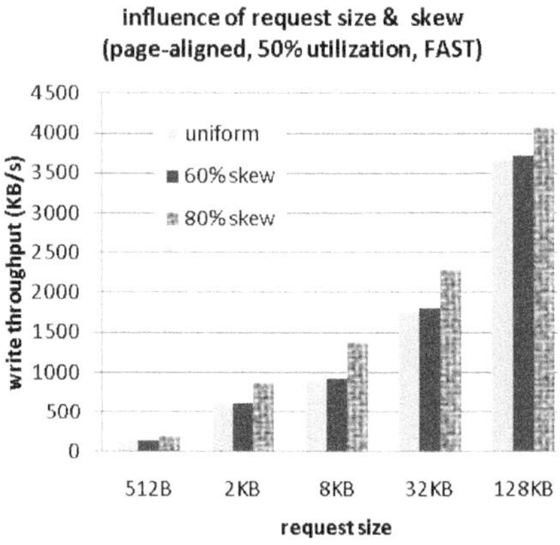

Fig. 7. Influence of skewed write (FAST)

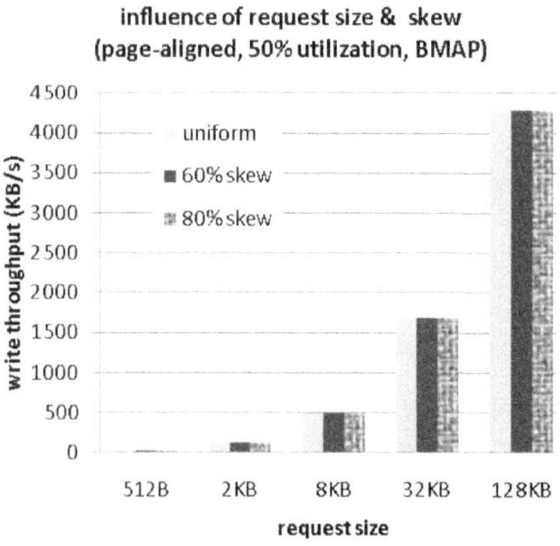

Fig. 8. Influence of skewed write (BMAP)

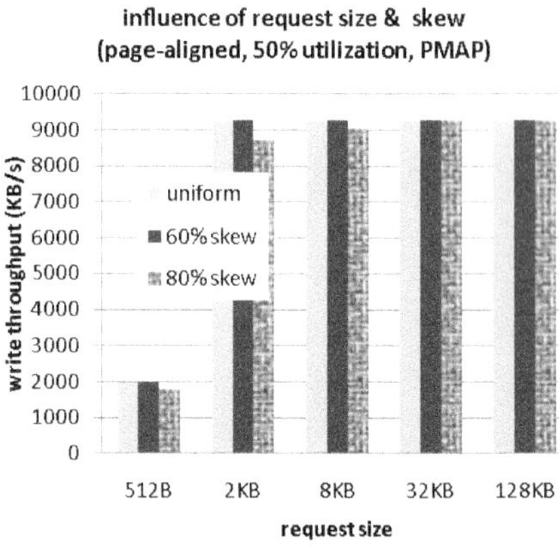

Fig. 9. Influence of skewed write (PMAP)

Figures 6-9 show the influence of skewed write probability of the BAST, the FAST, the block mapping, and the page mapping, respectively. X axis of each figure is the request size, which varies from 512 bytes to 128 KB. Y axis is the average write throughput. The write requests are NAND page-aligned and only 50% of the partition was used. Uniform means that the used region was written with the same probability, and 60% skew mean that 60% of the write requests occurred in the 40% of the used region. The results show that the influence of the skew of write probability is low in the block mapping and in the page mapping. In the hybrid schemes, skewed access pattern delivers a better performance because the utilization of log block increases when the write requests are concentrated. However, its impact is not as serious as the request size.

5 Conclusion

From the experiments, the most influential factor was the request size. It considerably influenced on the performance of the entire sector mapping schemes. In addition, the influences of page-alignment and skewed write probability were decreased as the request size increased. Thus, to improve NAND-based storage, file systems should use a large allocation unit, or SSD can use the internal buffer to increase the request size by absorbing small-sized write requests.

The influences of page-alignment and skewed write probability were restrictive. The page-alignment mainly influenced on the page mapping scheme, and the skewed write pattern was advantageous only in the hybrid mapping schemes that use log blocks.

The future work is to apply the result to the implementation of file systems. We plan to evaluate the performance improvement of NAND-based storage by using a large allocation unit and the internal buffer of SSD.

Acknowledgments. This work was supported by Basic Science Research Program through the National Research Foundation of Korea (NRF) funded by the Ministry of Education, Science and Technology (2010-0003938).

References

1. Ban, A.: Flash file system optimized for page-mode flash technologies. United States Patent, No. 5,937,425 (1999)
2. Ban, A.: Flash file system. United States Patent, No. 5,404,485 (1995)
3. Kim, J., Kim, J.M., Noh, S., Min, S., Cho, Y.: A space-efficient flash translation layer for compactflash systems. IEEE Transactions on Consumer Electronics 48, 366–375 (2002)
4. Lee, S., Park, D., Chung, T., Choi, W., Lee, D., Park, S., Song, H.: A log buffer based flash translation layer using fully associative sector translation. ACM Transactions on Embedded Computing Systems 6(3) (2007)
5. Shin, I.: Light weight sector mapping scheme for NAND-based block devices. IEEE Transactions on Consumer Electronics 56, 651–656 (2010)
6. Shin, I.: Reducing computational overhead of flash translation layer with hashed page tables. IEEE Transactions on Consumer Electronics 56, 2344–2349 (2010)
7. HY27UF084G2M series 4Gbit (512Mx8bit) NAND flash, Hynix Corp. (2006)

Semi-automatic Semantic Service Annotation for SOAP and REST Web Services

HyunKyung Yoo, YooMi Park, and Hyunjoo Bae

Service Convergence Research Team
Electronics and Telecommunications Research Institute (ETRI)
Daejeon, Republic of Korea
{hkyoo,parkym,hjbae}@etri.re.kr

Abstract. Until now, most service annotation has been added the semantics to WSDL, that is a description of SOAP based web services. But REST services have been widely used because of simplicity and usability. In order to discover the most suitable services among various web services and compose them, the integrated service annotation of SOAP and REST web services is necessary. In this paper, we present semantic service framework which is designed for user's goal based service discovery and composition. And we present the semi-automatic service annotation for SOAP and REST web services. The proposed annotation approach deals with functional semantics, non-functional semantics, and data semantics from web service description and web service portal. Based on this service annotation, it is useful to discover and compose services that satisfy the user's goal.

Keywords: semantic web services, service annotation, data semantics, functional semantics, non- functional semantics, SOAP, REST.

1 Introduction

Web services specify the description of service functionality and the invocation method. With these service descriptions, users discover, compose, and execute the web services. But because of no semantics like QoS(Quality of service), availability, and security in service descriptions, there is a limit to find the services that satisfy the user's goal more accurately.

Semantic web services are web services whose properties, capabilities, interfaces, and effects are encoded in an unambiguous, and machine-interpretable form[1]. They are essential to facilitate the automated discovery and composition of web services on the basis of comprehensive semantic information. Most of all, semantic service annotation is basic step for automated discovery and composition of semantic web services.

There are 4 types of semantics in web services: data semantics, functional semantics, non-functional semantics, and execution semantics[2]. Data semantics are formal definition of data in input and output parameters of a web service. They are used in service discovery and interoperability between web services. Functional semantics are formal definition of the capabilities of a web service like service name,

E. Ariwa and E. El-Qawasmeh (Eds.): DEIS 2011, CCIS 194, pp. 70–77, 2011.

category, and provider. They can help the discovery and composition of web services. Non-functional semantics are formal definition of quantitative or non-quantitative constraints like QoS requirements like minimum cost and policy requirements like message encryption. They are used in discovery, composition and interoperability of Web services. Execution Semantics are the formal definition of the operational behavior of a system. They describe how the system behaves, what the semantics are of the execution of the system. They are used in process verification and exception handling.

We focus on the semantic annotation of web services, especially considering data semantics, functional semantics, and non-functional semantics about UC(Unified Communication) domain.

In this paper, we propose the architecture of semantic service framework which is designed for user's goal based service discovery and composition. And we present semantic service annotator that supports the semi-automatic service annotation for SOAP and REST web services. Our annotation approach deals with functional semantics, non-functional semantics, and data semantics from web service description and web service portal.

This paper is organized as follows. In the next section, we go into the architecture of semantic service framework and the each function's role. Section 3 describes main semantic information of web services and our semantic service annotator's operation method. We conclude in Section 4 and give an outline for future work.

2 Semantic Service Framework

Generally, lifecycle of web service has 5 steps: service publication, discovery, selection, composition, and invocation. Service publication includes service annotation and it makes available the description of the capability of a service. Service discovery locates different services suitable for a given task. Service selection is to choose the most appropriate services among the available ones. Service composition combines services to achieve a goal. Service execution is to invoke services following programmatic conventions.

This Semantic Service Framework (see Fig. 1) is designed for user's goal based service discovery and composition. It consists of Semantic Service Annotator, Integrated Service Registry, Application Creator, Goal Ontology, and Semantic Service Discovery function.

Semantic Service Annotator function provides the semantic annotation of web services using data semantics, functional semantics, and non-functional semantics. And annotated services are published to Integrated Service Registry. When Application Creator function receives user's goal input, it requests and responses synonyms of input to the Goal Ontology function. Receiving the synonyms of request goal, Application Creator function requests goal-driven service discovery to Semantic Service Discovery function. Semantic Service Discovery function discovers and selects the matched service lists. Finally, Application Creator function receives service discovery result and performs service invocation.

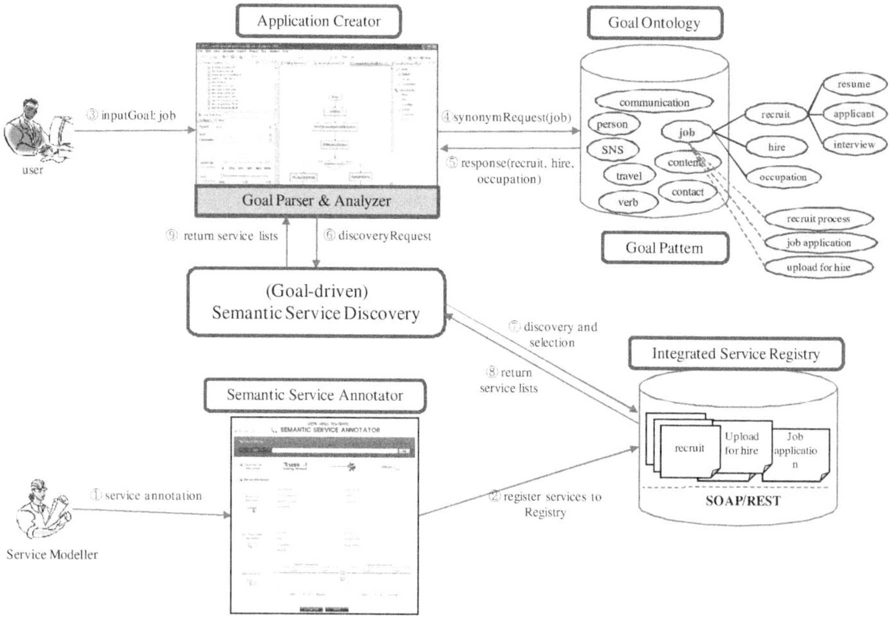

Fig. 1. Semantic Service Framework

We apply semantic service framework to UC domain. So we annotated UC services like call, message, e-mail, group, presence, directory, discussion, and job. And we defined keyword based goal ontology and goal pattern. In service discovery process, we used job related goal ontology and goal pattern.

3 Semantic Service Annotator

Currently, no annotation standard for web services exists. However, there exist a range of proposals for such a standard, the most prominent ones are[3]:

- OWL for service, OWL-S(Semantic Markup for Web Services)[4], a collaborative effort of academic and industrial partner within DARPA Agent Markup Language program(DAML).
- WSDL[5] for service, WSDL-S[6], a specification by IBM and the METEOR group at the University of Georgia.
- Web Service Modeling Ontology, WSMO[7], an extension and refinement of the Web Service Modeling Framework, WSMF.

These researches on semantic web services suggest new service model and description language with ontology for goal-based computing. However, the semantic description of web services using the new model and languages requires expertise on ontology and lots of manual work even for expert. In addition, they dealt with SOAP based web services rather than REST web services which are currently widely accepted. These limitations make it difficult to respond fast to the dynamically changing web service environment that exist more than 30,000 services[8].

For solving these problems, we provide a semi-automatic semantic service annotation environment by supporting automatically crawled the semantics of each web service and a step-wise annotation web user interface. To extract the essential semantic information, we analyzed semantic information defined in WSMO, OWL-S and UDDI[9].

WSMO service descriptions consist of functional, non-functional, and execution semantics of web services. WSMO considered category, capability(precondition), and capability (effect) in functional semantics and accuracy, financial, network-related QoS, performance, reliability, robustness, scalability, security, transactional, trust in non-functional semantics[10]. UDDI is an industrial initiative to create an internet wide network of registries of web services for enabling businesses to quickly, easily, and dynamically discover web services and interact with one another[11]. Similar to UDDI, OWL-S profile allows web service to define their service name, categories, description, contact information, service classification etc. And OWL-S profile element has a corresponding UDDI element described in [11]. For example, the contact information element is present in both OWL-S Profile and UDDI.

In our current work, we have extended the OWL-S/UDDI mapping to WSMO semantics. Figure 2 shows mapping relation of WSMO, OWL-S profile, and UDDI. Service category, precondition, effect, and QoS elements are common semantics in WSMO, OWL-S profile, and UDDI.

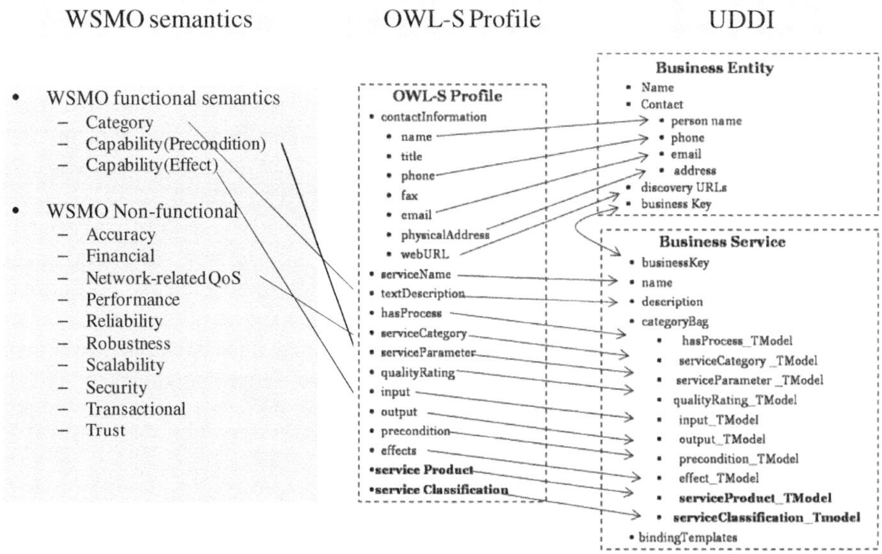

Fig. 2. Mapping relation of WSMO, OWL-S profile, and UDDI

Based on mapping relation of WSMO, OWL-S profile, and UDDI, we defined main semantic fields as following table 1. In this table, we surveyed whether each field of semantic type is defined in SeekDa and ProgrammableWeb which are public

Table 1. Main Semantics

	Field	SeekDa	Program mableweb	main factor	reference
Data semantics	input[2)3)]	input	×	O	WSDL or UseNow in SeekDa
	output[2)3)]	output	×	O	WSDL or UseNow in SeekDa
Functional semantics	serviceName[2)3)]	title	API name	O	
	serviceCategory[1)2)3)]	×	category	O	
	serviceProvider[2)3)]	provider	provider	O	
	serviceURL[1)2)3)]	WSDL File	API home	O	
	description[1)2)3)]	description	summary	O	
	country	country	×	(optional)	
	effect	×	×	(optional)	User Tags(keyword) in SeekDa
Non-functional semantics	protocol[1)]	protocol	protocol	O	SOAP or REST
	availability[1)]	availability	×	(optional)	response time
	cost[1)]	×	usage fees	(optional)	
	security[1)]	×	security	(optional)	no token, token, SSL support
	rating[1)]	user rating	×	(optional)	user rating in SeekDa
	serviceType	×	×	(optional)	atomic service or composite service
	responseTime	×	×	(optional)	availability graph in SeekDa

[1)] semantic information defined in WSMO
[2)] semantic information defined in OWL-S
[3)] semantic information defined in UDDI

web service portals. They provide the semantic information of registered web services. And we defined main factors in our semantic service annotator.

Data semantics we considered are input and output parameter names and types. They can be parsing from WSDL or useNow in SeekDa. Functional semantics are service name, service category, service provider, service location(URL/URI), description, country, and effect. Service name is defined to title in SeekDa and API name in ProgrammableWeb. Service category is not defined in SeekDa but defined to category in ProgrammableWeb. Service provider is defined in SeekDa and ProgrammableWeb. Service location is defined to WSDL in SeekDa and API home in ProgrammableWeb. Also description field is defined to descrption in SeekDa and summary in ProgrammableWeb. Country is only defined in SeekDa, so we use this field optionally. Effect is not defined in SeekDa and ProgrammableWeb, but this field indicates additional service description optionally. Almost functional semantics can be crawled from web service portal.

Non-functional semantics are protocol, availability, cost, security level, user rating, service type, and response time. Protocol is defined to protocol in SeekDa and ProgrammableWeb, and shows whether service is SOAP or REST. Availability is only defined in SeekDa and it can be estimated from response time. Cost is only defined to usage fees in ProgrammableWeb and it is optional field. Security level is only defined to usage fees in ProgrammableWeb and shows whether specific service supports no token, token, or SSL security. User rating is only defined in SeekDa and it shows whether service users like a service or not. Service type is atomic or composite service and not defined in SeekDa and ProgrammableWeb. Also response time not defined in SeekDa and ProgrammableWeb but can be extracted from availability graph in SeekDa. Almost non-functional semantics are not defined in SeekDa and ProgrammableWeb, but these semantic fields are useful so we use them optionally.

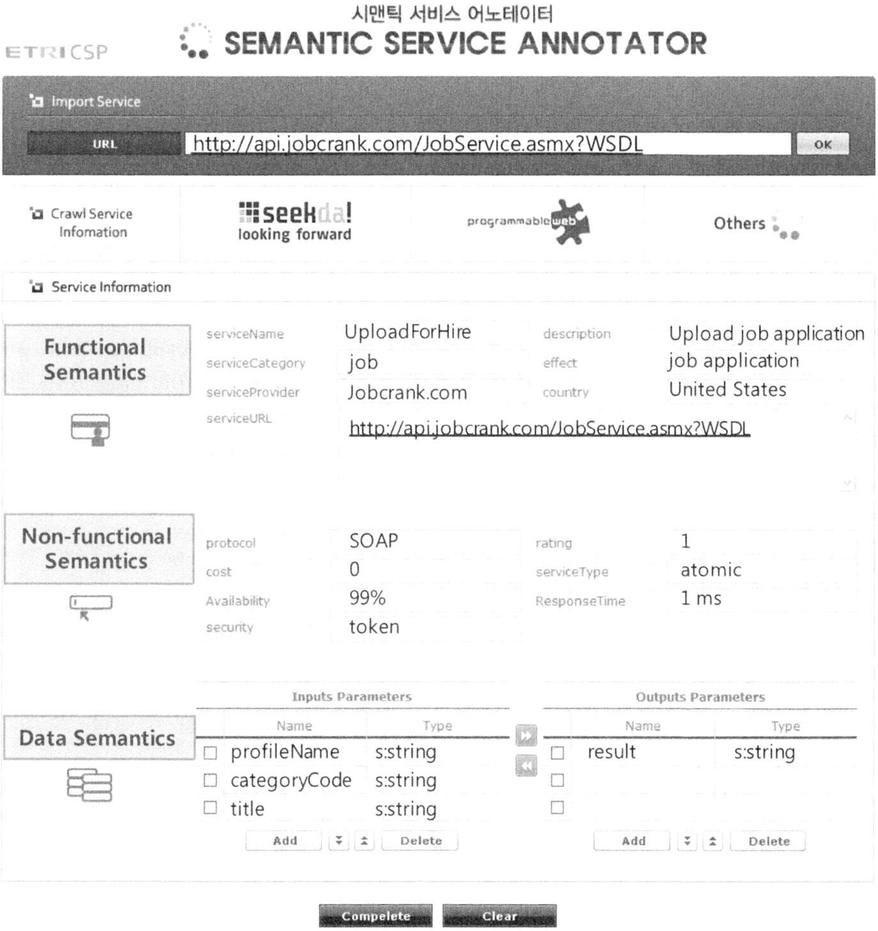

Fig. 3. Semantic Service Annotator UI

Fig.3 shows Semantic Service Annotator UI. It is composed of Import Service, Crawl Service Information, and Service Information part. Service Information consists of functional semantic fields, non-functional semantic fields, and data semantic fields.

In Import Service menu, user inputs SOAP service URL or REST service URI and sees service description. By parsing semantic fields described in service URL/URI, service name, service description, and input/output parameters field are automatically annotated.

In Crawl Service Information menu, when user clicks SeekDa or ProgrammableWeb, semantic fields registered in web service portal can be crawled. From crawled semantic information, service category, provider, and country field in functional semantics are automatically annotated. Also protocol, availability, cost, security, and rating field in non-functional semantics are automatically annotated. For Import Service and Crawl Service Information process, automatic annotation is performed. And then user can annotate manually the unfilled semantic field like service type and response time.

In this semantic service annotator UI, we give an example about job services. From WSDL, service name is uploadForHire, service description is upload job application, and input/output fields are automatically annotated. From SeekDa, service provider, country, protocol, availability, and rating fields are automatically annotated, too. And then we manually annotated effect, cost, security, service type, and response time.

After completion of annotation, user publishes service annotation to service registry for semantic discovery and composition.

Our semantic service annotator has 3 features. First, the integrated annotation for SOAP or REST services is possible. Second, it performs semi-automatic service annotation by crawling semantic information from web service description and web service portal. Third, it provides not only functional semantic information, but also non-functional semantic information like availability, rating, response time which accumulated at runtime. It is useful architecture to goal-based service discovery.

4 Conclusions

In this paper, we presents semantic service framework which is designed for user's goal based service discovery and composition. We apply semantic service framework to UC(Unified Communication) domain. So we annotated UC services like call, message, e-mail, group, presence, directory, discussion, and job. And we defined keyword based goal ontology and goal pattern.

We propose the semi-automatic semantic service annotation for SOAP or REST services. Based on semantic information defined in WSMO, OWL-S and UDDI, we re-defined the essential semantic information. It deals with functional and non-functional semantic information crawled from web service description and web service portal. It is useful to discover, and compose for SOAP or REST services.

For further study, we have a plan to employ semantic service mediation technology for service discovery and composition of SOAP and REST services.

Acknowledgments

This research was supported by the KCC(Korea Communications Commission), Korea, under the Development of Customer Oriented Convergent Service Common Platform Technology support program supervised by the KCA(Korea Communications Agency) (KCA-2011- (**09913-05001**)).

References

1. McIlraith, S.A., Son, T.C., Zeng, H.: Semantic Web services. IEEE Intelligent Systems, Special Issue on the Semantic Web, 46–53 (March 2001)
2. Oren, E.: WSMX Execution Semantics: Executable Software Specification. In: WIW 2004 Workshop on WSMO Implementations (2004)
3. Gruber, J.: Semantic Description of Parameters in Web Service Annotations. Artificial Intelligence (September 2006)
4. Martin, D., Burstein, M., Hobbs, J., Lassila, O., McDermott, D., McIlraith, S., Narayanan, S., Paolucci, M., Parsia, B., Payne, T., Sirin, E., Srinivasan, N., Sycara, K.: OWL-S: Semantic Markup for Web Services. W3C Member Submission (November 2004), http://www.w3.org/Submission/OWL-S/
5. Roberto, C., Jean-Jacques, M., Arthur, R., Sanjiva, W.: Web Services Description Language (WSDL) Version 2.0 Part 1: Core Language. W3C Recommendation (June 2007), http://www.w3.org/TR/wsdl20/
6. Akkiraju, R., Farell, J., Miller, J.A., Nagarajan, M., Sheth, A., Verma, K.: Web Service Semantics - WSDL-S. W3C Member Submission (November 2005), http://www.w3.org/Submission/WSDL-S/
7. Lausen, H., Polleres, A., Roman, D.: Web Service Modeling Ontology (WSMO). W3C Member Submission (June 2005), http://www.w3.org/Submission/WSMO/
8. Park, Y.-M., Jung, Y., Yoo, H., Bae, H., Kim, H.-S.: EasyApp: Goal-driven Service Flow Generator with Semantic Web Service Technologies. In: ESWC (May 2011)
9. Clement, L., Hately, A., von Riegen, C., Rogers, T.: Universal, Description, Discovery and Integration (UDDI). OASIS UDDI Spec. (October 2004)
10. Fensel, D.: The Web Service Modeling Ontology(WSMO). STI-Innsbruck course material (April 2009)
11. Srinivasan, N., Paolucci, M., Sycara, K.: Semantic Web Service Discovery in the OWL-S IDE. In: Proceedings of the 39th Annual Hawaii International Conference on System Sciences (HICSS 2006), p. 109 (2006)

E-Commerce Adoption in Nigeria

Francisca Egbokhare, Kingsley Ukaoha, and Stella Chiemeke

Department of Computer Science, University of Benin, Edo State, Nigeria
fegbokhare@yahoo.com

Abstract. E-commerce, the buying and selling of goods and services over the Internet and other digital technologies has attracted much research especially in developing countries within the last two decades. Findings from such researches focused more on the barriers to e-commerce with very little on the extent of adoption. This paper utilized the findings from past studies and the explanatory case study methodology to describe the extent of e-commerce adoption in Nigeria. Recent attempts to transcend known e-commerce barriers and the role of banks and available ICT technologies are also discussed.

Keywords: E-commerce, online-banking, payment methods, GSM technology.

1 Introduction

There are several definitions for the term e-commerce: [1] describe it as a term that consist primarily of the distribution, marketing, buying and selling of products or services, and transfer of funds over electronic systems such as the internet; business transactions that take place via telecommunications networks [2]; buying and selling of information, products and services via computers and telecommunication networks[3]; technology-mediated exchanges between parties (individuals or organizations) as well as the electronically based intra or inter organizational activities that facilitate such exchanges [4]. In this paper, we adopt the definition by [5] that define e-commerce as the process of buying and selling goods and services electronically using the Internet and other digital technologies. E-commerce has contributed to shape the global economy and has also transformed many businesses from low level to global levels. Benefits of e-commerce [6] include exposure to wider markets, convenience, increase in wealth creation and reach, competitive advantage, business transformation, low cost, anytime anywhere access to markets, etc. Despite the numerous benefits gained from e-commerce adoption, available literature show that the level of adoption is low in developing countries. [7] discussed barriers to e-commerce adoption from three perspectives: economic, socio-political and cognitive. Slow Internet diffusion, unavailability of credit cards and logistic challenges were identified as the main economic challenges. The socio-political barriers explained in terms of formal and informal institutions included preference for face-to-face interactions, legal, policy and environmental issues. The cognitive barriers enumerated by the author centred on lack of awareness, computer illiteracy and language barriers since the most common language of communication on most websites is English. [6] identified cost, lack of skilled human resources and

E. Ariwa and E. El-Qawasmeh (Eds.): DEIS 2011, CCIS 194, pp. 78–86, 2011.

environmental factors as additional barriers to e-commerce adoption in developing countries. [8] in [9] staged e-commerce development into three categories as follows: Readiness, Intensity and impact. The first stage deals with the readiness of people, businesses, and infrastructure for e-commerce activities. The second stage focused on the extent to which a country undertakes e-commerce activities while the last stage is concerned about the impact of e-commerce on business activities and the nation's economy. According to [9] most developing countries are on the first or second stage of economic development and thus studied the behavioural factors that influence e-commerce adoption in developing countries. Cost, Internet complexity and infrastructural issues were identified as the major challenges to e-commerce adoption in developing countries. [10], in a study of e-commerce adoption in Nigeria identified poor perception of the security of online transactions and payment methods as the major barriers. These findings were consistent with those identified from previous studies on developing countries. Most research on e-commerce in developing countries tend to focus on the barriers and very little have been published on the extent of e-commerce adoption in developing countries despite these barriers. This paper therefore focuses on the second stage of e-commerce development in Nigeria.

2 Traditional Commerce in Nigeria

Nigeria is one of the nations described as a 'cash-based' economy. Until recently, most business transactions for goods and services were carried out by 'face – to – face" negotiations in open markets with payments through cash or cheques. The culture adopted by most Nigerians is to physically inspect goods, negotiate and if satisfied pay. The resultant effect of this commerce culture is that most business entrepreneurs are forced to travel within and outside the country to purchase goods and services carrying physical cash. Apart from the high cost of travelling, carrying physical cash also exposed them to other types of risks which often resulted to loss of business capital. In August 2001, The Global System for Mobile Communication (GSM) technology was introduced into the Nigerian economy. This enhanced communication and improved business transactions in Nigeria. Business associates could transact business over the phone without the risk of travelling. Payment for goods and services from remote locations was still a major barrier until the year 2005 when the banking sector witnessed a technological transformation. The concept of e-banking emerged. [11] defined e-banking as a service that allows customers to use some form of computer to access account-specific information and possibly conduct transactions from a remote location - such as at home or at the workplace. E-banking is used in this paper as the delivery of new and traditional banking products and services through electronic delivery channels that permit customers to access their accounts from any branch of the bank in Nigeria. Initially, only a few banks in Nigeria provided e-banking services and such banks were termed 'new generation' banks. Since the new generation banks offered 'better' services through the use of various forms of ICTs, there was a drift to these banks which led to increased competition in the banking sector and today, to retain old customers and attract new ones, all Nigerian banks offer e-banking services.

E-banking improved and boosted commercial activities in Nigeria. Business managers began to gradually understand the tremendous benefits offered by e-banking and this increased the adoption of online banking channels for commercial activities. To minimize the queues in banking halls and reduce the physical presence of people in banking halls, debit cards (popularly called ATM cards) were introduced. Today, most bank customers in Nigeria (literate or illiterate) own and use debit cards. This changed the way people keep and use money. The ability to withdraw quick cash from the closest ATM spot to make payments helped the business community (these cards can be used for direct payments but most Nigerians do not use this facility).

3 Methodology

To provide a holistic and in-depth explanation of the extent of e-commerce is adoption in Nigeria, a multiple case study approach was used to gather data. This was to enable the authors to collect and examine data within the specific context of e-commerce adoption in Nigeria. [12] defined the case study research method as an empirical inquiry that investigates a contemporary phenomenon within a real – life context when boundaries between phenomenon and context are not clearly stated. Yin further classified case research into three main types: exploratory, descriptive and explanatory. Exploratory case studies explore any phenomenon in the data which serves as a point of interest to the researcher. Descriptive case studies attempt to describe a natural phenomenon which occurred within the data in question while exploratory case studies examine the data closely both at the surface and at a deep level in order to explain the phenomena in the data. An explanatory case study approach was adopted in this research.

Three cases: a University, an SME and an individual entrepreneur were studied using Key Informant Interviews (KII) and participant observation. Key Informant Interviews were considered significant in collecting data because they give the interviewer greater flexibility in the questioning process and allow the respondent greater depth of response. Also, the interviewer has freedom to probe more deeply and to extend the responses of the sample [13], [14].

The choice of these organizations was based on the fact that they use digital devices to conduct business. Open end questions were used in the interview to enable the respondents express their opinions freely. The interviews were conducted at the respondents sites where the authors could observe some of the activities. The responses were recorded so that no information would be lost.

4 Findings

4.1 Case Study 1

The University of Benin (Uniben), a Federal Government owned institution in Nigeria with an enrolment of over 40,000 student in the full-time and part-time programmes shared among ten (10) faculties was the first case study in this research. Three (3) staff from the Information Communications Technology (ICT) centre and thirty (30) students randomly selected from the ten (10) faculties of the University were interviewed. (i). why the institution adopted the portal system for course registration (ii) the resources available in the portal and how e-commerce activities are performed. The students' interviews related to the infrastructure used to access the portal and how payments were made.

Prior to the year 2003 most activities relating to students course registration and fees payment were manual. The manual process was slow, prone to fraud and students had to be physically present at specific points for registration. To fulfil one of the main objectives of the University, which is to keep students abreast with the latest technology, the management of the University, introduced the Student Registration Portal (Fig. 1) in the 2003/2004 academic session.

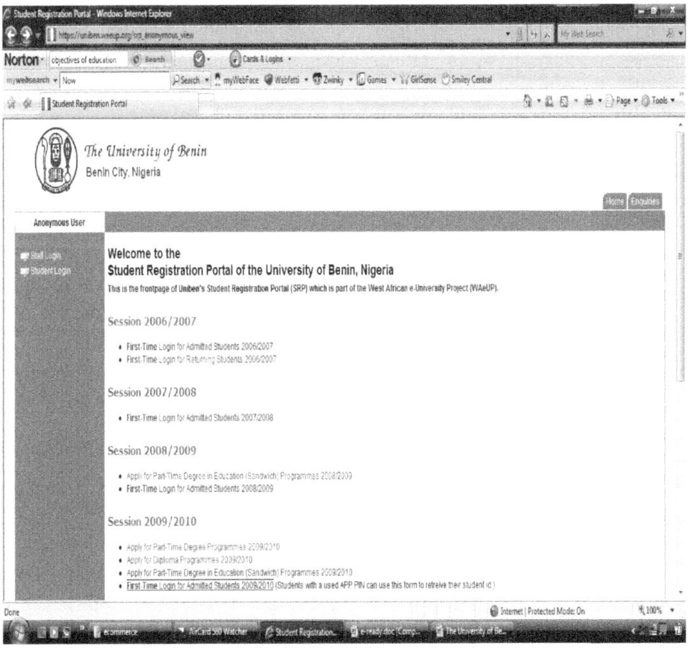

Fig. 1. The University of Benin Portal (source: http://uniben.waeup.org)

The portal (https://uniben.waeup.org) provides an avenue for potential, current and old students of the institution to access the resources provided by the institution. Services provided in the portal can be grouped into two main categories: academic and business. The academic services include:

i. Admission requests
ii. Admission processing
iii. Clearance
iv. Course registration
v. Course advising
vi. Generation of matriculation numbers

vii. Inter/Intra faculty transfers
viii. Uploading of results
ix. Processing of transcripts.

The business services, which is the main focus of this research include:

i. Purchase of forms
ii. School fees payment
iii. Payment for hostel accommodation
iv. Payment for transcripts, etc.

There is a direct relationship between these two sets of activities. Until a student fulfils his/her financial obligations to the University and logs into the portal, the academic activities cannot commence. This paper focused on the business activities.

4.1.1 Business Transactions via the Uniben Portal

The introduction of the portal helped to restructure how business transactions are performed within the Institution. Findings from the study show that most students have debit cards (called ATM cards) which are used to withdraw quick cash, check account balances and to charge their mobile phones but the cards are not used for any form of e-payments. Also, most students own mobile phones with WAP services which are used to access the University portal though some also access the portal by paying an affordable fee at cyber cafes. Cyber cafes (as used in this paper) are private individuals that provide Internet access to the public at an affordable fee.

One of the major business activities within the portal is application for admission. Prior to the placement of the adverts, the institutions would liaise with authorised banks to produce a limited number of debit cards (also called scratch cards) valued at the amount a potential candidate pays to obtain an application form. Advertisements are placed by the University at its website, national dailies and other electronic media, etc announcing the availability of programmes and requests for applications from interested candidates. The adverts contain information to direct interested applicants to banks where payments are made into the institution's bank account in exchange for a 'debit card'. The card (called a scratch card) contains a 'pin' code which serves as an access code for the candidate to log into the institutions' portal for business transactions. Specific instructions on how to access the site are contained on the scratch card. Once an applicant logs into the portal the business transaction begins. Applications are submitted and the admission is processed and the status of applications (Admitted or not admitted) is communicated to the candidate via the portal.

Another important business activity on the portal is payment of school fees (tuition) and hostel accommodation fees by students. This is also done via scratch cards obtained from stipulated banks after cash payment worth the debit amount stored on the card. The beauty of the portal system is that students can register their courses anytime anywhere. It is only when the student logs into the portal via the pin code obtained from the scratch card that the appropriate transaction will be initiated. For example, clearance/course registration for fresh students commences upon payment of the clearance fees at the bank and then the student logs into the portal to initiate clearance. After the clearance exercise, the student is directed on how to obtain the school fees scratch card to log in and proceed with course registration. Course level advisers and students communicate via mobile phones and e-mail messages.

4.2 Case Study 2

The second case study is a Small and Medium scale Enterprise (SME) that purchased goods and services from global markets via e-commerce websites. We define an SME as a limited liability business organization that employs less than 50 people and is registered with the Corporate Affairs Commission in Nigeria. The major activity performed by this organization is importation of large quantities of goods with retail outlets in major cities of Nigeria. The manager of this organization was interviewed and the questions centred on how business contacts are established and the payment methods used for online purchases. Business contacts are established via e-commerce websites on the Internet. Most payments made for e-commerce transactions were through bank guarantees. The manager interviewed had debit cards (Visa and Master Cards), but the responses showed that the respondent used this cards for business transactions worth only a specific amount. When payments involve huge amounts, they do not trust the sites to be secure enough for card transactions. Thus bank intervention is sought at this point as mediators to act as payment guarantees for e-commerce transactions using Domiciliary accounts. A Domiciliary Account is a special account in foreign currency especially in US dollars opened in a local bank that allows account holders to make international bulk payment in form of bank wire transfer for goods or services online. A Domiciliary account comes handy when dealing in Mega transactions which customers might not want Master Cards or Visa Cards to handle.

When e-commerce transactions advance to payment points, the banks are contacted with the necessary payment details to make payments. According to the manager, using banks (believed to be established institutions with strong legal frameworks) as payment guarantees is more 'secure' than exposing debit card information to an unknown 'agent' at the other end of the transaction. The bank is given the necessary payment details and the customer (manager in this interview) has to sign some legal/contract documents with the bank. According to the manager, this is necessary to protect both the bank and the customer. The bank need the legal document to protect it because if the customer claims that the information details are correct and the bank is to work with those details, if the money posted does not reach its destination, the transaction must be traced. This will attract some cost. The customer bears the cost by the term of the agreement if the information provided was wrong otherwise, the bank does. When asked if he was comfortable with such strict legal agreement, the manager still said it was better than exposing the card information to a site that he cannot trust.

4.3 Case Study 3

The third case study was a private entrepreneur NIKSEG involved in catfish production in Nigeria. The owner/manager and five (5) 'retailers' were interviewed to elicit data on the tools used for business transactions/negotiations and the method of payments used. The farm has a capacity to produce about 5,000 catfish quarterly. The owner has a database containing the names and telephone numbers of buyers. When it is time to harvest the, buyers are contacted via their mobile phones to inform them about product availability, the harvest date/time, the price per kilogram of fish and a bank account number where buyers can make payments before visiting the farm with a copy of the payment teller. Because these organizations expect payments from customers, the banks usually send credit alerts via mobile phones to the organizations stating the payment details (As part of the security mechanisms for proper implementation of e-banking in Nigeria, most bank account numbers are tied to customers' mobile phone numbers so that transaction information can be forwarded instantly to account owners). Necessary steps are taken by the organizations to deliver the products to customers as soon as the payment alert is received. As much as possible, cash payments are discouraged at the farm. Customers can also periodically contact the farm to inquire if fish is available. A customer contacts a business organization via a mobile phone for commercial activity. Negotiations commence and at the end of the transaction, the customer receives a bank account number and some other payment details. The buyers interviewed own ATM (debit) cards but they are only used for cash withdrawals and to check account balances. The idea of using cards for payments sounds 'strange' to them.

Business transactions using Mobile phones (M-commerce) is turning out to be one of the most common e-business models utilized in Nigeria because the teledensity is above 55% [15].

5 Discussion

The findings from the study show that e-commerce acceptance is increasing in Nigeria with e-banking that allows customers to conduct Bank transactions online, from the convenience of their homes or offices. The trend in e-commerce from the cases studied in this paper present a business model depicted in Fig. 2. The model consists of three main entities: The customer, the business organization and the bank. Banks are used as payment guarantees for most e-commerce transactions both at the local (within the country) and global levels. The model also shows that there exists a communication channel between the major actors in the model – The customer communicates with the business organization and the bank; the bank communicates with the business organization for payments and the business organization communicates with both the customer and the bank.

At the local level, Mobile phones are widely used in Nigeria for e-commerce. Most business negotiations and payment confirmations are performed using mobile phones. According to the ITU, as at December 31, 2007, there were 135.31 million mobile lines in sub-Saharan Africa out of which 46.97 million were resident in Nigeria. This shows that Nigeria has 34.72 per cent of the total mobile lines in the sub-region. According to the head of the Nigerian Communications Commission (NCC), today the nation records 50 per cent teledensity which translates to over 70 million telephone lines [15]. This shows that the Global System for Mobile Telecommunications (GSM) technology is well established in Nigeria.

The main challenge slowing down the pace of e-commerce adoption still centres on payment methods. Most business transactions are still cash based [16] and requires physical appearance at the Banks to make cash payments. Most online payment methods such as e-cash, e-checks, smart cards and encrypted credit cards are not too popular in developing countries like Nigeria. The automatic teller machine (ATM), which is the most widely used e-Payment instrument in Nigeria is shunned by many cardholders because of the identity theft and the incessant cases of ATM card frauds reported daily in the national print and electronic media [16, 17, 18]. Wider e-commerce patronage is dependent on the availability of trusted and secure payment systems [19]. Trust, security, speed and convenience are factors that need consideration when proposing e-commerce payment methods in Nigeria.

6 Conclusion

There is a bright future for e-commerce in Nigeria. The adoption of electronic commerce is rapidly changing for the better. Findings from this study show that there is increased awareness of the benefits of electronic commerce in Nigeria. This has prompted businesses to transcend existing barriers by exploring and utilizing other available alternatives. Most barriers and problems of e-commerce adoption in developing countries may be blamed on the culture, traditions and mindset inherited from past generations. Today, over 70% of Nigerian Universities have introduced the portal system for all business transactions between students and the Universities, with several secure and online payment solutions such as e-transact, e-cash, etc. We therefore believe that the labour market will soon be flooded with a new breed of professionals exposed to a totally different culture (surrounded by both fixed and mobile digital devices) that 'trust' and use ICT devices as tools to identify, purchase and pay for goods and services. Also, the National Information and Telecommunications Development Agency (NITDA), the body charged with the development and implementation of ICT policies for development in Nigeria, is currently working on modalities to provide a good legal system to provide a secure and safe environment for e-commerce. With the efficient and strong Information Technology (IT) network provided by GSM technologies, the numerous e-banking services involving card payments being proposed by most together with a proposed partnership between Nokia Mobile Phones, Finland and the Nigerian Government there will be increased e-commerce participation in the country through the use of mobile devices. M-commerce and mobile banking may dominate the future e-commerce model for the country, since customers will then be able to link up with markets and make payments without the high dependence on banks as payment guarantees.

References

1. UNCTAD. E-commerce in Nigeria - What the Future Holds, http://www.cipaco.org/spip.php?article11582
2. Turban, E., Lee, J., King, D., Chung, H.M.: Electronic Commerce. In: A Managerial Perspective. Prentice Hall, New Jersey (2000)

3. Lawrence, E., Lawrence, J., Newton, S., Dann, S., Corbitt, B., Thanasankit, T.: Internet Commerce; Digital Models for Business. John Wiley and Sons, Chichester (2003)
4. Rayport, J., Jaworski, B.: Introduction to e-commerce. McGraw-Hill, New York (2003)
5. Laudon, K., Laudon, J.: Management Information Systems: Managing the Digital Firm, 10th edn. Pearson, Prentice Hall (2007)
6. Apulu, I., Latham, A.: Information and Communication Technology Adoption: Challenges for Nigerian SMEs. TMC Academic Journal 4, 64–80 (2009)
7. Kshetri, N.: Barriers to e-commerce and competitive models in developing Countries: A case study. TMC Academic Journal 4, 64–80 (2003)
8. Uzoka, F.E., Shemi, A.P., Seleka, G.G.: Behavioural Influences on E-Commerce Adoption in a Developing Country Context. The Electronic Journal on Information Systems in Developing Countries 31, 1–15 (2007)
9. UNCTAD. E-commerce and Development Report. United Nations, Geneva (2001), http://www.unctad.org/en/docs/ecdr2001_en.pdf
10. Folorunso, O., Awe, O.G., Sharma, S.K., Zhang, J.: Factors Affecting the adoption of E-commerce: A study of Nigeria. Journal of Applied Sciences 6, 2224–2230 (2006)
11. Insley, R.: What is eBanking?, http://www.bankersonline.com/ebanking/gurus_eb030402b.html
12. Yin, R.K.: Case Study Research: Design and Methods. Sage Publication, California (1984)
13. Robson, C.: Real World Research: a Resource for Social Scientists and Practitioner-Research. Blackwell, Oxford (1997)
14. Cohen, L., Mannion, L., Morrison, K.: Research Methods in Education. Routledge Falmer, London (2000)
15. Africa Manager, http://www.africanmanager.com/site_eng/articles/14192.html
16. Ayo, C.K., Ukpere, W.I.: Design of a secure unified-payment system in Nigeria: A case study. African Journal of Business Management

The Role of Contextual Support in Increasing Information Systems Enrollments

Asli Y. Akbulut-Bailey

Department of Management
Seidman College of Business
Grand Valley State University
Grand Rapids, MI 49504
Tel.: (616) 331-7302; Fax: (616) 331-7445
akbuluta@gvsu.edu

Abstract. Over the last decade, enrollment in information systems (IS) related programs has plummeted worldwide and still remains low despite positive job market predictions. Given the significant negative consequences of low enrollments on both academia and industry, the IS community has focused its efforts on mechanisms to increase enrollments. This study investigates how such a mechanism – social support – influences students' aspirations to pursue an IS degree. More specifically, the study suggests that social support, self-efficacy, outcome expectations, and interests are expected to independently and cumulatively affect students' choice of IS.

Keywords: careers, enrollment crisis, education, information systems, majors, social support, student recruitment.

1 Introduction

Over the last decade, enrollment in information systems (IS) related programs has plummeted worldwide and still remains low despite positive job market predictions. In the United States, student enrollment has fallen by as much as 75 percent since 2000 [1]. Many universities in Europe have also reported similar sharp drops in enrollments both at the undergraduate and graduate levels [2, 3]. At the same time, employment projections indicate that career opportunities in the field are strong and the demand for information technology (IT) professionals continues to increase [2, 3, 4]. However, due to declining enrollments, it is estimated that there will not be enough graduates with IT skills to fulfill this increasing demand [5]. This paradoxical situation is not just a U.S. or European concern. Similar trends are observed worldwide regarding the supply and demand of IT professionals.

Given the significant negative consequences of low enrollments on both academia and industry (such as program/department closures, faculty layoffs, tenure failures, inability to fulfill the demands of companies that are desperately seeking qualified IS graduates), the IS community has focused its efforts on different mechanisms to increase enrollments [1, 6; 7,8; 9; 10]. Some of these initiatives focus on marketing and promotional efforts to build awareness about IS degrees and careers and to

E. Ariwa and E. El-Qawasmeh (Eds.): DEIS 2011, CCIS 194, pp. 87–98, 2011.

change the image of the profession by busting the prevailing myths. Other initiatives emphasize revamping university curriculum to make IS programs and courses more attractive and valuable to today's students.

Even though these initiatives appear to be potentially profitable approaches aimed at curtailing declining enrollments, there is very limited empirical evidence to prove whether implementing these mechanisms would actually result in an increase in the number of students pursuing IS degrees and careers. Therefore, these different approaches that are recommended in the literature must be confirmed and validated through qualitative and quantitative studies. Moreover, existing recommendations are largely based on how educators perceive the enrollment issue from a macro perspective. In order to facilitate a more comprehensive understanding of the situation, it is necessary to understand the mechanisms by which students are compelled to seek IS degrees from their perspective. This study will address this important research gap by developing and testing a research framework that could be used to explain how and why a key contextual support factor that has been repeatedly mentioned in the literature, social support, influences major selection in the IS discipline from students' perspective.

Contextual supports refer to the environmental factors (e.g., financial support, availability of facilities, social support, existence of role models, etc.) that people perceive as having the potential to facilitate their efforts to implement a particular educational or occupational goal [11]. While there are many potentially profitable factors to consider, this study focuses on the role of one specific contextual support factor, namely social support, in steering students toward the IS major. In terms of social support, students who perceive high levels of support from the people who are important to them, such as family, friends, advisors, etc. might become more confident in their abilities to pursue an IS major, expect to receive valued rewards from majoring in IS, develop greater interest in the IS discipline, and acquire aspirations to choose IS as their primary field of study [12].

Despite its intuitive appeal, no evidence to date has empirically linked perceived social support to student uptake. Moreover, a theoretical model has yet to be put forth to explain the means by which social support sways students to select IS as a major. Understanding these underlying mechanisms has significant implications for explaining and eventually modifying student choice behaviors. To proceed toward the development of successful intervention strategies aimed at attracting larger pools of students to the IS field, it is vital to understand the interplay among the various factors affecting students' major choices. Therefore, the specific objectives of this current study are: [1] to empirically validate whether perceived social support improves student interest in the IS discipline and [2] to derive and test a theoretical model that can be used to explain how and why social support influences major selection.

2 Theoretical Background

This study utilizes Social Cognitive Career Theory (SCCT), which was developed in the vocational psychology literature. SCCT represents a conceptual framework aimed at understanding the mechanisms through which individuals develop goals to pursue a particular educational or occupational path, make choices among available opportunities, and perform in their selected fields of pursuit [11, 13]. SCCT represents a comprehensive set of personal, environmental, and behavioral variables that influence career choice behaviors over time. According to SCCT, people enter contextual situations with a set of abilities, expectations, traits, histories, emotions, and cognitive resources to deploy during their interactions with the environment. Environmental forces (including contextual supports and barriers) can preclude, enable, inhibit, or promote certain types of behavior. When considering prospective behaviors, individuals assess their ability to engage in these behaviors by integrating perceptions of themselves, the environment, and the particular behavior in question. Behavior in a given situation is, therefore, mutually determined by environmental and personal components [14].

[12] leveraged SCCT to develop a model (IS Major Choice Goals Model) that describes the core factors affecting student decisions to major in IS. The Model consist of four interrelated factors: self-efficacy, outcome expectations, interest (personal factors), and choice goals (behavioral factor). Even though the Model provides an explanation of the main factors that motivate students to choose a major in the IS field, it does not incorporate all the factors that could potentially influence students' major or career decisions. Moreover, the core model does not include any environmental factors. This current study extends the IS Major Choice Goals Model by including an environmental factor, social support.

Personal Factors. Individuals posses certain traits, histories, and cognitive resources to deploy during their interactions with the environment. Central to SCCT are the concepts of self-efficacy, outcome expectations, and interests [13]. Self-efficacy refers to a perception of one's ability to organize and execute courses of action to accomplish a particular task [15]. Self-efficacy functions by providing individuals with a set of beliefs regarding their capabilities to exercise control over their actions and the environment. Self-efficacy plays a central role in computing, including training [16, 17], technology acceptance [18], and technology use [19, 20] to name a few. Since self-efficacy judgments are situational and task-specific [21], this study focuses on a context-specific form of *self-efficacy*, which is defined as an individual judgment of one's capability to perform effectively as an IS major.

Outcome expectations capture the perceived likelihood that favorable consequences will occur as a result of a particular action [15, 22]. Although rewards ultimately materialize after one has acted, individuals do consider the prospective likelihood that their actions will produce favorable results before engaging in the activity. Individuals are more likely to undertake behaviors that they expect to result in favorable outcomes. Unless one expects the behavior to produce favorable outcomes, the individual may lack the necessary motivation to undertake the behavior [15, 22]. Outcome expectations can be categorized into three major forms – social (e.g. recognition), self-evaluative (e.g., sense of accomplishment), and physical (e.g., angst) [see 15]. Like self-efficacy judgments, outcome expectations target the outcomes that transpire as a result of performing specific behaviors. Therefore, in the context of the current study, *outcome expectations* refer to the perceived likelihood that valued rewards will be received as a result of pursuing an IS major.

Interest refers to an emotion that arouses attention to, curiosity about, and concern with a particular educational path [13]. In this study, the target of interest specifically focuses on majoring in IS. Even though individuals may try out and pursue many different activities throughout their formative years, they ultimately develop distinctive patterns of academic and career interests, as certain activities differentially intrigue people to varying degrees over time [13, 15].

Environmental Factors. Environmental factors encompass the temporal and spatial forces beyond an individual's boundaries [15]. These factors can influence and be influenced by behavioral and personal factors. According to SCCT, individuals do not make educational and career choices in a vacuum, as they are cognizant of particular environmental circumstances. Therefore, environmental factors are expected to pervade every stage of the academic and career development process [13].

The literature has identified several environmental factors that individuals perceive as aiding their efforts to implement a particular educational or occupational goal. For instance, a variety of support factors have been mentioned in the literature including social support, role models, instrumental assistance, and financial resources [6, 11]. While there are many important support factors to consider, this study focuses on the role of social support in steering students toward the IS major. *Social support* refers to a student's perceptions that most people who are important to him would approve and encourage his decision to major in IS. Social support can come from a variety of people including family, friends, advisors, peers, and the like [23].

Social support enables students to develop a strong sense of professional identity, leading to positive results [24]. For example, it is plausible that students who perceive high levels of social support would become more confident in their abilities to pursue an IS major, expect to receive valued rewards from majoring in IS, develop greater interest in the IS discipline, and acquire aspirations to choose IS as their primary field of study. Moreover, these students would be more likely to be satisfied with their decision to pursue the IS major. Therefore, I expect social support to play an influential role in student psychology and behavior in the context of IS major choices.

Behavior. In the context of career-related choices, the behavior in question is operationalized as choice goals, which can be defined as the determination to engage in a particular educational or occupational activity [15]. Specific to this study, *choice goals* refers to a students' aspirations to choice IS as a major. According to the SCCT, choice goals play an important role in the self-regulation of behavior. People set goals to organize and guide their behavior, as well as to increase the likelihood that desired outcomes will be attained. Goals play an important role in decision making theories, including career choice decisions. In this respect, career plans, aspirations, and expressed choices are considered as goal mechanisms [13].

3 Research Model and Hypotheses

Figure 1 below represents the research model utilized in this study. As illustrated, social support, self-efficacy, outcome expectations, and interests are expected to independently and cumulatively affect choice goals. The following sections describe the hypotheses in detail.

According to SCCT, environmental support factors such as social support play an important role in promoting certain behaviors. Research has shown that individuals will be more determined to be engaged in a particular course of action when they perceive that behavior will be approved and supported by the important people in their lives [24].

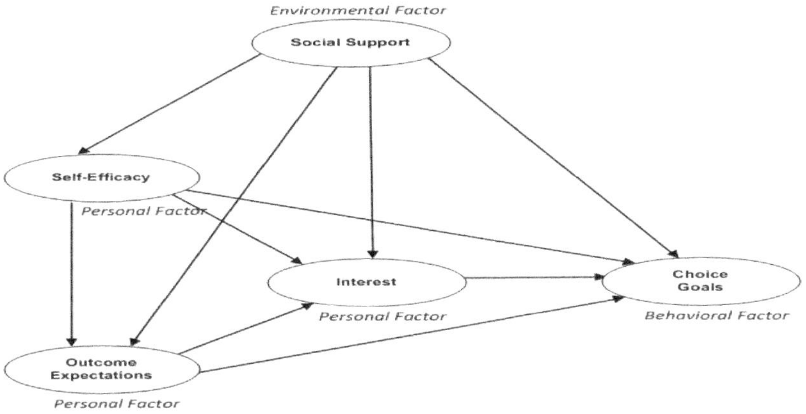

Fig. 1. Research Model

[25] suggested that environmental support factors may affect individuals' choice goals directly. As such, it is reasonable to assume that students would be more determined to select a major in a field in which they feel their decision would receive support from the important people in their lives. Therefore, the following hypothesis is offered:

H_1: Social support will have a significant positive influence on choice goals.

Discussing the interplay among personal and environmental factors on behavior, research points out that most external influences affect human functioning through intermediary self processes [26, 27]. Along these lines, Lent et al. suggested that environmental support factors may indirectly affect choice behavior through personal factors (i.e. self-efficacy, outcome expectations, and interest) [25]. The degree of social support available to students might promote student interest in a particular subject, as individuals, such as family, friends, peers, and teachers, can expose students to a wider variety of relevant topics, activities, and advice, which might also encourage students to become more inquisitive. Therefore, the following hypothesis is offered:

H_2: Social support will have a significant positive influence on interests.

According to SCT, environmental factors can have a profound influence on self-efficacy and outcome expectations [15, 22]. Research has shown that social support for career choices has a tremendous influence on a person's expectations and values connected with these choices. Since students who perceive high levels of support about a particular major would be better equipped individuals to perform certain behaviors, we expect that social support will affect students' self-efficacy perceptions. Students who are supported by the important people in their lives are more likely to develop higher levels of confidence in their abilities to perform as an IS major. Therefore, the following hypothesis is offered:

H_3: Social support will have a significant positive influence on self-efficacy.

Similarly, social support may promote outcome expectations. Family, friends, peers, teachers might provide information and clues about the consequences that may occur as a result of pursuing an IS major [19]. When students perceive that they are being supported, they are apt to believe that they are more likely to obtain rewards as a result of majoring in the IS field. Therefore, the following hypothesis is offered:

> *H_4: Social support will have a significant positive influence on outcome expectations.*

The relationship between self-efficacy and outcome expectations has been repeatedly studied in the IS literature. Research has shown that self-efficacy beliefs influence outcome expectations [19, 20, 28, 29]. People expect to achieve desirable outcomes in activities at which they deem themselves as capable. In essence, an individual who possesses a strong sense of efficacy is more likely to believe that favorable consequences will arise from her or his actions. Therefore, it is reasonable to assume that students who have higher levels of self-efficacy will develop robust outcome expectations.

> *H_5: Self-efficacy will have a significant positive influence on outcome expectations.*

[13] has demonstrated that perceptions of self-efficacy play an important role in the formation of educational and vocational interests and behaviors. People tend to form enduring interests in activities in which they view themselves as capable [30]. Thus, it is reasonable to assume that students with higher levels of self-efficacy will be more interested in pursuing majors and careers within the field of IS.

> *H_6: Self-efficacy will have a significant positive influence on interest.*

Self-efficacy beliefs are also assumed to have direct effects on choice goals. [15] has proposed that self-efficacy affects an individual's goals to perform a specific behavior. When high self-efficacy prevails, individuals are more likely to set goals to engage in a particular behavior. As such, students who are confident in their abilities to perform as an IS major would be more likely to develop aspirations to major in the IS field. Therefore, the following hypothesis is offered:

> *H_7: Self-efficacy will have a significant positive influence on choice goals.*

Similar to self-efficacy, an individual's expectations about the consequences of pursing educational and vocational paths shape interests [13]. In essence, when a student expects pursuing a major or career in the IS field will result in favorable outcomes, he or she will be more likely to find that IS field compelling and develop an interest. Therefore, the following hypothesis is offered:

> *H_8: Outcome expectations will have a significant positive influence on interest.*

Outcome expectations can also affect choice goals directly. People develop goals, in part, based on the rewards they expect to receive. The higher the likelihood of obtaining valued outcomes, the more likely that people will adopt particular career goals. Therefore, the following hypothesis is offered:

> *H_9: Outcome expectations will have a significant positive influence on choice goals.*

In addition to self-efficacy and outcome expectations, I anticipate that interest will influence choice goals. Research indicates that people tend to select academic and career options that match their primary interests [31]. Emergent interests lead to cognized choice goals for further activity exposure (i.e. intention plans, or aspirations to engage in a particular academic or career direction), fostering the development of goals to choose particular actions (e.g., declaring a corresponding major) [13]. Therefore, students who are interested in the IS field will be more determined to major in the IS discipline.

H_{10}: Interest will have a significant positive influence on choice goals.

4 Methodology and Analyses

Study participants consisted of students enrolled in an introductory level management information system course at a large state university. A web-based survey was used to collect the data. A total of 318 usable responses were obtained. Forty five percent of the respondents were female and respondents averaged 21.4 years of age ($SD = 2.14$).

A total of five scales were required to test the research hypotheses. Previously validated scales were used. These scales were adapted from previous studies [11, 14]. Partial Least Squares (PLS) was used for data analysis [32, 33]. More specifically, PLS-Graph Version 3 was utilized [34]. The psychometric properties of the measurement model were confirmed prior to estimating structural model parameters, as discussed in the following sections.

Measurement Model Analysis. Reliability and validity of the indicators and constructs were examined in three stages. Reliability of each construct was examined to ensure that the items collectively measured their intended construct consistently [35]. Reliability was assessed by examining the reliability of individual items (Cronbach's α) and the composite reliability of constructs [32, 36]. As shown in Table 1, both Cronbach α's and composite reliability scores were well above the recommended level (0.70) for acceptable reliability [32, 36]. As such, the reliability of the scales was confirmed.

Convergent validity was also assessed at the individual item and construct levels by examining the individual item loadings and the average variance extracted (AVE) respectively [36]. All individual items exhibited adequate loadings (greater than 0.707) and no unacceptable cross loadings emerged. As shown in Table 1, the AVE score for each construct is also well above the recommended (0.50 or greater) level [36]. Therefore, convergent validity was confirmed.

Discriminant validity was assessed by comparing the AVE values associated with each construct to the correlations among constructs [32]. The discriminant validity analysis is provided in Table 1. For each construct, the AVE exceeded the correlations between constructs, confirming discriminant validity.

Given the results of the reliability and validity analysis, it was concluded that the scales exhibited excellent psychometric properties.

Table 1. Descriptive Statistics, Reliability, Correlations, and Discriminant Validity

				Constructs				
Construct	∝	CR	AVE	CG	INT	OE	SE	SS
CG	0.979	0.984	0.940	**0.970**				
INT	0.950	0.961	0.833	0.691	**0.913**			
OE	0.967	0.972	0.780	0.335	0.508	**0.883**		
SE	0.974	0.979	0.885	0.487	0.516	0.415	**0.941**	
SS	0.960	0.971	0.894	0.290	0.414	0.602	0.335	**0.946**

[a]Diagonal elements (in bold) represent the square root of the average variance extracted (AVE). Off-diagonal elements represent the correlations among constructs.

Note: ∝ = Cronbach's alpha. CR = composite reliability. AVE = average variance extracted. SE = self-efficacy. OE = outcome expectations. INT = interest, CG = choice goals, SS = social support.

Structural Model Analysis. The results of the structural model analysis are represented in Figure 2.

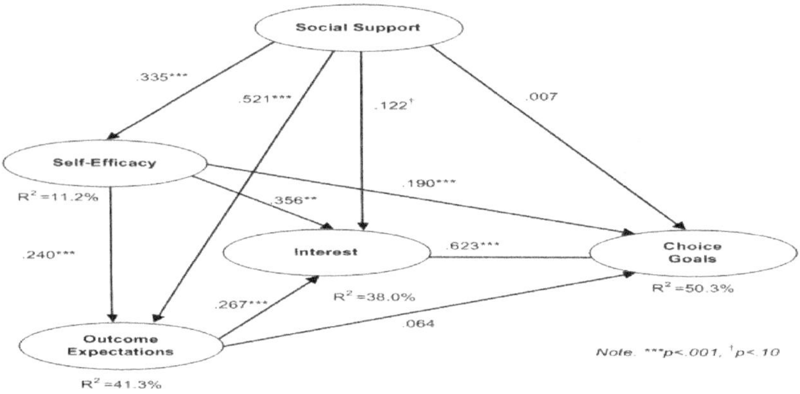

Fig. 2. Structural Model Results

The results indicate that the model explains a sizeable proportion of the variance in choice goals (50.3 percent), interest (38 percent), outcome expectations (41.3 percent), and self-efficacy (11.2 percent).

Despite expectations, social support was not a significant predictor of choice goals (0.007, *ns*). Therefore no support was offered for H_1. As expected, social support was a significant predictor of interest (0.122, p<0.1) self-efficacy (0.335, $p < 0.001$) and outcome expectations (0.521, $p < 0.001$), supporting hypotheses H_2, H_3, and H4.

Self-efficacy was found to be a significant predictor of outcome expectations (0.240, $p < 0.001$) and interest (0.356, $p < 0.001$). Therefore, hypotheses H_5 and H_6 were supported. Self-efficacy also served as a significant predictor of choice goals (0.190, $p < 0.001$). As a result, hypothesis H_7 was also supported

Outcome expectations was a significant predictor of interest (0.267, $p < 0.001$), supporting hypothesis H_8. However, in opposition to expectations, outcome expectations did not have a significant influence on choice goals (0.064, *ns*). Therefore, hypothesis H_9 was not supported. Finally, interest was found to be a significant predictor of choice goals (0.623, $p < 0.001$), supporting hypothesis H_{10}.

5 Discussion

Over the past few years, there has been a decline in the number of students pursuing IS degrees. In order to overcome this situation, the IS community has started to look for mechanisms to re-fuel student interest in the discipline. To address this important issue, I investigated how such a mechanism – social support – influences students' aspirations to pursue an IS degree. As such, my findings have important implication for IS programs, as the information gained herein can be utilized to design and implement a specific intervention strategy to attract larger pools of students to the IS discipline.

Specifically, findings indicate that perceived social support plays an important role in student uptake. Social approval and encouragement increases students' self-efficacy and outcome expectations. Social support of important people not only enhances students' confidence in their ability to successfully perform as an IS major, but also elevates students' expectations that valued rewards will be received by majoring in IS. Moreover, social support directly affects student interest. The effects of social support on choice goals are channeled indirectly through self-efficacy, outcome expectations, and interests. In essence, strong self -efficacy and outcome expectations foster student interest in the IS discipline. Therefore, it is reasonable to assume that students are more likely to develop an interest in the IS discipline when they feel efficacious and expect to receive valued rewards. However, the results did not provide support for the direct effects of outcome expectations on choice goals. In contrast, choice goals develop through strong interests, which evolve, in part, form a robust sense of efficacy and outcome expectations. It was also found that self-efficacy leads to more robust outcome expectations. Not surprisingly, students who deem themselves as capable of majoring in IS perceive that value rewards are more likely to be obtained. Finally, findings also provided strong support for the positive relationship between interests and choice goals, confirming that interest serves as the primary mechanism though which goals to choose IS major emerges.

6 Conclusion

As a result of this study, we have gained a theoretical understanding of the role social support can play in the student recruitment process. The model not only supports the notion that social support can be used to attract larger pools to the IS discipline, but also explains how and why social support influences student aspirations. It is clear from the findings of this study that university educators can utilize social support to boost student confidence (i.e., self-efficacy) and expectations of value rewards (i.e., outcome expectations). In turn, these factors elevate student interest, which ultimately influences students' aspirations to choose IS as a major. This recommendation is consistent with the findings in the IS literature, which states that domain-specific self-efficacy and outcome expectations can be increased through training mechanisms and support structures [19, 37], like social support. The knowledge gained as a result of this study demonstrates the importance for higher education institutions to provide social support to students in introductory IS courses through university advisors, peers, career services, and the like.

Despite the knowledge gained herein, some cautions are warranted. The constructs in the research model represent a relatively limited subset of the factors that could plausibly affect student choices. In order to develop a more comprehensive set of intervention strategies targeted at student recruitment, a wider range of support factors needs to be considered and validated. The research model can be readily adapted to study these factors and potential barriers that might be impairing student enrollments. In addition, I utilized a survey to examine the relationships among the variables in the model. Although the measures exhibited sufficient levels of reliability and validity, it is plausible that self-reported data could have resulted in common method variance, artificially inflating the relationships among the variables. Therefore, future studies should utilize additional methods using complementary samples to identify the boundary conditions of the findings.

It is important to note that even though this study focused on the positive aspects of perceived social support, research indicates that social support can have negative consequences as well. For example well-intended attempts to give social support can be harmful if students think they are excessive, improper, or given at an inappropriate time (24). Therefore, future studies should examine the potential negative influences of perceived social support on students' decisions to major in IS related disciplines.

References

1. Street, C., Wade, M., Bjørn-Andersen, N., Ives, B., Venable, J., Zack, M.: Reversing the Downward Trend: Innovative Approaches to IS/IT Course Development and Delivery. Communications of the Association for Information Systems 22(28), 515–524 (2008)
2. Panko, R.R.: IT Employment Prospects: Beyond the Dotcom Bubble. European Journal of Information Systems 17, 182–197 (2008)
3. Leeuwen, J.V., Tanca, L.: Student Enrollment and Image of the Informatics Discipline Informatics Europe. The Association of Informatics / Computing Departments and IT Research Institutes in Europe Report IE-2008-01 October 2008 Working Group Report for Informatics Europe, Introduction, 2-3 (2008)
4. Lomerson, W.L., Pollicia, L.: CIS Enrollment Decline: Examining Pre-College Factors. In: Proceedings of the 2006 Southern Association for Information Systems Conference, pp. 93–103 (2006)
5. Lynch, T.: Reducing IT Labor Shortage Vulnerabilities through Strategic Staffing. Sapphire Technologies (2007), http://www.sapphire.com/Portals/0/Research%20Files/Worker%20Shortage%20Whitepaper.pdf (accessed on August 2, 2008)

6. Akbulut-Bailey, A.Y.: A Measurement Instrument for Understanding Student Perspectives on Stereotypes of IS Professionals. Communications of the Association for Information Systems 25(29) (2009)
7. Dick, G., Granger, M.C., Jacobson, M., Van Slyke, C.: Where Have All the Students Gone? Strategies for Tackling Falling Enrollments. AMCIS 2007 Proceedings Paper 334 (2007)
8. Firth, D., Lawrence, C., Looney, C.A.: Addressing the IS Enrollment Crisis: A 12-step Program to Bring about Change through the Introductory IS Course. Communications of the Association for Information Systems 23(2), 17–36 (2008)
9. Galletta, D.: If We Rebuild IT Will they Come Back? CNAIS and Microsoft Academic Days Cruise (2007), http://galletta.business.pitt.edu/galletta/presentations/IfWeReBuildITWillTheyCome.ppt (accessed on July 31, 2008)
10. Akbulut, A.Y., Looney, C.A.: Improving IS Student Enrollments: Understanding the Effects of IT Sophistication in Introductory IS Courses. Journal of Information Technology Education (8), 87–100 (2009)
11. Lent, R.W., Brown, S.D., Talleyrand, R., McPartland, E.B., Davis, T., Chopra, S.B., Alexander, M.S., Suthakaran, V., Chai, C.: Career Choice Barriers, Supports, and Coping Strategies: College Students' Experiences. Journal of Vocational Behavior (60), 61–72 (2002)
12. Akbulut, A.Y., Looney, C.A.: Their Aspirations Are Our Possibilities: Inspiring Students to PursueComputing Degrees. Communications of the ACM 50(10), 67–71 (2007)
13. Lent, R.W., Brown, S.D., Hackett, G.: Toward a Unifying Social Cognitive Theory of Career and Academic Interest, Choice, and Performance. Journal of Vocational Behavior (45), 79–122 (1994)
14. Looney, C.A., Akbulut, A.Y.: Combating the IS Enrollment Crisis: The Role of Effective Teachers in Introductory IS Courses. Communications of the Association for Information Systems (19), 781–805 (2007)
15. Bandura, A.: Social Foundation of Thought and Action: A Social Cognitive Theory. Prentice Hall, Englewood Cliffs (1986)
16. Agarwal, R., Sambamurthy, V., Stair, R.M.: Research Report: The Evolving Relationship between General and Specific Computer Self-Efficacy - An Empirical Assessment. Information Systems Research 11(4), 418–430 (2000)
17. Johnson, R.D., Marakas, G.M.: Research Report: The Role of Behavioral Modeling in Computer Skill Acquisition: Toward Refinement of the Model. Information Systems Research 11(4), 402–417 (2000)
18. Taylor, S., Todd, P.A.: Understanding Information Technology Usage: A Test of Competing Models. Information Systems Research 6(2), 144–176 (1995)
19. Compeau, D.R., Higgins, C.A.: Application of Social Cognitive Theory to Training for Computer Skills. Information Systems Research (6), 118–143 (1995a)
20. Compeau, D.R., Higgins, C.A.: Computer Self-Efficacy: Development of a Measure and Initial Test. MIS Quarterly (19), 189–211 (1995b)
21. Marakas, G.M., Yi, M.Y., Johnson, R.D.: The Multilevel and Multifaceted Character of Computer Self-Efficacy: Toward a Clarification of the Construct and an Integrated Framework for Research. Information Systems Research (9), 126–162 (1998)
22. Bandura, A.: Self-Efficacy: The Exercise of Control. W. W.H. Freeman and Company, New York (1997)

23. Kovach Clark, H., Murdock, N., Koetting, K.: Predicting Burnout and Career Choice Satisfaction in Counseling Psychology Graduate Students. The Counseling Psychologist 37(4), 580–606 (2008)
24. Inglehart, M., Brwon, D.R.: Social Support for Career Choices and Academic Achievement: An Emirical Investigation. In: 97th Annual Meeting of the American Psychological Association, New Orleans, LA, August 11-15 (1989)
25. Lent, R.W., Brown, S.D., Nota, L., Soresi, S.: Testing Social Cognitive Interest and Choice Hypotheses across Holland Types in Italian High School Students. Journal of Vocational Behavior (62), 101–118 (2003)
26. Bandura, A.: Social Cognitive Theory of Personality. In: Pervin, L., John, O. (eds.) Handbook of Personality, 2nd edn., pp. 154–196. Gailford Press, New York (1999)
27. Bandura, A.: Exercise of Human Agency through Collective Efficacy. Current Directions in Psychological Science (9), 75–78 (2000)
28. Compeau, D.R., Higgins, C.A., Huff, S.: Social Cognitive Theory and Individual Reactions to Computing Technologies. MIS Quarterly (23), 145–158 (1999)
29. Looney, C.A., Valacich, J.S., Todd, P.A., Morris, M.G.: Paradoxes of Online Investing: Testing the Influence of Technology on User Expectancies. Decision Sciences 37(2), 205–246 (2006)
30. Bandura, A., Schunk, D.H.: Cultivating Competence, Self-Efficacy, and Intrinsic Interest through Proximal Self-Motivation. Journal of Personality and Social Psychology (56), 805–814 (1981)
31. Holland, J.L.: Making Vocational Choices: A Theory of Vocational Personalities and Work Environments, 2nd edn. Prentice Hall, Englewood Cliffs (1985)
32. Barclay, D., Higgins, C., Thompson, R.: The Partial Least Squares Approach to Causal Modeling: Personal Computer Adoption and Use as an Illustration. Technology Studies (2), 285–324 (1995)
33. Wold, H.: Systems Analysis by Partial Least Squares. In: Nijkamp, P., Leitner, L., Wrigley, N. (eds.) Measuring the Unmeasurable, pp. 221–251. Marinus Nijhoff, Dordrecht (1985)
34. Chin, W.W.: PLS Graph, Version 03.00, Department of Decision and Information Systems, University of Houston (2003)
35. Gefen, D., Straub, D.W., Boudreau, M.C.: Structural Equation Modeling and Regression: Guidelines for Research Practice. Communications of the AIS 4(7), 1–77 (2000)
36. Fornell, C., Larker, D.F.: Evaluating Structural Equation Models with Unobserved Variables and Measurement Error. Journal of Marketing Research (18), 39–50 (1981)
37. Stephens, P.A.: Decision Support System for Computer Literacy Training at Universities. Journal of Computer Information Systems 46(2), 33–44 (2005/2006)

Analysis of the DBLP Publication Classification Using Concept Lattices

Saleh Alwahaishi[1], Jan Martinovič[2], and Václav Snášel[2]

[1] King Fahd University of Petroleum and Minerals,
Department of Accounting and MIS
salehw@kfupm.edu.sa
[2] FEECS, VŠB- Technical University of Ostrava,
Department of Computer Science
{jan.martinovic,vaclav.snasel}@vsb.cz

Abstract. The definitive classification of scientific journals depends on their aims and scopes details. In this paper, we present an approach to facilitate the journals classification of the DBLP datasets. For the analysis, the DBLP data sets were pre-processed by assigning each journal attributes defined by its topics and then the theory of formal concept analysis is introduced. It is subsequently shown how this theory can be applied to analyze the relations between journals and the extracted topics from their aims and scopes. The result is a concept lattice that contains information on journal-topic relational context depending on how they are associated. It is shown how this approach can be used to facilitate the classifications of scientific journals.

1 Introduction

Formal Concept Analysis (FCA) was invented in the early 1980s by Rudolf Wille as a mathematical theory [1]. FCA is concerned with the formalization of concepts and conceptual thinking and has been applied in many disciplines such as software engineering, knowledge discovery and information retrieved during the last two decades. The mathematical foundation of FCA is described in [2].

FCA is a mathematical theory for concepts and concept hierarchies that reflects an understanding of "concept". It explicitly formalizes extension and intension of a concept, their mutual relationships, and the fact that increasing intent implies decreasing extent and vice versa. Based on lattice theory, it allows deriving a concept hierarchy from a given dataset. FCA complements thus the usual ontology engineering approach, where the concept hierarchy is modeled manually.

FCA considers the extensional and the intensional part equally important, whereas the other formalisms are biased towards the intensional aspect of concepts. FCA is thus complementing other conceptual knowledge representations; and the combination of FCA with other representations has been the topic of many publications. For instance, several approaches combined FCA with description logics [3, 4, 5, 6] and with conceptual graphs [7, 8, 9]. In this paper, we describe how we used FCA to create a visual overview of the DBLP scientific journals classification based on their aims and scopes. As a case study, we zoom in on the top journals based

E. Ariwa and E. El-Qawasmeh (Eds.): DEIS 2011, CCIS 194, pp. 99–108, 2011.

on their impact factors. The remainder of this paper is composed as follows: In section 2 we introduce an overview of the Digital bibliography and Library project (DBLP). Section 3 visualizes, with an example, the literature using FCA lattice. In section 4 we explained the classification criterion of journals and applied the concept lattice on the selected journals. Section 5 concludes the paper.

2 Digital Bibliography and Library Project (DBLP)

Digital libraries are collections of resources and services stored in digital formats and accessed by computers. Studying them offers an interesting case study for researches for the following reasons: Firstly, they grow quickly, Secondly, they represent a multidisciplinary domain which has attracted researchers from a wide area of expertise. DBLP (Digital Bibliography & Library Project) is a computer science bibliography database hosted at University of Trier, in Germany.

It was started at the end of 1993 and listed more than one million articles on computer science in January 2010. These articles were published in Journals such as VLDB, the IEEE and the ACM Transactions and Conference proceedings [10, 11]. Besides DBLP has been a credible resource for finding publications, its dataset has been widely investigated in a number of studies related to data mining and social networks to solve different tasks such as recommender systems, experts finding, name ambiguity, etc. Even though, DBLP dataset provides abundant information about author relationships, conferences, and scientific communities it has a major limitation that is its records provide only the paper title without the abstract and index terms.

2.1 Using DBLP Dataset in Recommender Systems

In addition to using the DBLP dataset for finding academic experts, it has been used extensively in academic recommender systems. A number of studies were conducted to recommend academic events and collaborators for researchers using different methods and techniques. For example, a recommender system for academic collaboration called DBconnect was presented in [12], the authors of this paper used DBLP data to generate bipartite (author-conference) and tripartite (authorconference-topics) graph models, and designed a random walk algorithm for these models to calculate the relevance score between authors. And in another study [13] a recommender system for events and scientific communities for researchers was proposed based on social network analysis.

2.2 Other Uses for DBLP Dataset

Querying large datasets produces large sets too, which makes the user unable to decide from where he has to start looking at the results. To solve this problem clustering and ranking were suggested in many papers. A system to visualize author information and relationships simultaneously was presented in [14]. The authors applied two types of clustering, keyword clustering and author clustering to visualize the relationships and groupings of authors and after that the results obtained from both techniques was combined by using a multiclustering technique. In [15] document clustering was applied to provide an overview of the recent trends in data mining activities. The authors in [16] proposed two tools, the dynamic and the streaming tensor analysis (DTA and STA) to mine and summarize large tensors and detect patterns. Clustering and ranking are often applied separately but in [17] a novel framework called RankClus was proposed to integrate them. To increase the accuracy of IR clustering the authors in [18] proposed transferring knowledge available on the word side to the document side, they introduced a model based on nonnegative matrix factorization to achieve it.

3 Formal Concept Analysis

Formal Concept Analysis can be used as an unsupervised clustering technique. The starting point of the analysis is a database table consisting of rows G (i.e. objects), columns M (i.e. attributes) and crosses $I \subseteq G \times M$ (i.e. relationships between objects and attributes). The mathematical structure used to reference such a cross table is called a formal context (G, M, I).

Table 1 shows a formal context example of color mixing for illustrative purposes. The formal objects are orange, violet, green and brown while the formal attributes are blue, yellow, red, and white. A formal concept of this context will consist of an ordered pair (A, B), where A is a subset of the four formal objects and B is a subset of the four formal attributes. The intent should contain exactly those attributes shared by all objects in the extent, and conversely the extent should contain exactly those objects sharing all attributes in the intent. Both its extent and its intent therefore determine a formal concept.

Table 1. Cross table of color mixing formal context

	Blue	Yellow	Red
Orange		X	X
Violet	X		X
Green	X	X	

In order to formalize the definition of a formal concept we introduce the derivation operator. In a formal context (G, M, I) the set of all common attributes of a set $A \subseteq G$ of objects is denoted by:

$$A' := \{m \in M \; (g, m) \in I \text{ for all } g \in A\}$$

Analogously the set of all common objects of a set $B \subseteq M$ of attributes is:

$$B' := \{g \in G \; (g, m) \in I \text{ for all } m \in B\}$$

Based on the above example, the following sets could be derivate: {Orange}'={Yellow, Red}

{Blue, Yellow}' = {Green}. Using the derivation operator, a formal concept of the context (G, M, I) can be defined as a pair (A, B) where $A \subseteq G$, $B \subseteq M$, $A'=B$ and $B'=A$, A is the extent and B is the intent of the concept (A, B). The resulting ordered set of all formal concepts forms a complete lattice, which is known as concept lattice.

Figure 1 visualizes the concept lattice of the color mixing concept by a line diagram with nodes representing formal concepts and edges representing the relations between formal concepts. The extent of a concept node is the set of all objects that label this node or other nodes on a path going downward, while the intent of a concept node is the set of all attributes that label this node or other nodes on a path going upward.

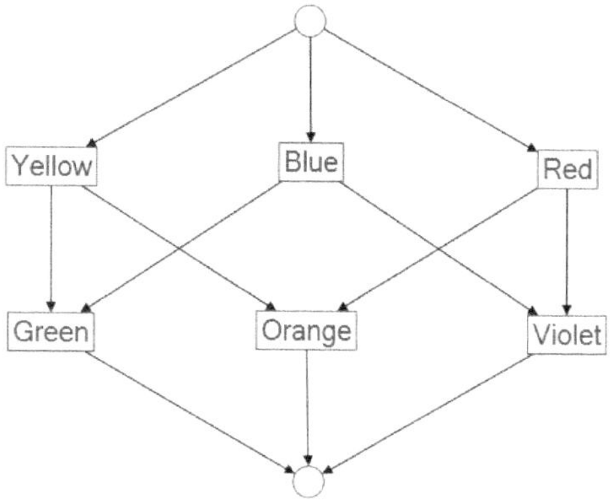

Fig. 1. Concept lattice for color mixing

The object label is attached below the node of the smallest concept whose extent contains the object, while an attribute label is attached above the node of the largest concept whose intent contains the attribute.

4 Concept Analysis of Journals Classification

This section describes how formal concept analysis is employed to analyze the DBLP's journals classification. A group of interested similar journals, which covered the scope of computer science, were selected. The list of selected journals was obtained from well-known DBLP database that contains information about the published articles and their authors as well. The selected list of links to journals has the size of 115 items. The next step was to identify main topics, which each of the journals covers. From the journal web sites we have found the aim and scope of each journal, and have manually extracted the main topics, such as Pattern Recognition, Image Processing, etc.

4.1 Journals Selection and Categorization

Each journal has been identified by an existing classifier by company due to the problem with using their own names or similar names of topics. The used classifier that contains about 1224 sub disciplines classified to disciplines and those classified

Table 2. Journals' main topics and subfields

Abbreviation	Main Topic	Subfields
AIIP	Artificial Intelligence and Image Processing	Adaptive Agents and Intelligent Robotics
		Neural, Evolutionary and Fuzzy Computation
		Simulation and Modeling
		Computer Vision
		Pattern Recognition and Data Mining
		Signal processing
		Image Processing
CTM	Computation Theory and Mathematics	Computer Graphics
		Other Computation Theory and Mathematics
		Numerical Computation
		Applied Discrete Mathematics
		Computational Logic and Formal Languages
		Analysis of Algorithms and Complexity
CS	Computer Software	Software Engineering
		Operating Systems
		Computer System Security
		Bioinformatics Software
ISLIS	Information Systems and Library and Information Studies	Database and Database Management
		Information Retrieval and Web Search
		Inter-organizational Information Systems and Web Services
		Information Systems Management
		Information Systems Development Methodologies
DF	Data Format	Data Encryption
		Data Structures
DC	Distributed Computing	Mobile Technologies
		Distributed Computing
CT	Communications Technologies	Computer Communications Networks (computer network)
		Wireless Communications
		Other Communications Technologies (telecommunications)
CA	Computer Architecture	
DIP	Data and Information Processing	
STVV	Software Testing and Verification & Validation	

to discipline field, e.g. sub discipline Pattern Recognition is in disciplines Artificial Intelligence and Image Processing and that is in Information and computing sciences [19]. We selected only sub disciplines in the field Technology and Information and computing sciences. Our manually extracted topic from journals in many cases correspond the classified disciplines, but in some cases it was necessary to assign the extracted topic to sub discipline, which was almost similar. Therefore, journals were classified into a list of topics based in their relation to the topic. The classification process ends up with ten main topics that have twenty nine subfields or disciplines. Table 2 shows the main topics and their subfields.

4.2 Lattice Construction for Journal-Topic Matrix

A journal is represented as a list of topics. The topics are the disciplines that being covered by all journals, based on the extracted data from their aims and scopes. Each topic is assigned a weight of 0 or 1. A topic's weight for a journal expresses the coverage possibility of the topic by the related journal. A value of 1 denotes that the journal covers the column's topic and 0 denotes the lack of coverage.

Formally, these data can be represented as a matrix of journals by topics whose m rows and n columns correspond to m journals and n topics, respectively. The elements of the journal-topic matrix are the weights of each term for a particular document, that is:

$$\boldsymbol{Y} = \begin{bmatrix} y_{11} & \cdots & y_{1n} \\ \vdots & & \vdots \\ y_{m1} & \cdots & y_{mn} \end{bmatrix}$$

Where y_{ij} denotes the weight assigned to topic T_j for journal J_i.

The formal concept analysis of the data starts with the creation of a formal context. The formal objects of the formal context are the journals J_i that were retrieved from DBLP database. The set of these journals is denoted by J. Using the information that was extracted from the aim and scope of the journals in J. The coverage possibility T_j that shows the topic coverage by the journals in J, constitute the formal attributes of the formal context. The set containing these attributes is denoted by T.

The cross table of the resulting formal context has a row for each journals in J, a column for each topic in T and a cross in the row of J_i and the column of T_j if the corresponding weight y_{ij} is 1. To minimize the cross table size, journals impact factors will be considered to decrease the number of tested journals. The journals with an impact factor of 3.0 and above will be enlisted in the matrix, dropping the number of selected journals to be 18 as shown in Table 3. After the formal context is constructed, formal concept analysis is applied to produce the concept lattice.

Table 3. Journals' impact factors and abbreviations

Abbreviation	Journal	Impact Factor
A	Nucleic Acids Research	6.878
B	IEEE Transactions on Pattern Analysis and Machine Intelligence	5.96
C	International Journal of Computer Vision	5.358
D	Computer Applications in the Biosciences	4.328
E	Journal of Selected Areas in Communications	4.249
F	Transactions on Medical Imaging	4.004
G	Transactions on Information Theory	3.793
H	BMC Bioinformatics	3.78
I	Transactions on Neural Networks	3.726
J	Journal of Chemical Information and Computer Sciences	3.643
K	Transactions on Fuzzy Systems	3.624
L	Journal of Computational Chemistry	3.39
M	Transactions on Graphics	3.383
N	Transactions on Mobile Computing	3.352
O	Transactions on Image Processing	3.315
P	Pattern Recognition	3.279
Q	Automatica	3.178
R	Information Sciences	3.095

Table 4 represents the formal context. A cross in the row of J_i and the column of T_j indicates that T_j is believed to be a covered topic by the journal of J_i.

The formal concepts of the contexts are shown as extent-intent pairs, where the extent is a subset of the journals and the intent is a subset of the topics.

({F,G,J,Q,R}, {AIIP,CTM})
({F,Q,R}, {AIIP,CTM,CS})
({A,D,F,H,L,Q,R}, {CTM,CS})
({C,G,J,Q}, {AIIP,CTM,CS,ISLIS})
({G,N,R}, {CS,CT})
({G,O,R}, {AIIP,DF})
({B,F,Q,R}, {AIIP,CA})
({G}, {AIIP,CTM,ISLIS,DF,CT})
({H}, {CTM,CS,STVV})
({Q}, {AIIP,CTM,CS,ISLIS,CA,DIP})
({R}, {AIIP,CTM,CS,DF,CT,CA})

The intent of each formal concept contains precisely those topics covered by all journals in the extent. Conversely, the extent contains precisely those journals sharing all topics in the intent.

Table 4. Formal context

	AIIP	CTM	CS	ISLIS	DF	DC	CT	CA	DIP	STVV
A		x	x							
B	x							x		
C	x			x						
D		x	x							
E							x			
F	x	x	x					x		
G	x	x		x	x		x			
H		x	x							x
I			x							
J	x	x		x						
K	x									
L		x	x							
M	x									
N			x			x	x			
O	x				x					
P	x									
Q	x	x	x	x				x	x	
R	x	x	x		x		x	x		

The line diagram of the concept lattice, showing the partially ordered set of concepts is shown in Fig 2, has the minimal set of edges necessary; all other edges can be derived by using reflexivity and transitivity. Journals and topics label the node that represents the formal concept they generate. All concept nodes above a node labeled by a journal have the journal in their extent. All concept nodes below a node labeled by a topic have the topic in their intent. The extent of the concept node labeled by the topic "STVV" for example is easily found by collecting the journal H labeling this concept node on a path going downward.

The intent of this concept is found by first collecting the topic "STVV" and by going upward to collect the topic "CTM", and "CS" labeling the two concepts found on paths going upward. The resulting extent-intent pair of this concept is ({H}, {CTM,CS,STVV}).

The concept generated by the topic "DF" is a sub concept of the concept generated by the topic "AIIP", for the extent of the former concept is contained in the extent of the latter concept. All journals classified by the topic "DF" were also classified by the topic "AIIP", suggesting that within the given formal context "DF" is a more specific topic than "AIIP".

Another multi constructed example is found in the extent of the concept node labeled by the topic "DIP", which is found by collecting the journal Q labeling this concept node on a path going downward. The intent of this concept is found by

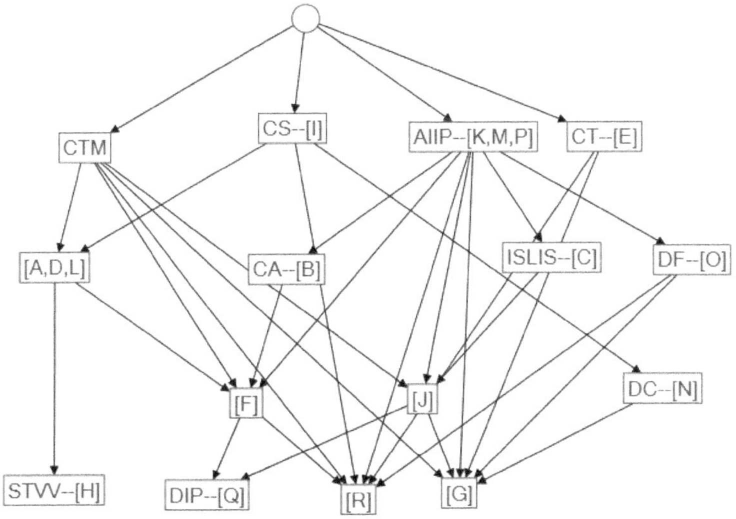

Fig. 2. Concept lattice for journals classification

collecting the topics "CTM", "CA", and "ISLIS" labeling the three concepts found on paths going upward. The latter two topics, however, are sub concepts of the concept generated by the topic "AIIP". The resulting extent-intent pair of this concept is ({Q}, {AIIP,CTM,CS,ISLIS,CA,DIP}).

5 Conclusion

The concept lattice uncovers relational and contextual information. Journals' topic categorizations are put into relational context depending on how they are associated by the journals' aims and scopes. The topics "Computer Theory and Mathematics – CTM", and "Data and Information Processing –DIP" for example are shown as related because these topics share a similar classification context. The implicit structures revealed help researchers to classify journals more efficiently. This approach has the potential to support the emergence of new knowledge by identifying concept relations, making these explicit and enabling researchers to inspect these concept relations.

Concept lattices are not intended to build or substitute traditional static ontologies, rather they aim to support specifications of less rigorous relations, or associations [20], which might be more intuitive to knowledge workers and lead to more interesting links via associations.

The first author would like to thank KFUPM for its support of this work.

References

1. Wille, R.: Restructuring lattice theory: an approach based on hierarchies of concepts. In: Rival, I. (ed.) Ordered Sets, pp. 445–470. Reidel, Dordrecht (1982)
2. Ganter, B., Wille, R.: Formal Concept Analysis: Mathematical foundations. Springer, Heidelberg (1999)

3. Beydoun, G.: Using Formal Concept Analysis towards Cooperative E-Learning. In: Richards, D., Kang, B.-H. (eds.) PKAW 2008. LNCS (LNAI), vol. 5465, pp. 109–117. Springer, Heidelberg (2009)
4. Beydoun, G., Kultchitsky, R., Manasseh, G.: Evolving semantic web with social navigation. Expert Systems with Applications 32, 265–276 (2007)
5. Maddouri, M.: A Formal Concept Analysis Approach to Discover Association Rules from Data. In: Belohlavek, R. (ed.) CLA, 10-21 (2005)
6. Priss, U.: Formal Concept Analysis in Information Science. In: Blaise, C. (ed.) Annual Review of Information Science and Technology. ASIST, vol. 40 (2006)
7. Ganter, B., Kuznetsov, S.O.: Scale Coarsening as Feature Selection. In: Medina, R., Obiedkov, S. (eds.) ICFCA 2008. LNCS (LNAI), vol. 4933, pp. 217–228. Springer, Heidelberg (2008)
8. Stumme, G., Bestride, Y., Taouil, R., Lakhal, L.: computing Iceberg Concept lattices with TITANIC. Data and Knowledge Engineering 42(2), 189–222 (2002)
9. Stumme, G., Wille, R., Wille, U.: Conceptual knowledge discovery in databases using Formal Concept Analysis Methods. In: Żytkow, J.M. (ed.) PKDD 1998. LNCS, vol. 1510, pp. 450–458. Springer, Heidelberg (1998)
10. Ley, M.: The dblp computer science bibliography: Evolution, research issues, perspectives. In: Laender, A.H.F., Oliveira, A.L. (eds.) SPIRE 2002. LNCS, vol. 2476, pp. 1–10. Springer, Heidelberg (2002)
11. http://en.wikipedia.org/wiki/DBLP
12. Zaiane, O.R., Chen, J., Goebel, R.: Dbconnect: mining research community on dblp data. In: WebKDD/SNA-KDD 2007: Proceedings of the 9th WebKDD and 1st SNA-KDD, Workshop on Web Mining and Social Network Analysis, pp. 74–81. ACM, New York (2007)
13. Klamma, R., Cuong, P.M., Cao, Y.: You never walk alone: Recommending academic events based on social network analysis. Complex (1), 657–670 (2009)
14. Chan, S., Pon, R., Cardenas, A.: Visualization and clustering of author social networks. In: Distributed Multimedia Systems Conference, pp. 174–180 (2006)
15. Peng, Y., Kou, G., Shi, Y.: Recent trends in data mining: Document clustering of dm publications. In: International Conference on Service Systems and Service Management, vol. 2, pp. 1653–1659 (2006)
16. Sun, J., Tao, D., Faloutsos, C.: Beyond streams and graphs: dynamic tensor analysis. In: KDD 2006: Proceedings of the 12th ACM SIGKDD International Conference on Knowledge Discovery and Data Mining, pp. 374–383. ACM, New York (2006)
17. Sun, Y., Han, J., Zhao, P., Yin, Z., Cheng, H., Wu, T.: Rankclus: integrating clustering with ranking for heterogeneous information network analysis. In: EDBT 2009: Proceedings of the 12th International Conference on Extending Database Technology, pp. 565–576. ACM, New York (2009)
18. Li, T., Ding, C., Zhang, Y., Shao, B.: Knowledge transformation from word space to document space. In: SIGIR 2008: Proceedings of the 31st Annual International ACM SIGIR Conference on Research and Development in Information Retrieval, pp. 187–194. ACM, New York (2008)
19. Obadi, G., Drazdilova, P., Hlavacek, L., Martinovic, J., Snasel, V.: A Tolerance Rough Set Based Overlapping Clustering for the DBLP Data. In: IEEE/WIC/ACM International Conference on Web Intelligence and Intelligent Agent Technology, pp. 57–60 (2010)
20. Krohn, U., Davies, N.J., Weeks, R.: Concept lattices for knowledge management. BT Technology Journal 17(4), 108–116 (1999)

A Multivariate Mathematical Model to Analyze the Market Prices Correlation at Regional Level

Andreea Iluzia Iacob[1] and Costin-Ciprian Popescu[2]

[1] Department of Statistics and Econometrics,
The Bucharest Academy of Economic Studies, Romania
aiacob@ase.ro

[2] Department of Mathematics, The Bucharest Academy of Economic Studies, Romania
ciprian.popescu@csie.ase.ro

Abstract. In this work is presented the total least squares algorithm and its application in the economic field, whose calculation can be performed using certain software packages. This approach can be also used to analyze the dependence between various economic indicators, especially for the situation in which the direction of the causality between the model variables is unknown. The model is employed for studying the relation between wheat market prices for three Romanian historical regions, which are some of the most important cereal producers for Romania. The final result consists in a unified formula, which provides a global pattern of the national wheat market as a whole.

Keywords: singular value decomposition, total least squares, correlation, market price.

1 Preliminaries

The total least squares (at short: TLS) is one of the most interesting algorithms used in Statistics. It has a wide area of applications: Geophysics [1], Environmental science [9], Economics [4], [7]. In the rough, TLS can be used for finding a mathematical relation, namely a equation, between some statistical variables $x^{(1)},...,x^{(m)}$. In the case of two variables, $x^{(1)},x^{(2)}$, the problem can be solved in the Euclidean plane. After a formal notation: $x^{(1)}=x$, $x^{(2)}=y$, the variables can be measured on the two axis of a Cartesian coordinate system xOy: Ox and Oy. Suppose that at n different moments, some experimental measurements are known: $(x_1, y_1),...,(x_n, y_n)$. In some cases (if the ordinary least squares (LS) is used, for instance), before applying the regression algorithm, it is necessary to assign the direction of dependence. If x is the independent variable, and the relation is assumed to be linear,

$$y = ax + b \tag{1}$$

the parameters a,b must be estimated. If x is the dependent variable, then the relation becomes:

$$x = cy + d\,. \tag{2}$$

E. Ariwa and E. El-Qawasmeh (Eds.): DEIS 2011, CCIS 194, pp. 109–115, 2011.

In both cases, the result is a fitting line. By applying LS, the previous two equations are not equivalent. This is a major disadvantage, because the practical cases, when the type of dependence cannot be specified, are various. TLS gives the possibility to overcome such an impediment. Instead of minimizing the sum of squared errors in a LS sense, TLS algorithm minimize the sum of squared distances from the points $(x_1, y_1),\ldots,(x_n, y_n)$ to the fitting line. In this way, the final result is not influenced by an initial assumption regarding the direction of dependence. Consider, for example, the following data points: $P_1(1,2)$, $P_2(2,5)$, $P_3(3,4)$, $P_4(4,6)$, $P_5(5,8)$, $P_6(6,6)$, $P_7(7,9)$. By applying LS, we obtain the following solutions:

$$y = 0.96429x + 1.8571 \tag{3}$$

when x is the independent variable, and

$$x = 0.80769y - 0.61538 \tag{4}$$

when x is the dependent variable. TLS method gives a unique solution for both cases:

$$0.74163x - 0.67081y + 0.86669 = 0\,. \tag{5}$$

The line obtained by TLS lies between the LS conjugate lines (Fig. 1). For m variables, $x^{(1)},\ldots,x^{(m)}$, the method can be extended to more than two dimensions, when the final result is a hyperplane:

$$H = \left\{\left(x^{(1)},\ldots,x^{(m)}\right) \middle| q_0 + q_1x^{(1)} + \ldots + q_mx^{(m)} = 0\right\}. \tag{6}$$

If the experimental measurements $x_i^{(1)},\ldots,x_i^{(m)}$ (for $i = 1,\ldots,n$) are known, the parameters $q_0,\ldots,q_m$ are obtained such that they are minimizing the sum of squared distances from points $\left(x_i^{(1)},\ldots,x_i^{(m)}\right) \in \mathbf{R}^m$ to H.

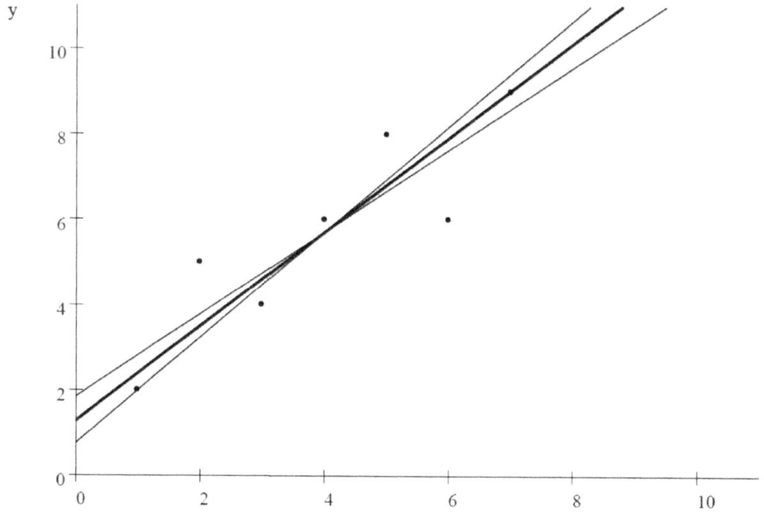

Fig. 1. LS and TLS solutions

2 The Model

For two dimensional TLS, the solution can be determined by algebraic, geometrical or even analytic arguments [8]. Moreover, for $m \in \{2,3\}$ there are some MATLAB procedures [6], [7], [8]. Yet, for an arbitrary number of dimensions, TLS is based on a matrix factorization method, called singular value decomposition (SVD). If A is a real $n \times m$ matrix, then there exists the factorization $A = Q_1 \Sigma Q_2^T$, where Q_1 is an $n \times n$ orthogonal matrix, Σ is an $n \times m$ nonnegative diagonal matrix (including the more general rectangular diagonal type) and Q_2 is an $m \times m$ orthogonal matrix. This factorization has some interesting properties [3], [10]. For solving TLS, the matrix Q_2 has a more significance than the others. For example, if A is an 7×2 matrix with columns

$$col_2^1 = (-3,-2,-1,0,1,2,3)^T \tag{7}$$

and

$$col_2^2 = (-3.7143,-0.7143,-1.7143,0.2857,2.2857,0.2857,3.2857)^T \tag{8}$$

then Q_2 is an 2×2 matrix with columns $(0.67081,0.74163)^T$ and $(0.74163,-0.67081)^T$.

The importance of TLS mainly derives from a few characteristics, as follows:

- Due to the fact that the reasoning is related with the fitting hyperplane instead of the axis of dependent variable, the assumptions regarding causality don't influence the final result (see the previous example and [5]);
- Because is based on orthogonal distances, the method is independent of the type of coordinate system; also non-Cartesian coordinates can be chosen [7];
- Singular value decomposition and TLS can be used for an arbitrary number of variables: $m \in \mathbf{N}$, $m \geq 2$.

The steps for obtaining the fitting hyperplane in a general case (m variables: $x^{(1)},...,x^{(m)}$) can be briefly described as in the following lines [2], [3], [11]. At first, a single point in $\mathbf{R}^m$, $C\left(x_C^{(1)},...,x_C^{(m)}\right)$ (which is called the centroid) is determined by the formula:

$$x_C^{(j)} = n^{-1}\left(x_1^{(j)} + ... + x_n^{(j)}\right), \tag{9}$$

for all $j = 1,...,m$. For our example (the points from $\mathbf{R}^2$: $(1,2)$, $(2,5)$, $(3,4)$, $(4,6)$, $(5,8)$, $(6,6)$, $(7,9)$) the centroid is $C(4,5.7143)$. Then, the matrix A is computed such that its columns $\mathbf{a}^j$ $\left(j = \overline{1,m}\right)$ are as follows:

$$\mathbf{a}^j = \left(x_1^{(j)} - x_C^{(j)},...,x_n^{(j)} - x_C^{(j)}\right)^T. \tag{10}$$

Hereinafter, A is decomposed by SVD:

$$A = Q_1 \Sigma Q_2^T . \tag{11}$$

The parameters $q_1, \ldots, q_m$ are the components of the Q_2 column, which corresponds to the smallest singular value of A. At last, q_0 is computed by taking into account that the centroid belongs to the fitting hiperplane (line, when $m=2$ and plane when $m=3$). For instance, in the case of previous example, A was determined for the points $P_1, \ldots, P_7$. In this situation, q_1 and q_2 are the components of the second column of Q_2.

3 Computational Results

Due to its unique characteristics (mainly independence from initial assumptions regarding the causality and the capacity to work with a large number of statistical variables), TLS is very useful when we search a pattern, a mathematical relation between various economic measurements. Thus, the evolution of some indicators can be traced and forecasted as a whole. Petras and Podlubny [7] have used TLS for $m=3$ in the process of modeling national economic evolution; Iacob et al. [4] applied the bidimensional TLS for studying some social and economic issues. The models for $m \in \{2,3\}$ are more representative and intuitional due to the possibility to build-up some graph charts. In the following, we will use the three-dimensional TLS to analyze the jointly evolution of wheat market prices (expressed in euro/ton, according to the Romanian Ministry of Agriculture and Rural Development) on three significant Romanian markets (namely, three historical regions: Banat, Oltenia and Muntenia). We use the notation: $x^{(1)} = x$, $x^{(2)} = y$, $x^{(3)} = z$, which are the wheat prices for Banat, Oltenia and Muntenia respectively. The initial data (Fig. 2) refers to the first ten weeks of the year 2010, as in the following table.

Table 1. Regional prices

Week	Dimension 1 (x) Banat Region	Dimension 2 (y) Oltenia Region	Dimension 3 (z) Muntenia Region
1	107.43	104.11	129.06
2	107.06	118.43	124.79
3	113.18	100.55	132.99
4	116.32	126.19	128.82
5	113.03	123.73	128.12
6	114.97	102.13	132.72
7	119.88	113.88	128.51
8	113.72	101.85	141.56
9	116.18	117.76	130.67
10	122.58	108.64	124.90

At first, the centroid C is computed. Its space coordinates, x_C, y_C, z_C, are given by the formulas:

$$x_C = 10^{-1}(x_1 + ... + x_{10}),\ y_C = 10^{-1}(y_1 + ... + y_{10}),\ z_C = 10^{-1}(z_1 + ... + z_{10}). \tag{12}$$

After performing the calculus, we obtain the point $C(114.44;111.73;130.21)$ (Fig. 3).

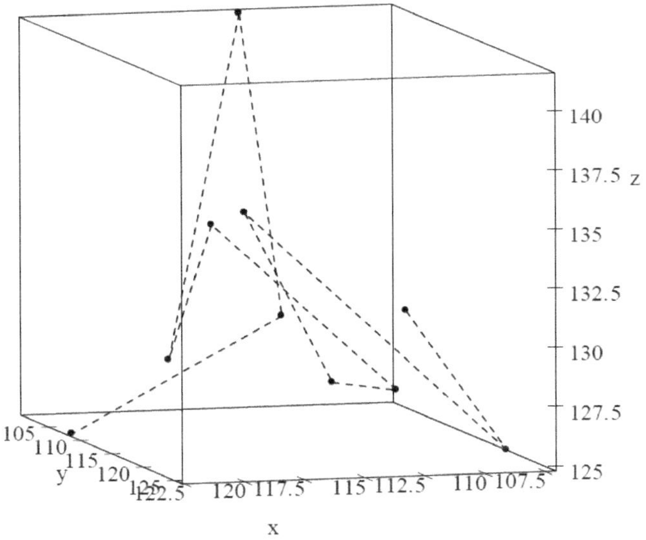

Fig. 2. Space position of real data

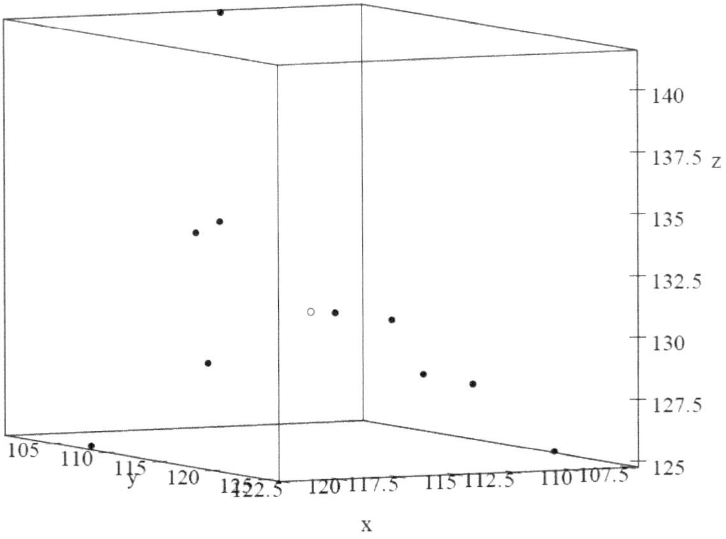

Fig. 3. The initial datapoints and the centroid (circle)

Consider now the 10×3 matrix A, computed as in the previous theoretical description. Singular value decomposition for A gives the factorization:

$$A = Q_1 \Sigma Q_2^T \tag{13}$$

where the third column vector of Q_2 is:

$$\mathbf{q}_2^3 = \left(6.0987\times10^{-2};0.30902;0.94910\right)^T . \tag{14}$$

Also, it is the normal vector on the regression plane, H (Fig. 4). Finally, by using the fact that $C(114.44;111.73;130.21)$ belongs to H, it results that the fitting plane has the equation:

$$6.0987\times10^{-2}x + 0.30902y + 0.94910z - 165.09 = 0 . \tag{15}$$

This last equation also represents the mathematical relationship which gives a global perspective about the simultaneous variation of regional market prices, even if we don't know which of them can be considered as dependent variable.

This method can be also applied to study the relation between various economic indicators, especially for the situation in which the direction of the causality is unknown.

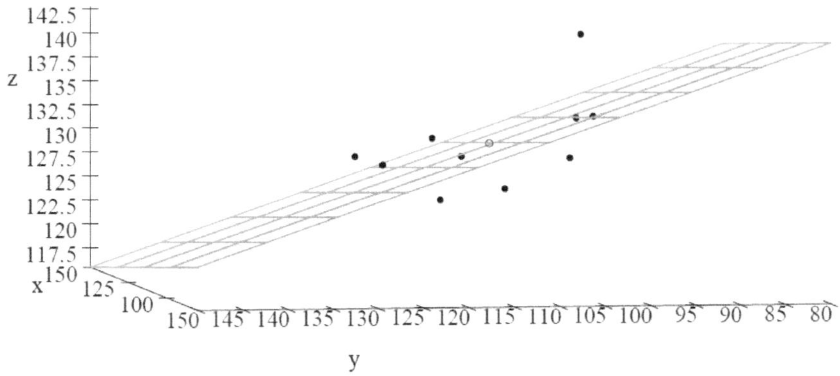

Fig. 4. The initial datapoints and the fitting plane

4 Conclusions

In this work we studied the orthogonal regression and its application in the economic domain, whose calculation can be performed using MATLAB routines or other software. The choice of TLS algorithm instead of other estimation methods is justified by two major advantages. In the case of a higher number of statistical variables for which we don't know from the beginning their status in the regression equation (independent/ dependent variable) we can obtain a general mathematical relationship which describes their simultaneous evolution. This is not possible if other methods are applied. Secondly, the obtained mathematical relationship can be used as a starting point to perform a complex analysis involving various parameters in order to achieve a global view on an economic phenomenon. Such a phenomenon may be considered the evolution of a given product price on a major market at country level. Instead, in some cases, this price may not be unique on such a large market, because it has distinct regional components. By applying TLS, we can obtain a unified formula, which characterizes the whole market, although we used data at regional level. This one gives a global pattern of an entire national market concerning a certain product.

Acknowledgments. This work was supported by CNCSIS – UEFISCDI, project number PNII – IDEI code 1793/2008, financing contract no. 862/2009.

References

1. Bifulco, I., Raiconi, G., Scarpa, T.: Computer Algebra Software for Least Squares and Total Least Norm Inversion of Geophysical Models. Computers & Geosciences 35, 1427–1438 (2009)
2. De Groen, P.: An Introduction to Total Least Squares. Nieuw Archief Voor Wiskunde, Vierde Serie 14, 237–253 (1996)
3. Golub, G.H., Van Loan, C.F.: Matrix Computations. Johns Hopkins University Press, Baltimore (1996)
4. Iacob, A.I., Popescu, C.C., Dimian, G.C.: Tracking Changes in the Regional Social-Economic Activity by a Geometric Fitting Model: The Romanian Case. In: Pirtea, M., Mazilu, M., Strouhal, J. (eds.) Selected Topics in Economy and Management Transformation, vol. 1, pp. 428–433. WSEAS Press (2010)
5. Nievergelt, I.: Total Least Squares: State of the Art Regression in Numerical Analysis. SIAM Review 36(2), 258–264 (1994)
6. Petras, I., Podlubny, I.: Orthogonal Linear Regression in 3D-Space by Using Principal Components Analysis. A Function for MATLAB. MATLAB Central File Exchange (2006)
7. Petras, I., Podlubny, I.: State Space Description of National Economies: The V4 Countries. Comp. Stat. & Data Anal. 52(2), 1223–1233 (2007)
8. Pozzi, F.: Orthogonal Linear Least Squares on a Two-Dimensional Plane. MATLAB Central File Exchange (2008)
9. Ramos, J.A.: Applications of TLS and Related Methods in the Environmental Sciences. Comp. Stat. & Data Anal. 52(2), 1234–1267 (2007)
10. Strang, G.: Linear Algebra and its Applications. Thomson Learning (1988)
11. Van Huffel, S., Vanderwalle, J.: The Total Least Squares Problem: Computational Aspects and Analysis. SIAM, Philadelphia (1991)

IT Project Selection Model Using Real Option Optimization with Fuzzy Set Approach

Shashank Pushkar[1] and Akhileshwar Mishra[2]

[1] Dept. of Computer Science and Engineering, Birla Institute of Technology, Mesra, Ranchi, India-835215
shashank_pushkar@yahoo.com
[2] Dept. of Computer Applications, National Institute of Technology, Jamshedpur, India-831014
amishra_8@yahoo.com

Abstract. Optimal selection of interdependent IT projects for funding in multi-period has been challenging in the framework of Real Option analysis. This paper presents a mathematical model to optimize the fuzzy Option value for multi-stage portfolio of IT projects. A fuzzy Option model is used to maximize the Option value of each IT project. The IT portfolio selection problem is formulated as a fuzzy zero–one integer programming model that can handle both uncertain and flexible parameters to determine the optimal project portfolio. The idea of optimizing the fuzzy real option value of the portfolio is to maximize the overall value and to minimize the downside risk of the selected portfolio for funding. A transformation method based on qualitative possibility theory is developed to convert the fuzzy portfolio selection model into a crisp mathematical model from the risk-averse perspective. The transformed model can be solved by an optimization technique .The optimization model and solution approach can help IT managers in optimal funding decision making for projects prioritization.

Keywords: IT project portfolio management, Fuzzy logic, Real option, Fuzzy set optimization, Financial evaluation.

1 Introduction

The companies that select IT projects face an important problem of selecting a project portfolio for funding. The purpose of project portfolio decision is to allocate a limited set of resources to projects in a way that balances risk and reward. Since the IT project portfolio decision deals with future events and opportunities, much of the information required to make portfolio decisions is at best uncertain and at worst very unreliable. However, even with this doubtful information, the project portfolio decision still must be made. Moreover, resource or budget availability may be flexible because additional budget may be reallocated from other budget categories or projects within the company.

Fuzzy set theory has been used to model imprecise and preference information in many applications. It can also be used to represent uncertain project information. Pereira and Junior [1] formulated a simple fuzzy multi-criteria R&D portfolio

E. Ariwa and E. El-Qawasmeh (Eds.): DEIS 2011, CCIS 194, pp. 116–128, 2011.

selection problem that represented project appraisals for each criterion as fuzzy set and developed an algorithm to get non-dominated solutions. Machacha and Bhattacharya[2] modelled uncertain critical factors involved in the information system project selection by fuzzy sets and developed a fuzzy logic approach to emulate the human reasoning process and make decisions based on vague or imprecise data. Mohamed and McCowan [3] applied fuzzy set theory to handle the inherent uncertainty of both momentary and non-momentary aspects in construction projects and used a fuzzy ranking index to rank and select construction projects. Hsu et.al.[4] applied the fuzzy AHP approach to select government-sponsored frontier technology R&D projects and indicated the adequacy of fuzzy approach in selecting R&D projects. Fuzzy set theory is also applied to model uncertain and flexible project information. Wang [5] has used fuzzy set theory to describe uncertain and flexible project information.

The objective of this paper is to develop a fuzzy portfolio selection model to optimize the IT portfolio for the risk-averse decision maker in an uncertain environment. Since traditional project valuation methods often underestimate the risky project, a fuzzy Options model is used to maximize the Option value of each IT project. The IT portfolio selection problem is formulated as a fuzzy zero–one integer programming model that can handle both uncertain and flexible parameters to determine the optimal project portfolio. A transformation method based on qualitative possibility theory is developed to convert the fuzzy portfolio selection model into a crisp mathematical model from the risk-averse perspective. The transformed model can be solved by an optimization technique .An optimal IT portfolio can be obtained by solving the transformed model using an optimization technique. Depending on the resource flexibility, the decision maker can perform sensitivity analyses to evaluate the appropriateness of the project portfolio selected.

We conclude that the proposed approach can assist decision makers in selecting suitable IT portfolios, while there is a lack of reliable project information.

2 Dependency View of IT Projects

Here the collection of IT projects is a portfolio of projects to be prioritized for funding. The projects are implemented separately but they can have following types of dependency [6],[7],[8]:

1. Total dependency(Hard dependency)
2. Partial dependency(Soft dependency)

Hard dependency of project i on project j indicates that the capabilities developed for project j is also required by i, i.e. j creates an Option to implement i and i can be implemented either together with j or after implementation of j but not before j's implementation. If i is implemented after implementation of j, the idea of Real Option analysis says that the project creates an Option for the implementation of i. Therefore the Option value of i should be added to the DCF value of project j to get the total value of j.

Soft dependency of project i on j indicates that the capabilities developed for project j supports or enhances the capabilities required by project i but there is no strict requirement of project i to be implemented together with j or after j's implementation. If i is implemented after the implementation of j, the benefit level of i would be increased by certain fraction depending on the level of dependency of project i on project j. Therefore, according to Real Option valuation, if i is implemented after j, Option value of i should be added to the DCF value of j to have the total value of j, but the Option value of i to be added to the DCF value of j will be only in proportion to the dependency level of i on j . If a project j has no dependency on i the capabilities developed for j and i are independent and they do not effect each other in generating benefits irrespective of their period of implementation and neither of them will generate Option for the other project. In the fig. 1 given next α1, α2 .etc. .are all investment projects. The solid arrow indicates total dependency (e.g. α2 is totally dependent on α1). Dashed arrow indicates partial dependency (e.g. α6 is partially dependent on α5). The project that has no dependency on any other projects are independent and without arrow.

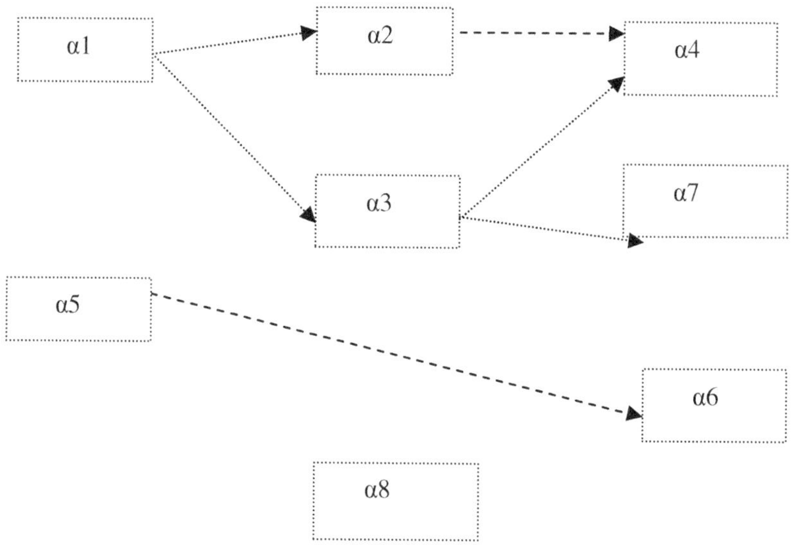

Fig. 1. Dependency graph for portfolio of eight IT projects

3 Modelling Uncertain and Preference Parameters in Portfolio Management

Fuzzy set theory has been widely used to represent uncertain or flexible information in many types of applications, such as scheduling, engineering design, and production management [9]. It may provide an alternative and convenient framework for handling uncertain project parameters (e.g., project value, cost, etc.), while there is lack of certainty in data or even lack of available historical data. This is because the possible range of a project parameter and the most plausible value within that range can be estimated and specified by experts based on their experiences. For computational efficiency, trapezoidal or triangular fuzzy numbers [9] are used to represent the above uncertain project parameters.

A trapezoidal fuzzy number $\tilde{A} = (m_1, m_2, \alpha, \beta)$ is defined as:

$$\mu_{\tilde{A}}(x) = \begin{cases} (m_1 - x)/\alpha, & x \leq m_1 \\ 1, & m_1 \leq x \leq m2 \\ (x - m_2)/\beta, & x \geq m_2 \end{cases} \quad (1)$$

where, m_1 and m_2 are the left and right modal values. And, α and β are the left and right spreads, respectively. A triangular fuzzy number is a specialized trapezoidal fuzzy number with $m_1 = m_2$ and is usually denoted as $\tilde{A} = (m_1, m_2, \alpha, \beta)$ or $\tilde{A} = (m_1, \alpha, \beta)$. For example, an uncertain project value can be represented by a trapezoidal fuzzy number $\tilde{v}$ (see Fig. 2). The membership function $\mu\ \tilde{v}\ (x)$ represents the grade of possibility that the project value will be realized in x. The values within the range [m1, m2] (core) are the most certain rewards and the value outsides the range [m1 $-\alpha$, m2 + β](support) are the least possible ones. The values outside the core and inside the support of $\tilde{v}$ are in between.

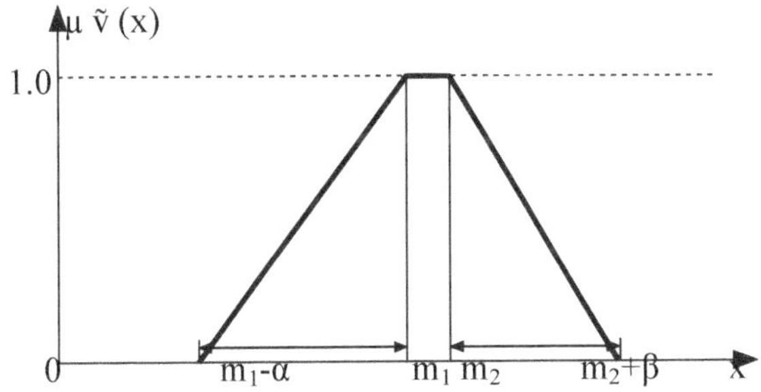

Fig. 2. Uncertain project value with fuzzy set

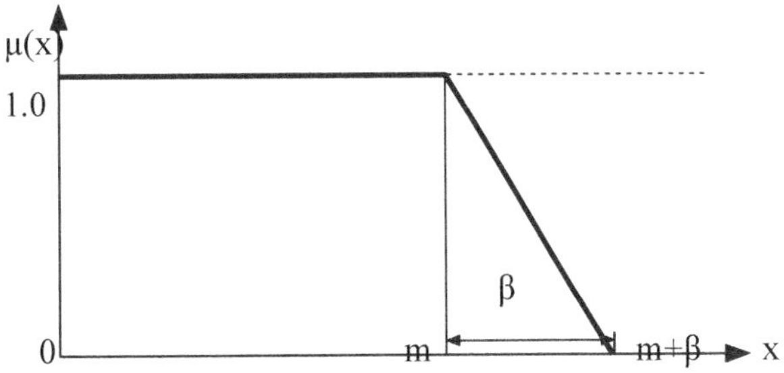

Fig. 3. Preferred budget spending with fuzzy set

In addition, there often exists certain flexibility in making the portfolio decision. For example, the available budget may be flexible [10].They are often determined by the preference of a decision maker and can also be represented by fuzzy sets. This is because there is an opportunity to seek limited additional funding if it is justified by an expected value of the selected projects. An example of the preferred budget spending $\tilde{B}$ = (0, m, 0,β) is shown in Fig. 3 and it denotes the degree of satisfaction of the budget spending. If the budget spending is less than m, then the decision maker is completely satisfied. However, if the budget spending is greater than m, then the degree of satisfaction decreases. When the budget spending is greater than m + β, the degree of satisfaction becomes zero.

The fuzzy arithmetic operations including the addition and subtraction used in this chapter are defined next. Let $\tilde{A} = (a, b, \alpha, \beta)$, $\tilde{B} = (c, d, \delta, \gamma)$ denote fuzzy numbers. Then,

$$\tilde{A} \oplus \tilde{B} = (a+c, b+d, \alpha + \delta, \beta + \gamma) \quad (2)$$

$$\tilde{A} \ominus \tilde{B} = (a \quad d, b - c, \alpha + \delta, \beta + \gamma) \quad (3)$$

where ⊕ and ⊖ are addition and subtraction operators, respectively. The detail can be referred in Klir and Yuan[9]. In addition, the possibilistic mean and variance of Ã are defined as [11]:

$$E(\tilde{A}) = (a + b)/2 + (\beta - \alpha)/6 \quad (4)$$

$$Var(\tilde{A}) = (b - a)^2/4 + (b - a)(\alpha + \beta)/6 + (\alpha + \beta)^2/24 \quad (5)$$

Now, the qualitative possibility theory [10] has been introduced that used in this paper to handle the fuzzy constraint involving both uncertain and flexible parameters. The basic concept of qualitative possibility theory which provides a good framework to handle this type of fuzzy constraint is introduced as follows:

Let U be a set of states and X be a set of possible consequences. Suppose that the decision maker has some knowledge of the actual state and some preference on the consequences of his/her decision. Let a possibility distribution represent the incomplete knowledge on the state on U and μ be the possibility distribution representing the preference of decision maker on X. The utility of a decision d whose consequence in state u is x = d (u) for u ∈ U can be evaluated by combining the plausibilities π(u) and the utilities u(x) in a suitable way. Two quantitative criteria were proposed by Dubois and Prade [10] to evaluate the worth of decision d regarding uncertain information.

Pessimistic criterion:

$$U_*(d) = \inf_{u \in U} \max(1-\pi(u), \mu(d(u))) \quad (6)$$

Optimistic Criterion:

$$U_*(d) = \sup_{u \in U} \min(\pi(u), \mu(d(u))) \quad (7)$$

In this research, the pessimistic criterion is used to determine the satisfaction degree of the fuzzy constraint that contains uncertain parameters on its left-hand side and flexible parameters on its right-hand side. Let $\tilde{R}$ be the possible consequences of decision d and $\tilde{B}$ be the preference of decision maker about the consequences, where the degree of possibility or the degree of preference is characterized by the membership degree of a fuzzy number. The satisfaction degree of the decision d can be defined as a function of $\tilde{R}$ and $\tilde{B}$:

$$C_d(\tilde{R},\tilde{B}) = \inf \max(1 - \tilde{R}(u), \tilde{B}(u)) \quad (8)$$

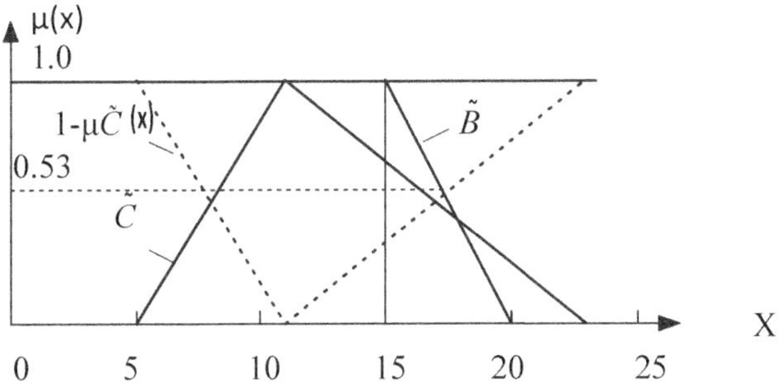

Fig. 4. Example of satisfaction degree of fuzzy budget constraint

The following example is used to illustrate the concept.

Example. Assume that an IT manager intends to fund for a set of IT projects within a pre-defined budget. Because of uncertainties lies in IT projects, it is difficult to estimate the cost of IT projects accurately by a single value. It may be represented by the fuzzy number $\tilde{C}$ =(11, 11, 6, 12). In addition, the preferred value of budget spending is specified as the fuzzy number $\tilde{B}$ =(0, 15, 0, 5). The satisfaction degree of the constraint that the development cost should be less than or equal to the allocated budget spending is 0.53, according to Eq. (8). From figure 4, the satisfaction degree of the constraint is determined by the intersection of the inverse of the right edge of $\tilde{C}$ and the right edge of $\tilde{B}$; in other words, the satisfaction degree is determined from the pessimistic perspective. As the uncertain project cost $\tilde{C}$ increases, the satisfaction degree of the fuzzy budget constraint decreases.

4 Methodology for Optimizing IT Projects Portfolio

Usually, the present value of expected cash flow can't be characterized by a single number. However, Carlsson and Fuller [11] say that the managers are able to estimate the present value of expected flows by using a trapezoidal possibility distribution of the form:

$$\tilde{S}_0 = (s1, s2, \alpha, \beta)$$

i.e. the most possible values of the present value of expected cash flows lie in the interval [s1, s2] (which is the core of the trapezoidal fuzzy number $\tilde{S}_0$) and (s2+β) is the upward potential and (s1-α) is the downward potential for the present value of expected cash flows.

In the similar manner one can estimate the expected costs by using the trapezoidal possibility distribution of the form:

$$\tilde{X} = (x1, x2, \alpha, \beta),$$

i.e. the most possible values of expected cost lie in the interval [x1 , x2] (which is the core of the trapezoidal fuzzy number $\tilde{X}$), and (x2 + β,) is the upward potential and (x1 - α) is the downward potential for expected.

In fuzzy cost and fuzzy value circumstances, Carlsson and Fuller[11] suggests the following formula for computing the fuzzy Real Option:

$$FROV = \tilde{S}_0 e^{-\delta T} N(d1) - \tilde{X} e^{-rT} N(d2) \tag{9}$$

Where,

$$d\,1 = (\mathrm{In}(E(\tilde{S}_0)/E(\tilde{X})) + (r-\delta+\sigma 2/2)T)/\sigma\sqrt{T}$$

$$d\,2 = d1 - \sigma\sqrt{T}$$

and where $E(\tilde{S}_0)$ denotes the possibilistic mean value of the present value of expected cash flows, $E(\tilde{X})$ stands for the possibilistic mean value of expected costs and $\sigma = \sigma(\tilde{S}_0)$ is the possibilistic variance of the present value of expected cash flow, r is the annualized continuously compounded rate on a safe asset with the same maturity as the expiration of the Option, T is the time to maturity of the Option (in years) and where δ denotes the dividends paid out during the life-time of the Option, σ denotes the standard deviation of the annualized continuously compounded rate of return.

Now, seeing the above formulation we can see that the FROV (Fuzzy Real Option value can be calculated based on the formula (2), (3),(4) and(5) mentioned earlier in this section.

On the basis of Fuzzy Real Option value mentioned above we can formulate the model to maximize the FROV of IT projects portfolio similar to the concept of maximization of Real Option Value.

Here we are taking the problem to select a set of IT projects from a pool of candidate projects to maximize the Real Option value within the given budgetary and sequencing constraint. Each candidate project has certain sequence for funding which depends on the other dependent projects. The sequencing characteristics of IT projects have been shown in the figure 1 and explained in section 2 of the paper.

Since the imprecision and flexibility are encountered in making IT projects portfolio as mentioned the earlier sections, a fuzzy zero-one integer programming model has been proposed here to optimize IT portfolio funding decisions in uncertain environment.

Notation:

n = the total number of candidate projects.

$\tilde{V}i$= the fuzzy Real Option value of candidate project i due to its dependent projects.

$\tilde{B}$= Fuzzy budget available.

$\tilde{c}i$= Fuzzy investment cost of candidate project i.

D i = Set of projects directly dependent on project i (D i $\subset$ P).

$\tilde{R}i$ = Present value of return from project i.

Xi = Binary value indicating the funding of project i;

$$= \begin{cases} 1, \text{if it is funded,} \\ 0, \quad \text{otherwise.} \end{cases}$$

$$Yij = \begin{cases} 1, \text{if i is to be implemented prior to the implementation of j,} \\ 0, \quad \text{otherwise.} \end{cases}$$

$$RQi = \begin{cases} 1, \text{if project i is required to be implemented,} \\ 0 \quad \text{otherwise.} \end{cases}$$

d i j = Level of dependence of project i on project j, defined as follows:

d i j = 0 , if i is not directly dependent on j;

0< d i j <1 , if i is partially dependent on j;

d i j = 1 , if i is totally dependent on j.

Problem Statement:

$$\text{Max } \sum_{i=1}^{n} \sum_{j \in Di} Yij * (\tilde{V}i) * Xi$$

S.t.

$\sum_{i=1}^{n}(\tilde{c}i * Xi) \preccurlyeq \tilde{B}$ (Budget Constraint)

$Y_{ij} . d_{ij} < 1, \forall j \in Di, \forall i$ (Sequencing constraint)

$\sum_{i=1}^{n} RQi * Xi \geq \sum_{i=1}^{n} RQi, \forall i$ (Condition for selecting mandatory projects)

Here, the objective is to maximize the Fuzzy Real Option value of IT project portfolio for the prioritization of IT projects for funding. With the maximization of Real Option in fuzzy environment with the fuzzy budget, fuzzy cost and fuzzy Net Present Value can intern minimize the risk because it will select those projects first which have the high Option values and are providing infrastructure to the other dependent projects. Since, in this formulation, we have taken budget as a preference parameter and cost as an uncertain parameter (Fuzzy Real Option value would be uncertain if we take cost and NPV as uncertain parameter),in the next section we are specifying an approach based on quantitative possibility theory briefly presented in previous section.

Since the proposed IT portfolio model involves the fuzzy objective value and fuzzy constraints containing uncertain and flexible parameters on their left- and right-hand sides, respectively, here we introduce an approach based on qualitative possibility theory to determine the optimal solution for the fuzzy IT portfolio selection model. The portfolio selection model can be considered as the following form:

$$\text{Max} \quad \sum_{i=1}^{n} \widetilde{V}i * xi$$

$$\text{S.t.} \sum_{i=1}^{n} \tilde{c}i * xi \preccurlyeq \widetilde{B}, \quad xi \epsilon [0,1]$$

Here, coefficient $\widetilde{V}i, \tilde{c}i$ are uncertain parameters, and $\widetilde{B}$ is a flexible parameter, where all of them are characterized by fuzzy numbers.

Inuiguchi and Ramik [12] proposed the possiblistic linear programming approach that can handle the fuzzy linear programming model with uncertain objective function and parameters on the left-hand side of each constraint, where all uncertain parameters are restricted by fuzzy numbers. Using possibility theory [14], the fuzzy linear programming problem was transformed into a crisp mathematical model that can be solved by an optimization technique. The above approach was applied for transforming a fuzzy optimization model into a crisp integer programming model by Wang and Hwang [13] for R&D portfolio.

Here, the approach of Wang and Hwang[13] has been extended to handle the fuzzy constraint and fuzzy objective function containing both uncertain and preference parameters. Through the above approach, the fuzzy IT portfolio selection model is transformed into an integer programming model which can be solved by an optimization technique.

Let us consider an inequality constraint of the above problem:

$$\tilde{c}1x1+\tilde{c}2x2 +...+\tilde{c}nxn \leq \widetilde{B}$$

If the decision maker feels that the satisfaction degree of the constraint needs to be greater than or equal to λ , the constraint can be reformulated based on pessimistic criterion according to equation equation(8)

$$C(\tilde{c}1x1+\tilde{c}2x2 +...+\tilde{c}nxn ,\widetilde{B})\geq\lambda$$

The satisfaction degree of the constraint is determined by the intersection of the inverse of the right edge of $\sum_{i=1}^{n} \tilde{c}i * xi$ and $\widetilde{B}$(see figure 5 next).

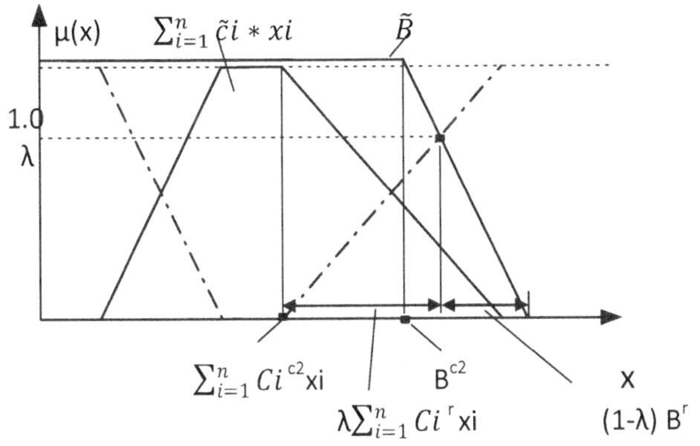

Fig. 5. Graphical interpretation of fuzzy constraint $C(\tilde{c}1x1+\tilde{c}2x2+...+\tilde{c}nxn, \tilde{B})\geq\lambda$

Now the constraint can be transformed into

$$\sum_{i=1}^{n} Ci^{c2}xi + \lambda \sum_{i=1}^{n} Ci^{r}xi \leq B^{c2} + (1-\lambda)\ B^{r}$$

Where, Ci^{c2}, B^{c2} are the right modal values of $\tilde{c}i$ and $\tilde{B}$. And Ci^{r}, B^{r} are their right spreads, respectively .

In the other words, given the required satisfaction degree λ, the right modal value of $\sum_{i=1}^{n} \tilde{c}i * xi$ plus the factor λ of its right spread should be less than the right modal value of $\tilde{B}$ plus the factor (1-λ) of its right spread. Therefore, all fuzzy constraint involving uncertain and flexible parameters can be transformed into crisp constraints. The value of λ can be selected based on resource flexibility. The larger the value of λ , the smaller will be resource available.

Similarly, we can transform the fuzzy objective function into crisp objective function. Assuming that the decision maker feels that the satisfaction degree of objective function should be greater than or equal to γ , the objective function can be transformed as follows:

Max V

S.t.

$C(\sum_{i=1}^{n} \tilde{V}i * xi), V)\geq\gamma$,

Which is equivalent to(see the figure 6 next)

$$\text{Max}\quad V\ \text{s.t.}\ \sum_{i=1}^{n} Vi^{c1}\,xi - \gamma\sum_{i=1}^{n} Vi^{l}\,xi \geq V$$

Since the problem is the maximization problem, the left edge of $\sum_{i=1}^{n} \tilde{V}i * xi$ is used based on pessimistic criterion to determine the satisfaction degree of the portfolio value that is greater than V regarding the projects selected.

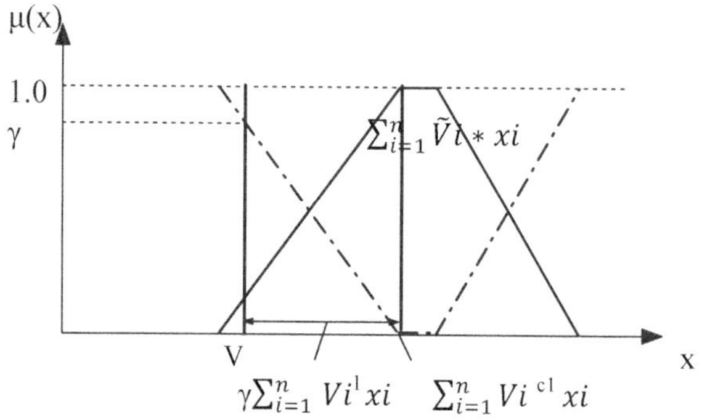

Fig. 6. Graphical interpretation of fuzzy objective function($C(\sum_{i=1}^{n} \tilde{V}i * xi), V) \geq \gamma$)

The above objective function is equivalent to :

$$\text{Max} \quad \sum_{i=1}^{n} Vi^{cl}\, xi \; - \; \gamma\sum_{i=1}^{n} Vi^{l}xi$$

The value of γ can be selected according to the pessimistic attitude of the decision maker. The larger the value of γ, the more risk-averse the decision maker is.

According to the approach describe above, the fuzzy IT portfolio selection model can be transformed into crisp mathematical model that can be solved by available optimization techniques. The following simple example is used to illustrate the approach.

Example:

$$\text{Max} \quad \tilde{V}1x1 + \tilde{V}2x2 + \tilde{V}3x3$$

S.t.

$$\tilde{c}1x1+\tilde{c}2x2 + \tilde{c}3x3 \leq \tilde{B}$$

Table 1. Fuzzy coefficients for the given example

$\tilde{c}1$	(2,1,1)
$\tilde{c}2$	(3,1,1)
$\tilde{c}3$	(2,1,1)
$\tilde{V}1$	(10,2,2)
$\tilde{V}2$	(15,1,1)
$\tilde{V}3$	(20,3,3)
$\tilde{B}$	(6,1,1)

All coefficients are represented as fuzzy number in table 1 above.

Let , $\lambda = 0.85$, and $\gamma = 0.9$,Using the above approach, the problem is transformed as follows:

Max 8.2 x1+14.1x2+17.3x3

s.t. 2.8x1+3.85x2+2.85x3≤6.15

x1,x2,x3∊{0.1}

The best solution is 25.5 for x1=x3=1, x2=0.

5 Conclusion

This paper develops a fuzzy portfolio selection model to optimize the IT portfolio for the risk-averse decision maker in an uncertain environment. Since traditional project valuation methods often underestimate the risky project, a fuzzy Real Option model is used to maximize the Option value of each IT project. The IT portfolio selection problem is formulated as a fuzzy zero–one integer programming model that can handle both uncertain and flexible parameters to determine the optimal project portfolio. A transformation method based on qualitative possibility theory is developed to convert the fuzzy portfolio selection model into a crisp integer programming model from the risk-averse perspective. The transformed model can be solved by an optimization technique. Therefore, an optimal IT portfolio can be obtained by solving the transformed model. The future directions can be Finding the effect of incorporation of fuzzy dependencies among the IT projects' portfolio optimization models. Another direction could be proposing multi-criteria decision making models in IT portfolio by integrating the objectives of the above models in the framework of fuzzy Real Option.

References

1. Pereira, O., Junior, D.: The R&D project selection problem with fuzzy co-efficients. Fuzzy Sets and Systems 26, 299–316 (1988)
2. Machacha, L.L., Bhattacharya, P.: A fuzzy-logic-based approach to project selection. IEEE Transactions on Engineering Management 47, 65–73 (2000)
3. Mohamed, S., McCowan, A.K.: Modelling project investment decisions under uncertainty using possibility theory. International Journal of Project Management 19, 231–234 (2001)
4. Hsu, Y.G., Tzeng, G.H., Shyu, J.Z.: Fuzzy multiple criteria selection of government-sponsored frontier technology R&D projects. R&D Management 33, 539–551 (2003)
5. Wang, J.: A fuzzy robust scheduling approach for product development projects. European Journal of Operational Research 152, 180–194 (2004)
6. Pushkar, S., Sharma, R.R., Mishra, A.: Dynamic Programming approach to optimize portfolio of Interdependent IT projects. CiiT International Journal of Artificial Intelligent Systems and Machine Learning 1, 127–131 (2009)
7. Bardhan, I.R., Kauffman, R.J., Sanjeewa, N.: Optimizing an IT Project Portfolio with Time-Wise Interdependencies. In: HICSS 2006 Proceedings of the 39th Annual Hawaii International Conference on System Sciences, vol. 8, p. 168 (2006)

8. Pushkar, S., Mustafi, A., Mishra, A.: A Meta-heuristic Approach for IT Projects Portfolio Optimization. Journal of Computer Science and Engineering 1, 42–47 (2010)
9. Klir, G.J., Yuan, B.: Fuzzy sets and fuzzy logic theory and applications. Prentice-Hall, Englewood Cliffs (1995)
10. Dubois, D., Prade, H.: Qualitative possibility theory and its applications to constraint satisfaction and decision under uncertainty. International Journal of Intelligent Systems 14, 45–61 (1999)
11. Carlsson, C., Fuller, R.: A fuzzy approach to real Option valuation. Fuzzy Sets and Systems 139, 297–312 (2003)
12. Inuiguchi, M., Ramik, J.: Possibilistic linear programming: a brief review of fuzzy mathematical programming and a comparison with stochastic programming in portfolio selection problem. Fuzzy Sets and Systems 111, 3–28 (2000)
13. Wang, J., Hwang, W.L.: A fuzzy set approach for R&D portfolio selection using a real option valuation model. Omega 35, 247–257 (2007)
14. Dubois, D., Prade, H.: Possibility theory an approach to computerized processing of uncertainty. Plenum Press, New York (1988)

New Engagement Model of IT Governance and IT Management for the Communication of the IT Value at Enterprises

Carlos Juiz

University of the Balearic Islands, Department of Computer Science, Carretera de Valldemossa, km. 7.5, 07122 Palma, Spain
cjuiz@uib.es

Abstract. The power of IT and business alignment that has the use of a communication model of the IT value should be based on the ability to engage IT governance models and IT management models, respectively. This engagement should provide a clear view both board members, users and IT staff. Thus, our research provides this communication model that explains explicitly how IT projects, the board's strategy and business units should go together and in the same direction. In addition, our implementation of this model alerts the CIO when IT assets are not really aligned to the principles and objectives of the board or the budget is spent on just technology, not investing it in valued solutions. Our research methodology is based on the ISO/IEC 38500 standard model, although important features have been added based on our IT governance experience and the use of a tool that implement the model itself.

Keywords: IT Governance, IT Management, ISO/IEC 38500.

1 Introduction

IT Governance has been historically difficult in comparison with to govern other corporate assets. This difficulty may be originated due to the pressure forces from business units asking for new IT solutions and due to the misperception of IT services [18]. Other difficult factors for implementing IT Governance may be the undefined value of IT or even the unclear roles of the CIO and the CTO at the organization [17]. Anyway, whatever the origin of the problem, when the communication between the board and IT staff of an organization is not effective, the image the board has about IT is that they arrive always late, are expensive and not entirely competent [19]. Additionally, the IT Governance tasks are partially recursive, that is, the corporate board and the CIO should establish an IT governance framework and should specify the specific field of IT Governance activities different to other levels of management or operation, but IT Governance being included within the framework itself. This last feature complicates the understanding of IT Governance at enterprises. All the difficulties explained above motivate the generation of proposed model in this paper.

E. Ariwa and E. El-Qawasmeh (Eds.): DEIS 2011, CCIS 194, pp. 129–143, 2011.

1.1 IT Governance Goals and Implementation

The system of IT governance has several layers (including itself) corresponding to three different kinds of different but complementary tasks [14]:

- IT Operation, which deals with the continuity and competence of the IT infrastructure and the IT staff of the organization. Their duties are mainly to implement the business projects, to run the infrastructure and to standardize the architecture and the corresponding operations, while maintaining the IT services deployment.
- IT Management, which aims to achieve the credibility in the design and management of the infrastructure and architecture of the IT and also the IT personnel management.
- IT Governance, which aims to achieve the commitment and the evidence that IT is a strategic element that provides value to the organization. It includes the establishment of framework of governance seeking the compliance with business units and corporate objectives, in the context of the business processes and IT assets.

Thus, the most important objective of the IT Governance is the valorization of IT activities through the alignment between business and IT. However, the key question for the board is whether IT investment is harmonized with its strategic objectives, while producing business value. Since some companies spend more than half of all capital investment on IT assets, most of the company boards remain skeptical about whether their IT investments are paying off [9]. Boards are usually frustrated with their IT staff, and they respond by putting pressure on IT costs and CIOs ability to solve this huge alignment problem [10].

Therefore, IT Governance communication requires also a conceptual model to engage the IT Operations and the IT Management to ensure the performance and conformance of IT products, operations and services. We believe that our model improves the communication among the board and IT staff through this CIO governance framework. Companies that can communicate effectively about the value of IT are able to create continuously more value from IT assets. When CIOs make IT's performance and decisions transparent, everyone, from seasoned technology experts to non technical staff, can better understand their roles in line operation and managing IT. This state of harmony that we call Value of Alignment (VoA) is characterized by complex, multifaceted and never completely achieved set of relations captured by the model we have developed.

The model presented here not only helps to communicate the principal governance structures, the major IT decisions and the alignment, but it is a governance framework that indicates how they are related and also how to engage the three main tasks of above in the three layers of implementation of IT Governance.

Our model does not prevent the adoption of any standard of governance or management of IT, on the contrary, it allows a leisurely adoption, to workaround the symptoms of poor communication and implementing the standards selected by the organization at a later stage of governance maturity, by increasing the scope of ISO/IEC 38500 standard but including it in its core.

In addition, our model has been proved by implementing a dashboard tool [13], this tool help CIOs not only in the third layer (Governance) but also in the other two (Operations and Management) related through performance indicators and measurements.

The paper is as follows: sections 2 to 4 serve to understand the scope of our model. Section 5 reminds previous engagement modelling of IT Governance and IT Management by simply addition of the Thorp [15] model to ISO/IEC 38500 model. In section 6 we develop our main contribution for communicating the value of IT coming from IT governance and IT management engaging mechanisms. Section 7 devotes to the research implementation and experimentation of our proposed model of engagement. The paper ends with our conclusions, the open problems and the bibliographical references.

2 IT Governance and ISO/IEC 38500

The IT governance is to specify the decision rights and accountability framework to produce the desired behavior in the use of IT at the organization [9]. Also the IT governance has been identified as the responsibility of executives and senior management that consists of leadership, organizational structures and processes that ensure that IT assets are supporting and extending the company objectives and strategies of the organization [5]. There are other IT governance definitions, but all converge on the rights and decisions framework about IT at the company.

After all, the definition of IT governance comes from the general definition of governance. Thus, the IT governance should not be very different of governing other assets, such as financial, personnel, intellectual property, administration, facilities, etc. However, the day-by-day work at many companies seems to be quite different. It seems natural that the CIO to continuously justify each minor decision, which is not the case in other governance assets. That is, this continuous reevaluation does not happens with other traditional assets, where is almost impossible to think about this continuous justification of simple projects, tactic goals, IT department strategy, IT budgeting, etc. that CIO typically suffers.

Therefore, one of the basic mistakes in an enterprise is to confuse the governance with the management (and even operation) of IT. The reason of this misunderstanding is because the layer frontiers may be somewhat diluted. Indeed, this error has been widely promoted by some IT management de facto standards, which include some governance mechanisms. It is not the nature of this paper the debate about standards, but we may conclude that COBIT [6] and ITIL [8] are currently regarded IT management frameworks with some governance features. Both standards contain parts that refer to the IT governance, explicitly or implicitly, as a subset within the management of IT systems. The same applies to the standard ISO/IEC 20000 [2, 3] which is also a management framework of IT.

We may conclude that there was only one standard for IT governance until 2005, corresponding to the Australian Standard AS8015 [7], on which the ISO/IEC 38500 [4] is based. In figure 1, the conceptual model for IT governance (and its relation with IT management is simply depicted. The informal interpretation of figure 1 is as follows:

- IT managers and technical staff should guarantee the development of IT projects and their corresponding operations to maintain QoS of business processes.
- These projects should be directed from the strategic plan and policies coming from the board, in which the CIO must be included to improve communication with the business units and IT staff.
- Thus, business units and IT units must work together to propose new projects that CIO and other governance structures should evaluate to be included in the applications portfolio that implement the strategic plan.
- To close the virtuous cycle, once the projects become a reality and they serve to operate business, infrastructure or architecture processes, IT staff should measure their performance and conformance.
- The CIO must monitor these values in order to have enough information to consider new proposals coming from lower IT layers again.

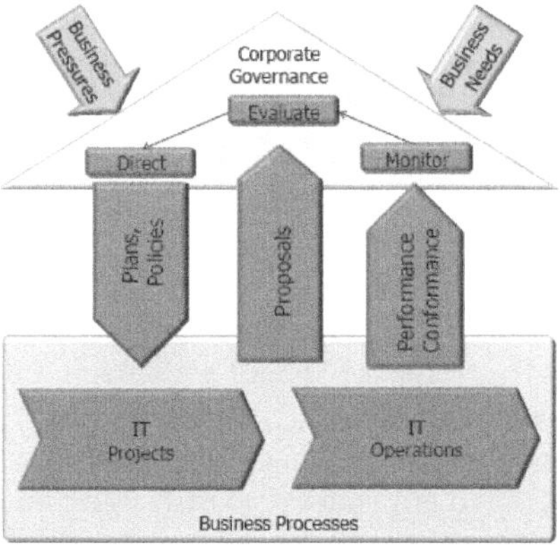

Fig. 1. Model for corporate governance of IT ISO/IEC 38500 as appears in [14]

The core of our model is implemented taking into account this virtuous cycle and also to provide enough information to align plans with IT projects and to keep an eye on performances metrics coming from IT operations and projects. But this core is not enough and must be extended as we explain in next sections.

3 IT Governance Decisions

In addition to the IT governance framework of ISO/IEC 38500, according to [9], the five types of decisions to be taken by the layer corresponding to the governance of IT are as follows:

- IT principles: that is to clarify the role of IT in the business.
- IT architecture: that tries to define the requirements of integration and standardization.
- IT Infrastructure: determining shared and allowed services.

- Need for business applications: specifying the needs of business units either to acquire them or to develop them internally.
- Investment and prioritization of IT: to select which initiatives are funded and how much is spent on them (applications portfolio).

In our communication model, the five decision types are explicitly shown but in different layers, because the infrastructure and the architecture are usually close related to IT management execution while the principles, the applications portfolio and the priorisation of investments are normally related to IT Governance planning. These decision types are not explicitly shown in ISO/IEC 38500 model.

4 IT Performance and Conformance Metrics

The board must use IT operations to obtain value for the institution. In order to ensure this value, the CIO has to keep an eye on [12]:

- IT managers and staff have implemented practices and processes required to maximize the value of IT to the business.
- IT investments are made based upon a balance between risks and benefits and those budgets are adequate.
- IT projects arrive on time and within budget.
- IT staff improves reputation, product leadership and the appearance of profitability
- IT activities provide customer (or user) confidence and gain competitive time periods to bring a product or service to market.

Additionally, IT managers and the rest of the IT staff also must measure performance by defining and inspecting along with the execution measurements to verify that targets are compliance, so as to remove contingencies. CIOs also have to know some metrics about risk management in order to evaluate proposals. IT staff should ensure that management has put processes, technology and trust in places right to security of the information. Thus, transactions are reliable services are usable and can appropriately resist attacks and recover from fault.

CIO should monitor the use of IT resources needed to achieve the objectives and ensure that there is a proper balance in IT investments to provide growth to the organization. As shown in Figure 1, CIO need to monitor the performance of the IT staff; through the proper metrics and IT staff should provide a simple and efficient way to understand these metrics. Thus, these metrics should help the CIO to decide whether the infrastructure and architecture that has implemented the IT staff responds to business initiatives and to ensure the operation in terms of value, not in technical terms (which is in turn the responsibility of the IT operation and the IT management layers).

4.1 IT Management and IT Operation Goals

The mission of IT staff is to provide an information processing capability that benefits the company business. In order to fulfill this mission, IT management and IT

Operation must provide the following services, while managing costs and prioritizing requests to optimize value:

- Operate and support the infrastructure required to process, store, secure, and communicate information.
- Operate and support the business applications that process information.
- Provide technology consulting, training, and planning services.
- Employ, train, and deploy staff required to provide these services.
- Plan, develop/purchase/acquire, test, and implement new infrastructure to fix problems or provide enhanced information processing capabilities to the business.

We can find a complete description of these tasks in the standard ISO/IEC 20000 and other de facto standards. This paper is not to go further into these activities as the proposed model is a general framework which identifies as link them to specific tasks of IT Governance.

In any case, [11] is an example of the data elements for measuring IT performance by related categories. Some of the metrics represent averages while others are reported in the form of a graph. By reporting these metrics on a regular basis (monthly is the minimum recommended reporting period), trends can be observed across the reporting periods. In many cases the trends are more important than the actual value. IT Management has to capture most of these indicator categories:

- Availability of existing Processing Capabilities
- Utilization of Available Staff Resources Efficiently
- Timely Response to Business Requests for New Features or Services
- Successful implementation of system and service changes
- Management of the cost of delivering IT services and optimization of their investment

5 Engaging IT Governance and IT Management together

In figure 1, the IT governance is situated on top of the management of IT by the realization of three main tasks: managing the plans and policies are established for IT, evaluating the proposals that are coming from business processes on the current and future use of IT, and finally monitoring the operations implemented to make that planning to be real (by evaluating this monitorisation).

However, the tasks of IT management, which are below the tasks of IT governance, are consisting mainly of planning how to implement these proposals for current and future use of IT, build and run IT projects that implement those operations. Obviously, these tasks are modeled following ISO/IEC 38500. As can be seen, there is a strong relationship between IT Governance and IT Management through projects and operations. This strong relationship sometimes confuses the roles of CIO and CTO in many organizations that have not yet matured understanding of the ISO/IEC 38500 model. Thus, in figure 1, it can be seen that the system for governance of IT oversees, controls and receives information from a suite of interconnected management systems uniquely configured to serve the needs of the organization. This confusion is our main motivation for the present work.

On the other hand, Thorp identifies seven key aspects of management responsibility [15]:

- Strategic planning: setting direction for effective, efficient and acceptable use of IT.
- Enterprise architecture: planning and management of the overall design and interaction of components within the business system, including people, process, structure and technology – the latter including infrastructure, software systems and data structures.
- Portfolio management: selection of the most appropriate investment options;
- Program management: overall supervision of the works required to deliver agreed investments.
- Project management: specific planning and implementation of a single approved initiative.
- IT asset management: ensuring that software systems and infrastructure remain efficient, effective and acceptable, and that they are appropriately retired and/or replaced when they no longer meet these criteria.
- Operational service delivery: providing sustained effective efficient and acceptable delivery of the IT operational capability required by the organization, this discipline is now widely referred to as IT Service Management and it is fully developed in ISO /IEC 20000 [2, 3] and ITIL [8].
- Information security: understanding and treatment of risk to the availability, integrity, privacy and authenticity of information that the organization creates and collects during the course of business. This issue is general covered extensively in the ISO /IEC 27000 series.

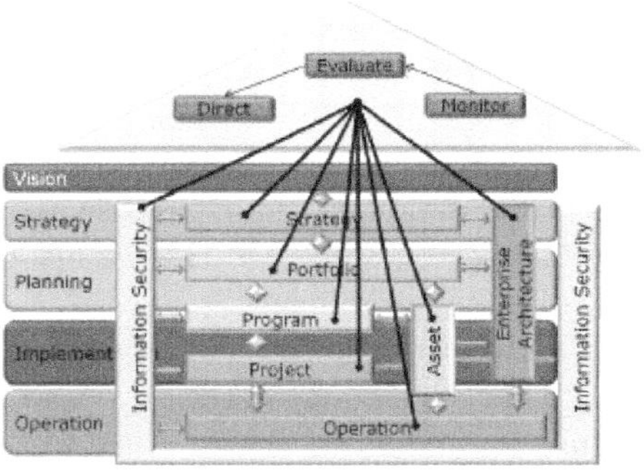

Fig. 2. Governance – Management engagement as appears in [14]

Toomey [14] proposes a more generalised view of how governance and management are integrated in an overall system. Thus, we can now visualise an evolved version of the ISO/IEC 38500 model for governance, where the three fundamental steps in the management cycle are now replaced by the eight key disciplines, mapped over the four primary management systems. In this way, we can now begin to develop a clearer understanding of how governance and management roles and tasks are related, and how they are both distinct and inter-dependent.

Although this model of engagement seems appropriate to combine, in a simple manner, the standard ISO / IEC 38500 with the Thorp's model, it can lead to the same ambiguities of confusion between the three levels of Governance, Management and Operation (particularly in first two) that boards usually experience. In addition, five types of Governance decisions proposed by Weill and Ross [9] are partially diluted in figure 2 (principles and investments are crucial and not shown).

6 New Engagement Model for the Communication of IT Value Coming from IT Governance and IT Management

In order to simplify the communication for IT Governance issues, we propose a new layered model for communicating the engagement for IT Governance and IT Management. This model not only includes in its core the ISO/IEC 38500 (as the Toomey's one), and the Thorp's essential key aspects for Management responsibility, but also it considers how communicate to the board (and the rest of the organization) that the Value of Alignment (VoA) could be extracted from even from the day-to-day Operation.

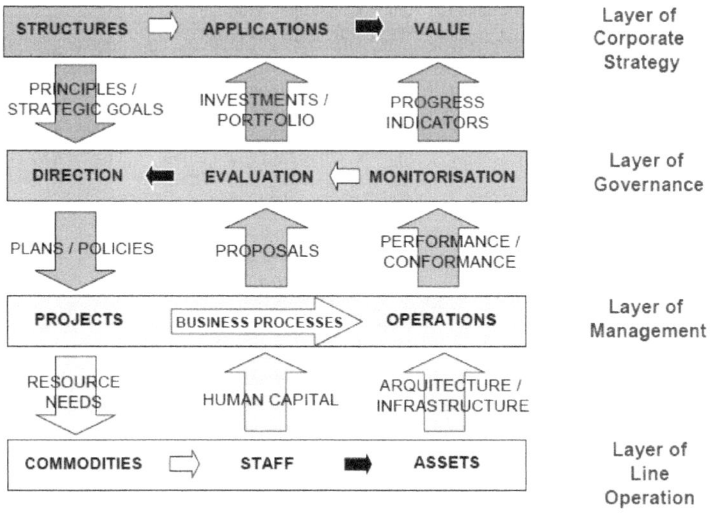

Fig. 3. Extended ISO/IEC 38500 model for the communication of IT value

Our layered model may be implemented through different instruments of alignment in order to monitoring and follow up decisions about IT. The model served to develop AlineaTIC [1]. This tool, we created for helping CIOs to keep IT aligned, and to hold the Value of Alignment (VoA) in their respective organizations. We experienced that our model better communicates IT Governance issues and may substitute the one shown in figure 2, complementing also the ISO/IEC 38500 information.

Figure 3 shows our model for improving communication of the value of IT at enterprises by enlarging the ISO/IEC 38500 picture. As you can observe, our model consists of four layers of IT, from top to bottom:

- The layer of IT Line Operation, including personnel, assets and utilities (buildings, computers, networks, air conditioning, etc.).
- The layer of IT Management, which corresponds to the transformation of IT projects, which are made to improve business processes, to daily operations, these operations include maintenance.
- The layer of IT Governance, which corresponds to the direction of IT Management based on the evaluation of project proposals, and monitoring the operations. The IT Management and IT Governance layers are identical to the standards ISO/IEC 38500 and AS8015 [7].
- The layer of Corporate Strategy, which aims to get value from IT in terms of applications that are requested from governing structures in order to produce value of IT, which is the result of the Value of Alignment (VoA) that is the model motivation.

As can be seen, each layer contains a transformation, so we have:

- Commodities (buildings, computers, networks, air conditioning, etc.) are transformed in IT assets through IT staff knowledge and training in the Line Operation layer.
- IT Projects are transformed into IT Operations contributing to IT Services, when business processes are implemented at the layer of IT Management. This transformation is exactly shown as in ISO/IEC 38500.
- Operation trends are monitorised in order to be evaluated transforming the observation into new directions at IT Governance layer. This is also identical to the ISO/IEC 38500.
- Governance (not only IT) structures at enterprise are seeking IT value by transformation of IT applications and solutions.

In order to interconnect the four layers different instruments are used (left to right in figure 3):

- The board and other governance structures at the enterprise establish business principles and high-level strategic objectives and the CIO must translate them into IT principles and IT strategic goals.
- These goals are further developed into tactic goals in detailed plans and IT policies.
- The projects should be originated from this direction plans and should need additional resources.
- The IT staff training and formation understand de business processes and catch the requirements of business to fill out standard project forms.
- These standard forms are evaluated and some of them will constitute the project portfolio and the investments will be rolled out to be applications that the board visualises.
- At the same time, IT infrastructure and IT architecture hold the operations.

- These operations are monitorized providing IT Management indicators and metrics providing progress and advance, giving alignment and value (see section 4.1).

As you may realize, in our model there are several virtual cycles to promote in the IT Governance framework that covers the main decisions depicted in [9] (see figure 3 and follow the cycles):

- The different structures (board, committees, commissions, interest groups, etc.) express the strategic business principles or objectives that the CIO should transform into principles and strategic objectives. These principles must be transformed into plans and IT policies. The projects to be implemented by IT Management must be aligned with those plans and policies, which could potentially require a series of new IT assets.
- The IT architecture that attempts to define the requirements for programs and data integration, and IT infrastructure that determines shared services, allow developing the projects and transforming them into daily operations that keep business processes.
- Business processes may require further improvement through proposals that should be evaluated by the IT Governance and redirect policies and plans, if necessary. At the same time, the operational performance and conformance should be measured and the metrics must be monitored so that they help to make decisions about new business proposals or even lead to other proposals.
- New proposals often require investments, which can only be explained if they are aligned with the principles, plans and needs, and consistent with the assets and management levels. Otherwise, it is almost impossible for the rest of the enterprise thinking about the expensiveness of IT and they are not aligned with the business, or even worst they do not provide value.
- The investments allow new applications required in terms of business and that are delivering value. The CIO must monitor the progress of that value, which is in line with plans and policies previously directed.
- The two virtual cycles already identified in the ISO/IEC 38500 (see figure 1) remain: the projects must follow the plans and IT governance policies and their transformation through business processes arises new proposals. Such proposals should be assessed in accordance with the plans. On the right, operations arising from the exploitation of the projects are monitored to track their performance and conformance, to be assessed for new projects (if they are in accordance with the plans and policies).
- At line operation layer, the resource needs of new staff may change the architecture or the information infrastructure that permit new projects and operations for business processes.
- At the corporate strategy layer, the investment needed to deploy applications that produce value may depend on monitoring their progress. After the evaluation of this progress, CxOs may determine a change in such investments.

However, the IT staff and the CIO are not the only ones that suffer misunderstanding of IT Governance and IT Management relationship. Because IT is as critical to business success as other assets, the entire enterprise suffers when the executives do not see the value of IT. The problem is how communicate value from IT. Our model helps CIOs to communicate the IT value, not only with the rest of the company but also with IT staff which is usually reluctant to be evaluated and monitored without seeing why they should be governed.

Moreover, the basic types of decisions [9]: principles, architecture, infrastructure, application needs and investments can not be isolated from each other. If the IT Governance framework are well designed, decisions reinforce one to another ensuring that business goals. Each of the type of decisions requires individual attention but nothing can be done in isolation. The same may be applied for IT Governance mechanisms (structures, communication and alignment) are not operating in isolation because their impact depends on the interactions between them.

Additionally, IT Management enables IT Governance to track a large number of metrics performed with tactical aims of the organization. We try to put together all this concepts in a model to improve communication between IT Governance and IT Management issues, and also between IT and the rest of the enterprise. Our communication model helps to understand the IT turnaround:

- Communicating how to improve IT management processes
- Communicating how to improve governance as a means to manage application demands
- Communicating how IT value is obtained

Our model does not guarantee the successful alignment or IT value at the enterprise, it just helps to communicate how the different layers are related and engaged. However, we also consider the different factors that may influence their successful application (or the opposite) in the same model (boxes with arrows surrounding our model in figure 4).

In [14], Toomey considers that in the context of organizational change (which is main goal of any kind of governance), it will also require business specialists who will design processes, controls, structures, job roles, environments; who will prepare and prove work instructions; who will design, build and deliver training for people at all levels of the organization affected by the change; and who will oversee the new capability in operation to ensure that it is operating as intended.

Thus, there are some resources that may be required to enable effective organizational change. We believe that these resources are common factors of success/failure of our model, e.g. the organization design clearly affects the number and the quality of the governance structures at the enterprise.

Another example crucial for the success on direction at the layer of IT Governance is the intensity of the business pressure to force the alignment of strategy and plans. The services' delivery capacity of IT Management should be essential for integrating new operations with the required SLA. We can not extend the paper more with the other factors due to the space limits of the article, but it is clear that any of the four levels are affected by them.

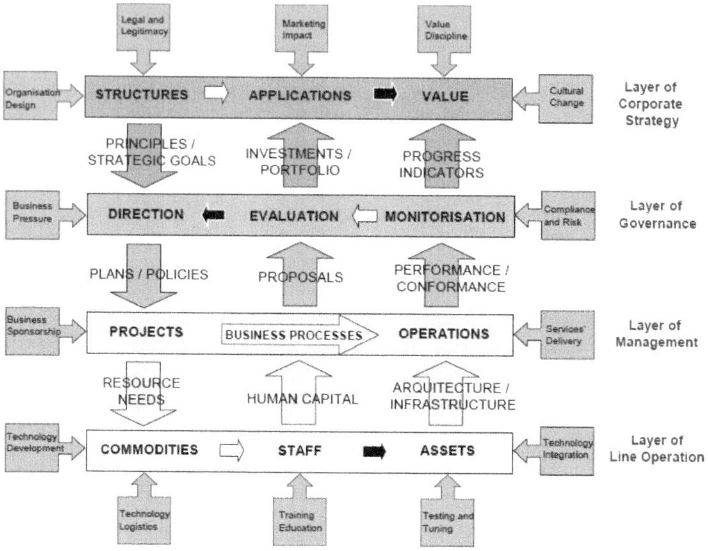

Fig. 4. Factors of success/failure of implementation of the model for the communication of IT value engaging Management and Governance together

7 Experimentation and Implementation

In order to validate our model we performed two different tasks in parallel:

- On one hand, our research group have developed a software tool (now in beta test), namely AlineaTIC [1, 13]. AlineaTIC provides a complete framework on which store the five key types of decisions for IT Governance as appears in [9], and the IT Management and IT Operation metrics as appears in [11]. In short, AlineaTIC is a dashboard for annotating principles, objectives and project portfolio and their features e.g. deadline, budget, description. Additionally, governance structures and their corresponding meeting minutes may also being stored in AlineaTIC database. So that, CIOs should browse all the IT Governance components in the same framework on which IT managers may store the metrics and indicators of services and operations.
- On the other hand, because the author of this work also performs the tasks of IT Governance at the University of the Balearic Islands as Vice President of Information Technologies, we are starting to experiment and validate our engagement model to communicate IT value at our institution. This good practice is necessary as long as the conference of Spanish Rectors should implement ISO/IEC 38500 in the coming years at Spanish universities [16]. In order to implement the model shown in figure 5, we are developing several instruments of communication, e.g. an IT principles list, the publication of strategic and tactical goals, the investment portfolio and the project portfolio, the set of performance/conformance indicators and the

business value indicators, among others. We believe that the communication of these instruments together with the model itself and the utilization of AlineaTIC will improve the communication of the IT value at UIB.

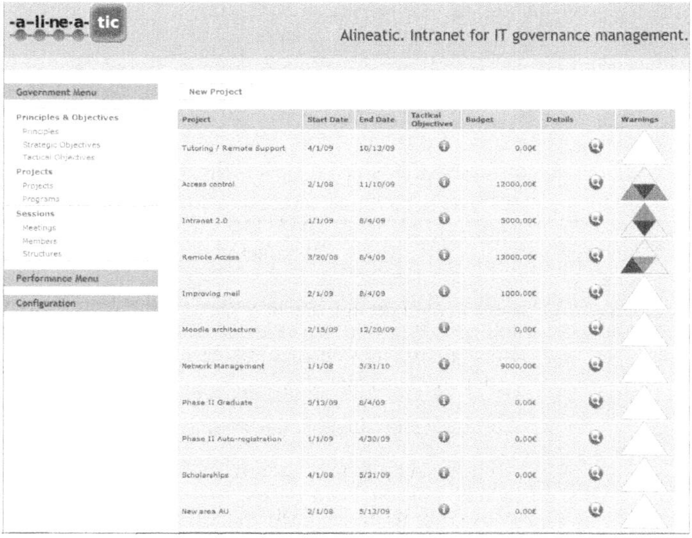

Fig. 5. AlineaTIC screenshot showing project warnings and tactical objectives alignment

8 Conclusions and Open Problems

One of the main problems faced by the CIO is the difficulty of communicating effectively to the rest of the company how IT Governance and IT Management contributes to the value of IT. Furthermore, the difficulty of distinguishing the roles of IT Governance and other IT Management motivated the publication of ISO/IEC 38500, based on the AS8015 standard. However, although the ISO/IEC 38500 model aligns projects, operations and plans, makes no explicit reference to other decisions that affect the alignment of business and IT, such as, for example, the principles, architecture, infrastructure and investment. Our model takes includes the standard and these decisions, together. Moreover, the model explicitly shows how the value of IT is related with the business alignment which the rest of the enterprise is expecting from CIO activity.

This conceptual model of communication of IT value coming from the engagement of IT Governance and IT Management helps the CIO to explain how the implementation of projects is really following the strategy developed by the board.

In short, IT assets need to be aligned with board objectives to produce IT value, so that they support appropriately the enterprise and to provide their IT services on time, with the right functionality and expected benefits, to enable the organization to grow with the introduction in new markets, increasing customer retention and driving strategies to be competitive. Thus, IT staff is assigned to explicit responsibilities in the organization for each assessment and establish value measures between business and IT. For example, designing a balanced scorecard of IT to include these measures, developed under the supervision of the board and the easy approval the three layers of the IT Governance system. Our model helps to CIOs to align goals and projects and also to manage performance and conformance indicators of operations coming from the lower layers.

The CIOs should identify which are the IT metrics they need and how they can be related with the scorecard of the enterprise. They are also responsible for verifying that the risks associated with IT projects are controlled by IT staff and that their budgets are realistic. Specifically, CIOs are responsible for integrating IT budgets in the corporate financial plan. The CIO must manage budgets and IT investment and provide a performance monitoring system in the remaining executives and business managers. The evaluation of the IT progress at the organization should include indicators linking direct with business objectives and therefore the organization's overall. The model presented in this paper serves to communicate the most important performance and conformance values coming from IT administration and IT operations in order to keep IT production (maintenance and services) continuously improving.

Theoretically, the IT Governance, like most other managerial issues, is strongly associated to executive management in a cooperative manner. However, due to the extreme specialization of IT, CIOs must rely heavily on lower layers of the organization (IT Operations and IT Management) to obtain the necessary information for making assessments and decisions. To achieve effective governance of IT, the lower layers need to apply the same principles as the CIO for setting goals, giving and receiving instructions and to provide and evaluate performance measures. In summary, the practices with the Governance of IT need to be implemented at all levels of the company. Our proposed model also helps to communicate not only the alignment of board objectives with IT projects but also the performance and conformance of IT operations which should be managed by IT staff.

Another interesting feature in our engagement model is that is an extension of the ISO/IEC 38500, not only by adding two more layers but also because of the five basic decisions that [9] identifies (principles, architecture, infrastructure, applications and investments) are also included in the model.

Finally, we are experiencing the value of the model in our institution and we have developed a tool not only for our enterprise but also a commercial product that develops the model presented here. So that, we hope in the short term that we shall have improved communication between layers of the IT Governance and will make proper surveys and interviews into the board and intermediate levels of the our institution to know whether the implementation of the model is successful. At the same time, we are going to comercialise AlineaTIC as a helpful tool for CIOs in any kind of organization that needs to show explicitly the value of IT, which are practically all enterprises. AlineaTIC was born based on the model here presented.

Acknowledgment. This work was partially funded by Spanish Ministry of Science and Innovation through the national project TIN2007-60440.

References

1. Vicens, J., Pérez, C., Jiménez, J., Juiz, C.: AlineaTIC: A Tiny Tool for IT Governance Alignment at Universities. In: de Compostela, S. (ed.) Proceedings of EUNIS 2009, vol. 148, pp. 60–61 (2009) ISBN 978-84-9887-138-8
2. ISO/IEC 20000-1, Information technology - Service management Part 1: Specification (2005), http://www.iso.org/iso/catalogue_detail?csnumber=41332
3. ISO/IEC 20000-2, Information technology - Service management - Part 2: Code of practice (2005), http://www.iso.org/iso/iso_catalogue/catalogue_tc/catalogue_detail.htm?csnumber=41333
4. ISO/IEC 38500, IT Governance Standard (2008), http://www.38500.org
5. Board Briefing on IT Governance, 2nd Edition. IT Governance Institute (2009), http://www.itgi.org/Template_ITGIc9a4.html?Section=About_IT_Governance1&Template=/ContentManagement/ContentDisplay.cfm&ContentID=6658
6. COBIT 4.1. IT Governance Institute (2008), http://www.itgovernance.co.uk/products/897
7. AS 8015-2005 Corporate governance of information and communication technology. Standards Australia (2005)
8. Taylor, S., Lloyd, V., Rudd, C.: ITIL Service Strategy, 3rd version. The Stationery Office Books, United Kingdom (2007)
9. Weill, P., Ross, J.W.: IT Governance: How Top Performers Manage IT Decision Rights for Superior Results. Harvard Business School Press, Boston (2004)
10. Hunter, R., Westerman, G.: The Real Business of IT: How CIOs Create and Communicate Value. Harvard Business School Press, Boston (2009)
11. Spanos, N.: 100 IT Performance Metrics. Computer Aid Inc. (2009)
12. Fernández, A.: Análisis, Planificación y Gobierno de las Tecnologías de la Información en las Universidades. PhD. Dissertation, Universidad de Almería (2009)
13. Vicens, J., Pérez, C., Jiménez, J., Juiz, C.: Una herramienta simple para la implementación del alineamiento en el gobierno de las tecnologías de la información y las comunicaciones (TIC). In: Proceedings of ITSMF 2009, Spain (2009) ISBN 978-84-692-9919-7
14. Toomey, M.: Waltzing with the Elephant: A comprehensive guide to directing and controlling information technology, Infonomics Pty Ltd. (2009)
15. Thorp, J.: Rethinking IT Governance - Beyond Alignment to Integration: The Thorp Network (2005)
16. Fernández, A., Llorens, F. (eds.): Gobierno de las TI para las Universidades. Conferencia de Rectores de las Universidades Españolas (2011) ISBN: 978-84-935509-8-1
17. Smith, G.S.: Straight to the top, becoming a world-class CIO. John Wiley & Sons, Chichester (2006)
18. Wyatt-Haynes, R.: ALIGNIT. In: Business Impact Through IT. John Wiley & Sons, Chichester (2007)
19. Covey, S.R.: The 7 habits of Highly Efective People. Simon & Schuster, New York (1989)

P2P Queries Routing Using Distributed Knowledge

Anis Ismail[1,2], Aziz Barbar[2], and Ziad Ismail[3]

[1] Lebanese University,
University Institute of Technology
Saida – Lebanon
anismaiil@ul.edu.lb
[2] American University of Science & Technology
Alfred Naccash Avenue - Ashrafieh
Beirut, Lebanon
aai003@students.aust.edu.lb,
abarbar@aust.edu.lb
[3] TELECOM ParisTech
Paris, France
ismail.ziad@enst.fr

Abstract. The growing interest in Peer-to-Peer systems (such as Gnutella) has inspired numerous research activities. The problem in a schema-based Peer-to-Peer (P2P) system is how to locate Peers relevant to a given query. Different methods proposed routing strategies of queries taking into account the P2P network at hand. In this paper, we propose an architecture, based on (Super-) Peers, and we focus on query routing. Our approach considers that (Super-) Peers having similar interests are grouped together for an efficient query routing method. In such groups, called Super-Super-Peers (SSP), Super-Peers submit queries that are often processed by members of this group. A SSP is a specific Super-Peer that contains knowledge about: 1. its Super-Peers and 2. The other SSP. Knowledge is extracted by using data mining techniques (e.g. decision tree algorithms) starting from queries of Peers that transit on the network. The advantage of this distributed knowledge is that, it avoids making semantic mapping, between heterogeneous data sources owned by (Super-)Peers, each time the system decides to route query to other (Super-)Peers. The set of SSP improves the robustness in queries routing mechanism and scalability in P2P Network. Compared with a baseline approach, our proposed architecture shows that data mining technique increase performance with respect to response time and precision.

Keywords: P2P, Schema, Query Routing, Data Mining.

1 Introduction

The Peer-to-Peer computing paradigm is viewed as a novel approach for people to share resources such as files and computing cycles, or to support collaborative tasks. The popularity of Peer-to-Peer systems in the last couple of years illustrates how the

E. Ariwa and E. El-Qawasmeh (Eds.): DEIS 2011, CCIS 194, pp. 144–157, 2011.

internet is gradually shifting toward a distributed system that supports more than unique client-server application. Peer-to-Peer (P2P) systems are distributed systems in which nodes of equal roles and capabilities exchange information and services directly with each other. In recent years, P2P has emerged as a popular way to share huge volumes of data. The key to the usability of a data-sharing P2P system, and one of the most challenging design aspects, is efficient techniques for search, route queries and retrieval of data. The major problem in such networks is query routing, i.e. deciding to which other (Super-) Peers the query has to be sent for high efficiency and effectiveness. The traditional P2P systems offer support for richer queries, it provides the option to search by identifier, such as a keyword search with regular expressions. Search techniques for these systems must therefore operate under a different set of constraints than techniques developed for persistent storage utilities.

However, such systems that broadcast all queries to all Peers suffer from limited efficiency and scalability. In hybrid P2P systems [1][2], composed of (Super-)Peers, when a Peer submits a query, this Peer becomes the source of this query. Then the query is transmitted to its Super-Peer (SP). The routing policy in use determines the relevant neighbors (SP) quickly, based on semantic mappings between schemas of (Super-)Peers, and to which neighbors, the query is sent. When a SP receives a query, it will process the query over its local collection of data sources of different Peers. If any results are found, the SP will send a single response message back to the query source. An important factor to the user is the time he must wait for the results to arrive. This is due mainly to the mediation process which remains difficult to realize in such a context when the number of (Super-)Peers increases. Response times tend to be slow in hybrid P2P networks, since the query travel through several SP in the network and whenever the SP is forced to look for connections (i.e. mappings) in order to route the query. Satisfaction time is simply the time that has elapsed between the submission of the query by the user, and the time he receives the overall results.

Data mining has recently become very popular due to the emergence of vast quantities of data. In this paper, A practical issue about data mining in P2P network is discussed. The motivations behind P2P data mining include the optimal usage of available computational resources, privacy, and dependability in order to eliminate critical points of service.

In this paper, we present the effect of data mining in P2P query routing. Our proposed method focuses on how the query is routed to relevant Peers with minimum query processing at SP level in order to improve answering time of the queries by using data mining technique. The important advantage of our approach is scalability.

Our approach consists of grouping together (Super-)Peers that have similar themes for an efficient query routing. Each obtained group, called Super-Super-Peers (SSP), contains domains, composed of Super-Peers (the responsible of domains) and their corresponding Peers (the members), that submitted queries that are often processed by members of this group. Each SSP operates with an index, obtained by applying decision tree algorithms, that keeps track of locations of contents concerning a query: when a SSP receives a query from a Super-Peer (in its group), it consults directly its index (without making any mappings) in order to determine 1. In its group all Super-Peers (or domains) that are able to answer this query and 2. In other groups (i.e. other SSP), all Super-Peers which are relevant to this query.

The following section presents work related to our topic. Section 3 recalls briefly principal concepts of P2P networks and shows the context of our work. Section 4, introduces the Super-Super-Peer (SSP) network with decision tree. Section 5 presents our simulator to evaluate our approach. Section 6 presents Experiments and Evaluations. In Section 7, we present the conclusions.

2 Related Work

P2P networks are quickly emerging as large-scale systems for information sharing. Through networks such as Kazaa, e-Mule, BitTorrents, consumers can readily share vast amounts of information. While initial consumer interest in P2P networks was focused on the value of the data, more recent research such as P2P web community formation argues that the consumers will greatly benefit from the knowledge locked in the data [3][4].

Query routing in a Peer-to-Peer network is the process of routing a query to a number of relevant Peers and not broadcasted to the whole network. The problem of query routing is the discovery of relevant Peers to a given query after we denoted which Peers are considered as relevant. Surely in Peer-to-Peer systems, the network topology and the category of P2P determine to a large extent the applied routing strategy. Hence, before describing a routing algorithm, we have to look at the characteristics of the Peer-to-Peer network that it will be applied to. An efficient query routing aims to limit network bandwidth consumption by reducing messages across the network and reducing total query processing cost by minimizing the number of Peers that contributes to the query's results. Finally, routing in P2P networks is crucial for the scalability of the network. In the next subsections we describe the dominant approaches at query routing and their applied Peer-to- Peer environment.

Raahemi, Hayajneh and Rabinovitch [5] present a new approach using data-mining technique, and in particular, decision tree, to classify Peer-to-Peer (P2P) traffic in IP networks by capturing Internet traffic. They built several models using a combination of various attribute sets for different ratios of P2P to non-P2P traffic in the training data.

Bhaduri, Wolff, Giannella and Kargupta [6] propose a P2P decision tree induction algorithm, in which every Peer learns and maintains the correct decision tree compared to a centralized scenario. This algorithm is completely decentralized, asynchronous, and adapts smoothly to changes in the data and the network. [6] It offers a scalable and robust distributed algorithm for decision tree induction in large Peer-to-Peer (P2P) environments. Computing a decision tree in such large distributed systems using standard centralized algorithms can be very communication-expensive and impractical due to synchronization requirements.

An important problem in data mining over multiple data sources includes applications in different areas, such as data streams, data-warehouses, and bioinformatics. However, the computation and communication complexity of such solutions render them impractical when a large number of data sources are involved. F. Emekci, O.D. Sahin, D. Agrawal, and A. El Abbadi [7] consider a scenario where multiple data sources are willing to run data mining algorithms over the union of their data, as long as each data source is guaranteed that its information that does not pertain to another data source will not be revealed. In particular, they focus on the classification problem, and present an efficient algorithm (ID3 algorithm) to build a decision tree over an arbitrary number of distributed sources in a privacy preserving manner.

Medview [8] was designed earlier to support the learning process in oral medicine and oral pathology. The purpose of Medview was to provide a computerized teaching aid in oral medicine and oral pathology. MEduWeb is a web-based educational tool that allows students to search in the database and generate exercises with pictures of real patients [8]. It uses the MedView database containing several thousand patient examinations where Khan, Anwer, Torgersson and Falkman use Data mining technique (Decision trees) on this data base [8].

3 Semantic Network – Baseline

3.1 Network Configuration

A new Peer P_j advertises its expertise by sending, to its Super-Peer, a domain advertisement $DA_j = (PID;\ E^j_{XP},\ T_j\ ;\ \varepsilon_{acc}\ ;\ TTL)$ containing the Peer ID denoted PID, the suggested expertise E^j_{XP}, the topic area of interest Tj , the minimum semantic similarity value (ε_{acc}) required to establish semantic mapping between the suggested expertise E^j_{XP} and the theme of its Super-Peer. When receiving an expertise E^j_{XP}, a Super-Peer SP_a invokes the semantic matching process to find mappings between its suggested schema and the received expertise.

3.2 Baseline Approach

A Peer submits its query on its local data schema. This query is sent to its Super-Peer; the responsible for the domain (see Figure 1). The Super-Peer in its turn suggests, based on the index obtained by the process of mediation (first level), the Peers of its domain or the other Super-Peers that are able to treat this query. Each submitted query received by a Super-Peer is processed by searching connections (second level of mappings) between the subject of this query and expertise of Peers (of the same domain) or the description of themes of other Super-Peers. In its turn, a Super-Peer from the nearby domain, having received this query, researches among Peers (in its domain) that are able to answer this query. The major problem of this approach is the mediation at the two levels cited above: if we take thousands of Peers or Super-Peers, this approach cannot be scaled due to the mappings at both levels. The following sections describe our approach in order to avoid Super-Peer, when it's too busy to treat all users' queries, to process the second level of mapping. This approach improves response time of queries and scalability in P2Ph context by restructuring the network dynamically. In order to achieve this goal, we introduce the concept of Super-Super-Peer (SSP).

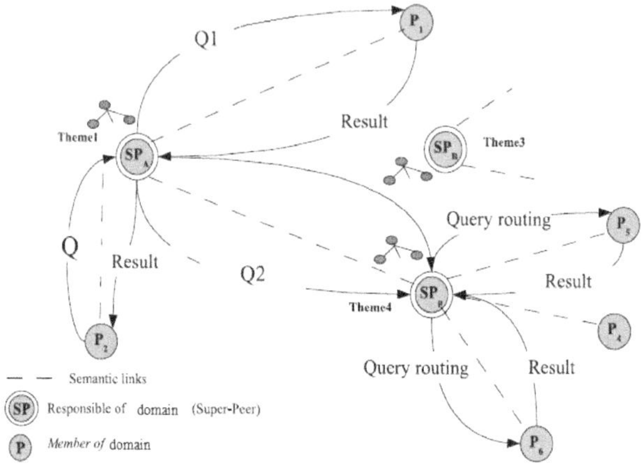

Fig. 1. Network configuration and query routing (Baseline approach)

4 Super-Super-Peer Network

4.1 Topology

A Super-Super-Peer (SSP) network is a semantic of Overlay Network (SON) with adding a new layer (SSP) representing our work. The SSP number j is defined as follows:

$$\mathrm{SSP}^{j} = \cup_{l=1}^{|M|}(SI_e^l C) \qquad |M| \leq |T| \tag{1}$$

Where M is the number of Super-Peer in SSP^j and $|M| \leq |T|$ (total number of Super-Peers). $SI_e^l C$ is the Semantic Inter- domain of the Super-Peer number l.

A Super-Super-Peer is represented physically with a specific Peer. This Peer, representing the Super-Super-Peer number j, is noted as follows:

$$\mathrm{SSP}^{j} = (\mathrm{PS} \cup \mathrm{SP}_{\mathrm{TJ,DJ}}, \mathrm{EXP}(\mathrm{P_S}), \mathrm{K}^{j}, \mathrm{RSC}^{J}, \mathrm{RSI}^{J}, \ \mathrm{IND}^{j}) \tag{2}$$

where $P_S \subseteq P$ is a subset of Peers having very close center of interests denoted T J = {T1,..., Ts}, EXP (P_S) is the set of expertise of Peers interested by at least one of themes in T J, $SP_{TJ, DJ}$ (belong to SP) is the set of Super-Peers responsible of domains which have very close domain interests, DJ = {D1, ..., Ds} represents the description of themes in T J (D_J describes T_J). $K^j \subseteq K$ is the set of overlay links between each Super-Peer $SP_{Tj, Dj} \in SP_{TJ,DJ}$ and 1. The Peers connected to it (within its domain); 2. The other Super-Peers; 3. The Super-Super-Peer SSP^j itself. RSC^J is the set of semantic Intra-Domain of the Super-Peers $\in SP_{TJ, DJ}$. RSI^J is the set of semantic Inter-Domain for each Super-Peer in $SP_{TJ, DJ}$. IND^j is the index obtained using a decision tree algorithm to identify directly the most relevant (Super-) Peers, without going through mappings, to provide good results when a query is submitted by a Peer.

Our proposed System (See Figure 2) is an hybrid P2P system based on an organization of Peers around Super-Peers, according to their proposed themes, where Super-Peers are connected to a Super-Super-Peer (SSP), the engine that specifies the Super-Peers having Peers which may have relevant data to answer queries with minimum query tasks. This improves answering time of the queries.

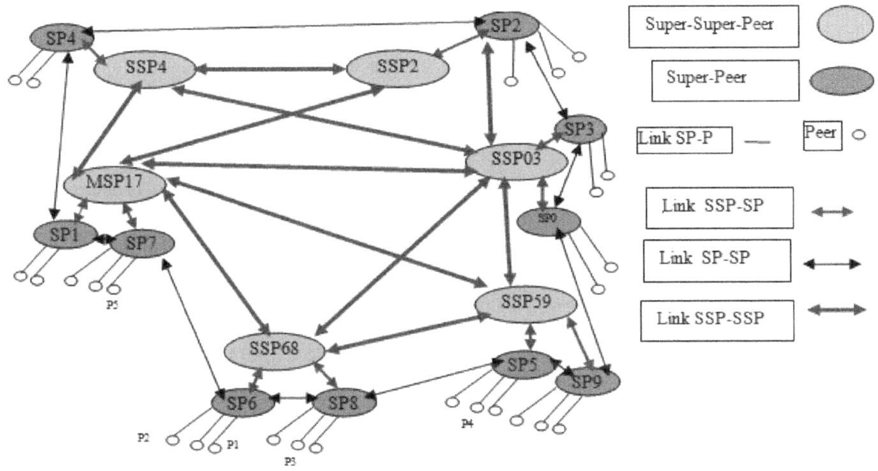

Fig. 2. Baseline with Knowledge

The Super-Peer architecture allows the heterogeneity of Peers by assigning more responsibility to Peers able to assume them. Therefore, certain Peers, called Super-Super-Peers, have an additional computing power and greater bandwidth, resources, performing administrative tasks. They are responsible for routing queries to relevant Super-Peers. That allows, not only to reduce efforts of compilation of queries, but also to prevent the spread of queries in the network.

In each domain, there is a Super-Peer connected to a Super-Super-Peer with an index to identify Super-Peers that are most relevant to provide good results of queries. Otherwise, if the Super-Super-Peer didn't find the relevant Super-Peers form its index for a given query, it returns the query to its parent to work with the baseline to find the answer to this query. We suggest to run our simulations in two configurations, one with the baseline connection between the Super-Peers (Hybrid architecture) (See Figure 2), and the other with non connection with the Super-Peers (Grouping-knowledge architecture (GK)), to see the effect of data mining (decision tree) in the baseline architecture.

The building block (SSP) of the current P2P systems in the architectures (Grouping Knowledge – GK and Hybrid) is the notion of a Super-Peer-group, or a number of nodes (Super-Peer) that participates with each other for a common purpose to minimize the load in the SSP to communicate with other SSP.

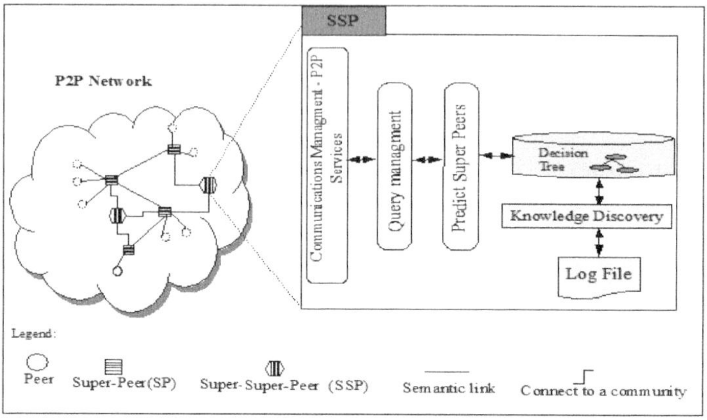

Fig. 3. Architecture of a SSP (all fields)

4.2 SSP Architecture

In this section, we present the logical architecture of a Super-Peer holding knowledge, also known as SSP (Super-Super-Peer). We distinguish the different components related to a SSP: the log file, the discovery of knowledge, a component to predict relevant Super-Peers, and Query management. The second component is the construction of decision trees. Decision trees are often used for classification and prediction. It is a simple and powerful representation of knowledge. The models produced by decision trees are represented as tree structures. We used an implementation of an existing algorithm in the WEKA platform to build the decision tree from the log file (log). The last component can predict, based on the decision tree, all Super-Peers relevant to a query. The query management entity receives a query from a Super-Peer in the domain-group (SSP) and returns the result of the prediction (the relevant Super-Peers) to this Super-Peer.

The general architecture of a Super-Super-Peer is described in Figure 3. Each SSP contains the following components:

- Query Manager: this module differs from that defined by the semantic mediation approach, in the fact that the routing application is based on the decision tree. This allows the prediction of Super-Peers to which candidates will be forwarded the query to be processed.
- Logfile: file containing the queries processed by a Super-Peer domain. It contains the components of the application, and the Super-Peer who responded to the query. When several Super-Peers respond simultaneously to a query, many lines will be added to the file Logfile of the domain, where each line consists of the components of the query, followed by a Super-Peer chosen among those who responded to the query. Hence, we add many lines as Super-Peers who responded to the query.
- Method of construction of knowledge: it is the algorithm for constructing the decision tree by analyzing the queries handled by domain-group members and is stored in the Logfile. We used in our experiments the algorithm J48 WEKA platform to induce the decision tree.

- Predication: this module uses the decision tree to predict, for a given query Q, the Super-Peers that are relevant candidates to process the query Q. Contrary to the general case where the tree used to predict a single value of the class (Super-Peer), we infer here all likely values of each class with its own probability. This list of class values is the set of Super-Peers likely to process the query.

4.3 Decision Tree

Learning by reasoning is one of the approaches used by Dang [9] to solve problems of extracting knowledge from data. This approach appears in various applications, such as in classification, prediction, by rule extraction from data etc. Several methods have been used, for example: neural networks, decision trees, Bayesian networks etc.. We are particularly interested in the decision tree method to extract knowledge from useful data.

Currently, the algorithms to build decision trees (J48, NBTree, ...) allow uniform treatment of almost all types of attributes: numerical, symbolic, fuzzy or probabilistic [9]. Algorithms also adapt to different problems: the presence of missing, incorrect, inaccurate, unreliable date, etc.. The advantages of methods based on decision trees have been well detailed in [10]. These methods are very attractive according to the result that provide. The predictive model of decision tree is easy to analyze, and can be applied to large databases. It also has the advantage of being applicable to digital qualitative data. The characteristics and functioning of this technique are detailed in the work of CART [11], ID3 [12] and its extension C4.5 [13]. The construction of a generic decision tree is presented by Algorithm 1.

Algorithm 1. Construction of decision trees in general

Input: DB (X, Y, Z) is a database,
$Cl = (Cl_1, Cl_2, ..., Cl_p)$ The set of classes

Output: decision tree DT result

Initialize the empty tree DT;
The current node is the root of the empty tree;
Do
  If the current node is terminal **then**
  Assign a class to the current node;
  Otherwise
    Select a test attribute;
    Create subtree of DT associated with the test attribute;
Until All the leaves are labeled;

For each domain-group Ci, we will associate a Logfile Li, Which gathers the queries processed by at least one of its Super-Peers. Then, a knowledge extraction algorithm is triggered to extract the hidden knowledge in the Logfile.

Therefore, the decision tree predicts a Super-Peer from the components of a query. In general, the Super-Peer returned is the one with the highest probability. We use in this paper a probabilistic inference that can exploit the decision tree and return a list of possible Super-Peers each one with its own probability. The launching of the construction of the decision tree is performed periodically according to the number of new queries added to the Logfile Li. Thus, when the number of queries exceeds the threshold θi then the tree Ti is rebuilt, taking into account new queries of the logfile of the domain-group.

4.4 Query Routing Based on Knowledge

Query routing in a P2P network is the process by which a query is directed to a number of Peers, instead of being broadcast to the entire network. The routing algorithm of query in the architecture GK (Algorithm 2) find the relevant Super-Peers that have Peers can answer this query. A Peer Pi formulates query Q and then sends it to his godfather (Super-Peer) SP_Q. Then it applies to its group (SSP), to determine the Super-Peers that are relevant for this query. For this, we use knowledge (decision tree associated with the group G_i) to find the Super-Peer probable predicted to be relevant to process the query Q. Each predicted Super-Peers receive the query and search Peer P_k belonging to it and can answer the query Q:

Algorithm 2. Calculating the answers to Q using the Grouping-knowledge

Entry: Query Q
Output : RQ, AQ

SP_Q: Super-Peer that receives the query Q
G_i: group SP
L_i: Logile G_i
T_i: Tree associated to G_i
SP_List: list of Super-Peers that can process the query Q
SP_List = T_i(Q) / / prediction of Super-Peers likely to treat Q
AQ = {}, {} = RQ
For SP∈ SP_List **Do**
  Send (Q, SP) // if the Super-Peer belongs to several GROUPS.
  // Search the Peer SP that can process Q: Local Search
  If ∃ son(P_k, SP) capable of processing Q //using the concept of capacity of Peers
    AQ = ∪ {SP @ P_k}
    RQ = ∪ Treat (Q, P_k) // P_k processes the query Q and returns the answer RQ
  EndIf
EndFor
Return QA, QR.

The treated query is directed to each Super-Peer that is likely predicted by the decision tree. However, it is possible that all set of predicted Super-Peers is empty. In this case, we can always calculate an answer to this query using the baseline approach.

5 Simulator Architecture

Since the beginning of P2P-applications, there has been a discussion over the usage of P2P-networks, whether they offer legal or illegal content. It is not a secret that most of the shared data in common P2P-networks consists of illegal content. On the other hand, companies see potentials in P2P-technolgie. RedHat, i.e., distributes their Linux-Images over BitTorrent, because it would be too expensive to provide the necessary server-infrastructure including the server hardware and bandwidth capacity. This is only one example. There are many ways to use P2P-technologie for legal content distribution. P2P still grows in popularity. Thus, it is important to improve new P2P technologies and make them more efficient. Unfortunately, it is not possible to test or simulate P2P-networks like a client-server architecture where always a complete overview over the destination network segment is ensured. P2P networks consist of a constant flow of Peers connecting and disconnecting to the network. And this is just one example of the complexity of P2P. Due to these problems it is nearly impossible to assess the performance of a new P2P application or algorithm without simulation. There are several Peer-to-Peer simulators available:

OverlayWeaver [14] is a Peer-to-Peer overlay construction toolkit written in Java which can be used for easy development and testing of new overlay protocols and applications. The toolkit contains a so-called Distributed Environment Emulator which invokes and hosts multiple instances of Java applications on a single computer. This allows the simulation of up to 4,000 nodes. Since simulations have to be run in real-time and there is no statistical output, its use as an overlay network simulator is very limited.

PlanetSim [15] is an object-oriented simulation framework for overlay networks and services written in Java. It has a well-structured and modular architecture and makes use of the Common API [16]. In addition to the overlay protocols Chord [17] and Symphony [18], there are several services like CAST and DHT available on the application layer. PlanetSim offers only limited support to collect statistics and has a very simplified underlying network layer, without consideration of bandwidth and latency costs. This makes it difficult to simulate heterogeneous access networks and terminal mobility. It is possible to visualize the overlay topology at the end of a simulation run, but there is no interactive GUI. A more comprehensive survey of Peer-to-Peer network simulators can be found in [19], where the authors show that most available Peer-to-Peer network simulators have several major drawbacks limiting them in use for research projects.

When implementing a P2P simulation it is important to consider Peer behavior, bandwidth and network topology. Locating the content usually affects the properties of the architecture and therefore the simulation model, as well as different other aspects such as dynamic changes in network size, Peer capabilities, characteristics of the shared files, human behavior etc. For our implementation and simulation, we used the Java programming language, the SimJava package. SimJava [19] is a process based discrete event simulation package for Java. Based on a discrete event simulation kernel, SimJava includes facilities for representing simulation objects as animated icons on screen. A SimJava simulation is a collection of entities each running in its own thread. These entities are connected together by ports and can communicate with each other by sending and receiving event objects.

Our simulator is based on a set of tools such as WEKA that is a data mining platform (See Figure 4).

We have developed the necessary tools to interface the simulator with the various external components without any user intervention. We start by initializing the parameters of the system. This leads to the generation of a SON network with a level of Super-Peer (domain) which is juxtaposed to the Peer's level. A third level domain-group complements the previous two levels the trust (confidence) between the Super-Peers to clarify the domain-group which is characterized by the knowledge using WEKA. Trust between two Super-Peers depends on the number of semantic links connecting them. The trust is useful where a Super-Peer SP leaves the network: Peers attached to SP will then be attached to the Super-Peer with the highest degree of trust with SP. Then the simulation sending query begins and it is the characterizations of domain-groups that are used to route queries to the relevant Super-Peers. The aggregation of all results returned by each Super-Peer that has processed the query, constitute the response to the submitted query. The generation of applications is ensured by Peers. In fact, each Peer P can generate a query by selecting elements of expertise that become components of the query Q. We say that a Peer P is relevant to the query Q, if the expertise of P contains at least a fraction of the components of Q. This is determined using the ability of a Peer P to resolve a query Q. So each Peer generates a number N of queries that are derived from its expertise. After this phase, Peers send their queries to their Super-Peers.

All queries exchanged within the network are stored in a global file LogFile. Thus, for a query Q, the file LogFile contains the following information: the identifier of the Peer (P), which submitted the application, its Super-Peer (SP), the query (Q) itself and the Super-Peer which responded favorably to this query.

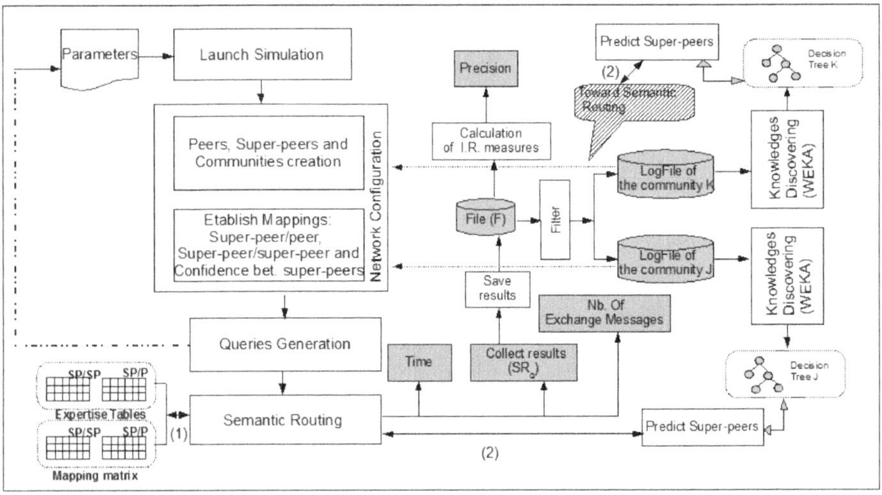

Fig. 4. General Architecture of our simulator

6 Results and Discussion

Evaluating the performance of P2P network is important to understand how useful it can be in the real world. As with all P2P applications, the first question is whether P2P is scalable. Our systems were evaluated with different set of parameters i.e. number of Peers, number Super-Peer etc. Evaluation results were quite encouraging. There are many dimensions in which scalability can be evaluated: one important metric is the time it takes the Answer of a given query. We run simulations on P2P network of different sizes. Each Peer sends Query to its SP that in its turns sends the query to a SSP in order to precise which Super-Peer(s) can answer the given query in both architectures. In the first architecture, we modified the number of Peers (1000, 2000, ..., 8000 Peers) and Super-Peers (15, 20, 25, 30, 35, ..., 50) in both architecture to measure the execution time. Second, The most popular measure for the effectiveness of our systems is the precision.

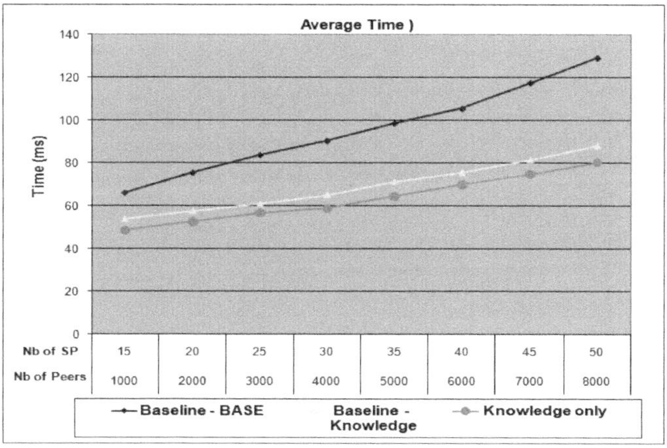

Fig. 5. Execution time

Precision = (relevant answered Peers in our architecture GK))/(relevant answered Peers in architecture GK-baseline).

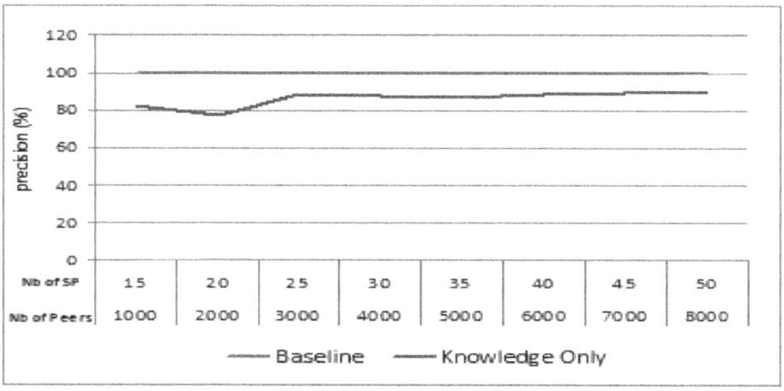

Fig. 6. Precision rate

Figures 5 and 6 show the result of our simulations. It demonstrates the performance of using the Super-Super-Peer with a decision tree for routing Queries to relevant P2P domains (SP). In the first observation, the difference in the execution times between 1000 and 2000 Peers in the architectures baseline with knowledge and knowledge only is small (See Figure 5). The considered time is affected by the increase of the increase of the repository size. Measurements shown in Figure 6, show that the publishing time increased in the architecture where knowledge is less than architecture-baseline, and in architecture with knowledge at 5000 Peers, the response time decreases about 35 % as for the architecture-baseline. This is due to the processing of queries at SP level in the baseline architecture, otherwise in the architecture with knowledge and with the knowledge only, the processing of queries at SSP level using decision trees (Prediction Mechanism), while we can see that the time in the architecture knowledge only is also less then the architecture with knowledge, this depends on the classification of the Peer in the architecture-knowledge and the need of the baseline architecture in the architecture with knowledge, but in the architecture with knowledge only we win some time but we loose some precision concerning the queries responses. Measurements in Figure 6 have shown a decrease in the execution time when the number of Peers and Super-Peers (domains) increased. This means that our architectures are scalable. Measurements in Figure 6 have shown the precision of the architecture with knowledge only compared to the architecture-Base which is our baseline. We could observe that there is almost a linear line in precision between these architectures, which means that our architectures are stable when the number of Peers and Super-Peers increase. This experiment was also designed to measure the accuracy of data (since precision is not affected completely by the network size).

Finally, our Prototype in grouping P2P domains (P2P) raises some interesting performance issues. We performed experiments to demonstrate how the presence of grouping domains affects their performance, and to illustrate how grouping domains can improve the scalability of the overall system.

7 Conclusions

In this paper, we proposed an architecture using distributed classification for P2P networks. We captured the traffic of queries and their answers in the baseline architecture, preprocessed and labeled the data, and built several models using a combination of different attributes in the training-data set. We observed that the accuracy of the classifier increases significantly when we take a bigger size of the network in the baseline architecture. This implies that the accuracy of the classifier increases when we get more information about the domain of Peers. To detect domains of Peers, the decision-tree algorithm (J48) needs to be implemented in an added level called SSP.

One important area for improvement is performance. Some of the options for improving performance were discussed in the evaluation of P2P Network and include:improvements in the Answering time of a given query. In the analysis of the results of the experiments; we demonstrated that the integration of the data mining in the P2P context will improve performance, and therefore, it is scalable.

References

1. Ioannidis, S., Marbach, P.: On the Design of Hybrid Peer-to-Peer Systems. In: SIGMETRICS 2008, Annapolis, Maryland, USA, June 2-6, pp. 157–168 (2008)
2. Annapureddy, S., Guha, S., Gkantsidis, C., Gunawardena, D., Rodriguez, P.R.: Is high-quality VoD feasible using P2P swarming? In: Proceedings of the 16th International Conference on World Wide Web, WWW 2007, pp. 903–912 (2007)
3. Liu, K., Bhaduri, K., Das, K., Nguyen, P., Kargupta, H.: Client-side Web Mining for domain Formation in Peer-to-Peer Environments. SIGKDD Explorations 8(2), 11–20 (2006)
4. Bhaduri, K., Kargupta, H.: Distributed Identification of Top-l Inner Product Elements and its Application in a Peer-to-Peer Network. IEEE Transactions on Knowledge and Data Engineering (TKDE) 20(4), 475–488 (2008)
5. Raahemi, B., Hayajneh, A., Rabinovitch, P.: Peer-to-Peer IP Traffic Classification Using Decision and IP Layer Attributes. International Journal of Business Data Communications and Networking 3(4), 60–74 (2007)
6. Bhaduri, K., Wolff, R., Giannella, C., Kargupta, H.: Distributed Decision Tree Induction in Peer-to-Peer Systems. Statistical Analysis and Data Mining Journal 1, 1864–1932 (2008)
7. Emekci, F., Sahin, O.D., Agrawal, D., Abbadi, A.E.: Privacy preserving decision tree learning over multiple parties. Data & Knowledge Engineering 63(2), 348–361 (2007)
8. Ahad Shahbaz, K., Rao Muhammad, A., Olof, T., Göran, F.: Data Mining in Oral Medicine Using Decision Trees. Proceedings of World Academy of Science, Engineering and Technology 27, 225–230 (2008)
9. Dang, T.H.: Mesures de discrimination et leurs applications en apprentissage inductif, Thesis, Paris 6 (2007)
10. Gay, D.: calcul de motifs sous contraintes pour la classification Supervisée, Thesis, Université de la Nouvelle Calédonie (2009)
11. Breiman, L., Friedman, J.H., Olshen, R.A., Stone, C.J.: Classification and Regression Trees. Wadsworth and Brooks, Belmont (1984)
12. Ross Quinlan, J.: Induction of decision trees. Machine Learning 1, 81–106 (1986)
13. Quinlan, J.R.: C4.5: programs for machine learning. Morgan Kaufmann, San Francisco (1993)
14. Li, J., Stribling, J., Morris, R., Kaashoek, M., Gil, T.: A performance vs. cost framework for evaluating DHT design tradeoffs under churn. In: INFOCOM 2005, 24th Annual Joint Conference of the IEEE Computer and Communications Societies (2005); Proceedings IEEE 1, 225–236 (2005)
15. Garca, P., Pairot, C., Mondjar, R., Pujol, J., Tejedor, H., Rallo, R.: Planetsim: A new overlay network simulation framework. In: Gschwind, T., Mascolo, C. (eds.) SEM 2004. LNCS, vol. 3437, pp. 123–136. Springer, Heidelberg (2005)
16. Dabek, F., Zhao, B., Druschel, P., Kubiatowicz, J., Stoica, I.: Towards a common api for structured Peer-to-Peer overlays. In: Kaashoek, M.F., Stoica, I. (eds.) IPTPS 2003. LNCS, vol. 2735, pp. 33–44. Springer, Heidelberg (2003)
17. Stoica, Morris, R., Liben-Nowell, D., Karger, D., Kaashoek, M., Dabek, F., Balakrishnan, H.: Chord: a scalable Peer-to-Peer lookup protocol for internet applications. IEEE/ACM Transactions on Networking 11(1), 17–32 (2003)
18. Manku, G., Bawa, M., Raghavan, P.: Symphony: Distributed hashing in a small world. In: 4th USENIX Symposium on Internet Technologies and Systems, pp. 127–140 (2003)
19. Naicken, S., Basu, A., Livingston, B., Rodhetbhai, S.: A Survey of Peer-to-Peer Network Simulators. In: Proceedings of the Seventh Annual Postgraduate Symposium, Liverpool, UK, pp. 70–76 (2006)

Electronic Payment Use and Legal Protection

Echo Huang[1] and Fachang Chen[2]

[1] Department of Information Management
[2] Graduate Institute of Science and Technology Law,
National Kaohsiung First University of Sci. & Tech.,
2 Juoyue Nantz Kaohsiung, Taiwan, ROC
{echoh,fachang}@nkfust.edu.tw

Abstract. This study examines why consumers accept and continue to use e-payment for online purchase, specifically, the relationship between their perceived benefits, legal protection, risk avoidance, and satisfaction with prior experiences. The analytical results presented in this study indicate that beliefs (benefits, legal protection and risk allocation) differentially affect e-payment use behavior. Notably, consumer beliefs and confirmation affect satisfaction with e-payment use and continuance intention. Finally the practical and theoretical implications of this study are discussed.

Keywords: e-Payment Use, Perceived Risk, Perceived Benefits, Perceived Legal Protection, Risks Allocation.

1 Introduction

Accompanying the rapidly growth of the Internet population, more and more innovative Internet payment methods have been developed to address the needs for greater speed and convenience [1]. New Internet payment methods based on wired and wireless Internet channels, along with related technologies such as smart cards, e-money, virtual currency and P2P payment(PayPal), are together termed "e-payments." Ways to make payments through the Internet or mobile phones have proliferated in the past few years. Various types of services exist, some of which are new methods of accessing existing payment arrangements, while others including both completely new payment arrangement and new methods of accessing existing payment arrangements, but all are ultimately linked to existing payment and banking channels [2]. Two major payment processing methods exist: (1) in-house processing: when a customer visits a merchant web site makes an electronic payment and the payment is processed on the web server of the merchant; (2) outsourced processing: where merchants outsource the payment to an independent electronic payment service provider to avoid security concerns and the need to provide their own payment processing software.

An emerging technology, e-payment plays a critical role in the development of B2C e-commerce, since the lack of e-payment standards hinders the successful implementation and acceptance of B2C e-commerce [3]. Introduction of e-payment does not automatically lead to usage. A large number of new payment methods have

E. Ariwa and E. El-Qawasmeh (Eds.): DEIS 2011, CCIS 194, pp. 158–171, 2011.

poor acceptance among consumers. Thus, it is important to identify consumer expectations regarding e-payment. Recently both technological advances and online stimulation have increased customer expectations. Therefore, it is unsurprising that managing customer expectations have become both increasingly challenging and more essential than ever before. Consumer expectations potentially can significantly influence the perceived benefits of the use of new products/services [4]. How are consumer needs reflected in today's web environment? An understanding of consumer perceptions of new technology contributes to a healthy e-commerce development. Online merchants who develop effective strategies can potentially enhance e-payment success.

User perceptions of information systems are currently a more critical issue than ever before, especially in the context of Internet applications. Various well-known technology acceptance theories, including the technology acceptance model (TAM) [5], theory of planned behavior (TPB)[6], theory reasoned action(TRA)[7], and diffusion of organizational innovation(DOI)[8] have been used to examine the variables that motivate consumers to accept and revisit the web. However, the characteristics of a real purchase behavior are more complex than simply accepting or visiting a website. A real purchase is accompanied by payment preferences including matters of payment size, method and timing. Those preferences are based on prior experience of different degrees of perception of the benefits and risks associated with e-payment. This study thus posits that by combining the attitude and expectation approaches, the strong theory linking attitudes to behaviors can be exploited in social psychology theories, with the expectation literature being used to help identify the antecedents that affect satisfaction. This approach is very similar with the continuance model of Bhattacherjee[9], and thus this study attempts to adapt the original continuance use model with three constructs, perceived benefits, legal protection, especially in relation to risks allocation, and risks to explore the effect of consumer's post-consumption expectations on e-payment loyalty. Furthermore, the findings of this study help future researchers understand how to utilize the continuance model and examine the continuance of particular information systems from the perspective of adopters.

2 Legal Issues Related to E-Payment

Various methods exists for performing electronic payments, including smart cards, electronic checks, credit cards, internet payment, etc. Since these payment tools are electronic, theoretically they can be used in the internet environment. Despite the existence of numerous issues relating to these payment tools, including issues relating to privacy, transaction security, and so on., this paragraph focuses on allocating payment risk allocation for electronic payments on line because correct allocation risk is crucial to providing legal protection for such transactions. As this study demonstrates, a tendency exists for ordinary electronic payment users (product users) to hold limited or no liability towards possible risks while the risks allocation among the transferring financial institutions (in a transfer situation) is primarily based on the agreement among them financial institutions. Furthermore, the jurisdiction issue is ignored on the assumption identical solutions will be reached in different jurisdictions. This paragraph describes the introduction of a mechanism for dealing with the above issues in the United States and Taiwan, in an attempt to picture current trends regarding risks allocation for online electronic payments.

The discussion of payment risk allocation for online electronic payments is divided into two parts: product user liability, and possible risk allocation among the transferring financial institutions. Product user liability is discussed in the Section 3.3, which deals with perceived legal protection. Besides product user liability, numerous electronic payment situations involve credit transfers among different financial institutes. Just like in the first part, issues exist regarding the risks allocation between financial institutions transferring funds. The United States and Taiwan lack federal laws governing risks allocation among financial institutions transferring funds(credits). While Article 4 of the Uniform Commercial Code and the Mode Law on International Credit Transfers contain guidelines for financial institutions with regard to the above issues; neither are legally binding. According to the Uniform Commercial Code(U.C.C. § 4A-211) and the Mode Law on International Credit Transfers(Mode Law on International Credit Transfers, Art. 12), payment orders cannot be revoked following acceptance or execution by another financial institution without an agreement among the parties involved allowing such revocation. Thus provided there is no wrong doing on the part of the recipient of the payment order the sender of the payment will bear the risks associated with ensuring the online payment is honored. This approach offers a good reference for Taiwan in dealing with the same situation.

3 Theoretical Background

3.1 IS Continuance Model

The focus of this research, IS Continuance mode[9] is a parsimony model of the well-known expectation and confirmation theory (ECT) which posits that user satisfaction is determined by two constructs: expectation of the service/product and confirmation of expectation following repurchase [10]. Per Oliver's expectation and confirmation theory, users' IS continuance intention is determined primarily by their satisfaction with prior experiences. Bhattacherjee[9] adapted two well-grounded theories, ECT and technology acceptance model (TAM), then proposed an IS Continuance Model to explain the cognitive structure of consumer intention to reuse information system is retained in memory from prior experience and ex post expectation (see Figure 1).This approach considers post-consumption phase to assess an IS reuse behaviors. In the post-consumption phase, there are four major variables --- perceived usefulness, confirmation, satisfaction, and continuance intention. Perceived usefulness is defined as ex post expectation, because it is a cognitive belief salient to

IS use[5], and a long-term attitude which affects the consumer behavior towards information system [5, 11]. The consumption resulted in perceived usefulness that was influenced by these expectations.

Per IS Continuance Model, consumers' reuse intention of e-payment is determined primarily by their post-consumption expectation. If online merchants and e-payment providers target consumers and entice their loyalty to using e-payment, it is necessary to understand the effects of post-consumption expectation on e-payment and confirm how the accumulated expectations affect the decision to reuse e-payment. After reviewing previous literatures, we decompose three post-expectations of e-payment into perceived benefits, perceived legal protection and perceived risk. The details are discussed in the next section.

3.2 Perceived Benefits

In spite of the risks of e-commerce, B2C has recently increased significantly. Jarvenpaa &Todd[12] and Furnell & Karweni[13] argued that security issues have not stopped people from shopping online. One reason why e-commerce has grown so much despite the associated risks is the associated advantages, which include a faster shopping experience, wider selection, and lower prices. The most prominent benefits of cybermalls appear to be convenience, time savings [1], ease of use, prices and cost savings, and selection of goods[14]. Lecleric, et al[1] found that people are less willing to waste their time than their money, since lost time is more difficult to recoup. Beckwith[15] also suggested that technological advances and improved services had reduced the willingness of consumers to wait. Essentially as the pace of life has increased, consumers have come to expect the speed of services to keep pace]. Consequently, the delivery of all types of goods is heading towards quick response and instantaneous interactions. Besides, incentives and economic advantages are also important] in explaining user behavior regarding purchase decisions in addition to the known determinants of e-payment selection such as factor preference, convenience, and technologies.

3.3 Perceived Legal Protection

In the United States, the Electronic Fund Transfer Act (15 U.S.C. § 1693g (2004).) stipulates that if the identity of product users (consumers) can be verified by signature, photograph, or fingerprint, or by electronic or mechanical confirmation, the risk allocation of product users owing from being unable to verify(probably because of identity theft) cannot exceed the lesser of $50 or the unauthorized amount before the financial institutions reasonably realize the situation, except where the product users fail to report within sixty days (or in some extenuating situations: within a reasonable time) of transmission of the statement or fail to report within two business days after learning of the loss or theft of a card or other means of access(or in some extenuating situations within a reasonable time). In the case of exceptions mentioned above), the liability of product users cannot exceed $500 or the unauthorized amount between two business days after their learning of the loss or theft and the time they notify the financial institutions, whichever is less. The regulation also places the burden of proof on the financial institutions.

In addition to the Electronic Fund Transfer Act, another similar regulation is Regulation Z of the Truth in Lending Act (12 C.F.R. 226.12 (2006).). The Truth in Lending Act deals with credit card use. According to this regulation, the liability of a cardholder for an unauthorized credit card transaction shall not exceed the lesser of $50 or the quantity of money, property, labor, or services obtained by the unauthorized use before the card issuers was notified of the loss] Using credit cards on line can create questions regarding the jurisdiction whose law applies. Because of this possibility, Regulation Z expresses that Electronic Fund Transfer Act will have priority in issues regarding liability for unauthorized use of credit cards in internet transactions. In the Collins[16] case, the plaintiff alleged that his Internet banking account had been emptied of funds by unauthorized transactions by a Ms. Theresa Baker while he was in the jail. The court found that neither party was at fault and 1693g should be applied in this situation provided the transactions truly were unauthorized. Furthermore, in the Heritage Bank[17] case, the court said the statutory regulation could not be modified except by mutual agreement among the two parties involved.

In Taiwan, although no specific law exists regarding risk allocation between product users and financial institutions, and theoretically it appears that no court is able to apply traditional property risk allocation concepts involved in situations involving online electronic payments], the issues of risk allocation for online electronic payments most likely depend on mutual agreement between two parties. Generally, Taiwanese financial institutions are willing to take responsibility for risk allocation in relation to online electronic payments[18]. Particularly, in the case of a sample of individual Internet banking contracts promulgated by the Financial Supervisory Commission, if product users can notify financial institutions immediately after identifying an unauthorized transaction, the financial institutions will bear the loss. The above demonstrates that most likely because of the strong ability of financial institutions to undertake risk[19], our administrative branch is more lenient towards product users(the consumers). This leniency may arise from a motivation to promote the online industry driving this policy.

3.4 Perceived Risk

Numerous risks are associated with online transactions. Ring and Van de Ven[20] classify risk into two types: environmental and behavioral. Environmental risks derive from underlying infrastructure, while behavioral risks result from trading partners. These risks derive primarily from the open nature of the Internet, which is beyond the full control of consumers. Although merchants stress the security of transactions provided they are protected via methods such as encryption, authentication, firewalls, and so on, possibilities still exist for imperfect monitoring and the disclosure of private, credit card, and personal information[21]. Koyuncau and Bhattacharya[22] reported that the main concerns of customers include credit-card fraud, release of private information, risk of non-delivery of goods following payment, and lack of any guarantee of the quality of goods and services purchased in the absence of visual inspection.

Hancock and Humphrey[23] argued that fraud, operational, and systemic risks exist in all payment systems. Fraud risk is addressed through proper internal payment processing procedures and insurance. Moreover, operational risk is addressed by limiting access to sensitive facilities, especially for large-value payment networks, and through establishing back-up or duplicate computer facilities. Molesworth and Suortti[24] argued that consumer were concerned regarding payment method for large online transactions since they normally paid for online purchases using credit cards, which were not suitable for expensive items. Systemic risk involves the potential for a domino-like series of failures among participants in a payment network resulting from unexpected failures of one or more participants to settle their intra-day net debit. Jarvenpaa and Todd[12] indicated that in the context of e-commerce, consumer perceived personal risk (through misuse of credit cards, etc) is the most significant of the overall risks. Furthermore, consumers are frequently resistant to new methods of conducting financial transactions, particularly when they believe that they may lose control[25].

3.5 Research Model and Hypotheses

The IS continuance model has been criticized for low explanatory power, and consequently various empirical studies have suggested integrating it with other constructs or theories to improve its predictive power[9, 26]. Though previous studies[12, 24] have contributed to our understanding of technology continuance, these previous studies also demonstrate the complexity of the issue. This investigation follows the trend of focusing on integrating additional constructs to predict continuance intention from different perspectives. Basing itself on the Continuance model], the research model contains two ex post expectations, namely perceptions of benefits and risks]. Since the Continuance Use Model is adopted in this investigation as the theoretical base, hypotheses H1 and H5 were formulated based on Bhattacherjee's [9] hypotheses.

This study measures positive attributes using a single dimension, namely perceived benefits. Thus this study presents hypotheses H2, H6 and H9. The possibility of legal protection reduces consumer feelings of insecurity. Consumers are traditionally at a disadvantage when dealing with financial institutions with regard to some issues, for example, privacy, transaction security, risk allocation, and so on, and thus governments are willing to interfere in relation to such issues. This positive attribute is measured under perceived legal protection. Thus, this leads to hypotheses H3, H7, and H10. Again, the negative concerns are measured under a single dimension called perceived risk. Concern regarding risk is a negative value state, which leads to three hypotheses: H4, H8, and H11. The hypotheses of the proposed model are listed as follows.

H1. Consumers' continuance intention is positively associated with consumers' level of satisfaction with e-payment use.

H2. Consumers' continuance intention is positively associated with their perceived benefit of e-payment use.

H3. Consumers' continuance intention is positively associated with their perceived risks allocation of e-payment use.

H4. Consumers' continuance intention is negatively associated with their perceived risk of e-payment use.
H5. Consumers' extent of confirmation is positively associated with their satisfaction with e-payment use.
H6. Consumers' perceived benefits of e-payment are positively associated with their satisfaction with e-payment use.
H7. Consumers' perceived risk allocation of e-payment is positive associated with their satisfaction with e-payment use.
H8. Consumers' perceived risk of e-payment is negatively associated with their satisfaction with e-payment use.
H9. Consumers' extent of confirmation is positively associated with their perceived benefits of e-payment use.
H10. Consumers' extent of confirmation is positively associated with their risks allocation of e-payment use.
H11. Consumers' extent of confirmation is negatively associated with their perceived risk of e-payment use.

4 Research Methodology

This study used survey as the main methodology for obtaining data. The respondents comprised individuals with experience of using e-payment for online transactions and who were aware the processes involved in e-payment systems developed by the banking sector or related organizations. A questionnaire was developed primarily based on previous literatures for measuring the relevant constructs.

Table 1. Definition of Constructs

Construct	Definition	Adapted from
Continuance intention	Consumers' intention to continue using virtual currency.	Parasuraman et al.[9] loyalty intention scale.
Satisfaction	Consumer's feeling with previous virtual currency use.	Lin,et al[26] satisfaction scale.
Confirmation	Consumer's perception of the congruence between expectation of virtual currency use and its actual performance.	Bhattacherjee[9] confirmation scale.
Perceived benefits	Perceived benefit is defined as 'the extent to which the consumer expected to result from using virtual currency'.	LaRose & Atkin [29], Eastin[30] perceived benefit scale.
Perceived legal protection	The risks allocation between the products users and the financial institutes.	Adapted from the legal attitudes in the United States and Taiwan.
Perceived risk	Perceived risk is defined as 'the extent to which the consumer is uncertain about the consequences of using virtual currency'.	Pavlou[14], Bensaou & Venkataman[28], Ring & Van de Ven[20] perceived risk scale.

4.1 Measurement

The principal constructs were developed based on existing measures whenever possible or on similar scales, as shown in Table 1. Although all the items were based on previous studies, the scale was modified to adapt to the context of this study and the questions were translated into traditional Chinese. Face validity must be performed to ensure that the questionnaire measures what it is supposed to measure. Face validity may be determined by experts in the appropriate areas, and an adequate literature review is helpful in this regard. Consequently, a preliminary version of the instrument was assessed for content validity by two e-commerce scholars and revisions were made as necessary. According to Zmud and Boynton[32] refining the instrument through pre-testing and pilot testing of typical respondents satisfied the face validity criteria. Therefore, a pilot study was performed to verify the instrument through administration to 30 online consumers. These pre-test subjects had recent experience in either offline or online payment. The necessary refinement was implemented and the final instrument was thus obtained.

4.2 Subjects

The research subjects were individuals with experience in using e-payment for online transactions. A survey of e-payment users was performed at a website, focusing on 1000 users randomly selected from the member list, and eliminating users without e-payment experiences, resulting in a final sample of 500 individuals. The participants were informed in advance that they would gain reward credits after completing the online questionnaire. Non-response and incomplete questionnaires were discarded, leaving 467 usable cases. Table 2 lists the respondent characteristics.

Table 2. Descriptive statistics of respondents' characteristics

Measure	Items	Frequency	Percent
Gender	Male	123	26.3
	Female	344	76.7
Age	16-25	378	80.9
	26-35	73	15.6
	36-45	13	2.8
	46-55	3	0.6
Education	High school	145	31.0
	Two-year college	89	19.1
	Bachelor	211	45.2
	Master	22	4.7
Income	<5000	230	49.3
	5001-10000	136	29.1
	10001-20000	48	10.3
	20001-40000	41	8.8
	Over 40000	12	2.6
Years of Internet experience	<3 years	35	7.5
	4-6 years	191	40.9
	7-9 years	181	38.8
	9-11 years	35	7.5
	>11 years	25	5.4

4.3 Data Analysis and Assessment

To analyze the dimensions of expectation factors, we conducted the exploratory factor analysis without any priori constraints on the estimations of components or the number of components to be extracted. Items were loaded for two factors at around 0.65 factor loading and emerged with no-cross construct loadings above 0.5. Perceived benefits and perceived legal protection loaded on one factor only. The results show that the measures of perceived benefits and legal protection would be expected to have similar profiles in user continuance of e-payment. As we focus on the positive expectations including benefits and risks allocation, we integrate the benefits and risks allocation as one factor renamed it as 'perceived benefits and protection'.

Per Anderson and Gerbing [33] suggestion, confirmatory factor analysis(CFA) was employed to evaluate the convergent validity for modeled constructs. Data analysis for this study was performed with SPSS and EQS. Each scale item can be modeled as a reflective indicator of it corresponding hypothesized construct. To examine the goodness-of-good-fit of the overall CFA model, Bentler[34] suggested that chi-square normalized by degrees of freedom($\chi^2/df.$) should not exceed 5. Additional indexed of fit, Bentler-Bonett Non-Normed Fit Index(NNFI), Comparative Fit Index(CFI), Normed Fit Index (NFI), and Incremental Fit Index (IFI), and Standardized Root Mean Square Residual (SRMSR) , should both exceed 0.9. [34]. Using these measures, we assessed the measurement model and determined whether the measured variables reliably reflected the theoretical constructs. Data analysis proceeded in two stages: the measurement model was first examined for validating and refining the research instrument, followed by an analysis of the structural equation model for testing the associations hypothesized in our research.

Convergent validity refers to the confirmation of the existence of a construct determined by the correlations exhibited by independent measures of the construct. Evidence of convergent validity is thus reflected in the strength of factor loadings and their associated significant t-values along with estimated of the average variance explained(AE). Construct validity for the five measurement scales was assessed via CFA. For acceptable construct validity, each item should have a minimum factor loading of 0.60 on its hypothesized construct [35]. Therefore, two items with loadings less than 0.5 were dropped. After the refinement, a rerun of the CFA model on the shortened scales found that 24 of the remaining 25 items had factor loadings exceeding 0.6; sat5 had a loading just under the 0.6 norm, and was considered acceptable.

Scale reliabilities were estimated using Cronbach α, three scales (perceived benefit and risk allocation, confirmation, and satisfaction) had Cronbach α exceeding 0.80, other two scales (perceived risk, intention) had Cronbach α exceeding 0.90. As shown in Table 5, the composite reliabilities ranged between 0.86 and 0.90. AVE ranged from 0.50 to 0.62. The factor correlation matrix indicated that the largest squared correlation between any pair of construct was 0.53 (satisfaction and confirmation), while the smallest AVE was 0.50. Hence, the test of discriminate validity also met the suggested value [36]. The goodness-of-fit of the structural model was comparable to the previous CFA model. Overall, the statistics indicated the model fits the empirical data, the relative chi-square ($\chi^2/d.f.$) is 4.62 (χ^2 = 50.916; $d.f.$ = 11), NFI is 0.90, IFI is 0.90, CFI is 0.90, and SRMSR is 0.09. Although the χ^2 value is significant, all other statistics are within the range, suggesting a good fit.

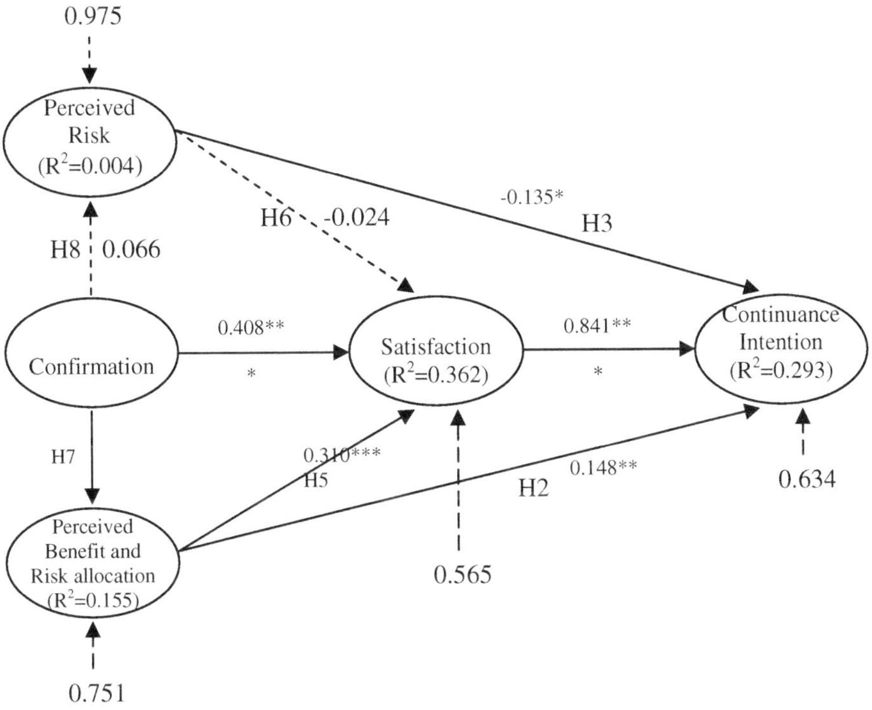

Fig. 1. Path coefficient analysis

Model fit: χ^2 =50.916 (d.f. =11, p<0.01), NFI = 0.90, CFI = 0.90, IFI = 0.90, SRMSR = 0.09.

4.4 Hypotheses Testing

The eight hypotheses listed above were tested collectively using the structure equation modeling(SEM), a multivariate statistical technique used to examine the direct and indirect relationships between measures and latent variables. According to the research model, all parameters were specified in the EQS program for model estimation. Model fit may be assessed by examining the results of the analysis, comparable to that of the previous CFA model. The EQS model used a covariance matrix as input. The path analysis is used to examine the significance and strength of hypothesized effects in the research model. The standardized path coefficients and path significances are shown in Figure 3. The R^2 values represent the percentage of variance in the dependent variable that all the proposed independent variables explain.

SEM permits the direct and indirect effects of each parameter from the perspective of the entire model to be found. In this model, as depicted in Figure 1, most path coefficients were as hypothesized, except H9 and H11. Continuance intention was predicted by satisfaction(β=0.841), perceived benefits and risks allocation(β=0.148), and perceived risk(β=-0.135). In addition to these three direct effects, confirmation, perceived benefits and risks allocation, and perceived risk also had small indirect effects on continuance intention via satisfaction with corresponding β=0.408, β=0.310, and β=-0.024 respectively. Results showed that the model accounts for 29.3% of the variance in intention and 36.2% in satisfaction.

5 Discussion and Implications

This study examined whether IS continuance theory could explain the post-consumption expectation and satisfaction formation process for e-payment users. Within the confirmation/satisfaction paradigm, e-payment user needs and expectations were examined as confirmation standards. In general, e-payment user satisfaction was conceptualized as comprising two independent sources --- satisfaction with perceived benefits and risk allocation, accompanied with e-payment and satisfaction with the perceived risk of e-payment transactions. Both sources were hypothesized to contribute independently to overall e-payment user satisfaction. The analytical results *here* show that perceived benefits, legal protection and risk of e-payment are important predictors of e-consumer repeat purchase intention. The results presented here also demonstrate that beliefs (perceived benefits, risk allocation and perceived risk) differentially affect consumer behavior.

The analytical results here also suggest that satisfaction with the e-payment benefits and risk allocation may be more important for overall satisfaction than satisfaction with the perceived risk. That is, if the online payment is perceived to be risky and security services are poor, but the user requires the benefits of e-payment and believes that possible losses will be refunded via legal channels, that user will continue to use e-payment. Restated, if online shoppers know they will obtain the benefits they require by using e-payment, they will utilize e-payment, even if system or services are perceived to have low reliability. From a legal perspective, the certainty of risk allocation between products and financial institutions is also an important consideration. This finding is consistent with Stroborn, et al [27], who found that benefits sought are more important to e-payment users than the possible risk. Also, from a consumer perspective, if e-payment provides different benefits to match consumer needs and provides them with risk-free guarantees, consumers will continue to use e-payment for online purchases. These findings indicate that increased efforts should be focused on developing attractive benefits of e-payment versus emphasizing better online security environments. The results presented in this study are consistent with those of Jarvenpaa &Todd[12] and Furnell & Karweni[13].

This study validates the Continuance Model as a theoretical basis for studying IS/IT continuance behavior and helps academics understand the relationships between perception-confirmation-satisfaction-intention. The findings of this study also help clarify the predicators of benefits and the influence of risks on purchase abortion behaviors by online consumers. The findings of this study have several practical implications. Understanding important benefits, legal protection and risk of e-payment can guide e-payment providers, participants, and banks in fine-tuning their services. E-payment providers can satisfy customer needs by offering tangible benefits (for example economic advantages) and intangible benefits (for example convenience, time saving, and psychological factors) through the e-marketing mix they offer], and can also remain mindful of the need for risk-free guarantees that consumers derive from improved content delivery and display. For merchants studying consumer expectations and segmentation, better understanding of underlying consumer behavioral tendencies of benefit seeking and risk avoidance can enable merchants to better manage the customer experience and associated e-payment services. Some businesses offer online payment mechanisms using credit cards. However, many people are concerned about using credit cards for online payment. Financial transaction systems thus have been developed to overcome this problem, for instance "internet payment systems" [37]. Customers can accomplish transactions in a single click. The need for repeated information and multiple forms can be minimized by using "software agents" that automate tasks [38].

Increased e-payment continuance may also depend on effective risk control and improved settlement arrangements. Although consumers cannot control Internet fraud and deception, they can at least take action to recognize, avoid, and report such problems. FTC proposes that the government should encourage consumers to protect themselves through behaviors such as using a secure browser, checking site privacy policies, read and understanding refund and shipping policies, keeping personal information private, giving payment information only to businesses they know and trust, keeping records of their online transactions and checking their e-mails, and reviewing their monthly credit card and bank statements. E-payments are unlikely to significantly impact monetary policy, but they do raise regulatory issues regarding consumer rights and protection. To address this concern, online merchants should continue to strive to ensure safe transactions and align their communications accordingly.

6 Conclusion and Limitations

This study presents an important contribution to the theory by extending IS Continuance to address post-expectation of its two belief constructs with legal issues. To help explain the analysis model, besides providing legal protection against infringements by third parties, the tendency in dealing with risk allocation between product consumers and the financial institutions is to be lenient towards product consumers. In a sense, the risks-allocation legal approach reduces consumer perceived risk. The proposed model integrates consumer psychology and legal perspectives both of which have previously received little attention. Furthermore research is required to elucidate the processes involved in cognitively matching consumer goals to continuance intention. However, the theoretical and empirical work performed in this study provides a solid basis for related future studies. In conclusion, e-payment continuance remains a complex, elusive yet extremely important phenomenon. However, research on continuance behavior has made significant progress towards revealing some of its mysteries.

Despite its contributions, this study has several significant limitations. First, the present study posits an extension to the Continuance Model for e-payment. Several issues are raised by the e-payment study, including generalizability of the results to other settings and technologies, and operationalization of the study constructs. Second, the conceptual model should be carefully interpreted when applied to predict frequent buyer behavior or when the results are extended to other consumers. In this study, only 2.8% of respondents had over ten transactions per month, possibly leading to contrasting cognitive impacts when assessing individual perception recognition between different segments. We suggest conducting further research to examine this issue.

References

1. Leclerc, F., Schmitt, B.H., Dube, L.: Waiting time and decision making: Is time like money? Journal of Consumer Research 22(1), 110–119 (1995)
2. Allen, H.: Innovations in retail payment: e-payments. Bank of England Quarterly Bulletin 43(3), 428–439 (2003)
3. Teo, T.S.H., Yeong, Y.D.: Assessing the consumer decision process in the digital marketplace. Omega 31, 349–363 (2003)
4. Miller, H.: Managing customer expectations. Information Systems Management 17(2), 92–95 (2000)
5. Davis, F.D.: Perceived Usefulness, Perceived Ease of Use, and User Acceptance of Information Technology. MIS Quarterly 13(3), 319–342 (1989)
6. Ajzen, I.: The Theory of Planned Behavior. Organisational Behaviour and Human Decision Processes 50, 179–211 (1995)
7. Fishbein, M., Ajzen, I.: Belief, attitude, intention, and behavior: An introduction to theory and research. Addison-Wesley, Reading (1975)
8. Rogers, E.: Diffusion, of Innovation, 4th edn. Free Press, New York (1995)
9. Bhattacherjee, A.: An empirical analysis of the antecedents of electronic commerce service continuance. Decision Support Systems 32, 201–214 (2001)
10. Oliver, R.L.: A cognitive model for the antecedents and consequences of satisfaction. Journal of Marketing Research 17, 460–469 (1980)
11. Karahanna, E., Straub, D.W., Chervany, N.L.: Information technology adoption across time: a cross-sectional comparison of pre-adoption and post-adoption beliefs. MIS Quarterly 23, 183–213 (1999)
12. Javenpaa, S.L., Todd, P.A.: Consumer reactions to electronic shopping on the World Wide Web. International Journal of Electronic Commerce 1(2), 59–88 (1997)
13. Furnell, S.M., Karweni, T.: Security implications of electronic commerce: a survey of consumers and businesses. Internet Research 9(5), 372–395 (1999)
14. Richmond, A.: Enticing online shoppers to buy- A human behavior study. Computer Networks and ISDN Systems 28, 1469–1480 (1996)
15. Beckwith, N.: Organization for Economic Cooperation and Development. The Oecd Observer 238, 28–31 (2003)
16. Collins, V.: Missouri Electric Cooperatives Employees Credit Union, WL 2189693, E.D.Mo (2006)
17. Lovett, V.: Heritage Bank 613 N.W.2d 652 (2000)

18. Ting, L.Y.: The application of credit cards on internet transaction and related issues. Science & Technology Law Review 44(13), 58 (2001)
19. Baxter, T.C.: Problems and Gaps in the UCC Coverage of Payment Systems. SD30 ALI-ABA 73 (1998)
20. Ring, P.S., Van de Ven, A.H.: Developing processes of cooperative inter-organizational relationships. Academy of Management Review 19, 90–118 (1994)
21. Pavlou, A.P.: Consumer Acceptance of Electronic Commerce: Integrating Trust and Risk with the Technology Acceptance Model. Information Journal of Electronic Commerce 7(3), 101–134 (2003)
22. Koyuncu, C., Bhattacharya, G.: The impacts of quickness, price, payment risk, and delivery issues on online shopping. Journal of Socio-Economics 33(2), 149–241 (2004)
23. Hancock, D., Humphrey, D.B.: Payment transactions, instruments, and systems: A survey. Journal of Banking & Finance 21(11), 1573–1579 (1997)
24. Molesworth, M., Suortti, J.-P.: Buying cars online: The adoption of the Web for high-involvement, high-cost purchases. Journal of Consumer Behaviour 2(2), 155–169 (2002)
25. Plouffe, C.R., Hulland, J.S., Vandenbosch, M.: Research report: Richness versus parsimony in modeling technology adoption decisions – Understanding merchant adoption of a smart card-based payment system. Information Systems Research 12(2), 208–228 (2001)
26. Lin, C.S., Wu, S., Tsai, R.J.: Integrating perceived playfulness into expectation-confirmation model for web portal context. Information & Management 42, 683–693 (2005)
27. Stroborn, K., Heitmann, A., Leibold, K., Frank, G.: Internet payments in Germany: a classificatory framework and empirical evidence. Journal of Business Research 57, 1431–1437 (2004)
28. Bensaou, M., Venkataman, N.: Inter-organizational relationships and information technology: A conceptual synthesis and a research framework. European Journal of Information Systems 5, 84–91 (1996)
29. LaRose, R., Atkin, D.: Audiotext and the re-invention of the telephone as a mass medium. Journalism Quarterly 69(2), 413–421 (1992)
30. Eastin, M.S.: Diffusion of e-commerce: an analysis of the adoption of four e-commerce activities. Telematics and Informatics 19, 251–267 (2002)
31. Parasuraman, A., Zeithaml, V.A., Malhotra, A.: E-S-QUAL: A multiple-item scale for assessing electronic service quality. Journal of Service Research 7(3), 213–233 (2005)
32. Zmud, R.W., Boynton, A.C.: Survey Measures And Instrument in MIS: Inventory and Appraisal. In: Kremer, K. (ed.) The Information Systems Research Challenge: Survey Research Methods, pp. 149–180. Harvard Business School Press, Boston (1999)
33. Anderson, E.W., Sullivan, M.W.: Strengthening the satisfaction-profit chain. Journal of Service Research 3, 107–120 (2000)
34. Bentler, P.M.: EQS Structural Equations Program Manual. BMDP Statistical Software (1989)
35. Nunnally, J.C.: Psychometric Theory. McGraw-Hill, New York (1978)
36. Fornell, C., Larcker, D.F.: Structural Equation Models with Unobservable Variables and Measurement Error: Algebra and Statistics. Journal of Marketing Research 18(3), 382–389 (1981)
37. Shon, T.-H., Swatman, P.M.C.: Identifying effectiveness criteria for Internet payment systems. Internet Research 8(3), 202–217 (1998)
38. Riggins, F.J., Rhee, H.-S.: Toward a unified view of electronic commerce, Association for Computing Machinery. Communications of the ACM 41(10), 88–96 (1999)

Bridging between SAML-Based Payment and Other Identity Federation Payment Systems

David J. Lutz

Rechenzentrum Universität Stuttgart,
Allmandring 30, 70550 Stuttgart, Germany
lutz@rus.uni-stuttgart.de
http://www.rus.uni-stuttgart.de

Abstract. Identity Federations are increasingly being used to establish convenient and secure attribute-based authentication and authorization systems. During the last few years, a third aspect has become important within these federations: i.e., payment. Thus, several payment approaches have been designed and used in Identity Federations. However, when more than one federation is being combined into an inter-federation association, federation bridges have to be established to translate messages between the participating federations. Whilst the problem of bridging identity information between federations has already been considered in many research activities, the problem of how to bridge payment data still remains unsolved. Therefore, this paper presents a solution to bridge between a SAML-based payment enabled Identity Federation and four other kinds of payment solutions used by Identity Federations.

Keywords: Identity Federation, ePayment, Inter-Federation Bridges.

1 Introduction

Identity Federations are increasingly being used to transmit identity information between different entities. Although this concept provides many benefits to the federation participants, it also has some limitations: firstly, Identity Federations usually have strict borders. Thus, if identity information should be transmitted between participants in different federations, a federation bridge approach has to be deployed. Secondly, Identity Federations focus only on authentication and authorization and are, therefore, missing methods of payment. However, both concepts have been investigated during the last few years and, currently, solutions for federation bridges and payment approaches in Identity Federations have been introduced. However, combining both concepts by bridging the payment approaches, has yet to be achieved. Obviously, this leads to a major drawback: if an Identity Federation has deployed payment mechanisms, the strict federation borders prevent payment data transmission to participants in other federations. Thus, this paper provides five solutions for bridging between different payment approaches to allow the participants of SAML-based payment federations using the concept of federation bridges not only for identity information, but also for payment data.

E. Ariwa and E. El-Qawasmeh (Eds.): DEIS 2011, CCIS 194, pp. 172–186, 2011.

The remainder of this paper is structured as follows: to familiarise the reader with the concepts of Identity Federations, several kinds of federation concepts are highlighted, followed by a description of the challenges to be met when bridging between them. Then, five different approaches for payment within Identity Federations are identified. This is followed by a discussion on how to bridge between a SAML-based payment enabled Identity Federation and other kinds of federation payment. Finally, in conclusion, the results are discussed and summarized.

2 Identity Federations

Within an Identity Federation, several Service Providers (SP) agree to allow user authentication not on their systems, but at the user's home institution, e.g., the user's university or his/her telecom operator. This home institution, the so-called Identity Provider (IdP), furnishes, upon request, authentication and attribute data about a specific user to federated Service Providers. Therefore, the Service Providers are able to check, based on the data received, whether the user is allowed to have access to a specific resource or to consume a specific service.

To provide a quick look at several kinds of such federations, the following subsections briefly explain the three major Identity Federation concepts: Shibboleth, Liberty Alliance and WS-Fed. A more detailed overview on further Identity Federation concepts can be found in [1].

2.1 Shibboleth

Shibboleth [2] is a package of several supporting functions for Web Single Sign-On (SSO) across or within organizational boundaries. It is based on the Security Assertion Markup Language (SAML) and represents one of the most used federation support packages within the academic arena.

A Shibboleth federation consists typically of one or more Identity Providers, which host user data, of one or more Service Providers that offer restricted resources to users, and of users who wish to access protected SP-resources using Web-browsers. Additionally, Shibboleth provides an optional discovery service, which identifies the user and the user's IdP.

Authentication is carried out as follows: the user accesses the restricted website and is redirected to a Discovery Service, where he/she has to chose his/her IdP. After selection, the Discovery Service redirects the user to his/her IdP where he/she has to authenticate himself/herself. The IdP validates the user's credentials and sends either a POST or a redirect to the user, depending on which of the two profiles (POST or artifact) is used. The POST Profile demands a post-message that includes the SP's address in its *action* tag and the base64 encoded SAML Authentication Assertion in its hidden target tag. By using the POST command, the Assertion Consumer Service (ACS), which is a part of the SP, receives the assertion. If more user attributes are required, in order to facilitate a decision for the user's access request, the ACS can send a SAML Attribute Request using SOAP to the IdP's Attribute Authority. Here, the user's attributes are sent to the SP, filtered by an Attribute Release Policy, which specifies those attributes that the IdP is allowed to release to the requesting SP. Based on the received SAML Attribute Assertion and the already obtained SAML Authentication Assertion, the Policy Decision Point (PDP) of the SP can now grant or deny access to the restricted resource. For the Artifact Profile, the IdP sends a redirect command instead of the POST to the user's browser. That redirect command includes the parameter *SAMLart*, whose value is a SAML Artifact [3]. The ACS has now to resolve the artifact by contacting the IdP's Artifact Resolution Service (ARS) via SOAP. The ARS responds with a SAML Authentication and the process continues just as has been described for the POST profile.

2.2 Liberty Alliance

Whilst the Shibboleth approach is mainly used within an academic context, Liberty Alliance was formed by several commercial organizations and vendors. Unlike the Shibboleth consortium, the specifications that the Liberty Alliance Project has provided are not just specific to supporting only a basic Identity Federation. Indeed, the Liberty Alliance consortium has written numerous specifications. However, although many of them can be used to enhance an Identity Federation, of these specifications, only two are relevant regarding Identity Federation establishment: the Liberty Alliance ID-FF 1.2 Specifications, describing the architecture of an Identity Federation (ID-FF), and the Liberty Alliance ID-WSF 2.0 Specifications for setting up a framework for a higher-level Web service architecture associated with identity.

Liberty ID-FF. Liberty ID-FF [4] is an approach for building circles of trust between Identity Providers and Service Providers, thus, enabling Identity Federations. Before user-initiated processes can start, both IdP and SP have to be federated, which means that an explicit trust relationship has to be established between them and that they have to create handles for each other, to be used later.

The Single Sign-On process in a Liberty Alliance Identity Federation is very similar to Shibboleth's process. This SSO process is defined as follows: the user visits an SP by using his/her Web-browser and is, after selecting the correct IdP for login, redirected to this IdP with an embedded parameter indicating the originating SP. The user authenticates himself/herself at the IdP and receives, after a valid login, another redirect command, this time back to the SP, together with either a SAML Artifact or a POST-form with the embedded SAML Authentication Assertion. For the Artifact Profile, the SP contacts the IdP and requests a full assertion using SOAP [5]. The ID-FF Architecture does not focus on the transmission of attributes for authorization purposes, but [5] specifies a possible approach to transmit attributes in the same way as proposed by Shibboleth Identity Federations: as a SOAP connection between the SP and the IdP using the ID-FF architecture and SAML Attribute Assertions.

Liberty ID-WSF. Whilst Liberty ID-FF describes the basic Identity Federation architecture, ID-WSF [6] specifies a Web-based federation at a higher level.

Again, using a SOAP binding profile, a SOAP-based invocation framework for identity services is provided. A Discovery Service, which is one of the core identity services, is used to discover the users' registered identity services. Thus, the user is not seen as having his/her account only at one Identity Provider. It is possible to merge different identity information from different identity hosts. Liberty ID-WSF uses SAML as a language for identity and concordant security information. The ID-WSF protocol will not be described in detail here, since it follows the concept of ID-FF with some extensions.

2.3 Web Service Federation

Web Services Federation (WS-Fed) [7] is part of an overall effort by IBM and Microsoft to build a Web services security framework, or WS-Security.

The main components in a WS-Federation are the Requestor, which wishes to have access to a restricted resource, the resource itself, which may have specific restrictions relating to its access, and an Identity Provider combined with a Security Token Service (STS). Other components are the Attribute Services and the Pseudonym Services, which are of less importance. The requestor uses either his/her Web-browser or a requestor service to request access to the resource. The Identity Provider performs authentication and provides identity confirmations by issuing security tokens. Attributes are received from an Attribute Server, which can be combined with the Identity Provider. If pseudonymity is required at the resource, the Attribute Service is enhanced by a Pseudonym Service, which aligns the requestor's attributes with a pseudonym. The authorization is carried out by an Authorization Service, a specific instance of an STS that operates in a decision brokering process.

The process of accessing a protected resource within the WS-Fed environment may be seen as follows: when a requestor initially asks for access at a Resource Provider using his/her Web-browser, he/she is redirected (in some cases with the Resource Provider's IdP as an intermediate component) from the resource to his/her IdP. The information about the requestor's IdP should be received by interacting with the requestor, if not already known at the resource. After the requestor authenticates at his/her IdP, this IdP issues a security token and sends it in another redirect to the Resource Provider, where the security token is examined in order to decide access. If the resource provider needs the user's attributes, the same method (contacting the user's IdP by a Web-redirect) is chosen. Information about the required attributes as well as token information are stated in the redirect command. To avoid the need to request a security token each time the requestor seeks access, artifacts can be stored as cookies in the requestor's browser. Additionally, WS-Fed also provides a mechanism to use SOAP instead of HTTP as the underlying protocol for accessing the resources.

3 Bridges between Identity Federations

The transmission of identity information between federation entities, as described in Section 2, can only be carried out within a specific federation. However, if entities located in different federations have to communicate, a so-called federation bridge has to be established in order to link the federations. Such a federation bridge has to fulfil three tasks: firstly, it has to establish a trust relationship between the federations involved. Secondly, it has to translate from the protocol being used in one federation to the protocol being used by the other federation. Thirdly, if different languages for attribute descriptions are being used, a translation between these languages must also be done. This section identifies three concepts for such federation bridges and describes how they can solve the given tasks.

3.1 eduGAIN

eduGAIN [8] has been designed as a bridging approach for academic federations around Europe. Currently, within almost every country in Europe an academic Identity Federation has been deployed. However, for inter-federation connectivity between these federations, a new solution has to be found. Therefore, the aim of eduGAIN is to enable different federations to interact.

To enable such interaction, federations, having accepted the eduGAIN policies, are able to access the eduGAIN Metadata Service, which provides the metadata for all participating federations. In addition, the WAYF (Where Are You From) components have been enhanced to WFAYF (Which Federation Are You From) that forces the user to select his/her home federation. Bridging elements are able to translate messages that have been created by the protocol of one federation into a confederation formatted message, which can then be transmitted to the bridging element of the destination federation.

Currently, eduGAIN is deployed in a pilot phase with 13 federations, but it is expected that more federations will follow.

3.2 STORK

Whilst eduGAIN bridges academic federations, STORK [9] focuses on bridging eID federations. An eID federation is seen as a governmental federation that enables eID validation in one country. Therefore, the infrastructure in each country that has established an eID validation approach, is such an eID federation. Users in an eID federation are able to prove their identity just by presenting their eID cards. The service provider, to whom the card is presented, is able to validate the identity of the user by using the electronic eID validation infrastructure provided by the user's country of origin.

However, similar to the problem in academic federations, this concept needs enhancements if a cross-border eID validation is required. Therefore, STORK provides a solution on how to enable inter-federation connectivity between different eID federations. To achieve this goal, STORK proposes Pan-European Proxy Services (PEPS) that act as federation bridges. When a foreign citizen requests an eID validation, he/she will be redirected to a foreign national PEPS, which, in turn, forwards him/her to the PEPS in his/her own country. From the home PEPS, the citizen is redirected to an authentication portal, where he/she carries out the authentication. After successful authentication, the national PEPS in the home country is able to contact an Attribute Provider, which releases, based on privacy policies, attributes about the citizen. The information released from the Authentication Portal and the Attribute Provider are combined into a digital identity by the home PEPS and sent to the PEPS in the foreign country, which forwards the message to the service provider, at which the citizen wishes to authenticate.

3.3 SEMIRAMIS

SEMIRAMIS [11] foresees not only inter-federation communications as focused in eduGAIN and STORK, but also communications between different kinds of federations, such as eID and academic federations. Since the current approaches usually cover only inter-federation communications between federations of the same kind, e.g. between academic federations or between eID federations, a new concept had to be designed. Thus, SEMIRAMIS has refined the eduGAIN and STORK technology as well as the Identity Aggregator concept from SWIFT [10]. These refinements combined with a powerful federation proxy, which is able to translate between different kinds of federations, enable communications not only between similar federations, but also between dissimilar federations.

4 Concepts for Payment within Identity Federations

Usually, Identity Federations focus only on the transmission of identity information. Thus, when a service requires payment, a solution for this has to be found. However, these solutions cover a wide area, from such concepts as bank transfers or credit card payments, which do not correspond with the federation technology, to SAML-based payments, which combines Identity Federation and payment technologies into one approach. To provide a detailed view on several of these concepts, this section describes five different payment approaches that may be used to enable payment within an Identity Federation.

4.1 Bank Transfer

The bank wire transfer [12] is one of the most commonly used solutions to transfer money from one account to another. Whenever two banks have a relationship that enables wire transfer (such institutions do not need to have a contract with each other - a link to a centralized organization such as the Society for Worldwide Interbank Financial Telecommunication (SWIFT) is usually enough), customers of those banks can transfer money as follows: if the payer wishes to transfer the money to the payee by bank wire transfer, he/she instructs his/her bank to send the money to the specified account at the payee's bank. The payer's bank transmits a secured message to the payee's bank, which contains all relevant information. To transfer the money, both banks should have a reciprocal account with each other, in which case the payer's bank can transfer money from the payer's account to the account of the payee's bank and the payee's bank transfers the money from the account of the payer's bank to the account of the payee.

If a reciprocal account does not exist, both banks have to use an intermediary financial institution that has accounts at both banks in order to transfer the money.

4.2 Credit Card and SET

Electronic payment using credit cards is usually supported by Secure Electronic Transaction (SET), which is a protocol for securing credit card transactions over the Internet [13]. Within the SET framework, four major roles have been identified with a secure transaction:

- The Cardholder is the person who has the credit card. He/she has a contract with the Issuer in which he promises to pay the debt.
- A Merchant within the SET framework is a person or organization that sells goods or services. It has a contract with the Acquirer to which it has agreed to receive payment processing services in return for a fee.
- The Issuer is the company that has issued the card to the Cardholder and is responsible for the payment of the debt - usually by charging the user's account. The Issuer has contracts with the Cardholder and the credit card associations in which it accepts the risk of card debt.
- The Acquirer is an organization that provides card authorization and capture services for Merchants. It is the bridge between the Merchants and the credit card associations. It has contracts with the Merchants and with the credit card associations in which it agrees to their general terms and conditions of business.

The paying process defined within the SET framework is as follows: when a customer wishes to buy something from a Merchant, he/she places an order and receives in turn the Merchant's X.509 certificate and the Acquirer's Payment Gateway X.509 certificate. Both certificates can be validated by the established PKI. The customer returns the payment information to the Merchant. This information contains the order as well as payment information. The order information is encrypted with the Merchant's public key, the payment information with the Acquirer's Payment Gateway public key. Thus, it is impossible for the Merchant to receive the customer's credit card information and it will not be possible for the credit card company to receive information about the goods the user has bought.

The advantage of this approach is higher security and privacy than in most other credit card based payment protocols. Non-repudiation, achieved by the PKI, and following the need-to-know principle are also reasons for the widespread use of this solution.

4.3 PayPal

PayPal [14], established in 2000 and now a subsidiary of eBay, is currently often used to transfer money for online business transactions. To use PayPal, both buyer and seller must have a PayPal account. After an acquisition, the merchant informs the customer about his/her PayPal account and the customer uses PayPal to transfer money to the merchant's PayPal account, either from his/her PayPal account or by submitting his/her credit card details to PayPal. If a money transfer using a credit card is chosen, the transaction from the customer's bank account to PayPal follows the schema for credit card transfer. To have PayPal act as an intermediary institution enables trust, privacy and security. Both parties should trust PayPal, since they have accounts there and PayPal benefits from its reputation. Privacy is enhanced, because only PayPal has knowledge about the user's bank information, and due to PayPal's security implementation (use of SSL; a 'Buyer Protection Policy' and a 'Seller Protection Policy'), security is also enabled within the money transaction.

4.4 Attribute Assertion Payment

The first step towards the complete integration of payment processes into the Identity Federation infrastructure was carried out by Jennings [17] by proposing to use SAML Attribute Assertions for payment of SIP sessions.

To integrate a payment approach into SAML, Jennings extended the usual federation architecture, consisting of User, Service Provider and Identity Provider. He introduced the Payment Provider (PP), a component that hosts the User's account and that is allowed to send his/her money to merchants when the user is required to pay within that federation.

After receiving a payment offer from a merchant in an attribute assertion payment federation, the User contacts his/her PP to request a payment assertion. The PP initiates the payment process by examining the User's authentication and checks if he/she is authorized for the payment process. If so, the PP generates a payment receipt and the account of the User is charged in relation to the contractual agreement between the User and the PP, either at this point or at a specified time later. Depending on the chosen mode, the receipt is either a SAML Payment Assertion or a SAML URI Reference that acts as a pointer to the assertion stored at the PP. The Payment Receipt is then sent to the user, who presents it to the SP as proof of payment. If the PP uses the assertion as a receipt, the SP can examine the assertion directly; otherwise it has to contact the PP requesting resolution of the URI. The core of such a payment assertion is an attribute statement, which can look as follows:

```
<saml:AttributeStatement>
   <saml:Attribute
       NameFormat="urn:oasis:names:tc:SAML:2.0:attrname-
           format:uri"
       Name="urn:ietf:params:xml:ns:payattr">
       <samlAttributeValue
           xsi:type="payattr:PaymentReceiptValueType"
           payattr:merchantBits="MDE1Mw=="
           payattr:pspBits="abc"
            payattr:serviceUrl="https://psp.example.com/
                paymentService"
            payattr:currencyNamespace="currency:
                namespace:..."
            payattr:currencyDivisor:1000
```

```
            payattr:currency="USD"
            payattr:amount="300"/>
    </saml:Attribute>
  </saml:AttributeStatement>
```

The assertion's elements that comprise this attribute statement will not be explained in detail in this section, since most of it is part of the standard SAML assertion definition [18]. All payment related information is in the attribute statement block of the assertion conveyed within the `<saml:AttributeStatement>`

4.5 SAML-Based Payment

The concept of SAML-based Payments allows the combination of a SAML-based Identity Federation with payment processes [1]. In contrast to the Attribute Assertion-based payment, the SAML-based payment solution specifies a new type of assertion: the SAML Payment Assertion. Furthermore, the usual Identity Federation architecture has been enhanced by a Payment Provider to support payment at the Identity Federation layer.

The first process relating to federation payment is the generation and issuing of payment data by the payer's Payment Provider. The payer sends a request for payment data to his/her Payment Provider, where the transmitted data (e.g., authentication data and attributes) are evaluated and the payer's account is checked. If all security checks are passed successfully, the Payment Provider generates the data, stores locally some information about its creation and sends the signed payment data to the payer.

The main process is the actual payment. The payer signs, being informed about the required payment, the already issued payment data and sends it to the payee. The payee initially checks the security data such as digital signatures as well as the amount and its currency as supplied within the data. For further validation, the payee could also contact the issuing Payment Provider who may inform the payee about any tampering or overspending with respect to the payment data.

The major element used during the SAML-based payment is the newly designed SAML Payment Assertion, which has been specified based on the already defined SAML Assertions [19] and may look as follows:

```
<saml:Assertion
    xmlns:SAML Payment Namespace
    Version="2.0"
    ID="_a75adf55-01d7-40cc-929f-dbd8372ebdfc"
    IssueInstant="2008-09-15T20:03:25.32Z"
    <saml:Issuer> https://payment.provider.com/
    </saml:Issuer>
    <!-- SIGNATURE OF ASSERTION -->
    <ds:Signature xmlns="http://www.w3.org/2000/09/
         xmldsig#"> PP Signature
     </ds:Signature>
     <saml:Subject>comsumer@payment-provider.com
     </saml:Subject>
     <saml:Conditions>
         NotBefore="2008-09-15T20:03:25.32Z"
         NotOnOrAfter="2009-09-15T20:03:25.33Z"/>
     <saml:PaymentStatement>
```

```
        <saml:PaymentAttribute Name="amount">
            <saml:PaymentAttributeValue xsi:
                type="xsd:string">5.45
            </saml:PaymentAttributeValue>
        </saml:PaymentAttribute>
        <saml:PaymentAttribute Name="currency">
            <saml:PaymentAttributeValue xsi:
                type="xsd:string">EUR
            </saml:PaymentAttributeValue>
        </saml:PaymentAttribute>
    </saml:PaymentStatement>
</saml:Assertion>
```

The third process in the chain of payment related processes is the reimbursement of the payment data into real money, usually requested by the payee at the issuing Payment Provider. The PP validates all the pieces of data (digital signatures, amount and currency, checks for overspending and tampering, optional SP authentication) and if the validation passes successfully, it credits the required amount to the payee's account.

5 Bridges between SAML-Based Payment Identity Federation and Other Payment-Enabled Identity Federations

Obviously, the only payment concept described in Section 4, which is fully integrated into Identity Federation technology, is the SAML-based payment approach. Therefore, a federation equipped with this technology would offer its participants a convenient payment solution. However, if one of the payment partners is located outside of the Identity Federation, a bridge has to be established, not only for the transmission of identity information, but also for the transmission of payment data. Thus, this section describes a solution for a payment-bridge between a SAML-based payment federation and the payment solutions described in Section 4.

5.1 Bridge to Bank Transfer Identity Federation

As described in Section 4.1, two bank accounts, identified by bank and account numbers, are required for a bank transfer.

If money is transferred from a participant of the SAML-based payment federation to a bank account federation, the payer requests a SAML Payment Assertion at his/her Payment Provider and sends it to the federation bridge. Additionally, the payer provides the federation bridge with the bank account details of the payee. Now, the federation bridge requests assertion reimbursement to its own account and then carries out a bank transfer from its account to that of the payee. However, in both cases, the money sent by the payer will be finally transfered to the payee's bank account.

If money is transferred from a participant of a bank account federation to a SAML-based payment federation, the payer carries out a bank transfer to the account of the federation bridge and specifies the identity of the payee. Then, the federation bridge requests a SAML Payment Assertion at its Payment Provider containing the accordant amount and currency. This payment assertion is finally sent to the payee.

However, as described above, the federation bridge requires only little additional information to carry out the transfer between both federations. In the first case, it needs to know the bank account of the payee, which has to be provided by the payer, and in the second case, the identity of the payee within the federation has to be known, which can be included in the bank transfer message.

5.2 Bridge to Credit Card Identity Federation

When considering a credit card payment using SET, as described in Section 4.2, the federation bridge has to interrupt the communications between Cardholder, Merchant and Acquirer.

If money is transferred from a participant of the SAML-based payment federation to an SET-enabled federation, the payer requests a SAML Payment Assertion at his/her Payment Provider and sends it to the federation bridge. However, to be able to send an SET-supported message, the federation bridge further needs the merchant's certificate, acquirer's payment gateway certificate and information about the order and payment as well as the merchant's access point. Since the payer should be aware of this information, they have to be provided to the federation bridge by himself/herself. As soon as the federation bridge has received the payment assertion and the additional information, it requests an assertion reimbursement at the accordant Payment Provider and the money will be transferred to the federation bridge's account. Afterwards, the federation bridge uses the merchant's public key to encrypt the order information and the acquirer's payment gateway public key to encrypt the payment information, using its own credit card data. After that, the federation bridge sends the message, which now conforms to the SET format, to the merchant. The merchant, in turn, will proceed with the usual steps for an SET-based credit card payment.

If money is transferred from an SET-enabled federation to a participant within a SAML-based payment federation, the federation bridge has to be established with a merchant's credit card interface. The payer is provided by the payee with the usual SET information, but the federation bridge is specified as being the merchant. Therefore, the payer encrypts the offer information, provided by the payee, with the federation bridge's public key and the payment information with the public key of that payment gateway defined by the federation bridge's acquirer. Now, the SET message is sent to the federation bridge, combined with additional information belonging to the offer data and the payee's identity within the SAML-based payment federation, which was already given to the payer by the payee. When the federation bridge receives such a message, it proceeds with the usual SET payment steps and sends the encrypted payment data to the specified acquirer's payment gateway. Then, the federation bridge requests a SAML Payment Assertion at its Payment Provider and sends this assertion to the payee.

To summarize: the federation bridge needs additionally the payee's certificate, the acquirer's payment gateway certificate, the offer information, the payment data and the payee's access point to translate a SAML Payment Assertion into an SET message. If an SET message has to be translated into a payment assertion, the federation bridge has to know the payee's identity in the SAML-based payment federation.

5.3 Bridge to PayPal Identity Federation

The major step in a PayPal payment, as described in Section 4.3, is the transfer of monetary funds from one account to another in a similar fashion to that during a bank transfer.

If money is transferred from a SAML-based payment federation participant to a PayPal-enabled federation, the payer requests a SAML Payment Assertion at his/her Payment Provider, sends it to the federation bridge and informs the federation bridge about the PayPal account of the payee, which has been provided to him/her during the bargaining process. Then, the federation bridge requests assertion reimbursement at the accordant Payment Provider and credits in this way the money to its account. Now, the federation bridge has two possible solutions to proceed: firstly, it can use PayPal to transfer money from its credit card account to the payee or, secondly, it can transfer the money from its PayPal account to the PayPal account of the payee. However, whatever solution is chosen by the federation bridge, the money will be finally transferred to the payee's PayPal account.

If money is transferred from a PayPal federation to a participant of a SAML-based payment federation, the federation bridge has to be equipped with a PayPal account. During the bargaining process, the payee informs the payer about the PayPal account of the federation bridge and about his/her identity in the SAML-based payment federation. Then, the payer uses PayPal to transfer the money from his PayPal account to the PayPal account of the federation bridge and, additionally, provides the federation bridge with the identity of the payee in the SAML-based payment federation. Afterwards, the federation bridge requests a payment assertion at its Payment Provider and sends this assertion to the payee.

Therefore, such a federation bridge needs the following additional information: if money is to be transferred to a PayPal federation, the federation bridge has to know the payee's PayPal account, and if money is to be transferred from a PayPal-enabled federation to a SAML-based payment federation, the federation bridge needs the payee's identity in the SAML-based payment federation.

5.4 Bridge to Attribute Assertion Payment Identity Federation

Although payments with attribute assertions, as described in Section 4.4, and that using payment assertions is very similar, there exists some differences: the attribute assertion requires the additional attributes *merchantBits*, *pspBits*, *serviceURL*, *currencyNamespace*, and *currencyDivisor*, whilst the payment assertion approach does not require these attributes.

If money is transferred from a participant of a SAML-based payment federation to an attribute assertion payment federation, the payer has to request all the required attributes from the payee. In addition to those specified above, the identity of the payee in the attribute assertion payment federation has to be known by the payer. However, when the payer has received all required information, he/she requests a SAML Payment Assertion at his/her Payment Provider and sends it, together with the additional required information, to the federation bridge. Now, the federation bridge requests assertion reimbursement at the accordant Payment Provider and receives the monetary funds on its account. Then, it requests a SAML Attribute Assertion from a Payment Provider in the attribute assertion payment federation and includes the additional required information in its request. However, after having received the requested attribute assertion from the Payment Provider in the attribute assertion payment federation, it sends the assertion to the payee.

If money is transferred from an attribute assertion payment federation to a participant in a SAML-based payment federation, the payer is informed about the identity of the payee and then sends the requested attribute assertion combined with information about the identity of the payee to the federation bridge. The attribute assertion contains more information than is needed to request a payment assertion - the federation bridge needs only the identity of the payee in the SAML-based payment federation to request a SAML Payment Assertion at its Payment Provider. After having requested the payment assertion, the federation bridge sends the assertion to the payee.

Focusing only on the additional information, in the first case the federation bridge needs knowledge about the identity of the payee in the attribute assertion payment federation, about the merchantBits, the pspBits, the serviceURL, the currencyNamespace, and the currencyDivisor. If a payment message shall be translated from an attribute assertion payment federation to a SAML-based payment federation, only the identity of the payee in the SAML-based payment federation has to be known additionally by the federation bridge.

5.5 Bridge to SAML-Based Payment Identity Federation

Although, when bridging between two SAML-based payment federations, as described in Section 4.5, nearly all the major information remaining the same, additional information has to be considered. Whenever a money transfer is being carried out between two SAML-based payment federations, the payer has to be aware of the payee's identity in the target federation. However, if such a transfer is made, the payer requests a SAML Payment Assertion at his/her Payment Provider and sends this assertion to the federation bridge together with the payee's identity information in the target federation. Now, the federation bridge requests assertion reimbursement at the Payment Provider in the source federation and, then, requests a new SAML Payment Assertion at a Payment Provider in the target federation. This new assertion is sent to the payee, who

Table 1. Overview of additional information when bridging from/to a SAML-based payment federation

Federation	From SAML-based Payment	To SAML-based Payment
Bank Transfer	Account Number and Bank Number of the payee	Identity of the payee
Credit Card	Merchant's Certificate, Acquirer's Certificate, Payment Information, Merchant's Access Point	Identity of the payee
PayPal	PayPal Account of the payee	Identity of the payee
Attribute Assertion	Identity of the payee, merchantBits, pspBits, serviceURL, currencyNamespace, currencyDivisor	Identity of the payee
SAML-based Payment	Identity of the payee	Identity of the payee

can either request reimbursement at the accordant Payment Provider or use the assertion for further payments within the federation. Obviously, as additional information, only the identity of the payee in the target federation is required.

6 Conclusions

This paper has provided solutions to bridge between SAML-based payment federations and other payment mechanisms that may be deployed within Identity Federations. After having described the basic concepts, such as Identity Federations, federation bridges and five kinds of payment approaches for Identity Federations, an approach has been presented how to bridge between those payment approaches and the SAML-based payment approach, which has been identified as most suitable for the federation technology. Table 1 highlights the additional data required when bridging between these payment mechanisms. Therefore, this paper enables the users of SAML-based payment solutions to enhance the concept of federation bridges to not only bridge identity information, but also to bridge payment data. Having these possibilities, the SAML-based payment approach receives more benefits.

Further research could provide more capabilities of the SAML-based payment federation bridge, e.g., by examining more payment approaches than these described here. Additionally, apart from SAML-based payment, other Identity Federation payment approaches may be seen as the source of monetary transactions and, therefore, bridges between those approaches may be investigated.

Acknowledgements

The research leading to these results has received funding from the European Communitys Competitiveness and Innovation Framework Programme (CIP-ICT-PSP) under grant agreement nr. 250453 (SEMIRAMIS) [11].

References

1. Lutz, D.: Payment Processes for Identity Federations: The SAML-based Payment Approach. Shaker, Aachen (2011)
2. Internet2. About Shibboleth, http://shibboleth.internet2.edu/about.html (last visited: May 9, 2009)
3. Maler, E., Mishra, P., Philpott, R.: Bindings and Profiles for the OASIS Security Assertion Markup Language (SAML) /security (2003), http://www.oasis-open.org/committees (last visited: May 19, 2009)
4. Wason, T., et al.: Liberty ID-FF Architecture Overview, http://www.projectliberty.org/resource_center/specifications/liberty_alliance_id_ff_1_2_specifications (last visited: May 19, 2009)
5. Cantor, S., Kemp, J., Champagne, D.: Liberty ID-FF Bindings and Protocol Specification, http://www.projectliberty.org/resource_center/specifications/liberty_alliance_id_ff_1_2_specifications (last visited: May 19, 2009)
6. Tourzan, J., et al.: Liberty ID-WSF Web Services Framework Overview, http://www.projectliberty.org/resource_center/specifications/liberty_alliance_id_wsf_2_0_specifications (last visited: October 13, 2009)
7. Lockhart, H., et al.: Web Services Federation Language (WS-Federation), Version 1.1. IBM Corporation (December 2006), http://www.ibm.com/developerworks/library/specification/ws-fed/ (last visited: May 9, 2009)
8. Howlett, J., Nordh, V., Singer, W.: EduGAIN Service Definition and Policy Initial Draft, http://www.geant.net/Media_Centre/Media_Library/Media%20Library/GN3-10-081-DS3_3_1_eduGAIN_service_definition_and_policy.pdf (last visited: January 14, 2011)
9. Leitold, H.: Challenges of eID Interoperability: What we learn(ed) from the STORK Journey?, http://www.cs.kau.se/IFIP-summerschool/slides/herbert.pdf (last visited: January 14, 2011)
10. Secure Widespread Identities for Federated Telecommunications (SWIFT), http://www.ist-swift.org/ (last visited: January 21, 2011)
11. SEMIRAMIS project: Semiramis Website, http://www.semiramis-cip.eu/ (last visited: January 11, 2011)
12. Mann, R.: Payment Systems and other Financial Transactions. Aspen Publishers, Inc., New York (2006)
13. IBM International Technical Support Organization. Secure Electronic Transactions: Credit Card Payment on the Web in Theory and Practice. Redbook, IBM Corporation (June 1997)
14. PayPal Inc. The PayPal Website, https://www.paypal.com (last visited: May 19, 2009)
15. Nokia Corporation, SUN Microsystems. Deploying Mobile Web Services using Liberty Alliance's Identity Web Services Framework (ID-WSF). White Paper.
16. Fulup Ar Foll. Liberty Alliance - From Usecases to Specifications. Sun Microsystems.
17. Jennings, C., Jun, G.: Payment for Services in Session Initiation Protocol (SIP) 2007, http://www.ietf.org/ID.html (last visited: May 19, 2007),
18. Ragouzis, N., et al.: Security Assertion Markup Language (SAML) V2.0 Technical Overview (October 2006), http://www.oasis-open.org/committees/download.php/14361/sstc-saml-tech-overview-2.0-draft-08.pdf (last visited: May 19, 2009)
19. Cantor, S.: at al. Assertions and Protocols for the OASIS Security Assertion Markup Language (SAML) V2.0 (2005), http://docs.oasis-open.org/security/saml/v2.0/ (last visited: March 17, 2009)

ERP Implementation's Risk Factors in State Owned Company in Post-Socialist Transitioning Country

Adnan Kraljić, Denis Delismajlović, and Tarik Kraljić

Information Technology Department
International Burch University
Sarajevo, Bosnia and Herzegovina
{akraljic,tkraljic,ddelismajlovic}@ibu.edu.ba

Abstract. The main objective of this paper is to present the ERP implementation's risk factors in state owned company in post-socialist transitioning country as Bosnia and Herzegovina is. Paper will treat selected risks factors according to their impact on implementation process. This study presents observations/remarks based on experience of authors in ERP implementation projects in public sector in Bosnia and Herzegovina. This paper aims to generate list of ERP implementation factors that will provide structural knowledge for all stakeholders involved in the process of ERP implementation in public sector. Also it could be approached as a ground base for professionals to foster its implementation practices and focus on critical factors.

Keywords: enterprise resource planning (ERP), implementation, owned company, post socialist transitioning country, Critical Risk Factors (CRFs).

1 ERP in General

One of the most significant concepts in today's business information systems is Enterprise systems (ES), also known as Enterprise Resource Planning systems (ERP). ERP can be defined as software architecture designed in order to expedite the information flow as well as the information sharing between various departments in a company, and also to provide to decision-makers an enterprise-wide view of all information that they may need to assist them in decision-making. So, the main feature of ERP is computer-based integration of the whole organization into one system and database. It means that the data entered in one module of the system are automatically available for other organization's functions, which allows higher efficiency (i.e. data are entered only once in the system), as well as real-time reporting.

Many people often think that ERP is software. No, it is not. ERP is a concept. It is an enterprise-wide set of management tools that balance demand and supply, link customers and suppliers into a complete supply chain, providing high degrees of cross-functional integration among all business functions. Indeed, ERP is commonly implemented by a complete set of applications with the use of single, unified database to store data for various modules. [2] The target of each ERP implementation in organization is to benefit by improving business operations and ease decision making

E. Ariwa and E. El-Qawasmeh (Eds.): DEIS 2011, CCIS 194, pp. 187–196, 2011.

process. Shang and Seddon (2002) [3] created a framework to sum up the benefits from enterprise systems (including ERP systems). The benefits of an ERP system can be classified into five different dimensions:

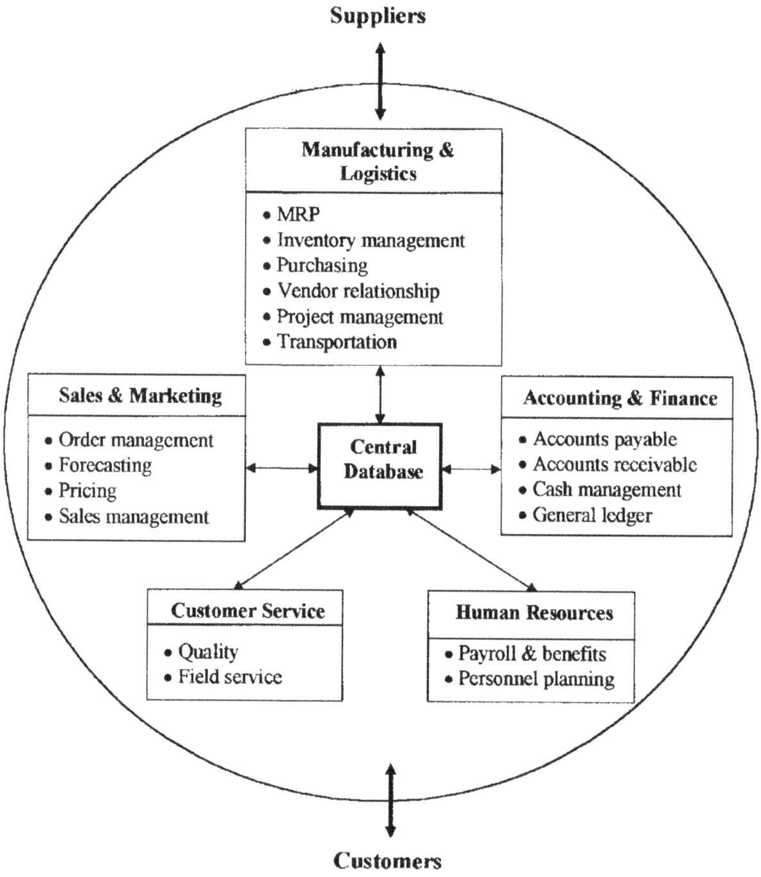

Fig. 1. An overview of ERP system [1]

(1) *Operational benefits*: Generally, the purpose of ERP system is automation of business processes. Often ERP implementation is seen as prerequisite for business process changes, in other words, business process reengineering. It is expected to provide the benefits in terms of cost decrease, cycle time reduction, productivity improvement, quality and service improvement. According to Shang and Seddon this is the most important benefit – improving core business functionalities. It is ground base for all other benefits listed in next paragraphs.

(2) *Managerial benefits*: With ERP system organization may achieve better asset management; improve decision making process and planning. Technical benefit of

implementing modern ERP system is centralized database system that provides integrated view of the organization. Data integration is prerequisite for relevant managerial reports, and relevant decision making process.

(3) *Strategic benefits*: ERP system could provide benefits for supporting business growth, business acquisitions, cost management and external linkages. However, this is theoretical approach of Shang and Seddon framework of summarize benefits. In practice, ERP implantation struggles to provide this strategic benefit to company. There is no standardized way to measure this aspect of ERP implementation.

(4) *IT infrastructure benefits*: ERP system provides business agility and flexibility for current and future changes; IT costs cut, IT infrastructure improvement. This is the benefit which can be provided very fast with current technologies and availability oftechnology (servers, routers, cables etc.), and it is really tangibleasset of ERP implementation.

(5) *Organizational benefits*: ERP system should improve working patterns, improve business processes, empower workers and build common vision. This is the part of ERP implementation that emphasis the idea of ERP not as a software but rather a concept. ERP as software can fulfill organizational needs completely, but it does not mean that it will improve organization's process, working patterns, and organization's vision.

In general an implementation is seen as successful if it is completed within budget and time with meeting all the implementation deliverables as measured by ROI, KPIs etc. In any ERP implementation lots of variables are involved like personnel (business side, technical side, support side, users), implementation partner (for example local integration software PeopleSoft, JD Edwards, Salesforce.com etc.), and implementation strategy. [4] With a number of issues that arise together, in a few months to a year or so for implementation, it is important to address critical factors that shape an implementation. Also, as we mentioned previously, it is important not to underestimate the nature of public institution and all bureaucracy you have cope with during the implementation.

2 CRFs in General

CRFs have been analyzed by various authors in several academic papers. Sumner classifies specific risk factors for implementing ERP. Summary of Sumner's research [5]:

In another research done by Huang et al. 28 risk factors are defined and those factors are categorized into the six risk factor clusters previously recognized by Sumner. The authors then made survey among 198 members of a Chinese Enterprise Resource Planning Society (CERPS) and prioritize the risk factors. The results were analyzed and resulted in the following table [6]:

Table 1. Risk factors by Sumner

Risk category	Risk factor	Unique to ERP
Organizational fit	Failure to redesign business processes	Yes
	Failure to follow an enterprise-wide design which supports data integration	Yes
Skill mix	Insufficient training and reskilling	Yes
	Insufficient internal expertise	Yes
	Lack of business analysts with business and technology knowledge	Yes
	Failure to mix internal and external expertise effectively	Yes
	Lack of ability to recruit and retain qualified ERP systems developers	
Management structure and strategy	Lack of senior management support	
	Lack of proper management control structure	
	Lack of a champion	
	Ineffective communications	
Software systems design	Failure to adhere to standardized specifications which the software supports	Yes
	Lack of integration	Yes
User involvement and	Insufficient training of end-users	
training	Ineffective communications	
	Lack of full-time commitment of customers to project management and project activities	
	Lack of sensitivity to user resistance	
	Failure to emphasize reporting	
Technology planning/integration	Inability to avoid technological bottlenecks	
	Attempting to build bridges to legacy applications	Yes

Following their claim, we can also conclude that public owned companies in countries like Bosnia and Herzegovina can have specific risk factors that can be crucial in ERP project implementation.

Table 2. Top ten risk factors of ERP risk

1.	Lack of senior manager commitment to project
2.	Ineffective communications with users
3.	Insufficient training of end-user
4.	Fail to get user support
5.	Lack of effective project management methodology
6.	Attempting to build bridges to legacy applications
7.	Conflicts between user departments
8.	The composition of project team member
9.	Fail to redesign business process
10.	Unclear/Misunderstanding changing requirements

3 Country Specific Issues of Public Sector

Although the ERP term is usually associated to manufacturing companies and processes, it has become quite common in the public sector as well. In Bosnia and Herzegovina there are also some big public sector companies that implemented an ERP or are in the process of implementation. According to SAP User Community in Bosnia and Herzegovina SAP ERP is the main ERP vendor for big public companies. If it could be useful information for someone we will name those companies: EPBiH, BH Telecom, JP EPHZ HB, HT Mostar, Clinical center University of Sarajevo. All those companies are big companies with thousands of employees. It is important to stress this "huge" because researchers have concluded that small and medium organizations have distinctive and unique needs compared to large organizations (Raymond 1985; DeLone 1988; Lai 1994) and therefore, the research findings of large organizations cannot be generalized to small to mid-sized firms. [7][8][9] Also implementation in huge and public companies has set of specific critical risk factors that are often not properly address during the implementation phase and could cause an implementation failure. In next paragraph we will describe more specifically public sector in Bosnia and Herzegovina.

One of the issues of public sector in Bosnia and Herzegovina is very complex stakeholder structure due to political system as a result of post conflict situation. (Dayton and Paris political agreement resulted in four different levels of government – 14 governments, 180 ministers; 1 prime minister per 300 000 people, one the most complex and expensive governmental body in the world). According to the 2005 CMI report, this bloated public sector accounts for 54% of the annual GDP - more than in any other European country. [10] These different layers of government produced confusion over legislature and competencies and generate a heavily administrative system that lacks transparency and provides many opportunities for abuse of office and diversion of public funds.

Another issue is widely spread corruption as a one of the common characteristics of post socialist developing country. After the war in Bosnia and Herzegovina and privatization which was proceed doubtfully and obscure hundreds of state owned companies finished in bankruptcy. However, still few state owned companies, mainly utility and telecom companies, are the backbone of country's economy. Unfortunately,

Table 3. The proposed critical risk factors for public companies in Bosnia and Herzegovina

Phase	Risk factors	Unique to state owned companies
Planning	• ***Lack of top management support*** • Lack of a proper management structure for the project • Lack of a champion • Lack of strategy for IT development of organization	• Inadequate tendering procedure • Incompetent team members for defining requirements • Corruption and bribery involved in decision making process
Implementation	• Failure to redesign business processes • Failure to follow an enterprise-wide design that supports data integration • Lack of 'business' analysts • Failure to adhere to standardized speciation which the software supports • Lack of data integration • Insufficient training and reskilling of the IT workforce in new • maintenance technology • Insufficient 'internal' expertise • Failure to mix internal and external expertise effectively • Unsuccessful attempts to integrate ERP with legacy applications	• Time consuming decision making flow process (from bottom to top) • Working habits of management and employees. • Legislation changes due to often law adjustments to EU • Non business oriented environment (life time employment, its better not to work rather to work and make mistake, no evaluation of work) • Business processes inherited from past with no initiative for improvements
Use and maintenance	• Inadequate support	• Lack of local support • Lack of investment in further employee education (corruption could be reason)

public sector in Bosnia and Herzegovina is very complex and due to the last surveys one of the most corrupted in Europe, especially in its employment policy. The country routinely performs very poorly in **TI's Corruption Perceptions Index (CPI)**. In 2009, consistent with previous iterations of the index, Bosnia and Herzegovina scored 3, 0 on a scale of 0 (highly corrupt) to 10 (highly clean), ranking 99 out of the 180 countries assessed, suggesting widespread and endemic forms of corruption. [11]

As mentioned previously 54% of GDP is consisted of public sector what implies the importance of this sector and long term consequences if fraud is part of it. Same report states that corruption pattern in Bosnia and Herzegovina is characterized by (a) high level of public concern with corruption, (b) low level of public trust in the governments, (c) state capture and conflict of interest, (d) public administration inefficiencies reflected in widespread bribery in public offices, (e) distorted business environment and (f) a significant burden on poor households, exacerbating poverty and inequality. Public tenders (defined by public procurement law) could provide opportunity for corruption if they are done with a lack of transparency. [12] Also process of choosing the bid winner is complex with not strict definition of vendor selection criteria. According to the World Bank report, in the most cases in Bosnia and Herzegovina, tender policy is that price values for more than 70% of possible points that vendor can earn. This leads to artificially low price that ensures wining the bid, but do not ensure the quality of service.

4 Strives in Public

To conduct this paper we used qualitative methods, including contact with employees of companies that implemented ERP system and author's observations as participants of several ERP implementations in public sector companies in Bosnia and Herzegovina (conducted in period of two years). We focused our research on specific critical risk factors for public companies in Bosnia and Herzegovina. Obviously we could not segregate the influence of ex socialist society factors that are incorporated in public companies in Bosnia and Herzegovina. Although, the use of perceptual measures in assessment of specific critical risk factors of ERP implementation could be in the literature described as subjective we are sure that it can provide thoughtful insight in this specific topic. We have listed Critical Risk Factors in following table.

5 Research Results

Inadequate tendering procedure - The Public Procurement Law adopted in 2004 generally complies with the main principles of the EU public procurement system. [13] However, in practice procurement process for public companies still provide significant space for fraud. One of the most questionable aspects of public tendering law is determining price as the most important factor in bidding. So winning the bid is based significantly, if not exclusively on price. This leads to artificially dropping the price of some offers so companies are in the risk to become uncompetitive if the price is set according to the real market price for the project scope. In this case the offer with the lowest price will win the bid, but the quality of proposed solution is questionable and, as it is sometimes happening in practice, it results in over-budgeting of the ERP implementation project and project delay.

Incompetent team members responsible for defining requirements and deliverables in tendering documentation – By law, tender documentation provided by public company in Bosnia and Herzegovina must be prepared by in-house commission consisted from employees who have knowledge and experience to define the needs and requirements for their organization. Also, if project is significant and the nature of company does not provide in-house experts, company is allowed to involve third party consulting company in order to provide appropriate tendering documentation. In practice, both, company employees and third party consultants, could be unskilled for the role they are in charge, so they provide poor requirements and deliverables definition in tendering documentation. For example, in one project in Bosnia and Herzegovina, third party consulting company made an estimation of the number of SAP licenses needed for the organization. However, during the project the number of licenses needed raised over 3 times. It had direct effect on budget and time scope of project.

Corruption involved in decision making process - The country routinely performs very poorly in TI's Corruption Perceptions Index (CPI). In 2009, consistent with previous iterations of the index, Bosnia and Herzegovina scored 3, 0 on a scale of 0 (highly corrupt) to 10 (highly clean), ranking 99 out of the 180 countries assessed, suggesting widespread and endemic forms of corruption. [14] It is not unusual that decision making body (formed by executive managers), in tendering procedure, after the presentation of solutions by vendors, come with one vendor as favorite, but another vendor is chosen as a winner of the bid. Even if the decision making body made their clear statement regarding the best possible solution and vendor, the final decision can be influenced by different interest groups led by their short term benefits.

Time consuming decision making flow process (from bottom to top) – Decision making process in such companies can be very slow. One reason could be very complex and deep organization structure. Specific to some public companies is lack of using of modern information infrastructure, like e-mails.Another example is using of internal mail service for paper notices delivery.Also, the nonprofit approach is deeply rooted in employees of public companies in Bosnia and Herzegovina (no real responsibility and valuation by working achievements).

Working habits of management and employees - Bosnia and Herzegovina is a former communist country, and some of the habits from that period have remained in the public sector companies. These habits could include: no real authority of the management, work is not valuated by achievement but personal relations; there is no incentive by employees to make some efforts to improve their work environment because they are not paid by their working performance and commitment (salary is determinate by salary coefficients for each working position. Coefficient is provided by legislation and internal company HR documents and it could be steady for years). Another problem is unqualified employees with lack of knowledge and practice in business domain they are hired for. The reason for this could be corruption in employment process (some public companies advocate publicly that they prefer daughters and sons of their current employees in hiring process.

Legislation changes due to often law adjustments to EU - Legislation changes in Bosnia and Herzegovina are quite frequent. The main reason is being up to EU standards that have been required in the process of becoming EU member. Due to bigger risk of corruption, public companies can be under higher pressure then other companies.

Lack of local support - The life cycle of ERP system is more than just implementation phase. Lack of decent local support is common issue that companies are facing, and it can raise costs of support by hiring non-local consulting companies.

Also, education of employees is one of crucial point in support of companies operations. Very often managers underestimate long term benefits of employee education. It can lead to negative outputs; inadequate internal support and high cost of external support. High cost of maintenance jeopardize further ERP system improvement and investments.

6 Conclusion

As it is stated in abstract the purpose of paper is to address critical risk factors specific for ERP implementations in public sector in Bosnia and Herzegovina as a post socialist country. Exploring the literature we found a number of papers describing the critical risk factors of implementation in companies in general, but none of them considers those factors in public and post socialist environment. Additional value of this paper is author's working experience derivate from SAP ERP implementation projects in post conflict business environment. Addressing critical risk factors specific to ERP implementation in state owned and post socialist companies we provide insight in this specific environment. It could be useful in further ERP implementations and research. We could bring the effect in two main points:

- Success of each ERP implementation in state owned company is conditioned by political system and environment.
- Provided critical risk factors in ERP implementations for state owned companies could be useful for researchers and ERP integrators. Managing these risk factors could improve ERP implementation.

References

1. Sheu, C., Yen, H.R., Krumwiede, D.W.: The effect of national differences on multinational ERP implementation: an exploratory study. TQM & Business Excellence 14(6), 641–657 (2003)
2. Case #2: SAP ERP Implementation for State Owned Electricity Company, `http://julian.asia/2011/02/01/case-2-sap-erp-implementation-for-state-owned-electricity-company/`
3. Shang, S., Seddon, P.B.: Assessing and managing the benefits of Enterprise systems: The business manager's perspective (2002), `http://onlinelibrary.wiley.com/doi/10.1046/j.1365-2575.2002.00132.x/abstract`

4. Bhagwani, A.: Critical Success Factors In Implementing SAP ERP Software. An EMGT Field Project Report Submitted to the Engineering Management Program and the Faculty of the Graduate School of The University of Kansas (2009)
5. Sumner, M.: Risk factors in enterprise-wide/ERP projects, School of Business, Southern Illinois University. Journal of Information Technology 15, 317–327 (2000)
6. Huang, S.M., Chang, I.C., Li, S.H., Lin, M.T.: Assessing risk in ERP projects: Identify and prioritize the factors. Industrial Management and Data Systems 108(8), 681–688 (2004)
7. DeLone, W.H.: Firm Size and the Characteristics of Computer Use. MIS Quarterly 5(4), 65–77 (1981)
8. Raymond, L.: Organizational Characteristics and MIS Success in the Context of Small Business. MIS Quarterly 9(1), 37–52 (1985)
9. Lai, V.S.: A Survey of Rural Small Business Computer Use: Success Factors and Decision Support. Information & Management 26(6), 297–304 (1994)
10. Corruption and Anti-Corruption in Bosnia and Herzegovina (Bosnia and Herzegovina), http://www.u4.no/helpdesk/helpdesk/query.cfm?id=221
11. Corruption and Anti-Corruption in Bosnia and Herzegovina (Bosnia and Herzegovina), http://www.u4.no/helpdesk/helpdesk/query.cfm?id=221
12. Bosnia and Herzegovina Diagnostic Surveys of Corruption, World Bank, http://www1.worldbank.org/publicsector/anticorrupt/Bosnianticorruption.pdf
13. SIGMA, Support for Improvement in Governance and Management, A joint initiative of the OECD and the European Union, principally financed by the EU, http://www.sigmaweb.org/dataoecd/28/61/46401690.pdf
14. Corruption and Anti-Corruption in Bosnia and Herzegovina (Bosnia and Herzegovina), http://www.u4.no/helpdesk/helpdesk/query.cfm?id=221

Factors Influencing ERP Implementation in Australia

Joseph Dagher and Joze Kuzic

Monash University, Melbourne Australia
JosephD@netspace.net.au,
Joze.Kuzic@monash.edu

Abstract. This research investigates the Factors influencing Enterprise Resource Planning implementations in Australia. It is accomplished through five case studies conducted in five companies in Australia. Five senior managers were interviewed, each of whom was involved in ERP implementation in their respecting companies. Some of the findings of this research show that business factors are the most important cause in initiating ERP implementations within business organisations, followed with personnel and technology factors. The research has also indicated that the user engagement is very important to the success of ERP implementation, and it can have an effect on the success and failure of ERP projects.

1 Background

The implementation of an ERP system in general involves sophisticated business processes and high level of integration between various departments within the same organisation. The level of integration of applications and flows in ERP systems will enable organisations to streamline these business processes. Markus, Tanis, and Van Fenema (2000) state that ERP systems provide structured information to the whole organisation which help improve business process. ERP systems integrate these business processes using common database platforms, shared data warehouses and information. According to Davenport (1998) ERP implementations involve large groups of internal and external people.

The research shows that the ERP market in the United States alone could generate billions of dollars for ERP vendors and consulting firms (Willcocks and Sykes 2000). The trend of ERP implementation is fast growing globally and across various sectors, industries and company sizes. Off the shelves products such as SAP, PeopleSoft, Oracle, SyteLine, JD Edwards, Pronto and MFG/PRO are configurable, packaged software that provide integrated suite of information resources, systems and processes and suit a wide range of businesses and business functions and activities (Bagchi 2003, Stefanou 2001).

While ERP systems were mainly perceived to suit large corporations, the trend of Small-to-Medium Businesses ("SMB") adopting and implementing ERP systems is also growing and many vendors have developed products that fit this growing market. Australia is not an exception to this trend. The research reported in this paper looks at small to medium sized organisation (SMEs), more particularly the ERP implementation issues in them.

E. Ariwa and E. El-Qawasmeh (Eds.): DEIS 2011, CCIS 194, pp. 197–205, 2011.

2 Literature Review

ERP systems assist organisations in managing their business operations by effective management of their various functions including finance, customers, suppliers, sales, purchasing, production, distribution, warehousing and supply chain. ERP systems offer many benefits to organisations, however their implementations are complex and require a high level of coordination within functional hierarchies Markus et al (2000).

Wilder and Davis (1998) have reported that in the 1990s not many companies have completed their ERP implementation on time and on budget. There have been many publicised SAP failures which affected ERP reputations in general. Research by InformationWeek cited that the top three reasons of failures in the 1990s were poor planning or project management (77%), failure to align IT with business goals or change in business goals during the project (75%) and lack of management support (73%).

Research on ERP adoption and implementation has been divided into two major categories: organisational and technological factors (Bagchi et al 2000). Organisational factors affect the determination of adoption issues and can further be split into two set of factors: business and personnel issues. This review focuses on these issues separately despite their inseparable effect in an attempt to demonstrate the variance and importance of human factors such as user acceptance and commitment on ERP implementation, in addition to broader business factors such as culture, business processes, management support and project teams on ERP adoption.

Technological factors affect the infrastructural issues to adoption and link between human and operational sub systems which affect the outcome of ERP implementation. Technological and organisational factors are equally important to the success of ERP projects. Davenport (1998) argued that the lack of formation between human and business systems add to the risk of failure. Therefore the choice of hardware, technological infrastructure and software configuration can impact on the overall success of the project especially if they were not bring into line with the organisation's structure, strategy and operations (Markus et al 2000).

Willcocks and Sykes (2000) addressed the issue of Information Technology ("IT") to the organisation and that companies still consider IT to be a cost to the business rather than a "strategic resource". According to them such management attitude affects the overall success and failures of ERP implementation.

Failing to take note of organisational socio-technical make up of any organisation affects underlying infrastructure, culture, and interaction between organisational norms and technological development will affect the success and failure of ERP implementation plans (Davenport 1998, Pan et al 2004, Scarbrough 1999).

According to Wei et al (2005) as organisations adapt their business processes to the new ERP system, this effort of change management may cause an ERP implementation to fail to achieve the anticipated benefits. Resolving misalignment problems usually requires technological and organisational change in order to achieve full and successful ERP adaptation.

An important ERP implementation issue is the formation and structure of the project team. According to Kim & Pan (2006) a project team should attempt to strike a balance between business activities and IT activities by ensuring a cross-functional team membership and cross functional operations. Conflict between business and IT functions and operations cause a risk in ERP implementation and success (Schmidt et al 2001). The organisation should hence assign the best skilled members to participate in these cross functional project teams.

Organisational culture has also been identified as a critical factor in any ERP implementation and a successful culture will affect the overall outcome of the project (Davenport 1998, Scott and Kaindall 2000). Organisational culture has been identified as a paramount in the development of ERP project and can affect its success through its effects on ERP adoption, user commitment and communication within a team (Bagchi 2003, Davenport 1998).

The very nature of the ERP implementation can be seen as problematic and it can affect user involvement, acceptance, participation, commitment and utilisation of ERP projects. In their research, Kawalek et al (2002) define user participation as a critical factor in determining success of ERP projects. User participation provides the implementation team with added benefits and increase rates of success. It can improve roll out success, understanding of specific functional, departmental, cultural, legacy and historical concerns and issues and help resolve them and manage them.

Users' participation and input are critical to the success of the project and cannot be isolated. Bagchi, Kanungo and Dasgupta (2003) studied links between users' attitudes and involvement and the links with ERP implementation. The authors concluded that different forms of influencers are required when marrying ERP processes with organisation processes as the change created poses a difficult challenge in work, communication, workflow and information processes.

Technical issues are also an important factor in any project success especially in ERP implementation. One of the fundamental reasons in technological failures is contributed to the use of modular design in ERP systems which contradict the traditional SDLC approach. The new approach, referred to as 'operation process', involves "integrating the business internal operation information to streamlining the information flow among all functional departments" (Huang 2004, 102). This entails the implementation of vendor's ERP packaged modules to speed up implementation time and increase success. This involves aligning internal processes to fit in with the packaged ERP processes rather than the other way around.

Huang (2004) found that the major technical problems that are still facing organisations when implementing ERP systems are related to issues such as customisation and integration with existing or third party applications or software.

Factors that influence success of ERP implementation vary according to organisational type, project type, scope, ERP brand, business processes, culture, vendor, software modules, level of integration and types of data. It is paramount however to find out how these factors drive success or failure of various ERP implementations. Somers and Nelson (2001) developed a list of 22 CSFs that affect and impact on ERP implementations, following their review of 110 ERP implementation cases. CSFs vary according to organisational type, project type, scope, ERP brand, business processes, culture, vendor, software modules, level of integration and types of data. It is paramount however to find out how CSFs drive success or failure of various ERP implementations. Some of the above mentioned CSF are presented below.

Goals and objectives should be clear and specific (Akkermans et al 2002). Goals should be defined at the start of the project and should encompass the three primary objectives of project management, namely scope, time and cost (Somers et al 2001). However as ERP projects are more complex than average IT projects "it is often very difficult to determine them (goals and objectives) in a clear-cut manner" (Akkermans et al 2002, p36).

Cooperation between all departments and business units is imperative for the success of the implementation project (Stefanou 1999, Willcocks et al 2000 and Akkermans et al 2002). Zhang et al (2002) found that as ERP systems are company-wide systems, support and cooperation between all departments during implementation has a positive impact on the success of the ERP project. This is evident as ERP processes cover all functional areas and departments within the business.

The Project champion, as a member of the senior management team of the organisation (for example, the CIO, CFO or CEO), is very important as he/she plays the role of a change manager throughout the life of the project. He or she has the ability to make high level decisions and to initiate significant organisational changes (Willcocks et al 2000). According to Beath (1991) in Somers et al (2001) project champions are transformational leaders who have the power and ability to facilitate and promote the project to the rest of their organisation.

As a new ERP system is being implemented, external implementation consultants should pass on knowledge and skills of the new application, functionalities, features and processes to internal employees (project team and others). Therefore every staff member within the organisation who uses the new ERP system needs to be trained during the early stages of the implementation to ensure a smooth transition towards the end (Davenport 1998 and Summer 1999).

Failing to educate and train users in understanding the implications a new ERP system has on their business processes can disturb the ERP implementation and cause serious problems for an organisation (Crowley 1999, Esteves et al 2001 and Al-Mashari 2002). According to Zhang et al (2002, p6), training should cover "the following three aspects: logic and concepts of ERP, features of the ERP system, and hands on training". It is argued that the re-skilling and development of all users, including onsite training, in preparation of the new system is crucial (Summer 1999). Bhatti (2005, p3) noted that training should not only cover using the new system "but also new processes and understanding the integration within the system and how the work of one employee influences the work of others".

3 Research Methodology

This research was conducted within five Australian companies who implemented ERP systems in recent years. Each of the five companies belongs to small to medium size companies. Their main business is focused on sales and distribution of outsourced consumer or commercial products. The customers they are dealing with are primarily resellers and distributors. All five participating companies operate in Australia and have branches around Australia.

All five senior managers from these companies have had direct involvement in their company's ERP implementation projects. All had more than three years of experience in their positions and were involved in all phases of ERP implementation projects. An outline of the five companies and interviews is presented in Table 1.

Table 1. Summary of companies and interviews

	Company A	Company B	Company C	Company D	Company E
Interviewee	Managing Director	GM Finance & Admin	Systems Accountant	Project Manager	Group IT Manager
Number of Staff	40	130	220	75	300
Annual Turnover	< $50M	$50-$100M	$50-$100M	< $50M	>$100M
Number of IT Staff	0	2	3	5	7
Number of ERP Team	0	6	12	12	15
ERP Implemented	SAP Business One	Pronto	MFG/PRO	SAP All-In-One	Syteline
Date of Completion	Sep-07	Nov-07	Jun-05	Aug-06	Jul-03
Duration of Project	12-24 mth	<6 mth	<6 mth	<6 mth	6-12 mth
Customisation Level	High	Low	Low	Low	Low
Use of Standard Process	No	Yes	Yes	Yes	Yes
Project Outcome	Failure	Success	Success	Success	Success
Level of Success (out of 10)	4	9	9	7	10
Level of Total Satisfaction	Low	High	High	Medium	High
Met Original Expectations	No	Yes	Yes	Yes	Yes
Completion On Time	No	Yes	Yes	No	Yes
Completion On Budget	No	Yes	Yes	No	Yes
Implementation Cost	$500K-$1M	<$100K	<$100K	$500K-$1M	$500K-$1M
Cost Ratio					
Hardware	10%	0%	20%	25%	8%
Software	10%	90%	25%	20%	25%
Training	inc in Consulting	5%	5%	5%	20%
Consulting	80%	5%	50%	50%	47%
Customisation Ratio	30%	5%	10%	25%	15%

The following research questions guided this research:

1. What factors initiate the need to implement ERP in Australia?
2. To what extent project management affect success and failures of ERP projects?
3. To what extent efforts and overall users' involvement affect success and failures of ERP projects?

In respect to the question number one, each interviewee was asked to score sequentially from 1 to 3 each of the three factors (Technological, Business and Personnel) in terms of their influence in initiating the need to implement their ERP systems (1 was the most influential and 3 the least influential). Respondents' answers were entered against each of the three factors.

In respect to the second question, each interviewee was asked to give a score from 1 to 5 to each of the three project management effort questions including the efforts of both internal and external project managers (where 1 was the highest and 5 was the lowest). Answers of the five companies were entered against each of the three questions. Company averages of the three questions were calculated by dividing each company total by the total number of questions.

In respect to the third question, each interviewee was asked to give a score from 1 to 10 to each of the five users engagement questions (where 1 was the highest and 10 was the lowest). Answers of the five companies were entered against each of the five questions. Company averages of the five questions were calculated by dividing each company total by the total number of questions.

4 Findings and Discussions

Regarding the initiating factors in ERP implementation, it can be seen from Table 2 that business factors are the main drivers behind ERP implementations. Eighty percent of the cases ranked business factors as their number one driving factor.

Table 2. Influencing factors for ERP implementations

Factors	Company A	Company B	Company C	Company D	Company E	Factor TTL	Factor Ave	Factor Median
Technological	3	3	1	2	3	12	2.4	3
Business	1	1	2	1	1	6	1.2	1
Personnel	2	2	3	3	2	12	2.4	2

All five managers supported these arguments. Issues and challenges such as customer and market pressures, external forces (administrative and legislative), changes in business models, supporting expansion and growth strategies, stock management and control, advanced warehousing and shipping, standardisation of processes and meeting customer demands were some of the examples given by the interviewees.

This indicates that senior management aim to place their companies in positions where they are capable to respond and react to their external environment (being customers, suppliers, government, competition etc). It also confirms the reliance that these organisations place on information systems to provide the tools and mechanisms in an efficient and effective manner.

Personnel issues came second, indicating that companies do place a high reliance on users' satisfaction and involvement. Hence in the five ERP implementation projects, it was evident from the data collected that users' opinions and engagement were significant. All five cases had a companywide steering committee representation. Project teams worked very closely with management as well as users, involving them in project updates and engaging their interest and feedback throughout the life of the project.

The technology factor ranked as the least important factor in this organisation clearly separates systems and technology. Technology is perceived as the infrastructure or vehicle that makes everything work. As technology becomes easier and cheaper to obtain and maintain, the attitude towards it is also shifting, and it appears to be more accepted in business operations and is increasingly utilised across all staff levels. However it is also seen as easily changeable and expendable, hence it was not listed highly as a factor especially in ERP implementations.

Project management efforts in ERP projects involve three characteristics: on-time performance, on-cost performance and within scope. Data in Table 3 indicate that a low score means a higher "project management efforts" within the implementing organisation.

For the five companies in this study, this means that the closer the company's "project management efforts" are to a figure of 1, the higher the chances for ERP implementation success. Reversely, the further a result is from the number 1 figure, the higher the chances of ERP implementation failure.

Company E, for example, has rated project management efforts as well as internal project manager's effort as number 1. It has rated external project manager's effort as 2, on a scale from 1 to 5. Thus, Company E with a score of 1.3 can be said to have higher chances of project success than company A with a score of 3.7. The three remaining companies B, C and D scored an almost similar result in their project management efforts. Therefore it can be noted that their project management efforts should enable them success in their implementation efforts. While company D did face some issues with increases in cost, this did not however prevent the final success of the project. The analysis of the data indicates that it can be concluded that project management efforts have an effect on the success and failure of ERP projects.

Table 3. Project Management Efforts

Project Management Efforts: 1-5 (highest to lowest)	Company A	Company B	Company C	Company D	Company E
How do you define the project management efforts?	4	1	1.5	2	1
How do you define the internal project manager's efforts?	4	1	1	2	1
How do you define the external project manager's efforts?	3	3	2	1	2
Average	3.7	1.7	1.5	1.7	1.3

User engagement in ERP projects involves characteristics such as users' participation, acceptance, involvement and current utilisation. Data in Table 4 indicate that a low score means a higher "user engagement" within the implementing organisation.

For the five companies in this study, it meant that the closer the company's "user engagements" is to a figure of 1, the higher the chances for the success of the ERP implementation. Conversely, the further the score is a figure of 1, the higher the chances of ERP implementation failure.

Table 4. Users Involvement

Users Involvement: 1-10 (highest to lowest)	Company A	Company B	Company C	Company D	Company E
Overall users' participation?	n/a	3	3	3	1
Overall users' acceptance (pre & post)?	6	2	2	4	2
Overall users' commitment (pre, during & post)?	7	3	3	2	4
Overall users' involvement (pre & during)?	7	3	3	2	2
Overall users' current utilisation?	4	1	1	2	1
Average	6	2.4	2.4	2.6	2

Company E with a score of 2 can be said to have higher chances of project success than company A with a score of 6. This was also an issue as company A had no staff at the time of the implementation. The three remaining companies B, C and D scored another close result to each other, namely 2.6 and 2.4 respectively. Therefore it can be noted that their user engagement should enable them to succeed in their implementation efforts. It can therefore be concluded that user engagements have an effect on the success and failure of ERP projects.

5 Conclusions and Further Research

This research analysed five Australian companies who recently implemented ERP systems. It aimed to further understand the complexity of ERP systems implementation. The research has highlighted that business factors are the most important cause in initiating ERP implementations within business organisations, followed with personnel and technology factors.

The research has also indicated that project management efforts in all companies should enable them success in their implementation efforts.

Finally, the research has indicated that the user engagement is very important to the success of ERP implementation, and it can have an effect on the success and failure of ERP projects.

This research included five organisations who have similar business models but who do not operate in the same industry. Future research may replicate this study using specific industries and evaluating trends that are specific to these industries or sectors. Furthermore, this research examined implementations of five different ERP systems. Future studies may consider a vertical approach where customers of one ERP vendor are analysed and studied.

References

1. Markus, M., Tanis, C., Van Fenema, P.: Multiple ERP implementations. Communications of the ACM 43(4), 42–46 (2000)
2. Davenport, T.H.: Living with ERP. CIO Magazine 12(5), 30–31 (1998)
3. Davenport, T.H.: Mission Critical – Realising the Promise of Enterprise Systems. Harvard Business School Publishing, Boston (2000)
4. Willcocks, L.P., Sykes, R.: Enterprise resource planning: the role of the CIO and its function in ERP. Communications of the ACM 43(4), 32–38 (2000)
5. Bagchi, S., Kanungo, S., Dasgupta, S.: Modeling use of enterprise resource planning systems: a path analytic study. European Journal of Information Systems 12, 142–158 (2003)
6. Stefanou, C.: Supply chain management and organisational key factors for successful implementation of enterprise resource planning (ERP) systems. In: Proceeding of the American Conference on Information Systems, Milwaukee, WI, pp. 800–802 (1999)
7. Stefanou, C.J.: A framework for the ex-ante evaluation of ERP software. (online copy, 2001)
8. Wilder, C., Davis, B.: False starts, strong finishes. InformationWeek, 41–53 (November 30, 1998)
9. Pan, S.L., Flynn, D.: De-escalation of commitment to information systems projects: a process perspective. Journal of Strategic Information Systems 13(3), 247–270 (2004)

10. Wei, H., Wang, E., Ju, P.: Understanding misalignment and cascading change of ERP implementation: a stage view of process analysis. European Journal of Information Systems 14, 324–334 (2005)
11. Kim, H.W., Pan, S.L.: Towards a process Model of Information Systems Implementation: The Case of CRM. Database for Advances in Information Systems 37(1), 59–76 (2006)
12. Schmidt, R., Lyyntinen, K., Keil, M., Cule, P.: Identifying Software Project Risks: An international Delphi study. Journal of Management Information Systems 17(4), 5–36 (2001)
13. Scott, J.E., Kaindal, L.: Enhancing functionality in an enterprise software package. Information & Management 37, 111–122 (1998)
14. Kawalek, P., Wood-Harper, T., et al.: The Finding of Thorns: User Participation in Enterprise System Implementation. Database for Advances in Information Systems 33(1), 13–22 (2002)
15. Huang, S.M., Hung, Y.C., Chen, H.G., Ku, C.Y.: Transplanting the best practice for implementation of an ERP System: a structured inductive study of an international company. The Journal of Computer Information Systems 44(4), 101–110 (2004)
16. Somers, T., Nelson, K.: A Taxonomy of players and activities across the ERP project life cycle. Information & Management, 1–22 (2003)
17. Akkermans, H., van Helden, K.: Vicious and virtuous cycles in ERP implementation: a case study of interrelations between critical success factors. European Journal of Information Systems 11, 35–46 (2002)
18. Zhang, L., Lee, M.O., Zhang, Z., Banerjee, P.: Critical Success Factors of Entreprise Resource Planning Systems Implementations Success in China. In: Proceedings of the 364th Hawaii International Conference on System Sciences, HICSS (2002)
19. Beath, C.A.: Supporting the Information Technology Champion. MIS Quarterly 15(3), 355–372 (1991)
20. Summer, M.: Critical success factors in enterprise wide information management systems projects. In: Proceedings of the Americas Conference on Information Systems, AMCIS (1999)
21. Crowley, A.: Training Treadmill – A Rigorous Plan of End User Education is Critical to Whipping ERP Systems into Shape. PC Week Online (1999)
22. Esteves, J., Pastor, J.: Analysis of critical success factors relevance along SAP implementation phases. In: Proceedings of the 7th Americas Conference on Information Systems, Boston (2001)
23. Al-Mashari, M.: Enterprise resource planning (ERP) systems: a research agenda. Industrial Management & Data Systems 102(3), 165–170 (2002)
24. Bhatti, T.R.: Critical Success Factors for the Implementation of Enterprise Resource Planning (ERP): Empirical Validation. In: The Second International Conference on Innovation in Information Technology, p. 110 (2005)

BUSCLIS for Construction Industry

Ahmad Noraziah[1], M. Affendy Omardin[2], Noriyani Mohd Zin[1], Roslina Mohd. Sidek[1], Mohd Helmy Abd Wahab[3], and Jiwat Ram[4]

[1] Faculty of Computer Systems & Software Engineering, University Malaysia Pahang, Malaysia
[2] Faculty Civil Engineering and Earth Resources, University Malaysia Pahang, Malaysia
[3] Faculty of Electric & Electronic, Universiti Tun Hussein Onn Malaysia
[4] University of Adelaide, Australia
noraziah@ump.edu.my

Abstract. In this research, we focus on software namely Building Submission Checklist System (BuSCLIS) that has been developed to be use in construction industry. An objective of developing BuSCLI is to simplify the management of submission data of building plan approval through online system for the Local Authority (LA) or State Town and Country Planning in Malaysia. We presents the data management of the system through the data dictionary include login, user, contractor, consultant, checklist, location and project. BuSCLI facilitates user by computerized the forms and provide fast, efficient, transparent, effective service to the engineer, architect and contractor. Relevant and timely information managed by sophisticated BuSCLI with the database management system, MySQL.

Keywords: BuSCLIS, building plan, RAD, data dictionary.

1 Introduction

A mechanism is required to promote knowledge sharing among its diverse industry players. To set up a knowledge database for the construction industry would require a huge amount of resources especially in the application of information and communication technology or ICT. Regardless of the potential of Enterprise Resource Planning systems to increase productivity and internal ICT efficiency, construction companies hesitate to adopt these ICT solutions [1]. The construction sector is also not making full use of the potential of collaborative systems for information sharing and coordination with external partners while construction companies do not take advantage of ICT solutions for digital information exchange and sharing documents on-line. Therefore mostly of activities or process in construction industry still using conventional system. The construction industry has been one of the last industries to harness the power of information and communication technology (ICT). With the view that construction is a business like others and clients now expect quality product, this perception should begin to change. Advance in ICT are causing dramatic changes in construction and built environment. Using ICT may helps construction industry such as facilitate integration of various processes in the construction, standardization

E. Ariwa and E. El-Qawasmeh (Eds.): DEIS 2011, CCIS 194, pp. 206–217, 2011.

of information and faster and fewer flow of information in industry. Most activities or processes in construction industry still using conversional system. Because of utilizing of ICT become wisely, some changes need to do in activities and process in constructions industry.

In Malaysia, application of ICT become wisely because rapid developments of computer technologies have change the way of working environment. To assist in the process, the utilization of ICT and automated software can provide efficiency and effective solutions to the problems of mass data and information handling [1,2]. Object-oriented software engineering methodology the idea object model for the business relates to the use case model of the supporting information system [2]. One of the changes that have to make in construction industry is submission of building plan approval checklist. Before the advent of system, organization kept all their data in manual or conventional files. Basically, the manual system workflow is very inefficient and ineffective. Submission of building plan approval in manual use many forms and consumes time. Thus, it is error prone in endorsement the form.

The need for the system arises as the result of set problem faced by user in the conventional system way of performing the related task. Using conventional system, there are some problems happened. The current practice of a construction project, which involves submission of building checklist plans to the local or municipal authority for approval, is a very tedious and time-consuming process. The time involved can range from weeks to months until the approval time. Besides, Local Authority did not save any data regarding to their client. The submission of checklist process of the building plans to the relevant authorities will require several forms before submission. Such as, standard checklist for building plan approval which accordance to building categories, the fees for temporary building and other forms that related. This will waste time and sometimes user makes mistakes by fulfill the wrong document. User has to bring bundle of checklist paper and related document to be checked. This will damage the papers if it is in bad condition (rainy day) or may lost some of the checklist. By using conventional system, user cannot view the updated report for the approval submission. They have to wait until the approval time.

In this paper, we focus on the software namely Building Submission Checklist System (BuSCLI). BuSCLI facilitate users by computerized all the forms accordance to the building categories, submission, endorsement or approval through online. Heuristic and software engineering method are deployed while developing this system.

2 Literature Review

The submission of building plans to the local or municipal authority for approval in the current practice of a construction project is a very tedious and time-consuming process. The compliance process of the building plans to the relevant authorities require the authorities involved to check in particulars on the building plan for building by-laws non-compliance [8].

Building Plan Approval: Building plan approval is a stage of the approval process spans a whole range of legislative and procedural rules and requirements and necessitates the input of a host of professionals, designer and specialist. There are some variations in the submission and approval procedures between the different States although in the final analysis the basic requirement and steps quite similar [3]. In Malaysia the development approval process involves principally the following main stages which are:

- Land use conversion and subdivision approval stage
- Planning permission or Development Order approval stage
- Building plan approval stage
- Construction monitoring and enforcement stage
- Certificate of fitness for occupancy approval stage
- Maintenance and management stage

The authorities involved in the approval process, these are dictated by the locality of the project, whether it is State or city based, as the difference in the relevant authorities. A common list of such authorities would include Agriculture Department, Department of Environment, Department of Civil Aviation, District Land Office, Fire Service Department, Local Planning Authority and others related authorities.

An **electronic Submission** (or **e-Submission**) is an existing computerized system. It is a set of registration files submitted in electronic form during an approval or variation or renewal procedure (Centralized, National, Mutual, And Decentralized). It could be a set of files (Portable Document Format (.pdf), Microsoft® Word files (.doc) or Rich Text Format (.rtf) and picture files like jpeg, or png, etc.) usually submitted in folders. The basic concept of the e-submission is to enable the public to submit planning application to the Local Authority (LA) or State Town and Country Planning and receive the answer via the electronic or Internet. This process will minimize human contacts thus provide fast, efficient, transparent and effective service to the public [3]. The effectiveness with which this process activities is undertaken depend on the availability and appropriate utilization of information of different types which are obtain from various sources.

In Malaysia, the electronic environment is picking up pace rapidly with the implementation and development of the electronic hub of Malaysia, the Multimedia Super Corridor (MSC). Several systems that related to submission and approval system has been reviewed. Some of another system also reviewed to know the system characteristic, provided facilities, and module in the system. The systems are E-submission [3], E-government [4] and CWorks [5]. E-submission system is a web application system which all the submission through online system. One of the applications is e-Bangunan which is implemented in the Majlis Perbandaran Sepang (MPS).

MPS takes advantage of ICT's benefits and Geography Information System (GIS) to develop a system to ease user deal with them. E-Bangunan used by people who involved in submission of building plan with MPS. Several modules have been develop to make the system meets the user needed and make the process and activities in submission and approval become more efficient. This system allowed user to make application on new project and review the current status of their application in MPS through online. E-government is a web application system. It has improved both how the government operates internally as well as how it delivers services to the people of Malaysia. It seeks to improve the convenience, accessibility and quality of interactions with citizens and businesses; simultaneously, it will improve information flows and processes within government to improve the speed and quality of policy development, coordination and enforcement. Poorly, E-government have some problems in security, credibility and technology knowledge. CWorks Free is a Computerized Maintenance Management System (CMMS). It is a Maintenance Software for Plant and Facility Management and its stand alone system that did not use internet. Its purpose is to ease people start on maintenance software to track and record their maintenance activities. Fig. 1 shows the main page of E-government, while Fig. 2 shows the main page of CWorks.

Fig. 1. Main page of E-government

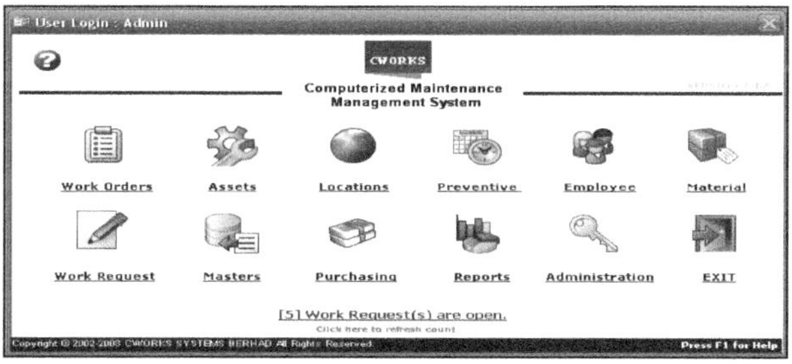

Fig. 2. Main page of CWorks

The submission process of the building plans to the relevant authorities will require the authorities involved to check in details on the building design for building by-laws non-compliance [6]. The Submission System of Urban Construction Archives (SSOUCA) [7] is a software that now used by the Urban Construction Archives Agency of Shaoguan City and Zhenjiang City of China. It is developed with Windows Presentation Foundation (WPF) technology. WPF act as a fundamental platform in running SSOUCA. The WPF supports both online and offline work and is very suitable to be based on developing remote submission system. The platform of web server system used in SSOUCA is ASP.Net 3.5 and IIS 6.0, and one open source of WebGIS server is MapGuide used to render the spatial information within submitted archived. OpenLayers 2.8 is one of the open source Geographical Information System (GIS) viewer in JavaScript, is used to present archive map in the browser. The flow of the complete submission process is illustrated in Fig. 3.

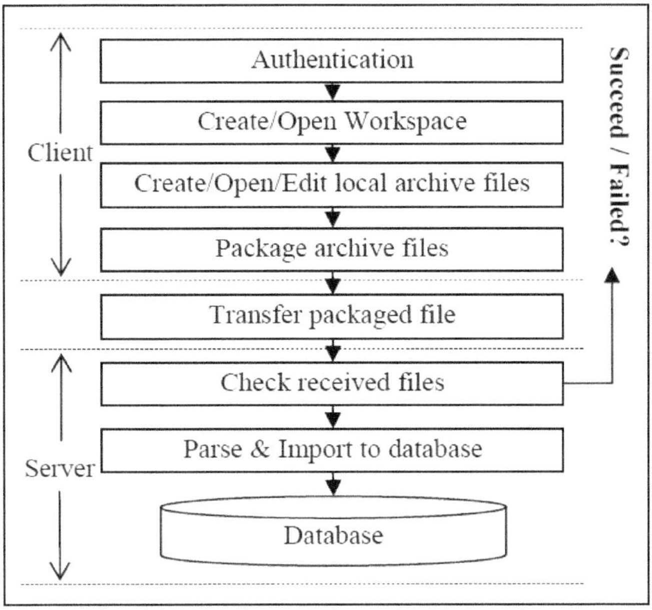

Fig. 3. Flowchart of the SSOUCA System

In [8] opportunities of IT in construction industry of Iran are investigated in three categories. There are pre-construction phase, construction phase and earthquake disaster mitigation. Studies show that information technology can be used in these items for reducing the losses and increasing the benefits [8]. Through management of documents that provides information about all aspects of project and to determine how processes can be managed to greatest effect using concurrent engineering frameworks. It is necessary to understand the performance and behavior of the structures during the earthquake and consequences arising after structures damage and IT can be used as a tool for educating people and minimizing the losses of earthquake [8].

3 Methodology

Rapid Application Development (RAD) is one of methodology development lifecycle designed to give much faster development and higher quality than the traditional lifecycle [9]. It includes developing and refining the data models, process models, and prototype in parallel using an iterative process. RAD methodology was chosen in developing BuSCLI system because:

Time constraint: Request from the users of the system estimate the development of the system between three to four months. Since submission of the applications and checklists is main thing in order to get approval for development of building, users needs the system develop as fast as possible to ease the process and activities submission and approval of customer projects. RAD methodology design for a faster development and higher quality because RAD model provides "high-speed" development process.

Medium size of system: BuSCLI is developing for OSC staff in MPK and people that involved in the construction industry such as contractor, consultant and architect.

Ability to identify and repair problems in early stage: In developing this system, developer and user are worked together to get the best result of the system, therefore, if user needs changes on the requirement, developer will do the changes at any stages to fulfill the user requirement. This method improved working relationship and trust between developers and clients in order to get the best system result and the system meets the user requirement. RAD consists of four phases as shown in Fig. 4.

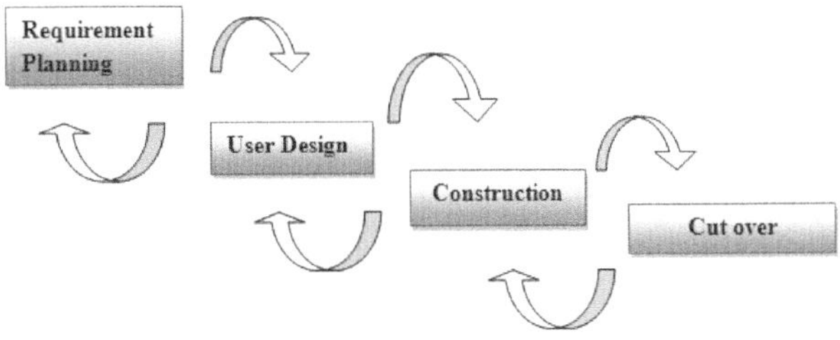

Fig. 4. Rapid Application Development (RAD)

4 System Description

Building Submission Checklist System (BuSCLI) is a web application system which develops for staffs in Operational Submission Center (OSC) in Majlis Perbandaran Kuantan (MPK), Malaysia. This computerized system helps user in manage the submission of checklist for building plan by user such as contractor, architect, and engineer in construction industry.

The objectives of this project are:

i) To develop Building Submission Checklist System for Operational Submission Centre (OSC);
ii) To generate updated report on submission approval.

Meanwhile, the scopes of this project include:

a) Main user for this system is Operational Submission Centre‘s staff in Local Authority (LA) in Majlis Perbandaran Kuantan (MPK) where One Stop Centre will handle all the submission of building plan;
b) Contractor in construction industry.

Using programming language PHP and MySQL database, this system is an online system, where user sharing their data using internet. Other software had been used include xampp as Apache Web Server to support the database, Acrobat Professional to design the interface for the form and Microsoft Word and Microsoft Project to make documents.

5 System Design

Computerize system is more reliable and accurate. Data analysis will be process very fast and safe. But most software is delicate: even the slightest error, such as changing a single bit, can make it crash [10]. Thus, development techniques emphasis on *design* should be managed correctly to overcome this fragility [11]. In particular, to make a clearer understanding on how data management of BuSCLI, we present its data dictionary. The Data dictionary or data repository is a central storehouse of information about the system's data. Data dictionary is used to collect data. The data dictionary also defines and describes all data elements and meaningful combinations of element. There are seven (7) tables exist in BUSCLI which are the login, user, contractor, consultant, checklist, location and project. These tables hold the data that is related. Table 1 – Table 7 show data dictionary and the items that are defined in BuSCLI system.

Table 1. Login Data Dictionary

Field Name	Description	Data Type	Data size
userID	User ID	Varchar	8
Pass	User Password	Varchar	6
UserLevel	User level	Int	-

Table 2. User Data Dictionary

Field Name	Description	Data Type	Data size
LG_ID (FK)	User ID	Varchar	6
Password	User Password	Varchar	6
Nama	User Name	Varchar	30
Alamat	User Address	Varchar	30
Notelefon	User Contact No	Int	10
NoTelefo Bimbit	User Contact No	Int	10
Poskod	User Postcode	Int	5

Table 3. Contractor Data Dictionary

Field Name	Description	Data Type	Data size
No_projek (FK)	No of project	Varchar	20
No_daftarpemaju (PK)	Contractor_ID	Varchar	6
Nama_pemaju	User IC No	Int	12

Table 4. Consultant Data Dictionary

Field Name	Description	Data Type	Data size
No_daftar_perunding (PK)	No of Consultant	Varchar	10
Nama_syarikat	Name of company	Varchar	12
Nama_perunding	Consultant name	Varchar	50
No_projek (FK)	Project no	Varchar	10
Nokeahlian	Member no of consultant	Date	

Table 5. Checklist Data Dictionary

Field Name	Description	Data Type	Data size
CK_RefFileNo (PK)	Reference File No of checlist	Varchar	25
CK_BuildTypes	Types of Building	Varchar	
CK_BuildFileNo	Building file No	Varchar	20
CK_Noitem	No of Document in checklist	Varchar	

Table 6. Location Data Dictionary

Field Name	Description	Data Type	Data size
L_ID (PK)	Location ID	Int	10
No_projek (FK)	Application Fail No	Int	10
Mukim	District of location	Varchar	
Bandar	Town location	Varchar	
Nolot	Location Lot Number	Int	6
Keluasan lot	Size of lot	float	
Namapemiliklot	Owner name	varchar	50
Jalan	Name of road	varchar	10

Table 7. Project Data Dictionary

Field Name	Description	Data Type	Data Size
No_projek (PK)	No of project	Int	10
No_daftar_pemaju	No of contractor registration	Varchar	100
Tajuk_projek	Application category	Varchar	20
Kategori_permohonan (FK)	Category of application	Date	
Tarikh_permohonan	Date of application	Int	10
No_fail_kebenaran_merancang	Category of building	Varchar	10
No_fail_kejuruteraan	No of fail engineering	Varchar	
Jenis_pembangunan	Application types	Varchar	
L_ID (FK)	Location ID	Varchar	6
Kategori_pembangunan	User IC	Int	12
Terperinci Bangunan (FK)	Details of building	Varchar	8

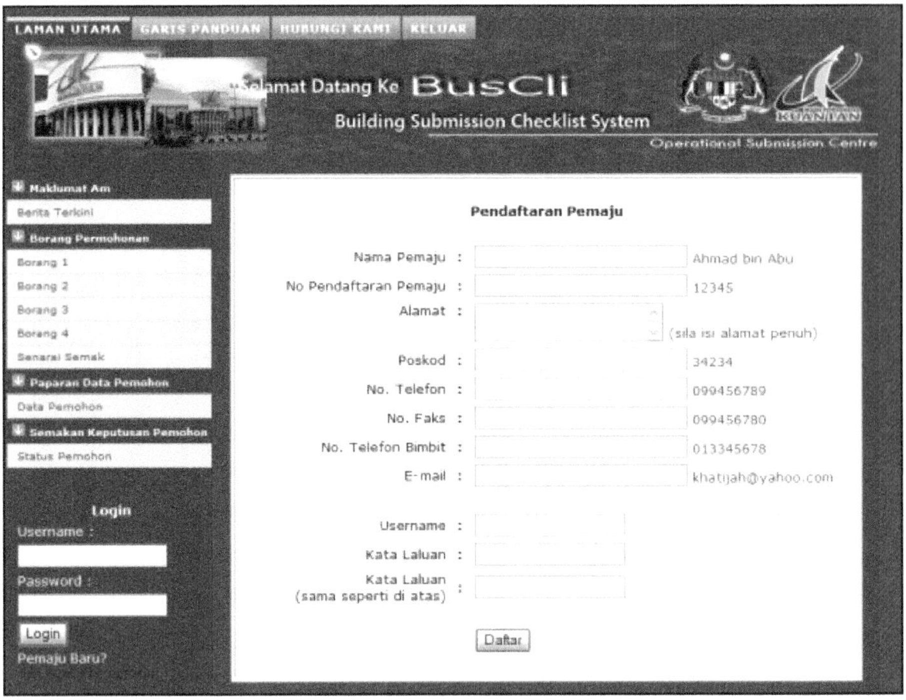

Fig. 5. Contractor Registration Module

6 Implementation

In this phase, the method of the interface design detail explained. Macromedia Dreamweaver 8 has been used as a tool in designing the interface for BUSCLI. Interface plays the important role in interaction between human and computer. Good interface design makes user feel comfortable while accessing the system. In Building Submission Checklist System several of 10 Heuristic Usability by Jacob Nielsen that suitable in the system has been implemented.

a) Match between system and the real world

   BuSCLI is a web based application that developed for Operational Submission Centre (OSC) in Majlis Perbandaran Kuantan, Malaysia. This system has followed the manual form that OSC provided for their client. Besides, makes the management in the OSC more efficiency in managing the submission of form by client.

b) Consistency and standards

   In developing the interface for BuSCLI, consistency and standard of the interface has been carefully designed. Besides, consistency and standard in designing the interface help user feel they monopoly the system. Consistent in color layout, font and icons applied in this system

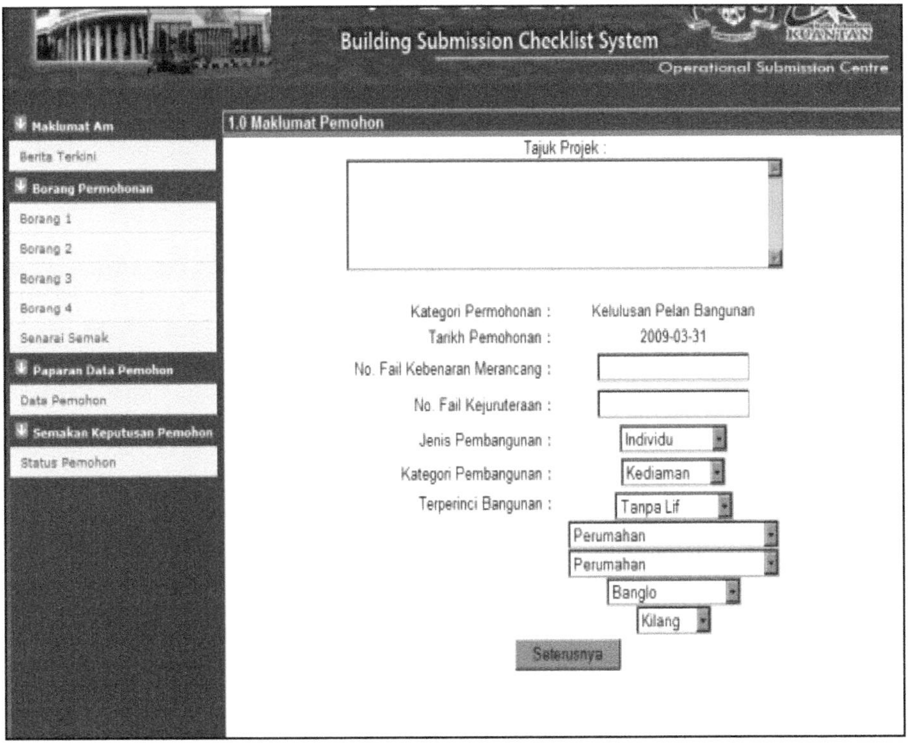

Fig. 6. Project information form

Fig. 5 shows the registration module is used by new contractor which is did not have account before. After the contractor fills all the required information, they have to fulfill the information related to the application such as project information, location, owner, and consultant that involved in the project, as shown in Fig. 6.

7 Conclusion

In this study, we present the new novel contribution in software design of Building Submission Checklist System (BuSCLI). We have elaborates on the system description, review the conventional system and existing computerize system, present the methodology and propose system design of BuSCLI. By using RAD methodology, this system developed to solve the problem occurs in manual or current operation in submission of application in building plan. Through the proper system design, BuSCLI is able to manage information properly. Thus, it can reduce time and make the approval process become faster, accurate with effective data control and support files sharing in network. This system approach allows users to access data in a flexible manner. In future, all process that related to the submission in building plan can be computerized and not only limited to the checklist.

Further research and development can be done to enhance the system by developing a more user friendly front end. Enhancement can be done at the database. Besides, some module can be added into the system like submission all the items or form in JPEG file or data can save in PDF file. For future development the other process and activities in the submission of building plan can be computerized, not only for the checklist and computerized certain forms. Besides, this system can make data sharing between Local Authority (LA) in Malaysia

References

1. Moody, D.L.: Metrics for evaluating the quality of entity relationship models. In: Ling, T.-W., Ram, S., Li Lee, M. (eds.) ER 1998. LNCS, vol. 1507, pp. 211–225. Springer, Heidelberg (1998), doi:10.1007/b68220
2. Connolly, T.M., Begg, C.E.: Database Systems: A Practical Approach to Design, Implementation and Management, 5th edn. International Computer Science Ser. Pearson, London (2010)
3. Harbans Singh, K.S.I.: Engineering and Construction Contracts Management. Auerbach Publication, Malaysian Construction Industry Master Plan (January 2011), http://www.cidb.gov.my
4. Jelani, A.M.: The Implementation of E-Government at the Local A thorities Level with Emphasis on Planning and Development Approval Process. Ke Note Address at Leadership Seminar on Urban Management (2003)
5. CWorks - The Easy Route to Maintenance Reports, http://www.cworks.com.my/ (January 24, 2011)
6. Sulaiman, M.J., Weng, N.K., Theng, C.D., Berdu, Z.: Intelligent CAD Checker For Building Plan Approval. In: International Council for Research and Innovation in Building and Construction CIB w78 Conference 2002, Aarhus School of Architecture, June 12-14 (2002)

7. She, J., Jiang, H., Xu, W., Xiao, K., Chen, J.: Urban Construction Archive Submission System with WPF Technology. Supported by Specialized Research Fund for the Doctoral Program of Higher Education of China (No.: 20050284009), the Science and Technology Plan of Ministry of Housing and Urban-Rural Development of China (No.: 2009-S5-6), and by Surveying and Mapping Research Fund of Jiangsu Province of China (No.: JSCHKY200803, No.: JSCHKY200908)
8. Hemmati, A., Kheyroddin, A.: Sustainable Development in Construction. World Academy of Science, Engineering and Technology 59 (2009)
9. Shelly, C., Rosenblatt: System Analysis and Design, 4th edn. Course Technology, United States of America (2001)
10. Noraziah, A., Norhayati, R., Abdalla, A.N., Roslina, A.H., Noorlin, M.A., Affendy, O.M.: A Novel Database System Model Design for Tender Management System. Journal of Computer Science 4(6), 463–466 (2008)
11. Roy, P.V.: Self Management and the Future of Software Design. Electronic Notes in Theoretical Computer Science 182, 201–217 (2007)

Development of Online Fuel Consumption Cost Calculator

Ahmad Noraziah[1], A.S. Ahmad Solihin[1], Tutut Herawan[1], Roslina Mohd Sidek[1], Eyas El-Qawasmeh[2], and Ezendu Ariwa[3]

[1] Faculty of Computer Systems & Software Engineering, University Malaysia Pahang, Malaysia
[2] King Saud University, Saudi Arabia
[3] London Metropolitan University, United Kingdom
noraziah@ump.edu.my, kidphantom89@gmail.com

Abstract. Recently, fuel price becomes as hot topic and never ending issue especially the demand of fuel is very high. Malaysia Government has stood up in helping citizens by giving certain amount of money per vehicle owner to reduce their burden. However, the solution of reducing the total amount of fuel cost and consumption seems to be more helpful if the citizens can plan their fuel expenditure efficiently without unnecessary spend. Therefore, new software namely Online Fuel Consumption Cost Calculator (OFCCC) has been developed to help user plan and calculates the total amount of fuel cost for a car to travel based on the distance given, driving speed, weight capacity and current market fuel price cost. This software has been developed by using Microsoft Web Expression 2 and SQL Server database system. The result shows that the users can obtain a minimum cost towards the desired destination by using OFCCC.

Keywords: OFCCC, database, software, fuel.

1 Introduction

A The debates of fuel price becomes as hot topic and never ending since the demand of fuel especially petrol is very high. In Malaysia, the fuel prices are currently unstable due to increasing and dropping price this few years. At least thirdteen (13) times of rising and six (6) times of reducing fuel cost happened in Malaysia since year 1990 [1, 2]. The price of fuel will also trigger the price of other things such as food, clothes, and many other daily essential needs. Hence, this become as a serious problem towards the middle and lower income families when the increasing of fuel price. Even though the government stood up to assist citizens by giving certain amount of money per vehicle owner to reduce their burden, but the solution of reducing the total amount of fuel cost and consumption seems to be more helpful if the citizens can plan their fuel expenditure efficiently without unnecessary spend. Therefore, necessary steps to reduce the fuel consumption cost are very important to save our money towards unnecessary spend.

Before an obtainable of estimation system, the citizens tend to spend their money towards fuel without specific planning. Online Fuel Consumption Cost Calculator

E. Ariwa and E. El-Qawasmeh (Eds.): DEIS 2011, CCIS 194, pp. 218–228, 2011.

(OFCCC) provides the simulation result by support the calculation based on the user input data. To assist in the process, the utilization of Information Communication Technology (ICT) and automated software can provide effective solution to the problems of mass data and information handling [3, 4]. Object-oriented software engineering methodology the idea object model for the business relates to support the information system [3]. In addition, estimating methods represent important processes for calculation total fuel consumption cost [5]. In this paper, Online Fuel Consumption Cost Calculator (OFCCC) has been developed to calculate the total fuel consumption cost. The development of OFCCC involves the database technology that capable to manage the driver's information. The user's can input data and able to choose the outstanding result as their guide to reduce the fuel consumption and save their money in everyday life.

2 Literature Review

2.1 Study on Fuel Consumption

Federal Test Procedure (FTP) is an identical laboratory test scheme for new vehicles that deployed in United States of America and Canada. Preferred pre-production prototypes of new vehicle models are "run in" for about 6000 kilometers before testing. All vehicles, including four-wheel (4x4) and all-wheel drives (AWD), are tested in two-wheel drive mode. Tests are adjusted to reflect the increased weight and engine load using 4x4 and AWD systems. Fuel consumption ratings are generated according to test cycles and correction factors that involve the aerodynamic efficiency, weight, rolling resistance and drive mode of different vehicles and the achievable real-world driving conditions in Canada. Other adjustments are made to reflect the average fuel consumption of vehicle configurations, options and sales mixes sold in Canada. FTP considered two tests which are the city test and the highway test [6].

In simulated city course, the city test simulates 12 kilometers, stop-and-go trip. An average speed is 32 km/h, while a top speed of 91 km/h. The test runs for 23 minutes and includes 18 stops. About 4 minutes of test time are spent idling, to represent waiting at traffic lights. The test begins from a cold engine start, which is similar to starting a vehicle after it has been parked overnight during the summer. When the test is completed, the test cycle starts again with a hot engine start, and the first 8 minutes of the test are repeated. This simulates restarting a vehicle after it warmed up, drive and stopped for short time. Meanwhile, simulated highway course considers the highway test simulates a 16-km trip with an average speed of 77 km/h and a top speed of 97 km/h. The test runs for 13 minutes and does not include any stops. However, the speed varies to simulate different kinds of rural and highway roads. The test begins from a hot engine start.

2.2 Existing Systems

Canadian Fuel Consumption Calculator (CFCC) from Office of Energy Efficiency (OEE) of Canada Government has focus on the way to conserve energy and save money in order to make environment healthier [7]. This included the fuel consumption guide on how to reduce the usage of fuel as well as saving tips. CFCC can track the fuel economy for every trip. With a couple of data inputs that are distance traveled and liters of fuel purchased, CFCC can determine the fuel consumption in liters per 100 kilometers. Even though CFCC affords comparison of different vehicles, it cannot provide for variances in vehicle condition, driving habits and etc. The ratings indicate what fuel efficiency users can achieve, if the users keep their vehicle properly maintained and drive with fuel efficiency in mind. User need to record the odometer reading, number of liters purchased, and the price paid each time the fuel tank is fulfilled. Subtract of the previous odometer reading is required from the new one to in order to determine the distance traveled. Figure 1 shows the data input for CFCC.

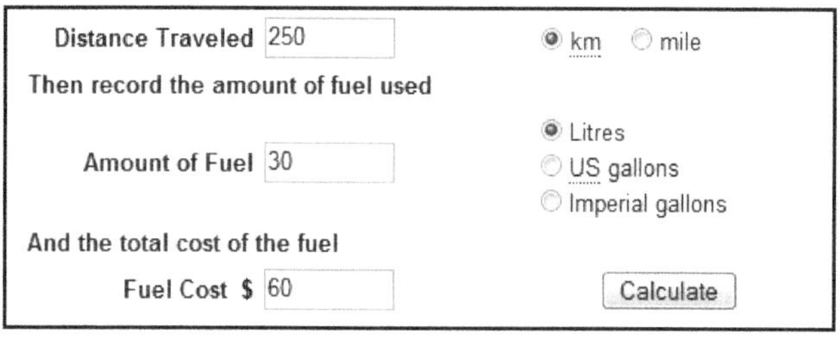

Fig. 1. Data Input for CFCC

Australian Annual Fuel Cost Calculator (AAFCC) focus on the way to estimate potential saving money by calculates annual fuel cost [8]. To give a hint of potential savings, a difference in fuel consumption of one L/100km will cost or save the average motorist about $195 a year. This is assuming the motorist travels 15,000 kilometers during the year and petrol costs $1.30 a liter. If the price of fuel per liter increases by 10 cents, the difference in annual fuel costs increases by $15. The differences of reduction amount cost greatly depicts when total cost of estimation is calculated per annum. The system multiply by 12 months to approximate the annual fuel cost per year. Figure 2 depicts an example of calculation using AAFCC.

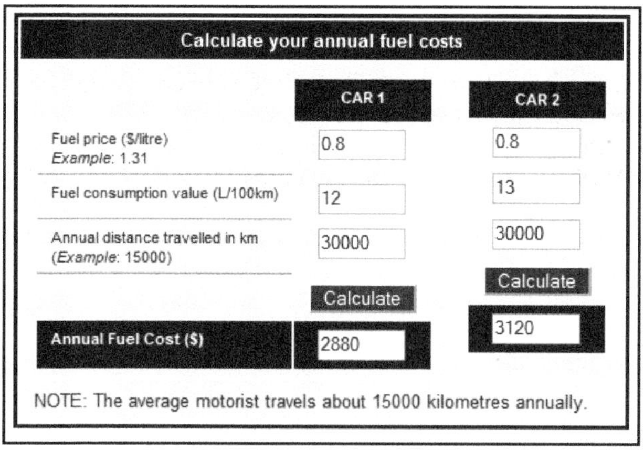

Fig. 2. Australian Annual Fuel Cost Calculator (AAFCC)

Smart Fuel Consumption Cost Estimator (SFCCE) do the calculation based on the user input data and provide a result on fuel consumption [9, 10, 11]. The calculation is based on several factors such as include transmission type, driving style, average speed on road, passenger and luggage weight capacity, air conditional status. The system is good to be used in terms of planning, but it is a standalone system. EFCCS is developed using Visual Basic .NET and SQL Database Server. The interface is designed using Visual Basic .NET. Figure 3 shows the calculation result of SFCCE.

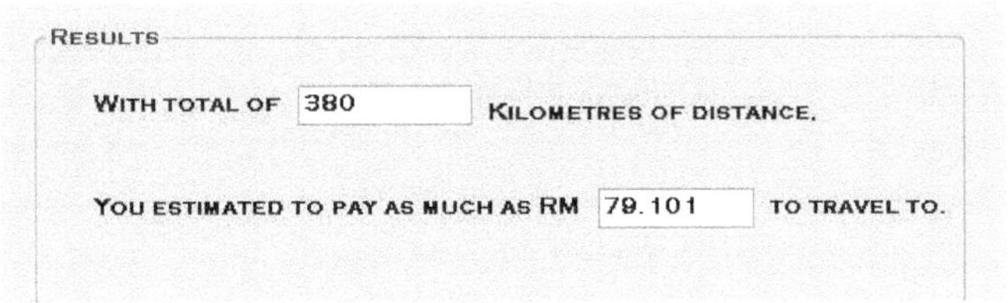

Fig. 3. Calculation result of SFCCE

3 Methodology

When we plan to develop, acquire or revise a system we must be absolutely clear on the objectives of that system. The objectives must be stated in terms of the expected benefits that the business expects from investing in that system. The objectives define the expected return on investment. SDLC (System Development Life Cycle) has three primary business objectives:

- Ensure the delivery of high quality systems;
- Provide strong management controls;
- Maximize productivity.

In other words, the SDLC should ensure that we can produce more function, with higher quality, in less time, with less resource and in a predictable manner. The development of OFCCC follows the SDLC. Figure 4 shows the phases in SDLC.

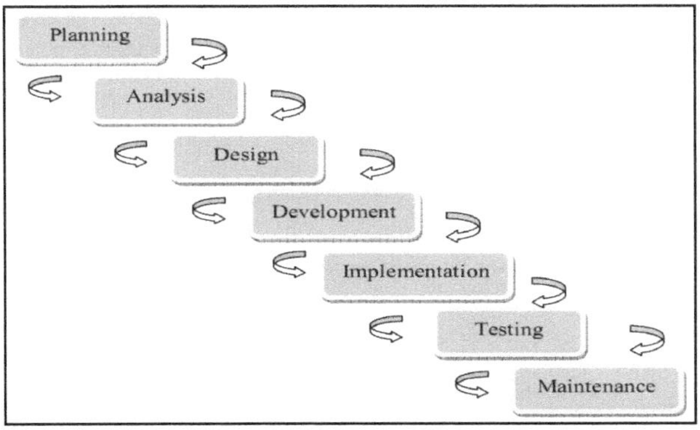

Fig. 4. Phases in SDLC

The process of development consists of 4 types which are:

1. Design the Interface
2. Using suitable coding
3. Design the Database
4. Develop the Estimation Formula

Online Fuel Consumption Cost Calculator (OFCCC) is developed using Web Based Application. The interface is designed using Microsoft Office Web Expression. All the forms in this system are Windows forms application and run in Microsoft Windows platform. Table 1 shows the details of the software that has been used for this development.

Table 1. Software tools

Software Tools	Purpose
Microsoft Office Web Expression	Design, coding and testing.
Window 7 Professional 2007	As the platform for the whole development phase.
Microsoft Office Word 2007	Documentation the project.
Microsoft Office Power Point 2007	Present the project.
Microsoft Office Visio 2007	Drawing and mapping charts.
Microsoft Office Project 2007	Drawing Gantt chart and planning project.
Google chrome	Searching information.
AVG 9.0	Protection from viruses.
Foxit Reader	View the document.
SQL Server 2000	Database platform.

Table 2 listed all the hardware facilities to be used in the development of this project.

Table 2. Hardware tools

Hardware Tools	Specification	Purpose
Laptop	Type : Dell Name : Dell Inspiron 1420 Processor : Intel® Core™ 2 Duo RAM : 2.00 GB System type : 32-bit Operating System Clock speed : 1.83 GHz	1. Offline and online research 2. Platform to run the application, software and project. 3. Use for overall project development.
Printer	Type : Canon Name : Canon MP 110 Features: 1) Photo print quality 4800x1200 dpi	1. Printing documentation

4 System Description

Online Fuel Consumption Cost Calculator (OFCCC) was build to help all car drivers especially students, staff, and lecturers at University Malaysia Pahang (UMP) to reduce the fuel usage consumption and to save money as maximum as we can. This system will analyzed, make calculation based on the path that has been set and then will make the calculation based on the criteria's that has been chosen that are the speed of the car, the engine power (cc), car transmission, how many the driver stop the car before reach to its destination, and distance of the travel. Lastly, the system will convert the amount of fuel usage and calculate the current cash converter such as Ringgit Malaysia (RM), pound sterling, yen and euro. The objectives of this project is to develop the Online Fuel Consumption Cost Calculator (OFCCF) and by considering enhancement of the Smart Fuel Consumption Cost Calculator (SFCCF) and also by considering current fuel price.

Meanwhile, the scopes of this project include:

1) The system can be used by all people especially UMP community such as students, lecturers and staff.
2) There will be top 3 of the Malaysian's most popular car to be used in this system which based on their ranking.
3) Car tested were Perodua Myvi, Perodua Viva and Proton Saga BLM.
4) This system estimated the current types of petrol that are Ron '95 and Ron '97 only.

Microsoft Office Web Expression and SQL Server 2000 as its database have been used in the development of this application. OFCCC is an online system, where user can share data by using internet.

5 System Design

Firstly, the user will enter and insert their username and password, if they're not registered, they will proceed into registration form and register into the system. Next, the system will retrieve the user's data once they successfully logged into the system. They will prompt into fuel consumption retrieve data form and need to select several fuel consumption factors that they desired. Next they will need to insert their driving information before insert the distance to the destination. For the distance, user will get the distance by using Google Maps technology. Once all factors have been decided, they will calculate data for the result. If the user does not satisfied with the result, he/she can retry with the different driving information. Furthermore, if the user is satisfied with the result, he/she can convert the total amount into the other currency such as Dollars, Yen, Euro and Pound.

Some development processes that had to be done were listed below:

i. Develop the interface
The interface will be developed based on the requirement and the design before.
ii. Develop the database

Next, the development of database will proceed and will be developed by using SQL Server 2000.

iii. Finding suitable formula

After the interface has been developed, the formulas for fuel cost and travel cost must be define.

iv. Develop the program

Finally, the system Online Fuel Consumption Cost Calculator (OFCCC) will be fully developed by using Microsoft Office Web Expression.

6 Implementation

OFCCC use database system to manage the driver's information. The software has been design to manage the driver's account, find the factors of affecting fuel consumption, handle the process of estimation that consider the total time consume and summary from driver's data. Briefly, this system deploys JavaScript, PHP script, and SQL Server, and Microsoft Web Expression 2 in order to develop the OFCCC. All the forms in this system are Windows forms application and run in Microsoft Windows platform.

6.1 Development of Inteface

Interface is one of the most important things in developing systems. This is because an interface allow user of the system to interact with system which provides mean of input and output. Input is allowing user to manipulate the system while output allowing the system to produce effect's of the user's manipulation. Login module is the first module that has been created. To open an existing project, run Easy PHP as shown in Figure 5.

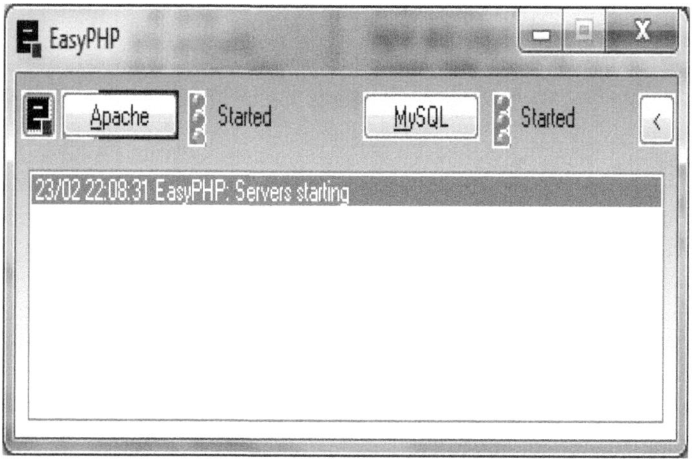

Fig. 5. Run Easy PHP

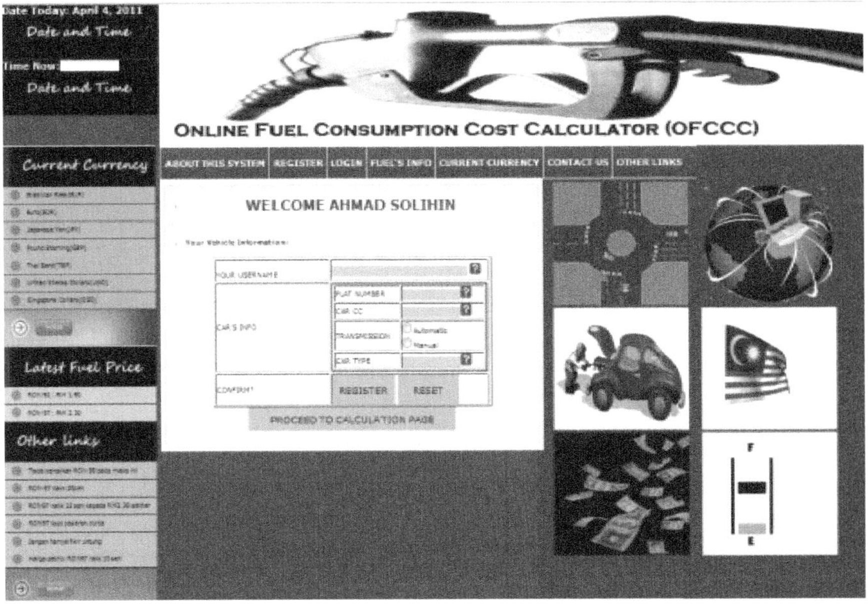

Fig. 6. Interface for retrieve form

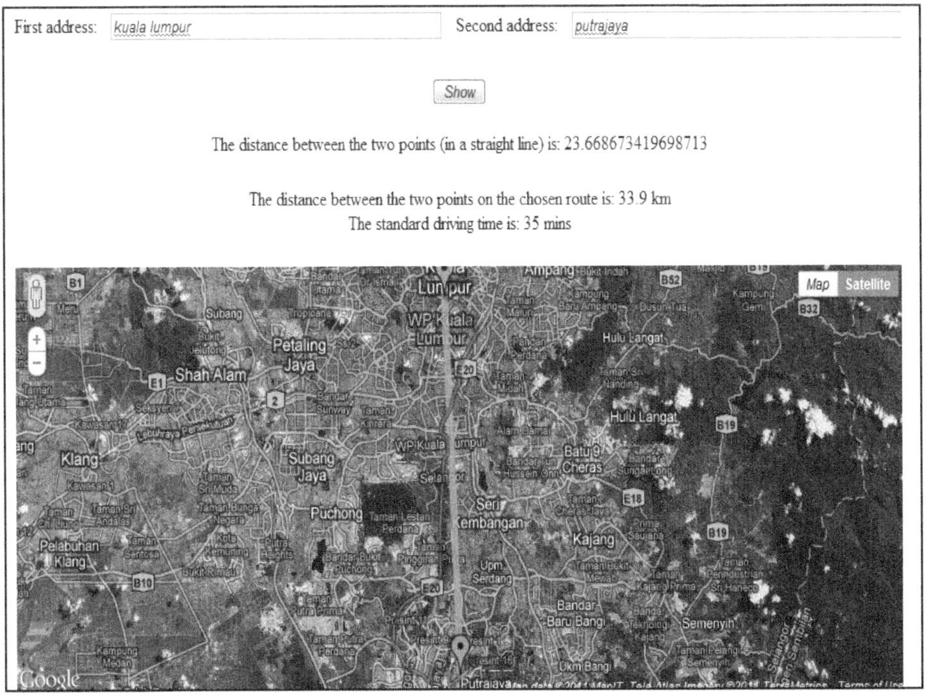

Fig. 7. Result to get the distance

User can retrieve the information if they already registered. OFCCC retrieves the user information based on the username registered, whereas the vehicle information based on the car plate selected by the user. The vehicle information retrieved consists of the car model, engine cc and transmission type as shown in Figure 6. Meanwhile, Figure 7 shows an example of OFCCC obtains the distance between two points to travel in certain place.

OFCCC integrate with Google Map in order to find the distance between two points.

6.2 Development of Database

Input, output and process has been focused in the design and development phases. As such, what programs are needed and how they are going to interact with each other. OFCCC overall structure has been designed to ensure the reliable, accurate, maintainable system. One of the significant design elements includes specifying the data model. The emphasis of logical database model is on logic, which is a readable method and useful for representing the knowledge [11, 12]. The core of logical database design is Entity Relationship (E-R) models [13, 14]. This database design is most frequently deployed since it establishes a simple data form for each relation and for many-to-many relationships [15]. The concept of database management system is applied in OFCCC. For example, frequent users of OFCCC that register more than 1 vehicle may only enter their car plate number to retrieve the vehicle's data such as engine cc and vehicle model and etc. E-R Diagram for OFCCC has three entities, include *User*, *Vehicle* and *Travel*. Data dictionary of OFCCC includes *User*, *Vehicle* and *Travel*. Data dictionary for *User* is deployed to store user's personal information such as first name, last name, home address and etc. Next, data dictionary *Vehicle* is used to store user's vehicle information such as engine cc, car model, transmission and also car plate number. Finally, data dictionary *Travel* has been designed to store the summary of the system such as travel date, travel time, travel cost, travel speed and etc.

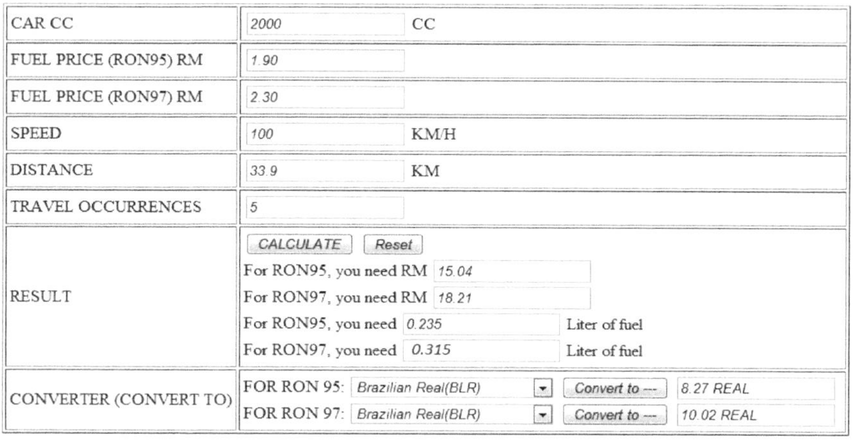

Fig. 8. Example of the result and output

6.3 OFCCC Calculation

The calculation is based on several factors such as vehicle's engine cc, transmission type, driving style, average speed on road, passenger and luggage weight capacity, air conditional status, vehicle service and distance covered. OFCCC calculates by converting each of the factors into a certain value to produce an estimation of fuel consumed. Thus, the exact amount of price needed to spend to reach towards the destination can be stated. Figure 8 shows example of the result and output of OFCCC.

7 Conclusion

The system was fully implemented in programming language with SQL codes to manipulate the data. OFCCC has been successfully developed and tested in the single client server environment. The system is capable of:

1. Manage the driver's and vehicle information.
2. Converting fuel consumption factors into a certain value.
4. Calculating the total amount of fuel consumed to reach a certain destination.
5. Obtain distance needed using the help from Google Maps
6. Convert the total price from Ringgit Malaysia (RM) into other currency.

OFCCC helps the car drivers to plan the fuel expenditure cost at the same time manage to estimate the arrival time towards the destination. Hopefully, this OFCCC at least help can help the low to average income families to save up little more money in their everyday spending. Currently we are working on adding extra function towards the system such as exact estimation upon departure and arrival time, annual fuel consumption saver and several other factors.

References

1. Malaysia Petrol Since (1990), `http://www.motorcar-malaysia.com/2007/11/malaysia-fuel-price-since-1990.html` (retrieved on February 23, 2011)
2. Malaysia Petrol & Diesel Price Chart since (1990), `http://casualzone.blogspot.com/2008/12/malaysia-petrol-price-chart-in-2008.html` (retrieved on February 25, 2011)
3. Daniel, L.: Metrics for Evaluating the Quality of Entity Relationship Models. In: Ling, T.-W., Ram, S., Li Lee, M. (eds.) ER 1998. LNCS, vol. 1507, pp. 211–225. Springer, Heidelberg (1998)
4. Connolly, T.M., Begg, C.E.: Database System A Practical Approach to Design, Implementation and Management, 5th edn. International Computer Science Series. Addison Wesley, London (2010)
5. Slater, D.: Consumer Culture and Modernity, 6th edn. Polity Press, Cambridge. ISBN: 0745603033 9780745603032
6. EnerGuide, Fuel Consumption Guide 2007. Natural Resources of Canada (article in press) (rerieve on July 2008)

7. Energy Publications, Fuel Consumption Calculator. Natural Resources Canada's Office of Energy Efficiency (retrieved on April 2010)
8. Greenhouse Office, Fuel Consumption Guide Database 2006. Department of Environment and Water Resource, Australianm (retrieved on April 2010)
9. Noraziah, A., Amer, M.A., Abd Alla, A.N., Zanariah, S.: Fuel Consumption Cost Estimator (FCCE). Research Journal of Applied Sciences 3(7), 496–499 (2008)
10. Noraziah, A., Azhar, M.A.M., Sidek, R.M., Wahab, M.H.A.: Development of Expediency Fuel Consumption Cost Simulator. In: 2010 2nd International Conference on Education Technology and Computer (ICETC 2010), vol. 4, pp. 553–556. IEEE Xplore, China (2010)
11. Noraziah, A.: Specific Data Model of Smart Fuel Consumption Cost Estimator. In: International Conference on Computer Technology & Development 2009 (ICCTD 2009), vol. 1(1), pp. 429–431. IEEE Xplore, Malaysia (2009)
12. Joseph, B.: The Importance of Business Process Modeling in Software Systems Design, doi:10.1016/j.scico.2008.01.002
13. Noraziah, A., et al.: A Novel Database System Model Design for Tender Management System. Journal of Computer Science 4(6), 463–466 (2008)
14. Lin, C., Hong, C.: Using Customer Knowledge in Designing Electronic Catalog, Expert Systems with Applications. ScienceDirect 34(1), 119–127 (2008)
15. Noraziah, A., Noorhuzaimi, M.N., Junaida, S.: Smart Electronic Visitor Information Management System with Biometric Verification. Journal of Digital Information Management System 7(5), 318–322 (2009)

The Effect of Private Valuation on E-Auction Revenues

Timothy Leung and William Knottenbelt

Department of Computing,
Imperial College London,
Exhibition Road, London SW7 2AZ
United Kingdom
{tl908,wjk}@doc.ic.ac.uk,
timothy.leung08@imperial.ac.uk
http://www3.imperial.ac.uk/computing

Abstract. In recent years, Internet auctions have become increasingly widespread. The Independent Private Values (IPV) model is widely used in the studying of auction behaviour and plays a fundamental role in many analyses of Internet auction performance. This model assumes privacy and independence, meaning that the private values of buyers are drawn from a common distribution, or in probabilistic terms, the series of values are independent and identically distributed. Since a general stochastic analysis is intractable, the IPV model has a significant impact on auction behaviour. In this paper, we study auction performance using an auction process simulator, considering both the hard close and soft close types of Internet auctions. From our experimental findings, we are able to establish quantitative relationships between the different auction process parameters, and also to deploy suitable IPV distributions in modelling the characteristics of different communities of bidders.

Keywords: Online Auctions, Internet Auctions, Auction Income, Auction Duration, Hard Close, Soft Close.

1 Introduction and Related Work

Instead of companies selling items to consumers, consumers are now selling items among themselves, with a common mechanism of achieving this being the auction. In fact, auctioning allows for a departure from the fixed price model, which some regard as too rigid to be able to respond rapidly to supply and demand fluctuations and changes. The pervasiveness and ubiquity of the Internet has played a pivotal role in catalysing the widespread acceptance of such a variable pricing model.

Internet auctions exhibit characteristics which are not often shared with conventional auctions, e.g. auctions of fixed duration which encourage sniping (bidders submit their bids moments before the close of an auction thereby preventing other bidders from submitting counter-bids), the acceptance of multiple bids in a single auction, and a maximum threshold whereby the auction will terminate at that price point. A detailed comparison is made between the two in Table 1. Due to lack of regulation, the size of the market and the volume of bidders and sellers, Internet auctions are better suited to incorporating algorithms of increased complexity as

E. Ariwa and E. El-Qawasmeh (Eds.): DEIS 2011, CCIS 194, pp. 229–242, 2011.

opposed to the more established procedures at traditional auction houses. For example, while eBay runs what essentially amounts to an English auction with a fixed duration, Swoopo runs what is known as a penny auction, where each bid incurs a fee and also extends the length of the auction by a short amount (10-20 seconds).

Table 1. Comparison Between Internet and Conventional Auctions

Internet Auctions	Conventional Auctions
Vickrey auctions dominant	Tend to be first-price auctions
Sniping	No sniping
Can have absolute pre-determined end-time	Pre-determined fixed end-time usually not acceptable
Can run for days or weeks	Usually run for no more than minutes or hours
Timely submission of bids depends on network speed and reliability	No such dependency
Concealed information – highest bid not known	Often without concealed information – highest bid known
Buy-It-Now (BIN) option common	Buy-It-Now option uncommon
Seller Ratings – a key consideration	Seller Ratings – largely unimportant

One way to view an auction is to regard it as the determination of bidders' valuations by the seller with the hindrance of concealed information from bidders [1]. The value of the object being sold (or lot) can either be the same for everyone and bids will vary according to the accuracy of the information a bidder holds, or each bidder will have his own private valuation that is unaffected by the valuations of those around him, whether known to him or not. The Independent Private Values model [2] include the assumptions of privacy and independence where the value of the commodity in question is private to the individual buyers, and that different buyers do not know the values other buyers attached to the commodity. In addition, these values are drawn from a common distribution, which is known to the buyers. In probabilistic terms, this essentially amounts to a series of values, which are independent and identically distributed. A common distribution used is the uniform distribution [3]. In this paper, through the use of simulations, we show that the results of auctions, measured through metrics such as average auction income and average auction duration, remain largely insensitive to the underlying private value distribution because the auction incomes tend towards a similar value for high bid rates.

There has been substantial work done on auctions, with several books written on the topic [4-7]. A stochastic number of bidders is studied in [8] where first-price sealed-bid auctions having constant absolute risk aversion is analysed. As a result of the stochastic analysis, the authors conclude that the seller should conceal the number of bids in order to maximise the selling price. Stochastic models of bid arrival characteristics are studied in [9,10] where the so-called BARISTA (Bid ARrivals InSTAges) model that makes use of non-homogeneous Poisson process is proposed. The probabilistic and statistical properties of these models are analysed and studied and the usefulness of these models for auction modelling is illustrated and discussed.

A stochastic approach to Internet auctions is given in [11], where bid arrivals also follow a Poisson process, with successive bids increasing in value and the seller's problem is to decide when it should accept a bid. After each bid, the seller waits for some random decision time to determine whether to accept the offer. If a new bid arrives before that time expires, then the process is repeated for this new bid. However, if a new bid does not arrive before this time expires, then the seller accepts the current bid. If the seller accepts the offer too quickly, then the price obtained may be low with respect to the price that the seller would have received had he or she been more patient. On the other hand, if the seller waits a long time before accepting an offer, a higher price may be obtained but at the expense of wasting more time. After selling the good, the seller rests for some random time before initiating a new auction. Characteristics of this mechanism include decision time, rest time, and maximum bid value. These may be adjusted, which will affect the auction duration. Similarly, in this paper, we simulate the bid arrivals as a Poisson process, and we follow the commonly adopted Independent Private Values approach in which the buyers valuations are drawn independently from a common distribution. Unlike the assumptions in [11], however, there are no overheads relating to decision time or rest time in our model, which more realistically models real-life Internet auction mechanisms. We focus on the key performance metrics of income per auction and the duration of an auction in order to compare auctions that involve bidders with underlying private values that are distributed uniformly, exponentially, normally, exponentially truncated, and normally truncated.

Studies of Internet auction bidding behaviour have been undertaken in [12-14]. In [14], different properties of online auctions such as consumer surplus, sniping, bidding strategy and their interactions are studied, where a significant correlation between sniping and surplus ratios is found. It also examines the efficiency of online auctions, where Pareto efficiency is used as the optimality criterion. In [13], it is suggested that the strategic advantages of sniping are eliminated or severely eroded in auction mechanisms that apply an auction extension rule, and that there is noticeable difference between sniping on eBay and Amazon in proportion to user experience.

Experimental studies of Internet auction behaviour have been undertaken in [15, 16, 3]. In [16], laboratory experiments with human subjects are also conducted, and the operational efficiency of Internet auctions is studied. Collusion behaviour such as shilling, in which the seller plays a part in the bidding process, is studied in [17], where two types of shilling strategies are examined, which deploys competitive bidding and reserve price mechanism and each of these exhibits a characteristic pattern of behaviour. While an auction can be defined as a market institution whereby offers are made only by the buyers, i.e. bids, or only by the sellers, i.e. asks, a double auction is one where both buyers and sellers are able to make offers [18]. Viewing the interlinking relationship between bidders and sellers as networks is proposed in [19], and the competitions in auctions is investigated in [20]. Price variation characteristics and consumer surplus are studied in [21, 22].

2 Stochastic Behaviour of Private Values and Auction Performance

In a typical auction, buyers compete for items or services, with the price going up over time, and the items or services for sale are displayed and specified in a particular website (e.g. uBid.com). We denote the private values distribution by $f(v)$, and we assume that the bids arrive over time in a Poisson manner with rate λ, and that the bids $\{Q_k\}$ are independent ascending ordered values taken from $f(.)$. We shall study both *hard close* and *soft close* Internet auction mechanisms. In the former, the auction time is fixed with duration T, while in the latter, the auction only closes on the expiration of a given no bid interval of length α. The fixed inactivity window α may be adjusted, and for meaningful operation, it should not be significantly smaller than the bid inter-arrival time; a high value for α will produce a higher income but the auction will take longer.

As indicated previously, the hard close mechanism, while common in Internet auctions, is seldom practised in conventional auctions. Let N be the number of bids received, and the largest bid $Q_{(N)}$ received over the time interval $(0, T)$ will be accepted on the close of the auction. A high value for T will produce a larger average accepted bid but the auction duration will be longer. For practical meaningful auction operation, T should be significantly greater than the mean bid inter-arrival time $1/\lambda$, i.e. $T >> 1/\lambda$.

2.1 Uniformly Distributed Private Values

The uniform distribution for private values is commonly employed in auction studies [3]. It possesses the following desirable features that are widely used to characterise Internet auction behaviour.

- *It is naturally capped by a finite value:* in most auctions, the private values do not go to infinity but is bounded by a certain upper limit. Since bids can often start at a very low value, the range of values permitted by uniformly private values may be presented by $(0, L)$, so that with the probability that a bid falling into a small value interval is given by $\Pr[x < Q_j < x+\Delta x] = \Delta x/L$.
- *It represents that no information is available and no bias exists concerning the inclinations and behaviour of the underlying bidder group, as well as no interaction or correlation between bids:* any value is possible and they happen with equal probability. This property is also useful in expressing a wide cross-section of bidder valuation spreading over different geographical regions, disparate cultures, personal preferences and perceptions – typically found on the Internet – and with little or no communication or agreements among the bidders.

Key performance metrics are the average income per auction and the average duration of an auction. Since for hard close auctions, the auction duration is fixed, this quantity is of interest mainly for the soft close case, where the duration is a random variable. For each parameter setting, we carry out 100 auction experiments and the measurements collected are averaged. Figure 1 shows the average auction income for different values of λ for hard close auctions when $T = 10$, and $L = 100$. We see that the increase in bid rate up to about $\lambda = 1$ produces rather steep average auction income improvement. There seems to be a critical bid rate at around $\lambda = 1$, above which the improvement in income becomes less pronounced.

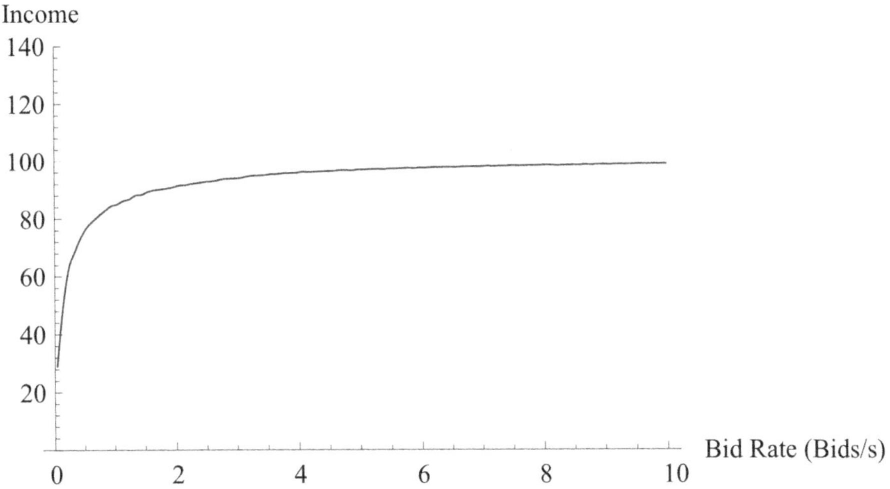

Fig. 1. Auction income for uniformly distributed private values for hard close auctions

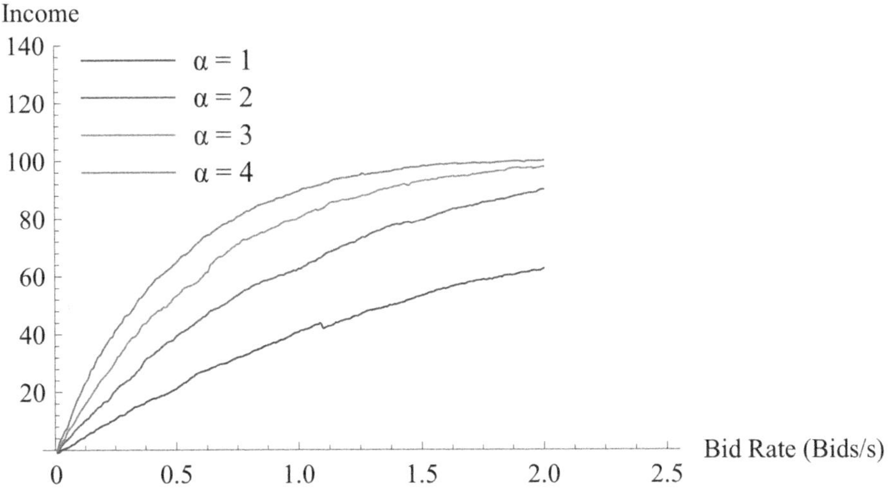

Fig. 2. Auction income for uniformly distributed private values for soft close auctions

Figure 2 shows how auction income varies for soft close auctions with λ for = 1, 2, 3 and 4. We see that average auction income increases gradually for small values of λ but accelerates for large values. As the bid rate increases, there is reduced chance of a no bid interval occurring, and the difference between $\alpha = 1$ and $\alpha = 4$ tends to widen as $\alpha \rightarrow 1$, but slowly narrows afterwards, especially between $\alpha = 2$, $\alpha = 3$ and $\alpha = 4$. Depending on the specified length of the no bid interval α, the auction duration for soft close auctions can show considerable divergence for high bid rate, which is shown in 3. We observe that for larger values of α (e.g. $\alpha = 4$), it can shoot up to very large values for high bid rates, which seems to be due the fact that under such circumstances, having no arriving bid in an interval of $\alpha = 4$ becomes increasingly unattainable, leading to almost an indefinite continuation of the auction.

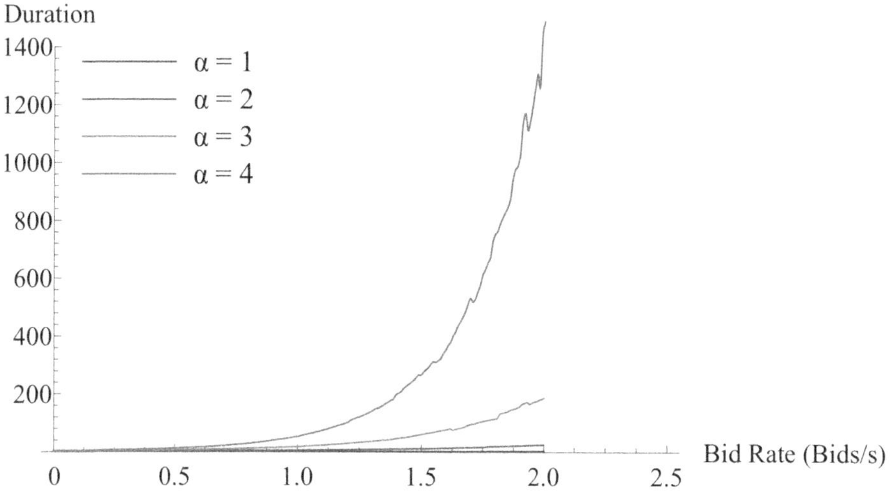

Fig. 3. Auction duration for uniformly distributed private values for soft close auctions

2.2 Exponentially Distributed Private Values

The exponential distribution $\mu e^{-\mu v}$ is one of the most widely used distributions in stochastic modelling. Compared with the uniform distribution, it has an added natural advantage of representing private values since private values are not allowed to go negative, and the exponential random variable is always positive. Since for the exponential distribution, the smaller values has a higher probability of occurring than higher values, i.e. for $u < v$ and an arbitrary interval of length k,

$$\Pr[u \le Q_i \le u+k] = \int_u^{u+k} \mu e^{-\mu t}\,dt$$

$$>$$

$$\Pr[v \le Q_i \le v+k] = \int_v^{v+k} \mu e^{-\mu t}\,dt$$

which is a consequence of the inequality $e^{-\mu\mu} > e^{-\mu v}$. Thus the exponential private values distribution represents a situation where people are looking for bargains from the auction, since the lower values are favoured. Figures 4 and 5 give the auction performance of the exponentially distributed private values; for effective comparison with the uniformly distributed private values, here we set $1/\mu = L/2 = 50$. The graph for the auction duration for soft close auctions is omitted as it is the same as Figure 3, because the bid arrival process is independent of the private values. We see that the average auction income I for hard close auctions increases rather steeply at first but the increase slows down for higher bid rate. This is interesting as, unlike the uniform distribution, there is no cap on the private values. Again, unlike the uniform distribution, where the auction income is bounded by $L = 100$, the auction income here reaches to well over 200. For the soft close cases, it is particularly noteworthy to observe that, unlike the nonlinear behaviour for hard close auctions, the average auction income here increases approximately linearly with respect to the bid rate. In fact, for $\lambda = 2$, the average auction income appears to follow the relationship:

$$I = 100 \times \alpha. \quad (1)$$

Indeed, more generally, the relationship between income and bid rate appears to follow the equation:

$$I = \frac{\alpha\lambda}{\mu}. \quad (2)$$

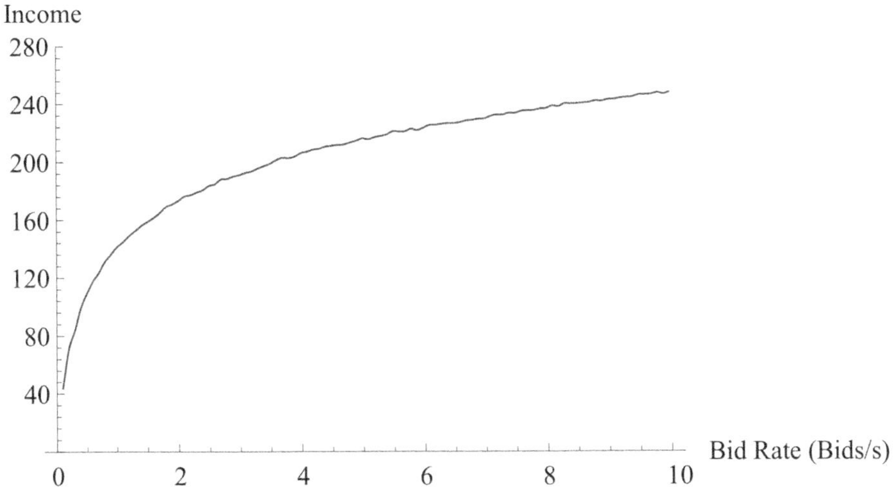

Fig. 4. Auction income for exponentially distributed private values for hard close auctions

As it stands, however, the ordinary exponential distribution in representing private values is not sufficiently realistic as it allows arbitrarily large values to be used, which is often not the case for practical auction processes. For example, for $\alpha = 4$, the average highest bid can go up to 400, which is over four times the auction income for the uniformly distributed private values case, even though both have the same mean private value. For a more realistic representation of private values, we make use of the truncated exponential distribution over the same interval as the uniform case, namely, the interval $(0, L)$, i.e.

$$f(v) = \frac{\mu e^{-\mu v}}{1 - e^{-\mu L}}, \text{ for } 0 < v < L, \quad (3)$$

and vanishes outside the interval $(0, L)$. Figures 6 and 7 give the auction performance for truncated exponentially distributed private values. We see that the performance behaviour of the ordinary exponential distribution and the truncated exponential distribution is rather different. However, there is a remarkable similarity in the auction income behaviour between the truncated exponential private values and the uniform private values. In the uniform case, the ceiling of 100 is approached faster than in the truncated exponential case, which as indicated above may be due to the fact that the bidders in this case is looking for bargains and there is a greater tendency (probability) to bid for the lower values than the higher ones, whereas in the uniform case, all the values happen equally likely.

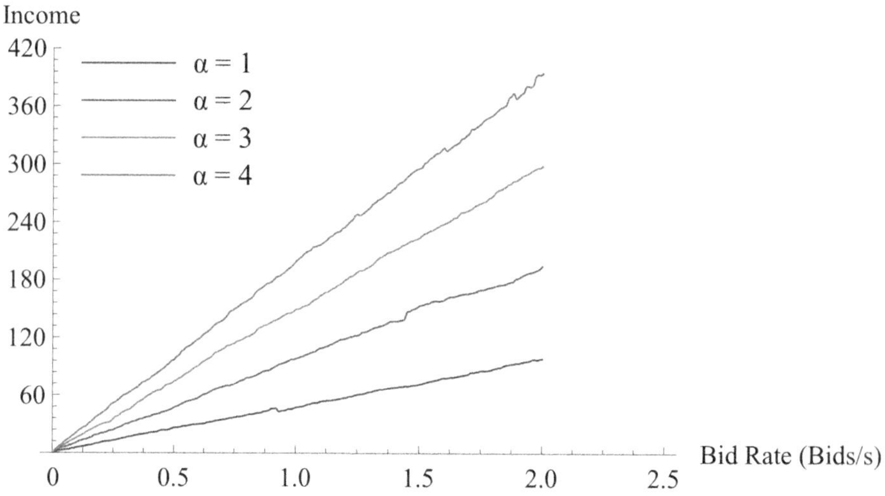

Fig. 5. Auction income for exponentially distributed private values for soft close auctions

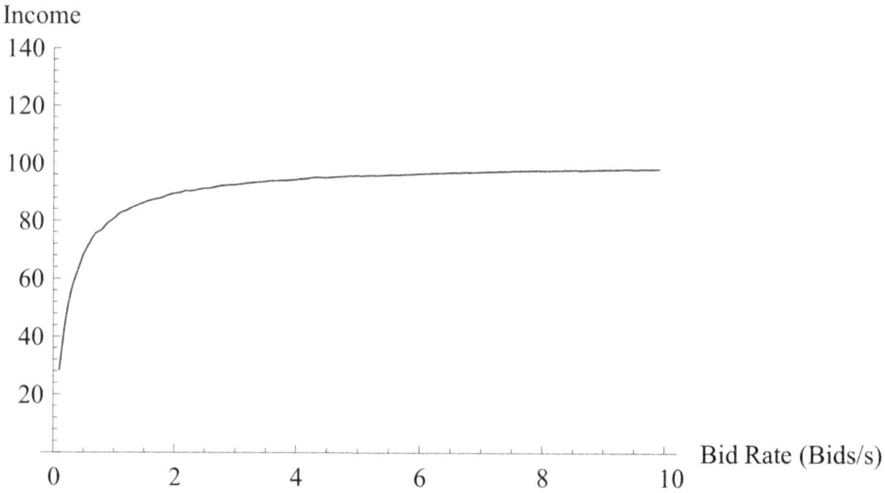

Fig. 6. Auction income for truncated exponentially distributed private values for hard close auctions

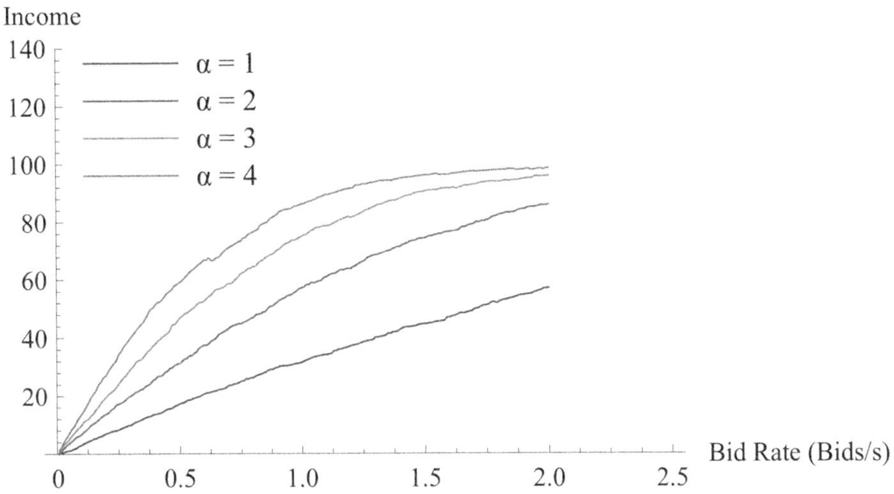

Fig. 7. Auction income for truncated exponentially distributed private values for soft close auctions

2.3 Normally Distributed Private Values

The normal distribution is highly versatile and is representative of a variety of social and physical phenomena. Here, it represents some measure of implicit agreement concerning the value of the auction item among the bidder population, since there is a mode value, which they roughly agree upon. In addition, there may even be some degree of indirect interaction or communication among the global community of bidders, perhaps through various forms of social networking. Here, we take the mean of the normal distribution η to correspond to the mean of the uniform distribution, which is $L/2 = 50$, and likewise we take the variance σ^2 to also correspond to the variance of the uniform distribution, which is $L^2/12 = 833.33$.

Figures 8 and 9 give the auction performance of the normally distributed private values. We see that, while the auction income definitely goes above 100, it is much more subdued compared with the exponential case for hard close auctions. Similar performance behaviour is also evident for soft close auctions. These are probably due to the strong clustering around the mean/mode. Unlike the exponential case, however, there is no simple linearity relationship observed, but rather a sub-linear relationship may be inferred.

However, the ordinary normal distribution has two properties, which limits its usefulness for auction processes. First, it can go up to $+\infty$, which as indicated earlier for the exponential distribution, is often not realistic. Second, it can go down to $-\infty$, which means that negative values are unavoidable no matter how far we shift the mean to the right, and this again is not permitted in auction processes. As for the exponential case, we make use of the truncated normal distribution confined to the interval $(0, L)$, i.e.

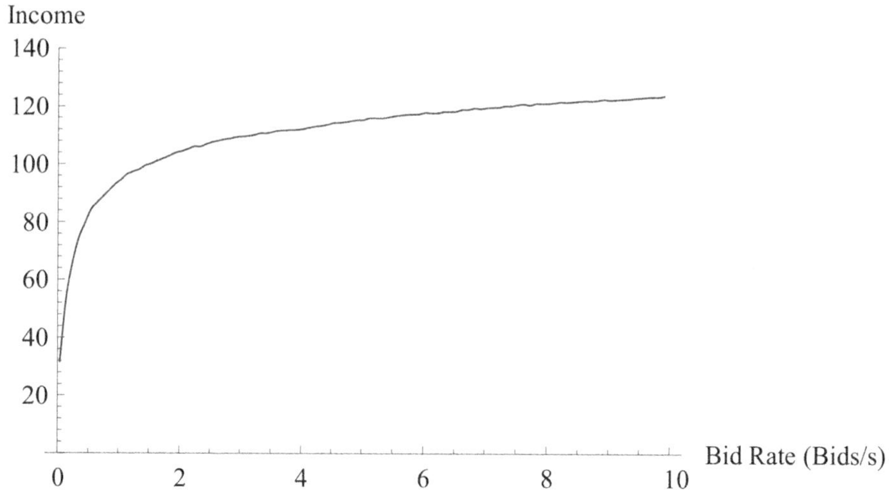

Fig. 8. Auction income for normally distributed private values for hard close auctions

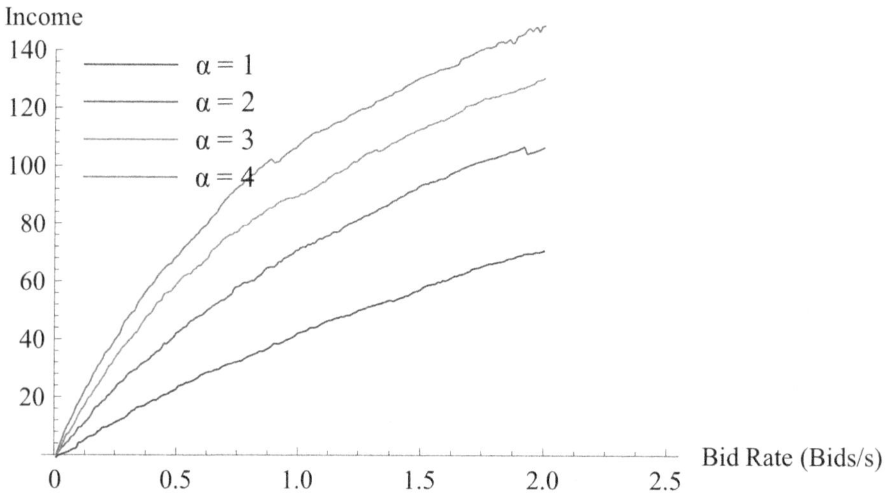

Fig. 9. Auction income for normally distributed private values for soft close auctions

$$f(v) = \frac{\exp\left[-\dfrac{(v-\eta)^2}{2\sigma^2}\right]}{K\sqrt{2\pi\sigma^2}}, \text{ for } 0 < v < L, \tag{4}$$

but vanishes outside the interval $(0, L)$, and K is the constant

$$K = \frac{1}{\sqrt{2\pi\sigma^2}} \int_0^L \exp\left[-\frac{(t-\eta)^2}{2\sigma^2}\right] dt. \tag{5}$$

Figures 10 and give the auction performance for truncated normally distributed private values. Here, we also see that the performance behaviour of the ordinary normal distribution and the truncated normal distribution is rather different, and there is also a remarkable similarity in the auction income behaviour between the truncated normal private values and the uniform private values. Similar to the remarks for the truncated exponential case, in the truncated normal case, the ceiling of 100 is approached slower than in the uniform case which may be due to the clustering of values around the mean/mode that limits its scope in going up to very high private values.

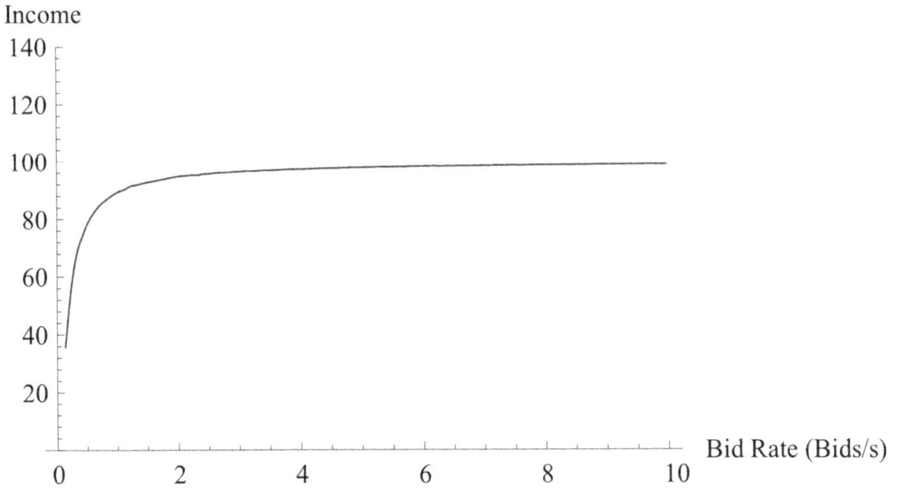

Fig. 10. Auction income for truncated normally distributed private values for hard close auctions

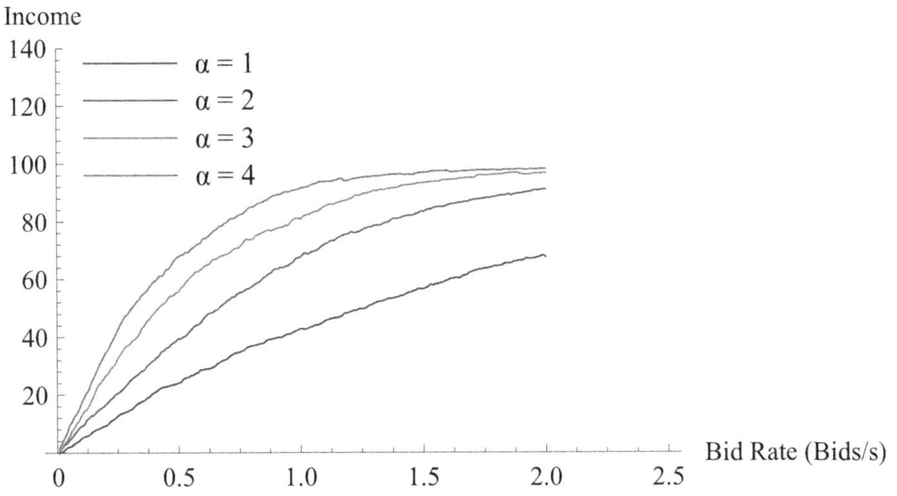

Fig. 11. Auction income for truncated normally distributed private values for soft close auctions

We thus see that in the modelling of private values, the uniform distribution as well as the truncated versions of the normal and exponential distributions are more realistic and versatile. The average auction incomes for these three distributions exhibit similar behaviour in response to the bid level. It is interesting to compare how quickly the ceiling of L is approached in these cases. Table 2 shows the different bid rates in attaining 70%, 80%, and 90% of the ceiling L for the hard close auctions. From the sellers' point of view, the preferred private values distribution is the uniform, since it attains a high average income more quickly than the other two distributions. The least preferred is the truncated exponential distribution since it is the slowest among the three private values distribution to attain high average income, probably due to the reluctance of the underlying bidder community in bidding reasonable values.

Table 2. Comparison Between Internet and Conventional Auctions

Private Values Distribution	0.7L	0.8L	0.9L
Uniform	$\lambda = 0.3$	$\lambda = 0.5$	$\lambda = 1.0$
Truncated exponential	$\lambda = 0.6$	$\lambda = 1.0$	$\lambda = 2.5$
Truncated normal	$\lambda = 0.4$	$\lambda = 0.7$	$\lambda = 1.9$

3 Architecture of Simulation System and Experimental Methodology

To simulate the stochastic model, an auction process simulator has been constructed in C++ which samples values from the uniform and exponential distributions for the private value of bidders and the rate of bids respectively utilising the Boost C++ Library. In particular, we use the `variate_generator` with the `uniform_01` and `exponential_distribution` headers, which is implemented on top of the `mersenne_twister` psuedo-random number generator. Ten averages of a hundred trials each are run for each lambda, which is sampled at 0.01 intervals in the units concerned over the desired interval. The standard deviation of the results in the previous section average 0.573 income units in auctions with a hard close, while auctions with a soft close have an average standard deviation of 2.730 income units.

Within the simulator, an auction house/website runs one or more auctions which have parameters determining whether it is first-price or k-price, whether it can accept multiple bids, and whether the auction has a hard or soft close. Furthermore, each auction takes place by auctioning off a lot, which is transferred from one owner (the seller) to another owner (the buyer), each of which has an associated reputation and wealth. Sellers can also set a reserve price on a lot, while each buyer has a valuation of each lot (consisting of an associated utility and confidence in that utility), which determines the amounts that the buyer should bid for those lots.

4 Summary and Conclusions

The impact of the Independent Private Values (IPV) Model on Internet auction performance is analysed through the use of an auction process simulator. A variety of

Internet auctions processes are studied which include First Price Auctions, Vickrey Auctions, and Multiple Bid Acceptance Auctions. Both hard close and soft close auctioning mechanisms are evaluated and quantified.

We have studied IPV distributions that admit a finite range of positive values, which include the uniform, truncated normal, and truncated exponential distributions. The uniform distribution may be used to represent bidders of whose IPV very little is known, with all values within the range occurring with equal probability. On the other hand, the truncated normal distribution may be used to represent the community of bidders in which there is some degree of agreement on the value of the item being auctioned. Since consumers are often looking for bargains in Internet auctions (as opposed to obtaining the good through conventional channels), many tend to bid at the lower end of the spectrum of values, and such social behaviour may be represented by the truncated exponential IPV distribution, where the lower value clusters have a greater probability of occurring. For these distributions, we have found that their performances exhibit a remarkable similarity in their pattern of increase. In all such IPV distributions, the average auction income tends to rise rather steeply at first and then gradually settles to approach the ceiling value. In these cases, the experimental data suggest that the average auction income would appear to have a component containing a term of the form $1\text{-}e^{-\lambda b}$, while for soft close auctions, the average duration of an auction typically shows an exponential increase and would seem to have a component containing a term of the form $e^{\lambda c}$. Of these three IPV distributions, we have found that the rate of convergence to the ceiling is fastest in the uniform distribution, followed by the truncated normal distribution, with the truncated exponential distribution converging the slowest.

While the present experimental study is able to give some significant results concerning the impact of the IPV distribution on auction performance, in future it will be useful to make use of theoretical analysis to derive and confirm some of these findings.

References

1. Cowell, F.: Microeconomics: Principles and Analysis. Oxford University Press, Oxford (2006)
2. Parsons, S., Rodriguez-Aguilar, J.A., Klein, M.: Auctions and bidding: A guide for computer scientists. ACM Comput. Surv. 43, 10:1–10:59 (2011), http://doi.acm.org/10.1145/1883612.1883617
3. Katok, E., Kwasnica, A.: Time is Money: The effect of clock speed on sellers revenue in Dutch auctions. Experimental Economics 11(4), 344–357 (2008)
4. Cramton, P., Shoham, Y., Steinberg, R.: Combinatorial Auctions. MIT Press, Cambridge (2006)
5. Klemperer, P.: Auctions: Theory and Practice. Princeton University Press, Princeton (2004)
6. Krishna, V.: Auction Theory (2002)
7. Milgrom, P.R.: Putting Auction Theory to Work. Cambridge University Press, Cambridge (2004)
8. McAfee, R., McMillan, J.: Auctions and bidding. Journal of Economic Literature 25(2), 699–738 (1987)
9. Shmueli, G., Russo, R., Jank, W.: The barista: A model for bid arrivals in online auctions. Annals 1(2), 412–441 (2007)

10. Russo, R., Shyamalkumar, N., Shmueli, G.: Models of bidder activity consistent with self-similar bid arrivals. Statistical Methods in E-Commerce Research, 325 (2008)
11. Gelenbe, E.: Analysis of single and networked auctions. ACM Transactions on Internet Technology (TOIT) 9(2), 1–24 (2009)
12. Ockenfels, A., Roth, A.: The timing of bids in internet auctions: Market design, bidder behavior, and artificial agents. AI Magazine 23(3), 79 (2002)
13. Ockenfels, A., Roth, A.: Late and multiple bidding in second price Internet auctions: Theory and evidence concerning different rules for ending an auction. Games and Economic Behavior 55(2), 297–320 (2006)
14. Wenyan, H., Bolivar, A.: Online Auctions Efficiency: A Survey of eBay Auctions. In: Proceedings of WWW 2008 Conference, Beijing, China, pp. 925–933 (2008)
15. Lucking-Reiley, D.: Using field experiments to test equivalence between auction formats: Magic on the Internet. American Economic Review 89(5), 1063–1080 (1999)
16. Vragov, R.: Operational efficiency of decentralized Internet auction mechanisms. Electronic Commerce Research and Applications 9(2), 111–125 (2010)
17. Kauffman, R., Wood, C.: The effects of shilling on final bid prices in online auctions. Electronic Commerce Research and Applications 4(1), 21–34 (2005)
18. Friedman, D.: The double auction market institution: A survey. The Double Auction Market: Institutions, Theories, and Evidence, 3–25 (1993)
19. Dass, M., Reddy, S.: An analysis of price dynamics, bidder networks and market structure in online auctions. In: Jank, W., Shmueli, G. (eds.) Statistical Methods in eCommerce Research (2008)
20. Haruvy, E., Popkowski Leszczyc, P., Carare, O., Cox, J., Greenleaf, E., Jank, W., Jap, S., Park, Y., Rothkopf, M.: Competition between auctions. Marketing Letters 19(3), 431–448 (2008)
21. Bapna, R., Jank, W., Shmueli, G., Hyderabad, G.: Consumer surplus in online auctions. Information Systems Research 19, 400–416 (2008)
22. Jank, W., Shmueli, G., Wang, S.: Forecasting Online Auctions using Dynamic Models. In: Workshop on Data Mining for Business Applications, Citeseer, p. 1 (2006)

CLOUD COMPUTING: Comparison of Various Features

Nawsher Khan[1], Ahmad Noraziah[1], Mustafa Mat Deris[2], and Elrasheed I.Ismail[1]

[1] Faculty of Computer Systems & Software Engineering, University Malaysia Pahang
[2] Faculty of Computer Science and Information Technology,
Universiti Tun Hussein Onn Malaysia
Tel.: +6012-3456789, Fax: +609-87654321
nawsherkhan@gmail.com

Abstract. Cloud computing is fundamentally altering the expectations for how and when computing, storage and networking resources should be allocated, managed, consume and allow users to utilize services globally. Due to the powerful computing and storage, high availability and security, easy accessibility and adaptability, reliable scalability and interoperability, cost and time effective cloud computing is the top needed for current fast growing business world. A client, organization or a trade that adopting emerging cloud environment can choose a well suitable infrastructure, platform, software and a network resource, for any business, where each one has some exclusive features. In this paper, we managed a comprehensive classification for describing cloud computing architecture. After this classification, easy to choose a specific cloud service out of several existing cloud computing services developed by various projects globally such as Amazon, Google, Microsoft, Sun, force.com etc. Using this survey results not only to identify similarities and differences of the various aspects of cloud computing, but also identifying some areas for further research.

Keywords: Cloud Computing, Classification, Virtualization, Large Scale Data.

1 Introduction

Cloud computing is being heralded as the next-generation shift that combines the Internet and computing so that software, content and data can be stored in remote servers run by other companies or by a client and accessed by computers, phones and TVs through the Internet from anywhere in the world. Many consumers are already using cloud applications such as Google Earth, Google Docs, Gmail, Hotmail, Yahoo, iTunes, Online Operating System, Flicker, Facebook, etc. Hence Cloud computing is Web-based processing, whereby shared resources, software and information are provided to computers and other devices on demand over the Internet. Cloud Computing is hinting at a future in which we won't compute on local computers, but on centralized facilities operated by third-party compute and storage utilities. Needless to say, cloud computing is not a new idea. In fact, back in 1961, computing pioneer John McCarthy predicted that "Computation may someday be organized as a public utility" and went on to speculate how this might occur [21].

E. Ariwa and E. El-Qawasmeh (Eds.): DEIS 2011, CCIS 194, pp. 243–254, 2011.

"Cloud Computing" is a big revolution in Grid computing. Vision is same for both, to reduce the cost of computing, increase reliability and increase flexibility by transforming computers from something that we buy and operate ourselves to something that is operated by a third party. Now things are different than they were 10 years ago. With the passage of time, we have a new need to analyze huge data, thus motivating greatly increased demand for computing. We have being spent multiple billions of dollars by various services i.e. Amazon, Google, and Microsoft to create real commercial large-scale systems containing hundreds of thousands of computers [1, 2].

2 Background

Today, the most recent paradigm to emerge is that of Cloud computing, which promises reliable services delivered to the end-user through next-generation data centers which are built on virtualized compute and storage technologies [6]. Consumer will be able to access desired service from a "Cloud" anytime anywhere in the world on the bases of demand. Computing services need to be highly reliable, scalable, easy accessible and autonomic to support ever-present access, dynamic discovery and composability, consumers indicate the required service level through Quality of Service (QoS) parameters, according to Service Level Agreements (SLAs). All of these paradigms, the recently emerged Cloud computing paradigm appears to be the most promising one to leverage and build on the developments from other paradigms [7].

There are so many definitions of Cloud by various researchers. Ian Foster defines cloud computing as " A large-scale distributed computing paradigm that is driven by economies of scale, in which a pool of abstracted, virtualized, dynamically-scalable, managed computing power, storage, platforms, and services are delivered on demand to external customers over the Internet" [3, 1].

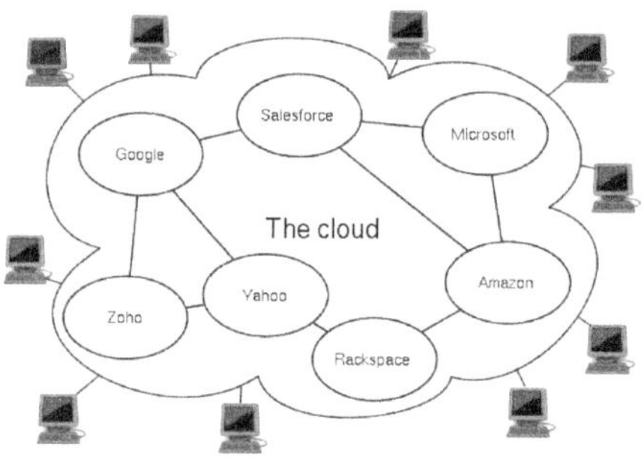

Fig. 1. Simple Structure of Cloud Environment

Here are some definitions [4] and Buyya's [5] work defines Clusters and Grid as:

"A **Cluster** is a type of parallel and distributed system, which consists of a collection of inter-connected stand-alone computers working together as a single integrated computing resource".

"A **Grid** is a type of parallel and distributed system that enables the sharing, selection, and aggregation of geographically distributed `autonomous' resources dynamically at runtime depending on their availability, capability, performance, cost, and users' quality-of-service requirements".

"A **Cloud** is a type of parallel and distributed system consisting of a collection of inter-connected and virtualized computers that are dynamically provisioned and presented as one or more unified computing resource(s) based on service-level agreements established through negotiation between the service provider and consumers".

We add yet another definition to the already saturated list of definitions for Cloud Computing:

A large-scale distributed computing paradigm, which provides Data Storage Service, Computing Power and Data Transferring Service, with capabilities of elasticity Software (SaaS), Infrastructure (IaaS), Platform (PaaS), Network (NaaS), Business (BaaS) and Organization as a Service.

There are two main factors contributing to interests in Cloud Computing:

1. Rapid reduce in hardware cost and rise in computing power and storage capacity, and the arrival of multi-core architecture and modern supercomputers consisting of hundreds of thousands of cores.
2. The exponentially increasing data size in scientific instrumentation and Internet publishing and archiving. The wide-spread adoption of Services Computing and Web 2.0 applications, etc.

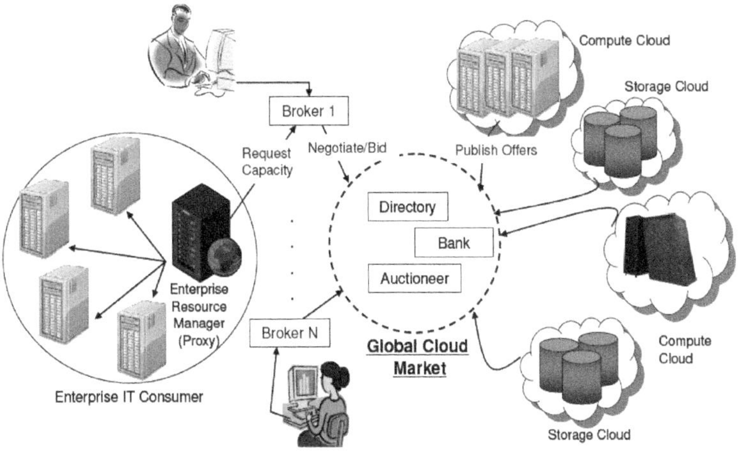

Fig. 2. Global Cloud exchange and market infrastructure [7]

For further explanation of the above definitions, we need to discuss the characteristics and compare Cluster, Grid and Cloud Computing [7].

Table 1.

Characteristics	Computing Environment / Systems		
	Clusters	**Grids**	**Clouds**
Population	Commodity computers	High-End computers (Servers, Clusters)	Both and also web-base storage
Scalability	100s	1000s	100s to 1000s
Service Negotiation	Limited	Yes, SLA based	Yes, SLA based
User Management	Centralized	Decentralized and also virtual organization based	Centralized or can be delegated to third party
Resource Management	Centralized	Distributed	Centralized/Distributed
Capacity	Stable and Guaranteed	Varies, but high	Demand-base Provisioned
Pricing of Services	Limited, not open market	Dominated by public good or privately assigned	Utility pricing, discounted for larger customers
Node Operating System (OS)	Standard OS (Windows, Linux)	Standard OS (Dominated by Unix)	A hypervisor (VM) which can run multiple OSs
Failure Management (Self-Healing)	Limited (Often failed task/application are restarted)	Limited (Often failed task/application are restarted)	Strong support for failover and content replication. VMs can be easily migrated from one node to other.
Ownership	Single	Multiple	Single
Interconnection Network/Speed	Dedicated, high-end with low latency and high bandwidth	Mostly Internet with high latency and low bandwidth	Dedicated, high-end with low latency and high bandwidth
Discovery	Membership service	Centralized indexing and decentralized info services	Membership services

Table 1. *(continued)*

Security/ Privacy	Need Traditional login, Medium level of privacy-depends on user rights	Public/private key base authentication and mapping a user to an account. Limited support for privacy.	Each user/application is provided with a virtual machine. High security/privacy is guaranteed.
Allocation/ Scheduling	Centralized	Decentralized	Both Centralized/ Decentralized
Standards/ Interoperability	Virtual Interface Architecture (VIA)-based	Some Open Grid Forum Standards	Web Service (SOAP and REST protocols)
Single System Image	Yes	No	Yes, but optional
Interworking	Multi-clustering within an organization	Limited adaptation, but being explored through research efforts such as Gridbus InterGrid	High potential, third party solution providers can loosely tie together services of different Clouds
Application Drivers	Science, business, enterprise, computing, data centres	Collaborative scientific and high throughput computing applications	Dynamically provisioned legacy and web application, content delivery
Potential for Building 3rd-Party or Value-Added Solution	Limited due to rigid architecture	Limited due to strong orientation for scientific computing	High potential can create new services by dynamically provisioning of compute, strong and application services and offer as their own isolated or composite Cloud services to users.

Generally, we have three types Public and Private Hybrid clouds. When a Cloud is made available in a Pay-As-You-Go manner to the public, we call it a *Public Cloud*, the service being sold as Utility Computing. Current examples of Public Utility Computing are Amazon Web Services, Google AppEngine and Microsoft Azure. We use the term *Private Cloud* to refer to internal datacenters of a business or other organization that are not made available to the public. *Hybrid* is the combination of both. Thus, Cloud Computing is the sum of SaaS and Utility Computing, but does not normally include Private Clouds. The advantages of SaaS to both end-users and service providers are well understood. Service providers enjoy greatly simplified software installation and maintenance and centralized control over versioning and end-users can access the service "anytime, anywhere", share data and collaborate more easily, and keep their data stored safely in the infrastructure. [5, 7].

The vision of computing utility based on the service provisioning model anticipates the massive transformation of the entire computing industry in the 21st century whereby computing services will be readily available on demand, like other utility services available in today's society. Similarly, computing service users (consumers) need to pay providers only when they access computing services. In addition, consumers no longer need to invest heavily or encounter difficulties in building and maintaining complex IT infrastructure. Hence, software practitioners are facing numerous new challenges toward creating software for millions of consumers to use as a service, rather than to run on their individual computers [7, 18].

3 Importance, Needs and Expectation of Cloud

Gartner Executive Programs Worldwide Survey of More Than 2,000 CIOs Identifies Cloud Computing as Top Technology Priority for CIOs in 2011. According to Mr. McDonald "The resource realities indicated in the 2011 CIO Agenda Survey raise the urgency and importance of adopting new infrastructure and operations technologies, such as cloud services and virtualization. These technologies were selected by CIOs the most often and the top-two technologies for 2011 and are well-suited for this budget reality, as they offer similar service levels at lower budget costs." [19]. The vision of cloud, in very near future, will decrease the density of hardware and user will be able to access any service just through one screen, because cloud will provide all software as well as hardware services.

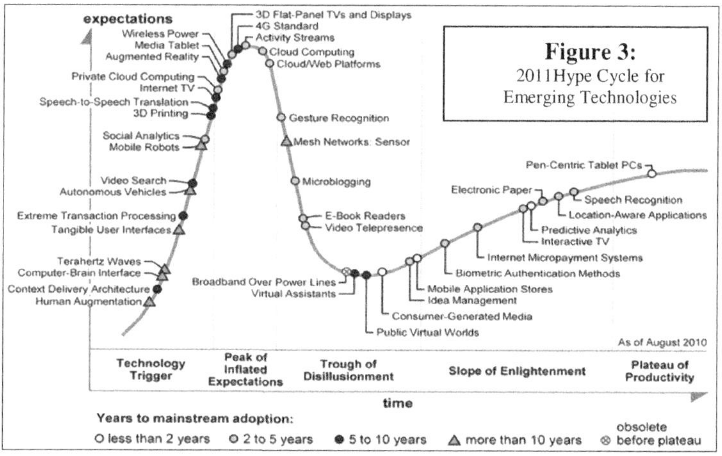

Figure 3: 2011Hype Cycle for Emerging Technologies

4 Failure of Cloud

Cloud computing provides so many services (SaaS). Anything can be a SaaS, therefore anything can be a cloud. "Cloud will never go down", but a service can.

When Gmail or some other hosted service has an interruption, it does not indicate a cloud failure, it's a service failure. Providers such as Amazon, Google, Microsoft, Salesforce.com, IBM and Sun Microsystems have begun to launch new data centers for hosting Cloud computing applications in various locations around the world to provide redundancy and ensure reliability in case of site failures [5, 7]. This research gives the following table with more detail with duration about the outage of various services of cloud. Table 2.

Table 2. Outage in Cloud

Service	Duration Hours/Minutes	Date
Twitter	24 h	Dec 6-7, 2010
Gmail and AppEngine	2.5 h	Feb 24, 2009
Google Search Engine	40 m	Jan 31, 2009
Microsoft Azure	22 h	Mar 13-14, 2008
Gmail	1.5 h	Aug 11, 2008
AppEngine	5 h	Jun 17, 2008
Simple Storage System	2 h	Feb 15, 2008
Simple Storage System	6-8 h	Jul 20, 2008
FlexiScale	18 h	Oct 31, 2008
Amazon S3	1.5 h	Feb 15, 2008

5 Cloud Services

Cloud computing can provide three kinds of services, IaaS, PaaS and SaaS. *SaaS* means the service provided to client is the applications running on the cloud computing infrastructure. It can access by thin client interfaces such as browser etc. *PaaS* refers to deploy the applications created by the development language and tool say Java, python, .net etc. provided by the service providers to the cloud infrastructure. *IaaS* refers to the services provided to the users is to lease the processing power, storage, transpiring, network and other basic computing resources, with which users can deploy and run any software including operating systems and applications. To all these services, there is no need for users to manage or control the cloud infrastructure, including network, server, operating system, storage and even the functions of applications.

5.1 Cloud Infrastructure as a Service (IaaS)

Computing is being transformed to a model consisting of services that are commoditized and delivered in a manner similar to traditional utilities such as water, electricity, gas, and telephony. In such a model, users access services based on their requirements without regard to where the services are hosted or how they are delivered. Several computing paradigms have promised to deliver this utility computing vision and these include cluster computing, Grid computing, and more recently Cloud computing. Thus, the computing world is rapidly transforming towards developing software for millions to consume as a service, rather than to run on their individual computers [7, 17]. IPs manages a large set of computing resources, such as storing and processing capacity. Through virtualization, they are able to split, assign and dynamically resize these re-sources to build ad-hoc systems as demanded by customers as well as SPs. They deploy the software stacks that run their services, which is the Infrastructure as a Service (IaaS) scenario [8, 9, 17].

At present, it is common to access content across the Internet independently without reference to the underlying hosting infrastructure. This infrastructure consists of data centers that are monitored and maintained around the clock by content providers. Cloud computing is an extension of this paradigm wherein the capabilities of business applications are exposed as sophisticated services that can be accessed over a network. Cloud service providers are incentivized by the profits to be made by charging consumers for accessing these services. Consumers, such as enterprises, are attracted by the opportunity for reducing or eliminating costs associated with "in-house" provision of these services. However, since cloud applications may be crucial to the core business operations of the consumers, it is essential that the consumers have guarantees from providers on service delivery. Typically, these are provided through Service Level Agreements (SLAs) brokered between the providers and consumers [7].

Providers such as Amazon, Google, Salesforce, IBM, Microsoft, Sun Microsystems and GigaSpace have started to establish new data centers for hosting cloud computing applications in various locations around the world to provide redundancy and ensure reliability in case of site failures. Since user requirements for cloud services are varied, service providers have to ensure that they can be flexible in their service delivery while keeping the users isolated from the underlying infrastructure. Recent advances in microprocessor technology and software have led to the increasing ability of commodity hardware to run applications within Virtual Machines (VMs) efficiently [9, 11].

5.2 Cloud Platform as a Service (PaaS) Features

In our Global village, there are various cloud computing platforms; each has its own characteristics and advantages. For better understanding, we analyze these platforms and give comparison from different implementation aspects. Table 3. [9].

User requirements for cloud services are varied, service providers have to ensure that they can be flexible in their service delivery while keeping the users isolated from the underlying infrastructure. Recent advances in microprocessor technology and software have led to the increasing ability of commodity hardware to run applications within Virtual Machines (VMs) efficiently. VMs allow both the isolation of applications from the underlying hardware and other VMs and the customization of the platform to suit the needs of the end-user.

PaaS offerings may include facilities for application design, development, testing, deployment and hosting as well as application services such as team collaboration, web service integration and database integration, marshalling, scalability, security, persistence, storage, application versioning, state management, application instrumentation and developer community facilitation. These services are provisioned as an integrated solution over the web [8].

PaaS offerings facilitate deployment of applications without the cost and complexity of buying and managing the underlying hardware and software and provisioning hosting capabilities, providing all of the facilities required to support the complete life cycle of building and delivering web applications and services entirely available from the Internet [17]. This is denoted as Platform as a Service (PaaS) i.e. Amazon Elastic Compute Cloud (EC2), Google Apps Engine, Microsoft Azure, Sun Network.com (Sun Grid) and GRIDS Lab Aneka etc.

Table 3. Comparison of Some Cloud Computing Platforms

Property	**Different Platforms**				
	Amazon Elastic Compute Cloud (EC2)	Google App Engine	Microsoft Azure	Sun Network.com (Sun Grid)	GRIDS Lab Aneka
Focus	Infrastructure	Platform	Platform	Infra-structure	Enterprise clouds
Service Type	Compute, Storage (Amazon S3)	Web Applic-ation	Web and non-web application	Compute	Compute
Virtua-lization	OS level running on a Xen hypervisor	Application container	OS level through fabric controller	Job management system (Sun Grid Engine)	Resource manager and scheduler
Dynamic negoti-ation of QoS	None	None	None	None	SLA-base resources reservation
Web APIs	Yes	Yes	Yes	Yes	Yes
User Access interface	Amazon EC2 command-line tools	Web-based administrati on	Microsoft windows azure portal	scripts, Sun Grid web portal	Work-bench, web-based portal
Value-added service providers	Yes	No	Yes	Yes	No
Progr-amming frame-work	Amazon Machine Images (AMI)	Python	Microsoft.N ET	Solaris OS. Java, C, C++, FORTRAN	APIs supporting models in c# .Net

5.3 Cloud Software as a Service (SaaS)

Saas offers the fastest time to value for generic business processes. SaaS is most appropriate for those business areas where the processes are standardized. In many cases, however, these processes are "different" because they are actually substandard. If businesspeople would adopt standardized business processes and the pre-built SaaS packages that can automate those standardized processes, they would significantly improve their business. In those cases where the data is too sensitive to trust offsite with a SaaS vendor, then the SaaS application often can be hosted within the enterprise's data center. SaaS is a part of cloud computing, and enterprises should consider internal, private and public options for cloud computing, as their security requirements dictate [7].

Finally, there are services of potential interest to a wide variety of users hosted in Cloud systems. This is an alternative to locally run applications. An example of this is the online alternatives of typical office applications such as word processors. This scenario is called Software as a Service (SaaS) [9, 17].

6 Pricing Structure

Several Cloud Computing and Conventional Computing datacenters are being built in seemingly surprising locations, such as Quincy, Washington (Google, Microsoft, Yahoo! etc) and San Antonio, Texas (Microsoft, US National Security Agency etc). The motivation behind choosing these locales is that the costs for electricity, cooling, labor, property purchase costs and taxes are geographically variable and of these costs, electricity and cooling alone can account for a third of the costs of the datacenter. Even prices are changing, but we compare currently prices below.

As a successful example, Elastic Compute Cloud (EC2) from Amazon Web Services (AWS) sells 1.0-GHz x86 ISA "slices" for $0.10 per hour, and a new "slice" or instance can be added in 2 to 5 minutes. Amazon's Scalable Storage Service (S3) charges $0.12 to $0.15 per GB/Month, with additional bandwidth charges of $0.10 to $0.15 per GB to move data IN and OUT of (AWS) over the Internet. Table 4.

Table 4. Platforms Pricing Structure

Platforms	Storage $/GB/Month	Transfe r $/GB	CPU $/GHz/ h
Amazon	0.055	0.10	0.100
Google	0.150	0.11	0.100
Microsoft	0.150	0.13	0.120

7 Conclusion and Lights to the Future

Cloud Computing is the fifth utility after water, electricity, gas and telephony, and it is the promising paradigm for delivering IT services as computing utilities. This paper present a comprehensive comparison of different aspects of cloud computing. After this analysis user can better understand the characteristic and will be able to do better selection of cloud platform, implementation and deployment requirement. In current cloud still we have challenges i.e. continuously availability, portability, consistency guaranty, data security and privacy. In current cloud environment, user can't fine the status of their data may be someone is using these data for his/her own purposes and also if server goes down for an hour, users are hit with the crises and user are handicapped.

Our future work lies in the areas of data replication and data scheduling in cloud computing as well as on the combination of these both, replication and scheduling techniques.

References

1. Foster, I., Zhao, Y., Raicu, I., Lu, S.: Cloud Computing And Grid Computing 360-Degree Compared. IEEE Grid Computing Environments, Gce (2008)
2. Silvestre, J.: Economies And Diseconomies Of Scale. The New Palgrave: A Dictionary Of Economics 2, 80–84 (1987)
3. Twenty Experts Define Cloud Computing. Sys-Con Media Inc., `http://cloudcomputing.sys-con.com/read/612375_p.htm` (January 25, 2011)
4. Pfister, G.F.: In search of clusters, 2nd edn. Prentice Hall, Upper Saddle River (1998)
5. Buyya, R. (ed.): High Performance Cluster Computing: architectures and systems, vol. 1. Prentice Hall, Upper Saddle River (1999)
6. Weiss: Computing in the clouds. Networker 11 (4), 16–25 (2007)
7. Buyyaa, R., Yeoa, C.S., Venugopala, S., James, B.A., Brandic, I.: Cloud computing and emerging it platforms: vision, hype, and reality for delivering computing as the 5th utility. Future Generation Computer System (2008), doi:10.1016/j.future
8. Peng, J., Zhang, X., Lei, Z.: Comparison of several cloud computing platforms. In: International Symposium of Information (2009)
9. Rimal, B.P., et al.: A taxonomy and survey of cloud computing system. In: International Joint Conference on Inc. (2009)
10. Chang, F., Dan, J., Ghemawat, S., Hsieh, W., Wallach, D., Burrows, M., Chandra, T., Fikes, A., Gruber, R.: Bigtable: A distributed storage system for structured data. In: Proceedings of the 7th Usenix Symposium on Operating Systems Design and Implementation, osdi 2006 (2006)
11. Decandia, G., Hastorun, D., Jampani, M., Kakulapati, G., Lakshman, A., Pilchin, A., Sivasubramanian, S., Vosshall, P., Vogels, W.: Dynamo: Amazon's highly available key-value store. In: Proceedings of Twenty-First ACM Sigops Symposium on Operating Systems Principles, pp. 205–220. ACM press, New York (2007)
12. Hamilton, J. Cost of power in large-scale data centers, `http://perspectives.mvdirona.com Inlargescaledatacenters. Aspx` (January 22, 2011)
13. Stanley, M.: Technology Trends, `http://Morganstanley.com/institutionaltechresearch/pdfs/techtrends062008.pdf` (January 17, 2011)
14. Keahey, K., Foster, I., Freeman, T., Zhang, X.: Virtual Workspaces: Achieving quality of service and quality of life in the grid. Sci. Programming 13(4), 265–275 (2005)

15. Opennebula Project, http://www.opennebula.org/ (January 5, 2011)
16. Amazon Elastic Compute Cloud (ec2), http://www.amazon.com (January 22, 2011)
17. Google App Engine Web Site. Web Resource (January 7, 2011)
18. Kleinrock, L.: A vision for the internet. St. Journal of Research 2(1), 4–5 (2005)
19. Gartner executive programs worldwide survey of more than 2,000 cios, http://www.gartner.com/it/page.jsp?id=1526414 (January 21, 2011)
20. Gartner's hype cycle special report evaluates maturity of 1,800 technologies (2010), http://www.gartner.com/it/page.jsp?id=1447613 (January 9, 2011)
21. Life in the cloud, living with cloud computing, http://computinginthecloud.wordpress.com/2008/09/25/utility-cloud-computingflashback (January 12, 2011)

Atlas: A Knowledge-Based Collaborative Framework for Handling Logistics Procedures

T. Tamisier, Y. Didry, and F. Feltz

Department Informatics, Systems, Collaboration (ISC)
Centre de Rercherche Public - Gabriel Lippmann
41, rue Brill, L-4422 Belvaux, Grand-Duchy of Luxembourg
tamisier@lippmann.lu

Abstract. Owing to their ability to easily organize and update heterogeneous knowledge, Decision-Support Systems form a promising approach for the optimization of logistics businesses. The management and visualization of the knowledge base of these systems are in this regard crucial to ensure a proper functioning and to keep an intuitive view of their expected behavior. This paper introduces Atlas, a customizable automated tool for assisting / improving the supply chain with respect to miscellaneous aspects such as secure collaboration, traceability, or multimodality. The operational knowledge of Atlas is accessed through 2 different views. In an analytical view, the knowledge is modeled on elementary if-then rules, which are processed by a resolution engine written in the Soar architecture. A synthetic view offers a pictorial representation of all the knowledge, and in particular, shows the inter-dependence of the rules and their procedural references. In addition to allowing an efficient processing, the system checks the coherence of the knowledge and produces a justification of the decision with respect to relevant operational procedures.

Keywords: Supply-chain optimization; decision-support; knowledge management; information retrieval.

1 Introduction

Automated reasoning systems have shifted from experimental trials within a specialized community to multipurpose tools, used in a wide variety of real domains. The purpose of these advanced tools is to provide a model of the reasoning, as well as a means to perform it, in a mechanical, standardized, and justified way[1,2]. They have in fact taken a significant importance in solving problems that can be formalized through inference rules and combinational cases, notably for identification, planning, optimizing, and decision making tasks. In particular, decision support tools are gaining ground both in large companies and public administrations, especially for the efficient and equitable handling of dynamic operational requests, such as the (re-) ascribing of tasks [3].

A historical crossroad in Eastern Europe, the Grand-Duchy of Luxembourg is nowadays characterized by the interconnection between rail, air and route transportation and an increasingly huge traffic. The project Atlas (Assistance to

E. Ariwa and E. El-Qawasmeh (Eds.): DEIS 2011, CCIS 194, pp. 255–262, 2011.

Transportational Logistics by Automated System) is concerned with the use of Decision-Support Systems to sustain the growth of the country as a prominent logistics place. Atlas seeks to offer tailored solutions for transport management, and dedicated to all economic actors of the supply chain, whether seeking the best way to comply with administrative, legal, and business constraints, or willing to improve on important features such as secure collaboration, traceability, or multimodality. In particular, the decision system will help dealing with the EU-shaped freight framework, notably characterized by the development of multimodality, aids to take off road transport, and new working rules for truck drivers.

As a main result, we develop a collaborative expert system aimed at processing regulation and operational rules related to multimodal freight transportation and involving the European and national contexts. To ease the integration in the working infrastructure of the larger number of related business and administration services, Atlas is deployed as an aggregation of web services supporting collaborating work inside and between organizations. The operators access them, according to specific rights depending on their pre-recorded user profiles, to share and manage their tasks, and to edit or update the knowledge base without the help of a computer specialist. Owing to the flexibility of its reasoning scheme, of its deployment, and of its usability Atlas can therefore be viewed as multi-purpose professional reasoning architecture.

2 Guidelines

The starting point for building Atlas are on the one hand the operational constraints and on the other hand the legislation regarding transportation. This knowledge consists however not in a monolithic structure, but forms a constellation of commercial offers, national laws, supra-national decisions, and international regulations.

Modeling texts into logical formalism has been proposed, in particular to directly apply inference mechanism in reference with legal contexts. Several formalisms and resolution algorithms are available and well-tried, such as the first-order and backward-chaining architecture of Prolog, the modal or deontic logics [4]. However, in Atlas, the heterogeneous nature of the knowledge and the numerous implicit definitions that are used make the translation into a formal and univocal computer language a very long and minute challenge. Consequently, instead of a whole mathematical modeling of references, we decided to concentrate on the explicit drawing of the mental procedures that governs the daily business, and the relations between these procedures to operational constraints, or legislation. The operating knowledge of Atlas is therefore a procedural modeling of the heterogeneous textual references.

An example of a procedure can be: "If goods are perishables, and the expiry date is after 30 days, goods can transit by rail". Such a procedure is modeled in the shape of a multi-valued acyclic n-ary graph, with nodes representing a factual state (e.g. railroad inter-connection available) used as a condition, and the edges denoting the necessary steps (e.g. testing the expiry date) to enter the state. Moreover, we ensure that a state is always unique in the graph (there are not 2 nodes with the same label), though it is fully possible to go to the same state by different ways. Figure 1 illustrates the graph-based modeling of procedures. The root node is associated with goods to be sent. The concluding leaves decide on accepting or rejecting the possibility to transit by rail.

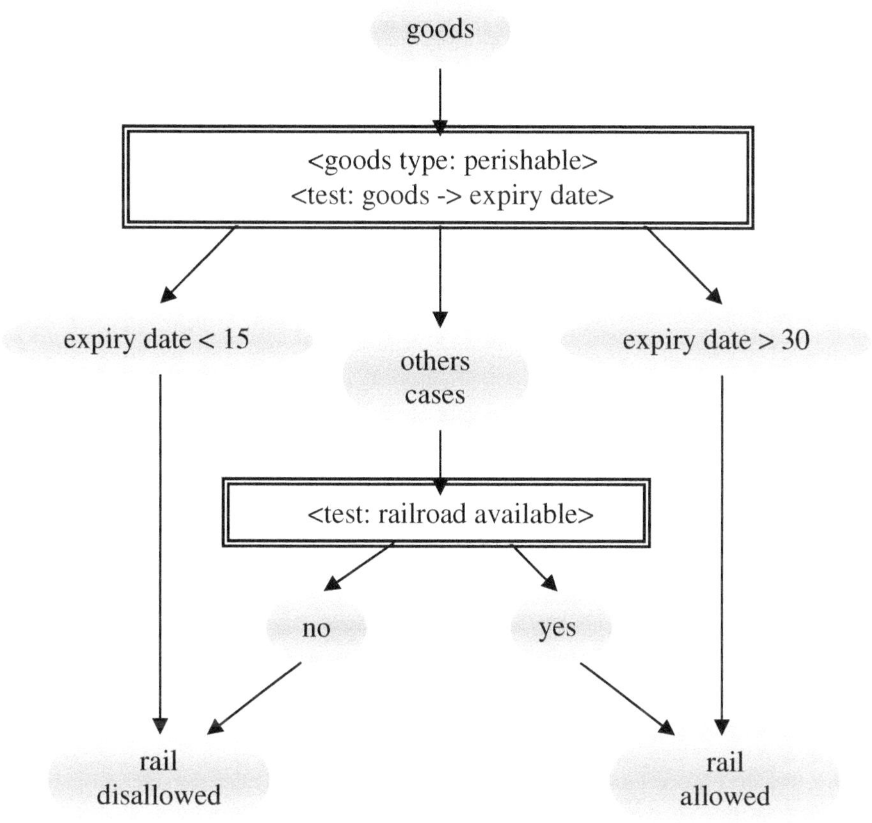

Fig. 1. Atlas procedures

3 Implementation

Our graph-procedural modeling has guided our choice relative to the technology used to model the procedures and infer with them. The reasoning on a concrete case consists, indeed, in proceeding from one state to another according to the procedures and the conditions (labeling the edges) that are satisfied. All the paths and all the states must be effectively checked, in order to ensure that no case for a given application is left. This consideration orientates our choice towards a rule-based inference system proceeding by parallel forward chaining (contrary to the Prolog like scheme, which proceeds by backward resolution in a depth-first manner).

The resolution kernel of Atlas is therefore developed on top of the Soar IA architecture. Soar is a general-purpose rule language whose inference engine is based on the Rete algorithm [5], and works in a forward-tracking manner: the rules (also called productions) are "if A then B" statements whose meaning is: "if the situation A is satisfied, then create (or produce) the situation B". The purpose of Soar is to propose a Unified Theory of the Cognition [6], and the system is backed as the most suitable language for intelligent agents programming [4]. One advantage of Soar is that it can communicate in many ways (through sockets or procedural routines), and allows us to place in the rules requests for information concerning the allowance demand or the claimant data.

However, because of its general purpose, writing rules in the Soar language can soon become intricate, relatively to the syntax itself as well as to the management of the inference algorithm [7]. Moreover, when slightly modifying the rule base, the behavior of the whole base can change drastically, in a way that the understanding of the change is not intuitive. For this reason, the heart of Atlas is an intermediate language with simplified syntax that is compiled into true Soar formalism. This upper-level layer is designed to provide the user with useful or necessary subroutines in view of the specialized topic of the program. All the subroutines are documented with a stable and proven behavior, corresponding to the expected modeling of the procedures. In particular, the intermediate language implements the required controls on the Soar resolution engine in order to manage the notion of state used within the procedures, and on-the-fly communications.

This high-level language makes also possible to run a graphical editor in which the procedures are directly modeled in the shape of graphs. This editor is based on the tool Jgraphpad [8], developed on Jgraph, the Java core graph visualization library that features a powerful array of graphical functionality, and notably allows to easily draw graphs and export them into miscellaneous formats. In Atlas, graphs drawn with Jgraphpad are exported into GXL (Graph eXchange Language) [9], written in the XML standard.

Atlas provides two basic components needed to implement this procedural model. The first component, Data Manager, provides textual and graphical tools to model the knowledge into procedural rules. The second component, Rule Manager, consists of a set of reasoning rules working with this modeled knowledge and the operational data required in order to apply the rules. The rules from the Rule Manager are operated in two modes. The first mode processes single cases by calling the operational data of problems, while the second mode performs mass simulations on operational data samples. This second mode is particularly useful for business and financial analysis with respect to traffic evolutions. We will now review the architecture of both components in detail, and discuss the subjacent rationales.

4 Data Manager

The Data Manager component provides tools for drafting and maintaining a domain-specific data model used into business decision-making procedures. From extended operational collaborations, we gather that business experts in charge of writing decision procedures, when using software-oriented modeling tools, get into difficulty about the knowledge representation used in the persistence layers of a software application (namely databases). The reason is that they need then to conceive of the procedures in a different level of abstraction as they do when working manually. Atlas therefore provides a business-oriented Data Manager, which brings 3 main advantages.

First, a knowledge representation of data at a business level drastically increases the speed and precision of the modeling of decision procedures, it is also less error-prone and more. Second, such a model, independent from the software-oriented persistence model, allows hiding low-level implementation features outside the competencies of business experts. Distribution of the knowledge in databases as well as changes in the specific encodings of information become transparent, while the fundamental concepts used in the procedures are preserved. Third, the business-oriented data model opens large possibilities of performing a fine-grained logical verification of the procedures, made of early checks that enable the experts to actively track conceptual or modeling mistakes, before the model is used in production.

The Atlas proprietary language for specifying business-specific knowledge follows the modern object-oriented language design, with conceptual entities consisting in typed fields and inheriting from parents ones. Moreover, each entity is by itself a new type that can be used in another as a field type. Simple types include truth-values, ranges over integer or real numbers, and enumeration. Inheritance allows factorizing common data shared by entities of the same type, and that are generally spread over different columns inside the databases. In whole, this approach thus facilitates the understanding and the maintenance of the knowledge model.

Since in general, the data are dispatched inside one or several databases, a link between the conceptual description of the data and the data actually stored in the databases is also required. We opted for a mechanism based on SQL queries that maps a pool of variables in the Data Model with the corresponding information inside the databases. For the sake of performance and maintenance, the implementation of queries is based on the fact that the data corresponding to a pool of specific variables in the conceptual data model can be recovered with one query. These mappings however must be conjointly written with the databases managers since they require fine knowledge about the data structure.

5 Rule Manager

The Rule Manager component contains tools for maintaining and using a software-oriented model computed from the knowledge entered through the Data Manager. The knowledge modeling is done using a Java SWING graphical editor. This editor allows the creation of modules that are composed of a set of If-Then rules. Basically, a module can have multiple I/O and can be composed of other modules. This approach allows us to divide the knowledge into reusable subgroup of rules. The goal is to avoid inefficient repetitiveness in the modeling process and to promote the use of modularity. This Rule Manager consists in two different components. The first groups the data contained in the rules of all modules, while the second maintains textual references for the rules, and is used to justify the answer of the reasoning core of Atlas. In the integration of Atlas in the CNPF, the content data represents the information required in a given juridical procedure (e.g. the age of a child, the validity date of a given certificate, the nationality of a beneficiary…) while the reference data consist of excerpts from legal and administrative texts (e.g. chapter, section, article, alinea…).

From an operational point of view, it is often required to organize the rules in a processing and decision workflow [10]. Atlas offer to edit workflows in a dedicated view, according to Sugiyama Layout hierarchy [11] and implemented based on the Jung API. It is also possible to implement any other layout algorithm according to the design of the workflows. Moreover, a set of tools built on top of Choco CSP library is integrated in the Rule Manager to perform logical checks (e.g. completeness, determinism and path consistency) of this Atlas operational workflow in the same way as what is offered for the business model in the Data Manager.

Atlas is organized around a three-part architecture that clearly separates the activities of designing decision procedures, mapping them with the actual data stored in distributed databases, and binding the procedures steps with additional information that can be interpreted at analysis time. This section focuses on the different ways of working with the procedures modeled through the previous components.

Basically, Atlas analyses the decision procedures of its knowledge base and instantiates the variables of the rules with the data provided by the Data Manager. It then returns a decisional verdict or a suggestion along with a trace containing all fired rules. In addition, every rule can be associated with documentation and reference data, to ease the interpretation and customization of the results.

The decision procedures implemented reflect closely the mental decision workflows of the operators. To optimize the processing, Atlas uses two analysis engines: one is specialized and optimized to perform analysis on workflows and the other is more general and deals with general decision rules. In the usual way, running an analysis over a given decision procedure returns a trace of the rules applied with a final state summarizing the result of the analysis. However, final states can also return a typed data that can be recursively used inside another procedure. Last, the final state of a procedure can be marked as inconclusive, which means that given the instantiation data provided by the Data Manager Component, the decision procedure cannot conclude because of the absence of important data.

The information and material supplied through the application is formalized and passed as inputs to the engine processing the rules. Upon completion of the inferences, Atlas gives an optimized traffic solution, or it may ask for more information or additional documents. The answer provided by Atlas must be deterministic, and justified. Due to either intrinsic incoherence or errors in the translation into computerized procedures, the knowledge of Atlas can be erroneous, or incomplete. In the traditional manual handling, the incoherence is detected and solved by the operator or the hierarchy. With an automatic processing, the situation could lead to unwanted responses. It is therefore necessary to proceed with a set of rules and an inference mechanism that guarantee the exactness of the knowledge and the uniqueness of the returned decision. Moreover, the reasoning process is in every case traceable. In addition, links are maintained from the rules to a database of legal references, in order to exhibit a justification of the decision.

Atlas can be queried in two ways: Allocation Query for analyzing a given set of procedures on one pool of data, corresponding to the information of one beneficiary; and Mass Simulation for performing the same analysis on a given set of procedures, but with a large set of beneficiary data. Allocation Query is the standard way to use the tool. Given a decision procedure designed inside the Rule Manager Component, the tool uses the binding information inside the procedure to retrieve the data values throughout the Data Manager, and analyses the rules according to the correct engine. The result is constituted by the sequence of all fired rules, and a final state describing the final point reached by the engine. During Mass Simulation, one set of procedures is targeted as a bunch of data is loaded through the Data Manager Component. Instead of producing one analysis, the Mass Simulation collects the analysis of every case to synthesize a statistical answer. Mass simulation can be really convenient to study the impact of several rules.

The analysis engine is designed to allow interrupting the analysis when special rules are fired or states are reached, in order to perform specific actions. This instrumentation framework is moreover sufficiently flexible to allow other kind of instrumentation like resuming the analysis in another state. From the result point of view, interrupting the analysis at one point and resuming it with new specific data that can reduce the search space for further rules does not change the result itself: the trace simply includes the new data and the result state integrate them explicitly.

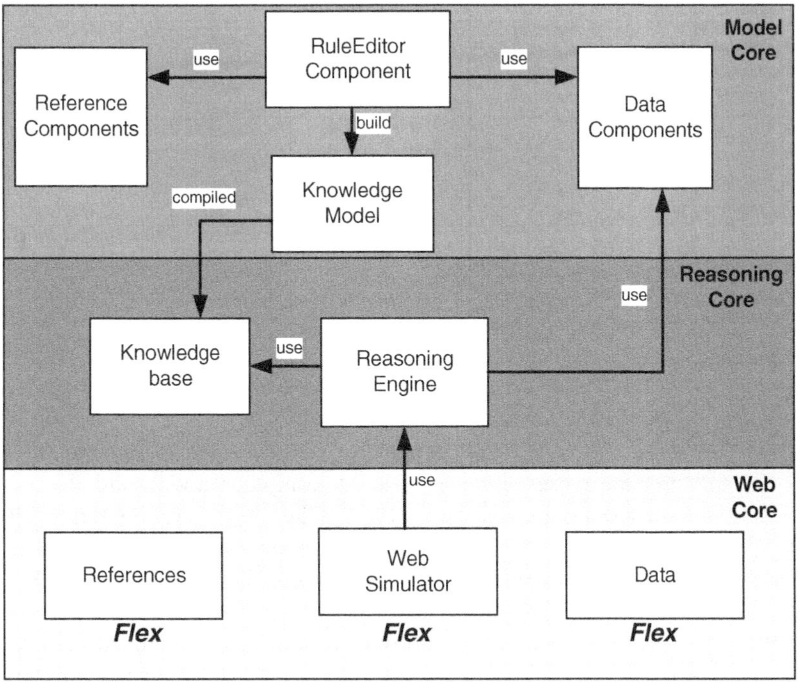

Fig. 2. Atlas overall architecture

6 Conclusion

A decision system for processing planning procedures automatically has been presented. This customizable system will be used for the optimization on multimodal freight involving Luxembourg. The raw knowledge of Atlas is a comprehensive set of operational and administrative procedures. However, though references are necessary in some intricate cases and for justifying the results, direct interpretation of textual references can be avoided in most cases. This article has discussed the feasibility of a method based on the modeling of the knowledge framework into light procedures. This approach is completed by a graphical visualisation of the juridical knowledge and an operational integration in a computerized infrastructure. Future works include a macro-editing package of the knowledge working from the graphical representation, in order to ease the update of Atlas without rewriting separate rules.

References

1. Gordon, T.: From Jhering to Alexy - Using Artificial Intelligence Models in Jurisprudence. In: Jurix Conference (1994)
2. Fehling, M.R.: Unified Theories of Cognition: Modeling Cognitive Competences. Artificial Intelligence 59(1-2) (1993)
3. The Softlaw Expert-System, `http://expert.Softlaw.com.au/fdss`
4. O'Callaghan, T.A., et al.: Building and Testing the Shyster-Mycin Hybrid Legal Expert System, `http://cs.anu.edu.au/software/shyster`
5. Eijlander, P.: The Possibilities and Limitations of Using Intelligent Tools for Drafting Legislation. In: Jurix Conference (1994)
6. Forgy, C.L.: Rete: a Fast Algorithm for the Many Pattern Many Object Pattern Match Problem. Artificial Intelligence 19 (1982)
7. Laird, J., et al.: SOAR: an Architecture for General Intelligence. Artificial Intelligence 33(1) (1987)
8. Jgraph, `http://www.jgraph.com/jgraphpad.html`
9. GXL, `http://www.gupro.de/GXL`
10. Di Battista, G., Eades, P., Tamassia, R., Tollis, I.: Graph Drawing: Algorithms for the Visualisation of Graphs. Prentice Hall, Englewood Cliffs (1999)
11. Sugiyama, K., Tagawa, S., Toda, M.: Methods for Visual Understandings of Hierarchical System Structures. IEEE Trans. in Systems Man & Cybernetics 11(2) (1981)
12. Radwan, A., Girgis, M., Ghanem, A.: A Study of Barycentre Algorithm for Hierarchical Graph Crossing Minimization. International Journal on Intelligent Cooperative Information Systems 2(2) (2002)

An Agent-Based Supplier Selection Framework: A Case-Based Reasoning Approach

Alireza Jahani, Masrah Azrifah Azmi Murad,
Md. Nasir Sulaiman, and Hasan Selamat

Faculty of Computer Science and Information Technology
Universiti Putra Malaysia
43400 Serdang Malaysia
jahani@fsktm.upm.edu.my,
{masrah,nasir,hasan}@fsktm.upm.edy.my

Abstract. In a competitive environment, those enterprises that always look forward and implement customer-winning supply chain competencies are more profitable than those that do not have such. Existing approaches have not considered customers' needs in the supplier selection and negotiation processes. This paper aims to present a systematic agent-based framework for supplier selection based on the case-based reasoning approach to evaluate material offers, and negotiate with the suppliers and customers on the price, volume, quality grade, and delivery date of supply materials. The main objective of this research is to take the customers' needs into consideration and provide them with alternative products which are closest to their first order if their first order was out of stock or they couldn't get supply from the suppliers. Based on the proposed framework, a numerical example of the known case study is illustrated for highlighting the effectiveness of the approach.

Keywords: Supply Chain Management, Intelligent Agents, Supplier Selection, Recommendation, Case-Based Reasoning.

1 Introduction

The Supply Chain Management (SCM) represents a critical competency in today's global market. A supply chain is a worldwide network of organizations and their associated activities like procurement, manufacturing and distribution, that work together to produce value for the customer [1]. Competitive advantage in tomorrow's environment will go to those enterprises that can consistently anticipate and implement customer-winning supply chain competencies [2]. Hence, the long-term objective of SCM is to increase customer satisfaction, market share, and profits for all organizations in the supply chain's stakeholders [3]. Therefore, to realize these objectives, tight coordination among the organizations in supply chains is needed [4].

In supply chains, since suppliers are manufacturer's external organizations, the coordination between a manufacturer and suppliers is very important, because the failure of coordination results in excessive delays, and ultimately leads to poor customer services [5]. Hence, there is a need for integrated systems for cooperation

E. Ariwa and E. El-Qawasmeh (Eds.): DEIS 2011, CCIS 194, pp. 263–274, 2011.

and information exchange. With such systems which make the suppliers more competitive than other suppliers, the performance will be improved while the costs decreased. Thus, supplier development is a vehicle that can be used to increase the competitiveness of the entire supply chains [6]. As more manufacturers become interested and involved in forming supplier partnerships, a guide is needed to help these manufacturers in selecting potential partners and in developing and implementing the partnership [7].

For development of SCM system, the benefits of adopting agent technology have been recognized in an increasingly wide variety of applications. The agent technology facilitates the integration of the entire supply chain as a networked system of independent echelons that utilize their own decision making procedure [8]. Agents are also capable of solving the problem of matching supply to demand and carrying out negotiations and coordination [9]. Negotiation refers to the process by which a group of agents (human or software) communicate with one another in order to reach a mutually acceptable agreement on resource allocation (distribution) [10]. The agents need to be able to exchange related information, resolve uncertainties, and revise preferences. Then, there is a need for an automated and integrated system for cooperation and information exchange that can receive orders from customers, generate production plans and material requirement specifications, check the inventory, make a build or buy decision, call suppliers for proposals, receive and evaluate bids, negotiate to finalize the bid, and satisfy the requirements of the negotiating parties. This can be useful for all the stakeholders, especially customers who are more crucial for any company's survival. This paper aims to present a framework for an agent-based supply chain system by using the case-based reasoning approach for supplier selection. Such framework should enable decision makers to evaluate material offers, and negotiate with suppliers and customers on the price, volume, quality grade, and delivery date of each order in the negotiation process.

The remainder of the paper is organized as follows: section 2 discusses the related works. An agent-based framework for supplier selection is proposed in section 3. Section 4 presents a case study with numerical examples of the method that was used for supplier selection. Finally, the conclusion and discussion are summarized in section 5.

2 Related Works

A number of researchers have attempted to apply agent technology to manufacturing enterprise integration, manufacturing scheduling and control, material handling, supply sourcing, supply chain management, mass customization, negotiation, information transfer and knowledge sharing within a supply chain. Saad et al. [11] proposed a Production Reservation approach by using a bidding mechanism based on the Contract Net protocol to generate the production plan and schedule. In AARIA [12], the manufacturing capabilities (e.g. people, machines, and parts) are encapsulated as autonomous agents. Each agent seamlessly inter-operates with other agents in and outside its own factory.

In the late 90's and early 00's, researchers found out the importance of supply chain integration which not only involves internal parts of organization, but also includes suppliers and customers. Hence, recent studies have led to significant advances by placing more emphasis on complexity and dynamics of supply chains and developing networks of distributed and cooperative entities to improve agility and global performance of supply chains. Barbuceanu and Fox [13] proposed to organize the supply chain as a network of cooperating agents, each performing one or more supply chain functions, and each coordinating their actions with other agents. Maturana et al. [14] have developed a hybrid agent-based mediator-centric Framework, called MetaMorph, to integrate partners, suppliers and customers dynamically with the main enterprise through their respective mediators within a supply chain network via the Internet and Intranets. Min and Bjornsson [15] presented a conceptual model of agent-based supply chain automation, in which a project agent gathers actual construction progress information and sends them to subcontractor agents and supplier agents, respectively, over the Internet. Jiao et al. [16] applies the multi-agent system paradigm to collaborative multi-contract negotiation in a global manufacturing supply chain. Wentao [17] has designed an agent-based negotiation model for the sourcing of construction suppliers based on the design of a new parallel bargaining protocol and Bayesian learning model has been integrated into the whole negotiation model to improve the efficiency. Lu and Wang [18] applied a multi-agent approach to study the supply chain framework in network economy. The information transfer process and cooperation between agents are two key issues in their framework. Kim and Cho [19] have used agent negotiation as a way to allocate numerous orders to many participants for supply chain formation in which all the participants, including buyers, manufacturers, and suppliers, are able to attain their own profits.

However, most of the above works, have not applied the customers' needs in the supplier selection and negotiation processes. Failure to account for that may either lead to unsatisfied customer demand and loss of market share. Therefore, in order to keep customers, there is a need for a proper mechanism which can offer alternative products to the customers. Typically, the supplier selection is a multi-criteria decision problem [20-21]. The suggested methods in the related literature can be classified into two categories: mathematical programming models and weighting models. The mathematical programming model has a problem in dealing with qualitative criteria that are very important in the decision making, especially for supplier partnership policies [21]. Therefore, in this paper, due to the multi-criteria decision making nature of supplier selection, we use case based reasoning approach which is in the subset of weighting models.

3 Framework and Mechanism

In supply chains and networked organizations, integration and cooperation of internal parts of organization are crucial for them to accomplish their tasks and exchange information and raw materials with each other. Hence, there is a need for an appropriate framework which can determine the position and relationships of different agents in the supply chain precisely to achieve tight coordination between internal and external parts. First, this paper aims to present an agent-based Supply Chain Framework in order to select the best suppliers based on the proposed case-based reasoning approach. Such framework should enable decision makers to evaluate material offers, negotiate with suppliers and customers on the price and terms of quotation in the negotiation process. Second, this framework enables one to make successful agreements with the final supplier on the price and other issues regarding the supply content. Finally, the main goal of this research is to take the customers' needs into consideration and provide them with alternative suppliers which offer closest materials to the customers' first order, if the manufacturer is unable to supply their first order. Hence, a real "win-win" situation can be achieved and the mentioned problems like costs and ease of customer loss can be reduced and the performance of supplier selection process will be improved.

3.1 An Agent-Based Supply Chain Framework

The proposed agent-based supply chain framework can generate a flexible, reconfigurable and coordinated approach to perform supplier selection process both across enterprises and within an enterprise. This framework is illustrated in Fig. 1 and major components of the proposed framework are described below:

In this framework, there is a FIPA-compliant multi-agent system composed of a seller agent, a design agent, a procurement agent, and a buyer agent. Also there is a case-based for keeping suppliers records. Each agent performs one or more supply chain functions independently, and each coordinates its action with other agents. Their functionalities are described below:

- *Seller agent* provides an intelligent interface for the customers to place their personal orders. It is responsible for acquiring orders from customers, negotiating prices or due dates and handling customer requests for order modification or cancellation. It also gathers customer preferences.
- *Design agent* is responsible to gather all the incoming orders from the seller agent and eliciting relevant information regarding customer choices, preferences and specifications. Another task of this agent is product planning and placing material requirement specification (MRS) into the case structures.
- *Procurement agent* takes MRSs from the design agent and then generates call for proposals (CFP) and advertises them through the buyer agent to all the potential suppliers. It analyses the whole production plan and decomposes the material requirements into specific categories in order to communicate the outgoing proposal's information with certain suppliers.
- *Buyer agent* provides an intelligent interface for the suppliers to bid for the outgoing CFPs of material requirements. It is responsible for inviting supplier to bid and to fulfill the material requirements and proclaiming the award of the bid. It is also responsible to manage suppliers' information and choose the most suitable and reliable suppliers based on the Suppliers' Case-Base and the material requirements of each order received from customers.
- *Suppliers' Case-Based* keeps supplier information files as cases and gather information on the past and new suppliers in order to identify alternative suppliers. Supplier information files include the name of each supplier, a list of materials available from each supplier with their attributes, the supplier's delivery history, the supplier's quality records, the supplier's overall desirability, and general information concerning the supplier's plant and management. Based on such information, both the current suppliers and the supplier candidates are included in this analysis as the alternatives.

3.2 The FIPA Contract Net Protocol

The FIPA Contract Net protocol [22] is used at the inter-enterprise collaboration level for the selection of suppliers. In general the negotiation process in the multi-agent paradigm is divided into three consecutive phases: inviting, bidding and awarding.

A contract net protocol defines the basic messages in accordance with these phases and how each message is to be processed. Whenever an order comes to a buyer agent, it invites potential suppliers to bid. Then the buyer agent collects and evaluates all the bids and selects the one with the maximal utility as the winner, and thus the winner supplier is awarded the contract. In other words, the buyer agent initiates a negotiation process by sending a ''call for proposal'' or ''call for bidding'' message to seller agents of suppliers. A few rounds of conversation may take place, where several proposals and counter-proposals are exchanged. The negotiation between agents ends when one party accepts or rejects the other party's proposal, or when any party terminates the negotiation process on its own.[16]

3.3 Order Management and the Supplier Selection Mechanism

Here, major activities in the workflow are briefly presented in Fig. 1 for better understanding of the proposed framework. Here is the description of the workflow steps:

1. The customer places an order through the seller agent to the design agent.
2. The design agent will formulate the material requirement specification (MRS) and make a case structure for the ordered product and then send it to the procurement agent.
3. The Procurement agent checks the inventory regarding stocked finished products and raw materials based on MRS structure. If the stock has enough resources, then there is no need for supplying.
4. Otherwise, the procurement agent must supply and provide raw materials, as much as needed, from suppliers.

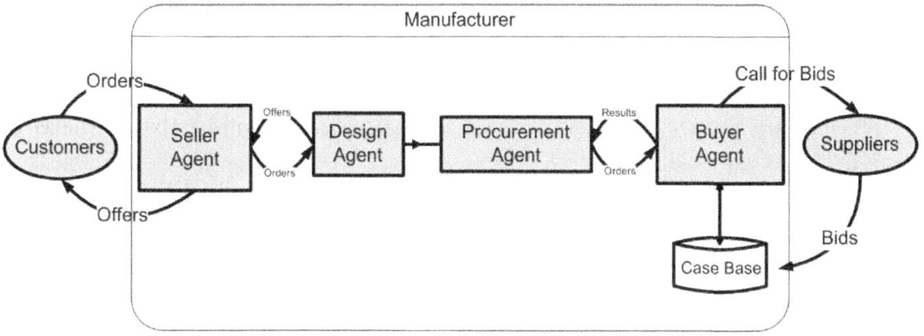

Fig. 1. Multi-agent based supply chain framework

5. The procurement agent advertises its outgoing orders through the buyer agent for all the potential suppliers.
6. After receiving the CFPs, the potential suppliers make the decision of bidding and then bid on the case-based of buyer agent.

7. After receiving all the bids, the buyer agent will give a comprehensive evaluation of the suppliers in consideration of price, due date, quality grade, volume, and so on, and then chooses the most suitable suppliers according to the evaluation results.
8. If some or all supply materials of the customer's first order could not be found during the supplying process, the procurement agent will try to generate alternative product recommendations based on the received bids and present them to the customers and negotiate with them regarding new offer.
9. If the customer accepts the new offer, then the buyer agent will choose the suppliers who bid the alternative product's materials.
10. The buyer agent proclaims the award of bid and gives necessary replies to the un-chosen suppliers.
11. The supplier who has won the bid carries out manufacturing to fulfill the incoming orders.
12. The supplier delivers its finished products to the manufacturer.

3.4 Case-Based Reasoning (CBR) Approach

One of the most important contributions of this paper is showing how buyer agents can check orders with received bids from its associated case-based to respond to requests from the procurement agent. On the other hand, when a new request is encountered, the buyer agent sends CFPs to the suppliers. After receiving all the bids and storing them in the case base, the buyer agent retrieves from the case base, cases that are identical or at least most similar due to the features of the new order's case.

According to [10], the process of CBR strategy includes four steps: retrieve, reuse, revise and retain, which constitute the CBR cycle. However, before the cycle can be run, another step, case description, should also be performed for both case base construction and application of case knowledge.

Case Description

The CBR mechanism starts with the description of a new order which corresponds to a new case. Case description is concerned with deciding what contents are to be stored in a case. It is important for the new case to be adequately described so that the retrieval of appropriate previous or newcomer's cases from the case base is possible. By considering order constraints which contain material requirement specifications for ordered products, this research adopts the case structure as shown in Table 1 to describe each case.

Table 1. Case structure and content

Case Attribute	Attribute Value
Product ID	Integer, from 01 to n
Product name	text
Price	Integer, from 1 to n
Volume	Integer, from 1 to n
Quality Grade	Integer, from 1 to 5
Delivery Time	Integer, number of days

1) *Product ID:* Numbers a certain product for its own and required materials are numbered from 01 to n.
2) *Product name:* Indicates the name of the product's required material.
3) *Price:* The price for a specific product which will be offered to customers or suggested by customers in an incoming order for negotiation.
4) *Volume:* Requested quantity of ordered products from customers or bidding quantity from suppliers.
5) *Quality Grade*: Specifies the requested quality for each material with 1 to 5.
6) *Delivery Time:* The requested delivery time by customer for each order. For suppliers, it indicates the possible delivery time for their bids.

Case Retrieval

Case retrieval is finding the most similar case from the case-based according to features of the new case. A CBR system seriously depends on this step to find the order's matches of incoming bids from suppliers. The nearest neighbor algorithm, one of the methods widely used to identify the similarity between cases, is employed here to perform the retrieval task. For the nearest neighbor algorithm, the similarity of two cases is calculated according to the following formula:

$$similarity\ (O,B) = \frac{\sum_{i=1}^{n} w_i \times sim(O_i, B_i)}{\sum_{i=1}^{n} w_i} \tag{1}$$

In (1), O is new order, B is incoming bid, Oi and Bi are the feature i of O and B respectively, wi is the weight of feature i, and $sim(O_i, B_i)$ is the similarity function of feature i. The value of $sim(O_i, B_i)$ is calculated as in

$$sim(O_i, B_i) = 1 - \left| \frac{O_i - B_i}{|O_i| + |B_i|} \right| \tag{2}$$

The weights of the features, which obtained from the customers, are applied to select the closest suppliers' bid to the customer's order. The role of the supplier selection mechanism is to calculate the similarity of each feature of the bids during the supplier selection and to rank the alternative suppliers.

Case Reuse

Once the same case or the most similar case to the incoming order is selected from the received bids, then, it will be used as a suggested case and will be offered to the customer. For the same cases, the suggested case can be reused by direct copy. But for most situations which have different values in their attributes, the seller agent can offer the retrieved case as an alternative to the customer who can either accept or reject it.

4 Case Study

For illustrating the proposed method of this paper, we use the case study of Moxober, a leading mobile phone manufacturing company in Finland which has also been used by [16]. Figure 2 shows Moxober's product structure at three levels: component parts, subassemblies and the final product. Nearly all the components parts were produced by Moxober, but with the development of global economy and booming telecommunication market, it has changed to a global manufacturing strategy focusing on key technologies and its core competency while outsourcing major component manufacturing activities such as the manufacturing of peripherals like batteries and chargers, memory chips and LCD panels. [16]

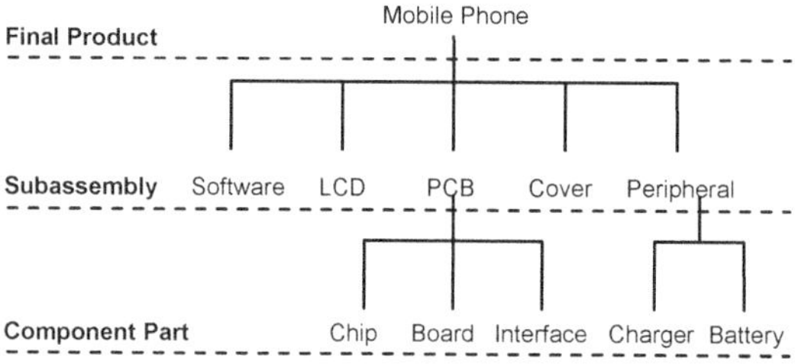

Fig. 2. BOM structures of Moxober mobile phones [16]

In Moxober's supply chain network, customers and suppliers are spread worldwide. The mobile phone company plays the role of the manufacturer. Its direct suppliers which are labeled Supplier I provide resources like software, PCB, LCD, cover and peripheral. Its suppliers' suppliers which are labeled Supplier II provide sub-resources like chip, board, interface, charger, and battery to the corresponding Supplier I. The next issue is to determine a specific configuration of the global manufacturing supply chain network for each individual customer order of a particular product model.

We will analyze the operation of this specific supply chain network by means of an agent-based supply chain framework and will also give a numerical example for using CBR in the supplier selection process. In fact, actual employment of a supplier should be consistent with the product fulfillment process of a specific customer's order in order to achieve customer satisfaction.

Now suppose a customer order from Wenzhou China. The customer places his order through the Seller agent of the mobile phone company. Through interaction, the customer can configure various ordering parameters such as product features like quality grade, quantity, price, and delivery date. The order information then goes to the design agent for product planning and determining a set of *Material Requirement Specifications* (MRSs) for each order along with the defined constraints by the design agent. Then, the MRSs will be organized into three case structures for LCD, Cover and Peripheral, and will be forwarded to the procurement Agent.

In order to accelerate the delivery, the procurement agent decides to allocate the final assembly of this order to Xiamen plant in China, a process which involves the requirement specification of three material types: LCD, Charger and Battery. The software design and PCB assembly operations are still held in Finland. The buyer agent will broadcast the material requirements to the potential suppliers who will bid on the platform of this agent to win the supplier selection procedure. Table 2 shows the case structure of an incoming order (ID=#13) related to MRSs in addition to the defined weight for each attribute by the customer.

Table 2. Case structure values

Case Attribute	MRS1	MRS2	MRS3	W
Product ID	01;013	02;013	03;013	-
Product name	Charger	Battery	LCD	-
Price	20-30	50-80	100-120	2
Volume	600-800	1200-1600	1000	4
Quality Grade	3-5	2-4	4-5	5
Delivery Time	20	15	12	4

Here are the defined constraints by [16]:

$$C_1 : MRS_1.Charger.Volume = MRS_2.Battery.Volume/2,$$
$$C_2 : MRS_2.Battery.DD \leq MRS_3.LCD.DD + 5$$

Since that customer defines the range of his order, this order will be counted as two cases with highest values and lowest values for each MRS attribute. This is done due to considering more cases and finding more suitable alternative products. For example, the lowest and highest values for MRS1 are:

$$Order_{high} = (01;013;Charger;20;\&800;5;20)$$
$$Order_{low} = (01;013;Charger;30;\&600;3;20)$$

Now, for the nearest neighbor algorithm which is used to find the most similar bid, the similarity of highest and lowest values of orders that have been identified by customers with each bid is calculated as follows. For example, the similarity of highest value of order 1 and supplier 1's bid for MRS1:

$$sim_p(O_{1_{High}}, B_1) = 1 - \left| \frac{20 - 25}{|20| + |25|} \right| = 0.888$$

$$sim_v(O_{1_{High}}, B_1) = 1 - \left| \frac{800 - 1000}{|800| + |1000|} \right| = 0.888$$

$$sim_q(O_{1_{High}}, B_1) = 1 - \left| \frac{5 - 5}{|5| + |5|} \right| = 1$$

$$sim_{dd}(O_{1_{High}}, B_1) = 1 - \left| \frac{20-20}{|20|+|20|} \right| = 1$$

$$Similarity(O_{1_{High}}, B_1) = \frac{(0.888 \times 2) + (0.888 \times 4) + (1 \times 5) + (1 \times 4)}{2+4+5+4}$$

$$Similarity(O_{1_{High}}, B_1) = \frac{1.776 + 3.552 + 5 + 4}{15} = \frac{14.328}{15} = 0.955$$

Table 3 and 4 show all the results of similarity function calculations for highest values and lowest values of received orders and suppliers' bids for each MRS. Table 3 assumes that the weight of each attribute is equal to 1 and table 4 assumes different weights for each attribute. The results show that weighted attributes play an important role in the awarding process which is based on the similarity function and the satisfaction of MRS constraints. For instance, if w=1, the bid of supplier 2 with the highest similarity for MRS1 would be selected, else if w=1 to 5, the bid of supplier 1 with the highest similarity for MRS1 would be selected. Therefore, the selected bid is compatible enough to users' preferences. Hence, customers' loss can be reduced.

Another task which must be done is checking the consistency of the selected bid with other bids. If the bid violates certain constraints, the bid is unqualified and the next bid with highest similarity would be selected. In this case, table 3, supplier 2 cannot be selected because it violates constraint C1.

Table 5 presents the results of similarity function calculations in comparison to [16] utility values for each MRS and also lists the winner of the bids for each MRS. In [16] for MRS, S1 was selected, but in this paper S2 is being selected due to the proposed mechanism and considering different weights for different attributes.

Table 3. The similarity function results for w=1

Weight	W=1					
Order & Supplier	$O_{hi}S_1$	$O_{hi}S_2$	$O_{hi}S_3$	$O_{low}S_1$	$O_{low}S_2$	$O_{low}S_3$
MRS 1	0.944	0.958	0.736	0.852	0.865	0.842
Order & Supplier	$O_{hi}S_4$	$O_{hi}S_5$	$O_{hi}S_6$	$O_{low}S_4$	$O_{low}S_5$	$O_{low}S_6$
MRS 2	0.891	0.969	0.852	0.830	0.836	0.844
Order & Supplier	$O_{hi}S_7$	$O_{hi}S_8$	$O_{hi}S_9$	$O_{low}S_7$	$O_{low}S_8$	$O_{low}S_9$
MRS 3	0.966	0.926	0.917	0.961	0.931	0.923

Table 4. The similarity function results for w=1 to 5

Weight	W=1 to 5					
Order & Supplier	$O_{hi}S_1$	$O_{hi}S_2$	$O_{hi}S_3$	$O_{low}S_1$	$O_{low}S_2$	$O_{low}S_3$
MRS 1	0.955	0.948	0.854	0.837	0.872	0.875
Order & Supplier	$O_{hi}S_4$	$O_{hi}S_5$	$O_{hi}S_6$	$O_{low}S_4$	$O_{low}S_5$	$O_{low}S_6$
MRS 2	0.906	0.978	0.826	0.805	0.696	0.871
Order & Supplier	$O_{hi}S_7$	$O_{hi}S_8$	$O_{hi}S_9$	$O_{low}S_7$	$O_{low}S_8$	$O_{low}S_9$
MRS 3	0.975	0.913	0.910	0.950	0.938	0.936

Table 5. The overall results and winners

MRS	Bid	[16] Utility	CBR (w=1)	CBR (w=1 to 5)	Winner
MRS 1	Bid11: (Supplier01; Charger; Volume|1000, price|25, DD|20)	0.68	0.944	0.954	S1
	Bid12: (Supplier02; Charger; Volume|800, price|20, DD|18)	0.73	0.958	0.948	
	Bid13: (Supplier03; Charger; Volume|1000, price|15, DD|22)	0.75	0.736	0.854	
MRS 2	Bid21: (Supplier04; Battery; Volume|1400, price|70, DD|10)	0.65	0.891	0.906	S5
	Bid22: (Supplier05; Battery; Volume|1600, price|60, DD|16)	0.72	0.969	0.978	
	Bid23: (Supplier06; Battery; Volume|2000, price|45, DD|18)	0.69	0.852	0.826	
MRS 3	Bid31: (Supplier07; LCD; Volume|1000, price|120, DD|11)	0.77	0.966	0.975	S7
	Bid32: (Supplier08; LCD; Volume|1200, price|100, DD|10)	0.71	0.926	0.913	
	Bid33: (Supplier09; LCD; Volume|900, price|90, DD|15)	0.69	0.917	0.910	

5 Conclusion Remarks

For any supply chain, there is a critical need for an automated and integrated system that can receive orders from customers and try to provide their orders by selecting the most suitable suppliers and negotiating with them to finalize the bid. The satisfaction of the requirements of the negotiating parties can be useful for all the stakeholders, especially customers who are more crucial for any company's survival, because, customer's loss would be risky for any company's competitive condition.

This paper presented an agent-based Supply Chain framework for supplier selection. Such framework enables agents to evaluate material offers, and negotiate with suppliers and customers on the price, volume, quality grade, and delivery time in the negotiation and supplier selection processes. Sometimes the manufacturer is unable to supply and provide their customers' first order. Therefore, the main contribution of this research is to take the customers' preferences into consideration and provide them with alternatives which are most similar to their first order from various suppliers. The second contribution is to use the CBR approach for finding the most similar alternatives by using nearest neighbor similarity function. During the ordering process customers can define the features' importance of their orders by weights. Hence, in the case retrieval level, these weights can help to find the most similar received bids and offer alternative products to the customers based on their desires. The results of the numerical example show that the proposed approach is robust enough to find the closest bid to the received order and rewards the winner supplier. The improvement and development of the prototype of the proposed framework should be submitted to further studies.

References

1. Wang, M., Liu, J., Wang, H., Cheung, W.K., Xie, X.: On-Demand e-Supply Chain Integration: A Multi-Agent Constraint-Based Approach. Expert Systems with Applications 34, 2683–2692 (2008)
2. Ross, D.F.: Introduction to e-Supply Chain Management: Engaging Technology to Build Market-Winning Business Partnerships. St. Lucie Press (2003)
3. Tan, K.C., Kannan, V.R., Handfield, R.B.: Supply Chain Management: Supplier Performance and Firm Performance. International Journal of Purchasing and Materials Management 34, 2–9 (1998)
4. Lee, H.L., Billington, C.: Managing Supply Chain Inventory: Pitfalls and Opportunities. Sloan Manage. Rev., 65–73 (1992)

5. Lee, E.-K., Ha, S., Kim, S.-K.: Supplier Selection and Management System Considering Relationships in Supply Chain Management. IEEE Transactions on Engineering Management 48, 307–318 (2001)
6. Hartley, J.L., Choi, T.Y.: Supplier development: Customers as a Catalyst of Process Change. Business Horizons 39, 37–44 (1996)
7. Ellram, L.M.: A Managerial Guideline for the Development and Implementation of Purchasing Partnerships. Journal of Supply Chain Management 31, 9–16 (1995)
8. Gjerdrum, J., Shah, N., Papageorgiou, L.G.: A Combined Optimization and Agent-Based Approach to Supply Chain Modelling and Performance Assessment. Production Planning & Control: The Management of Operations 12, 81–88 (2001)
9. Blecker, T., Graf, G.: Multi Agent Systems in Internet Based Production Environments—An Enabling Infrastructure for Mass Customization. In: The Second Interdisciplinary World Congress on Mass Customization and Personalization (2003)
10. Lu, S.-Y.: CIRP working group on engineering as collaborative negotiation (2004), `http://mspde.usc.edu/ecn`
11. Saad, A., Kawamura, K., Biswas, G.: Performance Evaluation of Contract Net-Based Heterarchical Scheduling for Flexible Manufacturing Systems. In: Proceedings of the 1995 International Joint Conference on Artificial Intelligence, Workshop on Intelligent Manufacturing, pp. 310–321 (1995)
12. Parunak, H.V.D., Baker, A.D., Clark, S.J.: The AARIA Agent Architecture: An Example of Requirements-Driven Agent-Based System Design. In: Proceedings of the First International Conference on Autonomous Agents (1997)
13. Barbuceanu, M., Fox, M.S.: Integrating Communicative Action, Conversations and Decision Theory to Coordinate Agents. In: Proceedings of the First International Conference on Autonomous Agents, pp. 49–58. ACM, Marina del Rey (1997)
14. Maturana, F., Shen, W., Norrie, D.H.: MetaMorph: An Adaptive Agent-Based Architecture for Intelligent Manufacturing. International Journal of Production Research 37, 2159–2173 (1999)
15. Min, J.U., Bjornsson, H.: Agent-based Supply Chain Management Automation. In: Proceedings of the Eighth International Conference on Computing in Civil and Building Engineering (ICCCBE-VIII), pp. 1001–1006 (2000)
16. Jiao, J., You, X., Kumar, A.: An Agent-Based Framework for Collaborative Negotiation in The Global Manufacturing Supply Chain Network. Robotics and Computer-Integrated Manufacturing 22, 239–255 (2006)
17. Wentao, L.: An Agent-based Negotiation Model for the Sourcing Of the Condtruction Suppliers. PhD. The University of Hong Kong, Hong Kong (2008)
18. Lu, L., Wang, G.: A Study on Multi-Agent Supply Chain Framework Based on Network Economy. Computers & Industrial Engineering 54, 288–300 (2008)
19. Kim, H.S., Cho, J.H.: Supply Chain Formation Using Agent Negotiation. Decision Support Systems 49, 77–90 (2010)
20. Weber, C.A., Current, J.R., Benton, W.C.: Vendor Selection Criteria and Methods. European Journal of Operational Research 50, 2–18 (1991)
21. Ghodsypour, S.H., O'Brien, C.: A Decision Support System for Supplier Selection Using An Integrated Analytic Hierarchy Process and Linear Programming. International Journal of Production Economics 56-57, 199–212 (1998)
22. Pan, A.C.: Allocation of Order Quantity Among Suppliers. Journal of Purchasing and Materials Management 25(3), 36–39 (1989)
23. Rosenthal, E.C., Zydiak, J.L., Chaudhry, S.S.: Vendor Selection with Bundling. Decision Sciences 26(1), 35–48 (1995)
24. FIPA. The Foundation for Intelligent Physical Agents (2005), `http://www.fipa.org`

Credit Scoring Using Soft Computing Schemes: A Comparison between Support Vector Machines and Artificial Neural Networks

Nnamdi I. Nwulu[1], Shola Oroja[2], and Mustafa Ilkan[3]

[1] Electrical and Electronics Engineering Department, Near East University, Lefkosa, Mersin 10, Turkey
[2] School of Computing and Technology, Eastern Mediterranean University, Gazimagusa, Mersin 10, Turkey
[3] Director, School of Computing and Technology, Eastern Mediterranean University, Gazimagusa, Mersin 10, Turkey
ninwulu@ieee.org, oroja.shola@yahoo.com,
mustafa.ilkan@emu.edu.tr

Abstract. The recent financial crisis that has devastated many nations of the world has made it imperative that nations upgrade their credit scoring methods. Although statistical methods have been the preferred method for decades, soft computing techniques are becoming increasingly popular due to their efficient and accurate nature and relative simplicity. In this paper a comparison is made between two prominent soft computing schemes namely Support Vector Machines and Artificial Neural Networks. Although a comparison can be made along various criteria, this study attempts to compare both techniques when applied to credit scoring in terms of accuracy, computational complexity and processing times. In order to assure meaningful comparisons, a real world dataset precisely the Australian Credit Scoring data set available online was used for this task. Experimental results obtained indicate that although both soft computing schemes are highly efficient, Artificial Neural Networks obtain slightly better results and in relatively shorter times.

Keywords: Credit scoring, Soft computing schemes, Support Vector Machines, Artificial Neural Networks.

1 Introduction

Credit scoring has overtime become one of the most concise measures of the credit worthiness of individuals or groups. Records of individuals or groups are stored and analyzed and a score is given. Typically a higher credit score infers that the applicant is more suitable to do business with and a lower credit score denotes the fact that the applicant isn't really suitable for business dealings or is high risk. In [1] four basic types of credit scoring are defined. They are application scoring where the applicants demographic, social and other important information are evaluated at the time of application. This kind of credit scoring basically assesses whether a new applicant is qualified to be given credit. The second class of credit scoring is behavioural scoring

E. Ariwa and E. El-Qawasmeh (Eds.): DEIS 2011, CCIS 194, pp. 275–286, 2011.

which is quite similar to application scoring, the only difference being that unlike application scoring which is for new applicants, behavioural scoring is for old or returning applicants. The third type of credit scoring is collection scoring which is concerned with categorising customers into different strata of insolvency or bankruptcy. The essence of collection scoring is to distinguish customers who are in varying levels of bankruptcy and identify those who need urgent action from those where action can be deferred. The fourth and final type of credit scoring identified is fraud detection which is primarily concerned with the degree to which an application is fraudulent.

In this work we are primarily concerned with application scoring. This class of credit scoring has been investigated in a lot of prior works in the literature with varying degrees of success. In [1] the authors propose a missing data imputation method and subagging an ensemble classification technique for credit scoring using a real world dataset consisting of a sample of IBM's Italian customers. The authors apply several classifiers namely kernel support vector machines, nearest neighbors, decision trees and Adaboost and compare results with their corresponding subagged versions. Results obtained indicate that subagging significantly improves the classifiers performance and results.

In another recent work [2] an SVM model was developed for predicting the degree of default in payments for technology based Small and Medium Enterprises (SME) in Korea. The model used input factors that consisted of company economic indicators, financial ratios and technology indicators. Results obtained in this work indicate that SVM outperforms neural networks and logistic regression models. In [3] authors utilized a generalized classification and regression tree (CART) for forecasting consumer credit risk for customer samples of a major commercial bank in the United States (US). The period studied is from January 2005 to April 2009 and the study determined that their machine learning model accurately forecasted credit events 3 to 12 months ahead. In [4] the author designed different types of Artificial Neural Networks (ANN) for municipal credit rating classification for municipalities in the US. The ANN's designed are feed-forward neural networks (FFNN), Radial basis function neural networks (RBFNN), Probabilistic neural networks (PNN), Cascade correlation neural networks (CCNN), Group method of data handling (GMDH) polynomial neural networks and Support Vector Machines (SVM). Results obtained from this study show that the Probabilistic neural networks (PNN) happened to be the best performing neural network model as it provided the highest classification accuracy amongst the other tools.

Recent research in the field of credit scoring seems to indicate that a hybrid credit scoring approach or utilizing ensemble classification techniques yield better results. In [5] authors propose four hybrid SVM models for credit scoring. In each case SVM is combined with other tools and the resulting hybrid system is tested on two different datasets. The other tools used in combination with SVM include conventional statistical Linear Discriminate Analysis (LDA), Decision tree, Rough sets and F-score approaches. The results obtained from this experiment seem to indicate that LDA with SVM outperforms SVM alone. Another example of a hybrid approach is in [6] where four different hybrid models were investigated. The models consisted of two classification techniques, two clustering techniques, a clustering technique used in conjunction with a classification technique and finally a classification technique used in conjunction with a clustering technique. All the developed hybrid models were evaluated using a real world dataset from a bank based in Taiwan and the obtained results from this experiment indicate that the two classification hybrid models (logistic regression and ANN's) outperformed the other hybrid models in terms of prediction accuracy.

Examples of the use of ensemble models for credit scoring are in [7], [8] and [9]. In [7] a host of several ensemble methods based on Least Square Support Vectors Machines (LSSVM) are developed and tested on two real word datasets. In [8] a comparison is made of three ensemble methods namely Bagging, Boosting, and Stacking. The ensemble methods are built on Logistic Regression Analysis (LRA), Decision Tree (DT), Artificial Neural Network (ANN) and Support Vector Machine (SVM). In [9] a novel vertical bagging decision trees model (VBDTM) is proposed for credit scoring. The ensemble model is built on several base learners that consist of various types of machine learning single models, rule extraction models, two stages models, hybrid models and aggregation models and experimental results indicate that the novel ensemble method (VBDTM) outperforms other methods.

It is noteworthy that researchers using hybrid and ensemble methods often claim that single models often have some inductive bias (in the case of SVM) and grapple with the problem of local minima and overfitting (in the case of ANN's), hence the need for ensemble classification techniques or hybrid models. The problem with hybrid and ensemble methods however lies in the fact that they involve a fair amount of computational complexity which subsequently increases processing times (time costs) and furthermore there is no conclusive evidence that they obtain better performance than single models.

Single soft computing models with the right amount of care in data pre processing and choice of network or model topology can deliver highly accurate judgments on credit scoring and in short processing times. To this end in this paper we utilize a single model of a Back Propagated Neural Network (BPNN) and a Radial Basis function (RBF) Support Vector Machine (SVM) and perform a comparative analysis between these two soft computing models for credit risk scoring. The comparative analysis used in this paper relies on a similar yardstick employed in [10] and seeks to determine amongst the two techniques:

- The model that returns a higher classification rate with minimal error.
- The model that obtained higher classification results with minimal time and computational costs
- The model that returned the highest accuracy with data it had not hitherto been exposed to (testing or validation data).

Furthermore in this paper we experiment with different scaling or normalization techniques and determine the best scaling/normalization technique that yields a higher accuracy rate. The paper is therefore arranged as follows; In section two we briefly detail the real world Australian credit scoring dataset, section three details the steps taken in data preprocessing prior to learning. Section four briefly describes the architecture or topologies of the ANN and SVM learners. In section five we provide the results of implementing the experimental setups of both soft computing schemes and the paper is concluded in section six with suggestions on areas for future research.

2 Credit Scoring Dataset

The credit scoring dataset used in this work is the Australian credit scoring dataset publicly available from the University of California online machine learning repository [11]. The dataset actually consists of details of real individuals which have been changed to symbols and numbers in order to protect customer confidentiality. There are 690 customers in the dataset with 307 customers having a positive credit score which means it is advisable to do business with them and 383 with a negative credit score meaning business dealings are not advisable or is risky. Each customer or case has 6 categorical and 8 nominal values in response to 14 attribute questions and an output of accept/reject or positive/negative. Table 1 provides a summary of the dataset's input attributes and their types of values.

Table 1. Credit Scoring Dataset Input Attributes and Characteristics

Attribute	Attribute Characteristics
1	Categorical. Formerly (a,b) Now (0,1)
2	Continous
3	Continous
4	Categorical. Formerly (p,g,gg). Now (1,2,3)
5	Categorical. Formerly (ff,d,i,k,j,aa,m,c,w,e,q,r,cc,x). Now(1,2,3,4,5,6,7,8,9,10,11,12,13,14)
6	Categorical. Formerly (ff,dd,j,bb,v,n,o,h,z). Now (1,2,3,4,5,6,7,8,9)
7	Continous
8	Categorical. Formerly (t,f). Now (0,1)
9	Categorical. Formerly (t,f). Now (0,1)
10	Continous
11	Categorical. Formerly (t,f). Now (0,1)
12	Categorical. Formerly (s,g,p). Now (1,2,3)
13	Continous
14	Continous

The raw data is fed to the soft computing models (ANN and SVM) but prior to network learning of the different models it is necessary that data pre processing be performed. The steps taken in data pre processing and the different techniques employed are described in the next section.

3 Data Pre- processing

A careful analysis of the raw Australian credit scoring dataset would reveal that the numerical values span a wide range and therefore the data cannot be fed into the soft computing models the way they are and therefore need to be normalized. Typical normalization approaches consist of determining the maximum numerical value in the whole dataset and dividing all the numbers by that maximum value. The problem with that approach for this dataset as espoused in [10] is the fact that the maximum value in the Australian dataset is 100001 which is an outlier value as it is far greater than other numbers. Dividing all the numbers in the dataset by 100001 would make learning for soft computing models difficult if not impossible as all the numerical values would be slightly greater than zero meaning that there would be insufficient information representation. This is partly responsible for the average classification results obtained by other single model soft computing learners. Table 2 shows the Australian credit scoring dataset prior to normalization for the first 10 cases. In this paper we utilize three different normalization techniques and they are briefly described in the next sub sections.

Table 2. Credit Scoring Dataset Input Attributes Prior to Normalization

	INPUT ATTRIBUTES														
NO.	1	2	3	4	5	6	7	8	9	10	11	12	13	14	OUTPUT
1	1	22.08	11.46	2	4	4	1.585	0	0	0	1	2	100	1213	01
2	0	22.67	7	2	8	4	0.165	0	0	0	0	2	160	1	01
3	0	29.58	1.75	1	4	4	1.25	0	0	0	1	2	280	1	01
4	0	21.67	11.5	1	5	3	0	1	1	11	1	2	0	1	10
5	1	20.17	8.17	2	6	4	1.96	1	1	14	0	2	60	159	10
6	0	15.83	0.585	2	8	8	1.5	1	1	2	0	2	100	1	10
7	1	17.42	6.5	2	3	4	0.125	0	0	0	0	2	60	101	01
8	0	58.67	4.46	2	11	8	3.04	1	1	6	0	2	43	561	10
9	1	27.83	1	1	2	8	3	0	0	0	0	2	176	538	01
10	0	55.75	7.08	2	4	8	6.75	1	1	3	1	2	100	51	01

3.1 Customer or Horizontal Normalization

In this normalization technique, we move across the dataset horizontally and automatically determine the highest numerical value for each individual customer or case, and divide all other numerical values by that maximum value. Thus we end up with 690 maximum normalization values one for each customer. Table 3 shows the maximum normalization values for the first 15 customers and Table 4 shows the first 10 cases of the final dataset using customer or horizontal normalization.

Table 3. The maximum numerical value for each customer used to normalize other input values

Customer	1	2	3	4	5	6	7	8	9	10	11	12	13	14	15
Max. Value	1213	160	280	21.67	159	100	101	561	538	100	858	470	211	1001	320

3.2 Attribute or Vertical Normalization

This normalization technique works by determining the highest numerical value for each of the 14 attributes and dividing all the other numerical values by that maximum value. Table 5 shows the maximum values for all the 14 attributes. These are the values all other input attributes are divided by. Table 6 shows the first 10 cases of the final dataset using attribute or vertical normalization.

Table 4. First 10 Cases of the Credit Scoring Dataset after Customer/Horizontal Normalization

	INPUT ATTRIBUTES														
NO.	1	2	3	4	5	6	7	8	9	10	11	12	13	14	OUTPUT
1	0.0008	0.02	0.009	0.002	0.003	0.003	0.001	0	0	0	0.001	0.002	0.1	1	01
2	0	0.14	0.044	0.013	0.050	0.025	0.001	0	0	0	0	0.013	1	0.006	01
3	0	0.11	0.006	0.004	0.014	0.014	0.004	0	0	0	0.004	0.007	1	0.004	01
4	0	1	0.531	0.046	0.231	0.138	0	0.046	0.046	0.51	0.046	0.092	0	0.046	10
5	0.0063	0.13	0.051	0.013	0.038	0.025	0.012	0.006	0.006	0.09	0	0.013	0.4	1	10
6	0	0.16	0.006	0.020	0.080	0.080	0.015	0.010	0.010	0.02	0	0.020	1	0.01	10
7	0.0099	0.17	0.064	0.020	0.029	0.039	0.001	0	0	0	0	0.020	0.6	1	01
8	0	0.10	0.008	0.004	0.019	0.014	0.005	0.002	0.002	0.01	0	0.004	0.1	1	10
9	0.0019	0.05	0.002	0.002	0.003	0.015	0.006	0	0	0	0	0.004	0.3	1	01
10	0	0.56	0.071	0.02	0.040	0.080	0.068	0.010	0.010	0.03	0.010	0.020	1	0.51	01

Table 5. The maximum numerical value for each attribute used to normalize other input values

Attribute	1	2	3	4	5	6	7	8	9	10	11	12	13	14
Max. Value	1	80.25	28	3	14	9	28.5	1	1	67	1	3	2000	100001

Table 6. First 10 Cases of the Credit Scoring Dataset after Attribute/ Vertical Normalization

	INPUT ATTRIBUTES														
NO.	1	2	3	4	5	6	7	8	9	10	11	12	13	14	OUTPUT
1	1	0.28	0.41	0.67	0.29	0.44	0.06	0	0	0	1	0.67	0.05	0.012	01
2	0	0.28	0.25	0.67	0.57	0.44	0.01	0	0	0	0	0.67	0.08	0.00001	01
3	0	0.37	0.06	0.33	0.29	0.44	0.04	0	0	0	1	0.67	0.14	0.00001	01
4	0	0.27	0.41	0.33	0.36	0.33	0	1	1	0.16	1	0.67	0	0.00001	10
5	1	0.25	0.29	0.67	0.43	0.44	0.07	1	1	0.21	0	0.67	0.03	0.001	10
6	0	0.20	0.02	0.67	0.57	0.89	0.05	1	1	0.03	0	0.67	0.05	0.00001	10
7	1	0.22	0.23	0.67	0.21	0.44	0.004	0	0	0	0	0.67	0.03	0.001	01
8	0	0.73	0.16	0.67	0.79	0.89	0.11	1	1	0.09	0	0.67	0.02	0.006	10
9	1	0.35	0.04	0.33	0.14	0.89	0.11	0	0	0	0	0.67	0.09	0.005	01
10	0	0.69	0.25	0.67	0.29	0.89	0.24	1	1	0.04	1	0.67	0.05	0.001	01

Table 7. Credit Scoring Dataset Input Attributes After Scaling to the -1: 1 Interval

	INPUT ATTRIBUTES														
NO.	1	2	3	4	5	6	7	8	9	10	11	12	13	14	OUTPUT
1	+1	-0.749	-0.18	1	-0.54	-0.25	-0.89	-1	-1	-1	+1	1	-0.9	-0.976	-1
2	-1	-0.731	-0.5	1	0.08	-0.25	-0.99	-1	-1	-1	-1	1	-0.84	-1	-1
3	-1	-0.523	-0.88	-1	-0.54	-0.25	-0.91	-1	-1	-1	+1	1	-0.72	-1	-1
4	-1	-0.762	-0.18	-1	-0.38	-0.5	-1	+1	+1	-0.672	+1	1	-1	-1	+1
5	+1	-0.807	-0.42	1	-0.23	-0.25	-0.86	+1	+1	-0.582	-1	1	-0.94	-0.997	+1
6	-1	-0.937	-0.96	1	0.08	0.75	-0.89	+1	+1	-0.940	-1	1	-0.9	-1	+1
7	+1	-0.889	-0.54	1	-0.69	-0.25	-0.99	-1	-1	-1	-1	1	-0.94	-0.998	-1
8	-1	0.351	-0.68	1	0.54	0.75	-0.79	+1	+1	-0.821	-1	1	-0.96	-0.989	+1
9	+1	-0.577	-0.93	-1	-0.85	0.75	-0.79	-1	-1	-1	-1	1	-0.82	-0.989	-1
10	-1	0.263	-0.49	1	-0.54	0.75	-0.53	+1	+1	-0.910	+1	1	-0.9	-0.999	-1

3.3 Normalization / Scaling to the -1: 1 Interval

In this normalization technique we scale all the values to the range of -1 to 1. Thus in this procedure unlike the prior scaling methods we have both positive and negative values in the final dataset. Table 7 shows the first 10 cases of the final dataset using this normalization or scaling procedure.

4 Soft Computing Training Phase

After data pre processing, the next procedure is training using the soft computing schemes. In this work Artificial Neural Networks (ANN) and Support Vector Machines (SVM) are the utilized soft computing schemes. The subsequent sub sections briefly describe the training or learning procedures employed.

4.1 Support Vector Machines Training

The C-SVM model with an RBF kernel was used for SVM training using the LIBSVM software [12]. Furthermore in this work the cross validation approach was used. The cross validation procedure is used to avoid the problem of over fitting data. This approach allows us to determine suitable parameters (C and γ) for our RBF kernel. In v-fold cross-validation (which was used in this work), the training dataset is divided into v equal subsets. Sequentially one subset is tested using the SVM classifier trained on the remaining (v – 1) subsets. The obtained cross-validation accuracy is the percentage of data correctly classified.

The highest cross validation accuracy is obtained and the parameters which produce the best results are saved and then used to train the SVM learner. The saved model is then used on the out of sample data or data it has not been exposed to before (testing set). In this work v=5. The parameter search range for C was conducted from ($2^{-100} - 2^{100}$) while for γ it was also from ($2^{-100} - 2^{100}$). The best C obtained was 0.0625 while γ was 0.0221. These values of C and γ were those that obtained the highest validation accuracy and they were then used for training the SVM learner.

4.2 Neural Network Training

For neural network training the learning algorithm used is the back propagation learning algorithm. Fig. 1 shows the architecture of the proposed credit scoring neural network model. Our ANN input layer has 14 neurons which corresponds to the number of the input attributes with each input neuron receiving a normalized attribute numerical value. There is one hidden layer containing 10 neurons while the output layer has 2 neurons where 1 0 represents a positive credit score and 0 1 denotes a negative credit score.

Since there were two methods of normalizing the neural network input data (customer and attribute normalization) we end up with two neural networks where NN1 is the network for the customer normalized data and NN2 is the network for attribute normalized data.

The initial weights of both neural networks were randomly generated with values between -0.35 and +0.35 and during training the learning co efficient and momentum rate were adjusted and the values that achieved the highest training accuracy rate were saved.

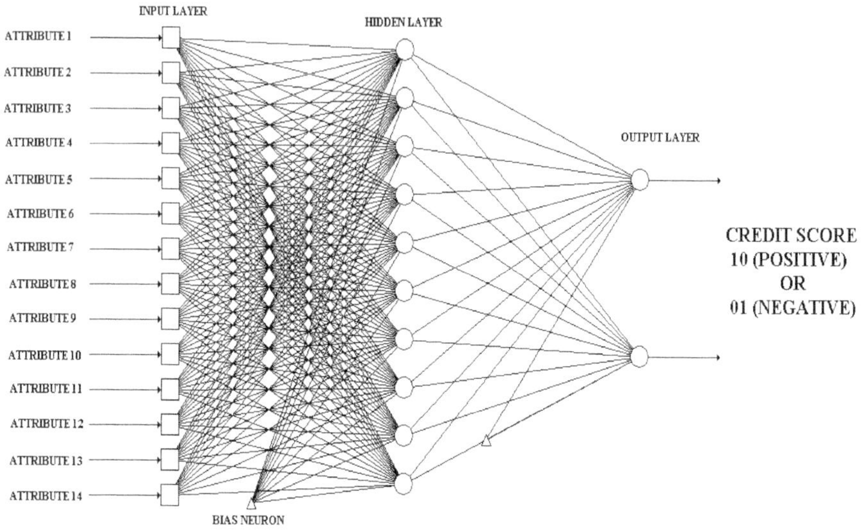

Fig. 1. Architecture of the proposed credit scoring neural network model

5 Experimental Results and Discussions

The results of the soft computing credit scoring models were obtained using a 2.2 GHz PC with 2 GB of RAM, Windows XP OS and LIBSVM v 2.9.1 for the SVM model and MATLAB v 7.9.0 (R2009b) for the ANN model. Since there are a total of 690 cases in the dataset we utilized training to testing ratio of 50%: 50%. Thus there are 345 cases for training the soft computing models and 345 cases for testing the trained models. The reason an equal training to testing ratio was used is to ensure that the soft computing models are not exposed to more training data than testing data thereby ensuring an unbiased model.

The following were the obtained results for the developed neural models: NN1 learnt and converged after 1000 iterations and within 214.89 seconds (training times), whilst the running time for the neural network after training and using one forward pass was 0.58×10^{-4} seconds (testing time). The training dataset accuracy rate was 87.2% while the testing dataset yielded an accuracy rate of 78.08%. Combining both accuracy rates (training and testing) yields an overall accuracy rate of 82.64%. For NN 2 error convergence was after 1000 iterations and within 200.83 seconds (training times), whilst the running time for the neural network after training and using one forward pass was 0.672×10^{-4} seconds (testing time). The training dataset accuracy rate was 90.14% while the testing dataset yielded an accuracy rate of 84.64%. Combining both accuracy rates (training and testing) yields an overall accuracy rate of 87.39%. Table 8 lists the final parameters of the successfully trained neural network models and their accuracy rates and training times and Fig. 2 and Fig. 3 shows the error versus iteration graph for NN1 and NN2.

The trained SVM modelling system delivered the following results: using the training dataset yielded 87.5362 % accuracy rate while the testing dataset yielded an accuracy rate of 86.087%. Combining both accuracy rates (training and testing) yields an overall accuracy rate of 86.8116%. Table 9 lists the final parameters of the successfully trained SVM model.

A comparison of all the obtained results along the criteria defined hitherto in this paper suggests that the ANN system achieves better accuracy rates while the SVM learner learnt in shorter time period. It is our opinion however that the ANN modeling system would be more suitable for practical applications due to its obtained higher accuracy.

Table 8. The Final Parameters of the Credit Scoring Artificial Neural Network Models

	NN1	NN2
Number of Input Neurons	14	14
Number of Hidden Neurons	10	10
Number of Output Neurons	2	2
Weights Values Range	-0.35 to +0.35	-0.35 to +0.35
Learning co-efficient	0.00021	0.00795
Momentum Rate	0.77	0.81
Obtained Error	0.0055	0.004624
Performed iterations	1000	1000
Training time(s)[1]	214.89	200.83
Run Time(s)[1]	0.58×10^{-4}	0.672×10^{-4}
Training dataset accuracy rate	87.2%	90.14%
Testing dataset accuracy rate	78.08%	84.64%
Overall accuracy rate	82.64%	87.39%

1. Using a 2.2 GHz PC with 2 GB of RAM, Windows XP OS and MATLAB v 7.9.0 (R2009b)

Table 9. The Final Parameters of the Credit Scoring Support Vector Machine Model

Number of Features	14
Number of Classes	2
C Parameter Search Range	$2^{-100} - 2^{100}$
γ Parameter Search Range	$2^{-100} - 2^{100}$
C	0.0625
γ	0.0221
V	5
Type of SVM used	C-SVM
Kernel	RBF
Training optimization time(s)[1]	0.05
Training dataset accuracy rate	87.5362%
Testing dataset accuracy rate	86.087%
Overall accuracy rate	86.81%

1. Using a 2.2 GHz PC with 2 GB of RAM, Windows XP OS and LIBSVM v 2.9.1.

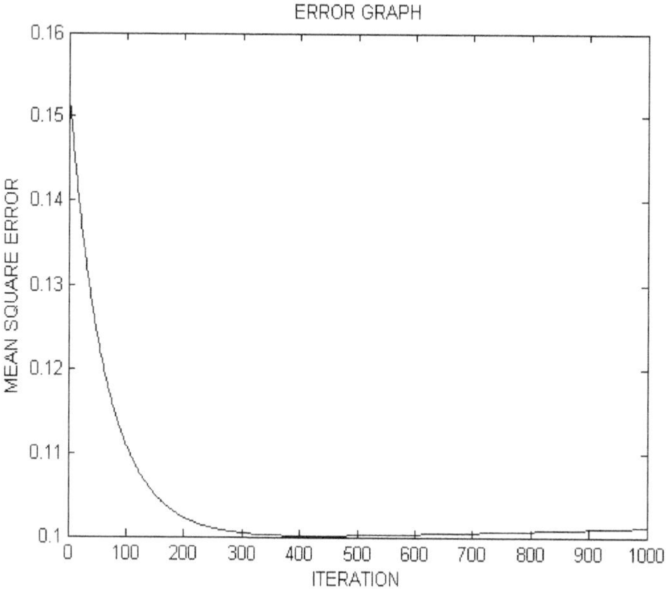

Fig. 2. Error versus Iteration Graph for NN1

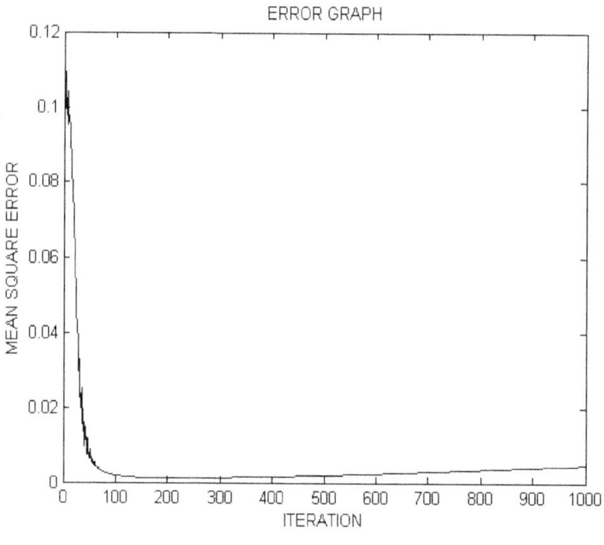

Fig. 3. Error versus Iteration Graph for NN2

6 Conclusion

This work provided an evaluation between Support Vector Machines (SVM) and Artificial Neural Network (ANN) when applied to the task of credit scoring. The aim of this work is provide a comparative analysis of ANN and SVM models when applied to credit scoring in terms of accuracy, computational complexity and processing times. For this task the Australian credit scoring dataset which is a real world dataset and contains 690 cases of various customers and their credit scores was used. This work has hitherto been attempted with various single soft computing models and various ensemble classification algorithms and hybrid systems with varying results.

Prior to feeding our developed system with the data, we performed data pre processing specifically we normalized the data using three different methods and techniques, giving us three variations of the Australian credit dataset which we fed to three different soft computing models (2 were ANN based with the remainder SVM based).

Both developed ANN models used a 3-layer supervised learner based on the back propagation learning algorithm while for the SVM learner we utilized C- SVM using the RBF kernel and v-fold cross validation mechanism. Experimental results obtained show that the better ANN system outperforms the SVM system (87.39% to 86.81%) while the SVM system requires a shorter training time than the ANN system (0.05 s to 200.83 s). The 0.05s obtained does not however include the parameter search range which is a time consuming process. In light of the above we conclude that the ANN system is the better system taking into consideration its better accuracy results and relatively shorter training times.

Future work will consist of designing a soft computing model that can determine if a customer is on the borderline. i.e. the customer is not exactly suitable to do business with and is also not high risk.

References

1. Paleologo, G., Elisseeff, A., Antonini, G.: Subagging for Credit Scoring Models. European Journal of Operational Research 201, 490–499 (2010)
2. Hong, S.K., Sohn, S.Y.: Support vector machines for default prediction of SMEs based on technology credit. European Journal of Operational Research 201, 838–846 (2010)
3. Khandani, A.E., Kim, A.J., Lo, A.W.: Consumer credit-risk models via machine-learning algorithms. Journal of Banking & Finance 34, 2767–2787 (2010)
4. Hajek, P.: Municipal credit rating modelling by neural networks. Decision Support Systems 51, 108–118 (2011)
5. Chen, F.L., Li, F.C.: Combination of feature selection approaches with SVM in credit scoring. Expert Systems with Applications 37, 4902–4909 (2010)
6. Tsai, C.F., Chen, M.L.: Credit rating by hybrid machine learning techniques. Applied Soft Computing 10, 374–380 (2010)
7. Zhou, L., Lai, K.K., Yu, L.: Least squares support vector machines ensemble models for credit scoring. Expert Systems with Applications 37, 127–133 (2010)
8. Wang, G., Hao, J., Ma, J., Jiang, H.: A comparative assessment of ensemble learning for credit scoring. Expert Systems with Applications 38, 223–230 (2011)

9. Zhang, D., Zhou, X., Leung, S.C.H., Zheng, J.: Vertical bagging decision trees model for credit scoring. Expert Systems with Applications 37, 7838–7843 (2010)
10. Khashman, A.: A Neural Network Model for Credit Risk Evaluation. International Journal of Neural Systems 19, 285–294 (2009)
11. Asuncion, A., Newman, D.J.: UCI Machine Learning Repository. University of California, School of Information and Computer Science, Irvine, CA (2007), `http://www.ics.uci.edu/~mlearn/MLRepository.html`
12. Chang, C.C., Lin, C.J.: LIBSVM: a library for support vector machines (2001), software `http://www.csie.ntu.edu.tw/cjlin/libsvm`

A Novel Social Network Model for Forming Relationships

Sreedhar Bhukya

Department of Computer and Information Sciences
University of Hyderabad, Hyderabad- 500046, India
sr3naik@gmail.com

Abstract. Recent studies on social networks are based on a characteristic which includes assortative mixing, high clustering, short average path lengths, broad degree distributions and the existence of community structure. Here, a model has been developed in the domain of 'formation of relationships' which satisfies all the above characteristics, based on some existing social network models. In addition, this model facilitates interaction between various family groups. This model gives very high clustering coefficient by retaining the asymptotically scale-free degree distribution. Here the community structure is raised from a mixture of random attachment and implicit preferential attachment. In addition to earlier works which only considered Neighbor of Initial Contact (NIC) as implicit preferential contact, we have considered Neighbor of Neighbor of Initial Contact (NNIC) also. This model supports the occurrence of a contact between two initial contacts if the new vertex chooses more than one initial contacts. This ultimately will develop a complex social network rather than the one that was taken as basic reference.

Keywords: Social networks. Random initial contact. Neighbor of neighbor initial contact. Tertiary contact. Forming relationship.

1 Introduction

Formation of relationships is an essential part of our life. Most of our relationships, if not all, are based on trust in one or other form. Trust is a crucial factor in formation of relationship in real life. The importance of trust is still not completely exploited in the social networking domain. Through this paper, I would like to draw a model which captures 'trust' in the formation of relationships in social networks. Here we developing a model on formation of marriage relationships based on trust in Indian context. This model works well within the communities and can also be useful in formation of marriage relationships across different communities.

The earlier model [1] didn't discuss about various applications of social network formation. The earlier model is applying it to a particular context of marriage relationships based on trust, one may trust someone for providing good recommendations (referral trust or trust in belief) [2], a mechanism that replicates human trust in which trust is based on class [3] membership rather than prior knowledge in the entity.

Social networks are made of nodes that are tied by one or more specific types of relationships. The vertex represents individuals or family. Social networks have been

E. Ariwa and E. El-Qawasmeh (Eds.): DEIS 2011, CCIS 194, pp. 287–295, 2011.

intensively studied by Social scientists [4-6], for several decades in order to understand local phenomena such as local formation and their dynamics, as well as network wide process, like transmission of information, spreading disease, spreading rumor, sharing ideas etc. Various types of social networks, such as those related to professional collaboration [7-9], Internet dating [10], and opinion formation among people have been studied. Social networks involve Financial, Cultural, Educational, Families, Relations and so on. Social networks create relationship between vertices; Social networks include Sociology, basic Mathematics and graph theory. The basic mathematics structure for a social network is a graph. The main social network properties includes hierarchical community structure [11], small world property [12], power law distribution of nodes degree [13] and the most basic is Barabasi Albert model of scale free networks [14]. The more online social network gains popularity, the more scientific community is attracted by the research opportunities that these new fields give. Most popular online social networks is Facebook, where user can add friends, send them messages, and update their personal profiles to notify friends about themselves. Essential characteristics for social networks are believed to include assortative mixing [15, 16], high clustering, short average path lengths, broad degree distributions [17, 18].

The advantage of our model can be understood from the following example. Let us consider a family head (new vertex) contacting other person within a community for marriage alliance, and suppose that he/she didn't get suitable alliance from that person/family or form his/her neighbors, but he/she may or may not get suitable alliance from neighbors of initial contacted family. Then we are asking initial contacted family to consider its neighbor of neighbor family for suitable alliance for the person who is in search of alliance (new family). This model is very successful in real life environments where trust is given utmost priority. The trust of the person who is searching for alliance (new vertex) on the person with whom he/she goes for alliance (tertiary vertex) is based on trust in initial contacted family. The trust of initial person on tertiary vertex is based on his/her trust on neighboring family. The whole network is based on trust between different family groups within the community. Here we considering only caste based communities for marriage alliances. Communities can also be defined based on region, religion, gender etc.

The basic avenues /opportunities available for a person/family group for marriage alliance in a real environment are (1) Relatives (2) Colleagues (3) Friends (4) Neighbors or Colony people, and these four categories need not necessarily be mutually exclusive to each other.

Let us consider a person contacting us for some purpose and we are unable to help him, then we will try to help him by giving some contacts of our friends. The extreme case of this nature is that we may try to contact our friend of friend for this purpose. We have implemented the same thing in our novel model [1]. In the old model [19], information about friends was only used to be updated, where as in our present model, information about friend of friend also has been updated. Of course this model creates a complex social network model but, sharing of information or data will be very fast. This fulfills the actual purpose of social networking in an efficient way with a faster growth rate by keeping the community structure as it is.

2 Network Growth Algorithm

The algorithm includes three processes: (1) Random attachment (2) Implicit preferential contact with the neighbors of initial contact (3) In addition to the above we are proposing a contact between the initial contact to its Neighbor of Neighbor contact (tertiary). The algorithm of the model is as follows [1] here we consider a vertex is as a person or a family in the network. Here we consider m_r is Initial Contact (New family, i.e searching alliance), m_s is Secondary Contact (neighbor of initially contacted family), and finally m_r is Tertiary contact (neighbor of neighbor initially contacted family, i.e match for alliances)

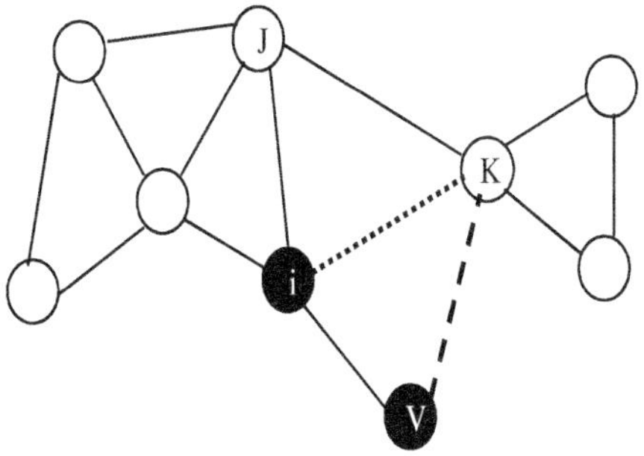

Fig. 1. Growing process for searching alliances in same community group, consider all vertices as persons or families, the new vertex 'V' family initially connect through some one as initial contact (*say i family*). Now i *family*, updates its neighbor of neighbor contact list and hence connects to k family. V' family connects to m_s number of neighbors (say k family) and m_t number of neighbor of neighbors of i family (say family k).

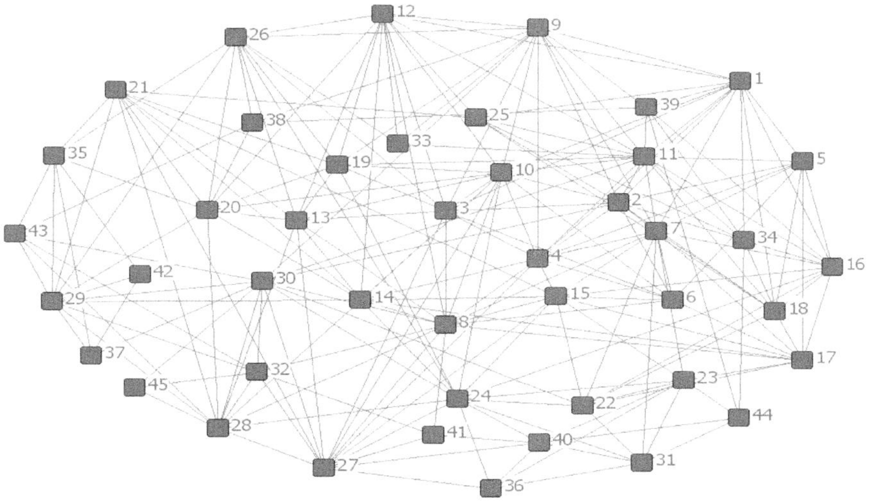

Fig. 2. Showing social network graph with 45 Families

1) Start with a seed network of N vertices
2) Pick on average $m_r \geq 1$ through some one as initial contacts
3) Pick on average $m_s \geq 0$ neighbors of each initial contact as secondary contact
4) Pick on average $m_t \geq 1$ neighbors of each secondary contact as tertiary contact
5) Connect the new vertex to the initial, secondary and tertiary contacts
6) Repeat the steps 2-5 until the network has grown to desired size.

In this application we tried 45 families and prepared a growing same community network.

3 Vertex Degree Distribution

We derive approximate value for the vertex (family) degree distribution for growing same community network model mixing random initial contact, neighbor of neighbor initial contact and neighbor of initial contacts. Power law degree distribution with p (k) ~ k^{γ} with exponent $2<\gamma<\infty$ have derived [13,20]. In this model also the lower bound to the degree exponent γ is found to be 3, which is same as in the earlier model.

The rate equation which describes how the degree of a vertex changes on average during one time step of the network growth is constructed. The degree of vertex v_i grows in 3 processes:

1) When a new vertex directly links to v_i at any time t, there will be on average ~ t vertices. Here we are selecting m_r out of them with a probability m_r/t.
2) When a vertex links to v_i as secondary contact, the selection will give rise to preferential attachment. These will be m_r. m_s in number.
3) When a vertex links to v_i as tertiary contact, this will also be a random preferential attachment. These will be $2m_r\, m_s\, m_t$ in number.

These three processes lead to following rate equation for the degree of vertex v_i [1]

$$\frac{\partial k_i}{\partial t}=\frac{1}{t}\left(m_r+\frac{m_r m_s+2m_r m_s m_t}{2(m_r+m_r m_s+2m_r m_s m_t)}k_i\right) \tag{1}$$

Based on the average initial degree of a vertex is

$$k_{init}=m_r+m_r m_s+2m_r m_s m_t$$

Separating and integrating from t_i to t, and from k_{init} to k_i, we will get the following time evaluation for the vertex degrees

$$k_i(t)=B\left(\frac{1}{t_i}\right)^{1/A}-C \tag{2}$$

Where

$$A=2\left(\frac{m_r+m_r m_s+2m_r m_s m_t}{m_r m_s+2m_r m_s m_t}\right), B=A\left(m_r+\frac{1}{2}m_r m_s+m_r m_s m_t\right), C=Am_r$$

From time evolution of vertex k_i (t), we can calculate the degrees of distribution p(k) by forming cumulative distribution F(k) and differentiating with respect to k. Since the mean field approximation[1] the degree $k_i(t)$ of a vertex v_i increases monotonously from the time t_i the vertex initially added to the network, the fraction of vertices whose degree is less than $k_i(t)$ at t is equivalent to the fraction of vertices that introduced after time t_i. Since t is evenly distributed, this fraction is $(t-t_i)/2$. These facts lead to the cumulative distribution [1]

$$F(k_i)=P(\tilde{k}\le k_i)=P(\tilde{t}\ge t_i)=\frac{1}{t}(t-t_i) \tag{3}$$

Solving for $t_i=t_i(k_i,t)=B^A(k_i+C)^{-A}t$ from (2) and inserting it into (3), differentiating $F(k_i)$ with respect to k_i, and replacing the notation k_i by k in the equation, we get the probability density distribution for the degree k as

$$P(k)=AB^A(k+C)^{-2/m_s+2m_sm_t-3} \tag{4}$$

Here A, B and C are as above. In the limit of large k, the distribution becomes a power law p (k) ~ $k^{-\gamma}$ with $\gamma=3+2/m_s$, $m_s>0$, leading to $3<\gamma<\infty$. Hence the lower bound to the degree exponent is 3. Although the lower bound for degree exponent is same as earlier model. The probability density distribution is larger compared to earlier model, where the denominator of the first term of degree exponent is larger compared to the earlier model.

4 Clustering

The clustering coefficient on vertex degree can also be found by the rate equation method [21]. Let us examine how the number of triangles E_i changes with time. The triangle around v_i are mainly generated by three processes

1. Vertex v_i is chosen as one of the initial contact with probability m_r/t and new vertex links to some of its neighbors as secondary contact, giving raise to a triangle.
2. The vertex v_i is chosen as secondary contact and the new vertex links to it as its primary or tertiary contact giving raise to a triangles.
3. The vertex v_i is chosen as tertiary contact and the new vertex links to it as its primary or secondary contact, giving raise to a triangles.

These three process are described by the rate equation [1]

$$\frac{\partial E_i}{\partial t}=\frac{k_i}{t}-\frac{1}{t}\left(m_r-m_rm_s-3m_rm_sm_t-\frac{5m_rm_sm_t}{2(m_r+m_rm_s+2m_rm_sm_t)t}k_i\right) \tag{5}$$

where second right-hand side obtained by applying Eq. (1) integrating both sides with respect to t, and using initial condition $E_i(k_{init}, t_i) = m_r\, m_s(1+3m_t)$, we get the time evaluation of triangle around a vertex v_i as

$$E_i(t) = (a+bk_i)\ln\left(\frac{t}{t_i}\right) + \left(\frac{a+bk_i}{b}\right)\ln\left(\frac{a+bk_i}{a+bk_{init}}\right) + E_{init} \tag{6}$$

Now making use of the previously found dependent of k_i on t_i for finding $c_i(k)$. solving for $\ln(t/t_i)$in terms of k_i from (2), inserting into it into (6) to get $E_i(k_i)$, and dividing $E_i(k_i)$ by the maximum possible number of triangles, $k_i(k_i-1)/2$, we arrive the clustering the coefficient

$$c_i(k_i) = \frac{2E_i(k_i)}{k_i(k_i-1)} \tag{7}$$

For this equation detail explanation on refer ref [1]

For large values of degree k, the clustering coefficient thus depend on k as $c(k) \sim \ln k/k$.

This has very large clustering coefficient compared to the earlier work where it was $c(k) \sim 1/k$.

5 Results

In this application we tried 45 sample families and prepared a growing same community network, where edge to vertex ratio and triangle to vertex ratio for 45 families has been prepared. The results are given in Table 1 here one can see an enormous increase in secondary contacts (for searching alliance). In addition tertiary contacts (families) also have been added in our model, which leads to a faster and complex growth of same community network.

Table 1.

Data on our application	Initial Contact (IC)	Secondary Contacts (SC)	Neighbor of Neighbor IC (NNIC)
Vertices	2.63	5.36	2.91
Triangles	0.6	6.450	7.35

5.1 Simulation Results

The below results have been represented graphically by calculating the degree (number of families) of a node. This also is shows an enormous growth in degree of nodes.

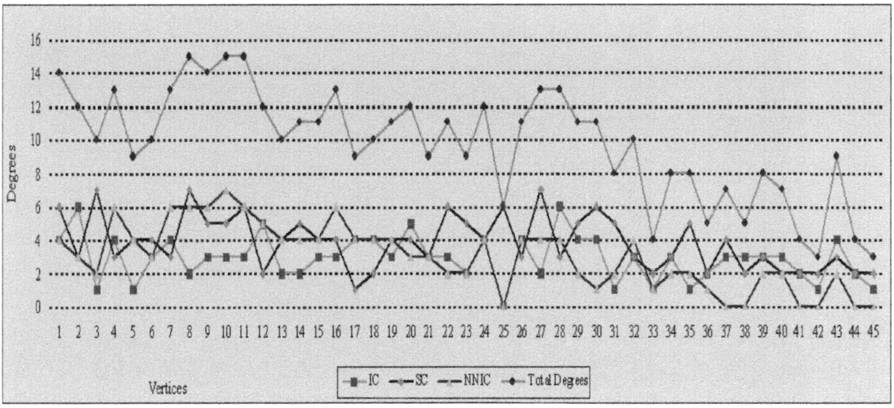

Fig. 3. Comparison results of growing network community: initial contacts are growing very slow rate compared to secondary contact i.e. ■ indicates initial contact, ♦ indicates secondary contacts, and ▲ indicates neighbor of neighbor of initial contact connects to the vertex v_i, Finally ● indicates degree of each vertices, when initial, secondary and tertiary contact connect to a vertex v_i. Our network community is growing very fast and complex when compared to existing model, vertices simulation results based on Table 1.

6 Conclusion

In this paper, a model which reproduces very efficient networks compared to real social networks has been developed. And also here, the lower bound to the degree exponent is the same. The probability distribution for the degree k is in agreement with the earlier result for m_t =0. The clustering coefficient got an enormous raise in growth rate of $\ln(k_i)/ k_i$ compared to the earlier result $1/k_i$ for large values of the degree k. This is very useful in the case of searching for marriage alliances within a community. This gives more and better options for a person/family looking suitable alliances based on trust. It also makes the process of searching easier and faster without losing any trust. This kind of social networking will be very much appropriate in the Indian context. With the help of a case study on formation of marriage relationships, we have successfully proved that earlier model works well in this case too. This model can be used to develop a new kind of social networking among various research groups.

Tool

We have used C language and run the program finally we got good results, UciNet, NetDraw these tools are very useful to Draw the graph and finally Excel tool for getting results and getting simulation results.

Notations

Notation	Description
m_r	Initial Contact (New family, i.e searching alliance)
m_s	Secondary Contact (family)
m_r	Tertiary contact (family, i.e match for alliances)
k_i	Degree of vertex i (neighbor relational families)
E_i	Number of triangles at vertex i (mutual family)
$P(k)$	Probability density distribution of degree k

Note: In India, Hinduism is the religion followed by majority of the people. Hindus are divided into different caste groups based on their birth and professions. Hindus marry within their own caste groups (similar endogamous marriages).

References

1. Bhukya, S.: A novel model for social networks. In: BCFIC, February 16-18, pp. 21–24. IEEE, Los Alamitos (2011)
2. Thirunarayan, K., Anantharam, P., Henson, C.A., Sheth, A.P.: Some Trust Issues in Social Networks and Sensor Networks. In: CTS-2010, pp. 573–580 (2010)
3. Al-Arayed, D.A., Sousa, J.P.: General Trust Management- GTM. In: SocialCom 2010, pp. 857–864 (2010)
4. Milgram, S.: Psychology Today, vol. 2, pp. 60–67 (1967)
5. Granovetter, M.: The Strength of Weak Ties. Am. J. Soc. 78, 1360–1380 (1973)
6. Wasserman, S., Faust, K.: Social Network Analysis. Cambridge University Press, Cambridge (1994)
7. Watts, D.J., Strogatz, S.H.: Collective dynamics of 'small -world' networks. Nature 393, 440 (1998)
8. Newman, M.: The structure of scientific collaboration networks. In: PNAS, vol. 98, pp. 404–409 (January 17, 2001)
9. Newman, M.: Coauthorship networks and patterns of scientific collaboration. In: PNAS, vol. 101, pp. 5200–5205 (April 6, 2004)
10. Holme, P., Edling, C.R., Liljeros, F.: Structure and Time-Evolution of an Internet Dating Community. Soc. Networks 26, 155–174 (2004)
11. Girvan, M., Newman, M.E.J.: Community structure in social and biological networks. Proc. Natl. Acad. Sci. USA 99, 7821–7826 (2002)
12. Newman, M.E.J.: The structure and function of complex networks. SIAM Review 45, 167–256 (2003)
13. Krapivsky, P.L., Redner, S.: Organization of growing random networks. Phys. Rev. E 63, 066123 (2001)
14. Barabási, A.-L., Albert, R.: Emergence of scaling in random networks. Science 286, 509–512 (1999)
15. Newman, M.E.J.: Assortative Mixing in Networks. Phys. Rev. Lett. 89, 208701 (2002)
16. Newman, M.E.J., Park, J.: Why social networks are different from other types of networks. Phys. Rev. E 68, 036122 (2003)

17. Amaral, L.A.N., Scala, A., Barth, M., Stanley, H.E.: Classes of small-world networks. In: PNAS, vol. 97, pp. 11149–11152 (October 10, 2000)
18. Boguna, M., Pastor-Satorras, R., Díaz-Guilera, A., Arenas, A.: Models of social networks based on social distance attachment. Phys. Rev. E 70, 056122 (2004)
19. Toivonen, R., Onnela, J.-P., Saramäki, J., Hyvönen, J., Kaski, K.: A model for social networks. Physica A 371, 851–860 (2006)
20. Evans, T., Saramäki, J.: Scale-free networks from self-organization. Phys. Rev. E 72, 026138 (2005)
21. Szabo, G., Alava, M., Kertesz, J.: Phys. Structural transitions in scale-free networks. Phys. Rev. E 67, 056102 (2003)

Towards User Experience Based Persuasive Systems

Ahmad Jawdat, Qasem Obeidat, and Alaa Aljanaby

Computer Science Section, College of arts and Sciences
University of Nizwa, Oman
{jawdat,qasem,alaa}@unizwa.edu.om

Abstract. Persuasive technology is a recent research field that combines the computing and human psychology aspects. The target is to develop persuasive systems that are able to change or reshape human behavior. Persuasive technology has quickly found a wide range of applications in many fields of research and development like marketing, health, safety and environment. Persuasive systems may also be used in other domains like religion, politics, diplomacy, military training, management, and education. Improving the persuasion process is a key element in the success of persuasive systems. The user experience is an important factor that should be included in the persuasion process. This paper reviews the current trends of persuasive technology and shows some example of the available persuasive systems. It then contributes by proposing a new and promising research direction for designing persuasive systems that take the user feedback as a main element in the persuasion process. Some of the systems that follow this approach have been proposed and illustrated.

Keywords: Persuasive Technology, Persuasive Systems, User Experience, Web and Mobile Persuasive, Ambient Persuasive, E-commerce, Web Advertising.

1 Introduction

Persuasive technology is defined as the use of computing technology to change or reshape the attitude or behavior of the users [1, 2, 3]. Persuasive technology is recently being used in many applications such as web-based applications, portable devices, stand-alone programs, computerized toys, games and robotics [4]. However, there are many other application areas that are candidate to use persuasive technology such as politics, religion, health, safety, self-improvement and environment protection [5]. The persuasive technology can be classified as tools, media or social actors' based on the functional role of the computing device [2, 3]. As tools persuasive technologies increase the ability of users to perform a target behavior by simplify the target. While as a media persuasive technology can allow people to experience information developed to sharp their opinions and as actors it can take on pseudo-human roles

Fogg has proposed a model for the human behavior called Fogg Behavior Model (FBM) [4]. The model was to make a better understanding of elements involved in human behavior and thus help in developing more efficient persuasive systems. Motivation, ability and triggers are the three factors that included in FBM. In order for

E. Ariwa and E. El-Qawasmeh (Eds.): DEIS 2011, CCIS 194, pp. 296–307, 2011.

a human to perform a target behavior, based on FBM, he should be motivated enough, has the ability and need to be triggered to do so. Examples of motivators are pleasure/pain, hope/fear and acceptance/rejection. The ability factor examples are time, money and physical effort while the triggers examples are spark, facilitator and signal. However, the persuasion process can also make advantage from the accumulated experiences of previous users who used some system and put their feedback. The user feedback can play main role in persuading future users to do or not to do the targeting behavior.

This paper studies the current trends of persuasive technology researches and briefly surveys some of the available persuasive systems. The contribution of the paper is to draw lines for developing more effective persuasive systems by proposing the approach of designing persuasive systems based on users' experiences. The rest of this paper is organized as follows. Some research domains of persuasive technology are first discussed in Section 2. Section 3 briefly surveys some recently developed persuasive systems. The new approach of using user experience as a key factor in developing persuasive systems is then discussed in Section 4. The measurement of the overall user satisfaction based on the new approach is discussed in Section 5. Section 6 concludes the paper.

2 Persuasive Technology Research Domains

Persuasive Technology has been used in many research domains. Ambient, games, web, and mobile are some examples of these domains. These domains have got a lot of research efforts in the few past years and they are briefly reviewed in next subsections.

2.1 Ambient Persuasive

The term ambient persuasive is part of a larger domain which is the Ambient Intelligence (AmI) that refers to embedding intelligent systems into the environment where they interact with the users everywhere and anytime in their daily lives. Ambient Intelligence is seen as the next step for Artificial Intelligence (AI). The AI techniques and methods are very useful in developing AmI systems [6]. Embedding persuasive systems within environment is called ambient persuasive or environmental persuasion [7]. Ambient persuasive systems are mainly installed in public places to make the most benefit from using them. Moreover, using ambient persuasive allows people to be persuaded, without being annoyed, in the right time and at the right place. This means that they will gain the most benefit from persuasion, especially if the message that will be delivered is simple and direct [8]. Ambient persuasive systems may be found in anyplace in home (e.g. energy consumption), factory (e.g. motivation and productivity), shopping malls (e.g. advertising or specific consumer behaviors), office, classroom, vehicle, hospital, etc.

Vehicle is a popular place where you can think of attaching a persuasive system. These systems targeted some behaviors like the driver speeding or attaching safety belt for more safety by alerting the driver using sound or light [9]. Many complex systems have suggested different approaches to ensure better economic driving behavior. EcoMatic system [10] automatically reduces the fuel consumption when it is activated by the driver and at the end of the trip it shows the amount of the saved fuel. It works by adjusting various parameters within the car such as changing the engine into an idle mode when the car stops moving. Another system that is used in vehicles is CommuterNews [11] which aimed to motivate the driver to listen to the news by providing questions and making competition.

WaterBot [12] is another clear example of ambient persuasive, where the information appear on a device that is attached to the sink itself; the information displayed are used to motivate people to turn off the tap when the water is not being used which will reduce the amount of wasted water. It relies on sound and light to motivate water savings. The CleanSink [12] system was also suggested adding a small display beside the sink that can persuade people to wash their hands properly by following the directions displayed. It was suggested to be used in hospitals, restaurants, and industrial clean rooms. In hospitals' examination rooms, CleanSink can control the room lights, so if the staff washes their hands the lights will turn on.

2.2 Web and Mobile Persuasive

Most of the persuasive systems available were developed as web sites, mobile systems, games or embedded systems within the environment. Using Web based systems, and mobile applications can give a great opportunity to spread persuasive systems and to interact with users, where they can be reached easily. One of the persuasive websites is the www.scorecard.org website; this website helps users to participate in protecting the environment [13]. There are many studies available on the Human Computer Interaction that discussed persuasion of the interface itself. Those studies concentrated on methods of making the user to trust the website and to take action rather than surfing only, and to persuade them to come open the website regularly. Persuasion and promotion are the key success for any new website.

A mobile phone application that alert person to call friends periodically [14] is an example of using persuasive technology in mobiles. Another mobile device application called SmartTrip [15] aims to combine multiple trips into a single trip in order to reduce driving. Also an environmental sustainability related application is the GreenScanner [16] which is a mobile application that can be used at stores to give detailed information about the environmental impacts of various products using their barcodes. Another mobile application introduced in [17] helps people to select healthy food by providing comparisons between two or more products on one aspect of dietary that the customer determines which gives simple information for healthier food.

2.3 Game Persuasive

During the last few years, games have founded as a common and one of the most important form of persuasive technology. Each game must has advantages to the players into different domain like health, education, religion, culture, business, etc. It is better if the game has a web-based game interface to reach a large number of people with a low cost [18]. By using game as persuasive technology help people (game players) to improve and change their attitudes or behaviors by given them knowledge that has affects in their real life.

Some games depend on the player movements of some parts of his/her body like Wii game or PlayStation; one can play tennis in Wii by using stick and move his hand and body as in the reality. Another game is Konami's Dance Dance Revolution (DDR) which is revolves around the concept of dancing. The dancer here moves on different places on floor bad to match the screen display marking. These games and others can be viewed as persuasive systems as they encourage player to be active, fitness and preventive measures against some illness [19].

The SuperKids game Drop & Catch is an educational computer game designed by Dole Food Company. This game teaches children the advantages of eating 5 to 9 different kinds of fruits and vegetables per a day. The kid player Bam-Nana got to pack super food snacks to give him the boost he will need. The super kid friend Brocco is giving him a hand tossing nutritious snacks as fast as he can. But his enemy Sat Fat wants to sabotage things with junk foods. Bam-Nana wins if he catches 5 super foods respectively; if he catches one of junk food he must start from the beginning and remove all super foods that he collected before, refer to www.dole.com.

3 Persuasive Systems

Many persuasive systems have been developed since the early work of Fogg [1, 2, 3]. Recommender systems are considered as collaborative filtering systems [20]. They use people opinions and data to build recommendations for other users who may share the same interests. Nowadays, they are used by many e-commerce websites. The researches in this area proved that the users showed interest of this kind of systems. Researchers now are investigating how to improve the value of recommendations and make them more persuasive for the users to make more benefit from them [21]. One of the good methods suggested for building recommendations depends on making groups of people who have similar profile of interests. The profile of interests is created by collecting data about users when they bid on, rate or buy a specific product. The system then uses these similar profiles to build recommendations [5]. Recommender Systems are very important in businesses especially in e-commerce. They can increase sales and help people find interesting items. One good application is the MovieLens, it has thousands of users and it is a web site for recommending movies where you can rate some of the movies you already seen and depending on your ratings the system will suggest movies to watch of your type [22].

Decision support systems help the decision makers and support them in the decision making process, these systems mostly refer to people in the high management positions. Some other references introduced them as consumer decision support systems which help online users make purchasing decisions in e-commerce web sites [23]. The reliance on decision support systems is optional, that's why it depends on how much persuasive they are. The persuasiveness of these systems will convince the decision maker to rely on the decision support provided. There are many factors that affect the overall persuasiveness of these systems, the complexity of the decision, the person using the system and the message delivered by the system [24]. An example is a system that assists consumers to reduce the number of unnecessary visits to health care facilities.

Self Monitoring systems allow people to monitor themselves to modify their behaviors to achieve a predetermined goal [3]. This type of persuasive system helps people continuing the behavior change process rather than convincing them to start changing the undesired behavior. For example UbiFit [25] is an interactive application that helps people monitors their daily physical activities. They can define a weekly target and view progress toward their predefined goal. UbiFit uses a display image for a garden with flowers that resides on the background screen of a mobile phone. The garden represents one week's activities and the flowers of different colors represent different types of activities. This image could be changed over time because it may get boring.

4 The Proposed Approach of User Experience Based Persuasive Systems

The persuasive technology is still in its beginning and there are so many ideas that could be implemented in a lot of fields. Persuasive applications can cover various domains, and many of them still need to be discovered and developed. In this section we will introduce some of our innovative ideas to share with the fellow researchers of this technology. To start with education for example; many ideas could be implemented to persuade people in order to read more, educate themselves, or encourage them to join a college. A mobile application that introduces information in a form of questions and answers, and uses ranking to motivate users to gain the knowledge is one example. Another important domain is politics; political parties may add an automatic negotiating agent in the web to convince people in order to join their party. These kinds of systems and many more use artificial intelligence techniques such as natural language processing and machine learning.

Furthermore, there are many other challenging applications that could be used to convince people to do or stop doing behaviors such as: drugs, alcohol and internet addiction. In addition, they could be used to promote healthy lifestyle activities like practicing, or to persuade employees to put more effort and time in their work. On the other side, applications could be developed to convince terrorists to stop bombing, or to influence someone with specific religious thoughts or ideas.

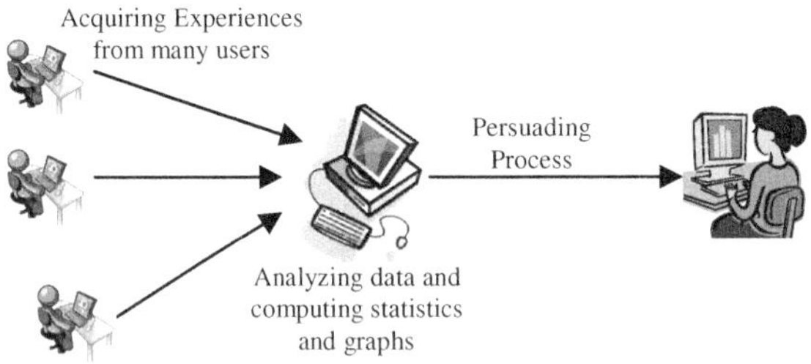

Fig. 1. User Experience Based Persuasive System

We suggest introducing experience based persuasive systems, refer to Fig. 1, which depend on other people personal experiences. The system automatically generates useful information based on the acquired experiences to help others in decision making. Using this idea we can make benefits from the knowledge of many people all over the world about a specific action or behavior. We believe that involving users in the persuasion process would give more credibility to the system. The system will automatically analyze the collected data, and compute statistics to create suggestions and recommendations. As a result these recommendations are used to convince other users to follow or to stop a specific action.. In next subsections we propose three applications where the new approach can be used effectively.

4.1 E-Commerce and Customers Persuading Process

People frequently seek professional advice before buying a certain product. They would usually ask a friend or a salesman or simply surf the web for the required information. In fact most of us need to be convinced about a specific product before buying it. This is one of the most important drawbacks of the E-commerce comparing with traditional trading process. With the use of persuasive system, we might reduce the effect of this factor. Using other people experience feedbacks for a specific product will give more confidence for the customer when he decides to buy it.

People proved through the experience of wikis and forums that they tend to share their knowledge with others. In e-commerce the lack for an appropriate platform is a major obstacle that prevents users from participating and sharing their own experiences. For internet customers, seeing statistics and information about a specific product is relieving before buying or participating in an auction because the product is intangible. The system should collect data about products from people who had used it; this will give more credibility for new customers to trust the system's output. Statistics and charts can be generated by the system and introduced in a simple and readable way to customers, in order to convince them to buy the product.

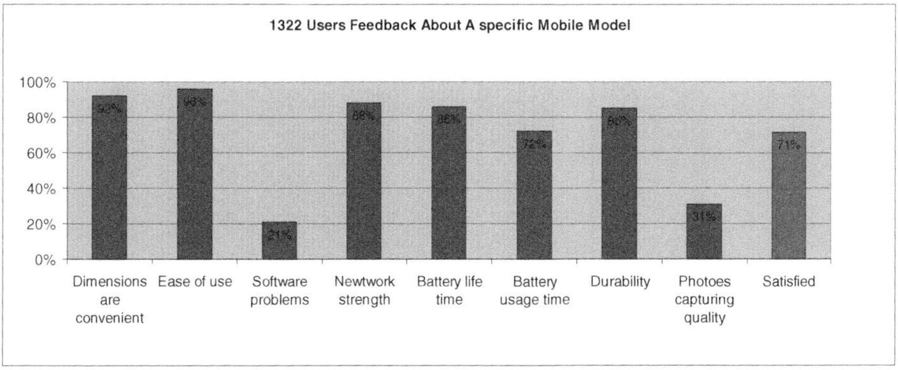

Fig. 2. Representing users' feedback in the form of a graph - Example 1

Fig 2 shows an example of how the user's experiences can be viewed as a column chart so it is easy to read by any customer. It shows two colors; the green indicates good feedback while the red indicates drawbacks. At the end there is a total satisfaction column showing the degree of users' contentment. On the title you can see the number of users who shared their experience while using this specific mobile phone, more users give more credibility and accuracy to the calculated statistics.

From the website owner's view, the persuasive system will help to increase the sales as the reputation and credibility of the website in giving advices and information about the product will be more. And will also provide feedback about the products for manufacturer's pro future development. This data in the system is valuable, since it reflects the degree of satisfaction of the customers about the products from real life use. Thus, the information is very important for manufacturers to induce the decision makers to enhance their production in general. They could change their materials or pay more for research groups or even change the whole product into a new improved version.

Another part that can be added to the persuasive system is a price reasonability system. This system shall be embedded within e-auction web sites. In auctions one of the customers' main concerns is that when should they stop bidding and whether the deal they won is a bargain or not. It is quite often that the customer might be interested in a specific item, and has no idea how much it is worth, especially used items. The pricing reasonability system helps customers to know whether the price of the item is reasonable or not by giving a green color or red for the auction price. The system can automatically calculate this value by comparing similar items already sold with the opportunity of showing details of those items.

Moreover, the system can generate the collected users' experiences and display it in the form of suggestions for customers who didn't decide exactly to buy a specific model of the product yet. For example, if a customer wants to buy a mobile phone, he can provide the system with his own requirements and expectations as shown in Fig. 3. The system then produces a list of suggestions to the customer sorted by the best results given by other users as shown in Table 1.

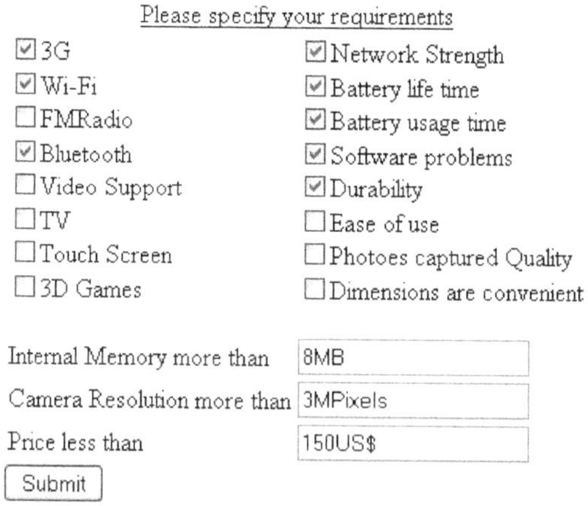

Fig. 3. Specifying User requirements

Table 1. Ranking according to users' feedback

Mobile	SW problems	Network strength	Battery life time	Battery usage time	Durability	Overall
HTC HD2	92%	93%	85%	82%	92%	88.8%
Samsung Mesmerize i500	87%	85%	86%	83%	86%	85.4%
Blackberry Torch 9800 Slider	56%	91%	86%	82%	78%	78.6%
Nokia N8	43%	80%	80%	88%	85%	75.2%
Sony Ericsson W8	21%	88%	92%	80%	81%	72.4%

4.2 Persuading Businesses to Participate in Web Advertising

Many of the available websites today depend on advertisement as a major source in their revenue model. The well known websites usually do not face major problems in attracting businesses to advertise using there websites. On the other hand, websites with a limited number of users may struggle to convince business decision makers to use their websites for advertising. The proposed system will benefit both types of websites to increase their total daily income from advertisements, using automated persuasive system to draw advertisers. Additionally, many of the small and medium businesses need to be convinced to spend more money on advertising. They need to be encouraged to spend more money on advertising by showing them that it will support their business and help them gain more profits.

Moreover a link could be added to the website to start the persuasive system. The system will mainly depend on other advertisers' statistics with the aim of showing how their businesses developed and their profits increased from putting advertisement on this website. Therefore, the system should allow current advertisers to share their experiences and explain the benefits they gained from advertising on that website. This could be done by adding numbers and statistics regarding the improvement they found on their profits taking into account the advertising fees to reveal if they were satisfied or not. Several methods could be exercised in order to encourage advertisers to constantly add their data to the system like; giving discounts on the total advertising costs, or giving higher priority for their advertisement in the system so it will appear more often on the customers' pages.

The system's major work is to collect the numbers and statistics added by advertisers and process these data entries to generate persuading procedures that could be used to convince other business owners to advertise on the website. Mainly, this process will depend on showing new advertisers how other businesses improved and gained more profit by advertising on this web site, using numbers and real data, in order to convince them that they can also enhance their income. The system may also show messages from all advertisers explaining their experiences using web advertising, and may also allow new advertisers to contact them for further information; however this depends on the approval from advertisers in advance.

4.3 Best Tourism Experience

Most tourists, who plan to visit a particular city, search the internet prior to their travel to get an insightful view and gain helpful information about their requirements. Like the places they should see, the activities they should do, hotel reservations, maps, transportation, restaurants, etc. The problem is that there is no real user experience in the internet to utilize it, rather all the information available are from private companies showing only one side of the story. And the small chunks of data available from users are distributed on forums and appear as comments on articles and news.

In this system residents of a specific city can share their familiarity and knowledge about the aspects of their city to benefit others. This may help visitors to live a great experience when visiting the city, and will also persuade more people to visit it on the long term. Tourists can also participate by sharing their experience after visiting this city. Not only will this data be useful for the residents and for visitors, it also will be useful for the private sector. A restaurant or a hotel for example will have a feedback from large number of users, and will use this data to improve its service. This will have great effects on the quality of life in that city on the long term.

The data in this system especially for the service sector should be calculated on a monthly basis with the ability to show the overall evaluation. As this is not constant and may change by time. New data for places and activities may be very important but still does not have the same number of recommendations from users as old data. So we can depend on the percentage of recommendations per month instead of the total.

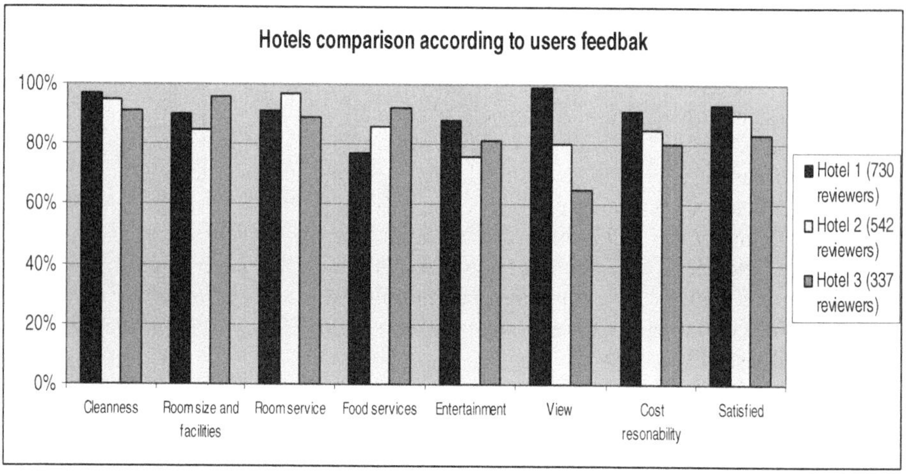

Fig. 4. Representing users' feedback in the form of a graph - Example 2

In the example shown in Fig. 4 the user has chosen three hotels to compare, depending on some pre-specified criteria like number of stars, or his budget, or hotel location, etc. The system will give the user a graph that shows other users opinions about different aspects in these hotels for the last month. Then the user can decide which hotel with the best characteristics that suit him, instead of choosing randomly.

5 Overall User Satisfaction Measurements

The emphasizing of the above proposed method is on the negative feedbacks, especially if the same feedback is repeated from more than one user. In this case these opinions gain a special weight and may indicate a real drawback in the evaluated subject. The user's overall satisfaction can be calculated and we introduce an example of such calculation in this section.

In order to calculate the overall satisfaction of users, an equation is used to emphasize certain disadvantages. If more users face the same problem in a particular mobile, then there is more possibility that new users are going to face the same problem if they buy that mobile. A weight is to be assigned to each feedback, and then the average of all weights is the overall evaluation result for a specific feature.

For example let's consider the 'software problems' feature, if we for instance have collected a feedback from 83 users and 28 users stated that they faced software problems in this mobile, while 55 users did not. The weight for the positive and negative users' feedbacks will be calculated as follows. $NW = \sum_{i=1}^{n} \frac{(i+1)}{2}$; where n is the total number of negative feedbacks and NW is the weight of negative feedbacks. $PW = \sum_{i=1}^{m} 1$; where m is the total number of positive feedbacks and PW is the weight of positive feedbacks.

The result of this case when n=28 is 203.5. On the other hand, the weight for each positive feedback is fixed and equal to 1, the result is calculated as follows. Result of satisfaction = Positive weight / (Positive weight + Negative weight) * 100% = 55 / (55 + 203.5) * 100% = 21%. In this example, only 28 people expressed their resentment on the mobile software performance. The overall percent of satisfaction where very low, it was only 21%. Despite that 55 people gave a positive feedback. This is how we concentrate on the negative feedback if they are repeated because they will be more likely to happen with other users. Table 2 shows the results of calculating the overall user satisfaction on facing "software problems" for different kinds of mobile devices and different samples of users.

Table 2. Overall user satisfaction on facing "software problems" for different kinds of mobile devices and different samples of users

Mobile	Number of users	Positive Feedback	Negative Feedback	Overall Satisfaction
HTC HD2	177	170	7	92%
Samsung Mesmerize i500	106	99	7	87%
Blackberry Torch 9800 Slider	198	175	23	56%
Nokia N8	147	122	25	43%
Sony Ericsson W8	83	55	28	21%

6 Conclusion

People should start participating in building a new dimension of the internet scope. This dimension depends on users as the main source of data, not as a receiver for information only. Everyone has his own experience in life that can be useful to others, if it is collected and analyzed correctly. Because this is the age of information revolution, even the smallest piece of information matters,. Based on these thoughts we suggested implementing a user experience based persuasive system which depends on building persuasive system using the collected knowledge from users.

Through out our paper we have shown three examples where various systems could be employed. The first example showed how this system can be very useful in E-commerce and E-auction, where it will provide the user with information from real users, rather than having information from the manufacturer or experts only. The second example was about improving web sites revenues from advertisements, and how to improve the web marketing sector. While the last example viewed how this kind of system can help in creating a great tourism experience by using the users feedback.

Likewise, the same idea represented in those examples could be implemented in almost any e-service available. Private universities can use persuasive systems using previous students input, in order to convince new students to join their university. Job search websites can also persuade companies to supply them with job vacancies and can also persuade job seekers to add and update their data. The same suggestion goes for hospitals, banks, insurance companies, etc.

An obvious concern regarding the users experience based persuasive systems is fraud and fake data, where some users might add fake data in order to promote a specific product, or a restaurant or anything else. This is an important issue that must be investigated and studied for every system alone, and solutions should guarantee the validity of the data. This problem is an important issue, because it may affect the credibility of the system and subsequently affect the results of the persuading process.

References

1. Fogg, B.J.: Persuasive computers: Perspectives and research directions. In: Proc. of the SIGCHI Conference on Human Factors in Computing Systems (CHI 1998), pp. 225–232 (1998)
2. Fogg, B.J.: Persuasive Technologies. Communications of the ACM 42(5), 26–29 (1999)
3. Fogg, B.J.: Persuasive Technology: Using Computers to Change What We Think and Do. Morgan Kaufmann Publishers, San Francisco (2003)
4. Fogg, B.J.: A Behavioral Model for Persuasive Design. In: Proc. of Persuasive 2009, California, USA (2009)
5. Cheng, R.: Persuasion Strategies for Computers as Persuasive Technologies. Department of Computer Science, University of Saskatchewan (2003)
6. Ramos, C., Augusto, J., Shapiro, D.: Ambient Intelligence - The Next Step for Artificial Intelligence. In: Ramos, C., Augusto, J., Shapiro, D. (eds.) IEEE Intelligent Systems Special Issue on Ambient Intelligence, vol. 23(2), pp. 15–18 (2008)
7. Mathew, A.P.: Using the environment as an interactive interface to motivate positive behavior change in a subway station. In: CHI 2005 Extended Abstracts on Human Factors in Computing Systems, pp. 1637–1640 (2005)

8. Intille, S.S.: Ubiquitous computing technology for just-in-time motivation of behavior change. In: Proc. of 11th Word Congress on Medical Informatics, Medinfo-2004, pp. 1434–1437 (2004)
9. Oinas-Kukkonen, H., Harjumaa, M.: Towards Deeper Understanding of Persuasion in Software and Information Systems. In: Proc. of the 1st International Conference on Advances in Computer-Human Interaction (ACHI 2008), pp. 200–205 (2008)
10. Meschtscherjakov, A., Wilfinger, D., Scherndl, T., Tscheligi, M.: Acceptance of Future Persuasive In-Car Interfaces Towards a More Economic Driving Behavior. In: Proc. of First International Conference on Automotive User Interfaces and Interactive Vehicular Applications (AutomotiveUI 2009), Essen, Germany, pp. 115–118 (2009)
11. Tester, J., Fogg, B.J., Maile, M.: CommuterNews: A prototype of persuasive in-car entertainment. In: CHI 2000 Extended Abstracts on Human Factors in Computing Systems, pp. 24–25. ACM Press, The Hague (2000)
12. Arroyo, E., Bonanni, L., Selker, T.: Waterbot: Exploring feedback and persuasive techniques at the sink. In: Proc. of the SIGCHI Conference on Human Factors in Computing Systems (CHI 2005), pp. 631–639 (2005)
13. King, P., Tester, J.: The Landscape of Persuasive Technologies. Communications of the ACM 42(5), 31–38 (1999)
14. Marcus, A., Chen, E.: Designing the PDA of the future. Interactions 9(1), 34–44 (2002)
15. Johnson, E.M., Koh, H., McAtee, J., Shoulders, S.: SmartTrip: Persuasive technology to promote conscious driving habits. In: CHI 2007 Extended Abstracts on Human Factors in Computing Systems (2007)
16. Tomlinson, B.: Prototyping a community-generated, mobile device-enabled database of environmental impact reviews of consumer products. In: Proc. of the 41st Hawaii International Conference on System Sciences, p. 154 (2008)
17. Intille, S.S., Kukla, C., Farzanfar, R., Bakr, W.: Just-in-Time Technology to Encourage Incremental, Dietary Behavior Change. In: Proc. of the AMIA 2003 Symposium (2003)
18. Khaled, R., Biddle, R., Noble, J., Barr, P., Fischer, R.: Persuasive Interaction for Collectivist Cultures. In: Proc. of the Seventh Australasian User Interface Conference (2006)
19. Khaled, R.: Culturally-Relevant Persuasive Technology. PhD thesis. Victoria University of Wellington (2008)
20. Herlocker, J.L., Konstan, J.A., Riedl, J.P.: Explaining collaborative filtering recommendations. In: Proc. of the 2000 ACM Conference on Computer Supported Cooperative Work, pp. 241–250 (2000)
21. Konstan, J.A.: Introduction to Recommender Systems: Algorithms and Evaluation. ACM Transactions on Information Systems 22(1), 1–4 (2004)
22. Cosley, D., Lam, S.K., Albert, I., Konstan, J.A., Riedl, J.: Is Seeing Believing? How Recommender Interfaces Affect Users' Opinions. In: Proceedings of the Conference on Human Factors in Computing Systems, pp. 585–592 (2003)
23. Zhang, J., Pu, P.: Performance Evaluation of Consumer Decision Support Systems. International Journal of E-Business Research 2(3), 28–45 (2006)
24. Alison, P.: Persuasive Decision Support: Improving Reliance on Decision Support Systems. In: Proc. of Pacific Asia Conference on Information Systems (PACIS 2009). Association of Information Systems, Hyderabad (2009)
25. Consolvo, S., Landay, J.A., McDonald, D.W.: Designing for Behavior Change in Everyday Life. IEEE Computer Society, Los Alamitos (2009)

Parallel Laplacian Edge Detection Performance Analysis on Green Cluster Architecture

Noor Elaiza Abdul Khalid[1], Noorhayati Mohd Noor[1], Siti Arpah Ahmad[1], Mohd Helmi Rosli[1], and Mohd Nasir Taib[2]

[1] Faculty of Information Technology and Quantitative Sciences
Universiti Teknologi MARA
40450 Shah Alam, Selangor, Malaysia
Tel.: +6019-2692717
elaiza@tmsk.uitm.edu.my
[2] Faculty of Electrical and Electronic Engineering
Universiti Teknologi MARA
40450 Shah Alam, Selangor, Malaysia

Abstract. The current trend of computer hardware declining and the speed of personal computer increasing had lead to opportunity of parallel programming. This paper presents the implementation of parallel Laplacian edge detection on cluster of four used personal computers. The algorithm was developed using C# language and had utilized the Message Passing Interface (MPI) library for parallel implementation. Comparison between sequential versus parallel implementation had been made based on sequential time taken for varies of images sizes. Results show significant time improvement as well as performance efficiency earned using parallel computing platform focusing on image processing Laplacian edge detection algorithm.

Keywords: Parallel computing, Image processing, Edge Detection, Cluster.

1 Introduction

As the computer hardware cost is declining, and the speed of personal computer is increasing, the potential of parallel computing usage and its application become inevitable [1-3]. As living in today's era which every application related to science and engineering has to deal with a large amount of data, thus demand real-time or near real-time performance. The aim at bridging together both theoretician and practitioners who dealing with information extraction techniques for large amounts of data make the parallel computing area become inevitable. Parallelism paves the way for near real-time performance [4].

The nature of image processing exhibits the potential for significant parallelism. The algorithms in image processing such as edge detection, contrast enhancement and segmentation usually deal with pixel by pixel manipulation and thousand of iterations, inherit the potential of parallelism [5]. Thus this work has focus on utilizing the implementation of Laplacian edge detection algorithm, one of the central tasks of the

E. Ariwa and E. El-Qawasmeh (Eds.): DEIS 2011, CCIS 194, pp. 308–316, 2011.

lower levels of image processing, on parallel platform and investigation is done on finding the most optimal image size that best optimized the infrastructure

Nowadays, digital image are so many that research activities in this area are very active [1-10]. The nature of image processing that inherit parallelism, cultivates the parallel computing paradigm in software and hardware based. Hardware base parallel computing had created the Graphics Processing Unit (GPU) [6]. However the software based parallel programming continue to evolve due to the cheaper personal computers (PC) and many of used PC [7].

Parallel implementation of edge detection algorithm, such as Sobel and Canny had been investigated by many [6][8-10]. Application of Fast Sobel edge detection of medical images for automatic diagnosis had been implemented on GPU platform using Compute Unified Device Architecture (CUDA) programming model [6]. Performance of parallel approach of Sobel edge detection had been investigated in [8] by focusing on the speed up and efficiency of their Beowulf Cluster. Comparison of Sobel edge detection and homomorphic filtering, implemented on GPU compared to implementation on CPU had been done in [9], resulting the conclusion of speed up increase with the image size increase. As for parallel Canny edge detector, the implementation are done on application towards agriculture field to focusing on distinguishing between the paddy and the weeds based on images [10]. However none of the papers look into the importance of image sizes comparison between sequential and parallel implementation. Most of them focused on the speed up factor [8-10], efficiency difference [8], memory utilization [10] and on thread differences performance between CPU and GPU [6].

Image sizes are one of important characteristic that cannot be avoided in research relating to image processing. With the advancement of technology today, bigger and bigger image sizes are produces every day. Based on this issue, one of the application of image processing that has potential in utilizing the parallel computing platform are algorithm that relates to medical image modalities [11-12]. For example, the automatic discrimination between normal and pathological region within analyze tissues on the breast cancer case require huge computational. Tissues structures had been divided into sub-images and the classification had been done on the parallel platform. Images of 3MB, 5 MB and 7 MB had been investigated and result shows that parallel execution time scales with the number of processes in almost linear trend [11]. Algorithm related to CT image reconstruction also required huge computational due to the three-dimensional data. Research by [12] had used GPU single instruction multiple data (SIMD) parallel computing type to accelerate the 2D algebraic reconstruction and their result also shows speeds up increases when the reconstruction image size increase [12].

Based on the above mention reviews, this work focuses on the investigation of 1KX1K, 2KX2K and 3KX3K sizes of general images implemented on sequential versus parallel platform.

2 Research Design and Development

This research used nine general images taken from the internet. Each of the images has three different sizes of 1KX1K, 2KX2K and 3KX3K. The images are colored and roughly are scenery, animals and part of car images. The sizes of the imagers are modified to the specified sizes using Adobe Photoshop software.

2.1 Parallel Architecture and Software Specification

The specific software that had been used in this project such as the operating system, the programming, graphics tools and parallel library are listed in table 1.

Table 1. Lists of software used

Software/Tools/Library	Description
Operating System	Windows XP Professional sp3
Programming	Visual Studio 2008 XML
Graphic	Adobe Photoshop CS5
Parallel Communication	Mpich2
Monitoring Tools	Rightmark
Documenting Software	Microsoft Office 2007

As for the hardware used, the specific of computer nodes and the network device used for this work are listed in table 2. The cluster architecture is divided into two phases. Phase one consists of only two nodes. One node as a master and worker and another is the worker only. Phase two consists of four nodes. One node is a master and worker and the other three nodes as a workers. Figure 1 and figure 2 are the two architectures. These computer nodes are taken from unwanted computers from the university's administration department. The computers still working but only the processors and random access memory (RAM) are only at 256 MB. This work aims to utilize old computers, thus the word "green" cluster architecture get the name.

Table 2. Lists of hardware used

No of Item	Specification
Four node of computers	Intel® Pentium® 4 CPU 2.40 GHz 256MB of RAM DDR1 40GB of HHD CD-ROM
One switch	EtherFast® 4124 24-Port 10/100 Ethernet Switch
Four Cables	UTP Cable RJ45

Fig. 1. Phase one network architecture

Fig. 2. Phase two network architecture

2.2 Methods

This research consists of image processing algorithm, evaluated on the sequential versus parallel manner. Image processing algorithm used is Laplacian edge detection algorithm. Lena image is used as the benchmark the output image produced in sequential and parallel manner. Ten images with of sizes of 1Kx1K, 2Kx2K and 3Kx3K. are used as experiment case. The performance are measured using speed-up, percentage of improvement and efficiency factors.

Edge detection is one of the common technique and widely study for image processing. The Laplacian edge detection techniques had been used to demonstrate the sequential and parallel processing performance in this work. The outline of the objects is detected by convolving a mask with a matrix centered on a target pixel. The Laplacian detects the edge using a mask as in Fig.1 [5].

0	-1	0
-1	4	-1
0	-1	0

Fig. 3. Laplacian Edge Detection Mask[5]

In sequential processing, a program execution is run on a single machine or single processor. The instruction is executed one after another on a single processor. The program is written in C#.

The parallel processing setup consists of simultaneous use of more than one processor to execute a program threads. In this study, the parallel processing is established using two connected machines for example a master and a worker which communicates using parallel communication software named Message Parsing Interface (MPICH2). Both master and worker nodes run on Windows XP. The image data is split into two smaller images which then processed independently by the two connected machines. After, the worker node has finished processing the smaller image, the output is passed to the master node for reassembling and final output. Figure 4 shows the summary of the parallel architecture.

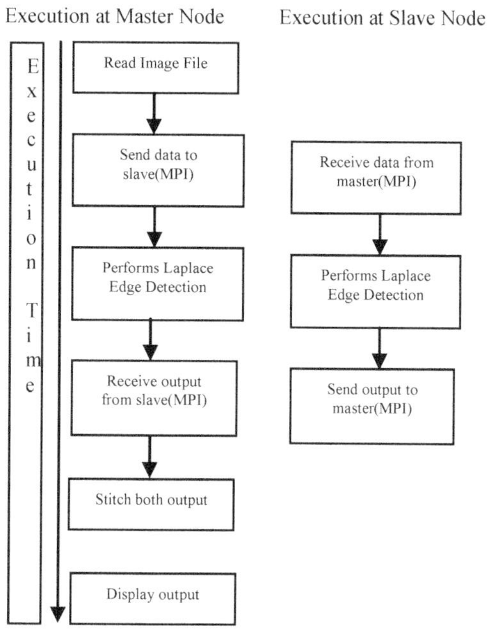

Fig. 4. Parallel Architecture of Laplacian Edge Detection

The evaluation of the parallel execution performance is measured with respect to speedup, performance improvement and efficiency with reference to the time taken for both sequential and parallel processing (Haron et al, 2010).

Speedup measures how much a parallel algorithm is faster than a corresponding sequential algorithm. The speedup calculation is based on equation (1) as below;

$$\text{Speedup} = \frac{\text{sequential(time)}}{\text{parallel(time)}} \tag{1}$$

The performance improvement depicts measurements relative improvement that the parallel system has over the sequential process. This performance is measured based on equation (2) below;

$$\text{Performance Improvement} = \frac{\text{sequential(time) - parallel(time)}}{\text{sequential(time)}} \tag{2}$$

Efficiency is used to estimate how well-utilized the processors are in solving the problem, compared to how much effort is wasted in communication and synchronization. As for efficiency, the calculation is based on equation (3) below;

$$\text{Efficiency} = \frac{\text{sequential(time)}}{\text{no of processor x parallel(time)}} \quad (3)$$

3 Results

The results are discussed using the following sequence; the first is the results of standard Lena images, implemented in sequential and parallel manner. The performance are analyzed based on speed-up factor, percentage of performance improvement and efficiency results of sequential, 2 node and 4 nodes

3.1 Visual Laplacian Algorithm for Standard Lena Image

Figure 5 below shows output of Lena image generated from the sequential and parallel processing. Both outputs are visually identical. This proves that both systems produce the same output. This test had been conducted before the performance evaluation between the sequential and parallel processing.

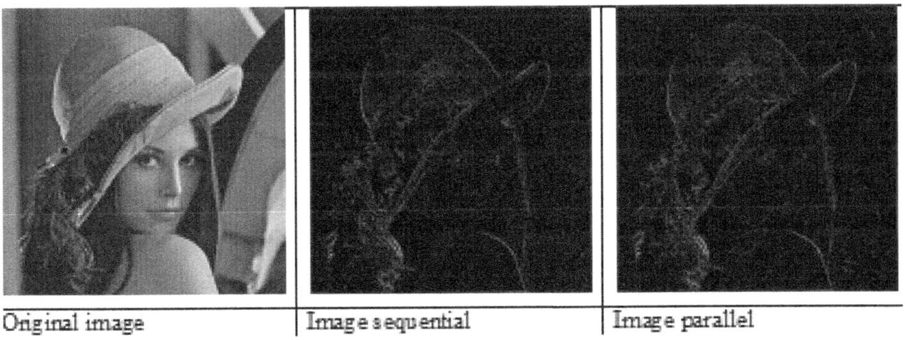

Fig. 5. Standard Lena images; sequential versus parallel implementation

3.2 Performance

The performance are measured based on the speed-up factor, performance improvement and efficiency based on function (1), (2) and (3) in the previous section. Figure 6 shows the speedup performances of parallel processes using duo and quad cluster. There speedup values for almost all the images processed with duo cluster are close to two which indicates reasonably good performance whereas the quad cluster shows the speedup values of around 3.5 thus showing slightly less efficient use of all the processors.

The second analysis is based on the performance improvement of the cluster against the sequential process as depicted in Figure 7. The performance significantly improve for duo cluster from image with 1Kx1K to 2KX2K, however it does not indicate much improvement between the 2Kx2K and 3Kx3K. It is also found that there is an average of about 0.45 for the duo cluster compared to the quad clustered process which is mostly above 0.70 for images of 2Kx2k and 3Kx3K. This indicates the increase the speed of processing is significantly improved with the quad clusters. The performance improvement increases from 1Kx1K and 2Kx2K, but reduces in 3kx3k in the quad cluster.

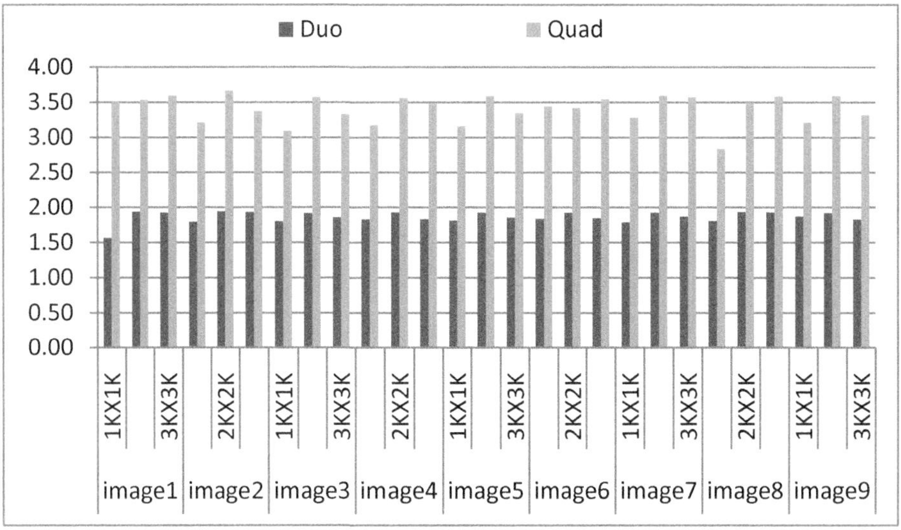

Fig. 6. The speedup performance of duo and quad cluster

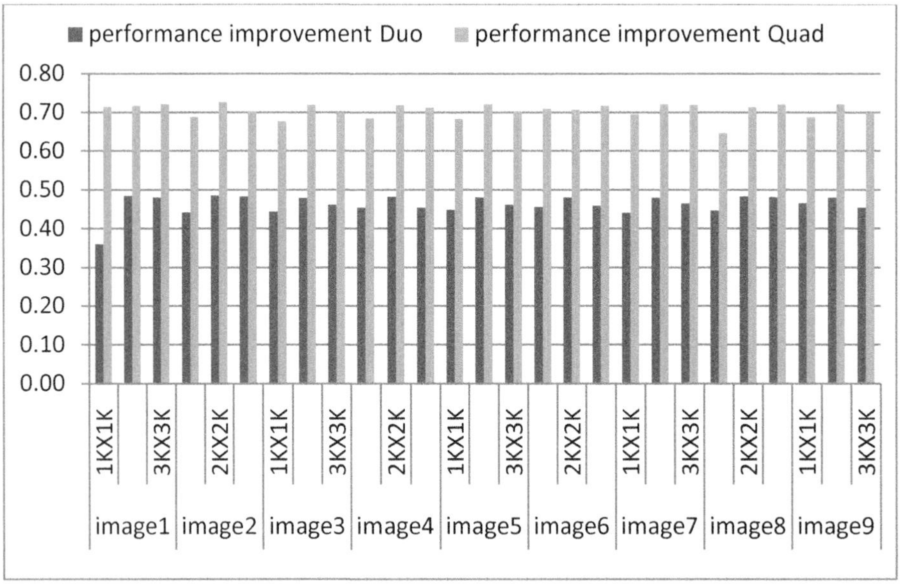

Fig. 7. The parallel performance improvement of duo and quad clusters

The third performance is based on the efficiency of the use of each of the CPU in the clusters. The results indicates almost the same trend where the CPU in the duo cluster is more efficiently used compared to the CPUs in the quad cluster. This trend can be seen in Figure 8.

Fig. 8. The parallel process efficiency of duo and quad cluster

This research is about utilizing used PC in organization by demonstrating its usability in parallel implementation of image processing algorithm. Laplacian edge detection algorithm had been successfully implemented in sequential and parallel manner. Basically both duo and quad have similar trends for all the method of performance such as speedup, performance improvement and the efficiency. Generally the performance measurement methods increases from 1Kx1K to 2Kx2k but reduces at 3Kx3K images. However, the parallel execution remains to outperform the sequential execution as indicated by the positive measurement for speedup, performance improvement and efficiency. This is obviously seen in Table 3.

Table 3. Speed, Performance Improvement and Efficiency Measurement

Image Size	Speedup		Performance Improvement		Efficiency	
	Duo	Quad	Duo	Quad	Duo	Quad
1KX1K	1.79	3.21	0.44	0.69	0.89	0.80
2KX2K	1.93	3.56	0.48	0.72	0.96	0.89
3KX3K	1.87	3.46	0.47	0.71	0.94	0.87

4 Conclusion

This research has proved that the Laplacian edge detection technique will perform at a higher speed in parallel environment than in sequential. Faster in the quad then in the duo but not necessarily efficient in utilizing the available CPUs. As a conclusion, this works shows that parallel implementation on the used PC still can be utilized especially in relation to image processing applications. However the limitation of this research is that the bureaucracy in getting the used/old PC and the supporting staff in maintaining and running cluster is quite challenging.

References

[1] Abbas, A.: Grid Computing: A practical Guide to Technology and Applications. Charles River Media, Hingham (2003)

[2] Mattson, T.G., Sanders, B.A., Massingill, B.L.: Patterns for Parallel Programming. Addison-Wesley, Reading (2004)

[3] Danelutto, M.: HPC the easy way: new technologies for high performance application development and deployment. Journal of Systems Architecture 49(10-11), 399–419 (2003)

[4] Rajasekaran, S.: Special issues on parallel techniques for information extraction. Journal of Parallel and Distributed Computing 68, 1–2 (2008)

[5] Wilkinson, B., Allen, M.: Parallel Programming Techniques and Applications Using Networked Workstations and Parallel Computers. Prentice Hall, Englewood Cliffs (2005)

[6] Johnson, A.L.: A Parallel Algorithm for Fast Edge Detection on the Graphics Processing Unit, Thesis for Honors in Computer Science, The Faculty of the Department of Computer Science Washington and Lee University (2010), `http://www.gpucomputing.net/?q=node/554`

[7] Han, C.T., Hong, J.T.K., Akma, F., Shamsir, M.S.: BirgHPC: Creating Instant Computing Clusters for Bioinformatics and Molecular Dynamics. Oxford University Press, Oxford (2011)

[8] Haron, N., Amir, R., Aziz, I.A., Jung, L.T., Shukri, S.R.: Parallelization of Edge Detection Algorithm using MPI on Beowulf Cluster. Innovation Science and Software Engineering (2010)

[9] Zhang, N., Wang, J., Chen, Y.: Image Parallel Processing Based on GPU. In: 2nd International Conference on Advanced Computer Control (ICACC), pp. 367–370 (2010)

[10] Osman, M.A., Mohamad, M.Y., Abdullah, R.: Parallelizing en edge detection algorithm for image recognition to classify paddy and weeds leaf on Sun Fire Cluster System. In: Proceedings of the 7th WSEAS International Conference on Software Engineering, Parallel and Distributed Systems, World Scientific and Engineering Academy and Society, pp. 56–60 (2008)

[11] Galizia, A., Clematis, A., Viti, F., Milanesi, L.: A dynamic parallel approach to recognize tubular breast cancer for Tissue Micro Array (TMA) image building. In: 2010, 18th Euromico Conference on Parallel, Distributed and Network-based Processing, pp. 403–410 (2010)

[12] Xiao, Y., Chen, Z., Zhang, L.: Accelerated CT Reconstruction Using GPU SIMD Parallel Computing with Bilinear Wrapping Method. In: The 1st International Conference on Information Science and Engineering (ICISE 2009), pp. 95–98 (2009)

Performance Evaluation for DSQRM: A Domain-Based Query Routing Mechanism for P2P Networks

Ghada Hasssan, Hamidah Ibrahim, Md. Nasir Sulaiman, and Rasali Yakob

Faculty of Computer Science and Information Technology University Putra Malaysia, Serdang, Selangor, 43400, Malaysia
oghada@hotmail.com, {hamidah,nasir,razali}@fsktm.upm.edu.my

Abstract. An important challenge in peer-to-peer (P2P) networks is locating the peers that can provide the answer for user query. To cope with this challenge, the proposed mechanisms have their own weaknesses to be a successful solution. In this paper, we propose a new query routing mechanism to improve the search performance in such networks. The mechanism consists of domain based architecture for grouping peers in the network into domains based on their contents. In each domain, interconnected groups of peers are constructed based on attributes analysis process. The mechanism provides the required methods for specifying the interaction between the peers in the same or different groups. A comparative analysis is performed to compare the proposed mechanism with two representative baseline routing approaches. To validate this analysis; an experimental study is conducted. The results show that the proposed mechanism achieves better performance with respect to the reduction of average number of messages, the average search path length, and response time.

Keywords: Query routing, Peer-to-peer (P2P) Network, routing mechanism, distributed search, Content-based routing.

1 Introduction

Over the last few years, introduction of the Peer-to-Peer systems have revolutionised the way of information exchange and information retrieval in distributed systems. In contrast to traditional client-server computing models P2P systems are decentralized distributed systems consisting of logically distinct computing elements called peers. The peers are connected to some other peers they know or discover. In such systems the user issues queries against an arbitrarily chosen peer and expects that the answer will include relevant data stored in all P2P connected data sources. These peers have comparable roles and responsibilities. They share or consume services and resources amongst each other [1].

Nodes in P2P environment form a virtual network (called overlay network) located above a physical network (i.e. the Internet).The topology of a P2P system indicates how its peers are situated on the virtual network. This topology has a strong impact on the query routing efficiency in terms of the number of exchanged messages, on one hand, and the answer quality on the other hand[2].

The importance of P2P searches has motivated several proposals for performing these operations efficiently in the last decade. Among them are hybrid systems of

E. Ariwa and E. El-Qawasmeh (Eds.): DEIS 2011, CCIS 194, pp. 317–330, 2011.

different types. However, those search systems are either unscalable, unreliable, slow response time or lack robustness. Usually they are based on one of the following techniques: flooding [3], random walk [4], central index [5], distributed index [6, 7, 8], and super peer [9, 10, 11]. The description of these techniques and their drawbacks is as follows.

In the flooding mechanism, queries are propagated along to all peers in the network. the advantages of this mechanism are the low maintenance cost, making it relatively easy to handle membership and data content changes, but it results in many redundant computations performed by each of the underlying peer, as well as many redundant network accesses and data transfers, which limit the system scalability and cause unnecessary traffic in the network.

To improve the flooding technique by reducing the redundant messages, the random walk mechanism is proposed. In this mechanism, the queries are forwarded to k randomly selected neighbours. Those neighbours in turn forward the query to k randomly selected neighbours until the request is answered or a maximum number of flooding steps occur (i.e. Time-To-Live (TTL)). The performance of random walk depends on the choice of k and TTL value. Choosing low values of k and TTL for searching objects with low popularity would result in low query hit rate and high delays, since the average number of peers required to be probed for discovering any object is inversely proportional to the popularity of the object[12]. On the other hand, choosing high values of k and TTL for searching objects with high popularity would result in excessive bandwidth consumption. Generally this mechanism reduces the network load but increases the search latency compared with the flooding mechanism [14].

The objective of peer indexing is to allow peers to select from an index the best neighbor to send the query to, rather than flooding or random selection. In a centralized index, a single server keeps references to data on many peers. This method scales poorly and when the node that holds the central index fails, the system will crash. In Distributed index techniques, such as Distributed Hash Table (DHT), each data item is identified by a key and nodes are organized into a structured graph topology that maps each key to a responsible node. The data or a pointer to the data is stored at the node that is responsible for its key. This mechanism is suitable in searching for rare objects to avoid searching the entire network to find them, but it incurs large overhead to reorganize the network when the peers join or leave the network.

Super-peer is a node that acts as a centralized server to a subset of client peers. Clients submit queries to their super-peer and receive results from it. Moreover, super-peers are also connected to each other, routing messages among them, and submitting and answering queries on behalf of their clients. Super-peers introduce a single-point of failure for its clients, and still there is a need to make them more reliable.

Object replication in p2p network refers to keep a copy from the object in many locations in the network. This method is good to improve the system availability and performance. Also, it improves the system scalability significantly because it reduces the number of hops traversed to find an object. Two ways exist for replication, the first one is replication for the actual data and the other one is replicate only pointers to the data, which is used by super-peer mechanism. This method is undesirable from the viewpoint of decentralization and peer autonomy. Moreover, it produces more complicated issues like storage load balancing, network load balancing, and replica consistency.

Accordingly, the current routing mechanisms tend to be very inefficient, either generating too much load on the system, providing a single-point failure, costly resource-consumption, or extremely unscalable.

Based on the proposed query routing techniques and their drawbacks, we come to a conclusion that additional research is needed to address the issues of query routing, especially for large scale systems, and to present a new solution that improves the efficiency of query routing techniques for such systems. Accordingly, this paper provides a new routing mechanism to overcome the weaknesses of the previously proposed mechanisms.

This paper is organized as follows. The next section describes the proposed query routing mechanism, and provides the details of its architecture and algorithms. Section 3 gives the details of the comparative analysis that it used to evaluate the performance of the proposed mechanism. Section 4 presents the details of the experimental study and the results. Section 5 provides the related work. Section 6 concludes the paper.

2 Domain-Based Semantic Query Routing Mechanism (DSQRM)

Previous researches have shown that users in P2P-networks are interested in subsets of all available content and they are often only interested in some content categories only [15]. Proceeding from this fact, we propose Domain-based semantic query Routing mechanism (DSQRM). The fundamental idea in DSQRM is to limit the search space to a given query around the related peers. This is done by grouping the peers in the overly network based on their contents. Each group represents domain that has its own schema and attributes. The leadership of each domain is assigned to one peer with relatively high capacities to hold the schema that encompasses all possible attributes in its domain. We name this peer the header of the domain.

In this Mechanism, the user query is routed directly to the domain where it can be answered and within that domain the query is directed to one or more selected groups of peers that may answer the query.

DSQRM is composed of architecture and two algorithms, which are Inter-Domain Routing algorithm (IDRA) and Cross-Domain Routing Algorithm (CDRA). IDRA is used by the peers that belong to the same domain to collaborate with each other to answer the query that its answer can be produced from their domain. CDRA is used between the different domain headers to forward the query that its answer can not be fully produced from the same domain where the query is posted.

2.1 DSQRM Architecture

The architecture of DSQRM (see Fig. 1) is a distributed architecture that consists of multiple classes of peers and domains. The identified classes of peers are normal peers, super peers, and main peers. These components are distributed at three levels as follows.

- Domain level: This level includes the peers that represent the normal network nodes, which are distributed in multiple sites. The domain is a logical grouping for peers that hold the same content or belong to one discipline. Each domain has a header that represents the peer with relatively high capacities than the other peers in the domain. The header of each domain acts as a method of interaction of its domain with the other domains. The interaction refers to the forwarding of a specific set of user queries that their answers can not be obtained from the domain where the query is post to the other domains, or the forwarding of the query answers back to the origin domains. The header of each domain is called super peer.

- Super domain level: In this level, the headers of the different domains (i.e. super peers) are grouped into super domains. In each super domain, the headers are linked together into ring topology. Each ring has maximum number of n headers. The different rings of the different super domains are linked together through the main peer that acts as an intermediate between them.
- Main level: This level contains the main peers. These peers have the widest view of all domains in the network. This is because each main peer stores the metadata of a full version of the domain's schema. The main peer acts as intermediate between the underlying super peers for forwarding their queries and answers.

In this architecture, initially, the set of all data sources of a particular field (e.g. biological field) are registered and grouped into Domains. The grouping is performed based on the topics that are provided by these sources. After domain grouping stage, the constructing of the headers ring stage starts. When the number of headers in each ring exceeds n, new ring must be constructed and so on. Finally the main peers are elected and linked together.

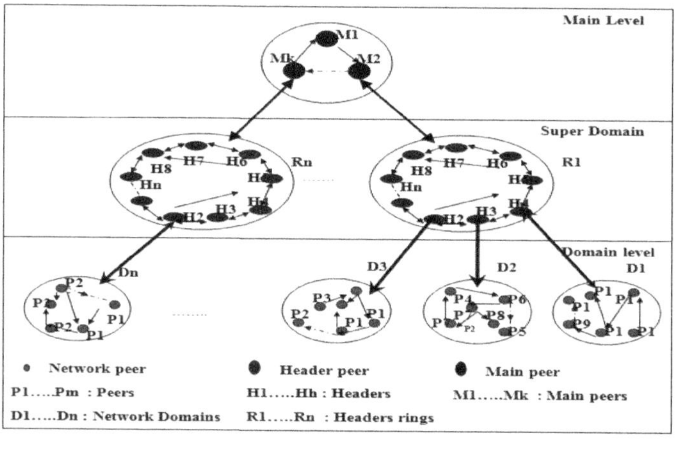

Fig. 1. The architecture of DSQRM

2.2 Inter-Domain Routing Algorithm (IDRA)

This algorithm is dedicated to be used by the peers that belong to the same domain in the domain level of the architecture.

Each domain in our proposed system has its own schema. This schema is represented by a list of its attributes. If we assume D_1 schema has 20 attributes (A_1,...A_{20}), we can classify these attributes into groups according to their occurrences together. For example (G_1:first name, last name, G_2:professor name, filed of study, department).

Accordingly, D_1 schema can be represented as groups of attributes as follows:

G_1:A_1,A_2,...A_6
G_2:A_7...A_{10}

Each new joined peer in the network sends its own schema information to the header of the domain. The header determines the attribute groups that belong to this peer. Accordingly for each peer in its domain, the header records the following information about the attribute groups:

P_1: G_1, G_3
P_2:G_4, G_2

Based on this information, the following facts can be deduced (~ means appear in):

G_1~P_1, P_5, P_{10}, P_4
G_2~P_4, P_8, P_3

Accordingly, additional interconnected groups of peers are produced inside each domain (e.g. D_1 (G_1, G_2, G_3,....)).see Fig. 2. (*b*) For more clarification.

For each produced group, a coordinator is elected. This coordinator has a link to its group's peers and the domain header. Each peer when it joins the system, it will have links to the coordinators of the groups and the header.

Based on the aforementioned description, the CDRA algorithm is as follows.

- *Each peer tests the received query against its domain schema*
  - *If it can be answer through it, then*
    - *It determines the attribute groups that the query belongs to it.*
    - *Forward the query to the corresponding groups' coordinators.*
    - *The group's coordinators flood the query to its group peers.*

  Else
    - *Forward the query to the domain header.*

2.3 Cross-Domain Routing Algorithm (CDRA)

This algorithm is dedicated to the super domain level. In this algorithm, each group of header peers is organized into a ring topology. Each peer node has associated number *NN* ($1<NN<n$), where n is total number of headers in each headers ring. n is associated with the last header in the series and 1 is associated with the first header.

Each header has knowledge only about the contents of the two direct neighbors (i.e. the successor and predecessor) and stores only one address for remote header called partner header. Each header has two types of links: Direct-neighbor-link (*DL*) and Partner-link (*PL*). *DL* is used to link the header with its direct neighbors and the *PL* is used to link the header with its partner header. The message forwarding between partner headers will be in one direction, i.e. the anticlock wise direction. see Fig. 2. (a) For more clarification.

In the following, we illustrate how to compute the direct successor (*DNs*) and the direct predecessor (*DNp*) neighbors and the partner neighbor (*PN*) for each header node:

$$DNs = | NN+1 | \bmod n,\ 1<NN<n$$

$$DNp = \begin{cases} |NN-1| \bmod n, 1 < NN \leq n \\ n, NN = 1 \end{cases}$$

$$PN = | NN+3 | \bmod n$$

The maximum number of hops between two headers (*H-Max*) in this level is calculated as follows.

H-Max =trunck((n-2)/3), where n is number of nodes in the super-domain ring.

To strictly guarantee that the query forwarding is not exceeding the maximum number of hops for this level, the Descending Factor (*DF*) is proposed. Before the first forwarding for the query through the headers ring, the query must be tagged with *DF* and the value of *DF* is equal to *H-Max*. *DF* must be decreased by (one) in each forwarding for the query through the ring. Therefore, in each forwarding the *DF* must be checked if *DF*>0 can be forwarded to the next partner and if *DF*<= 0 it must be forwarded to the main peer.

Based on the aforementioned description, the CDRA algorithm is as follows.

- ❖ *Each header determines the source of the received query.*
- ❖ *If the query source = the main peer, then*
  - ❖ *the header checks it against its local schema*
    - ❖ *if the query can be answered through it, then*
      - ❖ *it forwards the query to its underline peers.*
    - *Else*
      - ❖ *it checks its local knowledge about the direct tow neighbor schemas.*
      - ❖ *If it can be answered, then*
        - ❖ *it directly forwards it to the specific direct neighbor.*
      - *Else*
        - ❖ *it will be forwarded through the partner link.*
- ❖ *If the query source = one of its underline peers, then*
  - ❖ *the header checks it against its local knowledge about the neighbor schemas.*
  - ❖ *if it can be answered through one of them, then*
    - ❖ *it directly forwards it to the specific direct neighbor.*
  - *Else*
    - ❖ *it will be forwarded through the partner link.*
- ❖ *If the source of the query= one of its neighbors, then*
  - ❖ *the header checks it against its local schema*

❖ *if it can be answered through it, then*
❖ *it forwards the query to its underline peers.*
Else
❖ *it checks its local knowledge about the direct tow neighbor chemas.*
❖ *If it can be answered, then*
❖ *it directly forwards it to the specific direct eighbor.*
Else
❖ *it will be forwarded through the partner link*

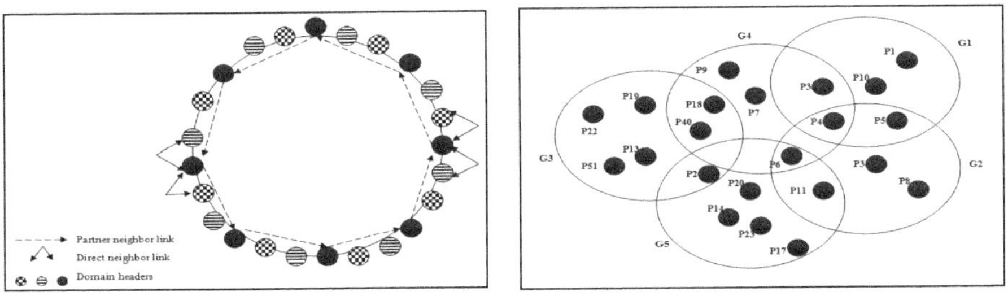

Fig. 2. (a) The Super domain level architecture; (b) The Domain level architecture

3 Comparative Analyses

In this section, we present the comparative analysis that is used to compare the proposed routing mechanism (DSQRM) and two representative baseline routing approaches, which are: super-peer based routing [16,17] and flooding based routing [18, 19, 20]. The purpose of the comparison is to evaluate the different routing mechanisms with regard to achieving the reduction of the total number of messages and the number of hops. This reduction is achieved through routing query messages using minimum number of both messages and hops [21,22]. Accordingly, in this comparison, two relevant performance metrics are considered as follows.

1. M_MAX is the maximum number of messages that are generated during the routing from the source node to the destination.
2. H_MAX is the maximum number of hops between the source and the destination.

Based on the definition of the two metrics, they are measured by using analytically developed equations that are based on considering the worst case for each mechanism with regard to routing a query from its source node to the destination node that contains the answer.

The worst cases for the three compared mechanisms are considered as follows.

- **DSQRM Mechanism:** The source node exists in the first domain, which belongs to the first super domain ring, and the node that contains the answer is assumed that it exists in the last domain that resides at the last super domain ring.
- **Super-Peer based Mechanism:** In the worst case, the source node connects to the first super peer, while the destination node connects to the

last super peer in the system. The super peers that represent the parents of both the source and destination are assumed that they exist in two different ends of linear bus geometry where routing is performed between them through all super peers that exist between these super peers. This is by assuming that each super peer forwards the query to the next closest neighbor in the direction of the destination.

❖ **Flooding Mechanism:** We assume as in [23] an N vertex strictly binary tree whose depth is about ($\log_2 N$) and that the source of the query is at the root. For the worst case, we assume that the destination exists in the last depth (level) of the tree, and the query forwarding follows the Breadth-first search algorithm.

Different equations are used to evaluate the values of H_MAX and T_MAX in the worst case for the compared mechanisms. These equations are summarized in Table 1. The mechanisms are compared by varying the number of nodes (N), which leads to the variation of the other parameters: number of super-peers, number of main peers, TTL (number of levels in Flooding). Table 2 summarizes the parameters and their values.

Table 1. The equations that are used to evaluate the values of H_MAX and M_MAX

	H_MAX	M_MAX
DSQRM	Trunc(S/3) +1, S≤20 7+M+1, S>20	H_MAX + 1
Super-peer	O(S) [1,2]	H_MAX + 1
Flooding	Log_2 N [23,19,20]	$\sum_{t=1}^{TTl} 2^t$ [23,18]

Table 2. The parameters and its values

Parameter	Value	Description
N	1,000-10,000	Total number of nodes in the network
S	10-100	Total number of super-peer in the network
TTL	number of levels in Flooding	Time to Leave
M	1-5	Total number of main-peer in the network

The three mechanisms are compared based on the values of both M_MAX and H_MAX by varying the number of nodes (N). The impact of this variation on M_MAX is as shown in Fig. 3. DBSQRM achieves an average of reduction in the number of messages with percentages 65.8% over the super-peer mechanism, and 99.1% over the flooding mechanism. Similarly, H_MAX is affected by the variation of the number of nodes, and the result is as shown in Fig. 4. DBSQRM achieves an average of reduction of the number of hops for different network sizes with percentages 81.1% over the super-peer mechanism, and 34.6% over the flooding mechanism.

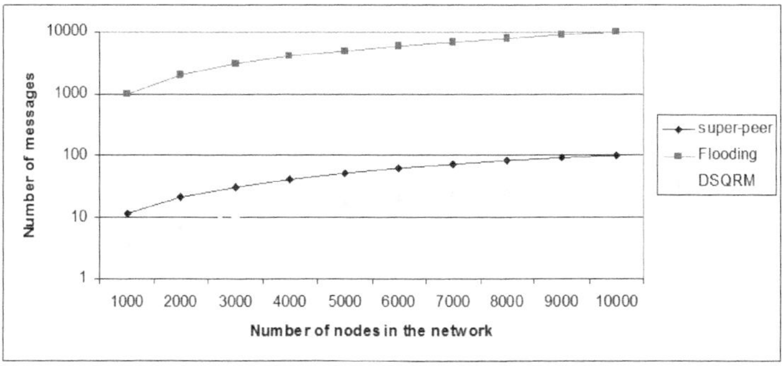

Fig. 3. The network load per query in the worst case

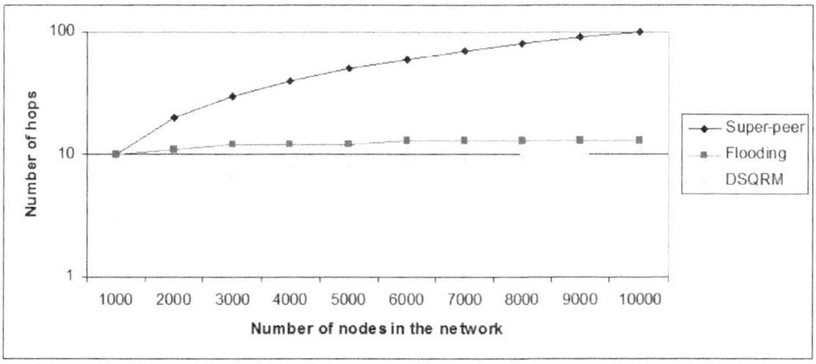

Fig. 4. The query path length in the worst case

4 Experimental Study

In our experimental study, we compared the performance of our proposed mechanism with the flooding mechanism, which is used as a baseline in the evaluation of P2P search systems [24, 25].

We describe the performance evaluation of our routing mechanism with a OMNET++ Version 4.1 [26]. All experiments were run on a machine Core 2 Duo 2.10 GHZ with 4 GB RAM, 500 GB Hard disk and Windows 7 operating system. In this section, we present the experimental setup, performance metrics and performance evaluation in our simulations.

4.1 Experimental Setup

We construct a network with 1,000...10,000 peers and distribute contents on the network according to a Zipf-like distribution. We generate ten queries according to the Zipf distribution. Each query is repeated 50 times and the averages are calculated. In this setting, we implement both the DSQRM mechanism and the Flooding based mechanism using binary tree topology.

4.2 Performance Metrics

There are many p2p search performance metrics. However, in the evaluation of DSQRM, we are mainly concerned with search path-length, network load, and response time to assess the efficiency of our approach. Query path-length is the number of hops that the query is passing through them before it reaches the target peer. This metric indicates how goal-oriented a query is routed and how fast answer may be returned [27]. The network load is the number of messages per query traces. This metric shows that to what extent the network is being flooded by one query[28]. The query response time is the time period from when a query is issued by a peer node until it receives the first response [29].

4.3 Performance Evaluation

Fig 5 shows the average search path length for DSQRM and the flooding mechanism. The search path length for Flooding starts with high value and increases slowly with the size of network but in DSQRM it starts and continues with small values for the most network sizes. In fact, the search path length of DSQRM is about 37% shorter compared to flooding mechanism at network size 10000 peer where the shortest difference between the two values of the average search path length is exist.

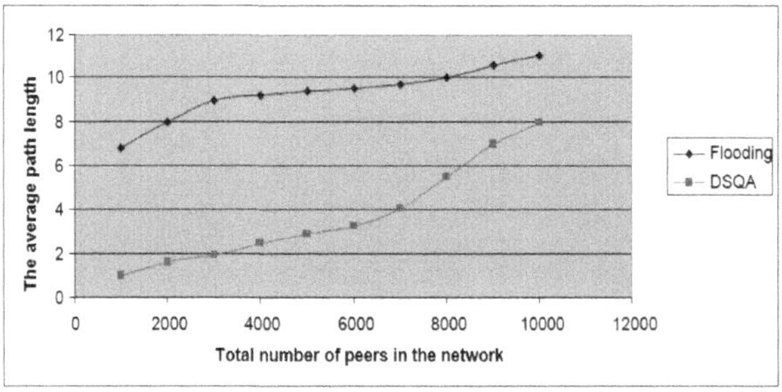

Fig. 5. The average search path length

We examine the network load traffic, in terms of the number of messages generated in the network to handle the user query. We compare the difference in traffic loadings between DSQRM and flooding under the same scenario for different network sizes without limit for TTL. Fig 6 shows the comparison results, the result shows clearly the variation in the numbers of messages between DSQRM and flooding mechanism. The flooding mechanism produces vast redundant messages, but DSQRM reducing network load, as fewer messages are required.

One of the important metrics in the evaluation of p2p search techniques is the query response time. In Fig 7, we show the result of the experiment that is used to study the performance of DSQRM in term of the response time. In this experiment we assume that the delay of all p2p network edges are equal and we set it to 10 ms. In this experiment, the average response time is faster by around 57% than the flooding mechanism.

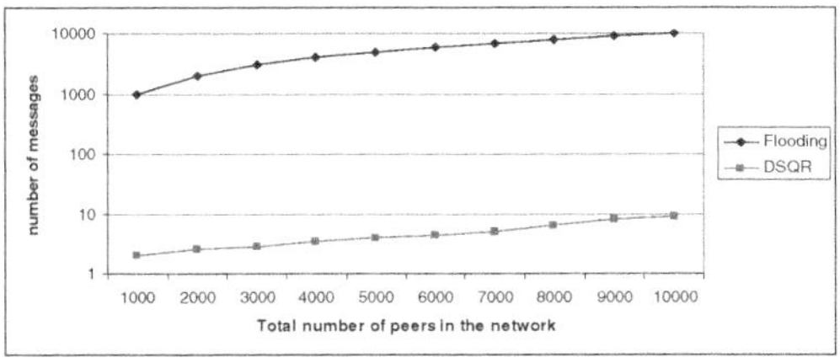

Fig. 6. The network load per query

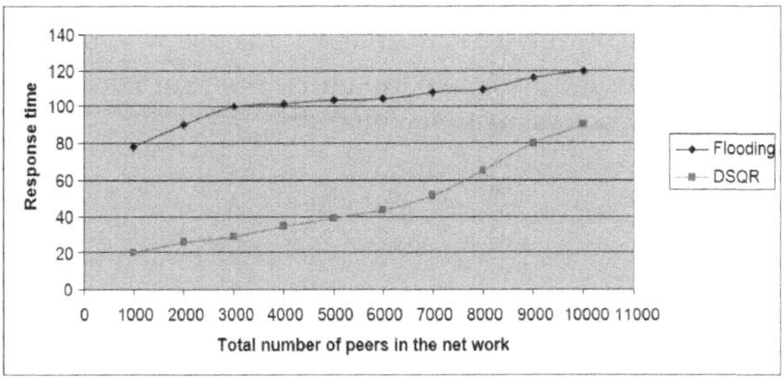

Fig. 7. The average response time

Finally, the aforementioned results demonstrate how much our technique, compared to flooding technique presents an advantage in the number of messages exchanged over the network and the average time needed to obtain responses. The Observation of the performance of the algorithm for large network size in these experiments, clearly demonstrates that DSQRM algorithm is more efficient than flooding for large scale P2P applications.

5 Related Works

Although the p2p technology provides attractive features for distributed data sharing like scalability, load balance, and fault-tolerance, still query processing in current P2P systems causes high cost and does not scale well. to improve the query performance, [30] proposes Semantic Overlay Networks (SONs), a flexible network organization that clustering the network nodes with semantically similar content together. This approach uses the flooding mechanism to perform the search in such architecture. So far, several approaches have been proposed based on SONs. Some of these approaches are described as follows.

Some approaches [31, 32, and 33] relay on one peer (super-peer) in each cluster that holds the metadata for all nodes in the cluster to direct the query to its destination. Search is performed by a peer contacting the super-peer responsible for the SON, and then the super-peer forwards the query to peers in the SON. The search at super-peer level is based on flooding [31], routing indices[33] or based on a topology link [32].

In [34,35], associative overlays approach is proposed. In this approach, each peer in the network maintains a list of the other peers that hold the same data item. This list is constructed in [34] using the information that is retrieved from the previous successful search. In [35], the list is constructed by each peer when it discovers the network.

[36,37, 38, 39] propose to use two types of links, which are neighbors link and acquaintance links to link the peer with its semantic related neighbors, and randomly selected neighbors, respectively. The search over the two links is performed using flooding. This approach has growing search cost with increasing of the number of nodes in the network.

[40,41] propose a new type of P2P networks, i.e. schema-based P2P networks that use the super-peer based topology. This method relies on predefined policies (schemas) that are defined by human experts to distribute peers to available super peers. The advantage of this approach is that it provides better scalability and load balancing, but queries are broadcasted to all peers and this consumes the network bandwidth, and the processing power at each peer.

Hierarchical SONs have also been proposed in the literature [42, 43] .[42] uses a structured P2P network (CAN) to distribute the indices through the P2P network hierarchically based on the generated semantics. [43] Relies on Hierarchical Summary Indexing Structure to summarize the information at different levels in the network.

6 Conclusion

Many distributed peer-to-peer applications need to determine the node that stores a data item. In this paper, we proposed the domain-based query routing mechanism to solve this challenging problem in a decentralized manner. DSQRM mechanism improves the efficiency of the peer-to-peer search system while keeping search costs low. It does this by grouping the peers with similar content into domains. Then, a process of attributes analysis is performed for the peers that belong to one domain to make interconnected groups of peers that contain semantically related information, in order to forward the queries that relevant to the cluster can be forwarded only to peers of that particular cluster. We presented the details of DSQRM architecture and the two query routing algorithms that perform the search process within the architecture

The benchmarking results show that the proposed mechanism outperforms the flooding using several performance metrics, i.e. response time of queries, network load, and average path length. We believe that DSQRM can effectively and efficiently supporting query processing in a multi-domain p2p data sharing system

References

1. Koubarakis, M.: Multi-agent Systems and Peer-to-Peer Computing: Methods, Systems, and Challenges. In: Klusch, M., Omicini, A., Ossowski, S., Laamanen, H. (eds.) CIA 2003. LNCS (LNAI), vol. 2782, pp. 46–61. Springer, Heidelberg (2003)
2. King, R.A., Hameurlain, A., Morvan, F.: Query Routing and Processing in Peer- To-Peer Data Sharing Systems. International Journal of Database Management Systems, Academy & Industry Research Collaboration Center (AIRCC) 2(2), 116–139 (2010)
3. Jurczyk, P., Xiong, L., Sunderam, V.: DObjects: Enabling distributed data services for metacomputing platforms. In: Proceedings of the VLDB Endowment, pp. 1432–1435 (2008)

4. Gkantsidis, C., Mihail, M., Saberi, A.: Random walks in peer-to-peer networks: Algorithms and evaluation. Performance Evaluation 63(3), 241–263 (2006)
5. Katchaounov, T.: Query Processing for Peer Mediator Databases, Doctoral Dissertation, Uppsala University (2003)
6. Gardarin, G., Dragan, F., Yeh, L.: P2P semantic mediation of web sources. LNBIP, vol. 3, pp. 3–16 (2008)
7. Ege, R.K., Yang, L., Kharma, Q., Ni, X.: Three-layered mediator architecture based on DHT. In: Proceedings of the International Symposium on Parallel Architcture, Algorithm and Networks (I-SPAN), Hong Kong, China (2004)
8. Huebsch, R., Chun, B.N., Hellerstein, J.M., Loo, B.T., Maniatis, P., Roscoe, T., Shenker, S.: The architecture of pier: an internet-scale query processor. In: Proceedings of 2nd Conference on Innovative Data Systems Research CIDR (2005)
9. Loser, A., Siberski, W., Wolpers, M., Nejdl, W.: Information integration in schema based peer-to-peer networks. In: Proceedings of the 15th International Conference on Advanced Information Systems Engineering, Klagenfurt, Austria (2003)
10. Halvey, A., Ives, Z.G., Mork, P., Tartarinov, I.: Piazza: data management infrastructure for semantic web applications. In: Proceedings of the Twelfth International Conference on World Wide Web, pp. 556–567 (2003)
11. Beneventano, D., Bergamaschi, S., Guerra, F., Vincini, M.: Querying a super-peer in a schema-based super-peer network. In: Proceedings of the 2005/2006 International Conference on Databases, Information Systems, and Peer-to-Peer Computing, Trondheim, Norway (2005)
12. Bisnik, N., Abouzeid, A.: Modeling and analysis of random walk search algorithms in p2p networks. In: 2nd IWHTP2PS (2005)
13. Xu, M., Shuigeng, Z., Guan, J., Hu, X.: A path-traceable query routing mechanism for search in unstructured peer-to-peernetworks. Journal of Network and Computer Applications 33 (2010)
14. Yang, B., Garcia-Molina, H.: Designing a super-peer network. In: Proceedings of the 19th International Conference on Data Engineering, Los Alamitos, USA (2003)
15. Crespo, A., Garcia-Molina, H.: Routing indices for peer-to-peer systems. In: Proceedings of the International Conference on Distributed Computing Systems. IEEE Press, Los Alamitos (2002)
16. Yang, B., Garcia-Molina, H.: Designing a super-peer network. In: Proceedings of the 19th International Conference on Data Engineering (2003)
17. Li, J., Vuong, S.: An Efficient Clustered Architecture for P2P Networks. In: Proceedings of the 18th International Conference on Advanced Information Networking and Applications (2004)
18. El-Ansary, S.: Efficient Broadcast in Structured P2P Networks. In: Proceedings of 2nd International Workshop on Peer-to-Peer Systems, pp. 304–314 (2003)
19. El-Ansary, S., Onana, L., Brand, P., Haridi, S.: A Framework for Peer-To-Peer Lookup Services based on k-ary search. SICS Technical Report (2002)
20. Trunfio, P.: Implementing Dynamic Querying Search in k-ary DHT-based Overlays. Grid Computing, 275–286 (2008)
21. Gummadi, K.: The impact of DHT routing geometry on resilience and proximity. In: Proceedings of the 2003 Conference on Applications, Technologies, Architectures, and Protocols for Computer Communications (2003)
22. Ghosh, S.: Distributed Systems: An Algorithmic Approach, 1st edn. Chapman and Hall/CRC (2006)

23. Wang, H., Lin, T.: On efficiency in searching networks. In: Proceedings of IEEE INFOCOM, Miami, FL, USA (2005)
24. David, F., Gilles, N., Patrick, V.: Semantic query routing in senpeer, a p2p data management system. In: NBiS, pp. 365–374 (2007)
25. Ismail, A., Quafafou, M., Nachouki, G., Hajjar, M.: Efficient super-peer-based queries routing. In: MEDES 2009, pp. 91–98. ACM, New York (2009)
26. http://www.omnetpp.org/
27. Li, M., Lee, W.-C., Sivasubramaniam, A.: Semantic small world: an overlay network for peer-to-peer search. In: ICNP, pp. 228–238 (2004)
28. Christoph, T., Steffen, S., Wranik, A.: REMINDIN': Semantic query routing in peer-to-peer networks based on social metaphors. In: Proceedings of the 13th Int. WorldWide Web Conference, WWW 2004 (2004)
29. Rostamia, H., Habibi, J., Livani, E.: Semantic partitioning of peer-to-peer search space. Computer Communications 32(4), 619–633 (2009)
30. Crespo, A., Garcia-Molina, H.: Semantic Overlay Networks for P2P Systems. Technical report, Stanford University (2002)
31. Liu, X., Wang, J., Vuong, S.T.: A category overlay infrastructure for peer-to-peer content search. In: Proceedings of IPDPS 2005 (2005)
32. Doulkeridis, C., Nørvåg, K., Vazirgiannis, M.: Peer-to-peer similarity search over widely distributed document collections. In: Proceedings of the 6th Workshop on Large-Scale Distributed Systems for Information Retrieval, LSDS-IR (2008)
33. Schlosser, M., Sintek, M., Decker, S., Nejdl, W.: HyperCuP – Hypercubes, ontologies and efficient search on P2P networks. In: Proceedings of International Workshop on Agents and Peer-to-Peer Computing (AP2PC), pp. 112–124 (2002)
34. Cohen, E., Kaplan, H., Fiat, A.: Associative search in peer to peer networks: Harnessing latent semantics. In: Proceedings of INFOCOM 2003 (2003)
35. Parreira, J., Michel, S., Weikum, G.: p2pDating: real life inspired semantic overlay networks for web search. In: Proceedings of SIGIR Wokshop on Heterogeneous and Distributed Information Retrieval (2005)
36. Cholvi, V., Felber, P., Biersack, E.: Efficient search in unstructured peer-to-peer networks. In: Proceedings of SPAA 2004 (2004)
37. Hui, K.Y.K., Lui, J.C.S., Yau, D.K.Y.: Small-world overlay P2P networks: Construction, management and handling. Computer Networks 50(15), 2727–2746 (2006)
38. Li, M., Lee, W.C., Sivasubramaniam, A.: Semantic small world: An overlay network for peer - to- peer search. In: Proceedings of the 12th IEEE International Conference on Network Protocols (ICNP), pp. 228–238 (2004)
39. Raftopoulou, P., Petrakis, E.G.M.: iCluster: A self-organizing overlay network for p2p information retrieval. In: Proceedings of the 30th European Conference on IR Research (ECIR), pp. 65–76 (2008)
40. Loeser, A., Naumann, F., Siberski, W., Nejdl, W., Thaden, U.: Semantic overlay clusters within super-peer networks. In: Proceedings of DBISP2P 2003 (2003)
41. Nejdl, W., Wolpers, M., Siberski, W., Schmitz, C., Schlosser, M., Brunkhorst, I., Loeser, A.: Super-Peer-based Routing and Clustering Strategies for RDF-based P2P Networks. In: Proceedings of WWW 2003 (2003)
42. Liu, F., Ma, F., Li, M., Huang, L.: Distributed information retrieval based on hierarchical semantic overlay network. In: Jin, H., Pan, Y., Xiao, N., Sun, J. (eds.) GCC 2004. LNCS, vol. 3252. Springer, Heidelberg (2004)
43. Shen, H.T., Shu, Y., Yu, B.: Efficient semantic-based content search in P2P network. IEEE Transactions on Knowledge and Data Engineering 16(7), 813–826 (2004)

A Highly Adaptable Information Dissemination Strategy*

A. Husain[1], S.K. Makki[2], L. Osborne[2], and B. Sun[2]

[1] Computer Science Department, SUNY Binghamton
[2] Computer Science Department, Lamar University
ahusian2@binghamton.edu,
{kami.makki,bo.sun,larry.osborne}@lamar.edu

Abstract. Wireless Sensor Networks have many real world applications. Accordingly, researchers and entrepreneurs are looking for a reliable, real time, and energy-efficient network structures. Traditional techniques of flooding the network with information have proved inept in all of the latter criteria. Others have made specific assumptions of how the network is used and thus make intelligent choices on data dissemination. This paper proposes a non-data centric and thus highly adaptable information dissemination protocol called the Irrigation Algorithm to efficiently route packet to base stations. To evaluate its performance this algorithm is compared with the Low-Energy Adaptive Clustering Hierarchy (LEACH) protocol.

Keywords: Communications, Frequency, Medium Access Control, Routing.

1 Introduction

The reduction of power consumption by sensor nodes is one of the major challenges in mobile wireless sensor networks. Since, these types of network operate based on the collaborative efforts of a large number of sensor nodes. The wireless sensor devices are portable and inexpensive, but suffer from a number of drawbacks, such as, stringent energy supply, limited processing and communications capabilities. There are a few ways to conserve battery life of a sensor device. One is to simplify the computations that a sensor device must carry out through implementing more efficient algorithms. The other possibility is to improve the system to transmit and receive less radio messages since sending and receiving radio messages consume most of the energy of a sensor device. In the next section we briefly investigate different ways that can reduce the consumption of sensor node energy. The remainder of this paper is organized as follow: Section 2 explains the related research work and the existing drawbacks. Section 3 explains our proposed algorithm called Irrigation Algorithm. Section 4 discusses the performance of our proposed algorithm which was analyzed and compared with a traditional solution – the leader based algorithm. Section 5 concludes the paper and discusses potential future work to help improve our proposed solution.

* This material is based upon work supported by the National Science Foundation under Grant No. 0851912 and 0922888. Any opinions, findings, and conclusions or recommendations expressed in this material are those of the author(s) and do not necessarily reflect the views of the National Science Foundation.

E. Ariwa and E. El-Qawasmeh (Eds.): DEIS 2011, CCIS 194, pp. 331–338, 2011.

Also, in this work, we consider that the sensors are stationary, and they start with the same energy level, and communicate only through broadcast messages. They also have the radios with the ability to change their broadcast strength (considering a known upper limit) and frequencies (e. g. at most four). Also sensors can change their detection range and identify their positions. In this wireless sensor network we consider only one base station which can only communicate with its physical neighbors (PNs). Through its PNs, the base station can begin a network setup protocol and receive incoming information packets in a timely manner. Similar to LEACH protocol, iterations of the algorithm are separated into rounds with a designated amount of time. This allows the base station to change its bridge to the network. Thus we combat the bottleneck of sensors near the base station would run out of energy early and reduce the networks lifetime.

2 Related Work

2.1 Dynamic Communication and Detection Range

With knowledge of sensor positions we can make the best decisions on sensing and communication range. As the prior researchers have assumed [12, 13, 14], we can vary the communication and detection range. We assume the communication range is at least twice the sensing range since this area coverage implies connectivity [11, 13]. Thus an accurate coverage area must now be calculated. With knowledge of each neighbor's position a sensor can make this calculation using geometric estimations using its detection range [7, 8]. Since any polygon created using three or four sensor midpoints can be decomposed into triangles, we can accurately model a physical network with a mesh virtual network as shown in Figure 1.

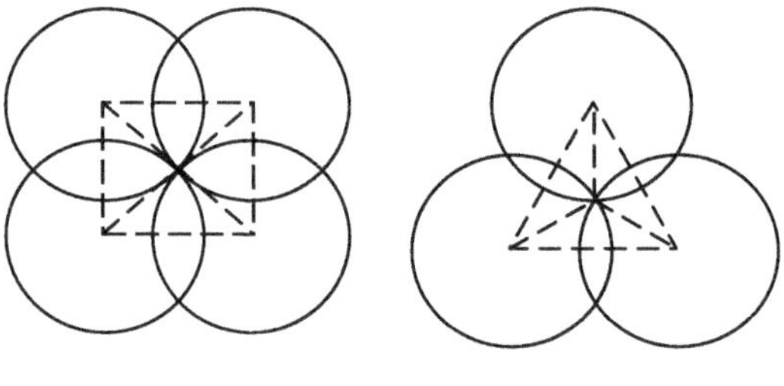

Fig. 1. Geometric Approximations

2.2 Mesh Networks

The physical and virtual network topology should be deemed separate entities. Regardless of the geographical layout and assuming that the virtual network is connected at network startup, a mesh network was determined the best virtual network topology. This choice was made because mesh networks are highly scalable and robust to individual node failure [6]. A node thus chooses up to 8 virtual neighbors (VNs) based on which physical neighbors have the furthest reliable communication link in each compass direction within a certain range.

2.3 WiseMac and PicoRadio

To setup an efficient Wireless Sensor Network we must implement an energy efficient Media/Medium Access Control (MAC), a data communication protocol. Tradition MACs spend more than 90% of their power on idle radio listening [4]. One such way to combat this is introducing sleep cycles where a sensor samples the medium for a preamble message when awake [3]. Another method is to embed hardware where a low power wake up channel can be implemented [4]. Sleep cycles can cause a sensor to be asleep when communication is required while a wake up message technique could save a significant amount of energy without sacrificing reliability [5].

2.4 Routing Techniques

Many packet routing techniques have been proposed in the past. The most basic and inefficient routing technique is flooding -- watching sensor sends its packet to all its neighbors and they send it to all their neighbors recursively. Without making further assumptions about how the network is being used, there are the improved routing concepts such as leader based (LEACH), negotiation based (SPIN), data based (Directed Diffusion) methods [10].

The leader based method (LEACH) uses clustering and randomized rotation of cluster leaders to route packets to the base station [9]. Only 5% of nodes have to act as cluster heads for LEACH to function [10]. Cluster leaders can communicate directly with the base station, and sensors within a cluster can only communicate directly with their leader. A sensor uses the following formula to determine whether it is a cluster head [9].

$$T(n) = \begin{cases} \frac{p}{1 - p * (R \bmod \frac{1}{p})} & \text{if } n \in K \\ 0 & \text{, otherwise} \end{cases} \qquad (1)$$

Where p is the preferred percentage of cluster heads (p=0.05, R is the current round, and K is the set of nodes that have not been cluster heads in the last $\frac{1}{p}$ rounds.

Sensors join a cluster when they receive an advertisement message from the leader node closest to them. To even out power consumption, after a designated amount of time, new leaders are chosen and the process begins again. This initialization assumes all sensors have the ability to communicate with the base station if designated as a leader. In addition, leaders have to keep their receiver on even if they receive no packet from their other cluster sensors. This is a major drawback of LEACH method.

3 The Proposed Algorithm

Our Proposed strategy called Irrigation Algorithm combined with PicoRadio and WiseMac technology should be an improvement upon the leader based LEACH method. Similar to LEACH, an iteration of our algorithm is run for an optimal time in which a base station's connection to the network does not expire.

At the beginning of each network setup sensors with power below a certain threshold are no longer considered as part of the network and do not participate in network setup. This allows for sensors to change their communication and detection range to match the networks deficiencies introduced by depleted sensors.

Our proposed Irrigation Algorithm uses Breath First Search Network Setup (BFS-NS) which is similar to the Minimum Cost Forwarding (MCF) algorithm [1]. In MCF there is a cost field that allows packets to flow along the minimum cost path. Starting from the sink, a cost value path is disseminated through flooding and no sensor node needs to store this minimum cost path.

The BFS-NS begins with the base station sending a packet with level = 1 to its virtual neighbors (for base station VN = PN). Each sensor that receives a "relevant" packet assigns itself to that level, increments the packet's level, and sends to all its neighbors. A "relevant" packet has level less than the current sensors level and has a level less than an arbitrary constant L (such that L < largest possible level in a network however, a sharp approximation of L yields better performance). After time T (based on delays of real world application), any packets received are ignored as shown in the partial pseudo code below. Even if the packet is "relevant", the length of the time it had taken to reach would imply that there is some probable delay in propagation along this route and should be avoided.

```
for (time T)
{
    if (packet level < sensors current level && packet level < L)
    {
        sensors current level = packet level;
         (packet level)++;
        send (packet);
    }
}
```

Generally nodes closer to base stations have faster energy depletion than the nodes that are farther from base stations. The reason is that, these nodes have to transmit the incoming messages from other parts of the network to base stations as well. This is a bottleneck in most routing algorithms. This problem can be overcome in one of two ways; moving base station (if there is only one base station) or alternating base stations (if there are multiple base stations). However, it is assumed that a base station's connection will remain alive through an iteration of our proposed algorithm.

Also, Multi-Frequency Media Access Control uses frequency assignment to make use of static properties of sensors [2]. To reduce communication interference, nodes within two hops are evenly assigned frequencies as shown in Figure 2. Additional hardware would be required to implement this frequency level association. However, the cost of additional hardware could dramatically improve a network performance that uses the Irrigation Algorithm. A sensor changes its receive-frequency to a value equal to (level modulo 3) and its send frequency becomes ((level-1) modulo 3).

3.1 Packet Level Flow

Through the using of BFS-NS and Frequency-Level Association steps, a watching sensor can effectively route to the base station. A watching sensor creates and sends a packet (every S seconds) on its send frequency so that it can be routed to the base station. A sensor keeps a hashed list with packet origins as the key and the number of packets as the value. If the stored value of received packets is less than the packet number then continue to send. This ensures that an already sent packet is not sent again.

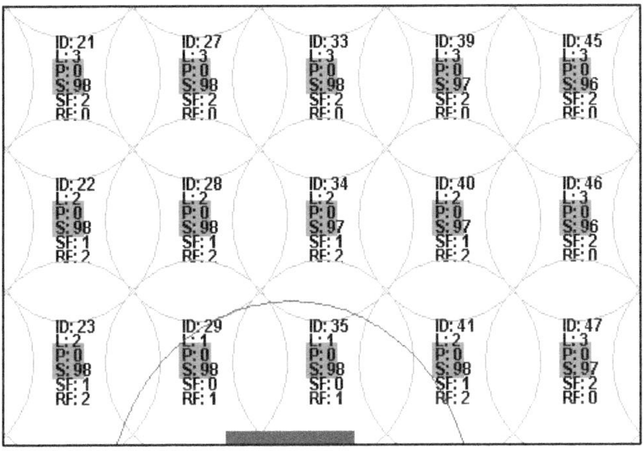

Fig. 2. Frequency Level Association
(L= level, SF=send frequency, RF= receive frequency)

4 Implementation (Simulators)

The LEACH Simulator (LS) and the Irrigation Algorithm Simulator (IAS) were written in Java with each sensor being a running thread. The simulations implement one iteration of each routing technique and collect data on power levels at end of an iteration (power consumption) and time from packet creation to base station (network delay). As the simulation follows ideal environment functioning one cannot accurately simulate reliability of sensors but one can extend the concept into a real world experiment to verify our purposed algorithm's claims for increased reliability. The arrangement of timeslots in LS and the preamble technique (WiseMac) [3] is not simulated in the IAS but rather we use synchronized receive methods. This assumes that timeslots and the preamble technique do not produce significant delays or consumption of power.

The area to cover is 950 units by 750 units, the default detection range is 75 units, the default communication range is 150 units, and a power of 100%. With these metrics the simulator places 63 sensors with 7 rows and 9 columns. A base station is arbitrary located on one side of this area (a purple rectangle at the bottom of Figure 2). At the default communication range a send costs 0.12%, a receive costs 0.10% and watching costs 0.5% of battery power. At first, a target is released randomly on the perimeter of the area. The target moves at a random speed up to 15 units per paint of screen and has a 10% chance of switching direction.

Using default communication range the leaders use flooding to advertise their existence. Based on a sensor's distance from a leader a sensor chooses the closest leader. The LS Advertisement and IAS Breadth First Search Setup last approximately 10 seconds. A base station uses flooding to assign levels by using its default communication range. Although previously stated that flooding is inefficient, this initial power cost increases overall efficiency of the future network. Altogether, the Advertisement Phase uses about 1-2% of a sensors power and the Breath First Search Setup uses about 1-3%.

IAS uses the default costs of communication and detection throughout its iteration. On the other hand, the leader based simulator needs new metrics to calculate power costs. To simulate data aggregation the cost to send from a leader to base station is 25% of a normal send packet at that distance. In addition, 40% of the receive cost is deducted for idle listening when a leader's receiver is on for each of his cluster sensor/s timeslot.

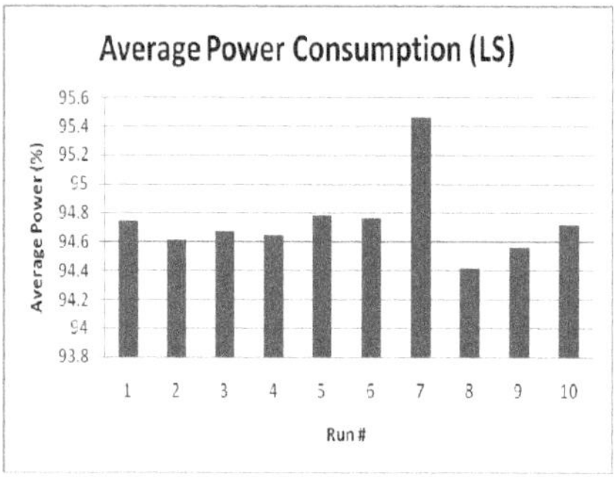

Fig. 3. Average Power Consumption (LS)

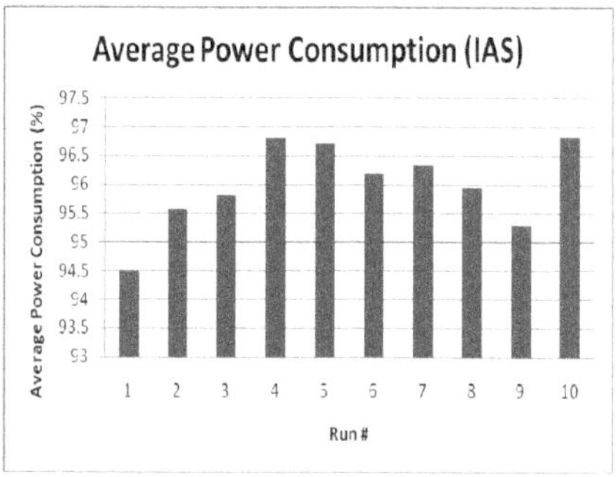

Fig. 4. Average Power Consumption (IAS)

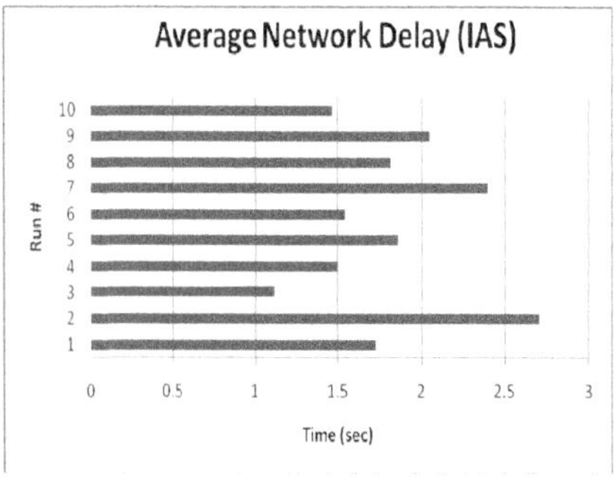

Fig. 5. Average Network Delay (IAS)

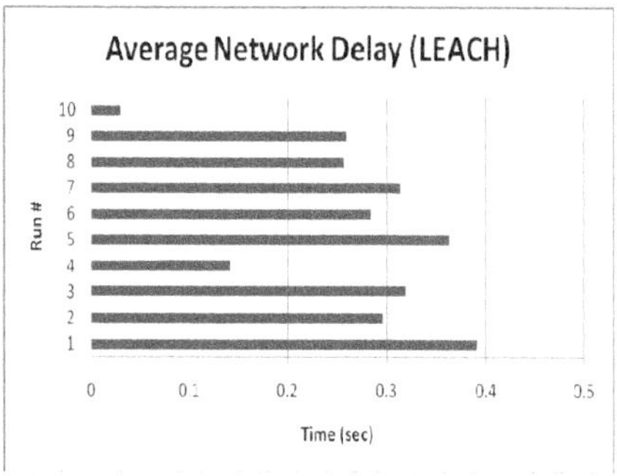

Fig. 6. Average Network Delay (Leach)

The Figures of 3 and 4 show the data collected for LS and IAS for energy consumption. The Figures of 5 and 6 show the data collected for LS and IAS for network delay. For LEACH we only consider runs where at least 5% or greater of the sensors are leaders. As leaders can watch a target and also have the ability to send packets directly to the base station, there are many packets that are instantly transmitted to the base station. While IAS had a greater network delay, the energy consumption by calculating average power was less in IAS. The greater network delay was predicted due to multi-hop routing and multiple copy routing. Yet this drawback should improve scalability and reliability.

5 Conclusion

The Irrigation algorithm finds an efficient way to route packets to the base station. From the simulation we see a tremendous improvement in energy efficiency mostly due to the application of PicoRadio. It is known that using multi-hop routing is far better for scalability and it was reiterated by the results of this simulation.

The technique is promising as the simulation demonstrates. Also, by using different frequencies, fewer unrelated sensors are interrupted through communication. This is a tremendous improvement upon techniques in which unnecessary sensors would wake up their receivers or spend extra energy on idle listening. There is also less radio interference due to many neighboring sensors operating on different frequencies. This increases reliability by avoiding collisions. Reliability is also increased by the use of multiple packet copies on multiple routes. Individual node failures thus do not affect the overall network.

For a future work, The Irrigation Algorithm can be extended to a system with multiple base stations. However, it requires to set up a decision making facility for a sensor that receives multiple level packets from different base stations to select the best one.

References

1. Ye, F., Chen, A., Lu, S., Zhang, L.: A scalable solution to minimum cost forwarding in large sensor networks. In: Proceedings of IEEE 10th International Conference Computer Communications and Networks, Scottsdale, Arizona (October 2001)
2. Zhou, G., Huang, C., Yan, T., He, T., Stankovic, J.A., Abdelzaher, T.F.: MMSN: Multi-Frequency Media Access Control for Wireless Sensor Networks. In: IEEE INFOCOM, Barcelona, Spain (April 2006)
3. El-Hoiydi, A., Decotignie, J.-D.: WiseMAC: An Ultra Low Power MAC Protocol for Multi-hop Wireless Sensor Networks. In: Nikoletseas, S.E., Rolim, J.D.P. (eds.) ALGOSENSORS 2004. LNCS, vol. 3121, pp. 18–31. Springer, Heidelberg (2004)
4. Rabaey, J., Ammer, J., Karalar, T., Li, S., Otis, B., Sheets, M., Tuan, T.: PicoRadios for wireless sensor networks: the next challenge in ultra-low power design. In: Solid-State Circuits Conference (2002)
5. Gu, L., Stankovic, J.A.: Radio-Triggered Wake-Up for Wireless Sensor Networks. Proceedings of Real-Time Systems 29(2-3), 157–182 (2005)
6. Lewis, F.L.: Wireless Sensor Networks. In: Cook, D.J., Das, S.K. (eds.) Smart Environments: Technologies, Protocols, Applications. Wiley, New York (2004)

7. Zalyubovskiy, V., Erzin, A., Astrakov, S., Choo, H.: Energy-efficient Area Coverage by Sensors with Adjustable Ranges. Journal of Sensors 9(4), 2446–2460 (2009)
8. Makki, S., Sun, B., Guidry, R., Hill, J.: Efficient Monitoring Strategy for Active Environments. Special Issue of International Journal of Software 6(4), 536–543 (2011)
9. Heinzelman, W., Chandrakasan, A., Balakrishnan, H.: Energy-Efficient Communication Protocol for Wireless microsensor Networks. In: Proceedings of the 33rd Hawaii International Conference on System Sciences (HICSS 2000) (January 2000)
10. Al Karaki, J., Kamal, A.: Routing Techniques in Sensor Networks: A survey. IEEE Wireless Communications 11(6), 6–28 (2004)
11. Karimi, M.: Wireless Communications and Fractal Antennas. In: Sixth International Latin American and Caribbean Conference for Engineering and Technology (LACCEI) (June 2008)
12. Madaan, A., Makki, S., Osborne, L., Sun, B.: An Intelligent Energy Efficient Target Tracking Scheme for Wireless Sensor Environment. In: Proceedings of the IEEE International Symposium on Wireless Pervasive Computing, ISWPC 2010, Palazzo Ducale, Modena, Italy, May 5-7, pp. 93–97 (2010) E-ISBN: 978-1-4244-6857-7
13. Zhang, H., Hou, J.: Maintaining Sensing Coverage and Connectivity in Large Sensor Networks. International Journal of Ad Hoc & Sensor Wireless Networks 1(1-2) (2005)
14. Gallais, A., Carle, J., Simplot-ryl, D., Stojmenović, I.: Localized Sensor Area Coverage with Low Communication Overhead. In: Proceedings 4th Annual IEEE International Conference on Pervasive Computing and Communications, PerCom 2006 (2006)

A Novel Binary Vote Assignment Grid Quorum Algorithm for Distributed Database Fragmentation

Ainul Azila Che Fauzi, Ahmad Noraziah, and Noriyani Mohd Zin

Faculty of Computer Systems & Software Engineering
University Malaysia Pahang
Pahang, Malaysia
ainulazila@yahoo.com

Abstract. Data replication is one of the mechanisms in data grid architecture since it improves data access and reliability. Therefore, the storage, availability, and consistency are important issues to be addressed in order to allow distributed users efficiently and safely access data from many different sites. This paper propose a new algorithm namely Binary Vote Assignment on Grid Quorum (BVAGQ) in order to handle data replication and transaction management. We address how to build reliable system by using the proposed BVAGQ algorithm for distributed database fragmentation. The result show that managing replication and transaction through proposed BVAGQ able to prepare data consistency.

Keywords: Data replication, Replication algorithm, fragmentation, BVAGQ, data grid.

1 Introduction

Organizations need to provide current data to users who may be geographically remote and to handle a volume of requests of data distributed around multiple sites in distributed environment. Therefore, the storage, availability, and consistency are important issues to be addressed in order to allow distributed users efficiently and safely access data from many different sites [1]. One way to provide access to such data is through replication. Replication is the process of copying and maintaining database objects in multiple databases that make up a distributed database system [2]. Replication provides user with fast, local access to shared data, and protects availability of applications because alternate data access options exist. A distributed database is distributed into separate partitions or fragments. Each partition or fragment of a distributed database may be replicated. Changes applied at one site are captured and stored locally before being forwarded and applied at each of the remote locations. Fragmentation in distributed database is very useful in terms of usage, efficiency, parallelism and also for security. This strategy will partition the database into disjoint fragments. If data items are located at the site where they used most frequently, locality of reference is high. In fragmentations, similarly, reliability and availability are low. But by combining fragmentation with replication, performance should be good. Even if one site becomes unavailable, users can continue to query or even update the remaining fragments.

E. Ariwa and E. El-Qawasmeh (Eds.): DEIS 2011, CCIS 194, pp. 339–349, 2011.

Data replication can be divided into three categories of fragmented replication scheme which are all-data-to-all-sites, some-data-to-all-sites and some-data-to-some-sites. The examples of all-data-to-all-sites protocols are Read-One-Write-All (ROWA) [3] and Hierarchical Replication Scheme (HRS) [4]. ROWA has been proposed for managing data in mobile and peer-to-peer (P2P) environment [3]. Meanwhile, replication in HRS starts when a transaction initiates at site 1. All the data will be replicate into other site. All sites will have all the same data. For some-data-to-all-sites category, voting protocol [5] became popular because they are flexible and are easily implemented. This technique has been applied to the front-end clusters for managing replicated data [6]. Besides voting, Tree quorum (TQ) [7] also some-data-to-all-sites category. TQ uses quorums that are obtained from a logical tree structure imposed on data copies. TQ has been proposed for persistent consistent distributed database commit in a dynamic a synchronous network, peer-to-peer network [8]. One more protocol in this category is Branch replication scheme [4]. Its goals are to increase the scalability, performance, and fault tolerance. Replicas are created as close as possible to the clients that request the data files. Using this technique, the growing of the replica tree is driven by client needs. Binary Vote Assignment on Data Grid (BVADG) [9] is one of the protocols in some-data-to-some-sites protocol. A data will replicate to the neighbouring sites from its primary site. Four sites on the corners of the grid have only two adjacent sites, and other sites on the boundaries have only three neighbours. Thus, the number of neighbours of each sites is less than or equal to 4.

The rest of the paper is organized as follows: Section 2 reviews data replication, database fragmentation concept and replication control protocol. Section 3 describes system model of the proposed BVAGQ algorithm. Finally, we conclude this paper in the last section.

2 Literature Review

2.1 A Study on Data Replication Concept

Replication is the process of sharing information to ensure consistency between redundant resources such as software or hardware components. This process helps to improve reliability, fault-tolerance, or accessibility of data [11, 12]. Data replication may occur if the same data is stored in multiple storage devices. Meanwhile, computation replication occurs when the same computing task is executed many times. A computational task is typically replicated in space, i.e. executed on separate devices, or it could be replicated in time, if it is executed repeatedly on a single device. Whether one replicates data or computation, the objective is to have some group of processes that handle incoming events. If we replicate data, these processes are passive and operate only to maintain the stored data, reply to read requests, and apply updates. When we replicate computation, the usual goal is to provide fault-tolerance. For example, a replicated service might be used to control a telephone switch, with the objective of ensuring that even if the primary controller fails, the backup can take over its functions [9].

2.2 A Study on Distributed Database Fragmentation Concept

Fragmentation in distributed database is very useful in terms of usage because usually, applications work with only some of relations rather than entire of it. In data distribution, it is better to work with subsets of relations as the unit of distribution. The other benefit from fragmentation is the efficiency. Data is stored close to where it is most frequently used and for data that is not needed, it is not stored. By using fragmentation, a transaction can be divided into several subqueries that operate on fragments. So, it will increase the degrees of parallelism. Besides, it also good for security as data not required for local applications is not stored. So, it will not available to unauthorized users. There are two main types of fragmentation which are horizontal and vertical. Horizontal fragments are subsets of tuples and vertical fragments are subsets of attributes as shown in Figure 1a and 1b.

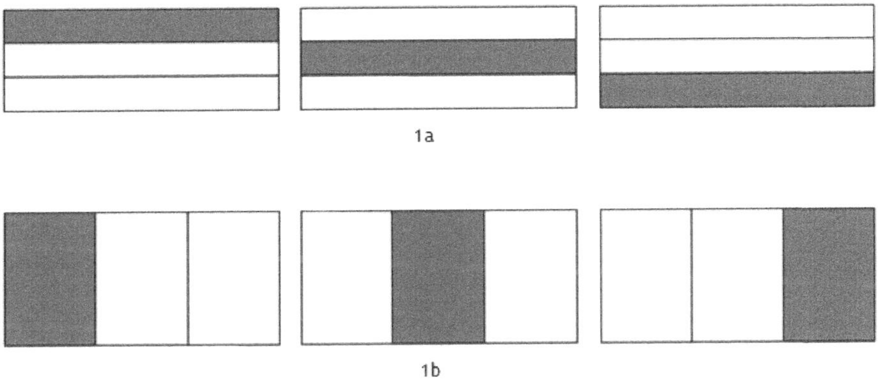

Fig. 1a and 1b. Horizontal and vertical fragmentation

2.2.1 Horizontal Fragmentation

Horizontal fragmentation groups together the tuples in a relation that are used by the important transactions [13]. A horizontal fragment is produced by specifying a predicate that performs a restriction on the tuples in the relation. It is defined using the Selection operation of the relational algebra. Given a relation R, a horizontal fragment is defined as:

σp (R)

Where p is a predicate based on one or more attributes of the relation.

2.2.2 Vertical Fragmentation

Vertical fragmentation groups together the attributes in a relation that are used jointly by the important transactions [13]. A vertical fragment is defined using the Projection operation of the relational algebra. Given a relation R, a vertical fragmentation is defined as:

$\Pi a1,\ldots,an$ (R)

Where a1,…,an are attributes of the relation R.

2.3 Replication Control Protocol

2.3.1 Read-One-Write-All (ROWA) Protocol

In ROWA techniques, replicas consistencies is guaranteed by the consistency of execution on one replica, but the client replicas are only updated and cannot provide accurate responses to queries. Synchronous replication methods guarantee that all replicas are maintained consistent at all times by executing each transaction locally only after all replicas have agreed on the execution order. Through this, a very strict level of consistency is maintained. However, because of the strict synchronization between replicas that is required for each transaction, synchronous replication methods have been deemed impractical and often times a centralized or client-server approach is preferred for systems that critically require strict consistency [3].

Any replicated database system needs to perform two main functions: execute transactions locally and make sure that the outcome of each transaction is re-erected at all replicas. The later task can be achieved in several ways. In the client-server approach, one server replica is in charge of executing/committing transactions locally before it disseminates the transactions to client replicas. This method is the closest to the single-server solution both in its performance [3].

2.3.2 Branch Replication Scheme (BRS) Protocol

Among BRS goals are to increase the scalability, performance, and fault tolerance. In this model, each replica is composed of a different set of subreplicas organized using a hierarchical topology. BRS use parallel I/O techniques [14, 15] in order to increase the scalability and performance of the system for read and write operations. The main features of BRS are root replica, parallel replication, fine grain replication, partial replication of popular file fragments and parallel data access better resource usage. This technique need low space per storage to support replica. So, small storage devices also can use to replicate data.

Replicas are created as close as possible to the clients that request the data files. The root replica grows toward the clients in a branching way, slip replicas into several subreplicas. Using this technique, the growing of the replica tree is driven by client needs. Hence, a replica is expanded toward the clients. When a replica or subreplica is replicated, two sites must be selected for the replication process. Replication does not have to be for the entire replica. Subreplicas can be also replicated following the former conditions. Assume that accesses to a file are not uniformly distributed and that, as a result, the subreplica Ri storage node is overloaded. BRS can replicate only this subreplica to discharge this node. Thus, the expansion of the replication tree might not be symmetric and different branches could have different depths [4].

2.3.3 Hierarchical Replication Scheme (HRS) Protocol

A hierarchical replication consists of a root database server and one or more database servers organized into a hierarchy topology [4].

Replication in HRS starts when a transaction initiates at site 1. All the data will be replicate into other site. All sites will have all the same data.

3 System Model

Binary Vote Assignment Grid Quorum (BVAGQ) technique will be used to approach the research. In BVAGQ, all sites are logically organized in the form of two-dimensional grid structure. For example, if a BVAGQ consists of twenty-five sites, it will logically organize in the form of 5 x 5 grids. Each site has a premier data file. In the remainder of this paper, we assume that replica copies are data files. A site is either operational or failed and the state (operational or failed) of each site is statistically independent to the others. When a site is operational, the copy at the site is available; otherwise it is unavailable [16]. For this research, 9 sites will be used which will be logically organize in the form of 3 x 3 grids as shown in Figure 2 below.

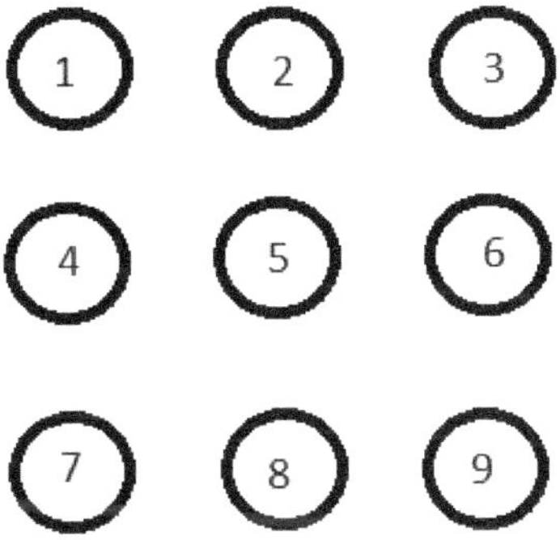

Fig. 2. BVAGQ sites

A data will replicate to the neighbouring sites from its primary site. Four sites on the corners of the grid have only two adjacent sites, and other sites on the boundaries have only three neighbours. Thus, the number of neighbours of each sites is less than or equal to 4. Refer to Figure 3, data from site 1 will replicate to site 2 and 3 which are its neighbours. Site 5 has four neighbours, which are sites 2, 4, 6 and 8. So, site 5 has five replicas. Meanwhile, site 6 replicates to site 3, 5 and 9.

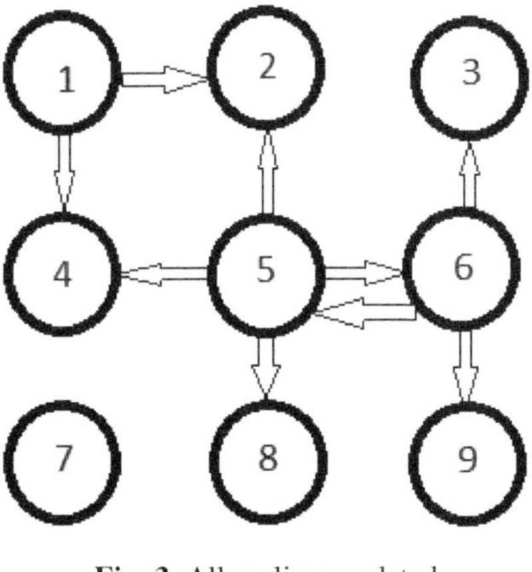

Fig. 3. All replicas updated

3.1 Algorithm

In this section, we proposed the new BVAGQ algorithm by considering the distributed database fragmentation.

Definition

The following notations are defined:

a) V is a transaction.
b) S is relation in database.
c) S_i is vertical fragmented relation derived from S, where i = 1,2,...,n.
d) P_k is a primary key
e) x is an instant in T which will be modified by element of V.
f) T is a tuple in fragmented S.
g) ${}^{Si}{}_{Pkxx}$ is a horizontal fragmentation relation derived from S_i.
h) P_i is an attribute in S where i = 1,2,...,n.
i) $M_{i,j}$ is an instant in relation S where i and j = 1,2,...,n.
j) i represent a row in S.
k) j represent a column in S.
l) η and ψ are groups for the transaction V.
m) $\gamma = \alpha$ or β where it represents different group for the transaction V (before and until get quorum).
n) V_η is a set of transactions that comes before V_ψ, while V_ψ is a set of transactions that comes after V_η.
o) D is the union of all data objects managed by all transactions V of BVAG.
p) Target set = {-1, 0, 1} is the result of transaction V; where -1 represents unknown status, 0 represents no failure and 1 represents accessing failure.
q) BVAG transaction elements $V_\eta = \{V_{\eta x,qr} \mid r=1,2,...,k\}$ where $V_{\eta x,qr}$ is a queued element of V_η transaction.
r) BVAG transaction elements $V_\psi = \{V_{\psi x,qr} \mid r=1,2,...,k\}$ where $V_{\psi x,qr}$ is a queued element of V_ψ transaction.
s) BVAG transaction elements $V_\lambda = \{ V_{\lambda x,qr} \mid r=1,2,...,k\}$ where $V_{\lambda x,qr}$ is a queued element either in different set of transactions V_η or V_ψ.
t) $\hat{V}_{\lambda x,q1}$ is a transaction that is transformed from $V_{\lambda x,qr}$.
u) $V_{\mu_{x,q_1}}$ represents the transaction feedback from a neighbour site. $V_{\mu_{x,q_1}}$ exists if either $V_{\lambda x,qr}$ or $\hat{V}_{\lambda x,q1}$ exists.
v) Successful transaction at primary site $V_{\lambda x,qr} = 0$ where $V_{\lambda x,qr} \in$ D (i.e., the transaction locked an instant x at primary). Meanwhile, successful transaction at neighbour site $V(\mu_{x,q_1}) = 0$, where $\mu_{x,q_1} \in D$ (i.e., the transaction locked a data x at neighbour).

Listing 1: The algorithm of Binary Assignment Grid Quorum

Algorithm

Start
V_η and V_ψ initiates lock
    If set $V\lambda_{x,}q_1 = 0$
        Then abort $V\lambda_{x,}q_{r+1}, \ldots, V\lambda_{x,}q_k$
        Execute $V\lambda_{x,}q_1, \lambda =_{\eta,\psi}$
    End if
V_η and V_ψ propagate lock.
If $V\lambda_{x,}q_1, \lambda =_{\eta}$ or $_{\psi}$ get quorum
    If (write counter of w $V\lambda_{x,}q_1 \in V_\eta$ is equal n/2)
        Then w $V\lambda_{x,}q_1 \in V_\eta$ get quorum.
        $V\lambda_{x,}q_1, \lambda =_{\eta}$ transform to $\hat{V}\lambda_{x,}q_1$
        $\hat{V}\lambda_{x,}q_1, \lambda =_{\eta}$ release lock. $\forall\, V\lambda_{x,}q_{1,}\, \lambda =_{\psi}$
        $\hat{V}\lambda_{x,}q_1, \hat{V}\lambda_{x,}q_1, \lambda =_{\eta}$
    Else if (write counter of w $V\lambda_{x,}q_1 \in V_\psi$ is equal n/2)
        Then w $V\lambda_{x,}q_1 \in V_\psi$ get quorum.
        $V\lambda_{x,}q_1, \lambda =_{\psi}$ transform to $\hat{V}\lambda_{x,}q_1$
        $\hat{V}\lambda_{x,}q_1, \lambda =_{\psi}$ release lock. $\forall\, V\lambda_{x,}q_{1,}\, \lambda =_{\eta}$
        $\hat{V}\lambda_{x,}q_1, \hat{V}\lambda_{x,}q_1, \lambda =_{\psi}$

    End if
End if
S is fragmented into S_i
S_i is fragmented into $^{Si}{}_{Pkxx.}$
$^{Si}{}_{Pkxx}$ divided into V_i
$\hat{V}\lambda_{x,}q_1$ update x.
Commit $\hat{V}\lambda_{x,}q_1$
End.

3.2 Experimental Result

To make it clearer on how we manage the transaction using BVAGQ, here we present the experiment result. Each node is connected to one another through an Ethernet switch hub. A cluster with nine replication servers connected to each other in the form of two dimensional 3 x 3 grid structures.

Using BVAGQ rules, each primary replica will copy database x to its neighbor replicas. Client can access database x at any server that has its replica. We assume that primary database a located in Server 1, primary database b will be at Server 2 and so on. Based on BVAGQ model, x for $V\lambda_{x,}q_1$ will be any instant a, b, c, d, e, f, g, h and i.

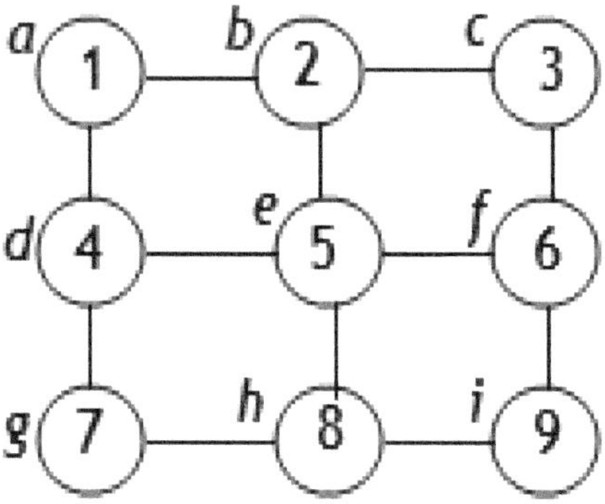

Fig. 4. Cluster with 3x3 replication servers

Table 1. Experiment Result

Time/Replica	Replica 1	Replica 2	Replica 4
0.1	unlock (a)	unlock (a)	unlock (a)
0.2	Begin transaction	Begin transaction	
0.3	write lock (a) counter_w(a)=1	write lock (a) counter_w(a)=1	
0.4	wait	wait	
0.5	$V_{\eta a,q1}$ propagate lock: 2	$V_{\psi a,q1}$ propagate lock: 4	
0.6	propagate lock: 2	$V_{\psi a,q1}$ get lock: 2 counter_w(a)=2 obtain quorum release lock: 1	
0.7	abort $V_{\eta a,q1}$, lock (a) from 2		
0.8		$V_{\psi a,q1}$ fragmented into S_2	
0.9		S_2 is fragmented into $^{S2}{}_{Pkxx}$	
0.10		$^{S2}{}_{Pkxx}$ divided into T_2 where T_1 = P_1 = Primary key T_2 = P_6 = instant a	
0.11		update a	
0.12	Commit $\hat{V}\lambda_{a,}q_1$	Commit $\hat{V}\lambda_{a,}q_1$	Commit $\hat{V}\lambda_{a,}q_1$
0.13	unlock (a)	unlock (a)	unlock (a)

If two sets of transactions, V_η and V_ψ initiates to update database *a* at replica 1 and 2, first it needs to request to update database *a* from primary replica 1 and 2. If $V\lambda_{x,}q_1$ = 0, the other transactions in queue will abort. Then, neighbor binary voting assignment is initiated. Transactions in both nodes, V_η and V_ψ will propagate lock. The first transaction that initiated will get the lock and other transactions will be aborted. So now Replica 1 and 2 have a transaction waiting but transactions cannot read or update database *a* at same time.

Primary nodes 1 propagate lock to its neighbor replicas 2 while primary nodes 2 propagate lock to its neighbor replica 4. Primary replica for $V_{\eta x,q1}$ propagates lock to its neighbor replicas 2 and 4. Primary replica for $V_{\psi x,q1}$ propagates lock to its neighbor replicas 1 and 4. The first transaction get majority quorum will be transform to $\hat{V}\lambda_{x,}q_{1.}$

3.3 Example Case

Refer Table 2 to Table 6; first the database will be fragmented using vertical fragmentation into S_i. Next, the fragmented database, S_i will be fragmented again but this time using horizontal fragmentation into ${}^{Si}{}_{Pkxx}$ leaving only instant for primary key and data that need to be update, *x*. Finally, the instant *x* is updated.

Table 2. Table S

P_1	P_2	P_3	P_4	P_5	P_6
$M_{1,1}$	$M_{1,2}$	$M_{1,3}$	$M_{1,4}$	$M_{1,5}$	$M_{1,6}$
$M_{2,1}$	$M_{2,2}$	$M_{2,3}$	$M_{2,4}$	$M_{2,5}$	$M_{2,6}$

Table S fragmented into S_1 and S_2 using horizontal fragmentation.

$S_1 = \Pi\, P_1, P_2, P_3, P_4, P_5\, (S)$

$S_2 = \Pi\, P_1, P_6\, (S)$

Table 3. Table S_1

P_1	P_2	P_3	P_4	P_5
$M_{1,1}$	$M_{1,2}$	$M_{1,3}$	$M_{1,4}$	$M_{1,5}$
$M_{2,1}$	$M_{2,2}$	$M_{2,3}$	$M_{2,4}$	$M_{2,5}$

Table 4. Table S_2

P_1	P_6
$M_{1,1}$	$M_{1,6}$
$M_{2,1}$	$M_{2,6}$

Table S_2 fragmented into ${}^{Si}{}_{Pkxx}$.

Table 5. Table ${}^{S1}{}_{Pkxx}$

P_1	P_6
$M_{1,1}$	$M_{1,6}$

Table 6. Table ${}^{S2}{}_{Pkxx}$

P_1	P_6
$M_{2,1}$	$M_{2,6}$

$T_1 = P_1 =$ Primary key

$T_2 = P_6 =$ instant x

4 Conclusion

In order to preserve data consistency and reliability of the systems, managing transactions is very important. In order to handle data replication and transaction management, we design a new model called Binary Vote Assignment on Grid Quorum. From the experiment result, we can say that managing replication and transaction through proposed BVAGQ able to preserve data consistency.

References

1. Mat Deris, M., Abawajy, J.H., Taniar, D., Mamat, A.: Managing Data Using Neighbour Replication On A Triangular-Grid Structure. International Journal of High Performance Computing and Networking 6(1), 56–65 (2009)

2. Mat Deris, M., Evans, D.J., Saman, M.Y., Noraziah, A.: Binary Vote Assignment on Grid for Efficient Access of Replicated Data. Int'l Journal of Computer Mathematics 80(12), 1489–1498 (2003)
3. Budiarto, S., Tsukamoto, M.: Data Management Issue Mobile and Peer-to-Peer Environment. Data and Knowledge Engineering 41, 183–204 (2002)
4. José, M.P., Félix, G.C., Jesús, C., Alejandro, C., Javier, F.: Branch Replication Scheme: A New Model For Data Replicatio In Large Scale Data Grids. Computer Architecture Group, Computer Science Department, Universidad Carlos III de Madrid, Leganes, Madrid, Spain (2010)
5. Gifford, D.K.: Weighted Voting for Replicated Data. In: Proceeding 7th Symposium on Operating System Principles, pp. 150–162 (December 1979)
6. Chen, I.R., Wang, D.C., Chu, C.P.: Analyzing User-Perceived Dependability & Performance Characteristics Of Voting Algorithms For Managing Replicated Data. In: Distributed and Parallel Databases, pp. 199–219. Kluwer Academic Publisher, Boston (2003)
7. Agrawal, D., El Abbadi, A.: The Generalized Tree Quorum Technique: An Efficient Approach For Managing Replicated Data. ACM Trans. Database Systems 17(4), 689–717 (1992)
8. Awerbuch, B., Tutu, C.: Maintaining Database Consistency In Peer-to-Peer Networks, Technical Report CNDS-2002-2 (2002)
9. Ahmad, N., Fauzi, A.A.C., Roslina, M. S., Zin, N.M., Beg, A.H.: Lowest Data Replication Storage of Binary Vote Assignment Data Grid. In: Zavoral, F., Yaghob, J., Pichappan, P., El-Qawasmeh, E. (eds.) NDT 2010. Communications in Computer and Information Science, vol. 88, pp. 466–473. Springer, Heidelberg (2010)
10. Wikipedia, the free encyclopedia, Replication (computer science) (January 22, 2010), http://en.wikipedia.org/wiki/Replication_computer_science
11. Noraziah, A., Mat Deris, M., Ahmed, N.A., Norhayati, R., Saman, M.Y., Zeyed, M.A.: Preserving Data Consistency Through Neighbour Replication On Grid Daemon. American Journal of Applied Science 4(10), 748–755 (2007)
12. ATLAS at the University of Chicago (2010), http://www.sciencedirect.com/science?_ob=RedirectURL&_method=externObjLink&_locator=url&_cdi=5638&_plusSign=%2B&_targetURL=http%253A%252F%252Fhep.uchicago.edu%252Fatlas%252F
13. Thomas, C., Carolyn, B.: Database Systems A Practical Approach To Design, Implementation, and Management, 5th edn.
14. Tang, M., Lee, B.S., Tang, X., Yeo, C.K.: The Impact on Data Replication on Job Scheduling Performance in the Data Grid. International Journal Of Future Generation Of Computer Systems (22), 254–268 (2006)
15. Jin, H., Cortes, T., Buyya, R. (eds.): High Performance Mass Storage and Parallel I/O: Technologies and Applications. IEEE Press and Wiley (2002)
16. Mat Deris, M., Mamat, R., Noraziah, A., Suzuri, H.M.: High Service Reliability for Cluster Server Systems, pp. 280–287. IEEE Xplore (2003)

Neighbour Replication on Grid Deadlock Detection Framework

Noriyani Mohd Zin, Ahmad Noraziah, and Ainul Azila Che Fauzi

University Malaysia Pahang, Malaysia
noriyanimz@gmail.com,
noraziah@ump.edu.my,
ainulazila@yahoo.com

Abstract. Data grid is a distributed computing architecture that integrates a large number of data and computing resources into a single virtual data management system. It coordinated the data from several of resources and enables the sharing of the data. In handling and managing data grid some of problems must be considered such as reliability and availability of the data to the user access, network latency, failures or malicious attacks during execution and etc. These problems can overcome by using replication technique. The data will replicate into several sites. If one of the sites has fail, it will fail independently and not affect to others node. The deadlock is the most important problem that must be manages when sharing any data in data grids. Furthermore, it can reduce the throughput by minimizing the available resources, so it becomes an important resource management problem in distributed systems. In this paper, we propose Neighbour Replication Grid Deadlock Detection (NRGDD) framework to detect the deadlock during transaction occur in Neighbour Replication on Grid replication model. Based on this framework it shows how the deadlock can be detected.

Keywords: NRGDD framework, replication, deadlock detection, probe message.

1 Introduction

Grid system and Peer to Peer network are the most commonly-used solutions to achieve the same goal: the sharing resources and services in heterogeneous, dynamic, distributed environments [1]. Data grid is a distributed computing architecture that integrates a large number of data and computing resources into a single virtual data management system [2]. It coordinated the data from several of resources and enables the sharing of the data. It also provide several of services in order to fit the needs of high-performance distributed and data-intensive [2], [3] computing. According to the type of resources shared, there are computational grids and data grids and both of them are not mutually exclusive. In fact, computational grids and data grids play important roles in grid environment and are complementary to each other [4].

E. Ariwa and E. El-Qawasmeh (Eds.): DEIS 2011, CCIS 194, pp. 350–357, 2011.

In handling and managing data grid is not an easy way, some problems must be considered such as reliability and availability of the data to the user access, network latency, failures or malicious attacks during execution and etc. These problems can be solving by using the replication technique. In data replications architecture, the data will be replicated into several sites. If one of the sites has failed, it will failed independently and not affect to others node. Therefore, the data replication will improve the reliability, availability and performance of the data. Replication in distributed environment receives particular attention for providing efficient access to data, fault tolerance and enhance the performance of the system [5-7].

In replication, the concurrency control and deadlock detection is the most important problem that must have manages when sharing any data in distributed systems. The lock mechanism is use when the transaction make request to get a data. If the data is available, the transaction that make a request will get a lock for that data, otherwise it will wait until the data is unlock or released then it can be acquired again. In this situation, a deadlock may occur in which every transaction involve in the deadlock are waiting to grant the data that has been lock by other transaction that make a circular wait until an action is taken to detect and resolve deadlock problems. Deadlock can reduce the throughput by minimizing the available resources, so it becomes an important resource management problem in distributed systems [8].There are two major deficiencies in deadlock where any other process cannot grant all the resources that held by the deadlocked processes and the deadlock persistence time will added to the reaction time of each process involved in the deadlock.

In this paper, we are not discuss on how to resolve the deadlock detection but we proposed Neighbour Replication Grid Deadlock Detection (NRDGG) framework to detect the deadlock during transaction occur in Neighbour Replication on Grid (NRG) replication model [9].

The rest of this paper is structured as follows. Section 2 presents the theoretical background of NRGDD. Section 3 we present the proposed framework for NRGDD and Section 4 the implementation of the system. The Section 5 concludes the paper.

2 Theoretical Background

Deadlock occurs when different set of transaction waiting for each other to obtain the same resource, consequently there is no operations can be done when the system become stuck. Without lost of generality we use transaction as a node in the explanation. This part describes Neighbour Replication on Grid Deadlock Detection (NRGDD) transaction model which involves T as a transaction, D is the union of all data object manages by all transaction T of NRG and x represents one data object (or data file) in D to be modified by an element of T_{α}, T_{β}, T_{γ}, T_{δ}, and T_{θ}. *Consider* $\lambda = \alpha, \beta, \gamma, \delta, \theta$ where it represent different group for the transaction T. Meanwhile, *PM* is a probe message. It contain a set of probe messages where *PM={InitID, VictimID, DepCnt, RouteString}*. Table 1 shows the probe message details description.

Table 1. Probe Message

Probe Message	Descriptions
InitID	Contains the identity of initiator of the algorithm
VictimID	A node or transaction that detects the deadlock sends the victim message to the node or transaction that cause of deadlock occurs. This node will be victimized for deadlock resolution.
DepCnt	The number of successor represent as a node or transaction which is waiting for resource.
RouteString	The node or transaction IDs visited by another node's (transaction's) probe message in order.

Each of NRG transaction elements $\{T_\alpha, T_\beta, T_\gamma, T_\delta, T_\theta\}$ have the probe message that use to communicate between them to request for a resources. Each node has a probe message storage structure also known as *ProbeS*. Only one probe message will be store on *ProbeS* at a particular time. The probe message will be erase from their *ProbeS* independently when the deadlock has been detected. Meanwhile, transaction $T_{\lambda x.PM}$ that detects the deadlock send a victim message to the transaction found to be victimized for the deadlock resolution. Victim message will be used for deleting probe message from *ProbeS*.

3 Proposed Framework

The different set of NRGDD transactions $T_\alpha, T_\beta, T_\gamma, T_\delta,$ *and* T_θ may request data object x simultaneously at any site of *S(B)* either at the same or different site. Each set of transactions communicate with each other by message passing. Each of them brings the elements of probe message or *PM*.

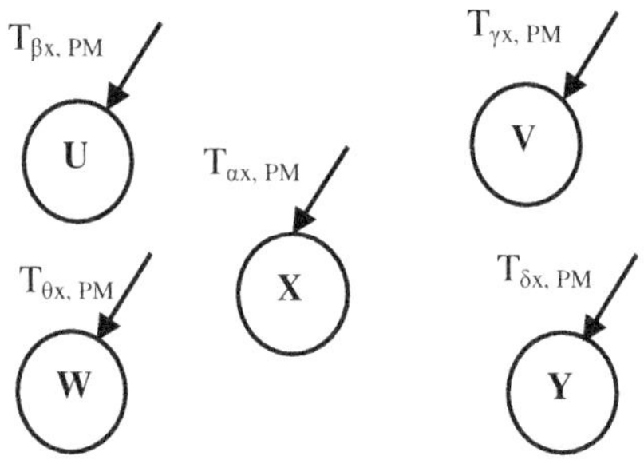

Fig. 1. Different set of transaction request a different site

An Illustration Example: Consider the situation shown in Fig. 1. A different set of transactions $T_\alpha, T_\beta, T_\gamma, T_\delta,$ *and* T_θ request a lock from a set of sited where $S(B_x) = \{U,V,W,X,Y\}$. Site X will replicate data x to site U, V, W, and Y. If the transaction of $T_{\alpha x.PM}$ get lock from site $i \in S(B_x)$ and other transaction will get lock from other site $j \in S(B_x) \mid j \neq i$.

Each sites $i \in S(B_x)$ has its own lock manager (LM). The LM will process a request for a lock from the transaction either the lock can be granted or not. The lock is granted immediately when it is free otherwise; the lock manager will send a reject message to the requesting transaction or node ID, then inserts it into the waiting list for the lock. Each node is uniquely identified by its {site id:process id} pair and for the simplicity of explanation a unique number has assigned using integer numbers (0, 1, 2, 3, ..., n)to all transaction or node. The transactions or nodes will create elements of probe message (*InitID, VictimID, DepCnt, and RouteString*), $T\lambda = \{T\ \lambda x, PM \mid PM = InitID, VictimID, DepCnt, RouteString\}$. Fig. 2 shows the framework for the NRGDD Transaction Model.

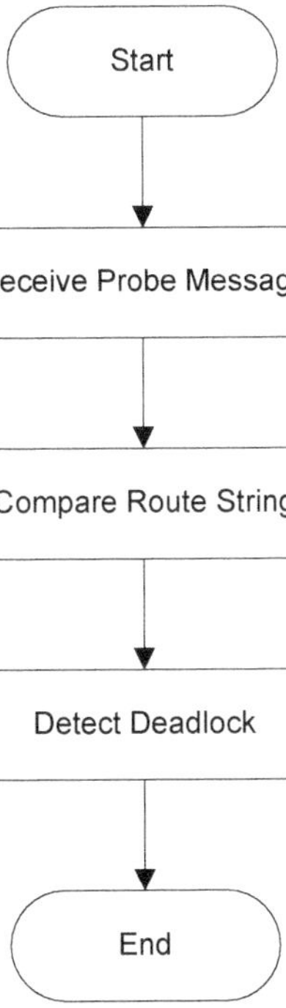

Fig. 2. Framework of NRGDD Transaction Model

We assume there are no failures occur during transactions. The different set of transaction can communicate between each other through passing message for a request of resources. In receiving the probe message T_λ will compare its route string with the sender's of the probe message. If the route string is prefix, the deadlock is detected.

4 Implementation

In this phase, we present the implementation of the system. In implementation phase, we consider there is no failure occure during transaction and based on the NRG model [15] we use a cluster with sixteen replication servers that are logically connected to each other in the form of two-dimensional 4 x 4 grid structure. Four different sets of transaction and sites will be use in this experiment. Data *b* in site *B* will be replicate to each site that adjacent with site *B*, which is site *A*, *C*, and *F*. Without lost of generality, five different set of transaction T_α, T_β, T_γ, and T_δ, come to update data *b* at replica *A*, *B*, *C*, and *F* shows in Fig. 3.

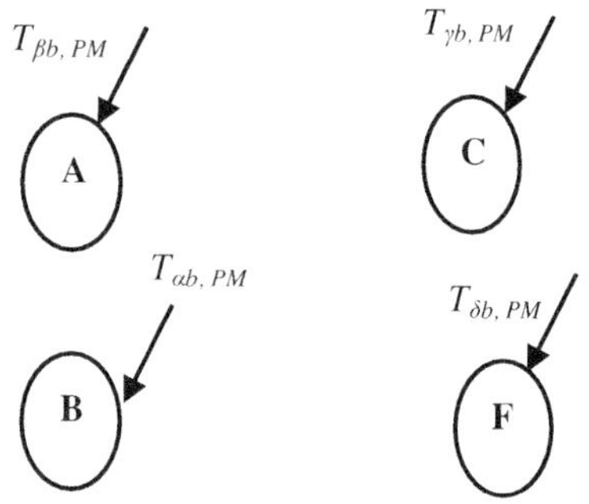

Fig. 3. Different set of transaction request to update data *b* at different sites

In forwarding the probe message to other nodes, a node must check the emptiness of its *ProbeS* first. It will compare its own *DepCnt* value with probe's *DepCnt* value when its *ProbeS* is empty. If this node's *DepCnt* is higher, then probe's *VictimID* and *DepCnt* values are updated with this node's ID and *DepCnt* values respectively; otherwise the values are kept intact. Before forwarding the *probe* message to all successors (the node that it's waiting) of this node, probe's *RouteString* field is updated by appending this node's ID at last of existing string (*i.e.*, concatenate operation). One copy of updated *probe* message is saved in *ProbeS* of this node. The Fig. 4 shows node 0, $T_{\alpha b,PM(0,0,1,\text{"}0\text{"})}$ has initiated execution and send *probe* message (0,0,1,"0") to its successor node 1, $T_{\beta b,PM(0,1,1,\text{"}01\text{"})}$. As node 1's *ProbeS* is empty and *DepCnt* value is 1, so the values are kept intact. Node 1 send its *probe* (0, 1, 1, "01") to its successors 2, $T_{\delta b,PM(0,1,1,\text{"}012\text{"})}$. Then Nodes 2 forwarded the probe message to node 3, $T_{\gamma b,PM(0,1,1,\text{"}013\text{"})}$.

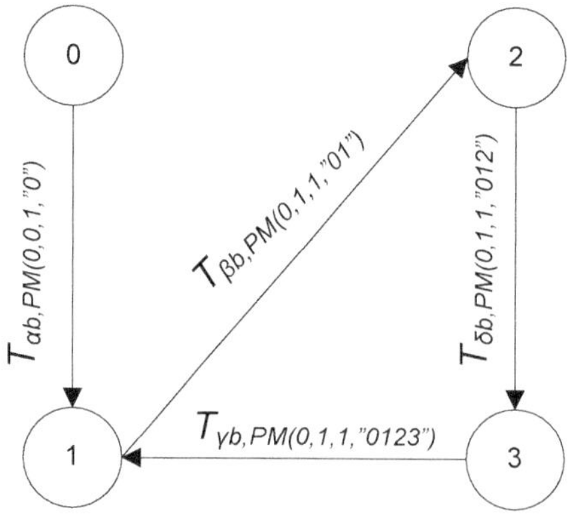

Fig. 4. Different set of transactions wait for each other to update data *b*

Deadlock is detected when *RouteString* of node 3, $T_{\gamma b,PM(0,1,1,"013")}$prefix with node 1, $T_{\beta b,PM(0,1,1,"01")}$ that start with "01". The probe message discards by the node that has detected a deadlock. Deadlock cycle can be detected at any node when the travelled path of *probe* message makes a dependency cycle. The Fig. 5 shows cycle of deadlock that has been detected, {1→2→3→1}.

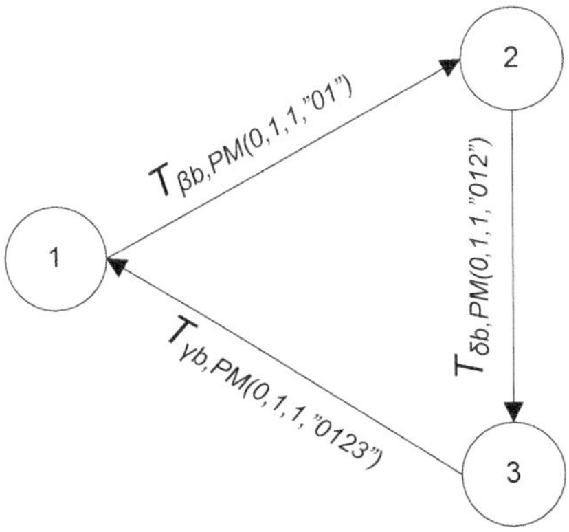

Fig. 5. Cycle of the deadlock

The Table 2 shows the experiment result that the NRGDD can detect the deadlock problems. At t7, node 3 at replica C has detected node 1 at replica A as a victim that cause of deadlock occur.

Table 2. The Experiment Result

Replica Time	A	F	C
t1	unlock(x)	unlock(x)	unlock(x)
t2	Begin_transaction	Begin_transaction	Begin_transaction
t3	Write lock(x), counter _w =1	Write lock(x), counter _w =1	Write lock(x), counter _w =1
t4	wait	wait	wait
t5	$T_{\beta b,PM(0,1,1,"01")}$ Propagate lock: F	$T_{\delta b,PM(0,1,1,"012")}$ Propagate lock: C	$T_{\gamma b,PM(0,1,1,"013")}$ Propagate lock: A
t6	wait	wait	wait
t7			Detect deadlock which is RouteString prefix with $T_{\beta b,PM(0,1,1,"01")}$, send victim message: $T_{\beta b,PM(0,1,1,"01")}$

The relation between resources and threads (processes) [10] is important in order to ensure the deadlock can detect for faster and accurate manner. If the number of processes more than number of resource and the number of process are equivalent to number of resources can detect deadlock in minimum time [10]. If we compare to [11], our algorithm is much faster than that. This is because in our algorithm, we use sixteen sites with 40 transactions or process and in this situation only four transactions will communicate with each other (see Fig. 4). In addition, only three transactions involve in deadlock situation (see Fig. 5), so it make faster than [11], because in [11] it is use 40 transaction with twenty sites. In this case more transactions will be involved in deadlock situation.

5 Conclusion

Managing transaction in data grids is important in order to ensure the transaction can occur properly. In this paper presents the NRGDD framework to detect deadlock during the transaction occur in NRG replication model. Deadlock will occur when different set of transactions may require the same resources that obtain by another transaction. NRGDD has resolved the deadlock problem by sending the minimum number of probe message to detect the deadlock. The relations between resources and processes use in detecting deadlock are important in order to ensure the minimize time require to detect this problem during transactions occur.

References

1. Stefano, A.D., Morana, G., Zito, D.: A P2P Strategy for QoS Discovery and SLA Negotiation in Grid Environment. Elsevier B.V., Amsterdam (2009) 0167-739X/$ - see front matter © 2009, All rigths reserved doi:10.1016/j.future.2009.03.001
2. Tu, M., Li, P., Yen, I.-L., Thuraisingham, B., Khan, L.: Secure Data Objects Replication in Data Grid. IEEE Transactions On Dependable and Secure Computing, 7(1) (January-March 2010); 1545-5971/10/$26.00 © 2010
3. Zhang, J., Lee, B.-S., Tang, X., Yeo, C.K.: A Model to Predict the Optimal Performance of the Hierarchical Data Grid. Elsevier B.V., Amsterdam (2009) 0167-739X/$ - see front matter © 2009, All rights reserved doi:10.1016/j.future,2009.05.010
4. Zhao, W., Xu, X., Wang, Z., Zhang, Y., He, S.: Improve the Performance of Data Grids by Value - Based Replication Strategy. In: 2010 Sixth International Conference on Semantics, Knowledge and Grids. IEEE, Los Alamitos (2010), 978-0-7695-4189-1/10 $26.00 © 2010 doi:10.1109/SKG.2010.48
5. Gao, M., Dahlin, A., Nayate, J.Z., Iyengar, A.: Improving Availability and Performance with Application-Specific Data Replication. IEEE Transaction. Knowledge and Data Engineering 17(1), 106–200 (2005)
6. Noraziah, A., Mat Deris, M., Man Norhayati, R., Rabiei, M., Shuhadah, W.N.W.: Managing Transaction on Grid-Neighbour Replication in Distributed System. International Journal of Computer Mathematics 86(9), 1–10 (2008), doi:10.1080/00207160801965198
7. Tang, M., Lee, B.S., Tang, X., Yeo, C.K.: The Impact on Data Replication on Job Scheduling Performance in the Data Grid. International Journal of Future Generation of Computer Systems (22), 254–268 (2006)
8. Srinivasan, S., Rajaram, R.: A Decentralized Deadlock Detection and Resolution Algorithm for Generalized Model in Distributed Systems. In: Distributed Parallel Databases. Springer Science plus Business Media, LLC (2011), doi:10.1007/s10619-011-7078-7

9. Noraziah, A., Mat, D.M., Ahmed, N.A., Norhayati, R., Saman, M.Y., Norhaslinda, D.C.: Neighbour Replication Transactions Processing in Distributed System. Advances in Systems Science and Applications. ISSN:1078-6236.
10. Abd El-Gwad, A.O., Saleh, A.I., Abd-ElRazik, M.M.: A Novel Scheduling Strategy for an Efficient Deadlock Detection. IEEE, Los Alamitos (2009) 978-1-4244-5844-8/09/$26.00 © 2009
11. Razzaque, M.A., Mamun-Or-Rashid, M., Hong, C.S.: MC2DR: Multi Cycle Deadlock Detection and Recovery Algorithm for Distributed Systems. In: Perrot, R., et al. (eds.) HPCC 2007. LNCS, vol. 4728, pp. 554–565. Springer, Heidelberg (2007)

A Learning Driven Model for ERP Software Selection Based on the Choquet Integral: Small and Medium Enterprises Context

Abdelilah Khaled and Mohammed Abdou Janati Idrissi

ENSIAS University, Avenue Mohammed Ben Abdallah Regragui
Madinat Al Irfane BP 713 Agdal, Rabat, Morocco
khaled@igf.finances.gov.ma, janati@ensias.ma

Abstract. Historically, Enterprise Resource Planning (ERP) systems were initially destined to large companies in order to standardize and streamline their key business processes. Recently, they have been increasingly adopted by Small and Medium Enterprises (SMEs). However, making strategic tradeoffs among the various marketplace solutions is a troublesome balance task for SMEs without the rescue of systematic decision approaches. This paper addresses the question of how to choose an ERP solution that best suits a given SME. It serves twofold objectives; firstly it defines a set of selection criteria related to SMEs' context. Secondly, it presents a selection methodology based on the construction of an induced decision model through capturing the decision maker's preferences. The key contribution of this paper is the introduction of a new iterative learning based approach destined to make enlightened decisions through the consideration of interdependencies among the adopted selection criteria thanks to the Choquet integral.

Keywords: ERP, SME, Selection, Evaluation, MCDA, Choquet integral, MACBETH, Fuzzy measures.

1 Introduction

An Enterprise Resource Planning (ERP) system is a set of integrated software packages that encompasses a large spectrum of business areas (e.g. finance, production, human resources…). Numerous organizations acquire this kind of software due to its ability to embed the world wide best practices adopted in different management domains. In addition, this packaged software is destined to streamline business processes, cut costs, raise quality, receive pertinent timely information, increase flexibility and improve customers' satisfaction. In this regard, the enterprises are now aware of the strategic benefits that could be gained from a high level of interaction with their business partners if the implementation is successfully done. However, it should be noted that not all ERP implementations have given satisfactory results. Actually, since the dawn of ERP projects, it has been widely reported that many of them fail to yield the expected payoffs ([1], [2]). Hence, the success rate is at alarmingly low level and these projects tend to be a very heavy burden on the

E. Ariwa and E. El-Qawasmeh (Eds.): DEIS 2011, CCIS 194, pp. 358–371, 2011.

organizations' budgets. In reference [3], the authors report that a great deal of the information about the success of such projects is based on the implementation reports coming from large companies. Historically, ERP systems were destined to large organizations that were willing and able to spend tens or hundreds of millions of dollars on an integrated software system ([4]). However, over the past few years, the ERP market has shown signs of saturation as large companies almost completed their significant ERP implementations. The time was ripe for the main vendors to steadily hold the challenge of Small and Medium Enterprises (SMEs). On the one hand, the vendors have started turning their marketing sights on the mid-market and redesigning their strategies to match its requirements. On the other hand, SMEs would unfavorably disrupt their business activities if they failed to upgrade their information systems to communicate with their supply chain partners or with their corporate headquarters ones ([5]).

The authors of reference [6] state that while large companies have the necessary financial and technical resources to be engaged in such large-scale investments, the case of smaller sized enterprises is far to be identical. In fact, SMEs have only limited budgets and experiences to address and overcome these matters ([7]). To tackle this issue, a great deal of importance should be attached to the selection stage related to the purchasing process. Indeed, integrated enterprise software's selection (e.g. ERP systems) has become a crucial step whenever an enterprise is faced with the prospect of acquiring a solution in order to support its management activities. Nevertheless, according to the authors of reference [8], the evaluation and selection of enterprise software has become increasingly difficult for the decision makers due the hundreds of software products available in the marketplace. The authors of reference [4] argue "*that methodologies developed for ERP selection for big installations may not all be applicable to the mid-tier customer base. Customers will have to be armed with the right tools to avoid serious errors and make purchases that will generate good returns*". Thereby, we suggest that a systematic approach is needed to help selecting the appropriate ERP system that best meets a given enterprise's requirements. The authors of reference [9] remark that an extensive part of the techniques used to select Commercial Off-the-Shelf (COTS) software are destined to reduce the potentially large number of comparisons needed to validate a piece of software against the initial requirements. According to the authors of reference [10], the selection of enterprise software is a typical MCDA (Multi Criteria Decision Aid) problem. This is due to its propensity to operate under multiple, often conflicting criteria and the discrete decision space in which the decision is made. They argue that by applying MCDA methods, justifiability and accountability will be improved considering that they are regularly seen as the pre-requisites of a complex and risky purchasing decision.

Many ERP software selection methodologies based on MCDA techniques have been proposed in the literature. An extensive part of the proposed methodologies suggest using Analytic Hierarchy Process (AHP) or Analytic Network Process (ANP) in order to decompose their decision problem into a hierarchy of more easily comprehended sub-problems ([11], [12]). However, due to the inherent uncertainties encountered when converting the human judgments to numerical values, many researchers turned to fuzzy sets in conjunction with multi criteria methods in order to consider the roughly estimated attributes ([13]). Nevertheless, the suggested decision models generate a high number of pairwise comparisons that sometimes could be overwhelming to the decision maker. Recently, many selection methodologies have tried to use artificial neural networks (ANN) in order to predict the optimal ERP system by iteratively training and refining decision networks ([14], [15]). However, these kinds of black box decision systems are not always appreciated by the top management. In addition, the proposed methodologies are very general and not always destined to the SME context. Actually, the selection criteria are not customized and the selection process is not totally covered.

This paper intends to develop a structured methodology for ERP selection applied to the SMEs' context. This methodology has the advantage of dealing with interdependent selection criteria and generalizing the decision maker's preferences in order to make an optimal and justifiable decision. Thus the remainder of this paper is structured as follows: In the first section, we start by defining a set of selection criteria that we judge it is important to consider in the SMEs' context. In the second section, we introduce our learning driven approach for ERP selection based on the defined criteria. This approach is based on The Measuring Attractiveness by a Categorical Based Evaluation TecHnique (MACBETH) to express the decision maker's preferences according to the adopted criteria. Likewise, the same technique is used to define a MACBETH scale of a set of fictitious binary ERP options. Owing to this, the Choquet integral is used as an interpolator of the expressed preferences to induce a general decision model. A heuristic is also suggested in order to reduce the number of pairwise comparisons proposed by the model.

2 ERP Selection Criteria for Small and Medium Enterprises

A software selection methodology is destined to narrow the initial list of the potential packages to a manageable bunch of solutions, which will be subjected to further scrutiny, until a choice is made ([16]). Actually, its main objective is to choose an optimal solution that provides the most adequate features that are mapped to the organization's requirements. The authors of reference [16] argue that most organizations lack a rigorous software procurement methodology with its salient selection criteria. Due to this, it is difficult to make effective and sound purchasing decisions ([17], [18]). They remark that the lack of understanding about how enterprises could evaluate the available packaged software could lead them to run the risk of making inappropriate acquisition decisions. On the other hand, the ERP vendors would either under-invest or over-invest in the wrong software attributes that the market doesn't truly appreciate.

A much acknowledged fact about ERP systems is that no solution could fit the various business contexts. Nevertheless, some solutions are more geared toward some environments than others. This hinges on the organization's activity sector and its operational and information technology models ([19]). Thereby, the question of identifying the appropriate criteria to evaluate the plethora of the commercially competitive ERP software products should be carefully addressed. Although the different selection methodologies remain generally the same regardless of the organization's size; some differences should be considered when addressing SMEs. They include the set of criteria used to assess the available packaged software. In this regard, in spite of what have been written in the prior research about ERP software selection criteria for SME context; no consensus seems to be reached to indicate which attributes managers choose to undertake the evaluation. The authors of reference [16], in their conjoint study of 1008 evaluation decisions completed in 126 organizations state that functionality, reliability, ease of use and ease of customization are considered to be the most important criteria. They report that ease of implementation and vendor's reputation shouldn't be considered as important as functionality and reliability which they get the most heavily weights. The authors of reference [20], in their integrative work of the set of criteria defined by ([21], [22] and [23]) presented 14 selection criteria for ERP selection. The most important criteria are as follows: Cost, technical aspects, functionality, support, vendor's vision, system reliability, integration, customization, vendor's market share, organizational fit, specialized industry knowledge, vendor's references, corporate compliance and implementation time. In addition, the authors of reference [4] find based on a sample of 80 small manufacturing and non-manufacturing companies that while reliability is rated highest by medium-sized companies, service and support are rated second and this fact confirms the findings of other researchers ([21], [22] and [24]). Moreover, compatibility arrives at the third position when selecting an ERP solution. Against all odds, the cost has received one of the lowest mean ratings in their findings related to SMEs. They conclude that many firms emphasize different priorities when defining the selection criteria. Indeed, as we mentioned before, smaller firms often lack financial resources that could enable them to bear the risk stemming from an inappropriate chosen system. Besides, their staff shortage doesn't encourage them to dedicate many working hours to an extensive IT development. Therefore, the cost of an ERP acquisition should be considered as an important criterion when taking the purchasing decision. It should be noted that the total cost of ownership (TCO) encompasses software and hardware acquisitions, implementation, maintenance and training costs incurred during the project's lifecycle. Actually, considering just the initial purchasing price will inevitably underrate the size of the real investment. Furthermore, "*software features and their functionality are the most significant issue of all*" ([24]). Indeed, organizations should carefully examine the functional coverage together with the sophistication of the provided functions ([25]). However, it should be noted that the marketplace's ERP solutions are generally mature enough that the differences between their basic functionalities are hardly noticeable. Hence, organizations should stress more on the aspects that would fulfill their real requirements that could provide them with a substantial competitive edge. Moreover, the authors of reference [22] point out that the customization ability of an enterprise system is judged as a fundamental feature by mid-size organizations. Indeed, 68% of respondents from SMEs rate customization as 'very important' as compared to 50% of respondents from large companies. In fact, customization helps reducing the timeframe and the cost incurred by additional custom development. The authors of reference [22] report that 100% of small-to-medium sized companies consider 'good support' as being very important (42.1%) or important (57.9%). In their study, they found that larger organizations put always a higher value on the 'vendor's market share' (35% rate this factor as 'very important'). The author of reference [26] argues that the vendor's reputation is the most important feature that should be considered under the 'Vendor – non-technical' aspects. Consequently, we suggest in our methodology, four generic criteria related to SMEs' context in order to evaluate the prospective ERP solutions. They consist of functionality, cost, customization and vendor's support

In the following section we develop our methodology for ERP selection based on the chosen criteria and the decision maker's preferences. The evaluation team could always adapt the set of the adopted criteria according to their specific contexts. In fact, the methodology remains the same whichever the adopted criteria.

3 Methodology for ERP Selection

Numerous methodologies for ERP evaluation have been proposed. They include scoring, ranking, mathematical optimization and multi-criteria decision aid (MCDA) approaches ([27]). The evaluation stage is influenced by multiple factors such as the decision-maker's conflicting objectives, the set of the candidate alternatives and the financial constraints. Thereupon, the ERP evaluation could be addressed as a kind of MCDA problem that implies the use of sophisticated methods. These methods aim to gather, analyze and disseminate information that will help the managers to make sound and justifiable decisions ([28], [29]). Actually, among the various multi criteria decision methods, the multiple attribute additive utility is the most well-known aggregation model of the Multi Attribute Utility Theory (MAUT). Indeed, it additively aggregates the multiple criteria into a single composite score. MAUT uses utility functions in order to convert attributes' scales into utility scales. It should be noted that an "Attribute" refers to a measure used to assess the achievement of an objective and a "Utility function" measures the degree of the obtained satisfaction/preference based on the value taken by the attribute. Then, MAUT assigns the attributes' weights and calculates the weighted average of each option as an overall utility score. Equations (1, 2) illustrate a multiple attribute additive utility function U:

$$\mathrm{U}(x_1, x_2, \cdots, x_m) = \sum_{i=1}^{m} k_i \mathrm{U}_i(x_i) \ . \tag{1}$$

Where $\mathrm{U}_i(x_i)$: Is the utility function of the attribute (i) and k_i : Is the weight of the attribute (i). The following constraints must be respected:

$$\begin{gathered} (k_1 + k_2 + \cdots + k_m = 1) \\ 0 \le \mathrm{U}(x_1, x_2, \cdots, x_m) \le 1 \end{gathered} \tag{2}$$

However, one of the critics advanced to the simplified additive utility model is that it ignores the interaction between criteria. Actually, this drawback is considered as a barrier to an accurate evaluation. For example, in order to evaluate an ERP package considering the chosen criteria of cost, functionality, customization and support, it is more likely that a negative interaction between functionality and customization would exist: Indeed, an ERP system with better functionalities has more chance of being more customizable. Hence, using the additive model to represent the decision maker's preferences would consider that the mutual importance of both criteria is simply the sum of each criterion's importance. But actually, it should be lesser. Indeed, the negative interaction is another way to express the redundancy among the criteria. Conversely, the importance of an ERP system with better functionalities and lower cost should be greater than the sum of the elementary importance of each criterion. In this case, we notice the existence of a positive interaction among the criteria representing a synergy among them. According to the authors of reference [30], within MCDA, the interdependencies among the criteria have been addressed through non-additive functions such as Choquet ([31]) and Sugeno ([32]) integrals.

In this section we propose a non-additive utility function based on of the Choquet integral. It represents the interaction among criteria. The use of the Choquet integral is justified by its ability to interpolate the decision maker's preferences based on a set of binary options. In addition, the Measuring Attractiveness by a Categorical Based Evaluation TecHnique (MACBETH) is also used to define elementary utility functions related to adopted criteria. Our proposed methodology encompasses the steps indicated in (Fig.1).

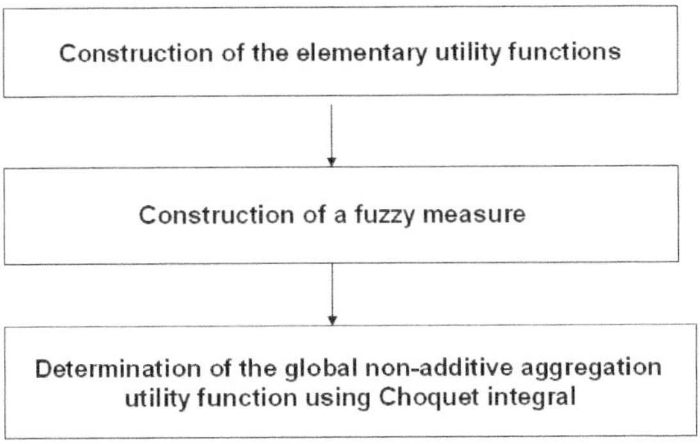

Fig. 1. The proposed evaluation process

Let C_1, C_2, C_3 and C_4 respectively represent the previously adopted set of criteria: functionality, cost, customization and vendor's support. Similarly, Let (V_1, V_2, V_3, V_4) denotes the utility values' vector taken by an ERP according to C_1, C_2, C_3 and C_4.

Construction of the elementary utility functions: The objective of this first step is to determine the preferences related to each criterion by the means of utility functions. The expressed preferences regarding each attribute are extracted using semantic scales such as the ones provided by MACBETH ([33]), AHP ([34]) or UTA ([35]). In our methodology, we suggest using MACBETH scales in order to define our utility functions as proposed by ([36]). MACBETH was introduced to direct how to determine the priority of a set of alternatives together with the criteria's relative importance in a multiple criteria decision-making problem. It has been widely discussed in its various aspects and it is based on a sound mathematical foundations. The major advantage of using MACBETH is the possibility to construct commensurable scales. Actually, commensurability assumes strong compensation among criteria. Hence, it allows for the relative ranking of the different solutions by aggregating their criteria's scores.

The determination procedure of the MACBETH scales relies on the definition of two fictitious values $\mathbf{0_i}$ and $\mathbf{1_i}$ for each criterion:

- $\mathbf{0_i}$ is defined as the minimal accepted value with respect to $\mathbf{C_i}$. An ERP system having a value less than $\mathbf{0_i}$ is automatically discarded.
- $\mathbf{1_i}$ is defined as the best value that an ERP system could have regarding $\mathbf{C_i}$, which is naturally more attractive than $\mathbf{0_i}$

Similarly, we denote by **ERP bad** and **ERP good** two fictitious **ERP** solutions respectively having $\mathbf{0_i}$ and $\mathbf{1_i}$ in each criterion:

- **ERP good** $(\mathbf{1_1, 1_2, 1_3, 1_4})$ denotes an ERP solution that has $\mathbf{1_i}$ in each criterion.
- **ERP bad** $(\mathbf{0_1, 0_2, 0_3, 0_4})$ denotes an ERP solution that has $\mathbf{0_i}$ in each criterion.

MACBETH is based on a questioning procedure in order to construct the cardinal scales. The questioning procedure is as follows:

Let **A** be the set of the prospective **ERP** systems that the decision maker has to choose from and **B** = *A* ∪ {**ERP bad, ERP good**}. For each **x, y** ∈ **B** and for each criterion $\mathbf{C_i}$, the decision maker is asked to verbally judge the difference of attractiveness between **x** and **y** regarding $\mathbf{C_i}$. When judging, the decision maker has to choose one of the following categories:

A0 - no difference of attractiveness
A1 - very weak difference of attractiveness
A2 - weak difference of attractiveness
A3 - moderate difference of attractiveness
A4 - strong difference of attractiveness
A5 - very strong difference of attractiveness
A6 - extreme difference of attractiveness

However, if the decision maker is unsure about the difference of attractiveness, they may choose the union of several successive categories among these above. ‘I do not know’ answer is acceptable and considered in MACBETH as a positive difference of attractiveness. The numerical scales are then obtained by the means of MACBETH judgment matrix. The consistency of this matrix is verified during the expression of the decision maker’s preferences. The M-MACBETH (http://www.m-macbeth.com/) software implements the extraction process of the MACBETH scales. The numerical scales are then extracted thanks to linear programming with the help of two boundary values on each criterion:

$$\text{Scale}_{\text{MACBETH}}(\text{ERP } bad) = 0 \text{ and } \text{Scale}_{\text{MACBETH}}(\text{ERP } good) = 1$$

Construction of a valid fuzzy measure: The second step of our methodology is destined to elicitate the decision maker’s preferences by the means of a fictitious set of binary ERP solutions. A binary solution in our case is an ERP system that either has **0** or **1** as criteria’s scores. For instance, **ERP1** (1,1,0,1) , **ERP2**(1,0,0,0) and **ERP3**(1,0,0,1) are examples of binary ERP solutions. Our objective is to indirectly extract a decision model by understanding how the decision maker appreciates the coalitions among the different criteria. According to the authors of reference [25], the methods based on indirect preference information are judged more practical. In fact, they require an easy cognitive interpretation in order to capture some preference information. Actually, the decision maker try to give some holistic preferences related to a reduced alternatives' set. Then the decision model's parameters are induced based on the extracted information. It should be noted that many valid decision models could be constructed.

To construct our model, let **A** denotes the set of the ERP binary options and $(A, \succeq)$ denotes an ordered set of the binary options with $\succeq$ is a binary preference relation: $x \succeq y$ means that **x** is at least preferred to **y** for each $x, y \in A$.

As ERP_{bad}, $ERP_{good} \in A$, it is possible to capture the decision maker's preferences through the ranking of the different binary ERP options on a MACBETH scale. Thus, for each **ERP** $\in$ **A**, a utility value will be assigned to it in the [-1, 1] interval.

In addition, let **N= {1, 2, 3, 4}** denotes a simplified notation of the four adopted criteria and $\mu : P(N) \to [-1,1]$ denotes the function that assigns values belonging to **[-1,1]** to each subset of **N** : For each $X \in P(N)$ $\mu(X) = \text{Scale}_{MACBETH}(1_X, 0_{N \setminus X})$ with $(1_X, 0_{N \setminus X})$ is an ERP system that has **1** in the criteria included in **X** and **0** otherwise. It is easy to notice that the function:

$\mu: P(N) \to [-1,1]$ verifies the following properties:

- $\mu(\emptyset) = 0, \mu(N) = 1$ (Boundary conditions)
- **For each** $S, T \subseteq N, S \subseteq T$ $\mu(S) <= \mu(T)$ (Monotonicity condition).

In the MCDA terminology the function μ is called a fuzzy measure or a capacity related to the criteria's set. It measures the importance of the criteria's coalitions.

Determination of the aggregation function: The purpose of the third step is to generalize the captured preferences' model to the prospective ERP options. Hence, we aim to construct a function **U** that verifies the following conditions:

- **U** carry each element in $[0, 1]^4$ to a value in **[-1.1]**
- For each $S \subseteq N$, $U(1_S, 0_{N \setminus S}) = \mu(S)$

In order to simplify the decision model, we suppose that the decision maker's preferences are linear. Owing to this, **U** should be constructed as a linear interpolation of the hyper cube's apexes (The binary options). As **U** is initially defined on $\{0, 1\}^4$, the interpolator should extend the definition's domain to $[0, 1]^4 \setminus \{0, 1\}.^4$

Furthermore, the author of reference [37] proved that in our case, the Choquet integral is the unique valid linear interpolator. The Choquet integral can be seen as a simple means to generalize the decision maker's rational. Therefore, the Choquet integral related to our **μ** capacity is defined in (Equations (3, 4)):

$$C_\mu(X) = \sum_{i=1}^{4} X_{\sigma(i)} \, [\mu(A_{\sigma(i)}) - \mu(A_{\sigma(i+1)})]. \tag{3}$$

For each $\mathbf{x} = (x_1, x_2, x_3, x_4) \in [0, 1]^4$
σ : A permutation on **IN** such as:

$$x_{\sigma(1)} \leq x_{\sigma(2)} \leq x_{\sigma(3))} \leq x_{\sigma(4)}$$

$$A_{\sigma}(i) := \{\sigma(i), \ldots, \sigma(4)\}, \text{ for each } i \in \mathbf{IN}, \text{ with } A_{\sigma}(5) = \emptyset . \tag{4}$$

However, the definition of **U** as a Choquet integral is totally defined by the determination of 2^n-2 parameters related to μ (i.e. fourteen parameters if (n=4)). In addition, the parameters' determination requires $(2^{2n} - n)$ pairwise comparisons using MACBETH. To put it differently, the number of pairwise comparisons is somewhat overwhelming to the decision maker. Actually, in order to reduce the computed parameters' number, one way is to consider the concept of the fuzzy k-additive measure. Indeed, a fuzzy measure is called k-additive if the interactions among any **k** criteria are solely considered. For example a 2-additive fuzzy measure considers exclusively the interactions between any criteria's couples and neglects any other interaction relationship. The authors of reference [30] point out that "*The use of 2-additive measures is justified by observing that the information on the importance of the single criteria and the interactions between couples of criteria are noteworthy. Moreover, it could be not easy or not straightforward for the DM to provide information on the interactions among three or more criteria during the decision procedure*". The interest of the 2-additive measures is that they drastically reduce the number of variables needed to define the fuzzy measure. They allow for a compromise between modeling ability and simplicity. For example, a 2-additive measure requires (n + n/2) parameters' determination.

Actually, the proposed methodology suggests a learning based approach in order to reduce the computed parameters' complexity. In fact, the decision maker is asked to provide their preferences related to a binary options' sample. A MACBETH scale and a fuzzy measure μ are then constructed in order to capture the decision maker's preferences. After the determination of the aggregation function (Choquet integral) based on the partially defined fuzzy measure μ, the decision maker is asked to validate the aggregation function against the remaining elements of the initial sample (The procedure of the construction of the aggregation function based on a partial definition of the fuzzy measure μ is defined below). In case of inconsistencies, the decision maker could adjust the parameters by iteratively reintroducing the inconsistent preferences into the decision model until it is accepted (Fig. 2).

In order to determine the Choquet integral aggregation function based on a partially defined fuzzy measure μ, we suggest using the least square approach developed by the authors of reference [38]. This approach minimizes the average quadratic distance between the Choquet integral's overall utilities and the satisfactions' degrees provided by the decision maker ([39]).

The least square approach is implemented within the KAPPALB package ([39]). KAPPALB stands for "laboratory for capacities". It is based on the GNU R statistical system and can be downloaded as free software from (http://www.polytech.univ-nantes.fr/kappalab).

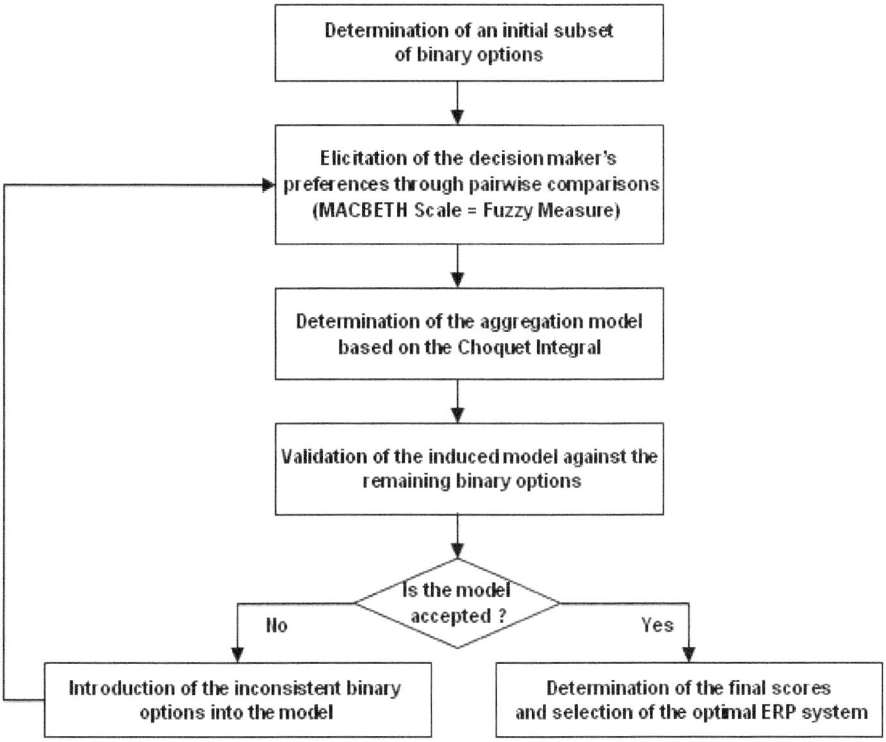

Fig. 2. The proposed iterative decision model

4 Illustrative Example

Let consider that an organization has to choose among three ERP systems having the following performance vectors: **ERP1** (50, 80, 60, 70), **ERP2** (80, 50, 20, 80) and **ERP3** (90, 20, 70, 40). In addition, we suppose that **ERP good** and **ERP bad** have the following performance vectors:

ERP good (100, 100, 80, 90) and **ERP bad** (40, 20, 10, 40)

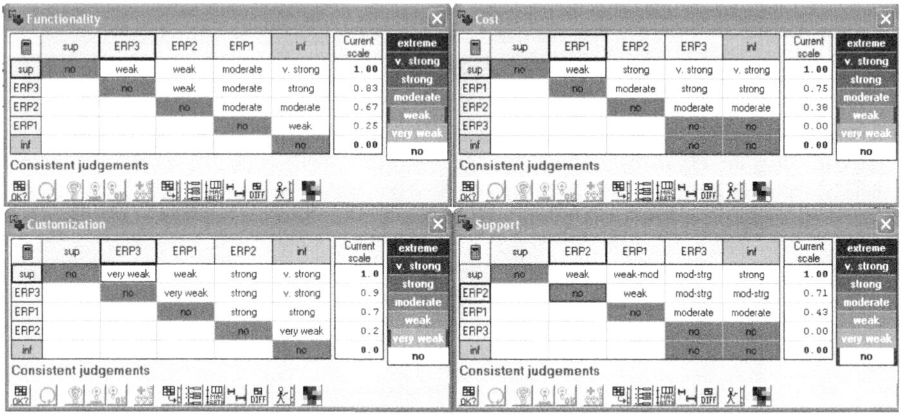

Fig. 3. The decision maker's judgment matrixes

As illustrated in (Fig.3), we use MACBETH to construct our cardinal scales through pairewise comparisons.

	sup	ERP(I)	ERP(F)	ERP(G)	ERP(B)	ERP(H)	ERP(E)	ERP(D)	ERP(C)	inf	Current scale
sup	no	moderate	mod-strg	strg-vstr	mod-strg	strong	strg-vstr	vweak-strg	v. strong	extreme	1.00
ERP(I)		no	moderate	strong	mod-strg	strong	mod-strg	strong	strg-vstr	vstrg-extr	0.95
ERP(F)			no	strong	strg-vstr	strg-vstr	strong	strg-vstr	v. strong	vstrg-extr	0.90
ERP(G)				no	strong	mod-strg	mod-strg	mod-strg	strong	strg-vstr	0.68
ERP(B)					no	strg-vstr	strg-vstr	strong	strong	mod-strg	0.47
ERP(H)						no	moderate	weak-mod	mod-strg	strong	0.25
ERP(E)							no	moderate	moderate	weak-mod	0.20
ERP(D)								no	mod-strg	weak-mod	0.15
ERP(C)									no	weak	0.03
inf										no	0.00

Fig. 4. The preferences' matrix

In the next step, we gather the decision maker's preferences related to a binary options' sample defined as follows:

Sup= ERP (1, 1, 1, 1) = **ERP good**; ERP (B) =ERP (1, 0, 0, 0)
ERP (C) =ERP (0, 1, 0, 0); ERP (D) =ERP (0, 0, 1, 0); ERP (E) =ERP (0, 0, 0, 1)
ERP (F) =ERP (1, 1, 0, 0); ERP (G) =ERP (0, 1, 1, 0); ERP (H) =ERP (0, 0, 1, 1)
ERP (I) =ERP (1, 0, 0, 1); **Inf** = ERP (0, 0, 0, 0) = **ERP bad**

MACBETH allows for computing a utility function that translates the decision maker's preferences related to the binary options' sample (Fig. 4). We construct then our partially defined fuzzy measure:

$\mu\{1,2,3,4\} = 1$; $\mu\{1\} = 0.47$; $\mu\{2\} = 0.03$
$\mu\{3\} = 0.15$; $\mu\{4\} = 0.20$; $\mu\{1,2\} = 0.90$; $\mu\{2,3\} = 0.68$
$\mu\{3,4\} = 0.25$; $\mu\{1,4\} = 0.95$; $\mu\{\emptyset\} = 0$

In the (Fig.5), we determine the fully defined fuzzy measure **μ**. It is obtained by using the least square approach.

```
                capacity
{}              0.000000
{1}             0.470000
{2}             0.030000
{3}             0.150000
{4}             0.200000
{1,2}           0.900000
{1,3}           0.653415
{1,4}           0.950000
{2,3}           0.680000
{2,4}           0.498592
{3,4}           0.250000
{1,2,3}         0.953994
{1,2,4}         0.976365
{1,3,4}         0.975135
{2,3,4}         0.855288
{1,2,3,4}              1.000000
```

```
> Choquet.integral(mu,ERP_A)
[1] 1
> Choquet.integral(mu,ERP_B)
[1] 0.47
> Choquet.integral(mu,ERP_C)
[1] 0.03000005
> Choquet.integral(mu,ERP_D)
[1] 0.15
> Choquet.integral(mu,ERP_E)
[1] 0.2000000
> Choquet.integral(mu,ERP_F)
[1] 0.9
> Choquet.integral(mu,ERP_G)
[1] 0.68
> Choquet.integral(mu,ERP_H)
[1] 0.2500000
> Choquet.integral(mu,ERP_I)
[1] 0.9499998
> Choquet.integral(mu,ERP_J)
[1] 0
```

Fig. 5. The overall fuzzy measure (KAPPALAB)

The constructed fuzzy measure is coherent with the initially defined values of **μ**. The **"Choquet.integral"** function is used to compute the various ERPs' performances including the prospective ones. Figure (6) shows the prospective ERP systems' computed performances.

ERP1 <-(0.83,0.75,0.9,0.71); ERP2 <-(0.67,0.38,0.7,0.43); ERP3 <-(0.25, 0, 0.2, 0)

```
> Choquet.integral(mu,ERP1)
[1] 0.810933
> Choquet.integral(mu,ERP2)
[1] 0.5900764
> Choquet.integral(mu,ERP3)
[1] 0.1541831
> |
```

Fig. 6. Computed performances (KAPPALAB)

According to previous results, the most optimal ERP system is ERP1with a score of 0.81. It should be noted that this model could be iteratively adjusted until it reflects the real decision maker's preferences.

5 Conclusions

In this paper, a comprehensive methodology for ERP selection is proposed in order to support SMEs in their purchasing decision. Firstly, this methodology is fairly intuitive, simple and covers the overall selection process. Secondly, owing to their dynamic and flexible nature, the adopted selection criteria are generic and practically adaptable to a wide range of firms. Thirdly, the proposed methodology is based on the construction of an induced decision model based on fuzzy measures and MACBETH scales. It introduces a new iterative learning driven approach destined to make enlightened decisions through the consideration of the importance of the criteria's coalitions. Finally, as future perspectives, we propose to validate our methodology against real study cases in order to improve it and make it more suitable.

References

1. Themistocleous, M., Irani, Z., O'Keefe, R.M.: ERP and Application Integration: Exploratory Survey. Business Process Management Journal 7, 195–204 (2001)
2. Willcocks, L., Petherbridge, P., Olson, N.: Making IT Count: Strategy, Delivery and Infrastructure. Butterworth, Oxford (2002)
3. Muscatello, J.R., Michael, H.S., Chen, I.J.: Implementing Enterprise Resource Planning (ERP) Systems in Small and Midsize Manufacturing Firms. International Journal of Operations and Production Management 23, 850–866 (2003)
4. Malie, M., Duffy, N., Rensburg, A.C.J.: Enterprise Resource Planning Solution Selection Criteria in Medium Sized South African Companies. South African Journal of Industrial Engineering 19, 17–30 (2008)
5. Chalmers, R.E.: Small Manufacturers Seek Best ERP Fit. Manufacturing Engineering Journal 123, 42–46 (1999)
6. Winkelmann, A., Klose, K.: Experiences while Selecting, Adapting and Implementing ERP Systems in SMEs: A Case Study. In: 14th American Conference on Information Systems, pp. 1–11 (2008)
7. Adam, R., O'Doherty, P.: ERP Projects: Good or Bad for SMEs? In: Shanks, G., Seddon, P., Willcoks, L. (eds.) Second-Wave Enterprise Resource Planning Systems: Implementing For Effectiveness, pp. 275–298. Cambridge University Press, Cambridge (2003)
8. Sen, C.G., Baracli, H., Sen, S.: A Literature Review and Classification of Enterprise Software Selection Approaches. International Journal of Information Technologies and Decision Making 8, 217–238 (2009)
9. Wybo, M., Robert, J., Leger, P.M.: An Optimization Model of the Business Applications Selection Process. Cahier du GreSI 5, 05–08 (2005)
10. Bernroider, E., Mitlöhner, J.: Characteristics of the Multiple Attribute Decision Making Methodology in Enterprise Resource Planning Software Decisions. Communications of the International Information Management Association 5, 49–58 (2005)
11. Wei, C.C., Chien, C.F., Wang, M.J.J.: An AHP Based Approach to ERP System Selection. International Journal of Production Economics 96, 47–62 (2005)
12. Ravi, V., Shankar, R., Tiwari, M.K.: Analyzing Alternatives in Reserve Logistics for End of Life Computers: ANP and Balanced Scorecard Approach. Computers and Industrial Engineering 48, 327–356 (2005)
13. Ayag, Z., Ozdemir, R.G.: An intelligent Approach to ERP Software Selection through Fuzzy ANP. International Journal of Production Research 45, 2169–2194 (2007)
14. Hu, Y.C., Tsai, J.F.: Back Propagation Multilayer Perceptron for Incomplete Pairwise Comparison Matrices in Analytic Hierarchy Process. Applied Mathematics and Computers 180, 53–62 (2006)
15. Matsuda, S.: A Neural Network Model for the Decision Making Process Based on ANP. In: International Joint Conference on Neural Networks, pp. 16–21 (2006)
16. Keil, M., Tiwana, A.: Relative Importance of Evaluation Criteria for Enterprise Systems: A Conjoint Study. Information Systems Journal 16, 237–262 (2006)

17. Shang, S., Seddon, P.B.: Assessing and Managing the Benefits of Enterprise Systems: The Business Manager's Perspective. Information Systems Journal 12, 271–299 (2002)
18. Appel, A., Dhadwaland, A., Pietraszek, W.: More Bang for the IT Buck. Mckinsey Quarterly 2, 130–141 (2003)
19. Tomas, J.L.: ERP and Integrated Management Product Software: From the Purchasing Decision to the Operational Utilization. Dunod, Paris (2002) (in French)
20. Baki, B., Çakar, K.: Determining the ERP Package Selecting Criteria: The Case of Turkish Manufacturing Companies. Business Process Management Journal 11, 75–86 (2005)
21. Hecht, B.: Choose the Right ERP Software. Datamation 43, 56–58 (1997)
22. Bernroider, E., Koch, S.: ERP Selection Process in Midsize and Large Organizations. Business Process Management 7, 251–257 (2001)
23. Verville, J., Halingten, A.: A Six Stage Model of the Buying Process for ERP Software. Industrial Marketing Management 32, 585–594 (2003)
24. Sahay, B.S., Gupta, A.K.: Development of Software Selection Criteria for Supply Chain Solutions. Industrial Management and Data Systems 103, 97–110 (2003)
25. Goldenberg, B.: Analyze Key Factors when Choosing Software. Marketing News 25, 23–23 (1991)
26. Chau, P.Y.K.: Factors Used in the Selection of Packaged Software in Small Businesses: Views of Owners and Managers. Information and Management 29, 71–78 (1995)
27. Wei, C.C., Chien, C.F., Wang, M.J.: An AHP Based Approach to ERP System Selection. International Journal of Production Economics 96, 47–62 (2005)
28. Wang, T.C., Hsu, S.C.: Multicriteria Decision Making with Incomplete Linguistic Preference Relations. In: 6th WSEAS International Conference on Applied Computer Science, pp. 19–24 (2007)
29. Chakraborty, S.: A Simulation Based Comparative Study of Normalization Procedures in Multiattribute Decision Making. In: 6th WSEAS International Conference on Artificial Intelligence, Knowledge Engineering and Data Bases, pp. 102–109 (2007)
30. Angilella, S., Greco, S., Matarazzo, B.: Non-additive Robust Ordinal Regression: A Multiple Criteria Decision Model Based on the Choquet Integral. European Journal of Operational Research 201, 277–288 (2010)
31. Choquet, G.: Theory of Capacities. Fourier Institute Annales 5, 131–295 (1953)
32. Sugeno, M.: Theory of Fuzzy Integrals and its Applications. PhD thesis, Tokyo Institute of Technology (1974)
33. Bana, C.A., Vansnick, J.C.: A Theoretical Framework for Measuring Attractiveness by a Categorical Based Evaluation Technique (MACBETH). In: 11th International Conference on Multicriteria Decision Making, pp. 15–24 (1994)
34. Saaty, T.L.: The Analytic Hierarchy Process. McGraw-Hill, New York (1980)
35. Jacquet-Lagreze, E., Siskos, Y.: Assessing a Set of Additive Utility Functions for Multicriteria Decision Making: The UTA Method. European Journal of Operational Research 10, 151–164 (1982)
36. Labreuche, C., Grabisch, M.: The Choquet Integral for The Aggregation of Interval Scales in Multicriteria Decision Making. Fuzzy Sets and Systems 137, 11–16 (2003)
37. Grabisch, M.: The Choquet Integral as a Linear Interpolator. In: 10th International Conference on Information Processing and Management of Uncertainty in Knowledge-Based Systems, pp. 373–378 (2004)
38. Mori, T., Murofushi, T.: An Analysis of Evaluation Model Using Fuzzy Measure and the Choquet Integral. In: 5th Fuzzy System Symposium, pp. 207–212 (1989)
39. Grabisch, M., Kojadinovic, I., Meyer, P.: A Review of Methods for Capacity Identification in Choquet Integral Based on Multi-Attribute Utility Theory: Applications of the Kappalab R Package. European Journal of Operations Research 186, 766–785 (2008)

SVM-SS Watermarking Model for Medical Images

Saliza Ramly[1], Syed Ahmad Aljunid[1], and Hanizan Shaker Hussain[2]

[1] Faculty of Computer and Mathematical Sciences,
Universiti Teknologi MARA, Shah Alam, Malaysia
sally_za213@yahoo.com, aljunid@tmsk.uitm.edu.my
[2] Faculty of Information Technology, Universiti Tun Abdul Razak,
Petaling Jaya, Malaysia
hanizan@pintar.unirazak.edu.my

Abstract. To ensure the crucial integrity and confidentiality of patients' information, this paper proposes a novel support vector machine (SVM) cum spread spectrum (SS) watermarking model to watermark medical images. In applying watermarking to secure medical images, there are generally three key stages, namely classifying the medical images into Region of Interest (ROI) and Region of Non-Interest (RONI), embedding the patients' information and other relevant information into the image, and lastly extracting that information from the watermark images. The classifying and embedding stages require specific techniques tailored to their different requirements while the third is usually done using symmetric algorithms applied in the embedding stage. Among the soft computing techniques, SVM excels in classification including image classification and has a high potential to be used in the watermarking to improve its performance. However, based on current works reviewed in medical image watermarking, none has applied SVM yet. Similarly, SS is robust to the most common of signal processing and geometric distortions have been successfully applied in image watermarking. Therefore, in our novel model, SVM will be applied in the first stage while SS will be applied in the second and third stages. Significantly, the model aims to secure medical images to resist distortion as well as to avoid medical images quality degradation. The patient confidential data will be embedded into the RONI of their medical images using grayscale JPEG format using the SS symmetric algorithm. The watermark images will be evaluated on robustness and imperceptibility. Experiments will be conducted to measure the similarity ratio (SR) to test the robustness and Peak Signal to Noise Ratio (PSNR) to test the imperceptibility. The results show a high quality robust and imperceptible watermarking has been achieved with SR of more than 0.98 and PSNR of more than 40dB.

Keywords: Watermarking, Soft Computing, Support Vector Machine, Medical Image, Spread Spectrum.

1 Introduction

Watermarking is a technique that embeds certain amount of confidential data or content-dependent information in the host or cover data file transparently to ensure its authenticity and protect the integrity of the stored information even in transmission.

E. Ariwa and E. El-Qawasmeh (Eds.): DEIS 2011, CCIS 194, pp. 372–386, 2011.

It is applied in many forms such as video, audio, text, 3D model and software code and is being used successfully in various applications such as authentication, copyright protection and commercialization as well as broadcasting [1][2]. Among the popular techniques in watermarking is digital image watermarking which is the technique for embedding and transferring certain amount of data into the host image. Zain et al. in [3] have stated that the main advantage of digital image watermarking is that the information is embedded directly to the image data. Therefore, the information can survive several modifications. In the digital image watermarking model, two processes are involved, which are embedding and extracting. The embedded data could be in form of text, another image as well as number [3][4].

One of the critical types of digital images is medical image. The medical image is used to store and record patients' information, which is very confidential. The stored information must be securely kept from any modifications or tampering [1][4][5][6]. Therefore, the security of the medical image is a must and it is normally separated into two parts, region of interest (ROI) and region of non interest (RONI) [7][8][9][10]. ROI is the significant part in medical image that must be protected and saved without the lost of any information even for long term storage. On the other hand, RONI contain less important information. Therefore, ROI must be strictly preserved while the RONI can be allowed for some modifications [11][12][13].

In medical images, watermark can be embedded either in spatial or transform domain. In the spatial domain, the watermark is embedded directly and the process is simple and fast but it is weak from the external attack, noise and JPEG compression. Transform domain method meanwhile is based on the spatial transformation and the coefficients processed in the frequency domain of the medical image. The transform domain is more preferable compared to spatial domain because it is more robust against several modifications such as compression, cropping and filtering [9][14][15].

In designing a good watermarking scheme, three main requirements need to be considered, which are robustness, imperceptibility and capacity. Robustness is the capabilities of watermarking image to resist malicious image processing attacks. Imperceptibility is to preserve the quality of the watermarked image while capacity is the number of bits used as watermark [1][16].

A trade-off issue among these requirements is challenging to obtain a high quality watermark. In applying watermarking to secure medical images, there is another important stage prior to embedding, which is classification. The stage divides the medical images into ROI and RONI. Among the soft computing techniques, namely neural network (NN), genetic algorithm (GA), fuzzy logic (FL), and support vector machine (SVM), SVM excels in classification including image classification and has a high potential to be used in the watermarking to improve its performance [17][18][19]. However, based on current works reviewed in medical image watermarking, none has applied SVM yet.

Among the embedding techniques in watermarking are spread spectrum (SS), least significant bit (LSB), patchwork and texture block coding. SS is commonly used in image processing and signal processing [20][21]. In fact, SS is one of the earliest technique but yet, it is still significant, relevant and continually being applied [22][23][24]. SS is frequently used together with the JPEG image format and normally applied in the transform domain [20][22][24]. Therefore, SS technique is proposed to be used in this research for the embedding and extracting processes. This technique has been chosen because it is more robust to the most common of signal processing and geometric distortions in order to secure the host images [20][21][22]. Another strength of SS is it will separate the watermark data over many frequency bins so that the energy in any one bin is so small and certainly undetectable [25]. Therefore, in our novel model, SVM will be applied in the first stage while SS will be applied in the second and third stages.

In the remaining section of this paper, we discuss the SC paradigms in section 2, followed by, the SC techniques in image watermarking in section 3 and the proposed novel SVM-SS image watermarking model in section 4. Section 5 concludes this paper.

2 SC Application in Image Watermarking

In this section, the application of SC in image watermarking is focused. Reviewed works shows that NN, GA, SVM and FL have and still continually been used in image watermarking. Each application will be discussed based on the three requirements of watermarking, i.e. imperceptibility, payload capacity and robustness, or these combinations.

2.1 Neural Network

The main goal of the works that involved NN focuses on the robustness [32][33][34][35]. Several types of NN commonly used in watermarking are such as Back-propagation Neural Network (BPNN), Radial Basis Function (RBF), Hopfield and full counter-propagation Neural Network (FCNN). Several works in NN are applied in the transform domain, especially in DCT. [33][35][40]. For example, Ahmad et al. [35] used the highest changeable threshold values of DCT coefficients to embed the watermark that is determined by the perceptual features of the original image. Most researches used JPEG image as the original image and binary image as the watermark info [32][33][34][39].

2.2 Genetic Algorithm

Basically, GA is employed to choose the best embedding positions in image watermarking. GA is frequently used to increase the watermark capacity and find the best strength of watermark while maintaining the quality of the image [41][42][43][44]. Generally, most works tend to use JPEG image and it have been done in the transform domain [42][46][47].

2.3 Fuzzy Logic

FL techniques has been used in watermarking such as fuzzy adaptive resonance theory [48] and fuzzy inference system (FIS)[49]. Generally, in most of these works, FL has been applied to preserve the imperceptibility of the watermarked image [50][51][52]. However, [53] used the FL to maximize the watermark strength by combining the FIS with human visual system (HVS). The watermarking strength is adjusted and embedded without degrading the image quality. FIS is also used in [52] to improve the robustness of the watermarked image.

2.4 Support Vector Machine

Most of works that involve SVM focuses on the imperceptibility. It is based on statistical learning theory which has the ability to overcome the weakness of neural networks [58]. SVM is also being applied successfully at different watermark stages such as embedding, detection and extracting. SVM can be trained and this trained model is obtained using a template sample. Watermark can be extracted based on the output of the SVM model [59]. Due to the good learning and generalization abilities of SVM, Yuanhai et al. [60] stated that this watermarking technique is better than traditional techniques against several attacks.

SVM also excels in classification; therefore, the classification problem before embedding the watermark can be potentially solved by SVM. Thus, the SVM based technique can help to improve of the conventional watermarking methods [61]. Yuanhai et al. [60] have used support vector regression to learn the characteristic of relationship between a random coefficient and its neighboring coefficient in the Discrete Multiwavelet transform domain. On the other hand, Tsai et al. [62] have trained SVM to memorize the relationship between watermark and image-dependent watermark. Then, the α-trimmed mean algorithm is used to remove noises. Another related work by Khan et al. [30] have combined SVM and NN based on machine learning to improve the watermarking system. Another very recent SVM-hybrid research is by Hussain et al. [63], which hybrid fuzzy c-means (FCM) and SVM in image steganography.

3 The Proposed SVM-SS Watermarking Model for Medical Image

Although numerous watermarking works have been applied using soft computing technique, none so far have applied SVM for medical images. Similarly, SS is robust to the most common of signal processing and geometric distortions have been successfully applied in image watermarking. Therefore, in our model, to ensure the crucial integrity and confidentiality of patients' information, SVM will be applied in the first stage while SS will be in the second and third stages. Fig. 1 shows the two stage watermark classifying-embedding processes.

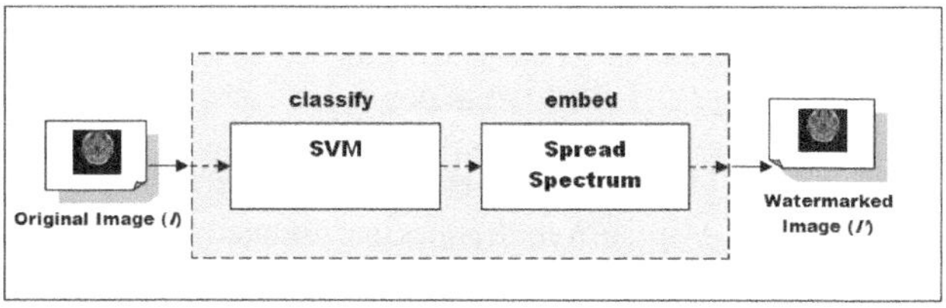

Fig. 1. The Two Stage Watermark Classifying-Embedding Processes

Initially, an original image (I) to be watermarked is preprocessed before embedding a watermark (W) (refer to Fig. 2). This process involves dividing the image into non-overlapping 8x8 blocks and then converts the image to the desired domain which is Discrete Cosine Transform (DCT). The watermark to be embedded is a bit stream gathered from the textual patient information that has been converted into binary form. The watermark (W) is then added on to the desired coefficients of the DCT. Each DCT coefficient will be classified before the embedding process. Therefore, only the coefficient that has been classified into RONI will be used to embed the watermark. The watermarked image(I') is the output of this process such that it is perceptually identical to I and is obtained by performing an inverse DCT on the altered transform coefficients. Mathematically, given E as the encoder function and K as the secret key, this can be written as:

$$E\ (I,W,K) = I' \tag{1}$$

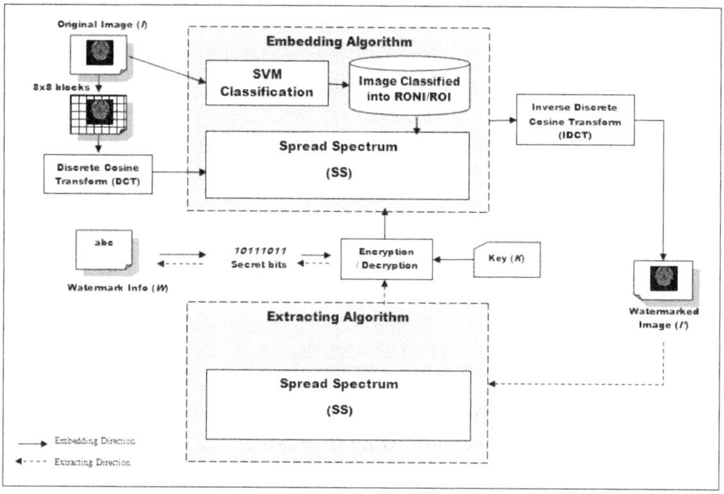

Fig. 2. SS-SVM Watermarking Model

During the extraction process, the embedded watermark will be extracted. A decoder function (D) takes watermarked image (I') to extracts a watermark (W') from the image by using secret key (K). Mathematically, this is written as:

$$D\ (I', I, K) = W' \tag{2}$$

The extraction process is the inverse of the watermark embedding process. In order to get back the watermark information, the original image is used. Both these images must be divided into 8x8 block pixels and then forward DCT will be applied. Secret key will be entered first in order to authenticate. Each image pixel array is compared for both images. If there is a difference between the original and watermarked image pixels, the data watermarked image pixel will be extracted and calculate to get the bit. All bits are combined and then converted into text. Consequently, only an authorized party can view the information.

3.1 SVM Classifying Stage

In the SVM classification, the original image will be used to extract the pixels. The pixels will be classified according to ROI and RONI. Fig. 3 shows the flow of SVM Based Image Classification.

During the training phase, the classification algorithm is presented with a set of labeled data. For example, the original image has been divided into two ROI and RONI. The classification algorithm uses this information to adjust its associated parameters in order to minimize the number of false positives and false negatives. In this research, a false positive corresponds to classifying a ROI as a RONI. Similarly, a false negative corresponds to classifying a RONI as a ROI. Both errors are important; however, since medical images are used, a false negative may be more costly than a false positive. Once the training phase is completed, the classification process must be tested using separate testing data.

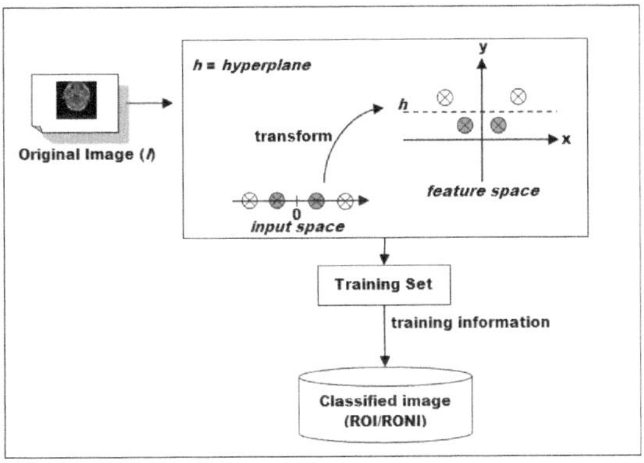

Fig. 3. The flow of SVM Based Image Classification

3.2 Spread Spectrum Embedding Stage

The SS used in this model to embed the watermark works by modulating a narrow band signal over a carrier. The spectral energy of the signal is spread over a wide band, thus decreasing its density that is often under the noise level. Therefore, the image is viewed as the high bandwidth that allows the watermark to be inserted together with the image without detection [64].

This technique uses a frequency domain transform to convert the input pixels into DCT domain (Refer to Fig. 4). In DCT domain, the sequence of DCT coefficient value c = c[1], …, c[n] is extracted. This sequence is the information carrier of the watermark and is modified. The watermark is a sequence of numbers w = w[1], …, w[n]. Each value w[i] is chosen independently according to N(0,1). There are several different formulas for embedding that depends on their embedding characteristics [65]. Equation (3) is the invertible function that will be used in the process based on Cox et al. [65]:

$$V'[i] = V[i](1+\alpha X[i]) \quad (3)$$

where to obtain V' as watermarked frequency, X represents the watermark, *V* represents the highest frequency of the DCT coefficient and α is the scaling parameter which is 0.1 that determines the extent to which X alters V. According to Cox et al., [65] the single parameter 0.1 is chosen because it provides a good trade-off between imperceptibility and robustness while *X* is a random number from the normal distribution, ~N (0, 1).

DCT is the frequency domain that separates the image into parts of differing importance. The image is separated into high, middle and low frequency components. Therefore, the watermark data is separated all over the image by using DCT coefficient technique.

Fig. 4 shows the transformation to DCT coefficient. The C(i,j) is the intensity of the pixel of the original image in row i and column j where as C(u,v) is the DCT coefficient in row u and column v of the DCT matrix.

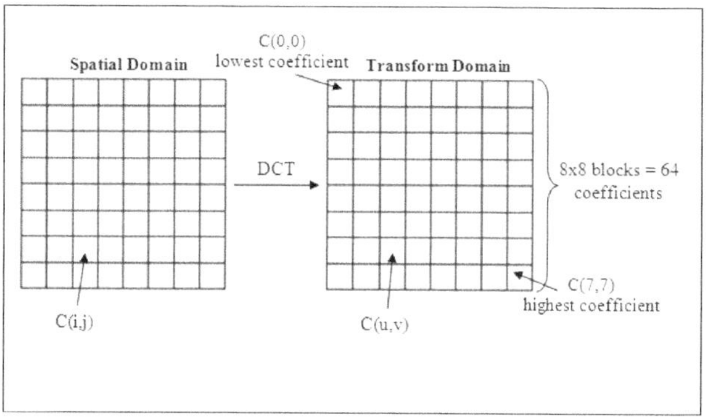

Fig. 4. Transformation to DCT Coefficient

In SS technique, the frequency domain which is the DCT coefficient is viewed as a communication channel and the watermark is viewed as a signal that is transmitted through it. Since DCT is the frequency domain that separates the image into parts of differing importance which are high, middle and low frequency components. The watermark bit will be embedded into the highest coefficient of each DCT block. Since the block is divided into 8x8 block, each of the block consist of 64 DCT coefficients. C(u,v) is represented for each coefficient and the block matrix is ranged from 0 to 7 while the lowest frequency of the original image block is located at the top-left coefficient C(0,0).

The frequency of DCT coefficient of image block will be getting higher throughout the sequence from left to right and top to bottom. Therefore, the highest frequency of DCT coefficient of the image block is located at the most right-bottom coefficient C(7,7). According to Cabeen and Gen [66], the human eyes are most sensitive to low frequencies rather than higher frequencies. This is why the watermark will be inserted into the highest coefficient of the block at C(7,7).

Since the data is embedded into frequency domain, the watermark is hard to be detected and damaged. If there is attempt to remove the watermark, the original data also will be corrupted.

4 Experiment

To ensure the crucial integrity and confidentiality of patients' information, a prototype of proposed model is developed and experimented with twenty of 256x256 JPEG grayscale images. The images used in this experiment are standard image database from MATLAB Central (http://www.mathworks.com/matlabcentral/) which has been used in various image watermarking works.

In SVM classifying stage, a total number of 20 dataset have been used in this stage. Each dataset is a grayscale image of 256x256 sizes. Therefore, the total number of data points for image is 65536. From this total number of data points, 2000 or 3% is used for training while the rest 65356 or 97% is used for testing. The luminosity and the edges value of the images are extracted and populated to be the features for the classification process. The best threshold is selected by testing certain value and the result is determined based on human eyes.

The effectiveness of SVM depends on the selection of kernel, the kernel's parameters, and soft margin parameter C. Since RBF kernel has been used in this classification process. The accuracy of the SVM classification is tested based on two parameter inputs which are cost (C) and Gamma (γ) parameters. Best combination of C and gamma is often selected by a grid-search with exponentially growing sequences of C and gamma. Based on the grid-search that has been done, the parameter's value has been determined which are 1000 for C and 1.0 for gamma. As a result, the pixels images have been successfully classified to ROI and RONI. The experiment results show that the average accuracy for SVM classification is 99.8487%.

In the SS embedding stage, after all locations with the highest coefficient for each DCT block are selected, the predicted label for these locations will be identified based on the result from the classification stage. Only locations with highest coefficient and labeled with -1 (RONI) will be used as embedding location. After the embedding process is done, the inverse DCT will be performed. The pixel gathered will be used to form the watermarked image.

Fig. 5 (a) shows the original image. The watermark information is a set of text that has been converted to binary form are embedded into the image. After embedding the watermark, the watermarked image that is produced and the original image cannot be distinguished by naked eye. Fig. 5 (b) shows watermarked image.

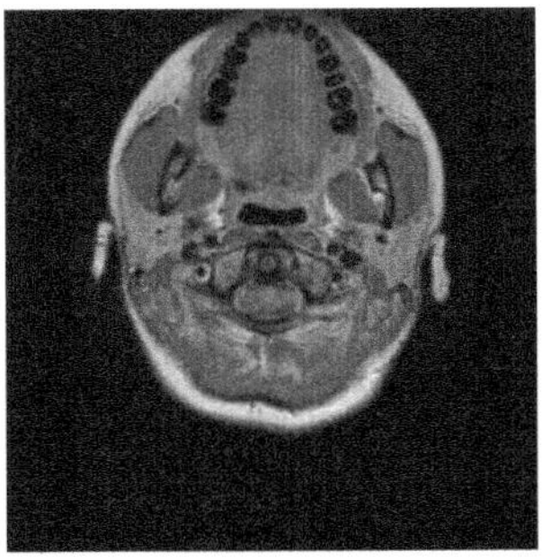

Fig. 5(a). Original Image

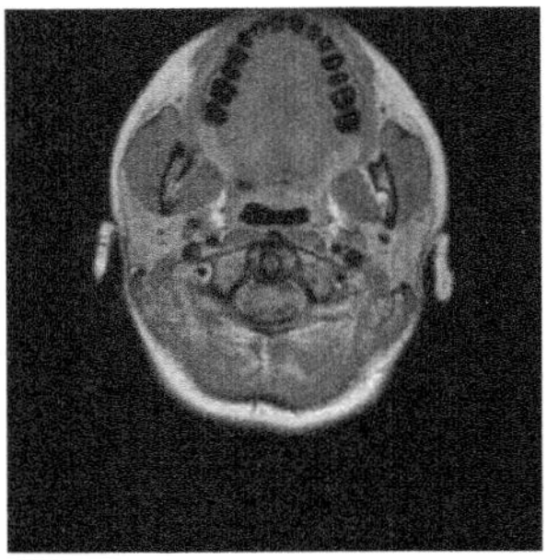

Fig. 5(b). Watermarked Image

To evaluate the crucial integrity and confidentiality of patients' information based on the proposed model, the robustness and imperceptibility of the watermarked images have been measured. The robustness will be tested by calculating the Similarity Ration (SR) between original and watermarked images. SR can be computed in order to make a comparison between extracted and original watermark. The equation is as follows:

$$SR = \frac{S}{S + D} \quad (4)$$

Where S indicates number of matching pixels values and D indicates of different pixel values. SR values ranges from 0 to 1, and SR values closer to 1 indicates that the number of matching pixels are high; thus implying that the watermark is more robust and hence the authenticity is preserved [67][68][69][70][71][72].

Table 1 shows the results of the SR that is measured by using several different sizes of watermark (capacities). When the size of the watermark information is increased, the corresponding SR value decreases. This is logical, as it implies that when the size of watermark information becomes larger, the robustness of the image is reduced.

Table 1. Similarity Ratio for Tested Sizes

Watermark Size	Similarity Ratio
40bytes	0.9951
60bytes	0.9939
80bytes	0.9927
100bytes	0.9878
120bytes	0.9853
Average	0.9910

By using the SVM classification, only the RONI area that are located in the highest coefficient of DCT block can be used to embed the watermark. Although his limit the size of watermark bits to be embedded, that end result is a more robust watermarked image. Otherwise, if the SVM classification has not been used, the watermark bits can be embedded into all highest coefficient of DCT blocks. This will not only allow too many watermark bits can be embedded that result to the low robustness of the watermarked image but more significantly, it will jeopardize the crucial integrity of the medical image.

Table 2. Comparison of Robustness SR Results

Works	SR
Method [67]	1.0
Method [69]	0.9181
Method [70]	0.8496
Proposed Model	0.991

Table 2 compares the robustness results of very recent previous works in [67][69][70] and the proposed model.. All these SR values are more than 0.8 while the proposed model value is 0.991, which is much closer to 1.0. This implies the robustness of the watermark is intact and hence the authenticity is preserved.

Table 3. Results for PSNR, Mean and Standard Deviation for Imperceptibility Testing

Original Images			Watermarked Images		MSE	PSNR (dB)
Name	**Mean**	**Standard Deviation**	**Mean**	**Standard Deviation**		
brain_001.jpg	42.184	55.071	41.445	54.865	0.952	48.554
brain_002.jpg	46.507	59.455	45.766	59.238	0.949	48.486
brain_003.jpg	46.450	60.995	45.708	60.783	0.934	48.720
brain_004.jpg	42.997	57.841	42.264	57.628	0.947	48.433
brain_005.jpg	43.750	59.346	43.026	59.132	0.950	48.577
brain_006.jpg	40.071	55.216	39.347	55.005	0.961	48.474
brain_007.jpg	44.562	58.942	43.832	58.720	0.968	48.416
brain_008.jpg	42.624	52.883	41.896	52.653	0.954	48.473
brain_009.jpg	50.271	60.184	49.541	59.947	0.955	48.530
brain_010.jpg	54.938	63.621	54.205	63.375	0.956	48.449
brain_011.jpg	56.557	64.658	55.832	64.406	0.944	48.633
brain_012.jpg	54.420	62.259	53.695	62.013	0.953	48.548
brain_013.jpg	56.041	64.935	55.316	64.688	0.955	48.527
brain_014.jpg	54.702	64.232	53.975	63.992	0.963	48.460
brain_015.jpg	50.259	60.643	49.523	60.412	0.943	48.434
brain_016.jpg	49.093	61.055	48.355	60.834	0.938	48.308
brain_017.jpg	43.286	56.190	42.547	55.975	0.939	48.678
brain_018.jpg	46.005	63.269	45.262	63.076	0.923	48.831
brain_019.jpg	39.181	57.918	38.437	57.737	0.927	48.792
brain_020.jpg	35.708	57.874	34.961	57.713	0.923	48.828
				Average:	**0.947**	**48.558**

The second criterion is the imperceptibility of the watermarked image, which is measured using the Peak Signal to Noise Ratio, as is defined in equation (5).

$$PNSR = 10\log_{10}\left[\frac{255^2}{MSE}\right](dB) \quad (5)$$

where MSE is the Mean Square Error between original image and watermarked image.

To measure the imperceptibility, the capacity of the watermark information used is constant (120bytes) and the same for all the tested images. Table 3 shows the results. The average PSNR value for the twenty medical images is 48.558 dB, which is more than the acceptable quality PSNR imperceptible value of 40dB. Thus, the results show that these watermarked images are of high imperceptibility. Based on the results of very recent works in [67][69][70], as illustrated in Table 4, although the achieved PSNR value of the proposed model is of high imperceptibility, there are other works which have performed better.

Table 4. Comparison of Imperceptibility PSNR Results

Works	PSNR
Method [67]	54.1047
Method [69]	42.14
Method [70]	59.1168
Proposed Model	48.558

Fig. 6 show the histograms for both the original and watermarked images. The standard deviation is 55.071 for the original image in Fig.6(a) and 54.865 for the watermarked image in Fig.6(b). It shows that the standard deviation is reduced after the watermark was embedded into the original image. This is because after the watermark is embedded, the values of selected pixels have been increased.

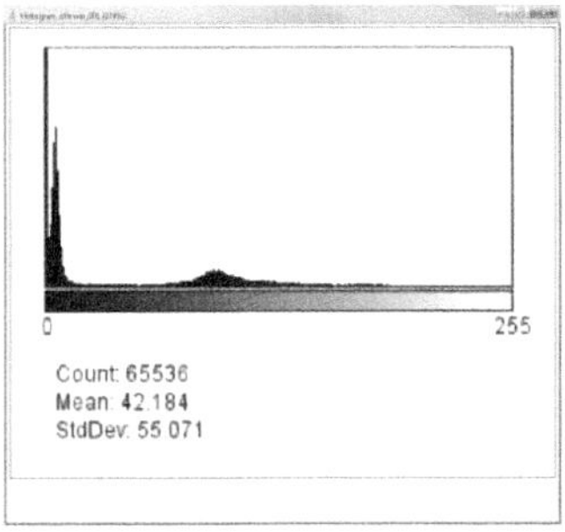

Fig. 6(a). Original Image Histogram

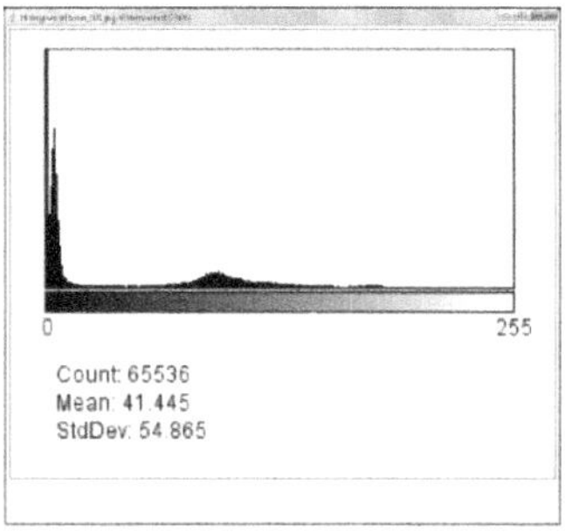

Fig. 6(b). Watermarked Image Histogram

In the SS extracting stage, both original and watermarked images are used in order to extract the watermark information. These images are compared and if there is a difference between original and watermarked image pixels, the value of watermarked image pixel will be extracted and calculated using inverse SS algorithm to get the bit. All bits are combined and then converted into text. As a result, the information extracted is same as the information that has been embedded.

5 Conclusion

Since medical images must have assurance in its crucial integrity and confidentiality, the security of these medical images must be not be breached. Among the soft computing techniques, SVM excels in classification including image classification. However, no work has so far applied SVM to medical image watermarking. Similarly, SS is robust to the most common of signal processing and geometric distortions have been successfully applied in image watermarking. Therefore, in our novel SVM-SS watermarking model, SVM is used in the first stage while SS will be applied in the second and third stages. Significantly, the model aims to secure medical images to resist distortion as well as to avoid medical images quality degradation. The patient confidential data will be embedded into the RONI of their medical images using grayscale JPEG format using the SS symmetric algorithm. The results show a robust and high quality imperceptible watermarking has been achieved with SR of more than 0.99 and PSNR of more than 48dB. Our future work is to experiment further this SVM-SS technique with various watermark attacks.

References

1. Zain, J.M., Clarke, M.: Security in Telemedicine: Issues in watermarking medical images. In: 3rd International Conference: Sciences of Electronic, Technologies of Information and Telecommunications, TUNISIA (2005)
2. Potdar, V.M., Han, S., Chang, E.: A Survey of Digital Image Watermarking Techniques. In: International Conference on Industrial Informatics INDIN (2005)
3. Zain, J.M., Clarke, M.: Reversible Watermarking Surviving JPEG Compression. In: EMBS 2005, pp. 3759–3762 (2006)
4. Planitz, B.M., Maeder, A.J.: A Study of Block-Based Medical Image Watermarking Using a Perceptual Similarity Metric. In: Proceedings in DICTA 2005, p. 70 (2005)
5. Raul, R.-C., Feregrino, -U.C., de Gershom, J.T.-B.: Data Hiding Scheme for Medical Images. In: Proceedings in: 17th International Conference on Electronics, Communications and Computers (CONIELECOMP 2007), IEEE Computer Society, USA (2007)
6. Giakoumaki, A., Pavlopoulos, S., Koutsouris, D.: Multiple Image Watermarking Applied to Health Information Management. IEEE Transactions on Information Technology in Biomedicine 10(4), 722–732 (2006)
7. Memon, N.A., Gilani, S.A.M., Ali, A.: Watermarking of chest CT scan medical images for content authentication. In: ICICT 2009, pp. 175–180 (2009)
8. Memon, N.A., Gilani, S.A.M., Qayoom, S.: Multiple watermarking of medical images for content authentication and recovery. In: IEEE:13th International, INMIC 2009. pp. 1–6 14–15 (2009)
9. Hyung-Kyo, L., Hee-Jung, K., Ki-Ryong, K., Jong-Keuk, L.: ROI Medical Image Watermarking Using DWT and Bit-plane. In: Asia-Pacific Conference, Communications, pp. 512–515, 5-5 (2005)
10. Siau-Chuin, L., Zain, J.M.: Reversible medical image watermarking for tamper detection and recovery. In: ICCSIT 2010: 3rd IEEE International Conference, vol. 5, pp. 417–420 (2010)
11. Maeder, A.J., Planitz, B.M.: Medical image watermarking for multiple modalities. In: Proceeding in Applied Imagery and Pattern Recognition Workshop, pp. 6–165 (2005)
12. Fallahpour, M., Megias, D., Ghanbari, M.: High capacity, reversible data hiding in medical images. In: Bayoumi, M. (ed.) Proceeding in: 16th IEEE (ICIP 2009), pp. 4185–4188. IEEE Press, Piscataway (2009)
13. Tzu-Chao, L., Chao-Ming, L.: Wavelet-based copyright-protection scheme for digital images based on local features. Information Sciences 179(19,9), 3349–3358 (2009)
14. Sung, J.L., Hae, M.M., Seung-Hoon, C., Sung, B.P., Yongwha, C., Min, H.C.: Dual Watermarking Method for Integrity of Medical Images. In: FGCN 2008, vol. 2, pp. 70–73 (2008)
15. Megalingam, R.K., Nair, M.M., Srikumar, R., Balasubramanian, V.K., Venugopala, V.S.: Performance Comparison of Novel, Robust Spatial Domain Digital Image Watermarking with the Conventional Frequency Domain Watermarking Techniques. In: Signal Acquisition and Processing, pp. 349–353 (2010)

16. Huang, S., Zhang, W.: Digital Watermarking Based on Neural Network and Image Features. In: ICIC 2009, vol. 2, pp. 238–240 (2009)
17. Cao, X.B., Xu, Y.W., Chen, D., Qiao, H.: Associated evolution of a support vector machine-based classifier for pedestrian detection. Information Sciences 179(8), 1070–1077 (2009)
18. Tsai, H.-H., Sun, D.-W.: Color image watermark extraction based on support vector machines. Information Sciences 177(2), 550–569 (2007)
19. Shao, Y., Chen, W., Liu, C.: Multiwavelet-based Digital Watermarking with Support Vector Machine Technique. In: CCDC 2008 (2008)
20. Cox, I.J., Kilian, J., Leighton, F.T., Shamoon, T.: Secure spread spectrum watermarking for multimedia. IEEE Transactions on Image Processing 6(12), 1673–1687 (1997)
21. Malvar, H.S., Florencio, D.A.F.: Improved spread spectrum: a new modulation technique for robust watermarking. IEEE Transactions on Signal Processing 51(4), 898–905 (2003)
22. Abdallah, H.A., Hadhoud, M.M., Shaalan, A.A.: A blind spread spectrum wavelet based image watermarking algorithm. In: ICCES 2009, pp. 251–256 (2009)
23. Altun, H.O., Orsdemir, A., Sharma, G., Bocko, M.F.: Optimal Spread Spectrum Watermark Embedding via a Multistep Feasibility Formulation. IEEE Transactions on Image Processing 18(2), 371–387 (2009)
24. Tian, H., Zhao, Y., Ni, R., Pan, J.-S.: Spread Spectrum-Based Image Watermarking Resistant to Rotation and Scaling Using Radon Transform. In (IIH-MSP) 2010, pp. 442–445, 15–17 (2010)
25. Todorov, T.: Spread spectrum watermarking technique for information system securing. In: Proceeding in CompSysTech 2004. ACM, New York (2004)
26. Yi, Q., Wang, K.: An Improved Watermarking Method Based on Neural Network for Color Image. In: Proceedings ofthe 2009 IEEE, International Conference on Mechatronics and Automation, Changchun, China (2009)
27. Seetha, M., MuraliKrishna, I.V., Deekshatulu. B.L.: Comparison of Advanced techniques of Image classification. Map World Forum (2007)
28. Lai, C.-.C., Hsiang-Cheh, H., Cheng-Chih, T.: Image Watermarking Scheme Using Singular Value Decomposition and Micro-genetic Algorithm. In: IIHMSP 2008, pp. 469–472, 15–17 (2008)
29. Kecman, V.: Learning and soft computing: support vector machines, neural networks, and fuzzy logic models. A Bradford Book. MIT Press, England (2001)
30. Khan, A., Tahir, S.F., Majid, A., Choi, T.: Machine learning based adaptive watermark decoding in view of anticipated attack. Pattern Recogn. 41(8), 2594–2610 (2008)
31. Shao, Y., Wei, C., Chan, L.: Multiwavelet-based Digital Watermarking with Support Vector Machine Technique. In: CCDC 2008, Beijing, China (2008)
32. Huang, S., Zhang, W.: Digital Watermarking Based on Neural Network and Image Features. In: ICIC 2009, vol. 2, pp. 238–240 (2009)
33. Liu, Q., Jiang, X.: Design and Realization of a Meaningful Digital Watermarking Algorithm Based on RBF Neural Network. In: WCICA 2006, vol. 1, pp. 2878–2881 (2006)
34. Jing, L., Liu, F.: Applying General Regression Neural Network in Digital Image Watermarking. In: ICNC 2008, vol. 5, pp. 452–456 (2008)
35. Ahmad, R., Naghsh, N., Ayoub, T.: New Robust Digital Image Watermarking Technique based on the Discrete Cosine Transform and Neural Network. Engineering Department of Isfahan University of Iran. IEEE, Los Alamitos (2008)
36. Yi, Q., Wang, K.: An Improved Watermarking Method Based on Neural Network for Color Image. In: International Conference on Mechatronics and Automation. IEEE, China (2009)

37. Huang, S., Zhang, W., Feng, W., Yang, H.: Blind Watermarking Scheme Based on Neural Network. In: Proceedings of the 7th, World Congress on Intelligent Control and Automation, China (2008)
38. Chang, C.-Y.: The Application of a Full Counterpropagation Neural Network to Image Watermarking. IEEE, Los Alamitos (2005)
39. Chang, C.-Y., Su, S.-J.: A neural-network-based robust watermarking scheme. Systems, Man and Cybernetics 3, 2482–2487 (2005)
40. Liu, Q., Jiang, X.: Design and Realization of a Meaningful Digital Watermarking Algorithm Based on RBF Neural Network. In: ICNN&B 2005, vol. 1, pp. 214–218 (2005)
41. Lai, C.-C., Huang, H.-C., Tsai, C.-C.: Image Watermarking Scheme Using Singular Value Decomposition and Micro-genetic Algorithm. In: IIHMSP 2008, pp. 469–472 (2008)
42. Kumar, S., Raman, B., Thakur, M.: Real Coded Genetic Algorithm Based Stereo image Watermarking. IJSDIA 1(1), 23–33 (2009)
43. Jagadeesh, B., Kumar, S.S., Rajeswari, K.R.: A Genetic Algorithm Based Oblivious Image Watermarking Scheme Using Singular Value Decomposition (SVD). In: NETCOM 2009, pp. 224–229 (2009)
44. Promcharoen, S., Rangsanseri, Y.: Genetic Watermarking with Block-Based DCT Clustering. In: ISCIT 2008, pp. 346–351 (2008)
45. Lai, C.-C., Tsai, C.-C., Pan, S.-T.: An SVD-Based Watermarking Scheme Using Improved Micro-Genetic Algorithm. Fuzzy-IEEE (2009)
46. Jung, H., Jeon, M.: Enhanced SVD Based Watermarking with Genetic Algorithm, vol. 56, pp. 586–593. Springer, Heidelberg (2009)
47. Sikander, B., Ishtiaq, M., Jaffar, M.A., Tariq, M., Mirza, A.M.: Adaptive Digital Watermarking of Images Using Genetic Algorithm. In: ICISA 2010, pp. 1–8 (2010)
48. Chang, C.-H., Ye, Z., Zhang, M.: Fuzzy-ART Based Adaptive Digital Watermarking Scheme. IEEE Transactions on Circuits and Systems for Video Technology 15(1) (2005)
49. Deng, C., Gao, X.-B., Tao, D.-C., Li, X.-L.: Digital Watermarking in Image Affine Co-Variant Regions. In: Proceedings of the Sixth International Conference on Machine Learning and Cybernetics, Hong Kong (2007)
50. Lande, P.U., Sanjay, N., Talbar, G.N., Shinde: A Fuzzy Logic Approach To Encrypted Watermarking For Still Images In Wavelet Domain on FPGA. International Journal of Signal Processing, Image Processing and Pattern Recognition 3(2) (2010)
51. Lande, P.U., Sanjay, N., Talbar, G.N., Shinde: Robust Image Adaptive Watermarking Using Fuzzy Logic An FPGA Approach. International Journal of Signal Processing, Image Processing and Pattern Recognition 3(3) (2010)
52. Coumou, D., Mathew, A.: A Fuzzy Logic Approach To Digital Image Watermarking. In: The International Workshop On Discrete-Event System Design, DESDes 2001, pp. 201–209 (2001)
53. Oueslati, S., Cherif, A., Solaiman, B.: Mimizing Strength of Digital Watermarks using Fuzzy Logic. SIPIJ 1(2) (2010)
54. Chen, W.-C., Wang, M.-S.: A fuzzy c-means clustering-based fragile watermarking scheme for image authentication. Expert Systems with Applications 36(2), Part 1, 1300–1307 (2009), doi:10.1016/j.eswa.2007.11.018, ISSN 0957-4174
55. Promcharoen, S., Rangsanseri, Y.: Genetic Watermarking with Block-Based DCT Clustering. In: ISCIT 2008, pp. 346–351, 21–23 (2008)
56. Kiani, S., Moghaddam, M.E.: A Fractal Based Image Watermarking for Authentication and Verification. In: CISP 2009, pp. 1–5 (2009)
57. Chen, W.-C., Wang, M.-S.: A fuzzy c-means clustering-based fragile watermarking scheme for image authentication. Expert Systems with Applications 36(2), Part 1 (2009)

58. Peng, H., Wang, J., Wang, W.: Image watermarking method in multiwavelet domain based on support vector machines. Journal of Systems and Software (2010) (in press)
59. Wang, X.-Y., Xu, Z.-H., Yang, H.-Y.: A robust image watermarking algorithm using SVR detection. Expert Systems with Applications 36(5) (2009)
60. Shao, Y., Chen, W., Liu, C.: Multiwavelet-based Digital Watermarking with Support Vector Machine Technique. In: CCDC 2008, Beijing, China (2008)
61. Tsai, H.-H., Sun, D.-W.: Color image watermark extraction based on support vector machines. Information Sciences 177(2), 550–569 (2007)
62. Tsai, H.-H., Tseng, H.-C., Lai, Y.-S.: Robust lossless image watermarking based on alpha-trimmed mean algorithm and support vector machine. Journal of Systems and Software (2009)
63. Hussain, H.S., Aljunid, S.A., Yahya, S., Ali, F.H.M.: A Novel Hybrid Fuzzy-SVM Image Steganographic Model. In: Proceeding of the 4th International Symposium on Information Technology (ITSim 2010), vol. 1, pp. 215–221 (2010)
64. Todorov, T.: Spread spectrum watermarking technique for information system securing. In: Proceeding in CompSysTech 2004. ACM, New York (2004)
65. Cox, I.J., Kilian, J., Leighton, F.T., Shamoon, T.: Secure spread spectrum watermarking for multimedia. IEEE Transactions on Image Processing (1997)
66. Cabeen, K., Gen, P.: Image Compression and the Discreet Cosine Transform. Student Project in Linear Algebra. College of the Redwoods (1998)
67. Sujatha, S.S., Sathik, M.: A novel pixel based blind watermarking algorithm by applying Fibonacci transform. In: Proceedings of the 1st Amrita ACM-W Celebration on Women in Computing in India (A2CWiC 2010), vol. 39, p. 6. ACM, NY (2010)
68. Ganesan, K., Guptha, T.K.: Multiple Binary Images Watermarking in Spatial and Frequency Domains. Signal & Image Processing: An International Journal (SIPIJ) 1(2) (2010)
69. Aggarwal, E.D., Kaur, S., Anantdeep, E.: An Efficient Watermarking Algorithm to Improve Payload and Robustness without Affecting Image Perceptual Quality. Computer Science - Computer Vision and Pattern Recognition (2010)
70. Sathik, M.M., Sujatha, S.S.: An Improved Invisible Watermarking Technique for Image Authentication. International Journal of Advanced Science and Technology (IJAST) 24 (2010)
71. Sathik, M.M., Sujatha, S.S.: Wavelet Based Blind Technique by Espousing Hankel Matrix for Robust Watermarking. International Journal of Advanced Science and Technology (IJAST) 26 (2011)
72. Kusyk, J., Eskicioglu, A.M.: A semi-blind logo watermarking scheme for color images by comparison and modification of dft coefficients. ACM Multimedia and Security Workshop (2005)

An Exploratory Study on the Trend of Smartphone Usage in a Developing Country

Mohd Azam Osman[1], Abdullah Zawawi Talib[1], Zainal Abidin Sanusi[2], Tan Shieng Yen[1], and Abdullah Sani Alwi[3]

[1] School of Computer Sciences, Universiti Sains Malaysia
[2] Center of Global Sustainability Studies, Universiti Sains Malaysia
11800 USM, Pulau Pinang, Malaysia
[3] Strategy Department & Creative Industrial Policy
MSC Malaysia 63000 Cyber Jaya, Selangor, Malaysia
{azam,azht}@cs.usm.my, zainals@usm.my,
tsy09_com036@student.usm.my, sanialwi@mdec.com.my

Abstract. The purpose of this study is to better understand the current dynamics of the Malaysian market for mobile content and applications. This paper presents the result of a survey on the trend of smartphone from the perspective of end consumers. The data was collected from 1814 respondents across major cities in Malaysia. This study has looked into the familiarity of users towards smartphones, choices of smartphone brand and service providers, and most importantly the determinants that influence their purchasing decision. Additionally, the consumers' preferences on smartphone specifications such as design, computing power, operating platform, and price are investigated. The statistics presented is to provide fundamental information regarding the status and trends in the smartphone market in Malaysia. Such information is useful for academics to the development of future works in the field, and for smartphone manufacturers, application developers and other stakeholders to plan their direction in the Malaysian smartphone market.

Keywords: Mobile phone, Smartphone, Market survey, Consumers study.

1 Introduction

Mobile phone usage has proliferated in recent years. Some areas of the world have enjoyed rapid deployment and high penetration of mobile telephony. 70% of the world's population own at least one mobile phone. Based on the statistics, children in United States now are more likely to own a mobile phone than a book, with eighty five % of kids owning a phone as to only 73% owning books [1]. Without exception, Malaysia is one of the countries riding the wave of telecommunication evolution. Mobile phone usage in Malaysia has gained the ever increasing momentum. It is reported that 85% of Malaysians own mobile phone(s) [2].

Most of the mobile phones nowadays are addressed as 'smartphone', as they offer more advanced computing power and connectivity than a contemporary mobile phone. Literally, the smartphone is a handheld computer, as it is powerful enough to

E. Ariwa and E. El-Qawasmeh (Eds.): DEIS 2011, CCIS 194, pp. 387–396, 2011.

deliver various functionalities comparable to a computer. The release of dual-core processors smartphone recently has further reaffirmed this assertion.

With the sheer size of smartphone market, it influences the economic growth in a country and provides job opportunities in the economic chain [3]. Regardless of the macro impact of the smartphone market, the demands largely depend on the individual consumers. Hence, an understanding of the smartphone market and trends from the perspective of consumers is valuable.

2 Problem Statements

Despite the pervasiveness of smartphone penetration in Malaysia, surveys that have been carried out is still less and far between. Moreover, most of the previous studies focused on the typical of mobile phone usage [4-6], the 'smartness' of the mobile phone are much neglected. Hence, the overall picture of smartphone market in Malaysia is unclear, and the statistics are hardly available. Hence, this study serves to provide the information on the smartphone trends and consumers' preferences in Malaysia.

Such information is vitally important for both academics and practitioners. From the academic viewpoint, the overview of the smartphone market in Malaysia provides them a foundation where they further design their research. On the other hands, practitioners such as mobile phone manufacturers, application developers, and relevant stakeholders in the industry would greatly appreciated the information as it can be used to strategize their marketing strategies, and plan for the future directions.

3 Research Methodology

3.1 Overview of Methods

In order to collect generalizable data that represent the whole population from the samples, questionnaire survey is adopted as a data collection method. Moreover, questionnaire survey is a common method used in similar researches. This study collects primary data through questionnaire survey that targets at individual users. Subsequently, the data collected is analyzed using appropriate non-parametric analysis method and presented the data in an intuitive and insightful presentation format.

3.2 Subject and Procedures

The data used in this study were collected via both online and offline self-administrated survey. The data was collected from the publics across the main cities in Malaysia. Publics in main cities are selected as the respondents because they constitute the major propositions of Smartphone user in Malaysia. Hence, it implies that the purposive sampling method is adopted in this study.

The questionnaire items are designed in such way that technical jargons are minimized, in order to enhance the understandability for the users from different knowledge backgrounds. At the end of data collection process, a total of 1814 sets of questionnaire have been successfully collected and usable. By acquiring this large sample size, the data collected is speculated to has low level of random errors, and the responses should be well distributed over all answer categories [7]. Thus, the quality of data is considered as fairly good, and suitable for data analysis.

4 Data Analysis

4.1 Profile of Respondents

Demographic variables indicate the profile of respondents, which could also be helpful for the understanding of the subsequent analysis of the outcomes. Table 1 shows the demographic of the respondents. The statistics shows approximately 90% of respondents are below 36 years old. This result is consistent to previous studies which found that majority of the smartphone users are teenagers and younger adults [8].

Table 1. Profile of Respondents

Item	Frequency	Percentage (%)
Gender		
Male	947	52.2
Female	867	47.8
Total	1814	100
Age		
16 and Less	77	4.2
17 – 26	1178	64.9
27 – 36	378	20.8
37 – 46	101	5.6
47 – 56	64	3.5
More than 57	16	0.9
Total	1814	100
Education level		
Secondary	740	40.8
Bachelor	856	47.2
Master	94	5.2
Ph. D	17	0.9
Others	107	5.9
Total	1814	100
Occupation		
Government	118	6.5
Professional	165	9.1
Self-Employed	146	8.0
Freelancer	793	43.7
Student	176	9.7
Executive	29	1.6
Management	143	7.9
Retired	71	3.9
Unemployed	22	1.2
Others	151	8.3
Total	1814	100

4.2 Familiarity towards Smartphone

Fig. 1 illustrates the familiarity of respondents toward Smartphone. The data shows that the approximately 72% of respondents are common users, about 17% are Smartphone fan, while about 11 % work in the field related to mobile. This implies that majority of consumers in Malaysia are common users, with a typical level of knowledge that is sufficient for typical usage of mobile phone such as making phone call, SMS, MMS, multimedia playing, and operating common applications.

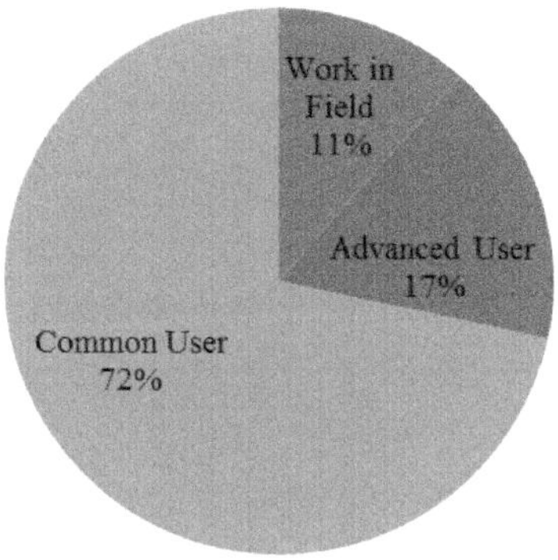

Fig. 1. Familiarity of Respondents towards Smartpohone

Fig. 2 has pointed out that male consumers tend to have higher familiarity towards smartphone compared to their female counterparts. It implies that smartphones as a kind of technologies do inherit the nature of general technology, in which male users are speculated to have higher interest and skills in technology [9].

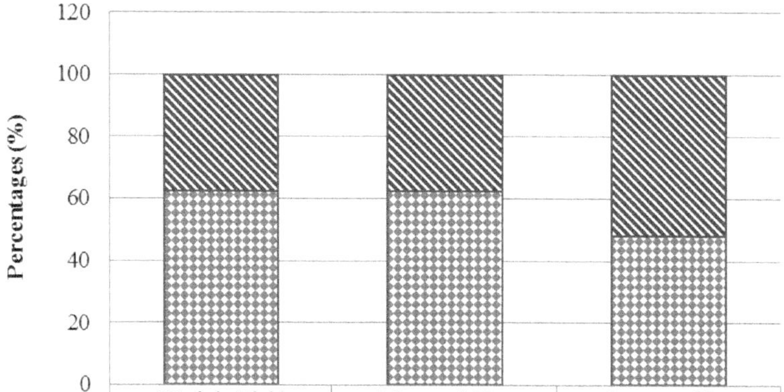

	Work in Field	Advanced User	Common User
Female	37.7	37.7	51.8
Male	62.3	62.3	48.2

Fig. 2. Familiarity Crosstab by Gender

4.3 Brands and Service Providers

Among the respondents, Nokia (40%) is the most popular brand, followed by Sony Ericsson (34%) and Apple iPhone (11%). Blackberry and HTC respectively constitute five percent and four percent of the total. As the brand is closely related to the operating platform, this information provides a hint to application developers about the common operating platforms in Malaysia.

In terms of service provider, majority of the respondents prefer Maxis (47%) and DiGi (39%), and a small %age prefers Celcom (13%). All of the service providers do provide 3G data services. DiGi offers unlimited data plan at approximately USD 27 dollars per month, while Maxis offers various data plans ranged from 3 gigabytes data limit at the price USD 27 dollars per month, to 12 gigabytes data limit at the price of USD 66 dollars per month. The prices of 3G data services have become reasonable and affordable by majority of the consumers. Hence, it is not irrational to posit that the competitive pricing of 3G data service has contribute to the popularity of 3G smartphone in Malaysia.

4.4 Preferences of Internet Connection Methods

The data also indicate that more respondents prefer to connect to Internet through Wi-Fi (62%) than 3G (38%). This implies that the Wi-Fi wireless network adapter is perceived as a necessity in the Smartphones. Moreover, 3G wireless data services are gaining momentum in Malaysia as the competitive price offered by service providers and the signal coverage areas are significantly expanded.

4.5 Determinants of Purchasing Decision

As a main interest of this study, the determinants of smartphone purchasing decision have been identified and discussed. Table 2 shows the percentage of total respondents that have chosen a particular determinant.

Table 2. Factors of Acquiring Smartphone

Determinants	Percentage (%)
Trend in community	35.6
Needs	34.4
Software	33.1
Cost of plan	28.8
Hardware	17.6
Signal reception	11.0
Others	3.5

For instance, 35.6% of the total 1814 respondents reported that the trend in community is important criterion that influences smartphone purchasing decision. This result implies that marketing and promotion remain as the vitally effective influencers that shape the trend of smartphone market. The next most important determinants are the needs for the smartphone and software preferences. The results suggest that consumers would adopt smartphone not because they actually needed the smartphone, but they were much influenced by the trends and norms in the society.

The crosstab analysis on the data shows 35.6 % of the respondents who perceived trend as a factor influencing their decision are fairly equal in in terms of gender. The same situation applies on needs, cost of plan, and others; they are all considerably equal in terms of gender.

Nonetheless, the percentage of male respondents who choose software and hardware as the purchasing determinant are obviously higher than the percentage of female respondents. For example, 61% of the respondents who agreed that hardware is important are male, whereas only 39% of those who agreed on this are female. It implies that male consumers tend to perceive hardware and software of smartphones as an important factor than the female consumers do.

4.6 Preferences of Smartphone Specifications

Additionally, the preferences of respondents on specification of Smartphone device are presented in the Table 3. Based on Table 3, the design of smartphones is reported as the most common specification that user considers when buying a smartphone, where 56% of all respondents feel that it is important. According to the statistics, built-in Wi-Fi adapter is the second most common specification that is important to consumers, and this is followed by computing power. Crosstab analysis on the Wi-Fi adapter by age suggests that consumers from all age groups are equally perceive Wi-Fi adapter as important to them (about 40%), with exception of those older than 57 year olds. Surprisingly, only 30.2% of the total respondents reported that price factor is a consideration in purchasing decision.

Table 3. Importance of Device Specifications

Specifications	Percentage
Design	56.0
Built-in Wi-Fi Adapter	38.5
Computing Power	34.2
Price	30.2
Screen Size	28.5
Music Player and Formats	28.3
Simplicity	24.5
Brand	22.2
Battery Life	19.7
Operating Platform	12.3
Business Supports	8.4
Other	2.7

Fig. 3 shows the percentage of respondents who agreed that design is an important factor, categorized by age groups. The result implies that the design is less important to the older consumers, compared to their younger counterparts. With regard to the operating platform, the data implies that male consumers tend to perceive operating platform as an important criterion to be taken into account. This assertion is supported by the data in which the respondents who agreed that operating platform is important constitute 70% male respondents, whereas only 30% female.

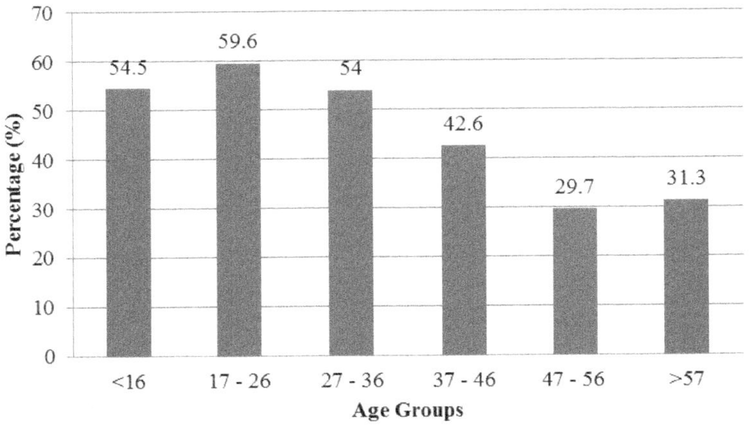

Fig. 3. Crosstab Analysis of Design by Age

The statistics in Fig. 4 indicate that computing power of the Smartphone is perceived to be more important by younger age groups, compared to their older counterparts. This might imply that younger adults are particular about the computing power of smartphone as they are heavy users of applications, games, flash, and media.

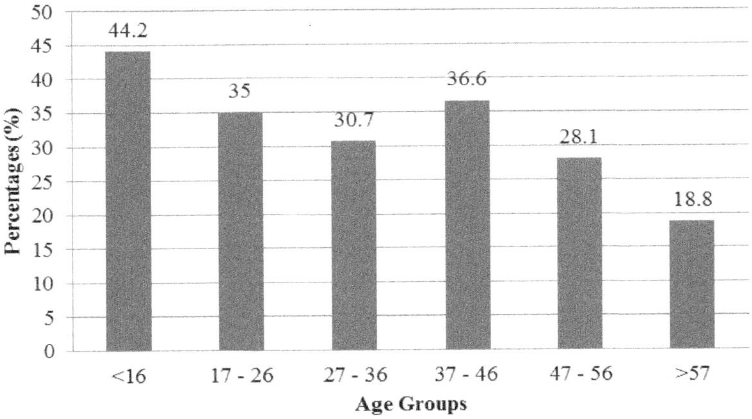

Fig. 4. Computing Power by Age

4.7 Usage of Smartphones

This study has examined the pattern of smartphone usage. The results are shown in Table 4. The most common usage of smartphone is still related to its core functionalities which are to make phone call, and SMS. Interestingly, the 40 % of the respondents have reported that they use smartphone for instant messaging daily. This would imply that consumers no longer solely depend on computer to send instant messages, but smartphone is another important platform for the consumers to interact with others through instant messaging.

According to the data analysis, entertainment is another major type of smartphone usage. Entertainment refers to the usage of music playing, movies, and games. Hence, the finding suggests that other than as a means of communication, smartphone is perceived by consumers as a source of entertainment.

Table 4. Usage Patterns of Smartphone

Usage	Daily	Few Times a week	Weekly	Rarely	Never
Make a phone call	82.45%	12.10%	2.05%	2.83%	0.55%
Check e-mail	21.43%	17.32%	7.88%	17.05%	36.31%
Business	15.77%	11.94%	10.16%	21.32%	40.81%
Entertainment	26.54%	23.82%	12.49%	20.04%	17.10%
Studying	18.54%	21.99%	12.27%	22.10%	25.10%
Browsing Web page	23.26%	18.38%	11.10%	20.77%	26.49%
SMS	85.23%	8.44%	2.44	2.11%	1.78%
Instant messaging	40%	16.55%	6.44%	14.27%	22.71%
GPS	11.16%	12.60%	8.55%	24.04%	43.64%
Read PDF/Word	10.77%	12.49%	8.72%	21.32%	46.70%
Others	14.32	3.22%	2.72%	7.61%	72.12%

5 Discussions

This exploratory study has discovered few main findings which have been discussed in this section. The statistics show that consumers from older age groups tend to be not particular about the technical specification of smartphone such as operating platform, computing power, and design. The plausible explanation would be, older consumers focus on the core functions of mobile phone such as making phone call and SMS. Thus, as long as the mobile phones support the basic usage and priced reasonably, they will go for the choice.

Hence, the result of this study suggests that the largest market for smartphones is consumers from younger age groups with purchasing power. Additionally, younger consumers, especially male would pay more attention on the technical aspects of the smartphone such as computing powers, operating platform, and software applications. This is reasonable as younger smartphone users are often the consumers of media and entertainment applications. Since these usages require high demand on computing power, the younger consumers will pay attention to the performance of the smartphone, in order to ensure smooth and delightful experience.

Furthermore, this study discovered that selling price is the most important factor that affects smartphone purchasing decision, whereas other factors such as design, features, and performance do influence the decision significantly as well. Interestingly, the report shows that trends in the society have more influence than the actual needs in the purchasing decision of a smartphone. In other words, smartphone is not merely a commodity to fulfill the communication requirements, but smartphone would be an indicator of status, prestige, and lifestyle.

6 Conclusion

This study has provided insightful overview of the smartphone trends and market in Malaysia, which could also be applicable to other developing countries in similar region. Based on these exploratory findings, future work can include refining the research to cater the specific domain of the smartphone study. For instance, empirical research can be conducted to systematically test and identify the determinants of smartphone purchasing decisions. Moreover, specific study can examine the influences of marketing strategies on the smartphone demands. For practitioners, the information provided here would be useful for them to have a better sense of the smartphone market in Malaysia and the region, and to inspire them to come out with effective commercial strategy.

Acknowledgments. This study is supported by MSC Malaysia and Universiti Sains Malaysia. We would like to acknowledge to all students who were involved in this study.

References

1. International Telecommunication Union, `http://www.itu.int/ITUD/ict/statistics/ict/index.html`
2. M.C.a.M. (ed.): Featuring the Handphone Users Survey In: Commission, Malaysian Communications and Multimedia Commission, Cyberjaya, Selangor Darul Ehsan (2007)
3. Garbacz, C., Thompson Jr., H.G.: Demand for telecommunication services in developing countries. Telecommunications Policy 31, 276–289 (2007)
4. Ishii, K.: Internet use via mobile phone in Japan. Telecommunications Policy 28, 43–58 (2004)
5. May, H., Hearn, G.: The mobile phone as media. International Journal of Cultural Studies 8, 195–211 (2005)

6. Yang, K.C.C.: Exploring factors affecting the adoption of mobile commerce in Singapore. Telematics and Informatics 22, 257–277 (2005)
7. Kothari, C.R.: Research Methodology: Methods and Techniques. New Age International Publishers, New Delhi (2002)
8. Wilska, T.-A.: Mobile Phone Use as Part of Young People's Consumption Styles. Journal of Consumer Policy 26, 441-463 (2003)
9. Comber, C., Colley, A., Hargreaves, D.J., Dorn, L.: The effects of age, gender and computer experience upon computer attitudes. Educational Research 39, 123 - 133 (1997)

Service-Oriented Enterprise: Taking the Next Step beyond Agility in the Digital Economy

Marinela Mircea

Economic Informatics Department, Academy of Economic Studies Bucharest, Dorobanti #15-17, Bucharest, Romania
mmircea@ase.ro

Abstract. In the digital economy, every enterprise has the tendency of becoming an intelligent enterprise and, through the means of innovational information technology solutions, of gaining competition advantage on the market. At the same time, management and service-oriented technology and principles caught the attention of researchers with the purpose of finding new methods to increase the enterprise agility. At present there are some problems regarding the transition to service-oriented architecture and the management of service-oriented enterprise. The study analyses the impact of service-oriented architecture on enterprise and some aspects regarding agile architecture for the service-oriented enterprise as an important factor in the economic development of enterprises within the knowledge-based society.

Keywords: agile enterprise, digital economy, service-oriented architecture, service-oriented enterprise, cloud computing, business process management, innovation management.

1 Introduction

The study will provide knowledge in the field of services-oriented enterprise (SOE) and some references to modern approach on ensuring enterprise agility. They will be created by starting from the present stage of the domain of expertise and taking into account the effect of synergy generated by the knowledge-based feature of modern society, with a major impact on the information system of grounding management decision within an organization. At the same time, the research will develop knowledge in the field of management and information and communications technology.

The reason behind the study results both from the goal of every enterprise, which is maximizing profit, and from the reason for which information exists and is produced in a society, namely grounding decisions as the main instrument of management. Furthermore, under the conditions of digital economy and of adoption on an increasingly larger scale of tactical and strategic management (beside operational management) within organizations, increasing business agility becomes an obvious objective, with real chances of becoming imperative at the level of enterprise. The key to business agility is service-oriented integration (SOI), and the key to SOI is the service-oriented architecture (SOA) [1]. Service orientation leads to new types of

E. Ariwa and E. El-Qawasmeh (Eds.): DEIS 2011, CCIS 194, pp. 397–409, 2011.

enterprise that requires a service-oriented management that enables encapsulation and composition. Migrating to a service-oriented architecture requires proactive management of the enterprise to achieve agility and requires knowledge regarding:

- *The impact of service-oriented architecture on enterprise*. The research made until now in the field of management and service-oriented technology led to a series of managerial recommendations with the goal of increasing the value of business using service-oriented technology (details in [2]). There have also been proposed elements of change in management and adjustment of business functions to service-oriented technology. We are presently facing the need of creating an environment for the adjustment of enterprise to service-oriented technology. The nature of business activities may critically determine the success of the services' paradigm.
- *Agile architecture for the service-oriented enterprise*. At present, there are a limited number of enterprise architectures, architectures of systems of applications and performance analysis environments for service-oriented environments. In addition, development methodologies, performance analysis and optimization models for service-oriented enterprises/networks of enterprises are rare and not very systematic. The element of novelty resides in the creation of an architectural model for service-oriented enterprises that should eliminate the gap between the level of the business and the level of the information system, and should allow transformation of organization knowledge into technical knowledge, needed by information systems in order to ensure interoperability between partners. The architectural model must comprise operation and development agile architecture for the integration of the enterprise within the service-oriented environment. The level of complexity resides in the collaborative context and in the effort to optimize the architecture of service-oriented enterprises.

2 Background

Management and service orientation drew the attention of researchers and systems developers within the past years when it comes to finding certain methods to gain *business agility* that can offer flexible business processes and greater business integration meant to increase the value of services offered to customers [3]. Service orientation can be applied across enterprises with beneficial effects on human resources, business management and information technology (figure 1). Achieving business agility involves monitoring the evolution of human resources, business processes and information systems. Thus, business agility can be achieved through agility of human resources, of business processes and of information technology.

Agility of human resources can be achieved through an organizational culture that provides a workforce intensively based on technological and business knowledge in all areas of business. The organizational culture must allow rapid adaptation of labor to the continuously changing business environment. *Agility of business processes* can be obtained through business process management (BPM) ensured by the enterprise's information systems.

Agility of information technology addresses mainly the technological architecture and infrastructure through the SOA. Technological agility currently represents a wide area of research as information technology creates most of the problems in

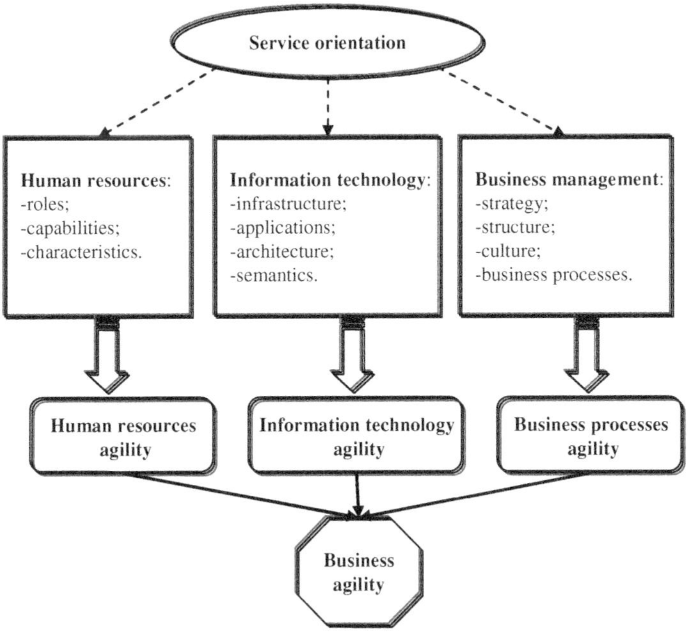

Fig. 1. The influence of service orientation

achieving agility. Moreover, integration in the enterprise represents the least mature category of capabilities, as for many enterprises it remains a goal to be achieved and not a reality. SOA can be seen as a paradigm for solving problems of integration at the application level. In addition, combined use of SOA and BPM has facilitated a new phase of development of flexible business processes, namely *service-oriented business processes*.

Taking into account the managerial recommendations and the practice in this field, in order to achieve success in the transition to SOA, one recommends that any organization should create a transition environment [2]. This particular environment should be based on management instruments for the existing knowledge within the organization, the elements under transition should be included into a management program and at the organization level, and a policy of organization change management should be developed.

Reengineering organizations' architecture by transition to SOA is a complex and long process, which demands rigorous analyses and well founded transition strategies. Strategies involve leadership engagement, roles and team structures, governance, skills and innovation management, adaptive culture. At present, there are few practical methods for engineering, reengineering and building of the architecture (details in [2]). Strategy of passing to SOA is not to be created for its own sake, but must follow the strategic goals of the organization.

Currently, enterprises are in various stages of migration to SOA. Thus, enterprises are likely to be encountered during starting stage (using web services in different departments, using service-oriented computing - SOC), using services between departments, between business, and at the organizational level. SOC is a new paradigm for delivering useful functionality in a cost effective way. It forms a new trend to be adopted by organizations in mitigating legacy system problems in order to maximize interoperability, reusability, flexibility and cost efficiency [4].

The trend in recent years is the migration to new types of enterprises, namely *service-oriented enterprises*. They exceed the SOA promises to increase agility, providing vision on demand. Service-oriented enterprise integrates the latest technologies with service-oriented business processes within an approach in which each participant can be seen as a provider and as a consumer of services. According to [5], within a service-oriented enterprise, everything is a service and the enterprise itself is a service and creates new space for agility and innovation for the enterprise. We can say that SOE is an enterprise that has applied service orientation in all core operations and business management.

SOE, SOA and SOC represent the result of a transition in several stages to the service-oriented environment (figure 2). Consequently, transition management is one of the most critical concerns in the long ramp-up to service orientation everywhere [6].

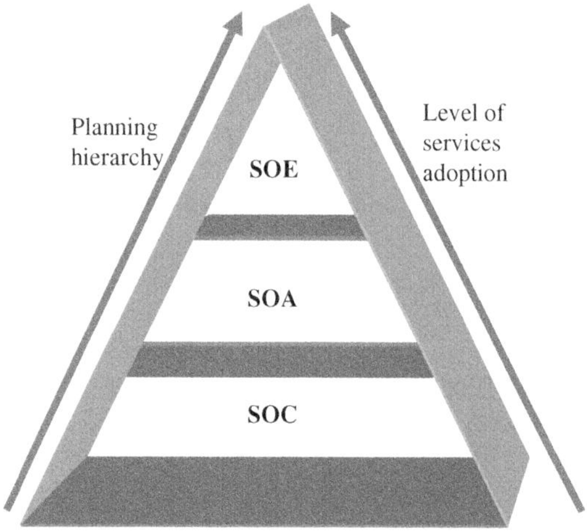

Fig. 2. Service orientation; level of adoption

3 Service-Oriented Enterprise – Modern Approach to Increase Agility in Digital Economy

The aim of any enterprise within the digital economy is becoming intelligent and obtaining advantage on the market through innovative approaches. At the same time, the collaborative environment involves the need for modern solutions to cope with the complex interactions between participants and the frequently changing market. In these circumstances, enterprises tend to go beyond agility and achieve a dynamic vision on demand. This can be achieved through the transition to SOE. Transition involves agile architectures and major effects at the organizational level.

The increasing popularity of SOA and web services is a step forward in considering the decision to integrate services in the organization or to migrate to SOE.

Although it offers many benefits recognized by many experts in the field, SOA is not a guarantee of success. SOA is a solution that generates complexity, costs of migration, involving important organizational resources that are often unavailable in organizations. Moreover, successful implementation depends on the organization and other factors considered critical in the decision to migrate.

In order to be successful in passing the SOE the following activities are required: identifying the impact of SOA on the organization; analyzing the opportunity of transition to SOE; identifying the most suitable/modern approach regarding organizational architecture; designing the architecture of the new enterprise; migration strategy; migration and efficient management of change; permanent audit of the solution. We shall analyze below the impact of SOA on the enterprise, with special focus on the management, and we shall present the elements of service-oriented enterprise architecture, with a special focus on the agility feature.

3.1 Impact of Service-Oriented Architecture on Enterprise

It is important to determine the impact of service-oriented architecture on the enterprise and the business models, and to identify solutions of adjustment of the management to service-oriented technology. The potential benefits of service-oriented architecture are recognized by many organizations in terms of [7]: a more agile business, shorter time in reaching the market, and more effective collaboration with suppliers and customers. In reality, realizing those benefits depends, in large measure, on whether executive leadership can effectively manage the long-term journey toward a SOA-based enterprise.

SOA brings major changes into the enterprise. One of the best approaches on managing changes and impact on enterprise is through clearly articulated service level agreements [8]. According to [8], this will ensure everyone concerned with the understanding of expectations regarding capabilities, capacity and availability. Incorporating organizational redesign is a complex task. This is done by modifying existing structures, by instituting new human resource and agility practices, by integrating new management principles, and by developing new organizational culture. All of these changes need to be performed without major disruptions and with efficient and proactive management. Some examples of effects and changes of SOA on enterprise are presented in table 1.

Organizations must translate their systems from the existing architectures to service-oriented architectures in a manner that does not impede the ongoing necessary functionality of the technology. Furthermore, the act of redesign is not sufficient to guarantee that the resulting business services will meet the needs of the business [1]. Transition to service-oriented enterprise requires loosely coupled enterprises that are based on the role of definitions of service consumers and service providers and the understanding of their relationships. The new organizational structure needs to be optimized to cater for business agility needs, streamline process and communication, minimize bureaucracy and provide results-driven output ([14], [15]).

Several specific change management activities and emphases will be particularly important for executing an overall SOA strategy and journey on the path to high performance [7]: leadership engagement, organization design, roles and team, structures, culture, governance, skills and talent management. While service-oriented

Table 1. Examples of enterprise changes

Element	Traditional enterprise	Service-oriented enterprise
Organization	functional and bureaucratic	cross functional and process centered
Ownership and control	sole, central control	shared, decentralized control
Responsibility	forced upon and divided	taken upon and shared
Management	top-down, power	meet in the middle
People	as resource of the enterprise	that are the enterprise
Work	traditional perspective	new perspective on work, more work based on knowledge
Culture	command, control, and conservative culture	reuse and adaptive culture
Information technology	management of traditional information technology infrastructures	- management of SOA services - dynamic and re-use application
Business process	traditional and connected business process	- business process can be created by using a composition of existing services in a new enhanced service [9] - new stage of business processes evolution, that of service-oriented business processes [10] - agile business process
Business process management	continuous improvement and optimize, but un-scalable and un-adaptive process [11]	- BPM in accordance with the principles of abstraction, specialization, in addition to the flexibility that service-oriented architecture promotes - the need for a different type of approach, such as Case Management [12] - the case-oriented BPM is considered to be the best solution of automation of Case Management [13]

enterprise enables and even drives organizational change, it also requires executives, enterprise architects and program managers to think and act differently or simply find themselves in possession of new problems with few or no new benefits [6].

Regarding the decision-making process, there are different types of organizations, according to the level of adoption of services (figure 3). In [16], Malone, identifies four different forms of decentralization that vary according to the decision-making process.

The organizations are being rethought, emphasizing on the flexibility and strong sensitivity to environment and the use of strategic systems in real time [17]. In addition, under conditions of recession businesses must use all the opportunities to maximize performance and minimize costs. In this context, the management passes through the transition from certain activities to the management under crisis conditions that requires innovation and ingenuity [18]. Therefore, each organization

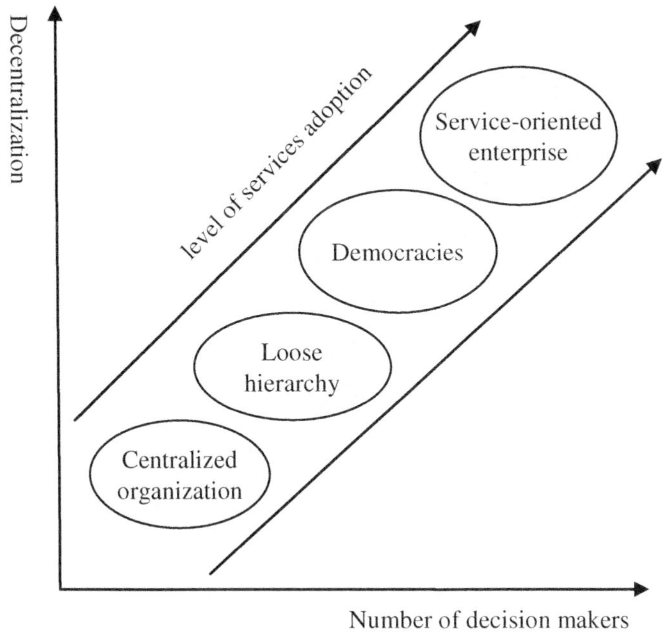

Fig. 3. Different types of organizations, according to the level of services adoption

tends to become an intelligent organization and to gain competition advantage on the market by the use of new and innovative business intelligence (BI) solutions for enterprise management.

Integration of a BI solution involves a large human and financial capital, for many small and medium-sized organizations, this representing an objective to attain and not a reality. In addition, service-oriented enterprise involve the use of BI solutions built on SOA that makes possible a seamless integration of technologies into a coherent business intelligence environment, thus enabling simplified data delivery and low-latency analytics [19]. Under these conditions, large investments in traditional BI solutions are often unpractical and unattractive, while popular solutions based on cloud computing, called Cloud BI or Software as a Services BI or BI services on demand are increasingly popular.

More details about aspects of the mix BI and cloud computing, putting the stress on the integration of a Cloud BI solution within organizations are presented in [17]. In addition, the opportunity of using a Cloud BI solution is analyzed in contrast with that of using a traditional BI solution, through the ROI (Return of Investment) indicator.

3.2 An Agile Architecture for Service-Oriented Enterprises

In order to be agile, the organization must continuously control the dynamics of the evolution of its business process, human resources and information system. At this level, agility requires a projection into the future, which must be instrumented via formal techniques, such as rational anticipation [20]. According to the Gartner Group, the agile organization must be "real-time, service-oriented and event-controlled". The agile organization requires agile architecture. The architecture must be analyzed in terms of service orientation in all its domains: ❶ business architecture, ❷ process architecture, ❸ data architecture, ❹ application architecture and ❺ technology architecture. Methods and practices of obtaining agility must be also identified for each domain.

According to [21], *business architecture* in a service-oriented enterprise is expressed by the following five models:

- business value model - describes the method of cooperation of the enterprise with other enterprises and the method of development of value;
- business structure model - expresses how an enterprise organizes its activity to non-overlapping functions;
- business behavior model - expresses how to determine the operations inside the business and shows behavior of business partners inside an ecosystem;
- business policy model - includes policies of business in supervising and leading all aspects of business architecture;
- business performance model - described the elements required for evaluation of performance of the enterprise based on performance indices.

An agile business architecture suppose understanding two main principles [22]: modularity ("process of identifying clusters of interdependent business activity and combining them into self contained modules") and end-to-end control ("all relevant module interface that enable service providers to fully shape the customer experience at all relevant touch points ").

The *process architecture* looks at processes (functions, activities, tasks, steps, flow, products) and events (triggers, cycles) and provides for the managers a comprehensive view on the activity of the organization. Process architecture includes elements like workflows, procedural rules, business cycles, functional decomposition.

As a response to the complex interactions between partners, integration of knowledge and business processes represents an important step in improving the agility of the organization [23]. For intensive knowledge based processes case management may be used, which provides a real time image on the current events and generates a rapid response to the organization's internal and external events. The dynamic capabilities provide agility through detection of patterns and rapid adjustment of business processes to events and agents (clients, businesspersons, analysts and programmers, process architects and analysts).

Data architecture includes those artifacts describing data and information (structuring data, information, knowledge, and intelligence dimensions as cohesive ontologies). Agile data architecture represents the methodology that allows a set of inter-related best practices to be coordinated and that provides the means by which to measure the success with the resulting solution [24].

Application architecture defining the desired future state, and formulating a realistic transition plan to achieve the service-oriented state (portfolios of systems of applications, interfaces, flows and structures of programs, software component architecture, portfolios of projects).

Technology architecture involves the selection and integration of software solutions, as well as the standards and infrastructure for achieving the service-oriented architecture (technological platforms, protocols and standards, networking topologies, software tools).

It is important to create an architectural model for SOE that eliminates the gap between the level of the business and the level of the information system, optimizes existing architectures, and increases enterprise agility. Architecture of the service-oriented enterprise is closely related to SOA, mounting to a bidirectional relationship between the two architectures (figure 4).

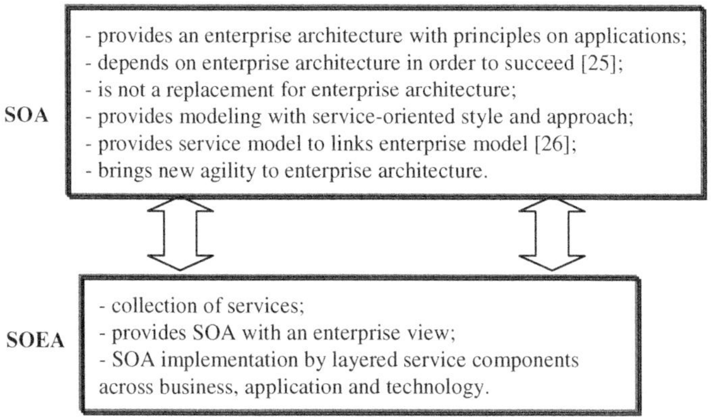

Fig. 4. The relationship between SOA and SOE architecture

Combining both paradigms, SOE/SOA becomes manifest in a three-stage model, consisting of the process model, service model, and technology model [27]. According to [27], "the process model corresponds to the previous business process modeling, the service model defines the services themselves and the relationship to the business processes, and the technology model defines the concrete implementation for realizing the services". Currently, with regard to business vision and the applicative architecture required to support it, three prevalent approaches collaborate complementarily in the search for the optimal solution:

- *BPM* is based on business modeling in order to optimize and adapt the whole set of activities [20]. BPM is considered to be a proactive instrument, allowing the organization to measure performance and make the necessary adjustments. In addition, BPM facilitates the gathering, simulation, and optimization of the knowledge on how people work and integrate them into the organization [23]. In order to achieve the business objectives, BI has to be included in each stage of the life cycle of business processes. Combining BPM and BI provides the input data for business decisions that execute the organization's strategy and in the end give the best results, applying intelligence into practice.
- *SOA* facilitates process instrumentation [20] and provides flexible software components that allow organizations to adapt quickly to the permanent demands for change of the market. SOA has the advantage of producing simple, modular, loosely

coupled components, therefore allowing for quick re-composition of the applicative frame of functionalities that they provide (details in [28], [29]).

- *Cloud computing* is considered the next step in the evolution of the internet, providing to the organization, against payment, the means of using information technology services, from infrastructure and capacities of calculation, applications and business processes to personalized collaboration [30]. Because they are complex platforms, it should be said that the agility of these solutions is difficult to test and validate.

SOA offers support in creating and managing shared services. Thus, several departments within the organization or/and organizations may create, maintain or operate common services accessible to everyone. SOA promotes the use of shared services provided locally or through cloud. The use of shared services offers benefits, such as costs reduction, fast access to the market, quality increase, but also challenges regarding security (number one challenge), loss of control, transition cost and others. The focus of cloud is in the provision and delivery of shared services by virtualizing the applications, platform and infrastructure so that the user of the service gets a seamless experience without being aware of the underlying provisioning methodology [31]. Cloud computing is helping organizations move towards an open and collaborative environment while reducing the costs of delivering and managing the needed services.

Cloud computing helps increasing SOA maturity in the organization through the cloud services. The new architecture of applications shall represent choreography of the best services created and/or selected through cloud. The enterprise architecture supports a service-oriented architecture in which information technology is provided through cloud. It supports a virtualized approach and assures the availability of the services, concerns regarding storage and system requirements. Also, by providing a virtual architecture, the capacity may be increased/diminished at request and the infrastructure resources used at high level. Cloud computing extends SOA environment at a virtual level, with increased capabilities of collaboration and efficiency increase.

Concerning the relationship between cloud computing and SOA/BPM it can be said that: ❶ at organization level cloud computing represents an extension of SOA and ❷ cloud computing is creating new opportunities for BPM product and service providers (details in [29], [32]). BPM combined with cloud computing technology may coordinate web services between users, information and systems, within/between organizations, the administration of business rules, real-time feedback in order to achieve tasks progress. It also may monitor results in relation to performance targets and may allow refining and permanent adjustment of flows for performance optimization [33]. Cloud computing combined with SOA also provides scalable services, universal access, models of new services, operational transparency and cost control. In addition, cloud is in many ways the next logical step beyond SOA [34]: ❶ "SOA applies the service principle to application software within the enterprise; ❷ cloud applies the same principle at the infrastructure and platform levels, as well as the application level, and between enterprises, as well as within them".

SOE architecture must allow aligning the business strategy with the information technology strategy. SOA offers alignment between the business processes and informational systems at the level of architecture, governance and communication. According to [35], SOA ❶ offers enterprise perspective, level of service granularity, architectural agility via decomposition for *alignment via architecture*, ❷ allows standard enforcement & performance measures, removing redundancy, streamlining operations, repository based, centralized information technology resource management, ease implementation based on service concepts for *alignment via governance* and ❸ offers service as a binding concept, social dimension for *alignment via communications*.

Using an integrated approach based on SOA, BPM and cloud computing may be a solution to obtain the agility and quick access to technology, with the achievement of savings at institution level. In addition, the solution may offer new opportunities to improve practices and attain innovation. The combination allows agile business that may confront the complex events that exist in the collaboration context. This entails the use of knowledge, processes, BI, cloud computing, SOA architectures with the purpose of ensuring enterprise's agility in a collaborative context in digital economy.

Considering that the simple adoption of information technology in the organization does not guaranty economic success, an analysis of the success in aligning information technology to the business requirements must be made. By using an evaluation environment may be established the degree in which information technology helps increasing the value added of the clients and reaching the organization objectives. At the same time, the evaluation and measurement of the costs and benefits for adopting the solution are important, these generally having major effects at the level of the business. Without a correct evaluation of the impact and implementation opportunity, the organization may confront itself with the situation of adopting a solution that does not lead to the expected results.

4 Conclusion and Future Research Directions

In the context of the digital economy, in order to ensure their development and especially their survival, enterprises must adapt on the way. Therefore, a SOA-based solution may be a response to rapid changes to which the enterprise is subject in the current business environment. Moreover, the use of SOA in combination with cloud computing may be a feasible solution to the challenges of the economic crisis. Through such a solution, the small, middle-sized or large enterprises may speculate market opportunities that under normal conditions would not be accessible.

Moreover, from the perspective of service characteristics, the adoption of solution based on SOA, BPM and cloud computing in business may be a prerequisite for the transition to a new form of innovative enterprises – the service-oriented virtual enterprise. Thus, by sharing resources and speeding up market integration, by speeding and streamlining business processes, migration to SOE may be a solution of adapting enterprises to the current social and economic conditions.

Regarding future direction of research related to this topic we mention:

- Creation of an environment for the migration to service-oriented technology, taking into account different factors, such as type of organization, objectives of the organization, the way of organization, the business environment and organizational culture, etc.
- Creation of an architecture for integration of the enterprise within the service-oriented environment. The level of complexity resides in the collaborative context and in the effort to optimize the architecture of service-oriented enterprises.

- Development of business intelligence architecture based on standards and oriented on services that should support solving integration problems and complex interactions between business partners. In order to achieve this objective, the strategies of engineering/reengineering of architectures shall be analyzed from the perspective of service orientation and a transition strategy of business intelligence architecture shall be proposed from the perspective of service orientation.

Acknowledgments. This work was supported by CNCSIS-UEFISCSU, project PN II-RU (PD), "Modern Approaches in Business Intelligence Systems Development for Service-Oriented Organizations Management", code 654/2010, contract no. 12/03.08.2010.

References

1. Bloomberg, J.: http://searchsoa.techtarget.com/tip/Why-service-oriented-management
2. Mircea, M., Andreescu, A.: Architecture Reengineering for Services Oriented Businesses. Journal of Applied Collaborative Systems 2, 55–66 (2009)
3. Demirkan, H., Kauffman, R.J., Vayghan, J.A., Fill, H.G., Karagiannis, D., Maglio, P.P.: Service-Oriented Technology and Management: Perspectives on Research and Practice for the Coming Decade. Electronic Commerce Research and Applications 7, 356–376 (2008)
4. Fang, C.F., Sing, L.C.: Collaborative Learning using Service-Oriented Architecture: A Framework Design. Knowledge-Based Systems 22, 271–274 (2009)
5. Graves, T.: The Service-Oriented Enterprise. Tetradian Books, England (2009)
6. Schekkerman, J.: What you all need to Know about Services Orientation! Structuring the Enterprise around Services. The Differences between Hype, Hope and Reality? In: IFEAD (2006)
7. Silverstone, Y., Nichols, D.: http://www.accenture.com/sitecollectiondocuments/pdf/SOA.pdf
8. Sweden, E.: http://www.enterprisearchitecture.info/Images/Documents/NASCIO_SOA_Research_Brief_2006.pdf
9. Maurizio, A., Sager, J., Jones, P., Corbitt, G., Girolami, L.: Service Oriented Architecture: Challenges for Business and Academia. In: Proceedings of the 41st Hawaii International Conference on System Sciences, pp. 315–340. IEEE Press, USA (2008)
10. Mircea, M.: Adapt Business Processes to Service Oriented Environment to Achieve Business Agility. Journal of Applied Quantitative Methods 4 (2010)
11. Madsen, M.: http://www.cgi.com/files/white-papers/cgi_whpr_67_soa_bpm_wp_e.pdf
12. Ghilic – Micu, B., Stoica, M., Mircea, M., Sinioros, P.: Cost - Performance Evaluation Environment for the Adoption of a Case Management Solution. Journal of Economic Computation and Economic Cybernetics Studies 1, 63–80 (2010)
13. Singularity, http://www.bptrends.com/publicationfiles/07-09-WP-CaseMgt-CombiningKnowledgeProcessWhite.doc-final.pdf
14. Bieberstein, N., Bose, S., Walker, L., Lynch, A.: Impact of Service-Oriented Architecture on Enterprise Systems, Organizational Structures, and Individuals. IBM Syst. J. 44, 691–708 (2005)

15. Cherbakov, L., Galambos, G., Harishankar, R., Kalyana, S., Rackham, G.: Impact of Service Orientation at the Business Level. IBM Syst. J. 44, 653–668 (2005)
16. Malone, T.: http://hbswk.hbs.edu/archive/4020.html
17. Mircea, M., Ghilic-Micu, B., Stoica, M.: Combining Business Intelligence with Cloud Computing to Delivery Agility in Actual Economy. Journal of Economic Computation And Economic Cybernetics Studies 1, 39–54 (2011)
18. Rosca, I., Moldoveanu, G.: Management in Turbulent Conditions. Journal of Economic Computation and Economic Cybernetics Studies and Research 2, 5–12 (2009)
19. Wu, L., Barash, G., Bartolini, C.: http://www.hpl.hp.com/personal/Claudio_Bartolini/download/soca07.pdf
20. Vickoff, J.P.: http://www.entreprise-agile.com/en/PumaIntroEN.pdf
21. Tohidi, H.: Modelling of Business Services in Service Oriented Enterprises. Procedia Computer Science 3, 1147–1156 (2011)
22. Lambrette, U., Gurley, H., Puopolo, S.: The Agile Business Architecture Creating Service Provider Value through Smart Sourcing. Cisco Internet Business Solutions Group, IBSG (2009)
23. Mircea, M., Ghilic-Micu, B., Stoica, M.: Combining Knowledge, Process and Business Intelligence to Delivering Agility in Collaborative Environment. In: Fischer, L. (ed.) 2010 BPM and Workflow Handbook, Spotlight on Business Intelligence, pp. 99–114. Future Strategies Inc., Florida (2010)
24. Lahanas, S.: Agile Data Architecture: Part 1 - Overview & Philosophy. Technical Report, Semantech Inc. (2007)
25. Greefhorst, D.: http://www.archixl.nl/files/lac2006_soea.pdf
26. Zhao, Y.: Service Oriented Enterprise Architecture and Service Oriented Enterprise. In: The 23rd Open Group Enterprise Architecture Practitioners Conference, Toronto, Canada (2009)
27. Siedersleben, J.: Component-Orientation in System Landscapes (Komponentenorientierung bei Systemlandschaften). Business & Information Systems Engineering (Wirtschaftsinformatik) 49, 110–117 (2007)
28. Mircea, M., Andreescu, A.I.: Agile Systems Development for the Management of Service Oriented Organizations. In: 11th International Conference on Computer Systems and Technologies, pp. 341–346. ACM Press, Sofia (2010)
29. Mircea, M., Andreescu, A.I.: Extending SOA to Cloud Computing in Higher Education. In: The 15th IBIMA Conference on Knowledge Management and Innovation: A Business Competitive Edge Perspective, pp. 602–615. International Business Information Management Association, Norristown (2010)
30. Cunningham, M.: Cloud Computing Enables Self-Serve BI. Technical report, Dashboard Insight (2010)
31. IMS Global Learning Consortium, http://www.imsglobal.org/soa/soawpv1p0/imsSOAWhitePaper_v1p0.pdf
32. Mircea, M.: SOA, BPM and Cloud Computing: Connected for Innovation in Higher Education. In: 2010 The International Conference on Education and Management Technology, pp. 456–460. IEEE Press, Chengdu (2010)
33. Barlow, G.: Business Process management and Cloud Computing. BPMinstitute.org (2009)
34. Hardin, C.: http://www.cioupdate.com/trends/article.php/11047_3863691_1/Service-Oriented-Architecture-and-the-Cloud.htm
35. Chen, H.M.: https://www.jyu.fi/it/laitokset/cs/en/infwest/hongmei

On Managing Services in Service-Oriented Architectures

Jürgen Dunkel and Carsten Kleiner

University of Applied Sciences & Arts Hannover, 30459 Hannover, Germany
{juergen.dunkel,carsten.kleiner}@fh-hannover.de

Abstract. In service-oriented architectures the management of services is a crucial task during all stages of IT operations. Based on a case study performed for a group of finance companies the different aspects of service management are presented. First, the paper discusses how services must be described for management purposes. In particular, a special emphasis is placed on the integration of legacy/non web services. Secondly, the service lifecycle that underlies service management is presented. Especially, the relation to SOA governance and an appropriate tool support by registry repositories is outlined.

Keywords: service management; service lifecycle; service semantics; service monitoring; service registry; service repository.

1 Introduction

Moving to service-oriented architecture (SOA) introduces a completely new structure of enterprise IT [1]. For each application in the enterprise reusable services must be defined encapsulating the implementation platforms and technologies used. Subsequently, these services can be orchestrated by process languages as BPEL [2] to compose complex and application spanning business processes that realize the different business strategies (see fig. 1).

Introducing SOA causes a paradigm shift: In SOA, reusable services are the crucial components of IT infrastructure. A service portfolio that is under continual development serves as the integration platform for enterprise-wide business processes. Managing the service portfolio is an essential task during IT operations. From a general perspective, moving to SOA let an enterprise substitute application and technology management by service management.

As one major goal SOA fosters the reuse of already existing services. Particularly, service management has to support all aspects of service-reuse. Especially, it has to deal with the following issues:

- *Finding a service*: Software developers and business process designers need decent support to decide whether the service portfolio contains an appropriate re-usable service. Otherwise, a new enterprise-wide usable service must be commissioned.
- *Selecting a service version*: If a suitable service has been found, the appropriate version of the service must be selected. Services will usually change over time so that different versions will co-exist. Version control

E. Ariwa and E. El-Qawasmeh (Eds.): DEIS 2011, CCIS 194, pp. 410–424, 2011.

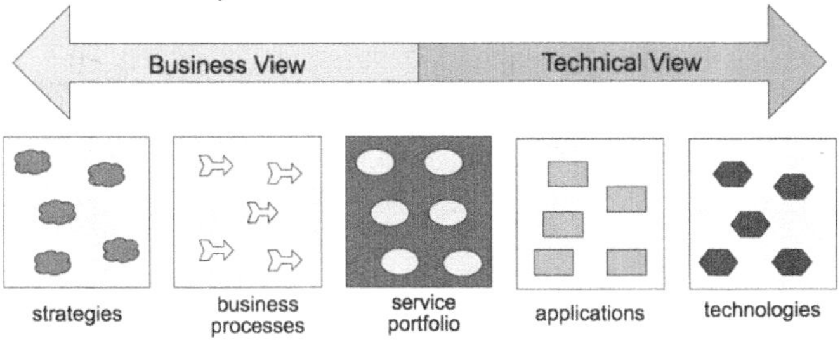

Fig. 1. Portfolio of services in a service-oriented architecture

regarding dependencies and incompatibilities between different service versions is indispensable for managing huge service portfolios. Therefore, change management is a significant aspect of service management.
- *Providing service access*: After the right version of a service has been chosen, the software developer must be provided with all information necessary to invoke the service, e.g. service signature, transport protocols and service endpoints.

To accomplish these objectives, service management has to overcome different challenges.

- *Service semantics*: The prerequisite of service-reuse is a complete understanding of the services provided. Firstly, semantics of each service must be precisely defined so that every service requester can understand all the effects and impacts of a service invocation. Furthermore, all non-functional aspects of a service such as quality of service (QoS) and service level agreements (SLAs) must be specified by formal contracts preventing differing interpretations. For instance, the security properties or performance characteristics of a service must be known in advance.
- *Heterogeneous technologies*: Big enterprises, especially in the financial sector are based on a heterogeneous IT infrastructure, including legacy systems, e.g. CICS transaction monitors or packaged systems like SAP. In a service-oriented architecture the services of the portfolio are implemented in different technologies running on different platforms. In real-world scenarios, a service-oriented architecture cannot only rely on Web services but must integrate legacy services based on proprietary protocols and technologies.
- *Tool support*: Big enterprises might have to administer several hundreds of services with a few thousands of operations. Due to the huge number of services, an appropriate tool support is indispensable. A service registry-repository must provide all necessary artifacts to find, understand and manage the services.

In summary, the real challenge in SOA-based enterprise IT is not developing a single service, but managing a huge amount of continuously changing services.

In this paper we want to present the results of a project we realized together with five enterprises from the financial sector. The main goal was to study and evaluate different concepts for service management. We laid the emphasis on a pragmatic approach, i.e. the objective was a service management process that could be easily established in the different enterprises. Furthermore, we investigated the particular requirements on an adequate tool support for service management.

The paper is organized as follows: In the next section we discuss how services in a service-oriented architecture can be described. In particular, different standards and formalisms for service description are discussed. In section 3, we outline the different aspects of service management related to the service life cycle. The subsequent section presents the requirements for SOA registry-repositories in some more detail. Finally, we summarize our results and provide an outlook on future lines of research and development.

2 Service Description

Many different aspects must be considered for using a service that is not self-implemented. First, the service description must specify the *service interface* providing the technical basis for service invocation. Furthermore, *non-functional aspects* such as quality of service (QoS) and service level agreements (SLAs) [3], [4] must be formally defined. For instance, details about the security mechanisms in place must be known before passing confidential data to a service. Other *management aspects* support life cycle management. For instance, version information with regard to service lifecycle has to be provided. Finally, the *semantics of a service* must be specified to decide if a certain service can fulfill the intended tasks. For Web services decent formalisms exist for most of these aspects of service descriptions. In this section, we will discuss how they can be applied for legacy services, which are services implemented by proprietary legacy technology.

2.1 Service Interface

Different middleware approaches provide well-established formalisms for describing service interfaces, e.g. Interface Definition Language (IDL) in Corba [5] and Web Service Description Language (WSDL) for Web services [6]. Especially WSDL allows a technology-independent description of all relevant technical aspects of a service. In WSDL four different parts are distinguished:

- The format of *input* and *output messages* that must be sent and received to interact with a service is defined by XML schema.
- All *operations* of a service are specified by the incoming and outgoing messages and the corresponding message exchange patterns (MEP) [6].
- The message format and the transport protocols are determined in the service bindings, e.g. message format (such as SOAP) and transport protocol (e.g. HTTP).
- Finally, the *service endpoints* describe the locations where the services reside.

A service description specifying these aspects is technically complete in the sense that the stubs classes responsible for service marshalling and demarshalling can be generated automatically.

For Web services, WSDL is the standard formalism for service description with a comprehensive tool support. However, for legacy services WSDL cannot be used directly. Nevertheless, WSDL is a good starting point for describing legacy services also, since WSDL is extensible and also because legacy system providers offer different tools to generate WSDL descriptions from legacy code.

- In legacy systems, the service operations with the corresponding input and output messages are described by proprietary data structures, e.g. by Cobol copybooks or 3270 screen buffers. To allow the usage of WSDL these legacy data structures must be defined by XML schema as in the type part of WSDL. Fortunately, there exist tools to convert legacy data to XML, e.g. CB2XML [7] or DFHLS2WS [8].
- Furthermore, the specification of the bindings and service endpoints must be adjusted to the technical characteristics of the legacy systems. The extensibility mechanisms of WSDL [6], [9] allow to incorporate arbitrary XML code in WSDL, e.g. to define legacy specific elements and attributes. For instance, to specify a Websphere MQ service endpoint, a technology-specific XML vocabulary determining queue names and delivery mechanisms can be defined.

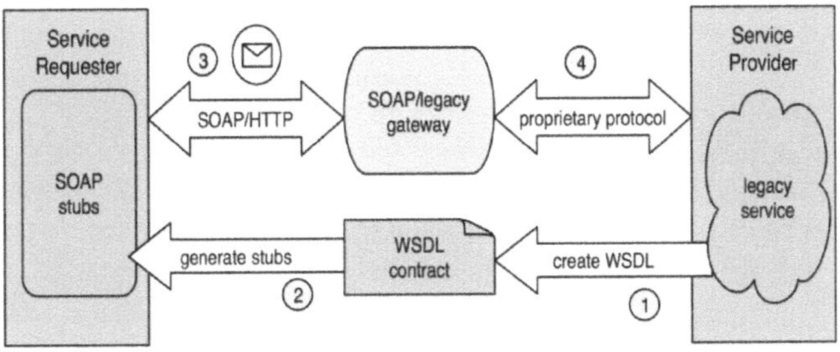

Fig. 2. Using SOAP/legacy gateways for integrating legacy services

Integration of legacy services can be accomplished by exchanging SOAP messages [10]. Figure 2 shows how a SOAP/ legacy gateway helps to integrate a legacy service in a service-oriented architecture.

1. A WSDL description is generated from the legacy service.
2. Stub classes are generated from the WSDL description.
3. The service requester invokes the legacy service using the stub classes that send the input data via SOAP messages to the gateway.
4. The gateway converts the SOAP message to legacy data (e.g. a Cobol copybook) and sends it via a proprietary protocol to the legacy system (e.g. to a Websphere MQ message queue).

Return values are sent back on exactly the opposite way to the service requester.

2.2 Non-functional Aspects

The usefulness of a particular service depends strongly on its non-functional properties [11]. Generally, we can distinguish constraints from service capabilities.

Constraints are conditions that the service requester has to fulfill. For instance, it might be necessary that the input message for a service contains a certain type of security token (e.g. a X.509 certificate). In contrast, *capabilities* describe a particular behavior that the service provider guarantees (under the condition that the requester satisfies all the constraints). For instance, it can be asserted that the response time is smaller than a threshold or that all data is encrypted according to specified mechanisms. The dependencies between constraints and capabilities can be defined in form of so-called Service Level Agreements (SLA).

It is crucial that non-functional aspects are described in a formal way for allowing service requester and server provider to rely on well-defined rules of service usage.

The WS Policy [12], [13] and the WS Policy Attachment [14] specifications address the description of non-functional aspects for Web services offering a rather general framework for specifying non-functional service aspects. WS Policy provides just formalisms for combing arbitrary assertions by using Boolean expression. However, formulating a specific assertion in a particular domain requires a domain-specific vocabulary. In some fields such a vocabulary has been already defined in corresponding WS* specifications, e.g. WS Security Policy [15] defines the vocabulary for security issues, and WS RM Policy Assertion [16], [17] that for reliability aspects. However, for many areas an own enterprise- or domain-specific vocabulary must be defined, e.g. for performance characteristics such as response time or throughput. Another example for missing standards is an assertion vocabulary for cost or billing aspects. Overall, even Web services are still lacking comprehensive standards for defining policies.

Legacy services can exploit WS Policy as a description language for non-functional properties without any problem, because WS Policy is completely technology-independent. However, the assertion-specific vocabulary defined in some WS* specs cannot be easily transferred to legacy services. Instead, legacy-specific vocabularies must be set up. One example is determining the transactional behavior of a service or defining the parameters for reliable message transport both of which might be technology-dependent.

2.3 Management Aspects

Management aspects cover all the necessary information for supporting lifecycle management. For each service its actual lifecycle state must be known: for instance, it is crucial, whether a service is just planned or already in operation. Because services are subject to further development and maintenance, different types of administrative information must be accessible. Examples for such management information are service *lease times*, and *version information*. Note, that services mutually rely on each other. Thus *dependencies* between different versions of services must be comprehensively defined.

Furthermore, each service must be *related to the organizational structure of an enterprise*. The usage of a particular service might be restricted to a specific group of persons. (For instance, a service for increasing the salary might only be accessible by people from the personnel office.) Therefore, for each service its appropriate access rights must be specified. Because SOA services are provided by different applications with their own user accounts, an enterprise-wide integration of user accounts in form of an *identity federation* is required.

For describing management aspects we can also make use of the WS Policy framework. Specific XML code can define state, version and dependency information. Unfortunately, there are no standards in this field yet, so that an enterprise-specific XML format has to be developed. Only for specifying authorizations a standard formalism already exists: the Security Assertions Markup Language (SAML) [18] allows the detailed specification of access rights for particular users in form of assertions.

2.4 Service Semantics

Each user of a service must completely understand its semantics, i.e. all of its impacts in a certain domain. Additionally, the service users must know all about its specific restrictions and specialties. Overall, semantic information about a service is the crucial criterion to choose the most appropriate out of a set of available services.

There are a lot of different ambitious approaches for describing semantics, e.g. using complex formalisms. Those are therefore mostly used in research projects. Instead, enterprises are looking for a pragmatic way to define service semantics. In general, a range of the following formalisms can be applied:

- *Informal textual descriptions*: Actually, only few enterprises use precise formalisms for service semantics. In our case study, all companies specified service semantics only informally by unstructured text documents. But they don't feel comfortable with this approach, because textual descriptions are imprecise and leave room for interpretations.
- *Design-by-contract*: One aspect of the semantical description of a service is a precise specification of the service interface. Design-by-contract uses pre and post conditions to describe the obligations of a service caller and the corresponding guarantees of the service provider. The Object Constraint Language (OCL) of UML [19] allows to formulate Boolean and temporal expressions for defining restrictions on operation parameters and return values. Actually, OCL is rather established in industry and most of the enterprises are planning to enrich the service description with OCL in the near future.
- *Ontologies*: An ontology is a semantic model to describe domain concepts including their properties, relations and dependencies. There are many different ontology languages. Well-known are e.g. RDF [20], RDF-S [21] and OWL [22]. Specialized on the semantic description of (Web) services are OWL-S [23] and WSMO [24]. For most enterprises approaches such as OWL-S or WSMO are too complex, difficult to understand and therefore too expensive [25]. A more pragmatic approach is the employment of Semantic Annotations for WSDL (SAWSDL) [26], which is a W3C standard allowing the annotation of WSDL language elements. In particular, the WSDL message types can contain pointers to an arbitrary conceptual model, which for instance is described in RDF-S, OWL or another ontology language.

In summary, it is challenging to introduce semantic service descriptions in an enterprise-wide service portfolio. But our case study has shown that an incremental process is promising. First, textual descriptions can be enriched by OCL pre and post conditions. Secondly, semantic annotations based on SAWSDL can be introduced, which presume that a conceptual domain model already exists. Finally, service ontologies could be developed. They allow advanced options such as using the RDF query language SPARQL [27], or exploiting inference mechanisms for intelligent reasoning.

3 Service Management during the Service Lifecycle

In a real-world enterprise IT adequate SOA governance must be in place making use of the service descriptions in all facets as described in the previous section. It is important to note that not only technical aspects are important for governance but the domain-specific business aspects alike. This can be inferred from the fact that SOA by its very nature is supposed to be accessible by both business as well as technology experts. Naturally, SOA should also be supported by appropriate software tools.

3.1 Prerequisite: SOA Governance

SOA governance is typically understood as the set of guidelines, rules and regulations within an organization on how the IT is structured and managed internally. It also consists of a set of processes that should be in place in order to enforce the aforementioned specifications.

Since SOA is both a technological as well as a business oriented pattern at least the first two steps in the development process differ significantly from traditional software development processes. This is due to the fact that the business departments are much more involved in the development process than before. Thus software tools used for service management have to be accessible by both technical as well as business experts. Ideally they are not only accessible but even improve and simplify the communication between those parties in the SOA process. In that way the software tools can be used to support all aspects of the process.

SOA governance does have to take all phases of the service lifecycle into account. The well-known (cf. [28]) simple lifecycle model which is sufficient for analyzing the governance aspects consists of three stages (Requirements & Analysis, Design & Development, IT Operations) which are depicted in fig. 3. It is important to stress that opposite to widespread belief, data from operations is also required in order to enable real management of a SOA. That is because services once in operation have to be monitored, their usage has to be controlled and other operations related information has to be analyzed. This analysis is often carried out by managing personnel. Thus software tools for SOA management have to provide an interface to managing personnel and also have to be integrated with IT operational systems. In fact, SOA specific extensions of those systems will be required in order to facilitate business activity monitoring.

Roles are often used within an organization in order to define responsibilities independent of particular beings. In SOA apart from the classical IT roles such as system analyst, application developer and IT administrator there is the need for defining an additional set of roles. In our case studies we identified the roles of domain owner, SOA architect, service developer (not to be confounded with application developer!) and metadata administrator. These roles seem to be of sufficient general importance even though an enterprise specific extension or adjustment may be required. In any case should software tools that support service management be able to

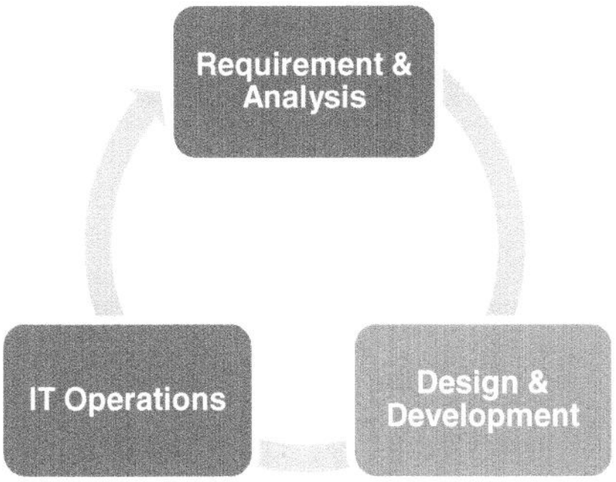

Fig. 3. Simple model of service lifecycle (cf. [28])

deal with such extended and flexible roles in a SOA. They should also support these roles and moreover be supportive of optimizing the cooperation between them.

3.2 Services Lifecycle

In order to be able to define the requirements for service management more precisely, it is necessary to look in more detail into the service lifecycle. We did that in our case study in cooperation with a wide range of companies, mainly from the financial sector. Though we received our empirical results solely in financial companies we feel that the foundation of our study is wide enough to lead to easily transferable results for other fields.

The more detailed lifecycle model that has been developed in our study is shown in fig. 4. Initially a service reaches the status *planned* after the idea is raised to offer a specific functionality as service. Note that the functionality does not have to be a new one; this model also applies to legacy functionality that is lifted to a service as well as external functionality to be integrated. The potential service is described in a concept paper which is then submitted to the local SOA managing board or SOA architect (depending on the particular organization), reaching the state *suggested*. The managing instance will then decide on the future development regarding this service:

- The concept may be approved if the service seems beneficial, is subject to implementation in the near future and thus entered into the development pipeline achieving the status *concept approved*.
- The service may seem beneficial in general, but the concept is not yet sufficiently detailed, completed or contains inconsistencies; in this case the service is returned to the suggesting party for an extended planning stage.
- The service is considered not relevant or already existing; in this case the service will not be considered for implementation and may be treated as *decommissioned*.

In the design and development phase a service will be implemented and thereafter is subject to testing and validation similar to traditional software components. It may either be considered ready for production moving to the *tested and implementation approved* status. Or the service still contains errors or deviates from the original concept in which case it is returned to the developers and moves back to the *concept approved* state.

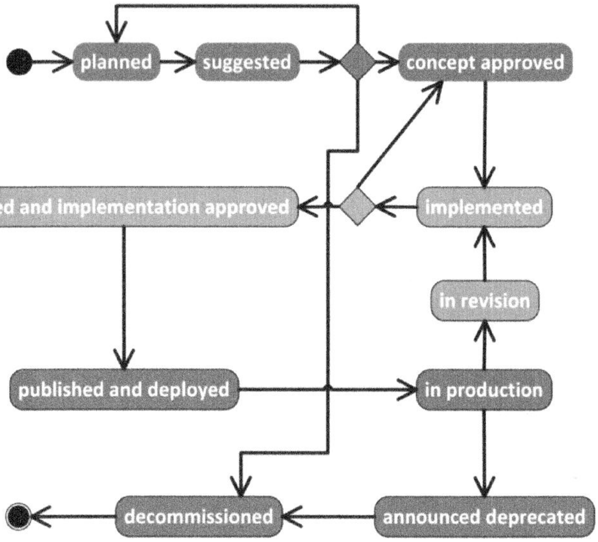

Fig. 4. Detailed model of service lifecycle

After successful testing a service is deployed and thus published to the IT operations stage. After operations has made the service available on a production system it reaches the *in production* status. This is the status where service monitoring takes place as described in the previous section, generating all necessary usage information for the services. This information should be stored in a central location ideally the same location which has been used for managing services throughout the previous stages of the lifecycle. Other developers and especially the SOA governing instance in the company may use such data for planning the future development of a service. There might be the need for certain adjustments which leads to the service going into the *in revision* state. In this state the next version of the service is planned and implemented while the current version may remain in production.

It might also be detected that a certain service is (no longer) required or used in which case it can be prepared for removing from the production system. This is expressed by the *announced deprecated* state. After a certain period of time the service is physically removed from the production system. The particular time interval depends on the service and company in question. This is expressed by the *decommissioned* state. At this time the service is no longer available but all meta-information assembled about the service is still available. This may be important for future services and SOA planning in general.

The increased complexity of the lifecycle coupled with the governance requirements from the previous section causes strong demand for advanced software support for service management. Tools that provide such functionality are typically called service registries and/or service repositories. In the next section we will describe requirements for these tools based on the discussion of service management in this section.

4 Using Registry Repositories for Service Management

4.1 Support during Service Lifecycle

As already discussed in the previous section a central software tool for managing all information about services in all different stages of the lifecycle is extremely beneficial. Such service registry-repositories (SOA-RR) are an important component of a SOA and support service management as well as governance throughout the full service lifecycle.

In particular a SOA-RR may be used for the following important tasks:

- In the requirements and analysis stage it may be used as a well-defined instance between the different parties involved in this part of the lifecycle (e.g. SOA board and service designers). It may assist in securing a redundancy-free SOA as well as conformance to the technological guidelines within the company. Moreover it facilitates a valid judgment of the business case for any given service by the managing board. Finally it may be used for enforcing a proper process model as well as conformance to the defined business strategy.
- During design and development it may increase reuse of basic services (cf. [1]) by the developers and may assist them in observing version-based dependencies between services. A SOA-RR supports the compliance with defined SLAs both on the basic service level as well as on the business service and process levels. Finally, it assists SOA board and lead developers in gaining an overview of the current implementation status of the company's SOA at any given time.
- In the operations stage information in the SOA-RR may be used for discovering rarely used services and to prepare decommissioning of services by e.g. identifying dependent services. It may also be used as a single point of storage for change requests to a given service. Finally, the information in the SOA-RR could also be used for accounting information in case the company internally or externally uses a charge model for the services.

Information for this final stage is in many cases based on data that is generated while services are in production. Monitoring life services and feeding the information back into the SOA-RR is a very important feature and is thus discussed in more detail in section 4.3.

4.2 Detailed Requirements for SOA-RR

In our study we also tried to evaluate existing commercial offerings of SOA-RR products. In order to do so we analyzed the requirements for SOA-RR described in the previous section. This leads to a functionality-oriented list of detailed requirements for SOA-RR in order to perfectly support service management.

We structured the necessary functions into four categories, namely basic functions, static functions, dynamic functions and technical functions which will be explained in more detail in the sequel.

Among the *basic functions* is the storage and management of all artifacts that are important for a SOA, namely services themselves, descriptions of interfaces, message formats, business processes and policies. All enterprises regardless their internal structures and processes require storage and management of full-text documents and arbitrary binary files. Of course all required metadata associated with any of these artifacts should also be managed by the SOA-RR. Finally it is not only required to store this information but also to be able to search for and visualize information. Note that services are not restricted to Web services in the context of most enterprises: other types of services integrated into the SOA such as legacy services should be equally manageable by the SOA-RR.

With *static functions* we denote all functionality that is not inherently related to operation of services in the production environment. Static functions support service developers, architects and the SOA board in the earlier stages of the lifecycle. Static functions include service discovery in order to increase the level of service reuse as well as dependency management between services and/or versions of services. These are already required during analysis and design in order to be able to improve the design of services. Moreover management of connections between different artifacts in a SOA such as versioning and classification of services is also necessary in the analysis and design stages already. It should again be noted that integration of legacy services (cf. [10]) is already very important in this set of functions as the SOA architects need a complete view on all services in the IT infrastructure in order to achieve the best possible overall design.

The IT operations part of the service lifecycle also has to be supported by a SOA-RR. Such *dynamic* or runtime *functions* may be of a very technical nature such as user, roles and rights management, access control, logging and monitoring of services and processes. They may also be of interest for the managing instances of a company considering e.g. support for change management, accounting of service usage and conformance information for given service levels and other types of policies. If required in a particular SOA the support for dynamic service discovery and binding also originates from dynamic functions supported by the SOA-RR.

Among the *technical functionality* to be provided by a SOA-RR are traditional database management system functions such as reliability, backup, recovery features and the option to operate it in a distributed environment. Also the potential for easy integration into the given IT infrastructure of the company is extremely important leading to requirements such as extensibility, support of well-known standards and publicly available API.

Altogether these requirements form a huge set of potential functions that almost no product will be able to fulfill without customized extensions. Therefore the complete list of functionality should be prioritized and weighted by each company individually in order to achieve a customized set of the most important functions in a given enterprise environment. Even if several of the listed functions do not seem immediately required for a given company they should be kept in mind, because it is very likely that they are required later on with increasing level of SOA maturity.

In our cooperation project we performed a market study to narrow the list of potential candidate products for our cooperating companies to a short list in a first step by analyzing system documentation. Note that parts of the individual priorities have already been used to determine the products on the short list. The products on that short list have been: Software AG CentraSite, IBM WebSphere Service Registry & Repository, Bea AquaLogic Service Registry (now: Oracle Service Registry), Systinet Registry (now part of: HP SOA Systinet). Finally for each cooperating company we used the individual priorities and weights to compare the products from the short list in detail in a second step. This comparison was based on concrete installations of the products and application to real-world services from the partners. The results strongly depend on the individual situation and thus no generally valid recommendation can be made.

4.3 Service Monitoring

Of particular importance for SOA management and governance is monitoring the current production operation of an enterprise's SOA. This is already obvious from the description of SOA governance tasks in section 3. The companies in our case study also considered this aspect to be so important that a follow-up project dedicated to the details of service monitoring in a SOA had been started.

An important aspect of the technical SOA management is detection of bottlenecks and performance tuning of the enterprise IT. To be able to do that information about the execution times of and average response time of services and processes as well as error rates and call frequencies is required. This information can be obtained while monitoring the operation of the services within a SOA. Monitoring information may also be used by the IT operation's management for capacity planning and infrastructure optimization.

Based on such atomic data derived information which is very important for the general SOA governance may also be inferred. Among that information may be the compliance with defined service level agreements, billing and accounting for commercial services and the conformance to defined security policies. This may go as far as monitoring call statistics for certain services and advertising these. Also business statistics might be generated from process monitoring information depending on the SOA maturity level of the organization.

Depending on the particular goals of service monitoring in an organization and the tools employed, several different architectural options are possible. In the simplest case each service would report the desired data to a central monitoring component in fixed intervals. This may be sufficient for simple monitoring information such as call frequency but is not really satisfactory as foundation for SOA governance.

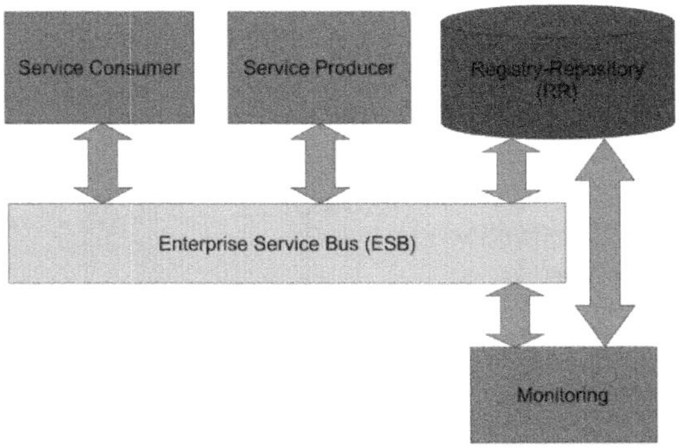

Fig. 5. Architectural model for SOA/service monitoring

Another option might be to define a fixed monitoring interface which every service has to implement. This interface would then be called by the monitoring component in certain intervals. The benefit over the first option is that a central monitoring component owns the monitoring process. Thus service errors or unfulfilled SLAs can be detected. The major drawback is that the service implementation itself has to be concerned with monitoring by implementing the interface. To overcome this, a loosely coupled architecture for monitoring should be preferred as shown in fig. 5.

In this architecture the monitoring component is independent of the services. It operates directly on the ESB to collect important execution information. It is also connected to the SOA-RR for two reasons: firstly the monitoring component operates based on the RR to obtain meta information required for proper operation. Secondly it assembles important monitoring information and stores it in the SOA-RR. This is required because the SOA-RR is the foundation for SOA governance (cf. section 3), i.e. the instance where the monitoring information will be evaluated.

5 Summary

In this paper we have discussed important aspects of managing services in a service-oriented architecture. The discussion and findings are based on a case study that we have performed in cooperation with several major companies from the financial sector in the Hannover region. Of specific interest for these companies is the integration of legacy/non-web services within their SOA.

In particular we have discussed which aspects of services need to be described for service management. For each of these aspects we have given example languages that can be used. Thereafter we have shown that service management in an enterprise environment requires SOA governance. Such governance has to be based on the specific service lifecycle in a SOA and should be supported by appropriate software tools. A specific lifecycle model which has been developed in our project has been presented and the SOA registry-repositories (SOA-RR) have been identified as the central piece in SOA governance. Also we have discussed why service monitoring and the feedback of results of this monitoring into the SOA-RR are very important for mature service management; this is still not standard in many products nowadays.

Consequently, SOA-RR tools have to support all the XML based languages used for service descriptions as well as all the requirements arising from supporting the service lifecycle. We have assembled all these requirements and shown that they can roughly be classified as basic, static, dynamic or technical. Advanced software tools are on the market and the best choice depends on the individual priorities of the particular enterprise. For the companies in our project we have developed a balanced scorecard. Based on this, each company is able to define its individual weights for the complete list of requirements. After defining such weights the best individual choice of a SOA-RR product at the time of writing can be concluded.

6 Future Work

Some parts of our research are subject to constant changes while others seem pretty stable. The general aspects of service description are not expected to change much whereas the particular languages used to describe them may change significantly in the near future. In particular the area of service semantics (maybe in a given domain context) might be subject to rapid improvement. Consequently, the requirements to support semantic service descriptions might increase.

The validity of the service lifecycle modeled in our project should be evaluated in real-world scenarios in other business sectors as financial. While the general stages seem pretty reasonable for every sector there might be some specific parts which are domain specific. Requirements for SOA-RR would have to be adjusted accordingly.

The tool evaluation results are undergoing constant change as the tools are improving constantly. Thus the partner companies of our project will need to monitor the market closely in order to be able to derive the most recent results at any time. Currently the companies are at different stages in the process of establishing a service management as described in this paper. Thus the time when a SOA-RR is required to establish a proper service management differs from immediate to medium-term.

Apart from service semantics we see the most potential for improvements in the near future in the area of service and business process monitoring. We are currently working on a project with the same companies in order to establish a service and process monitoring within their SOA. Particular focus in this project is on generation of monitoring information and the feedback of such data into the SOA-RR. This is required to establish a business process and service controlling based on monitoring.

Acknowledgement. The authors would like to thank the partner companies from the *competence center for information technology and management* (CC_ITM) for funding of this research project. In particular they would like to thank the companies for practical support and domain-specific cooperation during the project.

References

1. Krafzig, D., Banke, K., Slama, D.: Enterprise SOA: Service-Oriented Architecture Best Practices. PrenticeHall, Englewood Cliffs (2004)
2. OASIS, http://docs.oasis-open.org/wsbpel/2.0/OS/wsbpel-v2.0-OS.html
3. Lee, K., Jeon, J., et al.: QoS for Web Services: Requirements and Possible Approaches, http://www.w3c.or.kr/kr-office/TR/2003/ws-qos/
4. Wada, H., Suzuki, J., Oba, K.: Modeling Non-Functional Aspects in Service Oriented Architecture, http://www.cs.umb.edu/~jxs/pub/scc.pdf
5. Object Managemt Group. Common Object Request Broker Architecture, http://www.corba.org
6. Booth, D., Liu, C.K.: Web Services Description Language (WSDL) Version 2.0 Part 0: Primer, http://www.w3.org/TR/2007/REC-wsdl20-primer-20070626
7. CB2XML: Cobol copybook to XML converter, http://sourceforge.net/projects/cb2xml/
8. Williams, N., Herrman, R., Lopez, L., Ebbers, M.: Implementing CICS Web Services, IBM Redbook (2007), http://www.redbooks.ibm.com/redbooks/pdfs/sg247206.pdf
9. IBM: Write the WSDL extensions, http://publib.boulder.ibm.com/infocenter/iseries/v5r3/index.jsp?topic=/rzatz/51/webserv/wswsifattwsdl.htm.

10. Lawrence, C.: Adapting legacy systems for SOA, http://www.ibm.com/developerworks/webservices/library/ws-soa-adaptleg/
11. Wada, H., Suzuki, J., Oba, K.: Modeling Non-Functional Aspects in Service Oriented Architecture. In: Proc. of the 2006 IEEE International Conference on Services Computing, pp. 222–229. IEEE Computer Society, Los Alamitos (2006)
12. Vedamuthu, A.S., Orchard, D., Hondo, M., et al.: Web Services Policy 1.5 - Framework, http://www.w3.org/TR/ws-policy/#policy_expression
13. Vedamuthu, A.S., Orchard, D., et al.: Web Services Policy 1.5 Guidelines for Policy Assertion Authors, http://www.w3.org/TR/ws-policy-guidelines/
14. Vedamuthu, A. S., Orchard, D. et. al.: Web Services Policy 1.5 - Attachment, http://www.w3.org/TR/ws-policy-attach/
15. OASIS: WS-SecurityPolicy 1.2, http://docs.oasis-open.org/ws-sx/ws-securitypolicy/v1.2/ws-securitypolicy.html
16. OASIS: Web Services Reliable Messaging TC WS-Reliability 1.1, http://docs.oasis-open.org/wsrm/ws-reliability/v1.1/wsrm-ws_reliability-1.1-spec-os.pdf
17. OASIS: Web Services Reliable Messaging Policy Assertion (WS-RM Policy) Version 1.1, http://docs.oasis-open.org/ws-rx/wsrmp/200702/wsrmp-1.1-spec-os-01.pdf
18. OASIS: SAML V2.0 Executive Overview, http://www.oasis-open.org/committees/download.php/13525/sstc-saml-exec-overview-2.0-cd-01-2col.pdf
19. OMG: Object Constraint Language, http://www.omg.org/docs/formal/06-05-01.pdf
20. W3C: RDFPrimer, http://www.w3.org/TR/rdf-primer/
21. W3C: RDF Vocabulary Description Language 1.0, http://www.w3.org/TR/rdf-schema/
22. W3C: OWL Web Ontology Language Overview, http://www.w3.org/TR/owl-features/
23. W3C: OWL-S Semantic Markup Web Services, http://www.w3.org/Submission/OWL-S/
24. W3C: Web Service Modeling Ontology WSMO Submission/WSMO/, http://www.w3.org/
25. Lara, R., Polleres, A., Lausen, H., et al.: A Conceptual Comparison between WSMO and OWL-S, http://www.wsmo.org/2004/d4/d4.1/v0.1/20050106/d4.1v0.1_20050106.pdf
26. Farrell, J., Lausen, H.: Semantic Annotations for WSDL and XML Schema, http://www.w3.org/TR/sawsdl/
27. W3C: SPARQL – Query Language for RDF, http://www.w3.org/TR/rdf-sparql-query/
28. Durvasula, S., Guttmann, M., Kumar, A., et al.: SOA Practitioners' Guide Part 3: Introduction to Services Lifecycle, http://www.soablueprint.com/practitioners_guide

Planning for a Successful Corporate Wiki

Ioanna Lykourentzou[1], Younes Djaghloul[1], Katerina Papadaki[2], Foteini Dagka[3], and Thibaud Latour[1]

[1] Centre de Recherche Public Henri Tudor
29, avenue John F. Kennedy, LU 1855, Luxembourg, +3522425991703
{Ioanna.Lykourentzou,Younes.Djaghloul,Thibaud.Latour}@tudor.lu
[2] Bank of Greece,
21 E. Venizelos Avenue, GR 102 50, Athens, Greece, +302106799756
kpapadaki@bankofgreece.gr
[3] National Technical University of Athens, School of Electrical and Computer Engineering
Heroon Polytechniou 9, GR 15780, Athens, Greece, +302107722538
dagkaf@medialab.ntua.gr

Abstract. Corporate wikis are increasingly being adopted by enterprises as a solution to various organizational processes. Subsequently a significant number of research works have started focusing on providing results on both successful and unsuccessful corporate wiki implementations. Nevertheless, the scope of these studies is usually limited on a specific organizational case or focuses on a limited set of aspects of the wiki adoption, e.g. either the technological or the cultural one. Our objective in this work is to provide an overview of the key factors affecting the successful implementation of an organizational wiki, by analyzing thirty case studies reported in the research literature. The result of this analysis is the identification of a core set of common best practices to be taken into account by stakeholders when planning the integration of a wiki within a corporate context. In this way, the study aims at contributing to the planning and the realization of more successful corporate wiki implementations with enterprise environments.

Keywords: corporate wikis, computer-supported cooperative work, enterprise information systems, knowledge management.

1 Introduction

Since the early beginning of the 21st century, the world changed in a way that could hardly be imagined some years earlier. After the personal computer revolution of the 1980's and the boom of the World Wide Web in the 1990's, one even greater invention took place: web user collaboration. Indeed, up to that time, the idea of millions of interconnected people collaborating with one another had never, through the entire human history, been so widely implemented. And even better: this implementation works. The success of a variety of ventures, ranging from collaborative content creation communities – such as YahooAnswers – and social networking sites – such as MySpace and Facebook –, to content sharing applications, like Flickr and YouTube, proves it.

E. Ariwa and E. El-Qawasmeh (Eds.): DEIS 2011, CCIS 194, pp. 425–439, 2011.

The main feature of this new computing era, often called Web 2.0, is user collaboration. Among the most prominent paradigms of this movement stand wikis; a technology which enables distributed users to collaboratively work towards the creation of online content, by building and enhancing one another's contributions. The wiki technology is successfully used by one of the most influential and referenced sites of the web, namely Wikipedia. First appearing in 2001 and growing ever since, the Wikipedia model has proven that it is possible to effectively harness user knowledge into structured, qualitative content - and hence, it has opened the way to numerous other content collaboration efforts.

The success of Wikipedia, combined with the potential of producing significant knowledge value in a simple and efficient manner, soon attracted the attention of the corporate world, leading an increasing number of organizations to invest on the adoption of the wiki technology.

The advantages that they see in this investment are many. As indicated by a significant number of success stories [1-8], wikis can render corporate collaboration more inclusive and efficient, by actively involving employees and stakeholders into the organizational knowledge building process. They can also help build and maintain a solid experience base within the firm, a feature significantly appreciated, since expertise re-gaining is more than often translated into high costs, in terms of both time and resources. Wikis are also efficient in supporting organizational communication, as well as in complementing or, in some cases being an alternative to, other currently used business collaboration technologies.

As a result of the above, wikis are nowadays used to facilitate a broad range of organizational processes within the enterprise. These include the collaboration of dispersed corporate teams in document co-authoring efforts, the formulation of in-house communities of practice, the gathering of organizational tacit knowledge, as well as a number of more specific processes, such as customer relationship management, software development and project administration.

Despite the advantages they can gain an organization, the road to implementing a corporate wiki is not always obstacle-free. A number of non-successful ventures [9,10], indicate that, as with any technological solution, careful planning needs to take place prior to establishing a corporate wiki, in order to avoid the frustration, resource waste and innovation setback that a failed implementation might bring on.

Therefore, as the use of corporate wikis leaves the initial stages of enthusiastic acceptance and it faces reality, and in a time where knowledge is considered to be one of the most valuable assets for the survival of an organization in the global marketplace[11,12], a question that inevitably arises is: how can wiki-based user collaboration be effectively implemented so that it can really create value for the organization?

In seeking an effective means of implementing a corporate wiki, one may need to answer a number of related questions:

- Which should be the expectations and which are the anticipated constraints of using a wiki within a corporate context?

- Which are the important parameters that need to be taken into consideration by stakeholders and employees wishing to benefit from this new medium?
- What can the management do to support the implementation of a corporate wiki?
- How can the employees be motivated to use the newly introduced technology?
- Which technical characteristics need to be taken into account when selecting a wiki platform?
- Overall, is there a clear process to follow in order to simplify and to smoothen the integration of a wiki into the corporate working environment?

In this context, a considerable number of studies reporting on the issue of implementing a wiki within a corporation can be found in the research literature. Depending on their context and focus, i.e. whether they are applied or more theoretical, these studies provide significant results on a variety of aspects concerning the successful implementation of a wiki within a corporation. However, their results are usually limited on the specific organizational case that they describe. As such, they do not cover all the aspects that need to be taken into account when planning the adoption of an organizational wiki. In addition, depending on the scope of the case study, some works may focus more on the technological aspect of the wiki adoption, while others may deal with the cultural or motivational aspect of this implementation. Nevertheless, in their effort to plan for a sustainable corporate wiki, stakeholders need to have an overall view of the factors that have proven, according to previous experience, to affect this venture. A study, therefore, which would combine the results and observations of a diversity of case studies and viewpoints, to provide an overview of the key factors affecting the success of an organizational wiki would be of critical importance.

In this paper, and based on the results of analyzing thirty case studies reported in the research literature on the use of wikis in enterprise settings, we identify the factors that are most frequently reported to affect the success or failure of a wiki within a corporate context. The article thus aims at familiarizing stakeholders in a variety of organizational levels – including team leaders and project managers, organizational change or IT experts, communities of practice and individual employees – with the particularities that the use of the wiki technology most commonly presents and, in this way, to support the future implementation and sustainability of more successful corporate wiki stories. The rest of this paper is organized as follows: section 2 presents the most important findings of the related research literature and section 3 presents the research methodology followed for the identification and analysis of the selected case studies. Section 4 – constituting the main contribution of this paper – presents the identified best practices regarding the successful planning of a corporate wiki implementation. Finally, section 5 concludes with the main findings and future research directions of this work.

2 Related Literature

The most significant part of the available research literature on wikis focuses on either the educational domain or on Wikipedia, the popular wiki-based encyclopedia. It is only in the last few years that another type of studies, which pertains to the use of wikis on the corporate domain, has started to emerge. The focus of this latter type of works, a significant number of which constitute the set of the case studies analyzed by the present research effort, refers mostly to the implementation of a wiki on a specific corporation.

The studies that extend this focus on more than a single or a few enterprise cases, seeking to tap the broader picture and provide overall planning directions and guidelines are still very few. Among these, the study of Wagner [13] uses three media choice theories to evaluate the potential of enterprise wikis as a means of facilitating communication and collaboration within the enterprise. The study bases its results on 32 corporate wiki implementation case studies. It concludes that enterprise wikis present the potential of enabling and leveraging corporate communication, provided that specific aspects often related to their open nature, such as free-riding and conflict of values are adequately addressed.

Another multiple case study is the one performed by Stocker and Tochtermann [14]. This study draws its results from three corporate wiki implementation cases. It concludes that the examined corporate wikis indeed facilitated knowledge sharing among the employees and improved the corporate documentation processes.

Finally, the works of Poole [15] and Grudin [16], which categorize enterprise wikis into three categories, are also relevant to the scope of the present work in the sense that they perform a meta-analysis instead of providing direct implementation results. Specifically, the aforementioned studies provide a taxonomy of enterprise wiki genres, based on a corporate wiki application on a large organization. Three genres are in this context identified: single contributor wikis, which are used as personal information management tools, group wikis, which are used as tools to facilitate corporate team collaboration and in-house corporate encyclopedias, functioning as an enterprise-wide knowledge repository. These works also highlight three important commonly occurring issues of corporate wiki implementations, namely the need to align individual contributor and management expectations, the need to organize content in a flexible manner, as well as the requirement to position the wiki in the existing corporate culture.

The present work seeks to add to and extend the aforementioned research literature domain, by analyzing the results and the observations over thirty reported corporate wiki implementations, and in this way to identify a set of common patterns that influence the result of a corporate wiki implementation. By highlighting some of the most important factors affecting the problem-at-hand, the study therefore aims at facilitating the realization of more successful enterprise wiki ventures.

3 Research Methodology

To identify the enabling and restricting factors of applying and using a wiki within a corporation, the following methodological steps were applied:

1. Selection of the case study dataset

To select the dataset of the case studies that would be used as the basis of the study, initially an extensive search of the relevant recent academic literature was performed. The criteria that a study should fulfill in order to be included in the selected data set were that: a) the application domain of the described wiki implementation should specifically be an enterprise setting (thus not including settings such as the educational one or studies focusing on Wikipedia), b) the study should be an applied and not a theoretical one and c) it should provide results, either in a qualitative format, e.g. through interviews, reported user viewpoints or questionnaires, or in a quantitative format, e.g. through a log analysis of the wiki usage, or reports on the number of page views and edits. In addition, the study should clearly report on the perceived outcome, i.e. whether the corporate stakeholders and employees deemed the specific wiki implementation successful or not.

2. Basic profile building of each study

Thirty case studies were selected during step one [1-10,17-36]. Twenty six of the selected studies report beneficial, positive or successful results [1-8,17-23,26-36], while the results of the remaining four are reported not satisfactory or unsuccessful by the corporate stakeholders involved [9,10,24,25].

The next step included identifying the basic profile characteristics of each study, to determine the scope that could be covered by the fusion of their results. From all the features that could be used to characterize each study, a number of basic features were selected, on the basis that almost all the studies provided the respective information. Other features, for which a significant number of studies did not provide information, were not included. The profile of each study thus consisted of the following basic information elements:

- *Company size*. The selected studies were found to focus on small enterprises (less than 50 employees – 7 studies), medium (less than 100 employees – 11 studies) and large-sized (more than 100 employees – 12 studies) corporations.
- *Company specialization*. The studies were found to describe corporate wiki implementation experiences from a variety of different specializations including research (8 studies), manufacturing (1 study), consultancy (2 studies), educational services provision (2 studies), design (1 study), media/entertainment (3 studies), publications (2 studies), software development (8 studies), crisis management (1 study) and non-profit organizations (2 studies).
- *Target organizational task*. The purposes that the reported corporations implemented the wiki for also varied. Five different target wiki usage activities were identified, ranging from general company activities, such as knowledge codification (8 studies), or the facilitation of collaboration between the members of corporate communities of practice (4 studies), to more specialized corporate processes such as the ones related to the

development of information systems (10 studies). Other procedures include interaction with third parties (6 studies) and inter-organizational communication and collaboration (2 studies).

As one may observe, the studies cover a broad range of different organizational cases and corporate settings, providing the diversity potential that the present study seeks.

3. Extraction of the reported wiki enablers and constraints

The next step was to extract the enablers and constraints reported by each study regarding the specific wiki implementation performed. Initially, these factors were depicted using the language of the specific case study and then, when they referred to the same notion, they were codified using the same terminology.

4. Grouping and analysis of the identified enablers and constraints

The final step was the grouping and analysis of the identified enablers and constraints. During this step the extracted factors were used in conjunction with the respective study results, to identify common patterns of wiki success or failure across the examined cases. Some representative pattern strategies that were used to mark a specific factor as a common enabler of a corporate wiki implementation, are the following:

a) A study, characterized by specific factors, reports success, whereas another study, implicitly or explicitly reporting the lack of these factors, reports failure or partial failure.
b) A study attributes its success to one or more specific factors and the latter are also supported as success-contribution elements by other studies.
c) A factor has not contradictory meaning, i.e. there is no case of some studies supporting its success building capacity, while others supporting the opposite.

The success-enabling factors of a corporate wiki implementation, which were identified using the above pattern building criteria, are presented and analyzed in the following section, along with a reference to the case studies that support them.

4 Setting Up a Successful Corporate Wiki: Best Practices and Affecting Factors

Based on observations made over the successful and unsuccessful stories mentioned in the selected studies of the research literature, as well as on a specific set of studies focusing on the enablers and constraints of the use of wikis in corporate settings [13,16,37-40], one may distinguish four main categories of factors affecting the successful intergration of a wiki within a corporate setting: 1) the cultivation of a wiki culture within the enterprise, 2) the selection of the appropriate wiki platform to suit the needs of the organization, 3) the encouragement of user participation and 4) the maintainance of the achieved results (Figure 1).

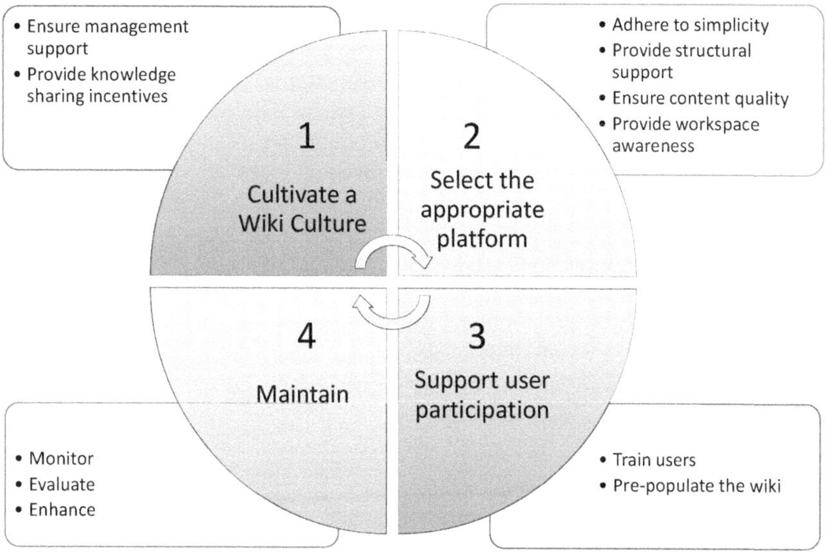

Fig. 1. Planning for a successful corporate wiki

4.1 Cultivate a "Wiki Culture"

The first important step in establishing a successful corporate wiki is the cultivation of an open, knowledge sharing culture inside the corporate environment. Overall, this step involves two main prerequisites: ensuring management support and providing users with the appropriate knowledge sharing incentives.

4.1.1 Ensure Management Support

Wikis typically function better within flat-based, rather than within strictly hierarchical knowledge structured organizational contexts. In other words, if knowledge is implicitly considered to be a personal, rather than a corporate asset, users will be reluctant to share, as this might limit the chances they stand towards inner competition. Thus, as a number of the examined case studies support [9,14,19-21,23,26,41], for the organization to actually benefit from the capabilities of a wiki system, the management should embrace the need for a non-hierarchical, open and bottom-up knowledge sharing culture, actively urge users to share their knowledge inside the corporation and promote interaction, dialogue and feedback among the prospective wiki users.

4.1.2 Provide Knowledge Sharing Incentives

Apart from realizing the need for establishing an open, sharing culture, the management is also important to provide prospective wiki users with incentives for sharing their knowledge [5,9,17,20,33,42]. The four incentives that seem to have the most impact include incorporating the wiki to the daily routine of the employees, providing recognition for one's contributions, building a safe-to-contribute environment and promoting team spirit.

The active integration of the wiki into the daily collaboration and communication processes of the organization is one of the most important factors of its success. To ensure this integration, one could follow two patterns: a) actively support the use of the wiki over other communication tools such as face-to-face meetings or e-mail exchanges and b) perceive the time that the employees will spent on contributing to the platform as productive work time and not as an extra activity, e.g. by allocating a specific number of working hours per month to tasks related to one's involvement with the corporate wiki.

The second important incentive refers to authorship recognition both by the management and by one's colleagues. Authorship recognition, e.g. in the form of "top participants", increases the perceived self-efficacy of the employees and their benefit they see in sharing their knowledge, and forms a strong sharing motivation [43,44].

Furthermore, a common employee concern, often leading to low corporate wiki participation levels, is that sharing work-in-progress may negatively affect the assessments they receive. Therefore, another incentive for knowledge sharing is the development of a working environment where the contribution of unfinished work is perceived as part of the development process and it is positively evaluated.

Another means of motivating employee sharing is to promote team spirit and to cultivate a sense of trust and identity inside the corporate wiki community. Possible ways to achieve this is by encouraging users to create personal profile pages and by promoting the building of closely connected, self-managed collaboration units inside the corporate wiki, such as communities of practice. Complementarily to positively affecting participation, the creation of a group identity has also been found to increase the social responsibility for one's actions and the commitment to common welfare, thus preventing "free riding", i.e. the situation in which the number of views is significantly higher than the number of user edits. Apart from fostering the development of team spirit, the trust levels that have already been established within the corporation can be used to promote the wiki acceptance [10]. Specifically, as a number of studies suggest [13,14], initially introducing the corporate wiki to small groups, which have already established a sense of trust, and then broadening its use to larger, more anonymous teams can prove significantly beneficial.

4.2 Select the Appropriate Platform

A second step towards a successful corporate wiki implementation refers to selecting the platform which is most appropriate for the needs of the organization. A number of issues that need to be taken into account to facilitate this selection include the level of complexity, structural support, quality assurance and workspace awareness provided by the platform. Based on the analysis of these issues, provided in the following, as well as using available web resources that present and compare the technical characteristics of a variety of wiki platforms [45-47], one may identify the platform that best suits their organizational needs.

4.2.1 Adhere to Simplicity - Customize If Necessary

Two additional aspects, important for the selection of a corporate wiki platform, are simplicity and customization. That is, the selection of the simplest possible wiki platform, which can meet the specified organizational requirements, can help reduce the complexity of learning to use the tool and in this way it can boost user participation [19,48].

A simple core platform can then be extended with the exact additional functionalities that the organization requires [7]. In fact, many organizations seem to prefer selecting a simple, usually open source, platform and to customize it to fit the needs of their own enterprise setting, rather than using a ready-to-use solution. A typical customization process, refers to extending a core wiki platform to support more complex file formats, compared to simple text, such as tables, spreadsheets, executable code, as well as enterprise simulation models [6,28].

Finally, instead of customizing a platform and owing the equipment that is necessary for its hosting and maintenance, another option is using already customized wiki solutions, which are offered as a hosted service by dedicated companies[49].

4.2.2 Provide Structural Support

A major issue often reported is the loose content structure that wikis inherently have [3,6,7,17,20,26,27]. Although the open editing nature of the wiki technology facilitates informal sharing, collaboration and innovation creation, yet it also tends to produce unstructured knowledge content, which in turn may result to difficulties in navigation and querying, as well as in the insertion and retrieval of useful information. On the other hand, enforcing a very strict information organization schema, e.g. through static intranet solutions, is by far not the optimal as it limits creativity and collaboration capabilities.

A variety of solutions exist to ensure structural support, while maintaining the open collaborative nature of the wiki. A first solution is the manual content maintenance, by a person or a core group of persons, often referred to as "wiki gardeners", responsible to ensure the correct classification of the inserted information and to maintain the consistency of the corporate experience base [3,17,26]. Another popular solution refers to enforcing a specified content structure through simple means, such as predefined topic taxonomies [29,30,33], or more advanced ones, like techniques that organize the wiki content based on a synergy of machine and human intelligence [50] or the utilization of semantic web technologies [2,22,31]. This latter solution, which facilitates context-based access through the provision of mechanisms such as tag-supported navigation and semantic querying, seems to successfully address the issue of structural support and for this reason it tends to be increasingly used by corporations wishing to integrate a wiki to their organizational activities.

4.2.3 Ensure Content Quality

One of the mostly often mentioned issues regarding the implementation of corporate wikis, refers to the need to ensure their content quality [2,3,8,20,25,26,41,51]. Ensuring quality of the wiki content is important for two reasons: it can help cultivate a notion of trust among users that the content they have contributed will not be misused and it can also ensure that one will find qualitative information that can indeed add value to their work. A first means to ensure content quality in a wiki platform include establishing membership criteria to restrict editing only to a specific community of corporate users [23,35,52]. This can help maintain the level of exchanged information high and on-topic, while it can also help avoid vandalism issues - often encountered in case the wiki is open to the wide public, e.g. in cases of corporate wikis used by news organizations. Differentiated group permissions can also be applied to further ensure content confidentiality, a factor important especially to large-scale enterprise settings.

Another means of ensuring content quality is using, manually or automatically assigned, quality tags [2-4]. In the manual form of this method, a central documentation team can monitor the wiki pages, mark them according to their quality and resolve arising quality issues. More advanced methods of automatic quality assurance, for instance through the use of peer review processes and automated expert identification mechanisms, can be also applied [53].

4.2.4 Provide Workspace Awareness

An additional important issue to consider when selecting a corporate wiki platform is the provision of workspace awareness, i.e. mechanisms that inform users regarding content changes, inserted comments or contribution dates [32]. Visualization techniques are a popular means of achieving this type of awareness and enhancing usability [1]. These techniques can be applied on document level, to enhance individual user collaboration, or across the wiki pages, to enable stakeholders, such as project managers, to better coordinate the processes served through the wiki. Finally, automatic notification mechanisms, such as RSS feeds, can also be applied to inform users regarding workspace changes, and thus to further strengthen the effectiveness of their collaboration within the platform [4,18,28,54].

4.3 Support User Participation

Having established an effective wiki sharing culture inside the organization and having selected the wiki platform that best suits the organizational needs, the next step towards a successful corporate wiki implementation is to ensure satisfactory user participation. Two main activities to ensure the above include effectively training the users and pre-populating the wiki with already existing corporate content.

4.3.1 Train Users

User training is reported to be a highly significant factor to the success of a corporate wiki platform and it should consist of guidance regarding both the cultural and the technological aspects of the tool[10,17,20,23,29,30,36].

As far as the cultural aspect is concerned, training should focus on introducing employees to the wiki knowledge sharing culture discussed above, so that they will be motivated to share experiences and ideas with colleagues and build the open environment necessary for the wiki platform to create value for the organization.

Apart from the cultural factor, training should also familiarize employees with the technical aspects of the wiki platform. This is important since even if the proper sharing culture has been established within the organization, employees and the stakeholders may still be reluctant to change the traditional collaboration means they have been using. Even in case that users eventually adopt the tool, if proper training has not been initially provided, then they are likely to interpret the wiki in terms of more familiar to them technologies [55] – such as static knowledge sharing solutions – a fact which may lead to its less effective use.

Technical training could include introducing users to the interface and functionalities of the wiki, to its navigation mechanisms, as well as to its content development syntax. This type of training can take place both prior to the launch of the wiki, through introductory sessions and workshops, as well as throughout its use, through the provision of guidelines, help pages and training areas, often referred to as "sandboxes", inside the platform [4,5,18,23,29,30,52]. Finally, the extent of the necessary training can be determined taking into account the level of familiarity with new technologies that the target user group already possesses.

4.3.2 Pre-populate the Wiki

Users are less likely to see future value and contribute to an entirely blank wiki platform and, thus, another means of boosting user participation – according to a significant number of studies – is to pre-populate the wiki prior to its launch [1,6,8,14,20,25,26,35]. The pre-population content can be retrieved from various sources potentially used within the organization, such as static HTML intranets, documentation databases, discussion forums or e-mail communications.

4.4 Maintain, Monitor, Evaluate and Enhance

The last step in establishing a successful corporate wiki, mentioned by almost all the examined case studies, is to constantly monitor, evaluate and maintain the results achieved, to ensure that the platform will produce long-term value for the organization. A number of means can, in this context be used to monitor the wiki integration in the corporate environment. These means include observing the user activity history, provided by most of the wiki platforms in a textual or visual way [1], or applying social network analysis to analyze and measure the activity levels inside the wiki and provide an insight to the collaboration aspects that need to be maintained, enhanced or supported.

5 Conclusion and Future Work

In this study, using results and observations drawn from thirty case studies of wiki implementations in corporate environments, we identify and analyze a number of issues that can affect or restrict the success of a corporate wiki. Overall, it seems that the effective implementation of a wiki in the enterprise is a mix of several factors, involving both a technological and a cultural aspect (Figure 2). The management should seek to support both these aspects in order to create the basis for a sustainable corporate wiki implementation, which will indeed create value for the organization.

Future work can include further extending this work to include potential additional factors revealed as new case studies are being published. In addition, this work focused on the identification of the common aspects that affect the adoption of wikis in an enterprise setting. Future work can include extending this analysis to different levels of granularity, e.g. depending on the company size, its specialization or its inherent organizational culture.

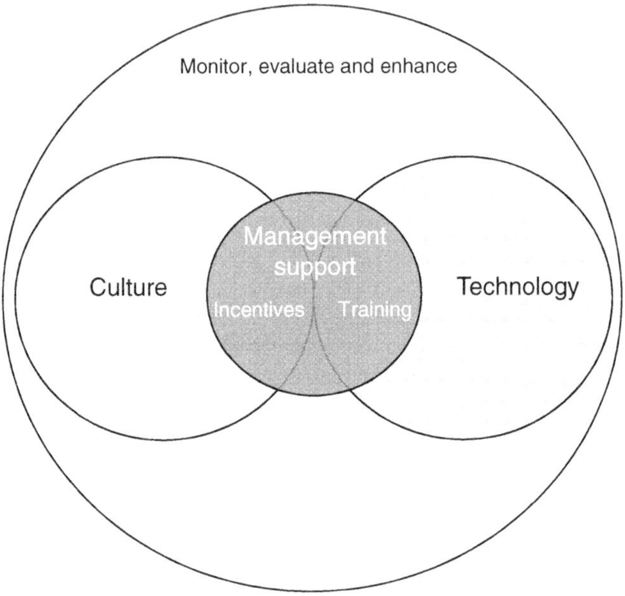

Fig. 2. An effective corporate wiki implementation involves both a cultural and a technological aspect

Acknowledgements

This work was carried out during the tenure of an ERCIM "Alain Bensoussan" Fellowship Programme at the Centre de Recherche Public Henri Tudor, Luxembourg.

References

1. Ding, X., Danis, C., Erickson, T., Kellogg, W.A.: Visualizing an enterprise Wiki. Paper Presented at the CHI 2007 Extended Abstracts on Human Factors in Computing Systems, San Jose, CA, USA (2007)
2. Rech, J., Bogner, C., Haas, V.: Using Wikis to Tackle Reuse in Software Projects. IEEE Softw. 24(6), 99–104 (2007), `http://dx.doi.org/10.1109/MS.2007.183`
3. Cammarata, V.: Wikibilty of Innovation Oriented Workplaces - The CERN Case. Master Thesis, University of Lugano, Lugano, Switzerland (2007)
4. Shepherd, E.: Documenting the Mozilla Project - A Practical Example of Wikis in Open Source Documentation. Paper Presented at the Third Workshop on Wikis for Software Engineering, WikiSym 2008 Conference, Porto, Portugal, September 8 (2008)
5. Munson, S.A.: Motivating and Enabling Organizational Memory with a Workgroup Wiki. Paper Presented at the The International Symposium on Wikis, WikiSym 2008, Porto, Portugal, September, 8-10 (2008)
6. Decker, B., Ras, E., Rech, J., Jaubert, P., Rieth, M.: Wiki-Based Stakeholder Participation in Requirements Engineering. IEEE Softw. 24(2), 28–35 (2007), `http://dx.doi.org/10.1109/MS.2007.60`

7. Feng, X., Chen, W., Feng, Y.Q.: Wiki-based Knowledge Managemen. In: Small and Medium Projects. Paper Presented at the International Conference on Construction and Real Estate Management, Bristol, UK, August 21-22 (2007)
8. Wagner, C., Majchrzak, A.: Enabling Customer-Centricity Using Wikis and the Wiki Way. J. Manage. Inf. Syst. 23(3), 17–43 (2007), http://dx.doi.org/10.2753/MIS0742-1222230302
9. Giordano, R.: An investigation of the use of a wiki to support knowledge exchange in public health. Paper Presented at the Proceedings of the 2007 International ACM Conference on Supporting Group Work, Sanibel Island, Florida, USA, November 4-7 (2007)
10. Leshed, G., Haber, E.M., Matthews, T., Lau, T.: CoScripter: automating & sharing how-to knowledge in the enterprise. Paper Presented at the Proceeding of the Twenty-sixth Annual SIGCHI Conference on Human Factors in Computing Systems, Florence, Italy, April 5-10 (2008)
11. Davenport, T., Prusak, L.: Working Knowledge: how organizations manage what they know. Harvard Business School Press, Boston (2000)
12. Huber, G.P.: The Necessary Nature of Future Firms: Attributes of Survivors in a Changing World. SAGE Publications, Inc., Thousand Oaks (2004)
13. Wagner, C., Schroeder, A.: Capabilities and Roles of Enterprise Wikis in Organizational Communication. Technical Communication 57(1), 68–89 (2010)
14. Stocker, A., Tochtermann, K.: Exploring the value of enterprise wikis: A multiple-case study (2009)
15. Poole, E.S., Grudin, J.: A taxonomy of Wiki genres in enterprise settings. Paper Presented at the Proceedings of the 6th International Symposium on Wikis and Open Collaboration, Gdansk, Poland (2010)
16. Grudin, J., Poole, E.S.: Wikis at work: success factors and challenges for sustainability of enterprise Wikis. Paper Presented at the Proceedings of the 6th International Symposium on Wikis and Open Collaboration, Gdansk, Poland, July 7-9 (2010)
17. Wiebrands, C.: Collaboration and communication via wiki: The experience of Curtin University Library and Information Service. Paper presented at the Australian Library and Information Association, Biennial Conference Perth, Australia, September 19-22 (2006)
18. Regolini, A., Berger, F., Ober, E.J., Dorren, L.: From tailored databases to Wikis: using emerging technologies to work together more efficiently. Interdisciplinary Journal of Information, Knowledge and Management 3, 103–113 (2008)
19. Hasan, H., Pfaff, C.C.: The Wiki: an environment to revolutionise employees' interaction with corporate knowledge. Paper Presented at the Proceedings of the 18th Australia Conference on Computer-Human Interaction: Design: Activities, Artefacts and Environments, Sydney, Australia (2006)
20. Stenmark, D.: Knowledge sharing through increased user participation on a corporate intranet. Paper Presented at the OKLC, Bentley College, Waltham, Massachusetts, USA, March 17-19 (2005)
21. Mestad, A., Myrdal, R., Dingsoyr, T., Dyba, T.: Building a Learning Organization: Three Phases of Communities of Practice in a Software Consulting Company. Paper Presented at the Proceedings of the 40th Annual Hawaii International Conference on System Sciences (2007)
22. Ghali, A.E., Tifous, A., Buffa, M., Giboin, A., Dieng-Kuntz, R.: Using a Semantic Wiki in Communities of Practice. Paper Presented at the Proceedings of the 2nd International Workshop on Building Technology Enhanced Learning solutions for Communities of Practice, Crete, Greece, September 17 (2007)

23. Lio, E.D., Fraboni, L., Leo, T.: TWiki-based facilitation in a newly formed academic community of practice. Paper Presented at the Proceedings of the, International Symposium on Wikis, San Diego, California (2005)
24. Majchrzak, A., Wagner, C., Yates, D.: Corporate wiki users: results of a survey. Paper Presented at the Proceedings of the 2006 International Symposium on Wikis, Odense, Denmark (2006)
25. Bradshaw, P.: Wiki Journalism: Are wikis the new blogs? Paper Presented at the The Future of Newspapers Conference, Cardiff University, September 13-14 (2007)
26. Mason, B., Thomas, S.: A Million Penguins Research Report Institute of Creative Technologies. De Montfort University, Leicester (2008)
27. Chau, T., Maurer, F.: A case study of wiki-based experience repository at a medium-sized software company. Paper Presented at the Proceedings of the 3rd International Conference on Knowledge Capture, Banff, Alberta, Canada (2005)
28. Al-asmari, K., Yu, L.: Experiences in Distributed software development with wiki. In: International Conference on Software Engineering Research and Practice & Conference on Programming Languages and Compilers (SERP 2006), pp. 293–389. CSREA Press, Las Vegas (2006)
29. Yang, D., Wu, D., Koolmanojwong, S., Brown, A.W., Boehm, B.W.: WikiWinWin: A Wiki Based System for Collaborative Requirements Negotiation. Paper Presented at the Proceedings of the 41st Annual Hawaii International Conference on System Sciences (2008)
30. Wu, D., Yang, D., Koolmanojwong, S., Boehm, B.W.: Experimental Evaluation of Wiki Technology and the Shaper Role in Rapid Interdisciplinary Requirements Negotiation. Paper Presented at the Hawaii International Conference on System Sciences (2009)
31. Auer, S., Jungmann, B., Schönefeld, F.: Semantic Wiki Representations for Building an Enterprise Knowledge Base. In: Antoniou, G., Aßmann, U., Baroglio, C., Decker, S., Henze, N., Patranjan, P.-L., Tolksdorf, R. (eds.) Reasoning Web. LNCS, vol. 4636, pp. 330–333. Springer, Heidelberg (2007)
32. Stubblefield, W.A., Carson, T.L.: Software design and engineering as a social process. Paper Presented at the CHI 2007 Extended Abstracts on Human Factors in Computing Systems, San Jose, CA, USA (2007)
33. Petter, S., Vaishnavi, V.: Facilitating experience reuse among software project managers. Inf. Sci. 178(7), 1783–1802 (2008), `http://dx.doi.org/10.1016/j.ins.2007.11.020`
34. White, C., Plotnick, L., Kushma, J., Hiltz, S.R., Turoff, M.: An Online Social Network for Emergency Management. Paper Presented at the Proceedings of the 6th International ISCRAM Conference, Gothenburg, Sweden, May 10-13 (2009)
35. White, C., Plotnick, L., Addams-Moring, R., Turoff, M., Hiltz, S.R.: Leveraging a Wiki to EnhanceVirtual Collaboration in the Emergency Domain. In: Proceedings of the 41st Annual Hawaii International Conference on System Sciences, pp. 322–322 (2008)
36. Raman, M.: Wiki Technology as A "Free" Collaborative Tool within an Organizational Setting. Information Systems Management 23(4), 59–66 (2006)
37. Yates, D., Wagner, C., Majchrzak, A.: Factors affecting shapers of organizational wikis. Journal of the American Society for Information Science and Technology 61(3), 543–554 (2010), doi:10.1002/asi.21266
38. Hester, A.J.: Increasing collaborative knowledge management in your organization: characteristics of wiki technology and wiki users. Paper presented at the Proceedings of the 2010 Special Interest Group on Management Information System's 48th Annual Conference on Computer Personnel Research on Computer Personnel Research, Vancouver, BC, Canada, May 20-22 (2010)

39. Holtzblatt, L.J., Damianos, L.E., Weiss, D.: Factors impeding Wiki use in the enterprise: a case study. Paper Presented at the Proceedings of the 28th of the International Conference on Human Factors in Computing Systems, Atlanta, Georgia, USA, April 10-15 (2010)
40. Kenney, B.: Seven Strategies for Implementing a Successful Corporate Wiki. Industry Week (2008)
41. Hasan, H., Meloche, J.A., Pfaff, C.C., Willis, D.: Beyond Ubiquity: Co-creating Corporate Knowledge with a Wiki. Paper Presented at the International Conference on Mobile Ubiquitous Computing, Systems, Services and Technologies, UBICOMM 2007, November 4-9 (2007)
42. Phuwanartnurak, A.J., Hendry, D.G.: Understanding information sharing in software development through Wiki log analysis. Paper Presented at the Proceedings of the 5th International Symposium on Wikis and Open Collaboration, Orlando, Florida (2009)
43. Osterloh, M., Frey, B.S.: Motivation, Knowledge Transfer, and Organizational Forms. Organization Science 11(5), 538–550 (2000), `http://dx.doi.org/10.1287/orsc.11.5.538.15204`
44. Wasko, M.M., Faraj, S.: Why should I share? Examining social capital and knowledge contribution in electronic networks of practice. MIS Quarterly, 35–37 (2005)
45. Wikimatrix (2011), `http://www.wikimatrix.org/` (accessed February 25, 2011)
46. Wikipedia, Comparison of wiki software (2011), `http://en.wikipedia.org/wiki/Comparison_of_wiki_software` (accessed January 10, 2011)
47. Wikipedia, Comparison of Wiki Farms (2011), `http://en.wikipedia.org/wiki/Comparison_of_wiki_farms` (accessed January 10, 2011)
48. Richter, A., Koch, M.: The enterprise 2.0 story in Germany so far. Paper presented at the International Conference on Computer-Supported Collaborative Work 2008, Workshop "What to expect from Enterprise 3.0: Adapting Web 2.0 to Corporate Reality", San DIego California, USA, November 8-12 (2008)
49. Socialtext (2011), `http://www.socialtext.com/customers/` (accessed January 12, 2011)
50. Kong, N., Hanrahan, B., Weksteen, T., Convertino, G., Chi, E.H.: VisualWikiCurator: human and machine intelligencefor organizing wiki content. Paper Presented at the Proceedings of the 16th International Conference on Intelligent User Interfaces, Palo Alto, CA, USA (2011)
51. White, K.F., Lutters, W.G.: Midweight collaborative remembering: wikis in the workplace. Paper presented at the Proceedings of the 2007 Symposium on Computer Human Interaction for the Management of Information Technology, Cambridge, Massachusetts (2007)
52. Plotnick, L., Ocker, R., Hiltz, S., Rosson, M.B.: Leadership Roles and Communication Issues in Partially Distributed Emergency Response Software Development Teams: A Pilot Study. Paper Presented at the Proceedings of the 41st Annual Hawaii International Conference on System Sciences (2008)
53. Lykourentzou, I., Papadaki, K., Vergados, D.J., Polemi, D., Loumos, V.: CorpWiki: A self-regulating wiki to promote corporate collective intelligence through expert peer matching. Information Sciences 180(1), 18–38 (2010)
54. Garrahan, M.: Disney's launches 'wiki' website aimed at parents. The Financial Times (2007)
55. Wilensky, H., Redmiles, D.: Adoption of Web 2.0 in the Enterprise: Technological Frames of KM Practitioners and Users. Paper Presented at the Computer Supported Cooperative Work, CSCW 2008, San Diego, California, USA, November 8-12 (2008)

Learning from the User: An Approach to Encouraging User-Generated Content within the Context of Social Media Communications

Isabel Anger and Christian Kittl

Evolaris next level GmbH, Hugo-Wolf-Gasse 8-8a,
8010 Graz, Austria
{isabel.anger,christian.kittl}@evolaris.net

Abstract. Internet phenomena like Facebook or Twitter hold great potential for companies. The 21st century's social networks are platforms for the (semi) public exchange of information. For an organisation, taking an active part in these conversations means gaining more trust, co-shaping its own image and obtaining knowledge from user-generated content. User-generated content can help optimise processes and act as a testimonial for the organisation's services and products. This paper offers a conceptional process model facilitating external knowledge management within organisational communication measures in Social Media.

Keywords: Marketing, Web 2.0, Social Media, Organisational Communications, User-generated Content.

1 Introduction

Platforms such as Facebook, Twitter or YouTube attract millions of people. The social network Facebook, for example, currently has more than 500 million active members who communicate and share multimedia content on the platform at least once a month. The great potential of the large quantity of publicly communicating persons is, however, often ignored by organisations. In Social Media – this term is a synonym for Web 2.0 and is used throughout this paper – users expect a certain amount of forthrightness and transparency by the communicating persons and organisations alike. The organisations, however, must act carefully in the process of sharing their knowledge as it is a crucial factor of economic success. In this area of conflict, companies must decide which information is published, how often and with what objective, to effectively use Social Media in their communication plans. The quickly and continuously evolving landscape of platforms and services and its use in organisational communications is, however, still largely unexploited in the scientific context.

This paper provides an approach to external communication in Social Media for the purpose of profiting from the knowledge of users. The publication of information by companies and the motivation of Social Media users to generate content are in focus. The following questions will be answered:

E. Ariwa and E. El-Qawasmeh (Eds.): DEIS 2011, CCIS 194, pp. 440–448, 2011.

- What information should be published?
- What content can be contributed by the users?
- What is the motivation of user-generated content?

Answering the questions will provide the basis for a conceptional process model.

The paper is structured as follows: After a brief explanation of the methodology, the theoretical basis which consists of a number of existing communication concepts and sociological research on Social Media is presented. In the second part, the conceptional process model which builds on the theoretical basis is introduced.

1.1 Definitions

In this paper, knowledge management is understood as a process of choosing, editing and distributing information [1]. In the context of Social Media communication this means that an organisation – whether it is non-profit or profit-oriented – shares and discusses information with an external target group. The objective is to gain new knowledge from interpersonal communication with the target group.

Social Media are platforms that facilitate this interpersonal communication, the publishing, discussing, rating and sharing of multimedia content without demanding high-level technical skills from the users [2]. Examples for Social Media platforms are Facebook, Twitter, LinkedIn or multimedia platforms such as Flickr or YouTube.

2 Methodology and Theoretical Basis

The conceptional process model presented in this paper is based on three existing models which provide steps to develop a strategy for using Social Media in organisational communications. Each model provides a different approach to communicating in digital social networks. These three approaches were analysed and split into their individual elements. The basis for the extraction of these elements esd the fundamental concept of a marketing plan [3] which includes the following steps: analysis of the starting point situation, objectives, strategy and activities, implementation and marketing mix, and finally, the measurement of results. The methods suggested for the different elements in the existing models (e.g. a Social Media SWOT analysis, the ACCESS model, the Lasswell formula) were compared and checked for integrity, feasibility and implementation in the overall context of organisational communications.

For each model, adequate case studies that were suggested by the authors of the respective model were analysed. With the insights gained from analysing the marketing concept and the case studies, the strengths and weaknesses of each existing Social Media concept were extracted and compared. Additionally, the insights gained from literature research on unique aspects of Social Media sociology, structures, technology and motivators for users to participate and generate content were considered.

Three concepts for organisational communications in Social Media were chosen from a variety of approaches for their clear structure and because they were equally based on theoretical research and practical experience. Each model has a unique approach and consists of different actions and methods for mastering each element in the strategy development process.

The first concept is a sales-oriented process model [4] which is closely aligned to the overall company objectives. The primary target groups are customers and potential new customers. The strength of this concept lies in its simplicity which enables companies without experience in the field of Social Media communications to engage in social networks quickly. It lacks, however, a method to conduct an analysis of the organisational starting point. The corresponding case study for this concept is the 2008 Social Media campaign of the current president of the United States, Barack Obama.

The second concept builds on the Lasswell formula [5] and extends it to comply with the netted structure of the web [6]. The focus is placed on reaching qualitative communication objectives and on providing a customer service oriented communication environment on Social Media. This concept provides a wide range of possibilities for measuring success. The case study for this approach is the Social Media strategy of computer manufacturer Dell.

The third concept offers a comprehensive three-phase model for devising a Social Media strategy [7]. In the first phase, different methods for analysing the organisational starting point are provided. The second phase is dedicated to creating adequate content for different platforms and target groups. In the third phase, the planned measures are implemented. Although it is very comprehensive, the concept lacks methods for measuring the success of the Social Media activities. The case study for this approach is the video campaign of the blender manufacturer Blendtec.

All three concepts lack approaches for setting up a budget for communication and only the three-phase model provides a guideline for setting up a time schedule for the communication activities.

2.1 Creating Content for Prosumers in Social Media

A prosumer is a Social Media user who produces and consumes content equally in the participatory environment of Social Media [8]. In Social Media, any user can become a producer of content without needing high-level technical skills. The only prerequisite for using Social Media is a valid e-mail address for signing up for the different services. The motivators for producing content and engaging in Social Media activities can be summarized with four main factors [7]:

- Communication: The prosumer fulfils his or her need for social interaction with the help of Social Media communication tools.
- Collaboration: The prosumer is part of a community and collaborates with other community members to reach a collective target.
- Education: The prosumer uses Social Media to gain and share information and knowledge.
- Entertainment: The prosumer consumes and produces entertaining content for a pastime.

Especially the factor *Collaboration* is important in the context of knowledge management. Collaboration implies that an equal share of input is contributed by each of the collaborating parties. For organisation, however, the publication of internal information and organisational knowledge might pose a critical. Although it might pose a value for the customer, the information secures economic success and should therefore be handled with care. Also, publishing information about customers or customer projects as well as personal information about employees without their consent is problematic. Therefore, guidelines that clearly define the rules for creating content and distributing it in digital social networks must be set up, explained and distributed to those in charge of officially communicating and thus acting as "the company voice" as well as to all other employees.

2.2 User-Generated Content

Information that provides value and is available for free is highly appreciated by the online community – as observed with the triumph of the open encyclopaedia Wikipedia. The users share valuable content (also seeking to positively influence their own status in the community), comment it and rate it positively. An organisation willing to listen to the users can profit from the published opinions and information. On the one hand, the organisation can optimise different areas of operation such as product design, product functionalities and communication according to customer feedback gathered on Social Media platforms. On the other hand, analysing the user-generated content on the web provides an overview on the sentiment and rating of the brand as well as trends and competitors.

User-generated content can be text, images, videos or audio generated and published by the users. The ideal type of prosumer produces and consumes content equally by definition. In practice, however, the Nielson 90-9-1 formula, the rule of participation inequality is more realistic: About 90 % of Social Media users are so-called *lurkers* who read or observe but do not contribute content. About 9 % of the users are *intermittent contributors* who contribute, edit and extend small portions of content. Approximately 1 % of the users are *heavy contributors* who supply most of the content [9]. For overcoming participation inequality or rather optimising the shares of lurkers, intermittent contributors and heavy contributors, the author provides a set of rules. These include creating an environment that encourages participation with continuous calls to action, providing rewards for participants without over-rewarding them and promoting quality contributors.

2.3 Motivators for User-Generated Content

As the creation of content for the web demands the dedication of time and thought, finding and utilizing the value of one's own content and leveraging the intrinsic and extrinsic motivators [10] for user-generated content plays an essential role in organisational communications. Intrinsic motivators are stimuli such as the desire to help others or to present oneself and establish one's status as an expert. These are motivators that the prosumer feels without external influence. Extrinsic motivators are any kind of reward expected or received from external entities but also praise or recognition which are situated in the upper levels of the hierarchy of needs, especially in the levels esteem and self-actualization [11].

The motivators for engaging in dialogue in Social Media are very similar to the motivators effecting social life offline as many behavioural patterns and norms known offline are transferred to online interaction situations. Intrinsic motivators online are self-presentation, social interaction, fun, curiosity and idealism. Extrinsic motivators consist of interest and praise from peers, belonging to a group and virtual or material rewards.

3 Conceptional Process Model

The conceptional process model presented in the following sections contains all elements from the initial analysis to performance measurement of the implemented Social Media activities. Figure 1 illustrates the process model.

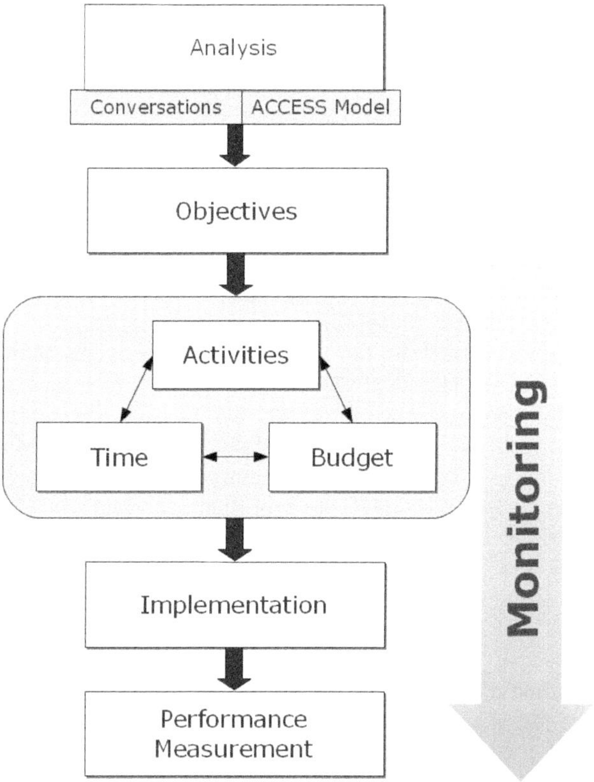

Fig. 1. Schematic illustration of the conceptional process model

3.1 Analysis

The first step in the concept is an analysis of the organisational starting point. This is the basis for all further steps and helps to determine whether an open communication structure is feasible and reasonable; and whether the concept of transparency is accepted by managers and employees alike. Additionally, the external starting point is analysed with the following methods:

Method 1: *Conversations* in Social Media according to the enhanced Lasswell model [5]: The Lasswell model describes the key elements of communication: "Who says what to whom in what channel to what effect." This is a linear approach to communication, channelling information and thus bringing it from the sender to the recipient. The enhanced Lasswell model [6] is "Who says what to whom in what channel to what effect then who hears what, who shares what with what intent to what effect." The enhanced model adds more actors to the communication process and blurs the boundaries between sender or content creator and recipient or consumer. This method allows the creation of a conversation landscape which visualises the current state of so-called "buzz" about a company or brand or keywords.

Method 2: The *ACCESS Model* [7]: This model includes six aspects of corporate communications that need to be considered when setting up a strategy.

- Audience: Evaluation of key target groups or segments on Social Media.
- Concept: Basic ideas on means of communication with the target groups including messages and channels.
- Competition: Overview of similar case studies in the same economic branch.
- Execution: Overview of all issues around the campaign such as legal concerns and human resources available for the campaign etc.
- Social Media: Selection of platforms suited for the desired audience and concept.
- Sales Viability: Business model underlying the concept.

3.2 Objectives

In the second step, the objectives are defined. Communication objectives can be divided into psychological and economic objectives. Psychological objectives are long-term goals including sustainable branding and image building. They cannot be measured in numbers and are determined by conducting market research. Economic objectives are short-term goals that can be expressed in numbers. Any objective must be clearly described, scheduled and measurable. An example objective is the increase of user-generated content on the organisation's Facebook page by 100 % within 12 months. Case studies of similar campaigns or from similar branches provide indicators for realistic objectives.

As Social Media, though unique in its communication demands, is an extension of existing communication channels, it is essential to align Social Media communication objectives with the objectives defined in the existing overall communication strategy.

3.3 Activities, Time and Budget

These three elements are strongly interconnected and must therefore be viewed as one step in the concept. The element "Activities" includes the selection of Social Media platforms (e.g. blogs, wikis, and accounts on social networks such as Facebook) and associated tasks. The element "Time" refers to a time schedule in which activity, objective and person in charge are listed. A 12-month time plan and an average spending of 30 minutes per day for the monitoring and care for the individual platforms is suggested for the initial implementation of Social Media communication [7]. The element "Budget" contains an estimation of all costs for the communication activities. As the use of most Social Media platforms is free, the largest part of the costs consists of personnel expenses.

3.4 Implementation

The next step is the implementation or execution of the devised measures. In this step processes within the organisation are gradually adjusted to meet the demands of Social

Media. Throughout the implementation process and the continuing communication on Social Media platforms, the development and evolution of new technologies or platforms that could have an impact on the organisation's communication plan must be supervised.

3.5 Performance Measurement

At the end of the communications campaign or at milestones of the communication process, a set of operating figures enables the organisation to determine the performance of the strategy. These operating figures are chosen according to the designated objective set up in step 2 of the process model. Two categories of operating figures can be distinguished: Level 1 figures (activity scores) and level 2 figures (quality scores). The first include basic indicators expressed in absolute numbers, e.g. amount of readers, followers or amount of content. Examples of level 1 figures are:

- *Raw Author Contribution* is the amount of own content published in Social Media.
- *Traffic, visitors* on different Social Media platforms.
- *Followers, Readers, Fans, Memberships* on different Social Media platforms.
- *Mentions, Links, Recommendations* from other users.
- Amount of *User-Generated Content.*

Level 2 figures are based upon level 1 figures, provide interpretation of level 1 figures and further insights into the quality of the organisation's performance. Level 2 figures include:

- *Interaction Ratio* describes the rate of interactions compared to the total amount of content published.
- *Mention Ratio* describes the amount of mentions, links or recommendations received in comparison to the total amount of content published.
- *Sentiment* (positive, negative or neutral) of comments and user-generated content.
- *Conversion Rate* is the amount of active contacts, acquired customers etc. (depending on the objectives) compared to the total amount of contacts.

The term raw author contribution refers to the amount of content created by the organisation itself. The content is the substance needed to trigger discussion and encourage dialogue. The publication of a large amount of quality multimedia content in combination with calls to action directed at the users to encourage dialogue demonstrates the organisation's will to communicate transparently and authentically and should therefore be seen as the basis for the performance measurement figures.

Additionally, key performance indicators from the field of knowledge management can be included in the performance measurement process. Example indicators for knowledge management are [12]:

- User Participation, generated ideas and extension of the organisational knowledge base.
- Costs for knowledge management, e.g. expenses for personnel.
- Usage of the knowledge base and intermediate effects on the organisation.
- Long-term effects on the organisational objectives.

Long-term performance measurement requires the use of more general performance indicators such as effects on revenue, profits, market share and image. In the long run, Social Media provide yet another tool for reaching organisational objectives.

3.6 Accompanying Process: Monitoring

Monitoring is the process of observing the Social Media landscape and conversations throughout the entire campaign. Identifying relevant conversations and trending topics enables the organisation to interact at the right places and at the right time. This can be done by subscribing to e-mail alert services but also by manual search. By monitoring performance figures such as interaction frequency and the development of follower figures, the effects of communication measures can be analysed. Reactions to released information, to calls to action or to discussions can be used as the decision basis for upcoming communication activities.

4 Conclusion

Social Media offers a lot of potential to broaden and optimise the knowledge and information basis and processes of an organisation. In the long term, this external knowledge management through Social Media communication supports the economic success of the organisation and also influences its image. A strategic procedure as presented in this paper enables the efficient and effective use of Social Media and its implementation within the overall context of organisational communications.

We have deliberately excluded a description or analysis of individual Social Media. It is important to set up a strategy based upon the basic pillars and principles of Social Media instead of focusing on individual services. Platforms may change, be shut down or evolve with time, urging users to move to new platforms. This may force organisations to abandon established accounts on less attractive platforms and migrate to other ones. The basic principles of Social Media, the idea of social knowledge exchange, openness and transparency, will remain.

If the content published by the organisation is valuable for the user, it will be discussed and shared. Any information that concerns non-disclosure agreements or personal information should, however, be handled with care and excluded from public communication in Social Media.

User-generated content can be encouraged by considering motivators and the unique characteristics of Social Media. Although the use of most Social Media platforms is free of charge, effective communication requires commitment and time and the willingness to be transparent and involve the target group into optimisation processes.

Finally, Social Media must not be understood as something an organisation is obliged to work with. Social Media pose a chance to participate and profit from the conversations about persons, companies and brands that are lead in Social Media in any case – whether on organisation takes part in them or not.

References

1. Schüppel, J.: Wissensmanagement. In: Organisatorisches Lernen im Spannungsfeld von Wissens- und Lernbarrieren. Gabler, Wiesbaden (1996)
2. Kaplan, A.M., Haenlein, M.: Users of the World, Unite! The Challenges and Opportunities of Social Media. Business Horizons 53(1) (2010), http://dx.doi.org/10.1016/j.bushor.2009.09.003
3. Pelz, W.: Strategisches und Operatives Marketing. In: Ein Leitfaden zur Erstellung Eines Professionellen Marketing-Plans. Books on Demand, Norderstedt (2004)
4. Meerman Scott, D.: The New Rules of Marketing & PR. In: How to Use Social Media, Blogs, News Releases, Online Video, and Viral Marketing to Reach Buyers Directly. John Wiley & Sons, Hoboken (2010)
5. Lasswell, H.: The Structure and Function of Communication in Society. In: Bryson, L. (ed.) The Communication of Ideas. Institute for Religious and Social Studies, New York (1948)
6. Solis, B., Breakenridge, D.: Putting the Public Back in Public Relations. In: How Social Media Is Reinventing the Aging Business of PR. FT Press, Upper Saddle River (2009)
7. Brake, D., Safko, L.: The Social Media Bible. In: Tactics, Tools & Strategies for Business Success. John Wiley & Sons, Hoboken (2009)
8. Beer, D., Burrows, R.: Sociology and, of and in Web 2.0. Some Initial Considerations. Sociological Research Online 12 (2007), http://www.socresonline.org.uk/12/5/17.html
9. Nielsen, J.: Participation Inequality. Encouraging More Users to Contribute. Jakob Nielsen Blog (October 9, 2006), http://www.useit.com/alertbox/participation_inequality.html
10. Barbuto, J.E., Scholl, R.W.: Motivation Sources Inventory. Development and Validation of new Scales to Measure an Integrative Taxonomy of Motivation. Psychological Reports 82(3) (1998)
11. Maslow, A.H.: A Theory of Human Motivation. Psychological Review 50(4) (1943)
12. North, K., Probst, G., Romhardt, K.: Wissen Messen – Ansätze, Erfahrungen und Kritische Fragen. Zeitschrift für Führung und Organisation 3 (1998)

Extraction of User Information by Pattern Matching Techniques in Windows Physical Memory

Funminiyi Olajide and Nick Savage

Department of Electronic and Computer Engineering,
University of Portsmouth, UK
{funminiyi.olajide,nick.savage}@port.ac.uk

Abstract. There have been few investigations into the amount of relevant information that can be recovered from the physical memory of Windows applications. Extraction of user information is vital in today's digital investigation and forensic investigators find it helpful to gain access to dispersal evidence stored over time in the physical memory of these applications. In this research, we present the quantitative and qualitative results of experiments carried out on the extraction of forensically relevant information from Windows computer systems. This process involves a pattern matching techniques of the original user input and the extracted memory dump strings processes. In conducting this research; we have identified the most commonly used applications on Windows systems, designed a methodology to capture data and processed that data. This research will report the amount of evidence dispersed over time in the physical memory when the application was running and user is not interacting with the system.

Keyword: User, information, pattern, matching, application, physical, Windows.

1 Introduction

For the purpose of incident response and analysis, volatile system memory is a valuable medium for the collection of digital evidence [1]. While traditional digital forensic techniques have focused on disk drives and other more lasting data sources [2], [3] system memory can provide a great deal of information about the systems runtime state at the time of, or just after, an incident [4], [5], [6]. These approach details running processes, loaded libraries, logged-in users, listening network sockets and open files in systems memory. In Windows volatile memory, there have been outstanding results into the research of application level evidence from the extracted memory dump processes of Windows applications based on user activities [7]. But, little has been done on the analysis of acquired evidence extracted from these commonly used applications. The recovery of user information from the physical memory of applications can be used to determine the amount of relevant evidence dispersed and as stored over time. This approach focused on memory imaging, when the application is still running and user is not interacting with the systems. In addition to this, the memory allocated to the extracted user information can be used to infer what the user has been using the applications for; the information which may not be

E. Ariwa and E. El-Qawasmeh (Eds.): DEIS 2011, CCIS 194, pp. 449–465, 2011.

visible when using traditional hard disk forensic investigation. By pattern matching techniques, the original user input information can be matched with the extracted memory dump string processes of the applications. This approach can visibly locate how the evidence is stored in the memory. The investigation of this information contained within the memory of the application and may become an essential tool for information assurance as well as solving crime and tracing fraud against people, where evidence may reside on a computer. For example, bank fraud, identity fraud, money laundering and child exploitation by paedophile uses social networking services like facebook and other twitted applications as a means of communication to commit various crimes.

In progress to this research, forensic investigation techniques for experiments have been designed to investigate the quantity and quality of information recovered from the physical memory of commonly used applications. This approach can reveal what user has been doing on the application and this, can provides additional relevant evidence when forensically investigating the volatile memory of Windows computer systems. In this research, the most commonly used applications have been identified and 100 sample data of the information retrievable from those applications had been conducted. The result of this investigation will facilitate the pattern matching techniques on physical memory of an application based on various user input. This will help in further analysis of the data found in the physical memory allocated to the application.

2 Related Work

The current tools and techniques for analyzing forensic data in the physical memory are limited. But, a framework was developed for automatic evidence discovery and correlation from a variety of forensic targets [8]. This demonstrates the integrated analysis and correlation of a disk image, memory image, network capture and configuration log files. A recent workshop on digital forensic highlighted the need of the forensic community for the development of tools and techniques for capturing data and analyzing the physical memory of computer systems [9]. The research idea is motivated on the facts that applications on physical memory content contain information that cannot be found on traditional hard disk forensic investigations. Olajide and Savage, identified seven most commonly used applications in Windows system and, design a methodology approach to the extraction processes of relevant evidence from physical memory [10]. This research facilitated the investigation and the analysis of data found in the physical memory content of the applications. The extended version of this research paper was presented on [11], which discusses on the identification of information extracted from the Windows physical memory. Although, Burdach describes that the memory extraction tools are not fully developed, [12], some tools do currently exist. Some of these tools required specialist hardware to be added to the computer system in order to extract the memory image. An example of this type of tool has been developed by Garcia, [13]. Garcia's tool is among the few hardware-based memory acquisition methods that use a PCI extension card to dump the memory content to an external device. Hardware based acquisition tools have advantages and is not requiring any additional software to be executed on the computer system when acquiring evidence. However, they do need to have the tool installed on every machine which may require investigation prior to that investigation. For this reason there has been much focus on software-based tools.

Msuiche has developed a command line tool that can be used on Windows to extract the physical memory of the computer system, [14]. It also reconstructs the virtual address space of the system process and other processes. In an attempts to find the most applicable tool to use, Memory dd developed by ManTech International Corporation was tested [15]. This tool is capable of revealing hidden and terminated processes and threads. Also, Windows Internal 5, covering Window server by using Win32dd [16], developed by Solomon and Russinovich was also tested during our investigation. However, Nigilant32 was very useful when tested. This tool allows an investigator to preview a memory image and take a snapshot of it. It has a small footprint, using less than 1 MB in memory when loaded and with a minimal impact during acquisition [17]. This tool was used to capture and or image the physical memory of computer systems.

There are few tools that can perform memory analysis. Some example are MemParser [18] and the Volatility Framework [19]. Of these two, the Volatility Framework is more extensive. This tool is capable of performing the analysis on a variety of memory image formats such as DD format, crash dump and Hibernate Dumps. Volatility is able to list OS kernel modules, drivers, open network socket, loaded DLL modules, heaps stacks and open files. Recently, a seminar addressed the need for more sophisticated tools on physical memory acquisition and analysis [20]. This is because external and internal intrusions will continue even in the robust security infrastructures of the best government and industry systems. But the key to successfully preventing and responding to any digital fraud investigations is the sound identification, collection, preservation and analysis of computer evidence. The workshop of [9], issued a memory analysis challenge to encourage research and tool development in this direction. Therefore, a method of [21] laid emphasis on the importance of forensic live response and event reconstruction methods. The extension of this work relies on the research of application level evidence from physical memory [7]. This research identified the important aspects of memory analysis and proposed an approach for application level evidence. A paper [22], identified the dispersal of time aspect of information stored on physical memory. This approach provides prospective information on how evidence is dispersed in the memory of some commonly used application during memory analysis. Olajide and Savage [23], discuses the methodology approach of extracting relevant information from the physical memory of Windows XP. This approach demonstrates the application process of user information on Windows applications. As a result of various research investigations that have been carried out on the extraction of relevant user information from the physical memory of Windows applications, it has become imperative to investigate into how original user input information can be matched with extracted memdump strings processes. This is a pattern matching techniques that we have implemented.

3 Methodology

The important aspect of this research is the identification of most commonly used applications on Window Systems of which to perform the experiments on. To ensure that our results are as applicable as possible, we attempted to identify which applications are commonly used by businesses. This is by contacting different institutions like banks, commercial retailer, telecommunication and public services to ask their technical support team which application were most commonly used on Windows systems. The most commonly used applications identified by this enquiry were Word 2007, Excel 2007, PowerPoint 2007, Outlook 2007, MS Access 2007, Internet Explorer 7.0 and Adobe Reader 8.0. In order to make our results as applicable as possible we tried to replicate a normal working environment while capturing memory images. In this, the computer would be turned on at the start of the day and then turned off at the end of the business day. When the computer is first turned on the application will be opened.

During the day user will interact with the applications recording exactly what was done and not using the computer for any other purpose. Example of 30 minutes blocks of user input information is shown in Table 1. The physical memory of the computer is captured every 30 minutes by Nigilant32. An example of this happening is shown in Figure 1. As earlier mentioned, there are seven applications studied in the overall research but, in this paper, we are presenting only the results of four of these; Outlook Email 2007, Internet Explorer 7.0, MS Access 2007, and Adobe Reader 8.0.

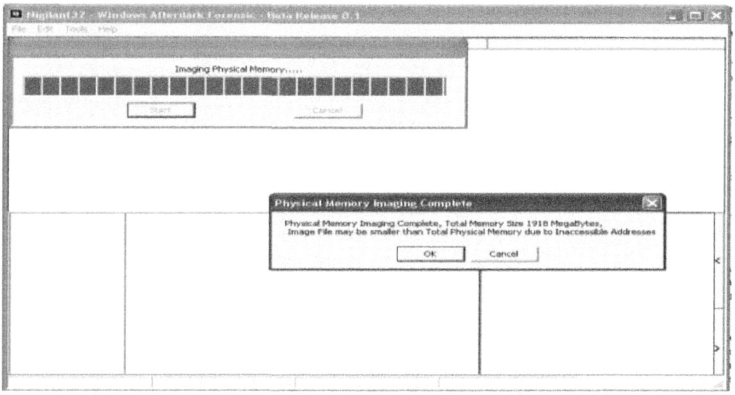

Fig. 1. Nigilant32 capturing physical memory

As describe in Table 1, is a typical flow of the evidence-based procedures that was formulised for the purpose of this research. Before we commenced the experiments using Nigilant32, windows machine was shut down and rebooted to ensure that the system was as clean as possible. This is to ensure that the memory allocated to each application had not previously been used to store unrelated data. Moreover, user inputs were made in each of the application at set interval of 30 minutes.

Table 1. Methodology Approach

Sample Application	User Action at every 30 minutes
Outlook 2007	Write a paragraph of text with commas, full stop, semi-colon, with subject headings. Send and receive email data to and from or do nothing. Save document or do not save. Various user input of information on the application at set interval.
Word 2007	Write paragraph of text, with commas, semi-colon, full stop, or do nothing on the document, save document or do not save document. Input alphanumeric, character 0-9, brackets closed or open and or, not. Long sentence or short.
MS Access 2007	Write text and numbers on database or do nothing, save document or do not save
Excel 2007	Lists set of numbers, draw a graph of the numbers or do nothing, save document or do not save. Input may contain alphanumeric, character 0-9, brackets close or open and or, not. Long sentence or short.
Adobe Reader 8.0	Highlights texts, search for texts or do nothing save document or do not save
PowerPoint 2007	Write a slide, slides of texts or do nothing, save document or do not save. User input may contain or type alphanumeric, character 0-9, brackets close or open and or, not. Long sentence or short.
IE70	Open or click on news. Click back or front, save or do not save. Highlights texts, search for texts or do nothing

As we can see from the Table 1, user actions on the application vary at interval. In some cases, no input users were made on applications but, images were captured at every 30 minutes. We ran series of test for ten days and this was continued until 100 images were captured on each application. As the physical memory in the computer was 2 Gigabytes (GB), this resulted in 200 GB of images being captured. After the collection of data, we make copies of images captured on each application for data storage and preservation purposes. In this experiment, our opinion was to identify what information can be recovered from only the RAM while the application is still running on Windows system and user was not interacting with the systems. Figure 2 describe the summary algorithms of experiment carried out in the first phase of our contribution.

Summary of experiment:

1). Windows systems were provided for the purpose of this experiment

2). Concurrently, opened the most commonly used applications on the Windows system.

3). As described in table 1, various user input and actions were then made on each of the application within a set period of time.

4). On target machine, we ran the trusted command shell of Nigilant32 to capture volatile images at every 30 minutes

5). Images were stored as captured on external disk and made copies of them.

Fig. 2. Summary of experiment

Furthermore, we consider components of user activities in the memory. The idea is to investigate the recovery process of information related to how a user is using the application. In this experiment, we developed series of self implemented code for evidence extraction, searching and pattern matching procedures. Firstly, we use volatility software to identify running processes on windows systems and sift through the selected applications. Secondly, we developed series of program written in python with the use of volatility software to convert raw images captured into dump processes. Also, we ran a python program to extract string processes from memory dump processes of the selected applications. Our intention is to ascertain recovery process of all information related to how a user is using the application in the physical memory.

Figure 3 described the algorithm summary of the experiment carried out in the second phase of this research. This includes the methodology approach of the automated executable program used for the memdump and extraction processes. Also, the approach of evidence searching and matching techniques was explored in the physical memory of Windows systems.

Summary of automated program for the evidence extraction

6). Run automated program written in python to dump memory

7).Run automated program written in python to extract strings processes for evidence searching

8). Run automated program written in python for evidence matching.

9) Run automated executable code to determine series of data base results of our findings

Fig. 3. Summary of program developed

As shown in Figure 3, series of automated executable program was developed. For this, a python code was installed and implemented on Windows systems using software like python, volatility software and string conversion tool. These tools can be used for memory analysis being an open source code. The approach is to match the original user input information with the extracted memory dump string processes of application. This resulted in a file that contains fragments of data that may be considered as evidence. Figure 4, describes a summary example of the step taken for pattern matching techniques.

Summary of pattern matching techniques

Run automated pattern matching technique written in Python code i.e. matches the original user input information with the extracted memdump strings processes of application as follows:

1. Open the initial log of user input evidence on application
2. Run a program code to read all data texts and search for exact character strings
3. Zero out an array to count character elements
4. Open memory dump strings processes in range of 10 characters
5. Find range of user input information in a range of 10 characters

Fig. 4. Summary of pattern matching technique

As investigated and implemented in this experiment, the extracted user information contains both partial and whole fragments of evidence. The next stage in processing the data is to identify those fragments extracted from memory that contain evidence which may be used to recreate what the user was using the application for. In order to do this, a pattern matching routine was developed using python code which identified partial fragments of evidence. In our experiment, strings of character were executed to assert that a certain piece of original user input data is equal to a certain pattern of the application processes that was extracted from the memory dump. In this, we match strings of user input that consists of letter first, and then a number. This is based on what a user is doing on the application. Basically, we compare partial fragments of the extracted memory with the saved user input to the application.

4 Result: Sample Quantitative Assessment

In this section, we present the quantitative assessment of user information that can be used as forensically relevant data. This information was extracted from the physical memory content of MS Access, Adobe, IE70 and Outlook Email. This investigation focused on the identification of user information and how much relevant evidence was dispersed in the physical memory. The memory image was captured at set interval while the application was still running and user is not interacting with the systems. In order to present the results, the following statistics which are indicative of the quantity of relevant user input information that was recovered was formulised. There are three scenarios we considered in the quantitative result analysis. These are mean evidence in repetitions, mean percentage of evidence found and mean evidence in a continuous block. *Firstly, the Mean Evidence in Repetition* is the average number of repeated evidence extracted and found in the physical memory of an application. This process can be used to match the original character of word information entered by the user and with the extracted memory dump strings processes. Then, it searches to count the identical characters that appears repeatedly in the memory allocated to that application. *Secondly, the mean percentage of evidence found* is calculated based on the number of character of the original user input and the extracted memory dump string data. This character was counted as it was stored in the memory and found relevant to the evidence searched for. Where evidence is not found, it resulted in zeros. The percentage of evidence found is the total numbers of evidence found without zeros. Thirdly, t*he mean evidence in a continuous block* is the length of evidence found in a continuous block in the physical memory of an application. The length of the character is 10 in a row. This character length was determined by the process of matching the original user input information with the extracted memory dump strings data. This process counts the lengths of identical character numbers of evidence found in the memory, where evidence was allocated and then, matched the evidence found with the original user inputs information. As described in Table 2, there are different percentages of evidence found on applications and mean average value of evidence in repetitions differs. Thus, the average length of evidence found in a continuous block varies as experimented on the sample applications.

Table 2. Result analysis sample applications

Element of Experiments	Outlook Email 2007	Adobe Reader 8.0	MS Access 2007	IE70
Mean Evidence Repetition	291.00	95.00	453.92	152.00
Mean % of Evidence found	95	35	39	99
Average Length of Evidence found in Continuous block	24.59	34.48	17.22	37.40

For example, in Adobe, we were able to recover the least amount of relevant information. The percentage of evidence found in this application was 35%. Original user input was described in Table 1. The result shows that not all the user input was visible in the memory. It is either dispersed in the memory or cannot be recovered. In the case of MS Access application, the percentage of evidence was recorded as 39%. This evidence found in the memory was based on various user input. The format function of this application usually takes an expression and returns it as formatted strings in the memory. MS Access allows user to either define owns format or use one of the named formats that has been predefined in the application database source. In this experiment, we discovered that user uses both. The predefined format shows that user write text and numbers on database or does nothing. User save document or do not save as described in Table 1. The user input information that was recovered was dispersed as stored over time. Further analysis indicated that not all user input can be recovered in the memory of this application.

Moreover, we have large amount of evidence stored over time on Outlook Email and IE70 applications. This information is relevant to various user actions on these applications. Series of experiments was performed for days; we investigated to find out how much the dispersal evidence was stored in the memory and how this evidence can be reconstructed for evidential purposes. Table 1 described user information and amongst all these applications, IE70 recorded a remarkable amount of 99.9% of evidence found and as dispersed in the memory. We discovered that all users input information was visible and can be recovered as stored over time in the memory. In the case of Outlook Email, user input information consists of alphanumeric characters of data texts. Of these applications and as stated in Table 1, this user input was made at set interval. The percentage amount of evidence found in Outlook Email application was 95%. This evidence information was also remarkable. The result of the experiments shows that where user input contained more of data texts strings than the numeric data then, the whole fragments of relevant evidence can be recovered in large content. In this approach, it was evident that large percentage amount of evidence was found and as stored over time in the memory content of these applications. We calculated the mean average value of evidence found in repetitions of these applications. Table 2, described the repeated evidence found in the physical memory of Outlook application as well as the evidence found in a continuous block. The amount of evidence found and repeated evidence may be important in digital investigation. This information can be useful to forensic investigators to justify the questions of who, when, what, where and how the evidence was allocated and how the evidences fond can be reconstructed in the memory. This user information can be classified as dispersal evidence and can be recovered in fragment of evidence.

5 Result: Sample Qualitative Assessment

In this section, we considered sample user information evidence that was extracted from the physical memory content of the four applications considered in this paper. These are Outlook Email, MS Access, Adobe Reader 8.0 and Internet Explorer 7.0. In this experiment, we clarify how evidence was dispersed in the memory, how the relevant information can be recovered as stored over time in the memory and how much user information can be reconstructed by pattern matching techniques. An example of qualitative fragments of evidence recovered from physical memory of Outlook Email is as shown in Figure 2.

5.1 Outlook Email Application

As described in Table 2 above, the percentage of evidence found on Outlook Email was 95%. This result shows the relevant user information and how this information related to what user was doing on the applications. The user evidence information can be recovered as stored over time in the physical memory. The evidence found is a remarkable based on the pattern matching techniques we have implemented in this research work. There are relevant amount of dispersal evidence found in the memory of Outlook Email. In this experiment, it was investigated that Outlook Email consists of predefined format of information like: *To, From and Subject.* This is the application predefined format that was embedded in Windows Outlook Email. It is evident that this type of information was not originally entered by the user but, when sending an email, it is compulsory for a user to enter relevant information on these predefined formats. Mostly, this information indicated where user is sending the information to and from where the information was received with a subject title of the email.

In the qualitative assessment of evidence found on Outlook Email, relevant user information was found repeated and appears consistently in a continuous block, in the physical memory of the application. We reconstructed this user input information with the extracted memdump strings evidence by pattern matching techniques. For example in Figure 5, user input information like "*Jonny Cole*". This information was found repeated in three different locations in the physical memory. Also, user input information like: *"Hung Parliament"*. This information appears repeatedly and reveal how it was stored over time in three different locations. In this perspective, the question of *where* the allocated evidence was found in the memory has been answered. The line numbers linked to this evidence in the memory is a typical example. Also, the original data texts information indicated *what* user was doing on the application. The questions of "*who*" *was* doing something on the application can be traced to the person that input data texts information on Outlook application.

Extracting Evidence from "Outlook Email Application" Date of Data Captured: 27/04/2010 Memory Dump String: Yes	
Original Text	Evidence Extracted From MEMDUMP STRINGS Partial / Whole Fragment with Line Numbers.
From: Jonny Cole Sent: 27 April 2010 09:21 To: jonnycole@hotmail.co.uk Subject: Hung Parliament Jade, The report has been made that hung parliament is not too good for economy and people should make their decision now and for all. There is little one can do in the need for people votes, but we would all see when people cast their votes and make their mind clear about the election Kallly	5616 Jonny Cole 5696 The report has been made that hung parliament is not too good for 6135 economy and people should make their decision now and for all. There is 6136 little one can do in the need for people votes, but we would all see 6137 when people cast their votes and make their mind clear about the 190356 The report has been made that hung parliament is not too good for economy and people should make their decision now and for all. There is little one can do in the need for people votes, but we would all see when people cast their votes and make their mind clear about the election 225722 Hung Parliament 236646 The report has been made that hung parliament is not too good for economy and people should make their decision now and for all. There is little one can do in the need for people votes, but we would all see when people cast their votes and make their mind clear about the election 237000 Jonny Cole 505774 Jonny Cole 505777 27 April 2010 09:21 505779 jonnycole @hotmail.co.uk 505781 Hung Parliament 505783 The report has been made that hung parliament is not too good for economy and people should make 505785 their decision now and for all. There is little one can do in the need for people votes, but we would all 505786 see when people cast their votes and make their mind clear about the election

Fig. 5. Outlook Email: Original Text / Extracted memdump evidence

Moreover, a user entered information on Outlook application and was stored over time in the memory. Also, it was found repeated and appears consistently in different locations. In this case, the questions of *when* the user input this information has been answered based on the allocated line numbers to this evidence in the allocated memory. As shown in Figure 5, the original user input data texts were contained in the *body texts* of sample Outlook Email sent. This evidence was found dispersed and appears repeatedly. For example the *line numbers: 190356 and 236646* indicated the whole fragments of evidence found and as repeated in the physical memory. This is the relevant user information extracted from the memdump of this application. Also, the questions of how evidence found can be reconstructed in the physical memory of Outlook Email become vital. For example, line numbers *505783, 505785 and 505786* illustrated the partial evidence found. This information can be reconstructed to form the whole fragment of the original user input information on the sample email sent. *Line number 505779* indicated where the body texts were sent to while line *505777,* illustrated when the information was sent to. This information has therefore; clarify the *"when"* question in memory analysis during forensic digital investigation. The result of the investigation shows that by pattern matching technique, we can reconstruct the event of user information. In this, both whole and partial evidence of original user input can be found as stored over time in the physical memory of the application.

5.2 Adobe Application

As described in Table 2 above, the percentage of evidence found on Adobe application was 35%. This result shows the least amount of relevant user information that can be recovered in the physical memory. This evidence information is related to what user was doing on the applications.

Figure 6 illustrated the least amount of information that can be recovered in the physical memory of this application by pattern matching techniques that we have implemented. Table 1 indicated "*what*" the user was doing on the application. The amount of evidence found was visible but was not repeated as in the case of other applications. There are no whole fragments of evidence found. The evidence found was not dispersed in the memory, but we discovered the partial fragment of evidence in the memory. For example, line numbers *221721 and 221780* are typical example of partial user information found. This information was stored over time in the memory of this application.

Extracting Evidence from "ADOBE READER 8.0 Application" Date of Data Captured: 27/04/2010 Memory Dump String: Yes	
Original Text	**Evidence Extracted From MEMDUMP STRINGS Partial /Whole Fragment with Line Numbers**
Open Reference Form Study be relevant to the needs of the oil Satisfactorily recommended In the applicant's participation	221721 Satisfactorily 221780 Recommended

Fig. 6. ADOBE: Original Text / Extracted memdump evidence

5.3 MS Access Application

In this experiment, the percentage of evidence found on MS Access application was 39% as shown in Table 2 above. This result shows the relevant user information that was recovered as stored over time in the memory

Figure 7, illustrated the qualitative results of user information in MS Access application. User input information was described in Table 1. There are no significant amounts of relevant information recovered from the physical memory. Original user input indicated alphanumeric characters but the extracted evidence found contained partial and some irrelevant data texts of user input. This was found repeated and appears consistently in the memory. In MS Access user input can be made on either the user defined owns format or use one of the named formats that have been

Extracting Evidence from "MS Access Application" Date of Data Captured: 27/04/2010 Memory Dump String: Yes	
Original Text	Evidence Extracted From MEMDUMP STRINGS Partial /Whole Fragment with Line Numbers
Open Item Category Condition Location Purchase Price Current Value Owner Acquired Date Attachments Open Banking (1) Category (2) Good (2) Location $881,114,775.00 $554,542,224,525.00 Fummy 24/04/2010 0 Open Administration (1) Category (2) Good (1) Location $558,223,382.00 $66,582.00 Petre 16/04/2010 0 Open Treasury (1) Category (2) Good (2) Location $55,245.00 $2,236,654.00 Petre 26/04/2010 0 Open Petroleum (1) Category (2) Good (3) Location $885.00 $889,754.00 Petre 23/04/2010 0 Open Coal (1) Category (2) Good (1) Location $6,692,238,850.00 $3,366,552.00 Petre 24/04/2010 0 5 $8,131,633,137.00 $554,548,784,067.00	718 Attachments 729 Attachments 39594 Acquired Date 62940 Purchase Price 62941 Current Value 62942 Attachments 63230 Purchase Price_Label 63232 Current Value 63234 Current Value_Label 159612 Attachments 159613 Attachments_Label 159614 Attachments 159615 AttachmentsAssetsAttachmentsAsset List.Assets.Attachments 159655 Current ValueAssetsCurrent ValueAsset List.Assets.Current Value 159663 Purchase PriceAssetsPurchase PriceAsset List.Assets.Purchase Price 159665 Acquired DateAssetsAcquired DateAsset List.Assets.Acquired Date

Fig. 7. MS Access: Original Text / Extracted memdump evidence

predefined in MS Access. We discovered that user uses both of these formats but, the amount of information recovered from the memory contained more of the predefined format than the user owns defined format. For example, the sample predefined format like *"Attachments"* was found repeated and appears consistently in the physical memory of this application. This information was found in five different locations as shown in line numbers: *718, 729, 62942, 159612 and 159615*. However, the user define format was used to input information like the amount of goods entere*d, $554,542,224,525.00* and the name attached to this database like *"Fummy"* are irrecoverable in the extracted memdump of evidence found on this application.

5.4 Internet Explorer 7.0 (IE70) Application

In this experiment, user actions were recorded as described in Table 1. The information can be relevant to what user was doing on the application. The percentage amount of information recovered was 99% as shown in Table 2. This is remarkable; the evidence recovered was stored over time in the physical memory of this application. Figure 8, illustrated the sample qualitative evidence of the extracted memdump information that was recovered from memory content of Internet Explorer 7.0 application.

We investigated to discover that there are two users' attempts on this application. It was recorded that user access two different WebPages and performed various actions as stated in Table 2. The investigative process of this experiment shows that user actions can be recovered. The user evidence information found was stored over time in the physical memory. The user information found was repeated and appears

<table>
<tr><td colspan="2">Extracting Evidence from "Internet Explorer (IE70) Application"
Date of Data Captured: 27/04/2010 Memory Dump String: Yes</td></tr>
<tr><td>Original Text</td><td>Evidence Extracted From MEMDUMP STRINGS
Partial /Whole Fragment with Line Numbers</td></tr>
<tr><td>From: <Saved by Windows Internet Explorer 7>
Subject: Katie Price Pregnant? Model Fuels Rumours After Pulling Out Of London Marathon On Doctor's Orders | Showbiz News | Sky News Date: Tue, 27 Apr 2010 09:52:11 +0100 _Orders. HEAD><TITLE>Katie Price =Pregnant? Model Fuels Rumours After Pulling Out Of London Marathon On =Doctor's Orders | Showbiz News | Sky News</TITLE> 3D"<p>Katie Price has fuelled rumours she may be pregnant after = pulling out of the London marathon on doctor's orders. </p>"=3D"Katie Price Pregnant? Model Fuels Rumours After Pulling Out =Of London Marathon On Doctor's Orders"=20name=3Dkeywords>

From: <Saved by Windows Internet Explorer 7>
Subject: London Marathon: Iraq War Veteran Phil Packer Beats His Record By 13 Days | UK News | Sky NewsDate: Tue, 27 Apr 2010 09:51:22 +0100
MIME-Version: 1.0Content-Type: multipart/related; type="text/html"; boundary="----
_NextPart_000_02F2_01CAE5EF.31DAAE80"
X-MimeOLE: Produced By Microsoft MimeOLE V6.00.2900.2180This is a multi-part message in MIME format.
http://news.sky.com/skynews/Home/UK-News/London-Marathon-Iraq-War-Veteran-Phil-Packer-Beats-His-Record-By-13-</td>
<td>1870
Katie Price Pregnant? Model Fuels Rumours After Pulling Out Of London Marathon On Doctor's Orders | Showbiz News | Sky News
3491
Katie Price Pregnant? Model Fuels Rumours After Pulling Out Of London Marathon On Doctor's Orders | Showbiz News | Sky News
3492
ws Internet Explorer
21829
Katie Price Pregnant? Model Fuels Rumours After Pulling Out Of London Marathon On Doctor's Orde - Windows Internet Explorer
Date: Tue, 27 Apr 2010 09:52:11 +0100
MIME-Version: 1.0 : http://news.sky.com/skynews/Home/Showbiz-News/Katie-Price-Pregnant-Model-Fuels-Rumours-After-Pulling-Out-Of-London-Marathon-On-Doctors-Orders/Article/201004215601764?lpos=Showbiz_News_Article_Related_Content_Region_5&lid=ARTICLE_15601764_Katie_Price_Pregnant_Model_Fuels_Rumours_After_Pulling_Out_Of_London_Marathon_On_Doctors9984
ndon Marathon: Iraq War Veteran Phil Packer Beats His Record By 13 Days | UK News | Sky News
102826
ndon Marathon: Iraq War Veteran Phil Packer Beats His Record By 13 Days | UK News | Sky News=News</TITLE>=3D"<p>A wounded Iraq war veteran has smashed his London marathon =20content=3D"London Marathon:
102862
ndon Marathon: Iraq War Veteran Phil Packer Beats His Record By 13 Days | UK News | Sky News News
Date: Tue, 27 Apr 2010 09:51:22 +0100
167978
<p>Katie Price has fuelled rumours she may be pregnant after pulling out of the London marathon on doctor's orders.</p>
171133
athon On Doctor's Orders | Showbiz News | Sky News
173605
<p>Katie Price has fuelled rumours she may be pregnant after pulling out of the London marathon on doctor's orders.</p>
173638
Katie Price Pregnant? Model Fuels Rumours After Pulling Out Of London Marathon On Doctor's Orders
234045
Katie Price Pregnant? Model Fuels Rumours After Pulling Out Of London Marathon On Doctor's Orders | Showbiz News | Sky News
234045
London Marathon: Iraq War Veteran Phil Packer Beats His Record By 13 Days | UK News | Sky News
Days/Article/201004415620262?lpos=UK_News_Second_UK_News_Article_Teaser_Region_4&lid=ARTICLE_15620262_London_Marathon%3A_Iraq_War_Veteran_Phil_Packer_Beats_His_Record_By_13_Days
"http://www.w3c.org/TR/1999/REC-html401-19991224/loose.dtd"><HTML lang=3Den-gb xml:lang=3D"en-gb"=20
436491
Katie Price Hit For Slander Damages
436491
Showbiz News
436534
Showbiz News
436534
Price Pregnant? Model Pulls Out Of Marathon
436549
Price Pregnant? Model Pulls Out Of Marathon
436549
Katie Price has fuelled rumours she may be pregnant after pulling out of the London marathon on doctor's orders.</td></tr>
</table>

Fig. 8. Internet Explorer (IE70): Original User Input / Extracted memdump evidence

consistently in the allocated memory. The evidence contained both partial and whole fragment of relevant user information. In some occasion, the evidence found was in a continuous block. For example, user opened two different type of internet information on subjects *like "Katie Price Pregnant"* and *"London Marathon: Iraq War..."* As shown in Figure 7, the whole fragment of information was recovered as stored in the physical memory. The question of *what* the user was doing has been answered. For example, user access *to "London Marathon:Iraq war"*. This user input information was recovered in both whole and partial fragment. In the extracted memdump evidence of this application, line numbers *like: 102826, 102862 and 234045* described "*what*" the user was doing. The question of "*when*" user input this information was shown with sample evidence linked to the line number *102862*. The question of "*where*" the evidence was stored over time is also linked to the *line numbers.* The question of "*who*" the user is can be answered as the user that opened the Internet Explorer 7.0 and access webpage information on *"London Marathon: Iraq war", line number 3492 and 171133 shows what the user was doing.* Also, we investigated to find out *"how"* this evidence can be reconstructed in the physical memory to ascertain the original user text input by the user. As shown in Figure 8, user actions can be reconstructed based on the event of activities that was performed in the physical memory. By pattern matching technique, this information was recovered as stored over time in the memory. The line numbers like: *234045, 102862 and 2492* was reconstructed to form the whole fragment of user input information on this application. The questions of *"how"* the evidence can be reconstructed have been answered. This information can be useful to forensic investigators in digital investigation and this approach can be applied to other social networking application services like MSN, Facebook, Twitter and LinkedIn.

6 Analysis

The result of the experiments consists of both quantitative and qualitative assessment of user input information on Windows application by pattern matching techniques. Table 2 described the quantitative assessment of result found on the sample applications like Outlook Email, Internet Explorer (IE70), Adobe Reader 8.0 and MS Access. There are three elements of experiments considered in the quantitative result as shown in Table 2. These three elements are the *percentage of evidence found* in these applications, *the average mean of evidence in repetitions*. This evidence can appear repeatedly and consistently in the physical memory. Also, the *average of the evidence found in a continuous block*. These three elements of experiments were carried out on these applications. Sample qualitative assessments are described in Section 5. The research work discusses the amount of relevant data found and stored in the memory. As investigated, Adobe application recorded the least amount of data stored over time. The amount of information recovered from the MS Access contained only the predefined format whereas, the user input on user define format are irrecoverable. In the case of Outlook email and Internet Explorer 7.0, the amount of data recovered was large. The evidence found was dispersed as stored in the physical memory. This research is in line with the long term of evidence preservation. The investigations approach focussed on the original user input information that was matched with extracted memdump strings processes. This process was achieved by pattern matching techniques that we have implemented. The purpose of the research focussed on the relevant user input in physical memory. This evidence recovered can be forensically relevant. The evidence dispersed can be reconstructed in the memory of these applications. Consequently, data evidence gained in each application is relevant to forensic investigators. This research work is based on the integrity, completeness and authenticity of the evidence found in the physical memory of four applications considered in this paper. As a practice in memory analysis, evidence is often saved in the memory for later use in the belief that it can be accessed anytime in the future.

This research detail the amount of dispersal evidence found and that can be recovered as in the allocated memory linked to the line numbers. As we can see from the above figures in *Section 5*, the extracted user information was dispersed and this evidence occurs repeatedly and consistently over time at different locations in the memory of an application. In some cases, only partial fragment was found on this application whereas, in other applications both partial and whole fragment of evidence can be recovered. We discovered that whole fragment of evidence can be found in a continuous block of the physical memory. For example in Figure 7, user opened Internet Explorer application and access two different web pages. The extracted memdump evidence indicated that user actions were stored over time with line numbers *102826 and 167978*. It is evident that this evidence is repeated and appears consistently in the memory of Internet Explorer. This information can be forensically relevant and can be used for evidential purposes. As illustrated in Section 5, the *Sample Figures 5, 6, 7, and 8* above can be described as qualitative aspect of evidence found, evidence dispersed and evidence found in a continuous block. In each of these figures contained two columns sessions. The left side contained the original user texts and the right side described the relevant user information extracted from the memdump of these applications. For example in Figure 5, the session of the original *"text"* answered the question of *"what"* the user was doing. The questions of "*who*" can be described as user that input information on each application or access WebPages on Internet Explorer 7.0. The questions of *"where"* evidence can be found can be traced to where user input was stored like line numbers. User input information on Windows applications; the questions of *"what"* the user was using can be answered as this. Also, the extracted evidence dispersed was allocated to different line numbers in the memory. The question of "where" the evidence was stored has been answered. The question of *"when"* can be answered as the time user access the web pages of an application or input information on the application. For example, in Figure 8, user access Internet Explorer 7.0. This action can be linked to line numbers *21829 and 102862*.

As illustrated above, the research experiment has clarified the important aspect of user activities on most commonly used applications. Finally, the question of *"how"* can be answered when user input information can be reconstructed. This is matching original user input information with the extracted memdump strings processes of information on each application. As earlier discussed in the *Section 3 and Table 1*, user input consists of alphanumeric data. This user input was made once at zero minutes. The application remains opened and user is not interacting with the applications but, images were captured at interval of 30 minutes. We assume that user may be doing something else. The Section 4, *Table 2* above described the summary of the quantitative results. The user input captured over time was investigated by strings pattern matching techniques. This was shown in the *Figures 5, 6, 7, and 8*. This evidence information may be crucial to forensic investigators to augment the percentage amount of user information stored over time and the amount of evidence dispersed in the physical memory. This research investigation follows the strings pattern matching techniques that we have implemented. These experiments have detailed how much evidence can be recovered when application was opened on Windows computer and images were captured at interval and, user is not interacting with the system.

7 Conclusion

In this research, we have presented a pattern matching model and the result analysis shows how much data can be recovered while the application is still running when image memory was captured at every 30 minutes and user is not interacting with the systems. Specifically, we have laid emphasis on the amount of relevant evidence found and the repeated evidence. Also the quantitative result shows the average length of evidence found in a continuous block of the physical memory. The experiment contains quantitative and qualitative assessment of information recovered from some Windows applications. In this paper, we introduce new methods for extracting relevant information from commonly used application on Windows system using pattern matching techniques that we have implemented. This process of experiments involved the use of automated executable program to dump the physical memory content of the applications; performed strings conversion processes and then, matched the original user input with the extracted memory dump strings processes. The approach we have taken can be found useful to forensic investigator to answer the most important questions of forensic digital investigations. This may includes the questions of who, what, when, where and how evidence was stored over time, how evidence was dispersed and how the evidence can be reconstructed. This approach can be used to describe the process of securing digital evidence resident in the physical memory.

8 Future Work

In the future, we will investigate on how much relevant evidence can be recovered when applications were closed and images were captured at set interval but, user was interacting with the systems. In this approach, user may be doing something else on the computer Windows systems. This investigation process will be based on how much data is lost over time in the physical memory.

References

[1] Petroni Jr., N.L., Walters, A., Fraser, T., Arbaugh, W.A.: FATKit: A framwork for the extraction and analysis of digital forenisc from volatile sysytem memory. Journal of Digital Investigation III(001), 197–210 (2006)

[2] Farmer, D., Venema, W.: The coroner's toolkit, TCT (August 2004), `http://www.porcupine.org/forensics/tct.html`

[3] Carrier, B.D., Grand, J.: A hardware-based memory acquisition procedure for digital investigations. International Journal of Digital Evidence (IJDE) I(01), 10–23 (2004)

[4] Farmer, D., Venema, W.: Forensic discovery, 1st edn. Addison-Wesley, Indianapolis (2005)

[5] Carrier, B.D., Spafford, E.H.: Automated digital evidence target definition using outlier analysis and existing evidence. In: Digital Forensic Research Workshop (DFRWS), New Orleans, LA, pp. 62–72 (2005)

[6] Stover, S., Dickerson, M.: Using memory dump in digital forensic; login. The USENIX Magazine 30(6), 43–48 (2005)

[7] Funminiyi, O., Nick, S.: Application level evidence from volatile memory. Journal of Computing in Systems and Engineering II(2), 70–78 (2009)

[8] Case, A., Cristina, A., Marziale, L., Richard, G.G., Roussev, V.: FACE: Automated digital evidence discovery and correlation. Journal of Digital Investigation V(008), 65–75 (2008)

[9] Digital Forensic Research Workshop (DFRWS) (July 2007), `http://www.dfrws.org/2007/challenge/index.shtml`

[10] Funminiyi, O., Nick, S.: On the extraction of forensically relevant information from physical memory. In: World Congress on Internet Security (WORLDCIS 2011), Technically Co-sponsored by IEEE UK/RI Computer Chapter, London, pp. 248–252 (2011)

[11] Funminiyi, O., Nick, S.: On the identification of information extracted from Windows physical memory. International Journal for Information Security Research (IJISR) II(2) (March 2011) ISSN 2042-4639

[12] Mariusz, B.: Windows memory forensic toolkit; finding digital evidence in physical memory. Journal of Information and Computing Systems 5(2), 45–75 (2007)

[13] Limon, G.G.: Forensic physical memory analysis: an overview of tools and techniques. In: TKK T-110.5290 Seminar on Network Security, Helsinki, Finland, pp. 305–320 (2007)

[14] Msuiche, Msuiche.net at: Capture memory under win2k3 or vista with win32dd (2008), `http://www.msuiche.net/2008/06/14/capture-memory-under-win2k3-orvista-with-win32dd` (accessed March)

[15] Memory, M.: ManTech international corporation. memory dd, `http://www.mantech.com/msma/MDD.asp` (accessed March 2010)

[16] Russinovich, M.E., Solomon, D.A.: Microsoft Windows internal covering Windows server 2008 and Windows vista, 5th edn. Microsoft Press, Washington (2009)

[17] Agile Risk Management.Nigilat32 small footprint, Agile, `http://www.agilerm.net/nigilant32` (accessed October 2009)

[18] Chris, B.: Mempaser analysis tool, memory forensics analysis tool for microsoft Windows systems. In: DFRWS 2005 Forensic Challenge Can be Accessed, MA, pp. 100–115 (2005), `http://www.dfrws.org/2005/challenge/memparser.shtml`

[19] Volatile Systems. The volatility framework: volatlile memory artifact extraction utility framework (April 2009), Can be accessed at, `http://www.volatilesystems.com/default/volatility`

[20] Harlan, C., Dave, K.: Windows forensic analysis incident response and cybercrime investigation secrets, 1st edn., vol. III(3), pp. 43–67. Syngress Publishing (July 2007)

[21] Funminiyi, O., Nick, S.: Forensic live response and events reconstruction methods in linux systems. In: PGNET - The Convergence of Telecommunications Networking and Broadcasting, Liverpool, UK, pp. 141–147 (December 2009)

[22] Funminiyi, O., Nick, S.: Dispersal of time aspect of information stored on physical memory. In: Cyberforensic - International Conference on Cybercrime Security and Digital Forensics, Glasgow, UK (2011)

[23] Funminiyi, O., Nick, S.: Digital forensic research and method of extracting relevant information from physical memory of Windows XP. In: Fourth International Conference on Internet Technologies and Applications (ITA11), Wrexam, Wales, UK (2011)

Label Size Increment of Bit String Based Labeling Scheme in Dynamic XML Updating

Meghdad Mirabi, Hamidah Ibrahim, Nur Izura Udzir, and Ali Mamat

Department of Computer Science, Faculty of Computer Science and Information Technology, Universiti Putra Malaysia, 43400, Serdang, Selangor, Malaysia
meghdad.mirabi@gmail.com,
{hamidah,izura,ali}@fsktm.upm.edu.my

Abstract. XML query processing based on labeling schemes has been proposed in the past several years. Based on labeling schemes, the structural relationships between XML nodes can be directly determined without the need of accessing the XML document. However, the existing labeling schemes have to re-label the pre-existing XML nodes or re-calculate the label values when a new node is inserted into the XML tree during an updating process. EXEL as a bit string based encoding and labeling scheme is able to remove the process of re-labeling for the pre-existing XML nodes efficiently. However, EXEL is unable to reuse the deleted labels for future node insertions. Also, another problem of EXEL is in the frequent skewed insertions where nodes always are inserted at a fixed place of an XML tree. In this case, the label size increases significantly. In this paper, we propose an algorithm to reuse the deleted labels for future node insertions and propose a strategy to solve the problem of frequent skewed insertion. The experimental results show that the proposed algorithm can reuse all the deleted labels for future insertions. Also, the proposed strategy can reduce the increment of label size in the case of frequent skewed insertions efficiently.

Keywords: Dynamic XML, Frequent Skewed Insertions, Reusability of Deleted Labels, XML Updating.

1 Introduction

XML [1] is a standard to represent and exchange the data on the Internet. In general, an XML document can be presented as an XML tree and elements in the XML document can be labeled based on the XML document structure.

The main operation in the labeling based XML query processing is to find all occurrences of structural relationships between nodes in an XML document. Many labeling schemes are proposed to efficiently determine the structural relationships between XML nodes when XML data are static which include studies by [2-7]. However, the process of re-labeling for the pre-existing XML nodes is necessary if the XML data are dynamic which cause degrading the XML query performance.

Moreover, several researches have been conducted to process the XML document updating in the case of ordering the XML data is not important which include studies

E. Ariwa and E. El-Qawasmeh (Eds.): DEIS 2011, CCIS 194, pp. 466–477, 2011.

by [4, 6, 8]. However, the maintenance of ordering the XML data is necessary because it influences the semantics of XML data. Therefore, several researches have been performed to maintain the XML document ordering when XML document has to update such as [4, 5, 7, 9-17]. These researches have proposed different labeling schemes to support XML node insertion and deletion without the need for the re-labeling process of the pre-existing XML nodes.

EXEL (Efficient XML Encoding and Labeling) scheme [10, 14] is an order based bit string encoding and labeling scheme which is able to remove the need for re-labeling process of the pre-existing nodes when the XML document is updated. In addition, the structural relationship between XML nodes can be computed effectively. However, the current problem of EXEL encoding and labeling scheme is label size increment. EXEL is unable to handle the reusability of the deleted labels for future node insertions. In addition, the label size of EXEL increases dramatically when new nodes always are inserted at a fix place of an XML tree.

The focus of this paper is to study the behavior of EXEL encoding and labeling scheme in the case of frequent skewed insertions as well as reusability of the deleted labels for future node insertions. Therefore, the main contributions of this paper are summarized as follows:

- We improve the MakeNewBitString algorithm proposed in [10, 14] which can reuse all the deleted labels for future insertions. Thus, we are able to control the label size increment when new nodes are deleted and inserted frequently in the dynamic XML updating.
- We propose a strategy to control the label size increment in the case of frequent skewed insertions.
- We conduct several experiments to verify that our proposed algorithm can efficiently control the label size increment in the case of frequent deletions and insertions as well as frequent skewed insertions.

The remainder of the paper is organized as follows: in Section 2, existing binary (bit) string based XML encoding and labeling schemes are investigated. In Section 3, EXEL encoding and labeling scheme is presented. In Section 4, our proposed algorithm to reuse the deleted labels and our proposed strategy to control the label size increment in the case of frequent skewed insertions are explained. Experimental results are illustrated in Section 5. Finally, the paper is concluded in Section 6.

2 Related Works

Dynamic Quaternary Encoding (QED) as a quaternary string based encoding scheme [12] and Compact Dynamic Binary String (CDBS) as a binary encoding scheme [15] remove the need of re-labeling process for the pre-existing XML nodes when the XML document is updated. Moreover, they can be applied to different labeling schemes which need to maintain the order of XML data. The key feature of QED and CDBS is that the labels are compared based on the lexicographical order rather than the numerical order.

The main problem of CDBS is overflow. If the number of inserted nodes is large, the length field size is not enough for new label. Thus, the process of re-labeling for all the pre-existing XML nodes is required. Even by increasing the size of length field, it still unable to completely remove the process of re-labeling.

The advantage of CDBS is in the XML updating process. In contrast with QED which the last 2 bits of the neighbor label must be modified, only the last 1 bit needs to be modified in CDBS. Thus, the update cost of CDBS is smaller than the update cost of QED.

In addition, the proposed algorithm in [18] is able to reuse the deleted labels of QED and control the increment of label size when nodes are deleted from and then inserted into the XML document frequently.

One solution to label the XML document which can remove the process of re-labeling is to leave some unused values for future insertions [2, 5]. However, when the unused values are used up later, they have to re-label the pre-existing XML nodes. The proposed algorithms in [12, 15, 18] do not need to leave some unused values for future insertions.

Improved Binary String Labeling (IBSL) proposed by [9, 17] is a binary string based prefix scheme which removes the process of re-labeling and re-calculation in dynamic XML updating. Moreover, the proposed algorithm suggested in [17] is able to reuse all the deleted labels when a large number of labels are deleted and then inserted into the XML document without worrying about degradation of query performance.

EXEL proposed by [10, 14] is able to insert a sibling or a parent as well as a child into the XML tree without the need for the re-labeling process of the pre-existing nodes. EXEL can save time during an updating process because of complete avoidance of re-labeling process for the pre-existing nodes. However, the problem of EXEL is the increment of label size when node insertions and deletions are performed frequently.

In our previous work [19], we proposed the algorithm to control the increment of label size when nodes are frequently deleted from and inserted into the XML tree but this paper is an extension of our previous work. We propose a strategy to control the label size increment in the case of frequent skewed insertions.

3 EXEL Encoding and Labeling Scheme

In this section, we present the EXEL encoding and labeling scheme and show how update to the XML document can be done without the need for the re-labeling process of the pre-existing XML nodes.

According to [10, 14], EXEL uses bit string codes to label the XML nodes. These bit string codes are ordinal as well as insert friendly. The key feature of bit string based labeling schemes is that labels are compared based on the lexicographical order rather than the numerical order. The definition of lexicographical order ($<$) of bit string codes is defined as follows:

Definition of Lexicographical Order (<):

If *LeftB* represents the left bit string code and *RightB* represents the right bit string code,

1. *LeftB* is lexicographically equal to *RightB* iff they are the same bit by bit.
2. *LeftB* is smaller than *RightB* (*LeftB* < *RightB*) iff at least one of the following condition is satisfied:
   a) The current bit of *LeftB* is '0' and the current bit of *RightB* is'1', if we compare them bit by bit from left to right.
   b) *LeftB* is the prefix of *RightB*.

The algorithm of generating the bit string codes for the XML nodes is illustrated in Fig. 1 which is the enhanced binary encoding algorithm in [10, 14].

Let N be the total number of nodes of XML tree,
For first bit string code $b(1), b(1) = \left(0^{log_2^N}\right)1$.
For $(i + 1)$ th bit string code $b(i+1), b(i+1) = b(i) + 10$.

Fig. 1. Bit string code generation algorithm

In order to encode N ordinal decimal numbers, the bit string code generation algorithm needs $[(log_2^N) + 1]$ bits for each bit string code. Thus, the total size for encoding N ordinal decimal numbers is $N[(log_2^N) + 1]$ bits. For example, in order to encode 18 ordinal decimal numbers, the size of the longest bit string code is 6 and the total size is 6 × 18 = 108 bits. Table 1 shows the bit string codes of 18 ordinal decimal numbers based on the bit string code generation algorithm.

Table 1. Bit string codes for 18 ordinal decimal numbers

Decimal Number	Bit String
1	000001
2	000011
3	000101
4	000111
5	001001
6	001011
7	001101
8	001111
9	010001
10	010011
11	010101
12	010111
13	011001
14	011011
15	011101
16	011111
17	100001
18	100011

EXEL uses the MakeNewBitString algorithm which is illustrated in Fig. 2 to generate a new bit string code between two pre-existing bit string codes. Example 1 illustrates the behavior of MakeNewBitString algorithm when new nodes are inserted in the XML tree.

```
MakeNewBitString (LeftB, RightB)
Begin
   If length (LeftB) > length (RightB) then
      newB := LeftB concatenate with 1;
   Else
      newB := (RightB with last bit changed to 0)
            concatenate with 1;
   Return newB;
End
```

Fig. 2. MakeNewBitString algorithm

Example 1: As shown in Fig. 3, assume that we use the MakeNewBitString algorithm to generate a new bit string code between the two pre-existing bit string codes "001001" and "001011". The new bit string code is "0010101". We cannot find any other bit string codes which are ended with "1" between "001001" and "001011" lexicographically with the small size. If we want to generate a new bit string code between "001001" and "0010101", the bit string code generated by the algorithm is "00101001". Moreover, the bit string code between "0010101" and "001011" generated by the algorithm is "00101011".

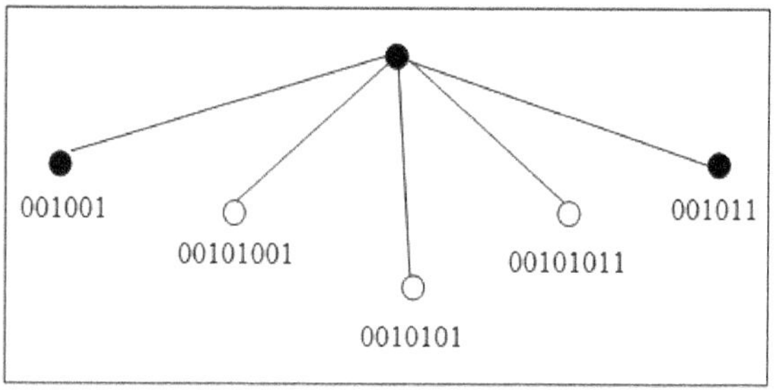

Fig. 3. Insertion of a new bit string code between two pre-existing bit string codes

According to Example 1, it is observed that for each bit string code insertion, the size of bit string code increases 1 bit. In other words, the label size increases linearly (O(N)) using the MakeNewBitString algorithm.

4 The Proposed Algorithm

The MakeNewBitString algorithm generates a new bit string code by increasing 1 bit in the label size. In order to control the label size increment, we modify the

MakeNewBitString algorithm. Our proposed algorithm is shown in Fig. 4. Example 2 shows the behavior of our proposed algorithm when new nodes are inserted into the XML tree.

Example 2: Assume that we want to insert a new bit string code between the two pre-existing bit string codes "001001" and "001011" as shown in Fig. 5. If we use the proposed algorithm to generate a bit string code between "001001" and "001011", the inserted bit string code is "0010101" similar to the previous algorithm. We cannot find any other bit string codes which are ended with "1" and are between "001001" and "001011" lexicographically with the small size. However, if we want to insert a bit string code between "001001" and "0010101", the bit string code generated by the proposed algorithm is "0010011". The result is different with the previous one which is "00101001". It saves 1 bit in the label size and reduces the storage space.

```
ModifiedMakeNewBitString (LeftB, RightB)
 Begin
   temp1 := LeftB + 10;
   temp2 := RightB - 10;
   If (LeftB < temp1) and (temp1 < RightB) then
      newB := temp1;
   Else If (LeftB < temp2) and (temp2 < RightB) then
      newB := temp2;
   Else
        If length (LeftB) > length (RightB) then
           newB := LeftB concatenate with 1;
        Else
           newB := (RightB with last bit changed to 0)
                  concatenate with 1;
   Return newB;
 End
```

Fig. 4. ModifiedMakeNewBitString algorithm

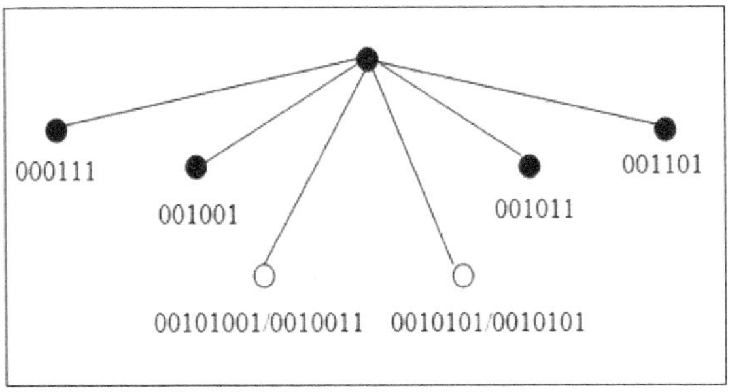

Fig. 5. Insertion of a new bit string code between the two pre-existing bit string codes

Based on Example 2, it is observed that the size of inserted bit string code increases 1 bit in the worst case for each bit string code insertion in the proposed algorithm. In other words, the label size increases linearly (O(*N*)) in worst case while it increases linearly (O(*N*)) in the previous algorithm for all cases.

Moreover, the proposed algorithm is able to reuse the deleted labels for future insertions. Example 3 shows this fact.

Example 3: Assume that the two bit string codes "001001" and "001011" are deleted. Now, we want to generate two new bit string codes between "000111" and "001101" as shown in Fig. 6. If we use the MakeNewBitString algorithm to generate two new bit string codes, the new bit string codes will be "0011001" and "00110011" while the two new bit string codes generated by the proposed algorithm are "001001" and "001011". Thus, the proposed algorithm is able to reuse the deleted bit string codes for future insertions as well as control the increment of label size.

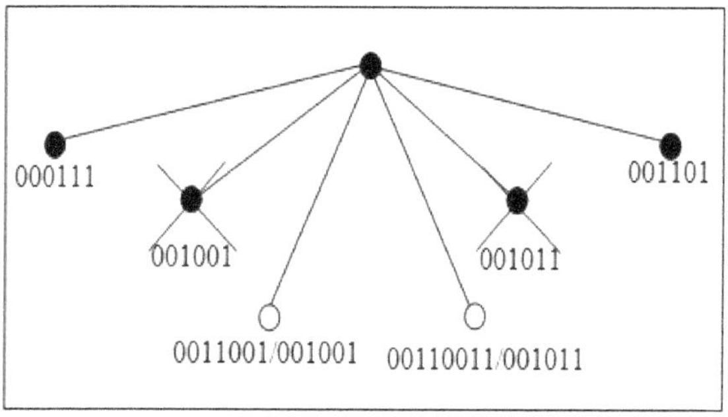

Fig. 6. Deleting and inserting bit string codes frequently

Another problem of the MakeNewBitString algorithm is its behavior in frequent skewed insertions. In frequent skewed insertions, nodes are always inserted at a fixed place of an XML tree. Thus, the size of bit string codes increases 1 bit for each bit string code insertion using the MakeNewBitString algorithm.

In order to control the increment of label size in the case of frequent skewed insertion, a solution is to leave some EXEL bit string codes for future insertions. In this case, it is required to estimate the total number of bit string codes that will be inserted as well as the place where bit string codes will be inserted. These estimations are based on the characteristics of XML document. Therefore, this solution is not a general solution because of its dependency to the XML document characteristics.

Our proposed strategy which is independent of the XML document characteristics is illustrated in Fig. 7.

Example 4: Assume that we want to insert 10 bit string codes between the two pre-existing bit string codes "001001" and "001011". In order to insert 10 bit string codes, the size of the longest bit string code is $[(log_2^{10}) + 1] = 5$ bits and the total size is $5 \times 10 = 50$ bits. These bit string codes are generated by the bit string code generation algorithm shown in Fig. 1 and stored in the *bitStringArray*. Table 2 shows the content of *bitStringArray* for the 10 generated bit string codes. Then, the ModifiedMakeNewBitString algorithm is invoked to generate the new bit string codes between the two pre-existing bit string codes "001001" and "001011". Therefore, "0010101" is generated and returned by the algorithm. This bit string code is assigned to *newB*. Now, based on our proposed strategy, the *newB* with the last bit deleted is concatenated with each of the 10 generated bit string codes. Table 3 shows the *newBitStringArray* for the 10 frequent skewed insertions.

/* *LeftB* represents the left bit string code and *RightB* represents the right bit string code and *N* is the total number of bit string codes which will be inserted at a fix place of an XML tree frequently. */

1. Generate *N* bit string codes based on the bit string code generation algorithm illustrated in Fig. 1 and store them in the *bitStringArray*;
2. *newB* := ModifiedMakeNewBitString (*LeftB*, *RightB*);
3. For *i* = 0 to *N*-1 do
   3.1. *newBitStringArray*[*i*] := (*newB* with the last bit deleted) concatenate with *bitStringArray*[*i*];

Fig. 7. The proposed strategy for frequent skewed insertions

Table 2. Content of *bitStringArray*

Index	Content
0	00001
1	00011
2	00101
3	00111
4	01001
5	01011
6	01101
7	01111
8	10001
9	10011

Table 3. Content of *newBitStringArray*

Index	Content
0	**001010**00001
1	**001010**00011
2	**001010**00101
3	**001010**00111
4	**001010**01001
5	**001010**01011
6	**001010**01101
7	**001010**01111
8	**001010**10001
9	**001010**10011

Analysis of Total Size of Bit String Codes: if the total number of pre-existing bit string codes is *N* and the total number of frequent skewed insertions is *m*:

- The total size of bit string codes in the MakeNewBitString algorithm after frequent skewed insertions is:

$$N[log_2^N + 1] + m([log_2^N + 1]) + (\frac{m(m+1)}{2})$$

- The total size of bit string codes in our proposed strategy after frequent skewed insertions is:

$$N[log_2^N + 1] + m([log_2^N + 1]) + m([log_2^m + 1])$$

5 Performance Study

In this section, the ModifiedMakeNewBitString algorithm proposed in this paper is compared to the MakeNewBitString algorithm proposed in [10, 14] in the case of reusability of the deleted labels. Also, our proposed strategy shown in Fig. 7 for frequent skewed insertion case is compared to the MakeNewBitString algorithm.

All the experiments were implemented in Java and were carried out on a 2.4 GHz Pentium 4 processor with 1 GB RAM running Windows XP Professional.

5.1 Performance Study on Reusing the Deleted Labels

Based on the bit string code generation algorithm in Fig. 1, we first generated 10,000 EXEL bit string codes and stored them into *bitStringArray0*. Then, we tested the case that the bit string codes are deleted then inserted at the *even* positions of *bitStringArray0* and stored these new bit string codes into *bitStirngArray1*; this is Case 1. Then, we tested the case that the bit string codes are deleted then inserted at the *odd* positions of *bitStringArray1* and stored these new bit string codes into *bitStirngArray2*; this is Case 2. Then, we tested the case that the bit string codes are deleted then inserted at the *even* positions of *bitStringArray2* (Case 3), the *add* positions of *bitStringArray3* (Case 4) and so on. This process was repeated 10 times (10 Cases).

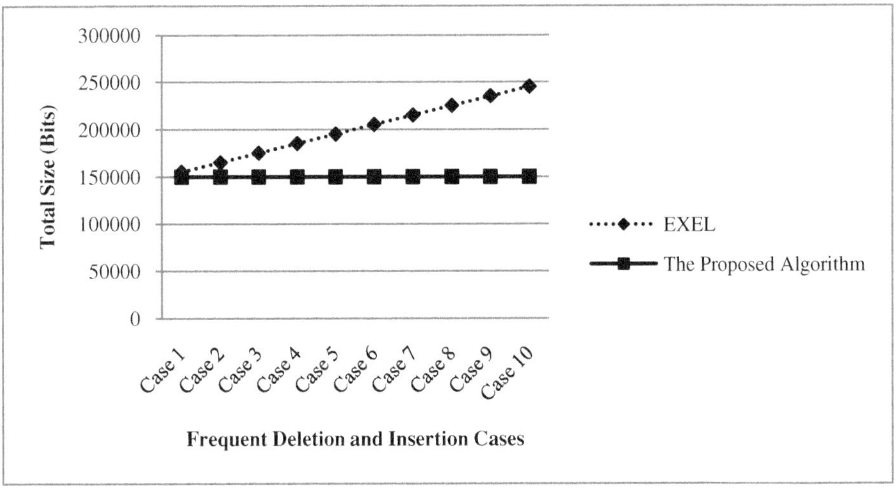

Fig. 8. Comparison of reusability of the deleted bit string codes

We compared the performance of MakeNewBitString algorithm to the ModifiedMakeNewBitString algorithm proposed in this paper. Fig. 8 shows that the total size of bit string codes in our proposed algorithm does not increase in all the ten cases. Thus, we reuse all the deleted bit string codes. On the other hand, the total size of bit string codes in the MakeNewBitString algorithm increases linearly for these ten cases. The experimental results confirm that our proposed algorithm can reuse all the deleted bit string codes for future insertions, thus it efficiently controls label size increment.

5.2 Performance Study on Frequent Skewed Insertion

Based on the bit string code generation algorithm in Fig. 1, we first generated 10,000 EXEL bit string codes. Then, we tested the cases that bit string codes are frequently inserted at a fix place. The location for insertions was selected randomly. We inserted from 1,000 bit string codes to 5,000 bit string codes with a 1,000 bit string codes interval.

We compared the performance of the MakeNewBitString algorithm to our proposed strategy illustrated in Fig. 7. Fig. 9 shows that our proposed strategy efficiently can control the increment of label size compared to the MakeNewBitString algorithm.

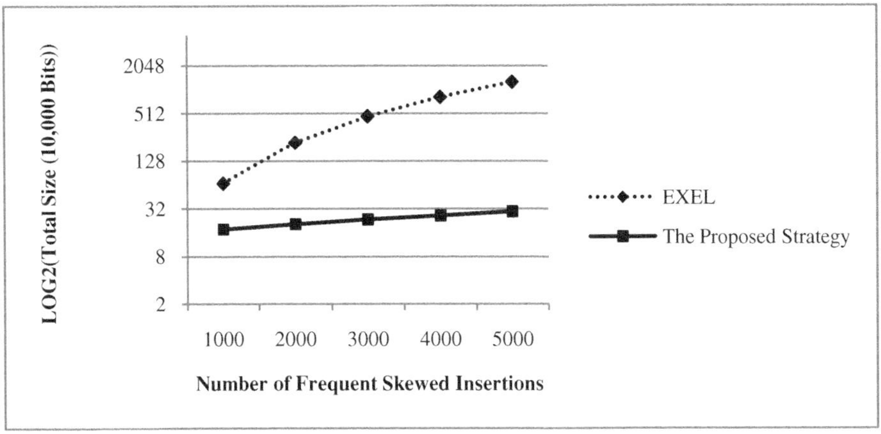

Fig. 9. Comparison of frequent skewed insertions

6 Conclusion and Future Works

In this paper, we improved the MakeNewBitString algorithm proposed in [10, 14]. Our proposed algorithm can reuse all the deleted labels for future insertions and therefore can control the label size increment. Also, the experimental results showed that the proposed algorithm can mainly reduce the increment of label size when labels are deleted and inserted frequently.

In addition, we proposed a strategy to control the label size increment in the case of frequent skewed insertion. The experimental result showed that our proposed strategy can efficiently reduce label size increment when labels are inserted frequently at a fix place of an XML document.

As a future work, we attempt to apply the EXEL encoding and labeling scheme to other applications involving updating process.

References

1. Bray, T., Paoli, J., Sperberg-McQueen, C.M., Maler, E., Yergeau, F.: Extensible Markup Language (XML) 1.0, 5th edn. W3C Recommendation (2008), http://www.w3.org/TR/REC-xml/
2. Li, Q., Moon, B.: Indexing and Querying XML Data for Regular Path Expressions. In: Proceedings of the 27th International Conference on Very Large Data Bases, pp. 361–370. Morgan Kaufmann, Roma (2001)
3. Zhang, C., Naughton, J., DeWitt, D., Luo, Q., Lohman, G.: On Supporting Containment Queries in Relational Database Management Systems. ACM SIGMOD Record Journal 30(2), 425–436 (2001)
4. Cohen, E., Kaplan, H., Milo, T.: Labeling Dynamic XML Trees. In: Proceedings of the 21th ACM SIGMOD-SIGACT-SIGART Symposium on Principles of Database Systems, pp. 271–281. ACM Press, Madison (2002)
5. O'Neil, P., O'Neil, E., Pal, S., Cseri, I., Schaller, G., Westbury, N.: ORDPATHs: Insert-Friendly XML Node Labels. In: Proceedings of the 2004 ACM SIGMOD International Conference on Management of Data, pp. 903–908. ACM Press, Paris (2004)
6. Tatarinov, I., Viglas, S.D., Beyer, K., Shanmugasundaram, J., Shekita, E., Zhang, C.: Storing and Querying Odered XML Using a Relational Database System. In: Proceedings of the 2002 ACM SIGMOD International Conference on Management of Data, pp. 204–215. ACM Press, Madison (2002)
7. Wu, X., Lee, M.L., Hsu, W.: A Prime Number Labeling Scheme for Dynamic Ordered XML Trees. In: Proceedings of the 20th International Conference on Data Engineering (ICDE 2004), pp. 66–78. IEEE Press, Boston (2004)
8. Tatarinov, I., Ives, Z.G., Halevy, A.Y., Weld, D.S.: Updating XML. In: Proceedings of the 2001 ACM SIGMOD International Conference on Management of Data, pp. 413–424. ACM Press, Santa Barbara (2001)
9. Ko, H.-K., Lee, S.: An Efficient Scheme to Completely Avoid Re-labeling in XML Updates. In: Aberer, K., Peng, Z., Rundensteiner, E.A., Zhang, Y., Li, X. (eds.) WISE 2006. LNCS, vol. 4255, pp. 259–264. Springer, Heidelberg (2006)
10. Min, J.-K., Lee, J., Chung, C.-W.: An Efficient XML Encoding and Labeling Method for Query Processing and Updating on Dynamic XML Data. Journal of Systems and Software 82(3), 503–515 (2009)
11. Amagasa, T., Yoshikawa, M., Uemura, S.: QRS: A Robust Numbering Scheme for XML Documents. In: Proceedings of the 19th International Conference on Data Engineering (ICDE 2003), pp. 705–707. IEEE Press, Bangalore (2003)
12. Li, C., Ling, T.W.: QED: A Novel Quaternary Encoding to Completely Avoid Re-Labeling in XML Updates. In: Proceedings of the 14th ACM International Conference on Information and Knowledge Management, pp. 501–508. ACM Press, Bremen (2005)
13. Silberstein, A., He, H., Yi, K., Yang, J.: BOXes: Efficient Maintenance of Order-Based Labeling for Dynamic XML Data. In: Proceedings of the 21st International Conference on Data Engineering (ICDE 2005), pp. 285–296. IEEE Press, Tokyo (2005)
14. Min, J.-K., Lee, J., Chung, C.-W.: An Efficient Encoding and Labeling for Dynamic XML Data. In: Kotagiri, R., Radha Krishna, P., Mohania, M., Nantajeewarawat, E. (eds.) DASFAA 2007. LNCS, vol. 4443, pp. 715–726. Springer, Heidelberg (2007)
15. Li, C., Ling, T.W., Hu, M.: Efficient Processing of Updates in Dynamic XML Data. In: Proceedings of the 22nd International Conference on Data Engineering (ICDE 2006), p. 13. IEEE Press, Atlanta (2006)

16. Yun, J.-H., Chung, C.-W.: Dynamic Interval-Based Labeling Scheme for Efficient XML Query and Update Processing. Journal of Systems and Software 81(1), 56–70 (2008)
17. Ko, H.-K., Lee, S.: A Binary String Approach for Updates in Dynamic Ordered XML Data. IEEE Transactions on Knowledge and Data Engineering 22(4), 602–607 (2010)
18. Li, C., Ling, T.W., Hu, M.: Reuse or Never Reuse the Deleted Labels in XML Query Processing Based on Labeling Schemes. In: Li Lee, M., Tan, K.-L., Wuwongse, V. (eds.) DASFAA 2006. LNCS, vol. 3882, pp. 659–673. Springer, Heidelberg (2006)
19. Mirabi, M., Ibrahim, H., Mamat, A., Udzir, N.I., Fathi, L.: Controlling Label Size Increment of Efficient XML Encoding and Labeling Scheme in Dynamic XML Update. Journal of Computer Science 6(12), 1535–1540 (2010)

Architectures to Implement In-Air Signature Mobile Authentication to Increase the Security of E-Commerce Applications and Opinion of End Users

Javier Guerra-Casanova, Carmen Sánchez-Ávila, Vicente Jara-Vera, Alberto de-Santos-Sierra, and Gonzalo Bailador

Centro de Domótica Integral
Universidad Politécnica de Madrid
Campus de Montegancedo, 28223 Pozuelo de Alarcón, Madrid, Spain
{jguerra,csa,vjara,alberto,gbailador}@cedint.upm.es

Abstract. This article proposes to include an in-air signature biometric technique in mobile e-commerce applications in order to increase the security of passwords and authenticate users directly from their mobile phones. Five architectures have been proposed to implement this technique as a complement of current authentication methods. Moreover, the opinion of end users has been considered assessed by a survey of 24 people. From the results of this survey it has been deducted that this authentication method seems useful, necessary and comfortable to complement the password authentication methods and increase the global security of e-commerce applications.

Keywords: e-commerce, mobile authentication, biometrics, gestures, in-air signature.

1 Introduction

Authentication is an essential part when users perform personal daily actions, like shopping, communicating or storing information. This problem has been solved typically memorizing passwords, so the one who knows the password is the one who is able to access the system. But this solution implies huge weakness, as passwords may be forgotten, stolen or copied.

In this context, different biometric techniques were born so that some physical or behavioral characteristics of people are the key of entering the system, avoiding the use of passwords and improving the security levels of different applications. [1]

Actually, different biometric techniques are already in use to get a higher level of security in different applications, avoiding the use of passwords anymore, and instead, different physical or behavioral characteristics of people are the key of entering a system.[2]

E. Ariwa and E. El-Qawasmeh (Eds.): DEIS 2011, CCIS 194, pp. 478–492, 2011.

Nowadays, from a mobile phone many operations may be performed needing user authentication, as private phone calls, connecting to the mail, starting up the device or accessing some Internet applications. Moreover, mobile phones include personal information, as agenda, mails received, personal applications or sms, whose content should not be accessible for anyone excepting the owner of the phone.

In all these contexts, mobile authentication is strongly required. But also, from a mobile device connected to Internet users are able to buy and execute different monetary operations including bank transactions and product acquisition in online shops. In these mobile e-commerce applications, authentication is an, even more, absolutely necessity.

Most of the e-commerce from mobile devices security issues still rely on passwords, but utilizing biometrics in mobile phones may be a solution to improve the required security guarantee.

At present there are different approaches trying to join several biometric techniques and mobile phones to enhance their security:

– Iris recognition through the cameras included in mobile phones. [3], [4], [5], [6].
– Face recognition by means of a camera (or video camera) embedded. [7], [8], [9].
– Voice recognition using the microphone of the phone when talking. [10], [11].
– Gait recognition of users walking with a phone embedding an accelerometer in their pocket. [12], [13].
– Genuine user recognition by keystroke analysis. [14], [15].

Obviously, in most of the works related trying to join biometrics and mobiles, researches tend to use identifying characteristics of users which may be easily extracted with sensors already included in the phones, as cameras, microphones, keys or accelerometers.

According to this idea, and due to the fact that handwritten signatures is a very extended technique to authenticate users when buying in traditional shops, we propose a biometric technique, similar to handwritten signatures, performed with the mobile phone itself, to authenticate users in e-commerce applications. This biometric technique is already introduced in [16] and is based on performing a signature in the air with the hand while holding the mobile device embedding an accelerometer. This technique is deeply explained in Section 2.

Following this, in Section 3 different architectures to implement this in-air signature biometric technique in e-commerce applications are described.

Actually, there are already some works applying biometric techniques in e-commerce applications:

– In [17] a keystroke analysis is applied to enhance the security of transactions when a PIN code is required.
– In [18] a global biometric framework is proposed within a PKI identification protocol including biometric issues for emergencies.

- In [19] a worldwide platform-independent mobile payment is proposed through iris scanning.
- In [20] a watermarking technique and an authentication protocol are proposed to be integrated on a mobile payment system, where the access key is obtained through the voice of the user.
- In [21] Web-based architecture is proposed using encrypted iris patterns as a biometric attribute for authentication of a customer for e-commerce transactions.
- In [22], as well, e-commerce transactions are protected through iris patterns including a web-based architecture in order to decrease credit card frauds over internet.

Besides, the opinion of mobile e-commerce users is asked through a survey in order to corroborate the necessity of security in mobile e-commerce applications and find at what extend an in-air signature biometric technique would be perceived as a good solution. This survey results are exposed in Section 4. Finally, the conclusions of this work are described in Section 5.

2 An Authentication Technique for Mobiles Based on Gestures

In this approach, we propose to authenticate users with their mobiles by performing a gesture (in-air signature) while holding their device on their hand. Those identifying gestures are chosen and created by users similarly to handwritten signatures.

Therefore, the main requirement of the technique is that the user should own a mobile phone embedding an accelerometer since it is the sensor needed to extract the information of the performance of the in-air signature. This demand is not a problem since leader mobile phones manufacturers are marketing devices fulfilling this task with a very growing sales volume. It is expected that in several years, most mobile phones integrate an accelerometer resulting this proposed biometric technique accessible for most of the population. For example, Apple sold more than 4 million iPhone mobiles, embedding an accelerometer, just in the three first months of 2009 [23].

To authenticate users within biometrics, it is necessary that users get enrolled in the system previously. Actually, in the enrollment phase of the authentication technique based on in-air signatures, users should repeat three times their identifying gesture to create their template of the gesture they will use as their signature to access the system. Creating a new personal gesture, easily to be repeated by the original user, but difficult to be reproduced by different people watching is not an immediate task. Indeed, most users chose to perform their own handwritten signature graph in the air, as signatures are usually complex lines that people are very used to repeat.

When accessing the system, users should repeat once their identifying gesture chosen at enrollment phase. Then, the gesture performed is compared with the template stored, and if matches, the access is granted.

Some of the characteristics of this biometric authentication technique that represent an advantage are:

- The execution of a gesture in three dimensions increases the difficulty of forging, as a person who visualizes a gesture does not have a reference plane, unlike in handwritten signature techniques where there is a fixed paper or tablet to sign on [24].
- This biometric technique combines the two general bases of biometrics. It depends both on something the user knows (the in-air signature) and how the user executes it. The main reason why a person may perform his/her own gesture in an apparently similar manner relies on some unique physical characteristics of each person: the manner the device is hold, how the arm and wrist are moved at executing the gesture, and also, wrist, hand and arm anatomy. These characteristics are so distinctive, that we suppose that even attackers knowing the required movement to entry the system will hardly success in the access.
- This approach proposes to authenticate the user directly in his/her mobile device (phone, PDA...) avoiding using an additional widget, so this recognition technique will be very comfortable for users, as they will not worry about other gadgets but their own mobile device.

Moreover, this authentication technique is expected to be widely accepted by people using their mobile phones to perform operations with a higher level of security. This assumption is based on the lack of invasiveness of the technique based on gestures, joined to the similarities to the high accepted and extended handwriting signature methods, and of course, the increase of security it provides.

Finally, in [16] an analysis of the fraud resistance of the technique to real attempts of falsification was presented, obtaining an Equal Error Rate value of 2.5% when analyzing a database of 34 in-air signatures. Each original in-air signature was attempted to be forged by three different people who studied the video record of the truthful user performing his/her identifying gesture.

3 Possible Architectures of In-Air Signature Authentication Technique in E-Commerce

According to the results presented in [16], the in-air signature authentication technique performance results (2.5% of EER) suggest that this technique should be used as a supporting method complementing the present use of passwords and contributing to an increase of the global security. The current state of the technique do not advise to substitute passwords with in-air signatures yet, but this option should be taken into consideration in the future.

Therefore, different solutions of architectures are proposed in this Section to include in-air signature authentication technique in mobile e-commerce applications in order to improve the security of all the monetary operations performed within a mobile phone with Internet access.

All these proposals are not required to be used separately; actually, better scenarios could be obtained with combinations of some of them. The architectures presented differ each other in the following aspects:

- Where the authentication process is executed.
- Whether the in-air signature goes out of the phone or not.
- Who stores the template of the in-air signature of users.

Following these considerations, the subsequent architectures to include in-air signatures in mobile e-commerce transactions are proposed:

3.1 Architecture 1: Authentication in the Mobile Phone

A possible architecture of application of in-air signature in mobile e-commerce transactions is considering a private key, stored inside the mobile device and linked to the owner of the mobile phone. This private key is released only when the biometric authentication succeeds, which means that the user of the phone has been able to repeat accurately the in-air signature of the owner of the phone.

Obviously, an enrollment phase is needed when the user buys a mobile card. In this moment, users must register themselves within their identity and also with their in-air signature. Therefore, whenever users perform their own in-air signature, the key stored in the mobile card would be released, and the identity of the user would be authenticated.

This key may be used directly to authenticate a user in an online shop or to encode a transaction through a PKI protocol.

This architecture includes a powerful advantage, which is the fact that the in-air signature never travels out of the phone of the user, reducing the possibilities of being intercepted and compromised.

3.2 Architecture 2: Authentication in the Online Shop Server

A second architecture option consists of including an in-air signature complementing a password when registering in an online shop.

In accordance with this, when new users desire to buy a product on an online shop from their mobile device, they should register in their web application filling the form presented with the personal data of users. Besides, an optional box should be presented asking whether the users should activate this higher security level through in-air signatures when the transactions are performed within his/her mobile device. If they check this option, an enrollment of in-air signatures should be performed and stored with the rest personal data of the users. Finally, whenever users try to buy a product in a previous registered online shop, they should authenticate themselves within their in-air signature as well.

This architecture involves the vulnerability that the in-air signatures are stored in the servers of the online shop, as often occurs with handwritten passwords. The solution of this problem should include a hash function to be able to compare whether the in-air signature performed coincides with the template stored, but without being able to recover the in-air signature from the template stored in the severs of the shop.

Besides, this architecture let users to create different in-air signatures for different online shops.

3.3 Architecture 3: Authentication in the Bank Server

Another option is to give the responsibility of storing the in-air signature template to the bank where the e-commerce transactions are charged. This architecture is appropriate for bank entities that would offer to their clients the possibility of including a higher security authentication on their transactions on Internet.

According to this, users who want to contract this service would enroll in the bank servers with their own in-air signature. Later on, whenever they perform an Internet transaction with their mobile, they would be asked to authenticate them also within their in-air signature.

Therefore, when users perform a monetary transaction on an online shop, this shop must access the bank servers to grant the operation of the user, asking about their monetary funds and whether their personal information is correct. Actually, the online shop inquires the bank to authenticate the user, so they redirect them to their bank web where the bank asks some personal information and a password to authenticate them. In this moment, if the transaction is performed within a mobile device and the higher security service is contracted, the bank web would inquire users to perform their in-air signature and compare it with the template already stored in the bank servers. If the in-air signature authentication success and the rest of personal information is correct, the bank would admit the transaction and tell the online shop that the operation is perfectly completed.

This architecture makes banks responsible of the most sensitive part of this biometric technique: the in-air signature template of the user. As bank entities are those who should grant the correct access to the money accounts of users, it seems quite understandable to provide them this information as well, in order to give banks more chances to protect e-commerce operations against fraud attempts.

3.4 Architecture 4: Virtual Wallet Application

Another option is to utilize the mobile device as a virtual wallet, that is charged within bank transfers. The virtual wallet application should be a downloadable program that should be installed in mobile phones. From any cash machine, a many transfer should be able to be performed to charge the virtual wallet with money.

The security of this virtual wallet is responsible of the application in the client, requiring for a password whenever a transaction of the money of the virtual wallet is required.

In this scenario, an in-air signature authentication technique is easily inclusive and would improve the security of requiring only a password to make the monetary operation. Therefore, when users download and install the virtual wallet application, the security of performing operations should be configured within no security, low security regarding passwords or high security adding in-air signatures.

Therefore, when users buy a product on an online shop within this virtual wallet, the authentication process consists of writing correctly their password and performing their in-air signature accurately in comparison with the template stored by the virtual wallet application.

This solution is quite comfortable since the amount of money which even might be compromised with the security of the architecture would be the one charged in the virtual wallet. Besides, the in-air signature never travels out of the mobile phone.

3.5 Architecture 5: Wallet of Passwords

The last architecture proposed in this paper does not utilize in-air signature authentication to protect a monetary transaction itself, but it provides a comfortable solution to manage with usual passwords, trying to solve the problem when they are forgotten due to the high number and the high difficulty of the passwords used by users at present.

This solutions is based on the idea of a password wallet, where all the passwords required are stored and are accessible when the in-air signature that protects them is executed accurately.

Following this idea, a hierarchical structure may be constructed, securing the most sensitive passwords with complex in-air signatures and the less ones with simpler in-air signatures.

It is remarkable that in this proposal, the in-air signature keeps inside the mobile device as well.

4 Users Acceptability

Considering the opinion of the final users, is a must aspect when adopting a new authentication scheme, since they are the ones who are going to utilize it. Thereby, it is essential to know previously whether there is a necessity on implementing this authentication scheme and to what extend the feeling of security of the users augment. Actually, users will not use a new authentication method unless they feel secure when using it, independently whether it would be really secure or not.

According to this, a survey has been developed and sent to people who had participated in the obtention of a database of in-air signatures utilized to study the performance of this authentication technique for mobiles. Results presented have been obtained from the responses of 24 people, who utilize habitually their mobile phones.

This survey evaluates firstly the need of security for different operations executed from mobiles. Then, an assessment of the security level provided by current authentication methods is presented, followed by the analysis of how biometrics could improve the security level. Finally, different aspects of the authentication technique based on in-air signatures are evaluated as well. Results are presented separately by the questions of the survey:

4.1 Need of Security on Mobile Operations

The first question proposed tries to evaluate to what extend users feel they need security in the different operations that may be performed from a mobile device. This includes:

- Mobile initialization.
- SMS access.
- Agenda access.
- Mail access.
- Applications download.
- Internet searches.
- E-commerce.

Figure 1 represents the percentage of answers corresponding to each operation and possible evaluation (1 very low - 5 very high).

From the previous figure, it can be derived that users are very worried about the security required for e-commerce applications, feeling monetary information the most sensitive when performing operations from their mobiles. Users demand

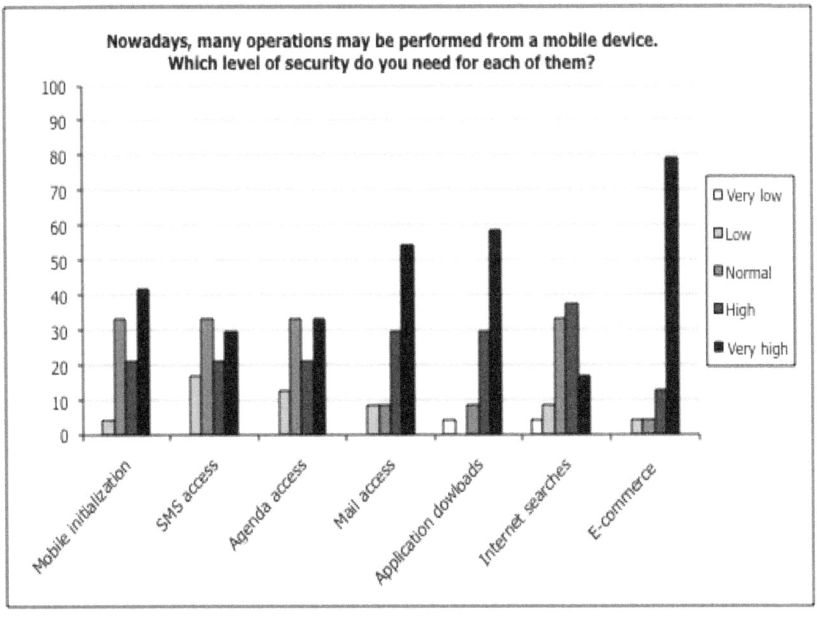

Fig. 1. Need of security on mobile operations

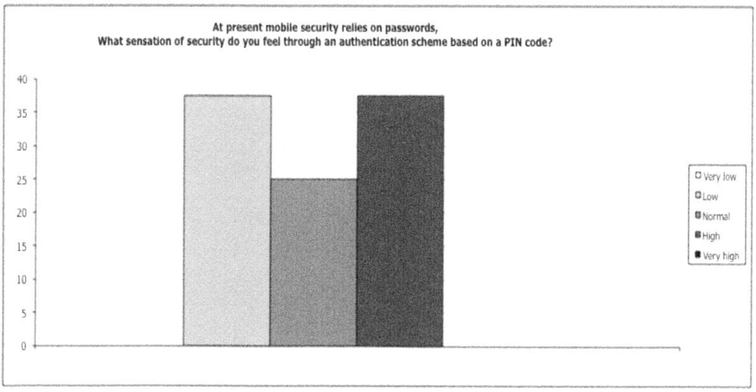

Fig. 2. Authentication based on passwords security sensation

as well a high level of security when their personal information is involved, whereas when no personal information is entailed users do not perceive security so important.

Summarizing, users demand a high level of security when operating from their mobile phones.

4.2 Password Security Sensation

At present, most applications for mobile devices relies their security in authentication schemes based on the repetition of a password or a PIN code. In this context, users have been asked to evaluate the security they feel on this authentication method. Results on percentage are presented on Figure 2.

According to the results of this question, it is derived that users find PIN code authentication as a method within normal security level.

4.3 Password Security Sensation for E-Commerce Applications

As a complementary of the previous question, users have been asked as well to assess the security of password authentication schemes when they perform an e-commerce operation. Results presented on Figure 3 claim that they feel a normal security level when executing a monetary transaction through this authentication method. These responses, in comparison with those in Section 4.1 state that security needs of users is not fullfilled yet by current authentication schemes based on PIN codes.

4.4 Feeling of Increase of Security through Biometric Authentication Methods in Mobile Devices

This question evaluates the sensation of including a biometric authentication technique in order to improve the level of security of all the operations considered in Section 4.1.

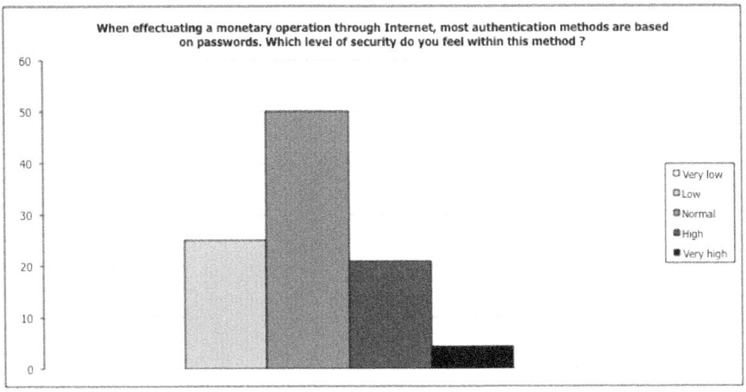

Fig. 3. Password security sensation for e-commerce applications

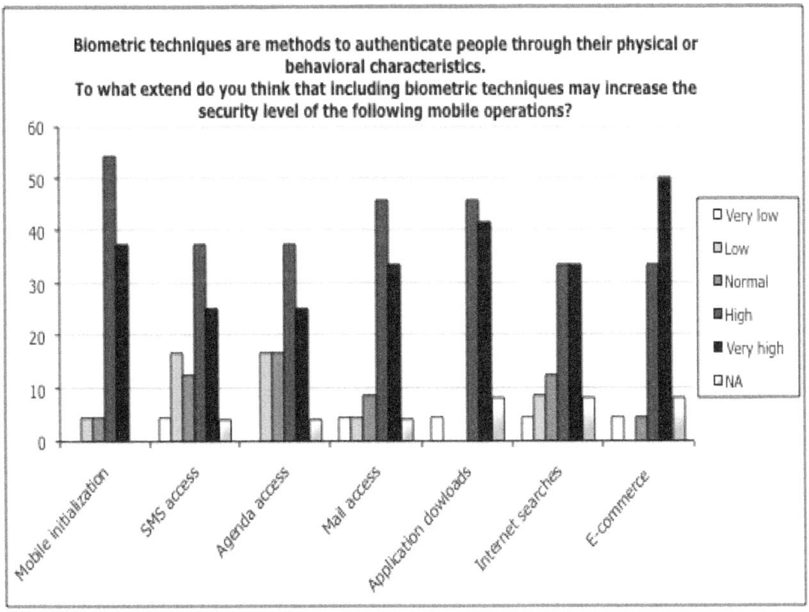

Fig. 4. Sensation of security increase on mobile operations through biometrics

From this figure, it is deducted that users do think that biometrics would help to satisfy the security requirements of the operations performed from mobile devices.

4.5 Feeling of Increase of Security through Biometric Authentication Methods in Mobile Devices

This section evaluates the opinion of users about the in-air signature as a method to increase the security of different mobile operations. It is remarkable that

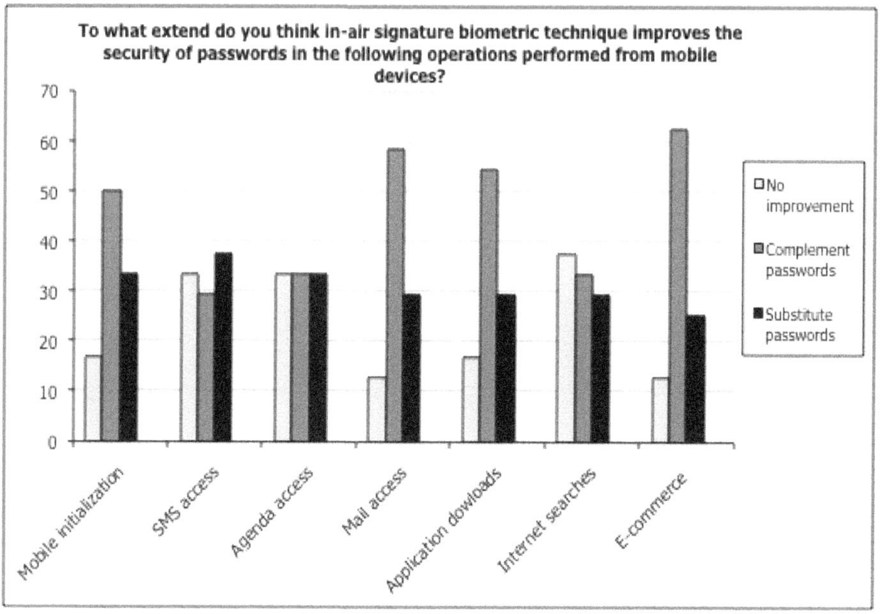

Fig. 5. Sensation of security increase on mobile operations through in-air signature authentication method

all of the users answering this survey have participated in the obtention of a database of in-air signatures with a mobile device, so they have repeated their in-air signatures several times, representing an enrollment phase and some access attempts. According to this, they have already get in contact with this biometric technique.

Figure 5 represents to what extend users trust in the in-air signature authentication technique to increase the security of different operations performed from a mobile device.

Therefore, most people consider in-air signature biometric technique as a complementary solution to increase the security of passwords. It is noticeable the results of e-commerce operations, where many people considered this authentication method as complementary and even substitutive of passwords.

4.6 Evaluation of Different Characteristics of In-Air Signature Authentication Method

Finally, other aspects of the in-air signature authentication technique have been taking into consideration:

- Confidence.
- Utility.
- Use difficulty.
- Comfortableness.

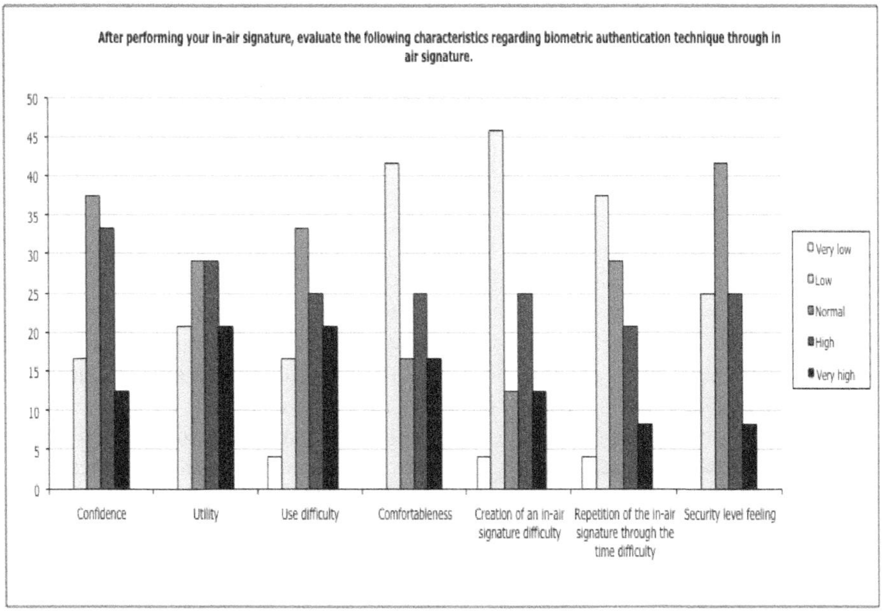

Fig. 6. Evaluation of different characteristics of in-air signature authentication method

- Creation of an in-air signature difficulty.
- Repetition of the in-air signature through the time difficulty.
- Security level feeling.

All the opinions about these features are represented in Figure 6.

According to this figure, it is remarkable the high comfortableness and ease felt when performing in-air signatures, as well as the high confidence, utility and security level perceived by the users.

5 Conclusion

Nowadays, transactions through Internet and other e-commerce operations are turned into usual actions for people. Besides, the growth of smartphones with Internet access makes most people possess an own mobile phone where monetary activities in Internet are easily performed.

Most of the e-commerce operation security relies on passwords that should be remembered by the owner of the phone. In this context biometrics may be a solution to help users and increase the security of the operations.

In this work an in-air signature technique is proposed as a technique to authenticate users by performing an identifying gesture in the air by holding the mobile on the hand. Some fraud resistance tests were previously performed evaluating the performance of the technique to a complementary to passwords method.

Different architectures have been proposed to implement the in-air signature authentication technique in real e-commerce applications. The architectures proposed consist of:

- Authentication in the mobile.
- Authentication in the server of the online shop.
- Authentication in the bank.
- Virtual wallet.
- Wallet of passwords.

Moreover, users have been taken into consideration the opinion of users, since they are the people who are going to utilize the authentication system. Therefore, a survey has been answer by 24 people after testing the in-air signature authentication system.

From this survey, the following conclusions may be inferred:

- People feel the necessity of a higher security, specially in e-commerce or monetary applications.
- People trust biometric techniques as methods to increase the security of e-commerce applications.
- People consider in-air signature technique as an useful method to complement password authentication technique in order to increase the security of e-commerce applications.
- People emphasize the comfortableness and ease of the in-air signature technique as a method to authenticate in e-commerce applications.

According to this, the in-air signature technique may be considered a good solution to be included in current e-commerce applications performed from a mobile device.

References

1. Chirillo, J., Blaul, S.: Implementing Biometric Security, 1st edn. Hungry Minds (2003) (incorporated)
2. Jain, A.K., Flynn, P., Ross, A.A.: Handbook of Biometrics. Springer-Verlag New York, Inc., Secaucus (2007)
3. ho Cho, D., Park, K.R., Rhee, D.W., Kim, Y., Yang, J.: Pupil and iris localization for iris recognition in mobile phones. In: International Workshop on Software Engineering, Artificial Intelligence, Networking and Parallel/Distributed Computing, International Conference on & Self-Assembling Wireless Networks, pp. 197–201 (2006)
4. Jeong, D., Park, H.A., Park, K., Kim, J.: Iris recognition in mobile phone based on adaptive gabor filter. In: Zhang, D., Jain, A.K. (eds.) ICB 2005. LNCS, vol. 3832, pp. 457–463. Springer, Heidelberg (2005)
5. Kurkovsky, S., Carpenter, T., MacDonald, C.: Experiments with simple iris recognition for mobile phones. In: Third International Conference on Information Technology: New Generations, pp. 1293–1294 (2010)

6. Jeong, D.S., Park, H.A., Park, K.R., Kim, J.: Iris recognition in mobile phone based on adaptive gabor filter. In: Proceedings of the Advances in Biometrics, International Conference, ICB 2006, Hong Kong, China, January 5-7, pp. 457–463 (2006)
7. Tao, Q., Veldhuis, R.: Biometric authentication for a mobile personal device. In: Annual International Conference on Mobile and Ubiquitous Systems, pp. 1–3 (2006)
8. yi Han, S., Park, H.A., Cho, D.H., Park, K.R., Lee, S.: Face recognition based on near-infrared light using mobile phone. In: Beliczynski, B., Dzielinski, A., Iwanowski, M., Ribeiro, B. (eds.) ICANNGA 2007. LNCS, vol. 4432, pp. 440–448. Springer, Heidelberg (2007)
9. Ijiri, Y., Sakuragi, M., Lao, S.: Security management for mobile devices by face recognition. In: 7th International Conference on Mobile Data Management, MDM 2006, pp. 49–49 (May 2006)
10. Shabeer, H.A., Suganthi, P.: Mobile phones security using biometrics. In: International Conference on Computational Intelligence and Multimedia Applications, vol. 4, pp. 270–274 (2007)
11. Lapère, M., Johnson, E.: User authentication in mobile telecommunication environments using voice biometrics and smartcards. In: Besson, M., Gobbi, R., Reed, R., Campolargo, M., Mullery, A. (eds.) IS&N 1997. LNCS, vol. 1238, pp. 437–443. Springer, Heidelberg (1997)
12. Mantyjarvi, J., Lindholm, M., Vildjiounaite, E., Makela, S.M., Ailisto, H.A.: Identifying users of portable devices from gait pattern with accelerometers. In: Proceedings of IEEE International Conference on Acoustics, Speech, and Signal Processing (ICASSP 2005), vol. 2, pp. ii/973–ii/976 (2005)
13. Iso, T., Yamazaki, K.: Gait analyzer based on a cell phone with a single three-axis accelerometer. In: MobileHCI 2006: Proceedings of the 8th Conference on Human-computer Interaction with Mobile Devices and Services, pp. 141–144. ACM, New York (2006)
14. Clarke, N., Furnell, S.: Authenticating mobile phone users using keystroke analysis. International Journal of Information Security 6, 1–14 (2007)
15. Saevanee, H., Bhatarakosol, P.: User authentication using combination of behavioral biometrics over the touchpad acting like touch screen of mobile device. In: International Conference on Computer and Electrical Engineering, pp. 82–86 (2008)
16. Guerra-Casanova, J., Sánchez-Ávila, C., de Santos-Sierra, A., del Pozo, G.B., Jara-Vera, V.: A real-time in-air signature biometric technique using a mobile device embedding an accelerometer. In: Zavoral, F., Yaghob, J., Pichappan, P., El-Qawasmeh, E. (eds.) NDT (1). CCIS, vol. 87, pp. 497–503. Springer, Heidelberg (2010)
17. Karnan, M., Krishnaraj, N.: Bio password keystroke dynamic approach to secure mobile devices. In: 2010 IEEE International Conference on Computational Intelligence and Computing Research (ICCIC), pp. 1–4, ID: 1 (2010)
18. Xing, S., Xue, H., Yan, X.: Research on model of biometric identification emergency response in electronic commerce. In: International Conference on Management of e-Commerce and e-Government, ICMECG 2008, pp. 185–188, ID: 1 (2008)
19. Lu, H., Claret-Tournier, F., Chatwin, C., Young, R.C.D.: M-commerce secured using web-enabled mobile biometric agents. In: 2007 IEEE/WIC/ACM International Conferences on Web Intelligence and Intelligent Agent Technology Workshops, pp. 480–483, ID: 1 (2007)

20. Wang, J., Yuan, S.: A novel security mobile payment system based on watermarked voice cheque. In: 2005 2nd International Conference on Mobile Technology, Applications and Systems, p. 4, ID: 1 (2005)
21. Vangala, R.R., Sasi, S.: Biometric authentication for e-commerce transaction. In: 2004 IEEE International Workshop on Imaging Systems and Techniques (IST), pp. 113–116, ID: 1 (2004)
22. Rahimi, A., Mohammadi, S., Rahimi, R.: An efficient iris authentication using chaos theory-based cryptography for e-commerce transactions. In: International Conference for Internet Technology and Secured Transactions, ICITST 2009, pp. 1–6, ID: 1 (2009)
23. Dowling, S., Nancy Paxton, J.H.: Apple reports first quarter results (2009)
24. Guo, J., Doermann, D., Rosenfeld, A.: Local correspondence for detecting random forgeries. In: International Conference on Document Analysis and Recognition, p. 319 (1997)

A Mobile Gaming Approach to Virtual Heritage Exploration

Kian Lam Tan, Chen Kim Lim, and Abdullah Zawawi Talib

School of Computer Sciences
Universiti Sains Malaysia
11800 USM Penang, Malaysia
andrewtankianlam@gmail.com, kim86_lavender@hotmail.com,
azht@cs.usm.my

Abstract. Virtual heritage is a computer-based interactive technology that provides formative stages of the educational experience of cultural heritage such as virtual tour of museums. With the fast growing technological advancement in mobile phone technology, it has become possible to create a virtual heritage application for edutainment for general public on mobile platform. In this paper, we present a virtual heritage application called M-Heritage Hunt that provides a technology-integrated environment that allows users to gain knowledge of heritage on mobile platform through panoramic views of the heritage sites and a game that combines the traditional games of Monopoly and Treasure Hunt. Based on the comparison and preliminary evaluation, the system has been found to be interesting, attractive and successful in delivering the heritage contents.

Keywords: game; mobile platform; panoramic view; virtual heritage; virtual reality.

1 Introduction

Virtual reality (VR) has been employed in many areas such as heavy industries, training and education. The technology is becoming unavoidable in the new emerging digital visualization fabric but it is still relatively unexplored on mobile device platform. In virtual heritage, VR brings a sense of reality to the users and provide the users with a clearer and more immersive view of the surroundings of a heritage building or site.

In this paper, we present an application of VR in virtual exploration of heritage sites on mobile platform that incorporates a game called M-Heritage Hunt. The main objectives of this game are to create an environment that provides panoramic view of various heritage sites, to attract and promote a particular heritage area and to increase the learning experience of a heritage area. M-Heritage Hunt is a novel game which is a hybrid of the traditional games of Monopoly and Treasure Hunt. Its main platform is the monopoly game which provides the outer view of a heritage area while the treasure hunt acts as a mini game within the Monopoly game that provides the inner view of a heritage building. A heritage gallery is also provided so that the users are

E. Ariwa and E. El-Qawasmeh (Eds.): DEIS 2011, CCIS 194, pp. 493–500, 2011.

able to view both the inner view and the outer view of a heritage building using panoramic view [2]. In our work, the UNESCO World Heritage Sites of George Town, Penang in Malaysia are chosen for the development of a demonstration system for the game.

2 Related Work

Squire [3] proposed that games can be an attractive medium for learning that should have attracted significant attention of educators. Furthermore, activities such as visiting and exploring a place, and playing a game can be used to gain new knowledge on the history, background, design and cultural perspective of a heritage building or site. Tan et al. [4] mentioned that using a game is a good model for learning and is applicable to all learners. Teachers or developers can make use of the game as a medium to convey the learning contents. Azan et al. [5] stated that learning history is difficult for most students, but if game is applied in the teaching, it will become easier and more interesting to learn.

Carr [6] has applied game in teaching physics and has successfully explained a complex physics theory (Einstein's Special Theory of Relativity) that is difficult to be comprehended by most students. Applying game in teaching is the best approach to be adopted in teaching especially in complicated and boring subjects.

Wenjun and Xiudong [7] presented a study on a good interface design for game applications. Song et al. [8] have developed a digital heritage application that serves as an edutainment tool that incorporates interactive storytelling techniques in order to enhance the process of exploring the virtual environment.

Toh et al. [9] presented a case study on adopting a combination of user research processes to produce the mobile augmented reality guide on design requirements from the tourist perspectives. In order to collect comprehensive user data, text recognition feature, user-friendly information, panorama photos, virtual contents (i.e. 3D characters, animation), push and pull content, augmented social experience (sharing of photos and memories) and group touring experience should be combined together into the mobile platform.

Heritage sites are full of historic entities. In general, the best way to attract the user's or visitor's attention to discover and appreciate these entities is by adopting a gaming approach. However, games have not been largely used in virtual heritage exploration. Normally, virtual heritage exploration involves virtual reality views and virtual guided tour. Therefore, an educational or leisure game should be incorporated in a virtual heritage application in order to increase the learning process and attract the user to learn more about a heritage site.

3 Game Design

The proposed game, M-Heritage Hunt is designed based on the classical board game called Monopoly together with the game of Treasure Hunt. In this board game, the player can control the virtual character (an icon) inside the game by rolling a dice to move around the path. The objectives of the game are to earn properties, to manage own resources and to visit historical buildings in a heritage area. The winner of the game is the player who have successfully monopolised the other players in the game. M-Heritage Hunt is not a single player game but a multi player game for two to four players. Moreover, before starting to play the game, the player can also visit various historic sites.

The framework of M-Heritage Hunt consists of two components namely Gallery and Game as shown in Fig. 1. The Gallery component consists of Information and Panoramic View of the heritage building and the surrounding area. The Information module contains information on the building such as pictures, descriptions and stories on the building. The Panoramic View module allows the users to monitor and control the view by themselves while viewing a heritage building or site. The Game component consists of Game Play and Treasure Hunt modules. The Game Play module is where players play Heritage Hunt and at the same time are able to visit the heritage sites. The Treasure Hunt module is where users are required to answer some questions based on the panoramic view in the Gallery.

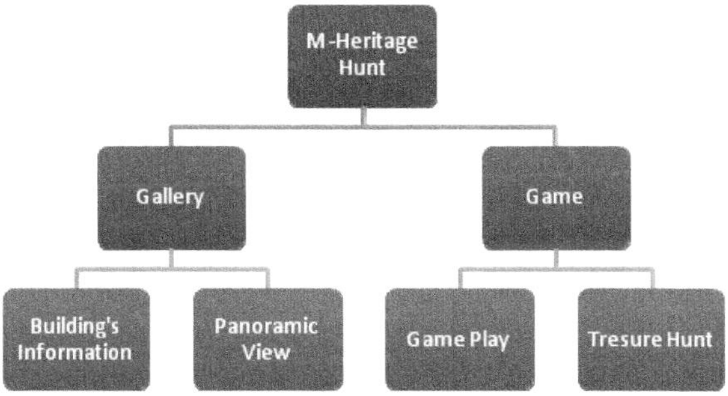

Fig. 1. The Overview of the Framework of M-Heritage Hunt

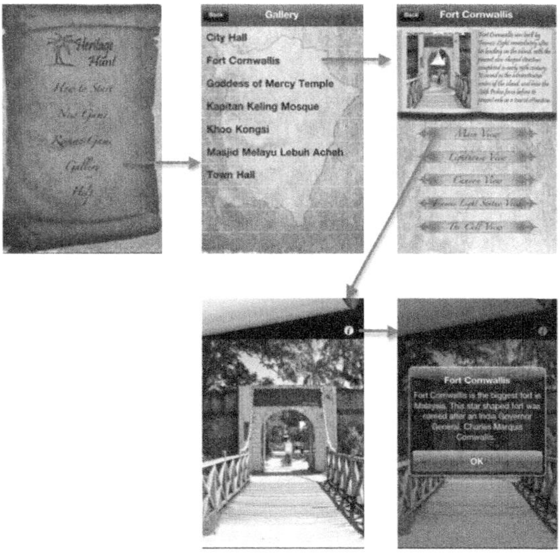

Fig. 2. Gallery Module

The Gallery module stores the views and information of a heritage building or site. The information is presented in a table format and each row in the table represents one building or site. Each of these buildings contains information such as pictures, descriptions and panoramic views as shown in Fig. 2.

The Game component is the section in which the Game Play module as shown in Fig. 3 and the Treasure Hunt module as shown in Fig. 4 are executed. Game Play consists of 40 movable cells. Four main cells are distributed at each corner of the board as in the game of monopoly, the other six cells are for the fate corner, another two cells are for the service tax and 26 cells are for the building objects, while the last two cells are for the public transport service. The four main cells represent the start point, the hospital, the free car park and the ambulance. In the cells of fate, there are three main types of fates namely the prize, the payment and the movement. The fate card consists of three possible actions based on the information of the fate card. The fate icon of the player is executed by the system automatically. The service tax card requires player to pay for the tax in the range of 100 to 200 depending on which type of icon the player steps on. The player is allowed to purchase the public transport service if the particular cell is not taken off by any other players. There is no other action that can be taken in this cell other than purchasing the transportation service.

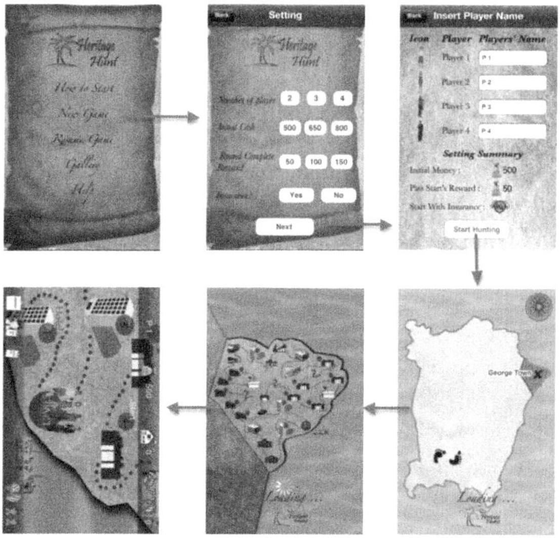

Fig. 3. Game Play Interface

As for the Treasure Hunt module, there are mini games for users to play. As shown in Fig. 4, the player is required to answer a series of questions in order to upgrade their property's value. If the player fails to answer the question, the hunt is considered as unsuccessful and the game is passed to the next player. Through the panoramic views in the Gallery module, the players would be able to understand better the buildings, background, culture, and architecture and thus able to answer correctly.

Furthermore, some hints are also given inside the questions to help the players to complete the treasure hunt as well as in learning the historical aspects of the heritage buildings or sites.

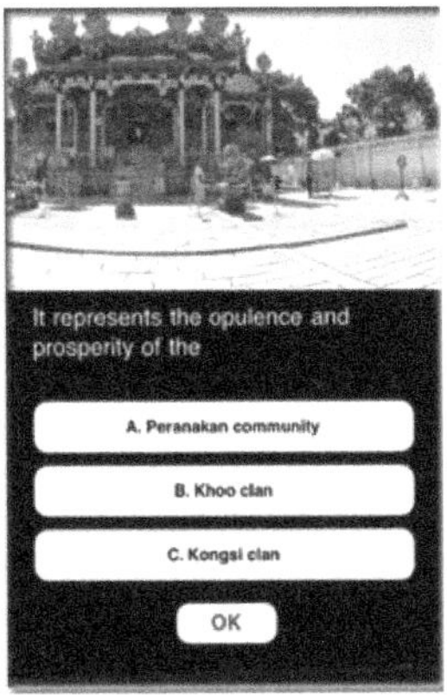

Fig. 4. Sample of Treasure Hunt

4 Implementation and User Interface

The game is implemented using the Objective C programming language and Apple X-Code as the Integrated Development Environment (IDE) to develop the game's platform. The graphics such as background pictures and panoramic views (the Gallery module) are constructed by using Adobe Photoshop CS5 together with a special stitching method for mobile platform.

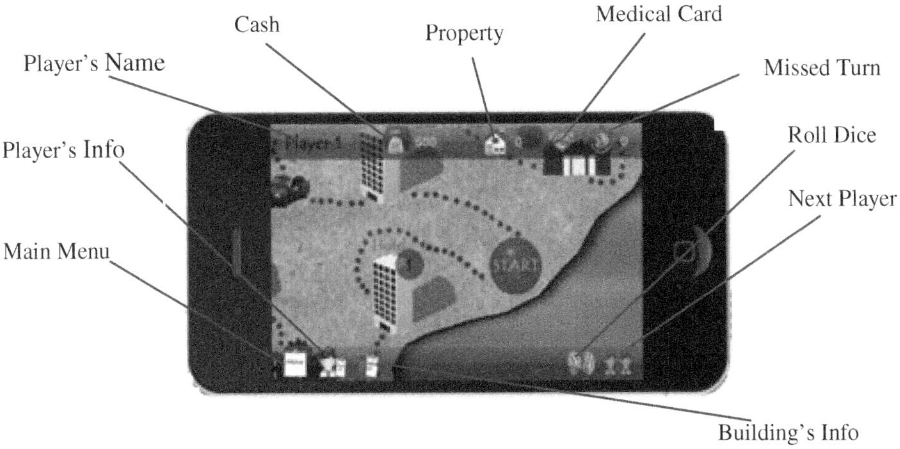

Fig. 5. Layout of M-Heritage Hunt

The layout of M-Heritage Hunt is as shown in Fig. 5. The main window is based on the monopoly platform. It is designed in such a way that the player would be able to play the game more easily. The monopoly map takes a huge portion of the screen so that the players have a proper view of the route.

The top bar of the layout displays the name of the current player (Player's Name), the total amount of money the player has in his/her possession (Cash), and the total number of buildings the player owns (Property). The top bar also indicates if the player owns any medical card (Medical Card). The card is used to let the player out of the hospital during the game. Besides, the top bar also displays the number of rounds the player has missed his/her turn that is the number of times the player could not roll the dice (Missed Turn).

The bottom bar of the layout enables the player to click on his/her information (Player's Info). A new frame displays a summary of the name of the buildings, the total amount of money and the medical card that the players own. Besides, it also includes the building information for the player if the player would like to view further information on the building (Building's Info). It will also direct the player to the Gallery component of M-Heritage Hunt. The bottom bar also contains icon that indicates the end of the player's turn that is when the game is passed to the next player (Next Player). It also has an icon for the player to roll the dice and the number of times the dice has been rolled will be shown next to it (Roll Dice).

5 Comparison and Preliminary Evaluation

Several virtual tour applications can be found in Apple Application Store such as Penang, Hong Kong 720° and Monopoly World. Penang and Hong Kong 720° applications are mainly for tourism purpose, while Monopoly World is for entertainment purpose. The summary of the comparison between M-Heritage Hunt and the above mentioned applications based on some attributes are given in Table 1. Only M-Heritage Hunt and Hong Kong 720° use virtual reality and provide panaromic views within the application. In M-Heritage Hunt, the view consists of both outer and inner 360° views of a site while Hong Kong 720° provides 720° view of only the outer view of a site. M-Heritage Hunt and Monopoly World include a game application while the others only provide virtual tour application. M-Heritage Hunt and Monopoly World do not require the Internet service because they are not location-based application. On the other hand, Penang and Hong Kong 720° need Internet in order to show the map and use GPS. M-heritage Hunt and Monopoly World also provide a map but it is only for game purpose.

In the preliminary evaluation of M-Heritage Hunt, twenty participants were invited to evaluate the game contents. The result of the evaluation is summarized in Table 2. 65% of the respondents have given an excellent rating (6 or 7) on whether the game is an interesting game. All respondents gave an excellent rating (6 or 7) (with 65% of them giving the highest rating) on whether they have gained any new knowledge after playing the game. For the third question on whether the game is easy to play, only a minority that is three respondents (15%) have given an average rating of 5 while the rest have given an excellent rating (6 or 7). For the last question, the majority of the respondents would like to play and buy similar game content in the future.

Also from the preliminary evaluation, some useful feedbacks on the effectiveness of the mobile game are obtained. Many respondents thought that the content is interesting with regard to the heritage information about George Town heritage area

Table 1. A summary of comparison between M-Heritage Hunt and three other applications

Attributes	**Mobile Application**			
	M-Heritage Hunt	**Penang**	**Hong Kong 720°**	**Monopoly World**
Virtual Reality	Yes	No	Yes	No
Panoramic View	Yes (Outer and Inner Views (360° view))	No	Yes (Outer Views only (720° view))	No
Game	Yes	No	No	Yes
Map View	Yes (for game purpose only)	Yes	Yes	Yes (for game purpose only)
Navigation System	Not Required	Required	Required	Not Required
Internet Service	Not Required	Required	Required	Not Required

Table 2. Result of preliminary evaluation

Rating Scale	**Questions**			
	1) Is the game interesting?	**2) Have you gained any new knowledge from the game?**	**3) Is the game easy to play?**	**4) Would you buy similar game?**
1	0	0	0	0
2	0	0	0	0
3	0	0	0	0
4	2	0	0	3
5	7	0	3	12
6	10	7	10	5
7	1	13	7	0
Total	**20**	**20**	**20**	**20**

and its environment and culture. The respondents also commented that the heritage site should include more buildings and places. On the learning content, many respondents agreed that M-Heritage Hunt has the ability to successfully deliver the educational content. In general, the majority of the respondents felt that the interface of M-Heritage Hunt is user friendly for game playing. Finally, the majority of the respondents have requested to install M-Heritage Hunt in their mobile device. They also proposed that M-Heritage Hunt should be made available on other mobile platforms such as Symbian, Window Mobile 7 and Blackberry.

6 Conclusion

We have shown that M-Heritage Hunt has great potential to be used as a virtual heritage exploration tool. The game which is a hybrid of the traditional Monopoly game and the Treasure Hunt game together with virtual reality would be able to impart better understanding of, and attract and promote a particular heritage area. The game is designed in such a way that the panoramic view of the heritage buildings and their descriptions are integrated with the game environment.

For future work, artificial intelligent players in the game will be implemented so that the players can play against them. Furthermore, Bluetooth or Wireless implementation will be developed to allow multiple players to play without having to share a single mobile device.

Acknowledgement

The authors would like to thank Tan Kian Guan, Poon Pui Yee, Kong Yng Jye and Chin Kew Yee for their contributions in the development of M-Heritage Hunt.

References

1. Liu, X., Qiao, J.: Research on Chinese Museum Design Based on Virtual Reality. In: Proceedings of the International Workshop on Modeling, Simulation and Optimization, pp. 372–374 (2008)
2. Xiong, Y., Pulli, K.: Fast Panorama Stitching for High Quality Panoramic Images on Mobile Phones. IEEE Transactions on Consumer Electronics 56(2), 198–306 (2010)
3. Squire, K.: Games, Learning, and Society: Building a Field. Educational Technology 47(5), 51–54 (2007)
4. Tan, P.H., Ling, S.W., Ting, C.Y.: Adaptive Digital Game Based Learning Framework. In: Proceedings of the 2nd International Conference on Digital Interactive Multimedia in Entertainment and Arts, pp. 142–146 (2007)
5. Azan, M.Z.N., Wong, S.Y.: Game Based Learning Model for History Courseware: A Preliminary Analysis. In: Proceedings of the International Symposium on Information Technology 2008, pp. 1–8 (2008)
6. Carr, D.: Visual Computer Game Features for Teaching Relativity. In: Proceedings of the 7th International Conference Computer Graphics, Imaging and Visualization 2010, pp. 35–40 (2010)
7. Wenjun, H., Xiudong, B.: HCI in Real-time Strategy Games: A Study of Principals and Guidelines for Designing 3D User Interface. In: Proceedings of the 7th International Conference Computer-Aided Industrial Design and Conceptual Design, pp. 1–6 (2007)
8. Song, M., Elias, T., Martinovic, I., Mueller-Wittig, M., Chan, T.K.Y.: Digital Heritage Application as an Edutainment Tool. In: Proceedings of the International Conference on Virtual Reality Continuum and its Application in Industry, pp. 163–167 (2004)
9. Toh, Y.-W., Jeong, J.-H., Pan, Y.-H.: A Combined User Research Process for Designing Mobile AR Guide in Cultural Heritage. In: Proceedings of the IEEE International Symposium on Mixed and Augmented Reality – Arts, Media & Humanities, pp. 71–72 (2010)

A Low-Cost Method for Generating Panoramic Views for a Mobile Virtual Heritage Application

Chen Kim Lim, Kian Lam Tan, and Abdullah Zawawi Talib

School of Computer Sciences
Universiti Sains Malaysia
11800 USM Penang, Malaysia
kim86_lavender@hotmail.com, andrewtankianlam@gmail.com,
azht@cs.usm.my

Abstract. Nowadays, with rapid advancement of technology, people can roam around the virtual world through the aid of the Internet. One of these advances is a photographic technique called panoramic view where images are captured with elongated field of view using specialized software or equipments. However, the computational cost of generating a panoramic view is high. One of the popular software for generating panoramic views is Apple Inc.'s QuickTime VR (QTVR). Nevertheless, iPhone Operating System (iOS) does not support the existing QTVR software. Therefore, in this paper, a low-cost method for generating panoramic views on mobile platform is proposed by storing finite images in an array in order to generate a 360o panoramic view. This method can be supported by all kinds of platform and therefore can be installed in any mobile devices without having to use any intermediate software to convert the format of the images. The outcome is a cylindrical panoramic view that allows the user to gain a 360o clear vision around historical monuments in a mobile virtual heritage exploration using lower computational cost but with similar quality of production.

Keywords: panoramic view; virtual heritage; image stitching.

1 Introduction

In the present society, people live in two distinct worlds which are the real world and the virtual world. The advancement of virtual reality (VR) becomes crucial in multidisciplinary areas such as simulation for education, entertainment, medical application and gaming [1]. Heritage is defined as our legacy inherited from the past, our traditions that we practice today, or our immaterial possessions that we are passing on to the next generations [2]. Each of the heritage buildings has its own historical stories. Some of the historical stories were told by our forefathers and others can be obtained from history books. On the other hand, virtual heritage is the technology that creates explicit visual representation of a heritage site such as monuments, artifacts and cultural buildings [3]. With virtual heritage, people can have an overall imagination of the heritage sites although they might have not visited some of the places before. Virtual heritage has also become a platform for improving the

E. Ariwa and E. El-Qawasmeh (Eds.): DEIS 2011, CCIS 194, pp. 501–512, 2011.

learning process of certain events and historical elements for use in an educational setting [4]. Panoramic view is a widely used technique to present virtual heritage since it gives a sense of immersion of the scene.

There are several representations of panoramas such as spherical, cubical and cylindrical panoramas as shown in Fig. 1. Spherical and cubical panoramas can be viewed from any directions from a current fixed position. Both types of panorama offer the users a 720° view that is a full view in both horizontal and vertical directions. However, spherical and cubical panoramas are difficult to capture compared to cylindrical panoramas since they also contain top view and the bottom view of the image. For cylindrical panorama, the observer's view in the vertical direction is limited but it offers a full 360° horizontal view. Yet, cylindrical panorama fulfills most of the requirements of virtual reality applications. Furthermore, the image format for cylindrical panorama can be saved as a normal photo format such as 'jpeg' and 'png'. Therefore, cylindrical panorama can fit most applications and reduce problems of format incompatibility with software devices. Besides, cylindrical panorama can also be unrolled into a planar image as shown in Fig. 2.

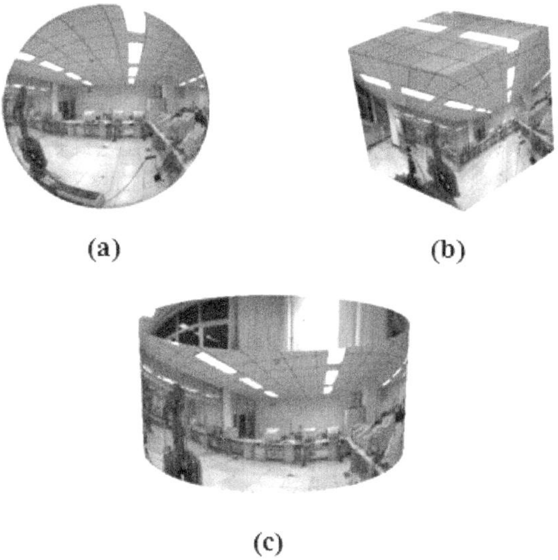

Fig. 1. Representations for Panoramas (a) Spherical (b) Cubical (c) Cylindrical [5]

Fig. 2. An Example of a Cylindrical Panoramic Image [5]

Virtual heritage applications combine real and virtual objects. So, cylindrical panorama is one of the most suitable techniques to be adopted in developing virtual heritage applications because it is possible for the users to navigate a 360° horizontal walkthrough. Therefore, users can now experience the heritage sites rather than merely looking at the photographs or reading the historical articles. The objective of this paper is to present a low-cost method of capturing and producing cylindrical panoramas for a mobile virtual heritage application. The virtual heritage area chosen in this study is the UNESCO heritage area of George Town, Penang in Malaysia. The city is filled with many historical monuments such as Kapitan Keling Mosque, Acheen Street Mosque, Fort Cornwallis, Goddess of Mercy Temple, Khoo Kongsi and many more. The normal photo of one of the heritage buildings obtained from the Internet is as shown in Fig. 3. With a cylindrical panorama, the photo as shown in Figure 4 can be viewed with a 360° view in horizontal direction using a high-end camera. In constructing a panoramic view, the individual images that make up the view have to be combined by using Adobe Photoshop. In order to view the panoramic view, the 'Cubic Converter' software is used to convert the view into the cubic format of Apple Inc.'s QuickTime Virtual Reality (QTVR) movie. QTVR is a real-time walkthrough system in which the image file format is only meant for the Macintosh platform. Since our proposed work was implemented on the iPhone Operating System (iOS) mobile device, we have to find an alternative method of producing panoramic views as QTVR is not supported on this platform.

Fig. 3. Normal photo of Kapitan Keling Mosque

Fig. 4. Cylindrical Panorama of Kapitan Keling Mosque

2 Related Work

Panorama was first introduced in the 1880s by Robert, B. and his son, Barker, H. A. [6]. Apple Incorporated has developed a well known QuickTime Virtual Reality system (QTVR) on the early Apple computers in 1995 which allow users to travel virtually and interactively through panoramic views [7]. Moreover, the techniques of panorama roaming and stereoscopic display have been developed for commercial application many years ago [6]. However, there are rooms for improvements such as by combining a traditional panorama captured by one camera and one viewpoint, with a stereoscopic panorama captured by two different viewpoints. In QTVR, the stereoscopic viewpoint problem of discrete viewpoints of panorama images has been solved [5]. Yet, there are problems that need to be solved when user walkthroughs between two viewpoints, and when the panoramic views are for mobile device as the iOS platform does not support QTVR. In order to prevent the unstable shifting of the viewpoint, the smoothness of virtual roaming world needs to be enhanced. Xianghua et al. [5] proposed an image transform technique that deals with the smoothness transaction problem.

Peleg and Ben-Erza [8] proposed a technique that produces the stereoscopic pair from one source panorama captured by a single camera instead of regular usage of at least two cameras. Although this technique is good, there are two obvious limitations. One of them is the fixed focal length that makes the user uncomfortable and the result is worse when the users are staring at a viewpoint with zero parallax. Parallax is the difference in the apparent position of an object that is viewed by two different lines of sight. The viewpoint is at zero parallax when the two views of an object are exactly superimposed on top of one another. The second limitation is the need to process one panorama in order to double up the panorama. This processing technique is not suitable for real time rendering. The rendering time determines the speed of image combinations and how effective the users can roam around the virtual environment.

Bourke [9] proposed a toe-in technique for capturing a pair of stereoscopic panoramas with zero parallax by using two rotating cameras. This method controls the parallax between two stereoscopic panoramas efficiently and permits zero parallax at a limited distance. However, this method also has a weakness. There is an unexpected heavy image load in practical development when the camera needs to be rotated 5 degrees per stereoscopic panorama in order to capture one panorama image.

According to Hongfei et al. [6], cylindrical panorama is the easiest way of capturing stereoscopic panorama and has the simplest rendering algorithm with a good roaming effect. At least six images are needed to produce a stereoscopic cylindrical panorama. A tripod is needed to fix a camera in order to obtain a well and accurate control of the rotation angles of the camera as shown in Figure 5(a). A pair of images needs to be captured at one viewpoint. One viewpoint represents the left eye while the other viewpoint represents the right eye. The solution needs twelve images to be captured at six viewpoints (turns at each viewpoint) as shown in Figure 5(b) [6]. The images {1, 5, 9, 4, 8, 12} are to generate the left eye panorama and {3, 7, 11, 2, 6, 10} are to generate the right eye panorama as shown in Figure 5(c).

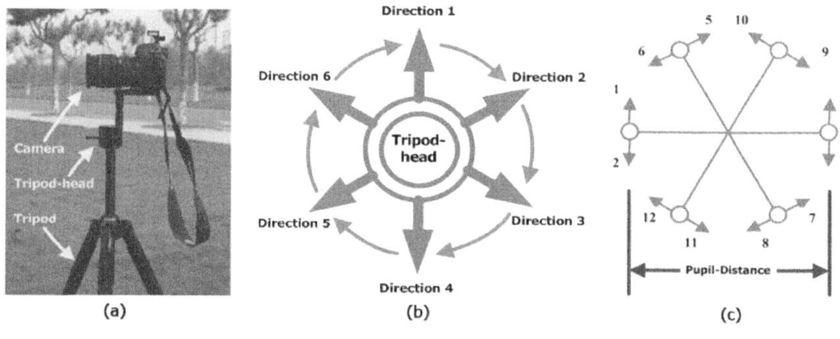

Fig. 5. A Method for Capturing a Stereoscopic Panoramic Image [6]

Virtual Reality has been used since the early 90's mostly in commercial field [10]. K. Kwiatek et al. [11] used virtual reality technique in reconstructing a heritage church – Charles Church. In order to create high resolution panoramas, they also used Digital Single Lens Reflex (DSLR) camera and a panoramic head, and basic 3D models of the interior view of the building were generated in Autodesk Image Modeler software. They exported the 3D files to 3D studioMax in order to generate a photorealistic visualization of the interior of the building. The sequence of spherical images is imported to QuickTime Pro in order to generate movie (MOV) files using H.264 codec which is compatible with Lucid Viewer or suitable for displaying on a 360° screen. Moreover, the 360° images are taken in both still and video motion as a preparation for an interactive storytelling following a story design. To display actors in the spherical panoramas, Chroma keying technique is used.

In another method, Hirayu et al. [12] constructed a virtual reality of a heritage site by starting with construction of the models of the building, and then capturing aerial photographs for color images using a helicopter. They also compressed the file of the images collected before constructing the building in 3D. This method is different from K. Kwiatek et al. [13] since the models are constructed, unlike the latter that uses video panoramas. However, both research works were carried out using the available source of information of the historical images.

3 Proposed Method

The proposed method of generating panoramic view is as shown in Figure 6. Firstly, in setting up the camera, the camera is adjusted based on the brightness of the environment. Then, the tripod is positioned at a suitable location before the camera is set up on the tripod. Next, horizontal 360° images are captured. The brightness of the images needs to be adjusted to prevent over exposure of the image. The horizontal 360° images are then stitched together to generate a cylindrical panoramic view. The next subsections describe in detail each of the steps of the method.

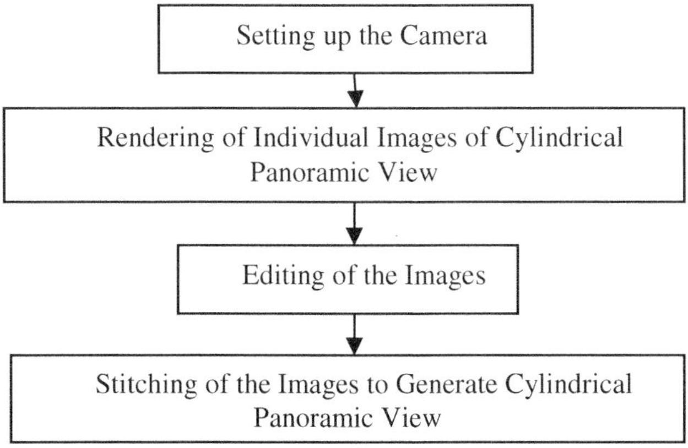

Fig. 6. Proposed Method of Generating Cylindrical Panoramic Image

3.1 Setting up the Camera

In the proposed method, Digital Single Lens Reflex (DSLR) camera is used since the image produced by this type of camera is higher in quality due to the higher number of pixels. When the images have higher number of pixels, they can be zoomed in for a clearer and more detailed view. The number of times zooming can be performed depends on the number of pixels in the images. Besides, DSLR camera is used because it can be adjusted to the manual mode to capture images. When capturing the images, the brightness would be different at different viewpoints. The higher the brightness of the environment, the higher the risk of over exposure of the images will be. The resulting panoramic view is directly influenced by the brightness of the images. The over exposure of the images can be prevented by manually setting the DSLR camera beforehand.

There are three important settings for the DSLR camera which are the aperture, the shutter speed and the International Standards Organization (ISO) speed. The aperture is used to control the area where light can enter the camera. The 'f' value represents the focal point of the image. The change in 'f' value or aperture can influence the sharpness and the focus for foreground's and background's landscape. When the 'f' value is small, the lens diaphragm opens wider. Thus, opening of the lens refers to lowering of the 'f' value and thus the focus area in the image is minimized. On the other hand, closing of the lens refers to a higher 'f' value and a larger focus area in the image. Besides, the sharpness or focus of the image's foreground and background can also be adjusted.

The function of the shutter speed of the DSLR camera is to control the duration of the exposure. The duration can be controlled by the camera sensor. When the camera sensor is opened or closed, the incoming light from the camera lens is determined by the shutter. The shutter speed refers to the period of time that the light is permitted to enter the camera. The faster the shutter speed is, the shorter the duration of the exposure time will be. The shutter speed can be adjusted to capture the different brightness of images that are needed. There is a contrast between the aperture and the shutter speed as shown in Table 1.

Table 1. Combining the aperture and the shutter speed that resulted in the same exposure

Aperture Setting	Example Shutter Speed
f/22	16 seconds
f/16	8 seconds
f/11	4 seconds
f/8.0	2 seconds
f/5.6	1 seconds
f/4.0	½ seconds

The ISO speed controls the sensitivity of the camera's sensor to a given amount of light. ISO is similar to shutter speed where it can influence the over exposure of the image. However, there is a difference between the ISO speed, the aperture and the shutter speed. A lower ISO speed is preferred because a high ISO speed can dramatically increase the image noise. By combining these three settings of the DSLR camera, the same exposure can be achieved. In general, the aperture affects the depth of field. Furthermore, the shutter speed may also cause motion blurring of the image. Finally, the ISO speed affects the image noise and thus the image quality is degraded.

3.2 Rendering of Individual Images of Cylindrical Panoramic View

The basic necessity in capturing individual images for cylindrical panoramic view is a camera's tripod. The tripod can prevent hand vibration and it is used to adjust the angles of viewpoints easily and accurately. Each and every image should be taken with the camera placed on a tripod at the same height.

There should be at least 1/3 overlapped area in every two subsequent images of a set. The image captured should have 1/3 of the previous image (from Figure 7(b)) as can be seen in Figure 7(c), and 1/3 of the image in Figure 7(a) have 1/3 of the next image in Figure 7(b). Therefore, in order to produce a 360° panoramic view, approximately nine to ten images are needed. As shown in Figure 8, each 40° plus or minus on a fixed position of one viewpoint produces a horizontal image.

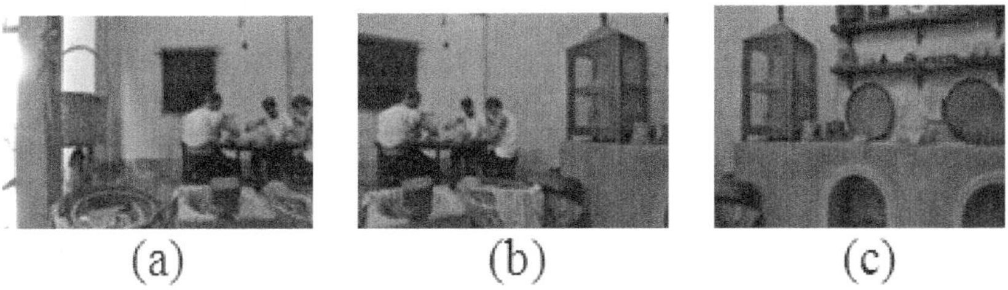

Fig. 7. Images from Khoo Kongsi

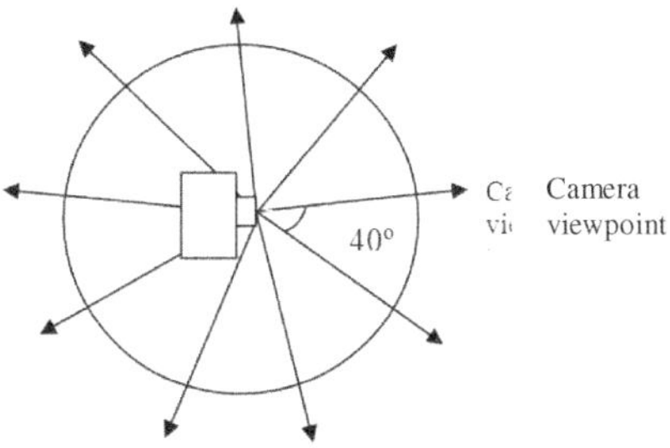

Fig. 8. Camera Viewpoints with an Interval of Approximately 40 degrees

3.3 Editing of Images

Although the DSLR camera is manually set before capturing an image, the image may also be exposed due to the fact that the brightness in the environment is different especially between those captured indoor and those captured outdoor. In our work, Adobe Photoshop is used to adjust the brightness of the images before stitching a panoramic image to prevent the exposure in the panoramic image. Photoshop can be used to adjust the brightness of the image by selecting the area of exposure. The image shown in Figure 9(a) is an example of an image that is exposed and with brightness adjusted by using Adobe Photoshop as shown in Fig. 9(b).

3.4 Stitching of Images to Generate Cylindrical Panoramic View

In this step the captured images are merged into one panoramic image. After all the images are edited, Adobe Bridge is used. Images as shown in Figure 10(a) until Figure 10(c) are pieces of images that are combined in reasonable sizes to generate three pictures respectively ((a), (b) and (c)). Instead of using QTVR which cannot be used on iOS device (.mov file is not supported on iOS device), these images are then arranged in an array with several repetitions of the edited images to produce an immersive effect with a 360° view. A finite loop of panoramic views is generated on the mobile device in order to allow the view to be scrolled continuously. Adobe Bridge is a strong media that provides centralized access and it is easy to organize, browse, locate and view. Next, Adobe Bridge is to be connected to Adobe Photoshop to activate the Photomerge function. These images can be combined automatically once the 'Panorama Mode' is switched to the Cylindrical Mode using Adobe Photoshop. After the cylindrical panoramic view is generated, the image is cropped before the user can have a 360° view in Cubic Converter as shown in Figure 11. The start and the end of the cylindrical panorama are also cropped accurately in order to match the image in the 360° view as shown in Figure 12.

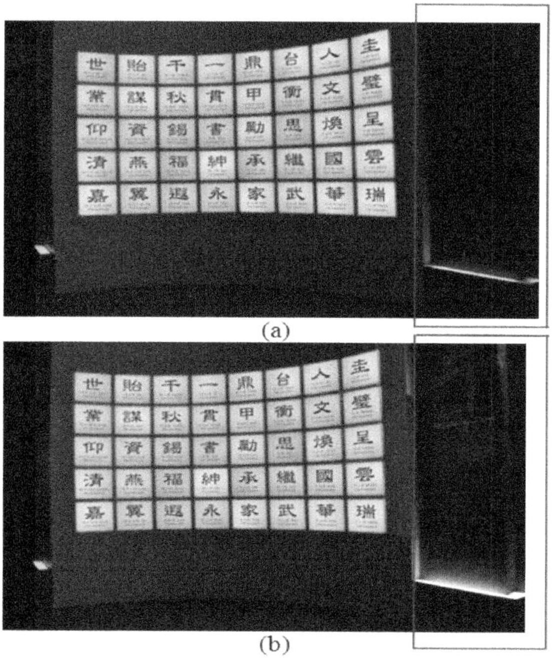

(a) (b)

Fig. 9. Image from Khoo Kongsi (a) Exposed (b) With Adjusted Brightness

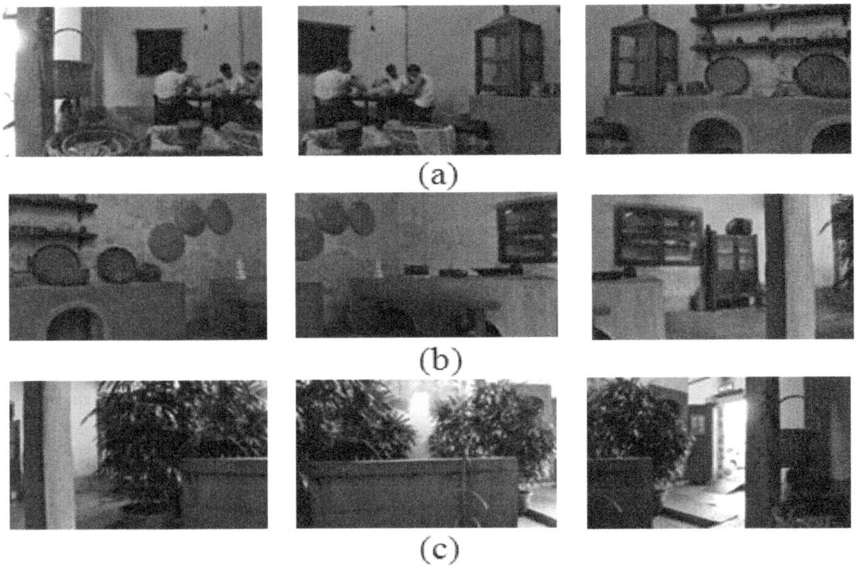

Fig. 10. A Complete Set of Images Captured from Khoo Kongsi for panoramic view

Fig. 11. A Sample of Cylindrical Panorama Before Cropping

Fig. 12. An Example of a 360^{0} Cylindrical Panoramic view

4 Comparison and Discussion

Three free trial image-stitching tools namely Adobe® Photoshop CS 5 from Adobe Systems Inc., Graphical User Interface for Panorama Tools (PTGui Pro) from New House Internet Services BV, and Panoweaver 7.0 from Easypano Holding Inc. were compared with our proposed method. Table 2 summarizes the outcome of the comparison.

Table 2. Comparison of Various Image-Stitching Tools

Feature	Image-stitching tools			
	Adobe Photoshop CS5	PTGui Pro	Panoweaver 7.0	The Proposed Method
Windows Compatible Without Using QTVR/Flash/Java Player	No	No	No	Yes
Macintosh Compatible (Including iOS)	No	No	No	Yes
Supported by iOS	No	No	No	Yes
Mobile Device	No	No	No	Yes
Hard Disk Space	752.8MB	36.3MB	146.1MB	14.2MB
RAM Required	1GB	256MB	512MB (Windows) 1GB (Macintosh)	128MB

From Table 2, all the three image-stitching software and our proposed method are supported on the Window platform. However, Adobe Photoshop, PTGui Pro and Panoweaver 7.0 cannot play the panoramic view on the Window platform if QTVR, Flash or Java player is not installed beforehand. As the eventual result of our proposed method is an image file in .JPEG format, the 360° panoramic view can be run on the Window platform without the aid of QTVR, Flash or Java player. Besides, Macintosh platform does not support Adobe Photoshop, PTGui Pro and Panoweaver 7.0 unless QTVR is used on the Macintosh platform even though the panoramic view generated by these three software systems is in .mov file format which is highly supported by the Macintosh platform.

The main reason of proposing this method is to ensure that iOS can play the 360° panoramic view without the aid of any intermediate software (QTVR/Flash/Java Player) in order to lower down the computational cost. Another reason is that iOS does not support .mov file as the panaromic views generated by Adobe Photoshop, PTGui Pro and Panoweaver 7.0 are in this format. Even on the mobile device, the output generated by these software systems cannot be played because all mobile devices do not support .mov file format unless QTVR, Flash or Java player is pre-installed. Our proposed method can be supported by all platforms including all mobile devices without the need to install any intermediate software.

The system requirement of our proposed method in terms of hard disk space and RAM is the lowest compared to the other image-Stitching tools. We have tested and evaluated these specifications based on iPhone version 1.1. This has shown that our proposed method is a low-cost method for generating panoramic view which can be used in particular in a mobile virtual heritage application.

5 Conclusion

The 360° view of cylindrical panoramic image is perfect for virtual heritage exploration because it allows the users to walkthrough the heritage sites by themselves. Furthermore, image with aid of historical stories can also be provided. Even though the iOS does not support the QTVR format, in our proposed method, by storing the image file format in an array using Adobe Photoshop we found a novel method of generating panoramic view with low memory and hard disk requirements and this method can be supported across all platforms. For future work, the fish eye lens of DSLR may be used to capture images to generate cubical panoramic view. Fish eye lens is a wide angle lens for DSLR camera that can take photographs in an extreme wide image and this lens is a special lens for the generation of distorted appearance of the images. In cubical panorama, users can roam 720° of the panoramic view.

Acknowledgement

The authors would like to thank Tan Kian Guan, Poon Pui Yee, Kong Yng Jye and Chin Kew Yee for their contributions in the development of the Gallery component of M-Heritage Hunt.

References

1. Noh, Z., Sunar, M.S., Zhigeng, P.: A Review on Augmented Reality for Virtual Heritage System. In: Chang, M., Kuo, R., Kinshuk, Chen, G.-D., Hirose, M. (eds.) Learning by Playing. LNCS, vol. 5670, pp. 50–61. Springer, Heidelberg (2009)
2. Russell, I.: Heritage, Identity and Roots: A Critique of Arborescent Models of Heritage and Identity. In: Smith, G., Messenger, P., Soderland, H. (eds.) Heritage Values in Contemporary Society. Left Coast Press (2009)
3. Stone, R., Ojika, T.: Virtual Heritage: What Next? IEEE Multimedia 7(2), 73–74 (2002)
4. Jianai, R., McDonough, J.P.: Preserving Born-Digital Cultural Heritage in Virtual World. In: Proceedings of the IEEE International Symposium on IT in Medicine & Education, vol. 1, pp. 745–748 (2009)
5. Ying, X., Peng, K., Zha, H.: Walkthrough In Large Environments Using Concatenated Panoramas. In: Proceedings of the 2009 IEEE International Conference on Robotics and Biomimetics (ROBIO), pp. 286–291 (2009)
6. Hongfei, F., Jinyuan, J., Hongkai, W., Luchen, T.: Immersive Roaming of Stereoscopic Panorama. In: Proceedings of the International Conference on Cyberworlds, pp. 377–382 (2008)
7. Chen, S.E.: QuickTime VR- An Image-Based Approach to Virtual Environment Navigation. In: SIGGRAPH 1995 Proceedings of the 22nd Annual Conference on Computer Graphics and Interactive Techniques, pp. 29–38 (1995)
8. Peleg, S., Ben-Erza, M.: Stereo Panorama with the Single Camera. In: Proceedings of IEEE Conference on Computer Vision and Pattern Recognition, vol. 1, pp. 395–401 (2002)
9. Bourke, P.D.: Synthetic Stereoscopic Panoramic Images. In: Zha, H., Pan, Z., Thwaites, H., Addison, A.C., Forte, M. (eds.) VSMM 2006. LNCS, vol. 4270, pp. 147–155. Springer, Heidelberg (2006)

10. Liu, X., Qiao, J.G.: Research on Chinese Museum Design Based on Virtual Reality. In: Proceedings of the International Workshop on Modeling, Simulation and Optimization, WMSO 2008, pp. 372–374 (2009)
11. Kwiatek, K., Woolner, M.: Transporting the Viewer into a 360 Heritage Story. Panoramic Interactive Narrative Presented on a Wrap-Around Screen. In: Proceedings of the 16th International Conference on Virtual Systems and Multimedia VSMM 2010, Seoul, South Korea, pp. 234–241 (2010)
12. Hirayu, H., Ojika, T., Kijima, R.: Constructing the Historical Villages of Shirakawa-go in virtual reality. IEEE Multimedia 7(2), 61–64 (2002)
13. Kwiatek, K., Woolner, M.: Embedding Interactive Storytelling within Still and Video Panoramas for Cultural Heritage Sites. In: Proceedings of the15th International Conference on Virtual Systems and Multimedia, VSMM 2009, pp. 197–202 (2009)

A Z Approach to Formalization and Validation of ORM Models

Amir Jahangard Rafsanjani and Seyed-Hassan Mirian-Hosseinabadi

Sharif University of Technology, Tehran, Iran
jahangard@ce.sharif.edu, hmirian@sharif.edu

Abstract. In this paper we present a formal definition of the basic concepts and notations of Object Role Modeling (ORM) using the Z formal specification language. Most of ORM concepts such as object and relationship types, value-types, objectification, reference schemes, sub-types, roles and constraints such as uniqueness, mandatory, cardinality, subset, equality, exclusive and ring constraints are specified formally. Population is specified as objects, relationships and roles instances. These are specified using Z axioms and diagram instances are specified using Z schemas. This would enable validation and reasoning on the formal properties of ORM diagrams such as detecting constraint contradictions and implications. All the specifications are validated and type-checked using Z/EVES.

Keywords: Data Modeling, ORM, Formal specification and verification, Z Specification Language.

1 Introduction

ORM has been successfully used as a database modeling methodology for more than 30 years. Recently it has become popular as a graphical notation in other areas such as modeling of business rules, ontology engineering, XML Schema design, requirement engineering and data warehouses. ORM's linguistic basis and role-based notation allows models to be easily validated with domain experts by natural verbalization and sample population. It has more expressive power for business rules and constraints than other popular notations such as ER or UML. ORM's graphical notation is more stable because it is attribute-free.

The most comprehensive work on formalization of ORM in first order logic was done by Halpin in [1] and [2]. Other formalization of ORM presented in [3], [4], [5], do not differ significantly from Halpin's work except that they make clearer distinctions between the role labels, their semantics and predicate names. There are other formalizations which try to map ORM to Description Logics [6], [7], [8]. Their main object is to enable automated reasoning on ORM diagrams. Most ORM constraints are supported in one DL Language or another, but none support all ORM constraints [9].

This paper proposes to formalize ORM using Z specification language [10]. Z has been previously used for formal specification of various models such as ER [11], relational data model [12], [13] and other data models such as ORA-SS [14] which is

E. Ariwa and E. El-Qawasmeh (Eds.): DEIS 2011, CCIS 194, pp. 513–526, 2011.

introduced to model semi-structured data. Most of ORM concepts such as object and relationship types, value-types, objectification, reference schemes (keys), sub-types, roles and constraints such as uniqueness, mandatory, cardinality, subset, equality, exclusive and ring constraints are specified formally. Population is specified as objects, relationships and roles instances. Some of them such as acyclic ring constraint have not been specified formally before. These are specified using various Z axioms, functions and relations. Diagram instances are specified using Z schemas. This would enable validation and reasoning on the formal properties of ORM diagrams such as detecting constraint contradictions and implications. All the specifications are validated and type-checked using Z/EVES [15].

The rest of the paper is organized as follows. Section 2 presents the background knowledge on ORM and Z formal language. Section 3 presents formal semantics of ORM in Z. In Section 4 the formal specification of a sample ORM schema is represented and some modeling inconsistencies are specified formally, and Section 5 concludes the paper and describes future work.

2 Background

2.1 Object Role Modeling

ORM is a conceptual modeling approach that views the world in terms of objects, and the roles they play. ORM allows a variety of data constraints to be defined such as mandatory role, subset, uniqueness, exclusion, cardinality and ring constraints.

Figure 1 shows an ORM diagram that models a 'Conference Paper' universe of discourse. This sample is taken from [16] and changed to ORM2 [17] notation.

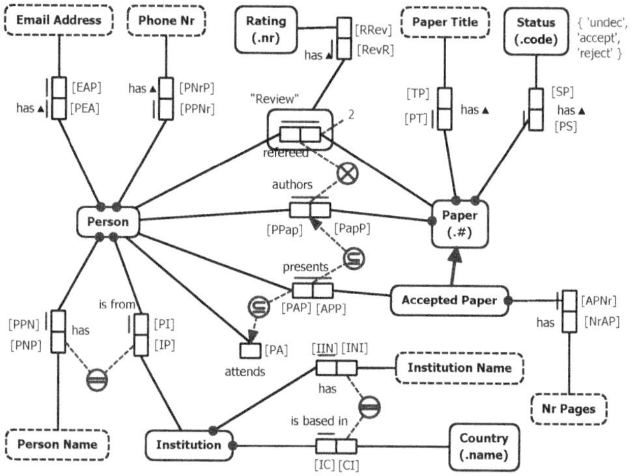

Fig. 1. 'Conference Paper' ORM Schema

In this diagram, object types are represented as named soft rectangles and relationship-types as named sequences of adjacent role boxes. Individual role names are written in square brackets near each role. A bar over a role or role sequence indicates an internal uniqueness constraint, and a circled underline or circled double underline denotes an external uniqueness (or primary uniqueness) constraint. Value constraints are represented as a braced list of values, and frequency constraints as a numeric range attached to one or more roles. Role and relationship subset constraints are shown as arrow with a circled subset notation, exclusion constraints as a circled 'x' between the relevant role-sequences, and subtype links as solid arrows between object types.

2.2 Z Formal Specification Language

Z is a formal specification language used for describing and modeling computing systems and is probably the most popular formal specification language currently available. Z is based on the standard mathematical notation used in axiomatic set theory, lambda calculus, and first-order predicate logic. All expressions in Z notation are typed, thereby avoiding some of the paradoxes of naive set theory. Z contains a standardized catalog (called the mathematical toolkit) of commonly used mathematical functions and predicates. Z/EVES is an interactive system for composing, checking, analyzing and theorem proving Z specifications.

3 Formal Semantics of ORM

3.1 Basic Types

In ORM a conceptual schema consists of a set of types. This set of types is split into two main types: relationship types and object types. Object types which are directly denotable are called value types whose instances have a direct denotation such as strings, numbers, etc. Relationship types have one or more roles each is played by an object type. We can use instances to populate the conceptual schema. These main concepts are defined using free types in Z:

$[TYPE, RO, OBJ]$

which represent *Object Types*, *Relationship* (*fact*) *Types*, *Roles*, and Object instances respectively. Object types are partitioned into two sets of value types and entity types:

$OT: \mathbb{P}\ TYPE$

$RT: \mathbb{P}\ TYPE$

$RT \cap OT = \varnothing$
$RT \cup OT = TYPE$

$ValueType: \mathbb{P}\ OT$

$EntityType: \mathbb{P}\ OT$

$EntityType \cap ValueType = \varnothing$
$EntityType \cup ValueType = OT$

Then the associations among these types are defined using axioms. The set of roles associated to a relationship type are defined using *Roles* function:

$Roles: RT \rightarrow \mathbb{P}_1 RO$

Each relationship type is mapped to at least one role. We define a function *Rel* which returns the relationship type associated with each role:

$Rel: RO \rightarrow RT$

$\forall ro: RO; r: RT \bullet Rel\ ro = r \Leftrightarrow ro \in Roles\ r$

Each role has an object type called the player of the role, which is provided by the function player:

$Player: RO \rightarrow OT$

3.2 Instances

In order to define instances (population) of types the following mappings are proposed. Function *OIns* is used to determine instances of an object type.

$OIns: OT \rightarrow \mathbb{P}\ OBJ$

Relationship type instances are rows of object instances where each row consists of assigning OBJs to the roles of the relationship type using a partial function; so a type ROW is defined:

ROW

$Row: RO \rightarrow\!\!\!\!\!+ OBJ$

$\forall x: \mathrm{dom}\ Row; o: OBJ \bullet Row\ x = o \Rightarrow o \in OIns\ (Player\ x)$

The predicate part says that to each role only objects from its player population can be assigned. The ROW type is used to specify relationship type instances:

$RTIns: RT \rightarrow \mathbb{P}\ ROW$

$\forall x: RT; y: \mathbb{P}\ ROW \bullet RTIns\ x = y \Rightarrow (\forall r: y \bullet \mathrm{dom}\ r\ .\ Row = Roles\ x)$

Each relationship type has a population which consists of a set of rows. The predicate part restricts the domain of each row to only roles of the relationship type.

RIns determines the instances of a role. It is defined by projecting the domain of the corresponding relationship type instances to the role:

$RIns: RO \rightarrow \mathbb{P}\ OBJ$

$\forall r: RO \bullet RIns\ r = \{\ row: ROW \mid row \in RTIns\ (Rel\ r) \wedge r \in \mathrm{dom}\ row\ .\ Row \bullet row\ .\ Row\ r\ \}$

Here we specify a relation called *InSameRow*. If there is a row in instances of the relationship type containing the roles *R* and *S* that maps *R* and *S* to object instances *X* and *Y* respectively, we say that ((*R*, *X*),(*S*, *Y*)) is a member of *InSameRow*.

$InSameRow: RO \times OBJ \leftrightarrow RO \times OBJ$

$\forall x, y: OBJ; r, s: RO \cdot (r \mapsto x, s \mapsto y) \in InSameRow \Leftrightarrow (\exists rt: RT \cdot rt = Rel\ r = Rel\ s$
$\quad \wedge (\exists row: RTIns\ rt \cdot (row\ .\ Row\ r = x \wedge row\ .\ Row\ s = y)))$

This relation is used in specification of uniqueness and ring constraints.

3.3 Subtypes

If instances of an object type are classified into a more specific type, this specialized type is known as a subtype. The main reason for using a subtype in modeling is to declare typing constraints. Another reason for subtyping is to encourage reuse of model components.

Subtypes in ORM are proper subtypes. For example, we say that *B* is a proper subtype of *A* if and only if the population of *B* is always a subset of the population of *A*, and $A \neq B$. Subtyping is specified in Z using partial function *ProperSubtype* that relates each object type to its supertype, if any exists:

$ProperSubtype: OT \rightarrow OT$

$\forall o_1: OT; o_2: OT \cdot ProperSubtype\ o_1 = o_2 \Rightarrow OIns\ o_1 \subset OIns\ o_2$

In order to identify objects of the same type the *SameType* relation is defined which relates two object types if and only if they are the same or they are direct or indirect subtypes of each other or they are direct or indirect subtypes of another object type. The *SameType* relation is not present in ORM language but it is used here to simplify other constraints specifications.

$SameType: OT \leftrightarrow OT$

$\forall x, y: OT \cdot (x, y) \in SameType \Leftrightarrow x = y \vee ProperSubtype^+\ x = y \vee ProperSubtype^+\ y = x$
$\quad \vee (\exists o: OT \cdot ProperSubtype^+\ x = ProperSubtype^+\ y = o)$

Various constraints can be defined on subtypes. These constraints are *total*, *exclusive* and *mandatory* constraints.

- **Total Subtypes**: The total constraint between subtypes means that the population of the supertype is exactly the union of the population of these subtypes. This is shown in Z using *TotalSubtype* function:

$TotalSubtype: \mathbb{P}\ OT \rightarrow OT$

$\forall oSet: \mathbb{P}\ OT; ot: OT \cdot TotalSubtype\ oSet = ot$
$\quad \Rightarrow (\forall o: oSet \cdot ProperSubtype\ o = ot) \wedge (\forall obj: OIns\ ot \cdot (\exists o: oSet \cdot obj \in OIns\ o))$

The predicate part says that for each object instance in supertype there exists an identical object instance in at least one of the subtypes.

- **Disjoint (Exclusive) Subtypes**: The exclusive constraint between subtypes means the populations of these subtypes are pairwise distinct, i.e. the intersection of the populations of each pair of the subtypes must be empty. This is shown in Z by *DisjointSubtype* function which maps disjoint subtypes to their supertype:

$$DisjointSubtype : \mathbb{P}\ OT \twoheadrightarrow OT$$

$$\forall oSet : \mathbb{P}\ OT;\ ot : OT \bullet DisjointSubtype\ oSet = ot \Rightarrow (\forall o : oSet \bullet ProperSubtype\ o = ot) \land (\forall o_1, o_2 : oSet \bullet OIns\ o_1 \cap OIns\ o_2 = \varnothing)$$

- **Partition (Mandatory) Subtypes:** If both total and exclusive constraints between subtypes exist it is called partition.

$$PartitionSubtype : \mathbb{P}\ OT \twoheadrightarrow OT$$

$$\forall oSet : \mathbb{P}\ OT;\ ot : OT \bullet PartitionSubtype\ oSet = ot \Leftrightarrow DisjointSubtype\ oSet = ot \land TotalSubtype\ oSet = ot$$

3.4 Uniqueness Constraints

Two types of uniqueness constraints are possible in ORM: *internal* and *external*. *Internal uniqueness constraints* are defined on instances of roles in a single relationship type. A set of role sets called *Unique* is defined to show roles that are unique in a relationship type population. When a role set is contained in Unique set it means that all that roles belong to a single relationship type and there are no two rows the relationship type population that contains same objects for the specified roles.

$$Unique : \mathbb{F}\ (\mathbb{F}\ RO)$$

$$\forall roles : \mathbb{F}\ RO \bullet roles \in Unique \Rightarrow (\exists_1 rt : RT \bullet roles \subseteq Roles\ rt \land (\forall r_1, r_2 : RTIns\ rt \bullet (roles \lhd r_1 . Row = roles \lhd r_2 . Row \Rightarrow r_1 . Row = r_2 . Row)))$$

External uniqueness constraints are defined on roles of two or more different relationship types. Here, we specify external uniqueness constraint on two roles using *InSameRow* relation defined previously. This definition can be extended to three or more roles.

$$ExtUnique2 : \mathbb{P}\ (RO \times RO \times OT)$$

$$\forall r_1, r_2 : RO;\ o : OT \bullet (r_1, r_2, o) \in ExtUnique2 \Rightarrow (\exists or_1, or_2 : RO \bullet or_1 \neq r_1 \neq or_2 \neq r_2 \land Rel\ r_1 = Rel\ or_1 \land Rel\ r_2 = Rel\ or_2 \land Rel\ r_1 \neq Rel\ r_2 \land Player\ or_1 = Player\ or_2 = o \land (\forall obj_1, obj_2 : OIns\ o;\ x : RIns\ r_1;\ y : RIns\ r_2 \bullet (((or_1, obj_1), (r_1, x)) \in InSameRow \land ((or_2, obj_2), (r_2, y)) \in InSameRow \Rightarrow obj_1 = obj_2)))$$

3.5 Objectification

In ORM2 a relationship type can be treated as an object type. So the object formed by objectification can be distinguished from original relationship:

$$Objectify : RT \twoheadrightarrow OT$$

$$\forall r : RT;\ o : OT \bullet Objectify\ r = o \Rightarrow o \in EntityType$$

3.6 Mandatory Constraints

- **Role Mandatory**: A role is called mandatory if its population is always identical to its player population, i.e. each instance in the role player population must play that role. The set of all mandatory roles is called *Mandatory* and is shown below:

$Mandatory: \mathbb{P}\ RO$

$\forall x: Mandatory \bullet OIns\ (Player\ x) = RIns\ x$

- **Disjunctive Mandatory:** The disjunctive mandatory constraint is used to constrain a set of two or more roles connected to the same object type. It means that each instance of the object type population must play at least one of the constrained roles. This is specified by the *DisjMandatory* set of role sets:

$DisjMandatory: \mathbb{P}\ (\mathbb{P}\ RO)$

$\forall r: \mathbb{P}\ RO \bullet r \in DisjMandatory \Rightarrow (\exists_1 o: OT \bullet (\forall x: r \bullet Player\ x = o) \wedge \bigcup \{\ x: r \bullet (RIns\ x)\ \} = OIns\ o)$

The predicate part says that all the roles in each role set belong to the same object type and the union of the roles instances sets is always equal to the object type instances set.

3.7 Reference Schemes (Keys)

In ORM each entity type must have a reference scheme, i.e. the set of value types which uniquely identifies each entity type. Two kinds of reference schemes are available in ORM: *Simple* and *Compound*. In order to specify these concepts we choose the explicated version of ORM model into account in which each simple reference scheme is a mandatory and 1:1 reference type.

Fig. 2. Explicating Reference Schemes

$SimpleReferenceScheme: EntityType \rightarrowtail ValueType$

$\forall o: EntityType; v: ValueType \bullet SimpleReferenceScheme\ o = v$
$\Rightarrow (\exists r: RT; r_1, r_2: RO \bullet Roles\ r = \{r_1, r_2\} \wedge Player\ r_1 = o \wedge Player\ r_2 = v \wedge r_1 \in Mandatory$
$\wedge \{r_1\} \in Unique \wedge \{r_2\} \in Unique)$

Here the predicate part enforces the existence of a mandatory and 1:1 relationship between the entity type and its identifying value type.

External uniqueness constraint is used to specify compound reference schemes. Here we specify compound reference schemes using two values but this can be easily extended to three or more values.

$CompoundReferenceScheme2: \mathbb{P}\ (RO \times RO \times OT)$

$\forall r_1, r_2: RO; o: OT \bullet (r_1, r_2, o) \in CompoundReferenceScheme2$
$\Rightarrow (r_1, r_2, o) \in ExtUnique2 \wedge (\exists r_3, r_4: RO \bullet (Player\ r_3 = Player\ r_4 = o \wedge Rel\ r_3 = Rel\ r_1$
$\wedge Rel\ r_4 = Rel\ r_2 \wedge r_3 \in Mandatory \wedge r_4 \in Mandatory))$

The predicate part indicates that the participation of entity type in relationship types must be mandatory.

3.8 Cardinality Constraints

In ORM, cardinality constraints can be defined on object types and roles.

- **Role Cardinality Constraints:** A fixed cardinality constraints *f* on a role states that each instance which plays the role, does so exactly *f* times.

$FixRoleFrequency: RO \rightarrow\!\!\!\!\!\!\!\quad \mathbb{N}$

$\forall r: RO;\ n: \mathbb{N} \bullet FixRoleFrequency\ r = n$
$\quad \Rightarrow (\forall o: OIns\ (Player\ r) \bullet \#\{\ row: ROW \mid row \in RTIns\ (Rel\ r) \wedge row\ .\ Row\ r = o\ \} = n)$

Role cardinality can be stated using lower or upper bounds or both. We have specified these constraints using *MinRoleFrequency*, *MaxRoleFrequency* and *MinMaxRoleFrequency* functions. Here because of space considerations we just present *MinMaxRoleFrequency:*

$MinMaxRoleFrequency: RO \rightarrow\!\!\!\!\!\!\!\quad \mathbb{N} \times \mathbb{N}$

$\forall r: RO;\ m: \mathbb{N};\ n: \mathbb{N} \bullet MinMaxRoleFrequency\ r = (m, n)$
$\quad \Rightarrow (\forall o: OIns\ (Player\ r) \bullet m \leqslant \#\{\ row: ROW \mid row \in RTIns\ (Rel\ r) \wedge row\ .\ Row\ r = o\ \} \leqslant n)$

- **Object Cardinality Constraints:** Fixed object cardinality constraint *n* on object type *A* states that each population of *A* includes exactly *n* instances:

$ObjectCardinality: OT \rightarrow\!\!\!\!\!\!\!\quad \mathbb{N}$

$\forall o: OT;\ n: \mathbb{N} \bullet ObjectCardinality\ o = n \Rightarrow \#\ (OIns\ o) = n$

Object cardinality constraints can be stated using lower or upper bounds or both:

$MinMaxObjectCardinality: OT \rightarrow\!\!\!\!\!\!\!\quad \mathbb{N} \times \mathbb{N}$

$\forall o: OT;\ m: \mathbb{N};\ n: \mathbb{N} \bullet MinMaxObjectCardinality\ o = (m, n) \Rightarrow m \leqslant \#\ (OIns\ o) \leqslant n$

3.9 Value Constraints

A value constraint in ORM indicates the possible instances for an object or a role. A value constraint is denoted as a set of objects:

$ObjectValueConstraint: OT \rightarrow\!\!\!\!\!\!\!\quad \mathbb{F}\ OBJ$

$\forall ot: OT;\ objSet: \mathbb{F}\ OBJ \bullet ObjectValueConstraint\ ot = objSet \Rightarrow OIns\ ot \subseteq objSet$

$RoleValueConstraint: RO \rightarrow\!\!\!\!\!\!\!\quad \mathbb{F}\ OBJ$

$\forall ro: RO;\ objSet: \mathbb{F}\ OBJ \bullet RoleValueConstraint\ ro = objSet \Rightarrow RIns\ ro \subseteq objSet$

3.10 Subset, Equality and Exclusive Constraints

The subset constraints can be defined on roles and relationship types. A subset constraint between two roles states that population of one is the subset of the other. In Z this is specified by partial function *RoleSubset* that determines the superset of each role, if any exists:

$RoleSubset: RO \rightarrow\!\!\!\!\!\rightarrow RO$

$\forall r_1: RO;\ r_2: RO \bullet RoleSubset\ r_1 = r_2 \Rightarrow RIns\ r_1 \subseteq RIns\ r_2$

A subset constraint can be defined between k roles of two n-ary relations. The relation *MultiRoleSubset* is defined to determine such constraints:

$MultiRoleSubset: \mathbb{F}\ RO \leftrightarrow \mathbb{F}\ RO$

$$\forall rSet_1, rSet_2: \mathbb{F}\ RO \bullet MultiRoleSubset\ rSet_1 = rSet_2 \Rightarrow \#\ rSet_1 = \#\ rSet_2$$
$$\wedge (\exists rt_1, rt_2: RT \bullet (rSet_1 \subseteq Roles\ rt_1 \wedge rSet_2 \subseteq Roles\ rt_2$$
$$\wedge (\forall r_1: RTIns\ rt_1 \bullet (\exists r_2: RTIns\ rt_2 \bullet rSet_1 \lhd r_1 . Row = rSet_2 \lhd r_2 . Row))))$$

For relationship types, a subset constraint states that population of one relationship type is subset of the other's. In Z this is specified by partial function *RTSubset* that determines the superset of each relationship type, if any exists:

$RTSubset: RT \rightarrow\!\!\!\!\!\rightarrow RT$

$\forall r_1: RT;\ r_2: RT \bullet RTSubset\ r_1 = r_2 \Rightarrow RTIns\ r_1 \subseteq RTIns\ r_2$

Equality constraints between roles or relationship types are defined similarly by *RoleSetEquality* and *RTSetEquality* functions:

$RoleSetEquality: \mathbb{P}\ (\mathbb{P}\ RO)$

$\forall r: \mathbb{P}\ RO \bullet r \in RoleSetEquality \Rightarrow (\forall r_1, r_2: r \bullet RIns\ r_1 = RIns\ r_2)$

$RTSetEquality: \mathbb{P}\ (\mathbb{P}\ RT)$

$\forall r: \mathbb{P}\ RT \bullet r \in RTSetEquality \Rightarrow (\forall r_1, r_2: r \bullet RTIns\ r_1 = RTIns\ r_2)$

Exclusion constraints between two or more roles or two relationship types state that populations of them are disjoint.

$ExclusiveRoles: \mathbb{P}\ (\mathbb{P}\ RO)$

$\forall r: \mathbb{P}\ RO \bullet r \in ExclusiveRoles \Rightarrow (\forall r_1, r_2: r \bullet (Player\ r_1, Player\ r_2) \in SameType \wedge RIns\ r_1 \cap RIns\ r_2 = \emptyset)$

$DisjointRTs: \mathbb{P}\ (\mathbb{P}\ RT)$

$\forall relationSet: \mathbb{P}\ RT \bullet relationSet \in DisjointRTs \Rightarrow (\forall rt_0, rt_1: relationSet \bullet RTIns\ rt_0 \cap RTIns\ rt_1 = \emptyset)$

3.11 Ring Constraints

In ORM ring constraints can be applied to a pair of roles in a relationship type that are connected directly or indirectly –via subtypes- to the same object type. Six types of ring constraints are supported by ORM:

- **Irreflexive Ring Constraint (ir):** This constraint states that an object instance cannot participate in a relationship with itself. For example no one can be the "Parent of" himself, so the relation "parent of" is irreflexive. The set of all role pairs that constitute an irreflexive ring constraints is defined by *irRing* in Z here:

$irRing: \mathbb{P}\,(RO \times RO)$

$$\forall x, y: RO \bullet (x, y) \in irRing \Rightarrow (Player\ x, Player\ y) \in SameType \wedge (\exists rt: RT \bullet (rt = Rel\ x = Rel\ y \wedge (\forall row: RTIns\ rt \bullet row\ .\ Row\ x \neq row\ .\ Row\ y)))$$

The predicate part states that players of the role pairs should be of same type (as defined earlier) and there exists no rows in the roles common relationship type population with the same object instance for them.

- **Symmetric Ring Constraint (sym):** This constraint states that if a relation holds in one direction it should also hold on the other. In case of ring constraint on role pair (x, y) in a relationship type, it states that if there is a row in the relationship type population that with o_1 as object instance of x and o_2 as object instance of y then there should be another row with o_2 as object instance of x and o_1 as object instance of y. This is defined by the following definition in Z:

$symRing: \mathbb{P}\,(RO \times RO)$

$$\forall x, y: RO \bullet (x, y) \in irRing \Rightarrow (Player\ x, Player\ y) \in SameType \wedge (\exists rt: RT \bullet (rt = Rel\ x = Rel\ y \wedge (\forall row_1: RTIns\ rt \bullet (\exists row_2: RTIns\ rt \bullet (row_1\ .\ Row\ x = row_2\ .\ Row\ y \wedge row_1\ .\ Row\ y = row_2\ .\ Row\ x)))))$$

- **Asymmetric Ring Constraint (as):** Asymmetric is the opposite of symmetric. If a relation holds in one direction it may not hold in on the other. In case of ring constraint on role pair (x, y) in a relationship type, it states that if there is a row in the relationship type population that with o_1 as object instance of x and o_2 as object instance of y then there cannot be another row with o_2 as object instance of x and o_1 as object instance of y. This is defined by the following definition in Z:

$asRing: \mathbb{P}\,(RO \times RO)$

$$\forall x, y: RO \bullet (x, y) \in asRing \Rightarrow (Player\ x, Player\ y) \in SameType \wedge (\exists rt: RT \bullet (rt = Rel\ x = Rel\ y \wedge (\forall row_1: RTIns\ rt \bullet \neg (\exists row_2: RTIns\ rt \bullet (row_1\ .\ Row\ x = row_2\ .\ Row\ y \wedge row_1\ .\ Row\ y = row_2\ .\ Row\ x)))))$$

- **Antisymmetric Ring Constraints (ans):** Antisymmetric is also the opposite of symmetric, but all asymmetric relations should be irrefelxive which is not the case for antisymmetric relations. In case of ring constraint on role pair (x, y) in a relationship type, it states that if there is a row in the relationship type population that with o_1 as object instance of x and o_2 as object instance of y then there cannot be another row with o_2 as object instance of x and o_1 as object instance of y unless $o_1=o_2$. This is defined by the following definition in Z:

$ansRing: \mathbb{P}\,(RO \times RO)$

$$\forall x, y: RO \bullet (x, y) \in ansRing \Rightarrow (Player\ x, Player\ y) \in SameType \wedge (\exists rt: RT \bullet (rt = Rel\ x = Rel\ y \wedge (\forall row_1, row_2: RTIns\ rt; o_1, o_2: OBJ \bullet (row_1\ .\ Row\ x = o_1 \wedge row_1\ .\ Row\ y = o_2 \wedge row_2\ .\ Row\ x = o_2 \wedge row_2\ .\ Row\ y = o_1 \Rightarrow o_1 = o_2))))$$

- **Intransitive Ring Constraint:** A relation is intransitive if, whenever it relates some A to some B, and that B to some C, it cannot relate that A to that C. In case of ring constraint on role pair (x, y) in a relationship type, it states that if there is a row in the relationship type population that with o_1 as object instance of x and o_2 as object instance of y and another row with o_2 as object instance of x and o_3 as object instance of y then there cannot be another row with o_1 as object instance of x and o_3 as object instance of y.

This is specified by the following definition in Z:

$itRing: \mathbb{P}\ (RO \times RO)$

$$\forall x, y: RO \bullet (x, y) \in itRing \Rightarrow (Player\ x, Player\ y) \in SameType$$
$$\wedge (\exists rt: RT \bullet (rt = Rel\ x = Rel\ y \wedge (\forall row_1, row_2: RTIns\ rt; o_1, o_2, o_3: OBJ$$
$$\bullet (row_1 . Row\ x = o_1 \wedge row_1 . Row\ y = o_2 \wedge row_2 . Row\ x = o_2 \wedge row_2 . Row\ y = o_3$$
$$\Rightarrow \neg (\exists row_3: RTIns\ rt \bullet (row_3 . Row\ x = o_1 \wedge row_3 . Row\ y = o_3))))))$$

- **Acyclic Ring Constraints(ac):** The acyclic constraint is a special case of the irrefelxive constraint. It states that a relation cannot directly or indirectly (through a chain) relates an object with itself. In ORM this constraint is preserved as difficult constraint. "Because of their recursive nature, acyclic constraints maybe expensive or even impossible to enforce in some database systems." [2] But in Z we can specify this constraint by using transitive closure of relations.

We use the closure of *InSameRow* relation to specify the acyclic ring constraint on two roles in a relationship. This insures that an object instance cannot be directly, or indirectly through a chain, related to itself.

$acRing: \mathbb{P}\ (RO \times RO)$

$$\forall x, y: RO \bullet (x, y) \in acRing \Rightarrow (Player\ x, Player\ y) \in SameType$$
$$\wedge (\exists rt: RT \bullet rt = Rel\ x = Rel\ y \wedge (\forall obj: RIns\ x \bullet ((y, obj), (x, obj)) \notin InSameRow^{+}))$$

Now we have a mathematical toolkit that enables us to specify an ORM model in Z specification language and verify various properties of the model. We use this toolkit specify an ORM model using Z schemas in next section 5 as a case study.

4 Validating ORM Models

We use the types and constraints defined in previous section to specify the sample ORM diagram shown in figure 1.

Please note that in this schema we have used the explicated version of the ORM schema shown in Figure 1; so value types like *PaperNr*, *StatusCode*, *RatingNr*, *CountryName* and the corresponding relationship types and roles are introduced in the Z schema.

ConferencePaperSchema

Person, Paper, Institution, Status, AcceptedPaper, Country, EmailAddress,
PhoneNr, Rating, PaperTitle, NrPages, InstitutionName, PersonName, Review,
PaperNr, RatingNr, StatusCode, CountryName: OT
Refereed, Authors, Presents, IsFrom, IsBasedIn, Attends, HasEmailAddress,
HasPersonName, HasPhoneNr, HasRating, HasPaperTitle, HasStatus, HasNrPages,
HasInstName, HasPaperNr, HasRatingNr, HasStatusCode, HasCountryName: RT
EAP, PEA, PNrP, PPNr, PPN, PNP, PI, IP, PA, PAP, APP, PPap, PapP, RevR, RRev,TP, PT, SP, PS, IIN, INI,
IC, CI, APNr, NrAP, PrPap, PaprP, PPNr, PNrP, SSc, ScS, RRNr, RNrR, CnameC, CCname: RO

undec, accept, reject: OBJ

ValueType = {*EmailAddress, PhoneNr, Rating, PaperTitle, NrPages, InstitutionName, PersonName, PaperNr, RatingNr, StatusCode, CountryName*}
Player = {*EAP* ↦ *EmailAddress, PEA* ↦ *Person, PNrP* ↦ *PhoneNr, PPNr* ↦ *Person, PPN* ↦ *Person, PNP* ↦ *PersonName, PI* ↦ *Person, IP* ↦ *Institution, PA* ↦ *Person, PAP* ↦ *Person, APP* ↦ *AcceptedPaper, PPap* ↦ *Person, PapP* ↦ *Paper, RevR* ↦ *Review, RRev* ↦ *Rating, TP* ↦ *PaperTitle, PT* ↦ *Paper, SP* ↦ *Status, PS* ↦ *Paper, IIN* ↦ *Institution, INI* ↦ *InstitutionName, IC* ↦ *Institution, CI* ↦ *Country, APNr* ↦ *AcceptedPaper, NrAP* ↦ *NrPages, PrPap* ↦ *Person, PaprP* ↦ *Paper, PNrP* ↦ *PaperNr, PPNr* ↦ *Paper,CnameC* ↦ *CountryName, CCname* ↦ *Country, RRNr* ↦ *Rating, RNrR* ↦ *RatingNr, SSc* ↦ *Status, ScS* ↦ *StatusCode*}
Roles = {*Refereed* ↦ {*PrPap, PaprP*}, *Authors* ↦ {*PPap, PapP*}, *Presents* ↦ {*PAP, APP*}, *IsFrom* ↦ {*PI, IP*}, *IsBasedIn* ↦ {*IC, CI*}, *Attends* ↦ {*PA*},*HasEmailAddress* ↦ {*EAP, PEA*}, *HasPersonName* ↦ {*PPN, PNP*}, *HasPhoneNr* ↦ {*PNrP, PPNr*}, *HasRating* ↦ {*RRev, RevR*}, *HasPaperTitle* ↦ {*TP, PT*}, *HasStatus* ↦ {*SP, PS*}, *HasNrPages* ↦ {*APNr, NrAP*}, *HasInstName* ↦ {*IIN, INI*}, *HasPaperNr* ↦ {*PNrP, PPNr*}, *HasCountryName* ↦ {*CnameC, CCname*}, *HasRatingNr* ↦ {*RRNr, RNrR*}, *HasStatusCode* ↦ {*SSc, ScS*}}
Mandatory = {*PEA, PPNr, PPN, PI, PapP, PT, PS, APNr, IIN, IC, PPNr, PNrP, CnameC, CCname, RRNr, RNrR, SSc, ScS*}
Unique = {{*EAP*}, {*PEA*}, {*PPNr*}, {*RevR*}, {*PT*}, {*PS*}, {*PrPap, PaprP*}, {*PPap, PapP*},{*PAP, APP*}, {*IIN*}, {*IC*}, {*APNr*}, {*PPN*}, {*PI*}, {*PPNr*}, {*PNrP*}, {*CnameC*}, {*CCname*}, {*RRNr*}, {*RNrR*}, {*SSc*}, {*ScS*}}
SimpleReferenceScheme = {*Paper* ↦ *PaperNr, Country* ↦ *CountryName, Rating* ↦ *RatingNr, Status* ↦ *StatusCode*}
ExtUnique2 = {(*PNP, IP, Person*), (*INI, CI, Institution*)}
CompoundReferenceScheme2 = {(*PNP, IP, Person*), (*INI, CI, Institution*)}
FixRoleFrequency = {*PaprP* ↦ 2}, *DisjointRTs* = {{*Refereed, Authors*}}
RTSubset = {*Presents* ↦ *Authors*}, *RoleSubset* = {*PAP* ↦ *PA*}
ProperSubtype = {*AcceptedPaper* ↦ *Paper*}
ObjectValueConstraint = {*Status* ↦ {*undec, accept, reject*}}, *Objectify* = {*Refereed* ↦ *Review*}

A major concern in modeling is to ensure there are no possible inconsistencies between various constraints defined in model. Having defined a formal semantics of ORM in Z, we can present and validate various inconsistencies formally. Here for space considerations we take some unsatisfiability patterns from [18] and specify them using our toolkit.

- **Top Common Supertype Pattern:** In this pattern, subtypes that do not have a top common supertype are detected. In ORM, all object-types are assumed by definition to be mutually exclusive, except those that are subtypes of the same supertype. Thus, if a subtype has more than one supertype, these supertypes must share a top supertype; otherwise, the subtype cannot be satisfied. For example object type "C" in figure 3.a cannot have any instance. Here is this pattern specified using a theorem in Z:

  theorem *TopCommonSupertypes*
  $\forall a, b, c: OT \cdot \{(a, b), (a, c)\} \subseteq ProperSubtype \Rightarrow (b, c) \in SameType$

- **Exclusive-Mandatory Pattern:** In this pattern, contradictions between exclusion and mandatory constraints are detected. For example in figure 3.b role "r1" cannot be played by any object instance. This pattern is specified as:

theorem *ExclusiveMandatory*
$\forall r: \mathbb{P}\ RO \mid r \in ExclusiveRoles \bullet \forall role: r \bullet role \notin Mandatory$

- **Subset-Exclusion-Equality Pattern:** In this pattern, contradiction between exclusion and subset constraints are detected. If there is an exclusion constraint between two roles, there can't be a subset or equality constraints between the relationship types of those two roles (Figure 3.c):

theorem *SubsetExclusionEquality*
$\forall r_1, r_2: RO \bullet (\exists r: ExcusiveRoles \bullet \{r_1, r_2\} \in r) \Rightarrow (Rel\ r_1, Rel\ r_2) \notin RTSubset \wedge (Rel\ r_2, Rel\ r_1) \notin RTSubset$
$\wedge \neg (\exists rSet: RTSetEquality \bullet \{Rel\ r_1, Rel\ r_2\} \subseteq rSet)$

- **Uniqueness-Frequency Pattern:** In this pattern, contradictions between value and frequency constraints are detected (Figure 3.d).

theorem *RoleUniquenessFrequency*
$\forall r: RO; m, n: \mathbb{N} \bullet MinMaxRoleFrequency\ r = (m, n) \wedge \{r\} \in Unique \Rightarrow m = 1$

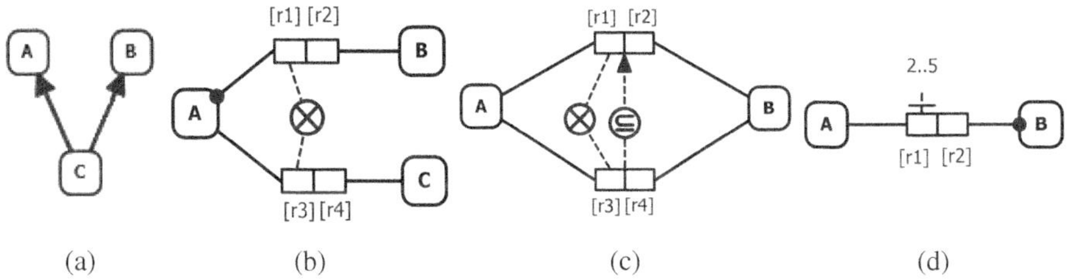

Fig. 3. (a) Subtype without a Top Common Supertype, (b) Exclusive and Mandatory Constraints Contradiction, (c) Subset and Exclusion Constraints Contradiction, (d) Uniqueness and Frequency Constraints Contradiction

It is obvious that the three inconsistencies specified in previous section are not present in the model. Proofs are omitted due to simplicity.

5 Conclusions

In this paper we presented a formal approach to ORM using Z formal specification language. We have tried to cover most of ORM concepts such as objects, relationships, roles and various constraints have been specified formally. This would enable validation and reasoning on the formal properties of ORM diagrams such as detecting constraint contradictions and implications. We provided some guidelines about validating models against certain unsatisfiability patterns. All the specifications were type-checked and validated using Z/EVES.

In the future, we plan to extend our work to cover some aspects such as data types in the specification. We are in the process of completing our guidelines for validating ORM models and we are porting our specifications and developing a theorem library to support validation of ORM models using HOL-Z proof environment. Furthermore we are going to develop a tool that automatically translates ORM models to their Z representations for machine validation.

References

1. Halpin, T.: A Logical Analysis of Information Systems: Static Aspects of the Data-Oriented Perspective. PhD Thesis, University of Queensland, Brisbane, Australia (1989)
2. Halpin, T.: Information Modeling and Relational Databases: From Conceptual Analysis to Logical Design, 2nd edn. Morgan Kaufmann, San Francisco (2008)
3. Hofstede, A.H.M., Proper, H.A., Weide, T.P.: Formal Definition of a Conceptual Language for the Description and Manipulation of Information Models. Information Systems 18(7), 489–523 (1993)
4. Hofstede, A.H.M., Proper, H.A.: How to Formalize It? Formalization Principles for Information System Development Methods. Information and Software Technology 40(10), 519–540 (1998)
5. Campbell, L.J., Halpin, T.A., Proper, H.A.: Conceptual Schemas with Abstractions: Making flat conceptual schemas more comprehensible. Data & Knowledge Engineering 20(1), 39–85 (1996)
6. Jarrar, M.: Towards Automated Reasoning on ORM Schemes. In: Parent, C., Schewe, K.-D., Storey, V.C., Thalheim, B. (eds.) ER 2007. LNCS, vol. 4801, pp. 181–197. Springer, Heidelberg (2007)
7. Jarrar, M.: Mapping ORM into the SHOIN/OWL Description Logic: Towards a Methodological and Expressive Graphical Notation for Ontology Engineering. In: Chung, S., Herrero, P. (eds.) OTM-WS 2007, Part I. LNCS, vol. 4805, pp. 729–741. Springer, Heidelberg (2007)
8. Keet, C.: Prospects for and Issues with Mapping the Object-Role Modeling Language into DLRifd. In: Proc. 20th International Workshop on Description Logics, pp. 331–338 (2007)
9. Keet, C.: Mapping the Object-Role Modelng language ORM2 into Description Logic Language DLRifd. Technical Report KRDB07-2, Free University of Bozen-Bolzano, Italy (2007)
10. Spivey, J.: The Z Notation: A Reference Manual. International Series in Computer Science. Prentice Hall, Englewood Cliffs (1992)
11. Josephs, M., Redmond-Pyle, D.: Entity-Relationship Models Expressed in Z: A Systhesis of Structured and Formal Methods. Technical Report PRG-TR-20-91, Oxford University Programming Research Group (1991)
12. Barros, R.: On the Formal Specification and Derivation of Relational Database Applications. PhD Thesis, University of Glasgow (1995)
13. Baluta, D.: A Formal Specification in Z of the Relational Data Model, Version 2, of E. F. Codd. M. Sc. thesis, Concordia University, Montreal, Canada (1995)
14. Lee, S., Sun, J., Dobbie, G., Li, Y.: A Z Approach in Validating ORA-SS Data Models. Electronoc Notes in Theoritical Computer Science 157, 95–109 (2006)
15. Saaltink, M.: The Z/EVES System. In: Till, D., Bowen, J.P., Hinchey, M.G. (eds.) ZUM 1997. LNCS, vol. 1212, pp. 72–85. Springer, Heidelberg (1997)
16. Bird, L., Goodchild, A., Halpin, T.: Object Role Modelling and XML-Schema. In: Laender, A.H.F., Liddle, S.W., Storey, V.C. (eds.) ER 2000. LNCS, vol. 1920, pp. 309–322. Springer, Heidelberg (2000)
17. Halpin, T.: ORM2. In: Chung, S., Herrero, P. (eds.) OTM-WS 2005. LNCS, vol. 3762, pp. 676–687. Springer, Heidelberg (2005)
18. Jarrar, M., Heymans, S.: Towards Pattern-based Reasoning for Friendly Ontology Debugging. International Journal on Artificial Intelligence Tools 17(4), 607–634 (2008)

Investigating the Correlation between Customer Retention Programs of CRM and Customer Retention in E-Banking Context

Alireza Nili[1] and Abbas Keramati[2]

[1] Department of Business Administration, Technology, and Social Sciences, Division of Industrial Marketing and e-Commerce
Lulea University of Technology (LUT), Lulea, Sweden/IUC, Chabahar, Iran
alireza.nili@yahoo.com
[2] Industrial Engineering Department, Faculty of Engineering, University of Tehran, Tehran, Iran
keramati@ut.ac.ir

Abstract. In this study, considering different perspectives and concepts about customer relationship management (CRM), we try to investigate the significance of the correlation between each of the customer retention programs of CRM (loyalty programs, customer service, customization, and community) and customer retention. Data from 286 top bank managers of two governmental and two private Iranian bank branches were gathered in a field survey. The results of data analysis show the positive and significant correlation between each of the customer retention programs of CRM and customer retention. The study also finds the most significant correlation between customer service and customer retention.

Keywords: Customer relationship management; CRM; customer retention programs; customer retention; electronic banking.

1 Introduction

The interest in focusing on long-term and profitable customers and the need to better understand their behaviors have changed the view of marketers about the marketplace. Traditionally, they have been trying to acquire new customers and the currently other firm's customers, which needed heavy price-oriented promotions and mass advertising. However, today, customers have access to a variety of products and when they do not meet their needs easily; they can choose other firms that provide them with fast and high quality products and services [4, 9, 12].

Now, firms know that absorbing and maintaining the customers is an art. They have realized that to reach this purpose using appropriate programs such as customer relationship management (CRM) which is a business philosophy that provides the organizations a vision to deal with their customers better, is inevitable. A CRM strategy delivers this vision by giving shape to customer service, marketing, and activities to analyze data and most firms view the final purpose of this vision,

E. Ariwa and E. El-Qawasmeh (Eds.): DEIS 2011, CCIS 194, pp. 527–536, 2011.

maximization of relationships with their profitable customers by increasing the value of these relationships [7, 21, 23, 25].

In today's competitive markets, like for any other industry, an aggressive competition between banks is seen more than in the past. They have realized that relationship with customers and its management are significant factors to win this race especially in e-banking in which face to face interactions does not exist. Therefore, in the banking sector, CRM is of strategic significance because of the important effects it has on customer retention [18, 5, 13, 18, 14].

The aim of this study is to investigate the correlation between each of the customer retention programs of CRM and customer retention in e-banking of Iranian banks. Iranian banks have used CRM and its programs more or less and proceeded to this issue with different rates of success. However, since there are not available studies that investigated the correlation between a comprehensive set of customer retention programs of CRM and customer retention in these banks especially in electronic environment, this research aims at getting a deeper insight to this issue. Based upon the above discussion, we have formulated the research problem as follows:

"How is the correlation between each of the customer retention programs of CRM and customer retention in electronic banking in Iranian banks?"

According to this research problem and the reviewed literatures in this study, the research hypothesizes are formulated as:

H1. There is a positive and significant correlation between loyalty programs and customer retention.

H2. There is a positive and significant correlation between customer service and customer retention.

H3. There is a positive and significant correlation between customization and customer retention.

H4. There is a positive and significant correlation between community of customers and customer retention.

Due to the structure of this study, we review and discuss the literature about CRM and customer retention in the second section. A comprehensive set of customer retention programs of CRM is presented in section 3. The fourth section presents the methodological choices made in this work. It also examines its validity and reliability. Section 5 analyzes the empirical data which are collected by the means of questionnaire to test the research hypothesizes. This study ends with section 6 in which the conclusions related to the formulated hypotheses will be stated.

2 CRM and Customer Retention

Different authors have described CRM in several ways which reflect variety of viewpoints about its definition. Some of them have described it as a philosophy or strategy, others as a process to maintain profitable customers [10]. However, most authors consider CRM as the combination of information systems and strategies in order to make the organizations more customer-centric. In this view, CRM is not considered as only technology, but as a tool which enables the organizations to store and analyze the data about companies and their customers [1, 11, 20, 22].

CRM creates long-term and profitable relationships with stakeholders and customers by uniting the IT and appropriate strategies for relationship marketing [1, 12, 23]. In addition, CRM supplies companies with this chance to use data to realize the customer's needs by cross-functional integration of operations, people, processes, and marketing capabilities that is enabled through applications, technology, and information [1, 21, 13, 25]. Regardless of the channel to interact with companies, CRM offers convenience of transactions, and customization for the customers [1, 23].

Indeed, many firms spend most of their energy, time, and marketing budgets to gain new customers. However, because the cost of acquiring new customers is much more than the cost of retaining existing ones, customer retention is very important to most banks and organizations [2, 3, 12, 14]. As in [2, 3], acquiring a new customer can be up to ten times more expensive than to retain a current one. Therefore, customer retention can be considered as the primary goal of the organizations practicing CRM strategies and applications [3, 15]. However, organizations can expect customer retention and maximization of profits by CRM efforts, if they focus on CRM strategies and programs which are inimitable and not substitutable by other companies. This is because CRM technologies can be easily purchased and duplicated by any entrants in the industry; thus, they can not provide competitive advantage for the organizations [8, 16, 24].

3 Customer Retention Programs of CRM

If the firms such as banks want to efficiently retain their profitable customers, they need to implement a comprehensive set of customer retention programs of CRM including: loyalty programs, customer service, customization, and community building [9].

3.1 Loyalty Programs

Loyalty program which is also called frequency program provides rewards to targeted customers in order to encourage them to buy products repeatedly [6, 9]. Customer loyalty in service industry especially in financial institutions (e.g. banks) providing e-services for their customers consists of three main dimensions including affective loyalty, behavioral loyalty, and cognitive loyalty. In descending order of significance, affective loyalty is influenced by customer satisfaction, cognitive loyalty, customer perceived value, and service quality. Moreover, determinants of behavioral loyalty include customer satisfaction, service quality, affective loyalty, customer perceived value, and cognitive loyalty. And finally, the only influencing factor of cognitive loyalty is the service quality [6]. However, loyalty programs can work effectively if firms increase customer switching costs and build barriers to entry [6, 9, 17].

3.2 Customer Service

Generally, a customer service encounter is defined as the contact or "touch points" that a customer has with a company [9]. These services are two types including *Reactive* and *Proactive* services by which companies can enhance their customer service [9, 12]. *Reactive* services are applied when a customer faces problem such as product failure, product return or question about a bill and contacts the firm to solve it or get more information about it. Today, most organizations especially the banks have used the technology and also trained their employees to deal with these situations through e-mails, faxback systems, telephone, etc. *Proactive* services are the situations where the firms do not wait for customers to contact them and are determined to hold a dialogue with their customers prior to use reactive solutions such as complaint handling. This can be done well where the sales force or other employees dealing with the customers are trained and interested to realize customers' expectations [9, 15, 24].

3.3 Customization

Customization is about creation of products and services based on individual customer's taste. In this way, each customer is able to choose a product from a list or order the item he or she really wants [9, 13]. Academicians call such customization, "versioning" which is easier and cheaper to do for services and intangible information goods than for physical products. However, banks can use the additional information gained from customers to tailor at least the appearance or ease of use of their website for the online services they provide for their customers [9].

3.4 Community

Using the Web, both online and offline companies can build online networks of customers in which they are able to exchange information about the products [9, 22] and also can interact between themselves and the company easier and more personally. This network of customers is called *community*. In this situation, the customer is committed to the company and therefore he or she is less likely to leave the family of customers [9].

4 Research Methodology

This research applies quantitative approach because of the concern about the representativeness and also to test and measure the research hypothesizes. Since we are going to focus on contemporary events and also there is no requirement to control over behavioral events, survey appears as the most suitable research strategy for this study. The way we collected data, designed questionnaire, determined the sample size, and studied the validity and reliability of this research are discussed in this section.

4.1 Data Collection

Since our research strategy is survey and also the sample is large, we used the questionnaire as the instrument to collect the primary data in this research. The questionnaire has been distributed to the top managers in each selected bank branch. To increase the response rate, meeting was the first method to give the questionnaires; however, due to the time and accessibility limitations, some of the respondents received the questionnaires by e-mail along with an explanation letter.

4.2 Questionnaire Deign

Scales for this survey were developed through the literature reviews. The questionnaire includes two types of questions. The first type consists of demographic questions about the top managers in each branch and the second type includes the different questions concerning their attitude about customer retention programs of CRM and customer retention in e-banking in the branch they are working in. The questions of the second type are divided into two groups of questions. One group is about customer retention programs of CRM and the other is related to the situation of current customer retention. All of the scales in the second type were measured using 7-point Likert scales. In the next step, in order to improve the validity and reliability of the data, the questionnaire has been modified after submitting it to eight academic and bank experts as a pilot test.

4.3 Sampling Method and Determining Sample Size

The population of this survey is all Iranian banks' managers (the top manager in each branch). However, because of the time limitation, we limited this population to all the top banks' mangers in the province of Tehran which is the heart of financial activities. In addition, according to [26], it has the highest rate of e-banking usage. In the next level, among all of the mentioned banks, we selected two governmental and two private banks. Among governmental banks, bank Refah and bank Maskan and among private banks, bank Pasargad and bank Saman have been chosen. We chose these banks because they are old and more pioneering in e-banking. In the final level, we used simple random sampling to choose the branches of each bank. Thus, from all the mentioned steps, we can say that we have used a probability stratified sampling method.

In this research, first we run 30 questionnaires and calculated the value of standard deviation (σ) which is 0.62062. Moreover, the calculated value for variance is 0.385. These values are very important to be used in Equation (1) [19].

In this formula, n is the total sample size for this research. Also total population is shown by N. The number of the branches of each bank is presented in table 1. Thus, according to this table, N is equal to 553. Also, it should be said that, for the 95% level of confidence, z value is 1.96.

$$n = \frac{N \times z^2_{\frac{\alpha}{2}} \times \sigma^2}{(N-1)\varepsilon^2 + z^2_{\frac{\alpha}{2}} \times \sigma^2} \tag{1}$$

$$n = \frac{553 \times 1.96^2 (0.62062)^2}{(553-1)(0.05)^2 + 1.96^2 (0.62062)^2} = \frac{817.90}{2.86} \approx 286 \cdot$$

Therefore, the total sample size based on the formula for this research is equal to 286. Table 1 presents the sample size for each of the four banks under study. We distributed the questionnaires to the respondents based on the calculated sample size for each bank in this table and finally, all of these questionnaires were collected.

4.4 Validity and Reliability Analysis

To calculate the reliability of the items, 30 questionnaires have been distributed to the respondents. After collecting all of these questionnaires, we calculated the Cronbach's alpha which for the variable of 'customer retention programs of CRM' is 0.97, for the variable of 'customer retention' is 0.95, and for all of the scales is equal to 0.970. Then, we deleted the first item and calculated the Cronbach's alpha again. This is done for the second, third, and all of the items respectively. The results show that in each of the mentioned steps there is no change in the value of Cronbach's alpha. Therefore, we can conclude that the designed questionnaire can be considered reliable.

Table 1. Sample size for each bank

Sampling Meathod	**Number of branches of each bank**	**Percentages of units in the population**	**Total sample size**	**Sample size for each bank**
	Refah: 147	0.266	286	0.266 * 286=76
	Maskan: 184	0.333		0.33 * 286 = 95
	Pasargad: 159	0.287		0.287 * 286= 82
	Saman: 63	0.114		0.114 * 286= 33
Total	553	100	286	286

Table 2. Rotated Component Matrix for the Questions Related to 'Customer Retention Programs of CRM'

Questions	Component			
	Customization	Loyalty programs	Community	Customer service
Customization 1	0.730	0.874	-0.041	0.407
Customization 3	0.841	0.246	0.298	0.145
Loyalty programs 1	0.407	0.805	-0.015	0.652
Loyalty programs 2	0.145	0.842	0.282	0.327
Loyalty programs3	0.652	0.557	0.206	-0.425
Loyalty programs 4	0.327	0.762	0.113	-0.320
Customer service 1	-0.425	0.743	0.105	0.849
Customer service 2	-0.320	0.085	0.778	0.779
Customer service 4	0.849	-0.030	-0.093	0.885
Customer service 5	0.779	0.251	-0.306	0.849
Customer service 8	0.756	-0.022	0.244	0.551
Community 1	-0.024	0.114	0.908	-0.024
Community 2	0.485	0.191	0.764	0.485
Community 3	0.259	0.026	0.816	0.485

To check the construct validity of the questionnaire and also to find out if all indicators of each variable (construct) measure what is expected, we used 'exploratory factor analysis'. The results showed that customer retention programs of CRM consist of four factors. It also led to delete the questions with little factor loads and communalities. Table 2 and Table 3 present the factor loads for the remaining questions calculated by Lisrel 8.5.

The questionnaire has content validity since the selection of scales is from literature and it is reviewed by eight academic and banks experts to remove the probable problems.

Table 3. Rotated Component Matrix for the Questions Related to 'Customer Retention'

	Component: Customer Retention
Customer Retention 2	0.847
Customer Retention 3	0.756
Customer Retention 4	0.854

5 Data Analysis

In this study we have used Pearson's correlation to measure the correlation between each of the customer retention programs of CRM and customer retention. In this regard, a positive value for this correlation implies a positive association, but a negative one, implies an inverse association. Also, a correlation value above 0.80 is considered pretty high [19]. Table 4 presents these values using SPSS 17.

Table 4. Pearson's Correlation

		Retention
Customization	Pearson Correlation	0.802
	Sig. (2-tailed)	0.000
	N	286
Loyalty programs	Pearson Correlation	0.815
	Sig. (2-tailed)	0.000
	N	286
Customer service	Pearson Correlation	0.877
	Sig. (2-tailed)	0.000
	N	286
Community	Pearson Correlation	0.858
	Sig. (2-tailed)	0.000
	N	286

5.1 The Correlation between Loyalty Programs and Customer Retention

Regarding the related significance number which is equal to 0.000 (Sig < 0.05), it can be said that the correlation between loyalty programs and customer retention is significant. On the other hand, the value of Pearson's correlation between loyalty programs and customer retention in table 4 is 0.815 which is positive and above 0.80. Therefore, we can conclude that the first hypothesis is accepted. Thus, there is a positive and significant correlation between loyalty programs and customer retention.

5.2 The Correlation between Customer Service and Customer Retention

Since the related significance number is equal to 0.000 (Sig < 0.05), the correlation between customer service and customer retention is significant. On the other hand, since the value of Pearson's correlation for these two variables is 0.877, it can be said that the second hypothesis is accepted. Therefore, there is a positive and significant correlation between customer service and customer retention.

5.3 The Correlation between Customization and Customer Retention

Since on one hand, the related significance number is equal to 0.000 and on the other hand, the value of Pearson's correlation is 0.802, we can say that the third hypothesis is accepted. Thus, there is a positive and significant correlation between customization and customer retention.

5.4 The Correlation between Community of Customers and Customer Retention

Like the three previous analyses, the related significance number is equal to 0.000 and the related value of Pearson's correlation is more than 0.80. Thus, the last hypothesis is accepted. Therefore, there is a positive and significant correlation between community of customers and customer retention.

Also, the results in table 4 reveal that the highest value of the Pearson's correlation is between customer service and customer retention. Thus, the correlation between these two variables is the most significant one.

6 Conclusions

This study first reviewed the previous researches in the literature on different perspectives and definitions of CRM and its relationship with customer retention. It shows that organizations can expect customer retention and maximization of profits by CRM efforts, if they design efficient CRM strategies and programs which are inimitable and not substitutable by other companies. In this regard, it provided a comprehensive set of customer retention programs of CRM including loyalty programs, customer service, customization, and community of customers. Then, it analyzed the correlation between each of these programs and customer retention in e-banking of two private and two public Iranian banks. The results of data analysis by means of Pearson's correlation show that there is a positive and significant correlation between all of the studied retention programs of CRM and customer retention. It also found that the correlation between customer service and customer retention is the most significant one. Therefore, we can conclude that to have a higher rate of customer retention, it is recommended that among the studied customer retention programs of CRM in this research, bank managers should invest and focus more on customer service to improve and develop it. In this regard, managers should note that these findings are applicable to any other industry. This result is the same as the result of multi-industry research done by Reinartz et al. (2004), which implies that the benefits of CRM are approximately the same across different organizations.

Finally, the most important limitation of this study stems from inaccessibility to the customers' opinions. Since the benefits of CRM are perceived by both the organizations and their customers, investigating the customers' views about CRM in e-banking will enable the future researchers to get more accurate findings. Future studies can also focus on different samples from different governmental and private banks in different provinces.

References

1. Dimitriadis, S., Stevens, E.: Integrated customer relationship management for service activities An internal/external gap model. Managing Service Quality 18(5), 496–511 (2008)
2. Lindgreen, A., Davis, R., Brodie, R.J., Buchanan-Oliver, M.: Pluralism in contemporary marketing practices. International Journal of Bank Marketing 18(6), 294–308 (2000)
3. Ang, L., Buttle, F.: Customer retention management processes: A quantitative study. European Journal of Marketing 40(1/2), 83–99 (2006)
4. Becker, J.U., Greve, G., Albers, S.: The impact of technological and organizational implementation of CRM on customer acquisition, maintenance, and retention. Intern. J. of Research in Marketing 26, 207–215 (2009)
5. Blery, E., Michalakopoulos, M.: Customer relationship management: A case study of a Greek bank. Journal of Financial Services Marketing 11(2), 116–124 (2006)
6. Juan, L., Yan, L.: Dimensions and influencing factors of customer loyalty in the intermittent service industry. Front. Bus. Res. China 3(1), 63–78 (2009)
7. Kim, H.S., Kim, Y.G., Park, C.W.: Integration of firm's resource and capability to implement enterprise CRM: A case study of a retail bank in Korea. Decision Support Systems 48, 313–322 (2010)
8. Melville, N., Kraemer, K., Gurbaxani, V.: Information technology and organizational performance: An integrative model of IT business value. MIS Quarterly 28(2), 283–322 (2004)
9. Winer, R.S.: A framework for customer relationship management. California Management Review 43(4), 89–105 (2001)
10. Zablah, A.R., Bellenger, D.N., Johnston, W.J.: Customer relationship management implementation gaps. Journal of Personal Selling & Sales Management XXIV(4), 279–295 (2004)
11. Chan, J.O.: Toward a unified view of customer relationship management. The Journal of American Academy of Business, 32–38 (2005)
12. Dominic, P.D.D., Goh, K.N., Wong, D., Chen, Y.Y.: The importance of service quality for competitive advantage – with special reference to industrial product. International Journal of Business Information Systems 6(3), 378–397 (2010)

13. Mithas, S., Ramasubbu, N., Krishnan, M., Fornell, C.: Designing web sites for customer loyalty across business domains: A multilevel analysis. Journal of Management Information Systems 23(3), 97–127 (2007)
14. Chou, D.C., Chou, A.Y.: Integrating change management and change auditing into information technology consulting practice. International Journal of Information Systems and Change Management 4(1), 15–41 (2009)
15. Chou, D.C., Chou, A.Y.: The complementary role of business process reengineering and information technology to total quality management practices. International Journal of Information Systems and Change Management 2(1), 21–29 (2007)
16. Al-Karaghouli, W., Fadare, E.B.: The impact of information lifecycle management process in the Nigerian financial sector. International Journal of Business Information Systems 6(1), 111–132 (2010)
17. Badamas, M.A.: Critical issues in the management of information systems in Nigeria: an empirical study. International Journal of Business Information Systems 3(1), 63–72 (2008)
18. Alikhanzadeh, A.: Electronic banking. Olume Rayaneh, Babol (2008)
19. Azar, A., Momeni, M.: Statistics and its application in management, 2nd edn. Samt, Tehran (2005)
20. Jianhong, Z., Yi, X.: Design of Customer Relationship Management Systems Based on Data Mining. In: The 2008 International Symposium on Electronic Commerce and Security (ISECS 2008), pp. 722–725. IEEE Computer Society, Washington, DC (2008)
21. Ghahfarokhi, A.D., Zakaria, M.S.: The impact of CRM on customer retention in Malaysia. In: The International Conference on Electrical Engineering and Informatics, Selangor, pp. 309–313 (2009)
22. Keramati, A., Mehrabi, H., Mousakhani, M.: The role of human, organization and technology in building competitive advantage with CRM: the case of Iranian internet service industry. In: The IEEE International Conference on Industrial Informatics (INDIN 2008), DCC, Daejeon, Korea, pp. 1279–1284 (2008)
23. Perumal, S.A.: Biometrics for Effective CRM in E-commerce. In: 2009 International Conference on Information and Financial Engineering (ICIFE 2009), pp. 104–107. IEEE Computer Society, Washington, DC (2009)
24. Huang, Y., Wang, J.: Services-oriented CRM system and enabling technologies for insurance enterprises. In: 2009 Second International Workshop on Knowledge Discovery and Data Mining (WKDD 2009), pp. 737–740. IEEE Computer Society, Washington, DC (2009)
25. Zhang, Z., Zhang, Z., Wang, Y.: The Research on Information Resources Management Framework for Enterprise. In: The 2008 International Seminar on Business and Information Management (ISBIM 2008), vol. 02, pp. 478–481. IEEE Computer Society, Washington, DC (2008)
26. Bank and Insurance manifest agency (2010), http://www.bima.ir/view-6918.html

Dynamic Geometry Technology in High School Classrooms*

Zhonghong Jiang

Texas State University, San Marcos, TX 78666, United States
zj10@txstate.edu

Abstract. This article describes the theoretical foundations and key elements of the dynamic geometry approach – an approach to high school geometry that utilizes dynamic geometry software and supporting instructional materials to help students construct mathematical ideas through active explorations and investigations. Due to its benefits to students' learning, this instructional approach should be implemented in as many classrooms as possible. The focus of the article is hence on how this approach will be operationalized in the classrooms.

Keywords: dynamic geometry; the DG approach; construct; explorations; investigations.

1 Introduction

Geometry is a weak spot in school mathematics education. Research has indicated that students entering high school have very little knowledge or experience of geometric properties and relationships; most are operating at the visual level of geometric thought [4]. These students can do little more than recognize different geometric shapes [12]. The problems that students have with perceiving a need for proof are well known to all high-school teachers and have been identified without exception in all education research as a major problem in the teaching of proof [3].

Curriculum content (what is taught) and the teaching approach (how the content is taught) are at the heart of the problem. Too often, school mathematics focuses more on the product than the process and fails to convey how mathematics has evolved as a logical system [15]. Specifically, Ref [6] claims that some geometry courses do not develop understanding but rather encourage memorization.

To improve this situation, the effective use of technology seems to be a solution. Dynamic Geometry (DG) is active, exploratory geometry carried out with interactive computer software such as the Geometers' Sketchpad [8] and Cabri-Geometry [9], which has been available since the early 1990's. As Goldenberg & Cuoco [5] point out, the term *dynamic geometry* has quickly entered the literature as a generic term

* This material is based upon work supported by the National Science Foundation under Grant No. 0918744. Any opinions, findings and conclusions or recommendations expressed in this material are those of the author and do not necessarily reflect the views of the National Science Foundation.

E. Ariwa and E. El-Qawasmeh (Eds.): DEIS 2011, CCIS 194, pp. 537–544, 2011.

because of its aptness at characterizing the feature that distinguished DG from other geometry: the continuous real-time transformation often called "dragging." This feature allows users, after a construction is made, to move certain elements of a drawing freely, observe other elements respond dynamically to the altered conditions, and explore the mathematical relationships that are invariant.

Along with the widespread use of DG software, many related research studies ([13], [10], [7], [15], [2], etc.) have been conducted. According to these studies, if DG software is used effectively, it can make significant difference to students' learning; when used as a cognitive tool, it can facilitate students' exploration and investigation activities, promote their conjecturing, verifying, explaining, and logical reasoning spirits and abilities, and enhance their conceptual understanding of important geometric ideas.

Due to all of these benefits to students' learning, an approach to high school geometry that utilizes DG software and supporting instructional materials to help students construct mathematical ideas through active explorations and investigations should be implemented in as many classrooms as possible. This instructional approach is referred to as the DG approach here.

This article will describe the theoretical foundations and key elements of the DG approach, and focus on how that approach will be operationalized in the classrooms.

2 The Theoretical Foundation of the DG Approach

The constructivist perspective suggests that knowledge cannot be passively transmitted from one individual to another but is actively constructed by the learners themselves ([1], [11]). The educational implications of DG tools for the learning of geometry are far reaching. The traditional approach to geometry instruction based on definitions, theorems, and their proofs makes little sense to students. An inductive approach based on experimentation, observation, data recording, and conjecturing, in which a deductive argument is viewed as an attempt at explanation rather than at verification, would be much more appropriate. Such an approach would give students the opportunity to engage in mathematics as mathematicians, not merely as passive recipients of someone else's mathematics knowledge. This is the only way children can learn mathematics from a constructivist point of view [12].

Ref [14] postulated that students progressed through a sequence of five discrete thought levels in geometric reasoning. The five levels are: *1. Recognition*: The student can learn names of figures and recognizes a shape as a whole; *2. Analysis*: The student can identify properties of figures; *3. Order*: The student can logically order figures and relationships, but does not operate within a mathematical system; *4. Deduction*: The student understands the significance of deduction and the roles of postulates, theorems, and proof; and *5. Rigor*: The student understands the necessity for rigor and is able to make abstract deductions. According to the van Hiele theory, the main reason the traditional geometry curriculum fails is that it is presented at a higher level than those at which students are operating [3]. The DG learning environment is a suitable environment in which students can explore geometry at their geometric thinking levels. Teachers can prepare activities that match students' current van Hiele levels so that students can continue their explorations with little help from their teachers and make the transition to the next highest level.

3 The Key Elements of the DG Approach

Emphasized by the DG approach, with the teacher's facilitation and intervention, students are expected to

- Construct dynamic geometric objects with DG tools;
- Construct dynamic representations of problem situations with DG tools;
- Perform actions (dragging, measuring, transformations, and/or animation) on the constructed objects/situations or the teacher provided DG environments;
- Observe what characteristics change and what remain the same;
- Investigate mathematical relationships and/or solutions in multiple ways;
- Formulate conjectures;
- Test conjectures;
- Receive immediate feedback from the software;
- Think mathematically and prove (or disprove) their conjectures.

4 Instructional Events of a Typical DG Lesson

In line with the key elements of the DG approach, a typical DG lesson should consist of the following instructional events:

1) Present a task (exploring concepts/relationships or solving a problem) to the class;
2) Instruct students to use DG tools to construct the related geometric object or problem situation (with help if necessary) or provide students with a prepared DG environment;
3) Ask students what conjecture(s) they can make based on their initial observation;
4) Instruct students to use dragging, measuring, transforming, and/or animation to experiment with the constructed or provided DG environment, and observe what characteristics change and what remain the same;
5) Ask students to make and test conjecture(s);
6) Instruct students to redo 4) and 5) in a new aspect or at a higher level, as appropriate;
7) Have students summarize and reflect on what they have conjectured;
8) Help students develop explanations to prove or disprove their conjecture(s).

For event 8, the teacher is expected to allow a significant amount of time for students to think on their own and share their ideas with other students. After that, if they can construct their own proofs, then they are encouraged to present the proofs to the class for a discussion. For students who have difficulties, a problem solving strategy - Using Subproblems - is applied to help them. The task of proving the conjectures is broken down into a series of subproblems (presented as questions) organized in a logical order. As the students finish solving all subproblems, the goal of developing a proof is achieved.

For a typical DG lesson, it would be ideal to conduct the instruction in a computer lab, or in the original classroom where a class set of laptops is available. Students either work one per computer or work in pairs (when possible, pair weaker students with stronger students). In either case, the teacher encourages students to share ideas with and help each other. The teacher circulates, observes (to monitor the progress), asks questions, and provides necessary help as students work. At the time when a class discussion is needed, the teacher should initiate it. During the whole lesson, assessment is an integral part of instruction that informs and guides the teacher as he/she makes instructional decisions.

Taking the heavy scheduling needs for school computer labs into consideration, such lessons will be scheduled (as appropriate) twice a week. During other class sessions, the instructional events described above can be modified as appropriate for the context of using whole-class presentations with a single computer.

5 An Example of a Typical DG Lesson

The objectives of this lesson are (for students) to develop a deep understanding of the properties of the perpendicular bisectors of a triangle, and to apply these properties to define the circumcenter and circumcircle of the triangle and explain (prove) their existence. With this understanding, the students will be able to explore on their own similar situations related to angle bisectors, medians, and altitudes of a triangle.

In this class session, the teacher is expected to do the following:

1) Present the following task and questions to the class:

Construct the three perpendicular bisectors of a triangle. What do you find? Does your finding hold for other shapes of triangles? Define the Circumcenter of a triangle. Can you prove your finding?

2) Instruct students to use the Geometer's Sketchpad (GSP) to construct an arbitrary triangle and its three perpendicular bisectors on their own (with help provided only when students need it).

3) Ask students what conjecture they can make based on their observations.

The students immediately observe that the three perpendicular bisectors intersect at a single point. When they drag any vertex of the triangle to change the shape and size of the triangle, they see that their finding always holds. By further observation, they also find that the intersection point is inside the triangle if it is acute, outside the triangle if it is obtuse, and on the hypotenuse (specifically, the midpoint of the hypotenuse) if it is a right triangle.

4) If the students haven't done so, instruct them to use the dynamic measurement feature of the software to measure and observe the distances from the intersection point to the three vertices, and ask them what conjecture they can make.

After measuring the distances, the students find that the intersection point of the three perpendicular bisectors is equidistant from all three vertices of the triangle, and this fact holds for all triangles as they see when dragging any vertex of the triangle to change its shape and size.

5) If the students haven't done so, instruct them to construct a circle, using the intersection point of the three perpendicular bisectors as the center and the distance from the center to any of the vertices as the radius, and ask them what conjecture they can make.

The students find that the circle circumscribes the triangle (i.e., all three vertices are on the circle). At this time, when the teacher introduces the terms "circumcircle" and "circumcenter", the students know where they come from and can make sense of them.

6) Ask the students to define the circumcenter of a triangle.

It is natural for the students to define the circumcenter of a triangle as the intersection point of the three perpendicular bisectors of the triangle (which is the center of the circumcircle of the triangle).

7) Have the students summarize what they have found/conjectured.

The students, through class discussion, arrive at a statement like the following: The three perpendicular bisectors of any triangle intersect at a single point, which is equidistant from all three vertices of the triangle. This intersection point is called the circumcenter – the center of the circumcircle of the triangle.

Through their GSP investigations, the students discover this important theorem on their own, without the knowledge transfer from the teacher. They must be excited with their findings, and this would arouse their curiosity to find out why the findings are correct, and stimulate them to work on a proof.

8) Lead the students to develop a proof (or proofs) of their findings.

The students are encouraged to come up with a proof as independently as possible and present their ideas to the class for a discussion. If students have difficulties to proceed, the teacher may intervene by asking a series of leading questions to help students to solve a set of subproblems consecutively. As students work to answer each of the questions, the teacher may circulate, observe, provide necessary help, and organize class discussions as appropriate. The following are suggested leading questions:

(1) The conjecture is about the perpendicular bisectors of a triangle. It might be better to consider the perpendicular bisector of a segment first. Construct a free point on the perpendicular bisector of a segment (see Fig. 1), and measure the distances from the point to the two end points of the segment. What do you notice?

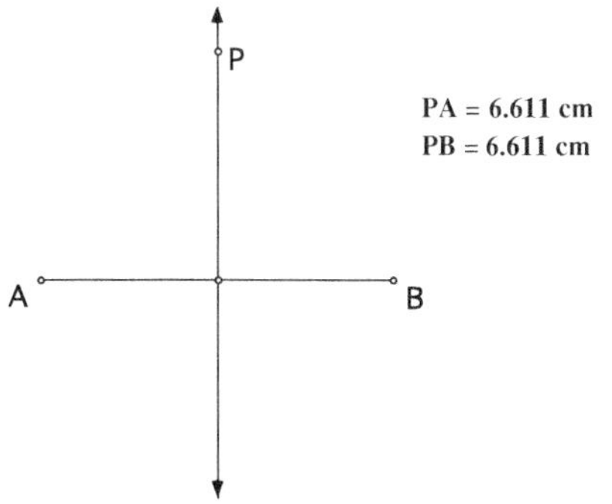

Fig. 1. Measuring the distances PA and PB

(2) Drag the free point anywhere along the perpendicular bisector. What do you notice now?

(3) What property of the perpendicular bisector of a segment has been shown? (Describe it by summarizing your answers to Questions 1 and 2.)

(4) Can you prove the property of the perpendicular bisector of a segment? (Hint: Use triangle congruence.)

(5) What is the converse statement of this property?

(6) Can you prove the converse statement? (Hint: Use triangle congruence.)

(7) In Fig. 2, point C is the intersection point of two perpendicular bisectors of ΔABD. What is the relationship between CB and CA? Justify your answer.

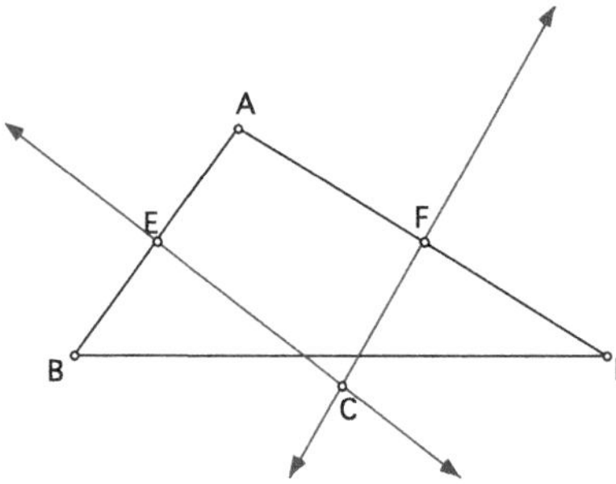

Fig. 2. C is the intersection point of two perpendicular bisectors of ΔABD

(8) What is the relationship between CA and CD? Justify your answer.

(9) What is the relationship between CB and CD? Justify your answer.

(10) What does your answer to Question 9 imply?

After students successfully answered Questions 1-10, they should be able to combine the answers to form a proof similar to the following one:

The property of a perpendicular bisector: Any point on the perpendicular bisector of a segment is equidistant from the two end points of the segment.

To prove this property, see Fig. 3 below:

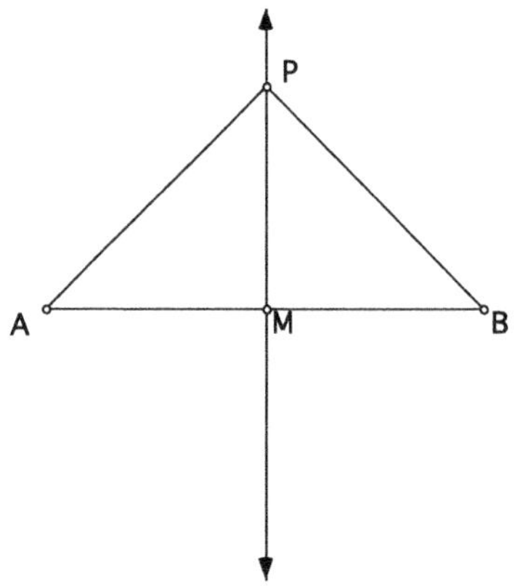

Fig. 3. For proving PA = PB

P is a point on the perpendicular bisector of $\overline{AB}$. Clearly, $\overline{AM} \cong \overline{MB}$ (M is the midpoint of $\overline{AB}$) and ∠AMP ≅ ∠BMP (both are right angles). $\overline{PM} \cong \overline{PM}$ (reflexive property). So ΔAMP ≅ ΔBMP (SAS). Hence $\overline{PA} \cong \overline{PB}$ (CPCTC). This indicates that PA = PB.

The converse statement of the property of a perpendicular bisector: Any point that is equidistant from the two end points of a segment is on the perpendicular bisector of the segment.

A proof for the converse statement:

Use the same figure (Fig. 3) in a slightly different way. This time, we have PA = PB implying that $\overline{PA} \cong \overline{PB}$. Construct the midpoint M of $\overline{AB}$, then $\overline{AM} \cong \overline{MB}$. $\overline{PM} \cong \overline{PM}$ (reflexive property). So ΔAMP ≅ ΔBMP (SSS). Hence ∠AMP ≅ ∠BMP (CPCTC). These two angles are a linear pair, and so each one must be a right angle. This implies that $\overleftrightarrow{PM}$ is perpendicular to $\overline{AB}$. Since M is the midpoint of $\overline{AB}$, $\overleftrightarrow{PM}$ is the perpendicular bisector of $\overline{AB}$.

Now let's come back to prove our conjecture about the three perpendicular bisectors of a triangle:

Let point C be the intersection point of two perpendicular bisectors of ΔABD shown in Fig. 2. Since C is on the perpendicular bisector of $\overline{AB}$, CB = CA by the property of a perpendicular bisector. Since C is also on the perpendicular bisector of $\overline{AD}$, CA = CD by the same property. By transitivity, CB = CD. By the converse theorem of the property of a perpendicular bisector, C is on the perpendicular bisector of $\overline{BD}$. In other words, the three perpendicular bisectors of ΔABD intersect at a single point C, which is equidistant from all three vertices of the triangle.

6 Conclusion

The goal of implementing the DG approach in the classrooms is to achieve better geometry teaching/leaning outcomes by engaging students in constructing mathematical ideas through experimentation, observation, data recording, conjecturing, conjecture testing, and proof as an attempt at explanation more than at verification. Using this approach, indicators of motivation – enjoyment, excitement, satisfaction, and perseverance – and of cognitive engagement – reflective statements, statements that involved shared meaning, or statements that drew on earlier interactions – would be apparent throughout the argumentations of the students [15]. Teachers should take full advantage of the potential of the DG approach to help their students to learn geometry (and mathematics in general) more effectively and successfully. With his colleagues, the author is conducting a research study (repeated randomized control trials) to investigate the efficacy of the DG approach with a grant from the US National Science Foundation.

References

1. Clements, D.H., Michael, T.B.: Constructivist Learning and Teaching. Arithmetic Teacher 38, 34–35 (1990)
2. Choi-koh, S.S.: A Student's Learning of Geometry Using the Computer. The Journal of Educational Research 92, 301–311 (1999)
3. de Villiers, M.: An Alternative Approach to Proof in Dynamic Geometry. In: Lehrer, R., Chazan, D. (eds.) Designing Learning Environments for Developing Understanding of Geometry and Space, pp. 369–394. Lawrence Erlbaum Associates, Hillsdale (1998)
4. Fuys, D., Geddes, D., Tischler, R.: The van Hiele Model of Thinking in Geometry among Adolescents. Journal for Research in Mathematics Education. Monograph 3 (1988)
5. Goldenberg, E.P., Albert, A.C.: What is Dynamic Geometry? In: Lehrer, R., Chazan, D. (eds.) Designing Learning Environments for Developing Understanding of Geometry and Space, pp. 351–368. Lawrence Erlbaum Associates, Hillsdale (1998)
6. Hoffer, A.R.: Geometry is More Than Proof. Mathematics Teacher 74, 11–18 (1981)
7. Hollebrands, K.: The Role of a Dynamic Software Program for Geometry in the Strategies High School Mathematics Students Employ. Journal for Research in Mathematics Education 38(2), 164–192 (2007)
8. Jackiw, N.: Geometer's Sketchpad, Version 5. Key Curriculum Press, Berkeley (2009)
9. Laborde, C.: Solving Problems in Computer Based. Geometry Environments: The Influence of the Features of the Software. ZDM 4, 128–135 (1992)
10. Myers, R.: The Effects of the Use of Technology in Mathematics Instruction on Student Achievement. FIU Electronic Theses and Dissertations (2009)
11. National Council of Teachers of Mathematics: Principles and Standards for School Mathematics. NCTM, Reston (2000)
12. Olive, J.: Opportunities to Explore and Integrate Mathematics with the Geometer's Sketchpad. In: Lehrer, R., Chazan, D. (eds.) Designing Learning Environments for Developing Understanding of Geometry and Space, pp. 395–418. Lawrence Erlbaum Associates, Hillsdale (1998)
13. Sinclair, N., Healy, L., Sales, C.: Time for Telling Stories: Narrative Thinking with Dynamic Geometry. ZDM 41(4), 441–452 (2009)
14. van Hiele, P.M.: Structure and Insight. Academic Press, Orlando (1986)
15. Vincent, J.: Interactive Geometry Software and Mechanical Linkages: Scaffolding Students' Deductive Reasoning. In: Masalski, W.J. (ed.) Technology-Supported Mathematics Learning Environment, pp. 93–112. NCTM, Reston (2005)

Automatic Subject Classification of Scientific Literature Using Citation Metadata

Abdulhussain E. Mahdi and Arash Joorabchi

Department of Electronic and Computer Engineering, University of Limerick, Ireland
{hussain.mahdi,arash.joorabchi}@ul.ie

Abstract. This paper describes a new method for automatic classification of scientific literature archived in digital libraries and repositories according to a standard library classification scheme. The method is based on identifying all the references cited in the document to be classified and, using the subject classification metadata of extracted references as catalogued in existing conventional libraries, inferring the most probable class for the document itself with the help of a weighting mechanism. We have demonstrated the application of the proposed method and assessed its performance by developing a prototype software system for automatic classification of scientific documents according to the Dewey Decimal Classification (DDC) scheme. A dataset of one thousand research articles, papers, and reports from a well-known scientific digital library, CiteSeer, were used to evaluate the classification performance of the system. Detailed results of this experiment are presented and discussed.

Keywords: Digital library organization, scientific literature classification, library classification schemes, Dewey Decimal Classification (DDC), library Online Public Access Catalogues (OPACs).

1 Introduction

Scientific digital libraries and repositories are a fast-growing concept within research and academic communities. The main aim of these services is to facilitate effective dissemination of research output among researchers by providing efficient centralized access points to large collections of research data in electronic format, mainly available in form of articles, papers, technical reports, thesis, and dissertations. Metadata, generally defined as data about data, plays a critical rule in digital libraries by providing structured data about characteristics of unstructured data resources. It can significantly improve the accessibility of resources by helping to describe, locate, and retrieve them efficiently. Hence, utilizing data mining and knowledge discovery techniques to create, enrich, and harvest metadata has been one of the main efforts of researchers working in the field of digital libraries. The focus of this work is on automatic generation of a specific type of metadata called classification metadata in scientific digital libraries, aimed at defining the content subject of archived resources according to a standard library classification scheme.

The rest of the paper is organized as follows: Section 2 discusses the role of classification metadata in digital libraries and reviews existing Automatic Text

E. Ariwa and E. El-Qawasmeh (Eds.): DEIS 2011, CCIS 194, pp. 545–559, 2011.

Classification (ATC) methods for generating classification metadata in digital libraries. Section 3 provides an outline of our proposed ATC method called Bibliography based ATC (BB-ATC). Section 4 describes a prototype ATC system which has been developed based on the proposed method in order to demonstrate its viability and evaluate its performance in organizing a scientific digital library. Section 5 describes the evaluation process and presents its results. Section 6 provides a conclusion along with a summary account of planned future work.

2 Classification Metadata

Medium to large-scale digital libraries contain tens to hundreds of thousands of items, and therefore require advanced querying and information retrieval techniques to facilitate precision search and discovery of archival materials. In order to deliver highly relevant search results, we need to go beyond the traditional keyword-based search techniques which usually yield a large volume of indiscriminant search results irrespective of their content. Subject classification of materials in digital libraries according to a standard scheme could improve the accuracy of information retrieval significantly and allows users to browse the collection by subject [1]. However, manual subject classification of documents is a tedious and time-consuming task which requires an expert cataloguer in each knowledge domain represented in the collection, and therefore deemed impractical in many cases. Motivated by the ever-increasing number of e-documents and the high cost of manual classification, Automatic Text Classification/Categorization (ATC) - the automatic assignment of natural language text documents to one or more predefined classes/categories according to their contents - has become one of the key methods to enhance the information retrieval and knowledge management of digital textual collections.

Since the early '90s, with the advances in the field of Machine Learning (ML) and the emergence of relatively inexpensive high performance computing platforms, ML-based approaches have become widely associated with modern ATC systems. A comprehensive review of the application of ML algorithms in ATC, including the widely used Bayesian Model, *k*-Nearest Neighbor, and Support Vector Machine, is given in [2]. In general, an ML-based ATC algorithm uses a corpus of manually classified documents to train a classification function which is then used to predict the classes of unlabelled documents. Applications of such algorithms include spam filtering, cataloguing news articles, and classification of web pages, to name a few. However, although a considerable success has been achieved in above listed applications, the prediction accuracy of ML-based ATC systems depends on a variety of factors, and no single ATC algorithm is adequate for all purposes.

On the other hand, as Golub [3], Yi [4], and Markey [5] discuss, there exits a less investigated approach to ATC that is attributed to the library science community. This approach focuses less on algorithms and more on leveraging comprehensive controlled vocabularies, such as library classification schemes and thesauri which have been developed and used for manual classification of holdings in conventional libraries. A library classification system is a coding system for organizing library materials according to their subjects with the aim of simplifying subject browsing.

Library classification systems are used by expert library cataloguers to classify books and other materials (e.g., serials, audiovisual materials, computer files, maps, manuscripts, realia) in conventional libraries. The two most widely used classification systems in libraries around the world today are the Dewey Decimal Classification (DDC) [6] and the Library of Congress Classification (LCC) [7], which since their introduction in the late 18th century have undergone numerous revisions and updates.

A promising avenue for the application of this approach is the automatic classification of resources archived in digital libraries, where using standard library classification schemes is a natural and usually most suitable choice because of the similarities between conventional and digital libraries. In general, ATC systems that have been developed based on the above library science approach can be divided into two main categories:

1. String matching-based systems: these systems do not rely on ML algorithms to perform the classification task. Instead, they use a method which involves string-to-string matching between words in a term list extracted from library thesauri and classification schemes, and words in the text to be classified. Here, the unlabelled incoming document can be thought of as a search query against the library classification schemes and thesauri, and the result of this search includes the class(es) of the unlabelled document. One of the well-known examples of such systems is the Scorpion project [8] by the Online Computer Library Centre (OCLC) [9]. Scorpion is an ATC system for classifying e-documents according to the DDC scheme. It uses a clustering method based on term frequency to find the most relevant classes to the document to be classified. A similar experiment was conducted by Larson [10] in early 90's, who built normalized clusters for 8,435 classes in the LCC scheme from manually classified records of 30,471 library holdings and experimented with a variety of term representation and matching methods. For more examples of these systems see [11, 12].
2. ML-based systems: these systems utilize ML algorithms to classify e-documents according to library classification schemes such as the DDC and the LCC. They represent a relatively unexplored trend which aims to combine the power of ML-based ATC algorithms with the enormous intellectual effort that has already been put into developing library classification systems over the last century. Chung and Noh [13] built a specialized web directory for the field of economics by classifying web pages into 757 sub-categories of economics category in the DDC scheme using *k*-NN algorithm. Pong et al. [14] developed an ATC system for classifying web pages and digital library holdings based on the LCC scheme. They used both *k*-NN and Naive Bayes (NB) algorithms and compared the results. Frank and Paynter [15] used the linear SVM algorithm to classify over 20,000 scholarly Internet resources based on the LCC scheme.

In this work, we propose a new category of ATC systems within the framework of the library science approach, which we call Bibliography Based ATC (BB-ATC) and is based on utilizing the citation networks among documents. We demonstrate and evaluate the application of the proposed method in the automatic generation of subject classification metadata for documents archived in scientific digital libraries.

3 Outline of Proposed BB-ATC Method

A considerable amount of documents have some form of linkage to other documents. For example, it is a common practice in scientific documents to cite related papers, articles, and books. It is also common practice for documented law cases to refer to other cases, patents to refer to other patents, and webpages to have links to other webpages. Leveraging these networks of citations/links among documents opens a new route for the development of ATC systems, known as collective classification [16]. Our proposed BB-ATC method falls into this route, and aims to develop a new trend of effective ATC systems that are based on leveraging:

1. The intellectual work that has been put into developing and maintaining extensive resources and systems for classifying and organizing the vast amount of materials archived in conventional libraries.
2. The intellectual effort of expert library cataloguers who have used the above classification resources and systems to manually classify and index millions of books and other materials in libraries around the world over the last century.

With the assumption that the majority of materials, such as books and journals, cited in a scientific document belong to the same or closely relevant classification category(ies) as that of the citing document, we can classify the citing document based on the class(es) of its references as identified in existing conventional library catalogues. The proposed BB-ATC method is based on automating this process using three main steps:

1. Identifying and extracting references in the document to be classified.
2. Searching for and retrieving the subject classification metadata of referenced materials from the online public access catalogues (OPACs) of conventional libraries.
3. Inferring and allocating a class(es) to the document based on the retrieved subject classification metadata of referenced materials with the help of a weighting mechanism.

This method of classification is applicable to any document that cites one or more published materials catalogued in at least one of the OPACs searched by the system. Examples of such documents include books, conference and journal articles, learning and teaching materials (e.g., syllabi and lecture notes), theses, and dissertations. In [17] the authors have described an ATC system designed and developed for automatic classification of electronic syllabus documents based on an early version of the BB-ATC method proposed here. Also, in [18] we have applied the underlying idea of the BB-ATC method to the problem of automatic keyphrase indexing of scientific documents which could be viewed as a multi-label text classification problem.

4 System Implementation and Functionality

In order to demonstrate the application of the proposed BB-ATC method for automatic generation of subject classification metadata in scientific digital libraries, we have developed a prototype ATC system for categorising the scientific documents archived in CiteSeer digital library [19] according to the DDC scheme. CiteSeer is a scientific literature digital library focusing primarily on the literature in computer science and information technology, and it contains over one million documents. We chose CiteSeer as our experimental platform for two main reasons:

1. CiteSeer is a well-known scientific digital library among the information science and digital library research communities and has been the subject of various studies in the areas of information retrieval and digital libraries.
2. It is an open-access and open-source project providing full access to all of its resources including: metadata records, archived items, and software source codes.

Our developed ATC system is effectively a metadata generator comprising a pre-processing, a data mining, and an inferring unit. The complete collection of CiteSeer's metadata records is freely available on the project's website[1] in the form of dump files. CiteSeer metadata records come in two different types: Open Access Initiative (OAI) records in Dublin Core XML format and bibliographic records in BibTex format. These two types of metadata records associated to each archived document contain a wide range of metadata about the document such as: type, title, authors, abstract, references, publishing date, publisher, source URL, format, language, etc. In order to easily access this large collection of metadata records we first developed a small software component to normalize and convert the CiteSeer BibTex records into XML format. Then the CiteSeer OAI and BibTex records in XML format were loaded into a native XML database called eXist-DB [20] which supports XML query languages, Xquery and Xpath, and facilitates efficient search and retrieval of CiteSeer metadata records.

The initial task of the pre-processing unit is to select a document from the CiteSeer archive for classification and retrieve its metadata from the CiteSeer metadata database for further processing. The selection can be sequential, random, or based on some criteria, such as publishing date, number of references, format, etc. Once a document is selected and its metadata is retrieved, the pre-processing unit compiles a list of titles of all the publications referenced in the document, such as articles, books, reports, etc., as per the list of references provided in the CiteSeer OAI metadata record of the document. The retrieved metadata of the document along with its list of references are then passed to the data mining unit.

The task of the data mining unit is two folds. In the first stage, it uses the Google Books Search (GBS) engine [21] to compile a list of publications that either cite the document to be classified or one of its references. This is done by submitting a number of URL queries to the GBS engine in the following format:

```
http://www.google.com/books/feeds/volumes?max-results=20&q=%22[title]%2C%22
```

For the first query, the variable *title* in above format is set to the title of the document to be classified, and in the subsequent queries the titles of the references in the document are used consecutively. The parameter *max-results* limits the number of returned matching results to twenty items. This parameter is set empirically to balance the bias in the search results in terms of the number of returned matching publications for different queries. The returned result for each query is an XML file containing the

[1] http://citeseer.ist.psu.edu/

metadata records of matching publications and each record contains a set of metadata elements such as: title, authors, ISBN, etc. At this point, we have a pool of metadata records for the publications that either cite the document to be classified or one of its references. In order to utilise the gathered metadata for inferring the DDC class of the document, we first need to discover the DDC classification numbers of the publications in the pool. This is achieved by the second stage of the data mining process, where the corresponding DDC numbers of publications in the pool are retrieved from the OCLC's WorldCat [22] database. WorldCat is a union catalogue of about 70,000 conventional libraries around the world. The data mining unit performs this task in two steps. First, it processes the metadata records of the publications in the pool to extract their corresponding ISBNs. These ISBNs are then used as unique identifiers for the publications to query the WorldCat database for their corresponding metadata records. The latter process is done by submitting the following URL query to the WorldCat Search API [23] per each ISBN:

```
http://www.worldcat.org/webservices/catalog/content/isb
n/[ISBN]%3Fwskey%3D[key]%3Dfull
```

The returned result for each query is and XML file containing the full bibliographic record of the publication in MARC 21 XML format [24]. Along with other metadata elements, this record contains a DDC classification number assigned to the publication by a professional library cataloguer in one of the 70,000 libraries that have merged their catalogue into the WorldCat catalogue.

The task of the inferring unit is to analyze the pool of metadata gathered by the data mining unit, which contains the DDC numbers potentially related to the document to be classified, and select a DDC number from the pool which is most probable to represent the document's core subject. The inference process is based on a weighting method designed to assign a relevance probability score to each unique DDC number in the pool according to its frequency distribution.

Initially, the weighting method assigns each unique DDC number in the pool three different weights: un-normalized local frequency, normalized local frequency, and global frequency. Each of these weights is designed to measure the relevance probability of a given DDC number in the pool in relation to the document from a unique perspective. We describe these weights and details of the inferring process in the course of the following example which gives a sequential account of how the proposed BB-ATC method is used to classify a sample document from the CiteSeer archive. The document used in this example is a research paper entitled "Statistical Learning, Localization, and Identification of Objects". The core subject of the document is AI-based computer vision and, therefore, it should be classified into the DDC class "Computer science, information & general works\Computer science, knowledge & systems\Special computer methods\Artificial intelligence\Computer vision" represented by the DDC number 00637. The classification process of this sample document would be as follows:

4.1 Pre-processing

The pre-processing unit retrieves the corresponding metadata records for the document to be classified from the CiteSeer metadata database. Table 1 shows some of the retrieved metadata for the sample document.

Table 1. Sample document's metadata

Metadata field	Font size and style
dc:title	Learning, Localization, and Identification of Objects
datestamp	1996-08-06
dc:description	This work describes a statistical approach to deal with learning and recognition problems in the field of computer vision…
dc:identifier	http://citeseer.ist.psu.edu/52.html
oai_citeseer:relation type="References"	<oai_citeseer:uri>oai:CiteSeerPSU:112462</oai_citeseer:uri>

4.2 Data Mining

As described earlier, this process involves compiling a list of publications that either cite the document to be classified or one of its references, and discovering their corresponding DDC numbers. As the last row of Table 1 shows, the document under classification either has only one reference, or the CiteSeer's citation extraction unit, ParsCit [25], which is responsible for extracting citations from the archived documents, has only managed to extract one of the references successfully. Therefore, the title of the document to be classified and the title of its single successfully extracted reference are the only available clues that can be used for mining a list of DDC numbers potentially relevant to the document. Table 2 shows the metadata gathered by the data mining unit for the publications that cite one of these two titles.

Table 2. Data mining results for the sample document

Publications citing the document to be classified titled: "Statistical Learning, Localization, and Identification of Objects"					
ISBN	DDC No.	ISBN	DDC No.	ISBN	DDC No.
0123797721	006.37	3540650806	006.3	0818681845	621.367
0123797772	006.37	3540629092	006.42	3540639314	621.367
3540646132	006.37	3540634606	006.42	0792378504	621.367
0780350987	006.37	389838019X	005.118	3540250468	629.8932
0769501648	Null	1558605835	Null	0780399781	Null
Publications citing the document's reference titled: "Learning Object Recognition Models from Images"					
ISBN	DDC No.	ISBN	DDC No.	ISBN	DDC No.
3540617507	006.37	1586032577	006.3	389838019X	005.118
0195095227	006.37	3540282262	006.3	1848002785	621.367
3540667229	006.37	3540634606	006.42	3540433996	629.892
3540404988	006.37	3540636366	006.7	0818638702	621.399
0120147734	537.56	0780399773	Null		

4.3 Inferring

The inference process starts by deriving the un-normalised local frequency, normalised local frequency, and global frequency weights for each unique DDC number in the pool, as per the following:

- The un-normalised Local Frequency (ULF) of a given DDC number, DDC_i, is defined as the summation of its frequencies in each of the search result sets, R_j, where $j = \{1,\ldots, m\}$ with m being the total number of search result sets:

$$ULF(DDC_i) = \sum_{j=1}^{m} Freq(DDC_{i,j}) \quad (1)$$

  The function $Freq(DDC_{i,j})$ returns the number of times that the DDC number, DDC_i, appears in the search result set j. For a given DDC number, DDC_i, which appears in the pool of search results at least once, $ULF(DDC_i)$ is an integer number greater than or equal to 1. For example, the result of data mining process for the sample document appearing in Table 2 shows that there are 15 publications citing the document to be classified and another 14 publications citing the document's only reference. Among this total of 29 publications, 8 are assigned the DDC number "006.37", and therefore the ULF value for this DDC number is equal to 8.
- In order to prevent a DDC number from unjustifiably biasing the inference result due to its overwhelming high frequency in a single or small number of search result sets, we have adopted a second weight called Normalised Local Frequency (NLF) defined as:

$$NLF(DDC_i) = \sum_{j=1}^{m} \frac{Freq(DDC_{i,j})}{|R_j|} \quad (2)$$

  where, $|R_j|$ represents the total number of DDC numbers in the search result set R_j. For a given DDC number, DDC_i, which appears in the pool of search results at least once, $NLF(DDC_i)$ is a positive real number greater than 0. For example, using the sample data given in Table 2, the NLF value for the DDC number "006.37" is $(4/12) + (4/13) = 0.64$.
- The third weight, Global Fequency (GF), aims to reflect how common a given DDC number is among all the search result sets irrespective of its frequency inside individual search result sets. The GF for a given DDC number, DDC_i, is defined as the total number of search result sets in which DDC_i appears once or more:

$$GF(DDC_i) = \sum_{j=1}^{m} \left[DDC_i \in R_j \right] \quad (3)$$

  where, $[DDC_i \in R_j]$ returns 1 if DDC_i appears in the search result set R_j at least once, and returns 0 otherwise. For a given DDC number, DDC_i, which appears in the pool of search results at least once, $GF(DDC_i)$ is a positive integer number, with a minimum value of 1 and a maximum value of m, with m being the total number of search result sets. Again, using the sample data given in Table 2, the DDC number "006.37", for example, appears in both R_1 and R_2 search result sets, and therefore its GF is equal to 2.

Having computed the ULF, NLF, and GF weights for a given DDC number, DDC_i, the formula in Equation 4 is used to derive a single Combined Weight (CW) for it:

$$CW(DDC_i) = GF(DDC_i) \times NLF(DDC_i) \times ULF(DDC_i)^{\frac{depth(DDC_i)}{10}+1} \quad (4)$$

where, $depth(DDC_i)$ returns the vertical position of DDC_i in the classification hierarchy. The formulas for the ULF, NLF, and GF weights of a given DDC number in the pool and the CW formula used to derive a single combined weight from them, have been empirically deduced to give the best inference results based on an extensive analysis of a preliminary dataset. The results of this analysis indicated that the impact of ULF on CW should be kept to a minimum for the DDC numbers at the first level of the DDC hierarchy and it should gradually increase as the depth/level of the given DDC number increases in the hierarchy. The last part of Equation 4 incorporates this condition. Sticking to the DDC number "006.37" in our example and using the data of Table 2, the CW for this DDC number is computed as: $2 \times 0.64 \times 8^{(5/10)+1} = 29.01$.

After computing the above weights for all the DDC numbers in the pool, the inferring unit builds a classification hierarchy tree from all the DDC numbers in the pool and their corresponding weights. This tree is then automatically inspected to find the most probabilistically relevant DDC number to the core subject of the document. The inferring unit uses Java Universal Network/Graph Framework (JUNG) [26], which is an open source software library for graph modelling, analysis, and visualisation, to build, crawl, and visualise the classification tree.

The automatic crawling process aims to find the strongest path in the classification tree based on the CW values of the nodes. It starts from the root/start node and moves to the child node which has the largest CW value as the probabilistically selected most relevant DDC number to the document in the first level of the DDC classification hierarchy. The same selection criterion is then applied to the children of the selected node and so on until a node with no children (i.e. a leaf node) is reached. In cases where all the children of a chosen node have equal CW values, the CWs of its grandchildren are compared and the grandchild which has the largest CW value along with its parent node becomes selected. If all the grandchildren of the chosen node have equal CW values, then the decision will be based on the CW's of its great grandchildren and so on. In rare cases where this selection criterion does not lead to a resolution and all of the descendents of the latest chosen node have equal CW values in their corresponding level of the classification hierarchy, the crawling process stops and the latest selected node becomes the final selected DDC number for the document.

During our preliminary experiments, we noticed some cases where there is a significant decrease in the CW value of a potentially chosen node in relation to its parent's CW value. In majority of studied cases, this sudden drop indicated that either the latest chosen node (i.e., the parent node of current potentially chosen node) is the most appropriate DDC number for the document or there is not enough evidence to confidently conclude otherwise. In these cases, the best policy is to stop the crawling process and output the latest confidently chosen node, i.e., the parent node, as the final selected DDC number for the document. This policy is incorporated into the inference process in the form of a thresholding mechanism which stops the crawling process if a potentially chosen node does not pass the criterion in Equation 5, and outputs the parent of that node as the final selected DDC number for the document.

$$CW(CN) \times depth(CN)^{children(PN)} > CW(PN) \tag{5}$$

where, *CW(CN)* is the *CW* value of the current potentially chosen node, *depth(CN)* is the depth of the current potentially chosen node in the DDC hierarchy, *children(PN)* is the number of the parent node's children (i.e., the number of the current potentially chosen node's siblings added by one), and *CW(PN)* is the *CW* value of the parent node.

The prototype BB-ATC system operates in two modes: unsupervised and semi-supervised/evaluation. In unsupervised mode, classification process of a document ends by adding its final chosen DDC number to its metadata record stored in the CiteSeer metadata database. In the semi-supervised mode, however, first, the built classification hierarchy tree and the inference result for the document are visualized and presented; and then the user is required to either confirm the DDC number suggested by the system for the document as the most appropriate, or enter the correct DDC number manually. Once the results are confirmed/corrected, both the DDC numbers chosen by the inferring unit and the user are added to the metadata record of the document stored in the CiteSeer metadata database. In parallel to that, when operating in evaluation mode, the system creates a HTML log file for each classified document containing its original metadata, data mining results, and manual and automatic generated subject classification metadata.

5 System Evaluation and Experimental Results

Evaluating the performance of the developed prototype BB-ATC system was the most challenging and time consuming part of this work. To start with, the CiteSeer digital library, used as the test platform in this work, does not provide any subject classification metadata for its archived items. In fact, to the best of our knowledge, there exit no digital library of scientific literature which classifies its collection according to a standard library classification scheme, such as the DDC or the LCC. This fact, as discussed in Section 2, can be attributed to two main obstacles: the first is the high cost of manual classification, and the second is the inefficiency of common ML-based ATC systems to cope with the sheer size of library classification schemes, containing thousands of classes. Therefore, in the absence of any suitable third-party test corpus, we had no option but to create our own.

To perform the evaluation, the pre-processing unit of the system was set to randomly retrieve the metadata records of one thousand documents from the CiteSeer metadata database to be automatically classified and manually examined by a group of five postgraduate students in our research group. The students were given access to the WebDewey[2] which is part of the Online Computer Library Centre (OCLC) [9] suite of cataloguing and metadata services and enables full browsing of the latest version of the DDC online. The students were first familiarized with the DDC scheme and its hierarchical nature, and then each were assigned a set of documents (as defined below) to examine and classify.

---

[2] `http://www.oclc.org/dewey/versions/webdewey`

In order to measure the effect of the number of references successfully extracted from documents on the classification performance of our system, the pre-processing unit was set to build the test corpus from five different subsets of documents grouped according to their number of references. Each subset is made up of 200 documents with equal number of references. The first subset contains the documents that have no references successfully extracted from them. The second, third, forth, and fifth subsets contain documents with 4, 8, 16, and 32 references, respectively. Also, we set the inferring unit of the system to work in the semi-supervised/evaluation mode, which requires the user to either verify or rectify the DDC number automatically assigned to the document, and logs all the data produced during the classification process of the document in a dedicated HTML log file, as explained previously in Section 5. The HTML log files for all of the 1000 test documents used in this experiment may be viewed online on our webpage[3].

We used the standard measures of Precision (*Pr*), Recall (*Re*), and *F1* to evaluate the classification performance of our system. Micro-average and macro-average are the two wildly used measures to evaluate the overall prediction performance of ATC systems. In micro-averaging, the above target performance measures (i.e. *Pr*, *Re*, and *F1*) are computed globally over all classes. Whereas, in macro-averaging, the performance measures are computed for each individual class locally and then the average over all classes is taken. Micro-averaging gives equal weight to each document, whereas, macro-averaging gives equal weight to each class. Due to the high subject sparsity of our test corpus, there is a substantial number of classes which contain only one or two documents, and that could result in biased performance measures if macro-averaging is used. Therefore, in order to obtain a true objective evaluation of the classification performance of our system, we adopted the micro-average measure which gives equal weight to each document regardless of its class. The overall micro-averaged precision, recall, and F1 for all the one thousand documents in the test corpus regardless of their number of references are 0.84, 0.78, and 0.81 respectively. In order to show the effect of the number of references in the documents on the classification performance of the system, Table 3 shows the micro-averaged performance measures for each of the five document subsets in the test corpus individually.

Table 3. Performance measures for each of the five document subsets in the test corpus

Subset	# of References	# of Docs	Micro-Avg. Precision	Micro-Avg. Recall	Micro-Avg. F1
1	0	200	0.72	0.52	0.61
2	4	200	0.84	0.82	0.83
3	8	200	0.84	0.83	0.84
4	16	200	0.88	0.86	0.87
5	32	200	0.89	0.88	0.89
Overall	0-32	1000	0.84	0.78	0.81

[3] `http://www.csn.ul.ie/~arash/BB-ATC1/HTML/index.html`

As a common practice in developing a new ATC method or system, it is always desired to compare its performance with that of others. However, it was not possible for us to conduct a true objective comparison between the performance of our system and that of other reported ATC systems due to the following:

1. To the best of our knowledge there has been no previous attempt to automatically classify a collection of digital scientific literature according to a standard library classification scheme.
2. Unlike our system which utilizes the full DDC scheme, other relatively similar reported ATC systems, due to their limitations, either adopt only one of the main classes in the DDC/LCC along with its subclasses as their classification scheme, or use an abridged version of the DDC/LCC by limiting the depth of the classification hierarchy to second or third level.
3. Some of the similar works had reported the performance of their system using measures other than the standard performance measures of precision, recall, and F1 used in this work.

Despite above, it is possible to provide a relative comparison between the performance of our system and those of similar systems reported in the literature. For example, Pong and co-workers [14] used both NB and *k*-NN algorithms to classify 254 documents according to a refined version of the LCC scheme which consisted of only 67 categories. They reported the values of 0.802, 0.825, and 0.781 as the best figures for micro-averaged F1, recall, and precision, respectively, achieved by their system. Also, Chung and Noh [13] reported the development of a specialized economics web directory by classifying a collection of webpages, belonging to the field of economics, into 575 subclasses of the DDC main class of economics. Their unsupervised string-matching based classifier achieved an average precision of 0.77 and their supervised ML-based classifier achieved an average precision and recall of 0.963 and 0.901, respectively. in [17] we used an early version of the BB-ATC method to automatically classify a collection of 200 computer science related syllabus documents archived in the Irish national syllabus repository according to the full DDC scheme. The achieved micro-averaged performance measures of precision, recall, and F1 were 0.917, 0.889, and 0.902, respectively.

6 Conclusions and Future Work

In this paper we proposed a new category of ATC systems based on a new route for leveraging conventional library classification systems and resources, which we refer to as the Bibliography Based ATC (BB-ATC) approach. Our proposed approach solely relies on the subject classification metadata of the publications citing either the document to be classified or one of its references, as catalogued in the OPACs of conventional libraries, in order to probabilistically infer the most appropriate class for the document. In order to demonstrate the application and evaluate the classification performance of the proposed BB-ATC approach, we developed a prototype ATC system for automatic classification of scientific literature archived in the CiteSeer digital library. The developed ATC system was evaluated using a test corpus of one thousand scientific documents and the classification results were presented and analysed with the aim of quantifying the prediction performance of the system and identifying the factors influencing its performance. We reported micro-averaged values of 0.84, 0.78, and 0.81 for the overall precision, recall, and F1 measures of our system, respectively, and provided a relative comparison between the performance of our system and those of similar reported systems.

Based on above, we believe that we have developed a new robust approach for automatic classification of scientific literature in digital libraries and repositories according to a standard library classification scheme, which offers a prediction performance competitive to that achieved by the ML-based and string matching-based system. As for future work, we have identified a number of enhancements that could potentially improve the prediction performance of our method:

- As discussed in section 4, in the first stage of the data mining process carried out by the data mining unit of our system, the GBS engine is used to gather the corresponding metadata of all the publications that either cite the document to be classified or one of its references. GBS enables the full-text search of books, journals, and other materials that Google and its library and publisher partners scan, OCR, and index. In October 2009, Google announced that they had over 10 million items searchable through GBS [27]. Google does not provide public access to the full content of the majority of these items due to copyright restrictions. However, the metadata record of each archived item includes a so called "word cloud" which contains a set of key terms that have been identified as statistically significant within the full textual content of the item. The majority of these key terms are domain-specific, semantically rich, and directly related to the core subject of the book, and we have already proved their application in automatic keyphrase extraction from scientific documents [18]. These key terms could be used to measure the relevance of a publication, which cites either the document to be classified or one of its references, to the document. Thus, we are currently working on an enhanced version of the BB-ATC system which searches the content of the document to be classified for these key terms and based on their total number and frequency in the document derives a relevance weight, which measures the subject similarity of the citing publications to the document. Incorporating this new weight into the inference process should eliminate or at least limit the negative effect of a minor number of citing publications, whose main subject does not match the subject of the document to be classified.
- As discussed in section 5, the number of references in the documents to be classified has a large impact on the prediction performance of the proposed method. The references are used as indicative clues which collectively point to the right class for the document and, therefore, the larger the number of the clues the more reliable and accurate the classification results. Based on this, we can expect our method to yield its best performance when applied to documents which have a large number of references, such as Electronic Thesis and Dissertations (ETDs). Therefore, the next version of the BB-ATC system incorporating the enhancements described above will be deployed and evaluated for classification of a large collection of ETD documents archived in a digital library, such as the Networked Digital Library of Thesis and Dissertations (NDLTD) [28].

References

[1] Avancini, H., Rauber, A., Sebastiani, F.: Organizing digital libraries by automated text categorization. In: Heery, R., Lyon, L. (eds.) ECDL 2004. LNCS, vol. 3232. Springer, Heidelberg (2004)

[2] Sebastiani, F.: Machine learning in automated text categorization. ACM Computing Surveys (CSUR) 34(1), 1–47 (2002)

[3] Golub, K.: Automated subject classification of textual Web pages, based on a controlled vocabulary: Challenges and recommendations. New Review of Hypermedia and Multimedia 12(1), 11–27 (2006)

[4] Yi, K.: Automated text classification using library classification schemes: trends, issues, and challenges. International Cataloguing and Bibliographic Control (ICBC) 36(4), 78–82 (2007)

[5] Markey, K.: Forty years of classification online: final chapter or future unlimited? Cataloging & Classification Quarterly 42(3), 1–63 (2006)

[6] Dewey, M.: Dewey Decimal Classification (DDC). (Online Computer Library Center (OCLC), 1876-2010) (cited February 2011), `http://www.oclc.org/us/en/dewey`

[7] Putnam, H.: Library of Congress Classification (LCC). (Library of Congress, Cataloging Policy and Support Office, 1897-2010) (cited February 2011), `http://www.loc.gov/catdir/cpso/lcc.html`

[8] Scorpion (OCLC Online Computer Library Center, Inc., 2002) (cited (February 2011), `http://www.oclc.org/research/software/scorpion/`

[9] OCLC (Online Computer Library Center (cited February 2011), `http://www.oclc.org/`

[10] Larson, R.R.: Experiments in automatic Library of Congress Classification. Journal of the American Society for Information Science 43(2), 130–148 (1992)

[11] Jenkins, C., Jackson, M., Burden, P., Wallis, J.: Automatic classification of Web resources using Java and Dewey Decimal Classification. Computer Networks and ISDN Systems 30(1-7), 646–648 (1998)

[12] Dolin, R., Agrawal, D., Abbadi, E.E.: Scalable collection summarization and selection. In: Proceedings of the Fourth ACM Conference on Digital Libraries. ACM, Berkeley (1999)

[13] Chung, Y.-M., Noh, Y.-H.: Developing a specialized directory system by automatically classifying Web documents. Journal of Information Science 29(2), 117–126 (2003)

[14] Pong, J.Y.-H., Kwok, R.C.-W., Lau, R.Y.-K., Hao, J.-X., Wong, P.C.-C.: A comparative study of two automatic document classification methods in a library setting. Journal of Information Science 34(2), 213–230 (2008)

[15] Frank, E., Paynter, G.W.: Predicting Library of Congress classifications from Library of Congress subject headings. Journal of the American Society for Information Science and Technology 55(3), 214–227 (2004)

[16] Sen, P., Namata, G., Bilgic, M., Getoor, L., Galligher, B., Eliassi-Rad, T.: Collective classification in network data. AI Magazine 29(3) (2008)

[17] Joorabchi, A., Mahdi, A.E.: Leveraging the legacy of conventional libraries for organizing digital libraries. In: Agosti, M., Borbinha, J., Kapidakis, S., Papatheodorou, C., Tsakonas, G. (eds.) ECDL 2009. LNCS, vol. 5714, pp. 3–14. Springer, Heidelberg (2009)

[18] Mahdi, A.E., Joorabchi, A.: A Citation-based approach to automatic topical indexing of scientific literature. Journal of Information Science 36(6), 798–811 (2010)

[19] Giles, C.L., Kurt, D.B., Steve, L.: CiteSeer: an automatic citation indexing system. In: Proceedings of the Third ACM Conference on Digital Libraries. ACM, Pittsburgh (1998)
[20] Meier, W.: eXist-DB. (exist-db.org, Released under the open source GPL licence, 2009) (cited February 2011), http://exist.sourceforge.net/
[21] Google Books Search (GBS) engine. (Google, 2004) (cited February 2011), http://books.google.com/
[22] WorldCat (Online Computer Library Center (OCLC), 2001-2010 2008) (cited (February 2011), http://www.oclc.org/worldcat/default.htm
[23] WorldCat Search API (OCLC - WorldCat, 2009) (cited (February 2011), http://worldcat.org/devnet/wiki/SearchAPIDetails
[24] MARC standards (Library of Congress Network Development and MARC Standards Office, 1999 December 5, 2007) (cited February 2011), http://www.loc.gov/marc/
[25] Councill, I.G., Giles, C.L., Kan, M.Y.: ParsCit: An open-source CRF reference string parsing package. In: Proceedings of the Language Resources and Evaluation Conference (LREC 2008), Marrakesh, Morrocco (May 2008)
[26] O'Madadhain, J., Fisher, D., Nelson, T., White, S., Boey, Y.-B.: JUNG 2.0. (Released under the open source GPL licence, 2009) (cited February 2011), http://jung.sourceforge.net/index.html
[27] Brin, S.: A Library to Last Forever (The New York Times, October 8, 2009) (cited June 2010), http://www.nytimes.com/2009/10/09/opinion/09brin.html?_r=1
[28] Networked Digital Library of Thesis and Dissertations (NDLTD, 1996-2010) (cited February 2011), http://www.ndltd.org

E-Learning Support for Logic Education

Marie Duží, Marek Menšík, Martina Číhalová, and Ludmila Dostálová

Department of Computer Science, FEI, VSB – Technical University Ostrava,
17. listopadu 15, 708 33, Ostrava-Poruba
marie.duzi@vsb.cz, {mensikm,m.tina.cihal}@gmail.com,
ldostal@kfi.zcu.cz

Abstract. In this paper we introduce two e-learning systems, namely eLogika and (LMS) ORGANON. Both systems are apt for teaching logic and should improve the quality of the teaching. The ORGANON system is primarily aimed at solving tasks and practicing logical formalisms by means of interactive exercises. The eLogika system is intended to support effective automated testing of students' knowledge together with automatic generation of suitable exam tests. We also describe the application of data-mining methods which can contribute to the improvement of e-learning systems by adjusting particular tests in accordance with students' capabilities and needs.

Keywords: Logic, teaching, e-learning, data-mining, test rating.

1 Introduction

E-learning systems have become a widespread tool for knowledge proliferation. The pros and cons of e-learning methods are in general well-known. The greatest advantage of these systems is the possibility to access a given system wherever and whenever the student needs to, provided he/she has access to the Internet. The greatest disadvantage is also obvious; hardly any computer system can fully compensate the direct human contact between teacher and student. As the teaching practice shows, this contact can never be fully dispensed with. Yet, teaching practice cannot be reduced only to the traditional face-to-face lectures presented by teachers. One of the reasons is the fact that education has currently become a matter of mass-scale production. For instance, at VSB-Technical University of Ostrava we have thousands of students in the so-called internal form and hundreds of students in the so-called combined form. These distance students are primarily a target group for e-learning methods, because much of their study is self-study. Every fortnight they can personally take part in lectures and seminars provided by their tutors. Though they have the possibility to discuss problems that may have emerged during their self-study with their tutors, the e-learning programs are indispensible for them. On the other hand, the tutors obtain feedback on the quality of a particular e-learning support. The crucial point here is the adequacy and adjustment of the e-learning support with respect to a particular subject. In other words, it should be tailored to the needs of the subject and the students. Not only that; the tutors also need e-learning support. It should facilitate an effective production and evaluation of exercises and exam tests.

E. Ariwa and E. El-Qawasmeh (Eds.): DEIS 2011, CCIS 194, pp. 560–568, 2011.

In this paper we concentrate on the subject of logic. The goal of this paper is twofold. First, we are going to introduce a method for test generation and evaluation. Second, we wish to demonstrate the merits stemming from combining e-learning with data-mining methods. In brief, this symbiosis is useful both for the tutors and the students. The tutors can adjust their methods according to the students' level of knowledge; the students get feedback on their weak points.

The paper is organized as follows. In Section 2 the *LMS Organon* system is described. In Section 2.1 we set out the reasons that motivated us to develop such a system. In Sections 2.2 and 2.3 the system itself is described together with the process of its development. Section 3 deals with the *eLogica* system. In Section 3.1 we concentrate on automatic test generation, and in Section 3.2 we discuss test evaluation methods. Finally, in Section 3.3 the application of data-mining methods to the test results and the way they are exploited is briefly described.

2 LMS ORGANON

In this section we are going to introduce the e-learning system *LMS ORGANON* designed for teaching logic. Unlike ordinary e-learning systems it is able to handle logic exercises including correcting, grading and providing elementary feedback. Moreover, it is able to handle administration of teaching, namely assigning individual homework, collecting delivered homework, grading, storing achieved results and providing data-mining. Hence the web tutor fulfils two requirements. Firstly, it helps students during their study to practice exercises on their own. Secondly, it helps teachers to diminish the burden of teaching administration and trivial consultations.

2.1 Motivation of the Project

Rudimentary logic courses are usually designed for large amount of students (groups of several hundred are not exceptional) who have no experience with handling formulae. Successful completion of such a logic course usually presupposes substantial portions of individual work because it rests on solving logic examples in order to obtain skills of how to work with formulas. Though solving examples is the best way to learn modern logic and become familiar with logic notation, there is a deplorable lack of relevant literature. Textbooks with sample solutions and a key for correct answers are very rare, if not entirely missing. Therefore, teachers not only have to create large amount of exercises each year themselves; they also have to correct and evaluate these exercises, and finally consult the results with students. Due to the mass-scale character of introductory logic courses, such a task is beyond the capacities of the teachers involved. However, the problems that students usually deal with and want to consult are of such a character that they can be easily solved and answered in an automatic way. So the appropriate computer-based assistance may solve the problem. For these reasons we decided to develop the Learning Management System (*LMS*) *ORGANON*.

The system should

- increase the efficiency of a student's homework by
    - providing permanent control while practicing exercises
    - answering student's questions immediately as they arise

- diminish the teaching burden by
  - reducing the amount of consultations
  - handling the administration and evaluation of students' assignments.

Originally we looked for some existing software that would be able to support a rudimentary course on logic. The number of didactic courseware packages oriented to introductory logic courses is quite large. Among them the most elaborate ones are presumably CSLI's courseware packages 'Tarski's Worlds', 'Language, Proof and Logic', 'Hyperproof', 'The Language of First-Order Logic', and 'Turing's World'.[1] Such software packages usually provide sophisticated didactics. However, they all ignore the administration of teaching, like correcting, grading and storing the achieved results. Moreover, they usually provide only a fixed structure for exercises. On the other hand, systems designed to satisfy the administrative requirements (e.g. e-learning systems) are able to deal with the administration of teaching, but they do not reflect the special needs of logic as a discipline. They were designed for those fields of study that have an encyclopaedic character, which is inadequate for logic exercises since the only way of practicing as well as testing is *via* test questions. Moreover, these systems usually do not make it possible to write logical symbols or draw diagrams. That is why we eventually decided to create a new e-learning system that will accommodate both these functions: it will be able to handle logic exercises (like specialized logical software) as well as manage the administration of teaching (in a similar way as e-learning systems do).

2.2 Description of the LMS ORGANON

The e-learning system *LMS ORGANON* has been primarily designed for introductory logic courses. Thus it satisfies the special needs of this discipline. Firstly, it is able to accommodate logic symbolism as well as the other sorts of visualizations like tables or diagrams. Secondly, it reflects the fact that logic exercises are not about memorizing knowledge (and thus cannot be practiced only by test questions); rather, they are of a computational, inferential and constructional character, which means that not only the solution but the whole process of solving the task at hand must be taken into account. The system consists of three segments:

- *The database of logic exercises*,[2] which
  - makes it possible to create an exercise structure according to the needs of the course
  - provides a number of exercises for individual practicing as well as testing
  - generates various fully comparable test variants

- *A grading module* to administer students' homework,[3] which
  - generates individual exercises for a graded assignment
  - facilitates electronic elaboration as well as submission of homework
  - manages to correct and evaluate homework

[1] For information on these packages, see, for instance, [4].
[2] For details on the database of logic exercises, see [3].
[3] For details on the Grading Module, see [2].

  - stores the achieved results including the record of the exercise, the student's solution, the results of automated correcting and grading
  - collects statistical data to provide feedback (data-mining)

- *A practicing module* that assists students in practicing the exercises;[4] this module can operate in three different modes:

  - To show (step by step) the *sample solution* of the exercise and provide relevant explications
  - To *consult* with students their own way of solving the exercise by
    - checking the equivalency of transformations when the step is finished (automatic)
    - alerting when a mistake like non-equivalence appears (automatic) as well as by showing the mistake (if required by a student)
    - providing hints for the next step or performing that step directly including the relevant explanation (if required by a student)
  - To *correct* the transformation when finished (not during transformation) and comment upon it in the same way as a graded assignment

2.3 The Development of the System

The prototype of the web tutor ORGANON was first used in the teaching process in the autumn of 2006, in the University of West Bohemia. Based on the experiences with this prototype a new version was introduced in the autumn of 2010. The database accommodates basic topics of modern formal logic and is gradually extended in order to accommodate also deduction and the application of logic in natural-language arguments (analysis and formalization, sentential negation, equivalence of sentences, validity of informal arguments).

The ORGANON system has no non-standard software or hardware needs. The only necessary facility is a browser. It is user-friendly and does not require any special abilities to be operated; all that is presupposed is that the user can handle and click a mouse. Thus it can be easily introduced at other universities and organizations. Currently we are preparing versions for other languages than just Czech in order to provide an international user interface.

Special attention has been paid to *user interface*. Firstly, it was necessary to accommodate a logic notation that respects common conventions, as well as solve the problem of compatibility between computers. Moreover, special interfaces were necessary for various sorts of exercises like truth-tables, diagrams, models and counterexample constructions. Finally, ORGANON is suitable for *disabled students*, in particular blind ones.

Since logic education is very much based on visualization of logical forms and most of the didactic mnemonic aids are visually based, we faced the problem of finding an alternative way to communicate logic and logic formalism to these students. It appears that an audio response might be a plausible solution and some positive results in this respect have been achieved.

---

[4] For details on the Practicing Module, see [2].

The ORGANON system has been primarily designed for practicing logical formalism. Thus the students become familiar with logical forms and diagrams and hopefully rid themselves of anxiety or even formalism-phobia. The precise structure of the database of exercises enables students to develop the skills required to handle special formal tasks. This is the first step on the way to becoming familiar with logic and logical thinking. Moreover, practical experience with the concepts of logic makes these concepts more familiar to students. Thus logical concepts will no longer remain incomprehensible entities for them. Conceptualization and formalization helps students to effectively organize and manage their knowledge.

In particular the students of the combined form who have no possibility to take part in regular practice lessons appreciate the help of ORGANON. The percentage of those students who make use of Organon and yet failed to pass the first exam attempt is now 10% lower than the percentage of those who do not make use of Organon. Thus we can expect that the use of the full version which is planed for the Autumn 2011 will notably increase the number of successful students.

Of course, an e-learning system cannot fully substitute a human teacher. Yet it can prove very useful by reducing the necessity to practice mechanical manipulations with formulas in lectures and seminars by providing an individual 24-hour service to each student. Thus it leaves space for discussing really interesting and inspiring topics during the lessons.

3 The eLogika System

Logic as an abstract, *a priori* discipline dealing with knowledge specification and correct reasoning is a very important component of all scientific disciplines. Thus lessons on logic appear in some form in almost all educational subjects. Logic is often an obligatory subject in the area of computer-science and mathematics, as it is also at VSB-Technical University Ostrava. Evidently, in mathematics and computer science logic is indispensable, because we deal here with theorem proving, knowledge representation and inferable/computable knowledge.

Our teaching practice makes it obvious that a successful command of logic develops the students' abilities of abstract thinking and valid argumentation. On the other hand, teachers need their students to provide feedback on weak/strong/difficult issues in teaching logic. Due to the large amount of students, an individual contact between teacher and student is almost impossible. In this situation an e-learning software can help a lot.

In what follows we are going to introduce our e-learning system *eLogika* as applied and used at VSB-Technical University Ostrava. This system has been developed at the Department of Computer Science and the results tested and consulted with the investigators of the joint project ORGANON, Learning Management System for logic, as described above.

3.1 A Brief Introduction to *eLogika*

eLogika is a web application so that Internet access is possible *via* browsers (Mozilla, IE). This system conveys didactic materials for courses on logic together with test generation and evaluation. Whoever wants to use the system must register and the process of authentication must be approved for the user. There are four roles for which a user can be registered: administrator, secretary, guarantor, and tutor. The administrator manages the system licence for other schools and registers the secretary. The secretary can register and edit courses and users within the registered school.

The guarantor is the unique role with all rights reserved for subject administration, students and testing. He/she registers tutors for the respective groups (teachers of the training courses), students and course graduation conditions. He/she has the right to generate exam as well as training tests and insert didactic material.

The tutor is a guarantor assistant; he/she has the right to generate training tests but not exam tests. These training tests serve for students to practice the subject without registering the results in the evaluation system. Tutors communicate with the students assigned to them and their main task is to assist students in solving their tasks. Though a student is a user with minimal rights, the system has been developed primarily for the needs of students. Students can use didactic materials and solve tests, thus in turn providing feedback to tutors.

3.2 Automated Test Generation and the Rating System

The e-learning system should facilitate the work of both the students and the teachers. Automatic generation and assessment of tests is a very useful facility for teachers. There are two main goals we want to achieve. First, we generate a large number of test variants for a common thematic topic, and second, we develop an effective test-rating and evaluation system.

eLogika has an open database that can be edited, updated and extended by a guarantor or tutor. The database consists of themed topic segments which in turn contain particular tasks. A task is usually presented to students as a question to which there are a number of correct and incorrect answers. The total number of answers is adjustable. The student's task is to tick the correct answers. When creating the test the user (guarantor or tutor) has to fill in the form with the test title, time limit, test blocks and total rating. Each block represents an adjustable percentage of total rating. The total sum of blocks must be 100%.

The user formulates a number of questions for each thematic block. Then the user has the option to choose one of the two possible ways of test generation, either manually or automatically. If the automatic variant is chosen then the selected test blocks are displayed. The user determines the number of questions and answers together with the type of an answer for each block. There are three types of answer: "exactly one correct answer", "at least one correct answer" and answering by "completing the form" (the students write down their answers into a pre-defined form). For instance, consider a question to which four incorrect and four correct answers are assigned. If the user picks the variant with four answers of the type "at least one correct answer", then the system generates from the question 58 different test variants. Hence another very useful aspect of the system is flexibility and a great variety of test variants belonging to a particular subject matter.

Another important and useful facility is an option to choose a theory elaboration. For instance, in the application used at VSB-Technical University Ostrava we usually go for [1]. After clicking on the 'theory' item in menu, the list of chapters is displayed. To each chapter there are references to those tests that serve to practice the content of the chapter. Thus it is possible to generate training tests tailored to the subject matter under discussion.

The second goal we follow is an effective test evaluation and rating. The well-known problematic issue of automatic testing is the fact that students can sometimes happen to answer correctly even though they do not know the correct answer. Thus it is important to adjust the rating system in such a way as to reduce random successful marking to a minimum. To this end we introduce the following evaluation strategy. In general, a correct answer yields positive credit points, whereas an incorrect answer results in negative credit points. Moreover, if the student marks all the answers as correct and some of them are incorrect, the resulting number of credit points becomes zero. Similarly, if the student does not tick any answers and some of the answers are correct, the resulting number of credit points also becomes zero.

As mentioned above, the questions are generated from the pre-defined blocks, each of which has a weight percentage assigned to it. Unless the resulting number is zero (due to the student's ticking either all the answers or none), each answer is evaluated separately with respect to the weight-percentage of the block. There are three strategies of calculating the positive/negative number of credit points:

(1) A correct/incorrect answer yields a positive/negative number that is calculated with respect to (a) the weight of the block, (b) the maximum number of credit points assigned to the whole test, (c) the number of questions in the block, and (d) the number of answers.

(2) The positive number assigned to a correct answer is calculated as *ad* (1). However, the negative number due to an incorrect answer is calculated with respect to the percentage pre-defined in the template of the block.

(3) In case the answer is of the form-completing type the students formulate their answer in prose using their own words. For this reason the evaluation cannot be automatic; rather it must be performed manually by the teacher who assigns to the answer a percentage of validity. The resulting number of credit points is then calculated with respect to this percentage.

> ***Example of rating:***
> Block weight = 20%
> Maximal test rating = 40 credits
> The number of questions in the block = 2
> The number of answers in the block = 4
> The number of credits per answer = ((20 / 100) * 40) / 2) / 4 = 1
>
> ---
>
> The number of credits per answer = 1

This evaluation system can yield a negative number of total credit points. In this case the negative number is replaced by zero. It turned out, in fact, that such an evaluation system serves our intended goals very well. The students soon realized that random clicking is to no avail, and that intensive studying is the best way to success.

3.3 Statistics and Data-Mining

The system collects information data from the student's test activities throughout the semester. For each question the following data are considered to be the most important ones in order to provide plausible feedback to teachers about the results and level of knowledge of their students:

- The number of attempts to solve the question
- How many times students changed their answers
- The time span students needed to solve the question

Some other important data that enter as input into the data-mining methods are as follows:

- Who the tutor is; who the guarantor is
- The day and time of problem-solving, the date and time of checking the test
- The number of questions and the number of answers
- The category of the question (topic)
- The final rating of the test
- The day and time when students have a practice course

The values of these attributes are then processed by particular data-mining methods, for instance, association and clustering.

Association methods are applied in order to propose to students a proper course throughout their process of studying. These methods discover categories of poor or sketchy knowledge and their mutual relations. Thus a student can be advised on which topics should be studied in more detail and which are his/her weak points. For example, the system may discover that a student has problems with semantics and for this reason does not understand the proof methods and cannot select an optimal one. In such a case the system has the student to thoroughly over the definition of interpretation, models and the notion of logical entailment as a necessary condition to master proving theorems well.

The clustering methods are useful for teachers (guarantors and tutors) because they group together students sharing a common category of problems. Thus the teacher can adjust training tests to tailor them to a particular group of students with sharing similar problems.

The development of the eLogika system started a year ago with the aim to make examination easier both for teachers and students. In case there are hundreds of students, it is very difficult for a teacher to effectively manage exam tests and the whole process of examination in general. On the other hand, the students who have little personal contact with their tutors are afraid of an automatic, non-human testing. In such a situation we need a system that would generate both training tests and exam tests; e-logica is such a system. Moreover, this automatic testing is always combined with a face-to-face oral examination. Thus we have a feedback and can adjust the the databse of tests in accordance to students' needs.

Before we decided to develop our own system, we looked around for existing ones, of course. First we tested our internal system Barborka, then Moodle, and others. Yet none of them proved to fit our needs well. The e-logica system is still a work in progress, and since we do not have much experience with its application in practice as yet, we cannot evaluate enough data to say that the system is really a success. Yet a notable progress has been observed in particular with respect to students' knowledge and abilities to explain their own solution, proof and logical reasoning in general.

Moreover, the two systems we introduced in this paper are mutually interconnected. The results of eLogika system are used for the ORGANON development, and vice versa.

4 Conclusion

In this paper we presented two e-learning systems for logic, namely *LMS ORGANON* and *eLogika*. The former is primarily focused on logical formalism and manipulation with formulas while the latter is oriented to test generation and evaluation. We also briefly described the application of data-mining methods in order to be able to adjust particular training tests in accordance with the strong and weak sides of individual students and groups of students. Both applications are web-oriented so that the students as well as the teachers can make use of them whenever and wherever they have access to the Internet. The systems are currently being applied in the course of Mathematical Logic, VSB-Technical University Ostrava, together with traditional methods, with a view to successfully accomplishing the stage of testing and fine-tuning the systems.

Acknowledgements

This research has been supported by the internal grant agency of VSB-TU Ostrava, Project No. SP2011/56, "Knowledge approach to the modelling, simulation and visualization of software processes", by ESF, Project No. CZ.1.07/2.2.00/07.0217, "ORGANON – Learning management system (LMS)", and by the Grant Agency of the Czech Republic, Project No. 401\09\H007.

References

[1] Duží, M.: Mathematical Logic. A textbook of the VSB-Technical University Ostrava (2002) (in Czech), `http://www.cs.vsb.cz/duzi/`

[2] Dostálová, L., Lang, J.: ORGANON - The Web Tutor for Basic Logic Courses. Logic Journal IGPL, doi:10.1093/jigpal/jzm021

[3] Dostálová, L., et al.: Odkud a jak brát stále nové příklady. ZČU, Plzeň (2009)

[4] The OpenProof Project. Stanford's Center for the Study of Language and Information (CSLI), Retrievable at `http://ggww.stanford.edu/NGUS/Openproof/`

Performance Analysis of Transport Control Protocol Flavours in the Existence of Packet Reordering Phenomena

Waheed Yasin, Hamidah Ibrahim,
Nor Asilah Wati Abdul Hamid, and Nur Izura Udzir

Faculty of Computer Science and Information Technology,
Universiti Putra Malaysia,
43400 UPM, Serdang, Selangor Darul Ehsan, Malaysia
waheedos80@yahoo.com, {hamidah,asila,izura}@fsktm.upm.edu.my

Abstract. The impact of packet reordering on the performance of TCP flavours is presented in this paper by analyzing four TCP flavours that are TCP-Reno, TCP-Newreo, TCP-SACK, and TCP-Linux. Thus, to do so an experiment is conducted based on simulation environment using Network simulator NS-2 version 2.33. The simulation results show that sending rate is decreased as a result of packet reordering phenomena; however, TCP-Linux performs better than other TCP flavours when there is more than one flow due to the large initial value of TCP-Linux slow-start threshold (ssthresh). These results demonstrate that packet reordering negatively affect the performance of TCP flavours. The finding of this paper can be summarized in that packet reordering may have a catastrophic effect on the performance of the TCP flavours, and the expected throughput from using these TCP flavours might not be achieved.

Keywords: TCP, Packet Reordering, Packet Loss, NS2.

1 Introduction

The Transmission Control Protocol (TCP) is one of the core protocols of the Internet Protocol Suite. TCP operates at a transport layer of the Open System Interconnection (OSI) reference model, which is responsible to provide reliable and ordered delivery of data from a program running on one computer called "Sender" to another program running on another computer called "Receiver". TCP is used in common applications as e-mail, file transfer, and web browsing. TCP controls segment size, the rate at which data is exchanged, and network traffic congestion [1].

Although TCP is the standard for Internet based communication networks, it has some limitations such as, consuming bandwidth in signaling, slow starting, which make it suffers from the under utilization in high speed networks [2]. For that reason and to address these drawbacks many high speed TCP variants were proposed in the last few years such as TCP-Reno [3], TCP-Newreno [4], TCP-SACK [5], and TCP-Linux [6]. These variants modify the congestion avoidance algorithms of TCP to be more suitable in high speed networks; however, they are still using the same fast

E. Ariwa and E. El-Qawasmeh (Eds.): DEIS 2011, CCIS 194, pp. 569–579, 2011.

retransmit and fast recovery algorithms used by the standard TCP, which enable TCP to detect and recover from packet loss earlier than the timeout period. It is well known that the fast retransmit and fast recovery algorithms of TCP may misinterpret packet reordering as packet loss. This misinterpretation leads to that TCP performs poorly in networks with severe packet reordering [7]. Consequently, packet reordering may have a bad impact on the performance of the TCP flavours. Thus, the expected throughput might not be achieved.

The aim of this work is to study the impact of packet reordering on the performance of some of TCP flavours. The organization of the paper is as follows: Section 2 presents packet reordering phenomenon and its major causes. The research methodology of this work is explained in details in Section 3. Section 4 presents the results of the experiments. Section 5 presents the discussion about the result. Some of the recent researches on packet reordering and its impact on TCP's performance are reported in section 6. Finally, section 7 presents the conclusion and findings of this work; also it gives some suggestions for future works.

2 Packet Reordering

In this section, the packet reordering phenomenon and its major causes are presented. Packet reordering is a phenomenon in which packets with higher sequence numbers are received earlier than those with smaller sequence numbers. For example, a TCP Sender sequentially sends four packets: P1, P2, P3, and P4. They may arrive at the TCP Receiver in the following order: P1, P3, P2 and P4, where P2 is reordered. Fig. 1 illustrates the packet reordering phenomenon.

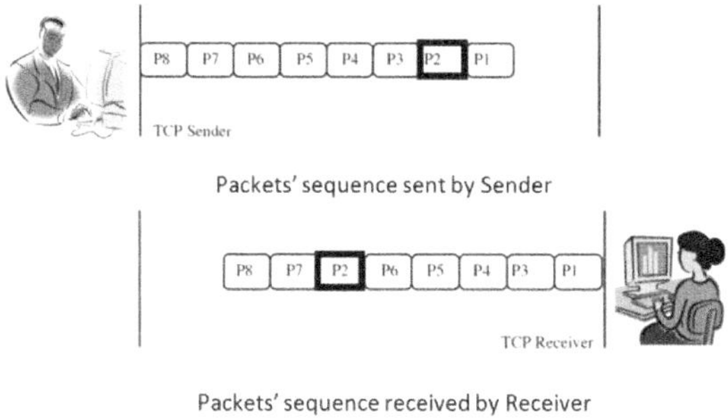

Fig. 1. Packet reordering phenomenon where P2 is reordered

2.1 Causes of Packet Reordering

The major causes of packet reordering are listed in [7] and [8] which can be summarized as follows:

- Multipath routing:

  Multipath routing is a strategy to spread the traffic load across the network in order to decrease network congestion. This strategy enables packets of a particular source to be forwarded over multiple routes to a particular destination.

Thus, these packets might be reordered on reaching the destination because of the differences in path delays [9].

- Route instability:

Route instability might happen as a result of many reasons such as shaky links, heavy load or burst traffic and unexpected changes in the wireless environment. Thus, route instability causes in forwarding packets on different paths and being reordered on arrival at the destination.

- Parallelism in current routers:

Current routers support a technique where packets belong to a particular traffic flow can be forwarded over cheaper multiple parallel links with lower capacity connected to the next router. Due to that packets might be of different sizes and the links' bandwidths might be different, packets might experience different transmitting time, which leads packets to arrive in different order. Also, some kind of integrated circuits which are used to accelerate the speed of transmitting might cause packets reordering.

- Retransmissions issued by Data Link layer:

Data Link layer of the OSI model has some retransmission mechanisms which have been proposed to overcome transmission errors experienced in wireless networks. These packets are retransmitted after the losses are discovered, which might be intermixed with other packets that were sent from the same traffic flow.

- The inactivity of router forwarding:

During updating routing tables, routers may block forwarding packets for a while, which may lead in interspersed between buffered packets and new packets causing packet reordering.

2.2 The Impact of Packet Reordering on TCP

As it is known, TCP relies on the use of a cumulative Acknowledgment (ACK) to declare the receipt of a segment [2]. The rate of receiving ACKs at Sender side determines the injection speed of TCP segments into the network and its associated destination. Due to a frequent packet reordering, TCP falsely retransmits segments and keeps its congestion window unnecessarily small. Moreover, it loses its ACK-clocking, and misinterprets the estimated Round-Trip Time (RTT) and Retransmission Time-Out (RTO). These are described in details in [8].

2.2.1 False Packet Retransmissions

An ACK is generated by a TCP Receiver to inform the TCP Sender the next sequence number that it is expecting to receive. TCP attempts to differentiate between packet reordering and packet loss using number of duplicate-Acknowledgments (dupACKs). RFC 2581 suggests that a TCP Sender should consider three or more dupACKs as a sign of that a packet has been lost. Due to packet reordering, TCP misinterprets it as a lost packet. Consequently, TCP unnecessarily invokes fast retransmit function to retransmit the packet that seems to be lost and fast recovery function to reduce the TCP sending rate. Therefore, TCP performs poorly in networks with severe packet reordering.

Let us consider the above example in Fig. 1; packets arrive at a TCP Receiver in the following order: P1, P3, P4, P5, P6 and P2. When P1 arrives, the Receiver sends an ACK to ask for the next packet which is P2, while P3 arrives, which indicates that P2 is missing.

Therefore, the Receiver sends an ACK for P2 again (this ACK is a dupACK). In this example, the reordered packet P2 causes only one dupACK; while referring to Fig. 1 P2 arrives after P6 does, then P2 triggers four dupACKs. Consequently, TCP Sender misinterprets it as a packet loss and P2 is retransmitted. Fig. 2 illustrates Packet loss Vs. Packet Reordering.

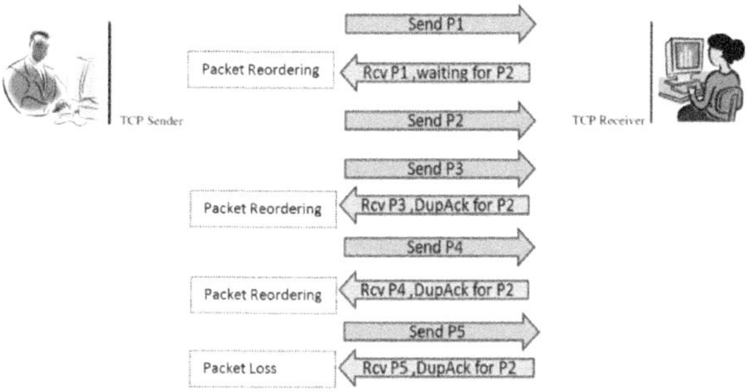

Fig. 2. Packet loss Vs. Packet reordering, where four dupACKs used as an indication that a packet has been lost

2.2.2 Making the Congestion Window Small without a Real Need

The fast recovery and fast retransmit functions are always triggered together. A false fast retransmission might lead to halve the congestion window, which causes in bandwidth under utilization.

2.2.3 ACKs Reordering

Packet reordering even causes ACKs to arrive at the Receiver out of order. In this paper, receiving segments out of order is called Forward-Path reordering, while ACKs reordering is called as Backward-Path reordering. An illustration of Forward-Path reordering and Backward-Path reordering is shown in Fig. 3. Assume segments are sent from Sender in the order P1, P2, P3, while P1 arrives after P2 at the destination. This represents a Forward-Path reordering. On the other hand, assume the ACKs sent by Receiver have the order as follows: A2, A3, and A1 arrive at Sender respectively, which describes the Backward-Path reordering. ACKs reordering may push TCP to inject more than one segment per ACK. This results in network congestions.

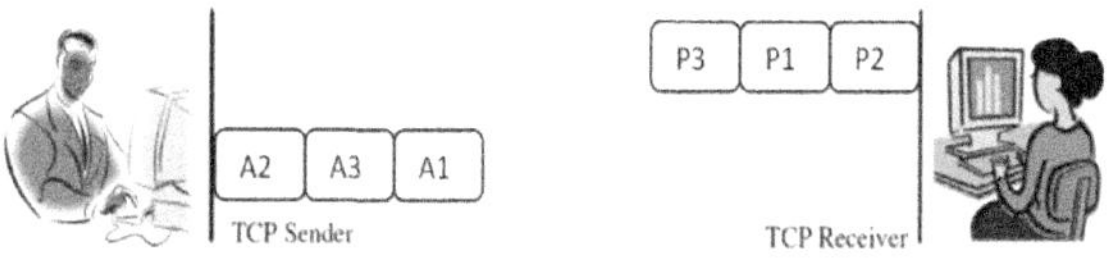

Fig. 3. Forward-Path Reordering and Backward-Path Reordering

2.2.4 Miss-Computing for RTT and RTO

A retransmitted packet might results in miss-computing of the RTT and RTO. That is because Sender becomes unable to determine whether ACK is declared according to the first packet transmitting or packet retransmitting.

3 Materials and Methods

In this section the research design is presented in details. Then we explain the TCP flavours which are used in this work. Finally, the simulations which are conducted in this work are explained.

3.1 Research Design

This research is a quantitative research, where we run an experiment to evaluate the impact of packet reordering on TCP. The design name is called "Static Group Comparison Research Design".

Pre-Experimental Design			
Group1 TCP-Reno	**Treatment** injecting packet reordering error	**Test** running simulations	**Observation** average throughput
Group2 TCP-Newreno			
Group3 TCP-SACK			
Group4 TCP-Linux			

Fig. 4. Research Design

The research design is illustrated in Fig. 4 where there are four groups. Each group represents a TCP flavour. These groups are presented in section 3.2. The treatment in our experiment is the packet reordering error rate injected in the network. The test here is running the simulation which is explained in details later. The average throughput of the network is the observation in our research design, which is also explained later.

3.2 TCP Flavours

Four TCP flavours are used in our experiment which are: TCP-Reno, TCP-Newreno, TCP-SACK, and TCP-Linux. In this subsection a brief explanation on the TCP flavours which are used in this work is given.

a. TCP-Reno: this flavour increases the Maximum Segment Size (MSS) by one as soon as it receives an ACK indicating the recipient of the packet. However, if three dupACKs are received, it halves the congestion window (cwnd), and invokes fast retransmit and fast recovery functions.
b. TCP-Newreno: this flavour has been proposed to improve retransmission when running the fast recovery function of TCP Reno, where for every dupACK, it continues sending new packets to keep the transmit window full. TCP-Newreno flavour assumes a pointer to a hole, and goes over to send packets follow this unacknowledged packet. These holes are filled whenever the RTO is reset.
c. TCP-SACK: TCP-Selective Acknowledgments or shortly TCP-SACK is a TCP flavour where, Receiver can inform Sender about all segments that have arrived successfully. Thus, the sender needs only to retransmit the segments that have really been lost.
d. TCP-Linux: A slow-start threshold (ssthresh) is used to enter the congestion avoidance stage when it is exceeded by cwnd. However, the initial ssthresh in TCP-Linux is large. Also, the first slow-start stage is completed after a loss. While, this ssthresh is updated at the end of each slow-start, subsequent slow-starts are activated by timeouts.

4 Simulations

The simulation tool which is used in this work is based on the Network Simulator (NS-2) version 2.33. NS-2 is an open source software, which is free and available on the Information Sciences Institute (ISI) web site http://www.isi.edu/nsnam/ns/.

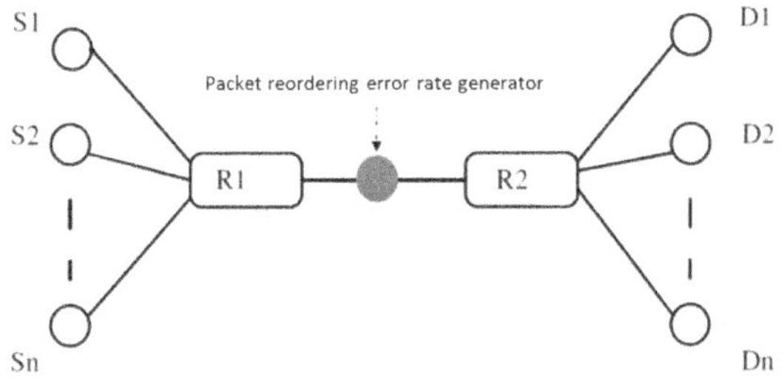

Fig. 5. Simulation Topology

In this work, Dumbbell topology is used, which is a general approach in computer networks. The Dumbbell topology consists of a number of nodes which are called Sources (S1, S2, ..., Sn) and Sinks (D1, D2, …, Dn), where n>2. The Sources are connected to a single router (R1). This router (R1) is connected to another router (R2) via a slow speed media. The router (R2) is connected to the Sinks. The Dumbbell topology is usually used to study some aspects of different network scenarios such as congestion control and fairness. The Dumbbell topology is illustrated in Fig. 5, where the packet reordering error rate generator is introduced between router R1 and R2. All sources and sinks are connected to the bottleneck link (R1-R2) through different links with different delays which are varied randomly from 0.1 to 0.9 ms in order to alleviate the phase effect. The application, which is applied between sources and sinks, is File Transfer Protocol (FTP) and the settings of the simulations are listed in Table 1.

We run the simulation for each TCP variants 12 times. Six of them were run with a number of flows equal to 1; and the rest with a number of flows equal to 4, where we chose these numbers randomly.

Table 1. NS-2 Simulations settings

Item	Setting
Bandwidth of the link between R1 and R2	10 Mbps
Link Delay between R1 and R2	50 ms
Queuing Type	DropTail
Bandwidth of the links between all Sources and R1	10 Mbps
Bandwidth of the links between R2 and all Destinations	10 Mbps
Link Delay of links between all Sources and R1	Random [0.1:0.9] ms
Link Delay of links between R2 and all Destinations	Random [0.1:0.9] ms
Reorder Error Rate	0.0, 0.2, 0.4, 0.6, 0.8, 1.0
Packet Size	1500 Bytes
Buffer Size	50 Packets

5 Results

The throughput is defined by the number of application bits transferred in seconds, and the average throughput is calculated by Equation (1).

$$\text{Average throughput} = \frac{\sum_{i=1}^{N} F(i)_{\text{throughput}}}{N} \tag{1}$$

where N is the number of flows, F(i)throughput is the throughput of flow number i. The average throughput is measured in bits per second. (In our experiment, N takes two values 1 and 4, which are chosen randomly.)

After running the simulation we considered that all TCP variants were affected by packet reordering phenomena.

Fig. 6 illustrates the simulation results of all the TCP variants when the number of flows is one (N=1). The packet reorder error rate varies from 0% to 10 %. Fig. 7 illustrates the simulation results of all the TCP flavours when the number of flows is four (N=4), while the packet reorder error rate varies from 0% to 10%. The packet reordering rate is the percentage of the traffic with reordering packets to the traffic without any reordering packets.

6 Discussion

Referring to Fig. 6, it can be observed that all the TCP flavours almost perform the same. At 2% packet reordering rate, the average throughput dropped severely from 46

Mbps to 1.5 Mbps for TCP-Linux and close to that for all variants. Then, they continue sending with low average throughput. This is because packet reordering results in triggering the packet loss which forced TCP to invoke fast retransmit function to retransmit the packet, and fast recovery function to decrease sending rate. This kind of impact is called false packet retransmissions which affects negatively the performance of TCP, which has been discussed earlier.

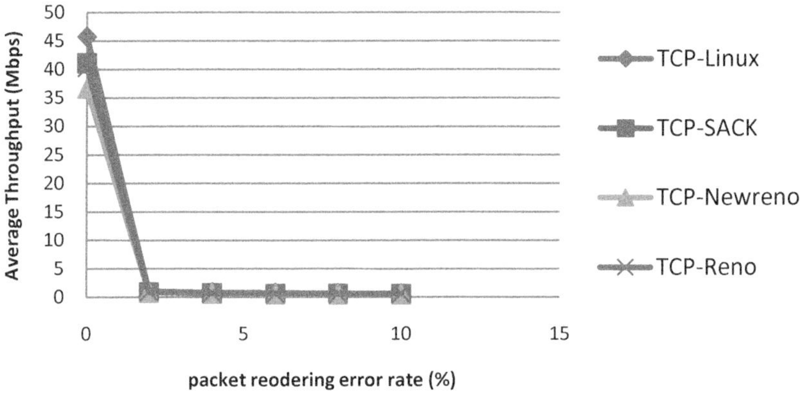

Fig. 6. Simulation results when N=1

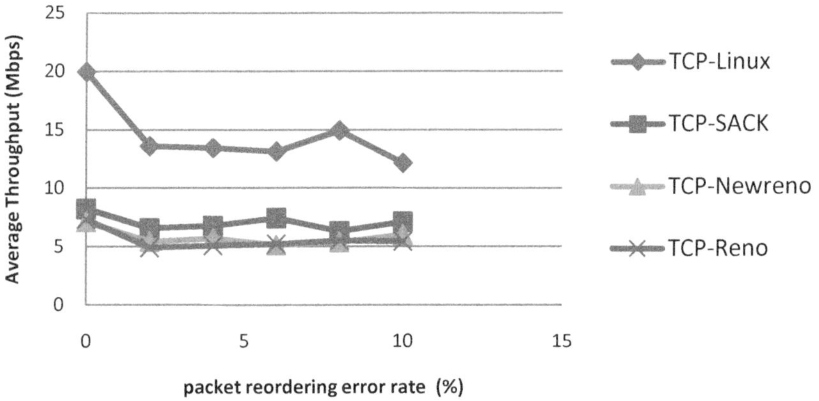

Fig. 7. Simulation results when N=4

Referring to Fig. 7, it can be observed that TCP-Linux is affected by packet reordering, where at 2% packet reordering rate, the average throughput dropped from 20 Mbps to 13 Mbps; however, for other variants the average throughput is below 7 Mbps. For TCP-Linux, at 8% packet reordering rate the average throughput increased slightly and dropped again. TCP-Linux performs 85% better than others because the initial ssthresh in TCP-Linux is large, as we mentioned earlier. Also, TCP-SACK performs more than 35% better than TCP-Newreno and TCP-Reno because Receiver can inform the Sender about all segments that have arrived successfully. Thus, the Sender needs only to retransmit the segments that have really been lost. For TCP-Reno and TCP-Newreno, a problem appears when a packet, which is reordered more than 3 times, is mistakenly interpreted as a packet loss. As a result of that, TCP activates fast retransmit and fast recovery functions. Thus, TCP performs poorly in networks with severe packet reordering error rate.

7 Related Works

Many researches have been conducted to show the effect of the packet reordering on the performance of TCP. In this section, some of the recent researches in this particular field are reported.

In [7], packet reordering phenomena in high speed networks and its impact on high speed TCP flavours have been studied, where it has been concluded that the network with a high packet sending rate experiences a high probability of packet reordering.

In [8], some of the key points that results in packet reordering have been presented. Also, taxonomy of packet reordering has been presented.

In [10], an algorithm which is based on the concept of Reorder Buffer occupancy Density (RBD) has been proposed, which gives information of buffer occupancy that is used to recover from reordering, measure packet reordering, and serve in identifying the causes of reordering.

In [11], an assumption that processing reordered packets in transport wastes time and consumes more resources has been adopted. Thus, a new mechanism called Sorting Reordered Packets with Interrupt Coalescing (SRPIC) has been proposed, based on interrupt coalescing mechanism. That is to reduce packet reordering in the receiver by sorting blocks of reordered packets before resending them.

Also other enhancements have been proposed for targeted applications to combat packet reordering. In [12], a modification to TCP-Friendly Rate Control (TFRC) mechanism has been proposed for multimedia applications that suffer from packet reordering. This modification based on Explicit Congestion Notification (ECN) ECN-TFRC performs better and it is more robust to packet reordering in the network.

In [13], an algorithm has been proposed to combat packet reordering which might be experienced due to moving from a slow access link to a fast one. This algorithm is based on changing the duplicate thresholds (duptresh). It decreases the Bandwidth Delay Product (BDP).

In [9], the effect of links heterogeneity, which is experienced due to the variation in links' delays, has been analysed. This analysis demonstrates that packet reordering over multiple links that are experienced in similar connections especially in wireless networks.

In [14], the effect of concurrency in network processors on packet ordering has been studied, and performed on Intel IXP 2400 processor model. This study also observed that the allocation scheme for the transmit buffer has an effect on packet reordering. Thus, a new scheme has been proposed, which is called "Packet Sort" which enhances the packet reordering up to 35% for Intel IXP 2400 processor.

A measurement study of packet reordering of User Datagram Protocol (UDP) traffic has been presented in [15]. It indicates that packet reordering is asymmetric, temporary, and site-dependent. This study assumes that packet size has no influence on packet reordering.

In [16], a new traffic splitting algorithm which is called Flow Chopped Load Balancing algorithm (FCLB) has been proposed based on the time slot between consecutive packets of the same flow. It has been shown that splitting a flow into multi paths might be performed without causing packet reordering.

The Internet Engineering Task Force (IETF) is currently developing new metrics, such as reorder density, to evaluate the characteristics of packet reordering and its factors in the internet [17] [18].

8 Conclusion and Future Work

In this work, the impact of packet reordering on the performance of TCP has been presented by analyzing four TCP flavours that are TCP-Reno, TCP-Newreno, TCP-SACK, and TCP-Linux. Thus, to show the impact of packet reordering on TCP flavours, an experiment has been conducted based on simulation environment using Network simulator NS-2 version 2.33. The simulation results show that sending rate has been decreased as a result of packet reordering phenomena; however, TCP-Linux performed better than other TCP flavours when there was more than one flow; this is due to the large initial value of TCP-Linux slow-start threshold (ssthresh). These results demonstrate that packet reordering negatively affect the performance of TCP flavours. Consequently, severe packet reordering may have a catastrophic effect on the performance of the TCP flavours, and the expected throughput from using these TCP flavours might not be achieved.

The limitation of this project is that we did not focus on the parameters of the packet reordering, and we use packet reordering as one parameter. Also, we focused on one application which is FTP. As a future work we attempt to study the parameters in the packet reordering such as reordering interval, reordering delay, and using different applications such as Voice over IP (VoIP), which its traffic characteristic is bursty. Also for future works, we attempt to evaluate the impact of packet reordering on different TCP variants such as TCP-BIC and TCP-NCR.

References

1. Charles, Kozierok, M.: The TCP/IP Protocol Suite and Architecture. In: TCP/IP Guide: A Comprehensive, Illustrated Internet Protocols Reference, 1st edn., pp. 121–138. No Starch Press, New York (2005)
2. Jain, R., Hassan, M.: New TCP Standards and Flavors. In: High Performance TCP/IP Networking: Concepts, Issues, Solutions, 2nd edn., pp. 264–279. Prentice Hall, USA (2003)
3. Meo, M., Casetti, C.: An Analytical Framework for the Performance Evaluation of TCP Reno Connections. Computer Networks 37(5), 669–682 (2001)
4. Bahk, S., Joo, C.: Analysis of Start-up Transition Dynamics of TCP NewReno. Computer Networks 36(3), 237–250 (2001)

5. Wu, L.-W., Sheu, T.-L.: An Analytical Model of Fast Retransmission and Recovery in TCP-SACK. Performance Evaluation 64(6), 524–546 (2007)
6. Kuznetsov, A., Sarolahti, P.: Congestion Control in Linux TCP. In: Proceedings of the FREENIX Track: 2002 USENIX Annual Technical Conference Table of Contents, pp. 49–62. USENIX Association, California (2002)
7. Feng, J., Ouyang, Z., Xu, L., Ramamurthy, B.: Packet Reordering in High-speed Networks and its Impact on High-speed TCP Variants. Computer Communications 32(1), 62–68 (2009)
8. Leung, K.-C., Li, V.O.K., Yang, D.: An Overview of Packet Reordering in Transmission Control Protocol (TCP): Problems, Solutions, and Challenges. IEEE Transactions on Parallel and Distributed Systems 18(4), 522–535 (2007)
9. Kaspar, D., Evensen, K., Hansen, A.F., Engelstad, P., Halvorsen, P., Griwodz, C.: An Analysis of the Heterogeneity and IP Packet Reordering over Multiple Wireless Networks. In: IEEE Symposium on Computers and Communications, ISCC 2009, Sousse, pp. 637–642 (2009)
10. Jayasumanaa, A.P., Barea, A.A., Nischal, T.B., Piratlab, M.: Reorder Buffer-Occupancy Density and its Application for Measurement and Evaluation of Packet Reordering. Computer Communications 30(9), 1980–1993 (2007)
11. Demara, P., Crawforda, M., Wu, W.: Sorting Reordered Packets with Interrupt Coalescing. Computer Networks 53(15), 2646–2662 (2009)
12. Chaudhary, R., Jacob, L.: Corruption and Reordering Robust TCP-Friendly Rate Control. Computer Communications 28(1), 97–107 (2005)
13. Daniel, L., Järvinen, I., Kojo, M.: Combating Packet Reordering in Vertical Handoff using Cross-Layer Notifications to TCP. In: IEEE International Conference on Wireless and Mobile Computing: Networking and Communications, WIMOB 2008, pp. 297–303. IEEE Computer Society, Avignon (2008)
14. Govind, S., Govindarajan, R., Kuri, J.: Packet Reordering in Network Processors. In: Parallel and Distributed Processing Symposium, IPDPS 2007, California, pp. 1–10 (2007)
15. Tinta, S.P., Mohr, A.E., Wong, J.L.: Characterizing End-to-End Packet Reordering with UDP Traffic. In: IEEE Symposium on Computers and Communications, ISCC 2009, Sousse, pp. 321–324 (2009)
16. Wang, X., Zhang, W., Chen, X., Niu, C.: Load Balancing Algorithm Using Flow Chopping to Avoid Packet Reordering. In: 2009 International Forum on Information Technology and Applications, IFITA 2009, Chengdu, vol. 2, pp. 193–197 (2009)
17. Bohacek, S., Obraczka, K., Lee, J., Hespanha, J.P.: Hybrid Modeling of TCP Congestion Control. In: Di Benedetto, M.D., Sangiovanni-Vincentelli, A.L. (eds.) HSCC 2001. LNCS, vol. 2034, pp. 291–304. Springer, Heidelberg (2001)
18. Chaudhary, R., Jacob, L.: Corruption and Reordering Robust TCP-Friendly Rate Control. Computer Communications 28(1), 97–107 (2005)

Online Analytical Processing Technique in Personalizing Student Academic Pattern Behavior for UniSZA Students' Results

Azwa Abdul Aziz and Wan Mohd Rizhan Wan Idris

Faculty of Informatics, Universiti Sultan Zainal Abidin, Gong Badak Campus, 21300 Kuala Terengganu, Terengganu, Malaysia
{azwaaziz,wmrizhan}@unisza.edu.my

Abstract. Business Intelligence (BI) refers to skills, processes, technologies, applications and practices used to support decision making. BI technologies provide historical, current, and predictive views of business operations which are normally used to analyze business data. Online Analytical Processing (OLAP) is one of the common BI approaches in quickly answering multi-dimensional analytical queries for analytical purpose. In this paper, we have proposed OLAP technique to be implemented in Academic area. Through this technique, UniSZA students' academic pattern behaviors can be analyzed. A set of data from students' examination results in relational DB is extracted into multi-dimensional model to support OLAP query processing. The results are grouped into several subject areas. Then, the analysis to recognize students' academic pattern behaviors is conducted. From the analysis, the groups of students who have the excellent skills or vice versa can be identified. It also optimizes the time dimension to perform current and historical data analysis. The weaknesses and strengths of the student can also be obtained. Finally, students' future potential areas can be predicted for the next level of educations.

Keywords: Data Warehouse, BI, OLAP, Multidimensional Model.

1 Introduction

Data Warehouse (DW) is databases devoted to analytical processing. They are used to support decision-making activities in most modern business settings, when complex data sets have to be studied and analyzed [1]. DW is processes of taking data from legacy and transaction of database systems and transforming data into organized information in a user friendly format. One of the main components in DW architecture is Business Intelligence (BI). BI refers to skills, processes, technologies, applications and practices which are used to support decision making [2]. BI software leverages on investment in data and systems to provide easy-to-use information that improves decision-making throughout an organization. Online Analytical Processing (OLAP) is one of the main functions offered by BI tools to support multi-dimensional model of DW.

Most of DW projects have been implemented in business sector whereby information is crucial in ensuring the companies' growth and maximizing their profits.

E. Ariwa and E. El-Qawasmeh (Eds.): DEIS 2011, CCIS 194, pp. 580–591, 2011.

Therefore the term 'business' refers to the BI tools such as Statistical Analysis Software (SAS), Business Object and Cognos. The problem is: Can these BI tools support education sector which consists of massive and rapid changes of data transactions? Can the multi-dimensional model support education data of universities which normally contains high volumes of data? How can we utilize the benefits of BI tools in education data? These problematic questions have motivated this research. In this paper, BI technologies are discussed in detailed to be utilized in education area for personalizing the students' academic data based on their results and assessments. Through this technique, the students' levels of strength and weakness upon the specific subject areas can be identified. Besides, the factors that influence the pattern of students' results can be obtained as well.

University Sultan Zainal Abidin (UniSZA) is one of the public institutions of higher learning in Malaysia. It contains of nine faculties including Faculty of Informatics (FiT) which becomes the case study of this research. FiT offers two diploma programs which are Diploma in Information Technology (Multimedia) (DITM) and Diploma in Information Technology (DIT). The data of students from existing transaction systems or any external sources has been taken to be converted into the multi-dimensional model in order to be used in OLAP analysis. The subjects of each program have been grouped into five main fields of computer science such as networking, multimedia, software engineering, programming and databases. The pattern of students' results for each semester can be analyzed using several data mining techniques. This pattern is important to determine the students' potentials on the subject area and to predict the best programs for the next level of students' educations. Furthermore, a list of factors that influence student result can also be obtained.

This study is important to determine whether OLAP technology can suit the requirement of education data. The previous researches show that the data mining has been widely used in business area and scarce in education area. It is because the data in educational field is very dynamic; the data can also be much different between the samples; and teachers or lecturers cannot afford the time and access to the expertise to do the tests on each sample especially in real time [3]. Another reason is in term of the size of data. If the tremendous amounts of data for the students' works are collected, the size of the data on one sample usually becomes small. Therefore, this study only focuses on personalizing the students' behaviors based on the results for each semester and several selected factors for determining students' achievements.

2 Related Research

Prior researches have focused more on implementing the pure data mining techniques and models to discover the educational data. Educational Data Mining (EDM) is an emergent discipline for developing methods to explore the unique types of data from the educational context [4]. In fact, EDM is an application of the data mining techniques implemented in the area of education for obtaining better comprehension on the students' learning processes and acknowledging the ways they participate in it, in order to improve the quality of the educational system [5].

Most of the EDM researches have utilized e-learning environments to implement the data mining algorithm [5, 6, 7, 8, 3]. It is because the collected data is more manageable and accurate since the online systems can record automatically the activities performed by the students. However, there are still studies conducted to analyze the educational data in the traditional learning environment [3]. Merceron & Yasef [3] have used the association rules to analyze the learning data. They have also conducted educational data mining case study for Logic-ITA student data [6]. Zorrilla et al. [5] have proposed a decision making system to help instructors study the pattern of student data in e-learning environment. The system has used Learning Content Management System (LCMS) databases to request a pattern and interpret the results. Talavera & Gaudiso [7] have performed the data mining model to characterize similar behavior groups on the unstructured collaborations spaces. While Hong & Zhang [8] have identified the behavior patterns of ninety eight undergraduate students in business course in Taiwan through the online learning processes.

However, the use of OLAP methods for educational data is still not widely implemented. For instance, Janson et. al. [10] have proposed a conceptual framework for DW approaches on Smart School System. The study has used a general method to apply DW systems into educational perceptive. The study has not focused on analyzing the students' performance behaviors or classifying students' patterns but it has implemented a normal DW architecture to improve school administration data.

In this paper, the benefit of OLAP in analyzing students' achievements and performance is utilized and discussed in detailed. It involves the studies on mining students' behaviors to obtain a pattern of each student individually. Consequently, the lecturers can be helped to use a proper teaching method in order to improve the students' achievements.

3 Proposed Architecture of Educational Data Warehouse (EDW)

DW is a collection of data separated physically from the operational environment that solves real business pain, and contains data of interest to multiple user groups. It comprises of data stored within well-defined period of time which is thus enabling a trend analysis to be carried out. Normally, DW is divided into three main layers in which data from one layer is derived from the lower layer [11]. The layers are data sources, staging area/data repository and presentation.

Data sources layer is the transactions data used for daily or basis operations to support an organization. In education perceptive, the data sources may come from online transaction system (OLTP) such as student result system, attendance system, registration course system or student enrollment system. It also may come from unstructured data such as excel records for student assignments. The data repository layer is DW repository, the core of DW system architecture. It contains of valuable data used for analytical purpose and data mining. It is designed in a star schema model which has dimension and fact tables [12]. Fact tables contain numeric values that present a measurement of business rules. Dimension tables are attributes of the fact tables. Presentation layer offers various functions and technologies in BI tools to manipulate data.

3.1 EDW Design

Fig. 1 shows the architecture of the proposed EDW for UniSZA case study. This design is assigned to personalize students' behaviors. The data for analyzing the students' performance may come from structured or semi-structured data. The structured data is aggregation or generalization of items described by elementary attributes defined within a domain. Relational tables and statistical data represent the most common type of structured data [13]. It is also well organized data stored in database management system (DBMS) such as student record system, student result system or student enrolment system. In UniSZA case, Information Technology Centre is responsible to handle all UniSZA application systems. In order to obtain the data, a set of procedures needs to be followed for the confidentiality of the data.

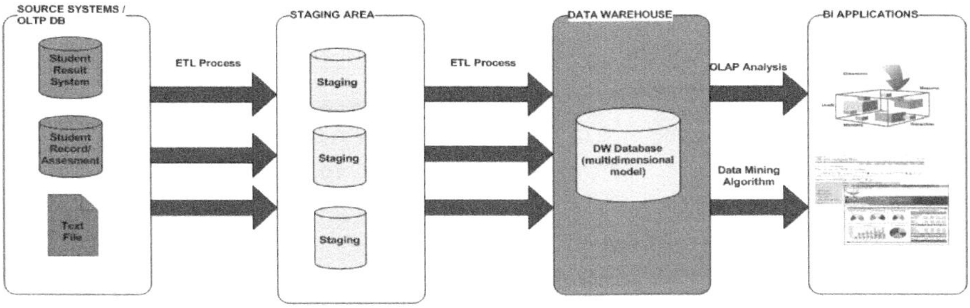

Fig. 1. EDW Architecture For UniSZA

The semi-structured data is data that has a structure with some degrees of flexibility [13]. The data may come from XML document or text file. For example, the lecturers may store the details of student assessment in their own files with different formats. One of the methods for collecting the semi-structured data is to provide a standard format to store data in text files.

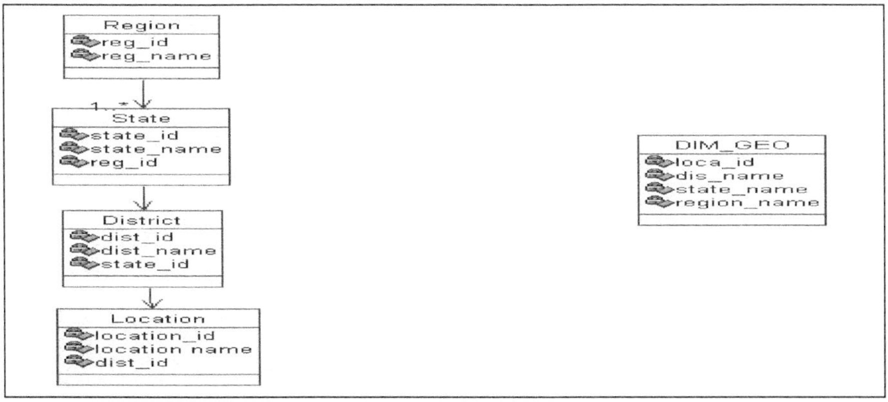

Fig. 2. The Conversion of the Normalized Geographical Information into Geographical Dimension

The selected data will be stored in staging area. The data staging area is everything between the operational source systems and the physical storage of DW. Once the data is extracted to the specified staging area, numerous potential transformations can be done such as cleansing of the data (correcting misspellings, resolving domain conflicts, dealing with missing elements, or parsing into standard formats), combining data from multiple sources, deduplicating data, and assigning warehouse keys [11]. Extract, Transform, Load (ETL) tools will be used to perform those processes/transformations. Once done, the data can be extracted from structured data (relational, statistical) to multi-dimensional model. For example, the relational tables which contain several normalized geographical information entities such as region, country, states, district, and location can be converted into geographical dimension. The primary key of the lowest group hierarchy (in this case location table) becomes the primary key for the dimension tables as shown in Fig. 2.

3.2 EDW Multidimensional Model

Operational databases offer an integrated view of the application, so that each entity of the real world is mapped into exactly a single concept of the schema [12]. The schemas are often represented at an abstract level through the entity relationship model (ERD). ERD needs to be normalized as highest as possible to avoid data redundancy or data inconsistency. The operational databases are optimized for preservation of data integrity and speed of recording business transactions through the use of database normalization.

In contrast, DW needs to become as simple as possible since it integrates a huge of data so that speed of data analysis can be optimally obtained. Frequently the data in DW is denormalized via multidimensional model (star schema). It contains of the facts and dimension tables. The fact tables contain numeric values that present a measurement of business rules. A row in a fact table corresponds to a measurement at the same grain such as the student's CGPA. The dimension table is a description of the fact tables such as student information, time dimension and geographical dimension.

For UniSZA case study, five dimension tables and one fact tables have been initialized for the early stage to analyze the students' performance. Geographical Dimension (D_{GEO}), Time Dimension (D_{TIME}), Program Dimension (D_{PROG}), Student Dimension (D_{STU}), Subject Dimension (D_{SUB}), Assessment Dimension (D_{ASM}) and Student Result Fact (F_{RES}) have been created to perform OLAP analysis. Each dimension may contain its own group of hierarchy. Fig. 3 shows the relationship between a table and former specification of the multidimensional model.

In order to support the OLAP analysis, a cube (C) relation can be described as follows:

$$C = (D_{GEO}, D_{TIME}, D_{PROG}, D_{STU}, D_{SUB}, F_{RES}) \quad (1)$$

Given a particular dimension table Di, the members of the dimension are the values in this table and they are arranged in a hierarchy denoted <i. Given an n-dimensional cube C = D1, . . . ,D_n, F), a cell reference (or reference for short) is an n-tuple (m_i, . . . ,m_n) where m_i is a member of dimension D_i for all i Є [1, n]. A cell is a tuple of cube (F) where cube (F) denotes the data cube [14] of the fact table F.

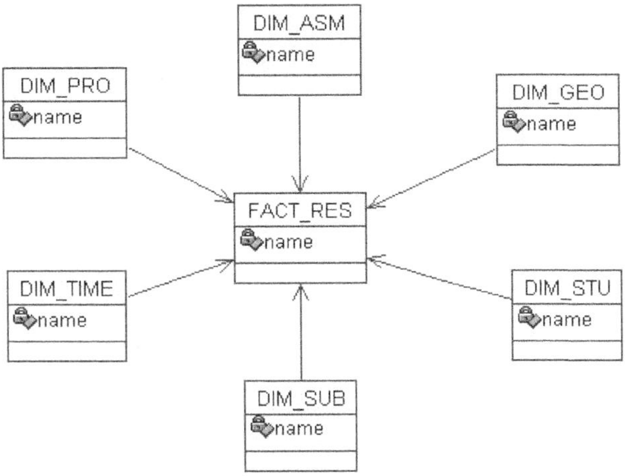

Fig. 3. UniSZA EDW Multidimensional Model

3.3 Descriptive and Predictive EDW Analysis

The data available in DW will be used for the analytical purpose. OLAP application has been used to provide the descriptive analysis. Through this application, the details of student performances over a subject and student achievement records can be obtained. For example, a query to obtain student performance on a specific subject group based on certain amount of time can be triggered by combining Subject Dimension (D_{SUB}), Time Dimension (D_{TIME}) and Student Dimension (D_{STU}) with Fact (F_{RES}).

```
SELECT * from DSUB, DTIME , DSTU, FRES  WHERE
DSUB. .ID = FRES. .ID AND DTIME.ID = FRES. .ID AND DSTU. .ID=
FRES.ID AND
FRES.ID = i
```

The query can be modeled in the relational algebra as follows:

$$\Pi_{pointer}\,(\sigma_{stu\_id = \text{“}i\text{”}}\,(F_{RES})) \tag{2}$$

Where i can be any relevant student ID number from databases

To obtain the description of student information or time dimension, the fact table can be linked to the dimension table as follows:

$$(\Pi_{ID}\,(F_{RES}) \cap \Pi_{ID}\,(D_{SUB}))\ \&\&\ (\Pi_{ID}\,(F_{RES}) \cap \Pi_{ID}\,(D_{STU}))\ \&\&\ (\Pi_{ID}\,(F_{RES}) \cap \Pi_{ID}\,(D_{TIME})) \tag{3}$$

The Predictive Analysis is used to forecast or predict the student achievement or to obtain the potential of student. This analysis must be based on the data gathered in the predictive analysis. Data mining techniques will be used to perform the predictive analysis. However the suitable model to be selected in this project is not decided yet. A study will be conducted to gather the best data mining model to be implemented in the multidimensional model such as AHP, TOPSIS and Fuzzy. The previous researches have utilized various techniques in educational data mining included using statistical classification, fuzzy rule induction and neural network to classify data [9], association rules [3], and clustering techniques [8].

Some major analyses that need to be conducted are:

i. Student Achievement Analysis based on the subject group

The objective of this analysis is to obtain the best subject group of student. Based on Information Technology (IT) subject groups (networking, multimedia, software engineering, programming and databases), the graph of the analysis result can be produced to perform the comparison and to view achievement captured on time frame. Acknowledging the best subject group is important in order to suggest the best computer field for the students to further their higher learning in future. In addition, performing mining techniques to find reason of each student's improvement or vice versa can be done. The fact result has many to one relation with dimension assessment. Each student's assessment (number of quiz taken, attendance, number of assignments done, and frequency of meeting lecturer) will be recorded to know whether the assessment can help the students improve their grades.

ii. Clustering Analysis

Clustering is a process of grouping physical or abstract objects into classes of similar objects. Both clustering and classification are data mining methods. Clustering is an unsupervised classification and classification is a supervised classification [15]. The goal of the clustering technique is descriptive rather than predictive [8]. It can be done by categorizing students into homogenous groups such as groups of programs (multimedia & IT), gender or pointer. Identifying students based on the similar group can help researchers perform more specific analysis against the group. Thus, decision can be made for choosing the best learning method to be applied to a particular group of students. Talavera & Gaudiso [7] have conducted the cluster profiling in mining student of E-Learning environment. Fig. 4 shows an example of clustering students based on several variables in unstructured collaboration spaces.

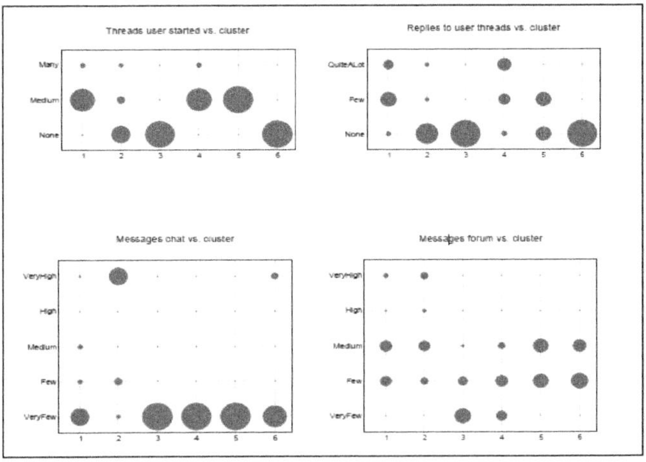

Fig. 4. Clustering Profiles of E-Learning Environment [7]

iii. Predictive Analysis

Predictive analysis is a process of predicting the pattern or future result based on current data available. It is important in Decision Support System (DSS) to make better decision. One of the famous methods in EDW for the predictive analysis is association rules. The association rules find relations between items [6]. Rules have the following form: $X \rightarrow Y$, *support* 40%, *confidence* 66%, which could mean '*if students meet lecturer for consultation more than 10 times, they get pointer more than 3.00 for the subject*", with a support of 40% and a confidence of 66%. Support is the frequency in the population of individuals that contains both *X* and *Y*. Confidence is the percentage of the instances that contains *Y* amongst those which contain *X*.

Let $I = \{I_1, , I_2, ..., I_p\}$ be a set of p items and $T = \{t_1, , t_2, ..., t_n\}$be a set of *n* transactions, with each t_i being a subset of *I*. An *association rule* is a rule of the form $X \rightarrow Y$, where *X* and *Y* are disjoint subsets of *I* having a support and a confidence above a minimum threshold [3].

Let us denote by $|X , Y|$ the number of transactions that contain both *X* and *Y*. The support of that rule is the proportion of transactions that contain both *X* and *Y*: $sup(X \rightarrow Y) = |X , Y| / n$. This is also called $P(X, Y)$, the probability that a transaction contains both *X* and *Y*. Note that the support is symmetric: $sup(X \rightarrow Y) = sup(Y \rightarrow X)$.

Let us denote by $|X|$ the number of transactions that contain *X*. The confidence of a rule $X \rightarrow Y$ is the proportion of transactions that contain *Y* among the transactions that contain *X*: $conf(X \rightarrow Y) = |X , Y| / |X|$.

An equivalent definition is: $conf(X \rightarrow Y) = P(X,Y) / P(X)$, with $P(X) = |X| / n$. Some variables that should be included in the project are shown in Table 1.

Table 1. Some suggested variables to be used in the project

Variable Name	Description
n_quiz	Number of quizzes taken (passed / failed)
n_assignment	Number of Assignment done (pass expected mark/ failed)
n_consultion_hour	The frequency of meeting lecturer to discuss
n_attendence	Number of attendance (class, lab,tutorial)
n_freq_KELIP	The frequency of students using KELIP(online notes/ exercises)
Tota_time_KELIP	Total times using KELIP
Total_carrymark	Total student carry mark

4 Software and Hardware Requirements

The costs of hardware and software involved in implementing DW projects are extremely high. The commercial BI software such as Cognos, SAS, Business Object and Hyperion usually costs thousand up to hundred thousand dollars. As budget constraint is one of the major issues in DW projects, we have decided to use Open Source BI/ETL tools. There are several open source BI and ETL tools available in the market. Most of the existing tools have began in 2005. Even though their capabilities are limited and having bugs compared to the commercial products, they are rapidly being enhanced and improved. The success of using open source tools in DW projects may dramatically reduces costs. As a result, small companies will gain opportunities to apply DW. Eclipse Business Intelligence and Reporting Tools (BIRT), Jesper Reports, Jfree Reports and Palo are examples of DW projects using the open source BI tools. Meanwhile ETL Talend Open Studio (TOS), Kettle ETL and Enhydra Octopus quite are examples of DW projects specifically for data integration and migration purposes.

Table 2. Source to Target Mapping

Source Tables	Conditions	SQL Statement	Target Tables
EMPLOYEES, JOBS	employees.job_id = jobs.job_id	*Select * from MPLOYEES,JOBS where employees.job_id = jobs.job_id*	DIM_EMP
DEPARTMENTS, EMPLOYEES	employees.employee_id =departments.employee_id	*Select * from EMPLOYEES, DEPARTMENTS where employees.employee_id =departments. employee_id*	DIM_DEPT
LOCATIONS, COUNTRIES, REGIONS	locations.country_id = countries. country_id **and** countries.region_id = region.region_id	*Select * from LOCATIONS ,COUNTRIES, REGIONS where locations.country_id = countries. country_id* ***and*** *countries.region_ id = region.region_id*	DIM_GEO
EMPLOYEES, DEPARTMENTS	employees.employee_id =departments.employee_id	*Select * from EMPLOYEES, DEPARTMENTS where employees.employee_id = departments. employee_id*	FACT_SLR

TOS has been used to design the data quality framework for DW [16]. TOS is an open source project for data integration based on Eclipse RCP [17]. TOS leverages the open source model to make data integration available to all types of organizations, regardless of their size, level of expertise or budgetary constraints. It may connect to all source and target systems. TOS is distributed under GPLv2 and has been launched in October 2006. In January 2008, it has been downloaded over 1 million times. In July 2009, the product is totaled 5 million downloads and used by over 300,000 users [18]. TOS operates as a code generator allowing data transformation scripts and underlying programs to be generated either in Java (since v2.0) or Perl (since v1.0).

Its GUI is made of a metadata repository and a graphical designer. TOS is a metadata-driven solution. All metadata is stored and managed in the repository shared by all the modules. The jobs are designed using graphical components. Some of the functionalities offered by TOS are synchronization or replication of databases, right-time or batch exchanges of data, ETL for analytics, complex data transformation and loading and data migration.

The project is developed to translate human resource relational DB into dimensional model for the salary fact table. Table 2 shows mapping tables from relational model to dimensional DW tables.

Then it is converted into ETL jobs as shown in Fig. 5 and Fig. 6 for creating DIM_GEO. Some reports produced from DW are employee's salary report and number of employees' based on region.

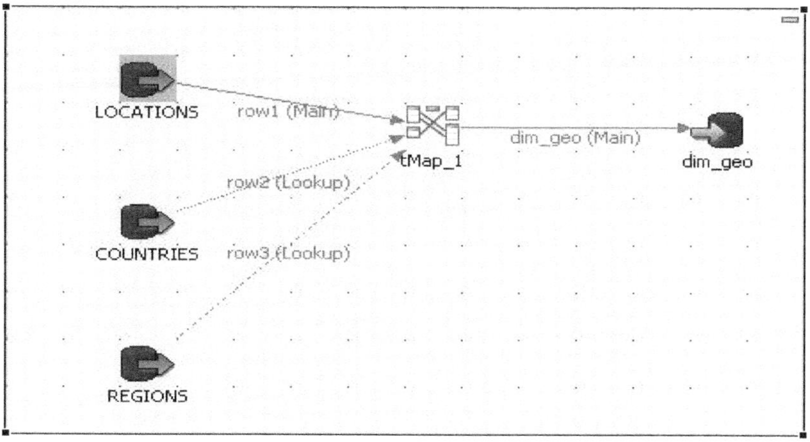

Fig. 5. Populate Data to DIM_GEO

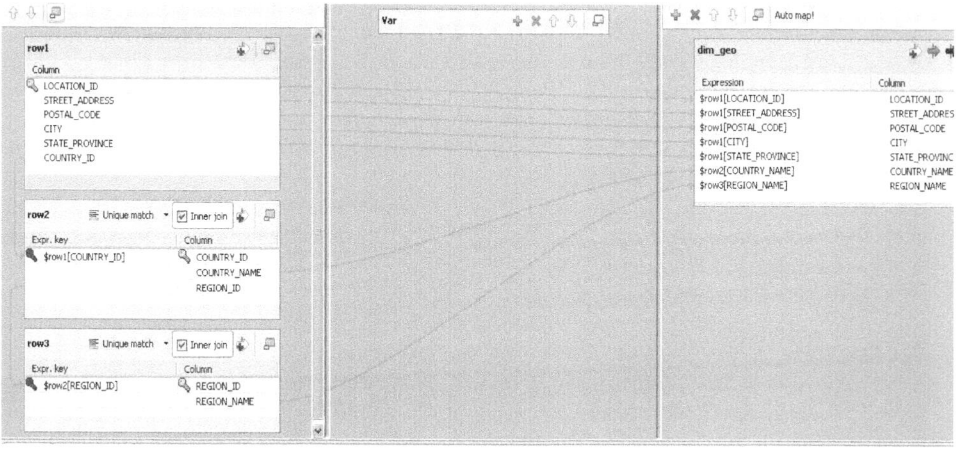

Fig. 6. ETL Job for DIM_GEO using TOS

5 Conclusion

Inspiring by research challenges arising in developing EDM, in this paper we have proposed an EDW architecture to analyze student performance behavior. Data from the transactions systems as well as external sources will be extracted to EDW to design the star schema model. Then the OLAP techniques can be utilized to obtain student achievement and perform descriptive analysis. Decision Support System (DSS) technique and algorithm can be applied in order to forecast the potential of student. We suggest association rules will be used as one part of predictive analysis techniques. It hopes we can derive the best teaching mechanism for a specific student. This project requires the involvement of many people in different computer backgrounds such as database, data mining, decision support system, information retrieval and so on. Future works can be focused on implementing the EDW architecture in more critical areas such as determining the most suitable course for secondary student to pursue study in a higher learning institution or helping in selecting candidates for public universities.

References

1. Angela, B., Cattaneo, F., Ceri, S., Fuggetta, A., ParaBoschi, S.: Designing Data Marts for Data Warehouse. Journal of ACM Transactions on Software Engineering and Methodology 10(4), 452–483 (2001)
2. Cognos: The Right Architecture for Business Intelligence. Cognos Inc., Burlington (2008)
3. Merceron, A., Yacef, K.: Interestingness Measures for Association Rules in Educational Data. In: 1st International Conference on Educational Data Mining (EDM 2008), Montreal, Canada (2008)
4. Romero, C., Ventura, S.: Educational Data Mining: A Survey from 1995 to 2005. Expert Systems with Applications 33(1), 135–146 (2007)
5. Zorrilla, M., Garcia, D., Alvarez, E.: A Decision Support System to Improve e-Learning Environments. In: Proceedings of the 2010 EDBT/ICDT Workshops (2010), doi:10.1145/1754239.1754252
6. Merceron, A., Yacef, K.: Educational Data Mining: A Case Study. In: Proceedings of Artificial Intelligence in Education (AIED 2005). IOS Press, Amsterdam (2005)
7. Talavera, L., Gaudioso, E.: Mining Student Data to Characterize Similar Behavior Groups in Unstructured Collaboration Spaces, In Workshop on artificial intelligence in CSCL. In: 16th European Conference on Artificial Intelligence Workshop on Artificial Intelligence in CSCL, pp. 17–23 (2004)
8. Hung, J., Zhang, K.: Revealing Online Learning Behaviors and Activity Patterns and Making Predictions with Data Mining Techniques in Online Teaching. Journal of Online Learning and Teaching 8(4), 426–436 (2008)
9. Romero, C., Ventura, S., Espejo, P.G., Hervas, C.: Data Mining Algorithms to Classify Students. In: International Conference on Educational Data Mining, Canada (2008)
10. Jason, O., Kannan, W.K., Asirvadam, S., Data Mining, V.S.: Warehousing Approaches on School Smart System: A Conceptual Framework. In: Proceedings of Knowledge Management International Conference, pp. 20–24 (2008)
11. Kimball, R., Caserta, J.: The Data Warehouse ETL Toolkit. Wiley and Sons, New York (2004)

12. Angela, B., Cattaneo, F., Ceri, S., Fuggetta, A., ParaBoschi, S.: Designing Data Marts for Data Warehouse. Journal of ACM Transactions on Software Engineering and Methodology 10(4), 452–483 (2001)
13. Batini, C., Cappielo, C., Francalanci, C., Maurino, A.: Methodologies for Data Quality Assessment and Improvement. ACM Computing Surveys 41(3), Article 16, 1–52 (2009)
14. Gray, J., Chaudhuri, S., Bosworth, A., Layman, A., Reichart, D., Venkatrao, M., Pellow, F., Pirahesh, H.: Data cube: A Relational Aggregation Operator Generalizing Group-By, Cross-Tab, and Subtotals. Data Min. Knowl. Discov. 1(1), 29–53 (1997)
15. Klosgen, W., Zytkow, J.: Handbook of Data Mining and Knowledge Discovery. Oxford University Press, New York (2002)
16. Aziz, A.A., Saman, M.Y.M., Hamzah, M.P.: Using Metadata Analysis and Base Analysis Techniques in DQ Framework for DW. American Journal of Economics and Business Administration 3(1), 112–119 (2011)
17. Talend Open Studio (TOS), `http://www.talend.com`
18. Open source start-up upgrades data integration software, `http://www.networkworld.com/news/2007/042407-talend-data-integration.html`

Performance Analysis of the Proposed Adaptive Gentle Random Early Detection Method under NonCongestion and Congestion Situations

Hussein Abdel-jaber[1], Jafar Ababneh[1], Fadi Thabtah[2], Amjad M. Daoud[1], and Mahmoud Baklizi[1,3]

[1] Department of Computer Information and Network Systems (CINS), The World Islamic Sciences and Education (W.I.S.E.) University, Amman, 11947, P.O. Box 1101
{hussein.abdeljaber,jafar.ababneh,amjad.daoud, mbaklizi}@wise.edu.jo

[2] Department of Management Information Systems (MIS), Philadelphia University, Amman, Jordan
ffayez@philadelphia.edu.jo

[3] Centre of Excellence, Universiti Sains Malaysia (USM) 11800, Penang, Malaysia
mbaklizi@nav6.org

Abstract. The developments in computer networks in recent days such as the internet have increased rapidly. Connections of these networks necessitate resources in order to send their data to their prospective destinations. Further, the connections require high speed router buffers which they route data in high speed. Congestion is one of the main issues that occur at the router buffer cause deterioration of the network performance, i.e. increasing average waiting time, decreasing throughput, etc. Gentle Random Early Detection (GRED) is one of the known congestion control algorithms proposed to detect congestion before the router buffer overflows. In fact, GRED improves the setting of the parameters for the maximum threshold position ($\max threshold$) at the router buffer and the maximum value for the packet dropping probability ($D_{\max}$). This paper proposes an Adaptive GRED algorithm that detects congestion at router buffers in an preliminary stage, and enhances the parameters setting of the $\max threshold$ and the $D_{\max}$. During congestion, the simulation results reveal that the Adaptive GRED drops fewer packets than GRED, and it marginally offers better performance results than that of GRED.

Keywords: Congestion Control, Gentle Random Early Detection (GRED), Adaptive GRED, Parameter Settings.

1 Introduction

With the rapid growth of computer network technologies, especially internet, congestion becomes one of the main issues that may affect the network's performance [13, 14]. Congestion occurs at router buffers of networks when the amount of arriving

E. Ariwa and E. El-Qawasmeh (Eds.): DEIS 2011, CCIS 194, pp. 592–603, 2011.

packets is larger than the available resources [12]. This can cause poor performance for computer networks [7] including the following:

- Increasing both the mean queue length (mql) and the mean waiting time (D) for packets.
- Degrading the amount of packet that are passed through the router buffer successfully (throughput (T)).
- Growing the packet loss probability due to overflow (P_L) result.
- Increasing the packet dropping probability (D_p)

In order to improve the network performance, a group of congestion control algorithms called Active Queue Management (AQM) have been proposed [1, 2, 3, 4, 5, 6, 8, 9, 10, 11]. Examples of AQM algorithms are Random Early Detection (RED) [9], Gentle RED [11], Adaptive RED [10], Random Early Marking (REM) [5], Dynamic Random Early Drop (DRED) [6] and some discrete-time queue analytical models [1, 2, 3, 4] which are built based on some of AQM methods. For instance, the analytical models of DRED, GRED and BLUE were built by analysing a single queue node using a discrete time queues approach [15].

One of the most known AQM methods is RED. Though, the performance of RED may deteriorate in the following many situations. For example, at a certain time, the arrival rate could increase, and as a consequence the RED router buffer builds up and overflows. The congestion measure of RED (aql) could be smaller than the minimum threshold position at the router buffer ($\min threshold$). Consequently, no packets will be dropped even though the RED router buffer is overflowing. Another obstacles of RED is it's dependency on the input setting ($\min threshold$, $\max threshold$, queue weight (qw), $D_{\max}$) [9]. These parameters must set to certain values in order to aderive a satisfactory performance [7, 10]. One possible solution to preventing RED's router buffer to build up quickly is to utilise the instantaneous queue length as a congestion detector rather than the aql. This gives the instantaneous queue length the opportunity to exceed the $\min threshold$ position, and to drop packets probabilistically before the router buffer overflows. DRED, BLUE and GRED algorithms are using the instantaneous queue length as a congestion detector. GRED algorithm was proposed primarily to deal with the the abovementioned limitations of RED. Precisely, GRED improves the process of setting the $\max threshold$ and the $D_{\max}$ parameters, and stabilises the aql at a position named T_{aql}. The T_{aql} position is half way from the $\min threshold$ and $\max threshold$ locations. Thus preventing the router buffer from filling up and becoming larger than the $\max threshold$ position, and as a result fewer packets are dropped.

This paper proposes a new algorithm called Adaptive GRED which aims to enhance the performance of GRED with reference to mql, D and P_L performance measures particularly during congestion. Unlike GRED, the D_{init} value of the proposed algorithm varies from $D_{\max}$ to 0.5 as long as the aql varies from $\max threshold$ to $double \max threshold$, whereas the D_{init} value of GRED varies from $D_{\max}$ to 1.0 as long as the aql value varies from $\max threshold$ to $double \max threshold$. This enables the proposed algorithm of providing further enhancements in setting the input parameters, e.g. $\max threshold$ and $D_{\max}$.

The organisation of this paper is as follows: Section 2 presents the GRED algorithm and the proposed algorithm is introduced in Section 3. The simulation information of GRED and proposed algorithm is provided in Section 4. Section 5 compares the performance evaluation results of GRED and Adaptive GRED, and finally, conclusions and future work are given in Section 6.

2 Gentle Random Early Detection (GRED) Method

GRED has been proposed in [11] to deal with some of RED's issues [6, 10, 11] discussed in the previous section. The pseudocode of GRED is presented in Figure 1, and description (definition) of the parameters used in the pseudocode is defined as follows:

Definition 1. $current\_time$: the current time.

Definition 2. $idle\_time$: the beginning idle time at the router buffer.

Definition 3. n : the number of packets transmitted to the router buffer through an idle interval time.

Definition 4. C : a counter that represents the number of packets arrived at the router buffer and have not dropped since the last packet was dropped.

Definition 5. D_p : the packet dropping probability.

Definition 6. D_{init} : the initial packet dropping probability.

Definition 7. $\mathrm{q\_instantaneous}$: the instantaneous queue length.

Definition 8. qw : the queue weight.

Definition 9. $D_{\max}$: the maximum value of D_{init}.

Definition 10. $q(time)$: the linear function for the time.

Definition 11. T_{aql} : target level for the aql.

Definition 12. $double \max threshold$ is set to $2 \times \max threshold$.

1. Initialisation stage
   $C = -1$;
   $aql = 0.0$;

2. for every arriving packet at a GRED router buffer:
   2.1 Calculate the aql for the arriving packet at the router buffer.
   2.2 Examine the queue status at the router buffer, e.g. empty or not.
   if (the queue at the router buffer = = empty)
   {
   Compute n, where $n = q(current\_time - idle\_time)$;
   $$aql = aql \times (1 - qw)^{n};$$
   }
   else
   $$aql = aql \times (1 - qw) + qw \times q\_instantaneous;$$
3. Determining the congestion status at the router buffer:
   $if\,(aql < \min threshold)$
   {
   $D_p = 0.0$; // No packets have dropped
   Set $C = -1$;
   }
   $elseif\,(\min threshold \le aql\ \&\&\ aql < \max threshold)$
   {
   $C = C + 1$;
   calculate the D_p value for the arriving packet as follows:
   $$D_{init} = \frac{D_{\max} \times (aql - \min threshold)}{(\max threshold - \min threshold)};$$
   $$D_p = \frac{D_{init}}{(1 - C \times D_{init})};$$
   drop arriving packet probabilistically in terms of its (D_p) value;
   Set $C = 0$;
   }
   $elseif\,(\max threshold \le aql\ \&\&\ aql < double \max threshold)$
   {
   $C = C + 1$;
   calculate the dropping probability (D_p) for the arrival packet as follows:
   $$D_{init} = D_{\max} + \frac{(1 - D_{\max}) \times (aql - \max threshold)}{\max threshold};$$

$$D_p = \frac{D_{init}}{(1 - C \times D_{init})};$$

Mark/drop arriving packet probabilistically in terms of its (D_p) value;

Set $C = 0$;

}

else // $if(aql \geq double \max threshold)$

{

Mark/drop every arriving packet with $D_p = 1$;

Set $C = 0$;

}

4. When the GRED router buffer becomes empty
   Set $idle\_time = current\_time$;

Fig. 1. The pseudocode of GRED algorithm

Figure 1 shows that whenever a packet arrives at the router buffer, the aql value is calculated as in RED [9], which it is given in the following equation:

$$aql = aql \times (1 - qw) + q\_\text{instantaneous} \times qw \tag{1}$$

If the aql value is smaller than the $\min threshold$ position, no packets will be dropped, and the D_p value is set to zero. On the other hand, if the aql value is larger than or equal to $double \max threshold$ position, a heavy congestion occurs, and subsequently every arriving packet will be dropped with D_p=1. Finally, when the aql value is between $\min threshold$ and $double \max threshold$ positions, a congestion occurs, and the router buffer drops the arriving packets probabilistically ($0 < D_p < 1$). The result of D_{init} varies between $D_{\max}$ and 1 as long as the aql value varies between $\max threshold$ and $double \max threshold$ positions [11]. This variance produces further tune to the parameter settings of $\max threshold$ and $D_{\max}$. The parameters of GRED, i.e. qw and $\min threshold$ have been set as in RED.

3 The Proposed Adaptive GRED

An adaptive GRED algorithm is proposed to improve the performance of GRED during congestion situations, i.e. deriving better quality results with reference to mql, D, and P_L performance measures. In addition, The proposed algorithm aims to enhance the parameter settings, e.g. $\max threshold$ and $D_{\max}$, of GRED. The Adaptive GRED drops arriving packets incipiently during the congestion. The congestion measure of the Adaptive GRED is aql, and it's parameters are the similar to those of GRED. The calculation of the aql in the proposed algorithm is also similar to that of GRED. Therefore, the Adaptive GRED decides whether to drop every arriving packet as in the GRED algorithm (see Figures 1 and 2). Figure 2 shows the pseudocode of the Adaptive GRED.

1. Initialisation stage
    $C = -1$;
    $aql = 0.0$;
2. For every arriving packet at an Adaptive GRED router buffer:
    2.1 Calculate the aql for the arriving packet at an Adaptive GRED router buffer.
    2.2 Examine the queue status at the router buffer whether empty or not.
    if (The queue at the Adaptive GRED router buffer = = empty)
    {
    Compute n, where $n = q(current\_time - idle\_time)$;
    $aql = aql \times (1 - \mathrm{qw})^{n}$;
    }
    else
    $aql = aql \times (1 - \mathrm{qw}) + \mathrm{qw} \times \mathrm{q\_instantaneous}$;
3. Determine a congestion status at the Adaptive GRED router buffer:
    $if(aql < \min threshold)$
    {
    $D_p = 0.0$; // No packets have dropped
    Set $C = -1$;
    }
    $elseif(\min threshold \le aql \&\& aql < \max threshold)$
    {
    $C = C + 1$;
    Calculate the D_p value for the arriving packet as follows:

$$D_{init} = \frac{D_{\max} \times (aql - \min threshold)}{(\max threshold - \min threshold)};$$

$$D_p = \frac{D_{init}}{(1 - C \times D_{init})};$$

Mark/drop arriving packet probabilistically in terms of its (D_p) value;

Set $C = 0$;

}

$elseif(\max threshold \le aql \;\&\&\; aql < double \max threshold)$

{

$C = C + 1$;

Calculate the marking/dropping probability (D_p) for the arrival packet as follows:

$$D_{init} = D_{\max} + \frac{\frac{(1 - D_{\max})}{2} \times (aql - \max threshold)}{\max threshold};$$

$$D_p = \frac{D_{init}}{(1 - C \times D_{init})};$$

Mark/drop arriving packet probabilistically in terms of its (D_p) value;

Set $C = 0$;

}

$else$ // $if(aql \ge double \max threshold)$

{

Mark/drop every arriving packet with $D_p = 1$;

Set $C = 0$;

}

4. When the Adaptive GRED router buffer becomes empty
   Set $idle\_time = current\_time$;

Fig. 2. The pseudocode of proposed Adaptive GRED method in detail

The main difference between GRED and the Adaptive GRED is in calculating the D_{init} value. The way of computing D_{init} in GRED is shown in Figure 1. Whereas the Adaptive GRED computes the D_{init} according to the following equation:

$$D_{init} = D_{\max} + \frac{(1 - D_{\max})}{2} \times \frac{(aql - \max threshold)}{\max threshold} \quad (2)$$

To clarify, when aql value is between $\max threshold$ and $double \max threshold$ positions, the calculated D_{init} value of GRED varies from $D_{\max}$ value to 1.0 as the aql value varies from $\max threshold$ to $double \max threshold$ position. However, in the Adaptive GRED, the D_{init} value increases from $D_{\max}$ value to 0.5 as long as the aql value increases from $\max threshold$ to $double \max threshold$ position. This gives more improvements for the parameter settings of $\max threshold$ and $D_{\max}$ than those of GRED. The proposed Adaptive GRED makes its router buffer overflows at times lower than those of GRED.

Furthermore, the Adaptive GRED also offers better P_L performance as well as slightly better performance of mql and D than those of GRED when a high congestion has occurred (see Section 5 for further details). Lastly, the running time of the Adaptive GRED is the amount of time of all events. i.e. packet arrivals and departures.

4 Simulation Information of GRED and Adaptive GRED

It has been assumed that α denotes the packet arrival probability at the router buffer in a fixed time unit called slot [15], and β denotes the probability of packet departure from the router buffer in a slot. The packet arrivals can be modeled using a Bernoulli process and packet departures can be modeled using a geometrically distribution. The geometrically distributed means $\frac{1}{\alpha}$ and $\frac{1}{\beta}$ are used for the packet inter-arrival times and service times, respectively. GRED and the proposed method

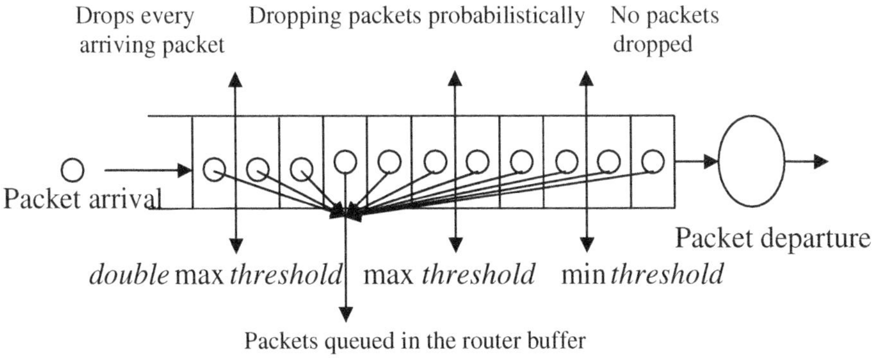

Fig. 3. The single router buffer for GRED and proposed Adaptive GRED

are simulated based on discrete-time queue [3, 15] that uses a slot as a time unit. In each slot, packet arrival and/or departure may exist. The compared algorithms are simulated by applying them in a network consisting of a single router buffer node (see Figure 3). Packet arrival and departure are implemented in a single mode. The scheduling mode is First Come First Served (FCFS). The GRED and the Adaptive GRED simulations are implemented in Java, on i7 processor machine with 1.66 GHz, and on 4 GB RAM.

5 Performance Evaluation Results

This section compares GRED and the Adaptive GRED with reference to different performance measures, e.g. (mql, T, D, P_L, D_p), in order to determine which algorithm offers better performance. The parameters of compared methods are similar and have been set as follows:

α and β were set to [0.18-0.93] and 0.5 respectively aiming to create noncongestion ($\alpha < \beta$) and congestion ($\alpha > \beta$) situations. The maximum number of queue node rooms (K) is finite and equal to 20, and this number can should generate accurate performance measure results at small queue sizes. $\min threshold$, $\max threshold$, $D_{\max}$ and qw have been set to 3, 9, 0.1 and 0.002, respectively as in RED [9]. $double \max threshold$ is set to 18 as in GRED [11]. In the simulation, a large number of slots have been used (2000000) in order to generate a warming-up period. The warming-up period ends when the system reaches a steady state.

The performance measure results are evaluated by varying the values of α. Hence, the decision which method provides better performance is only given based on the values of α. After the system reaches the steady state, the evaluations of performance measures can be achieved. For each α, the simulations are run ten times in which in each run, the seed value for the random number generator is changed aiming to delete a prejudice in the performance measure results. Also, the performance measure result for each α represents the mean of ten run times for that value. All performance measure results versus α values are shown in Table 1 and Figures (4-5). Table 1 displays mql, T and D results of the GRED and the Adaptive GRED versus α. While the results of P_L and D_p versus α are illustrated in Figures 4 and 5, respectively.

Table 1 shows that the GRED and the Adaptive GRED give similar mql, T and D results when no or light congestion ($\alpha < \beta$) is occurring. On the other hand, if heavy congestion occurs ($\alpha > \beta$), the Adaptive GRED offers slightly better mql and D results than those of GRED. This is since the Adaptive GRED's router buffer drops more packets than that of GRED in these circumstances, i.e. $\alpha > \beta$ (see Figure 5). It is observed from Table 1 that the compared algorithms generate similar T results regardless the congestion situation.

Table 1. mql, T and D performance results of GRED and proposed Adaptive GRED

	GRED			Proposed Adaptive GRED		
α	mql	T	D	mql	T	D
0.18	0.457	0.1787	2.5604	0.457	0.17866	2.5601
0.33	1.279	0.3277	3.903	1.279	0.3277	3.9038
0.48	6.1005	0.4689	13.009	6.088	0.4688	12.984
0.63	13.578	0.497	27.299	13.3645	0.4975	26.861
0.78	14.7936	0.49885	29.6551	14.3547	0.49909	28.761
0.93	14.9456	0.499	29.9316	14.4275	0.4995	28.8811

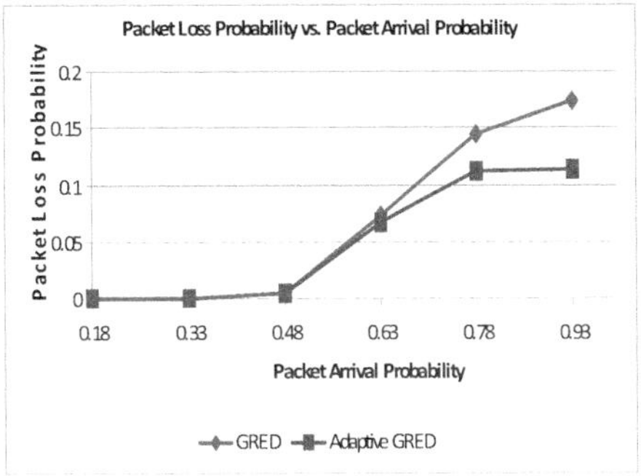

Fig. 4. P_L vs. α

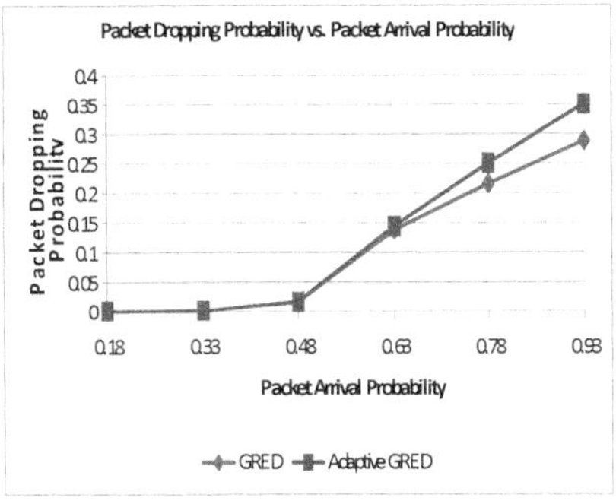

Fig. 5. D_p vs. α

Figure 4 depicts that the proposed algorithm loses fewer packets due to overflow (P_L) than GRED in congestion situations, and this is due to that it drops larger number of packets (D_p) than GRED (see Figure 5). This gives marginally smaller results of mql and D for Adaptive GRED than those of GRED. GRED's router buffer maintains it's aql at value lower than that of the Adaptive GRED when a heavy congestion has occurred. Therefore, Finally, both algorithms offer similar P_L and D_p results when no congestion or light congestion is present.

6 Conclusions and Future Work

An Adaptive GRED algorithm has been proposed to improve the performance of GRED when congestion situation occurs in the networks router buffer. the proposed algorithm slightly provides better mql, P_L and D results than that of GRED. Also, the Adaptive GRED improves the process of parameter settings of $\max threshold$

and $D_{\max}$. This is accomplished by varying the D_{init} value from the value of $D_{\max}$ from to 0.5 as long as the value of aql (its congestion measure) from $\max threshold$ value to $2\times\max threshold$ value. A comparison between GRED and the Adaptive GRED was conducted, the results of the comparison are the following:

- GRED and Adaptive GRED offered similar mql, T, D, P_L and D_p results in no or light congestion situations.
- The Adaptive GRED marginally outperformed GRED with reference to mql and D results in congestion situations.
- The compared methods provide similar T results in congestion situations.
- The Adaptive GRED presented better P_L results than that of GRED, whereas GRED provided better D_p results than that of Adaptive GRED.

In near future we intend to use other arrival processes such as Markov-modulated Bernoulli process (MMBP) in the proposed Adaptive GRED method aiming to determine the performance in bursty traffic and long range dependence.

References

1. Ababneh, J., Abdeljaber, H., Thabtah, F., Hadi, W., Badarneh, E.: Derivation of Three Queue Nodes Discrete-Time Analytical Model Based on DRED Algorithm. In: The Seventh IEEE International Conference On Information Technology: New Generations (ITNG 2010), pp. 885–890. IEEE Computer Society, Las Vegas (2010)
2. Abdeljaber, H., Thabtah, F., Woodward, M.: Traffic Management for the Gentle Random Early Detection Using Discrete-Time Queueing. In: Proceedings of the International Business Information Management Conference (9th IBIMA), Marrakech, Morocco, pp. 289–298 (January 2008) ISBN: 0-9753393-8-9
3. Abdeljaber, H., Woodward, M., Thabtah, F.: Performance Evaluation For DRED Discrete-Time Queueing Network Analytical Model. Proceedings of the Journal of Network And Computer Applications 31(4), 750–770 (2008)
4. Abdeljaber, H., Woodward, M., Thabtah, F., Al-diabat, M.: Modelling BLUE Active Queue Management Using Discrete-Time Queue. In: Proceedings of the 2007 International Conference of Information Security And Internet Engineering (ICISIE 2007), London, U.K., pp. 568–573 (July 2007)
5. Athuraliya, S., Li, V.H., Low, S.H., Yin, Q.: REM: Active Queue Management. IEEE Network 15(3), 48–53 (2001)
6. Aweya, J., Ouellette, M., Montuno, D.Y.: A Control Theoretic Approach To Active Queue Management. Computer Networks 36(2-3), 203–235 (2001)
7. Braden, R., Clark, D., Crowcroft, J., Davie, B., Deering, S., Estrin, D., Floyd, S., Jacobson, V., Minshall, G., Partridge, C., Peterson, L., Ramakrishnan, K., Shenker, S., Wroclawski, J., Zhang, L.: Recommendations On Queue Management And Congestion Avoidance in the Internet. RFC 2309 (April 1998)
8. Feng, W., Shin, K.G., Kandlur, D.: The Blue Active Queue Management Algorithms. IEEE/ACM Transactions on Networking 10(4), 513–528 (2002)

9. Floyd, S., Jacobson, V.: Random Early Detection Gateways For Congestion Avoidance. IEEE/ACM Transactions on Networking 1(4), 397–413 (1993)
10. Floyd, S., Ramakrishnan, G., Shenker, S.: Adaptive RED: An Algorithm For Increasing the Robustness of RED's Active Queue Management. Technical report, ICSI, August 1 (2001)
11. Floyd, S.: Recommendations On Using the Gentle Variant of RED (May 2000), `http://www.aciri.org/floyd/red/gentle.html`
12. Tanenbaum, A.S.: Computer Networks, 4th edn. Prentice Hall PTR, Englewood Cliffs (2002)
13. Thiruchelvi, G., Raja, J.: A Survey On Active Queue Management Mechanisms. International Journal of Computer Science and Network Security 8(12) (December 2008)
14. Welzl, M.: Network Congestion Control: Managing Internet Traffic, 282 pages (July 2005)
15. Woodward, M.E.: Communication and Computer Networks: Modelling With Discrete-Time queues. Pentech Press, London (1993)

Design Model to Select Suppliers for Multi Level – Multi Product Industries

Reza Allahyari Soeini[1], Laleh Tashakori[2], Javad Tashakori Bafghi[3], and Mohammad Mokhtari[4]

[1] Director of Development & Renovation Investment in Industrial Development & Renovation organization of Iran, P.O. Box 1999915511, Tehran, Iran
Allahyari@idro.org
Senior lecturer in Department of Information Technology Engineering, NOORETOUBA Virtual University, P.O. Box 1417964591, Tehran, Iran
Allahyarisoeini_reza@yahoo.com
[2]Department of Information Technology Engineering, NOORETOUBA Virtual University, P.O. Box 1417964591, Tehran, Iran
Tashakkori@ymail.com
[3] Senior lecturer in Department of Chemical Engineering, Yazd, Islamic Azad University, P.O. Box 155, Yazd, Iran
j.tashakori@ iauyazd.ac.ir
[4] Department of Industry Engineering, Science and Research Branch, Islamic Azad University, P.O. Box 19585-466, Tehran, Iran
mokhtari_iau@yahoo.com

Abstract. Supplier selection is a multi-criteria decision making problem which includes both qualitative and quantitative factors. In order to select the best suppliers it is necessary to make a trade-off between these tangible and intangible factors some of which may conflict. Buyer should decide about two problems: which suppliers are the best and how much should be purchased from each selected supplier. The majority of previous supplier selection techniques do not consider strategic perspective. Besides, uncertainty is one of the most important obstacles in supplier selection. For the first time, in this paper, the idea of the algorithm "Knapsack" is used to select suppliers. Moreover, an attempt has to be made to take the advantage of a simple numerical method for solving model. This is an innovation to resolve any ambiguity in choosing suppliers. This model has been tried in the suppliers selected in a competitive environment and according to all desired standards of quality and quantity. To show the efficiency of the model, an industry sample has been uses.

Keywords: Supply chain management, Supplier select, Knapsack, linear programming.

1 Introduction

Increasingly, companies are outsourcing portions of their business processes—from IT to raw material to after sales service to logistics and transportation. According to a recent survey carried out by Accenture, 80% of the companies' surveyed use some

E. Ariwa and E. El-Qawasmeh (Eds.): DEIS 2011, CCIS 194, pp. 604–615, 2011.

form of outsourcing and a majority of these companies are spending close to 45% of their total budget on outsourcing[1]. Manufacturing outsourcing began in 1970s and the 1980s when US jobs in steel and textile moved from Northern states to Southern states. Outsourcing is defined as purchasing ongoing services and parts from an outside company that a company currently provides, or most organizations normally provide for themselves [2]. In a survey carried out by Accenture, it was found that the primary reason for outsourcing is not cost-reduction rather it is the ability to focus on the core competencies. There are various reasons for outsourcing, most notably [3].

1. In many cases the third party can provide procurement services more efficiently. Outsourcing can provide access to specialized technology and operational platforms.
2. Outsourcing can help reduce the staffing levels.
3. The advancement in technologies has made procurement a very specialized service.

Companies try to reduce costs and manage risks. It is important to know that one of the major portions of the firms' expenses is elated to logistics activities which mostly are more than 50% of all companies' costs [4]. Therefore, companies try to manage purchasing tasks. Experts believe that supplier selection is one of the most prominent activities of purchasing departments [5]. But, supplier selection is a difficult problem for managers because the performances of suppliers are varied based on each criterion [6]. In the previous investigations, several methods have been suggested to solve the supplier selection problem. However, most of them have not paid attention to the strategic perspective.

Basically there are two kinds of SSP (supplier selection problem):

(1) Single sourcing. Constraints are not considered in the supplier selection process. In other words, all suppliers can satisfy the buyer's requirements of demand, quality, delivery, etc. The buyer only needs to make one decision, which supplier is the best.

(2) Multiple sourcing. Some limitations such as supplier's capacity, quality, delivery are considered in the supplier selection process. In other words, no one supplier can satisfy the buyer's total requirements and the buyer needs to purchase some part of demand from one supplier and the other part from another supplier to compensate for the shortage of capacity or low quality of the first supplier. In these circumstances buyers need to make two decisions: which suppliers are the best, and how much should be purchased from each selected supplier?

The vast majority of the decision models applied to the supplier selection are linear weighting models and mathematical programming models. The proposed decision model is more comprehensive and competitive rather than other published MCDM models for supplier selection due to its dynamic nature and strategic oriented.

In this model the idea of a backpack algorithm is used. Suppose that the tourist wants to fill their Knapsack with the states may choose from a variety of devices that provide maximum comfort for him. This can be the means of numbers from 1 to n and define a vector of binary variables (Binary) (j = 1,2, ... n) is formulated as math. This means that:

If my object j is selected, otherwise when the tool is easily rate j provides the address and the weight and c is the size of a Knapsack We take the issue of choosing between the binary vectors x, which is provided the limitation. As its objective function takes the maximum value.

This model has been implemented in a company that manufactures Moisture insulation. The company intends to buy products from multiple supplies. Furthermore, we utilize a proposed linear programming model to determine the order quantity from each supplier. The majority of previous models suppose that there is a single product, but our model has been designed for multiple products. In addition, the capacity of warehouse is taken into account as a constraint.

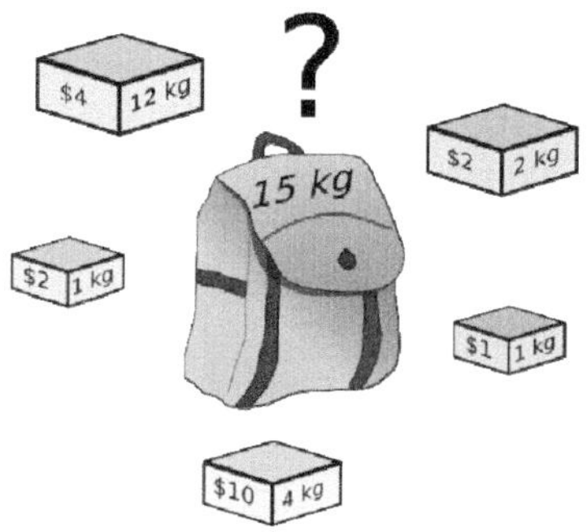

Fig. 1. Knapsack supplier

The organization of this paper is as follows: Section 2 discusses the literature review. Supplier selection model is presented in Section 3. In Section 4, a case study is illustrated. In the first phase, suppliers are assessed based. Then, the order quantity is determined by a linear programming model. Finally, conclusions are presented in Section 5.

2 Literature Review

Supplier selection is a multi criteria decision-making problem. Criteria and decision-making techniques are two important elements in a supplier selection problem. The first research was conducted in 1996, identified 23 different criteria to select suppliers based on questionnaires sent to directors of North American companies. These criteria include quality, delivery, performance, warrant and claim policy, production facilities and capacity, net price, and technical capabilities. Hence supplier selection problem (SSP) is a multiple criteria problem and it is necessary to make a trade-off between conflicting tangible and intangible factors to find the best suppliers. SSP is complicated by the fact that various criteria must be considered in the decision making process. SSP is further complicated by the fact that individual suppliers may have different performance characteristics for different criteria. For example, the supplier who can supply an item for the lowest per unit price may not have the best quality or service performance among the competing suppliers. Supplier selection is therefore an inherent multi-objective decision that seeks to minimize procurement cost, maximize quality and service performance concurrently. Often complicating the

SSP for the buyer is the presence of price discounts, offered by supplier, that depend on the total value of sales volume, not on the quantity or variety of products purchased over a given period of time. In traditional quantity discount pricing schedules, price breaks are a function of the order quantity which existed for each product, irrespective of the total purchasing volume over a given period of time. With the advent of just-in-time (JIT) purchasing, the strategy that calls for ordering smaller lot-size is more practical and feasible. So suppliers are finding it more meaningful to give discounts based on the total value of multi-product orders (i.e. total business volume) placed by a given buyer [7].

In 1973, model was presented a review where focused on industry applications of computer-assisted supplier selection models [8]. In 1991, the literature on supplier selection was categorized by reviewing 74 articles and price, delivery, quality, facilities and capacity, geographic location, and technology capability were identified [9].

In 2001, more research identified four stages in supplier selection problem which consist of problem formulation, formulation of criteria, qualification and final selection. In this study was stated that the majority of authors have focused on final selection stage [10]. In 2004, was presented some published supplier selection models and compared their relative efficiency using the total cost of ownership [11]. Also a model was presented a framework for assessing the flexibility of a supply chain including the flexibility of product delivery system, production system, product development and supply system [12].

In 2007, researchers have presented another literature review according to the purchasing process. Proposed classification is based on single and multiple items and periods [13].

Some authors not only solve the supplier selection problem, but also they determine how much should be purchased from each selected supplier. The majority of these papers have written in manufacturing environments. Researchers combined analytical hierarchy process (AHP) and linear programming to consider both tangible and intangible factors in supplier selection problem [14]. However, their model is deterministic and does not consider uncertainty in human though. In this paper, we extend their model.

In 2000, was utilized DEA for evaluating the suppliers and multi-objective programming for determining the vendor order quantity [15]. Researchers considered a supply network consisting of a manufacturer and its suppliers. They formulated a nonlinear programming model and determined how much of each raw material and component part to order from which supplier according to the capacity of suppliers and manufacturer. It is assumed that demand is stochastic. However, they only determined the order quantity and they did not select the suppliers [16].

In 2007, was proposed a multi-objective supplier selection model under stochastic demand conditions. Stochastic supplier selection has been determined with simultaneous consideration of the cost, quality, delivery and flexibility according to the limitations of capacity [17]. In the same year, presented a new method based on analytical hierarchy process improved by rough sets theory and multi-objective to determine the number of suppliers and the order quantity allocated to these suppliers.

In addition, was considered discount [18]. More research scholars optimized Price, lead-time and rejects (quality) to select the best vendor in the field of outsourcing. They applied quantity discount in the model [19].

3 Supplier Selection Model

3.1 Parameters in the Model

MAX_{Profit_s}	Show that this matrix, each of which suppliers have produced the raw material and what points are earned according to the algorithm.
P_i	Price per unit of raw material i.
G_i	Returns the amount of raw material i.
P_{max_s}	Maximum price of raw materials provided by the supplier s.
C_i	Amount of raw material i needed to make unit of product j.
dem_j	Predicted value for the product j.
r_s	Supplier price discount rate s.
d=1,2,…,D	Desired criteria for supplier selection.
i=1,2,…,I	Raw material
s=1,2,…,S	Supplier
j=1,2,…,J	The criteria for selecting suppliers.
T	Period
$stor_i^t$	Storage Capacity
$capacity^t$	Production capacity
Line	Production line
H_j^t	Production capacity of each production line
W_s	Supplier Rating Owner.
B_s	Vector producing value for supplier selection.
Cu	
M	Maximum points are looking for supplier selection.
X	If $W_d \leq Cu$ then $X_d = 1$ else $0 \leq X_d < 1$

3.2 Variables in the Model

F_j	Amount of product j produced.
$Q_{s,d}$	Total amount of raw materials purchased from supplier s.
$O_{i,s}$	If the material i is supplied by supplier s equal one, otherwise is zero.
V_s	Trade volume with the supplier s.
Profit	The value obtained for the supplier according to criteria d.
Q_s	Total amount of material purchased from supplier s.

3.3 Mathematical Formulation of Supplier Selection Model

Step 1:

Research the key factors of internal and external criteria for supplier selection: the key factors consist of both benefit and cost metrics. The academics collected a list of metrics that have been utilized frequently in international scientific journals. These criteria comprise both qualitative and quantitative ones. These criteria may be different for the purchase of raw materials or standards changes in different conditions. D vector in this model represents criteria.
(d = 1,2,3, ..., D)

Step 2:

Determine the weights of qualified criteria for buyer and each suppliers: B & W vector to produce the selected criteria. According to the buyer will impact how much the selected criteria for choosing their supplier from 1 to 7 are used to form the vector W. According to the criteria selected, each candidate is a supplier of absence from 1 to 7 we use to express these conditions and form a vector B.

Very Low=1, Low=2, Medium Low=3, Medium=4, Medium High =5, High=6, Very High=7

Step 3:

In order to express the criteria for selection which will be B or W and the vector which are superior to selection criteria, for each criterion in the above vectors obtains ratio $\frac{B_d}{W_d}$ Based on the $\frac{B_1}{W_1} \geq \frac{B_2}{W_2} \geq \cdots \geq \frac{B_D}{W_D}$ We evaluated the model.

Means for each measure is bigger than it is the criteria for excellence. If this ratio is equal to two criteria, which criterion is select that the vector D is expressed earlier.

Step 4:

For each producer to be resolved under the model with initial values:
$X_d = 0$, $\text{Profit} = 0$, $Cu = M$.

$$M = \sum_{d=1}^{D} B_d \tag{1}$$

$$\text{MAX}_{\text{Profit}} = \sum_{d=1}^{D} \begin{cases} X_d = {Cu}/{W_d} \\ \text{Profit} = \text{Profit} + X_d \times W_d \end{cases} \quad \Bigg| \; W_d > Cu \tag{2}$$

$$\begin{cases} X_d = 1 \\ Cu = Cu - B_d \\ \text{Profit} = \text{Profit} + W_d \end{cases} \quad \Bigg| \; W_d \leq Cu \tag{3}$$

$$\sum_{d=1}^{D} X_d W_d \leq M \tag{4}$$

MAX_{Profit} represents is a privilege for any supplier what intended to conditions obtains with regard to measures and it is used to select Providers. For convenience put the results of the above algorithm in a matrix. Rows are the raw materials and columns are providers. Score for the provider put in front of material that can provide. Any supplier who bring gotten more points, will be selected to provide the desired ingredients.

Step 5:

According to the matrix MAX_{Profit} we form the matrix $O_{i,s}$ them. The matrix $O_{i,s}$ put one the name in front of what selected supplier for raw material desired and treat the rest zero.

$$O_{i,s} \in \{1,0\} \tag{5}$$

Step 6:

To obtain the amount of materials purchased from selected suppliers, according to the amount of materials needed to build one unit of product, will operate as follows:

A first set of constraints express that demand must be satisfied for each product:

$$\textstyle\sum_r F_j = dem_j \qquad \forall j \tag{6}$$

Plant production capacity is equal to production capacity of each production line:

$$capacity^t = Line \times \textstyle\sum_j H_j^t \qquad \forall j \tag{7}$$

Demand should be less than the capacity of the factory:

$$dem_j \leq capacity^t \tag{8}$$

Define the total quantity of ingredients purchased from each supplier:

$$\textstyle\sum_d Q_s^t = \sum_i O_{i,s} \times \sum_j C_i F_j - G_i^t \qquad \forall s \tag{9}$$

If not part of the materials purchased in accordance Order (Raw Material Returns) must be less than the amount of trade volume with the supplier (Returns amount be deducted from the total amount purchased).

Total amount of materials purchased should be less than storage capacity:

$$Q_s^t \leq stor_i^t \tag{10}$$

Step 7:

Using Q_s Price for each unit provided by the supplier of raw materials, trade volume can be achieved with the selected supplier.

$$\sum_s V_s = \sum_i Q_s P_i \qquad \forall s \qquad (11)$$

$$V_s \leq P_{max_s} \times Q_s \qquad \forall s \qquad (12)$$

$$P_i \geq 0 \qquad (13)$$

Step 8:

Considering the volume of trade with selected suppliers and the amount of the Concession provider considers time fee, you can obtain what raw material purchase costs for the product or products.

$$\min cost = \sum_s (1 - r_s) \times V_s \qquad (14)$$

4 Case Study

Taking into account the quantitative, qualitative, tangible and intangible criteria, at this stage the decision maker has the choice between d1= geographical location, d2= cost, d3= Quality, d4= Mutual trust, d5=time delivery, d6= Management stability for the decision. These criteria make up vector D (D = [d1 ,d2 ,d3 ,d4 ,d5 ,d6]) .

Table 1. Information of supplier

materials	Suppliers	$B[d_1,d_2,d_3,d_4,d_5,d_6]$	B_d / W_d
	S_1	B_1=[7,1,6,5,5,7]	[1,0.14,6,0.83,1,1.4]
I_1	S_2	B_2=[7,7,6,5,5,1]	[1,1,6,0.83,1,0.2]
	S_3	B_3=[7,6,5,5,1,7]	[1,0.86,5,0.83,0.2,1.4]
	S_4	B_4=[7,7,6,5,1,5]	[1,1,6,0.83,0.2,1]
I_2	S_5	B_5=[1,5,6,7,7,5]	[0.14,0.71,6,1.17,1.4,1]
	S_6	B_6=[1,7,5,5,6,7]	[0.14,1,5,0.83,1.2,1.4]
	S_2	B_2=[7,7,6,5,5,1]	[1,1,6,0.83,1,0.2]
I_3	S_3	B_3=[7,6,5,5,1,7]	[1,0.86,5,0.83,0.2,1.4]
	S_7	B_7=[5,5,1,5,7,7]	[0.72,0.72,1,0.83,1.4,1.4]
	S_8	B_8=[6,5,5,7,1,7]	[0.86,0.72,5,1.17,0.2,1.4]
I_4	S_9	B_9=[1,5,5,7,6,7]	[0.14,0.72,5,1.17,1.2,1.4]
	S_{10}	B_{10}=[7,7,6,5,1,5]	[1,1,6,0.83,0.2,1]
	S_{11}	B_{11}=[7,7,5,1,6,6]	[1,1,5,0.17,1.2,1.2]
I_5	S_{12}	B_{12}=[5,1,5,6,7,7]	[0.72,0.14,5,1,1.4,1.4]
	S_{13}	B_{13}=[1,5,6,5,7,7]	[0.14,0.72,6,0.83,1.4,1.4]
	S_{14}	B_{14}=[7,1,6,7,5,5]	[1,0.14,6,1.17,1,1]
I_6	S_{15}	B_{15}=[7,6,5,5,1,7]	[1,0.86,5,0.83,0.2,1.4]
	S_{16}	B_{16}=[7,7,5,5,1,6]	[1,1,5,0.83,0.2,1.2]
	S_{17}	B_{17}=[1,5,7,7,6,5]	[0.14,0.72,7,1.17,1.2,1]
I_7	S_{18}	B_{18}=[7,6,1,7,5,5]	[1,0.86,1,1.17,1,1]
	S_{19}	B_{19}=[7,7,5,6,5,1]	[1,1,5,1,1,0.2]
	S_{20}	B_{20}=[7,7,6,5,5,1]	[1,1,6,0.83,1,0.2]
I_8	S_{21}	B_{21}=[7,6,5,5,1,7]	[1,0.86,5,0.83,0.2,1.4]
	S_{22}	B_{22}=[7,7,5,5,6,1]	[1,1,5,0.83,1.2,0.2]

Based on Vector D criteria, we depict vector W. Then we create vector B for each supplier. Vector B is indicated in Table 1. As can be seen in Table 1, for catering each raw material three suppliers are considered.

W=[7,7,1,6,5,5]

Based on the criteria vector $\frac{B_d}{W_d}$ ratio is calculated for each supplier, and are then sorted (Table 1) .

Having calculated the initial values M=Cu=3, $X_d = 0$, Profit $= 0$ to we set forward to obtain the amount MAX_Profit for each supplier. As can be seen in Table 2, more than one supplier could provide the raw material. Score for each supplier is placed against a raw material that can provide. Score of this supplier is marked in red in Table 2. The supplier is selected which earn more point. In case suppliers gain the same score, one with more points on quality is selected (Table 1).

Table 2. Matrix of supplier's point

MAX $_{profit}$	I_1	I_2	I_3	I_4	I_5	I_6	I_7	I_8
S_1	24.98	0	0	0	0	0	0	0
S_2	26.2	0	26.2	0	0	0	0	0
S_3	26.2	0	26.2	0	0	0	0	0
S_4	0	26.2	0	0	0	0	0	0
S_5	0	17.86	0	0	0	0	0	0
S_6	0	22.43	0	0	0	0	0	0
S_7	0	0	24.86	0	0	0	0	0
S_8	0	0	0	19.86	0	0	0	0
S_9	0	0	0	17.86	0	0	0	0
S_{10}	0	0	0	26.2	0	0	0	0
S_{11}	0	0	0	0	25	0	0	0
S_{12}	0	0	0	0	17.86	0	0	0
S_{13}	0	0	0	0	17.86	0	0	0
S_{14}	0	0	0	0	0	24.14	0	0
S_{15}	0	0	0	0	0	26.2	0	0
S_{16}	0	0	0	0	0	26.4	0	0
S_{17}	0	0	0	0	0	0	17.86	0
S_{18}	0	0	0	0	0	0	24.86	0
S_{19}	0	0	0	0	0	0	26.2	0
S_{20}	0	0	0	0	0	0	0	26.2
S_{21}	0	0	0	0	0	0	0	26.2
S_{22}	0	0	0	0	0	0	0	26.4

We put $\mathbf{O_{i,s}}$=1 against the raw material and the selected supplier in Table 2 (Table 3).

In this case study all purchases are assumed in cash $(r_s = 0)$ and returns on material is zero $(G_i = 0)$. Production value has been investigated in one month period (t=30).

For product A : $F_j = dem_j = 5570$ meter

For product B : $F_j = dem_j = 580$ meter

The total amount of fees paid is **Min cost=162,023,500 Rials(1$ U.S** = 10,454 Rials) for product A and product B (Table 4).

Table 3. Matrix of supplier selection

$O_{i,s}$	I_1	I_2	I_3	I_4	I_5	I_6	I_7	I_8
S_1	0	0	0	0	0	0	0	0
S_2	1	0	1	0	0	0	0	0
S_3	0	0	0	0	0	0	0	0
S_4	0	1	0	0	0	0	0	0
S_5	0	0	0	0	0	0	0	0
S_6	0	0	0	0	0	0	0	0
S_7	0	0	0	0	0	0	0	0
S_8	0	0	0	0	0	0	0	0
S_9	0	0	0	0	0	0	0	0
S_{10}	0	0	0	1	0	0	0	0
S_{11}	0	0	0	0	1	0	0	0
S_{12}	0	0	0	0	0	0	0	0
S_{13}	0	0	0	0	0	0	0	0
S_{14}	0	0	0	0	0	0	0	0
S_{15}	0	0	0	0	0	0	0	0
S_{16}	0	0	0	0	0	1	0	0
S_{17}	0	0	0	0	0	0	0	0
S_{18}	0	0	0	0	0	0	0	0
S_{19}	0	0	0	0	0	0	1	0
S_{20}	0	0	0	0	0	0	0	0
S_{21}	0	0	0	0	0	0	0	0
S_{22}	0	0	0	0	0	0	0	1

Table 4. Production Information (kg / Rials)

materials	Maximum production	C_i Product A	C_i Product B	Q^t_s	P_i	V^t_s
I_1	300000m/24 h	288.5	29	317.5	2,000	635,000
I_2	5000kg/24h	865.5	57	922.5	18,500	17,066,250
I_3	40000 kg/24h	865.5	0	865.5	46,500	40,245,750
I_4	1000000kg/24h	15002	1508	16510	5,350	88,328,500
I_5	100000kg/24h	1442.5	145	1587.5	400	635,000
I_6	20000kg/24h	1731	174	1905	4,000	7620,000
I_7	20000kg/24h	1154	116	1270	1,100	1,397,000
I_8	20000kg/24h	1731	174	1905	3,200	6,096,000
		Min cost				162,023,500

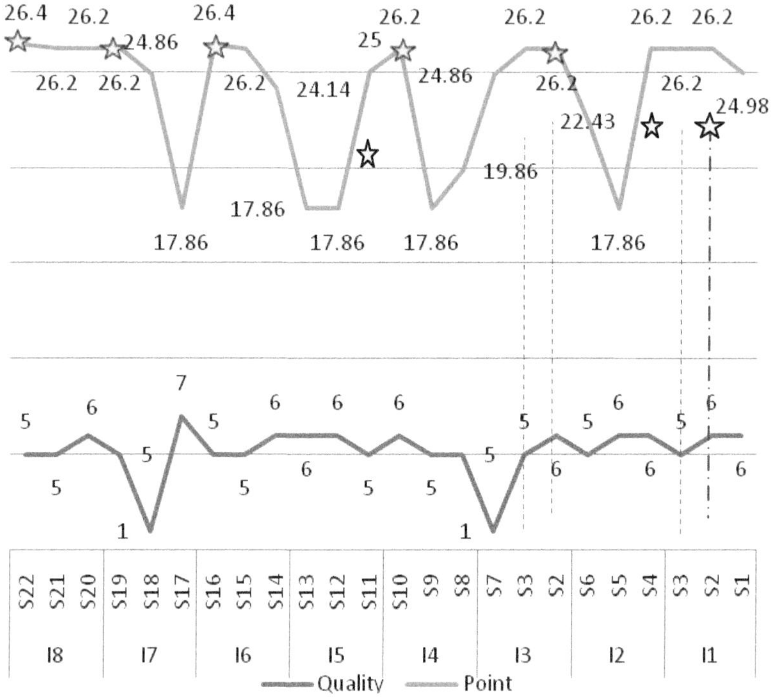

Fig. 2. Chart of Supplier Selection model

As shown in Figure 2 if the two providers obtain same scores, one with more points on quality is selected. (I_1 , I_3)

6 Conclusions

Select suppliers are difficult given the qualitative and quantitative criteria. This research is done in two phases. In the first phase, in a competitive environment to assess pay suppliers according to desired criteria. The second phase will determine the amount of the purchase of selected suppliers. Advantage of this algorithm can be pointed to the following:

Strategic vision in selecting suppliers, consider the qualitative and quantitative factors together, considering the amount of the order, storage capacity and production capacity as one of the selected parameters.

This algorithm can be easily implemented with a spreadsheet package and its computation is fast. Therefore, the proposed model can be applied easily in practical situations. Expertise, experience, authority, and the responsibilities of decision makers are not equal in practice. Furthermore, in the mathematical model, the weights of internal and external criteria are determined by decision makers. It is useful to propose a scientific method for determining these weights. In addition, this paper has focused on manufacturing environment. Another future research may be the proposing mathematical model with stochastic parameters.

Acknowledgments

The authors wish to express their gratitude to the company which provided the information and the data used in this case-study.

References

1. Accenture Consulting. Supply chain mastery in the global marketplace. In: 16th POMS Annual Conference, Chicago (2005)
2. Linder, J.: Outsourcing for radical change: A bold approach to enterprise transformation. AMACOM, New York (2004)
3. Camperi, F.: The hidden value and complexities of outsourcing. Mortgage Banking 65(8), 123–124 (2005)
4. Aissaoui, N., Haouari, M., Hassini, E.: Supplier selection and order lot sizing modeling: A review. Computers & Operations Research 34(12), 3516–3540 (2007)
5. Xia, W., Wu, Z.: Supplier selection with multiple criteria in volume discount environments. Omega 35(5), 494–504 (2007)
6. Liu, F.H.F., Hai, H.L.: The voting analytic hierarchy process method for selecting supplier. International Journal of Production Economics 97(3), 308–317 (2005)
7. Dickson, G.W.: An analysis of vendor selection system and decisions. Journal of Purchasing 2(1), 28–41 (1966)
8. Moore, D.L., Fearon, H.E.: Computer-assisted decision-making in purchasing. Journal of Purchasing 9(1), 5–25 (1973)
9. Weber, C.A., Current, J.R., Benton, W.C.: Vendor selection criteria and methods. European Journal of Operational Research 50(1), 2–18 (1991)
10. De Boer, L., Labro, E., Morlacchi, P.: A review of methods supporting supplier selection. European Journal of Purchasing and Supply Management 7(2), 75–89 (2001)
11. Degraeve, Z., Labro, E., Roodhoofi, F.: Total cost of ownership purchasing of a service: The case of airline selection at Alcatel Bell. European Journal of Operational Research 156(1), 23–40 (2004)
12. Pujawan, N.: Assessing supply chain flexibility: a conceptual framework and case study. International Journal of Integrated Supply Management 1(1), 79–97 (2004)
13. Aissaoui, N., Haouari, M., Hassini, E.: Supplier selection and order lot sizing modeling: A review. Computers & Operations Research 34(12), 3516–3540 (2007)
14. Ghodsypour, S.H., O'Brien, C.: A decision support system for supplier selection using an integrated analytic hierarchy process and linear programming. International Journal of Production Economics, 199–212 (1998)
15. Weber, C.A., Current, J.R., Desai, A.: An optimization approach to determining the number of vendors to employ. Supply Chain Management: An International Journal 5(2), 90–98 (2000)
16. Kim, B., Leung, J.M.Y., Taepark, K., Zhang, G., Lee, S.: Configuring a manufacturing firm's supply network with multiple suppliers. IIE Transactions 34(8), 663–677 (2002)
17. Liao, Z., Rittscher, J.: A multi-objective supplier selection model under stochastic demand conditions. International Journal of Production Economics 105(1), 150–159 (2007)
18. Xia, W., Wu, Z.: Supplier selection with multiple criteria in volume discount environments. Omega 35(5), 494–504 (2007)
19. Wadhwa, V., Ravindran, R.: Vendor selection in outsourcing. Computers and Operations Research 34(12), 3725–3737 (2007)

Application of Gradient-Based Control Methods in Efficient Oil Well Placement through Dynamic Fuzzy Neural Network Modeling

A. Ebadat[1], P. Karimaghaee[1], and H. Mahdiyar[2]

[1] School of electrical and control engineering, Shiraz University, Shiraz, Iran
[2] School of chemical, petroleum and gas engineering, Shiraz University, Shiraz, Iran

Abstract. This study presents an approach for determining optimal locations of oil wells in an oil field such that a predetermined production policy can be achieved. In the first step, Dynamic Fuzzy Neural Network (DFNN) is employed to generate an analytical and dynamic model of the reservoir. The model would be updated during the process due to current reservoir information. In order to determine optimal weights for DFNN, Orthogonal Least Square method is modified and applied. It will be shown that the method has more computational efficiency in comparison with other approaches. In the second stage, gradient-based approaches as one of the most common methods in control field are employed to determine well locations based on the generated model. The method can perform search without being obliged to use the simulator several times. Finally, simulation results show the abilities of the proposed procedure in both modeling and tracking control.

Keywords: Well placement; Dynamic Fuzzy Neural Network; Gradient Based algorithm.

1 Introduction

Recent growth of world population has significantly affected the energy demand [1]. This increasing demand necessitates recovering the existing hydrocarbon resources in an optimum way, which has led to emerging interest into the reservoir management problems. One of the key decisions in reservoir management is the determination of the optimal location of one or many wells during a field development plan. The well placement problem can be defined as finding the optimal location of one or more wells that can achieve the maximum Net Present Value (NPV) while minimizing operating costs, subject to various geological and economical constraints. Different factors such as reservoir geology, physical properties of the fluid and rock, aquifer characteristics, well type, surface facilities and economic parameters can influence well location.

In current industry various approaches have been proposed to solve this problem. Manual approaches which have trial and error nature have been usually used. In those methods experienced engineers consider numerical simulations to determine well locations but in most cases, especially in large reservoirs with the large number of

E. Ariwa and E. El-Qawasmeh (Eds.): DEIS 2011, CCIS 194, pp. 616–630, 2011.

wells, the procedure leads to non optimum solutions. Thus, in the recent years, there has been an increasing interest to solve this problem through systematic methods, which are provided by optimization algorithms.

The optimization problem can be stated as follows: Finding the optimal locations for drilling new wells, which minimize an economic or technical cost function (usually net present value or ultimate recovery) subject to different operational constraint such as bounded bottom hole pressure of wells and production/injection rates. Since this problem is nonlinear in nature and potentially has many local optimum solutions, evolutionary algorithms such as binary genetic algorithm (bGA), continues genetic algorithm (cGA), hybrid genetic algorithm (HGA)[2, 3], particle swarm optimization (PSO) [4], simulated annealing (SA) [5] have been extensively used in literature to tackle this problem [see6, 7, 8]. These algorithms search for a global solution. However, their underlying drawback is the numerous number of simulation associated with the search procedure. Therefore, deterministic methods, especially gradient-based algorithms were proposed in which monotonically increase in objective function in successive iterations is guaranteed. In other words, these methods perform the search with less simulation and are faster. Nevertheless, the main problem is the potential drawback of being stuck in local optima. It should be considered that in real cases especially in reservoirs with a large number of cells it is impractical to apply stochastic methods with hundreds of simulations thus deterministic methods would be more efficient for practical applicability. Discrete nature of the model that makes it impossible to compute gradients of objective function with respect to decision variables is another problem. In this respect, few approximation and problem reformulation are proposed by Handles et al. 2007 [9], Sarma and Chen 2008 [10]. Other suggested approaches are mathematical programming such as mixed integer programming [11], integer programming [12] and some other methods [see13].

As stated before, usually net present value (NPV) is considered as an objective function. However, it is obvious that although maximizing NPV is important, the way by which this maximum value is achieved is essential too. In other words, it should be considered what happens during time and what percentage of the profit in what percentage of the time is obtained. In addition usually there is an industrial demand for oil and gas production in oil and gas companies with respect to consumers needs. Therefore, there is no need to produce such that maximum oil is achieved. In such cases tracking a prespecified production curve could be a better choice.

In this paper, the optimal well placement problem is formulated as an optimal control problem in which well locations are input variables, and the field oil production total/rate is output. The target is to locate wells such that the output can track a desired prespecified curve which can be determined according to the industrial gas and oil companies' seasonal need. Thus, cost function is the error (or any function of it) between the reservoir response and desired output which is a time variant cost function. As stated above, gradient descent methods have some advantages like improvement of objective function in successive iterations and therefore fewer numbers of simulations. These characteristics make the method completely appropriate for well placement problem which is enormously CPU time-consuming. Therefore in the present work, gradient descent algorithm is used to minimize the cost function and track the desired oil production total/rate.

In order to apply the method to this problem, there is an urgent need to have a model which can describe output as a function of manipulated variables. In this regard, usually neural network and neuro-fuzzy modeling were used. In addition, because of reservoir uncertainties, dynamical approaches where the model would be updated during the process, could be more helpful.

Thus, we employed Dynamic Fuzzy Neural Network (DFNN) [14] for MIMO case and used the network to describe the error between the desired output and the real one as a function of well locations. Despite other proxies such as neural network and neuro-fuzzy, the proposed approach performs dynamically. Thereby, the model can be updated at any given iteration using current reservoir information. On the other hand, since the network starts with no hidden units, there is no need to generate input-output set of data for training purposes for which hundreds of costly and time-consuming simulations are required. To reduce output size in the network, which is crucial in network's training time; curve fitting tools are used and the curve's parameters are considered as network's outputs. For training purpose and weight adjustments, we modified Orthogonal Least Square (OLS) proposed in [15] and applied it to the problem. The method not only reduces the computational load, but also leads to more accuracy and there is no more need for inverse matrix calculation. Simulation results are used to adjust the parameters and structure of the network dynamically and therefore, the model will be updated locally and dynamically at each iteration after simulator run. Finally, an analytical model is achieved for which first and second derivatives exsists and it is possible to apply gradient-based method, directly. At last a 3D 3-phase reservoir model is used to represent the efficiency and practical applicability of the proposed approach in tracking desired field total oil production and production rate. Simulation results show that the required numbers of simulations reduce significantly and there is no more need to incur high computational load.

This paper is organized as follows. In Section 2, this problem is specifically defined and the benchmark model used for this study is introduced in Section 3. Then in Section 4, application of D-FNN for model generation is explained. After that, gradient-based algorithm, as our optimization method, is discussed in Section 5 and simulation results are presented in Section 6.

2 Problem Definition

In this paper, we attempt to locate the best drilling sites that minimize the error between a desired output curve and the real one. Thus, we formulate the problem as a control problem. A general control system block diagram is shown in Figure1. In this case, plant is the reservoir, inputs are well locations and plant's output is total oil production during a given period of the reservoir production life. The output signal is compared with the desired one and after error calculation; error signal is used as the controller input signal.

The first step in any problem is modeling. In reservoir problems modeling and simulation of the reservoir is one of the most important steps. Therefore, in the next parts first the reservoir simulation that is used to compute our objective function is described. We then explain application of D-FNN for model generation. Finally the gradient-based algorithm that was used as a solution is described.

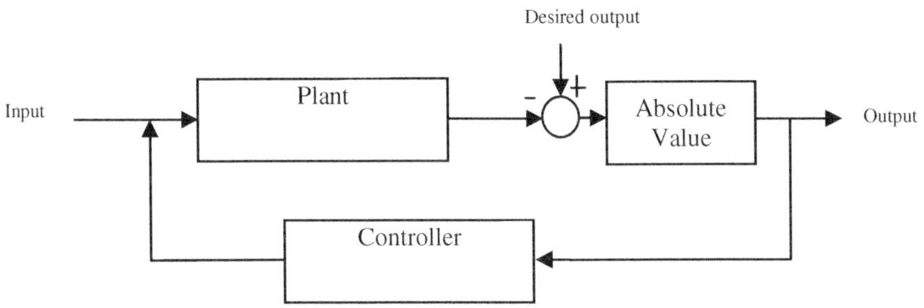

Fig. 1. Control Block Diagram

3 Plant Description

Naturally occurring hydrocarbon systems found in petroleum reservoirs are mixtures of organic compounds that exhibit multiphase behavior over wide ranges of pressures and temperatures [16]. Generally, reservoir model results from fluid movement in a porous medium. So the model can be formulated as a set of partial differential equations for the conservation of mass of each phase and Darcy's law. By combining equations, a nonlinear partial differential equation for each phase will be produced. On the other hand, relative permeability and capillary pressure are nonlinear functions of saturation in different phase which makes it so difficult to solve the problem through systematic methods. To solve equations through simulators, the model should be discretized in space. In this study ECLIPSE 100 commercial simulator which is developed at Schlumberger Company is used. ECLIPSE 100 is a three-phase, three-dimensional, general purpose black oil simulator that uses a fully implicit formulation solved at every time step. Program is written in FORTRAN77. To run simulator, geological and petro-physical data of the reservoir and production process are required. They are prepared in free format file using a keyword system and can be prepared to use any standard editor [8]. Visualization of output results can be made in different ways. In this paper, we used a link between Matlab and ECLIPSE to benefit from strong visualization power of MATLAB to analyze the numerical results.

4 Model Generation

Most of the real-world processes are dynamic, i.e. there are time dependencies between the output, past values of inputs and the states of the system so the exact order of the system is unknown. In such cases a sufficient model should be dynamic. This issue is also true for reservoir problems. In this paper Dynamic Fuzzy Neural Network (D-FNN) is used to describe the error between the desired output and the real one as a function of well locations. The network structure is based on extended Radial Basis Function (RBF) neural networks and performs Takagi-Sugeno-Kang (TSK) model-based fuzzy system [14]. Learning algorithm based on the D-FNN is used. The key idea is that the system starts with no hidden units. Then neurons can be recruited or deleted dynamically according to their significance to system performance so that not only the parameters can be adjusted, but also the structure can be self-adapted simultaneously[14]. Network's weights will be determined by using modified orthogonal least square method. In other words, by running simulator at each iteration, some new information is added to the problem and the model can be updated by using that information.

In summary, we can say D-FNN have been used as a model. The network maps a set of inputs to the objective function which is the absolute value of the error between the desired output and the real one. The network is trained with simulation results. After each iteration, when new simulation results are achieved, the parameters and structure of the network will be adjusted dynamically. So we can have a model updating at each iteration and there is no more need to generate input-output set of data for training purposes for which hundreds of costly and time-consuming simulations are required. The network's architecture is shown in Figure 2.

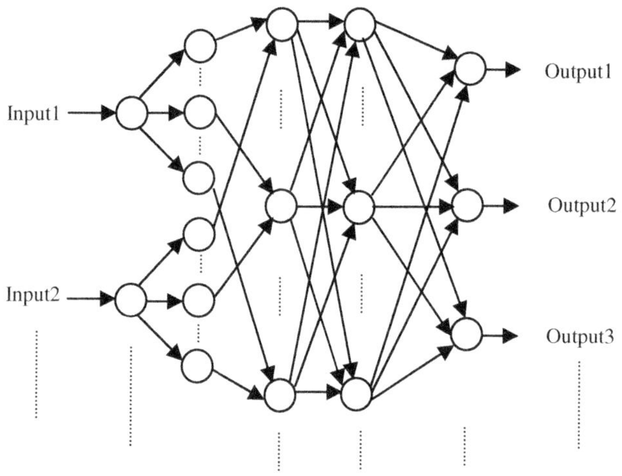

Fig. 2. DFNN structure

Network's inputs are well locations, which are discrete parameters that represent *I* and *J* indices of grid blocks where wells are located. The output could be the absolute values of the elements of error vector but in this case the output size will be too large and this results in time-consuming training process. Since we have time invariant inputs despite time varying output, using time index as a network input will cause problems. Finally to overcome the problem, curve fitting tools are used to approximate the error with a polynomial with a predefined degree n:

$$e(t) = a_1 t^n + a_2 t^{n-1} + \ldots + a_n t + a_{n+1}$$
$$\text{where} \quad e(t) = |Yd - Y(t)| \tag{1}$$

As a result, the network's outputs are the polynomial coefficients. The degree n may have different values in different cases and is determined with respect to problem complexity.

As discussed earlier, the main purpose of this part is model generation so in the following, we presented the network structure for MIMO case. The function that describes networks inputs and outputs relations is [14]:

$$y_i(X) = \frac{\sum_{k=1}^{u} w_{2k}^{i} \exp(-\frac{\|X - C_k\|^2}{\sigma_k^2})}{\sum_{k=1}^{u} \exp(-\frac{\|X - C_k\|^2}{\sigma_k^2})} = f_i(X) \qquad i = 1,\ldots,n+1 \ . \qquad (2)$$

where y_i is the value of *i-th* output variable which is the *i-th* coefficient in equation (1), $X = (x_1, x_2, \ldots, x_r)$ is input vector, C_k is the vector of centers of *j-th* RBF unit and w_{2k}^{i} is the weight of each rule for *i-th* output. u is number of membership functions. σ_k represents width of *k-th* Gaussian membership function of x_i, r is number of inputs, u is number of membership functions and $n+1$ is outputs nember.

For the TSK model:

$$w_j^{i} = k_{j0}^{i} + k_{j1}^{i} x_1 + \ldots + k_{jr}^{i} x_r \ . \qquad j = 1,2,\ldots,u \qquad (3)$$

The weights k can be determined by linear least square method [14] however; we modified orthogonal least square [15] method by which more accuracy can be achieved in comparison to linear least square and there is no need to calculate matrix inversion. In the article we first generalize DFNN proposed in [14] to the MIMO case and then modify the ROLS learning algorithm in [15] and use it for the learning of dynamic fuzzy neural network.

First we define:

$$\psi_j = \frac{\exp(-\frac{\|X - C_j\|^2}{\sigma_j^2})}{\sum_{k=1}^{u} \exp(-\frac{\|X - C_k\|^2}{\sigma_k^2})}, \qquad j = 1,2,\ldots,u \ . \qquad (4)$$

Then we have:

$$y_i = \sum_{j=1}^{u} w_j^{i} \psi_j \qquad i = 1,\ldots,n+1 \ . \qquad (5)$$

Suppose the *m-th* training pattern enters and all these m data are saved in $I \in R^{r \times m}, O \in R^{m \times n+1}$ as input and output matrices, respectively.

By defining:

$$W^i = \left(k_{10}{}^i \cdots k_{u0}{}^i k_{11}{}^i \cdots k_{u1}{}^i \cdots k_{1r}{}^i \cdots k_{ur}{}^i\right). \tag{6}$$

$$W = \begin{bmatrix} W^1 \\ W^2 \\ \vdots \\ W^{n+1} \end{bmatrix}. \tag{7}$$

$$Y = \begin{bmatrix} y_{1,1} & y_{1,2} & \cdots & y_{1,m} \\ y_{2,1} & y_{2,2} & \cdots & y_{2,m} \\ \vdots & \vdots & \cdots & \vdots \\ y_{n+1,1} & y_{n+1,2} & \cdots & y_{n+1,m} \end{bmatrix}. \tag{8}$$

$$\Psi = \begin{pmatrix} \psi_{11} & \cdots & \psi_{1m} \\ \vdots & \vdots & \vdots \\ \psi_{u1} & \cdots & \psi_{um} \\ \psi_{11}x_{11} & \cdots & \psi_{1m}x_{1m} \\ \vdots & \vdots & \vdots \\ \psi_{u1}x_{11} & \cdots & \psi_{um}x_{1m} \\ \vdots & \vdots & \vdots \\ \psi_{11}x_{r1} & \cdots & \psi_{1m}x_{rm} \\ \vdots & \vdots & \vdots \\ \psi_{u1}x_{r1} & \cdots & \psi_{um}x_{rm} \end{pmatrix}. \tag{9}$$

Where ψ_{jl} is the value of ψ_j for l^{th} sample ($l = 1,\ldots,m$).

Equation (5) can be rewritten in the following close form:

$$W\Psi = Y\ . \tag{10}$$

Orthogonal Least Square (OLS) will be used to determine the matrix weight, W [15]. The method uses matrix QR decomposition and frobenius norm to solve the matrix equation instead of matrix inversion calculation. Therefore, it has more computational efficiency. The weight W should be determined such that minimizing following cost function:

$$H(W) = \left\|O^T - Y^T\right\|_F = \left\|O^T - \Psi^T W_2^T\right\|_F\ . \tag{11}$$

$\|*\|_F$ represents the Frobenius norm which defined as $\|*\|_F{}^2 = trace(*^T *)$.

Because the Gaussian basis functions have distinct centers, Ψ^T is a full rank matrix so we can write:

$$\Psi^T = Q\begin{bmatrix} R \\ 0 \end{bmatrix}. \tag{12}$$

Where $Q \in R^{m\times m}$ is orthogonal matrix with the property of $QQ^T = Q^T Q = I$ and $R \in R^{(r+1)u\times(r+1)u}$ is an upper triangular matrix with the same rank as Q. Since an orthogonal transformation can preserve the F-norm of a matrix, the following cost function is achieved:

$$H(W) = \lfloor Q^T Y^T - Q^T \Psi^T W^T \rfloor . \tag{13}$$

Suppose:

$$Q^T Y^T = \begin{bmatrix} \hat{Y} \\ \tilde{Y} \end{bmatrix} . \tag{14}$$

Then we have:

$$H(W) = \left\| \begin{bmatrix} \hat{Y} \\ \tilde{Y} \end{bmatrix} - \begin{bmatrix} R \\ 0 \end{bmatrix} W^T \right\|_F = \left\| \begin{bmatrix} \hat{Y} - RW^T \\ \tilde{Y} \end{bmatrix} \right\|_F . \tag{15}$$

With $\hat{Y} \in R^{(r+1)u \times (n+1)}$.

Finally, optimum weights which minimize the cost function, *H(W)*, can be obtained by solving simple equation 16 in which $R \in R^{(r+1)u \times (r+1)u}$ is an upper triangular matrix:

$$RW^T = \hat{Y} . \tag{16}$$

Now the network can be used as a model that maps well locations to the objective function which is the absolute value of the error between the desired output and the real one so the cost function, $e(X,t)$; can be written in the form below where $f_i(X)(i = 1,..., n+1)$ are known functions described by equation (2):

$$e(X,t) = f_1(X)t^n + f_2(X)t^{n-1} + ... + f_n(X)t + f_{n+1}(X) . \tag{17}$$

As it can be seen in equation (17), by using DFNN the cost function can be stated as a nonlinear known function of input variables for which the first and second derivatives are existing. Therefore, any gradient based method can be applied easily to the problem.

Remark: The proposed DFNN can be used to describe any arbitrary cost function such as NPV as a function of manipulated variables.

5 Optimal Well Placement by Control Methods

Gradient based strategies iteratively search for a minimum value of cost function. The method of *Steepest Descent* is the simplest form of the gradient methods. The most important properties of the method are monotonically improvement in objective function in successive iterations and relatively low computational load. These characteristics make the method completely appropriate for well placement problem which is enormously CPU time demanding. In this part we use the model generated in section IV to apply the steepest descent method to well placement problem.

Consider the minimization of function $e(X,t)$ where X is r-dimensional vector. Suppose that $e(X,t)$ is smooth function for which first and second derivatives are exists then the direction where $e(X,t)$ decreases most quickly is in the direction opposite to $\nabla(e(X,t))$. The search starts at an arbitrary point and then slide down the gradient, until we are close enough to the solution.

Our cost function is time dependent. Thus, the gradient should be computed in each sampling time. In this case, the gradient in each time steps is multiplied by a coefficient gives different weights to the gradient of cost function in different time samples. So the algorithm can be written in the form below:

First we define the derivative of cost function with respect to inputs, i.e. I and J location of wells; in each time step:

$$\left.\frac{\partial e(X,t)}{\partial x_i}\right|_{t=t_m} = g_m(X,i) = \left(\frac{\partial f_1(X)}{\partial x_i} * t_m{}^n + \frac{\partial f_2(X)}{\partial x_i} * t_m{}^{n-1} + \ldots + \frac{\partial f_n(X)}{\partial x_i} * t_m + \frac{\partial f_{n+1}(X)}{\partial x_i}\right), \quad m = 1,2,\ldots,l \tag{18}$$

Where l is the number of time steps. Define:

$$\varphi_j = \exp\left(-\frac{\left\|X - C_j\right\|^2}{\sigma_j^2}\right) . \tag{19}$$

Considering equation (4), (5) and (19) we can have:

$$\frac{\partial f_1(X)}{\partial x_i} = \sum_{j=1}^{u}\left(\frac{\partial w^1{}_j}{\partial x_i}\psi_j + w^1{}_j\frac{\partial \psi_j}{\partial x_i}\right) = \sum_{j=1}^{u}\left(k^1{}_{ji}\psi_j + w^1{}_j\frac{\frac{-2}{\sigma_j^2}(x_i - c_{ij})\varphi_j\left(\sum_{k=1}^{u}\varphi_k\right)^2 - \varphi_j\sum_{k=1}^{u}\left(\frac{-2}{\sigma_k^2}(x_i - c_{ik})\varphi_k\right)}{\left(\sum_{k=1}^{u}\varphi_k\right)^2}\right) . \tag{20}$$

Then the gradient matrix can be calculated in the following form:

$$G(X,i) = \left[g_1(X,i) \quad g_2(X,i) \quad \ldots \quad g_{l-1}(X,i) \quad g_l(X,i)\right]^T . \tag{21}$$

The iterative procedure is:

$$x_{i,k+1} = x_i - \alpha_{i,k}\beta_{i,k}\,G(X,i)\big|_{X=X_k}, i = 1,2,\ldots,r . \tag{22}$$

Where r is the number of inputs, $\beta_{i,k} \in R^{1\times L}$ is the weight vector and $\alpha_{i,k}$ represents the step size that taken at each iteration.

Remark: There are other gradient based approaches which can be applied to the problem according to the problem complexity and nonlinearities.

6 Simulation Results

In this paper a 3D 3-phase black oil model is used. The reservoir is discretized by 20*40*12 corner point geometry grid [14]. Figure 3 illustrates the model in ternary saturation.

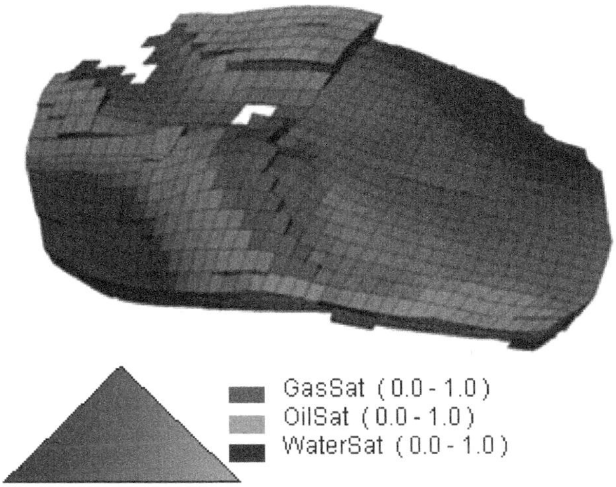

Fig. 3. Ternary saturation of the model

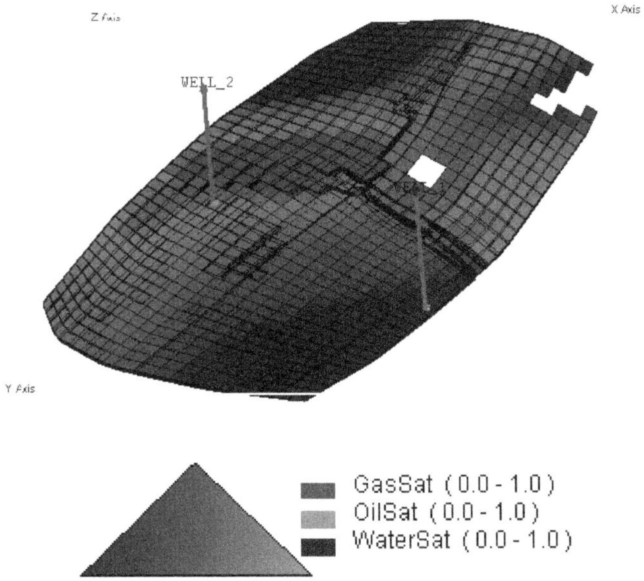

Fig. 4. Injection and production wells locations at initial condition

We use ECLIPSE 100 for reservoir modeling. The software is linked with Matlab. After each iteration, simulation results are available in the *.rsm file. The data is read by Matlab to generate inputs for the next iteration. The inputs save in a *.txt file and will be used by simulator for the next iteration. The procedure is repeated since output gets arbitrary close to the desired one.

Remark: In the following cases we assume a desired curve of field production is determined by development team with regard to companies' needs and reservoir protection issues. It should be considered that although we track a specified curve in the following examples, the method can track any other given curve through only a few numbers of iterations, as well.

Case I: In the first example the objective is to find an optimal location for one producer while keeping one injector and one producer locations fixed (Figure 4).

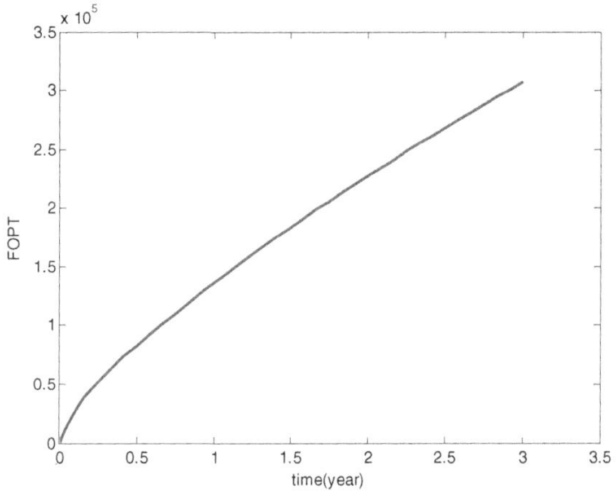

Fig. 5. Desired field oil production

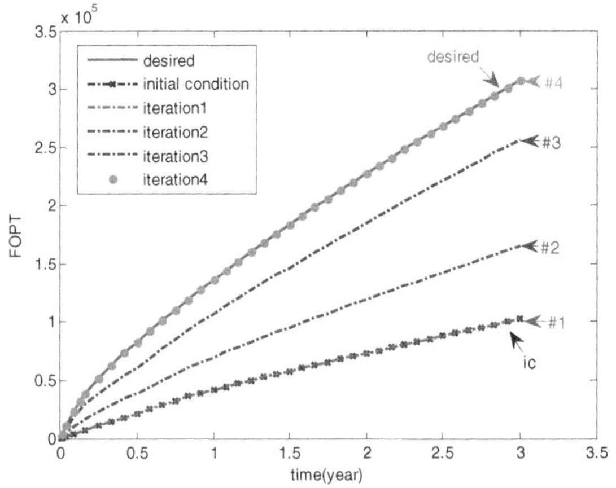

Fig. 6. Comparison of the desired output signal (solid line) and outputs in different iterations (dotted line)

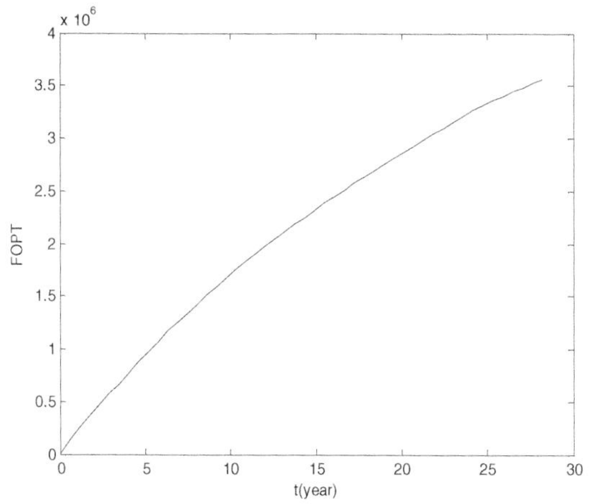

Fig. 7. Desired field oil production

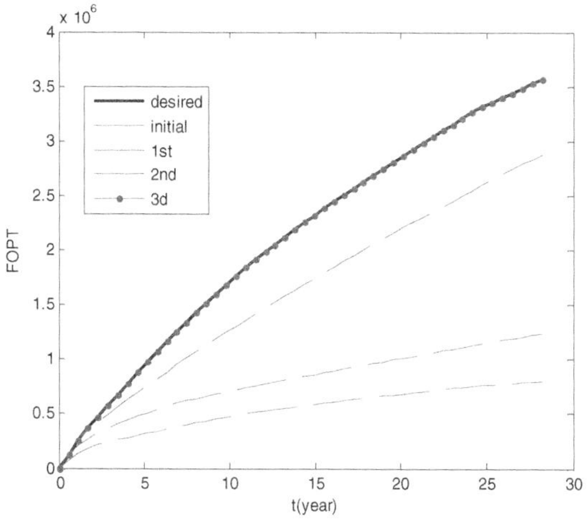

Fig. 8. Comparison of the desired output signal (solid line) and outputs in different iterations (dashed line)

Figure 6 illustrates good performance in tracking and compares desired output signal (solid line) and the output in different iterations (dotted line). As it can be seen finally we can track the desired output exactly. The cost function - absolute value of the error between the output and desired curve - decreases monotonically in successive iterations. Unlike stochastic methods, the proposed method requires only 5 simulations. This is an important issue especially for large-scales simulation models with many wells.

Case II: In the second example we assume the development team decided to place four vertical wells such that output can optimally track the desired FOPT curve. The reservoir is considered for 28 years. To prevent water production, if the value of water cut in each perforation of wells reach over 0.7 the connection will be blocked. Moreover, if the amount of GOR in any connection exceeds 5 MSCF/STB the connection will be blocked to have preservation production from the reservoir and to prevent pressure falling and gas coning phenomenon.

The desired prespecified output curve is shown in Figure 7. Figure 8 shows the output in different iterations (dotted lines) and compares it with the desired curve (solid line).

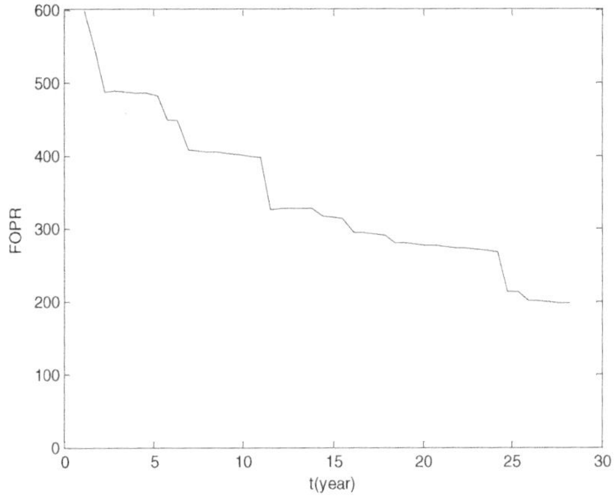

Fig. 9. Desired field oil production

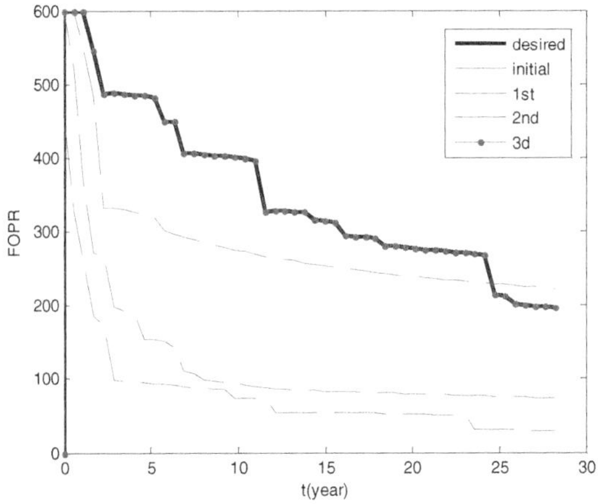

Fig. 10. Comparison of the desired output signal (solid line) and outputs in different iterations (dashed line)

Case III: In the third scenario, we place four vertical wells such that output can optimally track the desired FOPR (field oil production rate) curve which is more usual in industry in comparison with the second example. We used the same constraints as in case II. The desired prespecified output curve is shown in Figure 9. Figure 10 shows the output in different iterations.

7 Conclusion

In this paper the optimal well placement problem was formulated as a control problem. The target is to locate wells such that the output can track a desired prespecified curve which can be determined with respect to the industrial gas and oil companies' seasonal need. Since gradient-based approaches perform the search without being obliged to use the simulator several times and are faster due to increment of cost function at each iteration, they are completely appropriate for well placement problem which is enormously CPU time-consuming. Therefore in this paper gradient-based approach is used. In order to apply the method to this problem, dynamic fuzzy neural network is employed to generate an analytical function which can perform dynamically despite other proxies such as neural network and neuro-fuzzy. The model updates at each iteration using current reservoir information. In order to determine network's optimal weights, Orthogonal Least Square (OLS) method is proposed. On the other hand, since the network starts with no hidden units, there is no need for hundreds of costly and time-consuming initial simulator runs. Therefore, the required number of simulations will be decreased significantly. Efficiency of the proposed approach is investigated by applying it to a 3D 3-phase synthetic reservoir. The method was employed for three cases: placement of one well while there are other wells in the field, multi well placement for FOPT and FOPR curve tracking. Simulation results show the abilities of the proposed procedure in both modeling and tracking control.

Acknowledgements

The authors wish to thank Mohammad Sadegh Tavallali for his valuable discussion during the study.

References

1. OPEC, World Oil Outlook 2009. Vienna, Austria, Organization of the Petroleum Exporting Countries (2009)
2. Guyaguler, B.: Optimization of Well Placement and Assesment of Uncertainty, PhD thesis, Stanford University, Department of Petroleum engineering (2002)
3. Ozdogan, U.: Optimization of well placement under time-dependent uncertainty, Dept. of Petroleum Engineering., Stanford University. Master Thesis: xix, 88 pages, bound (2004)
4. Onwunalu, J.E., Durlofsky, L.J.: Application of a particle swarm optimization algorithm for determining optimum well location and type. Computational Geosciences, 1–16 (2009)

5. Johnson, V.M., Rogers, L.L.: Applying soft computing methods to improve the computational tractability of a subsurface simulation-optimization problem. Journal of Petroleum Science and Engineering 29(3-4), 153–175 (2001)
6. Bangerth, W., Klie, H., Stoffa, P.L.: On Optimization Algorithms for Reservoir Oil Well Placement Problem. Computational Geosciences 10(3) (2006)
7. Siemek, J., Stopa, J.: Optimizations of the wells placement in gas reservoirs using SIMPLEX method. Journal of Petroleum Science and Engineering 54(3-4), 164–172 (2006)
8. Zarei, F., Daliri, A., Alizadeh, N.: The Use of Neuro-Fuzzy Proxy in Well Placement Optimization. In: SPE 112214 Presented at the SPE Intelligent Energy Conference and Exhibition, Amsterdam, Netherlands (2008)
9. Handels, M., Zandvliet, M.J., Brouwer, D.R., Jansen, J.D.: Adjoint-based Well Placement Optimization under Production Constraints. In: SPE Paper 105797 Presented at the SPE Reservoir Simulation Symposium, The Woodlands, TX (2007)
10. Sarma, P., Chen, W.H.: Efficient well placement optimization with gradient-based algorithms and adjoint models. In: Society of Petroleum Engineers - Intelligent Energy Conference and Exhibition: Intelligent Energy (2008)
11. Rosenwald, G.W., Green, D.W.: Method For Determining The Optimal Location Of Wells In A Reservoir Using Mixed-Integer Programming. Soc. Pet. Eng. AIME J. 14(1), 44–54 (1974)
12. Vasantharajan, S., Cullick, A.S.: Well site selection using integer programming optimization. In: Third Annual Conference of the Intl. Assn. for Mathematical Geology (1997)
13. Cullick, A.S., Vasantharajan, S., Dobin, M.W.: Determining Optimal Well Locations From A 3D Reservoir Model. European Patent Application (2004)
14. Wu, S., Er, M.J.: Dynamic Fuzzy Neural Networks—A Novel Approach to Function Approximation. IEEE Transactions on Systems, Man, and Cybernetics 30(2) (April 2000)
15. Barry Gomm, J., Yu, D.L.: Selecting Radial Basis Function Network Centres with Recursive Orthogonal Least Squares Training. IEEE Transactions on Neural Networks 11(2) (March 2000)
16. Ahmed, T.H.: Reservoir engineering handbook. Elsevier/Gulf Professional, Burlington, Mass. (2006)
17. ECLIPSE 100 (Black Oil), Refrence manual and technical description. Schlumberger GeoQuest, Houston (2006)

Visual Data Mining: Using Self-Organizing Maps for Electricity Distribution Regulation

Hongyan Liu, Tomas Eklund, Barbro Back, and Hannu Vanharanta

Turku Centre for Computer Science (TUCS) / Åbo Akademi University,
Joukahaisenkatu 3-5 A, 20520 Turku, Finland
{Hongyan.Liu,Tomas.Eklund,Barbro.Back}@abo.fi
Pori School of Technology and Economics
Tampere University of Technology, Tampere, Finland
Hannu.Vanharanta@tut.fi

Abstract. The electricity distribution regulation and efficiency benchmarking practice in Finland has drawn attention because of its controversial regulatory scheme and arguably efficient electricity distribution sector. This study uses a computational intelligence tool, i.e., Self-Organizing Map (SOM), in the context of electricity distribution efficiency performance visualization. A SOM-model has been built based on collected data for 2001-2004. It allows the reader to discriminate between the Finnish DSOs' differing operating circumstances. Through clustering and visualization, an overall perspective of the efficiency performance of the DSOs in 2001-2004 is rendered. In addition, such a visualization approach connects the DSO's efficiency performance to its respective operating characteristics, which is otherwise not straightforwardly indicated by only studying efficiency scores. This application provides evidence that visual data mining with the SOM as a complementary approach in electricity distribution regulation and efficiency benchmarking has the potential to be expended to other regulatory practices (e.g., yardstick regulation).

Keywords: computational intelligence, visual data mining, artificial neural networks (ANNs), self-organizing maps (SOM), clustering, visualization, electricity distribution regulation, efficiency benchmarking, performance analysis.

1 Introduction

Electricity distribution is subject to regulation due to that it is considered to be a natural monopoly. Efficiency benchmarking of the electricity distribution system operators (DSOs) has been widely adopted as a regulatory tool. The aim is to encourage cost-cutting and enable efficiency improvement, in turn to secure electricity supply at a reasonable price. At the meanwhile, it provides indicators for the energy market authority to assess the regulatory policy such as the revenue / price cap or the return rate. There are different incentive regulation schemes in the OECD countries.[1] Accordingly, the benchmarking methods used by respective national regulation authorities vary, including: Data Envelopment Analysis (DEA), Corrected Ordinary

[1] For thorough discussion about various regulatory schemes, please see [1], [2], [3], [4], [5].

E. Ariwa and E. El-Qawasmeh (Eds.): DEIS 2011, CCIS 194, pp. 631–645, 2011.

Least Square method (COLS), Stochastic Frontier Analysis (SFA), and the so-called 'Network Performance Assessment Model' [6], [7], [8], [9], [10], [11].

The Finnish practice in electricity distribution regulation and efficiency benchmarking has drawn special attention because the Finnish Energy Market Authority (EMA) has implemented a controversial regulatory scheme – the rate of return (ROR) scheme – which is deemed to lack incentives for cost-cutting. Arguably, however, Finland has still achieved a more efficient electricity distribution system relative to many other European countries [12], [13]. The Finnish energy authority has adopted the DEA benchmarking method with the ROR scheme since 2000. The direct outcome of the DEA-model is a score on the scale between 0 and 1 for each DSO in a given year, with the score of 1 denoting the most efficient DSO. Nonetheless, the scores only indicate which DSO performed efficiently or inefficiently; but lack comprehensible connections to the actual operating characteristics of the DSOs, in terms of the selected measurements (i.e., *Operating Costs*, *Distributed Energy*, *Interruption Time*, *Network Length*, and *Number of Users*). For instance, while the fully efficient firms form the efficiency frontier, there can be several different inputs/outputs combinations (i.e., operating circumstances differ) reaching full efficiency (see Fig. 1).

The Self-Organizing Map (SOM), as one type of computational intelligence technique, has been extensively examined and successfully implemented for discovering hidden knowledge and visual benchmarking in business [14], [15], [16], [17]. Like other artificial neural networks (ANNs), the SOM is acknowledged for the robustness of handling non-linear and multivariate data space, especially with regards to dimension reduction. Additionally, as emphasized in [18], the SOM is a clustering, visualization, and abstraction method; and is different from statistical pattern recognition techniques. Compared to other clustering techniques, the SOM does not require predefining a desirable number of clusters, which means that little *a priori* knowledge of the data is required. While a normal distribution is usually preferred in statistics, the SOM does not make requirement on data distribution. Due to these advantageous features, therefore, this study seeks to apply the SOM in the field of electricity distribution efficiency performance visualization in the Finnish context. To our knowledge, the SOM has not been previously applied in this domain.

The purpose of this study is to examine the applicability of SOM-based visual data mining as a complementary approach in this specific domain, as well as to explore what insights and added value the SOM-model can offer in light of the Finnish DEA benchmarking. The questions of interest are: 1) *How many meaningful clusters can be extracted and what are the characteristics of the DSOs in each cluster?* 2) *Is it possible to visualize the connection between the efficiency performance and the selected measurements in a comprehensible manner?* 3) *What is the added value of applying visual data mining with the SOM as a complementary approach in electricity distribution regulation?*

Our study uses publicly available data. The examined period is from 2001 to 2004. This study follows a design science research methodology [19], [20], [21], in which a model is created and then evaluated. The evaluation is a so-called weak form, i.e., we use domain experts to interpret the results and evaluate the significance of the outcomes. It thus follows the traditional build-evaluate cycle of design science.

The rest of the paper is organized as follows. In the following section, the SOM algorithm, the DEA method, and the Finnish DEA benchmarking practice will be briefly discussed. The construction of the SOM-model is described in Section three. In Section four, the results will be presented and analyzed. In the final part, conclusions will be drawn and topics of future research are addressed.

2 Methodologies

2.1 The Self-Organizing Map (SOM)

The Self-Organizing Map (SOM) is a computational intelligence approach based upon Artificial Neural Networks (ANNs). ANNs are designed to mimic the basic learning and association patterns of the human nervous system, and consist of a number of neurons (simple processors) connected by weighted connection. ANNs learn by adjusting the weight of each connection, increasing or decreasing the importance of the input (information) being transferred, until a desired output is achieved. Essentially, they are non-linear, multivariate regression techniques, better able to handle erroneous and noisy data than parametric statistical tools [22].

The SOM is a two-layer ANN that uses the *unsupervised* learning approach, i.e., SOM does not require target output values for training [18]. The essence of the SOM is to map high dimensional data onto a spatial display (usually in the form of a two-dimensional lattice of hexagonal nodes). Each node i has an assigned parametric reference vector m_i with the same dimensionality as the input data vector x. In the very beginning of the training process, the map size (nodes) and dimensions (map ratio) are specified, and each node's reference vector is initialized (often based upon the principal components of the input data). The SOM uses the *competitive learning* algorithm, meaning that the nodes on the output layer compete with each other to be the best matching unit (BMU, i.e., the winner) whose connection weights to the input pattern are the closest in terms of the *Euclidian distance*. Once the BMU for each data vector has been located, the SOM algorithm allows the output nodes in the neighborhood of the BMU to adjust their weights accordingly. In batch training, the BMU's reference vector is substituted with the average of all the data vectors that it has won; then the surrounding nodes in the neighborhood learn from the BMU according to Gaussian function [23]. Theoretically, all the nodes on the output layer are the projection of the input data items. As such, the intrinsic relationships (e.g., similarities) of input data in the multivariate space are reflected on a two dimensional *topological map*, i.e., visual clustering is performed [24], [18]. In addition, the variables which are used for training the map are usually displayed in color as *feature planes*, with 'warm' colors representing high values while 'cold' colors for low values (see Fig. 3). Therefore, it is easy to visually interpret the characteristics of each cluster from the feature maps.

The Self-Organizing Map (SOM) has been extensively examined and successfully implemented in many applications in finance, medicine, and engineering [25]. In particular, the SOM has been used in the energy sector for e.g., power system stability assessment, on-line provision control, and load forecasting [26], [27], [28], [29]. In this study, Viscovery SOMine v.4.0 (http://www.eudaptics.com/) is used. SOMine uses an expanding map size and the batch training algorithm, allowing for very efficient training of maps [18]. SOM-Ward clustering method is also used to identify clusters based on operating circumstance similarities, which eliminates the need for subjective identification of clusters [23].

2.2 Data Envelopment Analysis (DEA)

Data Envelopment Analysis (DEA) is a non-parametric and frontier-based method for quantitative performance evaluation. It has been widely applied in management science, economics, and operations research for the estimation of production efficiency. For instance, in electricity distribution efficiency benchmarking, the regulatory authorities seek to induce cost-efficiency or to avoid the misuse of monopoly power by the firms who enjoy natural monopoly rights in their responsible regions [30]. The principle of the DEA method lies in using piecewise linear programming to calculate the best input-output ratio (the efficiency frontier) in a multiple input and output case. Then the DEA benchmarks the relative efficiency of the units within an organization or the efficiency across firms against the best practice (i.e., the frontier). A mathematical formulation is available in (1), which is originally presented by Charnes et al. [31].

$$\begin{aligned} &\text{Min } \theta \\ &\text{s.t. } \theta x_{j0} - \textstyle\sum_{i=1}^{n} \lambda i x j i \ \geq 0 \quad (j = 1, \ldots, p), \\ &\textstyle\sum_{i=1}^{n} \lambda i y k i \ \geq yko \quad (k = 1, \ldots, r), \\ &\lambda i \geq 0 \qquad\qquad (i = 1, \ldots, n). \end{aligned} \tag{1}$$

where :
θ: efficiency score for the assessed unit,
y_{ki}: observed output k of unit i,
x_{ji}: observed input j of unit i,
λ_i: weight of unit i in the reference point for the assessed unit,
subscript 0: refers to the assessed unit, but the unit preserves also its original index.

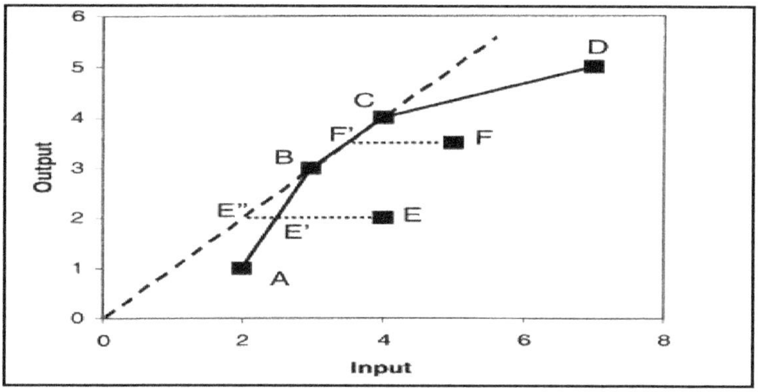

Fig. 1. Illustration of DEA based on a one-input/output case (adopted from [11])

On the one hand, the best practice frontier can be achieved through maximizing output for a given amount of input factors, the so-called output-oriented model. On the other hand, it can be obtained via minimizing the input factors required for a given level of output, named input-oriented model accordingly. Generally, the input-oriented model is used extensively in electricity distribution benchmarking [9]. With respect to electricity distribution benchmarking, the efficient firms will form a frontier (i.e., the solid line A-B-C-D), which envelops the inefficient firms (e.g. E and F), as shown in Fig. 1. Each firm's efficiency is represented by an efficiency score on the scale of 0 to 1, with the most efficient firms receiving the score of 1 [32], [11].

2.3 Finnish DEA Benchmarking

In practice, the DEA inputs and outputs vary in countries that have implemented this benchmarking method [8]. In Finland, the EMA has chosen *Operating Costs* as input, while *Interruption Time* and *Distributed Energy* consist of outputs, alongside two environmental factors (*Network Length* and *Number of Users*). The Finnish EMA has used the DEA-model as a part of the monitoring system in regulation of distribution pricing [11]. A mathematical presentation of the Finnish DEA model is shown in (2), as introduced by [33]:

$$\begin{aligned} &\text{Min } \theta \\ \text{s.t. } &\theta x_{j0} - \textstyle\sum_{i=1}^{n} \lambda i x j i \geq 0 \quad (j = 1, \ldots, p), \\ &z_{m0} - \textstyle\sum_{i=1}^{n} \lambda i z m i \geq 0 \quad (m = 1, \ldots, s), \\ &\textstyle\sum_{i=1}^{n} \lambda i y k i \geq y k o \quad (k = 1, \ldots, r), \\ &\textstyle\sum_{i=1}^{n} \lambda i = 1, \\ &\lambda i \geq 0 \qquad (i = 1, \ldots, n). \end{aligned} \tag{2}$$

where :
θ: efficiency score for the assessed unit,
y_{ki}: observed output k of unit *i*,
x_{ji}: discretionary input j of unit *i* (controllable),
z_{mi}: non-discretionary input m of unit *i* (non-controllable),
λ_i: weight of unit *i* in the reference point for the assessed unit,
subscript 0: refers to the assessed unit, but the unit preserves also its original index.

It is important to note that without regard to which measurements are designated as inputs or outputs, the DEA benchmarking outcome is simply a score between 0 and 1. It cannot provide a comprehensible connection between the efficiency performance and the respective operating circumstances for one to investigate further.

3 The SOM Model

3.1 Data and Dataset

The data used in this study are derived from the Finnish EMA data sources Tehokkuusluvut 2001-2004 (http://www.energiamarkkinavirasto.fi/). The use of the EMA data provides the best possible reliability and comparability across the examined years. There are in total 356 DSO samples included for training, with 94 in 2001, 90 in 2002, and 86 in 2003 and 2004 respectively. The variables in the SOM-model follow the Finnish DEA efficiency measurements, in order to make the analysis compatible. They are defined as in [11]:

Operating Costs – the amount of operating costs (teuro), controlled by the company;

Interruption Time – three year average of customers' total interruption time (h /year);

Distributed Energy – the amount of distributed energy weighted by the average national voltage-level-based distribution prices (teuro);

Network Length – the total network length of the different voltage levels (km);

Number of Users – the total number of customers.

These 5 variables will be referred to as *Cost*, *Interruption*, *Energy*, *Length*, and *Users* on the feature maps. A data distribution analysis was performed upon the dataset, and it shows that four variables (*Operating Costs*, *Distributed Energy*, *Network Length*, and *Number of Users*) are lognormal distributed while the variable of *Interruption Time* follows the general extreme value distribution.

3.2 Construction of the SOM Model

During the experiment, hundreds of maps were created with various combinations of the training parameters, including: Map Size (nodes) = 2000, 500, or 200; Tension[2] = 0.5, 0.3, or 0.02; Transformation[3] = *None*, *Sigmoid*, or *Logarithmic*; Scaling[4] = *Variance* or *Range*; Map Ratio[5] = *Automatic*. The variables were treated as equally important in the training process, meaning that no priority factor is assigned. Only one parameter was changed at each step while keeping other settings fixed to simplify comparison. For each set of parameter combinations, several runs were repeated. In turn, the trained maps were compared in terms of meaningful clusters, visual interpretability, average quantization error, and normalized distortion measure, in order to select a suitable set of training parameters. At this point, the domain expert was brought in to help evaluate the significance of the outcomes. Also the twistedness was tested by Ward clustering method in comparison with SOM-Ward clustering, and the topographic ordering was evaluated with the smoothness of neighborhood of each node.

Finally, a map with a satisfactory clustering result is selected, with Map Size = 2000, Tension = 0.3, Transformation = *Sigmoid*, Scaling = *By Default*, and Map Ratio = *Automatic*. The average quantization error is 1.773E-007. And the normalized distortion measure is 1.773E-007.

---

[2] Tension is used to denote the radius of neighborhood size in Viscovery SOMine.

[3] Two typical data transformation methods are logarithmic and sigmoid. The 'none' option refers to not applying any transformation.

[4] Each variable is scaled (normalized) by 'Variance' if its range is smaller than 8 times the standard deviation (i.e. $\max(x) - \min(x) < 8\sigma$); otherwise, the scaling is by 'Range', i.e., a simple linear scaling of the data between 0 and 1 (Viscovery SOMine Manual). The software is predefined with these principles as 'By Default'.

[5] Viscovery SOMine is capable of computing a suitable horizontal- vs. vertical- axis ratio based on the input data.

4 Results and Analysis

4.1 Identifying the DSOs in Clusters

As shown in Fig. 2, the selected map has eight clusters, which are labeled in alphabetic order. The characteristics of each cluster can be identified using the feature planes (Fig. 3[6]), as summarized in Table 1.

The compositions of each cluster are listed below. As many of the Finnish DSOs are municipality based, the company names are simplified accordingly. For example, Helsinki refers to Helsingin Energia, while Tampere stands for Tampereen Sähkölaitos.

Cluster A (2 DSOs) consists of Fortum and Vattenfall, which are two of the largest Nordic companies in the electricity industry, and have multi-regional operations in Finland.
Cluster B (3 DSOs) is made up of Helsinki, Espoo / E.ON, and Tampere, which operate in the metropolitan area of Finland.
Cluster C (3 DSOs) has Savon / Atro, Pohjois-Karjala, and Järvi-Suomi, which distribute electricity mainly in the north-eastern region and the big Finnish central Lakeland.

Cluster D (5 DSOs) is composed of Kainuu / Graning Kainuu, Kymenlaakso, and Uudenmaa, which are regional firms and whose operating area has low population density.[7]

Table 1. Characteristics of each cluster

Cluster	Efficiency Measurements				
	Operating Cost	***Interruption Time***	***Distributed Energy***	***Network Length***	***Number of Users***
A	Highest	Highest	Highest	Highest	Highest
B	Medium to high	Medium	Medium to high	Medium	Medium to high
C	Medium	Medium to high	Medium	Medium to high	Medium
D	Medium to low	Medium to low	Medium to low	Medium to low	Medium to low
E	Slightly low	Lower	Slightly low	Lower	Slightly low
F	Slightly low	Lower	Slightly low	Lower	Slightly low
G	Very low	Very low	Very low	Very low	Very low
H	Lowest	Lowest	Lowest	Lowest	Lowest

[6] The figures can only be interpreted in color format.

[7] Uudenmaa only existed in 2001 and 2002. Revo and Keski-Suomi merged with Vattenfall after 2001.

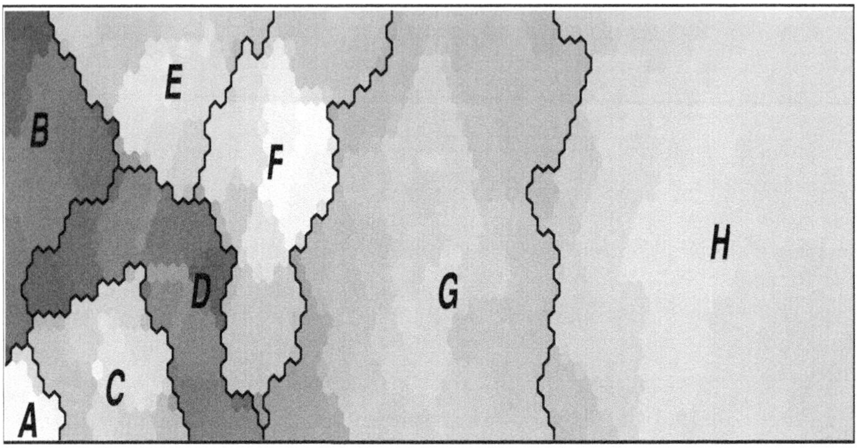

Fig. 2. General map with 8 clusters

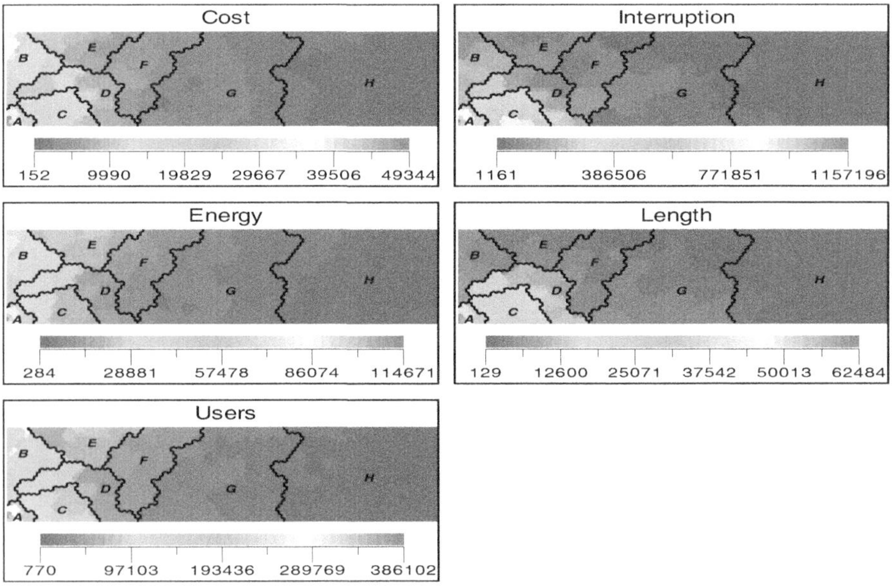

Fig. 3. Feature planes

Cluster E (4 DSOs) consist of major urban operators: Turku, Vantaa, Oulu, and Lahti.
Cluster F (6 DSOs) have Jyväskylä, Kuopio, Pori, Kouvola / KSS, Vaasa, and Lappeenrata, whose network responsibilities are in relatively small urban area.
Cluster G (22 DSOs) and *Cluster H* (46 DSOs) have mostly rural and small operators. Due to the size, it is difficult to list all of the DSOs within these two clusters.

To a great extent, this clustering result intuitively reflects the DSOs' geographical operating differences. For instance, the urban based DSOs in the cluster B, E, and F have relatively higher Operating Cost, Distributed Energy, and Number of Users, but shorter Network Length and Interruption Time. This is logical as in the urbanized area the population density, the energy demand, and uninterrupted electricity supply requirement are high, whereas the distribution network is concentrated and most likely favors underground cables over over-head lines, which in turn reduces the interruption probability by severe weather. When looking at the DSOs in cluster C which operate in the central lake and north-eastern area, it shows opposing characteristics, i.e., longer Network Length and Interruption Time, but lower user numbers.

4.2 Visualizing the Efficiency Performance of the DSOs

According to the Finnish DEA benchmarking, we import the efficient DSOs (whose efficiency score equals to 1) into the trained map year by year. As shown in Fig. 4-7, efficient DSOs can be located in almost every cluster.

It can be seen that a great number of DSOs performed stably efficiently from 2001 to 2004, such as Fortum in cluster A, Helsinki in cluster B, Järvi-Suomi in cluster C, Kymenlaakso in cluster D, Vantaa and Oulu in cluster E, Koillis-Satakunta, Rovakaira, and Tornionlaakso in cluster G, as well as Esse, Haukiputaa, Lehtimäki, Paneliankoski, Raahe, and Yli-Ii in cluster H.

Also, the maps illustrate the changes in each cluster across 2001-2004, with more DSOs becoming efficient. This implies that there has been a considerable efficiency improvement in the Finnish electricity distribution sector. One can as well identify which particular DSO improved their efficiency, such as E.ON, Jyväskylä, Rovaniemi, Jakobstad, Kemi, etc. The maps also reveal the unstable performance of certain DSOs. For instance, Atro from cluster C (2002) and Kainuu from cluster D (2002 and 2003) respectively appear as efficient, but only for those years.

The SOM-model allows the user to inspect the clusters (general map), the feature planes, and the values by cluster, node, or neighborhood simultaneously. It becomes possible to associate the individual DSO's efficiency performance with the 5 selected DEA efficiency benchmarking measurements. For instance, if we want to investigate the efficient performers Vantaa and Oulu in cluster E, the characteristics of cluster E, as well as the actual values of Vantaa and / or Oulu in a given year will be displayed in the value window in an interactive manner. However, due to the space limitation, these visualization results cannot be completely included in this paper.

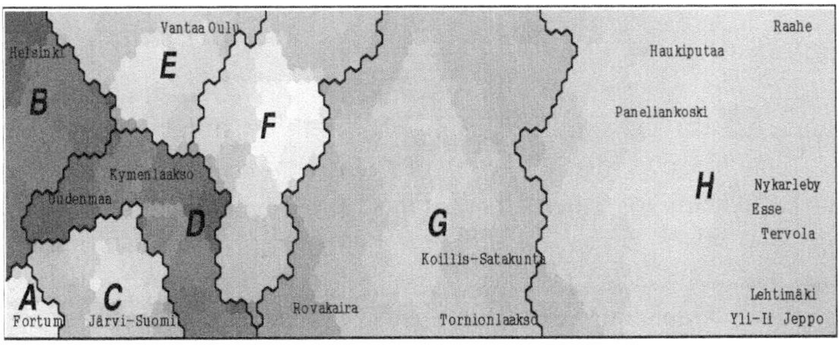

Fig. 4. Efficiency performance in 2001

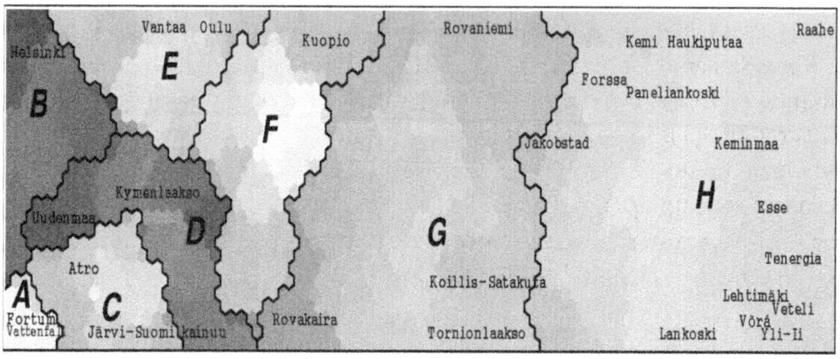

Fig. 5. Efficiency performance in 2002

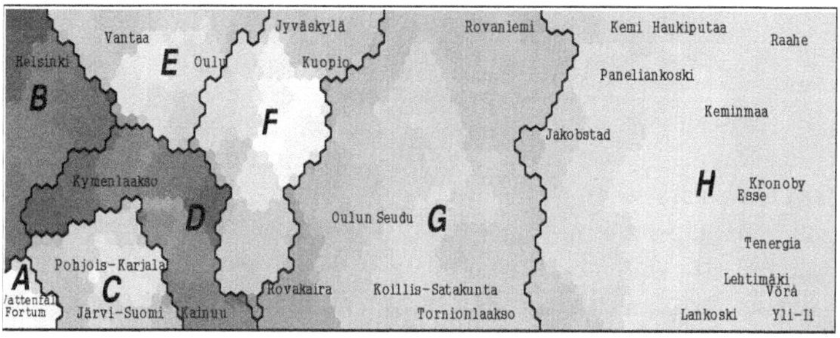

Fig. 6. Efficiency performance in 2003

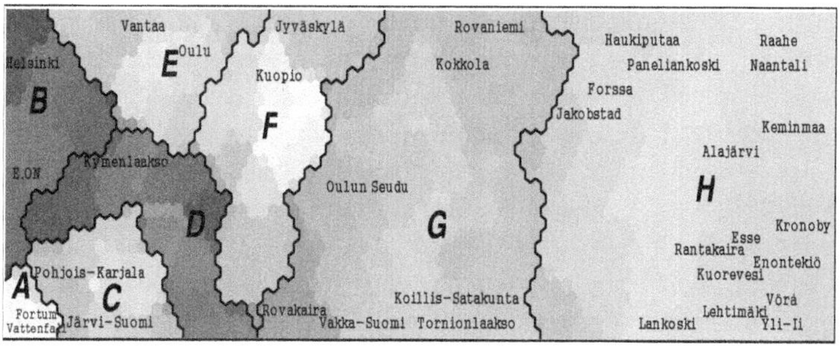

Fig. 7. Efficiency performance in 2004

Below (Fig. 8-11) are some snapshots for the purpose of illustration:

Since both Vantaa and Oulu performed efficiently in 2001, we can compare their respective efficiency profile with regards to the 5 DEA benchmarking measurements, from the perspective of both being within the same cluster. For instance, their Network Length values (Vantaa: 2,805 km; Oulu: 2,782 km) are at the lower band side of the cluster E they belong to (Min. 2,239 km; Mean 3,026 km; and Max. 7,793 km), whereas they are on the higher band side regarding the Number of Users (Vantaa: 84,760; Oulu: 72,325; cluster E: Min. 58,808; Mean 73,781; and Max. 93,209). On the other hand, the values of Interruption Time and Operating Cost reveal a mixed picture: they share a similar profile of short Interruption Time –Vantaa's is the cluster's minimum (37,012 h/year), while Oulu's (53,400 h/year) is below the group's mean value (69,943 h/year). On the contrary, Vantaa has relatively high cost attribute (8,222 teuro), which is above the group's mean value (8,042 teuro); whereas Oulu's Operating Cost is 5,230 teuro, close to the cluster's minimum (5,186 teuro).

If only comparing the 5 efficiency attributes between Vantaa and Oulu, it can be seen that Vantaa has higher value in almost all of the efficiency measurements than Oulu, except for that of Interruption Time (see Table II). The negative correlation between Operating Cost and Interruption Time which has been revealed in the case of Vantaa and Oulu raises the need for further investigation, but it is beyond the scope of this study.

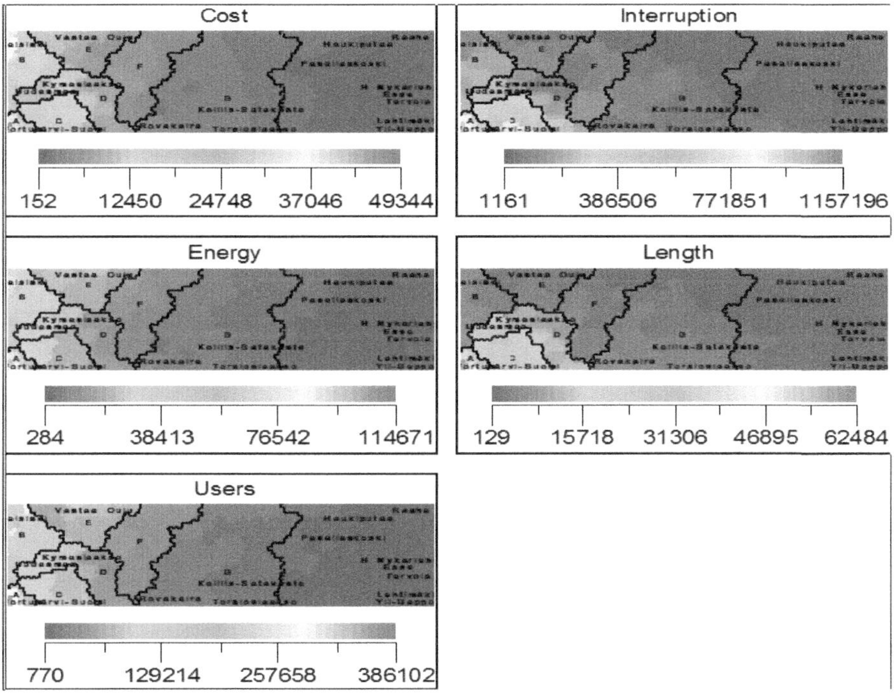

Fig. 8. Feature planes of efficiency performance in 2001

Range: Cluster X: 15 Y: 4 Nodes: 142 C 5: E, Oulu, Vantaa

Component	Mean	Std. deviation	Minimum	Maximum	Sum
Cost	8042	1904	5186	11151	128671
Interruption	69943	25015	37012	147822	1119090
Energy	22354	2158	17723	26008	357670
Length	3026	668	2239	7793	48416
Users	73781	8126	58808	93209	1180490

Fig. 9. Values for cluster E in 2001

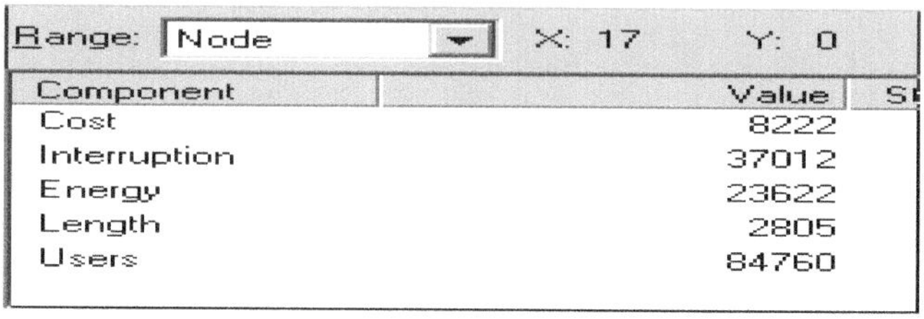

Fig. 10. Values for Vantaa in 2001

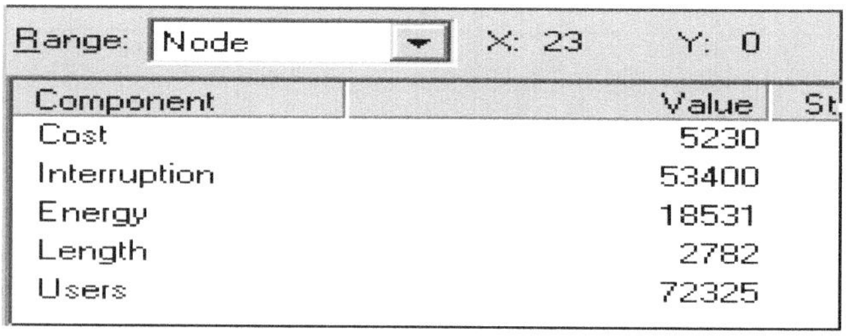

Fig. 11. Values for Oulu in 2001

Table 2. Attributes of Vantaa and Oulu

DSO	Efficiency Measurements				
	Operating Cost (teuro)	*Interruption Time (h/year)*	*Distributed Energy (teuro)*	*Network Length (km)*	*Number of Users*
Vantaa	8,222	37,012	23,622	2,805	84,760
Oulu	5,230	53,400	18,531	2,782	72,325

5 Conclusion

As discussed above, this study applied visual data mining with the SOM to perform clustering and visualization in the context of Finnish electricity distribution regulation and efficiency benchmarking. The data investigated are derived from the EMA database for the period of 2001-2004. The variables inspected are in accordance with the Finnish DEA efficiency benchmarking measurements. A SOM-model has been built. The contribution of such a computational intelligence driven approach can be concluded in the following:

Firstly, the 90 or so Finnish DSOs were grouped into 8 clusters. Based on the domain expert's evaluation, such a clustering result represents the operating differences of the Finnish DSOs. Through cluster analysis, the characteristics of DSOs in a particular group can be discriminated. Not only are the similarities and differences between clusters visible, but the correlations between specific measurements are also displayed. The SOM-model thus offers us an opportunity to study the Finnish electricity distribution sector on a comparable scale. To this end, we can draw the conclusion that the SOM is capable of clustering the Finnish electricity distribution sector in a meaningful manner.

Secondly, through visualization, the SOM-model makes the changes and trends in terms of efficiency performance and improvements in the Finnish context explicit. Additionally, it provides the possibility to investigate the efficiency performance in association with the DEA benchmarking measurements in a comprehensible and easy-to-use way. It implies the applicability of the SOM as a complementary analytical tool in Finnish electricity distribution benchmarking.

Thirdly, on a related note, the SOM-model would in particular make regulatory sense in connection with the yardstick scheme, used e.g., by Sweden and Spain. In yardstick regulation the goal is to identify a reference performance for utilities to compare with in terms of operating circumstances. The application of the SOM in this study demonstrates its capability to identify the DSOs with similar operating circumstances. Therefore, yardstick regulation may benefit from the application of the SOM for clustering of DSOs. This is considered as added value of applying visual data mining with the SOM as a complementary approach in electricity distribution regulation.

Finally, there are several issues emerging for future research consideration. At first, this study adopted a weak evaluation form based on the design science research framework. Therefore, interpreting and analyzing the outcomes could be further developed in the form of stronger validation. Next, the established SOM-model is based on the Finnish DEA-model measurements. It does not take into account factors such as capital cost and investments. In fact, such factors have an important impact in connection with regulation, benchmarking, and business strategies. It might be of interest to include these factors into the SOM approach in the future. On the other hand, this study has focused on the Finnish electricity distribution sector. The Finnish DSOs at large performed relatively efficiently. To some extent, it means that the observations are fairly homogeneous. Therefore, the applicability of the SOM in a highly heterogeneous energy market context needs further examination.

Acknowledgements. The financial support from the Finnish Funding Agency for Technology and Innovation (grant No. 40063/08) and the Academy of Finland (grant No. 127656) is gratefully acknowledged. We also would like to thank Peter Sarlin for his comments on training evaluation.

References

1. Comnes, G.A., Stoft, S., Greene, N., Hill, L.J.: Performance-Based Ratemaking for Electric Utilities: Review of Plans and Analysis of Economic and Resource Planning Issues, vol. I. University of California, Berkeley (1995)
2. Hall, G.L.: lectricity pricing and regulatory practice in a competitive environment. In: Workshop Paper No. 2: Analysis of Alternative Ratemaking Methodologies, Manila (2000)
3. Hill, L.: A Primer on Incentive Regulation for Electric Utilities. Technical Report, No. ORNL/CON-422, Oak Ridge National Laboratory, TN (1995)
4. Jamasb, T., Pollitt, M.: Benchmarking and regulation of electricity transmission and distribution utilities: lessons from international experience. In: Cambridge Working Papers in Economics 0101, Faculty of Economics. University of Cambridge (2000)
5. Joskow, P.J., Schmalensee, R.: Incentive regulation for electric utilities. Yale Journal on Regulation 4(1), 1–49 (1986)

6. Farsi, M., Fetz, A., Filipini, M.: Benchmarking and regulation in the electricity distribution sector. In: CEPE Working Paper No. 54, Centre for Energy Policy and Economics. Swiss Federal Institutes of Technology, Zürich (2007)
7. Honkapuro, S., Lassila, J., Viljainen, S., Tahvanainen, K., Partanen, J.: Effects of benchmarking of electricity distribution companies in Nordic countries – comparison between different benchmarking methods. In: Nordic Distribution and Asset Management Conference (Nordac 2004), Espoo, Finland, August 23-24 (2004)
8. Jamasb, T., Pollitt, M.: Benchmarking and regulation: international electricity experience. Utilities Policy 9(3), 107–130 (2001)
9. Jamasb, T., Pollitt, M.: International utility benchmarking & regulation: an application to European electricity distribution companies. In: Cambridge Working Papers in Economics 0115, Faculty of Economics. University of Cambridge (2002)
10. Kinnunen, K.: Pricing of electricity distribution: an empirical efficiency study in Finland, Norway and Sweden. Utilities Policy 13, 15–25 (2005)
11. Korhonen, P.J., Syrjänen, M.J.: Evaluation of cost efficiency in Finnish electricity distribution. Annals of Operations Research 121, 105–122 (2003)
12. Edvardsen, D.F., Førsund, F.R.: International benchmarking of electricity distribution utilities. Resource and Energy Economics 25, 353–371 (2003)
13. Kinnunen, K.: Investment incentives: regulation of the Finnish electricity distribution. Energy Policy 34, 853–862 (2006)
14. Back, B., Sere, K., Vanharanta, H.: Managing complexity in large data bases using Self-Organizing Maps. Accounting, Management & Information Technology 8(4), 191–210 (1998)
15. Debock, G., Kohonen, T.: Visual Explorations in Finance with Self-Organizing Maps. Springer, London (1998)
16. Eklund, T., Back, B., Vanharanta, H., Via, A.: Using the Self-Organizing Map as a visualization tool in financial benchmarking. Information Visualization 2(3), 171–181 (2003)
17. Kiviluoto, K.: Predicting bankruptcies with the Self-Organizing Map. Neurocomputing 21(1-3), 191–201 (1998)
18. Kohonen, T.: Self-organizing maps, 3rd edn. Springer, Berlin (2001)
19. Hevner, A.R., March, S.T., Park, J., Ram, S.: Design science in information systems research. MIS Quarterly 28(1), 75–105 (2004)
20. Järvinen, P.: On Research Methods. Opinpajan Kirja, Tampere (2004)
21. March, S.T., Smith, G.F.: Design and natural science research on information technology. Decision Support Systems 15(4), 166–251 (1995)
22. Bishop, C.M.: Neural Networks for Pattern Recognition. Oxford University Press, Avon (1995)
23. Vesanto, J., Alhoniemi, E.: Clustering of the self-organizing map. IEEE Transactions on Neural Networks 11(3), 586–600 (2000)
24. Haykin, S.: Neural networks: a comprehensive foundation, 2nd edn. Prentice Hall, Upper Saddle River (1999)
25. Oja, M., Kaski, S., Kohonen, T.: Bibliography of Self-Organizing Map (SOM) Papers: 1998-2001 Addendum. Neural Computing Surveys 3, 1–156 (2002)
26. Lendasse, A., Lee, J., Wertz, V., Verleysen, M.: Forecasting electricity consumption using nonliner projection and self-organizing maps. Neurocomputing 48, 299–311 (2002)
27. Nababhushana, T.N., Veeramanju, K.T.: Shivanna: Coherency identification using growing self organizing feature maps (power system stability. In: IEEE Proceedings of EMPD 1998 International Conference on Energy Management and Power Delivery, vol. 1, pp. 113–116 (1998)

28. Rehtanz, C.: Visualisation of voltage stability in large electric power systems. IEEE Proceedings Generation, Transmission and Distribution 146, 573–576 (1999)
29. Riqueline, J., Martinez, J.L., Gomez, A., Goma, D.C.: Possibilities of artificial neural networks in short-term load forecasting. In: Proceedings of the IASTED International Conference Power and Energy Systems, pp. 165–170. IASTED/ACTA Press, Anaheim, CA, USA (2000)
30. Bogetoft, P., Otto, L.: Benchmarking with DEA, SFA, and R. International Series in Operations Research & Management Science, vol. 157. Springer, Heidelberg (2011)
31. Charnes, A., Cooper, W.W., Rhodes, E.: Measuring the efficiency of decision making units. European Journal of Operational Research 2, 429–444 (1978)
32. Jamasb, T., Pollitt, M.: International benchmarking and regulation: an application to European electricity distribution utilities. Energy Policy 31(15), 1609–1622 (2003)
33. Banker, R.D., Morey, R.C.: Efficiency analysis for exogenously fixed inputs and outputs. Operations Research 34, 513–521 (1986)

The Intervening Role of Infrastructures in E-Learning Performance

Abbas Keramati[1], Masoud Afshari-Mofrad[2], Delnia Amir-Ashayeri[3], and Alireza Nili[4]

[1] Industrial Engineering Department, University of Tehran, P.O. Box 11155-4563, Tehran, Iran
[2] Information Tchnology Managemet Department, Tarbiat Modares University, P.O. Box 14115-111, Tehran, Iran
[3] Faculty of Managemet, University of Tehran, P.O. Box 11155-4563, Tehran, Iran
[4] Department of Business Administration, Technology, and Social Sciences, Lulea University of Technology, Lulea, Sweden / International University of Chabahr, Chabahar, Iran
{Keramati,M.Afshari}@ut.ac.ir, {Delnia67,Alireza.nili}@yahoo.com

Abstract. Although many researchers have studied different factors which affect E-Learning performance, there is little research on assessment of the intervening role of infrastructures in E-Learning performance. This study proposes a conceptual model to determine the role of infrastructures in the relationship between E-Learning factors and performance. A questionnaire was completed by 96 respondents. This sample consists of teachers at Tehran high schools who are utilizing a technology-based educating method. Hierarchical regression analysis is done and its results strongly support the appropriateness of the proposed model and prove that infrastructure plays a moderating role in the relationship between E-Learning factors and performance. Also latent moderated structuring (LMS) technique and MPLUS3 software are used to determine each variable's ranking. Results show that organizational infrastructure has the most important effect on E-Learning performance and teacher is the most important factor in E-Learning.

Keywords: E-Learning; Performance, Infrastructures; Moderating variable.

1 Introduction

During recent years, designing and implementing web-based education (E-Learning) systems have become ordinary for university students and lecturers [1] and this type of education is playing an important role in teaching and learning [2]. It is implementing as a new method of training which complements traditional methods [3] and its final ambition is to build an advanced society for citizens and support creativity and innovation [4]. In fact this new paradigm shifts education from teacher-centered to learner-centered [5]. There are many definitions for E-Learning. Some

E. Ariwa and E. El-Qawasmeh (Eds.): DEIS 2011, CCIS 194, pp. 646–652, 2011.

researchers have defined it as using all electronic media including: the internet, intranets, extranets, satellites, audio/video tapes, TV and CD-ROMs for instruction delivery [6]. In a narrow definition, E-Learning refers to delivery of learning material, course content and course communications assisted by technology. Advantages like cost reduction, elimination of time and space constraint and assisting the traditional instruction make it important and popular [7]. In addition, quality of education in distance education systems depends on the quality of electronic knowledge sources and other didactic materials instead of depending on teacher's quality and his ability to share knowledge [8]. The growth rate of E-Learning market is about 35.6% [9] and recent researches have shown that only in America, nearly $40 billion is spent annually on technology based training [10]. Considering such a great amount of investing in this system, it is essential to evaluate its different aspects and understand factors affecting its effectiveness [11]. Success in implementing and using this system is crucial because an unsuccessful attempt will be clearly revealed in terms of the return of investment [12]. One of the most important variables which can have a critical effect on E-Learning successful performance is infrastructure and schools have to set up or upgrade their infrastructures [13].

In general, two major approaches toward E-Learning infrastructures can be determined in the literature. In the first approach, some researchers tried to extract different infrastructures for implementing an effective E-Learning system. For instance, Kaur (2004) presented the factors of technological infrastructures, own level of readiness, etc [14]. Aydin and Tasci (2005) have focused on human resource infrastructures as an important variable in E-Learning effectiveness in emerging countries [15]. Darab and Montazer (2011) proposed an eclectic model for assessing E-Learning readiness and categorized infrastructures into three main groups [16]. Fathian et al. (2008) have evaluated e-readiness factors in Iran's environment. They have extracted organizational features, ICT infrastructures, ICT availability and security as critical issues for e-readiness assessment [17]. In the second approach, some researchers have considered infrastructure as an independent variable which affects E-Learning performance directly. For instance, Sun et al. (2008) have considered some infrastructures (such as: technology dimension and design dimension) as independent variables which affect E-Learning performance directly [9]. Also Johnson et al. (2009) have assessed the effect of technological infrastructures on E-Learning outcomes [10].

Although aforementioned researches evaluate different E-Learning aspects, there is little research on assessment of the intervening role of infrastructures in E-Learning performance. To overcome this shortcoming, in this study the role of infrastructures on the relationship between E-Learning factors and performance is assessed. In fact, there are some aspects of E-Learning (such as school's space) which don't have a direct impact on teachers' productivity but a better environmental condition will affect E-Learning performance indirectly.

In our model, based on previous researches, E-Learning factors were grouped into four groups including student, teacher, information technology and management support and commitment. Also we categorized infrastructures into three main groups including: technical, organizational and social factors.

Technical factors include: Hardware, software, content, internet access, bandwidth and school's space.

Organizational factors include: experts, organizational rules, organizational culture and management permanence.

Social factors include: society's conception of E-Learning, governmental rules and administrative instructions.

Radhakrirshnan et al. examined the effects of IT on value creation through enabling business processes capabilities [18]. Also, Albadvi et al. considered the role of organizational infrastructures (OIS) on the relationship between IT and firm performance [19]. As the results of these works imply, to have a better level of performance, it is essential to invest in intervening variables in addition to invest in IT. Accordingly, it is important to know which aspects of IT and infrastructures have the greater effect on performance. Such knowledge could be used to make wiser investments in IT. According to these researches this paper aims to assess the role of E-Learning infrastructures in the relationship between E-Learning factors and performance. To our knowledge, this is the first study which considered infrastructure as a moderating variable.

Considering the important role of infrastructure in E-Learning implementation will help managers and practitioners to promote its performance. So the following two main questions of this research are considered:

- Do infrastructures have a moderating effect on the relationship between E-Learning factors and performance?
- How much is the moderating effect of different aspects of infrastructures (which aspects are more important)?

2 Methods

Case studies and empirical researches are appropriate ways for IT researches [20]. This research is an empirical study by means of questionnaire in Iranian high schools. To recognize variables which affect E-Learning performance and identify research variables, 9 interviews were conducted with E-Learning experts in the IT sector of Training Bureau in Tehran. Based on an extensive review of interview transcripts and reviewing literature, research variables were recognized. An initial set of questions was developed to measure each variable. 2 academic experts viewed each of the items on the questionnaire for its content, scope and purpose (content validity).

A 5-point Likert scale (1 = completely disagree, 5 = completely agree) questionnaire was used to measure the variables of the model. 96 respondents answered research's questionnaires but four questionnaires were ignored since they were not complete. This sample consists of teachers at Tehran high schools who are utilizing a web-based educating.

Conceptual model of this study is depicted in figure 1. As shown in this figure, the model is composed from three variables including: E-Learning factors, Infrastructures and Performance. As mentioned before, this research tries to examine the moderating effect of infrastructures on the relationship between E-Learning factors and performance.

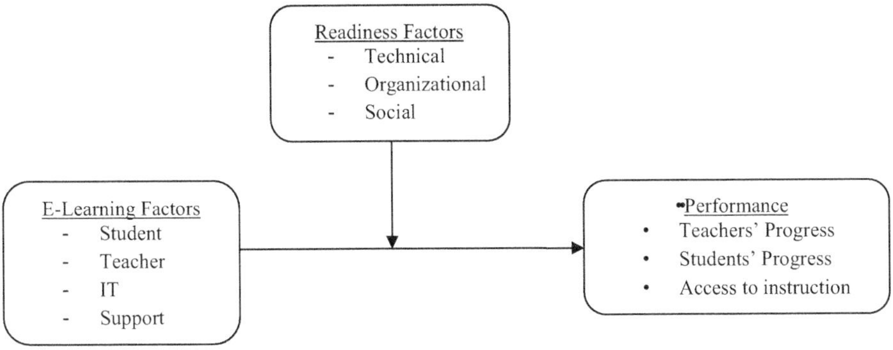

Fig. 1. Research's conceptual model

In this research, hierarchical regression analysis (HRA) is used to confirm the moderating role of infrastructures. Normality test of data is a prerequisite for using HRA. Kolmogrov-Smirnov (K-S) test is performed to test normality of data and since non-significant result (Sig value of more than .05) indicates normality, all variables (CSFs, Infrastructures and Performance) have normal data (E-Learning variable = 0.085, Infrastructures = 0.917 and Performance = 0.559). Also, using latent moderated structuring (LMS) technique and MPLUS 3 software, we rank infrastructure elements and each E-Learning factor. Figure 2 shows the complete structural model and effect of each element on performance.

3 Results

As stated earlier, hierarchical regression analysis is used to determine the moderating role of infrastructures. Table 1 shows the results of HRA.

Table 1. Hierarchical regression results

			t-test				F-Test	
Step	Measurement Scale	B	Statistics	Sig.	R square	• R Square	Statistics	Sig.
Technical: TECH								
1	TECH	0.374	1.974	0.000	0.099	0.099	8.240	0.000
2	ELNG	0.467	4.238	0.000	0.182	0.083	9.472	0.000
3	TECH*ELNG	0.711	4.564	0.000	0.345	0.163	14.73	0.000
Organizational: ORG								
1	ORG	0.515	4.735	0.000	0.209	0.209	22.418	0.000
2	ELNG	0291	2.409	0.018	0.260	0.051	14.744	0.000
3	ORG*ELNG	1.114	7.111	0.000	0.540	0.280	32.486	0.000
Social: SOC								
1	SOC	0.236	4.802	0.000	0.159	0.158	16.659	0.000
2	ELNG	0.366	3.348	0.001	0.255	0.096	14.920	0.000
3	SOC*ELNG	0.297	2.998	0.021	0.264	0.009	10.266	0.000
Infrastructure: IST								
1	IST	0.491	4.522	0.000	0.196	0.196	20.451	0.000
2	ELNG	0.323	2.789	0.007	0.265	0.069	14.940	0.000
3	IST*ELNG	6.046	1.018	0.000	0.491	0.227	26.409	0.000

As shown in this table, all significance levels are lesser than 0.05 and therefore all relationships are statistically significant.

In order to rank each element, the real effect of each factor is calculated considering all paths between that factor and PER, then the factors are ranked in the order of calculated values for their effect on PER.

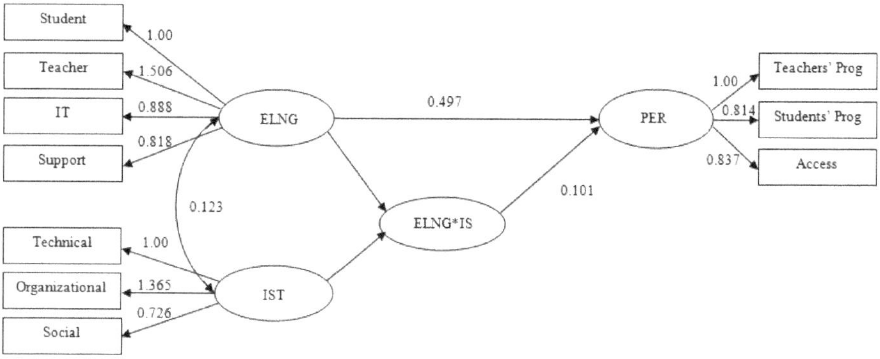

Fig. 2. Complete structural model

The rankings are shown in Tables 4 and 5 using the results from the model. The tables show the rank of the different factors based on the research model. For example, Total effect of STUDENT is calculated as:

$$\text{Total effect of STUDENT} = 1.00*0.497 + 1.00*0.101 = 0.598$$

In the above formula, the effect of STUDENT is calculated by the summation of the two possible paths from STUDENT to PER. The coefficient of 1.00 is gained from the measurement model, 0.497 is the direct effect of ELNG on PER and 0.101 is the effect of interaction of ELNG and IST on PER, calculated from the structural model.

Table 2 and Table 3 show the results of using MPLUS 3 software and LMS technique to rank different elements.

Table 2. Results of ranking different ELNG elements

Rank	E-Learning element	Total effect
1	Teacher	0.900
2	Student	0.598
3	IT	0.531
4	Support	0.489

Table 3. Results of ranking different IST elements

Rank	Infrastructure element	Total effect
1	Organizational	0.137
2	Technical	0.101
3	Social	0.073

4 Discussion and Conclusion

Although many researchers have studied different factors which affect E-Learning performances, there is little research on assessment of the intervening role of infrastructures. Based on Albadvi and Radhakrishnan ([18], [19]), this research tried to determine the intervening role of infrastructures in the relationship between E-Learning factors and performance. Based on Selim (2007), E-Learning factors grouped into 4 categories namely: Student, teacher, IT and support [21]. Also based on previous researches and authors' experiences, infrastructures grouped into three groups including: Technical, Organizational and Social. A survey conducted and 96 teachers In Tehran high schools filled research's questionnaire. Using hierarchical regression analysis, it is proved that infrastructure variable plays a moderating role in this relationship.

Also LMS technique and MPLUS 3 software were used to rank the effects of different aspects of variables. Results demonstrated that organizational infrastructure is the most important aspect which influences E-Learning performance. Technical infrastructure and social infrastructure are in lower levels of importance. The results of the ranking of different E-Learning elements show that in spite of previous researches which have shown that student is the most important element of E-Learning [15], teacher plays the most important role in E-Learning performance in Iranian high schools. This result revealed that to shift learning environment from teacher-centered to learner-centered, the first step is to train teachers and clarify advantages of this new paradigm for them. This is consistent with our interviewees' comments. They believed that one of the most difficulties in implementing and using E-Learning in Iran is lack of readiness in teachers.

References

1. Paechter, M., Maier, B., Macher, D.: Students' expectations of, and experiences in e-learning: Their relation to learning achievements and course satisfaction. Com. & Edu. 54, 222–229 (2010)
2. Franceschi, K., Lee, R.M., Zanakis, S.H., Hinds, D.: Engaging group E-Learning in virtual worlds. J. of Mgmt Info. Sys. 26(1), 73–100 (2009)
3. Gazinoory, S., Afshari-Mofrad, M.: Ranking different factors which affect E-Learning outcomes. In: International Conference on Information and Computer Applications, Dubai, pp. 400–403 (2011)

4. Kim, C.J.: Construction of E-Learning environments in Korea. ETR&D 53(4), 108–115 (2005)
5. Lee, B.C., Yoon, J.O., Lee, I.: Learners' acceptance of E-Learning in South Korea: Theories and results. Comp. & Edu. 53(4), 1320–1329 (2009)
6. Chang, T.Y., Chen, Y.T.: Cooperative learning in E-Learning: A peer assessment of student-centered using consistent fuzzy preference. Exp. Sys. with App. 36, 8342–8349 (2009)
7. Macgregor, G., Turner, J.: Revisiting e-learning effectiveness: proposing a conceptual model. Interactive Tech. and Smart Edu. 6(3), 156–172 (2009)
8. Cohen, E.B., Nycz, M.: Learning objects and E-Learning: an informing science perspective. Interdisciplinary J. of Knowledge and Learning Objects 2, 23–34 (2006)
9. Sun, P.C., Tsai, R.J., Finger, G., Chen, Y.Y., Yeh, D.: What drives a successful E-Learning?: An empirical investigation of the critical factors influencing learner satisfaction. Comp. & Edu. 50(4), 1183–1202 (2008)
10. Johnson, R.D., Gueutal, H., Cecilia, M.F.: Technology, trainees, metacognitive activity and E-Learning effectiveness. J. of Managerial Psych. 24(6), 545–566 (2009)
11. Schreurs, J., Sammour, G., Ehlers, U.: ERA - E-Learning Readiness Analysis: A e-Health case study of E-Learning readiness. In: WSKS. CCIS, pp. 267–275 (2008)
12. Govindasamy, T.: Successful implementation of E-Learning: Pedagogical considerations. The Internet and Higher Edu. 4(3-4), 287–299 (2001)
13. Wang, Q., Zhu, Z., Chen, L., Yan, H.: E-Learning in China. Campus-Wide Info. Sys. 26, 47–61 (2009)
14. Kaur, K.: An assessment of e-learning readiness at the Open University Malaysia. In: International Conference on Computers in Education, Kualalumpur (2004)
15. Aydin, C.H., Tasci, D.: Measuring readiness for E-Learning: reflections from an emerging country. Edu. Tech. & Society 8(4), 244–257 (2005)
16. Darab, B., Montazer, G.A.: An eclectic model for assessing e-learning readiness in the Iranian universities. Comp. & Edu. 56(30), 900–910 (2011)
17. Fathian, M., Akhavan, P., Hoorali, M.: E-readiness assessment of non-profit ICT SMEs in a developing country: The case of Iran. Technovation 28(9), 578–590 (2008)
18. Radhakrishnan, A., Zu, X., Grover, V.: A process-oriented perspective on differential business value creation by information technology: an empirical investigation. Omega 36(6), 1105–1125 (2008)
19. Albadvi, A., Keramati, A., Razmi, J.: Assessing the impact of information technology on firm performance considering the role of intervening variables: organizational infrastructures and business processes reengineering. Inter. J. of Prod. Research 45(12), 2697–2734 (2007)
20. Baroudi, J.J., Orlikowski, W.J.: The problem of statistical power in MIS research. MISQ 13(1), 87–106 (1989)
21. Selim, H.M.: Critical success factors for E-Learning acceptance: Confirmatory factor models. Comp. & Edu. 49(2), 396–413 (2007)

An Integrated Model of Technological and Behavioral Perspectives for Household Internet Adoption: An Empirical Study on Iranian Communities

Vahid Khatibi, Shima Mohebbi, and Abbas Keramati*

Industrial Engineering Department, Faculty of Engineering,
University of Tehran, Tehran, Iran
P.O. Box 11365-4563, Tehran, Iran
Tel.: +98 (21) 82084194
{vahid.khatibi,smohebbi,keramati}@ut.ac.ir

Abstract. The existing theories in the technology acceptance and Internet adoption fields could be classified to technological and behavioral approaches. In this paper, we propose an integrated household Internet adoption model combining both perspectives, so as the three primal models of technology acceptance model (TAM), theory of planned behavior (TPB) and uses and gratifications theory (U&G) are selected to construct the integrated model. The relations between the proposed model's constructs are then hypothesized based on the literature findings, and examined in a case study of Internet adoption among Iranian household users.

Keywords: Internet Adoption, Technology acceptance model (TAM), Theory of planned behavior (TPB), Uses and gratifications theory (U&G), Iranian communities.

1 Introduction

Information and communication technology (ICT) is the foundation for the development of the information society. The development of the household information technology has a deep impact on the development of social information [1]. Therefore, the starting point of the information society and dissemination of electronic applications begins from the consolidation of acceptance, access, and continuous usage of the ICTs by households and individuals. As the Internet gains wider acceptance, information society has begun to emerge and take form. Thus, the vast technological possibilities of the Internet cause the fast progress of the information society. The Internet can be used for very diverse purposes. It has become one of the most important means of new forms of cooperation and competition in the various subsystems of society. Anderson [2] concluded that Internet has a great influence on people's connections to friends, family, and their communities, on the social system of formal and informal support, and on the working of groups and

* Corresponding author.

E. Ariwa and E. El-Qawasmeh (Eds.): DEIS 2011, CCIS 194, pp. 653–666, 2011.

teams. Flanagin and Metzger [3] stated that the Internet can be seen now as the worldwide device for communications, which provides exchange of the text, graphics, audio and video information and access to the on-line services without boundaries. Furthermore, it is the valuable instrument of scientific, social, marketing researches, and businesses development. The Internet as an information and entertainment technology has affected education, government, publishing, the retail industry, banking, broadcast services, and health care delivery. The scope of Internet applications is therefore broad, and forces to deliver the Internet resource to households. Thus, the core indicators on accept and usage of Internet by households and individuals should be used in parallel with e-business activities blossom as a starting point of countries that are planning to implement the information society. Although many countries are attempting to build an information infrastructure and accelerate the adoption of Internet access technology, the results are not always satisfactory [4]. Further, in the Iranian communities, the percentage of Internet penetration is announced 43.2% in 2010, according to the Internet World Stats of Miniwatts Marketing Group (2010)[1] report.

In the Internet adoption field of study, there have been proposed several popular theories such as technology acceptance model [5], diffusion of innovations theory [6]; the theory of reasoned action [7]; social cognitive theory [8], and the theory of planned behavior [9] which can be classified into two categories: behavioral and technological models. The goal of this study is to propose an integrated household Internet adoption model combining both technological and behavioral perspectives. For this purpose, three primal theories of technology acceptance and usage behavior including technology acceptance model (TAM), theory of planned behavior (TPB) and uses and gratifications theory (U&G) are chosen such that an integrated model for household Internet adoption is proposed whose dimensions are defined based on the integration of the aforementioned theories' dimensions. The applicability of the proposed integrated model is examined for study of Internet adoption in the Iranian communities. The results of the current study will be helpful for various stakeholders that pursue household Internet penetration as a national policy and also will assist regulators, governments and the telecommunications providers to understand the broader issues of household Internet adoption such as the dimensions of adopters' internal beliefs, usage behavior, the intention to continued usage, and the factors affecting the acceptance of household Internet technology. Such findings can be applied to determine the appropriate facilitating and stimulating strategies for adopting household Internet at Iranian communities.

This paper is organized as follows. After introduction of technology acceptance and Internet adoption theories in Section 2, the integrated model for household Internet adoption have been proposed in Section 3. In the next pace, the research methodology including the measurement instrument, instrument development and reliability and validity analysis have been presented in Section 4. The empirical results of applying the proposed model on Iranian users based on structural equation modelling are presented in Section 5, and the case study's findings and implications are discussed in Section 6.

[1] http://www.internetworldstats.com/

2 Internet Adoption Theories

In order to measure users' acceptance of IT applications as well as factors affecting adoption of similar technologies, several models and theories with roots in IS, psychology, and sociology have been proposed including diffusion of innovations theory [6]; the theory of reasoned action [7]; social cognitive theory [8], and the theory of planned behavior [9]. Shan et al. [1] dichotomized this broad area of research. One important stream has focused on individual acceptance of technology, and employed intention-based models which use behavioral intention to predict usage. Such investigations mainly focus on the identification of the determinants of intention, such as internal beliefs of adopter, social influences, and facilitating conditions. Because of our concentration on both technological and behavioral perspectives, the three primal models of technology acceptance and usage behavior including technology acceptance model (TAM), theory of planned behavior (TPB) and uses and gratifications theory (U&G) are selected to develop the proposed model of research. It is worth mentioning that TPB and TAM stems from the Theory of Reasoned Action (TRA), which is based on the assumption that reasoned action is the motive behind behavioral intention [10]. TAM and TPB tailored to examine IT adoption on the job within organizational settings [10, 11, 12, 13] . Therefore, we advocate the similar concept and integrate the previous behavioral intention-based models including the TAM, TPB, and U&G Theory for constructing a conceptual model specific to household Internet adoption.

In the following, we briefly review the fundamentals of the above mentioned theories in the literature.

2.1 The Technology Acceptance Model (TAM)

TAM [5] is considered to be the most influential research model in studying, predicting, and explaining the determinants of IT acceptance and usage at the individual level [14, 15, 16]. It was tailored to IS context [10]. The TAM provides a foundation to outline the impact of situational and dispositional factors on internal beliefs, and behavioral intentions [15]. Also, Venkatesh and Davis [16] extended the original TAM model. TAM2 included additional determinants of the perceived usefulness and behavioral intention to use constructs, including social influence processes (subjective norm, image and voluntariness), cognitive instrumental processes (job relevance, output quality, result demonstrability), and experience as a moderating variable.

2.2 The Theory of Planned Behavior (TPB)

Although the TPB roots within organizational research, it is widely used by IS researchers to study IT adoption, implementation, and usage [12]. TPB extended the TRA, to account for conditions where individuals do not have absolute control over their behavior. The model of TPB asserted that attitude, subjective norm and perceived behavioral control are direct determinants of behavioral intention, which in turn affects behavior. TAM provided a more parsimonious set of constructs for predicting the adoption behavior of IT than the TPB while ignored some of the constructs that may be important in some other situations [4]. Therefore, many research efforts have been made to combine the TAM and TPB (e.g. [4, 14, 16, 17]).

2.3 The Uses and Gratifications (U&G) Theory

The U&G focuses on users' motives and their self-perceived needs [18]. Luo et al. [19] defined the motivations, usage behavior, and gratifications are three major U&G constructs which were extensively examined by communication researchers. Furthermore, U&G presupposes prior adoption of an innovation and concerns itself with the individual user's motivations to continued usage of that technology [18, 20, 21]. U&G has been used to assess a number of technologies such as, TV, radio, VCR, telephone, and cable TV media [20, 21]. The U&G perspective has also been suggested as a framework to study the motivations of individuals using the Internet in different areas (e.g. [18, 19, 22, 23]).

3 Proposed Integrated Model for Household Internet Adoption

After studying the existing theories in the technology acceptance and Internet adoption fields, we propose an integrated Internet adoption model in this section. The studied theories have taken some approaches to examine the adoption among users which can be classified in two categories: Technological and behavioral perspectives. Because of the importance of these perspectives, we mixed up the both perspectives to provide a holistic view on the subject. To achieve this purpose, we selected the three models of technology acceptance model (TAM), theory of planned behavior (TPB) and uses and gratifications theory (U&G) which are the most regular theories in the literature for studying the technological and behavioral perspectives. In following, based on the dimensions of the studied theories, some specific categories were defined to integrate these dimensions according to their similarities and appropriateness. After determination of the integrated model's dimensions, the relations between the studied models' dimensions to these categories were identified. In the next step, the most important measures to examine each of the integrated model's dimensions were obtained using a communal perspective on measures of the studied models' dimensions. The construction process of the integrated model has been exhibited in Fig. 1.

As noted before, this study is concerned with adoption and usage of household Internet which has already taken place. For this reason, we concentrate on the usage behavior and the future intention to continued usage of the household Internet based on the prior or current experience and subscription. In following, we focus on elaboration of the proposed model. For this purpose, we first determine the relations between the model' constructs based on the findings of the literature, and then examine their validity with the statistical investigations.

As illustrated in Fig. 2, the research model posits that household Internet usage behavior is influenced directly by three internal beliefs including individual perceived needs, perceived ease of use, and perceived availability of resources so that the last factor also influence directly on the behavioral intention to continuance usage

/subscription of household Internet. In addition, on the basis of the extended TAM, the usage behavior and intention to continued usage and subscription of household Internet are theorized to be influenced by external variables such as image and social norms. Hence, in our model, image has been considered as an external variable having direct influence on both usage behavior and intention to continuance usage. On the other hand, since satisfaction is a common measure of IS adoption success [24, 25], the fulfillment of needs, confirmation of expectations, and an important predictor of the intention to renewing the household Internet subscription in the future [26], it is also incorporated in the research model. A brief description of the aforementioned constructs and statistical hypothesis of the research are described below.

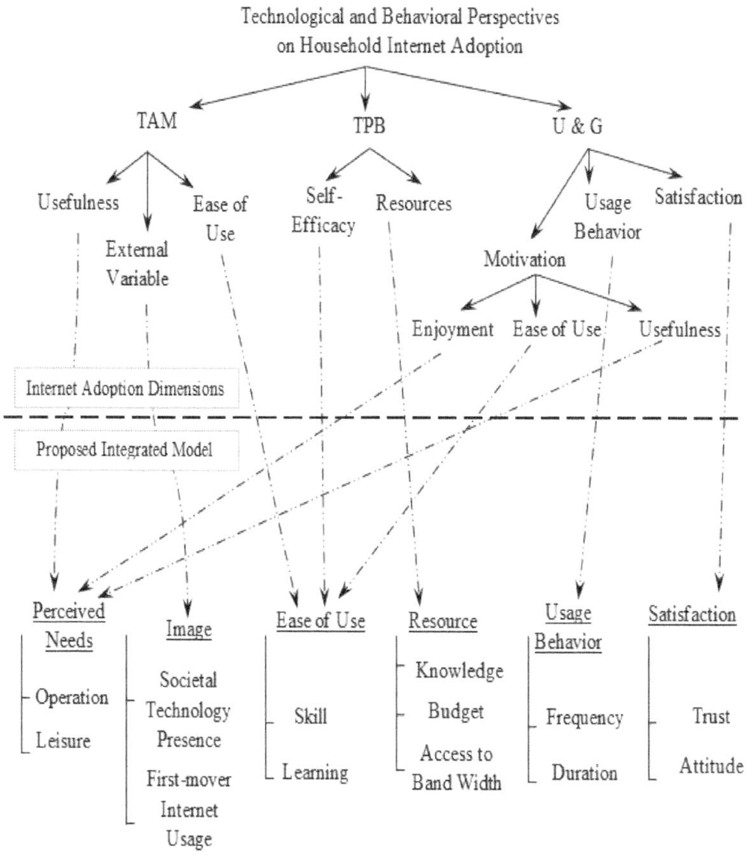

Fig. 1. Mapping Internet Adoption Dimensions to the Proposed Integrated Model

3.1 Perceived Needs (Motivations)

Adoption theory seeks to explain the organizational and individuals developing solutions to fulfill needs. Motivation theories also posit that an individual's behavior is driven by their needs; ultimately, the goal-directed action is to fulfill that individual's needs [19, 22]. Here, we refer to motivations of household Internet adoption as perceive needs, using the "Papacharissi and Rubin" scale of Internet usage motives. Therefore, researchers hypothesize:

H1: perceived needs have a positive influence on usage behavior of Iranian household Internet.

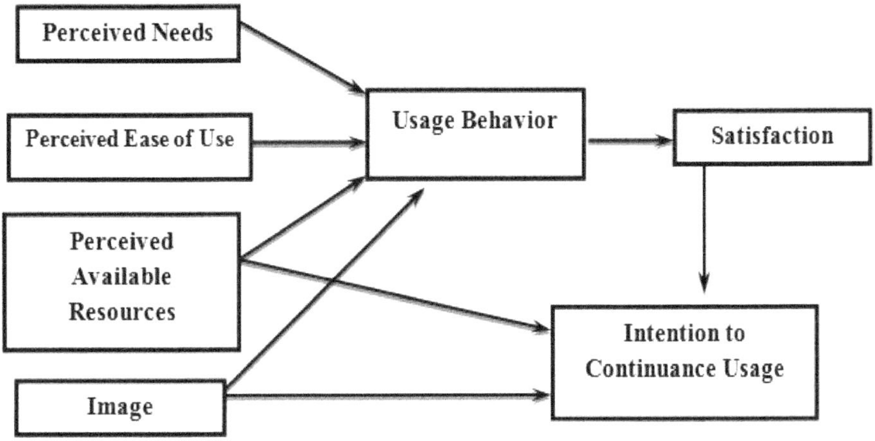

Fig. 2. Household Internet Adoption Model

3.2 Perceived Ease of Use

Perceived ease of use refers to "the degree to which a person believes that using a particular system would be free of effort. This follows from the definition of ease, which refers to freedom from difficulty or great effort. Thus, the proposition is as following:

H2: Perceived ease of use has a positive influence on usage behavior of Iranian household Internet.

3.3 Perceived Availability of Resources

This examines the availability of resources needed as perceived resources. Perceived resources refer to an individual's belief that he or she has the resources needed for adoption and using an information system or technology [27]. Therefore, this study tests the following hypotheses:

H3: Perceived availability of resources has a positive effect on usage behavior of Iranian household Internet.

H4: Perceived availability of resources has a positive effect on behavioral intention to continued usage of Iranian household Internet.

3.4 Image

Venkatesh et al. [10] described social influence as a direct determinant of behavioral intention was represented as image in Innovation Diffusion Theory (IDT). Image represents the degree to which usage of IT is perceived to enhance one's status in one's social system [28]. Therefore, researchers hypothesize that:

H5: Image has a positive effect on usage behavior of Iranian household Internet.

H6: Image has a positive effect on behavioral intention to continued usage of Iranian household Internet.

3.5 Usage Behavior, Satisfaction and Intention to Continued Usage

Ruggiero [20] Suggested that in order to use a certain ICT product or service, people derive gratification as their needs or wants are fulfilled. The terms satisfaction and gratifications both mean affective outcome derived from a specific behavior; as a result, they were sometimes used interchangeably in U&G studies [19, 20]. A number of technology adoption studies using TAM have employed user satisfaction as a measure of acceptance and adoption success [19, 24, 29, 30]. Therefore, this study hypothesizes that:

H7: There is a positive relationship between usage behavior and satisfaction.

H8: satisfaction has a positive effect on behavioral intention to continued usage of household Internet.

4 Research Methodology

4.1 Instrument Development

Here, in order to examine the research model and hypotheses, we employed the suggested measurements obtained from the integrated model so that individuals were asked to indicate their agreement or disagreement with several statements using a five-point Likert-type scale ranging from (1) strongly disagree to (5) strongly agree. The questionnaire included 18 questions items representing the 7 constructs identified in Table 1. In order to collect representative data of the target population with limited time and resources, a self-administered questionnaire was considered the most appropriate primary survey instrument in this study.

4.2 Data Collection

The participants were recruited in Tehran, the capital of Iran. In the light of the difficulty in obtaining any formal lists or information about the population, the selection of the target population was made according to the availability of those people who have been adopted and currently use the Internet in their homes.

The sample was randomly chosen from universities' teachers, household Internet adopters, and friends' networks, but the main category selected for this case study is young adults group. In this regard, It is worthy to note that the young adulthood stage in human development precedes middle adulthood and begins from the age of 20 and terminates at 40 [31]. Young adulthood is the period of achieving advanced knowledge such that the main focus is on applying the acquired knowledge in daily life. Human at this stage enter family life cycle and also re-evaluate the life structures and attempt to alter inappropriate components. Therefore, the authors believe that young adults can play the role of catalyst at community for Internet adoption as their behavioral patterns can influence directly on adolescents and indirectly on middle adults.

Table 1. Construct and Measurement of Household Internet Model

Perceived Needs
Internet is useful for entertainment and leisure. Internet is useful for acquiring information (news and etc.). Internet is useful for performing financial tasks such as checking bank accounts and paying bills. Internet is useful for participating in social networks and contacting other people (such as e-mail, chat, etc.)
Perceived Ease of Use
It is easy to be skillful at Internet. Internet is easy to learn.
Perceived Available Resources & Facilities
It would be within my budget to subscribe Internet. I have the knowledge of using Internet or there is always someone who could help me how to use it. I can have access to high speed Internet with ease.
Usage Behavior
How frequently do you believe you use the Internet? Infrequent Slightly Infrequent Frequent Slightly Frequent Extremely Frequent What is your degree of current usage of Internet? Less than 30 minute per day Between 30-60 minutes Between 1-2 hours Between 2-3 hours More than 3 hours
Satisfaction
I am satisfied with my usage of Internet. I support the idea of using Internet. Using the Internet is a secure and reliable tool for information exchange.
Image
Using emerging technologies such as Internet is momentous and symbolic in my society. Most of the prestigious people in my society use Internet for handling their works.
Intention to Continuance Usage
I would to continue the usage of Internet. I have access to high speed Internet.

In the first place, there is no arguments that if the parents plan to subscribe to Internet, their children can learn about the potential benefits of Internet and can simply know how to use it. In the second place, young adults can assure their parents, middle adults, about the security, cost-effectiveness, and easiness of Internet for performing daily works. As a result, change in attitude and perceived ability will be occurred gradually in a community. The researchers selected Tehran population's young adults as the best adopters of the emerging technologies in the country and, attempted to obtain samples covering various demographic backgrounds in order to reduce sampling bias caused by user characteristics. As a result, a total of 150 questionnaires were collected.

4.3 Reliability and Validity

The reliability analysis of a questionnaire determines its ability to yield the same results on different occasions and validity refers to the measurement of what questionnaire is supposed to measure [32]. In order to analyze reliability, we calculated Cronbach's alpha for all constructs, Need, Ease of Use, Resources, Image, Adoption, Satisfaction and Intention. Table 2 illustrates the reliability coefficients (Cronbach's alpha) of all constructs. These reliability coefficients are well above acceptable criterion of 0.70 [33], and indicate the reliability of constructs.

Construct validity of the questionnaire was assessed by means of principle component factor analyses of each construct separately. As shown in Table 2, each construct loaded on a single individual factor, because all of the Eigenvalues were considerably more than the accepted criterion of 1.0 (from 1.39 for the Image to 2.87 for the Need). Indeed, extracted single factors indicate the proper construct validity because the single individual factors accounted for about 62.00–89.00% of the total variance of each respective construct [33].

Table 2. Reliability and construct validity analysis

Constructs	Number of items	Alpha	Eigenvalue	Percentage of total variance
Need	4	0.86	2.87	71
Ease of Use	2	0.89	1.80	89
Available Resources	3	0.80	2.16	72
Image	2	0.74	1.39	69
Usage Behavior	2	0.80	1.67	83
Satisfaction	3	0.71	1.86	62
Intention to Continuance Usage	2	0.80	1.66	82

5 Empirical Results

When the validity and reliability of each criterion in the corresponding construct are specified, subsequent analysis can be done using different methods such as partial least square and multiple regressions. Here, in order to assess the model, Structural Equation Modelling (SEM) with Lisrel 8.8 is performed. LISREL examines the standardized path coefficients (direct effect) and these coefficients indicate the strengths of relationships between constructs. In SEM, two models are assessed, the measurement model and the structural model.

Table 3 illustrates descriptive statistics for each indicator and the results of the measurement model. It is specified that all the indicators have loaded highly on the relative constructs with significance levels of $p<0.01$. Convergent validity, which shows the degree of agreement in the indicators of a construct, can be assessed using variance extracted values. According to Fornell and Larcker [34], evidence of convergent validity occurs when the variance extracted values exceed 0.5 for one construct. Table 3 shows that all constructs have acceptable convergent validity.

Table 3. Results of Measurement Model

Model Construct	Measurement Criterion (Indicators)	Mean	Standard Deviation	Loading	Variance extracted
Perceived Need	N1	3.9	0.73	0.63	
	N2	4.16	0.82	0.77	
	N3	4.32	0.77	0.76	
	N4	4.38	0.74	0.99	
Total		4.19	0.76		0.71
Perceived Ease of Use	E1	3.94	0.76	0.81	
	E2	4.18	0.78	0.99	
Total		4.06	0.77		0.89
Perceived Available Resources	R1	4.32	0.79	0.87	0.72
	R2	4.44	0.72	0.65	
	R3	4.26	0.75	0.85	
Total		4.34	0.75		0.72
Image	I1	4.22	0.61	0.51	
	I2	4.28	0.83	0.98	
Total		4.25	0.72		0.69
Usage Behavior	UB1	3.86	0.88	0.84	
	UB2	3.96	1.04	0.85	
Total		3.91	0.96		0.83
Satisfaction	S1	4.26	0.59	0.52	
	S2	4.56	0.64	0.99	
	S3	4	0.72	0.61	
Total		4.27	0.65		0.62
Intention to Continued Usage	In1	4.57	0.7	0.95	
	In2	4.36	0.77	0.67	
Total		4.47	0.74		0.82

Further, the importance of each indicator within the corresponding construct can be analyzed. As shown in Table3, establishing communication and performing financial tasks through Internet exceeded from moderated level (4.19). Thereby, the highest amount of Internet usage is in communication (4.38) closely followed by financial affairs (4.32).This again points out the importance of person-to-person communication within the realm of ICTs. In other words, Internet as a tool for enjoyment and entertainment does not encourage individuals to adopt this technology. Further, the results imply that Iranian community pay considerable attention to the availability of resources so that this determinant can be considered as a pressure point for altering the usage behavior. Having required knowledge and financial resources for using Internet are exceeded from the moderated level (4.34) and hence are more important for the participants. Moreover, in this study, we asked the participant to rate the frequency of their Internet usage. The results demonstrate that most of them considered themselves as slightly frequent users. As for satisfaction, Table 3 shows that supporting the idea of using Internet for performing tasks is well above the moderate level (4.27). This reveals that cultural infrastructure is well established among Iranian communities.

Having assessed the overall model and aspects of the measurement model, we can now examine the estimated coefficients among the constructs. Here, the significance of the path coefficients is assessed by the t-values which should be greater than 1.96. The hypotheses tests are shown in Table 4.

According to the obtained path coefficients, the majority of the hypotheses to the relationships between the model constructs are supported. Perceived Needs, Perceived Ease of Use and Perceived Availability of Resources contributed significantly to the observed explanatory power of Usage Behavior, and indirect positive effect through its positive effect on an adopter Gratifications/ Satisfaction. The path coefficients are 0.45, 0.26, and 0.46 respectively. These finding are consistent with U&G perspective which claims the reasons of selecting, adopting continuously specific ICT in the voluntary choice are determined by the awareness of needs and the extent to which the technology helps to fulfil and satisfy/ gratify their felt needs or wants [19, 20, 22, 26].

Venkatesh and Davis [16] provided empirical evidence showing that ease of use becomes insignificant with increased experience. Furthermore, Venkatesh et al. [10] concluded that several constructs were initially significant, but then became not significant over time, including perceived ease of use. This explains the low significance level of perceived ease of use contribution to the usage behavior "Path coefficient=0.26"of those who has already adopted household Internet comparing with perceived needs "Path coefficient=0.45"and perceived availability of resources" Path coefficient=0.46". In the same vein, in contrast with Hypotheses 5 and 6, the obtained results illustrates that the external variable, image, has not significant direct positive effect both on Usage Behavior and Continuance Intention to Usage /Subscription. This indicates Iranian communities do not necessarily adopt Internet based on their subjective image. Although literature [1, 12, 16, 17, 35, 36] advocates the impact of social effects on ICT acceptance and adoption, our empirical study suggests that in Iranian communities other factors such as perceived usefulness and availability of resources, i.e. budget, knowledge and accessibility, are more influential than subjective image for adopting household Internet.

In addition, hypotheses 4 and 8 which postulate direct positive effect of adopter Gratifications/ Satisfaction and Perceived Availability of Resources on Continuance Intention to Usage /Subscription are supported.

Table 4. Test of Hypothesized Model

Hypothesis	Path	Standardized Path Coefficient	t-value	Test Result
H1	Need→ Usage Behavior	0.45	3.84	Supported
H2	Ease→ Usage Behavior	0.26	3.57	Supported
H3	Resource→ Usage Behavior	0.46	4.14	Supported
H4	Resource→ Intention	0.45	4.11	Supported
H5	Image→ Usage Behavior	0.01	0.14	**Not supported**
H6	Image→ Intention	0.07	0.82	**Not supported**
H7	Usage Behavior→ Satisfaction	0.89	6.25	Supported
H8	Satisfaction→ Intention	0.56	4.84	Supported

p-value< 0.01

6 Conclusions

In this paper, we proposed an integrated Internet adoption model based on the integration of three main models of technology acceptance and Internet adoption including technology acceptance model (TAM), theory of planned behavior (TPB) and uses and gratifications theory (U&G). Then, the relations between the proposed model's constructs were then hypothesized based on the literature findings, and examined in a case study of Internet adoption among Iranian users. The obtained results revealed that actual household Internet adoption among Iranian users are more affected by perceived need/usefulness and availability of resources rather than external variables such as subjective image.

References

1. Shan, A., et al.: Research of Home Information Technology Adoption Model. Homenet & Mobile Terminal 05, 10–16 (2008)
2. Anderson, B.: The Social Impact Of Broadband Household Internet Access. Information, Communication & Society 11(1), 5–24 (2008)
3. Flanagin, A.J., Metzger, M.J.: Internet use in the contemporary media environment. Human Communication Research 27(1), 153–181 (2001)
4. Oh, S., Ahn, J., Kim, B.: Adoption of broadband internet in Korea: the role of experience in building attitude. Journal of Information Technology 18(4), 267–280 (2003)
5. Davis, F.D.: Perceived usefulness, perceived ease of use, and user acceptance of information technology. MIS Quarterly 13(3), 319–339 (1989)
6. Rogers, E.: Diffusion of Innovations. Free Press, New York (1995)
7. Fishbein, M., Ajzen, I.: Belief, attitude, intention and behavior: An introduction to theory and research. Addison-Wesley, Reading (1975)
8. Bandura, A.: Social foundations of thought and action: A social cognitive theory. Prentice Hall, Englewood Cliffs (1986)
9. Ajzen, I.: The theory of planned behavior. Organizational Behavior and Human Decision Process 50(2), 179–211 (1991)

10. Venkatesh, V., et al.: User Acceptance of Information Technology: Toward a Unified View. MIS Quarterly 27(3), 425–478 (2003)
11. Choudrie, J., Dwivedi, Y.K.: A Comparative Study to Examine the Socio-economic Characteristics of Broadband Adopters and Non-adopters. International Journal of Services and Standards 3(3), 272–288 (2006)
12. Choudrie, J., Investigating, D.Y.K.: the Socio-economic Characteristics of Residential Consumers of Broadband in the UK. In: Tenth Americas Conference on Information Systems, New York (2004)
13. López-Nicolás, C., Molina-Castillo, F.J., Bouwman, H.: An Assessment of Advanced Mobile Services Acceptance: Contributions from TAM and Diffusion Theory Models. Information & Management 45(6), 359–364 (2008)
14. Chau, P.Y., Hu, P.J.: Information Technology Acceptance. Decision Sciences 32(4), 699–719 (2001)
15. Harris, K.D., Donaldson, J.F., Campbell, J.D.: Introducing Computer-Based Telemedicine in the Rural Missouri Counties. Journal of End User Computing 13(4), 45–60 (2001)
16. Venkatesh, V., Davis, F.D.: Theoretical Extension of the Technology Acceptance Model: Four Longitudinal Field Studies. Management Science 46(2), 186–204 (2000)
17. Taylor, S., Todd, P.A.: Understanding Information Technology Usage: A Test of Competing Models. Information Systems Research 6(4), 144–176 (1995)
18. Mondi, M., Woods, P., Rafi, A.: A 'Uses and Gratification Expectancy Model' to Predict Students' 'Perceived E-Learning Experience'. Educational Technology & Society 11(2), 241–261 (2008)
19. Luo, M.M.-L., Remus, W., Chea, S.: Technology Acceptance of Internet Based Information System: An Integrated Model of TAM and U & G Theory. In: Twelfth Americas Conference on Information Systems, Acapulco, Mexico (2006)
20. Ruggiero, T.E.: Uses and Gratifications Theory in the 21st Century. Mass Communication & Society 3(1), 3–37 (2000)
21. Stafford, T.F., Stafford, M.R., Schkade, L.L.: Determining uses and gratifications for the Internet. Decision Sciences 35(2), 259–288 (2004)
22. Papacharissi, Z., Rubin, A.M.: Predictors of Internet Use. Journal of Broadcasting & Electronic Media 44(2), 175–196 (2000)
23. Sun, T., Zhong, B., Zhang, J.: Uses and Gratifications of Chinese Online Gamers. China Media Research 2(2), 58–63 (2006)
24. Lin, H.-F.: Antecedents of Virtual Community Satisfaction and Loyalty: An Empirical Test of Competing Theories. Cyber Psychology and Behavior 11(2), 138–144 (2008)
25. Zviran, M., Erlich, Z.: Measuring IS User Satisfaction: Review and Implications. Communications of the Association for Information Systems 12(1), 81–103 (2003)
26. Al-Omoush, K.S., Shaqrah, A.A.: An Empirical Study of Household Internet Continuance Adoption among Jordanian Users. International Journal of Computer Science and Network Security 10(1), 32–44 (2010)
27. Mathieson, K., Peacock, E., Chin, W.: Extending the Technology Acceptance Model: The influence of Perceived Resources. The Data Base for Advances in Information Systems 32(3), 86–112 (2001)
28. Moore, G.C., Benbasat, I.: Development of an Instrument to Measure the Perceptions of Adopting an Information Technology Innovation. Information Systems Research 2(3), 192–222 (1991)
29. Adamson, I., Shine, J.: Extending the New Technology Acceptance Model to Measure the End User Information Systems Satisfaction in Mandatory Environment: A Bank's Treasury. Technology Analysis & Strategic Management 15(4), 441–455 (2003)

30. Wixom, B.H., Todd, P.A.: A Theoretical Integration of User Satisfaction and Technology Acceptance. Information System Research 16(1), 85–102 (2005)
31. Berk, L.E.: Development Through the Lifespan. Allyn & Bacon, Boston (2006)
32. Cooper, D.R., Schindler, P.S.: Business Research Methods. McGraw Hill, New York (2003)
33. Nunnally, J.C., Bernstein, I.H.: Psychometric Theory, 3rd edn. McGraw Hill, New York (1994)
34. Fornell, C., Larcker, D.F.: Evaluating structural equation models with unobservable variables and measurement error. Journal of Marketing Research 18(1), 39–50 (1981)
35. Brown, I., Letsididi, B., Nazeer, M.: Internet Access In South African Home: A preliminary Study on Factors Influencing Consumer Choice. The Electronic Journal on Information Systems in Developing Countries 38(2), 1–13 (2009)
36. Warren, M.: Farmers Online: Drivers and Impediments in Adoption of Internet in UK Agricultural Businesses. Journal of Small Business and Enterprise Development 11(3), 371–381 (2004)

Efficient Non-Quadratic Quick Sort (NQQuickSort)

Amjad M. Daoud, Hussein Abdel-jaber, and Jafar Ababneh

Department of Software Engineering,
The World Islamic Sciences and Education (W.I.S.E.) University,
Amman, Jordan
{amjad.daoud,hussein.abdeljaber,jafar.ababneh}@wise.edu.jo
http://www.wise.edu.jo

Abstract. In this paper, we present an engineered sorting algorithm, named NQQuicksort, which is efficient and non quadratic. To avoid the quadratic worst case, and degenerate partitioning performance, NQQuicksort adopts two pivot computations only. The first is the same as the pivot computation in median of three quicksort and the second is similar to that in binary quicksort (radix exchange). The pivot computations applied are quite different and non-related, such that when one pivot computation fails, it gives no indication to whether the second pivot computation step will, or will not succeed (fail). When the first pivot selected results in unbalanced partitioning, the second pivot computation is immediately applied in the next recursive call. NQQuickSort is faster than the tuned quicksort implementation of the Java class library engineered by Bentley and McIlroy [3]. The algorithm and its runtime behavior are discussed in detail. The performance of NQQuicksort is faster than quicksort as well as the fastest variant of radix sorting algorithms; the Least Significant Digit (LSD) radix sort[15].

Keywords: Sorting, QuickSort, Radix Sort, Recursion.

1 Introduction

Sorting is a computational process of arranging a collection of data items into order. Sorting is also one of the main problems studied in the field of algorithms design and analysis for many years and several books are written on this subject [1], [11], [18], [22]. Sedgewick in his book "Algorithms in Java" [21] presents a thorough treatment of the entire topic of sorting algorithms. Efficient sorting of large data sets is important for many applications and optimizing the worst case performance of sorting algorithms achieves speed-ups for computer software.

Sorting algorithms can be classified into sorting by data partitioning and sorting by comparison algorithms [17]. The basic operation in comparison sorting algorithms is a comparison operation between two different keys, using all the bits in the two keys. Sorting by comparison average case is $O(N \log N)$, where N is the input size. Quicksort is a fast sorting by comparison algorithm [8] that has

E. Ariwa and E. El-Qawasmeh (Eds.): DEIS 2011, CCIS 194, pp. 667–675, 2011.

an average case complexity of $O(N \log N)$, but it can go quadratic in the worst-case, when partitioning is degenerate. Quicksort body is very efficient relative to other sorting algorithms. When quicksort is implemented, the average case of $O(N \log N)$ is not guaranteed. Computing the pivot is critical to quicksort, affecting its efficiency and its running time complexity.

The ideal value for quicksort's pivot is the median value for the input data [20][21]. Computing the true median takes $O(N)$ operations, and results in a slow quicksort code [21]. The quicksort implementation in [20] computes the median using a three keys sample. A sample of three keys reduces the probability of the quadratic worst case, and improves the actual running time.

Recent quicksort implementations, attempt to improve performance and eliminate the quadratic worst case. Greater-than-less-than quicksort [4] attempts to compute the two child-partitions' pivots while partitioning a parent partition.

The Sumant and Goran algorithm repeats selecting a key value smaller than the current pivot, alternated with selecting a key value greater than the current key value. The selection is repeated K times, where K is a parameter to the algorithm.

Introspective Sort [19] cuts from median of three quicksort to the slower heap sort, to eliminate the quadratic quicksort. The median of three pivots [4] attempts to compute a more accurate pivot.

Our NQQuicksort pivot computing does not require larger sample sizes, or a prior computation of pivots like the quicksort algorithms above. The algorithm does not depend on non-quicksort algorithms to eliminate non-quadratic worst case, as Introspective Sort. In fact, the NQQuicksort depends on applying few pivot computation steps. When the current pivot computation step fails, we apply another (hopefully better) pivot computation recursively.

1.1 Paper Overview

In section 2, we survey related literature on quicksort. In section 3, we present the details of our algorithm. In section 4, we analyze the performance of our algorithm. In section 5, we present the experimental results of our algorithm and compare it to efficient implementations of the engineered Java quicksort implementation. Finally, in section 6, we summarize our research findings.

2 Background

An introspective quicksort algorithm is tested in [19] which does not go quadratic. This is because, the algorithm cuts to heap sort when the number of levels is $2 * \log(N)$. Introspective Sort is efficient when using the average function instead of the median function, varying the sample size adaptively, and increasing the sample size on degenerate partitioning. This would speed up Introspective Sort and make its quadratic worst cases less probable.

Our non quadratic NQQuicksort algorithm interleaves the execution of pivot computations instead of cutting permanently to a second sorting algorithm. The algorithm implements two different pivot computation steps and switches to the second pivot computation, when current partitioning fails. The two pivot computation steps applied are described as follows. The first is the same as the pivot computation in median of three quicksort and the second is similar to that in binary quicksort (radix exchange). The pivot computations applied are quite different and non-related, such that when one pivot computation fails, it gives no indication to whether the second pivot computation step will, or will not succeed (fail). On continuous failure, the algorithm continues switching to the second pivot computation step.

The common worst case is the killer of three test, which is a known worst case for quicksort [6]. In this test case, all keys are different and the distinguishing prefixes are maximal. Large distinguishing prefixes makes the killer of three test, a worst case for all radix-sorting algorithms, including binary quicksort [4] [21] applied in NQQuicksort. Radix sorting algorithms are sensitive only to distinguishing prefixes. The test results show that NQQuicksort deals with this case rather well. The distinguishing prefixes of a set of keys is the shortest prefixes of the keys that are pairwise different. Radix exchange, or binary quicksort [4] [21], is an implementation of quicksort, differing only in pivot computation. Binary quicksort, like quicksort has an average run time complexity $O(N \log N)$, where N is the input size.

The main advantage of binary quicksort over quicksort is that its run time in the worst case is bounded by $O(N * B)$ and does not go quadratic, where B is the number of bits representing the input keys. The original binary quicksort implementation, extracts the current left most bit and tests it, similar to radix sorting algorithms. Its worst case runtime complexity, $O(N * B)$ may be substituted by $O(N \log M)$, where M, the largest key value, is computed initially.

Our implementation of binary quicksort in NQQuicksort, investigates the worst case $O(N \log(M))$. We do not initially compute the largest key value. A partition's min and max key values are continually computed on partitioning and recursive calls. The pivot is the lower child partition's max and the upper child partition's min. The binary quicksort pivot computation step in NQQuickSort is independent of data. The pivot is defined as the mid value of the known input group min and max values, and may not appear in the input data.

3 Algorithm Details

The corresponding pivot computation in **algorithm SS step 1** given in Fig. 1, the *average*() function, apply the passed min and max, instead of the input's actual min and actual max. The input's known max values may be larger than the input's actual max values. Similarly, the input's known min values may be smaller than the input's actual min values.

This pivot computation makes NQQuickSort faster in adapting to non-uniform data than the original binary quicksort, which applies bit extractions, and is affected only by the length of the distinguishing prefixes.

In median of three quicksort [20], three keys, equidistant in the input array, are selected, and the median of the three values is assigned as the pivot.

The median computation is applied in **algorithm SS, Step 1** given in Fig. 1, *median_of_three*() function, and corresponds to the pivot computation in median of three quicksort. Combining the pivot computation steps of the two algorithms is such that NQQuickSort interleaves the executions of binary quicksort and median of three quicksort, by choosing and applying one of the two pivot computation steps.

The body code of binary quicksort and median of three quicksort is combined, in algorithm SS given in Fig. 1, and the efficient quicksort inner loop is coded inside the *partition*() function. The function partitions the input array, and returns the two partitions information in firstPartition, and secondPartition objects. A partition's object information includes the partition's left most and the right most element's indices. The partition () function returns the partitioning ratio in **algorithm SS, Step 2** given in Fig. 1.

The ration variable returned by the *partition*() function, is the size of the smaller of the two output partitions, to the size of the input array. If the returned ration is smaller than a preset constant, degenerate partitioning threshold (dpThreshold), we switch to the second pivot computation step in subsequent recursive calls.

In step 3, we toggle the boolean variable in recursive calls and use it to decide on a particular pivot computation. The dpThreshold constant is fixed throughout the algorithm at value 0.1. Using a reasonable degenerate partitioning threshold, in the range 0.001 to 0.3, is satisfactory in experiments. The computed pivot in **algorithm SS Step 1** given in Fig. 1, serves as the successive two child partitions' min or max values. For the lower partition, the computed pivot is the max known key value, and for the upper partition the computed pivot is the min known key value.

There is no explicit code in NQQuickSort to compute the partition's min and max values. We rely on pivots computed in Step 1, and consider pivots as child partition's min and max values. The pivot is passed to the next recursive level in **algorithm SS, Step 3** given in Fig. 1. Only if the median of three() function was applied in step 1, the actual lower range max and upper range min, are passed in recursive calls, as explained above. The following is the pseudo code of NQQuickSort.

The applied pivot computation steps in NQQuickSort are displayed next. The NQQuickSort pivot computation corresponding to binary quicksort is the average of the known partitions' min and max. This contributes to the speed of NQQuickSort, where the algorithm does not have to progress slowly. Binary quicksort tests the next bit for the total array at each complete recursive call, of many child partitions, whose union is the total array.

4 NQQuicksort Analysis

The running time of NQQuickSort in the worst case, is twice the worst case of binary quicksort. It is bounded by $2 * O(N * B)$, a non-quadratic running time complexity function, where N is the input size and B is the number of bits. Because binary quicksort implementation of quicksort does not go quadratic [21],

```
Uses constant: double dpThreshold ;
Parameters:
    int Array [],
    int left, int right, int min, int max,
    boolean s  select_pivot_computation

Step1:
if ( select_pivot_computation )
    pivot = median_of_three (Array[]);
else
    pivot = average_range (Array) similar to binary quicksort

Step2:
double ration = partition (Array, pivot , firstPartition, secondPartition);

Step3:
if ( ration < dpThreshold )
    s = !s;

Step4:
SS (Array, firstPartition.left, firstPartition.right, min, pivot, s );
SS (Array, secondPartition.left, secondPartition.right, pivot, max, s );
```

Fig. 1. Algorithm SS: NQQuickSort pseudo code

```
re_implemented_binary_qs_pivot = ((MaxKeyValue - MinKeyValue) / 2) + MinKeyValue) ;
median_3_qs_pivot = (Array[left] + Array[mid] + Array[right])/3
```

Fig. 2. Pivot Computation Steps

NQQuickSort does not go quadratic. Continually switching to binary quicksort, when partitioning fails assures or guarantees that NQQuickSort does not go quadratic. To elaborate, for a particular input array, assume that median of three quicksort partitioning is always futile. Then the number of recursion levels, in the worst case, is the same as that of binary quicksort multiplied by two. The partitioning of binary quicksort always alternates with futile partitioning of median of three quicksort. In implementation, we improve on the above worst case, where actual key values, selected as pivots, **algorithm SS Step 1** given in Fig. 1; the *median_of_three*() function, are passed as range min and range max, in recursive calls, as explained. In addition, the more usual optimization techniques in sorting algorithms are applied in NQQuickSort; insertion sort, is used to sort groups of size less than or equal to 10.

5 Experimental Results

We have run extensive experiments to validate our sorting algorithm and compared it with the Java built-in quicksort; a tuned implementation of

Table 1.

Java Tuned Sorting	NQQuickSort
Symbol JS	Symbol SS
Median (3) for small size groups	Alternate: Median of 3 key values,
Median (9) for large sized	Average (known min and max) groups

Table 2.

Random Data	Range [1..N]	Symbol = R
Inversely Sorted	Range [1..N]	Symbol = I
Sorted	Range [1..N]	Symbol = S
Killer Median of 3	Range [1..N]	Symbol = K

Table 3.

Size millions	Alg	R (msec)	I (msec)	S (msec)	K (msec)
2	JS	2910	1760	1760	2200
2	SS	2250	1100	830	1320
3	JS	4450	2700	2640	3400
3	SS	3400	1800	1430	2230
4	JS	5990	3790	3680	4610
4	SS	4830	2310	1750	3080
5	JS	7640	4830	4800	5870
5	SS	6050	2910	2310	3840

Bentley-McIlroy quicksort [3]. Bentley-McIlroy quicksort [3] takes the median of 9 equidistant keys for large arrays, where the sizes break point is determined empirically in [2]; partitions into three sub-arrays, containing keys with values less-than, equal-to and greater-than the pivot; and takes the median of 3 equidistant keys for smaller arrays. NQQuickSort, applies the median of three equidistant keys. Both algorithms are implemented in Java 2, and the algorithms symbols used for the tested algorithms are displayed in Table 1.

Uniform data is generated using the Java 2 function, Math.Random(), which gives double data type numbers in the range [01]. These numbers are scaled to the total ranges applied in the tests (32-bit positive integers). It is well known that any sorting method well suited for positive integers is well suited for sorting floating point numbers, text and more general data structures. The test data cases, and the range of key values used are displayed in Table 2.

Table 3 shows the running times in milliseconds for the algorithms in Table 1. In all tests, we report the average time of 5 runs for accuracy. Array sizes in Table 4 and Table 4 is in millions. The machine used in all the tests is Sony VIO 3000 MHz, 3GB RAM.(divide by 6)

Table 4.

Range	Alg	2	3	4	5
millions		(msec)	(msec)	(msec)	(msec)
2,147,483,647	JS	2970	4500	6040	7740
2,147,483,647	SS	2250	3350	4560	5770
2,00,000	JS	2910	4450	6050	7690
2,00,000	SS	2310	3350	4360	5820

We make the following conclusions, organized by case.

1. (R) Java tuned quicksort running time is about 127% times NQQuickSort running time.
2. (I) Java tuned quicksort running time is about 165% times NQQuickSort running time.
3. (S) Java tuned quicksort running time is about 200% times NQQuickSort running time.
4. (K) Java tuned quicksort running time is about 152% times NQQuickSort running time.

For the random uniform data, the running times of the two algorithms tested in Table 3, is not affected by the range, when the range is reasonable. The following table, Table 4, shows the running times of Java tuned quicksort and NQQuickSort for two ranges.

NQQuickSort is an adaptive implementation of radix exchange. The more important difference between NQQuickSort and radix exchange is the pivot selection step, where we allow the selection of a key from data, and therefore introduce adaptive-ness into the algorithm. The other difference is in computing the pivot using the division operator instead of a bit extraction. The latter difference allows using any range min and any range max in NQQuickSort.

In radix exchange as well as radix sorting algorithms, min and max depend only on the digit. The digit size in radix exchange is always one, and the pivot is of the form 2^B, where B starts at the index of the left most bit, and is decremented on recursive radix exchange calls. Radix exchange does not update the current min and max from actual data. This makes radix exchange very slow compared to NQQuickSort.

If we were to implement radix exchange using the averages function instead of the bit extraction function, NQQuickSort still differs from radix exchange in that it does not always compute the average of the minimum possible key value and the maximum possible key value. Keys are selected from data in recursive calls executing quicksort pivot computation.

In the following table, Table 5, we compare NQQuickSort with LSD for random uniform data. The digit size used in LSD is 16. It is known that LSD is the fastest radix-sorting algorithm, and that it is not in-place [21]. We see from Table 5, that using adaptive-ness and taking averages speeds up NQQuickSort.

Table 5.

Range	Alg	Time
	Alg	(msec)
0 .. 2 power 31	LSD	1750
0 .. 2 power 31	SS	2290
0 .. 2 power 63	LSD	4180
0 .. 2 power 63	SS	2910

Table 5 displays running times for random uniform distributions, for the positive integer 31 bits range, and the positive long 63 bits range. The array size is 2 millions. NQQuickSort is faster than radix sorting LSD for 63 bits data.

From Table 5 Using larger digit sizes in LSD radix sorting algorithms is not necessarily always a better strategy in radix sorting algorithms. Adaptive-ness results in better running times as we see above. In addition, LSD is not an in-place sorting algorithm.

6 Conclusions

NQQuicksort is a successful re-engineering of the quicksort algorithm that is carefully coded and its pivot computation steps are carefully selected. NQQuicksort adopts two pivot computations only. The first is the same as the pivot computation in median of three quicksort and the second is similar to that in binary quicksort (radix exchange). These two pivot computations are selected because they are quite different and non-related, so that when one pivot computation tends to go quadratic, the second pivot computation step will hopefully perform well with high probability. When one pivot computation results in unbalanced partitioning, the second pivot computation is immediately applied in the next recursive call; and the overall algorithm yields better performance. Our experimental results confirm that in many cases, NQQuickSort is twice as fast as the tuned quicksort implementation of the Java class library engineered by Bentley and McIlroy [3].

References

1. Aho, A., Hopcroft, J., Ullman, J.: The Design and Analysis of Computer Algorithms. Addison-Wesley, Reading (1974)
2. Anderson, A., Nilsson, S.: Implementing Radixsort. ACM Journal of Experimental Algorithmics 3(7) (1998)
3. Bentley, J.L., McIlroy, M.D.: Engineering a Sort Function. Software Practice and Experience 23(11), 1249–1265 (1993)
4. Bhutoria, S., Konjevod, G.: Quickening Quick-Sort. In: REAS 2003 (2003)
5. Cormen, T.H., Leiserson, C.E., Rivest, R.L., Stein, C.: Introduction to Algorithms, 2nd edn., pp. 145–164. MIT Press, McGraw-Hill (2001) ISBN 0-262-03293-7
6. Dean, B.C.: A Simple Expected Running Time Analysis for Randomized 'Divide and Conquer' Algorithms. Discrete Applied Mathematics 154(1), 1–5 (2006)

7. Dobosiewicz, W.: Sorting by Distributive Partition. Information Processing Letters 7(1), 1–6 (1978)
8. Hildebrandt, P., Isbitz, H., Mehlhorn, K.: Radix Exchange- An Internal Sorting Method for digital computers. JACM 6, 156–163 (1959)
9. Hoare, C.A.R.: "Partition: Algorithm 63," "Quicksort: Algorithm 64," and "Find: Algorithm 65". Comm. ACM 4(7), 321–322 (1961)
10. Hoare, C.A.R.: Quicksort. Computer Journal 5(1), 10–15 (1962) (reprinted in Hoare and Jones: Essays in computing science, 1989)
11. Knuth, D.E.: The Art of Computer Programming, 2nd edn., vol. 3, pp. 113–122. Addison-Wesley, Reading (1973) ISBN 0-201-89685-0
12. LaMarca, A., Ladner, R.E.: The Influence of Caches on the Performance of Sorting. In: Proceedings of the Eighth Annual ACM-SIAM Symposium on Discrete Algorithms, pp. 370–379 (1997)
13. Lau, K.K.: Top-Down Synthesis of Sorting Algorithms. The Computer Journal 35, A001–A007 (1992)
14. Martnez, C., Roura, S.: Optimal sampling strategies in quicksort and quickselect. SIAM J. Computing 31(3), 683–705 (2001)
15. Maus, A.: ARL: A Faster In-place, Cache Friendly Sorting Algorithm. In: Norsk Informatikkonferranse NIK 2002, pp. 85–95 (2002)
16. McIlroy, P., Bostic, K., McIlroy, M.: Engineering Radix Sort. Computer Systems 6(1), 5–27 (1993)
17. Douglas McIlroy, M.: A Killer Adversary for Quicksort. Software Practice and Experience 29(0), 1–4 (1999)
18. Mehlhorn, K.: Data Structures and Algorithms 1: Sorting and Searching. Springer, Heidelberg (1984)
19. Musser, D.R.: Introspective Sorting and Selection Algorithms. Software Practice and Experience 27(8), 983–993 (1997)
20. Sedgewick, R.: Implementing Quicksort programs. Communications of the ACM 21(10), 847–857 (1978)
21. Sedgewick, R.: Algorithms in Java, Parts 1-4, 3rd edn., pp. 1–4. Addison-Wesley, Reading (2003)
22. Sedgewick, R., Flajolet, P.: An Introduction to the Analysis of Algorithms. Addison-Wesley, Reading (1996)

Towards Building Weak Links between Persistent Digital Identity Documents: MetaEngine and Distance to Make Identity Less Visible

Ghazi Ben Ayed[1,2], Sami Sifi[2], and Mohamed Becha Kaanich[2]

[1] Faculty of Business and Economics, University of Lausanne, CH-1015, Lausanne, Switzerland
[2] EspriTec Research, Development & Innovation, ESPRIT School of Engineering, Tunis, Tunisia
ghazi.benayed@unil.ch,
{sami.sifi,mohamedbecha.kaaniche}@esprit.ens.tn

Abstract. Currently, metadata are being democratized and used for various purposes. We present a novel metadata-based mechanism to help making weak links between digital identity documents based on distance score that is generated by a distance function and performance. We identify two parameters of the distance function: elapsed time t and a random vector, which is defined by joint probability density for forgetting between two documents. The more the distance score is high the more the link established between parent and child document becomes weaker, therefore the child document becomes less visible. This would provide user more control over his identity and promote forgiveness in the digital age. We provided also an XRD implementation of the parent and child DigIdMeta documents.

Keywords: Digital identity hiding, identity attributes protection, metadata-based engine, distance, and weak links.

1 Introduction

"Imagine being able to remember every fight you ever had with a friend, every time someone let you down, all the stupid mistakes you've ever made (…) I never forget anything, good or bad, so it is hard to move on", says Jill Price, a Californian woman who can't forget and has a brain power and a flawless memory to perfectly recall every trivial detail of every day's life without using mnemonic tricks. She provided exact dates of Elvis Presley death, plane crash in Chicago, Easters from 1980 to 2003, and even broadcast's date of Dallas TV series episode that revealed who shot J.R. Neurobiologists at the University of California-Irvine have coined a new name for her condition, calling it "hyperthymestic syndrome". The term has Greek roots, "thymesis" for remembering, and "hyper", meaning more than normal [1, 2].

The digital age is promoting the spread of hyperthymestic syndrome, which may yield to "un-forgiving" syndrome. The digital footprints that we leave on the Internet cannot be erased and fuel the "un-forgetting" memories. At anytime, footprints that are perfectly remembered by the Internet could be easily recalled and used against us.

E. Ariwa and E. El-Qawasmeh (Eds.): DEIS 2011, CCIS 194, pp. 676–690, 2011.

The author of the book [3] notes that perfect remembering make us un-forgiving to both ourselves and others, thus, he warns societies about such syndrome from which its consequences would be seen in the near future. The same author provides a case to illustrate the un-forgiving consequence of un-forgetting memories. A 25-year-old single mother had completed her coursework and was looking forward to her future career in teaching. But she was denied her certificate, she was told because her behavior was unbecoming of a teacher. She had put a photo on MySpace showing her in costume wearing a pirate's hat and drinking from a plastic cup and captioned it "drunken pirate" for her friends to see. The university administration has argued that the photo was unprofessional. She considered taking the photo offline but the damage was done. Her web page had been catalogued by search engines and her photo archived by web crawlers. The Internet un-forgivingly remembered what Stacy wanted to have forgotten [3]. Therefore, Stacy has lost control her identity information, which implies irreversible and undesirable consequences: invasion of personal space, comfort and privacy, reputation harm, and openness to power abuses.

Personal data and security of identity information can be achieved by concept of identity hiding. Many tools, such as search engines, have been created to turn the Web into more visible and accessible platform but today users are requesting tools and features to have control over identity and particularly be less invisible. Web users are increasingly leaving trails on the net and most online service providers memorize, access and exploit 'Web of trails' for their own commercial benefits. As far service providers are processing identity information, as far users are losing control over their personal information that could compromise online security, privacy and trust [4-7]. One hundred million worldwide Facebook users are threatened by identity theft, cyber-stalking and cyber-bullying, and digital espionage as a repercussion of Facebook hack case [8], in which personal details have been collated from public Facebook people directory and published through file-sharing service. Not only people are posting personal facts on the Web but government agencies are steadily making databases available online. The databases may include birth, marriage and death certificates, credit histories, voter registrations and property deeds [9]. Stacy's profile in social network made her identity more visible and lost ownership and control over it since she couldn't make her photo invisible or delete it. In addition, digitizing dossiers promoted identity loss of control and easy accessing them, which in turn encouraged identity theft and fraud. Currently, users feel concerned and worried about security, but providing control over identity would inevitably establish a community of trust and foster collaboration between business parties. In this article, we aim to deal with the question of how to make identity in the digital age less visible in order to increase user control over it?

The remainder of the article is organized as follows. In Section 2, we introduce identity in the digital age and how it becomes more persistent. In Section 3, we explain the risk associated with digital identity strong persistent and how making it less visible and more volatile could provide privacy and user control. In Section 4, we explain the adoption of metadata associated with digital identity document (DigIdMeta) and metadata-based engine (MetaEngine) to make digital identity less visible; however, we identify parameters of the distance function in Section 5. In

Section 6, we present an XRD-based implementation of parent and child DigIdMeta documents. In Section 7, we explain the direction of future work and outlook and, finally, we conclude in Section 8.

2 Digital Identity

The notion of identity is evolving over time. Several decades ago, human identity was defined by geography, community, and family relationships. If an individual was born into a well-known and rich family or in a poor remote community, he or she would remain and would typically not be able to change their life pattern or economic status over time. The declaration of an individual's name, sometimes accompanied by the name of their city or village, was sufficient to prove his identity. Today, individuals are having greater choice for participation in different social circles, and more possibilities and freedom of social and economic mobility [10, 11].

2.1 Identity and Digital Identity

Identity is defined as a collection of attributes. Identity attributes are classified and organized into three groups. Each group maintains relationships with others, on which the perceived value is different. Attributes' group one derives from information and traits associated with a person that makes him unique such as personal characteristics, special interests, favorite activities, and hair color. Attributes' group two consists of context-specific attributes that are assigned to a person by others in the sake of identifying him temporarily within that context and based on some kind of relationship. Driver's license, credit card, health insurance card, library card are examples. However, attributes' group three deals with identity of persons' group or profiling. Marketing companies classify a person as a male over 50, a Swiss Air frequent flyer, and a Geneva resident. A person perceives the value and benefits of attributes' group two disclosure, which is usually established with his consent to meet a real need, however, attributes' group three are usually forced on us and may spawn issues such as unsolicited commercial email or spam [6].

Digitalization is allowing several digital representation of reality, including that of identity. Digital identity is seen as an intersection of identity and technology in the digital age. As more people live much of their lives online and they don't distinguish between online and offline, we consider the notions of identity and digital identity are the same. Instead of thinking of digital identity and real-space identity as separate things, they are maintained simultaneously and closely linked to one another to form the overall identity [12]. With the emergence of social networks within participative Web, digital identity is considered naturally social and defined as a social performance through a digital representation that a person presents across all the digital spaces, such as avatar, profile or pseudo. Performance denotes the person's activity involving agreement and disagreement, convention and innovation, communication and negotiation that occurs during a period of time [13]. In addition, the notion of identity has been extended not only to humans, but animals, machines, organizations, devices, and other objects or resources. We employ the term 'subject' to refer to an individual or a machine to which an individual has delegated a task [5, 6, 10, 14]. In addition, we consider the use of plural, digital identities, when referring to digital identity of several subjects.

2.2 Persistence of Digital Identity

Digital identity becomes more dynamic and persistent, thus, more visible. A person living in a remote village during the agrarian age could change many aspects of his personal identity as he wished such as choosing different clothes, expressing himself in a new way, and developing new habits and interests. He has not been able to control his social identity completely because family's status and gossip among neighbors could affect it. The person could change parts of social identity by associating with different people and adjusting social relationships but fellow villagers might still recall earlier versions of it. If he wanted to change or abandon aspects of social identity quickly, he can go beyond the small community where he grew up. Moving to a nearby village, there would likely still be some people who knew him, or knew of him through others and tell stories about him. In the agrarian age, it was possible for the person to completely abandon old social identity and cut off friends and family for good, if he were willing to travel far enough another city whose inhabitants had little communication with the residents of the town in which he had previously lived. The advent of Internet and digital technologies added new degrees of permanence to identity. He would not able to change his identity in a complete fashion. A photo of him, with a Photoshop-designed tattoo on his arm, posted in a blog could mark his identity in a persistent way. Moreover, digital identity is shaped by associations that are visible to onlookers at any moment, such as connections in social networks or blogrolls in blogs [12].

3 Strong Persistence and Loss of Control over Digital Identity

3.1 Forgetting and Remembering

In his book [3], the author explores remembering and forgetting over human history and into the digital age. "Since the beginning of time, for us human, forgetting has been the norm and remembering the exception". But this balance has shifted, because of widespread of digital technology and global networks, forgetting has become the exception and remembering the default. The author has questioned in the same book what the potential consequences of this shift are at the individual level and society level? What are the roles of forgetting and remembering in our society, and how these roles are changing? The author is questioning: is everyone who self-discloses information loses control over that information forever, and have no say about whether and when the Internet forgets this information? Do we want a future that is forever unforgiving because it is un-forgetting? He adds that the chilling effect of perfect memory alters our behavior [3]. While Jill Price admits that many of the memories bring her comfort, but she also faces frustrations because sometimes she wishes to forget certain unpleasant details. She mentions that constant memory recall is exhausting [1].

The human mind processes and filters a tremendous and huge amount of information before committing into long-term memory. To cope with the sea of stimuli, our brain uses multiple levels of processing and filtering before committing information to long-term memory. As our nerve cells process the incoming information, a tremendous amount of information is deliberately lost, which represents the first level of unconscious forgetting. If the information crossed the first level, it is then usually stored in short-term memory in which it can be easily retrieved but may fade in a matter of seconds. Short-term memory plays the role of a buffer of mental sketchpad for visual-spatial impressions, short audio-loop recordings, and episodic memory of experienced events. Short-term memory plays the role of information dispatcher through which information cross before being committed into long-term memory, called also "human memory". However, remembering is a two-step process: commit information to long-term storage and recall information from memory [3].

3.2 Loss of Control over Digital Identity

Maintaining control over digital identity fosters collaboration and trust. Internet users are increasingly losing control over digital identity. When browsing the Web, users are leaving online trails and disclosing more personal information either by choice or by force. Many online service providers businesses depend on the web trails such as social-networking sites. Ziki.com offers advertising services through Google ads based on the user's profile. Another example is Spock.com, which is a people finder engine on the web and more specifically people who have profiles on social networks Live Spaces, Friendster, Hi5, MySpace, and Wikipedia. Spock's mission is to aggregate the world's people information and make it searchable. It is devoted to finding, indexing and profiling people, thus, making digital identities more visible on the Internet. Digital identity is facing a retention/disclosure tradeoff. In one side, users refrain from sharing digital identity to prevent possible exposure and privacy breaches; and in another side they disclose digital identity attributes and other information to make online transactions, seek convenience, and have fun [6, 15, 16]. "This tension between individuals' interest in protecting their privacy and companies' interest in exploiting personal information could be resolved by giving people more control. They could be given the right to see and correct the information about them that an organization holds, and to be told how it was used and with whom it was shared" [17]. However, when disclosing attributes, they will be unforgettable like an etched tattoo [3]. The same author adds that making identity information less visible, or giving "the right to be let alone" [18], is an efficient way to provide user's control over identity and revive the forgetting in un-forgetting systems. In his book [19], the author explains the need differently. He argues that the word "trash" implies the remnants of something used but later discarded. It always contains traces and signatures of use such as monthly bills, receipts, personal papers, cellophane wrapping, price tags, and spoiled food. He stresses that future avant-garde practices will be those of trash and nonexistence, which is how does one develop techniques and technologies to make somebody unaccounted for? He illustrates with the example of laser pointer that can blind a surveillance camera when the beam is directed at the lens and as a consequence, the individual is not hiding but simply nonexistent to that node. For instance, Google Web history tool is a step towards providing more users' control over identity.

4 Digital Identity Metadata and MetaEngine

We assume that digital identity is represented by either a single document or a set of documents that comprises subject's attributes. Each digital identity document is linked with another document that comprises a set of metadata (DigIdMeta).

4.1 DigIdMeta Motivations

Metadata, information about information, called also "hidden data" [20] are being democratized and used from antiquity to codify knowledge and classify library materials. Assyrians attached small labels to clay tablets; Hittites and Ptolemies maintained catalogs of bibliographical entries and shelving information; and bookmarking catalogues usage in Chinese imperial library, Arabs 'halls of science', and renaissance's public libraries are all shining examples of keeping metadata-based classification system. Today, by aiming to organize the world's information, Google is adding metadata e.g. indexes and PageRank scores when crawling and indexing Web pages. With the advent of Web 2.0, Web users tag web sites, documents, photos and videos helping to label unstructured information so it can be easily found through folkminds such as Delicious URL[21], Diigo URL[22], and Technorati URL[23].

Ubiquitous and digital technologies are increasingly and easily producing metadata such as Amazon's popularity stars, bar codes and RFID labels. Moreover, photos uploaded to photos sharing websites or content management systems contain metadata such as when and often where they were taken, as well as the camera model.

Metadata can provide information about the owner and changes made on the document. Word processing and Adobe reader/writer manage metadata related to document updates tracking such as deleted passages, revision numbers and comments. DigIdMeta would help to know what is, when and who added, updated, and deleted digital identity documents.

Metadata usage is a common practice. Web developers and search engine optimization experts are enriching the <meta> tag in the head of Web sites.

4.2 DigIdMeta and MetaEngine

In opposition to many examples of using metadata as a mean of making digital identity more visible through recall capabilities such as casino's data fusion algorithms [20] and Microsoft's MyLifeBits research project [4], we propose in this article to use metadata as a mean to weak the links between digital identity documents, thus making them less visible.

A MetaEngine will manage metadata and would help subjects to maintain a less visible digital identity. We present in figure1, four environments where each is limited with an eclipse to represent metadata related to partial identities. Partial identity represents a subset of attributes that the subject can select for interacting with other parties. A traveler is asked to provide his passport at the counter of customs or immigration as a proof of his identity; and the same person, being a car driver, is asked to show his driving license to a police officer, who stopped him in the highway, for breaking the speed limit; a customer is asked to provide his credit card with fidelity saving card in a movie store to take advantage of DVD prices reductions; a student is requested to show his student card to have access to computer lab facilities; a patient's medical card must be provided to the hospital check-in personnel advisor to be eligible to receive health services; etc. In some mistrusted or policy restrictive environment, such as national security organizations, the person is asked to provide more than one identity proofs. The context will determine which partial identity needs to be communicated to establish trust and enable the transaction to go forward.

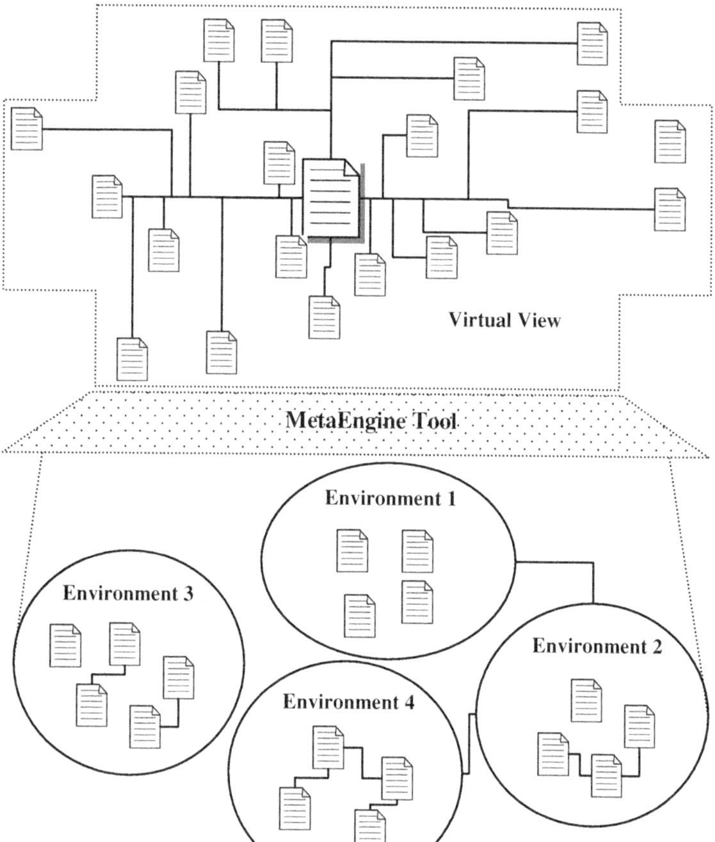

Fig. 1. DigIdMeta, MetaEngine tool and virtual view

The links across the environments represent links between any of DigIdMeta residing in different environments. The environment 3 is isolated and is not linked to any other environments to reflect a reality of a subject who has a limited set of attributes or striving to conduct anonymous activities. At the intra-environment level, the composite DigIdMeta could be linked to each others; a subset of them is linked; or not linked. The link between DigIdMeta represents the link between digital identity documents that the subject has established. The link between two or more digital identity documents could represent: a) the use of the same subject's account to access two or more services such as Google mail and YouTube. In this case, two distinct digital identity documents are created and generated comprising the same attributes but with different identifiers; b) attributes' values change and evolution over time such as subject's interests, home address, and employer. In this case, a new digital identity document is created comprising attributes' new values and linked to the former document; and c) a replication of static attribute in other digital identity documents, such as replication of ID number in driver's license document.

Privacy and data control advocates say that societies are committed to turn personal data from long-term memory into short-term memory and discourage the recall process. Brain's forgetting mechanism is inspiring research on making digital identity less visible. Researchers are closely studying how the brain forgets information that is stored in long-term memory. Some think that when we forget means that we have lost the link to that information like Web pages URLs. Others reckon and suggest that our brain constantly reconfigures our memory and they say that what we remember is based, at least in part, on our present preferences and needs [3]. Both ideas inspired us to consider adopting of MetaEngine tool that will provide management capabilities e.g. search, synchronization, and refresh of DigIdMeta to make digital identity documents less visible. MetaEngine may remind a rubber bulb of blood pressure sphygmomanometer. Instead of pushing/pulling air, it will pull DigIdMeta and digital identity documents from multiple sources and push a set of attributes to the requester. The requester could be a subject himself, trusted identity provider, or government. None of these requesters has access to all digital identity documents and associated DigIdMeta except the government or police to respond to critical national and/or international security needs. More specifically, MetaEngine functions as a collector of the available DigIdMeta and digital identity documents and push them into a virtual view, which is represented with a discontinuing-line shape in figure1. This is similar to data aggregation operation conducted via virtual directory in which collected data are maintained within non physical settings and the virtual view disappears whenever the operation is no longer needed. MetaEngine tool will quantify digital identity performance (see section 2.1) based on a set of parameters e.g. usage frequency and popularity rate. The identification of the parameters is out of the scope of this article and we assume here that MetaEngine is able to calculate a performance score for each digital identity document and write it in the associated DigIdMeta. In addition, MetaEngine elects DigIdMeta of the digital identity document that encloses the highest performance score as a parent DigIdMeta and places it in the center of the virtual view structure. The parent DigIdMeta in the center that is represented by a shadowed document in figure1 is surrounded by child DigIdMeta documents. The virtual view structure is similar to the central fact table surrounded by dimension tables in the data warehouse's star data schema. Moreover, the MetaEngine includes in parent DigIdMeta pointers to the surrounded child DigIdMeta documents and a distance score of each link in the associated child. The parent DigIdMeta does not enclose distance score because it has zero value.

The distance score would empower the "forgetting" capabilities. Distance score is calculated based on multiple criteria that will be detailed in section 5. As much the distance score is higher as far is the DigIdMeta child from the parent one. MetaEngine tool would make the digital identity document, which have a high distance score saved in the associated DigIdMeta, easy to access comparing to the one that has a low distance score. The latter digital identity document should be hard to retrieve and to be accessed. Operationally, disclosing a distant digital identity document could be followed by the subject's communication of his consent, or the requester has to request many times to be granted the access. To explain and illustrate the concept of distance, we provide two examples. Search engine provides an ordered list of Web links, based on popularity score, in response to a specific search request. The Web link that has the highest score appears in the top of the list and in the first search page, while the one that has a lower score appears down in the list in another page. Having the Web user looking for a Web link sequentially from search page1 to search page18 requires time and patience, which illustrates the notion of distance. The Web link in search page 18 is less visible and accessible. The concept of distance is seen also in public or university libraries. Without an efficient library management system, the books that are placed in upper-level shelves are considered distant and less visible, thus more inaccessible than a less distant book placed in lower-level shelves.

Moreover, MetaEngine tool conducts on-demand basis refresh operation, whenever the requester asks for digital identity document. It aggregates DigIdMeta, synchronizes the digital identity document duplicates, recalculates the scores, and reorganizes the links.

5 Distance Function

The author [3] suggests that the subject could set an expiration date to reduce the age of the digital identity document and thus, reviving forgetting and reducing recall capabilities in order to empower user control like disabling RFID chip. We believe that physical delete is hard to perform in the digital age and the value of the expiration date depends not only on the desire of the subject but also the other party agreement and/or legal and policy requirements. We propose to investigate what are the parameters that the human brain takes into account during information forgetting process. The parameters will be considered in identifying the distance function parameters.

Cooling functions (i.e. forgetting functions) model the apparent loss of information memorized by a human brain for machine computing. It is important to notice that the human brain tends to forget not because it has a limited capacity memory but rather information units tends to interfere with each other and be aggregated in a way that older information units become more and more inaccessible. However, when a recall or an active retrieval of information is performed, the brain updates his memory "internal storage" in order to decrease the likelihood of forgetting that information. It is important to retain those information units aggregation is conducted in a hierarchical manner: similar or related information units are stored together. In this way, when key information is recalled, the whole hierarchy of information units can be remembered easily. Therefore the process of memorization is interdependent, and so is the process of forgetting. More details about interference and forgetting are available in the reference [24]. In this paper, we want to design cooling function parameters in a manner that should reflect the natural process of forgetting. According to [25], the forgetting functions that are best-fitted with the process of forgetting are: the power function and the exponential function with time t scaled as $\sqrt{t}$. The author [25] claims that the exponential forgetting function is the most frequently used since it is the only function that has a constant rate of decrement. In our study, we want to use the exponential function as a probability density for each parameter of the digital identity considered as a random variable. More precisely, the probability density is a Poisson distribution over time t scaled as $\sqrt{t}$ and so each parameter follows a Poisson process. We believe that a forgetting parameter can be modeled by a Poisson process since there is no apparent relationship between forgetting information at a time t and forgetting it at another time t'. The parameters can be viewed as a multivariate random variable, which we can fit its expectation and covariance matrix by tuning the parameters of the probability density.

Given two documents, each has its own marginal probability density for forgetting and both have a joint probability density which defines the relationship of forgetting between the two documents. Assuming that X(t) is the forgetting random variable for the parent document and Y(t) is the forgetting random variable for the child document, the distance between the two documents is a function of $P(Y(t = t_0), X(t=t_0))$ which is the joint probability of forgetting the child document at time t_0 related to the parent document.

```
Function Distance ([X, Y], t0): output Distance_Score
```

The elapsed time t_0 is computed as $t_c - t_r$ where t_c is the current time of executing MetaEngine when establishing links between the DigIdMeta documents and t_r is the reference time which is the maximum between the creation dates of the two DigIdMeta documents. The Poisson random vector [X, Y] is constructed by using the Trivariate Reduction (TR) technique: given three independent Poisson random processes A, B and Z with parameters λ_1, λ_2, λ_3 respectively, the random vector components are defined as X = A+ Z and Y = B+ Z. The expectation of the random vector is given by (1) and the correlation between X and Y is given by (2).

$$E\left(\begin{bmatrix} X \\ Y \end{bmatrix}\right) = \begin{bmatrix} \lambda_1 + \lambda_3 \\ \lambda_2 + \lambda_3 \end{bmatrix} \tag{1}$$

$$\rho = \frac{\lambda_3}{\sqrt{(\lambda_1 + \lambda_3)(\lambda_2 + \lambda_3)}} \tag{2}$$

Thus, the joint probability of forgetting between X and Y is:

6 XRD Implementation of DigIdMeta

XRD, eXtensible Resource Descriptor, is a generic format for describing resources. It was recently published as an OASIS standard. It provides machine-readable information about resources (resource metadata) for the purpose of promoting interoperability. XRD provides XML format for describing resources. XRD is a document that is divided into two main sections: 1) document header section includes a description of the XRD document itself such as document's expiration date and XML namespaces; and 2) resource information section is divided into two subsections resource description and resource's associated links. The resource description subsection includes properties and aliases of the resource, and the other subsection lists linked other resources that can help utilize or understand the resource. If a requester's application wants to know and learn more about a digital identity document, identified by an URI, it retrieves its XRD document. XRD gives back characteristics and attributes enclosed between <property> tags; and the relationships to other resources and available associated services within <links> tags [26, 27]. We do not intend to provide whole XRD implementation of DigIdMeta, but the distance parameters, scores and links that are enclosed in parent and child DigIdMeta documents. The following code represents few elements of implementation of parent XRD DigIdMeta associated with digital identity document used as a profile in a favorite social network.

```
<XRD>
...
<Property type='http://favorite-social.net/gba/pfs'>
performance_score_value </Property>

<Link rel='update' type='text/html'
         href='http://favorite-social.net/gba/update'>
      <Title xml:lang='en-us'>Link to Updated DigIdMeta
      </Title> </Link>

<Link rel='duplicate' type='text/html'
         href='http://favorite-social.net/gba/duplicate'>
      <Title xml:lang='en-us'>Link to Duplicated
      DigIdMeta </Title> </Link>

<Link rel='child1' type='text/html'
         href='http://favorite-social.net/gba/child1'>
      <Title xml:lang='en-us'>Link to Child1 DigIdMeta
      </Title> </Link>
...

<Link rel='childn' type='text/html'
         href='http://favorite-social.net/gba/childn'>
      <Title xml:lang='en-us'>Link to Childn DigIdMeta
      </Title> </Link>
...
</XRD>
```

The next code represents elements of implementation of child XRD DigIdMeta associated with digital identity document used in a content sharing online service such as YouTube or Flickr.

```
<XRD>
...
<Property type='http://share-content.com/benag/pfs'>
performance_score_value </Property>

<Property type='http://share-content.com/benag/ 1'>
 1_value </Property>

<Property type='http://share-content.com/benag/ 2'>
 2_value </Property>

<Property type='http://share-content.com/benag/ 3'>
 3_value </Property>
...
</XRD>
```

7 Future Work and Outlook

We plan to extend this work in several directions. Since the parameter lambda3 controls the long run dependency between information and since data can't be treated in the same manner, we propose for future work to add variability through time. The goal is to define a time varying measure of risk which reflect the need to reinforce the connection between data and that's conditionally to the information generated by this dependence. The measure of risk is defined following principles of financial market volatility. Hereafter, we present definitions and models related to the volatility.

Volatility is statistical measure of the dispersion of returns for a particular security or market index. It refers to the amount of uncertainty or risk regarding the degree and size of changes in the value of a security. A higher volatility means that a security's value potentially can be spread out over a larger range of values. This means that the price of the security can change dramatically over a short period in either direction. A lower volatility means that a security's value does not fluctuate dramatically but changes in value at a steady pace over a period of time [28]. The volatility is also characterized by transitions between periods of high volatility and periods of low volatility. This is also known as volatility clustering. With volatility clustering, a turbulent trading day tends to be followed by another turbulent day, while a tranquil period tends to be followed by another tranquil period [29, 30]. The decision makers are especially interested on the length of the turbulence period, also known as the degree of persistence of the volatility. Volatility is said to be persistent if a volatility shock today has a meaningful influence on future volatilities. In practice the volatility persistence of an asset returns r_t is measured by the autocorrelation of the squared returns and/or the autocorrelation the absolute returns. For a strong persistence the autocorrelations remain positive for very long lags. This is also known as the long memory. For weak persistence the autocorrelation will decay in an exponential way to zero. A second measure of volatility persistence is the volatility half-life τ. This is the time taken for the volatility to move half-way back to its mean level V following a deviation from it [31].

Authors in [32] describe the most important features of volatility that a good volatility model should be able to capture. They particularly mention mean reversion, volatility clustering and persistence, and volatility half-life. For this purpose, the author [33] proposed the GARCH model, for which the future volatility depends on lagged value of returns and lagged value of volatility. Here we give a brief description of the first order GARCH model (Generalized Auto-Regressive Conditionally Heteroscedastic model):

$$r_t = \sigma_t . Z_t \tag{5}$$

$$\sigma_t^2 = \alpha_0 + \alpha_1 r_{t-1}^2 + \beta_1 \sigma_{t-1}^2 \tag{6}$$

Where σ_t^2 is conditional variance, σ_t is volatility, $Z_t \sim N(0,1)$ and α_0, α_1 *and* β_1 positive parameters. To guarantee the stationnarity of the volatility process and consequently its mean reversion, the model parameters must verify $\alpha_1 + \beta_1 < 1$. In addition to the volatility clustering, the GARCH model allows to model the persistence degree of volatility through the sum of the estimated parametersα_1 *and* β_1 . For $(\alpha_1 + \beta_1)$ close to one the actual volatility will have a strong effect on the future one, which is the case of strong persistence. The weak persistence corresponds to $(\alpha_1 + \beta_1)$ close to zero.

Another alternative to model the variation of dependency between DigIdMeta documents is to use the snowflake data schema instead of star data schema. The snowflake data schema would be more appropriate to take into consideration the phenomenon of interference in the human brain. The more we tend to forget information, the more it fuses with other information and therefore it becomes in deeper level in the snowflake data schema and vice-versa.

8 Conclusion

Dave Winer, an American software developer and web writer, highlights today's need for subject's control over digital identity by saying: "A quite simple, but powerful, technology is that empowers individuals to keep control over and manage their digital identities". We present a mechanism to help making weak links between digital identity documents based on distance score that is generated by a distance function and performance. We identified two parameters of the distance function: elapsed time t and a random vector, which is defined by joint probability density for forgetting between two documents. The more the distance score is high the more the link established through MetaEngine between parent and child document becomes weaker, therefore the child document becomes less visible. This would give the subject's more control over digital identity in order to increase trust and foster forgiveness in the digital age. We provided also an XRD implementation of the parent and child DigIdMeta documents. However, technical approach is not enough to make digital identity documents less visible; we need to develop a multidisciplinary and an integrated approach in which we take into consideration several other perspectives, e.g. legal, managerial, user-centricity.

References

[1] Kruglinski, S.: The Woman Who Never Forgets: Does AJ have the world's best memory? DISCOVER Magazine (2006), http://discovermagazine.com/2006/jun/j-woman-memory

[2] Adler, J.: Unable to Forget: The remarkable story of a woman who remembers every day of her life. Newsweek Magazine (2008), http://www.newsweek.com/2008/05/10/unable-to-forget.html

[3] Mayer-Schönberger, V.: Delete: The virtue of forgetting in the digital age. Princeton University Press, Princeton (2009)

[4] Bell, G., Gemmel, J.: A Digital Life. Scientific American Magazine, 58–65 (2007)

[5] International Telecommunication Union (2006), Digital Life. ITU Internet Report, http://www.itu.int/osg/spu/publications/digitalife/docs/digital-life-web.pdf

[6] Windley, P.J.: Digital Identity: Unmasking identity management architecture (IMA). O'Reilly Media, Sebastopol (2005)

[7] Cukier, K.: A special report on managing information. The Economist (February 23-March 5, 2010)

[8] Facebook 'hack' releases 100 million user details onto filesharing sites. Inforsecurity USA (2010), http://www.infosecurity-us.com/view/11343/facebook-hack-releases-100-million-user-details-onto-filesharing-sites/

[9] Fischetti, M.: Scoring Your Identity: New tactics root out the false use of personal data. Scientific American, 27–28 (2007)

[10] Noonan, H.: Identity. In: Stanford Encyclopedia of Philosophy (2009)

[11] Olson, E.T.: Personal Identity. In: Standford Encyclopedia of Philosophy (2008)

[12] Palfrey, J., Gasser, U.: Born Digital: Understanding the first generation of digital natives. Basic Books, New York (2008)

[13] Williams, S.: This is Me Digital Identity and Reputation on the Internet, http://www.slideshare.net/shirleyearley/this-is-medigital-identity-and-reputation-on-the-internet

[14] Center for Democracy & Technology, Privacy Principles for Identity in the Digital Age (Draft for Comment - Version 1.4) (2007), http://www.cdt.org/files/pdfs/20071201_IDPrivacyPrinciples.pdf

[15] Benantar, M.: Access Control Systems: Security, Identity Management and Trust Models. Springer Science + Business Media, Heidelberg (2006)

[16] Clauß, S., Kõhntopp, M.: Identity Management and Its Support for Multilateral Security. Computer Networks 37, 205–219 (2001)

[17] Cukier, K.: New Rules for Big Data: Regulators are having to rethink their brief. The Economist (February 23-March 5, 2010), http://www.economist.com/specialreports/displaystory.cfm?story_id=15557487

[18] Brown, P.: Privacy in an Age of Terabytes and Terror. Scientific American Magazine, 46–47 (2008)

[19] Galloway, A.R., Thacker, E.: The Exploit - A Theory of Networks. University of Minnesota Press (2008)

[20] Garfinkel, S.L.: Information of the World, UNITE! Scientific American Magazine, 82–87 (2008)

[21] Delicious, http://www.delicious.com
[22] Diigo, http://www.diigo.com
[23] Technorati, http://technorati.com
[24] Bjork, R.A.: Interference and forgetting. In: Byrne, J.H. (ed.) Encyclopedia of Learning and Memory, 2nd edn., pp. 268–273. Macmillan Reference, New York (2003)
[25] White, K.G.: Forgetting functions. Animal Learning & Behavior 29, 193–207 (2001)
[26] OASIS eXtensible Resource Identifier (XRI) TC, Extensible Resource Descriptor (XRD) Version 1.0 (OASIS Standard) (2010), http://docs.oasis-open.org/xri/xrd/v1.0/xrd-1.0.html
[27] Hammer-Lahav, E.: XRD Document Structure (2009), http://hueniverse.com/2009/03/xrd-document-structure/ (accessed December 9, 2010)
[28] Wikipedia. Volatility (finance), http://en.wikipedia.org/wiki/Volatility_%28finance%29
[29] Fama, E.F.: The Behaviour of Stock Market Prices. Journal of Business 38, 34–105 (1965)
[30] Mandelbrot, B.: The Variation of Certain Speculative Prices. Journal of Business 36, 394–419 (1963)
[31] Enders, W.: Applied Econometric Time Series, 2nd edn. John Wiley & Sons, Inc., Chichester (2003)
[32] Engle, R.F., Patton, A.J.: What Good is a Volatility Model? Quantitative Finance 1, 237–245 (2001)
[33] Bollerslev, T.: Generalized Autoregressive Conditional Heteroscedasticity. Journal of Econometrics 31, 307–327 (1986)

An Approach to the Integration of Cryptographic Services in the Cloud Computing Supported on a Standard Interfaces to the Execution of Cryptographic Processes on Demand. Study Case: Key Management Protocol Interoperability vs. RSA PKCS # 11 Standard

John Manuel Delgado Barroso, Luis Joyanes Aguilar,
Pablo García Gundín, and Jayguer Vasquezr

Universidad Pontifica de Salamanca, C/ Juan XXIII, Madrid,28022 España
{johnm.delgado,pablogundin,jayguer}@gmail.com
luis.joyanes@upsam.com

Abstract. Cloud Security is one of the biggest challenges that currently this technology is facing. Based on cryptography and keys used to protect information, this paper proposes the integration of key management model in the cloud KMIP with the cryptographic standard protocol PKCS11, responding to the problem of key management, no doubt, one of the main problems to solve when a model of this nature is thought in the cloud. The inclusion of cryptographic hardware reinforces this proposal, which is based in interoperable models that are compatible with high level of security devices like Hardware Security Modules.

Keywords: Key Management Interoperability Protocol, RSA PKCS#11, Hardware Security Module, Cloud Computing environments.

1 Introduction

Among all the elements related to the deployment of cryptographic operations in the cloud, this paper analyzes the elements that are involved with the key management, making a deep study of the state of the art on the current state of this technology. This is in order to take advantage of the best accessibility, key management, credential management[6] and interoperability models[6] of different patterns in favor of extending these models to the cloud computing architectures[14].

Cloud computing is a platform where services provided with computing capabilities and data processing are in the cloud. Inecitably needs to manage and control critical data. These services are directly related to processing of electronic mail, documents backup formats and implementation of online processes as cloud services.

Also, understanding that these services have implemented factors that cause them to be considered as highly critical services[8], it is when some privacy features are required in the implementation of cryptographic operations taking into account the

E. Ariwa and E. El-Qawasmeh (Eds.): DEIS 2011, CCIS 194, pp. 691–702, 2011.

number of intermediate operations that a cryptographic process can perform, like primality algorithms of the random number generators [NEWMA09] and how this affects both the performance in the key generation and in their level of reliability because knowing the key components, will result in the complete loss of confidence in the implementation of these processes.

Since it is impossible to ensure all components are being stored in a particular moment in a portion of memory, both volatile and physically, it is proposed the implementation of a new nature of security devices, that meet under the proper certifications, the perfect requirements to run, provide and store cryptographic objects in a secure environment on a platform supported with hardware devices for that purpose.

This type of hardware solutions, which, from now, will be defined as Cryptographic Storage Devices (Hardware Security Module, HSM in English) are responsible for performing delegated cryptographic operations supported in a completely separated hardware environment, tamper resistant and securized.

2 State of the Art

In reviewing the state of the art and its relationship with the cryptographic standards for projection into a cloud computing environment, the most striking elements denoted are: the key management models[14], regardless of their platform; cloud[14] infrastructure development models and the elements that must be taken in consideration in implementing RSA PKCS11 standards in the development of this project.

Three visions have been nested in the State of the art:

- One related to the conceptual elements associated with cloud computing[8], taking into consideration the security in the cloud, dividing this into its essential characteriscs, service models, deployments models, the factor associated with multipossesion, reference models that provides the cloud, the security domains and how they are reinforced using encryption technologies[12] for confidentiality and integrity and, finally, its relationship with the key management.
- From the second perspective, key management in the cloud[13] has been developed, likewise, it has been performed a review of the standards involved with this key patterns:

1. ANSI X9 Financial industry standards[4] [5].
2. ANSI/X9 X9.96-2004 XML Cryptographic Message Syntax (XCMS). [4] [5]
3. DMTF Working Group related to the Security Modeling
4. GlobalPlatform: Key Management System.
5. IEEE P1619.3 Security storage and key management by work group (SISWG).
6. IETF Proposal of use of symmetric keys (KEYPROV) [7]
7. KeyGen2. Proposal of Standard Management in cryptographic operations.

- From the third perspective, they are presented the RSA PKCS patterns as essential elements to integrate, as standard applications to cryptographic storage devices, as well as key protection management and performing task related to cryptography, in order to provide suitable mechanism for the deployment of encryption and digital signature processes in general.

3 Development of the Cryptographic Access Service

For the cryptographic service development, it has been implemented a key generation using the interoperable key management standard (KMIP) [1] [2], such standard presents the following command with the following attributes:

```
Object Type="00000002" (Symmetric Key),
Key Attributes:
Cryptographic Algorithm ="00000003" (AES),
Key Length="128"
Key usage Mask ="0000000C"
```

The key structure generation process consists of the following frame:

```
•    Tag: Request Message (0x420075), Type: Structure
(0x01), Data:
o    Tag: Request Header (0x420074), Type: Structure
(0x01), Data:
▪    Tag: Protocol Version (0x420067), Type: Structure
(0x01), Data:
▪    Tag: Protocol Version Major (0x420068), Type:
Integer (0x02), Data: 0x00000001 (1)
▪    Tag: Protocol Version Minor (0x420069), Type:
Integer (0x02), Data: 0x00000000 (0)
▪    Tag: Batch Count (0x42000D), Type: Integer (0x02),
Data: 0x00000001 (1)
o    Tag: Batch Item (0x42000F), Type: Structure (0x01),
Data:
▪    Tag: Operation (0x42005A), Type: Enumeration
(0x05), Data: 0x00000001 (Create)
▪    Tag: Request Payload (0x420076), Type: Structure
(0x01), Data:
▪    Tag: Object Type (0x420055), Type: Enumeration
(0x05), Data: 0x00000002 (Symmetric Key)
▪    Tag: Template-Attribute (0x42008E), Type: Structure
(0x01), Data:
▪    Tag: Attribute (0x420008), Type: Structure (0x01),
Data:
•    Tag: Attribute Name (0x42000A), Type: Text String
(0x07), Data: Cryptographic Algorithm
•    Tag: Attribute Value (0x42000B), Type: Enumeration
(0x05), Data: 0x00000003 (AES)
▪    Tag: Attribute (0x420008), Type: Structure (0x01),
Data:
```

- Tag: Attribute Name (0x42000A), Type: Text String (0x07), Data: Cryptographic Length
- Tag: Attribute Value (0x42000B), Type: Integer (0x02), Data: 0x00000080 (128)
- Tag: Attribute (0x420008), Type: Structure (0x01), Data:
- Tag: Attribute Name (0x42000A), Type: Text String (0x07), Data: Cryptographic Usage Mask
- Tag: Attribute Value (0x42000B), Type: Integer (0x02), Data: 0x0000000C (Encrypt, Decrypt)

And the command to send is shown as follows:

4200750100000120420074010000003842006701000000020420
068020000000040000000100000000420069020000000040000000000000
00004200D0200000000400000001000000004200F01000000D842005
A05000000004000000010000000042007601000000C04200550500000
0400000000200000000042008E01000000A842000801000000304200A0
70000001743727970746F6772617068696320416C676F726974686D00
42000B050000000040000000030000000042000801000000304200A070
000001443727970746F6772617068696320 4C656E67746800000000042
000B020000000040000000800000000042000801000000304200A07000
00018437279707446F6772617068696320557361676520 4D61736B4200
0B02000000004000000C00000000

The output command for the successful key generation is shown in the figure below:

Out: objectType="00000002", uuidKey

- Tag: Response Message (0x420078), Type: Structure (0x01), Data:
- Tag: Response Header (0x420077), Type: Structure (0x01), Data:
- Tag: Protocol Version (0x420067), Type: Structure (0x01), Data:
- Tag: Protocol Version Major (0x420068), Type: Integer (0x02), Data: 0x00000001 (1)
- Tag: Protocol Version Minor (0x420069), Type: Integer (0x02), Data: 0x00000000 (0)
- Tag: Time Stamp (0x42008F), Type: Date-Time (0x09), Data: 0x000000004AC0731C (Mon Sep 28 10:26:04 CEST 2009)
- Tag: Batch Count (0x42000D), Type: Integer (0x02), Data: 0x00000001 (1)
- Tag: Batch Item (0x42000F), Type: Structure (0x01), Data:
- Tag: Operation (0x42005A), Type: Enumeration (0x05), Data: 0x00000001 (Create)

- Tag: Result Status (0x42007C), Type: Enumeration (0x05), Data: 0x00000000 (Success)
- Tag: Response Payload (0x420079), Type: Structure (0x01), Data:
- Tag: Object Type (0x420055), Type: Enumeration (0x05), Data: 0x00000002 (Symmetric Key)
- Tag: Unique Identifier (0x420091), Type: Text String (0x07), Data: 46eca90a-4b20-423c-b968-750f299f0ca7

And the returned command can be defined by the following trace:

42007801000000C042007701000000484200670100000020420
068020000000400000001000000004200690200000004000000000000
000042008F0900000008000000004AC0731C42000D020000000400000
0010000000042000F010000006842005A050000000400000001000000
0042007C0500000004000000000000000042007901000000404200550
500000004000000020000000042009107000000243436656361393061
2D346232302D343233632D623936382D3735306632393966306361370
0000000

3.1 Object Oriented Design Model Scheme

In the implementation model, the following classes' deployment has been designed:

Fig. 1. Overview of the classes that perform the project

- es.openkmip.attributes: They are composed by the attributes that must have the secure objects that are made within the application; many of them are closely linked with the key deployment in business environments. Actually, these parameters are related to key parameters defined in RSA standards, used when a key is generated. Among them, type of algorithm or key length that the new generated key will have.
- es.openKmip.baseobject: They are objects that integrate most of the commands that the interoperable key management protocol deployment has. In this section are implemented credentials development for the recognition of who is performing the action and the associated permission with cryptographic processes.

- es.openKmip.ManagedObject: These are the templates integrated in the objects that will be managed in the protocol deployment. This class is entirely composed of key templates, its division is related to the type of cryptography which is associated to, i.e., if it is symmetric or asymmetric cryptography or if it's a public key linked to a certificate, among others.
- es.openKmip.messajecontents: These are all labels that are necessary to provide attributes to the processes of key generation. They are part of the dialog process performed between that client who wants perform an operation with Access to the cryptographic keys and functions supported by the key management server; they can be seen in the following figure:

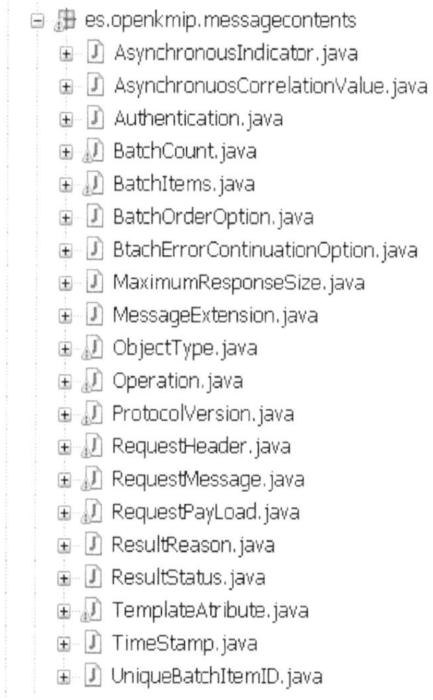

Fig. 2. Detail of labels used for client-server dialog in key management protocol

- Es.openKmip.operations: These are all operation supported by the key management protocol, such operations are designed to perform administration tasks, details of these features are shown in the following figure:
- Es.openKmip.pkcs11Bridge: Is a logical bridge that links attributes received from the proprietary protocol commands and are transferred to a generic interface (educational implementation) called IAIK. This is a cryptographic library which implements multiple cryptographic algorithms together with methods for handling them. All of this is under object-oriented programming philosophy.

Fig. 3. Details of labels used to execute client-server operations in key management protocol

This library is made to be used within Java applications and to be a provider of cryptographic functions of Java classes for working with information security. Among the multiple algorithms that IAIK implements, are included the following: key generation, both symmetric and asymmetric, data encryption and decryption, digest functions, certificate generation, etc. It is possible to find these algorithms and techniques: RSA, SHA, DES, triple DES, MD2, MD5, X509 certificates version 1, 2 and 3, IDEA among others.

The reason for using IAIK as a dynamic load library is because once the library is loaded and securely initialized, it provides the ability to deliver services, also it is possible to manage keys into devices that perform a compatible standard interface RSA PKCS#11. This element is one of the most important features that this platform provides, not being a direct development of cryptographic devices, but also applicable to cryptographic tokens and smartcards.

3.1.1 Standard Integration between Key Interoperability and RSA PKCS#11

The model implemented in the deployment of interoperable key management can be analyzed by observing the basic parameters of the sentence. This is so in order to see which is the minimum number of attributes must have that a key using this protocol to generate it:

Type of Key to generate.
Type of algorithm which will generate the key.
Key length.
Restrictions on use of key.

Considering this, to perform the correct integration between the attributes[10] of the interoperable key management protocol and RSA PKCS#11 standard, it has been analyzed the different attributes for key generation process used in RSA standard:

```
pkcs11KeyTemplate.getEncrypt().setBooleanValue(Boolean);
pkcs11KeyTemplate.getDecrypt().setBooleanValue(Boolean);
pkcs11KeyTemplate.getSign().setBooleanValue(Boolean);
pkcs11KeyTemplate.getVerify().setBooleanValue(Boolean);
pkcs11KeyTemplate.getWrap().setBooleanValue(Boolean);
pkcs11KeyTemplate.getUnwrap().setBooleanValue(Boolean);
pkcs11KeyTemplate.getExtractable().setBooleanValue(Boolea
n);
pkcs11KeyTemplate.getAlwaysSensitive().setBooleanValue(Bo
olean);
pkcs11KeyTemplate.getNeverExtractable().setBooleanValue(B
oolean)
pkcs11KeyTemplate.getTrusted().setBooleanValue(Boolean);
pkcs11KeyTemplate.getLocal().setBooleanValue(Boolean);
```

It can be seen that there are multiple attributes as well as differences between each of the attributes that manage the interoperable key management protocol and RSA PKCS#11 standard. These differences condition the design of the logical bridge between these two standards, taking into consideration that there are attributes closely related to the key security, how to export and with the assurance that provides a key if it is truly exportable or not. Attached to this point, it is important to consider the different certifications that the cryptographic hardware environment may have, since the attributes related to the key export are linked to the FIPS or not FIPS device configuration. In order to have an implementation laying down certified cryptographic key generation rules, key attributes can be configured using the following order, it is important the consideration to offer an additional configuration console from which can provide values for the security features, particularly those related to the key generation process.

BASIC attributes will be set in the following order:

```
pkcs11KeyTemplate.getEncrypt().setBooleanValue(Boolean);
pkcs11KeyTemplate.getDecrypt().setBooleanValue(Boolean)
pkcs11KeyTemplate.getSign().setBooleanValue(Boolean.TRUE);
pkcs11KeyTemplate.getVerify().setBooleanValue(Boolean.TRUE);
pkcs11KeyTemplate.getExtractable().setBooleanValue(Boolea
n.FALSE);
pkcs11KeyTemplate.getAlwaysSensitive().setBooleanValue(Bo
olean.TRUE);
pkcs11KeyTemplate.getNeverExtractable().setBooleanValue(B
oolean.FALSE);
pkcs11KeyTemplate.getTrusted().setBooleanValue(Boolean.TR
UE);
pkcs11KeyTemplate.getLocal().setBooleanValue(Boolean.FALS
E);
```

Consequently, for the designed prototype it has been integrated the attributes of key usage, which are fully compliant with interoperable key management protocol, while security patterns are applicable from access service to the cryptographic hardware, based on the RSA PKCS#11standard.

4 RSA PKCS#11 and Key Management Interoperability Protocol Integration Model Deployment

The deployment of this model is oriented to the key management technologies assessment, the cryptographic integration between RSA PKCS#11 standard attributes and the protocol chosen based on the performed criteria (KMIP Key Management Interoperability Protocol), as well as the development of a prototype aimed to key generation, to evaluate the most expensive operation as the base of for all key management model. This has, among its specific objectives, outline a key management mechanism integrated with a compatible standard RSA PKCS model, ensuring the implementation is fully compatible with standards and service providers focused in the cloud. For such purposes, it has been made the following operation model:

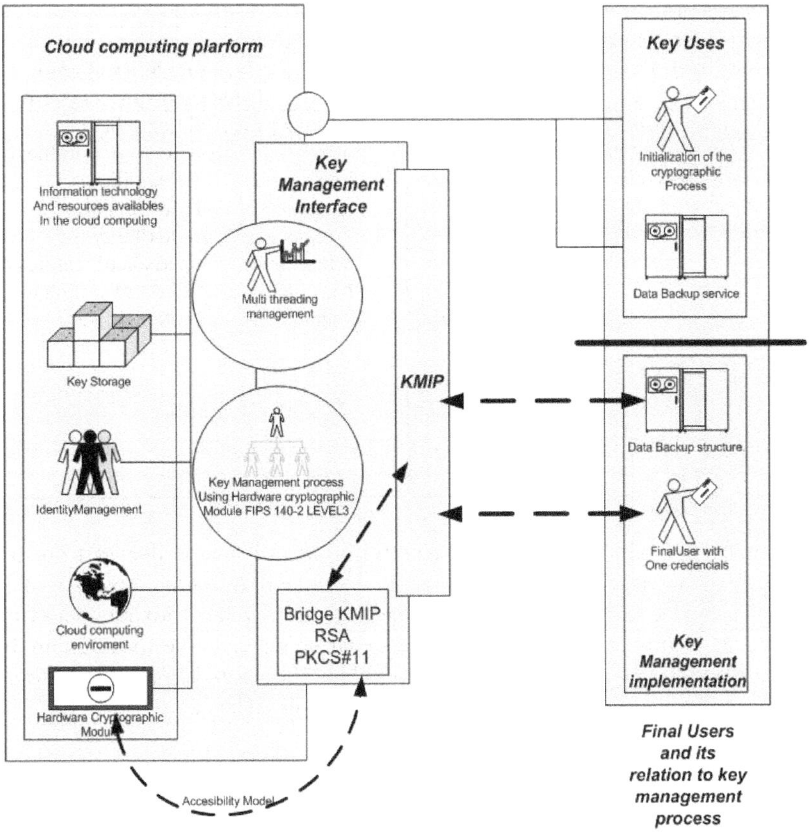

Fig. 4. Target solution deployment model: Cloud computing, cryptography –privacy operating environment

The proposed model has three elements of study:

- Key management consumers: They are responsible for operations related to data privacy and securing available data in the cloud. It has been proposed a clear distinction between the roles which perform key generation processes and, in general, all key management processes (destruction, redefinition, renew or querying secure objects within the environment) and those associated to the consumption of these keys for operational processes and deployment of solutions in the cloud.

  It is very important to make this distinction, because the key management interface does not perform cryptographic functions like electronic signature or data encryption or decryption, it is simply a secure objects management interface in the protected cryptographic hardware environment.
- Key management interface: This mainly consists of the defined link between devices which dialogues RSA PKCS#11 standard that exist in the cloud and the various requests that are performed by standard KMIP. Its function is providing a generic interface supported on the device to ensure the safekeeping and the trust structure which support data protection processes in the cloud. Furthermore, product of this unification, it is possible to see key management capabilities for accredited FIPS 140-2 certification and, at the same time, for considering it at the level of accessibility, taking into account the key services deployment model supported by a multithread service (tested under transactional and non-transactional conditions).

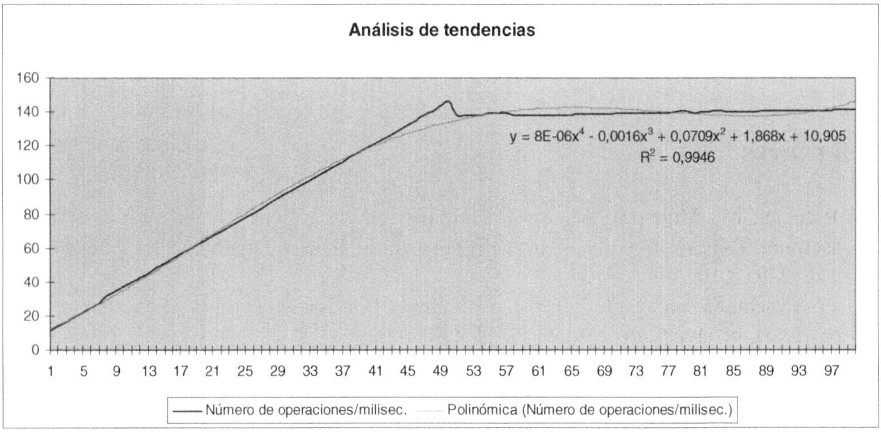

Fig. 5. Table of performance returned with 50 concurrent execution threads in 100 iterations

- Cloud computing platform: This is composed by informatics systems that interact in the makeup of the platform as its own operational support. Also, immersed in the cloud computing environment, the integration of safety guard elements, thanks to the existing cryptographic devices, key management operations can be natively executed within the platform. That mechanism of accessibility must be referred to a credentials model, which is directly implemented in KMIP, ensuring that the cryptographic functions access is safety guaranteed from KMIP credentials model and RSA PKCS#11standard, using the secure certified console that provides the cryptographic device.

5 Conclusions

Among the most important activities performed in this research, they are described the following:

- To have defined the most outstanding technologies in the key management.
- Cryptographic integration made between RSA PKCS#11 attributes and the protocol chosen under our criteria (KMIP Key Management Interoperability Protocol).
- To develop a prototype which performs, using the protocol, the selection of certain transactional operations, among them key generation was the selected one for the scope of this paper, due to it is the most complex and expensive and the base of every key management model.
- This prototype was tested in a multithread operating scenario, the target of this test is to see the compatibility between standards, as well as the differences in performance that brings the implementation of key generation functions oriented to decentralized architectures, abstracted from the cloud.
- The performance of the test was done on request process of 100 concurrent threads, this model propounds the possibility that, in fact, this standard application is operable, in addition to having a complete linkage between key generation of interoperability protocol and RSA PKCS#11 standard.

Also, it can be denoted that this study, in favor to obtain a mathematical structure which provides the way to estimate performance based on the number of concurrent threads. It has been possible to obtain a structure with a capacity of approximation of 99,46%, being this one of the most important elements of this study, since it can anticipate and predict performance based on the most transactional case studied in this paper. In cases with fewer simultaneous concurrent operations, R2 factors were very low, which gives us sufficient evidence that the estimation structures are unreliable in terms of the likelihood of the estimator.

References

1. Oasis, OASIS Members Form Key Management Interoperability Protocol (KMIP) Technical Committee (2009), http://www.oasis-open.org/committees/kmip/charter.php
2. Oasis, KMIP: Key Management Interoperability Protocol (2009), http://www.oasis-open.org/committees/kmip
3. Ansi, Interoperable Secure Key Exchange Key Block Specification for Symmetric Algorithms (2005), http://www.techstreet.com/standards/X9/TR_31_2005?product_id =1327251

4. Ansi, Retail Financial Services Symmetric Key Management Part 2: Using Asymmetric Techniques for the Distribution of Symmetric Keys Accredited Standards Committee X9 (2006), http://www.techstreet.com/cgi-bin/detail?doc_no=X9%7CX9_24_2_2006&product_id=1327211
5. Ansi, Framework for Key Management Extensions (2007), http://webstore.ansi.org/RecordDetail.aspx?sku=ANSI+X9.69-2006
6. Areito, J.: Seguridad de la Información: redes, informática y Sociedad de la Información. Cengage Learning-Paraninfo (2009)
7. Phillip, B.-H.: Overview of IETF KEYPROV (2009), http://tools.ietf.org/html/draft-ietf-keyprov-pskc
8. Elaine, B., Branstad, D., et al.: Cryptographic Key Management Workshop. NIST Focus Paper. NIST Key Management Workshop Sumary (2010), http://csrc.nist.gov/publications/nistir/ir7609/nistir-7609.pdf
9. Mathias, B., Christian, C., et al.: Design and Implementation of a Key-Lifecycle Management System. IBM Research (2009), http://www.zurich.ibm.com/~cca/papers/klm.pdf
10. Christian, C.: A Secure Cryptographic Token Interface. IBM Zurich Research Labs Research (2009), http://www.zurich.ibm.com/~cca/papers/mkms.pdf
11. Chakrabarti, A.: Grid computing security. Springer, Heidelberg (2007), http://www.amazon.com/Grid-Computing-Security-Anirban-Chakrabarti/dp/3540444920
12. Kimberly, G.: Encryption and Key Management Benchmark Report. Trust Catalyst (2008), http://idtrust.xml.org/news/2008-encryption-and-key-management-benchmark-report
13. George, H.: New Storage Security Specs Promote Hardware-Based Encryption. Byte and Switch (2009), http://www.networkcomputing.com/other/new-storage-security-specs-promote-hardware-based-encryption.php?type=article
14. Luther, M.: Federated Key Management as the Basis for Secure Cloud Computing (2010), http://www.scmagazineus.com/federated-key-management-as-the-basis-for-secure-cloud-computing/article/158089/

Optimizing One-to-Many Negotiation Agents in E-Commerce Using Aspiration Concept

Sahar Ebadi*, Md. Nassir Sulaiman, and Masrah Azrifah Azmi Morad

Department of Information System, Faculty of Computer Science and Information Technology, University Putra Malaysia, Serdang, Malaysia
Sah_ebadi@yahoo.com, Nasir@fsktm.upm.edu.my, Masrah.Azrifah@gmail.com

Abstract. With the growth of World Wide Web and increasing human demand on trading, e-commerce becomes an inseparable part of business. In the past decade a huge number of researches have been done in order to develop optimal negotiation agent systems in e-commerce. However, existing models are weak in supporting real world e-market conditions since most of them assume static conditions for environment and complete information about opponent agent's preferences. As a result, this work proposes an adaptive one-to-many negotiation model called Aspiration negotiation model. This model is proposed in order to assist agents to adapt to the dynamicity of opponent agent's preferences and environmental conditions. Proposed model is employed in order to optimize the negotiation outcome in terms of utility gained by agents. Experimental studies have been done to evaluate the performance of proposed model. Finally Aspiration model was able to outperform previous models in terms of seller, buyer and joint utility value.

Keywords: e-Commerce, Agent, Negotiation, Optimization, Genetic Algorithm, Aspiration, One-to-Many Negotiation.

1 Introduction

With the growth of World Wide Web and increasing human demand on trading, e-commerce becomes an inseparable part of business. Thousands of business companies are trading through Internet and create a vast global e-commerce place. Millions of transactions are accomplished daily between different buyers and sellers regardless of geographical locations. This process of buying and selling products or services on internet networks is called E-commerce.

Many research have been done to model the buying behavior in e-commerce although; all these researches defined six basic stages of buyer process [1]. They are product brokering, need identification, merchant brokering, negotiation, purchase and delivery as well as product brokering and evaluation [2].

* Corresponding author.

E. Ariwa and E. El-Qawasmeh (Eds.): DEIS 2011, CCIS 194, pp. 703–713, 2011.

1.1 Agents and Negotiation in E-Commerce

Among the six stage of the buying behavior, negotiation is the key component of e-commerce [3]. Negotiation is a process in which two or more parties with different criteria, constraints, and preferences, jointly reach an agreement on the terms of a transaction [4]. Generally, negotiation is between two types of negotiators namely, buyer and seller. Number of negotiator parties involve in negotiation could vary between at least two to many negotiator depending on the trading scenario. During the negotiation process buyer and seller exchange offers until they reach to a mutually acceptable offer. Offers are including issues such as price, quality and time. Once agents reach to a mutually acceptable offer they fast the deal and negotiation is done. There are obstacles in performing human-based negotiation which makes it impractical. Gathering negotiator parties in a specific place at a specific time, especially in international trading, this is practically inefficient. Negotiator's preferences are usually in conflict with each other. Therefore, finding a mutually acceptable offer is time consuming. During the past years, autonomous intelligent systems have employed on e-commerce application to overcome these difficulties.

Agent is a computer system that is situated in some environment, and is capable of autonomous action in this environment in order to meet its designed objective [5]. Agents are characterized by autonomy, social ability, reactivity and pro-activity. Concerning these characteristics agents are capable of building robust, fast and optimal system architectures in negotiation scenarios.

Many autonomous negotiation systems are developed using agents during last decade [4, 6-12]. Kasbah [8] is one of the primary negotiation systems proposed for negotiation in e-commerce. Kasbah is a one-to-one, single issue negotiation model. Anthony believes that negotiators focus on price issue rather than other issues. Therefore, parties are only conceding over price during negotiation. Beside all the advantages of Kasbah, limited number of issues and lack of intellectuality are the obvious drawbacks of this model. Later, Rahwan proposed a one-to-many negotiation model called ITA [4].

ITA agents were improved version of negotiation models in terms of number of issues and communicating terms as it presents a bilateral, multiple-issue negotiation model. ITA proposed four strategies to apply during negotiation. However, due to the pre-programmed nature of these strategies this model is not performing efficiently in dynamic environments.

One of the most outstanding negotiation models is e-CN [12]. E-CN is a concurrent one-to-many, multi-issue, bilateral negotiation system. E-CN negotiator agents are equipped with learning ability to classify their opponent agents according to their types. Also, agents are following three strategies, namely conceder, linear and tough. This model is popular because of its simplicity, applicability and its unique coordination system. Moreover, this system is currently being used in British Telecommunication projects.

1.2 Adaptability, a Vital Notion in E-Commerce

E-market places are filled by different agents coming from different sources and designs, characterized by various preferences and volatile deadlines. Due to these complexity, dynamicity and huge space of marketing places on Internet, finding an efficient negotiation model which performs efficiently under real world condition is impractical. Numbers of existing one-to-many negotiation models are faced a problem which we call it non-adaptability or blind negotiation.

Blind negotiation means negotiator agents are not taking into account their opponent preferences or the dynamicity of environmental conditions during negotiation. In other words, blind negotiators are not able to adapt themselves to the dynamicity of environmental condition. The adaptability of these negotiation agents to the dynamicity of environmental and opponent agent's preferences leaves an open issue for further improvement.

Although e-CN tries to learn the negotiator types using Bayesian learning but it was not successful in building a fully adaptive negotiation system. This non-adaptability of negotiator agents will result into a non-adaptive system and ends into a sub-optimal outcome of the system [13-17]. The non-adaptability of e-CN agents are potentially derived from the fragile decision policy of e-CN agents which traps the whole negotiation system in local optimum answers.

Final utility value of a non-adaptive, blind negotiation models like ITA [4] is around 0.60, while, for a semi-adaptive models like e-CN [18] is around 0.70.

1.3 Negotiation Optimization in E-Commerce

Optimization has been long the center of attraction in negotiation systems and e-commerce applications. A lot of studies have been done during the last decade in order to optimize a variety of negotiation agent models[1, 4, 9, 12, 18]. The aim of this research is to improve the non-adaptability problem of e-CN model. Therefore, a new negotiation algorithm is proposed which takes in to account the dynamicity of opponent agents and environmental conditions while decision making. The objective of this study is to improve the performance of e-CN negotiation model. Hence, a new negotiation model has been proposed which we call it Aspiration model. This new negotiation algorithm is based on the Aspiration concept and a new decision policy. Proposed negotiation algorithm improves agent's adaptability and helps agents to adjust to the environmental and opponent changes. This adaptability helps agents to find the best possible or pareto-optimum answers. Thus, by improving the adaptability of agents we are able to increase the utility gained by agents. In other words, the final performance of the system increases.

2 Negotiation Scenario

This study focuses on one-to-many negotiation scenario where one buyer agent is trying to find the best deal from one of the seller agents exist in e-market place. In order to build the foundation of Aspiration model, this study follows the same basic structures as e-CN model. Sequential Alternative Protocol (SAP) is chosen as agent communication protocol during negotiation.

In this scenario, each product is identified by five issues (attributes) called *Name, ManFac, Price, Quality, Deadline*. Accordingly, agent's preferences are represented in terms of these issues as follow: Name, represents the name of the product (e.g. CPU). Manfac, refers to the manufacturer of the product (e.g. Intel or IBM). Price, represents the price of the product. Quality, represents the quality of the product. Deadline, declares the due time for delivery (or payment). Among these five issues, only three issues are negotiable namely price, quality and deadline. Every negotiable issue (e.g. issue *j*) is declared by a tuple to represent its dimensions as $[X^{\alpha}_{jmin}, X^{\alpha}_{jmax}, W^{\alpha}_{j}]$. Issue's values are placed in an interval of $[X^{\alpha}_{jmin}, X^{\alpha}_{jmax}]$ which are the maximum and minimum boundaries of values for issue *j*. W^{α}_{j} shows the importance degree of this issue for agent α. In this work negotiation setup is as follow in Table1.

Table 1. Set up variables participating in negotiation model

Variable	Description	Value
X^{α}_{jmin}	Minimum bound for the value of issue J for agent α	[0-20]
X^{α}_{jmax}	Maximum bound for the value of issue J for agent α	[30-50]
W^{α}_{j}	Importance degree of issue j for agent α	1/m *
T^{α}	Is the hard deadline for agentα	[5-30]
N	Number of seller agents	[1-30]
M	Number of issues for product	5

*m is number of negotiable issues

Every agent has a hard deadline T^{α} which indicates the time that agent has to reach a deal. During this time agents try to sale or purchase a product which satisfies their preferences.

E-CN is following a very simple decision policy in its negotiation algorithm. E-CN decision policy is to accept offers that have higher utility than all the offers received up to now. Agents are encouraged to generate new offers if the offer is not acceptable and agent has not reached its deadline. Other than that, agent will reject the offer and terminates the negotiation. This rigid and non-flexible decision policy of e-CN agents builds a fragile negotiation algorithm which traps agents to fall into local optimum answers. As a matter of fact, e-CN agents are not able to take in to account the current situation and are not able to predict the opponent agent's actions. Therefore, they are not able to take the risk of rejecting local optimum answers in the hope of reaching higher benefit in the future.

3 Proposed Aspiration Negotiation Model

In order to overcome the non-adaptability problem of e-CN model a new negotiation model is proposed. The proposed negotiation model is called Aspiration model which includes new negotiation algorithm and new decision policy. This model is proposed to improve the adaptability of negotiator agents by considering the dynamic factors of the environment and opponent's preferences at the time. These improve the performance of negotiation model under dynamic e-Commerce environments and models. The proposed algorithm is explained in details in following section.

3.1 Aspirated Negotiation System Framework

In order to avoid these weaknesses of e-CN negotiation algorithm Aspiration model is proposing a new negotiation algorithm and embeds the aspiration level in the core of decision making policy of agent. Fig. 1 presents the system framework of Aspiration model.

Buyer agent is formed by two components namely Coordinator and Sub-buyers. Coordinator is acting as the central and higher level of buyer agent which informs sub-buyers from new reservation values and specifies a particular strategy to each sub-buyer after each round of negotiation[19]. Sub-buyer is acting as the negotiator which is directly in communication with seller agent. At the start of negotiation, Buyer agent searches the e-Commerce environment for potential sellers. For any amount of founded sellers, coordinator will generate a responsible sub-buyer to negotiate with seller agent through it.

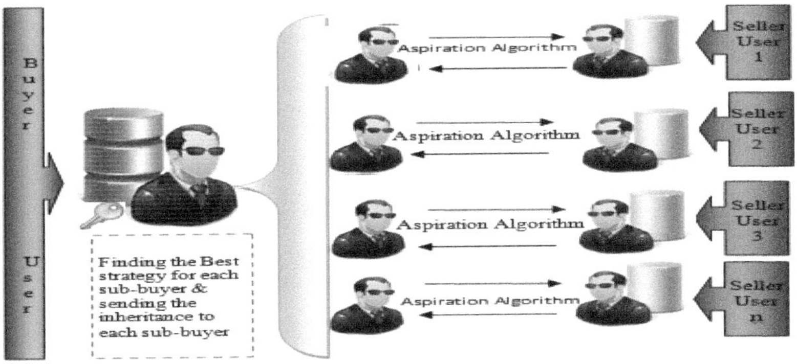

Fig 1. Aspiration model framework

Buyer agent inherits the reservation values obtained from buyer data base. Also, it coordinates all the sub-buyers by informing them from the new lowest utility value and specified strategies. Later sub-buyers will negotiate directly with seller agents through Aspiration negotiation algorithm. Each seller has its own preferences and database which will work individually in order to win in the negotiation. When seller receives the offer from buyer it replies through Aspiration algorithm which is explained in Fig. 2 in details.

3.2 Aspiration Concept

Aspiration level is a concept which represents the desire of agent for willing to deal, or minimum utility value acceptable by agent. Aspiration level is affected by several factors such as remained time for negotiation, type of agent and lowest utility value which an agent is willing to deal with at the moment. Aspiration level of each agent is calculated as follow:

$$AspirationLevel = 1+(LowestUtilityValue-1) * (Pcnt/deadline)^{\gamma} \quad (1)$$

When the lowest utility acceptable for agent is shown by (*LowestUtilityValue*) and *Pcnt* is the counter of negotiation rounds (time). *deadline* refers to the agent's time for negotiation. *(Pcnt/deadline)* represents the Time Pressure Factor (TPF) and shows for how long an agent is able to stands for its highest benefits. This parameter is located between [0, 1] and starts by 0 at the start of the negotiation, thus, keeps agent to the highest desired values. TPF increases by passing each round of negotiation. When the time pressure is equal to 1 agent will reduce to its lowest reservation value in order to fast the deal. Parameter γ depends on agent's strategy and is equal to 2, 0.5 and 1 respectively as it is obeying *conceder, tough* and *linear* strategies. γ affects the time pressure that agent is tolerating at the moment.

Therefore, agent can predict if the time pressure on agent should be considered seriously or agent can make a risk on it. For example, if buyer agent is following tough strategy means the seller agent is having conceder manner therefore seller agent will give up more benefit to the buyer agent through the time. This is the logic to allocate the highest value of 2 to the γ when agent strategy is tough. This allows buyer agent to take the risk of just accepting offers with high utility value. The time pressure factor *(Pcnt/deadline)* is considered to lower the aspiration level (risky behaviour) of agent while agent is near to the deadline. This fact allows negotiator agents to reach a deal if there is an overlap between agent's preferences.

As Equation 1 shows, aspiration level lowers through the time in order to make a deal. This is an important characteristic of Aspiration level which will guarantee reaching of agreement when there is a possibility. Thus, using aspiration level helps agents to adjust to the changes of opponent agent's type. Also, taking into account the remained time for negotiation avoids accepting low utility value offers and prevents agents to conduct a deal in sub-optimal conditions (local optima).

3.3 Aspirated Negotiation Algorithm

Now that agent knows at which level it is suppose to concede and risk the preferences, we can accurately decide whether a proposal is acceptable or there are potential upcoming deals to wait for. Aspiration model proposed its decision making policy based on aspiration concept. The final Aspirated negotiation algorithm is shown in Fig 2.

Fig 2. represents the procedure of Aspiration negotiation algorithm of agent, from the moment of receiving a message (call for proposal or proposal) up to the sending the reply message. When agent receives the opponent agent's offer (The incoming opponent agent's offer is shown by an inflow arrow terminated to "seller I receives a message by buyer j") it will calculate the utility value of that offer and updates the lowest utility value variable. Considering the recorded history of received offers agent will chose the best strategy to deal with opponent agent. Later, Aspiration level of agent is calculated as was explained in previous section. A new offer is generated using the best strategy. This offer generation is made using time-dependence strategies[20].

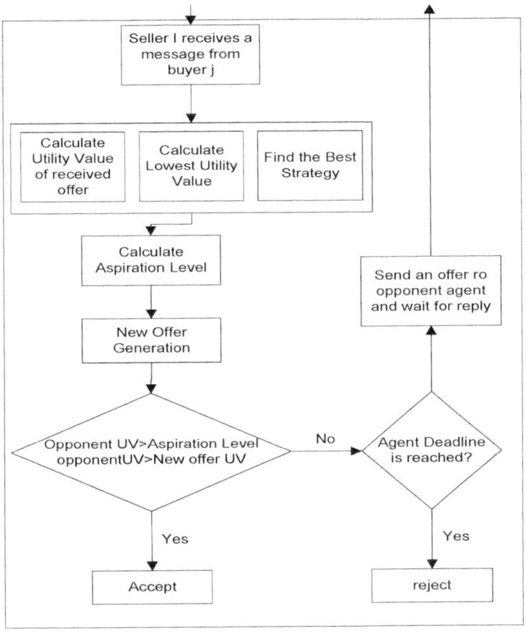

Fig. 2. Aspiration negotiation algorithm

As is indicated in Fig. 2 buyer decision making policy is based on two conditions:

- Condition 1: sellerOfferUV >AspirationLevel
- Condition 2: sellerOfferUV >NewOfferUV

An offer would be acceptable if it fulfils condition 1 or 2. If a proposed offer by seller was bigger than aspiration level (condition 1) it means that the utility value of this offer is already the highest amongst all the previous received offers (as it should hit the lowest utility value) and also agent is not expecting any better upcoming offer in the remaining time. Condition 2 is preventing from offering a proposal by agent which is lower than opponent proposed offer. This case usually happens when seller agent is under the pressure of short deadline or is experiencing conceder or linear strategy with low expectations.

In these two cases, buyer agent would accept the proposed offer by opponent agent and will terminate the rest of negotiation threads by refusing them. If these conditions were not met and agent deadline was not reached yet then agent will propose a new offer (shown in Fig. 2 by an outflow arrow begin from "send an offer to opponent agent and wait for reply").

4 Result and Discussion

Proposed Aspiration model is being compared with e-CN model in order to evaluate the final performance of the system. Mostly the performance of the negotiation system is evaluated based on utility value achieved by agent. In this research the utility value of each offer is evaluated using *U(x)* function calculated as follow:

$$U(x) = \sum_{j=1}^{m} w_j^{\propto} . \frac{x_j - x_{jmin}^{\propto}}{x_{jmax}^{\propto} - x_{jmin}^{\propto}} \quad (2)$$

Let, x be the accepted offer (or offer) to evaluate by agent α. Each offer is a combination different issues. Assuming that number of negotiable issues are $\boldsymbol{m}$ then an offer would be represented as follow (e.g. $= \{x_1, x_2, x_3, \dots, x_m\}$). The $x_{jmin}^{\propto}$ and $x_{jmax}^{\propto}$ are respectively the minimum and maximum reserved values for issue j of agent α. The importance degree of each issue for agent α is shown by $w_j^{\propto}$ which is equal to 1/m (as assumed in e-CN). The value of issue j for the offer to evaluate is represented by x_j. A present dynamic factor of environment is time which is dynamic through the time and is important in every e-commerce application and negotiation system. Therefore, we examine the performance and adaptability of our proposed model under different agent's deadlines (various time pressures). The represented utility values in the following graphs are corresponded to the utility value for the final deal.

Fig. 3 represents the Final utility value gained by Aspiration buyer agents vice versa Final utility value gained by e-CN buyer agents. As can be seen, due to the adaptability of Aspiration model, Aspiration buyer agents achieve higher utility value at all the time in compare with e-CN buyer agents. Aspiration buyer agents are able to control the effect of time pressure factor and heighten the Aspiration level of agents.

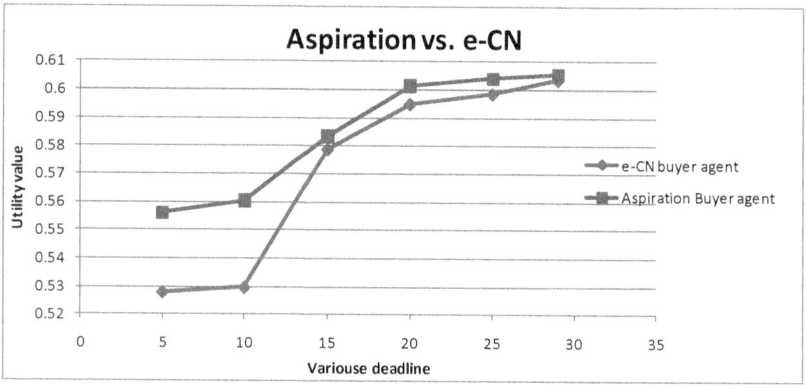

Fig. 3. Aspiration Vs. e-CN comparison in buyer agent utility value

Heightening the Aspiration level of agent increases its tolerance against low utility value offers in early rounds of negotiation. In other words, agents are able to increases their risky attitude considering the environmental condition (Long remained time for negotiation). Therefore, Aspiration buyer agents are able to outperform e-CN agents with a big difference in short deadlines (5 to 15).

For example, assuming buyer agent β's deadline is 25 and number of seller agents in environment is 5, after 5 rounds of exchanging offers seller agent may propose a local optima solution (an offer with 40% utility for agent). If lowest utility value received by buyer agent up to now was 39%, e-CN will accept this offer since 40% > 39%.

But Aspirated agents calculate the remained time for negotiation (time pressure factor).

Time Pressure Factor = *(Pcnt/deadline)=5/25=0.2*

Considering agents strategy is conceder, γ is equal to 2. Then, the aspiration value of agent β will be calculated as follow:

$$Aspiration\ level = 1 + (39\% - 1) * (5/25)^2 = 0.975$$

Aspiration level is equal to 0.975, since 40% < 0.975 agent will wait for upcoming chances to take. As can be seen Aspiration level helps agents to do not fall for low utility value or local optimum offers by increasing the aspiration of agent. This fact increases the risky attitude of agent by considering the environmental condition such as time in terms of *(Pcnt, deadline)* and also by taking in to account the opponent agent's preferences (such as opponents *type* and *strategy* and *LowestUtilityValue*).

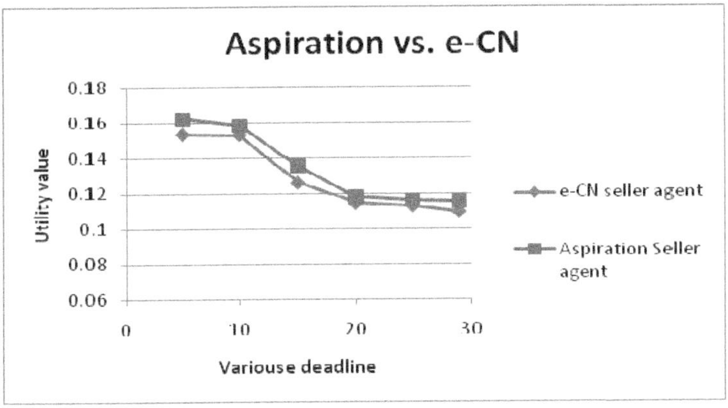

Fig. 4. Aspiration Vs. e-CN comparison in seller agent utility value

Fig. 4 represents the seller utility value in e-CN and Aspiration model. By increasing the Deadline parameter the utility gained by agents is decreasing. This is due to the fact that buyer with short deadline are under time pressure factor and have to give up some utility to seller agent. But buyers with long deadlines have less time pressure and therefore higher aspiration. This fact able seller agent to obtain higher utility in short deadlines but this time pressure will be lost by increasing the buyer deadline. So, in longer deadline seller will achieve lower utility value rather than shorter deadlines. Although, even in these cases Aspirated seller agents are able to gain higher utility than e-CN seller agents at all the times.

Another utility factor evaluated in different models is Joint utility value. Joint utility value is the sum of utility value gained by buyer and seller agent. Fig. 5 shows shows that joint utility value of Aspiration and e-CN model is increases by increasing the agent's deadline. The longer the agent has time to negotiate the higher the chance to find the best opponent to deal with. The longer the agent deadline is the more the whole utility gain is. Thus, also by increasing the agent's deadline, agent will have more time to find and converge to the mutually acceptable points.

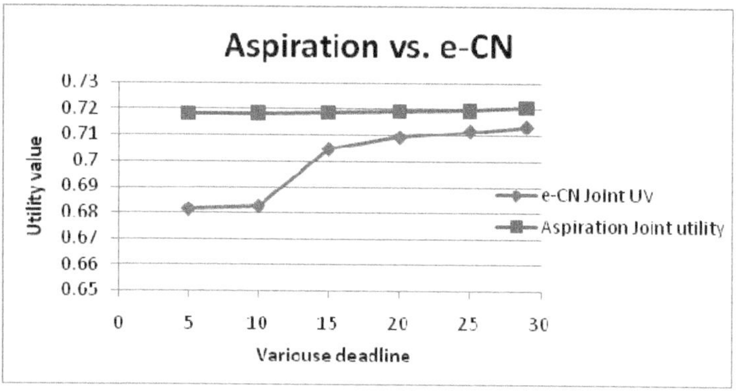

Fig. 5. Aspiration Vs. e-CN comparison in Joint utility value

Fig. 5 show that Aspiration model outperforms the e-CN model in all the times with 0.04% to 0.01% increase in the final outcome. As was explained Aspiration agents are able to gain far more utility than e-CN agents particularly in short deadlines.

5 Conclusion and Future Work

In order to overcome the non-adaptability of e-CN model a semi-adaptive negotiation algorithm is introduced. Proposed Aspiration model is able to adapt and control the risky attitude of agent by considering the time pressure factor and opponent agents type. Aspiration model is able to tackle the local optimum answers by heightening the risky attitude of agent and adapting the aspiration level of agent. This adapt ability of agent helps Aspiration model to gain higher utility value for buyer agent and seller agent. This results to the higher joint utility value which represents the final performance of the system. Aspiration model achieves higher performance than e-CN at all the times but in longer deadline Aspiration model was performing almost as the same as e-CN model. In order to improve the adapt ability of proposed agents an adaptive offer generation is being implemented by this author. Machine learning techniques have been proposed to be used in order to learn and adapt to the opponent preferences. We believe replacing the rigid and non-flexible offer generation by an adaptive mechanism will increase the performance of the system and decreases the time and cost of negotiation.

Another improvement would be to apply proposed Aspirated model on different datasets to evaluate the robustness of Aspiration model. Moreover, extending Aspiration one-to-many model to a many-to-many model would be another further improvement which is practical due to the nature of Aspiration system architecture.

References

1. Choo, N.S.: Machine learning approach for optimizing negotiation agents, p. 167. University Putra Malaysia, KL (2007)
2. Guttman, R.H., Moukas, A.G., Maes, P.: Agent-mediated electronic commerce: an MIT media laboratory perspective. International Journal of Electronic Commerce 4(3), 5–12 (2000)

3. Sandholm, T.: Atomated negotiation. Communication of the ACM 42(3), 84–85 (1999)
4. Rahwan, I., Kowalczyk, R., Pham, H.H.: Intelligent agents for automated one-to-many e-commerce negotiation. In: Proceedings of the Twenty-fifth Australasian Conference on Computer Science 2002. Australian Computer Society, Inc., Melbourne (2002)
5. Wooldridge, M., Jennings, N.R.: Intelligent Agents: Theory and Practice. Knowledge Engineering Review 10(2), 115–152 (1995)
6. Lau, R.Y.K.: An Evolutionary Approach for Intelligent Negotiation Agents in e-Marketplaces. Intel. Agents in the Evol. of Web & Appl. 167, 279–301 (2009)
7. Cheng, C.-B., Chan, C.-C.H., Lin, K.-C.: Intelligent agents for e-marketplace: Negotiation with issue trade-offs by fuzzy inference systems. Decis. Support Syst. 42, 626–638 (2005)
8. Anthony, C., Pattie, M.: Kasbah: An agent marketplace for buying and selling goods. In: Proceedings of the first International Conference on the Practical Application of Intelligent Agents and Multi-Agent Technology (1996)
9. Choo, N.S., Sulaiman, M.N., Selamat, M.H.: Machine learning approach in optimizing negotiation agents for e-commerce. Information Technology Journal 8(6), 801–810 (2009)
10. Ros, R., Sierra, C.: A negotiation meta strategy combining trade-off and concession moves. Autonomous Agents and Multi-Agent Systems 12, 163–181 (2006)
11. Dang, J., Huhns, M.N.: Concurrent Multiple-Issue Negotiation for Internet-Based Services. IEEE Internet Computing 10(6), 42–49 (2006)
12. Nguyen, T.D., Jennings, N.R.: Coordinating Multiple Concurrent Negotiations. In: Proceedings of the Third International Joint Conference on Autonomous Agents and Multiagent Systems, vol. 3. IEEE Computer Society, New York (2004)
13. Kakas, A., Moraitis, P.: Adaptive Agent Negotiation via Argumentation. In: AAMAS 2006, pp. 8–12. ACM, Hakodate (2006)
14. Ma, H., Leung, H.-F.: An adaptive attitude bidding strategy for agents in continuous double auctions. Electronic Commerce Research and Applications 6, 383–398 (2007)
15. David Pardoe, P.S., VanMiddlesworth, M.: TacTex 2005: An Adaptive Agent for TACSCM. LNCS, vol. 4452(52), pp. 46–61. Springer, Heidelberg (2007)
16. Fang, F., Wong, T.N.: Applying hybrid case-based reasoning in agent-based negotiations for supply chain management. Expert Systems with Applications 37, 8322–8332 (2010)
17. Lai, K.R., Lin, M.W., Yu, T.J.: Learning opponent's beliefs via fuzzy constraint-directed approach to make effective agent negotiation. Applied Intelligence 33, 232–246 (2010)
18. Nguyen, T.D., Jennings, N.R.: A heuristic model for concurrent bi-lateral negotiations in incomplete information settings. In: Proceedings of the Eighteenth International Joint Conference on Artificial Intelligence 2003, pp. 1467–1469 (2003)
19. Nguyen, T.D., Jennings, N.R.: Managing commitments in multiple concurrent negotiations. Electronic Commerce Research and Applications 4(4), 362–376 (2006)
20. Faratin, P., Sierra, C., Jennings, N.R.: Negotiation Decision Functions for Automated Agents. Elsevier Sience (1997)
21. Ebadi, S., Sulaiman, M.N., Murad, M.A.A.: A Review of Negotiation Agents in e-commerce. International Journal of Computer Science and Information Security 8(3), 11–20 (2010)

Algorithmic Method for Generating DC-DC Converter Circuits by Using Topological Matrix

Murad Ahmed Ali Taher

Department of Computer Engineering
Vice Manager of Information Technology Center "ITC"
Hodeidah University, Yemen
dr_muradabsi@yahoo.com

Abstract. This paper proposes a new method for syntheses DC–DC converters by using Main Topological Matrix MTM. The properties of MTM are described. The common properties for single-switch DC-DC converters are also given. The proposed method has a lot of advantages as opposed to other methods. This method is fully algorithmic and takes into account the design by pats. It is also shown by examples how this method is used for generating all sub-class (sub-family) of DC-DC converters with predetermined characteristics.

Keywords: DC-DC converter, topological matrix MTM, algorithmic method.

1 Introduction

Using digital and embedded systems in different fields are widespread due to their accuracy and high efficiency. The development and minimization of the digital systems are happening faster and faster due to new technology for fabrications of Integrated Circuits IC and the existence of theorems and algorithmic methods for their simplification and minimization [1]. Therefore we can say that the computer can help to simplify and minimize itself.

The main part of any electronic device and/or electric vehicle is its power supply, but the development and minimization of the power parts " DC-DC Converters " of any electronic or electric devices (Computers, Embedded Systems, ...etc) do not happen at the same speed as in their digital parts. This is due to the fact that the design (generation and development) of the DC-DC converter is based only on the skills and experience of the designer [2], [3]. There are new designed DC-DC converters which their implementation and topology are presented in [4], [5][6][7], and [8]. The different loads require different features and characteristics of DC-DC converters. The trends for all DC-DC converters are: high efficiency, increasing the switching frequencies for reducing the total size and weight, improved power density and dynamic performance, etc.

There are different series of designed DC-DC converters, but there are no fully algorithmic methods that can be translated into computer program for designing and generating DC-DC converter. This work proposes algorithmic method that can be translated into computer program for generating and implementing DC-DC converters with predetermined characteristics.

E. Ariwa and E. El-Qawasmeh (Eds.): DEIS 2011, CCIS 194, pp. 714–723, 2011.

2 Main Topological Matrix "MTM"

Any electrical circuit can be represented by graph [9] [10] [11], containing b-branches and n- nodes. Branches are divided into two topological groups; b_T- tree branches and b_L-links. A tree of the graph is a subset of the branches such that all graph nodes are connected by branches but without forming a closed path (b_T= n-1). Then these branches are the tree branches. The remaining branches (collectively called a co-tree b_L) are the links (b_L= b-b_T=b-n+1). Given a network graph with b branches and n nodes select a tree, we can obtain the Matrix of Independent Meshes MIM (KVL loop equations), and Matrix of Independent Nodes MIN (KCL equations). There are b–(n-1) KVL equations and n-1 KCL equations.

For the topological relations between MIM and MIN, we will consider basic step-up/ step- down converter shown in Fig.1. In Fig.2 the graph for this circuit is shown, in which the bold lines show branches and dashed lines show the links. Matrix of Independent Meshes and Matrix Independent Nodes MIM and MIN are shown in Fig3 and Fig.4 respectively. For the undirected graph, MIM and MIN are matching (Matrix transportations) as shown in Fig.5, a.

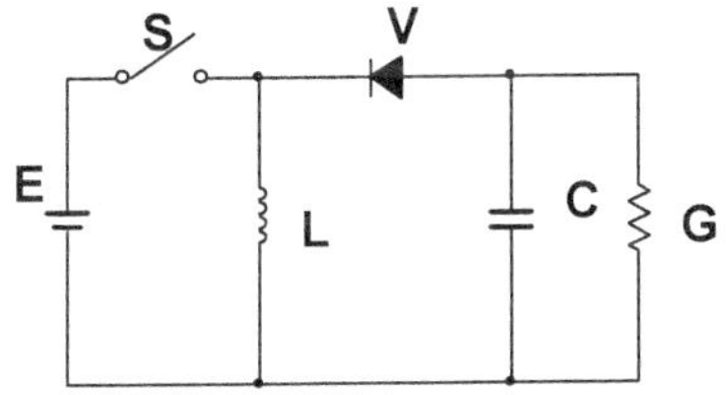

Fig. 1. The basic step-up/ step- down converter

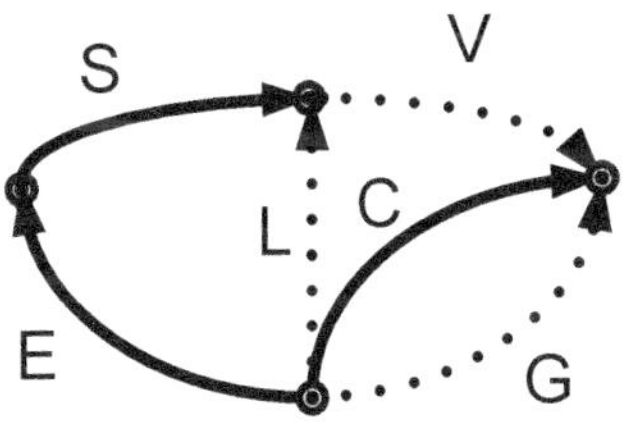

Fig. 2. The graph of the basic step-up/ step- down converter

L	V	G	S	C	E
1			1		1
	1		1	-1	1
		1		-1	

Fig. 3. The MIM matrix for basic step-up/ step- down converter

L	V	G	S	C	E
1	-1		1		
	1	1		1	
1	-1				1

Fig. 4. The MIN matrix for basic step-up/ step- down converter

L	V	G	S	C	E	
1			1		1	L
	1		1	1	1	V
		1		1		G
			1			S
				1		C
					1	E

a)

	S	C	E	
L	1		1	1
V	1	1	1	2
G		1		3
	1	2	3	

b)

Fig. 5. The structure of MTM for basic step-up/ step- down converter

With respect to the horizontal view (rows) of the Matrix of Fig.5,a we obtain Matrix Independent Meshes MIM (KVL loop equations) and for the vertical view (columns) we obtain the Matrix of Independent Nodes MIN (KCL equations). Unity sub- matrixes can be removed and we will obtain the Matrix that we will name the Main Topological Matrix "MTM" as shown in Fig.5,b. This MTM will be the tool for generating converter circuits;" MTM will be used for generating converter circuits" (backward using MTM).

2.1 Characteristics of MTM

Now, we will formulate the characteristics of MTM that will be used for formulation of the logical equations for the syntheses of our converters:

- Equality (identity) of MTM 's columns satisfies the corresponding elements in the series (E in series with S- see Fig.5);
- Equality (identity) of MTM's row satisfies the corresponding elements in parallel. Also the existence unity one in the row satisfies the corresponding elements of branch and link are linked in parallel (G in parallel with C - see Fig.5);
- Any other meshes (dependent mesh) can be obtained from logical addition (logical operation - X OR) two or more MTM's rows.
- Any other nodes (dependent node) can be obtained from logical addition (logical operation XOR) two or more MTM's columns.
- Isomorphic circuits have identical MTM. This means we have also a tool for the identification of isomorphism. ii
- Some terms and postulates for MTM: m[i,j] – element of MTM € {0,1}: 1- element exists in the corresponding mesh or node, 0- means the corresponding element is absent from the corresponding mesh or node (also we can designate it as $m_{i,j}$) . There are Column and Row matrixes for the MTM. For example in Fig.5, column C=[0 1 1] means m[1,2]=0, m[2,2]=1, and m[3,2]=1. Column matrix E= m[1 1 0] means m[1,3]=m[2,3]=1 and m[3,3]=0. Row Matrix L=[1 0 1] it means: m[1,1]=m[1,3]=1, and m[1,2]=0. Row Matrix G=[0 1 0] means m[3,1]=m[3,3]=0, and m[3,2]=1.

3 Formulating the Common Principles of DC-DC Converters Operation and Their Design Approach by Using MTM

The common operation principles for all DC-DC Converters (Single-Switch Switched Mode Power Supply SMPS) are the two timing intervals; some switches are "ON" in the first timing interval and others are "OFF". In the second timing interval will be vice versa. This means the switches that were "ON" in first interval will be "OFF" in the second timing interval and the switches that were "OFF" in first interval will be "ON" in the second timing interval (we can distinguish two equivalent circuits).

Si -designates the switch that will be "ON" in the first timing interval (S-type switch). The number of S-type switches is designated by s. VI will designate the switch that will be "ON" in the second timing interval (V-type switch) and their number will be designated by v.

For Single-Switch DC-DC Converters the number of Capacitors - c should equal the number of inductive elements- l (c=l), we will designate this parameter as q.

For Single-Switch DC-DC Converter's graph, the number of the independent meshes [9] is k= l+ v+ 1 – (1 - corresponding the load resistance) in the first timing interval of operation, and the number of independent meshes is k= l+ s+ 1 in the second timing interval of operation. Since the graph contains a fixed number of independent meshes, so v=s (number of S-type switches should be equal to the number of V- type switches). We will designate this parameter as p.

From the above the number of the Independent Meshes KVL equation for the graph circuits for Single-Switch DC-DC Converters: k= q+ p+1, and the number of the independent nodes (KCL equations) u= b- k, where b- is the number of circuit's elements.

We will follow the following approaches for all DC-DC Converters:

- Neglecting the losses in all the components of DC-DC converter - All switches, coils, transformers (multi-winding coils) are assumed ideal elements.
- S –type switch - the switches that transfer energy from DC source (switches that absorb energy from the energy source , these switches are ON in the first interval of the operation),
- V- Type switch - the switches that delivered the energy are stored in magnetic elements to the load.
- E – Input Voltage Source.
- L1, L2, , Ll –Inductive elements (transformers, single or multi-winding coils)
- C1, C2, Cc – Capacitors.
- The load resistance R =1/G - assumed in parallel with output capacitor(s) won't be shown in MTM.
- The MTM Matrix will be designated by m, and its cells by m [imp] or mi, j, where I≤ k, and j≤u.

3.1 Generating All Members of Single-Switch DC-DC Converters by Using MTM

❖ Subclass DC-DC Converters with two switches (s=v=1)

Generating subclass DC-DC converters with two switches (s=v=1), and two reactive elements (one Inductive element L and one output Capacitor C - c=l=1) will be as the following:

The structure of MTM for these sub-class converters are shown in Fig.6, the inductive element L- assumes a single-winding coil. From the above discussion the number of the independent Meshes is k= p+q+1=3. As the links of the graph we will choose the elements L, V, and G. The remaining elements S, C, and E will be the tree branches. Since the load conductance is always in parallel with the output capacitor C, G can be unconsidered in the MTM in this phase (generating phase procedure).

	S	C	E	
L	x	x	x	1
V	x	x	x	2

Fig. 6. Structure of MTM for basic DC-DC Converters

	S	C	E	
L	1	x	1	1
V	1	x	x	2
	1	2	3	

Fig. 7. Possible MTM's for basic converters (see text)

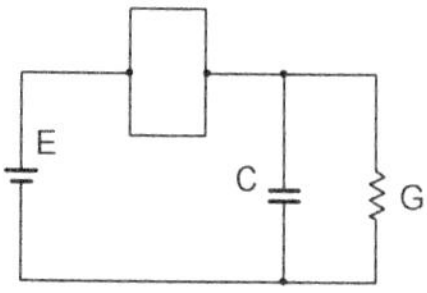

Fig. 8. This connection should be eliminated

When switch S is "ON" the energy is drawn from E and delivered to L, m [1, 1] =m [1, 3] = 1- to form the loop that contains the elements E, L, and S, as shown in Fig.7. When V is "ON" in the second timing interval it should create the mesh that contains elements L, C, V, but does not contain the switch S, which will be "OFF" in this timing interval. However this mesh is a dependent mesh and we can obtain this loop (mesh)by adding (logical operation- XOR) two rows of m, for this reason m[2,1]=1 from the logical equation: m[1,1]+m[2,1]=0 – a condition for removing S from the mesh that contains L, and V (sign + designates the logical operation XOR). m[1,2]+m[2,2]=1 – is a condition for existing the capacitor C in the mesh that contains L, and V. Column Matrix C=[m[1,2] m [2,2]] and Column Matrix E=[[1,3] [2,3]] should be different " equation: C+ E should be equal to 1 (C+ E =1)", if not so then C and E will be in series and the equivalent circuit will be as shown in Fig.8. In this case the output voltage will be equal to the input, or the output voltage will be zero. This connection should be eliminated, and the possible remaining combinations (with decimal codes) for Column Matrixes C and E that satisfy the conditions above are:

	a	b	c
C E=[1 2] [1 3]=	1	2	2
	3	1	3

In this way, we will obtain the three alternative circuits familiar as the basic DC-DC converters as shown in Fig.9 , a, b , c with their MTM "The load G- is always connected in parallel with the output capacitor C" .

	S	C	E	
L	1	1	1	1
	1	0	1	2
	1	2	3	

	S	C	E	
L	1	0	1	1
V	1	1	0	2
	1	2	3	

	S	C	E	
L	1	0	1	1
V	1	1	1	2
	1	2	3	

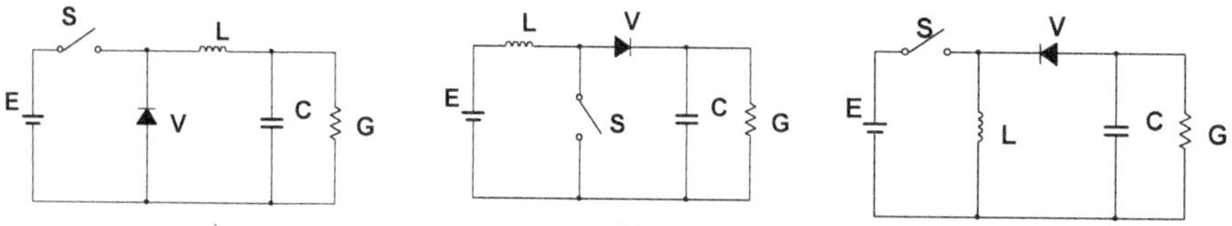

a) **b)** **c)**

Fig. 9. The basic DC-DC converters with their MTM

❖ Generating All Subclass Converter Members with Two Switches (q=1), and Four Reactive Elements (p=2)

The structure of this MTM is shown in Fig. 10. The subscripts 1, 2 correspond to the input and the output respectively. In the first timing interval when S is "ON", the energy is drawn from E and is delivered to L1. so m[1,1]=m[1,4]= 1 for forming the loop which contains elements E, and S. When V is "ON" in the second timing interval this should create the mesh which contains the elements L1, V, and C1, hence m[3,2] = 1. For eliminating switch S from the loops - L1V C1 and L2VC2, Column matrix S should be S= [1 1 1] "Switch S will be "OFF" in this timing interval". Since these loops are not independent loops, we can obtain these meshes by the logical addition of two rows of m (logical XOR). The logical equations; m12+m32=1 and m23+m33=1 - for the existence the capacitors C1 and C2 in the loop L1VC1 and loop L2VC2 respectively. Besides m12+m22=1 for the existence capacitor C1 in the mesh which contains elements L1, and L2 (mesh L1, L2..), otherwise this mesh will contain two elements E and C2, or one of them. In the first case the input and the output voltages will be equal whenever in the second case the average voltage in E or C2 will be zero, hence these two cases should be eliminated. Alternative values for the column matrix C1= [1 0 0] or [0 1 1], the value [1 0 0] should be eliminated otherwise the average current of L1 will be zero, hence C1= [0 1 1] as shown in Fig.10. By using decimal codes the alternative values for columns matrixes C2 and E will be [2,3,4,5] and [1,3,5,7], respectively. From these alternatives we have to eliminate the topology that does not satisfy the logical equation: (m13+ m23)+^m24= 1 - that satisfies the existence of element C2 and/or E in the mesh which contains the elements L1, L2 and C1, otherwise the average voltage on C1 will be zero (this value is not unacceptable). We also have to eliminate the non-regular matrixes by which we cannot build schemas [1] - (^x- means logical not x). So all the alternatives "all possible combinations" of MTMs that satisfy the conditions and logical equations stated above are shown in Fig.11. And all sub-class circuits of DC-DC converters according to these MTM are shown in the Fig.12.-

	S	C1	C2	E	
L1	1	0	X	X	1
L2	1	1	X	X	2
V	1	1	X	X	3
	1	2	3	4	

Fig. 10. The structure of the MTM for sub-class circuits of DC-DC converters with two switches, and four reactive elements

	S	C1	C2	E	
L1	1	0	0	1	1
L2	1	1	1	0	2
V	1	1	0	0	3
	1	2	3	4	

a)

	S	C1	C2	E	
L1	1	0	0	1	1
L2	1	1	1	1	2
V	1	1	0	0	3
	1	2	3	4	

b)

	S	C1	C2	E	
L1	1	0	0	1	1
L2	1	1	1	0	2
V	1	1	0	1	3
	1	2	3	4	

c)

	S	C1	C2	E	
L1	1	0	0	1	1
L2	1	1	1	1	2
V	1	1	0	1	3
	1	2	3	4	

d)

	S	C1	C2	E	
L1	1	0	1	1	1
L2	1	1	1	0	2
V	1	1	0	0	3
	1	2	3	4	

e)

	S	C1	C2	E	
L1	1	0	0	1	1
L2	1	1	0	0	2
V	1	1	1	0	3
	1	2	3	4	

f)

	S	C1	C2	E	
L1	1	0	0	1	1
L2	1	1	0	0	2
V	1	1	1	1	3
	1	2	3	4	

g)

	S	C1	C2	E	
L1	1	0	1	1	1
L2	1	1	0	0	2
V	1	1	1	0	3
	1	2	3	4	

h)

	S	C1	C2	E	
L1	1	0	1	1	1
L2	1	1	0	1	2
V	1	1	1	1	3
	1	2	3	4	

e)

Fig. 11. All generated MTM's for sub-class circuits of DC-DC converters with two switches, and four reactive elements

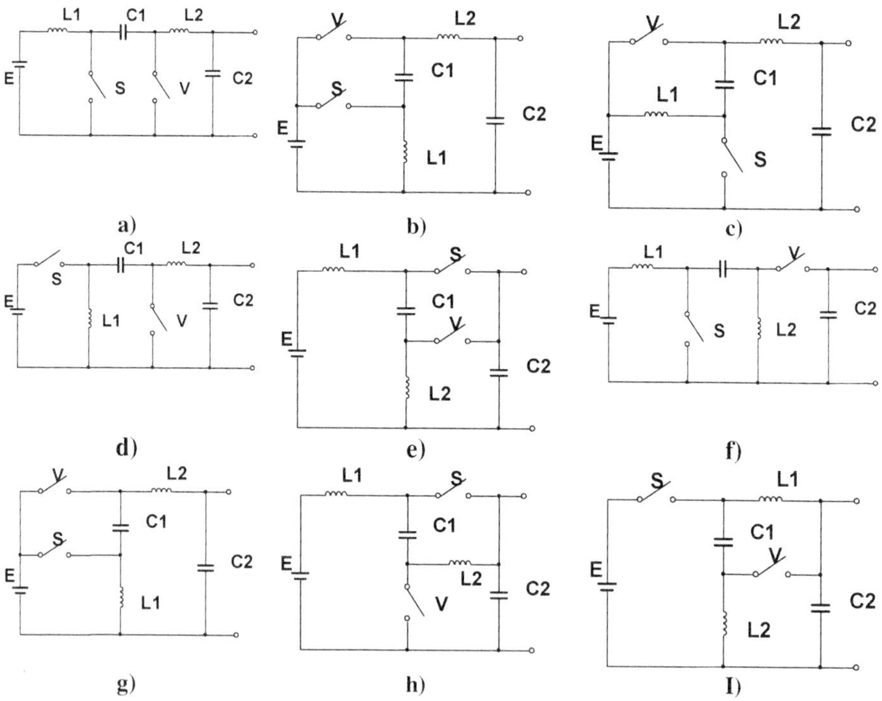

Fig. 12. All sub-class circuits of DC-DC converters with two switches, and four reactive elements

4 Algorithm and Software Implementation

The main tasks of the software were to: –

1. Receive the parameters p and q to determinate the dimension of MTM.
2. Generate all possible combinations of MTM's matrixes.
3. Print all possible topological MTM's combination matrixes that satisfy the logical equations for the determined sub-class of the circuits.

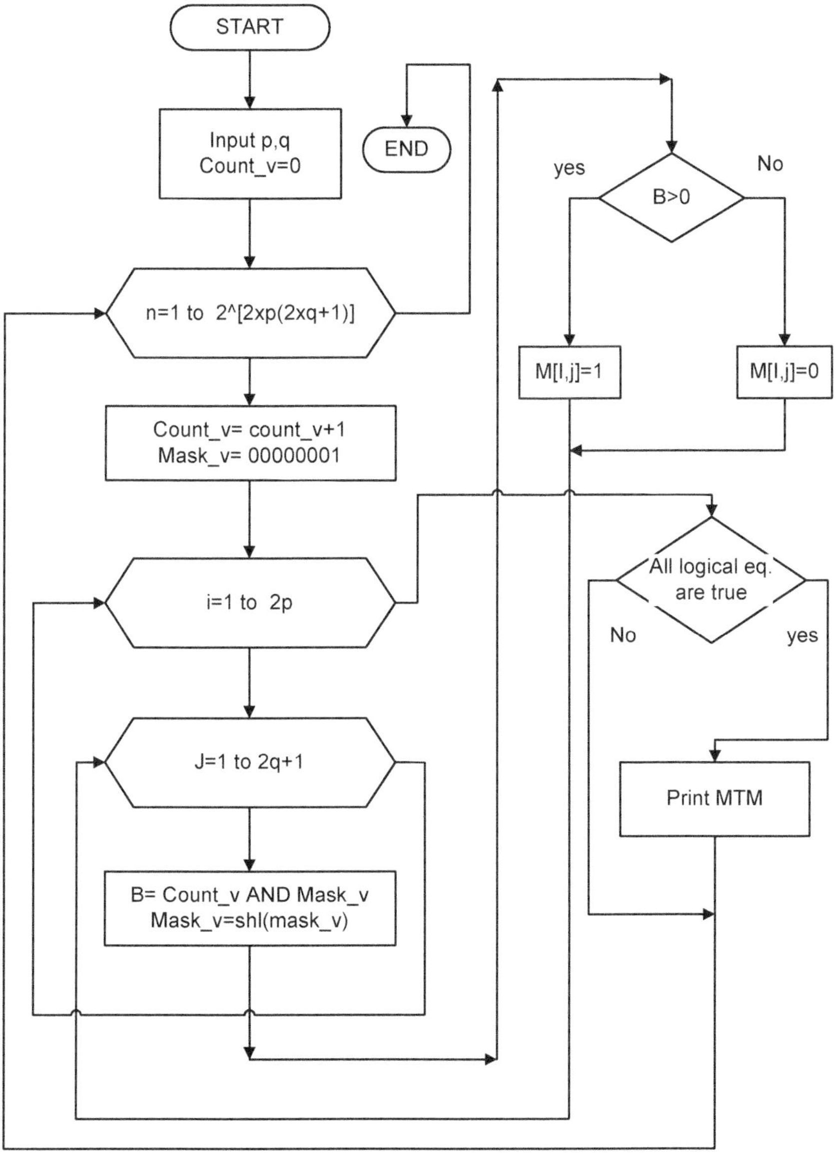

Fig. 13. Flow chart of the proposed algorithm for generating all members of sub-class circuits of DC-DC converters

The Flowchart Algorithms for this task is shown in Fig.13. It is beginning to receive the parameters p and q, generate all possible combinations of binary numbers to MTM (Count_v - count variable incremented from ...0000 to ....1111). The mask variable (mask_v) each time is shifted left so we can complete each cells in the MTM by 0 or 1. Next each completed MTM has to be checked for satisfying the logical equations, if so the software will print the MTM (the topological matrix of the circuit). These procedures are repeated until all combinations will be finished.

5 Conclusion

This paper develops and proposes a fully algorithmic method for synthesizing and generating DC–DC converters by using MTM. By using the topological matrix MTM we generate all sub-class circuits of the DC-DC converters with predetermined characteristics.

Due to the formation of logical equations for completion MTM and generation of all the sub-family of our circuits we can call this method – the design by parts for synthesizing and generating converter circuits with predetermined characteristics (characteristics of the synthesized converters are coded in the logical equations).

Isomorphic circuits have identical MTM, so we have also a tool for identification of isomorphism of the circuits.

This method can be developed for synthesizing and designing not only DC-DC converters, but also another circuits like filters circuits... etc, and can be translated to computer program for synthesis different classes of power electronic circuits.

Acknowledgments

Author wish to thank the anonymous reviewer for his helpful comments.

References

1. Calcutta, D., Cowan, F., Parchizadeh, H.: 8051 Microcontrollers - An Applications Based System Introduction. Newnes, Linacre House, Jordan Hill, Oxford OX2 8DP (2004)
2. Mitchell, D.M.: DC-DC Switching Regulator Analysis. McGraw-Hill Book Company, USA (1988)
3. Erickson, R.W.: Fundamentals of Power Electronics. Cluwer Academic Publishers, Boston (2004)
4. Su, G.J., Peng, F.Z.: A Low Cost, Triple-Voltage Bus DC-DC Converter for Automotive Applications. In: The IEEE Applied Power Electronics Conference and Exposition (APEC), Austin, Texas, March 6-10, vol. 2, pp. 1015–1021 (2005)
5. Dudrik, J., Oetter, J.: High-Frequency Soft-Switching DC-DC Converters for Voltage and Current DC Power Sources. Acta Polytechnic Hungarian 4(2), 29–46 (2007)
6. Rajarajeswari, N., Thanushkodi, K.: Design of an Intelligent Bi-Directional DC-DC Converter with Half Bridge Topology. Euro Journals Publishing 22(1), 90–97 (2008) ISSN 1450-216X

7. Kelley, R., Mazola, M., Draper, W., Cassidy, J.: Inherently Safe DC-DC Converter Using a Normally-On SiC JFET. In: Proc. of IEEE APEC, pp. 1561–1565 (2005)
8. James, P., Forsyth, A., Calderon-Lopez, G., Pickert, V.: DC-DC converter for hybrid and all electric vehicles. EVS24 University of Manchester, UK (May 2009)
9. Artemenko, M.E., Taher, M.A.: Synthesis transistor's Converters with determined characteristics. Technical Electrodynamics, Kiev, N4, pp. 43–47 (1994)
10. Deo, N.: Graph Theory with Applications to Engineering and Computer Science. PHL learning Prt, ltd (2004)
11. Diestel, R.: Graph theory, 3rd edn. Springer, Berlin (2005)

Maturity Assessment of Business/IT Alignment Using Fuzzy Expert System

Ahmad Nadali[1], Sanaz Pourdarab[1], Aliakbar Mazloumi[2], and Hamid Eslami Nosratabadi[3,*]

[1] Department of Information Technology Management, Science and Research Branch, Islamic Azad University
[2] Department of Mechanical and Manufacturing Engineering, University Putra Malaysia43400 UPM, Serdang, Malaysia
[3] Young Researchers Club, Science and Research Branch, Islamic Azad University
hamideslami.na@gmail.com

Abstract. Business/IT alignment means the degree to which the information technology mission, objectives, and plans are supported by the business mission, objectives, and plans. The aim of this research is the maturity assessment of Business/IT alignment by an intelligent system. Here, a Fuzzy Expert System has been designed in which main effective variables on Business and IT alignment have been considered as Inputs and level of maturity as output. Then, system rules have been extracted by the IT experts and the system has been developed with the use of FIS tool of MATLAB software. Finally, the presented steps have been run in an Iranian Bank as empirical study.

Keywords: Business IT Alignment, Strategic Alignment, Business Strategy, IT Strategy, Fuzzy Expert System.

1 Introduction

Although alignment is a top management concern, no comprehensive model of the construct is commonly used. A number of models of strategic business/IT alignment have been proposed till now from which the most well known are [1], [2]. The alignment of business and IT strategies has been utilized by organizations to create and improve efficiencies, reduce costs, create barriers to entry, improve customer and buyer/supplier relationships, and to create new products and business solutions. In the research of [3] concerning the alignment of business and IT strategies, they have found that there were at least four common themes which were repeated by respondents of a survey of the companies who were more aligned at all levels of IT/business strategy: Clear direction, Commitment, Communication and Cross-functional Integration. These themes are called "The four C's," and the alignment results are in cross functional integration. In fact the managers from organization that have aligned IT with business strategies argue that the integration was crucial to the organization's survival and its success and the IT units have added value to an

* Corresponding author.

E. Ariwa and E. El-Qawasmeh (Eds.): DEIS 2011, CCIS 194, pp. 724–738, 2011.

organization's effectiveness by acting as change agents, focusing on business imperatives, and helping to achieve effectiveness and efficiency. Another alignment model has been introduced to investigate the evidence of alignment between business and IT [4]. They expanded a model with two new components: the relationship management as an antecedent of alignment, and the balanced scorecard as the mechanism of alignment [5].While most of the literature has focused on the fit between a firms's IT and business strategy, the alignment issues need to be addressed at Strategic, Tactical, and operational levels. Strategic alignment helps meet an organizations' future IT needs; tactical alignment allows the organization to allocate its IT resources effectively; operational alignment ensures effectiveness and efficiency of IT in supporting the organization's operations on a daily basis. Organizations that have a higher level of alignment are more likely to achieve higher levels of performance and perceived business value from IT. The five factors that affected the social dimension of IT alignment identified by [5] included shared domain knowledge between business and IT executives, IT implementation success, communication between IT and business executives, connections between business and IT planning processes, and strategic business plans. A research of 256 UK manufacturing firms found that the major factors that influenced alignment were IT maturity, technical IT sophistication, and the CEO's software knowledge [6]. By applying the theory of knowledge integration, it provided a comprehensive framework that examined the relationship among integration behavior, alignment, IT planning and projects, and business impact of IT [7]. Their study asserted that business–IT alignment was influenced by IT managers' participation in business planning and business managers' participation in strategic IT planning. Furthermore, alignment was found to be positively associated with the success of IT planning and projects, which led to a positive business impact of IT. A framework called strategic alignment maturity (SAM) has been proposed to assess the extent to which business and IT functions align [8]. SAM provides organizations with a tool to evaluate the maturity of their strategic choices and alignment activities and identify areas in which they can achieve a higher level of alignment. Subsequent research included a benchmark study by [8] that used SAM at 50 Global 2000 companies to create a benchmark for business–IT alignment and identify specific recommendations for improving alignment. In another Paper, an operational model of strategic alignment is proposed and empirically validated through a mail survey of 110 small firms [9]. The purpose of this research is designing a fuzzy expert system which is able to assess the maturity level of business/IT alignment. The reminder of this paper is organized as follows. In Section 2, we review some key investigations in the area of Business/ IT alignment. In Section 3, the explanation of Fuzzy Expert System is presented. We detail, in Section 4, the system and present the results achieved using the system. Finally, we conclude the paper conveying final considerations and perspectives for future work in Section 5.

2 Business/IT Alignment

There is a definition of alignment as "the degree to which the information technology mission, objectives, and plans are supported by the business mission, objectives, and plans" [10].Another one define alignment as the "fit between an organization and its strategy, structure, processes, technology and environment" [11]. It has been stated that in business/IT alignment, IT is applied in an appropriate and timely way, in harmony and collaboration with business needs, goals, and strategies [12]. The importance of alignment is that it can help organizations in three different ways. The first is by maximizing the return on IT investment; the second is by enabling organizations to achieve competitive advantage through IS; and thirdly, it facilitates them to respond to new opportunities by providing direction and flexibility [13].To improve alignment, a research identified that having clear organizational goals, understanding the relationship between IT and business priorities, closing the gap between IT and business strategy, communication between IT staff and line manager, support from senior managers, strong management, IT control, trust, understanding the business environment are all enablers of alignment[14]. IT, when accompanied with BPR efforts, can provide business with a number of benefits, such as cost reduction, time elimination, and error minimization. However, there are other benefits that are mostly related to IT-enabled process orientation. These can be summarized in the following: *Enabling parallelism.* Moving from a sequential structure of processes into a parallel one reduces the processes' cycle time, problems resulting from delays, process disruptions, and handoffs. *Facilitating integration.* Moving from the division of labor approach into the "case management" approach eliminates unnecessary tasks and improves communication and quality of services. *Enhancing decision making.* Reducing the number of levels in an organization's hierarchies enhances the decision-making process. *Minimizing points of contact.* BPR, when combined with IT, eliminates intermediaries at different levels and reduces time and distance in the exchange of information required in any process [15]. MIT research on the utilization of IT within the enterprise context led to the development of a 'strategic alignment model'. With some changes of the terminology used, this model was published later by Henderson and Venkatraman and is shown in figure 1[1]. The model distinguishes between business and IT (columns) and the external versus internal focus (rows).Here, four cells or areas of attention are defined that are considered important for obtaining alignment. The unity between business and IT strategy is called 'functional integration' and that between the external and internal perspective the 'strategic integration'. For overall integration, multiple alignment perspectives concurrently play a role, as indicated by the arrows between the four areas of attention. Within these four areas, some sub-domains are indicated for which mutual alignment is considered important. Hence, one might refer to a multivariable, co-alignment perspective. The multiple facets are an indication of the difficulty of operationalizing the alignment concept practically, at least by means of these concepts [16].

Within the strategic alignment model, the *process* of alignment is understood as using a certain pattern to bring into unity the relationships between (remarkably only) three of the four areas of attention (alignment as *state*). Four patterns are distinguished, depending on the chosen starting point. That starting point is called the 'dominant alignment perspective'. The four alignment patterns are shown in figure 2. With the first pattern, the dominant alignment perspective is called *strategic execution.* The starting point is the business strategy, which subsequently defines the organizational infrastructure and processes that must be supported by the IT

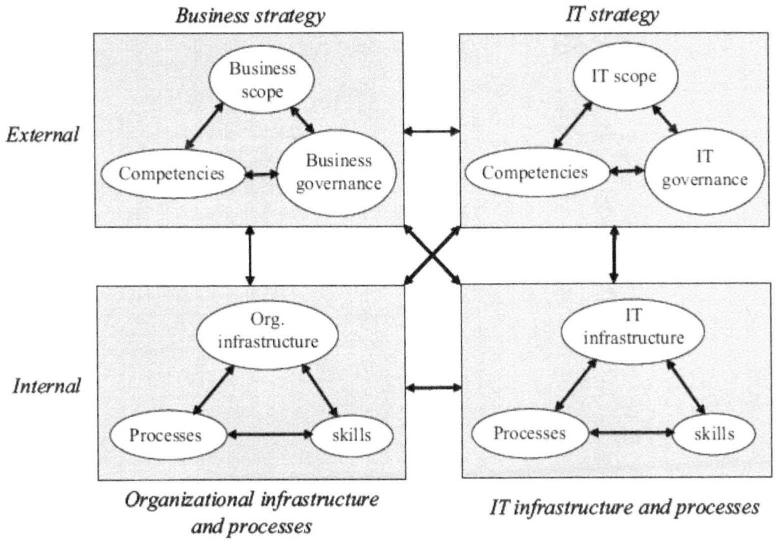

Fig. 1. Strategic alignment model [1]

infrastructure and processes. Notably an explicit IT strategy is not addressed within this dominant alignment perspective. The IT function is seen merely as a service and cost center. Possibilities and opportunities offered by IT for arranging the organizational infrastructure and processes differently are thus not considered within this perspective. The second dominant alignment perspective, and associated pattern, is labeled *technology potential*. Here too the business strategy is the starting point, but is used to formulate the IT strategy that subsequently defines the IT infrastructure and processes. Within this perspective the central issue concerns how to use technology for supporting the business optimally. The *competitive potential* is the third dominant perspective. In this case the IT strategy is the starting point, where the renewing possibilities and opportunities that IT can offer are utilized for defining an innovative and competitive business strategy. Subsequently, the business strategy defines the organizational structures and processes. Finally, the fourth dominant alignment perspective is labeled *service level*. Again, the IT strategy is the starting point, but unlike the third perspective, the focus lies with arranging the IT infrastructure and processes such that IT services can be delivered effectively and efficiently. One can also label this the IT supplier perspective, since the business strategy does not play a primary role. It is emphasized that the four perspectives (and associated alignment patterns) are dominant, but not necessarily exclusive. Given a certain dominant perspective, the other perspectives might play a role [16].

The term ''IT alignment'' refers to the coordination of a firm's IT strategy with its business strategy. This high level coordination has received extensive coverage in contemporary MIS literature. A research characterized business-IT alignment as applying IT in an appropriate and timely way, which is in harmony with business strategies, goals, and needs [2]. Another one stated that alignment is the degree of fit and integration among business strategies, IT strategies, business infrastructures, and

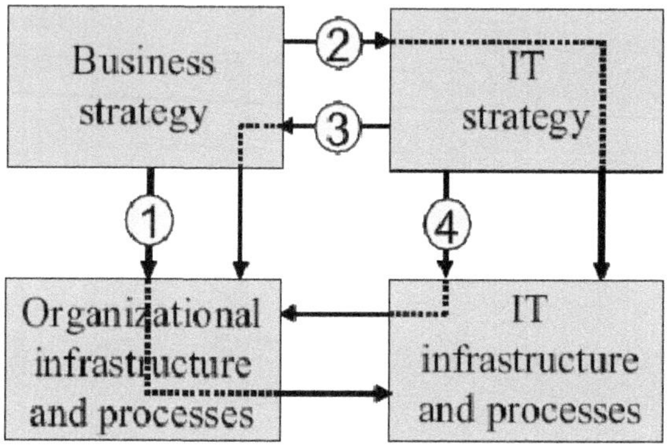

Fig. 2. Alignment perspectives[16]

IT infrastructures [1]. In an extensive review of alignment research, classified business-IT alignment along four dimensions, namely strategic/intellectual, structural, social, and cultural[17]. The strategic/intellectual alignment dimension offers organizations an opportunity to enhance its competitive capability. A survey asserted intellectual alignment as the state in which a set of high-quality interrelated business and IS plans exist [5]. This state emerges from internal consistencies and external validity between the outputs of business and IT planning. [18] Refers to structural alignment as the degree of structural fit between IT and business. Factors influencing structural fit include IS decision making rights, reporting relationships, the centralization and/or decentralization of IS services and infrastructure, the deployment of IS personnel, and the alignment of IT structures with competitive strategy. The social alignment dimension is the state in which IS and business executives understand, and are committed to the business and IS mission, objectives, and plans. The authors examined factors derived from the political behavior model, the resource dependency theory and the social construction theory that either enable or inhibit alignment. The cultural alignment dimension can be viewed through several lenses [19]. Successful planning between business and IT is a precondition of cultural fit and a strong company culture is a precondition to the type of informal structure that fosters alignment [19].

3 Fuzzy Expert System

A fuzzy expert system basically uses a group of fuzzy rules to solve problems. A fuzzy rule consists of two parts: an IF part (antecedent) and a THEN part (consequent). After defining fuzzy rules, the fuzzy inference procedure is then applied to get the fuzzy output. However, in the real word, we need a crisp value to solve the problems. Therefore, in most of cases, we need to transfer the fuzzy output to a crisp value. This is called ‘‘defuzzification procedure”. There are two main defuzzification methods used in fuzzy expert systems: the Mean of Maximum (MOM) method and the Center of Area (COA) method. Briefly, the procedure of a fuzzy expert system is described as follows:

1. Define problems with fuzzy variables and membership functions.
2. Generate fuzzy rules.
3. Input crisp values and transfer them to matching degrees using appropriate membership functions.
4. Conduct fuzzy inference and produce fuzzy output.
5. Employ the defuzzification procedure to get a crisp value based on the fuzzy output [20].

Fuzzy expert systems deal with phenomena that are uncertain and nonlinear in nature. Fuzzy logic provides the appropriate mathematics for sound reasoning under these conditions, and does not introduce unwarranted precision into the analysis.

Hence, a fuzzy-logic based expert system can overcome the shortcomings of traditional linear modeling. Moreover, the fuzzy expert system can interpret, and encompass as rules, the valuable project experiences gained by the system test team (Fig. 3).

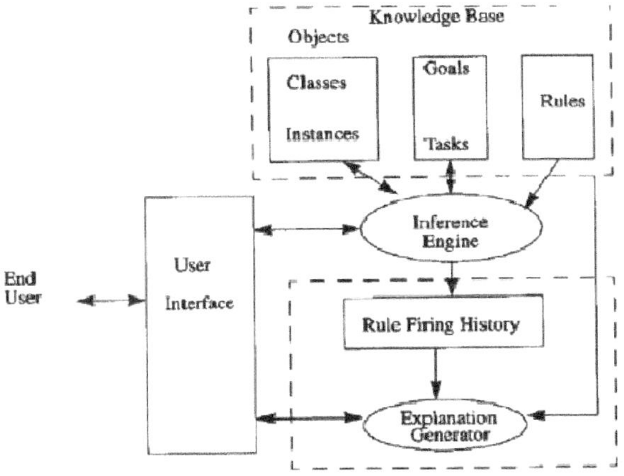

Fig. 3. Fuzzy expert system structure [22]

The fuzzy inference system is a popular computing framework based on the concepts of fuzzy set theory and fuzzy rules such as (x is A) AND (y is B) then (z is C), where the antecedent A(x),B(y), and the consequent C(z) can be fuzzy sets. The inference rule is a relation R(x, y, z) whose membership function is defined as:

$$\mu_R(x,y,z)=\mu_A(x)\times \mu_B(x)\times\mu_C(x) . \quad (1)$$

Where $\mu_A(x)$, $\mu_B(x)$, $\mu_C(x)$ are membership functions or characteristic functions of fuzzy sets A, B, and C. There are different manifestations of the conjunction operation ×. Mamdani proposed using the minimum operator for conjunction [21], and Larsen used the algebraic product operator for conjunction. Execution of a rule is based on composition where the antecedent A' is a fuzzy match of inputs with A, B' is a fuzzy match of inputs with B, and the inferred consequent is,

$$C' =(A' \cap B') \circ R \quad (2)$$

Where R is the fuzzy relation between A, B and C. There are different approaches to implement Eq. (2). Mamdani proposed a min–max method [21].When rules are organized in a hierarchical manner, the inference engine determines how pieces of knowledge are related together and matches them against relevant data. The inference procedures are based upon the modus ponens rule. For a given rule A→B, whenever the premise of the rule is true, the rule fires and its conclusion also becomes true. A chain of rules can be fired in sequence as x1→xn .There are three different inference methods: (1) forward chaining, (2) backward chaining, and (3) direct chaining. A chain that is searched or traversed from a problem to its solution is called a forward chain. A backward chain goes from a solution to the problem (hypothesis). Forward chaining can also be described as reasoning from facts to the conclusions that follow from the facts, while backward chaining can also be described as obtaining sub goals through the goal. The direct chaining inference procedure differs from the first two methods in that it uses a bit matrix, or a relational list, to infer x_n from any x_i Thus, the direct chaining inference process can begin at any point between the solution and problem.

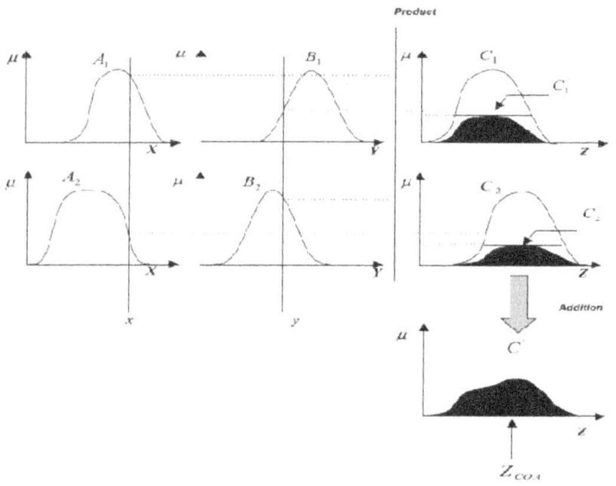

Fig. 4. The Mamdani fuzzy inference system using the product-sum method[22]

Defuzzification is a mapping from a space of fuzzy output into a space of single output. Once the inference engine performs the reasoning, an obtained fuzzy output, needs to be transformed into a single value representing the results of inference. There are various standard techniques available for this mapping process, including the max criterion, mean of maximum, and the center of area. The latter is the most common method, and is based on finding the center of gravity of the solution fuzzy sets as shown in Eq. (3). A discrete fuzzy set with N members yields a single result,

Z_{COA}, which is computed as:

$$Z_{COA} = \frac{\sum_{i=1}^{N} \mu_i d_i}{\sum_{i=1}^{N} \mu_i} \quad . \tag{3}$$

Where d_i is the value from the set that has a membership value$_{\mu i}$. Unfortunately, there is no systematic procedure for choosing a defuzzification strategy. And because some information is likely to be lost during defuzzification, additional research work is needed on how to use the information available in the solution fuzzy sets. The most important component of fuzzy expert systems is the set of rules and how the rules interact with each other to generate useful results. The rules are typically obtained from the domain experts so that the expert system can emulate the reasoning and inference process of a human expert. There is always an argument about using an expert's domain knowledge as a guideline for an expert system. Given the value of expert input, it is practical to start with an expert's guideline. Of course, a necessary feedback mechanism is needed for experts to adjust their judgment as the testing moves on [22].

4 The Proposed Fuzzy Expert System

This expert system is designed for assessing the maturity of IT Business alignment based on Luftman's criteria. Maturity categories were included: Communications, Competency/value measurements, Governance, Partnership, Technology scope, Skills [23]. Communications: The effectiveness of leveraging information for mutual understanding and knowledge sharing. This category evaluates such issues as whether business and IT understand each other's operating environment, whether a liaison is used to facilitate knowledge transfer between them, and whether there are rigid protocols that impede discussion and sharing of ideas. Competency/value measurements: The management decisions and strategic choices that an organization makes when determining the value and contribution of IT to the firm. This category evaluates such issues as whether an organization uses technical or business metrics for measuring IT success, whether the organization has formal benchmarking practices, and whether IT has contributed to the achievement of the organization's strategic goals. Governance: The choices organizations make when allocating decision rights for IT activities. This evaluates issues such as how IT projects are prioritized and how IT budgets are controlled. Partnership: Pertains to how IT and the business perceive each other's contribution. This evaluates issues such as IT's role in strategic business planning and how risk and rewards are shared by IT and business functions. Technology scope: The management decisions and strategic choices an organization makes when allocating resources toward its IT infrastructure. This evaluates whether the primary systems of the organization enable business strategy, whether business or IT changes are transparent across the organization, and whether the IT architecture is flexible in accommodating business and technology changes. Skills: The organization's cultural climate toward change and innovation. This evaluates issues such as the organization's ability to change, whether career crossover opportunities among IT and business professionals exist, and whether the organization has the ability to attract and retain the best business and technical professionals[23].The criteria used in the model are the most effective factors on maturity of IT/Business alignment including six major factors and thirty-eight attributes which being selected according to the background research that have been introduced by Luftman and presented as follows[2,24]:

- **Communications (Com):** Understanding of Business by IT, Understanding of IT by Business, Inter-/Intra-organizational leading, protocol rigidity, Knowledge sharing, Liaison(s) effectiveness.

- **Value Measurement (VM):** IT metrics, Business metrics, Balanced metrics, Service level agreements, Benchmarking, Formal assessment/reviews, Continuous improvement.
- **Governance (Gov):** Business strategic planning, IT strategic planning, Reporting/Organization structure, Budgetary control, IT investment Management, Steering committee(s), Prioritizing process.
- **Partnership (Par):** Business perception of IT value, Role of IT in strategic Business planning, Shared goals, Risk, Rewards/Penalties, IT program Management, Relationship/Trust style, Business Sponsor/Champion.
- **Scope & Architecture (SA):** Traditional, Enabler/Driver, External, Standards Articulation, Architectural integration, Functional, Enterprise, Inter-enterprise, Architectural transparency, Flexibility.
- **Skills (Sk):** Innovation and Entrepreneurship, Locus of power, Management Style, Change readiness, Career crossover, Education and cross-training, Social-political and trusting environment.

Here, the purpose is the maturity assessment of IT/Business alignment in Infotex[1] Bank according to situation of these main six factors. Since the obtained Ideas by the experts, managers and IT consultants, about the relation between the maturity level and each criterion, are not precise and have ambiguity, evaluation is done by linguistic variables. To do this, a Mamdani's Fuzzy Expert system has been designed. In this system, six main criteria of maturity have been considered as Inputs and maturity level as output. In Table 1 & 2, the Inputs and Output of the designed fuzzy expert system have been presented.

Table 1. The inputs of fuzzy expert system

Sign	Inputs	Interval	Type of membership function	Linguistic terms
Com	Communications	[0 1]	Gbell	VeryLow(VL), Low(L), Medium(M), High(H), VeryHigh(VH)
VM	Value Measurement	[0 1]	Gaussian	Low(L) Medium(M) High(H)
Gov	Governance	[0 1]	Gaussian2	Low(L), Medium(M), High(H)
Par	Partnership	[0 1]	Gaussian	VeryLow(VL), Low(L), Medium(M), High(H), VeryHigh(VH)
SA	Scope & Architecture	[0 1]	Gbell	Low(L) Medium(M) High(H)
Sk	Skills	[0 1]	Gbell	Low(L), Medium(M), High(H)

[1] Since the information of considered bank are confidential, The Authors have not been authorized to present The name of considered Band. So The name of the Bank is changed to protect its anonymity.

Table 2. The output of fuzzy expert system

Sign	*Output*	*Interval*	*Type of membership function*	*Linguistic terms*
ML	Maturity Level	[0 1]	Gaussian2	VeryLow(VL),Low(L), Medium(M) High(H), VeryHigh(VH)

This system according to the obtained rules from IT/IS experts about the relation between Input variables and Output, has been designed via MATLAB software. Table3 shows the obtained rules.

Table 3. The obtained rules from the experts for designing Fuzzy expert system

	Com	*VM*	*Gov*	*Par*	*SA*	*Sk*	*ML*
1	VH	L	H	H	H	H	H
2	M	H	H	M	H	M	M
3	L	M	L	VL	M	H	VL
4	H	M	M	H	L	L	L
5	M	H	H	L	M	M	M
6	VH	M	H	VH	H	M	VH
7	H	M	L	H	M	L	H
8	M	L	H	H	M	M	M
9	VL	H	M	M	L	H	M
10	M	L	M	H	L	M	L

After specifying Input and Output variables, membership functions by the experts have been defined for the variables which are shown in Fig 5 to Fig 11.

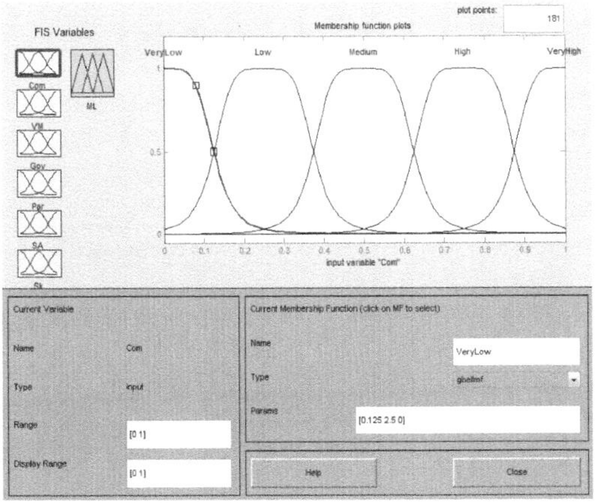

Fig. 5. Five Gbell Membership function for Communications

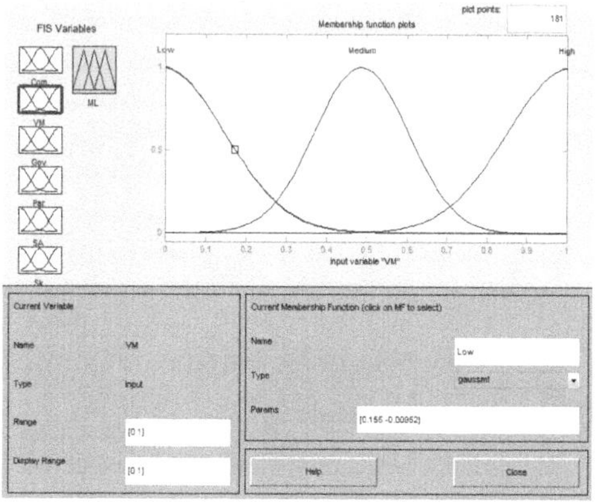

Fig. 6. Three Gaussian Membership function for Value Measurement

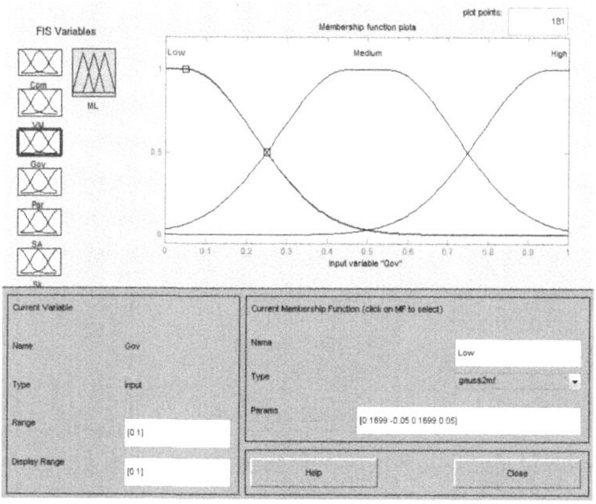

Fig. 7. Three Gaussian2 Membership function for Governance

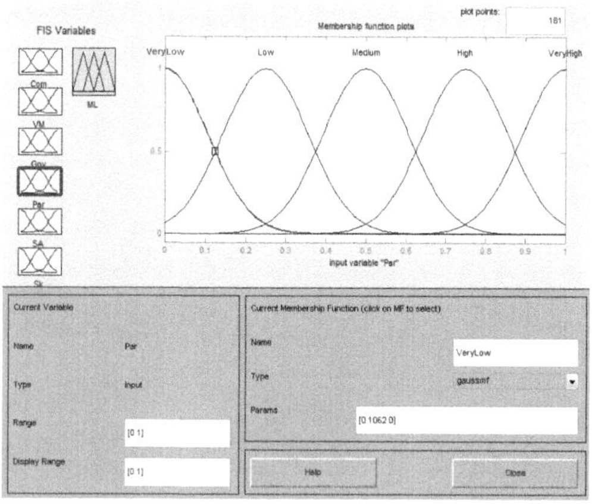

Fig. 8. Five Gaussian Membership function for Partnership

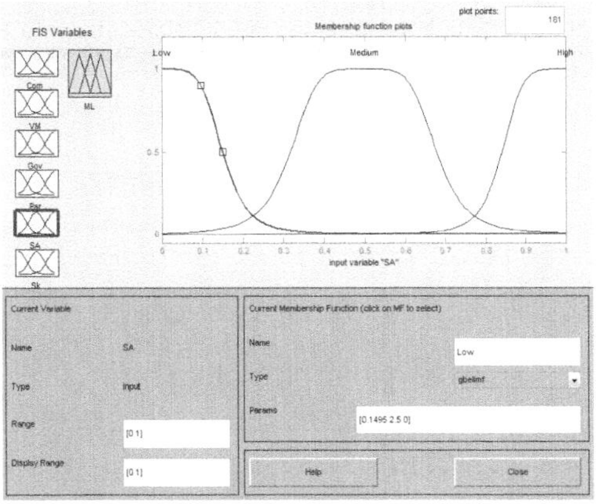

Fig. 9. Three Gbell Membership function for Scope & Architecture

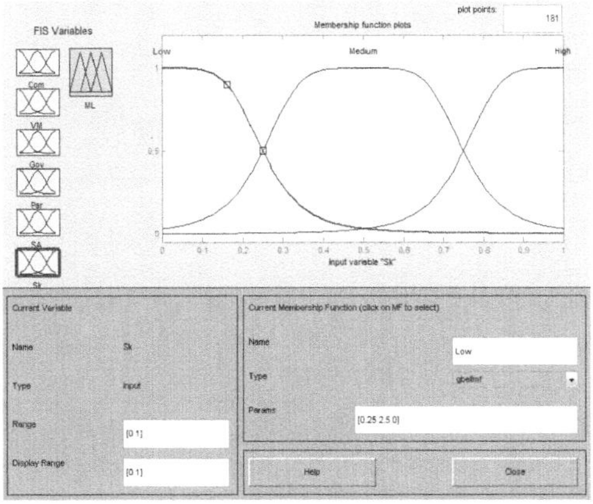

Fig. 10. Three Gbell Membership function for Skills

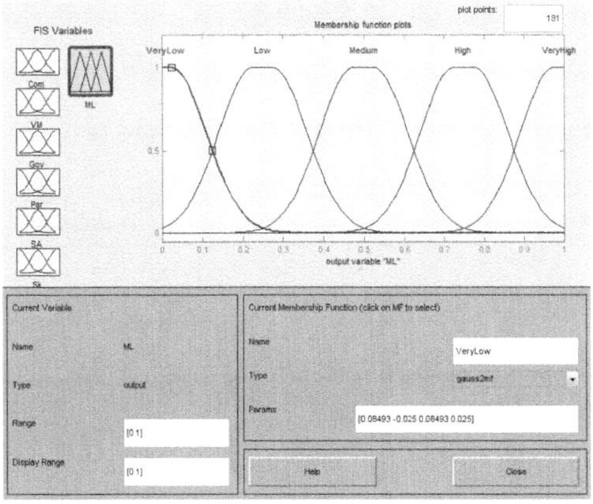

Fig. 11. Five Gaussian2 Membership function for Maturity Level

Here, Fuzzy Inference System (FIS) in MATLAB software has been used and some useful MATLAB commands to work with the designed FIS have been presented. To create a FIS, MATLAB fuzzy logic toolbox provides a user friendly interface in which they can choose the intended specification from drop-down menus.

```
>>fis = readfis ('BusinessITAlignment')
fis =
name: 'BusinessITAlignment'
type: 'mamdani'
andMethod: 'min'
orMethod: 'max'
defuzzsMethod: 'centroid'
impMethod: 'min'
aggMethod:'max'
input: [1*6 struct]
output: [1*1 struct]
rule: [1*10struct]
```

This system is able to determine the maturity level of IT/Business alignment based on the effective criteria. Regarding to the proposed fuzzy expert system, we have evaluated the maturity level of IT/Business alignment in the considered bank as Fig 12.

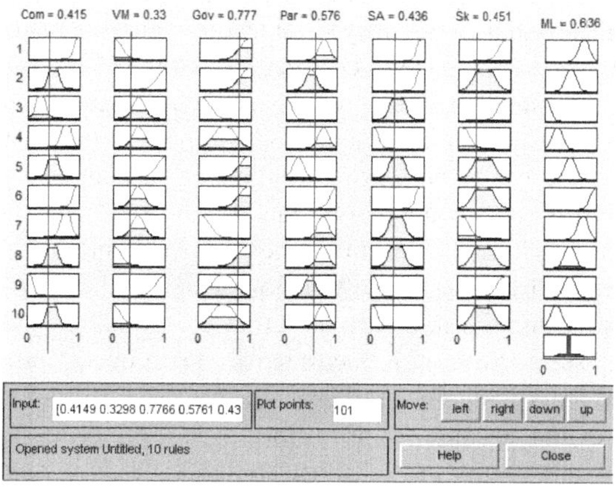

Fig. 12. Assessed maturity level of IT Business alignment by designed fuzzy expert system

According to the experts' opinions as the inputs, the following results have been identified:

Communications (Com): 0.41
Value Measurement (VM):0.33
Governance (Gov): 0.77
Partnership (Par): 0.57
Scope & Architecture (SA): 0.43
Skills (Sk): 0.45

As a result, maturity level (ML) of IT/Business alignment would be 0.694 out of 1. The final objective of this study was to present a Fuzzy Expert system to evaluate the maturity level of IT/Business alignment for companies or banks and as an empirical study, we have examined the current state of business–IT alignment of the Bank in IRAN. The findings of this study could serve as the starting point for developing a benchmark for companies/banks.

5 Conclusions

Assessing the maturity level of IT/Business alignment based on effective criteria is the major fundamental in this paper. To reach this goal, a Mamdani's Fuzzy expert system has been designed with considering the situation of six main effective factors on maturity level of IT/Business alignment as the Inputs and the maturity level as the output and Membership functions have been defined for the variables. Then, according to the rules obtained from consultants and IT managers as the experts, the fuzzy expert system has been designed. This system has the ability to determine the maturity level based on criteria levels as an evaluator system. The most important advantage for this Fuzzy Expert system is predicting the maturity level of IT/Business alignment. Finally, managers will be able to plan for future works with considering the obtained results of the proposed system to improve the maturity level of the IT/Business alignment.

Acknowledgement

Here, we appreciate from the IT Experts of the considered bank for their cooperation and sharing their knowledge and the data with us as the researchers.

References

1. Henderson, J.C., Venkatraman, N.: Strategic alignment: leveraging information technology for transforming organization. IBM Systems Journal 32(1), 4–16 (1993)
2. Luftman, J.: Assessing business-IT alignment maturity. Communications of AIS 4, art. 14, 1–50 (2000)
3. Weiss, J.W., Anderson, D.: Aligning technology and business strategy: issues & frameworks, a field study of 15 companies. In: Hawaii Proceedings, vol. 7 (2004)
4. Hu, Q., Huang, C.D.: Aligning IT with firm business strategies using the balance scorecard system. In: Hawaii Proceedings, pp. 2–5 (2005)
5. Reich, B.H., Benbasat, I.: Factors that influence the social dimension of alignment between business and information technology objectives. MIS Quarterly 1(24), 84–113 (2000)
6. Hussin, H., King, M., Cragg, P.: IT alignment in small firms. European Journal of Information Systems 11, 108–127 (2002)
7. Kearns, G.S., Sabherwal, R.: Strategic alignment between business and information technology: a knowledge-based view of behaviors, outcome, and consequences. Journal of Management Information Systems 23(3), 129–162 (2006)
8. Luftman, J.N.: Assessing IT/business alignment. Information Systems Management 20(4), 9–15 (2003)
9. Bergerona, F., Raymondb, L., Rivard, S.: Ideal patterns of strategic alignment and business performance. Information & Management 41(8), 1003–1020 (2004)

10. Reich, B.H., Benbasat, I.: Measuring the linkage between business and information technology objectives. MIS Quarterly 20(1), 55–81 (1996)
11. Kanellis, P., Lycett, M., Paul, R.J.: Evaluating business information systems fit: From concept to practical application. European Journal of Information Systems 8(1), 65–77 (1999)
12. Luftman, J.: Assessing IT/business alignment. Information Strategy 20(1), 7 (2003)
13. Avison, D., Jones, J., Powell, P., Wilson, D.: Using and validating the strategic alignment model. The Journal of Strategic Information Systems 13(3), 223–246 (2004)
14. Luftman, J., Brier, T.: Achieving and sustaining business-IT alignment. California Management Review 42(1), 109–123 (1999)
15. Mashari, M., Zairi, M.: Creating a fit between BPR and IT infrastructure: A Proposed Framework for Effective Implementation. The International Journal of Flexible Manufacturing Systems (12), 253–274 (2000)
16. Jan, A.P., Hoogervorst: Enterprise governance and enterprise engineering. Springer, Heidelberg (2009)
17. Chan, Y., Reich, B.H.: IT alignment: what have we learned? J. Inf. Technol. (22), 295–315 (2007)
18. Chan, Y.: Why haven't we mastered alignment?: The importance of the informal organization structure. MIS Q. Exec. (1), 97–112 (2002)
19. Singh, S.N., Woo, C.: Investigating business-IT alignment through multi-disciplinary goal concepts, vol. 14(3), pp. 177–207. Springer, London (2009), doi:10.1007/s00766-009-0081-0
20. Lin, C.C., Chen, S.C., Chu, Y.M.: Automatic price negotiation on the web: An agent-based web application using fuzzy expert system. Expert Systems with Applications 38(5), 5090–5100 (2011)
21. Mamdani, E.H., Assilian, S.: An experiment in linguistic synthesis with a fuzzy logic controller. International Journal of Man-Machine Studies 7(1), 1–13 (1975)
22. Xu, Z., Gao, K., Taghi, Khoshgoftaar, M., Seliya, N.: System regression test planning with a fuzzy expert system. Information Sciences (2010) (in press)
23. Chen, L.: Business–IT alignment maturity of companies in China. Information & Management (47), 9–16 (2010)
24. Luftman, N.J.: Measure Your Business-IT Alignment. Optimize: Business Execution for CIOs Magazine 26 (2003)

A Qualitative Enquiry to Explore the Concept of Users' Perception on Factors Influencing Flexible Traveling Behavior and Flexible Online Airline Reservation Systems

Arif Mushtaq*, Suziah Bt. Sulaiman, P.D.D. Dominic, and Sadia Riaz

Computer and Information Sciences Department
Universiti Teknologi PETRONAS
Tronoh, Perak, Malaysia
{mushtaq_arif,missriaz}@yahoo.com,
{suziah,dhanapal_d}@petronas.com.my

Abstract. Rigid and strictly defined business models do not support changes required to meet today's competitive business needs and demands. The business model must be adaptable and should have the agility needed to remain in such an environment. This implies that systems on which companies rely must therefore also be flexible and agile. However, in the case of Online Airline Reservation Systems (OARS), flexibility is undeterminable without accounting for traveler's flexible travelling behavior. In this paper we investigate and explore the concept of users' perception on factors influencing flexible traveling behavior and flexible OARS. A qualitative approach using grounded theory was conducted. Our findings show that users travelling behavior is molded by a number of important personality relevant determinants, both internal and external in characteristics. We conclude that flexibility of users and system are independent but still very much dependent on one another.

Keywords: Flexibility, Online Airline Reservation Systems, Flexible Traveling Behavior, Qualitative Enquiry.

1 Introduction

Flexibility is an important attribute to meet On Demand Businesses [1]. Today companies are continuously investing money and time to change their business strategies so as to become more agile in nature. Rigid and strictly defined business models do not support changes required to meet today's competitive business needs and demands. The business model must be adaptable and should have the agility needed to remain in such an environment. This implies that systems on which

* Arif Mushtaq received his MS (Digital Media) degree in 2006 from Hochschule Bremen, Germany. He is associated with Bahria University, Islamabad Pakistan as an assistant professor. At present he is pursuing doctorate studies in Computer and Information Sciences from Universiti Teknologi PETRONAS, Malaysia.

E. Ariwa and E. El-Qawasmeh (Eds.): DEIS 2011, CCIS 194, pp. 739–753, 2011.

companies rely must therefore also be flexible and agile [1]. However, in the case of Online Airline Reservation Systems (OARS), flexibility is undeterminable without accounting for traveler's flexible travelling behavior. Behavioral and heuristic approaches are fundamental in this context [2]. This drives need to investigate factors influencing upon flexible traveling behavior and flexible online airline reservation systems.

Theoretically, a traveler is categorized as flexible, if he/she possesses a flexible nature of traveling. This indicates he/she has a non-rigid schedule for traveling. Flexible travelers can travel on alternatively allocated itineraries and their traveling satisfaction comes mainly from heavy discounted fares provided by any airline. On the contrary, a traveler is categorized as inflexible, if he/she possesses an inflexible nature of traveling. This indicates he/she has a rigid schedule for traveling. Inflexible travelers only like to travel as per their indicated or preferred itineraries and their traveling satisfaction comes mainly from meeting their flying deadlines that are mostly based on reaching their destination as per their preferred itineraries [3]. However, clear understanding of consumer intent and behavior in the case of online airline ticket shopping and elsewhere cannot be achieved without considering the factors that affect purchase decisions [4]. The reason is selling products online are very different from selling in physical market and this requires a clear understanding of online customer interest [5], [6]. Internet marketing strategies can be adjusted if cyber marketers know what the consumers want and how they reach their decisions [7]. Similarly, such an understanding will help Web designers to develop sites making that are not only popular but also effective for sales [8].

This paper therefore specifically addresses the notion of flexibility in the context of users' flexible travelling behavior towards flexible online airline reservation system. The article is organized as follows: section 2 is dedicated to literature review. Section 3 covers methodology, while section 4 discusses detail accounts of data collection process. Section 5 is devoted to data analysis and findings. Section 6 discusses findings and section 7 concludes the study.

2 Literature Review

The user's flexibility is nothing but users' ability to rapidly change from one course of action to another, i.e. "flexible behavior", and it is referred as a hallmark of human cognition system [9]. Empirical research into cognition is usually scientific and quantitative, and involves formation of mental models to describe or explain certain behaviors. In context of flexible behavior of users, human cognition system may thus be examined from the perspective of cognitive psychology. Human-Computer Interaction (HCI) research is intended to explain interaction between humans and the computer technology. In order to provide a scientific explanation to human behavior (e.g. user interface design, information visualization, etc) many principles, theories and concepts from cognitive psychology are deployed in HCI, such as Perception, Categorization, Memory, Knowledge Representation, Language and Thinking [10].

The immense contribution of cognitive science to HCI is readily acknowledged by HCI researchers [11]. However, the fact remains that cognitive science and HCI share a deep rooted history originating from WWII. In WWII, it was required to essentially train manpower needed to fight the war. For the same purpose, academic researchers and psychologists worked very closely to devise faster training methods, and since then cognitive psychology remains an important aspect for understanding *human factors* in any discipline [12], [13].

Particularly in HCI, human factors are needed to understand the user and what cognitive processes they experience as a user. These experiences are viewed from user's perception of information, use of knowledge and decision making. So by developing an understanding of the user's behavior, HCI researchers prognosticate how interaction is taking place between the user and computer system. In absence of such an understanding, it will be almost impossible to optimize interaction effect of the user with the system [12].

A system is considered useable if users can accomplish their tasks easily. Similarly, a system is considered functional if it offers all the functions required by a user to perform their tasks [14]. Usability of the system can be evaluated on the basis of performance of its different functions and from literature we know flexibility of the system is one of the guiding principles that provide support to achieve, develop or improve its usability. Therefore, it is very critical for the organizations to design flexible systems that are easy to use and can accomplish all the requirements by way of offering customizability. And one should not overlook, that flexibility is mirrored in functional requirements as well. Typically, one need to–so to speak–add more buttons to make a system more flexible [15]. Therefore, system's flexibility translates into its customizability in achieving the defined usability objectives of the system which are effectiveness, efficiency and satisfaction.

Likewise, in context of user's flexibility different users may have different needs, interests and wishes to be served and system's effectiveness, efficiency and satisfaction may vary from one user to another based on their usability perception. For some users a system may be very effective but this may not be true for all. This drives the need of integrating cognitive ergonomics into the framework, to understand users' flexibility in designing of systems.

From literature we know that users' flexibility is reflected in their decision making behavior [16]. Decision making behavior is an outcome of once though process or thinking. Thinking refers to any intellectual or mental activity resulting in ideas or arrangements of ideas. Within HCI, thinking simulates human behavior, which is eventually translated as an action taken on part of users, in the form of making choices, performing logical operations, formation of concepts, problem solving and decision making. For understanding flexible human behavior, decision making is an important reflection of users thought process. Decision making is a mental process which results in selection of a course of action among several alternatives [17]. At the end of every decision making process, an output is produced in the form of a final choice or selection, which can be in the form an action, or an opinion of choice. Decision making process is an active research area since it examines decisions of users in context of their unique set of needs and preferences, therefore, reflection of users' flexible behavior can be seen in the decisions they make [18].

Numerous quantitative studies are identified in literature investigating flexibility of systems from different perspectives. For example, Stone [19] introduced quantitative characterizations to propose a mathematical framework to define, measure, and analyze embedded system functional flexibility. Similarly, Zhang [20] gave a quantitative model which can support the decision-making of selection of distribution system and flexible strategies. However, our literature review did not identify any qualitative study that provided theoretical justification to notion of flexibility from user's perspective as well as system's perspective. Gao and Zhang [21] investigated perception of leisure travelers by applying qualitative research methodology. This methodology was found to be relevant and suitable for achieving objectives of this research. Therefore it was imperative to undertake this study of online airline reservation systems using qualitative research technique to address this potential research gap.

3 Methodology

In order to gather an in-depth understanding of human behavior and the reasons that govern such behavior, qualitative research is conducted. This qualitative exploratory study adopted a grounded theory approach to investigate the users' perception on their flexible traveling behavior and flexible online airline reservation systems. Grounded Theory is a research method in which the theory is developed from the data, rather than the other way around [22], since it is an appropriate way to research a previously little studied area in IS research.

Moreover, this methodology provides an ideal and flexible guideline to analyze qualitative data and equips researchers with necessary understanding of underlying concepts to build theories through successive levels of data analysis [24]. Researchers [25] have recognized this method as an authentic research tool in qualitative data analysis due to its procedural credibility.

The population of this study consisted of travelers who had experience in purchasing tickets through airlines Self-Booking Tools (SBTs) and Online Traveling Agencies (OTAs). This was an important consideration, because travelers with experience in purchasing tickets through SBTs and OTAs could very well understand and relate to what being 'flexible traveling behavior' mean from users' perspective as well as from systems' perspective.

The data was collected from three methods. (1) Online travel forums, (2) semi-structured in-depth interviews and (3) Focus group. Use of online surveys to collect data has become a popular choice for researchers, with special reference to tourism data [26]. This is mainly due to the flexibility, reach and robustness offered by visual medium of internet. Likewise, in depth interviews and focus group were essentially required in this research, so as to build deeper understanding of respondents' perspective on flexible traveling behavior and flexible online reservation systems, which otherwise may not be possible to obtain through online travel forums alone. Moreover, in short interviews researcher is in a position to pick up non verbal cues and even rephrase questions so as to personalize them and make respondents feel at ease to answer them.

The analysis of interview transcripts was based on an inductive approach which is meant to identify emerging patterns in the data by using thematic codes. Inductive analysis looks for emerging patterns, themes and categories through analysis of data and opposes imposition of the same, prior to data collection and analysis [27, p.306].

In order to ensure study's trustworthiness, two methods were employed, (1) triangulation, and (2) negative case analysis.

With regards to triangulation, as mentioned above, three sources and three different data collection methods (1) Online travel forums, (2) semi-structured in-depth interviews and (3) Focus group were employed. This was important to see that data obtained from different independent data sources converged on something similar, or at least do not oppose each other [28]. The data was analyzed by two authors independently and then discussed together to derive emerging themes, categories and to also ensure credibility.

Negative case analysis was performed on the initial derived emerging themes [29], [23]. The purpose was to see if the characteristics of the derived emerging theme sufficiently inculcated the true essence of research and were applicable to all cases.

4 Data Collection

The data was collected from two online travel forums (1) http://www.travelblog.com and (2) www.travellerspoint.com/. The following questions were raised at these forums from July, 2010 to February, 2011

- Which factors influence upon your flexible traveling behavior?
- Which factors influence upon your perception of a flexible online reservation system?

14 respondents were from travelblog's forum, while 17 were from travellerspoint forum. The demographics of the respondents is shown in Table 1.

Table 1. Demographics of Online Travel Forums Respondents

	Travelblog (14)	**Travellerspoint (17)**
Male	9	10
Female	5	7
Average Age (Male)	37	41
Average Age (Female)	35	37
Countries of Origin	USA, China, Singapore, UK, Kenya, India, Peru, Indonesia, Spain, Thailand, Nepal, Romania, Canada	Japan, Malaysia, China, Singapore, Thailand, Australia, Indonesia
Rejected cases of ambiguous respondents	5	7

After data analysis of online travel forum discussion, the semi structured in-depth interview of actual travelers was conducted at Kuala Lumpur International Airport from 11 – 13th March, 2011. A realistic, flexible and ethically accepted approach was adopted to identify potential research participants. Since this research involved travelers and reservation systems, therefore, Kuala Lumpur International Airport (KLIA) was visited for consecutive three days in order to approach a number of volunteer travelers.

Table 2. Demographics of in-depth interview

No. of respondents (as per same Country of Origin)	Country of Origin	Gender		Age (Avg.)	Flying Frequency / Year (Avg.)	Purchase Experience with SBTs of Airline	Purchase Experience with any popular OTA
6	Malaysia	Male	4	34	Frequent (Twice a year)	Yes	Yes
		Female	2	30			
4	USA	Male	2	40	Very Frequent (more than twice a year)	Yes	Yes
		Female	2	37			
3	UK	Male	2	29	Very Frequent (more than twice a year)	Yes	Yes
		Female	1	26			
2	China	Male	1	36	Very Frequent (more than twice a year)	Yes	Yes
		Female	1	24			
2	India	Male	2	33	Frequent (Twice a year)	Yes	Yes
		Female	0	-			
2	Pakistan	Male	2	43	Frequent (Twice a year)	Yes	Yes
		Female	0	-			
2	Singapore	Male	0	-	Very Frequent (more than twice a year)	Yes	Yes
		Female	2	27			
2	Ireland	Male	1	25	Frequent (Twice a year)	Yes	Yes
		Female	1	20			
2	Thailand	Male	1	31	Frequent (Twice a year)	Yes	Yes
		Female	1	29			
1	Australia	Male	1	44	Very Frequent (more than twice a year)	Yes	Yes
		Female	0	-			
1	Sudan	Male	1	35	Not Very Frequent (Once a year)	Yes	Yes
		Female	0	-			
1	Mauritius	Male	1	29	Frequent (Twice a year)	Yes	Yes
		Female	0	-			

In total, 28 travelers were interviewed, and each interview lasted from 10-15 minutes. The contents of interviews were digitally recorded and transcribed, in addition to making handwritten notes. Moreover, extra efforts were put in to interview as much variety of travelers from different countries of origin as possible. Details of the travelers interviewed are summarized in Table 2.

Table 3. Demographics of Focus Group interviews

Meeting With Independent Airline Reservation Offices			
	No. of Manager	No. of Executives interviewed	No. of Technical Experts
Malaysian Airline	1	2	1
Fire Fly	1	2	1
Aero Asia	1	1	1

Finally, the focus group interviews were conducted with 3 managers, 5 junior executives and 3 technical experts of three local airlines, namely (1) Malaysian Airline, (2) Fire Fly, and (3) Aero Asia as shown in Table 3. The interviews were held from 15 – 25th March 12, 2011.

5 Data Analysis and Findings

A traveler is considered as flexible if he or she possesses a flexible nature of traveling. This indicates that the traveler has a non-rigid schedule for traveling. Flexible travelers can travel on alternatively allocated itineraries and their traveling satisfaction comes mainly from heavy discounted fares provided by airline [3].

5.1 Online Travel Forums

The responses received through online discussion forums were analyzed first as shown in Table 4. It identified some very basic key elements that instigate flexibility in a travelers' traveling behavior, especially if he or she is traveling on a non-rigid schedule. For instance, a promotional package offered by a particular airline makes it a lucrative option for travelers who are ready to travel at any alternatively allocated itinerary. Similarly, if an airline does not offer services and comfort to its customers, they are likely to become inflexible for opting to fly with it, even if it offers lower fares. Likewise, travelers flying purpose and flying frequency determines the extent to which he/she is ready to become a flexible traveler. External influences of travelers' family and friends also play an important role in shaping up their flexible traveling behavior.

Table 4. Results of Online Travel Forums

	Reasons
Which factors influence on users' flexible traveling behavior?	▪ Promotional packages offered by a particular airline ▪ Searching skills to look for best offers and deals online ▪ Budgetary constraints and leverages ▪ Traveling comfort in services offered ▪ Traveling purpose ▪ Flying frequency ▪ Family and friends
Which factors influence upon your perception of a flexible online reservation system?	▪ Simplicity ▪ Easiness ▪ Multiple options

As for the factors that influence upon perception of a flexible online reservation system, our analysis showed that a reservation system is perceived as being flexible if it offers easiness to users in terms of making reservations with minimal skills required, is not complicated in terms of operation and offers multiple features and options to users.

5.2 In-Depth or Semi Structured Interviews

The responses received through in-depth interviews were analyzed in the second phase. Table 5 provides additional information on users' flexible traveling behavior. In addition to key elements instigating flexibility in a travelers' behavior, factors such as airlines repute and travelers status consciousness contribute towards their flexible traveling behavior. Interestingly, customer loyalty, traveling mileage and patriotism also came into the limelight with our in-depth interviews with travelers. This indicates, if a traveler has a customer loyalty or earned traveling mileage from a particular airline it will influence upon his/her flexible traveling behavior, as well as, how patriotically associated the traveler feels with his/her country's airline. Finally, travelers who wish to live an eco-friendly life supported the idea of the green environment and they were of the view that if an airline supports eco-friendly policies, with lesser carbon emissions and lesser fuel consumption, it will influence upon their flexible traveling behavior as well as flying priorities.

Table 5. Results of in-depth interviews

	Reasons
Which factors influence on users' flexible traveling behavior?	▪ Airlines repute ▪ Standard conscious ▪ Promotional packages offered by a particular airline ▪ Searching skills to look for best offers and holiday deals ▪ Customer loyalty ▪ Traveling comfort in services offered ▪ Supporter of Green Environment ▪ Patriotism ▪ Traveling purpose ▪ Flying frequency ▪ Budgetary constraints and leverages ▪ Occupation ▪ Children holidays ▪ Traveling mileage ▪ Interest in recreation, leisure, and tourism
Which factors influence upon your perception of a flexible online reservation system?	▪ Provides alternative dates for flying ▪ Allows self-adjustments in itinerary ▪ Simplicity ▪ Easiness ▪ Multi-linguistic

Likewise, it was revealed that travelers flexible traveling is also dependent upon their interest taking in recreational and leisure activities. Respondents who indicated that they were frequent flyers attributed flexible traveling behavior directly to their interest in recreational and leisure activities. Some travelers also highlighted that flexible traveling behavior of a single person or an individual is different from the one who is traveling with his/her family. As families with children would prefer to travel mostly during the school breaks or holiday sessions, therefore, their flexible traveling behavior will be accordingly influenced by this factor. Travelers during discussion also pointed out the high influence of travelers' occupation on his flexible traveling behavior, as travelers who are associated or are in a job that gives them high work load, lesser breaks and requires more on-job working and lesser mobility, would be less flexible in their traveling behavior.

As for the factors that influence upon perception of a flexible online reservation system, our analysis showed that factors such as simplicity and easiness were again important determinants. From our in-depth interviews, it was found out that a flexible reservation system is considered to the one that can provide alternative dates for flying to the traveler and at the same time offers self-adjustment functionality, such as cancellation and changes, in the itinerary of the traveler. Some travelers, who were non-native English speakers, pointed that a system would be flexible to them if it supports multi-languages.

5.3 Focus Group

Our focus group participants were experts in online airline reservation businesses and system, with better and deeper understanding of travelers' flexible behavior as well as that of systems. Our in-depth interview results with our focus groups on factors influencing users' flexible traveling behavior were very much same as the once we have discussed earlier as shown in Table 6. However, additional factors that came into the scene included discounted airfares versus normal airfares and time frame, peak versus off travel season, chosen to fly also substantially influences upon flexible traveling behavior.

Table 6. Results of Focus Group

	Reasons
Which factors influence on users' flexible traveling behavior?	▪ Peak / off travel time ▪ Discounted versus Normal Fare ▪ Traveling mileage ▪ Traveling purpose ▪ Working hours ▪ Traveling comfort in services offered ▪ Children holidays ▪ Recreation, leisure, and tourism ▪ Promotional Schemes ▪ Airlines repute
Which factors influence upon your perception of a flexible online reservation system?	▪ Easiness ▪ Product presentation ▪ Post sale features ▪ User prompting for their guidance throughout reservation process ▪ Matrix display to sort airfares on different dates and destinations ▪ Low fare notifications ▪ Flexible and alternative date search ▪ Dynamic packaging ▪ Hotel search display, sort and reservation

Our focus group provided a more critical feedback on factors influencing upon perceived flexibility of an online airline reservation system and we were able to extract a number of important additional factors in our analysis. Our analysis showed that an online airline reservation system is perceived as flexible if it provides fare quotes, post-sale features and generates receipt. Likewise, if the reservation system can sort airfares on different dates and destinations, it will be perceived as flexible by users. Moreover, if the user is prompted throughout reservation process for his/her guidance, is timely notified on low airfares though flexible and alternative flying dates, it will influence upon user's perception of a flexible reservation system. Also by incorporating multiple traveling components in a single search, such as hotel search facility, the perceived flexibility of the reservation system will also be influenced.

6 Discussion

Following 6 themes emerged under factors influencing upon flexible traveling behavior and 3 themes emerged under factors influencing upon perceived flexibility of a reservation system after giving much thought process to results, reviewing literature, discussion with qualitative researchers.

6.1 Emerging Theme Analysis through Triangulation

The data collected from three different sources was examined for triangulation as shown in Table 7.

Table 7. Emerging themes on flexible traveling behavior and perceived flexibility

Emerging Themes	
Factors influencing upon flexible traveling behavior	**Factors influencing upon perceived flexibility of an online airline reservation system**
1. Travelers' flexible behavior is molded by their traveling consciousness. 2. Travelers' flexible behavior is molded by their belief that they have the required digital skills. 3. Travelers' flexible behavior is molded by their self-belief as flexible travelers. 4. Travelers' flexible behavior is molded by societal influences. 5. Travelers' flexible behavior is molded by how they attribute a cause to their traveling behavior. 6. Travelers' flexible behavior is molded by their prior traveling experiences.	1. Systems perceived flexibility is influenced by its perceived usefulness. 2. Systems perceived flexibility is influenced by end user support. 3. Systems perceived flexibility is influenced by comparison of features on the actual level of effect regarding to complete the reservation process.

It depicted a similarity pattern, especially in case of data collected from online travel forums and in-depth interviews of travelers at KLIA. Data analysis of later, however, provided a more detailed perspective of travelers flexible behavior by incorporating socio-economic factors and societal influences. The focus group, being technical experts, however significantly contributed towards identifying factors that may influence upon perceived flexibility of reservation systems.

Theme 1: Travelers' flexible behavior is molded by their traveling consciousness – Consciousness is a subjective experience of awareness. In context of flexible traveling behavior, our study showed that travelers have a certain form consciousness or awareness about their traveling behavior. This resulted in the emergence of first theme.

"I look for great deals through promotional schemes" (ID P2)

"Why I wouldn't travel with an airline that provides heavy discounts? I look for discounts all the time" (ID P6)

"I make cognizant traveling decisions. Do all background work first and then make a decision to purchase a ticket or not" (OTF P11)

"Airlines hefty discounts through their travel mileage schemes are very attractive and can make me to travel any time during the year" (FG P7)

Theme 2: Travelers' flexible behavior is molded by their belief that they have the required digital skills – Our study showed that having the digital skills to search for the best traveling deals, can influence upon once flexible traveling behavior.

Digital skills reflect upon travelers' self-efficacy and have resulted in evolution of our theme 2.

"I don't care traveling with any airline, as I can find best traveling online deals with much ease" (OTF P8)

"I don't waste time on googling what I am looking for, I know where to exactly go when I need to purchase an online ticket" (ID P26)

"It takes patience and perseverance to find out best traveling deals" (OTF P3)

Theme 3: Travelers' flexible behavior is molded by their self-belief as flexible travelers – This theme was categorized on the basis of how respondents reflected upon their self-identity as travelers. Two sub-themes emerged.

Sub theme 1: Traveling Motivation (traveling purpose, flying frequency, interest in recreation).

Motivation to travel is an important factor to influence upon travelers flexible behavior. For instance;

"It very much depends upon my traveling purpose and motivation" (ID P6)

"I love to travel, this is my biggest motivation" (OTF P1)

"As a sales man, if one has to travel around the year, his traveling motivation will be lower" (FG P15)

Sub theme 2: Socio-economic Position

Socio-economic standing of the traveler also influence upon flexible traveling behavior.

"depends on the job you are in" (OTF P4)

"...with limited financial resources, one can only long to take leisure trips" (ID P2)

"I am more flexible in traveling when I am paying for my ticket and can also compromise on comfort. This is not the case when my office is paying for me" (FG P9)

Theme 4: Travelers' flexible behavior is molded by societal influences – This theme emerged due to the social influences that influence upon a traveler's flexible traveling behavior. Social influences occur when a traveler's flexible behavior is affected by other people.

"We travel with our two sons. So our preference is to travel during their school holidays" (ID P16)

"We look for cheap deals as we have a large family to support and travel together" (OTA P17)

"My father reserves ticket for me when I travel or I call my friend in a travel agency. They decide for me. Simple!" (ID P14)

Theme 5: Travelers' flexible behavior is molded by how they attribute a cause to their traveling behavior – This theme emerged out a certain group of respondents who attributed a cause to their traveling behavior.

"We prefer Malaysian airlines over other airlines. It is our pride" (OTF P12)

"I prefer airlines with high repute, since they significantly enhance my traveling experience and pleasure" (ID P9)

"I am a supporter of eco-friendly living. I would be flexible to travel with an airline that supports this great cause" (ID P14)

"Airlines repute fascinates me a lot" (FG 8)

Theme 6: Travelers' flexible behavior is molded by their prior traveling experiences – Surely, traveler's prior traveling experiences influence upon their future traveling decisions. This theme has much to do with traveling comfort that one experiences.

"I prefer airlines with better leg space area and comfortable seats" (ID P30)

"Sometimes customers compromise on jet ways availability" (FG P18)

"Staff attitude is a traveling motivator" (OTF P11)

"We prefer airlines that serve Muslim halal food" (OTF P21)

Theme 7: Systems perceived flexibility is influenced by its perceived usefulness – A System will never be questioned for flexibility, if it satisfies users' expectations. Therefore, systems perceived flexibility is always dependent on the usefulness of a system.

"Searching for good packages using existing OTAs and SBTs is quite simple and easy" (ID P8)

"It requires the fewest steps to accomplish what users want to do" (FG 15)

"Users would prefer to use our system because they can make changes in their itinerary very easily" (FG 9)

Theme 8: Systems perceived flexibility is influenced by end user support – Our study showed that post-sale features are very essential in determining the perceived flexibility of a system. This theme has much to do with the user support.

"Every online reservation system has the capability to reserve a ticket...... for me a flexible system is the one which provides after sale service features" (ID 16)

"A flexible reservation system should support user prompting and guidelines throughout the reservation process" (FG P20)

Theme 9: Systems perceived flexibility is influenced by comparison of features on the actual level of effect regarding to complete the reservation process – This theme emerged due to the comparison features that influence upon systems perceived flexibility. Provision of multiple features in search of a better flight fare on different dates enhances the systems perceived flexibility.

"Me as a user would like to compare flight fares on different dates" (ID P22)

" It may (system) indicate about multiple destination options to users to choose from and accordingly point out fare changes" (FG P17)

"A system providing multiple searching options, like by dates, fares, destinations" (ID P14)

"If required, changes in itinerary can be made or at least recommended by the customer to the system" (ID P21)

6.2 Negative Case Analysis

Negative Case Analysis or deviant case analysis is the strength of qualitative research. It is a process for refining an analysis until it can explain or account for a majority of cases. The 8 themes that emerged from our analysis of factors influencing upon (i) flexible traveling behavior and (ii) perceived flexibility of an online airline reservation accounted for all of the cases. This ensured validity of our findings.

7 Conclusion

Flexibility is an important attribute to meet today's competitive business needs and demands. To meet the desired objectives, companies are continuously investing money and time to change their business strategies so as to become more flexible and agile in nature. However, in the case of Online Airline Reservation Systems (OARS), flexibility is undeterminable without accounting for traveler's flexible travelling behavior.

In this paper, we have attempted to define flexibility from two perspectives, i.e. from user's travelling behavior and flexibility of the reservation systems. Our findings show that users travelling behavior is molded by a number of important personality relevant determinants, both internal and external in characteristics. While, traveling consciousness, self-efficacy in digital skills and self-belief as flexible travelers are internal personality relevant determinants influencing directly upon travelers flexible behavior, societal influences, attribution and prior experiences are external personality relevant determinants that indirectly influence upon travelers flexible behavior. Moreover, external determinant may not necessarily always have the same influence every time, depending upon the situation the traveler is in.

As for system's flexibility, our findings show that system's perceived flexibility is reflected in its perceived usefulness. Perceived usefulness is a combination of system's effectiveness, efficiency and satisfaction. End user support or user prompting is considered to be a supporting characteristic that substantially augments efficiency and effectiveness of the system, while multiple options directly influence upon user satisfaction. If a system provides ranges of dates as flying and source destination options at different fares, flexibility of the system is enhanced in its perceived usefulness in the eyes of the users. This is because if a user chooses a flying option 'A' from a given one or two options, he has not made a flexible decision. But if he chooses the same flying option 'A' from a variety of given flying options, he is likely to enjoy extra satisfaction that he will get from the flexibility of the system and also in his purchase making decision. Likewise, if a system offers multiple flying options, they will also influence upon users' decision and make them change their mind to opt to fly from option 'B' instead of 'A'. This will again have positive influence upon user's satisfaction from the system – perceived usefulness.

This paper therefore concludes that flexibility of users and system are independent but still very much dependent on one another. While user's flexibility is related to their purchase making decisions, systems flexibility, although is reflected in its perceived usefulness, can influence upon user's travelling behavior by enhancing their satisfaction.

Acknowledgment. We thank all the travelers, executives, managers and technical experts of Malaysian, Fire Fly and Aero Asia airline carriers who participated in the focus group survey.

References

1. IBM: z/TPF – The Evolution of Transaction Processing to Open Standards. Enabling Transaction Processing for On Demand Business (October 2005)
2. Palma, A.D., Rochat, D.: Understanding Iindividual Travel Decisions: Results from a Commuters Survey in Geneva. Transportation 26, 263–281 (1999)
3. Mushtaq, A., Sulaiman, S., Dominic, P.D.D., Riaz, S.: Green Environment with Flexible Airline Reservation Systems. In: Proceedings of the ICIIT 2010, vol. 1, pp. 488–492 (2010)
4. Monsuwe, T.P., Dellaert, B.G.C., Ruyter, K.: What Drives Consumers to Shop Online? A Literature Review. International Journal of Service Industry Management 15(1), 102–121 (2004)
5. Olsen, K.A., Malizia, A.: Flexible User Interfaces for B2C Systems, Using Booking as a Case Study. In: Proceedings HCI, Las Vegas, USA (2005), `http://home.himolde.no/~olsen/artikler/FlexibleUserInterfaces.pdf` (accessed on July 19, 2009)
6. Malizia, A.: Adding Flexibility to B2C Booking Systems Using a Virtual Intermediate Travel agent. In: Proceedings of the 2005 IEEE Symposium on Visual Languages and Human-Centric Computing, pp. 337–338 (2005)
7. Limayem, M., Khalifa, M., Frini, A.: What Makes Consumers Buy from Internet, a Longitudinal Study of Online Shopping. IEEE 30(4) (2000)
8. Kowtha, N.: Choon: Determinants of Website Development: A Study of Electronic Commerce in Singapore. Information and Management 39(3), 227–242 (2000)
9. Bryck, L.R.: Flexible Behavior Under Control? Neural and Behavioral Evidence in Favor of a Two-Component Model of Task-Switching
10. Landauer, T.K.: Let's Get Real: A Position Paper on the Role of Cognitive Psychology in the Design of Humanly Usefid and Usable Systems. In: Baecker, R.M., Grudin, J., Buxton, W.A.S., Greenberg, S. (eds.) Readings in Human-Computer Interaction: Toward the Year 2000, 2nd edn., pp. 659–665. Morgan Kaufman Publishers, San Francisco (1995)
11. Preece, J., Rogers, Y., Sharp, H., Benyon, D., Holland, S., Carey, T.: Human-Computer Interaction. Addison-Wesley, Reading (1994)
12. Boring, R.L.: Human-Computer Interaction as Cognitive Science. In: Proceedings of the Human Factors and Ergonomics Society 46th Annual Meeting, pp. 1767–1771 (2002)
13. Human Factors and Ergonomics Society: Human Factors & Ergonomics: Designing for Human Use. Human Factors and Ergonomics Society, Santa Monica (1998)
14. Goodwin, N.C.: Functionality and usability. Communications of the ACM 30(3), 229–233 (1987)
15. Mushtaq, A., Sulaiman, S., Loviscach, J.: Issues with Flexibility: A Reason for not Using Online Reservation Systems? In: International Symposium on Information Technology, vol. 3, pp. 1076–1081 (2010)
16. Palma, A.D., Rochat, D.: Understanding Individual Travel Decisions: Results from a Commuters Survey in Geneva. Transportation 26, 263–281 (1999)
17. Herrera, F., Alonsa, S., Chiclana, F., Herrera-Viedma, E.: Computing with Words in Decision Making: Foundations, Trends and Prospects. Journal of Fuzzy Optimization and Decision Making 8(4), 337–364 (2009)
18. Shariff, N.M., Shah, M.Z.: Factors Influencing Travel Behavior and their Potential Solution: A Review of Current Literatures. Jurnal Alam Bina, Jilid 11(2) (2008)
19. Stone, A.: An Ontological Approach to Quantifying the Functional Flexibility of Embedded Systems. IEEE Systems Journal 5(1), 111–120 (2011)

20. Zhang, Z., Song, X., Gui, S.: The Quantitative Model of Flexibility Capacity of Distribution Logistics System Vased on PPC and Fuzzy Matter-Element. In: 2009 International Conference on Information Management, Innovation Management and Industrial Engineering, pp. 590–593 (2009)
21. Gao, B.W., Zhang, H.Q.: Dream Destination: A Concept of Perception of Leisure Travelers. International CHRIE Conference-Refereed Track. Paper 26 (2009), `http://scholarworks.umass.edu/refereed/Sessions/Friday/26`
22. Samik-Ibrahim, L., Rahmat, M.: Grounded Theory Methodology as the Research Strategy for a Developing Country [16 paragraphs]. Forum Qualitative Sozialforschung / Forum: Qualitative Social Research 1(1), Art. 19 (2000), `http://nbn-resolving.de/urn:nbn:de:0114-fqs0001198`
23. Strauss, A., Corbin, J.: Basics of Qualitative Research: Grounded Theory Procedures and Techniques. Sage, Newbury Park (1990)
24. Glaser, B.G., Strauss, A.L.: The Discovery of Grounded Theory: Strategies for Qualitative Research, p. 271. Aldine Pub. Co., New York (1967)
25. Charmaz, K.: Grounded Theory in the 21st Century. In: Holstein, Gubrium (eds.) Social Action Thousand Oaks, Sage, Cal (2005)
26. Schonland, A.M., Williams, P.W.: Using the Internet for Travel and Tourism Survey Research: Experiences from the Net Traveller Survey. Journal of Travel Research 35(2) (1996)
27. Patton, M.Q.: Qualitative Evaluation Methods. Sage, Beverly Hills (1980)
28. Decrop, A.: Triangulation in Qualitative Tourism Research. Tourism Management 20(1), 157–161 (1999)
29. Padgett, D.K.: Qualitative Methods in Social Work Research: Challenges and Rewards. Sage, Thousand Oaks (1998)

Author Index

GPSR Compliance

The European Union's (EU) General Product Safety Regulation (GPSR) is a set of rules that requires consumer products to be safe and our obligations to ensure this.

If you have any concerns about our products, you can contact us on ProductSafety@springernature.com

In case Publisher is established outside the EU, the EU authorized representative is:

Springer Nature Customer Service Center GmbH
Europaplatz 3
69115 Heidelberg, Germany

Batch number: 10838023

Printed by Printforce, the Netherlands